WAR IN THE SHADOWS

The Guerrilla in History

By Robert B. Asprey

Volume II

DOUBLEDAY & COMPANY, INC.
GARDEN CITY, NEW YORK

Grateful acknowledgment is made for permission to use excerpts from the following copyrighted material:

Dean Acheson, *Present at the Creation*, copyright © 1969 by Dean Acheson. Reprinted by permission of W. W. Norton & Company, Inc. and Hamish Hamilton Ltd.
Loeb Appian, *Appian's Roman History*, copyright 1912 by The Loeb Classical Library. Reprinted by permission of The Loeb Classical Library. (Harvard University Press and William Heinemann.)
Ronald Atkin, *Revolution! Mexico 1910–1920*, copyright © 1969 by Ronald Atkin. Reprinted by permission of The John Day Company.
John A. Armstrong, editor, *Soviet Partisans In World War II*, copyright © 1964 by the Regents of the University of Wisconsin. Reprinted by permission of The University of Wisconsin Press.
Donald L. Barnett and Karari Njama, *Mau Mau From Within*, copyright © 1966 by Donald L. Barnett and Karari Njama. Reprinted by permission of Monthly Review Press and Granada Publishing Limited.
Edward Behr, *The Algerian Problem*, copyright © 1961 by Edward Behr. Reprinted by permission of Hodder and Stoughton, Limited.
C. N. M. Blair, *Guerrilla Warfare*, copyright © 1957 by United Kingdom Ministry of Defence. Reprinted by permission of Ministry of Defence.
W. C. Bullitt, "A Report to the American People on China," October 13, 1947 issue of *Life*. Copyright © 1947 by Time Inc. Reprinted by permission of Time/Life Syndication Service.
Joseph Buttinger, *Vietnam: A Dragon Embattled*, copyright © 1967 by Joseph Buttinger. Reprinted by permission of Praeger Publishers, Inc. and Phaidon Press, Limited.
Bernard Callinan, *Independent Company*, copyright 1953 by Bernard Callinan. Reprinted by permission of William Heinemann, Ltd.
C. E. Callwell, *Small Wars and Their Practice*. Reprinted by permission of Her Majesty's Stationery Office.
F. Spencer Chapman, *The Jungle Is Neutral*, copyright 1949 by F. Spencer Chapman. Reprinted by permission of Chatto and Windus and the Author's Literary Estate.
Winston S. Churchill, *World Crisis*, copyright 1923, 1927 by Charles Scribner's Sons. Reprinted by permission of Charles Scribner's Sons and The Hamlyn Publishing Group, Limited.

iv

Contents

PART THREE Ho . . . Ho . . . Ho Chi Minh

CHAPTER 52   671
*A disrupted world • Soviet political aims • Western weaknesses •
Communist-inspired insurrections • The Cominform • American
reaction • Allied occupation of Vietnam • Conflict in the South •
The French take over • The Chinese in the North • Ho Chi Minh's
problems • His isolation • The French arrive in strength • Chinese exit • The French solution • Viet Minh opposition • Guerrilla warfare in the South • Trouble in the North • Outbreak of
insurgency*

CHAPTER 53   684
*Viet Minh strength • French counterinsurgency tactics • French
errors • Operation Léa • The political problem • General Revers's secret report • Vietnamese nationalism • Bao Dai's provisional government • The American position • Indochina's international importance • Truman's confusion • The French attitude
• The Élysée Agreements • Acheson's dilemma (I) • The lines
form*

CHAPTER 54   697
*Change in Viet Minh tactics • Vo Nguyen Giap • Mao Tse-tung's
influence • Communist tactics in the South • Viet Minh military
organization • The political base • Special Viet Minh units •
Guerrilla tactics • French countertactics • Terror tactics • Enter
Communist China • Viet Minh expansion*

CHAPTER 55   709
Viet Minh offensives • French disasters • La sale guerre *• General de Lattre de Tassigny • Giap's mistakes • Change in Com-*

*munist tactics • French strategy and tactics • De Lattre's "crusade"
• American intervention • American-French conflict • George
Kennan's warning to Acheson • Acheson's dilemma (II) • Gullion
and Blum dissent • Senator John Kennedy's position*

CHAPTER 56   722
*De Lattre's new tactics • General Salan takes over • Jean Letour-
neau • French political failure • Acheson's dilemma (III) •
Giap's problems • His shift in targets • Salan's countermoves •
Orde Wingate's ghost (I) • Continued French failure • Acheson
loses patience • Giap fans out • General Henri Navarre arrives*

CHAPTER 57   733
*The Greek civil war • Postwar confusion • Communist organiza-
tion and strength • Communist defeat • Markos changes tactics •
Growth of Communist strength • Government strength and weak-
ness • The balance sheet • Communist guerrilla operations •
Communist strength and weakness • Yugoslavia and Albania •
The Truman Doctrine • The American army's quantitative ap-
proach • Greek army offensives • Communist political errors •
Tito's defection • End of the war • The cost • Reasons for Com-
munist defeat • Western "victory"*

CHAPTER 58   746
*The Philippine problem • Postwar situation • The Huks • Basis
of Communist popularity • Communist tactics • Government
countertactics • American army influence • Success and failure •
Magsaysay takes over • His ultimate failure*

CHAPTER 59   759
*Rise of Indonesian nationalism • Allied occupation • Clashes with
the British • The Communist element • Negotiations break down
• The Dutch take over • A military solution • Guerrilla warfare
• Sukarno's problems • The Communist revolt • Dutch intransi-
gence • American intervention • The Dutch yield*

CHAPTER 60   768
*The Palestine problem • Historical background • The British role
• Jews versus Arabs • The Zionist position • Origin of Haganah*

• *World War II and the postwar situation* • *David Raziel: the militant element* • *Irgun and terrorism* • *Stern and the FFI* • *Menachem Begin* • *Guerrilla war* • *British countertactics* • *UN intervention* • *The British yield*

CHAPTER 61   781
Postwar Malaya • *Ch'en P'ing's Communist guerrilla army* • *Communist tactics* • *Government reaction* • *Counterinsurgency tactics* • *Ch'en P'ing's tactical adjustment* • *British problems* • *British tactical adaptation* • *The Briggs Plan* • *Guerrilla setbacks* • *Templer takes over: the qualitative approach* • *The tactical challenge* • *The cost*

CHAPTER 62   795
The Vietnam war • *Navarre's tactics* • *Chinese aid* • *The American position* • *Erroneous estimates of the situation* • *Genesis of the domino theory* • *On strategic values* • *"Strategic keys" versus "strategic conveniences"* • *Mark Clark's recommendations* • *General O'Daniel's mission* • *The Navarre Plan: ". . . light at the end of a tunnel"* • *Giap's response* • *Orde Wingate's ghost (II)* • *Dien Bien Phu* • *Giap's secret plans* • *Navarre's problems* • *Origin of the Geneva Conference* • *Navarre's continuing errors* • *American aid*

CHAPTER 63   809
Vietnam: French and American estimates • *Giap attacks Dien Bien Phu* • *Viet Minh tactics* • *The guerrilla effort* • *Crisis* • *Question of American military intervention* • *Dissenting voices* • *General Ridgway's warning* • *Eisenhower backs down* • *The fall of Dien Bien Phu*

CHAPTER 64   819
The Geneva Conference • *The American position* • *Dulles' defeat* • *The agreements* • *SEATO* • *Ngo Dinh Diem* • *His background* • *The refugee problem* • *American support* • *Eisenhower's letter* • *The Collins mission* • *Diem takes over*

CHAPTER 65   832
Diem's early government • The Fishel mission • Diem's house of power • "Communist"-suppression campaigns • The Diem dictatorship • Failure of Diem's reforms • The Montagnard problem • Question of general election • The American role • ARVN • MAAG's influence • The result

CHAPTER 66   848
Revolution in the South • Ho Chi Minh's problems • His attitude toward the South • Viet Minh tactics in the South • The National Liberation Front (NLF) • Non-Communist opposition to Diem • The 1960 revolt • Diem's refusal to effect reforms • His civil and military weaknesses • The American contribution

CHAPTER 67   862
The Mau Mau rebellion • Historical background • British colonization • Early native political movements • Rise of the KCA • Enter Jomo Kenyatta • Early Mau Mau activities • Government suppression • Mau Mau appeal • Organization and strength of Mau Mau • Kenyatta's arrest • The emergency begins

CHAPTER 68   877
Mau Mau terrorism • The government's response • British security forces • The tactical problem • British military tactics • Mau Mau mistakes • General Erskine's military solution • Forest guerrillas • Final operations • The tally

CHAPTER 69   887
The Cyprus rebellion • Historical background • The question of enosis • The 1931 rebellion • The postwar situation • Makarios and Grivas • Grivas' estimate of the situation • Origin of EOKA • Opening attacks • Early guerrilla operations • Harding's negotiations • He deports Makarios • His military solution • Organization and strength of EOKA • British counterguerrilla tactics • Grivas' critical analysis of British tactics • Attempts at a political solution • Fragile peace • The cost • Analysis of Grivas' tactics

CHAPTER 70   903

*The Algerian crisis • Historical background • The French con-
quest • French colonial policy • Growth of nationalism • The
1945 riots • Ahmed Ben Bella and the OS • Belkacem Krim's
guerrillas • The internal situation • FLN emerges • Outbreak of
rebellion • Soustelle's pacification strategy • Origin of SAS •
French military and political errors • La guerre révolutionnaire*

CHAPTER 71   914

*FLN growth • Rebel weaknesses • French strength increases •
The CNRA • The battle of Algiers • Jacques Massu and la guerre
révolutionnaire • French excesses • War in the countryside •
Guerrilla organization • The counterinsurgency task: destruction
and construction • French tactics • The Morice Line • Problem
of sanctuaries • Failure of the regroupement program • SAS difficulties • De Gaulle takes over • The Constantine Plan • French
tactical adaptation: the Challe Plan • Role of helicopters • De
Gaulle's peace offensive • Origin of OAS • A mutiny fails • Algerian independence • The cost*

CHAPTER 72   932

*The Cuban revolution • Special characteristics • Its psychological
impact on the United States • Historical background • Early
American presence • The Platt Amendment • American military
intervention • Gerardo Machado and the strong-man tradition •
Internal opposition mounts • Early rebellions • Washington intervenes • The Batista era • His strength and weakness • The political situation • The American position • Enter Fidel Castro • His
background • The 26th of July Movement • Trial, imprisonment,
release*

CHAPTER 73   948

*Castro in Mexico • Che Guevara joins • Return to Cuba • Early
disaster • The fugitives • Sanctuary in Sierra Maestra • Castro's
plan • Urban support • Early guerrilla operations • Castro's
problems • The Matthews interview • A myth begins • Guerrilla
tactics • Batista's countertactics • American army influence •
Dissension in Washington • Ambassador Smith*

CHAPTER 74   961
*Pact of the Sierra • Urban guerrillas • War in the countryside •
The balance sheet • The American position • Eisenhower's arms
embargo • The climax approaches • Operation Summer fails •
Castro's counterattack • The revolution spreads • Batista exits •
Castro takes over • Che Guevara on guerrilla warfare • His het-
erodoxy • His exodus • Che's Bolivian expedition • Capture and
execution • Che's failure analyzed*

CHAPTER 75   977
*John Kennedy inherits a war • General Lansdale's estimate of the
situation • Kennedy's strategic appraisal • His early errors • Lyndon Johnson's report • Hawks versus doves • Military versus political strategy • The Staley Plan • The Taylor mission • The
military solution • Kennedy's reservations • Roger Hilsman dissents • De Gaulle's warning • Kennedy acts • His relations with
Diem*

CHAPTER 76   993
*The situation in South Vietnam • NLF organization • The Peo-
ple's Revolutionary Party (PRP) • Hanoi's influence in the South
• NLF aims • "The Struggle Movement" • Agit-prop techniques
• Diem's failings • Increased American aid • American military
influence • Viet Cong setbacks • American optimism • Tactical
chimeras • The Viet Cong recovers • Disaster at Ap Bac • ARVN
failures • The strategic-hamlet program • Diem's increasing intransigence • The American commitment increases • Buddhist revolts • Shifting NLF strategy • Washington changes direction •
Diem's death*

CHAPTER 77   1015
*Kennedy's failure analyzed • The administration's ignorance con-
cerning South Vietnam • Ambition versus policy • Vietnam's low
priority • Pentagon and CIA influence • False reports • Kennedy's advisers • Guerrilla warfare and American armed forces •
Special Forces (the Green Berets) • CIA's role • The tactical
problem analyzed • General Griffith's warning • Quantitative versus qualitative warfare • The inevitable result*

CHAPTER 78   1029
*American military advisers • American dependence on technology
• Helicopters • ARVN tactics • The war escalates • Nolting's
and Harkins' dream world • Warnings from the field • Wishful
thinking in Saigon • American Government versus the press • The
Hilsman-Forrestal report • Kennedy condones the great deception •
Pierre Salinger's warning • McNamara's volte-face • Kennedy's
private doubts*

CHAPTER 79   1045
*Enter President Lyndon Johnson • Duong Van Minh's provisional
government • Political anarchy in the South • Revolutionary pressures • Nguyen Khanh takes over • McNamara's report (I) • Operation Plan 34A • Intelligence experts dissent • JCS hawks •
Nguyen Khanh's reforms • McNamara's report (II) • Renewed
VC offensives • The situation deteriorates • The Lodge plan: "carrot and stick" • Johnson backs the hawks • CIA rebuttal • Seaborn's mission to Hanoi • Hanoi hawks • Taylor relieves Lodge:
the military situation • The new Saigon team • The Tonkin Gulf
incident • William Bundy's Congressional resolution*

CHAPTER 80   1064
*General Taylor reports from Saigon • Seaborn's second mission to
Hanoi • William Bundy's program of escalation • Admiral Sharp's
recommendations • Taylor's operational plans • Pentagon voices
• Johnson: ". . . we still seek no wider war" • September meeting
in the White House • Enemy estimate of the situation • Douglas
Pike's analysis • Bias of the insurgency • Enemy strategic adjust-
ments • Edward Lansdale's analysis • The Bien Hoa attack •
John McNaughton's adjusted aims • "Fast full squeeze" and
"hot-blood actions" • Rostow on power • George Ball's doubts •
Taylor's pessimism • The intelligence panel dissents • Khanh's dictatorship • Dissent in Saigon • Tran Van Minh takes over*

CHAPTER 81   1085
*Fresh Viet Cong offensives • William Bundy's dilemma • Mc-
George Bundy's memorandum • The attack at Pleiku • McGeorge
Bundy's report • Sharp's "calculated risk" • The White Paper •
American marines land • Early results • Westmoreland demands*

more troops (*I*) • *Johnson's Baltimore speech* • *Hanoi's investment in the South* • *ARVN offensives* • *More American aid* • *The
enemy retreats* • *More American troops* • *Taylor dissents* • *Rostow's optimism* • *Renewed guerrilla offensives* • *The Thieu-Ky
dictatorship* • *Westmoreland demands more troops (II)* • *Senator
Fulbright's analysis* • *George Ball's secret warning* • *Clifford's and
Mansfield's pessimism* • *Ball's solution* • *Johnson's intransigence*
• *The deception continues*

CHAPTER 82   1110
The fighting escalates • *Viet Cong setbacks* • *American and
ARVN gains* • *The air war* • *Westmoreland's strategy* • *Search-
and-destroy tactics* • *The American build-up* • *Westmoreland's
four wars* • *The "other war"* • *American arms and equipment* •
Army operations in the central highlands • *Westmoreland's "spoiling" tactics* • *Operation Crazy Horse* • *Marine operations in I
Corps area* • *Walt's pacification program* • *PAVN crosses the
DMZ: Operation Hastings, Operation Prairie* • *Operations in III
Corps area* • *The air war escalates* • *The naval war* • *The "other
war": the Honolulu conference* • *Ky's Revolutionary Development
program* • *Elections in the South* • *The Manila conference* • *General allied optimism*

CHAPTER 83   1135
Blurs on the operational canvas • *Failure of Operation Rolling
Thunder* • *Increasing cost of aerial warfare* • *Shortcomings of
attrition strategy and search-and-destroy tactics* • *The refugee problem* • *Manpower facts* • *The numbers game* • *Russian and Chinese aid to the North* • *The ground war* • *Increasing American
costs (I)* • *The logistics picture* • *The Jurassic dinosaur*

CHAPTER 84   1149
More blurs on the canvas • *American tactical problems* • *The failure of Operation Crazy Horse* • *Colonel Emerson defines the tactical challenge* • *U. S. Marine Corps operations* • *Captain Miller's
observations* • *The intelligence failure* • *Mines and booby traps* •
VC intelligence network • *Captain Cooper's discovery* • *The pacification failure* • *Continued governmental abuses* • *ARVN's failure* • *Dissent in the U.S.A.* • *The Vietnam hearings* • *The*

thoughts of James Gavin and George Kennan • *The secret thoughts of Robert McNamara* • *Escalation pressures* • *The hawks win again*

CHAPTER 85   1176
The war continues • *President Johnson's optimism* • *The February bombing halt* • *Operation Cedar Falls* • *Task Force Oregon* • *Fighting in the highlands* • *The marine war* • *New tactical techniques* • *Khe Sanh defended* • *Air and naval wars* • *"The new team": Ambassador Bunker and pacification* • *South Vietnam's political progress* • *Allied profits for the year* • *". . . Light at the end of a tunnel"*

CHAPTER 86   1192
More blurs on the canvas • *Allied losses* • *Failure of Operation Rolling Thunder* • *The numbers game* • *Increasing American costs (II)* • *The fallacy of attrition warfare* • *The "other war" examined* • *The communications deficiency* • *Search-and-destroy versus pacification* • *"Have we killed all the enemy?"* • *Failure of the Revolutionary Development program* • *Komer's "indicators"* • *Government corruption* • *Failure of land reforms* • *Electoral restrictions and irregularities* • *Increasing opposition at home and abroad* • *Press and TV coverage* • *The experts dissent* • *Behind-the-scenes dissent* • *Westmoreland demands more troops (III)* • *John McNaughton: ". . . A feeling is widely and strongly held that 'the Establishment' is out of its mind."* • *McNamara's new policy paper* • *The President's "middle course"* • *The Clifford mission* • *Johnson's San Antonio offer* • *Westmoreland demands more troops (IV)* • *McNamara's final effort*

CHAPTER 87   1216
The Pueblo fiasco • *The Tet offensive* • *Enemy aims and accomplishments* • *Defeat or victory?* • *The Johnson-Westmoreland stand* • *General Wheeler's report* • *MACV objectives* • *Westmoreland demands more troops (V)* • *Hawks versus doves* • *Dean Acheson: ". . . With all due respect, Mr. President, the Joint Chiefs of Staff don't know what they're talking about."* • *The Clifford Group* • *Action in the North* • *The other war* • *Dissension within*

*America • Johnson's compromise • Westmoreland is relieved •
Johnson steps down • Paris peace talks • Saigon's intransigence •
The war continues • Increasing American costs (III) • Johnson
quits*

CHAPTER 88   1241
*The summing up (I): the Bible and the Sword • Not "reason good
enough" • Communists and dominoes • Inside South Vietnam •
Economics • Government versus press: America—the communications failure*

CHAPTER 89   1257
*The summing up (II): use of air power • The Douhet theory •
Strategic bombing in World War II • The paradox of nuclear stale-
mate • Lessons of the Korean War • American expectations in
North Vietnam • Historical factors • Harrison Salisbury reports
from the North • Bombs and international diplomacy*

CHAPTER 90   1274
*The summing up (III): the war on the ground • Westmoreland's
strategy • Westmoreland, Walt, and the enemy • The helicopter •
Khe Sanh • The tactical challenge • Never the twain shall meet •
King An Ya: ". . . The peasant despises nothing more than a fool"
• The school solution • CAP: Belisarius versus Narses*

CHAPTER 91   1296
*Richard Nixon's promise • His position on Vietnam • Enter Henry
Kissinger • His plan for disengagement • Combat operations continue • Abrams' tactics • The war escalates • Dissent on the
home front • The military and the Hellespont • Soedjatmoko
speaks out • Stalemate in Paris • Secret talks with Hanoi • Saigon
obstructionism • The President's new plan • First troop withdrawals • The Midway meeting • The Clifford plan (I)*

CHAPTER 92   1312
*The Hanoi scene • Emergence of the PRG • Combat action drops
• General Wheeler's stand • The doves reply • Nixon's decision •
Increasing American costs (IV) • Administration problems • CIA*

and Special Forces • Ho Chi Minh's death • Further troop withdrawals • Progress in South Vietnam • The President's November
address • The Thompson report • Blurs on the canvas • Hanoi's
position • Increasing dissent at home • Pacification problems •
Thompson's report examined • The Saigon government • End of
a year

CHAPTER 93   1328
Confused U.S. objectives • Congressional opposition mounts • In-
volvement in Laos • President Thieu's stand • President Nixon's
dilemma • The Cambodian invasion • Disappointing results •
Clark Clifford's new plan (II) • Renewed action in South Vietnam
• Nixon's dominoes • Administration reverses • Paris: peace plan
versus peace plan • The situation in South Vietnam: fact or fiction?
• Enemy offensive moves

CHAPTER 94   1350
The Nixon administration's new strategy • Hanoi's position • The
war in Cambodia • Opposition at home • ARVN invades Laos:
"the golden opportunity" • Battlefield alchemy: disaster • Reasons
why • Picking up the pieces • Flies in the Nixon ointment • The
Calley case • Captain Daniels writes the President • Thieu and Ky
fall out • The Pentagon Papers • South Vietnamese elections:
Thieu versus Thieu leaves Thieu • Enemy gains • Nixon's new
stand • Stalemate in Paris • Operation Rolling Thunder resumes
• Giap's spring offensive • ARVN reverses • The war escalates •
Nixon's new peace plan • ARVN's problems • Saigon's losses •
No win, no victory

CHAPTER 95   1369
The American failure • The public's role • Communications and
education • Citizen apathy • New voices searching • The public
trust • Official responsibility • Discretion versus dissembling •
Commager on power • Galbraith on duplicity • The Department
of State • Force versus diplomacy • Departmental problems • Reorganization and reform • The Department of Defense • Major
deficiencies • The Tuchman message • Anomaly and autonomy •
The Clearchos element • Interservice strife • Stab-in-the-back •

Congress and the press • *The tyranny of conformance* • Mene, mene, tekel, upharsin

Works Cited in This Volume   1392

Index   1405

List of Maps

Maps by Mary Potter

Volume II

43. CHAPTER 52:   681
Ho Chi Minh to Jean Sainteny, spring 1946: ". . . If we have
to fight, we will fight. You will kill ten of our men and we will
kill one of yours, and in the end it will be you who will tire of
it."

44. CHAPTER 54:   700
". . . The [Viet Minh] high command divided the country into
six interzones, each containing zones, provinces, districts, intervillages, and villages."

45. CHAPTER 55:   711
Bernard Fall: "When the smoke cleared, the French had suffered
their greatest colonial defeat since Montcalm had died in
Quebec."

46. CHAPTER 57:   743
". . . Unfortunately, American military commanders, primarily
army commanders, concluded that a Communist insurgency
could be defeated by conventional methods of warfare."

47. CHAPTER 58:   754
"Luis Taruc succinctly summed up the lesson: 'One thing seems
clear: no country—least of all a Christian land—can defeat Communism by the use of un-Christian methods.'"

48. CHAPTER 59:   761
1949: ". . . If the guerrillas, unlike Mao Tse-tung's forces, were
not strong enough to attack, neither was the enemy strong enough
to eliminate them."

49. CHAPTER 60:   779
". . . British security forces could disrupt various groups and

even cause [terrorist] operations to be suspended, but they could not eliminate the hard-core top command."

50. CHAPTER 61:   791

"The decisive tactical element in Malaya was not a troop unit (though troops were vital) but, rather, the village police post. . . ."

51. CHAPTER 62:   796

"Lessons learned from insurgencies in the Philippines, Greece, Indonesia, Palestine, and Malaya did not rub off on the French in Indochina."

52. CHAPTER 67:   864

". . . the story of an insurgency that need never have happened."

53. CHAPTER 69:   901

General George Grivas: ". . . our form of war, in which a few hundred fell in four years, was far more selective than most, and I speak as one who has seen battlefields covered with dead."

54. CHAPTER 71:   915

". . . the French army continued to rely on traditional techniques in fighting the Algerian war."

55. CHAPTER 72:   933

"The rebellion was peculiarly Cuban. . . . Castro's leadership proved important but revolution might have occurred without it. It could not have occurred without Batista's government."

56. CHAPTER 74:   973

Che Guevara: ". . . the Andes will be the Sierra Maestra of America, and all the immense territories that make up this continent will become the scene of a life-and-death struggle against the power of imperialism."

57. CHAPTER 81:   1091

March 1965: "The American public may not have known it, but their country had gone to war."

58. CHAPTER 82:   1111

Map 1: "In spring of 1966, at least four PAVN divisions were known to be immediately north of the DMZ."

59. CHAPTER 82:   1123

Map 2: ". . . The ground, naval, and air wars continued to escalate. More than ever, the U.S.A. seemed determined to win the war."

60. CHAPTER 85:   1187
"Despite improved tactics and techniques, as autumn gave way to early winter, [U.S.] army and marine commanders continued to dance to the enemy's tune."

61. CHAPTER 91:   1301
". . . American military operations . . . differed not in kind, but only in degree."

62. CHAPTER 93:   1333
". . . Paradoxically, while Nixon was speaking of further troop withdrawals, MACV was completing plans to invade Cambodia."

63. CHAPTER 94:   1354
"On February 8 [1971], an uneasy world learned that South Vietnam had invaded the panhandle of southern Laos."

PART THREE

Ho . . . Ho . . . Ho Chi Minh

. . . Marx, Engels, Lenin and Stalin are the common teachers for the world revolution. Comrade Mao Tse-tung has skilfully "Sinicized" the ideology of Marx, Engels, Lenin, and Stalin, correctly applied it to the practical situation of China, and has led the Chinese Revolution to complete victory.

Owing to geographical, historical, economic, and cultural conditions, the Chinese Revolution exerted a great influence on the Vietnamese revolution, which had to learn and indeed has learned many experiences from it.

HO CHI MINH

Chapter 52

A disrupted world • Soviet political aims • Western weaknesses • Communist-inspired insurrections • The Cominform • American reaction • Allied occupation of Vietnam • Conflict in the South • The French take over • The Chinese in the North • Ho Chi Minh's problems • His isolation • The French arrive in strength • Chinese exit • The French solution • Viet Minh opposition • Guerrilla warfare in the South • Trouble in the North • Outbreak of insurgency

NO WAR IN HISTORY solved so much and yet so little as World War II. No war so suddenly defeated ambitions of either victors or vanquished. No war opened such a Pandora's box, not to release winds but, rather, hurricanes of political, social, and economic change, which hurled existing structures into turmoil, confusion, and battle—what Cyril Falls, a lifelong student of warfare, has aptly called *sequelae*—morbid conditions following upon disease.[1]

In retrospect, the subsequent cold war between East and West is not difficult to understand. In 1945, however, the West held not the U.S.S.R. but Germany and Japan to be the real villains. Despite Stalin's increasing dissemblance and duplicity, still slight enough in view of the manifold problems on hand, at war's end sufficient of the Big Three spirit survived to kindle Western hopes for peace, a peace to be established and maintained by the new world body, the United Nations, supported alike by the Soviet Union and the United States.

1. Cyril Falls, *A Hundred Years of War* (London: Gerald Duckworth, 1953).

Fundamental to these hopes was the conceit that Stalin would behave in the Western definition of a civilized manner—the legacy, in part, of President Roosevelt but a legacy buttressed by American monopoly of the atomic bomb. That Stalin could not so behave, that heritage, temperament, and environment precluded such behavior, was generally overlooked. Voltaire once said, ". . . When you speak with me, define your terms." Had Stalin and his treaty makers been so pressed, American statesmen might have discovered a variance in contract law, including pertinent definitions, between East and West. Unfortunately, American statesmen did not so press our stubborn ally. The shock, then, was almost as great as the conceit when, shortly after Axis defeat, the relationship between East and West began deteriorating.

The rot resulted primarily from two major Russian political aims. Stalin wanted to establish a protective insulation of Communist-controlled border areas and states stretching from Finland down the Baltic coast to Germany, then across Europe to the Balkans and east to China. Partly to help free his hand for this task (by keeping the West off balance), partly to pave the way for traditional Russian expansionist ambitions, and partly to exploit the appeal inherent in Marxist-Leninist political destinies, he also wanted to foment the spread of communism in various war-torn countries.

Stalin accomplished his first aim more easily than the second. Unburdened by conscience and in full control of his ravaged country's domestic and foreign policies, he skillfully utilized his own strength in exploiting Western weaknesses. Various allied conferences during the war had conceded Eastern Europe to the Soviet sphere of influence, and Stalin did not hesitate in using preponderant Soviet military presence to reap the harvest carefully sown by Communist guerrilla activity during the war.

A vigorous and unified West might have blunted Stalin's sword in immediate postwar years, but such did not exist. France, Italy, and Holland lay shattered, England exhausted, economically *in extremis,* none able to cope effectively with such severe problem areas as Indonesia and Palestine—areas the result of crumbling colonial empires, areas remote from Communist control yet frictionally convenient to Stalin's Communist cause. Neither President Truman nor other American leaders leaped to accept the challenge of international leadership being inexorably thrust on them, and certainly nothing in Harry Truman's past career had prepared him to meet the complexities of the situation.

Forced politically into hasty demobilization of the armed forces, the American President thenceforth bargained from the unusable strength of the atomic-bomb monopoly and from the awkward peacemaking machinery of the United Nations. When neither served him well, when Stalin virtually ignored the unspoken threat of the atomic bomb to define borders, reparations, elections, and governments in terms foreign to Western understanding, Truman's growls, reluctant at first, lacked the teeth of either sufficient military presence or positive and determined policy, and he could find no effective voice in a temporarily strangled Europe.

Stalin's second goal, though more nebulous, complemented the first. To foment insurrection in various war-torn countries, the Soviet leader relied on local Communist guerrilla organizations. As we have seen, these included determined resistance fighters and those who scarcely fought at all. No matter the combat record, nearly all these indigenous forces ended the war with an effective and disciplined organization and with at least some arms and equipment—an insurrectionary capability strengthened both by chaotic and often anarchic local conditions and usually by carefully calculated and widely broadcast political appeals that subordinated Communist to nationalist aims.

Some readers will have forgotten the enormous threat posed by these forces in Europe alone. Not once, but several times, from 1946 to 1949, Communist movements threatened to capture the governments of France, Italy, and Austria. Their near success in Greece prompted the Truman Doctrine, of March 1947, the first of a series of drastic political, economic, and military measures that announced American determination to halt Soviet-inspired aggression, and that led ultimately to NATO and a relatively stabilized Europe.

But this healthful accomplishment did not stop Stalin from hanging the final drapes of the Iron Curtain. Nor did it prevent his pursuing the second aim elsewhere. He resembled, in these years, a skillful improvisator playing a political pipe organ. In Europe, he gave all support possible to local parties, and eventually established a restricted Comintern, the Cominform, for the long-range support task. In Greece, he played a waiting game; not only did he refuse to support the insurrection materially, but he did not hesitate to back away when the odds dramatically turned against it. In Manchuria, he offered partial, almost reluctant support to Chinese Communists. He did not support, at least materially, Communist insurrections in the Philippines, Indonesia, and Malaya, and he was careful with support in Vietnam.

Stalin nonetheless profited enormously from these activities, not least because of their continued demands on Western, and particularly American, resources. The United States was not prepared to cope with subtleties of political warfare. For a long period, she reacted rather than acted, dashing here and there like a delirious fire department confronted by a dozen professional arsonists. Forced to retain strong military forces in Europe while simultaneously reducing over-all military strength, she soon found herself overcommitted in trying to police the rest of the world. In time, this led to a serious weakening of so-called bastion areas such as Korea.

An important psychological element also entered. Desperately seeking friends to stem the Communist tide, the United States began to give military and economic aid to almost any declared anti-Communist government, some of which were decidedly reactionary if not totalitarian. Compounding this political anomaly, the U.S.A. was becoming increasingly tied to her European allies and, as one result, was slowly being forced to condone what amounted to colonial regimes in Southeast Asia. Soviet Communists naturally made capital propaganda from this, but that was to be expected. Far more serious: liberal and influential thinkers around the world began to contrast American foreign policy with her traditionally expressed libertarian ideals. In the U.S.A. itself, a divisive political movement began that would grow to serious rupture and, as a by-product, furnish excellent propaganda for Communist use.

Had basic assumptions of American foreign policy been correct, this would have provided no more than a temporary embarrassment easily absorbed by a country beginning to learn the truth of Admiral Mahan's somewhat cynical dictum: ". . . Defeat cries aloud for explanation; whereas success, like charity, covers a multitude of sins."

But fundamental to American foreign policy was the assumption of a Kuomintang-ruled China. When Chiang Kai-shek's government fell, in late 1949, American policy makers envisaged Southeast Asia as lying naked to the threat of Communist expansion. In seeking to clothe the area properly, the U. S. Government unfortunately chose only inferior materials from which to fashion a series of particularly ill-fitting and inappropriate suits.

Under terms of the Potsdam conference as confirmed at Yalta, Britain and China shared responsibility for occupying Vietnam: British forces moving in south and Chinese forces north of 16th parallel.

In the South, in Saigon, the British immediately collided with Tran Van Giau's hastily established Viet Minh regime, the Provisional Executive Committee of the South. Cunningly identifying itself with the allied cause, Giau's committee had assumed leadership of a tenuous local nationalist movement, the United National Front. One of Ho's more militant lieutenants, Giau already had partially alienated such important local groups as the Trotskyists and the two large and powerful religious sects, the Cao Dai and the Hoa Hao, an error repaired only in part by the time the first British troops arrived.[2]

Giau now met total rebuff from the British commander, Major General Douglas Gracey. To insure control of the area, Gracey fleshed out his small force not only by rearming some five thousand former French

2. George M. Kahin and John W. Lewis, *The United States in Vietnam—An Analysis in Depth of America's Involvement in Vietnam* (New York: The Dial Press, 1967); see also Robert Shaplen, *The Lost Revolution* (New York: Harper & Row, 1966); David Schoenbrun, *Vietnam* (New York: Atheneum, 1968); Joseph Buttinger, *Vietnam: A Dragon Embattled* (New York: Frederick A. Praeger, 1967) 2 vols.; Ellen J. Hammer, *The Struggle for Indochina 1940–1955* (Stanford: Stanford University Press, 1966).

prisoners of war, but by retaining the better part of seventy thousand Japanese soldiers under arms.[3]

Gracey answered civil disobedience by severe press censorship, martial law, and a strict curfew.[4] In late September, he widely exceeded his directive by allowing the local French commander, Colonel Jean Cédile, to eject Tran Van Giau's government from Saigon and to replace the republic's flag, a gold star on a red field, with the old and loathed tricolor.[5]

Tran Van Giau unwisely retaliated with mass terror methods, which resulted in large numbers of civil deaths, including those of some of his nationalist opponents, and widened the breach both between indigenous power groups and between those groups and the occupying powers. In late September, shooting started in the city and spread to the country. Gracey managed to bring both sides to the conference table only to learn what he already knew: that the French had no intention of yielding to the Viet Minh demand for independence. The talks soon broke down in favor of renewed fighting. In mid-October, French reinforcements arrived to join British and Japanese in clearing Saigon and environs of Viet Minh guerrilla resistance.

By late December, about fifty thousand French troops, commanded by General Leclerc, occupied the South, a good part of them Free French units (including twelve thousand men of the Foreign Legion) from Europe. Well organized, trained, and equipped, many of them combat veterans, their artillery shone and their armor gleamed; their tanks and trucks covered the countryside as their fighters and bombers (along with RAF planes) filled the skies. Nearly everyone in Saigon agreed that the fast-moving combat columns would quickly pacify the countryside to extend French control throughout Indochina, just as in the old days. Leclerc himself spoke of ". . . a simple 'mopping-up operation'

3. Hammer, op. cit.; see also Edgar Snow, *The Other Side of the River: Red China Today* (New York: Random House, 1961). Upon hearing of this action, General Douglas MacArthur allegedly exploded, ". . . If there is anything that makes my blood boil it is to see our Allies in Indochina and Java deploying Japanese troops to reconquer the little people we promised to liberate. It is the most ignoble kind of betrayal."

4. Hammer, op. cit.

5. Ibid.: ". . . The British commander [Gracey] was confronted with a political problem for which he had neither the background nor the advisers to deal with. He had been sent to Indochina on a military assignment and his instructions were strict: 'Sole mission: disarm the Japanese. Do not get involved in keeping order' "; see also Buttinger, op. cit.: "In a speech in 1953 . . . Gracey described how he treated the Vietnamese leaders who came to greet him as the Commander of the Allied troops. 'They came to see me,' he reported, 'and said "welcome" and all that sort of thing. It was an unpleasant situation and I promptly kicked them out' "; see also Hammer, op. cit.: Gracey's superior in Ceylon, Admiral Lord Louis Mountbatten, became increasingly concerned with Gracey's actions and only with difficulty did General Leclerc, the French commander-designate in Indochina, persuade him to leave Gracey in authority.

which would take more than four weeks."[6] The British, beset with empire commitments, left at year's end.

Developments in the North meanwhile moved at a slower tempo. Chiang Kai-shek and the Kuomintang had no intention of rejecting Ho's government in Hanoi as long as the Viet Minh did not interfere with the eating, raping, and looting habits of 180,000 Chinese soldiers worming their way down from Yünnan.[7] Chiang not only recognized Ho's *de facto* government, but his local commander refused to arm the thirty-five hundred French troops in Hanoi. Instead, he kept them ". . . in semi-internment," nor did he permit a thousand or so French guerrillas to re-enter Vietnam from China. Although he guaranteed ". . . law and order," he left ". . . most of the policing and all administration . . . in the hands of the Viet-Minh government."[8]

This was calculated policy on Chiang's part. China had suffered long decades of humiliation by the West, and the French, along with other Western powers, repeatedly had exacted profitable concessions at what amounted to gun point. Although Chiang knew that his presence in Vietnam was only temporary, he intended that the French would pay heavily for his departure (which is what happened). Meanwhile, he happily let the Viet Minh suffer the day's problems.

The Viet Minh faced plenty of problems. The Japanese surrender had left the north country in abysmal condition. Insatiable Japanese demands on the rice crop already had brought numerous deaths from starvation—locals said nearly 2 million deaths the previous year.[9] Widespread floods of the Red River, followed by severe drought, had ruined most of the current rice crop in Tonkin, and the bulk of what survived went to the voracious Chinese. Hundreds of thousands of people were starving; disease swept the land; the 1945–46 death toll would reach perhaps a million; millions more suffered helplessly, and the country looked to the Viet Minh for relief.

Having abolished ". . . the hated opium, alcohol, and salt monopolies," as well as ". . . the iniquitous head tax and the land taxes of the smaller owners," the new government also drastically reduced ". . . all the other land taxes, as well as the interest rates on loans."[10] As one result, the new government was broke. It was also decidedly factional, its Communist element a minority that survived mainly because of Ho's

6. Ibid.

7. Kahin and Lewis, op. cit.; see also Buttinger, op. cit., who points out that some of the Chinese troops were traveling north from Haiphong; Buttinger suggests 50,000 Chinese occupation troops.

8. Harold Isaacs, "Independence for Vietnam?" In Marvin E. Gettleman (ed.), *Viet-Nam—History, Documents, and Opinions on a Major World Crisis* (New York: Fawcett, 1965); see also Buttinger, op. cit.

9. Isaacs, op. cit.; see also Shaplen, op. cit., who reported one million deaths; Hammer, op. cit.: French authorities estimated 600,000 deaths.

10. Buttinger, op. cit.; see also Donald Lancaster, *The Emancipation of French Indochina* (London: Oxford University Press, 1961).

charisma, his appeal to non-aligned nationalists, and the disciplined organization of the Communist Party, as opposed to ineffectual leadership, organization, and traditional enmities of varied nationalist elements. Where possible, the Viet Minh brought these elements into its organization, one of the main instruments in the process being selective terrorism:

. . . Against people whose interests or political connections made them incorrigible enemies of the Vietminh, the Communists practised a policy of physical extermination from the very beginning of the revolution.[11]

Despite its chaotic and semi-bankrupt nature, the new government, without question, appealed to large numbers of peasants, not alone because of tax reforms but also because of a crash program against illiteracy: ". . . The measures, carried out enthusiastically by the educated of the country, produced greater results in one year than the French had been able, or rather had cared, to produce in more than sixty years.[12] The government similarly mobilized the people to attack flood and famine: ". . . in the spring of 1946, the people, although still undernourished, no longer died of starvation.[13] Nonetheless, by the end of 1945, rival parties, the VNQDD (*Vietnam Quoc Dan Dang*—The Vietnamese Nationalist Party) and the Dong Minh Hoi (Revolutionary League), controlled important provinces bordering the Chinese frontier, while elsewhere peasants found themselves subject to Viet Minh-imposed "voluntary" contributions and "public" subscriptions which ". . . turned out to be at least as heavy as the tax load imposed by the colonial regime."[14]

Outside Vietnam, the Viet Minh Government had almost no friends and a great many enemies. Contrary to what many persons in the West have assumed, the Kremlin at this time showed as much interest in helping Ho Chi Minh as it did the Republican Party in the United States. Nor could Mao Tse-tung, isolated in China's northwestern provinces, come to Ho's relief. The French Communist Party and the Socialists paid grudging lip service to the movement, but offered no material support. Ironically, Ho's greatest support came from the American command in Kunming, which refused to help De Gaulle's able representative, Major Jean Sainteny, in a grotesque attempt to replant the French flag in Hanoi, and from the small American military command that accompanied Chinese troops to Hanoi and continued OSS policy of supplying arms and equipment to the Viet Minh, a policy approved by Washington.

But this honeymoon would be short-lived. The French returned to Saigon with at least tacit approval of Washington, and Ho could not have

11. Buttinger, op. cit.
12. Ibid.
13. Ibid.; see also Hammer, op. cit.
14. Hammer, op. cit.

been pleased when Washington announced the sale of $160 million worth of surplus arms and equipment to the French Government.[15]

A very lonely Ho was also Communist Ho was therefore realist Ho. Having taken two steps forward, he took one step backward. In November, he dissolved the Indochina Communist Party, thus emphasizing the Viet Minh's nationalist character. He also began sending diplomatic flowers to the new French high commissioner, Admiral Thierry d'Argenlieu, a personal friend of De Gaulle—a part-time Carmelite monk who was so reactionary that a member of his staff described him as having ". . . the most brilliant mind of the twelfth century."[16] Ensuing negotiations can best be described as imperative diplomacy: Each side loathed the other, yet the state of confusion demanded some solution.

The Chinese presence posed the first problem. D'Argenlieu and his new deputy, Major Jean Sainteny, a hero of the French resistance and later De Gaulle's head of mission in Kunming, rid Vietnam of the Chinese incubus by renouncing French "special rights" in China as well as giving Chiang special railway and port rights in Tonkin.

With China out of the way, Sainteny hammered out an agreement with Ho Chi Minh, signed in early March 1946. Wanting to split Vietnam, France recognized the DRV as ". . . a free state, having its own government, parliament, army, and treasury, belonging to the Indo-Chinese Federation and to the French Union."[17] In return, Ho allowed fifteen thousand French troops to replace the Chinese garrison. The French were to train and equip the Viet Minh army, which would replace French occupation troops at a rate of three thousand per year for five years. French negotiators also agreed to hold a referendum to determine whether Cochin China ". . . should be reunified with Annam and Tonkin."[18] In mid-March, the first French troops arrived in Hanoi to commence what might have proved a workable solution to the Vietnam problem.

But a viable contract depends a great deal on the spirit of contracting parties. D'Argenlieu had been in Paris during the negotiations:

. . . after his return from Paris, d'Argenlieu openly criticized the moderate policy of Sainteny and Leclerc by expressing his amazement over the agreement of March 6. "Yes," he said, "that is the word, my amazement that France has such a fine expeditionary corps in Indochina and yet its leaders prefer to negotiate rather than to fight."[19]

Ho Chi Minh also had difficulty in persuading what he called "extremists" to accept the arrangement, which, he argued, was a necessary step

15. Shaplen, op. cit.
16. Bernard B. Fall, *The Two Viet-Nams—A Political and Military Analysis* (New York: Frederick A. Praeger, 1967).
17. Lancaster, op. cit.; Hammer, op. cit.
18. Kahin and Lewis, op. cit.; see also Lancaster, op. cit.; Buttinger, op. cit.
19. Buttinger, op. cit.

toward full independence. As a realist willing to compromise, Ho regarded the accords as an interim agreement, a temporary truce to be broken when he was strong enough to enforce a demand for unity and independence of all Vietnam. But Ho faced serious party opposition: Bellicose voices demanded immediate action, just as, in the South, D'Argenlieu was demanding French control of Indochina.[20]

D'Argenlieu was already feeling quite secure in Saigon. In late February 1946, General Leclerc proclaimed ". . . the total reestablishment of peace and order" throughout Cochin China and southern Annam.[21] He did not add that, by early March, French losses amounted to twelve hundred killed and thirty-five hundred wounded,[22] which demonstrated significant Viet Minh opposition despite the factious alliance of the Viet Minh with the Cao Dai and Hoa Hao sects. But if Leclerc exaggerated, he could at least point to French columns busily "pacifying" the countryside and to a force pushing into Laos. Saigon also had quieted: Although metal grill cages protected the better outdoor restaurants from grenade-throwing terrorists—the American correspondent Robert Shaplen noted that, in mid-1946, murders averaged fifteen per night! —the Viet Minh seemed increasingly subdued, the colony well on its way to prewar languor. Probably for this reason, the French delegation at the Dalat conference in mid-April proved particularly truculent regarding Vietnamese autonomy.

Scarcely had Ho and other Viet Minh political leaders, Communist and nationalist, sailed for France to work out a final agreement with the home government, when D'Argenlieu, under pressure from conservative colonialists and without authority from Paris, recognized the free state of Cochin China and its puppet president, Nguyen Van Tinh (who later committed suicide and was replaced with another French choice, Le Van Hoach). This marked the beginning of a major rift. Donald Lancaster, a British expert on Vietnam, later wrote:

. . . in spite of some local hostility towards the Tongkinese the population, who were conscious of their ethnic identity with the inhabitants of North and Central Vietnam, for the most part refused to support a movement considered to represent a French maneuver designed to split the nation in its struggle for independence.[23]

At the same time, D'Argenlieu ordered the army to occupy the Moi Plateaux, in the southern Annam central highlands, a provocative act that drew immediate protests from Hanoi.[24]

D'Argenlieu's unilateral act, reminiscent of the freewheeling Gallieni-

20. Ibid.; see also Hammer, op. cit. Each source offers a detailed analysis of the political situation.
21. Lancaster, op. cit.
22. Hammer, op. cit.
23. Lancaster, op. cit.
24. Ibid.; see also Hammer, op. cit.

Lyautey era of colonialism, contradicted the earlier agreement with the
Viet Minh and, taken with the French attitude displayed at Dalat, helped
torpedo the Paris talks. Since France had neither a government nor a
constitution at this time, these probably would not have resulted in
meaningful agreement on basic issues, but they could have laid the
groundwork for a later treaty.

But D'Argenlieu's action, which he compounded in August by calling
a federation conference without inviting the Viet Minh, led to a more
serious result. Ho's control of the Viet Minh was by no means assured
at this time. The Hanoi government, in some respects, resembled more
a coalition than a single-party Communist government, a fact acknowledged by Ho when, at the end of May, he created the Communist-
dominated Lien Viet Front. This did not fool all nationalist elements,
and such parties as the VNQDD and the Dong Minh Hoi continued to
control important northern provinces. After Ho's departure for France,
pro-Chinese elements of the Vietnam Nationalist Party and the Vietnam Revolutionary League began calling for direct action against the
French with such vigor that French forces temporarily allied with Viet
Minh forces to reclaim control of the Tonkin provinces and to chase
dissident leaders into exile in China. In Ho's absence, extremist Viet
Minh leaders, particularly the Minister of Interior, Vo Nguyen Giap,
opened war on other, non-Communist nationalists and on pro-French
Vietnamese. The net result was a greatly strengthened and unified Viet
Minh—the core of the larger Lien Viet, or Popular National, Front.[25]

Annoyed by French duplicity and possibly to dampen further criticism from Communist extremists, Ho became increasingly antagonistic
in negotiations with the French. Although, according to Jean Sainteny
and other observers, he seemed genuinely upset by continuing failure
of negotiations, he nonetheless remained a hard-core revolutionary who,
together with thirty of his comrades, had shared two hundred and
twenty-two years of imprisonment and exile, ". . . not to mention the
sentences to death in absentia and the years of imprisonment evaded by
those who escaped. . . ." Ho saw only a growth period ahead:

. . . Without the cold and desolation of winter
There could not be the warmth and splendour of spring.
Calamity has tempered and hardened me,
And turned my mind into steel.

A setback or two was acceptable:

. . . So life, you see, is never a very smooth business,
and now the present bristles with difficulties.

So now, at this crucial period, Ho Chi Minh realistically observed to
Sainteny, ". . . If we have to fight, we will fight. You will kill ten of our

25. Lancaster, op. cit.; see also Ellen J. Hammer, "Genesis of the First Indochina War: 1946–1950." In Gettleman, *supra*.

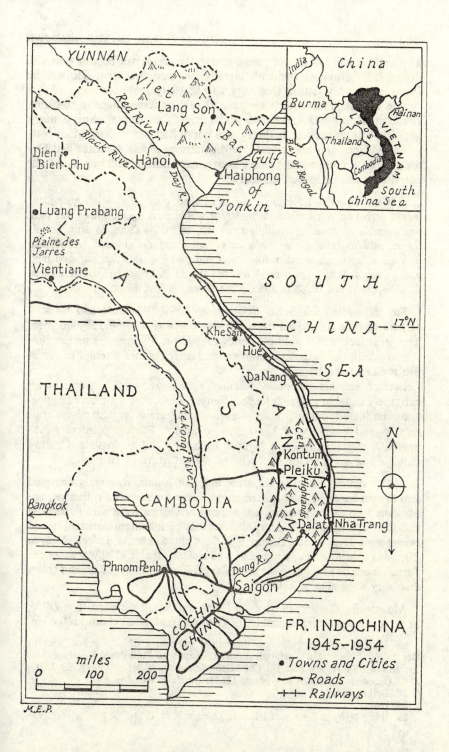

YÜNNAN

Viet
Lang Son

TONKIN Bac

Red River

Black River
Dien
Bien Phu
Hanoi
Day R.
Haiphong

Luang Prabang
Gulf
of
Tonkin

Plaine des
Jarres
Vientiane

L A O S

SOUTH

Khe San
17°N
Hué
CHINA

Da Nang
SEA

THAILAND

Mekong River

cen.

Kontum
N
Pleiku

Highlands

CAMBODIA
A
N
N
A
M

Dalat
Nha Trang

Bangkok

Phnom Penh

Dung R.
Saigon

COCHIN

CHINA

N

FR. INDOCHINA
1945-1954
• Towns and Cities
— Roads
+++ Railways

miles
0   100   200

Inset map:

India
China

Burma
Laos
Hainan

Thailand
VIETNAM

Bay
of
Bengal
Cambodia

South
China Sea

M.E.P.

682   WAR IN THE SHADOWS

men and we will kill one of yours, and in the end it will be you who will tire of it."[26] Shooting incidents already had occurred when Ho was in France; upon his return, they began to multiply.

The French, moreover, were consistently underreading the southern situation. Despite D'Argenlieu's and Leclerc's early optimism, a nasty guerrilla war continued. If the French controlled towns, Viet Minh controlled villages and countryside, particularly at night. A writer and historian who accompanied Leclerc's early expeditions, Philippe Devillers, pinpointed the main tactical result:

. . . If we departed, believing a region pacified, they [Viet Minh guerrillas] would arrive on our heels and the terror would start again. There was only one possible defense: to multiply the posts, to fortify them, to arm the villagers, and to train them for a coordinated and enlightened self-defense through a thorough job of information and policing. But this required men and weapons. What was needed was not the 35,000 men (of which Leclerc then disposed) but 100,000, and Cochin-China was not the only problem.[27]

Far more than additional troops were needed: Leclerc and his successors in time fielded an expeditionary corps exceeding 150,000 men. The great lack was a political policy to give the Vietnamese people reason to accept the Saigon government and deny Hanoi's attempt to establish a Communist regime.

Leclerc and his successor, Étienne Valluy, were fighting against an extremely capable guerrilla leader, Nguyen Binh, ". . . a man of apparently unlimited energy, bold decisions and great organizational talents"[28]—and a man who knew how to exploit French political weaknesses. A master of ambush, Nguyen Binh soon had his frustrated enemy indulging in mass terror methods including torture of suspects:

. . . The victims, often as not, were innocent people, frequently delivered into French hands by false denunciations. These tortures, and collective punishments such as the pillaging and burning of villages from which guerrillas had fired and disappeared, turned thousands of lukewarm nationalists and even people loyal to the French into their bitter enemies. Indeed, Nguyen Binh was able to excel as organizer and military leader chiefly because the French methods of fighting the guerrillas made many more Vietminh fighters than they were able to kill.[29]

Meanwhile, the breach between North and South widened. The DRV, at its second national assembly, in October, reasserted claim to Tonkin,

26. Shaplen, op. cit.; Ho wrote these lines when in a Chinese prison; see Ho Chi Minh, *Prison Diary* (Hanoi: Foreign Languages Publishing House, 1962). Tr. Aileen Palmer; see also Ho Chi Minh, *Selected Articles and Speeches 1920–1967* (London: Lawrence & Wishart, 1969). Ed. Jack Woddis.
27. Buttinger, op. cit.
28. Ibid.
29. Ibid.; Nguyen Binh was killed in Cambodia in 1951.

Annam, and Cochin China—that is, to all of Vietnam—and its new constitution significantly did not mention membership in either the Indochina Federation or the French Union.[30] Also significantly, Ho's new
cabinet contained five instead of the former two Communist seats.[31]
Political assassinations continued as the Viet Minh tightened its internal
organization: ". . . To be a young and vigorous revolutionary with an
independent political mind was more dangerous in 1946 than being a
'reactionary' had been in August, 1945. . . ."[32]

Just when either side decided to seek a military solution to the impasse is problematical. Such was the rampant mistrust and hatred that
a war probably was never far removed from either French or Vietnamese
minds. In his pioneering work *Street Without Joy,* Bernard Fall wrote
of this period:

. . . The French forces sent to Indochina were too strong for France to
resist the temptation of using them; yet not strong enough to keep the Viet-
Minh from trying to solve the whole political problem by throwing the
French into the sea.

The outbreak of the Indochina war can be traced back to that single,
tragic erroneous estimate. . . .[33]

That momentous autumn saw military forces of both sides acting with
an unhealthy arrogance that heightened tension everywhere. The explosion did not instantly occur. It began with a skirmish between French
soldiers and Viet Minh militia in Haiphong. It continued with stupid
and isolated attacks by the Viet Minh that killed twenty-three French
soldiers in Haiphong and six more in Lang Son. French military authorities now decided to teach the Viet Minh a "hard lesson." French raids
in Haiphong sent a civilian mob streaming from the town toward the
French air base at Cat Bi. The captain of a French cruiser mistakenly
believed that this mob intended to attack the air base. He opened fire and
killed about six thousand unarmed civilians.[34]

Although the tragedy brought an uneasy truce, Ho, prompted by Giap
and other militants, not to mention the belligerent French attitude, decided that the time had come for war. Faced with a French demand to
surrender their forces in Hanoi, on December 19 the Viet Minh attacked
French garrisons in Hanoi and elsewhere in Vietnam. The Indochina
war had begun.[35]

30. Hammer, *The Struggle for Indochina 1940–1955, supra.*
31. Buttinger, op. cit.
32. Ibid.
33. Bernard Fall, *Street Without Joy* (Harrisburg, Pa.: Stackpole, 1961).
34. Schoenbrun, op. cit.: offers 8,000 as the French figure, with unofficial estimates running as high as 40,000; see also Buttinger, op. cit.; Lancaster, op. cit.
35. Buttinger, op. cit., argues convincingly that the war began in September
1945.

Chapter 53

Viet Minh strength • French counterinsurgency tactics • French errors • Operation Léa • The political problem • General Revers's secret report • Vietnamese nationalism • Bao Dai's provisional government • The American position • Indochina's international importance • Truman's confusion • The French attitude • The Élysée Agreements • Acheson's dilemma (I) • The lines form

IN DECEMBER 1946, the Viet Minh army numbered about sixty thousand, of whom forty thousand possessed rifles.[1] Paramilitary and militia formations, such as the youth-oriented Tu Ve, numbered perhaps another forty thousand.[2] Although this force had received some training from Japanese and Chinese instructors, it was not an orthodox army capable of launching and sustaining co-ordinated offensives against units equipped with artillery and armor and supported by aircraft. Within a few weeks, French units had beaten off the various attacks and forced Viet Minh units to disperse. Ho and the main body almost immediately went into hiding in their old stamping grounds, the ideally defensive Viet Bac region, in upper Tonkin.

The French high command did not seem unduly disturbed by Viet

1. George K. Tanham, *Communist Revolutionary Warfare—From the Vietminh to the Viet Cong* (rev. ed.) (New York: Frederick A. Praeger, 1967).

2. Buttinger, op. cit.; see also John J. McCuen, *The Art of Counter-Revolutionary War* (London: Faber & Faber, 1966).

Minh attacks. More likely, they were relieved that the political game was over: The military could now clarify the situation in the best colonial tradition.[3] This meant occupying and defending important cities and towns and protecting lines of communication by a series of strong points. Local commanders began the arduous task of dividing assigned areas into small operational squares (the *quadrillage*) and trying to clear each of insurgents (the *ratissage*). To do this, unit commanders were to establish small operational bases in the disputed areas and commence *tourbillon,* or whirlwind-type, tactics essential to what Colonel McCuen has called "the territorial offense":

. . . that is, the detachments should keep constantly on the move within their assigned zones, attacking, ambushing, patrolling, searching, establishing an intelligence system, and, perhaps most important, contacting and assisting the people. . . .[4]

This was basically Marshal Lyautey's famous *tache-d'huile,* or oilspot, technique. Civil forces followed the military to clean out the insurgent apparatus and establish or re-establish civil government. Once military and civil forces had fashioned a secure strategic base, the military again moved out to repeat the process.

As we have pointed out (Chapter 17, Volume I), the tache d'huile is essentially a qualitative approach to the pacification problem. It was necessitated by limited forces operating in vast areas inhabited and defended by heterogeneous tribes. Not least of the reasons for its success were the social, political, and economic attractions offered by the pacified areas to primitive and insurgent tribesmen. In this sense, the tache d'huile was expansion by osmosis. It did not always work, but most of the time it did. At all times, it called for extreme patience and forbearance on the part of colonizers. On occasion, strong and homogenous tribes occupying naturally defensive terrain spelled a halt to the tache-d'huile process. Lyautey generally preferred to leave these "asleep" areas alone. If an enemy became too annoying and if his own strength justified it, he permitted raids in strength—the traditional *bouclage,* or "sealing-off," operation, which attempted to surround and destroy the enemy force. But he infinitely preferred to convert neighboring areas to his support so as to isolate the difficult areas, which then ". . . will fall into our hands by themselves. . . ."

3. Lancaster, op. cit.: Even the pacific Minister for French Overseas Territories, M. Moutet, agreed: ". . . Before a resumption of negotiations can be envisaged, a military decision is necessary. I regret the necessity, but you cannot commit with impunity acts of madness, such as those committed by the Viet Minh"; but see also Hammer (*Struggle*), *supra:* General Leclerc, who left Indochina in spring of 1946 and returned later that year as an official observer, warned his government against trying to seek a military solution to what he believed had become essentially a political problem.
4. McCuen, op. cit.

In 1946 and 1947, General Valluy, from a purely military standpoint, was on the right track in his use of the tache-d'huile technique. But he and his staff erred on several important points. First, they underrated both political and military strength of the Viet Minh, which meant that they moved too fast. Prompted by the colonial government and *colons,* they tried to do too much too soon. Neither military forces nor civil administration that followed won control of target areas. Instead, the French flag flew over main cities and towns, and roads remained open at least in daylight—but Viet Minh continued to control the countryside.

Considering the lack of political appeal, the limited numbers of French soldiers, heterogeneous French forces with concomitant internal conflicts and resentments, and the political organization of the Viet Minh, Valluy would have had his hands full in consolidating a strategic base in Cochin China alone. The situation called for a much slower and more methodical approach than ever Lyautey faced. Yet Valluy not only attempted to develop strategic bases in Cochin China, Annam, and Tonkin, but, in the fall of 1947, he decided on an all-out attack—the *bouclage*—against Ho and the main body of insurgents holed up in the naturally defensive Viet Bac region northwest of Hanoi.

Operation Léa began in October 1947. Involving fifteen thousand troops, or over a third of the total French force, it attempted to "seal off" an immense triangle of jungle and mountains in Tonkin.[5] French commanders spoke excitedly of "encirclement"—just as German commanders had spoken in the Soviet Union and Yugoslavia in World War II. Operation Léa fared no better than any of the German offensives designed to capture Tito: close, but no cigar. Although the French claimed eight thousand enemy dead and the capture of thousands of arms and tons of ammunition and equipment, the effort failed to capture Ho and his lieutenants or even to disperse for very long the Viet Minh command. By year's end, the French main force had returned to the lowlands, having established a string of vulnerable border outposts and forts more appropriate to Gallieni's 1884–85 strategy against insurgents and pirates than to a 1947 campaign against Viet Minh guerrillas.[6]

This combination of area pacification and sporadic attacks continued throughout 1948 and into 1949. Without a political impetus, it was doomed to fail. The French answer to the political problem—the dusting off of Emperor Bao Dai—would have become a meaningful weapon only if Paris had been serious about granting Vietnam independence and only if Bao Dai's followers had been capable of legitimate government. As it was, the political and military solutions formed a losing combination. The home government, faced with financial crises and veering dangerously toward Communist control, refused more than lukewarm support to the military campaign. Nonetheless, parties of the left did not join in

5. Fall, op. cit.
6. Ibid.; see also Buttinger, op. cit. (Vol. 2).

seeking a political solution to the Indochina problem, and influence of right and center parties remained strong: over half of the French military budget was being spent in Indochina.[7] Although the expeditionary force, which numbered around 150,000 including some Vietnamese troops, claimed to control much of Cochin China and the Tonkin Delta area, this control often proved illusory.

Despite optimistic reports from Saigon, the French Government grew increasingly worried about Chinese Communist victories and their effect on Indochina. In May 1949, the government sent out General Revers, Chief of the General Staff:

. . . In a secret report [soon obtained by the Viet Minh], he recommended the evacuation of the isolated garrisons along the Chinese border, which, lying in the midst of Vietminh country and being difficult to supply, were a drain on French resources and could probably not withstand a serious attack. General Revers, one of the first prominent Frenchmen to urge the rapid build-up of the Vietnamese Army, also insisted that before another offensive against the Viet Bac [Ho's stronghold] could be undertaken, the [Red River] delta had first to be completely pacified and its defense turned over to the Vietnamese Army. Not only did he recognize that without a strong Vietnamese Army to support the French, victory over the Vietminh would be difficult to achieve, but he also knew something about the political conditions that would make such an army effective. In this war, he said, "diplomacy" must have precedence over military considerations.[8]

French civil and military officials refused to admit the political elements at work. Yet the French army was facing a political movement undreamed of either by Gallieni or Lyautey, a nationalist movement that helped Ho to insinuate agents and cells throughout so-called controlled or pacified areas. This movement continued to grow while French strength and influence stood still and even declined. As Bernard Fall later wrote, only too few of the French

. . . recognized the fact that the Viet-Minh enjoyed exactly the same advantages with regard to the French as the French had enjoyed with regard to the Wehrmacht. By the time that recognition dawned and corrective measures were attempted, the situation had deteriorated beyond salvaging.[9]

The French high command failed to understand new and revolutionary political forces at work. No isolated failure this—as will shortly be

7. Buttinger, op. cit., offers a penetrating analysis of the relationship between the home parties and the colonial party.

8. Ibid.: ". . . His [Revers's] recommendations shared the fate of most later ones—being misunderstood or disregarded. In any case, they had no influence on either the military or political conduct of the war . . ."; see also Lancaster, op. cit., for a description of the ensuing government scandal.

9. Fall (*The Two Viet-Nams*), *supra*.

seen, the Dutch similarly erred in Indonesia, the British in Malaya, the Americans in Greece, the Soviets in Yugoslavia.

But nonetheless costly.

Had the French respected the Indochinese political climate of 1947, they possibly could have avoided a lengthy and ruinous war. The average Vietnamese peasant did not care about communism. He wanted *doc-lap*—a national independence—which he supposed would bring him and his family a better life (it could not bring a worse one). Japanese conquest and occupation of Southeast Asia had shattered the myth of white supremacy. The peasant may have known little about political forms and parties or even what the future was to hold under Vietnamese rule—but he wanted that rule, or, rather, he wanted an end to French rule. As Robert Shaplen noted in his masterful book *The Lost Revolution,*

. . . a revolutionary condition existed in Indo-China all along, one that should have been regarded from the start by the Western nations for what it was, a truly Asian revolution, representing the legitimate hopes of people throughout the region to be free of any domination, either that of their former colonial masters, of old or new native tyrants or satraps, or that of the Communists. Unfortunately, while the Communists were quick to take advantage of the revolutionary opportunities in Indo-China, the Western nations, especially France, did not face up to the realities of the situation.[10]

In March and April 1947, the French replied with studied coolness and but slight encouragement to Ho Chi Minh's expressed desire for a cease-fire and a political settlement. Nor did French policy encourage overtures by sophisticated Vietnamese who remained aware of the Communist threat to Vietnam's future. In May 1947, a group of moderate nationalists in Saigon established a National Union Front in support of the former emperor, Bao Dai, and attempted to come to political terms with the French. Such an arrangement would have spelled eventual Vietnam independence, and the French refused to consider it.

In September 1947, the new French high commissioner, Émile Bollaert, a veteran Radical Socialist who favored an independence policy more generous than his country would permit, was able to offer only ". . . liberty within the French Union," without a satisfactory definition of his terms.[11] In 1948, the French rejected a proposal by the nationalist Ngo Dinh Diem for dominion status of the country; instead, a Provisional Central Government of Vietnam emerged along with the concept ". . . of associated statehood within the French Union for each of the three states of Indo-China."[12]

By the time Bao Dai agreed to lead a Vietnamese Government— June 1949—most important nationalist leaders either had gone into exile

10. Shaplen, op. cit.
11. Hammer, op. cit.; see also Buttinger, op. cit.
12. Hammer, op. cit.

or joined Ho's camp in the North; others, such as Diem, who headed the powerful Catholic League, refused to serve on grounds that France had no intention of ever granting Vietnamese independence. On the other hand, whole hosts of nationalists, the *attentistes,* were sitting on the fence, refusing to commit themselves until one government or the other showed itself the probable victor. Continued French refusal to offer substantive terms to Bao Dai's provisional government angered Diem, who refused to serve the emperor as prime minister.

The important point to realize is that the *basic* French mistake was *political.* As one expert on Vietnam, Dr. George Tanham, wrote in his pioneering work *Communist Revolutionary Warfare:*

. . . To have underrated the force of nationalist feelings and to have disregarded all opportunities for genuine compromise may be called the basic French mistakes in Indo-China. Failing to realize in time the crucial importance of popular support in this type of war, they remained oblivious to the fact that their disregard of popular will helped their enemy to consolidate forces and led thus to the inevitable success of the Viet-Minh.[13]

Dr. Tanham did not comment on American complicity in the French failure, an important omission in view of subsequent events.

The reader will perhaps recall (see Chapter 45, Volume I) that President Roosevelt held positive feelings about the future of Indochina. At the time of his death, in April 1945, he was thinking in terms of an interim trusteeship leading to independence, a notion tentatively approved by Chiang Kai-shek and Stalin, but one that had drawn Churchill's disapproval at Yalta.

Roosevelt died without resolving the issue. At the Potsdam conference, in July 1945, the Big Three briefly revived it and agreed to an interim arrangement of British-Chinese military occupation. After Japan's surrender, this eventually gave way to the French return, which was scarcely surprising within the day's political context. And within that context, it is also difficult to see how the United States, beset with a host of other problems, could have prevented the French presence.

It was not even much of an issue.

The sad truth was the minimal importance of an artificial political entity called French Indochina (Laos, Cambodia, and Vietnam) in world affairs. Geographically, economically, and politically, the area was a cipher. This unpleasant fact was somewhat camouflaged by Japan's initial use of the country as a staging area—a strategic convenience in the days of short-range aircraft, but even then not a strategic necessity. Substantial French-Vietnamese resistance might have further camouflaged the fact, but as was the case with Lettow-Vorbeck's resistance in German East Africa in World War I, this would have provided more

13. Tanham, op. cit.

psychological than material value. It would not have altered war's course. Tactically and strategically, Indochina was less than a sideshow; it was a military neutrino—a whirling nothing. American interest in the area was as negative as American knowledge of the area. A senior Vietnamese diplomat recently told the writer the following: When General George C. Marshall was in Chungking in 1946, he spent an evening with a group of young Vietnamese nationalists and at one point remarked, ". . . Viet-Nam must be a very interesting country. Tell me, do you have your own language?"

In the hurly-burly of events accompanying the end of the war, Indochina grew from a nothing area to a nuisance area, a threat to allied and particularly American-French relationships. Truman apparently did not share Roosevelt's desire to exclude France from the area. In a meeting with De Gaulle in August 1945, he decorated the French leader, presented him with a new DC-4 airplane, and emphasized, ". . . my government is not opposed to the return of the French Army and French authority in Indochina."[14]

By not attempting to prevent the French return, indeed by seeming to support a renewed French presence, the American President found himself dangerously at odds with his purported belief in the principles of the Atlantic Charter. Here was a real dilemma—the frequent result when political idealism collides with political reality. Dexterous diplomacy probably could have resolved it, but unfortunately a number of factors inhibited the practice of dexterous diplomacy in this crucial period.

The first was turbulence within the Department of State itself, an orchestra of feuds and cabals cacophonously conducted first by old Cordell Hull, then by globe-trotting James Byrnes. Small at war's beginning and limited in imaginative policy by the isolation years, the department had swelled inexorably and often with as much purpose as a blowfish out of water. Concurrently, the American military had frequently pre-empted the State Department's traditional authority in the conduct of foreign affairs—an ugly habit continued into postwar years. Postwar confusion, which often gave rise to divided counsels, helped prevent the department from reasserting its authority, a state of affairs well described in two important books, George Kennan's *Memoirs* and Dean Acheson's *Present at the Creation*.[15] Finally, heavy demands on existing talent, both individual and organizational, meant stringent rationing, which resulted in slim diplomatic pickings for Indochina as well as many other areas.

International turbulence played a major role. From the moment Presi-

14. Charles de Gaulle, *War Memoirs* (Vol. 3—*Documents*) (London: Collins, 1955). Tr. R. Howar.
15. George F. Kennan, *Memoirs 1925–1950* (London: Hutchinson, 1968) Vol. 1; Dean Acheson, *Present at the Creation* (New York: Norton, 1969); see also W. W. Rostow, *The United States in the World Arena* (New York: Harper & Brothers, 1960).

CHAPTER 53   691

dent Truman assumed office, in spring of 1945, he faced far more urgent
challenges that, shortly after war's end, began turning to crises. As these
grew in importance and complexity, Vietnam remained a low-priority
area. By the time Ho Chi Minh attacked French garrisons, in December 1946, Stalin already had made clear his intentions to go about as far
as he could in Europe and the Middle East. Here the United States
and the West attempted to stop him. The Truman Doctrine, announced
in March 1947, flashed the first red light. George Kennan's realistic
statement of need for new principles of selected containment—the famous X article published in the July 1947 *Foreign Affairs*—called for
the political containment of Soviet power: ". . . a long-term, patient
but firm and vigilant containment of Russian expansive tendencies." The
U.S.A. and her allies were to establish red lights where necessary—
". . . the adroit and vigilant application of counterforce at a series of
constantly shifting geographical and political points."[16] Although Kennan was thinking primarily in political terms, the principles when applied
necessarily involved military action, and, during the next three years, the
deterrents differed considerably: the Truman Doctrine, the Marshall
Plan, the Berlin airlift, the North Atlantic Treaty Organization. Crumbs
from this table, both of effort and of money, fell to the other side of
the world, to China and the Philippines and Indochina; although they
sometimes were big crumbs, relatively speaking they were still crumbs.

These two factors helped to explain a third: the Franco-American
relationship in Indochina itself. No question existed in the mind of the
French Government—when there was one—as to the legality of the
French presence. Although De Gaulle had attempted to appease
Roosevelt at the Brazzaville conference on the subject of eventual self-
government for Indochina, his confreres scarcely shared his sentiments:

. . . The preamble of the political recommendations laid down that "the
aims of the work of civilization which France is accomplishing in her possessions exclude any idea of autonomy and any possibility of development
outside the French Empire bloc. The attainment of 'self-government' in the
colonies, even in the most distant future, must be excluded."[17]

Although the French Provisional Government, in March 1945, re-
examined the question and seemed to offer Indochina a liberal postwar rule, the French relinquished but slight control. Hers was the legal
government in Indochina, and she was in no mind to yield her hold in

16. "X" (George F. Kennan), "The Sources of Soviet Conduct," *Foreign Affairs,* July, 1947: This penetrating article was variously interpreted, as the author
makes clear in his *Memoirs, supra;* see also Walter Lippmann, *The Cold War—
A Study in U.S. Foreign Policy* (New York: Harper & Brothers, 1947); see also
Richard Leopold, *The Growth of American Policy* (New York: Alfred A. Knopf,
1965).
17. Lancaster, op. cit.

order to conform to the quaint American notion of self-determination
and eventual independence. Since her conquest of Indochina, she had
practiced a policy of "association," whereby she would continue to rule
the area as a colony, a policy opposed to that of "assimilation," which
ultimately could have yielded Vietnamese independence.[18]

Nor did the United States see fit to force the issue. As a traditional
ally of France, she had felt a genuine sympathy for France's defeat in
World War II and for the horrors of German occupation and loathsome
Vichy government. The U.S.A. also realized that the French return to
Indochina was in part a matter of *amour propre* and that to have contested it would have led to an ugly quarrel with a power whose co-
operation was essential to a stable Europe.[19] Moreover, the French
seemed to be working out a viable federation agreement with the Viet
Minh. By the time this effort failed and shooting started in earnest, the
international situation had changed to such a degree that the French
presence, far from proving embarrassing, was beginning to appeal to a
United States hard-pressed to provide economic and particularly military resources necessary to fight a world-wide cold war.

Later critics have suggested that French, and by implication American, diplomacy erred in not attempting to convert Ho Chi Minh into
an Asiatic Tito. A considerable number of facts have been adduced to
support the possibility. But several conditions would have had to exist
for even a trial run. The first was an imaginative French high commissioner working with a viable home government within the framework
of a liberal colonial policy. France possessed none of these. That the
idea did not occur to American officials is not surprising. In Western
eyes, this was the day of monolithic communism, this the day when some
outstanding intellects, driven by fatigue and fear into near panic, envisaged communism as a poisonous black cloud of no molecular structure quite capable of covering the sun of civilization. Although Tito's
defection and subsequent expulsion from Cominform, in June 1948,
suggested a cloud of factious elements, the worsening China situation
tended to obscure this significant development. In 1948, the West was
too far gone in worry for immediate reappraisal that could have led to
a qualitative rather than quantitative policy in combating the threat by
exploiting its essential weakness.

Pride also entered: the French had lost one war before it really
started; they were not going to lose another, and certainly not to a bunch

18. Dennis J. Duncanson, *Government and Revolution in Vietnam* (London:
Oxford University Press, 1968); see also De Gaulle (Vol. 3—*Documents*), *supra*,
for the complete French declaration made at the March 1945 conference.

19. Unfortunately, overburdened and, in some cases, frightened American policy
makers failed to realize that France needed American aid more than the United
States needed French co-operation. France would not have jeopardized her own
future position in Europe for the sake of her Indochina holding, particularly since
popular French sentiment did not support a costly colonial policy.

of peasants some of whom were not even armed. Fear formed still another factor. As Kahin and Lewis have written,

. . . the French saw Vietnam in terms of their empire as a whole, particularly with relation to their North African territories. They were apprehensive that if the Vietnamese were successful in wresting their independence from France, the already-restive nationalists in Algeria, Morocco, and Tunisia would be inspired to follow their example.[20]

Finally, and very important: In these formative and crucial years, the French army believed, as did American observers, that it was well on the way to defeating the Viet Minh. Few Frenchmen agreed with General Leclerc, who warned, ". . . in 1947 France will no longer put down by force a grouping of 24 million inhabitants which is assuming unity and in which there exists a xenophobic and perhaps a national ideal. . . . The major problem from now on is political."[21] In May 1947, the French Minister of War, M. Paul Coste-Floret, pointed to French control of ". . . most of the important cities and towns of northern and central Viet-Nam . . . [and] of virtually all strategic highways and waterways and of the area along the Chinese border." He concluded: ". . . There is no military problem any longer in Indo-China. The success of French arms is complete."[22]

Even after the failure of Operation Léa, in late 1947, and increasing evidence that the Viet Minh controlled a large part of the countryside, the French administration in Indochina and particularly the French military command (with some worthy exceptions) refused to reverse Coste-Floret's comforting conclusion.

Perhaps French commanders would have admitted some concern had the Viet Minh fielded its own army. Lacking direct confrontation, Valluy and his successors spoke in terms of "mopping-up" operations. They failed to realize either that the Viet Minh were building a regular army behind a screen of guerrilla operations, or that the Viet Minh were simultaneously mobilizing large parts of the population to fight a war beyond limits of their comprehension.

Continuing military stalemate and some setbacks in 1948 prompted President Vincent Auriol's government in Paris to re-examine the political question. Coupled with the deteriorating position of the Nationalist Chinese, this led to the Élysée Agreements, of March 1949, which formally created the Bao Dai government and made Vietnam an "associated state," along with Cambodia and Laos, in the French Union. The

20. Kahin and Lewis, op. cit.
21. Buttinger, op. cit.: General Leclerc refused the post of commander-in-chief and high commissioner primarily for this reason but, shades of William Tecumseh Sherman (see Chapter 11, Volume I), also because the government would not give him 500,000 troops to fight the Vietnam war.
22. Shaplen, op. cit.; see also Frank Trager, *Why Viet Nam?* (New York: Frederick A. Praeger, 1966); Buttinger, op. cit.

agreements also authorized for Vietnam ". . . its own army for internal security," a role ". . . in foreign and defense policies, and a [national] bank of issue."[23]

Had France been sincere, the agreements might have led to satisfactory political compromise with the Viet Minh. Unfortunately France relinquished precious little control over Vietnamese affairs with the agreements, which the National Assembly did not even ratify until February 1950. The net result of deed versus intent was a political sugar castle bound to deteriorate in fortune's rain. Kahin and Lewis have spelled out the unhappy result:

. . . So many of the substantive attributes of power were reserved to France that even on paper the new State of Vietnam was effectively and directly under French dominion. And, in fact, most of the very modest concessions granted under the agreements were never actually transferred to Bao Dai's "government," which continued to lack the attributes of independence necessary to attract nationalist support. Bao Dai emerged from the long process of negotiations with no increase in political prestige among the nationalist elements in Vietnam. Obviously dependent on France, his regime remained an unconvincing façade for a continuing French military and civil control that allowed few significant roles for Vietnamese. The only conclusion Vietnamese patriots could reach was that France, with Bao Dai as its agent, continued to run that part of the country not under the Vietminh. The effective range of political alternatives for these patriots remained quite as narrow as before—the Vietminh or the French—and this polarization grew more pronounced as the French now regularly labeled all those who resisted them or opposed Bao Dai as "communist." For more and more Vietnamese that word came to connote something good—a badge of honor, representing patriotic nationalism and courageous opposition to French rule. Thus did French intransigence in Vietnam further strengthen the ties between nationalism and communism there—a circumstance unique in southeast Asia.[24]

The Élysée Agreements also provoked international moves that widened the breach between East and West and made a political settlement even more remote. During negotiations, the Soviet Union and Communist China recognized Ho Chi Minh's DRV. A week after signing, Britain, the United States, and twenty-eight other governments recognized the three Associated States, but whereas Britain urged France to give greater independence to the new countries, the United States adopted a much more moderate attitude.

Privately, the Department of State feared a Viet Minh victory, as Secretary of State Acheson later wrote, ". . . unless France swiftly transferred authority to the Associated States and organized, trained, and equipped, with our aid, substantial indigenous forces to take over the

23. Acheson, op. cit.; see also Buttinger, op. cit.; Lancaster, op. cit.
24. Kahin and Lewis, op. cit.

main burden of the fight."[25] Unfortunately, neither Mr. Acheson nor his officials sufficiently stressed this opinion to the French Government, an omission only recently explained by the former secretary himself:

. . . Both during this period and after it our conduct was criticized as being a muddled hodgepodge, directed neither toward edging the French out of an effort to re-establish their colonial role, which was beyond their power, nor helping them hard enough to accomplish it or, even better, to defeat Ho and gracefully withdraw. The description is accurate enough. The criticism, however, fails to recognize the limits on the extent to which one may successfully coerce an ally. Withholding help and exhorting the ally or its opponent can be effective only when the ally can do nothing without help, as was the case in Indonesia. Furthermore, the result of withholding help to France would, at most, have removed the colonial power. It could not have made the resulting situation a beneficial one either for Indochina or for southeast Asia, or in the more important effort of furthering the stability and defense of Europe. So while we may have tried to muddle through and were certainly not successful, I could not think then or later of a better course. . . .[26]

The principal difficulty had appeared earlier: the conflict between American policy in Europe and the situation in Indochina. The problem already had become acute in American intervention in the Dutch-Indonesian wars. In January 1949, Walter Lippmann had astutely spelled it out in the New York *Herald Tribune*:

. . . Our friends in Western Europe should try to understand why we cannot and must not be maneuvered, why we dare not drift, into general opposition to the independence movements in Asia. They should tell their propagandists to stop smearing these movements. They should try to realize how disastrous it would be to them, and to the cause of Western civilization, if ever it could be said that the Western Union for the defense of freedom in Europe was in Asia a syndicate for the preservation of decadent empires.[27]

Unfortunately, the Western Union was leaning toward precisely that. The North Atlantic Treaty, signed in April 1949, had made France the most important member of new Europe. The Truman administration believed that the treaty, if it was to serve Western, including American, strategic interests, had to expand into some kind of political-military organization, a growth dependent in part on French co-operation.

Other events meanwhile were adding to the importance of the Western alliance. Fighting continued in Greece; in 1948, Communist rebels had tripped off emergencies in nearby Malaya, Burma, and Indonesia; the Hukbalahap insurgency in the Philippines was gaining ground. In

25. Acheson, op. cit.
26. Ibid.
27. George M. Kahin, *Nationalism and Revolution in Indonesia* (Ithaca, N.Y.: Cornell University Press, 1952).

696 WAR IN THE SHADOWS

1949, Ho Chi Minh put the DRV squarely in the world Communist movement, removing any moderate government officials and replacing them with hard-line Communists. In September of that year, explosion of an atomic weapon by the Soviets ended the security engendered by American monopoly of the weapon. Fears raised by this development gained fantasies from Chiang Kai-shek's fall and subsequent flight to Formosa.

As one result, the French effort in Indochina changed form still further in American administration minds. No longer did it seem such an embarrassing little colonial war. In late 1949 and early 1950, the United States, encouraged by France, began to paint the war in ideological colors: it started to become part of the free world's effort against communism. The U.S.A. now promised limited military and economic aid. Although she insisted on supplying economic aid directly to the three states—Vietnam, Laos, and Cambodia—she perforce supplied military aid to the French overseers, Vietnam not having an army worthy of the name. The outbreak of the Korean war, in June 1950, hastened the process of the American Government's mental conversion. On June 27, 1950, President Truman informed a group of legislators of steps he had taken to counter the new aggression. He added:

. . . I have similarly directed acceleration in the furnishing of military assistance to the forces of France and the Associated States in Indo-China and the dispatch of a military mission to provide close working relations with those forces.[28]

The United States was now hooked to help France fight a war the exact nature of which neither country had yet identified.

28. Harry S Truman, *Years of Trial and Hope* (Garden City, N.Y.: Doubleday, 1955); see also Acheson, op. cit.

Chapter 54

Change in Viet Minh tactics • Vo Nguyen Giap • Mao Tse-tung's influence • Communist tactics in the South • Viet Minh military organization • The political base • Special Viet Minh units • Guerrilla tactics • French countertactics • Terror tactics • Enter Communist China • Viet Minh expansion

HO CHI MINH and his military leader, Vo Nguyen Giap, had, themselves, seriously erred by attacking French garrisons in December 1946. Forced into precipitate retreat, they narrowly avoided capture in 1947. This was the perigee of their fortunes, and they owed much of their salvation to a realistic appreciation and acceptance of their peculiar situation.

The two leaders were familiar with Mao Tse-tung's theory of protracted warfare, but apparently had hoped to avoid the guerrilla phase of fighting called for by Mao. Even before the Japanese surrender, they had taken steps to convert their guerrilla force into a regular army, and they seem to have expected a favorable outcome from the December attacks.

In the event, they soon found themselves on the defensive, struggling to preserve the main body of troops while keeping alive the flame of revolution in the South. In their simple mountain hide-out northwest of Hanoi, they vaguely resembled Mao and his lieutenants hiding in the

Chingkang Mountains in 1927. And like Mao and his lieutenants, they spent the time in considerable soul-searching, which brought a conversion to Mao-style warfare—partly through the influence of the party's secretary-general, Truong Chinh, who in 1947 published a Vietnamese version of Mao's theory of protracted warfare, *The Resistance Will Win*.[1] To what extent Ho Chi Minh favored this and to what extent his hand was forced by more-militant Communists, Giap included, has never been satisfactorily determined by Western observers.

Vo Nguyen Giap took the lead in military thinking at this time. Giap was thirty-five years old, a socialist turned Communist, veteran of French jails, history teacher turned soldier. In 1950, he published a book, *La guerre de la libération et l'armée populaire* (*The War of Liberation and the People's Army*), which, seventeen years later, Dr. Tanham still considered ". . . one of the fullest expressions of Viet-Minh doctrine."[2]

After admitting the 1946 errors, Giap argued in favor of a three-phase, Mao-style war. The first phase called for a strategic defense, a passive resistance to wear the enemy down while both regular and irregular Viet Minh units reorganized and built up strength. Giap wrote that this phase ended in 1947 in favor of the second phase, active resistance and preparation for the counteroffensive. The second phase, still underway in 1950, called for extensive guerrilla attacks as well as a continued propaganda-subversion effort. The final phase, Giap wrote, would consist of a general counteroffensive designed to defeat the French army.

Some Western authorities have argued that the Viet Minh entered the second phase considerably later than 1947. This is possible—Giap might have offered the 1947 date to try to lessen the Viet Minh debt to China, which did not start sending arms and supply until 1950. In view of the fluid situation, the exact date does not much matter. The war in the South proceeded at a slower pace and in a different fashion from that up North, and even in the North the final phase of what Mao Tse-tung called "mobile," or orthodox, warfare was to be carried out with massive injections of guerrilla tactics.

As we have noted, Tran Van Giau's Committee of the South was waging guerrilla warfare by late 1945. Although Communist-inspired, this was frequently a nationalist effort. A veteran of the old nationalist

1. Buttinger, op. cit.; see also Tanham, op. cit.; Fall (*The Two Viet-Nams*), *supra*; Melvin Gurtov, *The First Vietnam Crisis—Chinese Communist Strategy and United States Involvement 1953–1954* (New York: Columbia University Press, 1967).

2. Tanham, op. cit.; see also Fall (*The Two Viet-Nams*), *supra*, for a different viewpoint; Vo Nguyen Giap, *People's War, People's Army* (New York: Frederick A. Praeger, 1967). Although written primarily for internal consumption and thus heavily propagandistic, General Giap's work nonetheless provides a wealth of information on Viet Minh organization, strategy, and tactics.

party, the VNQDD, and a dangerous terrorist, explained his motivation to Robert Shaplen:

. . . You see, this is not just a matter of a sudden conspiracy. We are like a spring that has been sat upon for nearly a hundred years and now has been released. Acts of "terrorism" for us have become a part of war, although we do not approve of throwing grenades so that innocent people are hurt or killed. Nevertheless, the people of Indo-china, despite mistakes we may make, support us because they will not accept the return of the French. This is true of the young people and the old ones. Children of ten and twelve are even trusted by us as liaison agents. Women help in our Red Cross and troop kitchens. Men who are too old to fight, or too ill, can often help by spying, or just by raising rice on their farms.[3]

Ho Chi Minh and his comrades had rightly recognized the necessity of harnessing this inspired nationalist attitude to the Communist effort, not alienating it as Tran Van Giau was doing. Shaplen later wrote:

. . . At the time of the Dalat Conference [April 1946], the Vietminh government in Hanoi sent a top organizer named Nguyên Binh to Cochin China to coordinate the resistance movement in the south, and he succeeded, in a matter of months, in establishing general unity, although some discordant elements remained. At this time, according to estimates I was given in Saigon, the guerrillas in Cochin China had about twenty thousand weapons of various kinds, mostly old French rifles and some Japanese guns. They operated in groups of ten or twelve men, and had already created small suicide squads, called *can tu*, which usually carried grenades and concentrated on hit-and-run tactics against French detachments or outposts. By the summer of 1946, the guerrillas were using terrorists in Saigon fairly regularly, and most of the cafes and restaurants . . . had put up some kind of protection. . . .[4]

While this effort continued, Ho and his associates concentrated on building a political-military organization throughout Vietnam with offshoots, in due course, in Cambodia and Laos. Although this was the main work of the formative years, it was not a phased effort but, rather, organic and continuing. It resulted in an organization of which some understanding is necessary if the reader is to appreciate fully the subsequent fighting and final French defeat, not to mention subsequent American political and military failures.

Basically, the Viet Minh depended on an organization similar to that forged by Chinese Communists, but one that, because of what Ho called ". . . geographic, historical, economic, and cultural conditions," differed in growth and activity.[5]

3. Shaplen, op. cit.
4. Ibid.
5. Ho Chi Minh, *Ho Chi Minh on Revolution. Selected Writings 1920–1966* (New York: Frederick A. Praeger, 1967). Ed. Bernard Fall.

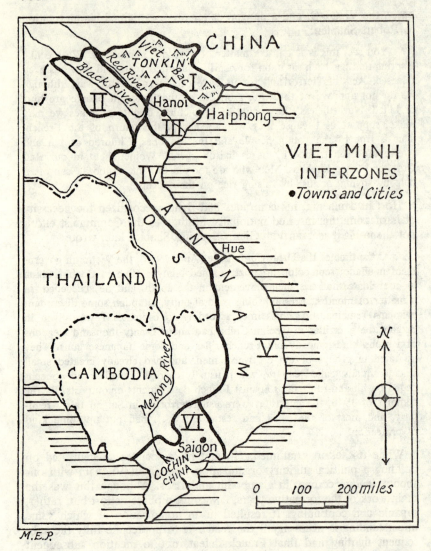

CHINA

Viet
TONKIN Bac
Red River
Black River
I
Hanoi
Haiphong
II
III
IV

VIET MINH
INTERZONES
•Towns and Cities

L
A
O
S

THAILAND

Hue

A
N
N
A
M

CAMBODIA

Mekong River

V

N

VI
Saigon
COCHIN
CHINA

0   100   200 miles

M.E.P.

The military machine consisted of three groups: regular army, regional forces, and popular troops. The Viet Minh recruited, organized, and trained regional and popular forces on a territorial basis. The high command divided the country into six interzones, each containing zones, provinces, districts, intervillages, and villages.[6] Where possible, zones,

6. Lancaster, op. cit.: The Viet-Minh relied mostly on radios for communications between interzones, but this often resulted in serious misunderstandings, particularly between North and South; see also Giap, op. cit.

provinces, and districts each raised and maintained provincial forces, while intervillages and villages raised and maintained popular forces. Impetus, however, stemmed from bottom upward, and this is the essential point: neither the regular army nor provincial forces could have existed for long without multifaceted support provided by villages and popular troops.[7]

Accordingly, the Viet Minh made every effort to win control of peasant hamlets and villages. From their mountain sanctuary northwest of Hanoi, Ho and Giap dispatched a steady stream of agitation-propaganda teams. These trained teams either contacted resident Communist cells working covertly or overtly to "develop" popular Viet Minh "bases" or they set about recruiting such cells.

What was their siren song?

The reader perhaps will be surprised to learn that it was not the virtues of communism. The pitch, as signaled by Ho in late December 1946, carefully avoids the word:

. . . Compatriots! Rise up!

Men and women, old and young, regardless of creeds, political parties, or nationalities, all the Vietnamese must stand up to fight the French colonialists to save the Fatherland. Those who have rifles will use their rifles; those who have swords will use their swords; those who have no swords will use spades, hoes, or sticks. Everyone must endeavor to oppose the colonialists and save his country.[8]

Revolutionary teams concentrated on the single issue of *doc-lap,* of independence, a magic word made into a vocal harp on which these agents skillfully played appealing variations on a theme.

These teams formed the Communist version of Lyautey's civil-military task forces, but instead of spreading brightly colored wares in the village market place, they spread words of hope and dignity in men's minds.

The Viet Minh agents cared.

They cared about high rents paid by peasants, usurious interest on loans, the lack of food that plagued the land, epidemics, illiteracy, lack of schools, teachers, hospitals, doctors. They condemned greedy landlords and rapacious tax collectors and corrupt officials who kept men indebted for life, debts that passed as legacy to survivors.

They discussed all these things and more, and they told the people that *doc-lap,* by returning the land to the people, would erase such injustices and allow everyone a happy and full life for the first time in anyone's memory.

How was *doc-lap* to be achieved?

As Uncle Ho said: by the people.

By peasant and worker, by people gathered listening to the song of

7. Tanham, op. cit.

8. Ho Chi Minh, op. cit.; see also *Mao Tse-tung, Basic Tactics* (New York: Frederick A. Praeger, 1966). Tr. with Introduction by Stuart R. Schram.

Viet Minh agents. The Viet Minh was the people's party; it was recruiting to fight the people's war.

Everyone had a task in the Viet Minh, young and old, able and infirm, men and women, boys and girls.

The Viet Minh needed men to fight as part-time guerrillas, to fight as village militia, to fight in regional forces, to fight in the regular army.

The Viet Minh needed support of all the people. As Uncle Ho said: The people would furnish food to the guerrillas, they would shelter them and care for them when wounded, give them information and money, act as messengers. They would spread the word to other people. Some would carry supplies for the regular army. Others would spy. All would lie. Some would kill. Each in his own way would fight. Some would fall; many would die. That was the price of *doc-lap*.

Where people responded, an organization emerged. The "popular forces" of a village or a complex of villages consisted of the Dan Quan,

. . . which theoretically included almost everyone . . . [and was] essentially a labor force with a tinge of military training. Though occasionally they performed sabotage, their main responsibility was to collect intelligence, serve as guards, make road repairs, build bases, fortify the villages, and—very important—act as porters. They wore no uniforms and had virtually no weapons, except for some sabotage materials.[9]

A smaller group, the Dan Quan Du Kich, "farmers by day—guerrillas by night,"

. . . had some arms and undertook guerrilla actions on a small scale. They received rudimentary military training and were expected eventually to become line soldiers. Though generally forbidden to assemble in large groups, they were called together in emergencies when it was essential to prevent French clearing operations or to intensify guerrilla activity.[10]

Members of Dan Quan and Du Kich carried on with normal civilian activities except in emergency cases. Controlled by a village committee, they spread the revolutionary word and furnished young fighters for provincial forces.

Provincial forces existed at district level, usually in company strength, and at province and zone levels, usually in battalion and, later, regimental strength. Though full-time soldiers, these troops wore a variety of uniforms and lacked heavy weapons and sophisticated equipment. This in no way diminished operational responsibilities:

. . . One of the primary duties of the regional forces was to protect an area and its population. They were the troops that met the French clearing operations, launched small attacks, and generally harassed the enemy; in

9. Tanham, op. cit.
10. Ibid.

short, they were the "mature guerrillas," who kept the enemy off balance and ambushed his reinforcements.

Their responsibilities extended both upward and downward in the total military organization. On the one hand, they trained and assisted the popular troops. On the other they were what might be called the guardians of the regular army. Not only did they constitute a reserve and supply reinforcements to the regular forces when needed, but they prevented interference in the army's training and planning, prepared the battlefield for impending operations, protected the regular forces in retreat and advance, and took over some of their defensive missions.[11]

Throughout this period, Ho and Giap carefully husbanded regular army units. Men who graduated from regional forces into the regular army received fairly systematic training in more or less orthodox military subjects including use of such heavy weapons as machine guns, mortars, bazookas, recoilless rifles. For a couple of years, the regular army consisted of battalions; in time, these battalions grew to regimental strength, and in 1950, to division strength (far inferior numerically to orthodox Western divisions).

The Viet Minh military organization was never far removed from political influence and control both inside and outside the army. Political officers from company level upward dealt with ". . . proper ideological indoctrination of the soldiers and the integration of military actions with political objectives."[12] Since the Communist aspect was still covert, a shadow party political organization also existed, operating through unit cells.

The system stressed the soldier's political training as much as if not more than his military training. As in China, he learned to depend on the people. One of the ten points of his oath was ". . . to respect and help the civilian population."

As Mao had done in China in the early stages of revolution, Ho also set the regular army to the recruiting task. In the work earlier cited, Giap wrote:

. . . Since popular "bases" were indispensable to the development of the guerrilla war, we dispersed the companies of each battalion and we permitted them the necessary liberty of action so that they could infiltrate different regions and cement their friendly relations with the local populace. Since the companies were relatively weak, they had no difficulty in understanding the necessity for firm popular bases. Thanks to their intimate acquaintance with the different regions, they easily won the support of the local population. Their close connection with popular bases gave a strong impetus to the armed conflict. When the guerrilla units acquired enough experience, when the local

11. Ibid.; see also Lancaster, op. cit.
12. Tanham, op. cit.; see also Giap, op. cit.

704 WAR IN THE SHADOWS

militia became powerful enough, the dispersed elements of the companies in the different localities gradually regrouped themselves.[13]

A reasonable idea of the activities of these soldiers can be gained from rules that Ho Chi Minh circulated to both soldiers and bureaucrats in April 1948. In working with people, Viet Minh agents were to follow certain "forbiddances" and certain "permissibles":

SIX FORBIDDANCES TO THE BUREAUCRATS AND SOLDIERS:
1. Not to do what is likely to damage the land and crops or spoil the houses and belongings of the people.
2. Not to insist on buying or borrowing what the people are not willing to sell or lend.
3. Not to bring living hens into the mountain people's houses.
4. Never to break your word.
5. Not to give offense to people's faith and customs (such as to lie down before the altar, to raise the feet over the hearth, to play music in the house, etc.).
6. Not to do or speak what is likely to make people believe that we hold them in contempt.

SIX PERMISSIBLES:
1. To help the people in their daily work (harvesting, fetching firewood, carrying water, sewing, etc.).
2. Whenever possible, to buy commodities for those who live far from markets (knives, salt, needles, thread, pen, paper, etc.).
3. In spare time, to tell amusing, simple, and short stories useful to the Resistance, but not betraying secrets.
4. To teach the population the national script and elementary hygiene.
5. To study the customs of each region so as to be acquainted with them in order to create an atmosphere of sympathy first, then gradually to explain to the people to abate their superstitions.
6. To show to the people that you are correct, diligent, and disciplined.[14]

Viet Minh leadership devoted equal care to political organization of the people. Each zone, province, district, and village fell under a separate committee command usually called the Committee of Resistance. At interzone or zone level, this committee ". . . dealt not only with the political, economic, and military aspects of the war but also with local problems of health and culture." Subordinate committees were less elaborate, those at the village level being responsible for ". . . the defense of the village and the day-to-day activities of the guerrillas." Where

13. Tanham, op. cit.
14. Ho Chi Minh (*Ho Chi Minh on Revolution*), *supra*.

covert cells existed, as was usual in French-occupied areas, the Viet Minh tried to establish shadow, or "parallel," governments.[15]

This system of what the French called *hiérarchies parallèles* was the key to Viet Minh control at each level of government. Based on Lenin's and Mao's teachings, it operated in two ways, either by utilizing ". . . existing administrative structures through the infiltration of subversive individuals, or the creation of altogether new clandestine structures designed to take over full administrative responsibilities when political and military conditions are ripe."[16]

The Viet Minh accomplished none of this organization overnight. Singers of the *doc-lap* song found a greatly varied reception. They were far more popular in the North, in the Red River Delta, than elsewhere. Mountain tribes surrounding their northern sanctuaries did not trust them (or anything else that was Vietnamese) and were pacified only with greatest difficulty. Various opposition nationalist groups, many in the South, wanted nothing to do with the Communist-dominated Viet Minh, even though rejecting French rule.

The Viet Minh countered a certain amount of this opposition by playing on the people's desire for independence. Once it controlled villages, it extended control by weaving the population together through the activities of Lien Viet, which, according to a French army report,

. . . included youth groups, groups for mothers, farmers, workers, "resistant" Catholics, war veterans, etc. It could just as well have included associations of flute players or bicycle racers; the important point was that no one escaped regimentation and that the [normal] territorial hierarchy was thus complemented by another which watched the former and was in turn watched by it—both of them being watched in turn from the outside and inside by the security services and the Party. The individual caught in the fine mesh of such a net has no chance whatever of preserving his independence.[17]

In addition to party representatives, who occupied key administrative positions at all administrative levels, the Viet Minh enforced discipline and extended control of the population by a civilian secret police force, the Cong An; a special military intelligence force, the Trinh Sat; and a special terrorist organization, the Dich-Van; which we will shortly examine more closely.

In these formative years, the Viet Minh suffered a considerable number of internal problems. From time to time, Ho complained of bureaucratic fumbling that resulted in waste and corruption. The armed forces lacked trained officers and specialists. Severe supply shortages also existed. Although weapons and other supplies arrived from Nationalist

15. Tanham, op. cit.
16. Fall (*The Two Viet-Nams*), *supra*.
17. Ibid.

China, Thailand, and the Philippines, these sources eventually dried up, to leave the Viet Minh mainly dependent on captured weapons or on "cottage production." This varied from factories employing as many as five hundred people and situated in sanctuary areas, to mobile shops of from ten to fifteen workers:

. . . Despite the shortage of precision tools, power, and raw materials, the Viet-Minh managed to produce fairly large quantities of materials. In the first six months of 1948, for instance, the Viets reported that shops in one intersector produced 38,000 grenades, 30,000 rifle cartridges, 8,000 cartridges for light machine guns, 60 rounds for a bazooka, and 100 mines. Another sector produced 61 light machine guns, 4 submachine guns, 20 automatic pistols, and 7,000 cartridges in the entire year 1948.[18]

Despite difficulties, the Viet Minh continued to grow in size and effectiveness. Although poverty of organization and strength confined operations to the guerrilla level—to raids on French outposts, ambush of patrols and convoys, and interdiction of roads—by 1948, these operations were displaying characteristics that made them increasingly difficult to counter.

Viet Minh raids were not slapdash affairs but generally well-thought-out and carefully planned operations in which mobility and surprise dovetailed to produce satisfactory results. They served both a political and a military purpose. Politically, they demonstrated that the Viet Minh intended to "liberate" an area from French control and thus added muscle to Viet Minh propaganda and helped to strengthen further the covert Viet Minh presence in that area. Militarily, they provided weapons and ammunition and also helped units to perfect infiltration and assault tactics. Finally, they exercised a demoralizing influence on the French.

Usually made at night, attacks were rarely prolonged. If successful, intruders gathered up weapons, perhaps a prisoner or two, and whatever ammunition and equipment they could carry. If a raid failed, attackers generally broke off action and fled, either to designated rendezvous areas or, if cut off, to friendly villages, where they merged with the population.

A successful raid depended in large part on accurate intelligence. Guerrilla teams not only wanted to strike the weakest outposts but the weakest part of a weak outpost. Here is where careful preparation of the population was paying off: French outposts were under almost constant scrutiny both from inside by various Vietnamese lackeys and from outside by peasants. Moreover, a friendly population supported Viet Minh agents and even combat teams who infiltrated into a target area to carry on the agitation-propaganda effort, organize the people, collect intelligence, and participate in attacks when necessary.

18. Tanham, op. cit.; see also Buttinger, op. cit.; Hammer, op. cit.: Forest "factories" also manufactured paper, chemicals, pharmaceutical products, and textiles.

A sympathetic population also greatly aided Viet Minh construction and security of defensive areas. In the North, these usually consisted of fortified villages. Guerrillas and villagers devoted thousands of man-hours to preparing underground labyrinths cunningly camouflaged and often stocked with food and water in case of prolonged occupation. A security network of innocent-looking peasants guarded these strong-holds against surprise, thus allowing guerrilla inhabitants the option of escape or ambush of an intruding French force. If outnumbered, or if other factors were unfavorable, the Viet Minh did not hesitate to abandon the village.

On the few occasions the French surprised the Viet Minh, the latter usually managed to break off action and escape. A case cited by Dr. Tanham, a surprise infantry and paratroop raid on Viet Minh headquarters in Cochin China in autumn of 1948, failed for the same reasons that the final German surprise raid failed on Tito's headquarters in World War II (see Chapter 36, Volume I): a guerrilla rear guard held off the attacking force long enough for the main body to escape, in this case to secret camouflaged positions, subterranean caves and riverbanks, or by melting into surrounding peasant areas.[19]

Obviously, the people's support, active or passive, was essential to continued success of Viet Minh operations or even to Viet Minh existence. This is why the Viet Minh devoted perhaps more effort to the agitation-propaganda-recruiting side of the war than to fighting the French.

Inept French tactics, for example clearing operations that destroyed huts, damaged crops, and maltreated peasants, greatly aided the Viet Minh in their effort to win the people's co-operation. Where French made progress in the pacification program, notably in the South, the Viet Minh used more-militant tactics to destroy the French influence. This was the task of the special terrorist organization, the Dich-Van, whose members did not hesitate to murder officials who co-operated with the French. In Viet Minh eyes, this was not wanton slaughter. Except in isolated and undisciplined cases, such murders served specific political goals: If the official was corrupt, his murder constituted a popular act; in any case, it served as a bloody warning that the French, despite martial trappings, did *not* control the area and that anyone impeding the fight for Vietnamese independence by trafficking with the French could and would be summarily dealt with.

We see here in these years the gradual appearance of all ingredients of an insurgency situation. Had the battle remained an internal affair confined to limited French and Viet Minh forces, it could perhaps have been resolved by political means—by some sort of standoff agreement similar to that reached in March 1946—before it broadened. Despite the intensity of the Viet Minh effort, their strength would probably not

19. Ibid.

have increased to the point where they could have undertaken the final, or mobile, phase of the war, anyway for many, many years.

But Communist China's victory, in 1949, greatly altered matters. The Viet Minh could now hope to enter the third phase of warfare. In late 1949, Ho Chi Minh's government proclaimed a national mobilization and began conscripting males between the ages of eighteen and forty-five. This guarantee of almost limitless porters, the promise of military aid from China and of sanctuary in case of defeat, and the peculiar vulnerability of French outposts in the North allowed Giap to become more tactically daring than his meager resources warranted. In anticipation of bigger things, in late 1949 he began attacking French outposts in the Black River Valley, northwest of Hanoi.

Chapter 55

*Viet Minh offensives • French disasters • La sale guerre •
General de Lattre de Tassigny • Giap's mistakes • Change in
Communist tactics • French strategy and tactics • De Lattre's
"crusade" • American intervention • American-French conflict • George Kennan's warning to Acheson • Acheson's dilemma (II) • Gullion and Blum dissent • Senator John
Kennedy's position*

T HE COMBINATION of superb intelligence gained from peasants,
meticulous planning, mobility, and surprise, which characterized the
Viet Minh's early guerrilla raids, was carried over to Giap's first major
offensive. Operation Le-Loi concentrated on destroying a series of small
French outposts located in the Black River Valley. By January 1950, fifteen Viet Minh battalions had overrun these small forts to drive a wedge
between the Thai Highlands and the Red River Delta.

Giap's success here, taken with the arrival of Chinese Communist
forces on the border, caused him to undertake the more ambitious operation of clearing the northern border area. In February 1950, Giap
declared that the second phase of the war, guerrilla warfare, was over
and that the third phase, mobile warfare, was to begin.[1] Giap now
opened Operation Le Hong Phong I.[2] Five Viet Minh regiments struck

1. Lancaster, op. cit.; see also Giap, op. cit.
2. Fall (*The Two Viet-Nams*), *supra*: The Viet Minh code name always carried
a psychological connotation; in this case, the operation was named after the first
secretary-general of the Indochinese Communist Party.

throughout the region and, after some sharp fighting, occupied major towns to leave French forces in northeastern Tonkin compressed into a string of forts stretching some one hundred and sixty miles along a single-lane highway, Route Coloniale 4, from Cao Bang to the Gulf of Tonkin. These were the forts that, in 1949, the French chief of staff, General Revers, had wanted evacuated.

Giap next turned his attention to these forts. Using fresh troops trained and equipped in China and supported by American artillery pieces that Communist Chinese had captured from the Nationalists, he attacked and briefly held the fort of Dong Khe. Throughout the summer, Viet Minh guerrillas interdicted the long and vulnerable French supply line. Giap meanwhile brought battle-tested regiments through China to the east, where they joined with ". . . ten newly formed Viet-Minh battalions, reinforced by a complete artillery regiment."[3] In September, he opened Operation Le Hong Phong II by again attacking and capturing Dong Khe, which effectively cut communications between Cao Bang, a key garrison eighty-five miles distant from the southern forts.

The French command in Hanoi reacted in two ways: It ordered the Cao Bang commander ". . . to blow up all his heavy equipment and all his motor transport and to march out of Cao-Bang"; simultaneously, it started a relief force of thirty-five hundred men marching north, where it would take Dong Khe and join the retreating Cao Bang garrison.[4]

This plan probably would have salvaged most of the troops, but the Cao Bang commander sabotaged it by refusing to abandon his artillery and transport. He thus tied his retreat to the jungle-flanked windings and flimsy bridges of Route Coloniale 4. He immediately struck a series of Viet Minh ambushes so fiercely executed that, according to Fall, ". . . after one day of arduous work, the force had covered *nine* miles."[5] Not until Giap's guerrillas chewed columns to shreds did he abandon transport and guns, but, by then, the relief force marching from the south was under heavy attack.

Remnants of the two forces met outside Dong Khe, where, despite reinforcement by three battalions of paratroopers, they were virtually annihilated. General Carpentier now evacuated the southernmost fort of Lang Son, leaving most of its thirteen hundred tons of supply to the Viet Minh. By the end of October 1950, ". . . almost the whole northern half of North Viet-Nam had become a Viet-Minh redoubt. . . ." Fall summed up the disaster:

. . . When the smoke cleared, the French had suffered their greatest colonial defeat since Montcalm had died in Quebec. They had lost 6,000 troops, 13 artillery pieces and 125 mortars, 450 trucks and three armored platoons, 940 machine guns, 1200 submachine guns and more than 8,000 rifles. Their

3. Ibid.; see also Buttinger, op. cit.
4. Fall (*The Two Viet-Nams*), supra.
5. Ibid.

NORTHERN VIETNAM
1950-1953
● Towns and Cities
•••• "de Lattre line"
— Routes 4 and 1

M.E.P.

abandoned stocks alone sufficed for the equipment of a whole additional Viet-Minh division.[6]

With the French troops falling back to the Red River Delta, where panic-stricken civilians greeted them with demoralizing rumors, it looked as if the Viet Minh would soon claim all of northern Vietnam. The disaster coincided with General MacArthur's serious reverse in Korea occasioned by Chinese entry into the war. French morale at home plunged. French Communists assumed a new militancy and started ". . . a campaign of strikes and demonstrations aimed at obstructing the transport of soldiers and war material to Indochina."[7] Such was the reaction to

6. Fall (*Street Without Joy*), *supra*; see also Giap, *op. cit.*
7. Hammer (*Struggle for Indochina*), *supra*.

what Communists termed *la sale guerre*—the dirty war—that important non-Communist voices began calling for French withdrawal.

One of them belonged to Pierre Mendès-France, a former Gaullist and future premier, who, in November 1950, laid basic issues on the line in the National Assembly:

. . . It is the overall conception of our action in Indochina that is false, because it relies both on a military effort that is too thin and weak to provide a solution through strength, and on a political effort that is too thin and weak to secure for us the allegiance of the population. . . . This cannot be on.

There are only two solutions. The first would be to fulfil our objectives in Indochina by force of arms. If we choose it, let us now give up illusions and pious falsehoods. In order to achieve decisive military successes rapidly, we will need three times as many forces on the ground and three times as many funds, and we will need them very quickly. . . .[8]

The effort would be expensive and would demand drastic sacrifices on the home front. The alternative

. . . is to seek a political agreement, an agreement, obviously, with those who oppose us. . . . An agreement means concessions, wide concessions. . . .

A choice must be made. . . . Apart from the military solution, the solution of force, there is only one possibility—negotiation. . . . Have we the means of escaping this outcome when we ourselves have made it unavoidable by our failures and mistakes?[9]

Mendès-France told the Assembly that concessions would include Vietnamese independence, negotiated withdrawal of French troops, and free, supervised elections.[10]

In the ensuing debate, Jean Letourneau, Minister for the Associated States, stated ". . . that the government of Premier René Pleven intended to carry out the March 8, 1949 [Élysée] agreements with the greatest liberalism. Virtually all of the administrative machinery would be in Vietnamese hands by January 1, 1951, he promised, and the French would hand over power as rapidly as possible to a Vietnamese army."[11] Having won Assembly approval, Pleven's government recalled Carpentier and Léon Pignon and appointed the forceful general Jean de Lattre de Tassigny to the dual civil-military command.

Although a sick man, De Lattre possessed considerable charisma, and his evident enthusiasm and tireless efforts brought a much needed boost to morale and army discipline. A cocky little fellow, called "Le Roi Jean"—King Jean—by some, De Lattre promised his troops no easy

---

8. Philippe Devillers and Jean Lacouture, *End of a War; Indochina, 1954* (New York: Frederick A. Praeger, 1969).
9. Ibid.
10. Ibid.
11. Hammer ("Genesis of the First Indochinese War"), *supra.*

road, but he also told them, ". . . No matter what, you will be commanded."[12]

De Lattre walked into an extremely crucial tactical situation. Giap's autumn victories had given him ideas made the more grandiose by initial Chinese successes in Korea and by an increasing flow of arms from Communist China. The Democratic Republic of (North) Vietnam was now unquestionably committed to the Communist camp—in early 1951, the government would re-create the Indochinese Communist Party, under the title of Lao Dong, and would begin the transformation of the state to a "people's democracy."[13] By late 1950, the army included heavy weapons, artillery, and even engineer units.[14]

As prelude to a push on Hanoi itself, Giap attacked the outpost of Vinh Yen with two divisions in mid-January 1951. This kicked off with a skillful diversionary effort that enticed a French mobile group into ambush and cost it some two battalions in casualties. But unexpectedly strong defenses at Vinh Yen, including well-directed artillery support and aircraft dropping newly introduced napalm, stopped the main effort. Giap foolishly ordered mass, or "human sea," tactics that sent wave after wave of infantry against determined defenders well dug in and supported by heavy artillery and air. Giap's logistics system was not up to this kind of warfare. Each of his divisions, of about twelve thousand men, depended on about fifty thousand human porters to support an offensive role.[15] Although he was said to have utilized 180,000 porters during the action, his primitive supply lines were unable to furnish resupply. Continuing intermittently for four days, the Viet Minh attacks suddenly ceased—a major setback which cost the Communists some six thousand killed, several thousand wounded, and five hundred taken prisoner.[16]

Apparently undeterred, Giap shifted his effort to the southeast, to the hill range around Dong Trieu. A successful attack here would open approaches to the coal-mining area and would cut the delta from the vital port of Haiphong. In late March, three divisions struck at Mao Khe. The small French garrison held out until reinforced by paratroopers, and once again the attack failed at considerable cost to the Viet Minh.

Giap struck next from the south, a surprise attack aided by a regiment he had infiltrated behind French lines. In late May, three of his divisions fell on Thai Binh. But their lines of communication ran across the Day River and here were interdicted by French river units and by planes dropping napalm. Thus hindered, assault units could not sustain the attack.

12. Fall (*The Two Viet-Nams*), *supra;* see also Buttinger, op. cit., and Lancaster, op. cit., for a more critical appraisal.
13. Lancaster, op. cit.
14. Giap, op. cit.
15. Edgar O'Ballance, *The Indo-China War, 1945–1954* (London: Faber & Faber, 1964).
16. Lancaster, op. cit.; see also O'Ballance, op. cit., who cites 7–8,000 wounded.

In mid-June, having lost about a third of their force, the Viet Minh abruptly broke contact and retreated to the mountains.

This series of battles produced important developments in each camp. As a Viet Minh failure, the actions caused Giap to reverse his thinking and postpone the third, or all-out offensive, phase. Rightly assuming that time was on his side, he spent summer of 1951 in rebuilding shattered divisions. He then turned to the Thai Highlands and Laos and in September began a series of nibbling actions against semi-isolated outposts.

Equally important developments occurred in French and American camps. The winter-spring battles, though far from "victories," removed much of the sting from earlier French defeats. By so doing, they combined with other factors—with De Lattre's conventional military background, with his dangerous belief in superiority of Western-style warfare in a guerrilla-warfare environment, perhaps with his illness—to blind him to the exact nature of the political challenge.

By spring of 1951, the French staff held ample evidence that France was fighting an extremely determined enemy whose operations depended in large part on co-operation of the Vietnamese people. Yet, no more than earlier administrators and military commanders, did De Lattre come up with a plan to steal this support and thus weaken his enemy perhaps irreparably.

Instead, De Lattre sought to inject enthusiasm into his forces and into the Vietnamese people, particularly the *attentistes,* or fence sitters, *not* by changing the nature of the political approach, but by changing the nature of the war, a task simplified by the East-West confrontation in Korea. The French historians Philippe Devillers and Jean Lacouture later wrote:

. . . While the [French] Chiefs of Staff Committee recommended a concentration of effort in southern Indochina, where the chief French interests lay, de Lattre maintained—and secured government support for his views—that the loss of Tonkin would lead to the West's loss of Indochina and Southeast Asia. Here was the bolt to the door, he claimed, and he added that a serious setback in the north might well cause the Vietnamese government simply to fade away. Having thus linked the fates of Indochina and Tonkin, he demanded absolute priority for this theater of war and the immediate dispatch of large reinforcements.[17]

De Lattre vigorously denied that his was a colonial war. Instead, in Robert Shaplen's words:

. . . De Lattre was convinced that he was leading a crusade against Communism. He told me that the French were in Vietnam "to save it from Peking and Moscow," and he predicted victory in fifteen months. He in-

17. Devillers and Lacouture, op. cit.

sisted that there was no longer an ounce of colonialism left in French
intentions. . . .[18]

In July 1951, De Lattre stated that the war

. . . no longer concerns France except to the extent of her promises to Vietnam and the part she has to play in the defense of the free world. Not
since the Crusades has France undertaken such disinterested action. This
war is the war of Vietnam for Vietnam.[19]

Whether De Lattre believed this or whether he realized the appeal that
his words would have to conservative members of the American Congress and public, it was palpable nonsense. One thing certain, his words
could not have convinced many Vietnamese, for as Shaplen pointed out:

. . . The French still owned practically all of the real wealth of Indochina,
and their investment was close to two billion dollars; they owned all the
rubber plantations, which, despite the war, were still operating . . . and they
owned two-thirds of the rice, all the mines, all the shipping, virtually all
the industry, and nearly all the banks. . . .[20]

Prompted by French and American governments, the former furnishing the authority, the latter most of the money, De Lattre also turned
to building a Vietnamese army, authorized by the Élysée Agreements
but so far consisting only of a few battalions. De Lattre began a widespread recruiting campaign designed to increase this force to thirty battalions. Due to hostility of French officialdom and Vietnamese apathy,
he only partially succeeded—under the circumstances, a major failure.
But he did succeed in obtaining some fresh troops from North Africa.[21]
Strategically, he insisted on continuing the war and again refused the
notion of withdrawing from the North. Wanting to deprive the Viet
Minh of the Red River Delta rice bowl, he attempted to seal off this vast
area, about seventy-five hundred square miles and eight million inhabitants, with a complicated complex of forts, some twelve hundred large
and small concrete structures, known as the "de Lattre Line."[22] At the
same time, he introduced the tactical innovation of mobile groups, special task forces of his best infantry, armor, and artillery units used
". . . as offensive striking forces to attack key Viet Minh installations
and force combat on . . . [De Lattre's] own terms."[23] De Lattre
mobilized seven of these *Groupes Mobiles*. Together with eight parachute battalions, they constituted his striking force, which was supposed
to check and defeat between six and seven Viet Minh divisions.

18. Shaplen, op. cit.
19. Buttinger, op. cit.
20. Shaplen, op. cit.
21. Devillers and Lacouture, op. cit.
22. Fall (*Street Without Joy*), *supra;* see also Lancaster, op. cit.
23. Tanham, op. cit.

Although De Lattre commanded a force of about half a million men, 350,000 of them ". . . were tied down in static assignments . . . or in noncombatant supply. . . ."[24]

De Lattre continued to rely on his air force and on two other tactical innovations. One consisted of Dinaussauts, or special river units of various-sized landing craft that patrolled numerous waterways. The other was an attempt to outdo the Viet Minh at their own game by sending special teams, consisting in part of "converted" Viet Minh prisoners, into Viet Minh territory to work up guerrilla resistance. The command of these units, called *Groupements de Commandos Mixtes Aéroportés,* or GCMA, went to a young paratroop major, Roger Trinquier, of whom we will hear more in the final chapter of this war. The units, which mostly parachuted into target areas, were supplied by airdrop while working with tribes loyal to the French.[25]

Thus armed, De Lattre set to work to "win" the war.

De Lattre's "victories" in winter and spring of 1951 also influenced American officials, both in Indochina and in Washington. The American attitude toward Indochina, if anything, had grown more ambivalent. Prime Minister Nguyen Phan Long had complicated matters in early 1950 by asking for economic and military aid directly from the United States. The prime minister optimistically argued that a grant of $146 million would allow him to build a national Vietnamese army that would defeat the Viet Minh in six months.[26] This drew a sharp retort from the French commander, General Carpentier:

. . . I will never agree to equipment being given directly to the Viet Namese. If this should be done, I would resign within twenty-four hours. The Viet Namese have no generals, no colonels, no military organization that could effectively utilize the equipment. It would be wasted, and in China the United States has had enough of that.[27]

The pending conflict, never satisfactorily solved, was noted by Walter Lippmann, who, in early April 1950, wrote:

. . . Everyone knows that the great majority of the people of Indo-China are bitterly opposed to the continuation of French rule, and that they could be united behind a government only if that government were clearly and certainly destined to make Indo-China as independent as Indonesia, the Philippines, India, Pakistan, and Ceylon. But if Bao-Dai or anyone else were promised independence, it is equally certain that the French army could not be induced to continue the war. The French officers and troops and the

24. Devillers and Lacouture, op. cit.
25. Roger Trinquier, *Modern Warfare—A French View of Counter-Insurgency* (New York: Frederick A. Praeger, 1964).
26. Lancaster, op. cit.
27. Ibid.; see also Hammer (*The Struggle for Indochina, 1940–1955*), *supra.*

French assembly may be willing to fight for the preservation of French interests in this rich colony. They cannot be counted upon to fight a dangerous, dirty, inconclusive war which is to end in the abandonment of the French interests in Asia. . . . Put bluntly but truthfully, the French army can be counted on to go on defending Southeast Asia only if the Congress of the United States will pledge itself to subsidize heavily—in terms of several hundred million dollars a year and for many years to come—a French colonial war to subdue not only the Communists but the nationalists as well.[28]

But when the United States agreed, in autumn of 1950, to help France raise a Vietnamese army, Ambassador Donald Heath, in Saigon, advised ". . . that the desired political and psychological effect [of a national army] could be obtained only if the Associated States were given a real role in the arrangements."[29] Shortly after, Secretary of State Acheson was advised by one of his lieutenants that ". . . Prince Bao Dai should be pushed to assume maximum effective leadership" and ". . . that although Indochina was an area of French responsibility, in view of French ineffectiveness it would be better for France to pull out if she could not provide sufficient force to hold; that we should strengthen a second line of defense in Thailand, Malaya, Laos, Cambodia, the Philippines, and Indonesia. . . ."[30] Just prior to Chinese intervention in Korea, still another lieutenant presciently warned the Secretary of State

. . . that the appearance of the Chinese in Korea required us to take a second look at where we were going in Indochina. Not only was there real danger that our efforts would fail in their immediate purpose and waste valuable resources in the process, but we were moving into a position in Indochina in which "our responsibilities tend to supplant rather than complement those of the French." We could, he added, become a scapegoat for the French and be sucked into direct intervention. "These situations have a way of snowballing," he concluded.[31]

Thus, American officials in Vietnam began to find the going increasingly frustrating. The aid question became a particularly sore point. During the 1950 negotiations, American officials wisely had held out for bilateral aid agreements between the United States and the three Associated States: Vietnam, Laos, and Cambodia. Most economic aid, which, up to July 1951, amounted to $23.5 million, went to Vietnam. But in administering funds, the head of the American aid program, Robert Blum, collided with French officialdom, which accused him of undermining French interests by fomenting Vietnamese nationalism. As one result, the French used obstructive methods to downplay the American effort and, at times, to nullify its most beneficial effects.

28. Lancaster, op. cit.
29. Acheson, op. cit.
30. Ibid.
31. Ibid.

A strong diplomatic stand undoubtedly could have rectified this un-savory situation, but external factors previously discussed continued to play a major role by dividing American councils. In Washington, George Kennan, by far the most prescient diplomat in the State Depart-ment, had become seriously alarmed by events in Indochina. In late Au-gust 1950, he wrote an official memorandum to Secretary of State Acheson that, unlike other advices of the time, offered a positive course of action based on grim reality:

. . . In Indo-China, we are getting ourselves into the position of guarantee-ing the French in an undertaking which neither they nor we, nor both of us together, can win. . . . We should let Schuman [French Foreign Minister Maurice Schuman] know . . . that the closer view we have had of the prob-lems of this area, in the course of our efforts of the past few months to support the French position there, has convinced us that that position is basically hopeless. . . . We should say that we will do everything in our power to avoid embarrassing the French in their problems and to support them in any reasonable course they would like to adopt looking to its liqui-dation; but that we cannot honestly agree with them that there is any real hope of their remaining successfully in Indo-China, and we feel that rather than have their weakness demonstrated by a continued costly and unsuccess-ful effort to assert their will by force of arms, it would be preferable to permit the turbulent political currents of that country to find their own level, unimpeded by foreign troops or pressures, even at the probable cost of an eventual deal between Viet-Nam and Viet-Minh, and the spreading over the whole country of Viet-Minh authority, possibly in a somewhat modi-fied form. We might suggest that the most promising line of withdrawal, from the standpoint of their prestige, would be to make the problem one of some Asian regional responsibility, in which the French exodus could be conveniently obscured.[32]

Unfortunately, Dean Acheson could not be persuaded to such a course. Committed to forging a defensive pact in Europe, he refused to antagonize the French by withdrawing support for their effort in Indo-china. Donald Heath, American minister (and later ambassador) in Viet-nam, ". . . did not believe in rocking the boat, and when De Lattre arrived, he fell completely under the General's spell."[33] Edmund Gul-lion, Heath's consul general and later minister counselor, opposed such a compliant attitude, as did Robert Blum, the aid chief, whose efforts to circumvent French obstructionism gained De Lattre's particular oppro-brium. But the impact of Gullion's and Blum's worthy efforts was largely absorbed by continuing American support of the French military effort. In December 1950, the American Government agreed that all military aid ". . . would be handed over to the French Command, while direct

32. George F. Kennan, *Memoirs 1950–1963* (London: Hutchinson, 1973), Vol. 2.

33. Shaplen, op. cit.

relations between the Associate States and MAAG were to be expressly precluded."[34] In 1951, the United States furnished French forces in Indochina over half a billion dollars' worth of military aid.

The United States could not satisfactorily identify with both the French and the Vietnamese. As Shaplen has pointed out, De Lattre may have been conducting an anti-Communist crusade, but ". . . as it developed, it was solely a French, and not a Vietnamese crusade." Neither De Lattre nor French and American officials who had donned armor and were marching on what they appeared to believe was a God-given mission could persuade the Vietnamese to enthusiasm, particularly since the Vietnamese were consigned to hold the horses of the French knights. The Vietnamese wanted independence, and, in autumn of 1951, they wanted the United States to help them gain it. Instead, she was obviously backing France. As Robert Blum sadly concluded, ". . . on balance, we came to be looked upon more as a supporter of colonialism than as a friend of the new nation."[35]

Blum's and Gullion's voiced concern was somewhat silenced by Ambassador Heath's policy of extreme co-operation with the French, but their portents nonetheless filtered into top Administration minds. Secretary of State Acheson later wrote these revealing paragraphs:

. . . Our military aid [to France in Indochina] mounted in the year 1951 to over half a billion dollars. General de Lattre came twice to Washington to demand more aid and faster delivery and to urge us to declare that loss of Indochina would be a catastrophic blow to the free world; yet he resented inquiries about his military plans and his intentions regarding transfer of authority to the three states. Too little seemed to be happening in Vietnam in developing military power and local government responsibility and popular support. While in 1951 the Vietnamese forces rose to four divisions, they had only seven hundred Vietnamese officers out of the two thousand required, and their military academy at Dalat was graduating only two hundred a year. Our offer of instructors from our military mission in Korea, which was mass-educating officers for twelve Korean divisions, was refused.

As the year wore on without much progress and we ourselves became bogged down in the negotiations at Panmunjom, our sense of frustration grew. A review of the situation in late August, before I left for a series of meetings in the autumn of 1951, brought warning from the Joint Chiefs of Staff against any statement that would commit—or seem to the French under future eventualities to commit—United States armed forces to Indochina. We did not waver from this policy.[36]

Considering ramifications of the situation, this negative approach could scarcely be termed viable policy. In truth, the United States did not have one, and by trying to establish the groundwork from which one

34. Lancaster, op. cit.
35. Shaplen, op. cit.
36. Acheson, op. cit.

could grow, Gullion and Blum reaped opprobrium of their seniors. De Lattre, who called Blum ". . . the most dangerous man in Indo-China," was instrumental in getting him relieved, in late 1951. Soon after his return to the United States, Blum summed up both the French and the American dilemmas:

. . . The attitude of the French is difficult to define. On the one hand are the repeated official affirmations that France has no selfish interests in Indo-China and desires only to promote the independence of the Associated States and be relieved of the terrible drain of France's resources. On the other hand are the numerous examples of the deliberate continuation of French controls, the interference in major policy matters, the profiteering and the constant bickering and ill-feeling over the transfer of powers and the issues of independence. . . . There is unquestionably a contradiction in French actions between the natural desire to be rid of this unpopular, costly and apparently fruitless war and the determination to see it through with honor while satisfying French pride and defending interests in the process. This distinction is typified by the sharp difference between the attitude toward General de Lattre in Indo-China, where he is heralded as the political genius and military savior . . . and in France, where he is suspected as a person who for personal glory is drawing off France's resources on a perilous adventure. . . .[37]

Blum went on to analyze the dichotomy of American participation in this colonial affair:

. . . It is difficult to measure what have been the results of almost two years of active American participation in the affairs of Indo-China. Although we embarked upon a course of uneasy association with the "colonialist"-tainted but indispensable French, on the one hand, and the indigenous, weak and divided Vietnamese, on the other hand, we have not been able fully to reconcile these two allies in the interest of a single-minded fight against Communism. Of the purposes which we hoped to serve by our actions in Indo-China, the one that has been most successful has been the strengthening of the French military position. On the other hand, the Vietnamese, many of whom thought that magical solutions to their advantage would result from our appearance on the scene, are chastened but disappointed at the evidence that America is not omnipotent and not prepared to make an undiluted effort to support their point of view. . . . Our direct influence on political and economic matters has not been great. We have been reluctant to become directly embroiled and, though the degree of our contribution has been steadily increasing, we have been content, if not eager, to have the French continue to have primary responsibility, and to give little, if any, advice.[38]

37. Shaplen, op. cit.
38. Ibid.

Blum's and Gullion's dissent was not altogether wasted, for their obvious sincerity in wanting to help the Vietnamese help themselves won the U.S.A. numerous friends in the area. Nor did their dissent go unnoticed at home. In 1951, a young senator, John F. Kennedy, visited Vietnam, where he listened to Edmund Gullion, among others. Upon his return to the United States, he stated:

. . . In Indo-China we have allied ourselves to the desperate effort of a French regime to hang on to the remnants of empire. . . . To check the southern drive of communism makes sense but not only through reliance on the force of arms. The task is rather to build strong native non-Communist sentiment within these areas and rely on that as a spearhead of defense rather than upon the legions of General de Lattre. To do this apart from and in defiance of innately nationalistic aims spells foredoomed failure.[39]

39. Arthur M. Schlesinger, Jr., *A Thousand Days* (Boston: Houghton Mifflin, 1965).

Chapter 56

De Lattre's new tactics • General Salan takes over • Jean Letourneau • French political failure • Acheson's dilemma (III) • Giap's problems • His shift in targets • Salan's countermoves • Orde Wingate's ghost (I) • Continued French failure • Acheson loses patience • Giap fans out • General Henri Navarre arrives

UNFORTUNATELY, Senator Kennedy's expressed pessimism concerning the Indochina scene represented a minority opinion—so often the natural corollary of fact. De Lattre and his fellow crusaders, French and American, clearly won the opening rounds. In spring of 1951, American officials, legislators, and faithful friends of Vietnam, riding the anti-Communist bandwagon, saw to it that De Lattre was well received in Washington, where press and television interviews ". . . did much to persuade the American public not only that effective national independence had been given to the Associate [sic] States but also that France's role in Indochina was disinterested."[1] He also won the promise of greatly increased military aid.

Flushed with this triumph and with renewed support from his own government, De Lattre, upon his return, embarked on a fresh tactical adventure. Impressed by the obstinacy of Viet Minh attacks at Thai Binh (see map, Chapter 55), he decided to try to woo Giap into another

1. Lancaster, op. cit.

"meat-grinder" situation where superior French firepower could tell. As bait, he chose the town and surrounding area of Hoa Binh, a key communications point between Viet Minh forces in the Northeast and a Viet Minh division in Annam that supported operations in Interzone Five, in central Vietnam.[2]

In mid-November, three battalions of paratroopers dropped into the area and, within twenty-four hours, secured all objectives—with minimum resistance. This alone was suspicious, but no one at De Lattre's headquarters seemed alarmed. Instead, his press officer announced to foreign correspondents that ". . . the conquest of Hoa-Binh represented a pistol pointed directly at the heart of the enemy."[3]

This sentence reflected considerable wishful thinking.

The conquest?

The conquest was occupation uncontested because Giap pulled back his units until he could send in reinforcements and reclaim the initiative; that is, until he could fight on his own terms.

The heart of the enemy?

The French task force interdicted a road flanked by dense jungle. But roads mean many things to many people. To armies dependent on motor transport and tanks, they are all-important. But Giap's supply traveled on very few trucks; indeed, it either rode to Annam on coolie backs or on coolie-pushed bicycles. Within a month, ". . . the Viet-Minh had (in its usual fashion) built a bypass road around Hoa-Binh."[4] In so far as effectively interdicting Viet Minh communications was concerned, the French battalions might as well have remained in Hanoi.

But what of De Lattre's main tactical objective?

De Lattre unquestionably brought the Viet Minh to combat, but with unforeseen results. Giap waited until his units had infiltrated the area in strength and then struck at French lines of communications. Although the Viet Minh employed a variety of guerrilla tactics to interdict De Lattre's supply lines, they did not hesitate to use costly assault tactics where necessary to eliminate key outposts. These attacks also took a heavy toll of French defenders. By the time that De Lattre, a sick man, suffering from terminal cancer, was evacuated, in December, he had already begun committing his limited reserves.[5]

His successor, General Salan, found the operation so costly that, in January, he terminated it. But, by now, the Hoa Binh task force was encircled! In the end, over three reinforced regiments spent eleven days fighting their way down twenty-five miles of road, a rescue effort that cost dearly in men's lives, precious vehicles, and time.[6]

In capturing, defending, and evacuating Hoa Binh, De Lattre and

2. Fall (*Street Without Joy*), *supra*.
3. Ibid.
4. Ibid.; see also Giap, op. cit.
5. De Lattre died in Paris in January 1952.
6. Fall (*Street Without Joy*), *supra*.

Salan had used about a third of their mobile forces, which weakened other areas and opened the delta to extensive infiltration by Viet Minh regulars. According to Fall, ". . . by March, 1952, the French were mounting combined operations involving several mobile groups *behind* their own lines in order to keep their communications open."[7]

Nothing epitomized the French dilemma more clearly than this situation, which directly resulted from refusal to equate force with mission. De Lattre and Salan were indulging luxury operations in an environment that called for strictest stringency. Ironically, the French command was concurrently supporting a number of *ratissage* operations much more in keeping with the tache-d'huile technique. Colonel John McCuen has described one such operation in the Red River area, a subsector assigned to an Algerian rifle battalion supplemented by a Vietnamese company, a force of about one hundred locally recruited Vietnamese guerrillas, and a river patrol of a few landing craft. Dividing his subsector into four parts, as dictated by terrain and enemy activity, the commander opened a vigorous territorial offense, what McCuen calls "nomadization," consisting of active and aggressive patrols and ambush operations:

. . . When the territorial offense began in early 1952, there was approximately a regular Vietminh Battalion in the area, reinforced by strong regional and local forces. The Sub-sector was in a state of decay which seriously threatened communications along the Red River. . . . Continuous nomadization seized the initiative from the guerrillas, assured security of the lines of communication and critical points, and exposed the Vietminh to attack by the mobile reserves. Within six months the estimated guerrilla casualties were 292 killed and 70 captured. Some 376 Vietminh political agents were arrested. Captured were 49 sampans and junks and numerous arms, including two 60mm mortars. The Sub-sector had been virtually cleared of regular, regional, and local Vietminh forces, most of which had sought safer havens. . . .[8]

So far, so good. At this advanced point in the pacification process, a civic action team should have entered the play. These teams, Mobile Operational Administrative Groups, or GAMO (*Groupes administratifs mobiles opérationnels*), were supposed to complete the pacification process: screen and clear the area of *all* Viet Minh military and civil agents and generate a viable local administration while temporarily supplying basic needs—food, clothing, shelter, medical treatment, and security (through local militia).[9]

Several factors hindered GAMO operations. The first was scarcity of properly qualified teams—again, a matter of matching resources and

7. Ibid.
8. McCuen, op. cit.
9. Ibid.; see also Lancaster, op. cit.: ". . . the teams . . . had been formed at the instigation of Nguyên Huu Tri, Governor of North Vietnam."

mission. The second was lack of political appeal: team members could tell peasants that the Viet Minh were evil, but peasants, from personal experience, knew that the Viet Minh were no more evil than the French administration with all its traditional injustices. Lacking political inspiration, teams perforce had to rely on superior performance, on setting up and running viable community services and continuing to protect the people until they could protect themselves. This frequently called for the regular military force; where this force had been transferred to a new area, the GAMO stood naked before renewed Viet Minh attacks.

In the case cited above, GAMO operations never did take place. McCuen described the inevitable result:

. . . Considering it [the area] pacified and needing the troops elsewhere, the French High Command called off its territorial offense in the Sub-sector by March 1953. The Algerian Rifle Battalion turned over its responsibilities to the civilian authorities with their National Guard and village militia. Vietminh military and political agents returned in strength to reinitiate their dormant operations among the unorganized and now unprotected people. The population started to decay. Vietminh regulars and regional units returned. Without popular support from the population or quick military support from nearby French regulars, the National Guard and village militia were no match for the tough, battle-hardened rebels. Within a few months, much of the Red River Sub-sector was again well on the way to becoming a Vietminh base.[10]

The devastating effect of the French political failure on military operations did not seem to strike the French high command.

De Lattre and his successors, Letourneau and Salan, persisted in dragging their feet on the issue of real Vietnamese independence, a move that undoubtedly would have spurred the pacification program. Similarly, a viable Vietnamese army would have solved, in large part, the military manpower problem. Yet, in January 1952, although thirty-six battalions of Vietnamese troops existed,

. . . only one division had been formed, and that was assigned to the defense of the Crown Domains, while the remaining three divisions, without staff, artillery, engineers, and communications sections, consisted merely of a mosaic of infantry battalions.[11]

Of seven hundred Vietnamese officers commissioned, only eighty held field rank and only four the rank of colonel. The first chief of staff, Nguyen Van Hinh, whom we shall encounter again, was an airman, a colonel in the French air force hastily promoted to brigadier general.[12] The upper classes did not willingly participate in a recruitment program, nor did conscripted students make the best officers. Too many of them

10. McCuen, op. cit.
11. Lancaster, op. cit.
12. Ibid.

claimed perquisites and privileges and ignored performance, often treating peasants with disdain:

> . . . the supercilious attitude of these scions of the bourgeoisie towards officers of the ill-armed and underpaid militia bodies was also a recurrent cause of friction and resentment, for many of the officers in the auxiliary forces, in spite of proven military capacity, were themselves debarred by lack of the requisite scholastic qualifications from access to the better-paid officer corps of the regular army.[13]

So it was that the French high command continued to fail both politically and militarily. Nor did the Truman administration intervene actively to force the French hand. In February 1952, the United States agreed to provide further military aid. In May, prior to Secretary of State Acheson's meeting with the French and British in Bonn, President Truman instructed him ". . . to avoid mentioning any specific amount of further aid and of internal changes in Indochina beyond the development of the forces. It was thought that such an agenda would keep the French to the points of immediate practical importance and avoid irritation on secondary and peripheral matters."[14]

It was these ". . . secondary and peripheral matters" that should have been discussed—and resolved. But factors present since 1946 had come of age to father new factors, all of them continuing to play a blocking role, as the Secretary of State later wrote:

> . . . cables from Paris and Saigon [i.e., American embassies in these cities] show the quandary in which we found ourselves. Paris told us that the French connected Indochina with the Tunisian-Moroccan problem and resented what they considered "United States intervention." Both Paris and Saigon agreed that Indochina needed to be "revitalized" or the drain on French resources might cause a decision to cut losses and withdraw. Bao Dai was not the man to pull Vietnam together, yet the French must go further to speed the evolution of the Associated States, just when de Lattre's death had removed effective French leadership. Saigon, while recognizing French sensitivities, believed that we should insist on information and action at the same time that the French asked us for aid. This, of course, is what we had been doing for two years.

Dutifully, in mid-June [1952] when Letourneau, who had succeeded de Lattre as High Commissioner, asked for more aid, I insisted, as my colleagues had suggested, that at a time when we were contributing more than a third of the cost of the campaign in Indochina it did not seem unreasonable to expect that we should be given the information to explain to our people why we were doing so and what progress was being made. Furthermore, friendly suggestions on the conduct of affairs from an ally so actively supporting them would not seem to be officious meddling. While Letourneau

13. Ibid.
14. Acheson, op. cit.

did not dissent, not much happened as a result. No one, however, seriously advised that, with the Bonn agreements awaiting ratification by the Senate and the French National Assembly and the situation in Indochina in its usual critical state, it would be wise to end, or threaten to end, aid to Indochina unless an American plan of military and political reform was carried out. Instead we recognized in a communiqué that the struggle in Indochina was a part of the worldwide resistance to "communist attempts at conquest and subversion," that France had a "primary role in Indochina," such as we had assumed in Korea, and stated that within the authority given by Congress we would increase our aid to building the national armies. Letourneau went home issuing optimistic statements of military and political progress in Indochina and the prediction that during the next six months American aid would increase to forty per cent of total French expenditures in Indochina.[15]

One reason, and a very good one, for French silence as to the military aspects was considerable ignorance. Where General Giap knew virtually every move contemplated by the French army, General Salan literally had no idea of Giap's next move. Typical was the post-Hoa Binh period. Although Giap could claim the upper hand in the Hoa Binh fighting, it was a fairly expensive claim. His casualties of just over a year probably topped twelve thousand dead, with many more thousands wounded. Not only were such losses difficult to replace, but they created a decided morale problem, and they also brought increasing criticism from party leaders beset with major agricultural and economic crises on the home front.[16] The French pacification effort was also beginning to cause Giap difficulty by depriving him of popular support that was essential to his tactics, particularly in predominantly Catholic areas. His concern is plainly shown in a directive of September 1952:

. . . In order to intensify guerrilla activity our attention must be focused not only on the regional troops but also on the armed bases of the communes and the communal guerrillas. The principal question is that of popular troops and the guerrillas. In certain regions one strives to reinforce these troops but is faced with great difficulties. The morale of the population [there] is not as solid as elsewhere. The bases of the popular troops and the cells of the party have been largely annihilated by the enemy and no longer present a satisfactory situation. These armed bases cannot perform their activities and are safeguarded only with great difficulty. Thus, our mission of first priority is to reinforce the popular bases.[17]

Until this happened, Giap wished to avoid further costly confrontations in the delta. Giap decided to strike instead in a less likely, and therefore, from the French standpoint, a more vulnerable area.

15. Ibid.
16. Hammer (*Struggle for Indochina*), *supra*.
17. Tanham, op. cit.; see also Giap, op. cit.

Beginning in 1950, the Viet Minh had been allied with the Communist-oriented Pathet Lao movement in nearby Laos. For some time, four Viet Minh battalions had been training Laotian cadres as well as spreading propaganda among Vietnamese living in Laos. Now, in autumn of 1952, Giap decided to push an army across the Thai Highlands in order to reach the Lao border (see map, Chapter 55).

In October, Giap started three divisions across the Red River. Within a week, they had overrun a series of small French outposts. But, in the interim, Salan organized defensive airheads at Lai Chau and Na San. In late November, the Viet Minh attacked Na San, where they expected little resistance. Instead, they encountered heavy fighting and, significantly, reverted to earlier and costly tactics, suffering an estimated seven thousand casualties in three unsuccessful attempts to overrun the position.[18] Giap now ordered his troops to bypass Na San. Although the French stand slowed the Viet Minh advance, the garrison subsequently failed to cut Giap's supply lines. Thus,

. . . the entrenched camp served principally to immobilize a force of from ten to twelve French Union battalions whose requirements in arms, ammunition, food, and comforts represented a heavy commitment for the French air force.[19]

Meanwhile, the Viet Minh advance forced Salan to evacuate other, smaller outposts, such as that at Dien Bien Phu (see maps, Chapters 52 and 62). By end of November, the Viet Minh army controlled much of the northwestern area and had reached the Laos border.

As Giap had foreseen, French artillery and armor had proved relatively useless against foot troops traveling in jungle, which also furnished excellent cover from French aircraft. Thus stymied, Salan reacted in two ways.

Despite failure of the Hoa Binh "meat-grinder" strategy, he and his staff were impressed at casualties inflicted on the Viet Minh, and they continued to think in terms of luring the enemy into attacking defended positions. The experience at Na San—Salan had hastily reinforced the garrison by airlift—encouraged the idea and led to establishing a series of *Bases Aéro-Terrestres,* or air-ground strong points, in the Northwest.

The reader will perhaps recognize a *Base Aéro-Terrestre* as the French version of Orde Wingate's "stronghold" concept (see Chapters 47–49, Volume I). A strong point consisted of a small garrison located in a remote mountain area, generally where local tribes had remained friendly to the French. Largely supplied by air, garrisons theoretically performed a psychological mission by maintaining French presence and a tactical mission by luring Viet Minh units to the attack. They also supported limited offensive action including support of GCMA units organized by De Lattre.

18. Lancaster, op. cit.
19. Ibid.; see also Fall (*Street Without Joy*), *supra.*

At the same time, General Salan thought to check Giap's drive toward Laos by a massive operation against his supply bases at Yen Bai and Phu Doan. Involving thirty thousand troops, ". . . by far the largest force ever assembled in a single attack in Viet-Nam," Operation Lorraine kicked off in late October, its first goal a hundred miles distant.[20]

Giap did not respond as Salan had hoped. Correctly reasoning that the French counteroperation would soon run out of steam, he kept his divisions on the Laos border while sending two regiments to fight a guerrilla-style delaying action. Although the French force "captured" the Phu Doan supply depots, the hard-pressed Salan called off the operation in mid-November. On the long road home, a Viet Minh regiment successfully ambushed two French mobile groups to cause heavy casualties.[21]

All this tactical activity personified protracted war, which at this stage clearly benefited the Viet Minh. The sad truth was that, while Ho Chi Minh and Giap relentlessly pursued limited and realistic goals, France continued to drag her heels both politically and militarily, the inevitable result of fecklessly pursuing an impractical, if not hopeless, ambition of retaining complete control of her Indochinese possessions. Not only was her increasing failure causing dangerous political explosions in France proper, but it was beginning to rile her most generous supporter —the United States. In mid-November 1952, when President-elect Eisenhower visited the White House, Secretary of State Acheson warned that ". . . we had been concerned for a long time about the course of action in Indo-China. There was a strong body of opinion in France which regarded this as a lost cause that was bleeding France both financially and by undermining the possibility of French-German equality in European defense."[22]

Despite Letourneau's promises to Acheson at their meeting in June 1952, no real information had been provided by the French, although it was obvious that the situation was deteriorating. The Secretary of State later wrote:

. . . In mid-December [1952] the Department [of State] noted the rising uneasiness in France about Indochina and a large gap in our government's information about the situation there and about French military plans, and it recognized as no longer valid an earlier French intention to so weaken the enemy before reducing French forces in Indochina that indigenous forces could handle the situation. It seemed clear to our observers that Vietnamese forces alone could not even maintain the existing stalemate. At the council Schuman pleaded for relief from France's "solitude" in Indochina and for volunteers to share the burden. He did not ask for troops, but for financial

20. Fall (*Street Without Joy*), *supra*.
21. Ibid.
22. Harry S Truman, op. cit.

help (we were already carrying forty per cent of it) and for recognition of the equal importance of the struggle in Indochina and Korea. Letourneau also spoke to the council, which responded with a resolution of support for the struggle against communism in Indochina but with no pledges of financial aid.[23]

At a later, private meeting of Acheson, Eden, Schuman, and Letourneau, the latter began an impassioned plea for aid which the American Secretary of State impatiently interrupted. Acheson was willing to provide a fact-finding military mission:

... I said it would go where Letourneau was; if he wanted to work with it in Saigon, that was satisfactory, but we would not struggle any longer to extract information from inferior officials who never seemed to have the authority to give it. He wanted aid; we wanted information. The next move was up to him.[24]

Jean Letourneau was in no position to have his Indochina books audited. He had installed as premier a rubber stamp named Nguyen Van Tam, who had failed, as had his predecessors, ". . . to build up any popular support, despite his talk of agrarian and other reforms."[25]

Militarily, he had become increasingly insolvent.

Although Vietnam forces had increased to sixty battalions comprising some 150,000 men, these were being organized, trained, and employed in the French tradition of conventional warfare, with French officers and (generally) NCOs in command. Yet the Vietnamese were playing an increasingly important combat role: in 1952, 7,730 of them were killed serving either with the Expeditionary Corps or in their own army, versus 1,860 and 4,049 Foreign Legion-African dead and missing.[26] Not unnaturally, the Vietnamese government and general staff wanted increased autonomy over its units. Significantly, in late 1952 the new Vietnamese general staff proposed a plan that, properly treated, would have solved many of Salan's problems.

The Vietnamese plan called for "light" battalions trained in guerrilla warfare and commanded by Vietnamese officers. These lightly armed, highly mobile units ". . . would be entrusted with the task of combating Viet Minh regional troops and pacifying areas from which enemy regular units had been expelled."[27] In the event, those units formed often consisted of unwilling and inadequately trained conscripts commanded by inefficient and often corrupt officers.

The national army suffered severely from lack of Vietnamese officers. In early 1953, only twenty-six hundred Vietnamese officers were serv-

23. Acheson, op. cit.
24. Ibid.
25. Shaplen, op. cit.; see also Buttinger, op. cit.
26. Lancaster, op. cit.
27. Ibid.

ing, with only a few above the rank of major; yet, over seven thousand
French officers served in Vietnamese units. Edmund Gullion later told
Shaplen: ". . . It remained difficult to inculcate nationalist ardor in a
native army whose officers and noncoms were primarily white Frenchmen."[28]

This military difficulty, lack of indigenous leadership, paralleled the
civil, or political, difficulty, and derived directly from it. Joseph Buttinger, in concluding that the major military deficiency ". . . was a lack
of competent [Vietnamese] officers," put his finger squarely on the
problem:

. . . The best elements of the Vietnamese educated middle class had no desire to serve in an army created to fight, still under French over-all direction,
for a regime they despised and against people who, even if led by Communists, were still known to be fighting primarily for national independence.
For these political reasons, which the colonial French mind failed to grasp,
the Vietnamese National Army never became much of a fighting force. It
remained indifferently trained, poorly led, and dubiously inspired. At the
end of the war, the French had at their disposal a Vietnamese force of 300,-
000 men, organized in various stages of training and availability for combat.
But not another square mile of territory had been pacified as a result of
its creation, and very few French troops had been relieved of their static
duties or become available for offensive action against the Vietminh.[29]

Because of failure to create a viable Vietnamese army, Salan continued generally on the defensive. The famed "de Lattre Line" (which
he privately called ". . . a sort of Maginot Line") had more holes
than a Swiss cheese, yet Salan continued to use some eighty thousand
troops to man ". . . more than 900 forts . . . using an armament of
close to 10,000 weapons, 1,200 mortars and 500 artillery pieces."[30] At
the time, Viet Minh strength *behind* the line continued to grow until
Giap's three regular regiments were working with fourteen regional, or
semiregular, battalions and an estimated 140 peasant militia companies
—some thirty thousand irregulars.[31] The French rightly termed this the
strategy of *pourrissement*—of "rotting away." As Giap now learned, it
was far more effective than that of meeting French forces head on—so
long as the French remained blind to the necessity of winning the population to their side.

With the bulk of French forces tied down, Giap continued to probe
into Laos while simultaneously expanding his control of central Vietnam. By spring of 1953, his units, working with various mountain tribes,
had reduced French control to a few beachhead areas such as Hué,
Da Nang and Nha Trang. In April, Giap's main force began infiltrating

28. Shaplen, op. cit.
29. Buttinger, op. cit.
30. Fall (*Street Without Joy*), supra.
31. Ibid.

into Laos. To gain time to build a central defense, Salan withdrew his outposts, two of the garrisons being badly mauled in the process. But, with help of an around-the-clock airlift, he organized a central defensive position on the Plaine des Jarres. Viet Minh attacks against this and against Luang Prabang failed, and in May, at onset of the rainy season, Giap called his divisions back to Vietnam. Important Viet Minh cadres remained behind, however, to continue working with the Pathet Lao.

If all this filled Foggy Bottom with alarm, it created something akin to panic in the Quai d'Orsay. In spring of 1953, a French Parliamentary Mission of Enquiry visited Vietnam and accused Letourneau of maintaining a ". . . veritable dictatorship, without limit or control," and of playing a game of ". . . power and intrigue."[32] Shortly after, a new French Government dismissed Letourneau and Salan, and appointed General Henri Navarre as commander in chief.

Navarre's appointment opened the final chapter in the French saga in Indochina. But before proceeding to those dramatic events, we must turn to equally vital guerrilla actions that were being fought elsewhere.

32. Buttinger, op. cit.; see also Hammer (*Struggle for Indochina*), *supra;* Lancaster, op. cit.

Chapter 57

The Greek civil war • Postwar confusion • Communist organization and strength • Communist defeat • Markos changes tactics • Growth of Communist strength • Government strength and weakness • The balance sheet • Communist guerrilla operations • Communist strength and weakness • Yugoslavia and Albania • The Truman Doctrine • The American army's quantitative approach • Greek army offensives • Communist political errors • Tito's defection • End of the war • The cost • Reasons for Communist defeat • Western "victory"

THE COMMUNIST-LED INSURRECTION in Greece broke out even before World War II ended (see Chapter 38, Volume I). Following German evacuation, a British force commanded by Lieutenant General Scobie landed in early October 1944; Prime Minister Papandreou and the government followed two weeks later.

Scobie commanded a hodgepodge force: two British brigades, British and American commandos, and some Free Greek units. Called III Corps, it numbered about twenty-six thousand men supported by five squadrons of aircraft—a weak army further diluted by erroneous command estimates that credited the Communist organization, EAM/ELAS, with co-operative intentions and with considerably less strength than they had.[1]

Scobie could do little more than occupy principal towns while

1. Edgar O'Ballance, *The Greek Civil War, 1944–1949* (London: Faber & Faber, 1966); see also C. M. Woodhouse, *Apple of Discord* (London: Hutchinson, 1948).

UNRRA [United Nations Relief and Rehabilitation Administration] units began the immense task of civil rehabilitation. EAM/ELAS used this confusing period to strengthen its ranks for all-out civil war. As Germans moved out, ELAS units filled vacuum areas and, in the North, established liaison with Albanian and Yugoslav Communist guerrillas. EAM already had organized a secret police (OPLA) and a gendarmerie (EP), both of which began to consolidate control of the countryside, major targets being hated Greek security battalions. EAM also used various delaying and obstructive tactics to prevent Papandreou from organizing a national army and a national guard. With the worsening situation apparent, Scobie called for reinforcements and received two Indian brigades.

The KKE Central Committee, the real authority behind EAM/ELAS, now came to a fateful decision that rested in large part on an arrogance derived from ignorance of the enemy's strength. Over the strong objections of Yioryios Siantos, who had led EAM during World War II, it decided to shift ". . . from infiltration and political intrigue to force."[2]

According to Major Edgar O'Ballance, whose excellent book *The Greek Civil War* I have largely relied on in this brief account, ELAS strength at the time had risen to above forty thousand, divided into two "armies": Army Southern, commanded by Siantos and Mandakas and comprising three divisions, or about eighteen thousand; and Army Northern, commanded by Saraphis and Aris and comprising five divisions, or about twenty-three thousand. While Army Southern drove the British from Athens to establish the new Communist government, Army Northern would destroy what was left of EDES resistance group.

Fighting broke out in early December 1944. Army Southern quickly gained the upper hand, separating and besieging British forces in Athens and Piraeus. But Scobie, hastily reinforced by a division from Italy, counterattacked in late December. Churchill and Eden also flew in and managed to bring dissident nationalist parties together in a new government under Plastiras, with Archbishop Damaskinos as regent.

Scobie quickly drove Army Southern from its positions, and a cease-fire, in mid-January, forced ELAS units to withdraw one hundred miles from Athens as well as from Salonika and the Peloponnese. ELAS foolishly refused to release civilian hostages, estimated between fifteen and twenty thousand, which greatly reduced its popularity in the country and allowed the Plastiras government to assume control of large areas.

These serious defeats jolted the KKE back to a covert strategy of infiltration. Under terms of the Varkiza Agreement, in February 1945, ELAS demobilized and disarmed its units, and released prisoners and hostages. The government reinstated regular army officers who had been serving with ELAS into the new national army, and it also legalized the

2. Edgar O'Ballance (*The Greek Civil War*), *supra:* The author suggests that Stalin might have been responsible for this decision.

KKE and promised to hold a plebiscite to determine whether monarchy should be restored and also a general election as soon as possible.[3]

Although a few ELAS units refused to disband and took to the hills, the main body turned in arms and went home. The uneasy peace soon broke down. The KKE accused the government of stalling. Rampant inflation, ". . . largely because of the influx of gold sovereigns through the Allied Military Mission," during the war,[4] helped Communists to foment unrest and demonstrations. The government, accusing ELAS of secretly burying arms and wholesale murder of hostages, instigated a repressive policy that included widespread arrest and detention of Communists, suspected Communists, and sympathizers. This policy helped to revive the Communist movement, as did return from German captivity of the former secretary-general of the KKE, Zakhariadis, in spring.

Throughout summer and autumn of 1945, charge and countercharge reverberated through the warm Greek air to intensify passions already inflamed by terrible human suffering. German occupation had left hundreds of thousands homeless and hungry, and, in the war's last months, only UNRRA relief shipments fended off mass starvation.

The end of World War II brought some relief to Greece, but the reconstruction task demanded a unified effort, with concomitant party and personal sacrifice. Instead, the country remained occupied by British troops whose commander attempted to reason with innumerable squabbling political factions, a pathetic caldron of internecine hatred fired by traditional, deep-seated, and often petty feuds fattened from the war years.

When the British, virtually frantic in frustration, asked Washington for financial help in autumn of 1945, President Truman gladly promised aid if the Greek Government would

. . . adopt a program of economic stabilization. I added that the extent to which we would help would depend on the effectiveness of the Greek action. . . .[5]

Although some progress resulted, nothing approximating good government appeared. Wanting to exploit the muddled situation, in December 1945 the KKE decided to reorganize scattered insurgent forces into a secret army capable of challenging the legitimate government. These groups now filtered across the border into Yugoslavia and Albania, which furnished training camps and some material aid. Although Stalin approved the decision, the Soviet Union subsequently furnished neither arms nor supply.[6]

While Nikos Zakhariadis launched this effort, he continued to pre-

3. Woodhouse, op. cit.
4. Ibid.
5. Harry S Truman, *Year of Decisions 1945* (London: Hodder & Stroughton, 1955).
6. O'Ballance (*The Greek Civil War*), *supra*.

side over a policy of infiltration and subversion of government. In March 1946, the KKE refused to participate in a general election, which overwhelmingly returned a rightist administration. Communists now stepped up disruptive tactics on two levels: in cities, by continued infiltration and obstructionism in government, armed forces, and labor unions; and in the country, by revival of small ELAS raids on villages.

In summer of 1946, the newly formed Republican Army began sending small guerrilla units over the border, mainly to carry out hit-and-run raids on villages to obtain food and also recruits.

In September, Markos Vaphiadis assumed command of the new army. A man of about forty years, Markos had joined the party in his teens, had been imprisoned, and had served with ELAS forces in Macedonia. Markos established small bases inside Greece and, aided by old EAM/ELAS village networks, stepped up guerrilla raids in quantity, depth, and purpose. In October, his groups began killing village policemen and progovernment peasants as well as taking hostages to insure later village co-operation.

How did the government react?

A confused official policy helped the Communist movement more than it hurt it. The initial error already had been made: a much too severe repressive policy, which allowed police, national guard units, and such paramilitary right-wing organizations as Colonel George Grivas' "X" group virtually a free hand in "cleaning up" ELAS remnants. By September, this policy had driven hundreds of people either to ELAS bands in the countryside or to Markos' new army across the border. And when a plebiscite, in September, returned a nearly 70 per cent vote to restore the monarchy, the new Tsaldaris government expanded its repressive policy by purging former ELAS officers from army and government service, closing down Communist and left-wing newspapers, and similar measures.

The government should have directed its zeal to the countryside, both to alleviate human suffering—numerous areas remained dependent on UNRRA supplies to avoid starvation—and to protect the people from guerrilla depredations. Partially influenced by British advice, the Tsaldaris government continued to think in "bandit" rather than "guerrilla" terms. To suppress "bandits," government relied on security forces totaling about thirty thousand—village gendarmerie, town police, and national guard units. Though not well organized, trained, or equipped, this total force, despite unco-ordinated operations, probably could have coped with bandits.[7] It could not cope with Markos' fast-moving guerrillas. Despite such measures as arming "anti-Communist" villagers—one can imagine the organization, training, and performance of this militia—the government continued to lose control of area after area.

In October, the government persuaded the British to go along with

7. Woodhouse, op. cit.

its committing regular army units. The Greek national army numbered only about a hundred thousand at this time and, like the national guard, was neither organized, trained, nor equipped for counterinsurgency operations. It also suffered from political controls: Powerful politicians insisted on guarding their own areas of interest, which meant tying up units in static defense; division commanders literally could not move units without permission from the army general staff in Athens, and the general staff itself was subordinate to a large, unwieldy, and politically divisive National Defense Council. In this respect, the Greek scene resembled that in Nationalist China and, as we shall see, the Philippines.

At this stage, then, winter of 1946–47, considerable red ink appeared in the Greek ledger: a continuing political anarchy that British efforts failed to ameliorate and that continued to hinder a proper attack on economic problems; a paucity of British aid, due to Britain's own severe economic problems; a repressive rather than progressive political policy, which drove some people to join the Communist insurgency; and a disorganized army and other security forces operationally hindered by severe deficiencies in organization, training, and equipment.

But black ink also appeared. In December 1946, in answer to formal complaint by Greece, the United Nations Security Council authorized a commission of inquiry to investigate and report on the allegedly Communist-provoked insurgency. This brought the problems of Greece into world focus. The United States simultaneously sent an economic mission to determine the country's needs. The people, themselves, remained amazingly resilient—a vast reservoir of strength, if only the government had recognized it: Despite the tragedy, sorrow, and hardship of four decades (indeed, of centuries), the fantastic spirit of the Greek people, particularly the rural people, with their love of freedom, never diminished. Significantly enough, a government amnesty policy (in refreshing contrast to over-all policy) had brought in several hundred deserters from Markos' ranks by end of 1946.

Nevertheless, red ink splashed over black, and government pusillanimity, fear, and corruption, prospered the Communist cause. Markos had started serious operations in September with about four thousand guerrillas divided into small, semi-independent units of about one hundred fifty men each. At year's end, his forces numbered perhaps seven thousand. In early 1947, this force (now called the Democratic Army) controlled a large area of northern Greece including perhaps one hundred villages. He next established general headquarters *inside Greece* at the junction of Albania, Yugoslavia, and Greece, the rugged terrain of the Grámmos and Vítsi mountain ranges. In March, he counted some thirteen thousand armed insurgents. In addition, the KKE in Athens, though operating underground, continued many subversive activities. Its highly secret terrorist organization, the OPLA, continued to intimidate and assassinate effective opponents. Of more importance to Markos was the country-wide organization known as YIAFAKA, which furnished his groups with intelligence, supply, recruits, and money, and sometimes performed propaganda and terrorist missions. Operating clandestinely, this organization probably had one or more "cells" in every town and village in Greece. Major O'Ballance estimated that, in mid-1947, it numbered some fifty thousand active members plus another quarter of a million sympathizers![8]

But red ink also appeared in the KKE ledger. As early as the end of 1946, the insurgency was falling between two stools of internal and external communism. The exile army needed material aid of Balkan countries, but, in exchange, Tito and Enver Hoxha demanded portions of northern Greece once the KKE won control. These guarantees caused a good deal of grumbling from the nationalist element of KKE, many of whom favored the Siantos theory of revolution from the inside.

Markos himself saw the danger of removing the revolution from the country, which was one reason he insisted on spreading operations throughout Greece, including the Peloponnese. But this also backfired, in that he needed at least fifty thousand armed rebels for the purpose. In trying to expand his meager force, he began impressing recruits, whom he held by threat of reprisals against village wives and families.

This proved a basic error—and on several counts. When unwilling recruits deserted, and they frequently did, Markos ordered reprisals, which further alienated the people from the insurgency. Unwilling recruits who remained in the mountains formed an abrasive element in a small guerrilla army whose ranks already were becoming disaffected by isolation, meager rations, physical discomforts, and inadequate arms and supply from parsimonious Yugoslavs and Albanians. Markos countered growing disaffection by sterner discipline and by circulating a false rumor that international brigades were on their way to aid the cause. Such palliatives only partially succeeded: By end of 1946, Markos faced a deserter problem.

The attempt to claim national affinity also explained in part transfer of Democratic Army headquarters to Greek territory (although Tito, anxious to free his diplomatic hand, urged removal of this insurgent incubus from Yugoslav territory). In taking this step, Markos established both an identity for the Athens government to exploit (particularly important from the standpoint of American public opinion) and a specific target for the Greek national army. Just as important, his move represented the first step in reverting to the earlier and unsuccessful doctrine of revolution by conventional warfare, which Siantos and Markos himself constantly argued against. But, in spring of 1947, Siantos died, and Markos perforce succumbed to pressure not only from a substantial element within the KKE but from Tito and Hoxha, who, so to speak, controlled the purse strings.

This new strategy might have worked had the Greek national army

8. O'Ballance (*The Greek Civil War*), *supra.*

remained dependent on its moribund British military parent. But, in February 1947, the Attlee government suddenly informed Washington that economic circumstances would force British withdrawal from Greece at the end of March. American advisers in Greece simultaneously warned Washington of an imminent Communist takeover. President Truman responded to the crisis with a massive military-economic aid program, announced in mid-March.[9]

The famous "Truman Doctrine" provided a much-needed shot in the arm to the Greek Government. In April, the army managed to round up fifteen thousand troops to launch a surprise offensive in the North. Although it caught Democratic Army units napping and inflicted reasonable casualties, the effort lasted only two weeks. But when Markos, goaded by Balkan allies, launched attacks on such towns as Flórina, Kilkís, and Kónitsa, local garrisons held until reinforced by neighboring units. This disappointing result caused the Democratic Army to revert temporarily to guerrilla tactics.

The KKE suffered another setback, in summer, when the Athens government launched a country-wide crackdown on known and suspected Communists. Although this got out of hand—some fifteen thousand persons were deported to the Aegean Islands—and brought down the government, it nonetheless disrupted and in some cases stopped the OPLA and YIAFAKA from supporting Markos.

Markos' strength continued to grow, however. In mid-1947, his forces numbered about twenty-three thousand, with perhaps seven thousand more in training. He now increased operational unit strength to about two hundred fifty men—some sixty-five to seventy "battalions" supported by a special area network, the ETA, whose units delivered supplies and evacuated wounded. His northern neighbors had also provided machine guns, mortars, and light artillery. His bands roamed virtually unimpeded over northern Greece, they were becoming increasingly active in central Greece, and one was even operating in the Peloponnese. According to Greek Government figures, in October 1947 the Democratic Army ". . . attacked and pillaged 83 villages, destroyed 218 buildings, blew 34 bridges and wrecked 11 railway trains."[10] Major towns managed to hold out, however, and Markos lacked strength and the necessary logistic setup for sustained attacks. He also lacked suitable officers and faced constant ammunition shortages. Moreover, he had lost command autonomy to a Yugoslav-dominated Joint Balkan Staff, which increasingly began to call operational signals.

Partly at Tito's and probably Stalin's instigation, the KKE announced formation of the "Free Democratic Greek Government" in December. Simultaneously, the Democratic Army attacked the major town of

9. Harry S Truman (*Years of Trial and Hope*), *supra*; see also Kennan (*Memoirs*—Vol. 1), *supra*.
10. O'Ballance (*The Greek Civil War*), *supra*.

Kónitsa, which was to serve as the new capital. Although Markos supported the attack with mortars, machine guns, and 105-mm. guns, it failed at considerably heavy cost: twelve hundred including deserters; as added mortification, not one ally recognized the new government, nor was it allowed to join the recently established Cominform.

The spirited defense of Kónitsa reflected some healthy changes in the Greek army, which showed both in increased firepower of infantry units and in air support. Massive shipments of military equipment from the United States had been arriving since summer. By end of March 1948, this aid totalled $71 million and included seventy-five thousand weapons, seven thousand tons of ammunition, twenty-eight hundred trucks and vehicles, and enough aircraft to support two squadrons.[11]

Simultaneously, an American military mission worked with the government in enlarging and reorganizing the Greek armed forces. This effort eventually resulted in an army of two hundred thousand supported by artillery, armor, and aircraft. The "fist" of this army consisted of an imposing eight infantry divisions, three independent brigades, and some special commando-type units trained in counterinsurgency warfare. To free the army for offensive operations, a reconstituted national guard numbering about fifty thousand and comprising some hundred battalions became responsible for local security.

The American organization responsible for this new look was a ponderous thing called the Joint United States Military Advisory and Planning Group (JUSMAPG), headed from February 1948 on by General James Van Fleet. JUSMAPG already had decided on a "military" solution of the insurgency problem, and neither Van Fleet nor the Greek National Defense Council objected. A combined Greek-American planning staff worked out a series of offensive operations, a co-ordination extended to the field via American officer advisers attached to Greek units.

In theory, the newly organized Greek army should have walked over Markos' twenty-three thousand guerrillas. In fact, nothing of the sort happened. Although local garrison defenses improved, which caused increased guerrilla casualties, large-scale government offensives, or "search-and-clear" operations, met only limited success. In June, for example, forty thousand troops attacked eight thousand guerrillas in the Grámmos Mountains area. In the ensuing fighting, Markos called in another four thousand guerrillas. But, late in August, when the national army was pushing in, Markos broke out. The government admitted eight hundred killed and five thousand wounded; they claimed three thousand guerrilla dead, 589 captured, and over six thousand wounded.

Meanwhile, JUSMAPG had been feverishly training fresh units; the magnitude of their effort was suggested by arrival from the United

11. Ibid.

States of 8,330 trucks and four thousand mules in June 1948. At the end of August, the army again attacked, with about fifty thousand troops, in the neighboring Vítsi Mountain area. Markos, with some thirteen thousand guerrillas, counterattacked and actually pushed the army back, although at the price of heavy casualties.

Considerable political action accompanied military give-and-take. In autumn of 1947, the Greek Government, prodded sharply by American authorities, cracked down hard on Communist elements. Actions included "total" conscription, with segregated political instruction or permanent detention for left-wing and Communist dissidents. Government police closed Communist newspapers, attempted to purge the civil service of suspects, and abolished the right to strike,[12] repressive measures continued throughout winter: In February, for example, the government publicly executed sixty-five Communists. In May, when Communist terrorists murdered the Minister of Justice, in Athens, the government replied with a bloodbath so severe that Britain and the United States finally protested.[13]

All this activity unfortunately furnished excellent propaganda both for the KKE and the Communist cause in general. Had the KKE acted more wisely, it could have been exploited into a powerful weapon. Instead, the KKE acted stupidly, by continuing to misuse the valuable weapon of terror. Markos' units displayed almost no discretion in dealing with villagers. Shortly after the civil war, this writer visited countless villages in Macedonia and Thrace, and the extent of wanton destruction and reported cruelties defied belief. In March, the KKE allowed Markos' units to spirit away nearly thirty thousand children for rearing in Cominform countries, a heinous act that caused widespread protest.[14] The murder of Justice Ladas in Athens was equally pointless, as were other random acts of terror, which only brought wholesale reprisals. But the biggest blow of all came in June and was no fault of the KKE: the Cominform suddenly expelled ingrate Yugoslavia.

Although Tito continued to support the insurgency, just how long his aid would last was anyone's guess. By late autumn, Markos' fiction of international brigades had become obvious to all, as had failure of the general population to rise inside Greece. Markos was forced to repair losses in the Grámmos-Vítsi campaigns only by brutal conscription. To add to his woes, Zakhariadis, the powerful secretary-general of the KKE, forced him to abandon protracted guerrilla strategy in favor of forming conventional units, small brigades of three or four battalions, the whole forming five "divisions." This fundamental split in the insurgent camp occurred in November 1948; it swiftly widened, and, at the end of January 1949, Zakhariadis replaced Markos in command of the Democratic Army.

12. Ibid.
13. Ibid.
14. Woodhouse, op. cit.

Meanwhile the national army had grown much stronger. The failure of the Grámmos-Vítsi campaigns had caused a basic change in tactics. Beginning in January 1949, the government lowered sights to concentrate on specific areas. By temporarily removing whole sections of population—a costly and onerous but highly effective process—it began to deprive guerrilla bands of intelligence and material support and led to some important gains.

By end of January, the army had cleared four thousand insurgents from the Peloponnese at a cost of fifty-eight killed (versus sixteen hundred insurgent dead). In February, the government appointed a new commander in chief of the army, the able and popular architect of the 1940 triumph over the Italians, General Papagos. Papagos accepted only after being promised that the National Defense Council would not intrude in field operations.

Although some heavy fighting lay ahead, the days of the Democratic Army were numbered. The final blow fell in July, when Tito closed his border to the insurgents. Papagos now attacked in six-division strength and, by end of August, cracked the Vítsi stronghold. In mid-October, Zakhariadis, possibly at Stalin's insistence, asked for a cease-fire.

The physical cost of the Greek civil war was enormous. The Greek Government later claimed that the war had taken nearly twenty-nine thousand Communist lives and that perhaps twice as many were wounded. Greek army losses included almost eleven thousand killed, some twenty-three thousand wounded, and thirty-seven hundred missing. Civilians suffered much-more-severe losses. Major O'Ballance estimated that, all told, 158,000 Greeks died, about half of whom were militant Communists.[15]

This tragic war also produced other losses, which paradoxically accrued as a result of what the West called "victory." The first such loss was Western failure to analyze the war accurately and learn thereby. Unfortunately, American military commanders, primarily army commanders, concluded that a Communist insurgency could be defeated by conventional methods of warfare. In subsequent years, army planners gave far too much credit to the importance of regular armies and increased firepower, and insufficient credit to the success of such methods as temporarily removing the civil population from guerrilla-infested areas and to the importance of a single, forceful commander not unduly restricted by civil control.

Neither did the enemy receive proper attention. If questioned on the cause of Communist defeat, most American officers today would mention Tito's defection and subsequent closing of the border, a misconception also held by the author of this book until he accompanied a U. S. Marine Corps mission to Greece in the early 1950s and discussed

15. O'Ballance (*The Greek Civil War*), *supra*.

the insurgency with numerous senior Greek officers and officials, in addition to traveling extensively in the north.

Tito was not the principal cause of Markos' defeat. Markos was beaten before he started. The KKE had never concentrated on establishing an identity with the people needed to support a protracted insurgency. As early as winter of 1941–42, Greek nationalists began to see through the fiction of EAM/ELAS, which, despite its coalitionist pretensions, would brook no minority opposition.[16] British SOE officers operating in Greece in World War II remarked on the cavalier behavior of ELAS leaders toward the civil population. ELAS' disregard increased

in the civil war, as evidenced by barbarous treatment of civilian hostages, rapacious behavior in villages, and kidnaping children and sending them from the country—stupid actions personally and feelingly described to this author by numerous villagers in Macedonia and Thrace not long after the war. This major miscalculation stemmed in part from the urban bias of Marxist-Leninist teachings (as opposed to those of Mao Tse-tung), teachings seemingly substantiated by immediate popu-

16. Woodhouse, op. cit.

larity and success of the insurgency, which unduly impressed the Soviet-oriented element of the KKE Central Committee; Zakhariadis was probably in large part responsible for this major error.

The second important Communist mistake also appeared during World War II, the attempt to acquire power by a military putsch. After the failure of EAM/ELAS to take power, in 1945, the KKE should have followed Siantos' advice to revert to infiltration and penetration tactics. Failing that, they should later have let Markos continue with guerrilla warfare; whether he could have survived with only Romanian and Bulgarian help is a moot question that probably would have involved the Soviet Union.

The West greatly overestimated the Soviet role in Greece. What Western leaders considered a great "victory" against Russian communism did not bother Stalin nearly as much as Tito's defection. *There* was a victory for the West—and one far removed from influence of Western arms.

Believing that it had won a victory in the conventional sense, the West could only have been disillusioned by subsequent events in Greece. The war did not eliminate Communist influence. Country people may have come to loathe Markos' guerrillas, but that does not mean they came to love their deliverers. Although a healthy political stability followed the end of the war—two prime ministers, or governments, in twelve years—the work of reconstruction proceeded slowly, partly the fault of fiscal demands of a military plant far too large for a small state to support. A plodding and generally feckless reconstruction naturally caused grumbling and, in time, turned some Greeks once again to the Communist cause.

As political conditions grew more unsettled, the government again exacerbated matters by invoking the traditional repressive policy that jailed thousands and eventually led to the loathsome dictatorship of the colonels.

The end result was hardly what President Truman and his advisers envisaged when he announced his brave doctrine in 1947. At that time, he told the American people

. . . that it must be the policy of the United States to support free peoples who are resisting attempted subjugation by armed minorities or by outside pressures.[17]

In words drowned by the irony of events, he told his vast audience that he wanted these free peoples to enjoy the American system:

. . . Our way of life is based upon the will of the majority, and is distinguished by free institutions, representative government, free elections, guarantees of individual liberty, freedom of speech and religion and freedom from political oppression.

17. Truman (*Years of Trial and Hope*), *supra*.

The second way of life is based upon the will of a minority forcibly imposed upon the majority. It relies upon terror and oppression, a controlled press and radio, fixed elections, and the suppression of personal freedoms. . . .[18]

18. Ibid.

Chapter 58

*The Philippine problem • Postwar situation • The Huks •
Basis of Communist popularity • Communist tactics • Government countertactics • American army influence • Success and
failure • Magsaysay takes over • His ultimate failure*

ONE OF PRESIDENT TRUMAN'S earliest official callers, in
April 1945, was the exiled president of the Philippine Islands, Sergio
Osmeña, who expressed concern for the postwar future of his country.
Truman hastened to assure him that he would ask Congress to support
a reconstruction effort for this American possession that had been
promised independence.[1]

The war left these islands in appalling condition: Over a million
Filipinos had been killed and hundreds of thousands wounded; disease
filled the barrios; millions of people were homeless and hungry; Manila and other important cities lay in ruins; the transport network essential to ship produce in a country predominantly agricultural had
been virtually destroyed, along with schools, hospitals, and villages.
The political framework essential to proper government had been
splintered by Japanese occupation forces and wartime collaborators.

1. Truman (*Year of Decisions*), *supra.*

The volatile nature of Filipino politicians caused further discord, as did the crying need for legislative reforms, particularly land reforms, a banner immediately hoisted by the Communist Huks, a group that survived the war in very real strength (see Chapter 40, Volume I).

The Huks did not attempt a putsch during the immediate reconstruction period. One reason was the powerful and popular presence of American military forces, which, as General MacArthur had promised, did return to liberate the islands. The obvious desire of the United States Government to grant independence also enhanced this popularity, as did human relief soon felt from a generous aid program.

But another, more subtle reason existed. In 1945–46, the Communist Party of the Philippines was not a cohesive political party controlled from either Moscow or Yenan. It contained socialist and Communist components, and each component contained members holding a variety of views generally expressed with nationalist bias. The Communist hierarchy included Mao-oriented Chinese members, but these were in a minority. Party officials had remained out of touch with each other for long periods, and no single voice dominated party councils. Luis Taruc, the *Supremo,* or commander in chief, of the Huks during and after the war, went so far in his memoirs as to write of autumn of 1945: ". . . As far as I could judge, there was no plan to prepare for a future revolution."[2]

Claiming to want a political solution, Taruc won a seat in the new Congress, elected in April 1946. Just what would have happened had Taruc and his fellows been allowed a minority function in the new government is anyone's guess. Disruptive they were, but they were scarcely alone in using strong-arm methods before and during the election. Their subsequent opposition to such legislation as the Bell trade agreement and a military-bases agreement with the United States should have surprised no one, particularly since Filipino and American non-Communist liberals also questioned the terms of these acts.

Although the Communists were disqualified from their congressional seats on grounds of using terrorism during the campaign, the trouble went much deeper. Taruc and his associates represented a distinct challenge to a hegemony exercised by immensely powerful landowners and industrialists spawned during four decades of American overlordship. This group, which included substantial American interests, had usurped the old landowning role of the Church, which had made itself hated by peasants. William Howard Taft's dreams of giving peasants a fair shake (see Chapter 14, Volume I) had disappeared into a day of real greed: In 1944, peasant farmers still owned only about 10 per cent of the land they tilled. They farmed remaining land on a tenant

2. Luis Taruc, *He Who Rides the Tiger* (New York: Frederick A. Praeger, 1967).

basis, with the average plot too small to support the farmer once his
rent, 50 per cent of the crop, was paid.

Nothing was secret about system or figures. They were over four
hundred years old. They explained four centuries of poverty punctuated by uprisings, and, in 1946, they explained a Communist popularity that a reactionary government was too greedy and frightened to
admit or accept.

Quiet analysis would have shown the fragile nature of this popularity,
which hard-core Communists suffered rather than enjoyed. It derived
from protest against perverted democracy, not belief in atheistic communism—abhorrent to good Catholics. It was a Red balloon highly vulnerable to puncture by proper leadership and corrective legislation, but
a balloon equally capable of expansion to unpleasant proportions. A
genuine land-reform bill in 1946 would have deflated the balloon virtually overnight and would have saved the government a long and costly
war that nearly resulted in Huk victory.

Instead of absorbing and then neutralizing opposition by legislation,
the government challenged the enemy. Charge collided with countercharge, the friction depositing powder that soon exploded into intimidation and murder. When the government unseated Communist members
of Congress, the Huks took to the hills and raised the standard of revolt.

This was not as forlorn as it sounds. Many Huks had buried World
War II weapons against such a contingency, and, in the back country of
central Luzon, had little trouble in finding relatively secure bases. The
Politburo in Manila ordered dissidents to revert to wartime organization
and establish Regional Commands or, Recos. Each of the half dozen
Recos occupied a specific area, where it operated in squadrons of varying size. The party had also kept alive its village network, which was
called the Barrio United Defense Corps or BUDC, the "farmers by day,
guerrillas by night." BUDC units normally operated ". . . in their own
locality, attacking targets of opportunity, assisting or reinforcing forces
from the higher strata, or simply maintaining the 'guerrilla presence,'
their domination of the local citizens."[3]

In short order, then, the Huks had a cause centered on the age-old
cry of "land for the landless," and they had a viable organization that,
for the moment, answered such urgent problems as food, clothing, and
shelter.

Where should they go from here?

The history of guerrilla warfare confirmed a potential, but it also
suggested weaknesses. One was need for food, clothing, shelter, and
security over a long period. Another was need for communications between units operating in six thousand square miles of primitive country
and between units and the underground Central Committee in Manila.

3. Valeriano and Bohannan, *Counter-Guerrilla Operations—The Philippines Experience* (New York: Frederick A. Praeger, 1962).

The guerrillas also required additional weapons and, most of all, information as to government strength and weakness.

The factor common to these needs was the peasant population. Although no figures exist, veteran observers have suggested that the Huks probably found about 10 per cent of the peasants actively favoring them, about 10 per cent actively opposed to them, and about 80 per cent neutral. This middle body, this frightened and apathetic 80 per cent, would have to furnish food, clothing, shelter, security, and information essential to Huk survival. They constituted Mao's famous water in which guerrilla fish were to swim.

The process of winning active or passive support of this group was immensely complicated, with one factor merging into another. The most important step, however, was *recognition* of need for this support. Literally every *action* of the Huks provoked a *reaction* from the peasant mass.

How did the guerrilla go about winning peasant support? He used to advantage his physical and armed presence in proclaiming a cause that struck a responsive note among many disgruntled peasants. The Huks oriented their appeal personally rather than politically. The honeyed words held a strong nationalist bias that associated people virtually devoid of hope and dignity with the freedom fighters of yesterday and today, the whole performance gaining force from contrast of the guerrilla presence with either minimum or no government presence.

But the guerrilla did not appeal by words alone. By successfully attacking police stations and small military outposts, the Huks encouraged the eager and intimidated the wary, and in the process, gained arms for new recruits. Nor did they hesitate to eliminate known opponents by using selective terrorism, usually torture and murder.

This consolidation process should have been a dangerous time for the Huk movement. Despite advantages gained by seizing the initiative, the Huks could not set up communication networks overnight; neither could they effectively broaden their support base in a short time. Had the government reacted skillfully, it might have ended the insurgency in short order. Unfortunately, its reaction was such as to help, and not hinder, the insurgent cause.

The Philippine Government was ill-equipped to cope with this insurgency. Police forces, along with other public services, were still being reorganized. The government's armed forces consisted only of a constabulary, the Military Police Command (MPC), equipped with small arms and supervised by American army officers. These company-size units lacked training and discipline, and in early raids on suspected Huk hideouts, they used little restraint either in rounding up suspects or in dealing with peasants.

This was partly the government's fault. President Roxas and his advisers failed to understand that the basic mission of democratic government is to represent the people and defend their interests. It follows that, in an insurgency situation, the first mission of government is to protect the people, not alone on humanitarian grounds but also because only the people can furnish information necessary to accomplish the corollary mission of destroying insurgent organization.

As two veterans of the Philippine insurgency, Colonels Valeriano and Bohannan, have pointed out in their invaluable book *Counter-Guerrilla Operations—The Philippine Experience*,[4] Roxas confused priorities and ordered the constabulary to eliminate the threat without due heed of either security or rights of peasants. He compounded this error by placing operational restraints on the constabulary. In effect, the government told the constabulary to suppress the rebellion by arresting rebels, but, at the same time, it refused to pass emergency legislation giving the constabulary sufficient powers to accomplish the task.

Under the writ of habeas corpus, a suspect could be detained only seventy-two hours. This meant, in effect, that the most carefully planned and humanely conducted raid was a waste of time. The government's problem was to provide ". . . a means by which troops could deal with prisoners and suspects in an acceptable, civilized way without releasing them. Politically speaking, this problem could not be solved unless the government enjoyed substantial public confidence. . . ."[5] Aware of its shaky foundations, the government did not act courageously, and the problem remained. The normal troop solution was to beat a suspect as warning. This, the theory of deterrence, had been exploded a thousand times in all countries, and is particularly dangerous if the suspect happens to be innocent.

The government also erred in ordering the MPC to place garrisons in towns and villages and on large estates of powerful politicians. This tied down units, and such was general behavior of troops that their presence further alienated the peasant population. Huk spies were everywhere, and soldiers could not move without their knowing it.

Deprived of information, the MPC could not begin to accomplish its mission. Initial failure produced frustration. The Huks, on the other hand, were daily gaining support and, with it, ample information on MPC plans and movements. As MPC patrols fell into ambushes and small outposts suffered surprise attacks, fear joined frustration to increase brutality toward people whom the soldiers were supposed to be protecting. Each instance of brutality converted more people to the Communist cause, a vicious circle that could only have been terminated by intelligent and decisive action at top governmental levels.

In the political sphere, the government relied on half measures that solved nothing. Valeriano and Bohannan offer a striking illustration of this in 1947, when the Huks demanded that the government guarantee a "fair share" of the rice harvest to tenant farmers. The Huks, most of

4. Ibid.
5. Ibid.

whom came from farm backgrounds, knew that an increased share of the harvest would not solve the peasant's economic plight. Tenant farms were mostly too small to support the tenant and his family, let alone the landlord as well. By enacting legislation that changed the fifty-fifty share arrangement to seventy-thirty in the tenant's favor, Roxas angered landlords without gaining peasant favor, and also showed himself prone to pressure of Huk propaganda (which the Huks quickly pointed out to the peasants).

If Roxas failed to assuage peasant dissatisfaction by legislative means, he positively encouraged it with his executive policy. He answered initial Huk successes by building an imposing (and expensive) national army, a policy encouraged by American military advisers and supported by the American Government.

Unfortunately, enlarged effort merely embraced old errors. The new battalion combat teams were splendid enough, supported as they were by armor, aircraft, artillery, and even war dogs, but they continued to fight guerrillas as if waging conventional war. Although search operations at times disrupted guerrilla communications and even, on occasion, trapped a few Huks, they more often than not disrupted and antagonized the native population.

The use of the *zona* is a case in point. Unable to obtain accurate information from alienated peasants, the army employed a technique of sealing off and "screening" one or more hostile villages. The *zona* was stupid psychologically, because the Japanese had used it frequently and people associated it immediately with horrible tortures and executions. If employed at all, it should have been but sparingly and then only by disciplined troops who would go out of their way to regain support of villagers. Instead, it was used frequently, and, all too often, to gratify baser instincts of soldiers, as described by Taruc:

. . . When the soldiers rounded up the barrio people, they would drive them at gun-point to the nearest town. Meanwhile, the raiders would be busy looting and burning. For a day or two, the troops would live well off the barrio people's poultry and domestic pets. . . . To cover their misdeeds, the soldiers would report that the vandalism was the work of the Huks who had "offered stiff resistance before finally running away." Or their story might be that the destruction they had left behind was the result of cross fire between themselves and the Huks who, of course, had suffered heavy losses, but had nonetheless succeeded in burning the barrio to cover their retreat and got away with their dead and wounded.[6]

Large-scale search-and-destroy operations also backfired. The army would spend weeks and sometimes months preparing a surprise attack in force against a guerrilla redoubt. Then several battalions suitably reinforced by artillery and air units would throw what communiqués

6. Taruc, op. cit.

called "a ring of steel" around the target area. These attacks rarely, if ever, achieved surprise. Taruc later wrote:

. . . If we knew it was going to be a light attack, we took it easy. If it might give us more trouble than we could handle, we slipped out quietly in the darkest hours of the night, abandoning the area of operation altogether. There were a few occasions when we were detected in our attempt to slip away and a running battle resulted. Occasionally, we carried out a surprise attack, achieving a lightning breakthrough and throwing our enemies into confusion. We were familiar with the terrain and had the advantage of light packs, the ability to move fast, and the support of the local people. Even the army's dog teams, cavalry, and motorized units were useless in the dark of night against an enemy that set out in small groups and dispersed in all directions, only to regroup again on the following day at a previously agreed meeting place. We were invariably successful in such fast, diversionary, tactical retreats.

When our ruse went undetected, it could be both amusing and saddening to watch the Philippine Air Force busily bombing and strafing, or to see thousands of government troops and civil guards cordoning our campsite and saturating, with every type of gunfire, the unfortunate trees and vegetation. Or we would watch them, worn and weary, scaling the whole height and width of a mountain, with not a single Huk in the area. After a week or two of such costly but useless efforts, we would often read glowing reports in the newspapers of the success of the operation. Such successes had to be claimed to justify the millions of pesos that were being wasted.[7]

Taruc claimed that six years of fighter-bomber attacks killed exactly twelve guerrillas!

These "ring of steel" operations inevitably involved peasant communities, whose villages sometimes became subject to *zona* treatment or even to outright attack. This merely deepened basic antagonisms, while false claims of success only heightened Huk prestige. The gulf between army (government) and people was so great that, by 1950, army units

. . . adopted the practice of entering every inhabited area in Huklandia in an exaggerated combat posture. Troops would move in by truck, obviously battle-ready, weapons pointing out in all directions as though they expected immediate assault.

From their demeanor, it was to be assumed that they felt they were among enemies, that they anticipated momentary attack. The psychological effect of this was deplorable. . . .[8]

Other gimmicks proved harmful to the objective of winning over the population. One was the absurd ". . . reconnaissance by fire—firing

7. Ibid.
8. Valeriano and Bohannan, op. cit.

into areas where guerrillas might be, without concern for the civilians who might equally well be there."[9] Similarly, the "open area" technique allowed troops in certain areas to shoot at anything that moved. Notices proclaimed this fact, but a certain percentage of any group "never gets the word" and the death of several innocent people, not to mention precious carabaos, scarcely increased army popularity. Road checkpoints further antagonized the populace, because, more often than not, the soldiers ". . . were collecting toll while disrupting thoroughly a great deal of commercial traffic."[10] Propaganda posters depicting Huk cruelties were so realistic that they frightened peasants not *away* from but *toward* the Huks.

More-sophisticated tactics also boomeranged. In theory, the Nenita units seemed unbeatable. This was a small detachment, Valeriano and Bohannan tell us, that was organized and trained ". . . to seek out and destroy top leaders of the Huk. Openly based in the heart of the strongest Huk area, it sought by disciplined ruthless action to strike terror into the Guerrillas and their supporters." In practice, ". . . the unit did succeed in capturing or killing many Huks, in substantially dampening the fighting spirit of many more, and in reducing the effectiveness of local support organizations." Alas, the operation was a success, but the patient died:

. . . the overall effect of the Nenita operation . . . was, on the whole, to increase support for the Huk. How could a government claiming concern for the welfare of the people and protection of their interests support a gang of ruthless killers, many of whose victims were not proved traitors? The political repercussions were serious, as might be expected in a democratic country. Even more damaging to the government was the condemnatory attitude of the press, cunningly intensified by Huk propagandists. In the end, many Filipinos were convinced that the government, by the use of such a force showed itself to be at least as bad as the Huk, and perhaps less deserving of support than the "agrarian reformers."[11]

Luis Taruc succinctly summed up the lesson: ". . . One thing seems clear: no country—least of all a Christian land—can defeat Communism by the use of un-Christian methods."[12]

Unfortunately, during this crucial period neither the Philippine Government nor its American advisers correctly analyzed the nature of the insurgency, which would have caused a rearrangement of priorities. As a result, clouds of confusion continued to cover the action, with a harmful and wasteful proliferation of official agencies. Valeriano and Bohannan pointed out the duplication of intelligence agencies. Constabulary, army, national police, and Manila police *each* maintained an

9. Ibid.
10. Ibid.
11. Ibid.
12. Taruc, op. cit.

M.E.P.

intelligence organization. ". . . Nearly a dozen other agencies, ranging from the special agents of the Office of the President to the Customs Secret Service, thought they had a proper role in the collection of intelligence about Communists, or the Huk, or both, and they too engaged in it."[13]

Naturally, the Huks prospered from this needless competition and from misplaced military zeal. While government troops harassed the people by day, ". . . every night the barrios were visited by Huk units, organizers, and propagandists who held impromptu meetings enlivened by revolutionary songs and short political skits."[14] Such grass-roots propaganda sessions allowed the Huks to disrupt communications between government and people by constantly contrasting official sayings with official doings. A Huk agent working in ruins of a village with firelight flickering on a corpse or two, the result of a government attack, did not have to be a William Jennings Bryan to alienate the peasant further from his government.

The Huks also continued to appeal by association, asking for and often receiving a penny or two; ". . . the farmer was asked, politely and

13. Valeriano and Bohannan, op. cit.
14. Taruc, op. cit.

humbly, if he could spare some food for the men who were fighting 'for his cause, on his behalf, and to establish the new peoples' democracy.' Thus guerrilla foraging was actually made to contribute to their propaganda campaign."[15]

Nocturnal visits also obtained young recruits for guerrilla units in the hills. Here the recruit usually attended school: ". . . a school for cadet officers, another for mass organizers . . . schools for intelligence officers, couriers, and medical workers. . . . The more advanced students attended classes in Philippine and world history, social and civic science, politics and government, mathematics." The Huks used group forums both to disseminate slanted news and for the weekly "production meeting"—". . . a criticism and self-criticism session of the type common in all Communist parties everywhere."[16]

Such methods resulted in steady growth of Huk strength, which Taruc later reported as ten thousand armed fighters and two thousand active sympathizers in 1948. Valeriano and Bohannan agreed with the figure of twelve thousand guerrillas, but concluded, ". . . perhaps 150,000 of the nearly two million people in the area [of central Luzon] were sympathizers and supporters of the Huk."[17] This did not include an undoubtedly high percentage of the passive population, which the Huks continued to intimidate in their favor.

Despite substantial Huk gains, the insurgency confined itself largely to central Luzon. Although the Central Committee in Manila grandly proclaimed formation of a People's Liberation Army, with ". . . a timetable for expansion and for the seizure of national power,"[18] the socialist and Communist factions already were arguing over long-term goals.[19] Neither the Central Committee in Manila nor the most united and determined Huk leadership in the field could overcome logistic and administrative problems in converting guerrillas to a semiregular force. Guerrillas lacked supporting arms and services of all types, and they possessed neither geographical proximity nor logistic means to gain these arms. They lacked safe areas in which to organize and train semiregular forces, and their supply system probably could not have supported the effort. An army would have ended the almost autonomous authority jealously protected by Reco commanders. Necessarily rudimentary communications also hindered disciplined and co-ordinated operations, and the Huks never did eliminate the bandit and criminal element that often hurt the insurgency by exploiting the environment for private gain.

Lack of co-ordinate command and growing dissension in higher ranks tended to panic some units into placing mistaken emphasis on terrorist methods, which culminated, in April 1949, with ambush and murder of

15. Valeriano and Bohannan, op. cit.
16. Taruc, op. cit.
17. Valeriano and Bohannan, op. cit.
18. Ibid.
19. Taruc, op. cit.

a motor party that included the popular widow of President Quezon:
". . . For the first time, widespread popular wrath flared against the
Huk."[20] The high command also incensed public opinion by ordering
all-out attacks on cities and army garrisons in 1950.

By this time, the insurgency had produced some excellent countertactics by the Philippine army and constabulary. By far the best army
tactic was the small patrol (as Americans had learned in 1898–1902).
Ranging from half-squad to platoon size, patrols carried out a variety
of missions. They extended the government's presence to villages, they
sometimes obtained intelligence on guerrilla movements, they set up
mobile checkpoints to disrupt guerrilla communications. Extreme mobility of patrols kept the guerrilla off balance and, not least, they allowed
the soldier an active and interesting role, as opposed to the deadening
garrison, or passive role, and thereby spawned new and sometimes effective tactical ideas.

The best army commanders practiced a variety of patrol tactics:

. . . regular patrols which passed through specified areas almost on a schedule, following roads or trails. There were unscheduled, unexpected patrols,
sometimes following an expected one by fifteen minutes. There were patrols
following eccentric routes, eccentric schedules, moving cross-country at right
angles to normal travel patterns, which often unexpectedly intercepted
scheduled patrols.[21]

In guerrilla-infested country, one patrol paralleled another so that either
could respond to an attack. Some commanders saturated an area with
patrols to overload the guerrilla intelligence service—rather like dropping strips of tinfoil to jam a radar screen.

Colonel Valeriano's constabulary company trained a force of four
officers and seventy-six men, Force X, as ". . . a realistic pseudo-Huk
unit that could, in enemy guise, infiltrate deep into enemy territory."
The reader may remember that General Funston employed a similar
device to capture the insurgent leader Aguinaldo in 1901 (see Chapter
14, Volume I). Valeriano heightened the illusion by including two
wounded men (volunteers) in the force and by staging mock battles
with the rest of the company. His sophisticated operation resulted in
spectacular successes. In addition to excellent "kills" of Huks, Force X
". . . found that most of the town mayors and chiefs of police were in
collusion with the enemy. They discovered that there were enlisted men
in the PC [constabulary] company on the other side of the swamps who
were giving information to the Huks. They learned that supplies were
left by women in selected spots along the road to be picked up at sundown by the Huk. . . ."[22] On occasion, Valeriano's regular company

20. Valeriano and Bohannan, op. cit.
21. Ibid.
22. Ibid.

would "capture" some of his Huks and turn them over to local police. In jail, they frequently obtained valuable intelligence on collaborators. Valeriano also tested loyalty of local officials by "kidnaping" peaceful farmers: If the local mayor or police chief failed to report the man's absence within five days, he was probably pro-Huk.[23]

Other units used civilian disguises to infiltrate villages and pick up valuable information. One unit acquired small panel trucks and filled the back end with soldiers—an unpleasant surprise for any Huk foraging patrol that stopped the vehicle. A commander well versed in old Moro campaigns remembered an American army habit of "losing" .45-caliber cartridges. Loaded with dynamite, they blew the Moro to bits when he fired them. This particular commander prepared cartridges that would blow up only the rifle, then inserted them into Huk supply channels with reportedly substantial "psychological and physical effects."[24] Some commanders left units behind to surprise guerrillas after a regular army "sweep"; others confused guerrillas into precipitate action by firing hundreds of flares.

Well-trained and -motivated soldiers will usually come up with shrewd and cunning battle practices, but these count for little if basic strategy is in error—and that was the case in the Philippines.

Fortunately for the future of that country, a natural leader finally tore himself from Manila's festering political womb to emerge in 1950. This was the famous Ramon Magsaysay, who became Minister of National Defense in the Quirino government.

Magsaysay was a peasant with a purpose hammered home by a determined but winning personality, which partially removed the sting from his decisive and sometimes ruthless actions. Believing that the power of his country lay in peasant hands, he insisted that first mission of government was to represent and protect peasants. In its simplest form, this meant returning government to people or, conversely, convincing the people that representatives of the government existed to serve their needs.

To the fury of many politicians, Magsaysay usurped the Communist call of "land for the landless" to make it the rallying cry for his party in the 1950 elections. Though his plans were later sabotaged, these were not empty words, and he went to a great deal of trouble explaining his reform program to the peasants.

Appointed Secretary of National Defense, Magsaysay turned to the immense task of effectively organizing the counterinsurgency for the first time. One of his early successes consisted in arresting the Politburo and Secretariat of the Communist Party in Manila. He then turned to teaching the army to associate itself with the people. He first introduced widespread internal reforms designed to check corruption and improve

23. Hosmer, *Counterinsurgency: A Symposium—April 16–20, 1962* (Santa Monica, Calif.: RAND Corporation, 1963).
24. Valeriano and Bohannan, op. cit.

discipline. At the same time, he tried to explain the government's mission to the military and show commanders how to carry it out. Magsaysay summarily eliminated such flagrant violations of human rights (and common sense) as "free-fire" areas, and he sharply curtailed the "combat-posture" of troops "at the ready" entering villages they theoretically were to protect. He changed the *zona* technique to a civilized interrogation, which insured the individual privacy and, just as important, left no doubt in the individual's mind that the purpose of the operation was his own protection. He insisted that the major aim of any military operation was to win civil co-operation—for, without it, the army would lack information and would not catch guerrillas. If a village was short of food because of its contribution, voluntary or forced, to the Huks, Magsaysay ordered the soldiers to replace the food.

As peasant hostility disappeared, military commanders began to receive valid and timely intelligence on which they based operations that soon yielded Huks—killed, captured, or surrendered. A generous amnesty program also attracted Huk defectors, particularly when pressure mounted from military operations.

Eighteen months after taking office, Magsaysay had brought the insurrection under control.

Magsaysay's political reforms did not work as well. In resigning his cabinet post, in February 1953, he wrote:

. . . Under your concept of my duties as Secretary of National Defense, my job is just to go on killing Huk. But you must realize that we cannot solve the problem of dissidence simply by military measures. It would be futile to go on killing Huk, while the Administration continues to breed dissidence by neglecting the problems of our masses.

The need of a vigorous assault on these problems I have repeatedly urged upon you, but my pleas have fallen on deaf ears. To cite an instance, some eight months ago I informed you that the military situation was under control, and I offered to leave the Department of National Defense in order to speed up the land-resettlement program of the government. My purpose was to shift our war on Communism to one of its basic causes in our country, land hunger. . . .[25]

25. Ibid.

Chapter 59

Rise of Indonesian nationalism • Allied occupation • Clashes with the British • The Communist element • Negotiations break down • The Dutch take over • A military solution • Guerrilla warfare • Sukarno's problems • The Communist revolt • Dutch intransigence • American intervention • The Dutch yield

So INTENSE the cold war, so mighty the issues, that it became tempting to blame all world problems on this quarrel of ideologies. To do so was to ignore recognized historical forces, particularly that of nationalism, which, decades earlier, had created and subsequently sustained a host of problem areas. In some instances, the Kremlin and local Communist parties attempted to exploit the condition. Other areas, however, held but peripheral connection to the conflict between the Soviet Union and the West, and almost no connection with communism. Such was the case with Indonesia and Palestine, whose peoples now used differing forms of guerrilla warfare to achieve specific political goals.

The Dutch never did regain balance in the East Indies. World War II left the Netherlands bruised and battered, unable to fill the power vacuum created by Japan's surrender. A powerful expeditionary force, acting promptly and effectively, would have had its hands full in reclaiming the islands from the new Sukarno-Hatta government. The Netherlands had no such force. Instead, she had to rely on Admiral Lord Mountbatten's South-East Asia Command, itself stretched thin in this vast area.[1]

Dutch attempts to have the Japanese govern by proxy proved futile. Clashes between Japanese soldiers and Indonesian nationals soon turned to heavy fighting.[2] The first allied officers who reached Djakarta, on September 8, 1945, reported that the nationalists ". . . controlled the public utilities of Jakarta and many more cities. The Republican government had set up ministries, was operating radio stations and newspapers, and regarded itself as the nation's functioning authority."[3] Professor Kahin noted ". . . throughout most of the area, in Java and Sumatra in particular, civil administration was operating at a level of efficiency that quite amazed the Allied forces."[4]

In mid-September 1945, a military mission arrived with Dutch representation, and toward the end of the month, Mountbatten sent in a company of troops. The Dutch wanted this mission to arrest the republican leadership, ". . . because apprehension of the leading persons and a show of force will strip the movement of its strength."[5] Refusing the request, Mountbatten advised Dutch officials to open negotiations with Sukarno's government, wise advice in view of Japan's legacy to Indonesia.

However empty Japanese words, the promise of independence, exploited variously by the Sukarno-Hatta government during the occupation, had claimed millions of minds. The Japanese also left the newly proclaimed republic with a militia-style army, the Peta, which numbered about 120,000. Finally, Japanese reliance on Indonesians during the occupation left a reasonable framework of government. In Dr. Otto Heilbrunn's words, ". . . The Indonesians were provided with a national will to independence, the military means to achieve it, and the administrative ability to sustain it."[6]

The Dutch refused this premise. A build-up in occupation forces, both British and Dutch, caused the newly appointed lieutenant governor, Dr. Hubertus J. van Mook, to insist on non-appeasement. His hand was strengthened in late October, when the British commander, Lieutenant General Sir Philip Christison, told Sukarno that the British recognized only the Netherlands government of the East Indies. Continuing clashes between Dutch and Indonesian nationals caused Christison, however, to prohibit more Dutch troops from landing in Java.

1. J. K. Ray, *Transfer of Power in Indonesia, 1942–1949* (Bombay: P. C. Manaktala & Sons, 1967).
2. Kahin (*Nationalism and Revolution in Indonesia*), *supra*.
3. Louis Fischer, *The Story of Indonesia* (New York: Harper & Row, 1959).
4. Kahin, op. cit.
5. Fischer, op. cit.
6. Abdul Haris Nasution, *Fundamentals of Guerrilla Warfare* (New York: Frederick A. Praeger, 1965). Introduction by Dr. Otto Heilbrunn.

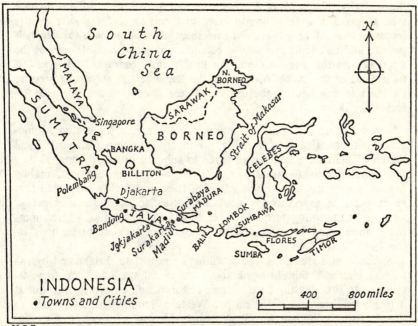

INDONESIA
•Towns and Cities

0   400   800 miles

M.E.P.

Christison's recognition of the Netherlands Government infuriated Indonesians. So did his use of Japanese troops in reclaiming cities from republican forces in Java, Sumatra, and Bali. When a British task force attempted to reoccupy the major port of Surabaya, in Java, some twenty thousand republican troops supported by a hundred twenty thousand civilians brandishing krises, clubs, and poisoned spears attacked a British Indian brigade.[7] British troops were actually being torn limb from limb when Sukarno and Hatta flew in and tried to stop the massacre. The British finally had to land another division, supported by air and naval gunfire—a battle that lasted until the end of November, when the Indonesians gave way.

This unfortunate period, in which other serious clashes occurred between Indonesian and British troops,[8] convinced the British more than ever that a solution had to be reached through negotiation:

. . . the battle of Surabaya was a turning point in their [Indonesians'] struggle for independence. It demonstrated to the British the fighting strength and the willingness to sacrifice life itself that were behind the popular movement they confronted. It awoke them to the fact that the Republic was backed by the Indonesian masses, not apathetically but positively and en-

7. David Wehl, *The Birth of Indonesia* (London: Allen & Unwin, 1948).
8. Ray, op. cit.

thusiastically. The Battle of Surabaya shocked the British into the realization
that, unless they were willing to bring to Indonesia and *expend* a greatly
increased strength of soldiers and equipment, they would have to alter their
policies and find some measure of common ground with the leaders of the
Republic. As this became clear, the British commenced to stiffen against
the refusal of the Dutch to deal with the Republic and put strong pressure
on them to negotiate to the end that peaceful compromise might be effected. . . .[9]

Although the Dutch army continued "pacification" operations, sometimes with considerable brutality, as in southwestern Celebes,[10] local
Dutch officials were inclined to agree to solution by negotiation. If they
detected a factional threat to the Sukarno-Hatta government, mainly
from Communists led by Tan Malaka, they nonetheless estimated that
seventy-five thousand troops would be needed to pacify the archipelago
—whatever the ruling party. At the end of 1945, their military force numbered about twenty thousand, with a promise of ten thousand more during 1946.

Sukarno and Hatta also were willing to negotiate. Frightened by extremist elements that brought about the Surabaya rebellion, they attempted to broaden the base of their government. They now introduced
a prime minister, the able and pro-Western Sutan Sjahrir, who was to
answer to a parliament, KNIP. Although this was a far cry from parliamentary democracy, Sjahrir introduced a modifying element both within
republican ranks and in the conflict with the Dutch.

The British, cautiously backed by the United States, brought contesting parties to the conference table in February 1946. Although talks began quite favorably, extremist elements of both flags soon brought on
an impasse. In the case of Indonesia, the obstruction came from the National Front, a Communist organization dominated by Tan Malaka. In
March 1946, Sukarno invited the Front to form a cabinet, and when it
failed to do so, he returned Sjahrir as prime minister. He answered the
Front's next attempt to overthrow the government by jailing its prominent leaders. He also successfully put down an attempted *coup d'état*
in June. The government, however, was walking on eggs and could not
afford to be too conciliatory in negotiating with the Dutch.

Despite all this trouble, Sjahrir had still introduced a workable proposal which got as far as a conference in the Netherlands in April. And
here the Dutch conferees proved intransigent. Their attitude befitted
the seventeenth century, not the mid-twentieth. Louis Fischer later
pointed out:

. . . a major difficulty was the permeation of Dutch politics by religious
ideas. Many Dutchmen believed in the divine right of the Dutch to rule

9. Kahin, op. cit.
10. Ibid.; see also Raymond Westerling, *Challenge to Terror* (London: William
Kimber, 1952).

the Indies. ". . . all authority derives from God," said Mr. Max van Poll, leader of the big Roman Catholic party, ". . . therefore, Dutch authority in the Netherlands East Indies is willed by God." Similarly, Mr. J. Meijerink of the Anti-Revolutionary (Calvinist) party, declared, "To maintain God's authority, the [Dutch] government may consider itself in God's service. . . . It must not hesitate to wield the sword if necessary."[11]

Mainly by threat of withdrawing all troops by November, the British again brought the Dutch to new talks at Linggadjati, on the northern coast of Java, in September 1946. To everyone's surprise, this meeting prospered from the beginning. After agreeing to a cease-fire, the two sides worked out an agreement in line with the Sjahrir proposals. The Netherlands recognized ". . . the Republic of Indonesia as exercising *de facto* authority over Java, Sumatra, and Madura."[12] The two governments were to co-operate in forming ". . . a sovereign democratic state on a federal basis to be called the United States of Indonesia." Together with the Netherlands, this would form a Netherlands-Indonesian Union.[13] Meanwhile, the republic would resist extending its contacts abroad.

Dutch and Indonesian representatives initialed the agreement in mid-November 1946. Although important political groups in both countries opposed the main provisions, the agreement is one of the might-have-beens of history. The Dutch Government, however, failed to sign the document until the end of March 1947. By that time, good-will engendered at Linggadjati was fast disappearing, and each government was violating one or more clauses.

Before the Linggadjati meeting, the Dutch had set up the puppet state of East Indonesia; they now established the states of West Borneo and West Java, and when the British evacuated their troops, in late 1946, extended control to coastal areas on Java and Sumatra that they soon held with ninety-two thousand troops. By late 1946, the Dutch Government was strong enough to undertake a "pacification campaign":

. . . In the areas where Indonesian resistance was most stubborn, authority was given to the savage Captain "Turk" Westerling to do what was necessary to break it. His most effective method was to have his troops round up village populations in the areas of principal resistance and arbitrarily pull men out of the crowd and shoot them, continuing this process until he was satisfied that the assembled villagers had yielded sufficient information concerning which of their members had been active in the resistance and the whereabouts of resistance forces. Probably between 500 and 1,000 Indonesians were killed in this manner, while probably at least 10,000 others were killed in the course of the whole campaign [that is, the pacification

11. Fischer, op. cit.
12. Ibid.
13. Ibid.; see also Kahin, op. cit.; Leslie Palmier, *Indonesia and the Dutch* (London: Oxford University Press, 1962).

campaign from mid-December 1946 to March 1947]. Most of those associated with the resistance who were not killed were jailed and for the most part remained in jail until after the transfer of Dutch sovereignty at the end of 1949. . . .[14]

In many instances, Indonesians reacted violently to this treatment, and incidents mounted. The republican government continued to sabotage the Dutch Government in East Indonesia, and also to extend contacts abroad in search of international support. Nor did the government seem in a hurry to ship rice necessary to feed Dutch-occupied areas of the large islands.[15]

The Dutch seized on this last issue as an excuse to solve the issue by military means: ". . . by maintaining that the Republican government did not exercise sufficient control over dissident extremist elements within its territory to implement agreements which it entered into."[16] In July 1947, the army launched a "police action"—a euphemism for a large-scale attack supported by aircraft and spearheaded by tanks that soon rolled over hundreds of miles to occupy cities, ports, and other key areas in Java and Sumatra.

Although republican forces numbered perhaps five hundred thousand, they included a good many disparate units neither organized, trained, nor equipped for modern warfare. Wisely, the Indonesian high command ordered all units to carry out scorched-earth tactics and retreat to woods and hills, there to wage guerrilla warfare as best they could.

By the time the United Nations brought about a cease-fire, the Dutch occupied nearly two thirds of Java and large areas of Sumatra and Madura. Fighting continued in numerous areas; under guise of "mopping-up operations," the Dutch seized large amounts of territory: ". . . Such actions and the refusal of the [UN] Security Council to contest them demonstrated to Indonesians how little in awe of the Security Council the Netherlands stood."[17]

A UN "Committee of Good Offices," consisting of Belgian, Australian, and American representatives, next brought antagonists together to hammer out the Renville agreement.[18] Although this saved the republic, it left the Dutch with its gains until various plebiscites could determine the people's wishes. The agreement favored the Dutch far more than the Indonesians, who signed under considerable pressure from Western powers; subsequent failure of the Dutch to abide by the agreement and failure of the Western powers to reinforce it caused most Indo-

14. Kahin, op. cit.; see also, Ray, op. cit.; Westerling, op. cit.
15. Fischer, op. cit.
16. Kahin, op. cit.; see also Alastair M. Taylor, *Indonesian Independence and the United Nations* (London: Stevens & Sons, 1960).
17. Kahin, op. cit.
18. Ibid.; see also Alastair M. Taylor, op. cit., for further discussion of this period.

nesian leaders to suspect Western, particularly American, motives.[19]

Sukarno's republic was now in bad shape. Compressed into one third of Java, the poor one third, its normal population of 23 million swollen by some seven hundred thousand refugees, the republic visibly faltered. Prime Minister Sjarifuddin, who had replaced Sjahrir, resigned in January 1948. Mohammad Hatta replaced him and at once began drastic surgery on economy and army, transferring hundreds of thousands of people to the land. He reduced the army from nearly half a million to a regular force of 160,000 plus some irregular, guerrilla-type units. He hoped eventually to reduce it to fifty-seven thousand regulars, a well-armed and well-trained force that

. . . would be prepared to operate at battalion strength in a mobile, hard-hitting guerrilla war against the Dutch, should they again attack. The old "static defense" would be changed into a "mobile offensive system" of shifting pockets that could not be mopped up. Supplementing this force of highly trained regulars would be a wide network of territorial militias made up of the local peasantry, who would be called upon to devote part of their time to military training.[20]

Hatta could do little, however, to repair material shortages incurred by a Dutch blockade or alleviate severe human hardships and inevitable inflation that arose from a distorted economy.

Hatta's reforms, coupled with the deteriorating domestic situation and the pro-Dutch attitude of the United States, made numerous enemies for Communists to exploit. Sjarifuddin, who was probably a secret Communist while serving as prime minister, openly joined the movement, which gained impetus from those headed by other Communist leaders such as Musso. In September, Communists rose in the city of Madiun and proclaimed a soviet government. Sukarno successfully rallied the rest of the country and managed to keep control of the army, which put down the rebellion. In late October, the last large rebel unit surrendered to republican forces. Musso was killed, Sjarifuddin executed. Such were the intricacies of Indonesian politics that the veteran Communist Tan Malaka had opted for the Sukarno-Hatta government. Released from jail, he was returned to house arrest when the revolt failed; he was later executed by a republican officer.

The Communist revolt further weakened the republican government. UN efforts to solve the impasse between the republic and the Dutch had come to nought. Observers reported frequent truce violations by each side. The Dutch steadily strengthened their economic grip on the islands and seemed particularly unwilling to co-operate and compromise over conflicting interpretations of various aspects of the Renville agreement.[21]

19. Kahin, op. cit.
20. Ibid.
21. Ibid.

But time was serving the republicans. The occupation was costing the Netherlands an immense sum of money—well over a million dollars a day—that she could ill afford. In December, the Dutch broke off UN negotiations and, presumably wanting to exploit Sukarno's immediate weaknesses, started the Second Police Action by a surprise bombing of his capital, Jogjakarta. Dutch troops quickly rounded up Sukarno and his principal officials and banished them to Sumatra.

This crass refutation of the Renville agreement triggered violent world reaction against the Dutch. The UN Security Council called for an immediate cease-fire and a release of republican leaders. When the Netherlands ignored the demand, the United States suspended Marshall Plan aid to the Dutch in the Indies and threatened to stop it to the home country. Governments around the world protested to The Hague, which at first denied responsibility, then attempted to defend the action.[22]

The Netherlands was fighting a losing battle. She could not afford to forfeit American aid. Her expenses in maintaining military forces in Indonesia in 1948 amounted to more than $400 million, which was approximately what the home country was receiving under Marshall Plan aid. Nor had her second offensive brought about the republic's collapse: ". . . by late January the 145,000 Netherlands troops in Indonesia were actually more on the defensive than on the offensive."[23]

In anticipation of the Dutch attack, the government had studied the earlier action carefully. As one result, it immediately enlisted its people in the new war. Citizens in Jogjakarta, for example, were ordered ". . . to obstruct and sabotage every effort to consolidate the Dutch government." Civil servants were to be ". . . 100 per cent noncooperative," their interim support if necessary assured by ". . . rich men and socially minded men." The people must hinder production of goods in every possible way; nor could they serve the Dutch politically: ". . . better to be jailed than to be a puppet and traitor."[24]

Another result of republican concern was army reorganization pushed through by Hatta, who also placed increased emphasis on guerrilla warfare. The chief of operations, thirty-year-old Abdul Haris Nasution, realized that the army could not stand against modern Dutch forces, but he also knew that ". . . to occupy Java down to the sub-districts, he [the Dutch] would need more than ten divisions, and it is certain that he is unable to form as many. With his actual strength of three to four divisions, he can occupy major towns and control communications, but

---

22. Ibid.: Professor Kahin offers a detailed analysis of these complex negotiations, with emphasis on the ambivalent American role; see also Fischer, op. cit.; Palmier, op. cit.

23. Kahin, op. cit.

24. Ibid.: Professor Kahin visited Jogjakarta at this time and found it, for the most part, ". . . a city of women, children and old men." Of some 10,000 indigenous civil servants, no more than 150 served the new Dutch administration, and most of these worked with republican approval.

he can never destroy the Indonesian forces if properly organized and dispersed."[25]

In essence, this is what happened in the Second Police Action. As usual, the Dutch high command underestimated staying power of the republicans. In early January the Dutch commander, General Spoor, announced ". . . that he would be able to crush the guerrillas within three months." His optimism soon faltered. As Dutch units moved into the country, occupying cities and towns and protecting lines of communication, they became increasingly immobile,

. . . nailed to hundreds, yes thousands, of stationary guard posts. In general they were tied to cities and highways and only seldom did they conduct a long and hot pursuit that would lead them to explore mountains and pockets, which indeed would have been disastrous for our morale.[26]

Guerrilla forces now began to surround enemy garrisons and increasingly to isolate them. If the guerrillas, unlike Mao Tse-tung's forces, were not strong enough to attack, neither was the enemy strong enough to eliminate them.

Here was a military stalemate that could have been solved only by greatly increased Dutch strength. But, for the Dutch, time and money were running out. The Netherlands could afford neither political isolation from the world nor economic refutation by the United States. In late April 1949, the Dutch Government agreed to release of prisoners and to new negotiations with the republican government.

A series of summer conferences yielded a cease-fire in August. Subsequent conferences at The Hague brought the republic into common cause with Holland and the other federal states to form a Republic of the United States of Indonesia—". . . a federal government formed of the Republic of Indonesia and the fifteen political units established by the Dutch."[27] On December 27, 1949, the Netherlands transferred full sovereignty to the new nation.

25. Nasution, op. cit.
26. Ibid.
27. Kahin, op. cit.

Chapter 60

The Palestine problem • Historical background • The British role • Jews versus Arabs • The Zionist position • Origin of Haganah • World War II and the postwar situation • David Raziel: the militant element • Irgun and terrorism • Stern and the FFI • Menachem Begin • Guerrilla war • British counter-tactics • UN intervention • The British yield

THE PALESTINE PROBLEM was nearly as old as Jerusalem hills. Orthodox Jews had never yielded spiritual claim to the Holy Land, where some brethren remained after Romans destroyed the Judean state. Through vicissitudes of ages, many Jews continued to look eastward: As early as the fourteenth century, Jewish refugees from Europe began trickling into Palestine.

Desire for a "national home" continued to grow, especially in European ghettos burdened with all too frequent pogroms. In the 1870s, a wave of anti-Semitism started new migration from central Europe. Then, in 1898, Theodor Herzl organized a Zionist international movement, aimed at ". . . establishing in Palestine a home for the Jewish People secured by public law."[1] The trickle of refugees into Palestine now increased. At the century's turn, the Jews there numbered perhaps forty thousand; in 1917, the figure reached eighty-five thousand.

1. Netanel Lorch, *The Edge of the Sword: Israel's War of Independence, 1947–1949* (New York: G. P. Putnam's Sons, 1961).

And now came the watershed: the Balfour Declaration, which pledged England's support of Zionist aims. Its origins are obscure. According to Lloyd George, it was made ". . . for propagandist reasons"—to win support of international, particularly American, Jewry to the allied side at a crucial time in World War I. In his provocative book *Promise and Fulfilment—Palestine 1917–1949,* Arthur Koestler calls it ". . . one of the most improbable political documents of all time. In this document one nation solemnly promised to a second nation the country of a third."[2] Whatever the case, the Paris Peace Conference and subsequent conferences converted Palestine into a British mandate (later approved by the League of Nations), and this encouraged further Jewish immigration during the 1920s.[3]

As might be expected, Palestine Arabs resented intrusion into what they regarded as their land. In 1920, Arabs attacked Jews in Jerusalem, in 1921 in Jaffa. British administration, which tended to favor the Arab population, and economic improvements brought by Jews somewhat mollified Arab grievances, but did not ameliorate the land question. In selling land to Jews, rich Arab and Turkish absentee landowners deprived some Arab tenants of ancestral homesteads; though they received compensation, this fundamental grievance was ignored by British administration. In 1929, an anti-Semitic nationalist, the British-appointed Mufti of Jerusalem, struck out by inciting a series of violent attacks against Jews.

The British Government now faced a major dilemma. It could not defend the Jewish cause without irreparably alienating Arab countries. In view of Western need for Middle Eastern oil, this would have created serious economic difficulties. To avoid a split and yet honor their pledge to Zionism, the British chose a compromise policy that often favored Arabs. But political pragmatism can sometimes become self-defeating: Attempting to walk a middle path softly, the British administration soon bogged down in Palestinian sands of intrigue. By attempting to satisfy everyone, the British satisfied no one.

While British policy maintained precarious peace, forces of discontent gathered strength. Hitler's anti-Semitic policy increased the refugee flow and added to Arab resentment. In 1932, the Jewish population numbered two hundred thousand; in 1935, nearly half a million.[4] Fighting broke out in 1936. The Arab rebellion continued to spread until suppressed two years later by a major British military effort (which, considering the European situation, Britain could ill afford).[5]

2. Arthur Koestler, *Promise and Fulfilment: Palestine, 1917–1949* (London: Macmillan, 1949); see also Christopher Sykes, *Cross Roads to Israel* (London: Collins, 1965); John Marlowe, *The Seat of Pilate—An Account of the Palestine Mandate* (London: Cresset Press, 1959).
3. Marlowe, op. cit.; Sykes, op. cit.
4. Koestler, op. cit.
5. Sykes (*Cross Roads to Israel*), *supra;* see also Christopher Sykes, *Orde Wingate* (London: Collins, 1959).

Various commissions meanwhile studied the problem, usually to recommend partition—that is, creating a small but separate Jewish state. Arab countries refused this solution, however, and such was their supposed importance to the coming international struggle that the British Government supported them. The famous Chamberlain White Paper of 1939 called for greatly restricted Jewish immigration—fifteen thousand a year at a time when tens of thousands were trying to escape concentration camps and ovens of central Europe—which would end altogether in five years; it also virtually prohibited land purchase by Jews; finally, it called for an Arab state within ten years, a state in which Jews would hold minority status.[6] A grossly unfair solution, the White Paper only added to smoldering Jewish discontent. When war broke out, however, the international Zionist organization and its executive, the Jewish Agency, chose to support Britain, as did the Jews in Palestine, the Yishuv.

Several factors explain the considerable forbearance shown by Jews in dealing with Arabs and the British administration. The Jewish Agency remained fully aware of basic antagonisms to the notion of a Jewish state: not only those of anti-Semitic gentiles, but of Jews themselves, of non-Zionists and anti-Zionists both in Palestine and the world. The two great Zionist leaders, Chaim Weizmann and David Ben-Gurion, were as much concerned with building and preserving as with administering. Money was as short as tempers; splinter movements were forever forming. To Weizmann and Ben-Gurion, only a policy of moderation could hold the movement together and retain support of international Jewry and sympathy of British and American governments.

The second factor was Jewish weakness in Palestine. In attempting to keep the peace, the British had never encouraged Jewish resistance. In the very old days, Jewish survival depended on assimilation with Arabs. As immigration continued and Jewish settlements developed, a sort of local militia sprang up. Then, in 1905, pogroms in Russia introduced new immigrants: tough, young men, for the most part socialist revolutionaries, who had experience in European arms and who founded ". . . the first country-wide para-military organization," Hashomer, or the Watchman—". . . a kind of Hebrew cowboy or Wild West ranger, highly respected among Arabs"—to protect lives and property.[7]

Hashomer slowly evolved into an underground Haganah (Defense Organization), ". . . a voluntary militia, organized in local units primarily for local defense."[8] The Haganah expanded during the 1936–39 Arab rebellion—as we have seen (Chapter 48, Volume I), Orde Wingate organized "Special Night Squads" from its reserve constabulary

6. Marlowe, op. cit.; Koestler, op. cit.; Sykes (*Cross Roads to Israel*), *supra*.
7. Koestler, op. cit.
8. Lorch, op. cit.

—but soon reverted to a protective role.[9] In 1941, the British allowed the Haganah to organize full-time guerrilla shock units, the Palmach, for fighting in Syria, but British policy continued to discourage a separate Jewish military force.[10]

The war nonetheless strengthened the Zionist hand. In 1942, Zionist leaders met in New York's Hotel Biltmore to censure the unpopular White Paper. The Biltmore Program, as it came to be known, called for unlimited immigration of Jews to Palestine, which, after the war, would become a Jewish commonwealth state.[11]

The war also strengthened the Haganah's military arm: Some thirty-two thousand Palestine Jews served in British forces, and, in 1944, the British authorized a separate Jewish Brigade Group. The brigade group dissolved at war's end, when a large British army occupied the area, but an underground Haganah army continued to exist. Commanded by a professional cadre of some four hundred soldiers, it consisted of Palmach guerrilla units totaling about twenty-one hundred men and women, backed by a small but ready reserve, and of a widespread territorial militia of some thirty thousand with many thousands of covert supporters.

Over-all weakness had caused the Jewish Agency and the Haganah to follow a defensive policy—the Havlagah—during the Arab rebellion, and a co-operative policy with the British during World War II. A good many Jews deeply resented what they deemed timid policies. In 1925, militant Zionists formed the Revisionist Party, under Vladimir Jabotinsky, who ". . . declared himself against any co-operation with Arabs until the Jews were their effective masters in Palestine, and he was pressing for the formation of a Jewish Legion to conquer the promised land."[12]

In 1935, the Revisionist Party splintered from the Zionist World Organization. Two years later, younger Revisionists formed a militant force, the Irgun Tsvai Leumi, or Etzel (National Military Organization), under a dynamic young leader, David Raziel.[13] A brilliant student, Raziel

9. Koestler, op. cit.
10. Sykes, op. cit.
11. Ibid.
12. Ibid.
13. Ibid.; see also Samuel Katz, *Days of Fire* (London: W. H. Allen, 1968). Katz places the origin of the Irgun, also called Haganah B, at an earlier year; Koestler, op. cit., offers a particularly interesting account: ". . . Its rank and file were recruited from the Revisionist Youth Organization *Betar,* and from the 'colored Jews'—Yemenites and Sephardis—for whom its flowery, chauvinistic phraseology had a particular appeal. These oriental Jews were eventually to constitute about one-half of Irgun's total strength, while the leaders were almost exclusively young intellectuals who had grown up in the Polish revolutionary tradition. This created the peculiar ideological climate of Irgun—a mixture of that quixotic patriotism and romantic chivalry which characterized the Polish student revolutionaries, with the archaic ferocity of the Bible and the book of the Maccabees. . . ."

switched from mathematics to military subjects in preparation for his messianic role:

> . . . He did not study military lore out of curiosity. He was consciously preparing himself to teach others. He wrote (together with his colleague, Abraham Stern) textbooks on the revolver and on methods of training. He conducted courses in the use of small arms and in the manufacture of home-made explosives. He was a scholar who could discuss the strategy and tactics of the Napoleonic wars, and write a commentary on Clausewitz. He fretted and chafed at the tardiness of the historical process. Although accepting Jabotinsky's leadership, he did not believe that party political action alone could achieve Jewish statehood. He was convinced that this could be attained only after an armed struggle with the British and he would have preferred to build the Irgun to meet the inevitable clash, rather than concentrate on retaliation against the Arabs.[14]

Under Raziel's inspired leadership, the Irgun concentrated first on smuggling illegal refugees into Palestine. Arab attacks on Jews in 1939 caused Irgun to open a terrorist campaign against the general Arab population. To protests of Zionist leaders, to the Jewish Agency and the Haganah, who pleaded the Sixth Commandment, "Thou Shalt Not Kill," the Irgun answered with Exodus xxi, 23–25: ". . . life for life, Eye for eye, tooth for tooth, hand for hand, foot for foot, Burning for burning. . . ."[15] The Chamberlain White Paper brought another change, this time to British military targets; when a police inspector tortured some Irgun leaders, Raziel had him murdered. Raziel and his coleader, Abraham Stern, were themselves arrested, but soon released.

The two leaders quickly resumed operations, but Stern, also a brilliant student, disagreed with Raziel's policy of wartime truce with the British. In 1940, Stern broke from Irgun to form the Lokhammei Kherut Israel (Fighters for the Freedom of Israel), or FFI. The Stern Gang, as it was generally known, concentrated on fighting the British by eliminating some Jewish moderates as well as gentiles: Anyone who opposed creation of a Jewish state became fair game. Raziel, in turn, agreed to work for the British army during the pro-German revolt in Iraq, and was killed in 1941, on his first mission. Stern fell to police bullets in 1942. A year later, another fanatic believer in the Jewish state, a Polish intellectual named Menachem Begin, took command of the Irgun. Stern's successor, a young scientist named David Friedman-Yellin, continued a policy of "unrestricted and indiscriminate terror"—from 1939 to 1943, Sternists killed eight Jewish, six Arab, and eleven British policemen, not to mention other victims.[16]

Continued British refusal to accept the Biltmore Program caused the

14. Katz, op. cit.
15. Koestler, op. cit.
16. Ibid.

Irgun, in 1944, to renounce its truce with the British and to form a loose, sometimes uneasy alliance with the Stern Gang in a new war for a Jewish state. In January 1944,

. . . The first large-scale commando-style attacks were launched on British civil installations. In three rounds of simultaneous assault the offices of the Immigration Department, the Income Tax offices and the CID headquarters throughout the country were blown up. One limiting decision was taken. As long as Britain fought Hitler, the Army was not to be touched.[17]

By early autumn, the Stern Gang had murdered fifteen men, mostly moderate Jews, and destroyed government installations including four police stations.[18]

Irgun strategy hinged on three considerations, as later clarified by Menachem Begin in his tormented book *The Revolt*. From a study of ". . . the methods used by oppressor administrations in foreign countries," the terrorists concluded that to destroy British prestige in Palestine would destroy British rule:

. . . The very existence of an underground, which oppression, hangings, tortures and deportations, fail to crush or to weaken must, in the end, undermine the prestige of a colonial regime that lives by the legend of its omnipotence. Every attack which it fails to prevent is a blow at its standing.[19]

Two other considerations strengthened this belief: the international situation and Britain's position therein, as well as Britain's internal strength. The terrorists concluded:

. . . As a result of World War II the Power which was oppressing us was confronted with a hostile Power in the east and a not very friendly power in the west. And as time went on her difficulties increased.

Begin and his fellows naturally counted on international sympathy and aid, particularly from the Hebrew Committee of National Liberation, in the United States.

A great many Jews, in and out of Palestine, disagreed with Irgun-Stern terrorism both on grounds of humanity and because they felt that evil acts would bring wholesale reprisals. Contrarily, terrorists shrewdly reasoned that a civilized power would find its retaliatory hands increasingly tied so long as the problem area claimed world attention:

. . . We never believed that our struggle would cause the total destruction of our people. We knew that Eretz Israel, in consequence of the revolt, resembled a glass house. The world was looking into it with ever-increasing

17. Katz, op. cit.
18. Sykes (*Cross Roads to Israel*), *supra*.
19. Menachem Begin, *The Revolt* (London: W. H. Allen, 1951). Tr. Samuel Katz.

interest and could see most of what was happening inside. . . . Arms were our weapons of attack; the transparency of the "glass" was our shield of defense. Served by these two instruments we continued to deliver our blows at the structure of the Mandatory's prestige.[20]

The Irgun drew a limit to terror, the Stern Gang did not. In November, two Stern Gang terrorists assassinated Lord Moyne, the Minister of State in Cairo. Public indignation, Jewish and gentile, ran high. The terrorist campaign already had alarmed the Jewish Agency and the Haganah, which believed that peaceful settlement could be made with England. Lord Moyne's death brought an open breach, with Agency and Haganah officials working with British authorities in rounding up and deporting nearly three hundred Stern and Irgun activists.[21] Since a good many Palestine Jews who deplored terrorist activities would still not turn in their fellows, the terrorists survived, though with greatly restricted means. Samuel Katz later wrote bitterly:

. . . The whole machinery of the Jewish Agency's security forces were now organized to wage war against the Irgun. The Haganah and the Palmach were sent into action. Hundreds of members of the latter were drafted into the towns from their kibbutzim [co-operative settlements]. Expulsions from schools, dismissals from places of work, kidnappings, beatings, torture, direct denunciations to the British, became the sole occupation of the action-hungry soldiers of the Haganah and the Palmach. In instinctive identification with the British overlord, they borrowed, from the tradition of the hunt, the term to describe this operation: it was called "the season."[22]

Zionist co-operation with the British did not reduce Zionist goals. In May 1945, after the German surrender, Dr. Weizmann wrote Prime Minister Churchill.

. . . demanding on behalf of the Jewish Agency the full and immediate implementation of the Biltmore resolution: the cancellation of the White Paper, the establishment of Palestine as a Jewish State, Jewish immigration to be an Agency responsibility, and reparation to be made by Germany in kind beginning with all German property in Palestine.[23]

The immigration issue headed the list. The Jewish Agency wanted unrestricted immigration for a hundred thousand Jewish, mostly Polish

20. Ibid.
21. Sykes (*Cross Roads to Israel*), *supra*; see also G. Costigan, "The Anglo-Irish Conflict, 1919–1922," *University Review*, Dublin, Spring 1968. Eliahu Bet Zouri, one of the assassins of Lord Moyne in 1944, had been taught in Tel Aviv by Esther Raziel, sister of David Raziel, commander of the Irgun. She had a plentiful supply of I.R.A. literature about the Irish conflict, and held up as heroes to her youthful Zionist pupils Robert Emmet and Michael Collins, as well as Garibaldi, Mazzini, and Washington.
22. Katz, op. cit.
23. Sykes (*Cross Roads to Israel*), *supra*.

survivors of German bestiality who languished in displaced-persons camps.[24] British delay, first by the Churchill government, then by Clement Attlee's Labour government, in treating this demand led to an extensive smuggling operation by the Haganah and, far more ominous, to an operational rapprochement between the Haganah, which claimed a country-wide membership of some forty thousand, and the Irgun-Stern groups, themselves steadily growing in strength and claiming thousands of passive sympathizers. Refugee smuggling increased, and, in October, the Haganah's clandestine radio station, Kol Israel, proclaimed the beginning of "The Jewish Resistance Movement":

. . . On the night of the 31st of October the "single serious incident" took place. Palmach troops sank three small naval craft and wrecked railway lines in fifty different places; Irgun attacked the railway station at Lydda, and the Sternists attacked the Haifa oil refinery. The attacks were accomplished with great skill and little loss of life, probably none intentionally. The operation had the desired effect of making the British Government think seriously about Palestine, but it also had the effect of solidifying yet further Bevin's resistance.[25]

The British now enlisted American aid in form of an Anglo-American committee of inquiry, but domestic politics in both countries slowed formation of this body. Illegal immigration activities continued to increase, as did ugly incidents between Palestinian Jews and British troops (which would soon number eighty thousand). In late December, Irgun units raided two police headquarters and an arms dump, killing nine British soldiers.[26] In late January 1946, the new high commissioner, Sir Alan Cunningham, ". . . promulgated severe emergency laws which among other provisions ordained death as the maximum penalty not only for taking part in a terrorist raid but for belonging to a terrorist society."[27]

The Anglo-American Committee's report merely exacerbated the situation by recommending immediate admission of a hundred thousand Jewish DPs. In refusing this and other proposals at a time when ". . . the situation was particularly propitious for carrying out Partition in a bloodless operation," Bevin and the Labour government were imprisoned by the old Arab complex that had restricted British policy for so long. The picture of the "Middle East going up in flames" seemed to paralyze realistic thinking, and in so doing, brought a near crisis in Brit-

24. Koestler, op. cit.: About a million Jews escaped death in German concentration camps. Of these, some 300,000 were living in Western Europe with a "fair chance of rebuilding normal life"; 100,000 of the remaining 700,000 "driftwood" lived in DP camps in the Western occupation zones. The record of the Western countries in absorbing these Jewish remnants is, at best, modest.
25. Sykes (*Cross Roads to Israel*), *supra.*
26. Ibid.
27. Ibid.: see also Katz, op. cit., who lists the regulations in detail.

ish relations with the Truman administration, itself acting far too cautiously as a result of domestic political pressures to solve a problem that the United States had helped create.[28]

Bevin and the Labour government were now on a collision course with disaster. In June, a new wave of sabotage swept over Palestine. In addition to usual attacks, terrorists destroyed twenty-two RAF planes at one airfield. The harassed British ". . . ordered the arrest not only of members of Palmach but of the Agency leaders. Ben Gurion was in Paris, or he would have been taken with the rest. There were widespread searchings by the military for Haganah, and especially Palmach arms. . . ."[29] During what Arthur Koestler has termed "Mr. Bevin's 18th Brumaire," the British also occupied the offices of the Jewish Agency, where they found documents that proved the Haganah's complicity in earlier terrorist operations.

Partly to destroy these documents and partly in keeping with its policy of reprisal, the Haganah agreed to an Irgun attack on British headquarters in the King David Hotel in Jerusalem. Although Irgun terrorists later claimed that ample warnings were given, the hotel was not evacuated, and the bombings claimed ninety-one British, Arab, and Jewish dead and forty-five wounded.

The deed shocked most of the civilized world, but what should have been a propaganda victory for the British turned sour when the British commander, General Barker, sent his officers a non-fraternization order at once intercepted and published by the Irgun. It reminded some observers of Gauleiter orders only too familiar from World War II:

. . . I am determined that they (the Jews) should be punished and made aware of our feelings of contempt and disgust at their behavior. We must not let ourselves be misled by hypocritical sympathy expressed by their leaders and representative bodies and by the protestations that they are not responsible and cannot curb the terrorists. I repeat that if the Jewish community really wanted to put an end to the crimes it could do so by co-operating with us. I have accordingly decided that as from the receipt of this letter all Jewish places of entertainment, cafes, restaurants, shops and private houses are out of bounds. . . . I understand that these measures will create difficulties for the troops, but I am certain that if my reasons are explained to them, they will understand their duty and will punish the Jews in the manner this race dislikes most: by hitting them in the pocket, which will demonstrate our disgust for them.[30]

Uproar over this ill-advised order more than neutralized adverse publicity reaped by the ghastly hotel attack.[31] Each incident, however,

28. Koestler, op. cit.; see also Sykes (*Cross Roads to Israel*), *supra;* Truman (*Year of Decisions 1945*), *supra.* Acheson, op. cit.
29. Sykes (*Cross Roads to Israel*), *supra.*
30. Begin, op. cit.
31. Ibid.

served the Irgun goal of focusing world attention on this torn and bleeding country.

In August, the British replied further with a massive raid on Irgun "headquarters" in Tel Aviv, which they sealed off with some twenty thousand troops supported by tanks.

. . . Life in Tel Aviv was brought to a halt. Every house and apartment was searched. The adult male population was led in groups to screening centers set up throughout the town. CID officers armed with lists and photographs identified more than a hundred thousand people. Among them were almost all the leaders and staff of the Irgun and the Lehi [Stern Gang], and the total Tel Aviv manpower of both organizations. Nearly eight hundred people were indeed led away to detention, and a British communiqué claimed the capture of many important terrorists.[32]

Katz later wrote that the British captured only two terrorists. Menachem Begin spent the emergency in a tiny cupboard and was not discovered.[33]

The worsening situation caused the Jewish Agency to lower its sights by requesting a reasonable partition arrangement. Fearful of Arab reaction, the British responded with a trusteeship plan, but the Attlee government also appointed a new Colonial Secretary, who was more sympathetic to Jewish aspirations and who initiated an appeasement policy by freeing Jewish Agency leaders. In return,

. . . Haganah dissociated itself from the terrorists and signalized the end of the alliance by issuing propaganda against them. The Central Executive of the Zionist organization condemned terrorism and called on the Yishuv to take action against the criminals.[34]

Something might have come of these moves but for the intransigence of the Arabs, who refused to countenance any partition plan; for the sympathy of the American Government to the Jewish plan, which infuriated the British; and for continued Irgun-Sternist activity.

By end of 1946, the Irgun-Sternist groups had killed 373 persons.[35] Although the police and army had imprisoned and deported some members, the organization continued to operate with at least tacit support of a large number of ordinary citizens. Considering the size of its full-time staff, never more than fifty persons, the task of running the Irgun to the ground was immense. British security forces could disrupt various groups and even cause operations to be suspended, but they could not eliminate the hard-core top command. Or, anyway, not without far better intelligence than they received. Instead of concentrating on improved intelligence procedures, which, among other things, required modera-

32. Katz, op. cit.
33. Begin, op. cit.
34. Sykes (*Cross Roads to Israel*), *supra*.
35. Ibid.

tion in dealing with the general population, the British high command frequently antagonized the people. In Christopher Sykes's later words,

. . . Exasperated by the crafty malignity of the terrorists whom they could defeat in the straight combat which for political reasons was denied them, and forced to endure defeat and humiliation while keeping order during a time of undeclared war; subjected to continual mockery and misrepresentation and frequent efforts to goad them into misconduct, the Army became an emotional dispenser of justice.[36]

It now began to use corporal punishment on suspected terrorists, a practice stopped when the Irgun kidnaped two British soldiers and gave them each eighteen lashes before sending them back to their units. Besides gaining world-wide publicity, instant retaliation caused the British to abandon this nefarious practice. The British next organized a counter-terror unit, but it soon died an ignominious, if gory, death. In early 1947, the British sentenced a young terrorist, Dov Grüner, to death by hanging, for his part in the murder of a policeman. His execution made him a popular hero and won many converts to the Irgun-Sternist cause both in Palestine and abroad. It was Ireland all over again (see Chapter 21, Volume I). In Jon Kimche's later words,

. . . With all their great experience of governing other people, the British here made the classical error of antagonizing the entire population in the attempt to subdue a small terrorist minority.[37]

As Begin and his fellows had foreseen, the British could take only limited action, action sufficient to turn people against them but not sufficient to end the terrorist movement. In Begin's later words,

. . . We often encountered the argument that the British Government if it so chose could take revenge by destroying us all and thus our operations were endangering the whole Jewish population. This was indeed a very serious question, perhaps the most serious we ever faced. General Cunningham, the last High Commissioner, referred to it in his report on the storming of Acre fortress. The General argued that there was no means of destroying the Jewish underground except by the application of the whole military might against the entire population.

But, added the General, the British, unlike the Germans, could not do such a thing. . . .[38]

Against this sordid background, the British Government continued efforts to effect a political compromise. But time was running out and criticism mounting on the British home front:

. . . In the House of Commons, at the height of the coal crisis, Winston Churchill warned that Britain could not sustain, morally or materially, a

36. Ibid.; see also Koestler, op. cit.
37. Sykes (*Cross Roads to Israel*), *supra*.
38. Begin, op. cit.

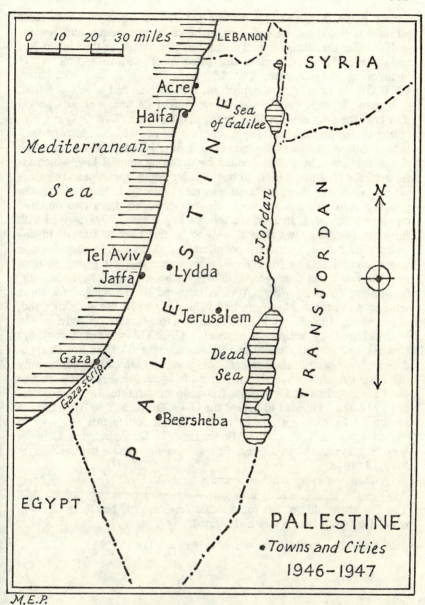

PALESTINE
• Towns and Cities
1946–1947

M.E.P.

long campaign in Palestine. He pointed to the expenditure of eighty million pounds in two years to maintain 100,000 soldiers there. She had no such interests in Palestine as to justify such an effort. . . .[39]

39. Katz, op. cit.

Ernest Bevin disagreed. Misreading the Jewish Agency's conciliatory attitude as weakness, he still thought he could bring Arab and Jew together under the British flag. To gain time, he turned to the United Nations in mid-February, a move that some interpreted as the first step in abandoning the mandate. The UN appointed a special committee, UNSCOP, to investigate the problem and recommend a new solution.

Meanwhile, terror and counterterror ruled Palestine, a ghastly period that kept the torn country in international headlines. Dov Grüner's execution brought widespread Irgun reprisals. In early March, terrorists attacked British installations and, in one day, killed or wounded some eighty soldiers. The British replied by declaring martial law, which infuriated the civil population without halting Irgun operations. The British also sentenced three captured terrorists to death. In May, Irgun units attacked Acre jail and released forty-one terrorists (and two hundred common criminals). In July, the refugee ship *Exodus 1947* arrived with forty-five hundred Jews aboard, only to be sent back to Europe to disembark its human, generally penniless, cargo on a Hamburg dock—a tragic event resulting from Bevin's intransigence, and giving militant Jews an enormous propaganda victory further exploited by Leon Uris' best-selling novel *Exodus*.[40] Also in July, the British hanged the three sentenced terrorists. The Irgun had kidnaped two British sergeants and, as promised, in retaliation hanged them on a tree outside Tel Aviv.

Undeterred by reciprocal savagery, UNSCOP worked throughout summer and autumn, finally to recommend an end of the British mandate in favor of still another partition plan, one reluctantly adopted by the Jewish Agency when the British made it clear that they intended to yield the mandate and withdraw troops in near future. In late November 1947, the UN voted to accept the UNSCOP plan. The Arab League responded by ordering attacks against Jewish settlements not only in Palestine but throughout the Middle East. In December, the Colonial Secretary announced that Great Britain would terminate its mandate on May 15, 1948.

By then the Haganah had secretly mobilized and Jew was fighting Arab as the beleaguered British garrison stood increasingly to one side. The British would remain for another few months, but their war was over. The Arab-Israeli war had started.

40. Leon Uris, *Exodus* (London: Allen Wingate, 1959).

Chapter 61

*Postwar Malaya • Ch'en P'ing's Communist guerrilla army •
Communist tactics • Government reaction • Counterinsurgency
tactics • Ch'en P'ing's tactical adjustment • British problems •
British tactical adaptation • The Briggs Plan • Guerrilla setbacks • Templer takes over: the qualitative approach • The tactical challenge • The cost*

SEEDS OF TROUBLE planted in prewar Malaya burst into discom-
fiting bloom not long after Japan's surrender. Here, as elsewhere in Asia,
a variety of elements enriched already fertile soil of dissatisfaction: Japanese victory over the white man, the white man's frantic effort to recover
initiative by political promises inherent in such documents as the Atlantic Charter, political and economic dislocation caused by Japanese
occupation, political awareness among all groups produced as defense
against brutal Japanese occupation policies, active opposition and con-
sequent improved organization of the Communist Party, the political
vacuum created by Japanese defeat, the British return with initial political confusion and economic hardship, delay in restoring tin mines and
rubber plantations to prewar condition.[1]

Soon after British troops returned to the peninsula, Whitehall an-

1. Lucian W. Pye, *Guerrilla Communism and Malaya—Its Social and Political
Meaning* (Princeton, N.J.: Princeton University Press, 1956) offers a detailed
political-economic analysis of this period.

nounced a new political arrangement known as the Union of Malaya. This was an attempt to juggle the three major ethnic groups (Malays, Chinese, and Indians)—some 5.5 million people—into a viable colonial state by improving the Chinese and Indian political position. It failed mainly because of opposition from powerful Malay sultans and the well-organized Malayan civil service. In December 1946, Whitehall began to consider a federation plan, not announced until 1948.

The political hiatus caused by bumbling bureaucracy suited the Communist Party of Malaya (MCP), which finished the war in a relatively strong position (see Chapter 46, Volume I). In 1945, it ostensibly disbanded its field army and turned in arms; in reality, it retained a cadre organization in form of an Old Comrades Association and buried a significant number of weapons. Its leader, Lai Teck, judged that he was not strong enough to seize power outright, a decision that some believe was occasioned by his being a British secret agent. The MCP did begin to attack by infiltration and subversion, however. Communist propaganda fell on willing ears, and Lai and his fellows successfully brought off numerous demonstrations and strikes.[2] Although these disrupted postwar recovery, they did not prevent it. As was and is quite common in Communist parties, a rift now developed: The Central Committee ousted Lai Teck, who disappeared, taking party funds with him.[3] His deputy in World War II, Ch'en P'ing, replaced him as party leader.

In February 1947, Ch'en P'ing was twenty-six years old. He had joined the MCP in 1940. At the time of the Japanese invasion, he was serving as party secretary in Perak state. During the war, he worked closely with the SOE (Force 136), an effort acknowledged by his being chosen to march in the Victory Parade in London and by being decorated with the Order of the British Empire![4] Ch'en P'ing brings to mind the young Burmese leader Aung San, who so impressed Field Marshal Sir William Slim. A British veteran of Malaya and expert on counter-insurgency warfare, Major General Richard Clutterbuck, later wrote, ". . . few people who have worked with him . . . deny that he is likable, intelligent and sincere."[5]

Unfortunately, in 1947 Ch'en P'ing was sincere only in bringing about a revolution in Malaya. Whether inspired by his own confidence, by an erroneous estimate of party strength, or by such outside influences as the Soviet Union and China is not known; he was never captured. He did send representatives to the Asia Youth Conference held at Calcutta

2. Julian Paget, *Counter-Insurgency Campaigning* (London: Faber & Faber, 1967): The author cites 300 major industrial strikes in 1947.
3. Pye, op. cit.; Special Operations Research Office (The American University, Washington, D.C.), *Casebook on Insurgency and Revolutionary Warfare* (Washington: The American University, 1962). Hereafter referred to as SORO.
4. Paget, op. cit.: By the time the decoration reached Malaya, in 1948, Ch'en had taken to the jungle and would soon have a price of £30,000 on his head!
5. Richard L. Clutterbuck, *The Long Long War—Counter-Insurgency in Malaya and Vietnam* (New York: Frederick A. Praeger, 1966).

in February 1948—a meeting that some authorities hold responsible for
the outbreak of "wars of liberation" all over Southeast Asia.[6] Probably
a combination of the three factors moved him to abandon infiltration
strategy in favor of Mao's three-step plan: a limited guerrilla phase to
wear down government strength while building MCP strength; an expansion phase with development of "popular bases" in towns and villages; a consolidation phase with conversion of guerrilla forces into an
army and subsequent defeat of government forces.

To accomplish this program, Ch'en P'ing reactivated his World War
II army of small guerrilla bands based in jungle areas. In 1947, the
Malayan People's Anti-British Army consisted of about four thousand
guerrillas, 90 per cent of whom were Chinese. Divided into eight regional regiments,

. . . they lived in large camps, normally of company size. These were well-
appointed, with parade grounds and classrooms in which the soldiers spent
more than half their time, attending indoctrination and self-criticism sessions,
lectures on current affairs, and classes in Mandarin Chinese. . . . The regiments operated in the early days mainly in the company groups in which
they lived, though there were also smaller raids and a number of larger
ones involving 200 or 300 men.[7]

Ch'en P'ing's army could not have functioned effectively without civilian support provided by an organization called the Min Yuen—the peace-
time version of World War II's Anti-Japanese Union. The Min Yuen
consisted of perhaps five thousand "formal" members assisted by thousands of Chinese rubber and tin workers living in villages bordering the
jungle. In each village, one or more Communist "cells" performed a variety of essential tasks such as furnishing guerrillas with intelligence,
recruits, food, medicine, clothing, and money. Armed members of the
Min Yuen—plantation workers by day, guerrillas by night—undertook
propaganda, sabotage, and terror missions. Administratively, the cells
formed shadow governments, what the French in Indochina called
"parallel hierarchies," at village, district, and province levels. This machinery enabled the Central Committee of the MCP to control Min Yuen
activities as well as provide an instant government for "liberated areas."
The Central Committee also organized bands of thugs called "Blood
and Steel Corps" for terrorist activities in cities.[8]

6. Psychologically a good year in that it was the centenary of the European
revolutions that so inspired Marx and Engels.
7. Clutterbuck, op. cit.; see also, Blair, op. cit.; Pye, op. cit., offers organizational and operational details including an interesting camp schedule.
8. Pye, op. cit.: A Central Committee member served as secretary of each State
Committee, and at least one State Committee member sat on the next-lower District
Committee, an overlap system that was supposed to insure continuity of policy.
In most cases, regimental commanders belonged to the appropriate State Committee, and important Min Yuen leaders sat on district committees.

Ch'en P'ing used his primitive but effective organization to unleash a mounting reign of terror: in cities, strikes, bombings, assassinations (particularly of Chinese Kuomintang leaders), extortion from merchants (particularly Chinese), bank robberies; in carefully selected country areas, theft, arson, murder of policemen and village officials, sabotage of rubber trees and tin mines. His purpose was twofold: By such means he partially financed his movement and broadened his base of support, besides gaining recruits and necessary arms and supply; at the same time, he hoped to induce popular revolts that would give him control of "liberated areas," essential to the next revolutionary phase.[9]

Ch'en P'ing nearly carried off this plan. The Malayan police force numbered only nine thousand constables, who were neither organized nor equipped to deal with this rash of violence, nor did thinly spread military units at first prove effective. The British Government, beset by problems at home and elsewhere in the Commonwealth, reacted only sluggishly. Encouraged by initial successes, and possibly under orders from Yenan or Moscow, Ch'en P'ing stepped up the tempo in early 1948 in anticipation of establishing the Communist Republic of Malaya in August.[10]

But Ch'en P'ing had underestimated both governmental and popular reaction. Despite numerous attacks and murders, many constables and officials proved extremely brave and loyal, and as a result, most villages remained politically viable. People may have been cowed and intimidated, but nowhere were there mass uprisings as foreseen by Ch'en P'ing.

Whitehall also pulled itself together to replace the moribund Union of Malaya with a federation scheme that introduced centralized direction of government and a formal recognition of the threat to legitimate government.[11] In June 1948, the high commissioner, Sir Edward Gent (soon after killed in an air crash), declared a state of emergency, and the legislature passed an Emergency Regulations Act, which, without

9. Ibid.: The British at first called the perpetrators "bandits," as had Chiang Kai-shek, Japanese military commanders, the Greeks, and the Filipinos; in Malaya, the authorities wisely changed to the more realistic term of Communist Terrorists, or CTs; see also Robert Thompson, *Defeating Communist Insurgency—The Lessons of Malaya and Vietnam* (New York: Frederick A. Praeger, 1966): The author offers an excellent account of the opening of the insurgency.

10. SORO, *supra.*

11. The new government provided limited autonomy to each of Malaya's eleven state and settlement rulers. Real power remained in the office of the high commissioner, a Whitehall appointee, who was assisted by a cabinet and a federal legislature. The high commissioner appointed cabinet and legislative members, and exercised veto power over the legislature. Although generally satisfying disgruntled Malayan sultans, the new plan provoked Chinese and Indian elements and undoubtedly cost the government some support. But most authorities agree that its virtues outweighed its shortcomings, although a promise of independence was needed in the end.

invoking martial law, nonetheless provided security forces with some sharp teeth.

Malaya's new laws called for country-wide registration of all citizens over twelve years of age, temporary abandonment of habeas corpus, right of search without warrant, heavy sentences including that of death for illegal possession of weapons, severe sentences for anyone assisting the Communist propaganda effort, right to impose curfews as needed. Later measures gave security forces the right to shoot anyone found in certain prohibited areas (a dubious practice) and also authorized courts to impose heavy sentences on persons supplying guerrillas.[12]

No one can deny the severity of these and other "control" laws, but, at that time in Malaya, no one could deny the severity of Communist threat to legitimate government. If the laws were harsh and if some defied principles of Western jurisprudence, they nonetheless brought home to the general populace the government's determination to restore and maintain law and order. The government's promise of immediate repeal, once proper government was restored, also caused the average citizen to co-operate in hopes of return to normality. The registration system further stressed the incentive aspect, since, without an identity card, the citizen could not ". . . obtain a food ration, space in a resettled village, a grant to build on it, an extra patch for growing vegetables, and many other things. . . ."[13] He was also assured of being asked blunt questions if he could not produce his card.

While the law temporarily subjected the citizen to arrest, detention, and interrogation at the government's pleasure, it did this to *all* citizens; further, it guaranteed the citizen against maltreatment or torture: In case of detention, a Public Review Board accepted appeals and periodically reviewed cases. A special Information Service attempted to mitigate the harshness of the laws by explaining the need for them in view of the Communist threat: During the emergency, the government distributed over thirty million leaflets in various vernacular languages, printed simple newspapers for rural areas, and sent twelve public-address/motion-picture units around the countryside.[14]

Thus armed, the government turned to its primary mission, providing security to the people, with secondary missions of separating the guerrilla from the people and then eliminating him. At first, this required a holding operation. The police could neither adequately protect the populace nor pursue the guerrillas. They had their hands full protecting themselves. Military forces, eleven battalions of British, Gurkha, and Malay troops, necessarily concentrated on providing static guards, mainly in plantation and mine areas. Malaya is a country larger than England, and the army quickly spread itself thin.

12. Clutterbuck, op. cit.
13. Ibid.
14. Department of Information, Federation of Malaya, *Communist Banditry in Malaya* (Kuala Lumpur: n.d.).

By holding or even retreating a little, the government won vital breathing space. One of its first steps was an enormous police-expansion program. Within six months, the police force grew from nine thousand to forty-five thousand; a part-time Home Guard augmented the police effort, and in time grew to about fifty thousand members. Military forces reached forty thousand, including twenty-five thousand troops from Britain and over ten thousand Gurkhas; they would number fifty-five thousand before the Emergency was over.[15]

During the government's build-up of security forces, guerrillas continued to raid almost at will. They struck plantations and police stations and small military posts; they threatened people and burned houses and stole money and supplies. In 1948, Ch'en P'ing's guerrillas killed 315 civilians, eighty-nine policemen, and sixty soldiers. Although the MCP was gaining support, Ch'en P'ing and his close associates still saw no signs of a general uprising.

The Communist leader now shifted tactics. Seeing that he faced a protracted war, which would require jungle bases, he reorganized his army (which now became the Malayan Races Liberation Army, or MRLA). Pulling perhaps two thirds of his force deep into the jungle, he left the remainder to operate among squatters and in rubber estates and tin mines. This failed to work—the number of terrorist incidents fell to less than half in summer of 1949—so, in late 1949, he again shifted tactics. Bringing his forces from the jungle, he attempted to form "liberated areas" along the jungle fringe. Terrorist activity rose sharply. In 1949, guerrillas killed 723 persons, including 494 civilians. In May 1950, terrorist incidents climbed to 534![16]

Government reaction still lagged. The police remained in throes of reorganization. Although reinforced by British veterans from the Palestine police, the greatly expanded force lacked sufficient leaders; recruit training was also understandably rudimentary. Ch'en P'ing's guerrillas continued to attack local police posts, not alone to kill policemen and steal arms but often to intimidate and sometimes even to recruit them. A favorite tactic was to disarm constables and warn them to keep to their compound at night, thus leaving the village under Communist control—often without authorities realizing it.[17]

The natural ally of the police, the military, was also suffering teething problems. The average operation from 1948 to early 1950 can be described as "too big and too late." This operational difficulty resulted mainly from trying to use conventional tactics in an unconventional situation—from trying to destroy the enemy in one fell swoop instead of breaking up his larger units in order to neutralize and destroy them piecemeal.

15. Clutterbuck, op. cit.; see also Pye, op. cit.; Department of Information, op. cit.
16. Department of Information, op. cit.
17. Clutterbuck, op. cit.

Military forces in the Philippines, Indonesia, and French Indochina were similarly erring. World War II commanders found it difficult if not impossible to adjust tactical values—to evaluate the new tactical environment and adapt to it. The World War II veteran usually failed, for example, to realize that concentration of force essential to an ordinary battlefield made little sense in a guerrilla environment. In the early days in Malaya, a commander, learning of a guerrilla attack on a police post or a village, responded by dispatching a battalion; by the time it reached the threatened area, it found the damage done: police killed, arms gone. A platoon, on the other hand, responded far more quickly, often checking an attack.

Nor was this particularly hazardous. The British soon learned that preponderant force was not usually a vital element in this type of war. A handful of guerrillas could not stand against a handful of well-trained and well-armed soldiers. Moreover, guerrillas did not know in what strength soldiers were approaching, and could not afford to stick around to find out.[18]

Similarly, in trying to eliminate the guerrilla, or at least to keep him off balance, the British erred with the quantitative approach:

. . . Initially, because of their previous training and experience, senior army officers were inclined to launch their units into the jungle in battalion strength —either in giant encirclement operations when a [guerrilla] camp was known to be in the area, or in wide sweeps based on no information at all. Neither of these types of operation had any success.[19]

One battalion, the Green Howards, spent most of the last four months of 1949 in the jungle; they killed *one* guerrilla.

The cumulative effect of this experience caused the military to decentralize control of operational units. General Clutterbuck later wrote:

. . . As we gained experience, infantry battalions were spread out in company-size camps, each company being responsible for patrolling the rubber estates and the neighboring jungle, and for aiding the village police posts in its area. These camps were not "forts" or "strong points"; they were merely living quarters for the soldiers.[20]

Battalion commanders perforce yielded tactical control of their companies. One veteran commander later noted: ". . . It would be almost a physical impossibility for a battalion commander to control every operation launched within his battalion area."[21] Similarly, company commanders often yielded control of an action to the platoon leader. The platoon leader, in turn, frequently utilized small patrols—generally self-

18. Ibid.
19. Ibid.
20. Ibid.
21. R. E. R. Robinson, "Reflections of a Company Commander in Malaya," *Army Quarterly*, October 1950.

sufficient, two-to-three day efforts commanded by sergeants and corporals.

Foreign as decentralized control at first seemed to regimental and battalion commanders (and their staffs), it soon began to pay off. As soldiers established closer contact with local functionaries and police posts, the flow of intelligence began to increase. Freed from higher staff delays, young officers learned to react quickly and effectively, not the least of the lessons being that ". . . only good battle drill and fire discipline will force a successful issue," while supporting arms will ". . . offer only indirect assistance."[22] As a natural corollary, unit commanders began to employ finesse in jungle operations by stressing tracking and listening operations. Instead of companies and battalions crashing through jungle to alert every guerrilla within a hundred miles, small patrols "disappeared" into jungle, where, in time and with the help of Dyak tribesmen from Borneo, they learned to track, observe guerrilla movements, set ambushes, and often locate and raid guerrilla camps.

These and other healthy changes were in the making when the counterinsurgency effort received a real boost. In April 1950, a recently retired general, Sir Henry Briggs, arrived to serve as director of operations.

The fifty-five-year-old Briggs introduced a new operational concept. The Briggs Plan, as it came to be known, recognized that the key to the situation lay in winning support of the civil population or at least in depriving guerrillas of that support. So long as guerrillas controlled large segments of the Chinese "squatter" population, police and troops would be deprived of intelligence concerning Communist village infrastructure and guerrilla movements; conversely, guerrillas would continue to receive intelligence regarding police and military movements.

How to prevent this?

Briggs answered this question with an imaginative resettlement plan that called for rounding up and moving almost half a million people into four hundred newly constructed villages. Like earlier segregation schemes that concentrated people in camps such as those the British introduced in the Boer war, the Briggs Plan aimed at collapsing the insurgency by depriving guerrillas of civil support. But the plan went further. As General Clutterbuck later wrote:

. . . In this first directive, Briggs put his finger on what this war was really about—a competition in government. He aimed not only to resettle the squatters but to give them a standard of local government and a degree of prosperity that they would not wish to exchange for the barren austerity of life under the Communists' parallel hierarchy; in other words, to give them something to lose.[23]

22. Ibid.; see also "Noll." "The Emergency in Malaya," *Army Quarterly,* April 1954.
23. Clutterbuck, op. cit.

Briggs also recognized need for a unified command. At federal, or top, level he introduced a War Council of civil, police, and military representatives. This was not a command organization, but a co-ordinating committee, with each voice heard in formulating plans. The same system operated at state and district levels by War Executive Committees (SWECs and DWECs). By eliminating duplicate operational efforts and by providing more rapid and effective exchange of intelligence, the area committee system also began to produce better operational results.[24]

None of these measures took place overnight. Civil deaths continued to rise, the guerrillas claiming about twelve hundred victims in 1950 and about a thousand in 1951 (including the high commissioner, Sir Henry Gurney, killed in a road ambush). The monthly incident rate remained high: By late 1951, guerrilla raids had caused about $27.5 million in damage to rubber plantations. One observer noted, ". . . at this time a marked drop in the confidence of the population, while reports showed considerable uneasiness over the situation in Government circles in Malaya."[25]

The government had not been idle, however. By autumn of 1951, over a quarter of a million people had been resettled at a cost of $21.5 million; the police numbered nearly eighty-four thousand including auxiliaries and special constables; the Home Guard counted another sixty thousand; troop strength reached fifty-five thousand and comprised over twenty-five battalions supported by several squadrons of aircraft including one of helicopters.[26] The government was also actively promoting an amnesty program for surrendered Communists, and three hundred of these had agreed to return to the jungle in special units to fight their brethren.[27]

As security forces cleared fringe areas, as more police and troops appeared in the field to work with village militia units in providing local security, as troops grew more adept in jungle operations, pressure against Communist communications and logistics slowly began to tell. As early as 1950, the guerrillas had abandoned "regimental" operations:

. . . By 1952 even the platoons were being broken up, and some of the sections were assigned to work directly with small Min Yuen groups. This process not only placed a greater strain on the party organization but made the District Committee level the critical point in the hierarchy.[28]

With central leadership giving way to state and district leadership, any semblance of a co-ordinated guerrilla campaign vanished. Despite

24. Ibid.; see also Thompson, op. cit.
25. Blair, op. cit.
26. Ibid.
27. Pye, op. cit.
28. Ibid.

"formal" directives, plans, and orders (often reaching jungle head-quarters months late), local guerrilla leaders increasingly turned to terrorism to survive.[29] Although the Min Yuen sometimes succeeded in reorganizing cells in resettled areas and among the Home Guard, the MRLA began to suffer distinct supply shortages. At first, guerrillas overcame this difficulty by direct purchase at inflated prices, but in-creased security measures began to dry up necessary money income from extortion and theft. Recruits no longer flocked willingly to the guerrilla banner. One well-informed source, in Selangor, ". . . estimated that by the end of 1952 about 80 per cent of all new recruiting was based on some combination of coercion and trickery."[30]

At this stage, a remarkably able commander appeared on the govern-ment scene. General Sir Gerald Templer arrived in early 1952 in the dual role of high commissioner and director of operations. If Briggs had struck the correct operational note, Templer brought with him the correct political tone: ". . . the policy of the British Government is that Malaya should in due course become a fully self-governing nation."[31] This promise of eventual independence, and particularly the optimism inherent in its expression at a critical time, cleared the air to an astonishing degree and virtually allowed Templer a dictatorial policy during the next two vital years, in which the guerrillas suffered military defeat.

These years recorded steady gains, a series of contacts and small battles that neutralized guerrilla operations by hindering communica-tions and reducing forces. Although a dynamic and, on occasion, ex-plosive leader, Templer was ". . . a great listener, particularly to the people with ideas, the policemen, platoon commanders, district officers, and rubber planters."[32] He insisted that ". . . the fighting of the war and the civil running of the country 'were completely and utterly interre-lated.'" He refused to allow a military takeover of what essentially re-mained a civil problem. As director of operations, he utilized a staff that *never exceeded nine officers,* its main element being ". . . a team of four officers of lieutenant colonel level—a soldier, an airman, a policeman, and a civil servant."[33]

Field operations followed a low tempo, with village security the pri-mary mission. This is the first of two points to stress, for local security is vital to waging successful counterinsurgency warfare. The decisive tactical element in Malaya was not a troop unit (though troops were

29. Ibid.
30. Ibid.
31. Clutterbuck, op. cit.; see also Robert Thompson, op. cit., and Robert Thomp-son, *No Exit from Vietnam* (London: Chatto & Windus, 1969).
32. Clutterbuck, op. cit.
33. Ibid.

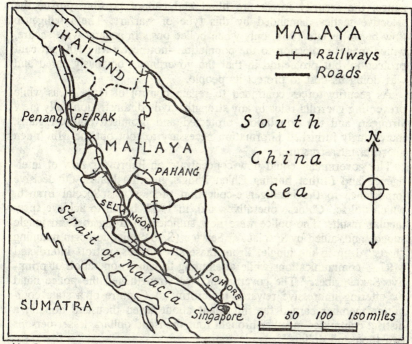

M.E.P.

vital) but, rather, the village police post, which, as General Clutterbuck has emphasized,

> . . . was the only thing that could provide security against the threat that really mattered in the villages—the man with the knife, who lived in the village and prowled the streets at night seeking out those people who had actively supported the Government or betrayed the guerrillas during the day. They were, I believe, far more frightened of this man than of any raid coming in from the outside. I believe that the primary function of the army during this period was to operate in such a way that the guerrillas could never attack in such strength that they could destroy the police post before help could arrive, and this, in general, was achieved.[34]

In early 1951, halfway through the resettlement program, construction of new fortified villages moved ahead of police expansion. After one or two ugly experiences, General Templer wisely delayed further occupation of new villages *until a police post was functioning in that village.*

Once local security was achieved, if only partially, real flow of intelligence began. This is the second point to stress, for, without intelli-

34. Richard Clutterbuck, letter to the author.

gence, the security forces are blind and cannot possibly pursue the selective tactics demanded by this type of warfare. The intelligence flow began in late 1951, only when police posts in general were secure, which meant protection to the population—not necessarily 100 per cent protection, but protection in that the government obviously cared and was doing its best to protect its people.

As security forces continued to regain control of large areas while preventing guerrilla raids in any strength, civil administration daily grew stronger, and the population, protected and promised political gains, increasingly furnished information necessary to root out the Min Yuen guerrilla infrastructure.

The government could now concentrate on improving flow of intelligence and further hurting Ch'en P'ing's guerrilla bands. Of decisive importance to the intelligence-collection process was Special Branch, which utilized Chinese operatives and, in 1952, began to achieve spectacular results. The police were now sufficiently strong to form jungle squads and, aided by Special Air Service (SAS) units, to begin manning "forts" deep in the jungle. From these strongholds, patrols interdicted MRLA communications while attempting to win co-operation of primitive Sakai tribes.[35] The government also strengthened the police hand by offering impressive rewards to informers: Capture of a state committee member earned the informant about seven thousand dollars; a district committee member brought four thousand dollars, lesser persons two thousand dollars.[36]

An enlarged police role allowed military forces to concentrate on exploiting intelligence furnished by Special Branch and other organizations. Valid intelligence alone enabled military commanders to ambush or attack remaining guerrillas, and where the commander lacked intelligence, he had to go without or procure it himself.

Like the rest of the emergency, the offensive phase was a time-consuming process that demanded enormous patience. Large-scale battalion and regimental "sweeps" had proved useless. Random shelling of open areas or suspected guerrilla areas had produced minimal results, as had Lincoln bombers and Hornet and Vampire fighters plastering various areas of the jungle. Instead, the war reverted to the small infantry unit, often operating entirely on its own. General Clutterbuck concluded:

. . . our best commanders in Malaya were the ones who set themselves the task of managing the war in such a way that their small patrols came face to face with the guerrillas on favorable terms; in other words, with good intelligence. This meant long hours of tactful discussions with police officers, administrators, rubber planters, tin miners, and local community leaders, get-

---

35. J. M. Woodhouse, "Some Personal Observations on the Employment of Special Forces in Malaya," *Army Quarterly*, April 1955.
36. Pye, op. cit.

ting them to co-operate with the soldiers and to promote the flow of information to them. Such commanders would regularly accompany their patrols, often placing themselves under the platoon commanders, so that they really understood the war and knew what was needed to win it.[37]

What *was* needed to win it?

Basically, a realignment of tactical thinking—away from conventional terms of "battle" and "victory" to much more sophisticated terms of "pressure" and "gain." Commentators then and later sometimes missed this essential requirement. One top American analyst later wrote that

. . . this failure of the MCP is significant as a demonstration that guerrilla warfare cannot achieve victories over an enemy vastly superior by conventional military standards. Although the Security Forces in Malaya have had a difficult and thankless task in fighting the Communists, they have proved that superior technology and resources provide the same advantages in irregular as in regular warfare.[38]

Nothing could be farther from the mark, yet this belief was to gain and hold considerable currency in U.S. military circles. It completely contradicted lessons offered by China, the Philippines, Indonesia, Greece, French Indochina, and Malaya.

In Malaya, superior technology and resources played a shadow second to human performance in a war that blended civil and military factors to an almost inexplicable degree. The airplane, the artillery piece, the psychological warfare program, the jungle "fort"—none approached the importance of the individual working among the people, his determination and brain his best weapons. Superior technology and resources did not "win" the Malayan war; they did help the government to establish an effective pacification program, and they did help the military carry out effective small-unit operations. But it was the pacification effort combined with the small-unit military effort that prevented the guerrilla threat from growing and finally countered it to the extent that guerrillas were unable to fight effectively any longer.

Tactically, patience had to replace impetuosity. At times, guerrillas holed up for weeks and even months. A young British officer, Arthur Campbell, later wrote a book, *Jungle Green,* that brought home the new tactical challenge faced by the Western soldier.[39] One ambush he described, a fifty-hour effort in a filthy, insect-ridden jungle swamp, succeeded in killing one guerrilla. Other ambushes trapped no one; sometimes guerrillas appeared but escaped into the night; sometimes his people scored several kills and broke up guerrilla camps. Similarly, police and soldiers, on occasion, spent months building information on locating an enemy camp which soldiers, after enduring appalling physi-

37. Clutterbuck, op. cit.
38. Pye, op. cit.
39. Arthur Campbell, *Jungle Green* (London: Allen & Unwin, 1953).

cal hardships, attacked only to discover that the enemy had fled to still another sanctuary. Disappointment caused by such fruitless efforts, each calling for extreme individual sacrifice, was overcome only by outstanding leadership.

Frustrating as these operations were, they eventually paid off. To accomplish his mission, indeed to survive, the guerrilla had to leave his jungle sanctuary sooner or later in order either to mount an attack or to receive food and supply from clandestine supporters. That was his vulnerability, and that was where the tactical force had to outdo him in patience—not an easy requirement, in view of the hurly-burly Western environment.

Yet patience and persistence, and a combination of small civil and military efforts from one end of the infected areas to the other, slowly cracked the insurgency. As the first, halting movements produced intelligence and machinery to exploit it properly, the effort became a crawl, and, as more intelligence flowed in to co-ordinated commands and as police and military tactics improved, the crawl became a walk. In two years, from 1952 to 1954,

. . . two-thirds of the guerrillas were wiped out, the terrorist incident rate fell from 500 a month to less than 100 and the casualty rate went from 300 to less than 40.[40]

Where once guerrilla leaders whistled and new guerrillas appeared, now they whistled in vain. The remainder found themselves increasingly cut off from support forces and increasingly under pressure from military units. Time favored security forces, for as strength, organization, and tactical abilities increased, the guerrilla could only suffer proportionally.

Yet the process was painfully slow and very expensive. The government's offensive phase did not end until 1955, and the consolidation phase continued until 1960. The twelve-year war cost the lives of nearly two thousand men of the security forces; guerrillas killed or kidnaped 3,283 civilians in the same period[41] and also did millions of dollars' worth of damage to the mines and plantations. The guerrillas themselves lost nearly six thousand killed, 1,752 surrendered, and 1,173 captured.[42] Ch'en P'ing and four hundred of his fellows escaped to the Malaya-Thailand border area, where, after a short hiatus, they resumed operations.

They remain active today.

40. Clutterbuck, op. cit.
41. Thompson (*Defeating Communist Insurgency*), *supra.*
42. Pye, op. cit.

Chapter 62

The Vietnam war • Navarre's tactics • Chinese aid • The American position • Erroneous estimates of the situation • Genesis of the domino theory • On strategic values • "Strategic keys" versus "strategic conveniences" • Mark Clark's recommendations • General O'Daniel's mission • The Navarre Plan: ". . . light at the end of a tunnel" • Giap's response • Orde Wingate's ghost (II) • Dien Bien Phu • Giap's secret plans • Navarre's problems • Origin of the Geneva Conference • Navarre's continuing errors • American aid

LESSONS LEARNED from insurgencies in the Philippines, Greece, Indonesia, Palestine, and Malaya did not rub off on the French in Indochina. Despite American and British appeals, France refused to push through political reforms that, in spring of 1953, might still have stolen nationalist thunder from Ho Chi Minh and the DRV Government.

Premier Laniel's new government offered only negative direction to its new commander in chief in Vietnam, fifty-five-year-old General Henri-Eugène Navarre, an armor officer, a military intelligence specialist, European-oriented, a reserved, somewhat colorless man, an art collector and cat-lover, of whom a friend said: ". . . There is an eighteenth century fragrance about him."[1]

Navarre was a mortal given an almost superhuman task. He was to expect no further troop replacements from France; his mission was to defend Laos while jockeying for a favorable negotiating position with the Viet Minh, but he was not to risk defeat of his forces. Navarre, him-

1. *Time,* September 28, 1953.

NORTHERN VIETNAM
1953–1954
• Towns and Cities
⁓ Roads

M.E.P.

self, remained under no illusions as to the military situation, secretly reporting to his government ". . . that the war simply could not be won in the military sense (just as the Korean War could not, without drawing Red China into it) and that all that could be hoped for was a *coup nul* —a draw."[2]

Like De Lattre and Salan before him, Navarre found himself tactically restricted:

. . . with an organized and better-equipped fighting force, almost twice the size of Giap's regular army, fewer troops were available to them for offensive action than to the Vietminh. Navarre estimated that of the total of 190,-000 men in the Expeditionary Corps, at least 100,000 were tied down in static defense duties. Lacouture and Devillers claim that of the 500,000 soldiers of which the French disposed after the build-up of the Vietnamese National Army in 1953, no less than 350,000 were assigned in "static duties." The Vietminh battle corps consisted of six divisions; the French had only the equivalent of three, including their eight parachute battalions. The other 350,000 were assigned to defending cities, holding isolated strong-points, accompanying convoys, patrolling highways, and conducting punitive

2. Fall (*The Two Viet-Nams*), *supra*.

actions against villages suspected of hiding and feeding the guerrillas, and of informing them about French moves. Alone sealing off and trying to pacify the [Red River] delta absorbed almost one-third of the Expeditionary Corps, a force obviously still insufficient for the task. When Navarre, in May, 1953, looked over the northern scene, he discovered that of the 7,000 villages in the delta, the French could boast of fully controlling no more than 2,000.[8]

Despite paucity of means, Navarre struck out variously at Viet Minh forces in the delta area. He also evacuated a series of outposts and garrisons, including the expensive airhead at Na San, which had been under siege since late 1952, and those ten battalions proved a welcome addition to his small operational force. By means of letters in the army newspaper, he exhorted troops elsewhere to adopt aggressive tactics:

. . . Your posts and blockhouses are only shelters. Shut up in them, you are besieged, without influence over the surrounding country and people. Bit by bit, climate and habit sap you of your aggressiveness.

Your best defense is to seek out the enemy. Reconnaissance is indispensable, not only to your security but to the accomplishment of your mission. By organizing frequent patrols and ambushes, you will restrict the enemy's freedom of movement and prevent him from undermining your sector, gathering intelligence and massing for surprise attacks. This is the only way by which you can gain the moral ascendancy essential to victory.[4]

These sound words produced no magic, nor did Navarre's tactical "jabs" result in lasting effect. An airborne raid near Lang Son, for example, destroyed ". . . some 5,000 tons of weapons, ammunition, explosives, and petrol," but encountered no enemy forces.[5] Other attacks, on occasion, hurt a few of Giap's units, but most of these avoided direct confrontation and continued to interdict French lines of communication. At this crucial period, Giap had five regiments operating in the delta, that is, behind the "de Lattre Line," where an estimated sixty thousand guerrillas, not to mention innumerable Viet Minh sympathizers, supported them.[6]

At the same time, the Korean cease-fire, signed in late July 1953, allowed the Chinese to provide instructors, arms, and equipment, much of it captured American equipment, which enabled the Viet Minh to increase their regular forces: ". . . the Viet-minh received trucks and

3. Buttinger, op. cit.; see also Lancaster, op. cit.: ". . . whereas the Viet Minh had at their disposal seven regular infantry divisions, which together with their independent regiments were now estimated to constitute an operational force with a strength equivalent to nine divisions, the French Union forces were only able to muster seven mobile groups and eight parachute battalions, or the equivalent of three divisions."; see also Giap, op. cit.

4. McCuen, op. cit.

5. Lancaster, op. cit.

6. Fall (*The Two Viet-Nams*), *supra*.

light and heavy weapons, including bazookas, mortars, and cannons, sufficient to outfit and transport heavy artillery units. . . ."[7] In mid-1953, the army boasted ". . . seven mobile divisions and one full-fledged artillery division, and more were likely to come rapidly from the Chinese divisional training camps near Ching-Hei and Nanning."[8]

This dismal picture stood at dramatic odds with French and American pronouncements. In May 1953, General Salan ". . . had predicted a 'shift' in the war to France's advantage within three years,"[9] an extraordinary statement, since, at the time, France controlled very little of the countryside. On the other hand, extensive American military aid was by then flowing into Saigon and Hanoi, an effort in keeping with the new, Eisenhower administration's determination to bring about French "victory"—an ambition, it should be said, more hotly pursued by Secretary of State Dulles, prompted in part by his own hatred of communism, in part by pressures from anti-Communist crusaders in government, military, and Congress, than by President Eisenhower himself.

Dulles was greatly concerned that a cease-fire in Korea would cause Communist China to turn southward. His was not a layman's opinion entirely, but, rather, the expressed fear of many senior military commanders. Whatever Eisenhower's real feelings, shortly after the Korean truce, in August 1953, he called attention, in a major speech, ". . . to the strategic, economic, and political importance of holding Indochina."[10]

The military opinion, which so largely influenced American actions, derived in part from fear produced by the Communist-monolith theory, in part from an exaggerated estimate of Communist China's aggressive intentions, and in part from warning reports submitted by members of the U.S. military aid group in Indochina. In 1953, most military analysts unfortunately were not impressed with developing strains in the Communist bloc: If a rift had not yet occurred between the Soviet Union and China, the rupture between the U.S.S.R. and Yugoslavia proved beyond doubt that communism meant many things to many people. The misreading of Communist China's aggressive intentions stemmed from the Korean war and a refusal to recognize that China's entrance therein resulted directly from General MacArthur's aggressive and incredibly inept strategy. As for reports from American officers in Indochina: not understanding the nature of the war, these observers, with some splendid but unheralded exceptions, failed to realize that Giap neither needed nor wanted Chinese troops to fight the French, so long as the French remained intent on defeating themselves.

The erroneous military estimate of the situation does not excuse the

7. Gurtov, op. cit.
8. Bernard Fall, *Hell in a Very Small Place: The Siege of Dien Bien Phu* (Philadelphia: J. B. Lippincott, 1967).
9. Gurtov, op. cit.
10. Hammer (*Struggle for Indochina*), *supra.*

administration's failure to make a more realistic strategic appraisal. But here two villains were at work. We have seen how Indochina, from the standpoint of American national interests, grew from a "nothing area" to a "nuisance area" to a "crucial area"—the result primarily of French intransigence coupled with the fall of Chiang Kai-shek. Having made political capital from Chiang's defeat, the Republicans fell prisoner to their own inflamed oratory. They had not only accused the Democrats of losing China, but had imputed the loss to sinister deeds of American officials. As one result, they could not think of losing even a portion of Indochina to the Communists.

To the villain of political opportunism, however, must be added that which afflicted the administration's military advisers: ignorance. In 1950, Representative Walter Judd had reported on a fact-finding mission to the Far East in part as follows:

. . . The area of Indochina is immensely wealthy in rice, rubber, coal, and iron ore. Its position makes it a strategic key to the rest of Southeast Asia. If Indochina should fall, Thailand and Burma would be in extreme danger, Malaya, Singapore, and even Indonesia would become more vulnerable to the Communist power drive. . . . Communism would then be in an exceptional position to complete its perversion of the political and social revolution that is spreading through Asia. . . . The Communists must be prevented from achieving their objectives in Indochina.[11]

This appraisal, an extension of William Bullitt's lopsided thinking in 1947 (see Chapter 51, Volume I), the genesis of the later, famous domino theory, was as impassioned as it was specious. As any interested CIA analyst could have testified, Indochina is not immensely wealthy in natural resources. In 1937, Doctor Virginia Thompson published vital and depressing statistics substantiated more recently by Gunnar Myrdal's comprehensive study of the Asian economy.[12] Vietnam's coal traditionally has gone from North to South, its rice from South to North. The French exported Vietnamese rice, as Joseph Buttinger has demonstrated, only at expense of the Vietnamese people's health. Rubber and coal exports were (and are) valuable to owners of French plantations and mines; they are not vital to Western production. Compared to Burma, Malaya, Thailand, and Indonesia, French Indochina is a poor area.

Just as inaccurate was Judd's assertion that Indochina forms ". . . a strategic key to the rest of Southeast Asia." In the first place, Vietnam belongs to East Asia, not to Southeast Asia—an intense rivalry has always existed between the Thai and the Vietnamese (see Chapter 42, Volume I). The second error is to call Indochina a "strategic key." If it

11. Gurtov, op. cit.
12. Virginia Thompson, op. cit.; Gunnar Myrdal, *Asian Drama—An Inquiry into the Poverty of Nations* (London: Allen Lane the Penguin Press, 1968), 3 vols.

were, it would follow that whoever held Indochina would control Southeast Asia, a falsehood repeatedly demonstrated by history.

The term "strategic key" should be used with great caution. Like "communism," it means many things to many people. A diplomat of the caliber of Ambassador George Kennan saw it in 1947 in terms of

. . . areas that I thought vital to our security and ones that did not seem to me to fall into this category. . . . There were only five regions of the world—the United States, the United Kingdom, the Rhine valley with adjacent industrial areas, the Soviet Union, and Japan—where the sinews of modern military strength could be produced in quantity. . . .[13]

A military planner concerned with armies and fleets and air armadas tends to demand certain geographical characteristics for a "strategic key." These usually concern control of communications—hence the geographer's terms "control cities" and "control points," for example Istanbul and Gibraltar, the Suez and Panama canals.

A "strategic key" logically should fit a door of national policy. A "strategic key (or necessity)" for one country is not necessarily a "strategic key (or necessity)" for another. Gibraltar, for example, would be a "strategic nothing" for a nation without a navy (unless the nation profited by granting base rights to a nation with a navy). Airfields in Morocco or Spain would scarcely serve the national interest of Basutoland, nor would Polaris-submarine bases in Scotland prove of interest to Ecuador.

Strategic values also change: Where once Gibraltar was a "strategic key" to British naval control of the Mediterranean, with the demise of the British Empire, it has become less important and Britain could comfortably survive without it, just as she survives without possession of the Suez Canal—a "strategic key" so long as national policy supported a Far Eastern empire. To take an example closer to home, the strategic value of the Panama Canal was far greater to the United States in the days of a one-ocean fleet than it is today. It is still important; it is not vital to the continued existence of the United States.

Technology also affects strategic values. Development of synthetic rubber in World War II, for example, almost canceled loss of the world's major rubber-producing areas to Japan. More recent development of super oil tankers cut sharply into strategic importance of the Suez Canal. Recent discoveries of rich oil fields in Alaska in time will reduce strategic importance of Middle Eastern oil fields to Europe, while, as Mr. Dean Acheson had suggested, development of a practical electric car—surely within the capability of nations that can place humans on the moon—would make Middle Eastern sheiks talk and act more circumspectly.

The majority of so-called "strategic keys" in reality are "strategic

13. Kennan (Volume I), op. cit.

conveniences." The difference is immense. Whereas a genuine "strategic key" is vital to a nation's existence, a "strategic convenience" is not vital, and acquisition or retention can be measured in terms of limited investment. Control of Albania, for example, would be a "strategic convenience" for the United States and the West—but invasion and possession essential to control are not worth the world war that they would undoubtedly bring about. In 1956, when Britain yielded control of the Suez Canal, it had become a "strategic convenience" to her and was not worth a threatened atomic holocaust—and recently Britain and the West have survived quite comfortably without it. American air bases in Libya and Morocco were "strategic conveniences" yielded without significant weakening of U.S. defense posture. In 1954, Britain deemed the island of Cyprus a "strategic key" to her Middle East position. When the cost of fighting for its control became too great, she reassessed its importance to recognize it as a "strategic convenience"; accordingly, she relinquished control to the United Nations in return for two base enclaves, which have served her military purposes adequately.

French Indochina has never formed a "strategic key." The area became a "strategic convenience" to the French for reasons discussed in Chapter 42, Volume I. Japan utilized it similarly in World War II. Both countries used the northern region to support incursions into southeastern China, and Japan also used it to support southern, eastern, and western incursions. The ease of her occupation and the abject French surrender only underlined Indochina's awkward geographic position from the standpoint of military defense, as did the subsequent allied blockade that effectively interdicted communications between Indochina and Japan proper. Also significant, Chiang Kai-shek and the Kuomintang government could have made a good case with the allied powers for acquiring control of the northern area; instead, Chiang contented himself with a temporary occupation followed by evacuation with profit.

No more is French Indochina a "strategic key" for Communist China. The prize of the Southeast Asian littoral is Burma, which borders China for over a thousand miles. A direct Chinese conquest of Burma would not depend on Chinese control of French Indochina, though, again, the area would be a "strategic convenience," as it would also be for a drive to the south. But, in 1953, China was not strong enough to drive either west or south, nor was there good reason for her to do so in view of continuing Viet Minh gains in Indochina and of the success of various subversion efforts elsewhere.

From the American standpoint, the area could scarcely form a "strategic key" unless the United States wished to invade southern China. In 1953, it did form a "strategic convenience" in that the French presence served to "contain" communism, or, put another way, continued to deny the area to the "enemy."

Had the Eisenhower administration regarded Indochina as a "strategic convenience" and no more, it might have charted a more realistic course. It might have questioned the psychological sacrifice of the United States identifying itself with a colonial power detested throughout Asia, North Africa, and the Middle East. It might have questioned the validity of the French effort to retain northern and even southern Vietnam (as George Kennan questioned it in 1950), an effort largely subsidized with American dollars. It might even have questioned the retention of southern Vietnam as essential to American interests, reasoning instead that a "strategic presence," an enclave or two similar to Guantánamo Bay, in Cuba, would suffice (and could be secured in return for continuing aid from the "legitimate" French Government). In answer to those who pleaded the cause of humanity—prevention of Communist "enslavement" of millions—the Administration might have answered that it had no intention of going to war to free the satellite millions of Europe, preferring instead to preserve a world while trying to free people by other means; it might have added that the bulk of peasants in Indochina, as in China, were probably as well if not better off than under former regimes; and it might have recommended that the few thousand prominent Vietnamese Catholics, good healthy Asian-Christian stock who would have suffered under Communist rule, could have been shipped to underpopulated Australia under an American-subsidized scheme.

That the Administration did not think in these terms is all too clear from the record. Nor did Secretary Dulles and his advisers, apparently, appreciate pertinent historical complexities. As Gunnar Myrdal astutely pointed out:

. . . it is worth bearing in mind a fundamental point that is commonly overlooked. Vietnam has been lumped together with the rest of Southeast Asia by many commentators, including ourselves . . . when by virtue of the political traditions, language, administrative system, and religious and philosophical outlook of its articulate strata, it belongs to East Asia. The Vietnamese have much the same culture, much the same ideals and ideas, and much the same attitudes and abilities as the Chinese. Yet for many centuries Vietnam defended itself against Chinese encroachment and sought a distinct identity. There is no reason to suppose that this tradition would not be kept alive under a Communist regime—unless, of course, people felt that they were the object of a relentless attack from the West.[14]

Failing to appreciate this inhibiting historical factor, the Eisenhower administration could not understand the natural and traditional hegemony exercised by China in this area, even though the United States exercised just such hegemony on another continent.

14. Myrdal, op. cit.

The Rolling Red Horde theory fathered a series of deeds designed to maintain the French "bulwark" against communism. In March 1953, General Mark Clark, commanding in Korea, visited Vietnam and concluded that ". . . the Vietnamese needed rifles, automatic rifles, machine guns, light mortars and transportation facilities that could carry them over the water-soaked rice paddies in the Delta sector. . . ." General Clark recommended that Washington supply these and other arms and equipment; in an attempt to remedy what he believed was a deficient French troop-training program for the Vietnamese, he also arranged the transfer of some American and Korean advisers to Indochina. In addition, he released transport aircraft, Flying Boxcars, to the French command.[15]

Then, in spring of 1953, the American military mission arranged by Acheson and Letourneau in December 1952 arrived in Indochina. Headed by Lieutenant General J. W. (Iron Mike) O'Daniel, it surveyed French military needs and recommended

. . . that in addition to the four hundred million dollars in aid set aside for Indochina, three hundred eighty-five million more should be made available before the end of 1954. On September 30, 1953, the United States pledged this aid and France promised to do (but did not do) all that we had been asking of her over the past two years.[16]

France, or anyway certain French officials, quickly fell in line with the American desire of saving Indochina. *Time* magazine's cover story of September 25, 1953, on Navarre, quoted him as saying: ". . . A year ago none of us could see victory. There wasn't a prayer. Now we can see it clearly like light at the end of a tunnel."[17] Not to be outdone, Secretary Dulles spoke grandly of "the Navarre Plan," which was designed to ". . . break the organized body of Communist aggression by the end of the 1955 fighting season."[18] In late November, Navarre advised his government that he did not believe the time had come to try to start peace negotiations. At month's end, the French high command in Indochina deigned to reply officially to an offer by Ho Chi Minh ". . . of direct negotiations with France based on a simple battlefield truce. . . ."[19] At the Bermuda conference, in December, the French Foreign Minister, M. Bidault, told President Eisenhower that the situation ". . . was better than it had been for a long time . . . for the first time they were thinking of winning eventually."[20]

15. Mark Clark, *From the Danube to the Yalu* (New York: Harper & Brothers, 1954).
16. Acheson, op. cit.
17. *Time*, September 28, 1953.
18. Fall (*The Two Viet-Nams*), *supra*.
19. Fall (*Hell in a Very Small Place*), *supra*.
20. D. D. Eisenhower, *Mandate for Change 1953–1956* (London: William Heinemann, 1963).

This verbal enthusiasm seemed to imply that, by some *deus ex machina,* France had suddenly reclaimed the military initiative. Nothing was farther from truth. As General Giap later wrote:

. . . After a careful study of the situation, the Party's Central Committee issued the following slogan to break the "Navarre plan": "Dynamism, initiative, mobility, and rapidity of decision in face of new situations." Keeping the initiative we should concentrate our forces to attack strategic points which were relatively vulnerable. If we succeeded in keeping the initiative, we could achieve successes and compel the enemy to scatter their forces. . . .[21]

While Navarre was rushing slim reserves about trying to plug holes in the "de Lattre Line" and prevent further losses in central Vietnam, Giap began striking at what the French were to call *zones excentriques,* that is, ". . . strategic points which were relatively vulnerable." He chose Laos, at first striking central and southern areas in addition to northern Cambodia, then attacking in greater strength in the North.

Navarre had to react to this new threat—it was a question of *how.* The most prudent tactic, considering his limited resources, would have been a withdrawal from northern Laos in favor of building a strong defensive complex in the South. In a later book, he explained that he rejected this course of action on grounds that the French Government, which had just signed a separate treaty with Laos, would not abandon Luang Prabang, the seat of the royal residence, or Vientiane, the capital.[22] He also rejected a defensive war of movement, which ". . . the nature of the terrain" and ". . . the lack of adaptation of our forces" made impractical. Instead, he decided on a "blocking action" by building a system of fortified camps, ". . . a mediocre solution" but the only possible way, in his mind, of preventing direct invasion.

In late November 1953, Navarre established a series of fortified airheads in the Northwest. He placed the largest of these in Dien Bien Phu, an immense valley of seventy-five square miles surrounded by partially jungle-covered hills. He ordered the French task force, about six thousand troops, to build a series of defenses around the airfield while designated battalions patrolled aggressively as prelude to linking up with French forces in nearby Laos; the base would also support GCMA units, which, the reader may recall, were specially trained guerrilla units operating with friendly tribes in this region.

This was precisely the system that Navarre had inherited from Salan and in part discontinued as an unproductive drain on his relatively meager resources. He nonetheless proceeded with what Wingate had attempted in Burma: building a fortified camp "behind" enemy lines to

21. Giap, op. cit.; see also McCuen, op. cit.
22. Henri Navarre, *Agonie de l'Indochine* (Paris: Librairie Plon, 1956).

support active operations against the enemy, a camp that was to be held "at all costs."[23]

In so doing, Navarre ignored three extremely valid arguments. The first already had been discreetly forwarded by President Eisenhower, who later wrote:

... the occupation of Dien Bien Phu caused little notice at the time, except to soldiers who were well acquainted with the almost invariable fate of troops invested in an isolated fortress. I instructed both the State and Defense Departments to communicate to their French counterparts my concern as to this move.[24]

Navarre's own commander of ground forces in northern Vietnam, General Cogny, presented a second:

... It seems that to the general staff (EMIFT), the occupation of Dien Bien Phu will close the road to Luang-Prabang and deprive the Viet-Minh of the rice of the region.

In that kind of country you can't interdict a road. This is a European-type notion without any value here. The Viets can get through anywhere. We can see this right here in the Red River Delta.

The rice surplus provided by Dien Bien Phu will only feed one division for three months. Therefore, it would only make a fractional contribution to an (enemy) campaign in Laos. . . .

I am persuaded that Dien Bien Phu shall become, whether we like it or not, a battalion meat-grinder, with no possiblity of large-scale radiating out from it as soon as it will be blocked by a single Viet-Minh regiment (see example of Na-San). . . .[25]

French intelligence reports presented the third: the presence in the area of an entire Viet Minh division. As Bernard Fall later wrote:

... The 316th Division was not the best of all Communist outfits, but it was excellently suited for operations in the highlands because two of its three infantry regiments . . . were recruited from among tribesmen who spoke the same language as the inhabitants of the T'ai highlands.

In addition to its three infantry regiments, Division 316 also had an artillery battalion, the 980th, equipped with recoilless rifles and heavy mortars. On the basis of this intelligence, it should have been obvious to the French that Dien Bien Phu was an unlikely choice as a mooring point for light, mobile guerrilla forces.[26]

As was his wont, Giap did nothing to stop the French from occupying and defending Dien Bien Phu. Only when the French plan became

23. Lancaster, op. cit.
24. Eisenhower, op. cit.
25. Fall (*Hell in a Very Small Place*), *supra.*
26. Ibid.

clear did Giap postpone his invasion of northern Laos in favor of an attack in strength against the new French position. His decision drew considerable argument from subordinate commanders, who remembered with distaste the cost of earlier Viet Minh attacks against French defensive positions. Giap answered these arguments by promising slow and methodical preparation that included careful training of assault troops and by secretly bringing up over two hundred heavy artillery pieces as well as anti-aircraft guns and ammunition to feed them.[27]

Giap thought he could achieve strategic and tactical surprise at Dien Bien Phu. Once he had made up his mind to attack—and undoubtedly he had to make a hard sell to Politburo comrades—he started concentrating three assault divisions plus a new artillery division equipped in part with pieces captured in Korea by the Chinese. Simultaneously, thousands of coolies went to work improving five hundred miles of road that led from the Chinese border to the target area. Provincial Road 41, which ran from the Red River to Dien Bien Phu,

. . . required nearly 20,000 coolies and tribesmen impressed from the nearby villages, who slaved for three months to rebuild the shattered remains of Road 41 and to widen its turns to accommodate the artillery pieces and the 800 Russian-built Molotova 2½-ton trucks which were to become the backbone of the conventional supply system.[28]

Meanwhile, French patrols, as called for in Navarre's original orders, began probing the periphery of the valley and beyond, operations that took place in the winter months and, due to repeated skirmishes, soon proved costly to the French. By February 1954, several painful facts had validated General Cogny's arguments against the operation.

The first was the immensity of the operational task in relation to assigned resources. The attempt to base offensive operations on Dien Bien Phu had failed. Costly probes had disclosed extensive Viet Minh positions, artfully camouflaged and defended in strength. Even worse, Navarre meanwhile had launched Opération Atlante, an attempt to clean out Viet Minh Interzone 5, in southern Annam. This effort, which soon came to a standstill, ". . . revealed both the poor quality of the recently raised and summarily trained light battalions and the inability of the Mobile Administrative Groups for Operational Purposes (GAMO) . . . to reorganize the administration of the occupied territory."[29] Like his predecessors, Navarre was trying to do too much with too little.

As for the proposed link-up between Dien Bien Phu and French garrisons in Laos, a road was out of the question: ". . . the 50-mile-long jungle track between Sop Nao and Dien Bien Phu was cut by deep ravines, crossed a 6,000-foot-high mountain range of sheer limestone

27. Giap, op. cit.
28. Fall (Hell), supra. See also Lancaster, op. cit.
29. Lancaster, op. cit.

cliffs, and was located hundreds of miles away from the nearest French heavy equipment bases."[30] One French commander reported that ". . . the jungle is so thick and the terrain is so fragmented that to establish a straight-line connection between Dien Bien Phu and Sop Nao, for example, would in all likelihood take several months."[31] Equally obvious, a few battalions could hope neither to secure a perimeter of some thirty miles nor, lacking construction materials and engineering know-how, to build adequate internal defenses.

Finally, Paris left little doubt that Navarre would be going it alone. In October and November, the Laniel government had made no secret of its desire to end the Indochina war, which, at home, was causing an extremely serious political riff. Toward the end of 1953, the British Foreign Minister, Anthony Eden, had interested the Soviet Union in trying to find a solution to the Southeast Asia problem. Due mainly to Eden's efforts, the Berlin conference of foreign ministers of Britain, France, the Soviet Union, and the United States, in late February 1954, agreed to ". . . a conference [at Geneva] to bring about a peaceful settlement in Korea and Indochina."[32] At long last, the big powers were opting for political settlement.

None of these facts seemed to impress General Navarre except to cause him to convert the purpose of Dien Bien Phu from that of supporting offensive operations to that of forming a tactical piece of sugar to attract and finally destroy Viet Minh ants, in others words to the Hoa Binh "meat-grinder" concept of offering the Viet Minh a suitable target and defeating their attacks by superior firepower.

Navarre's disastrous decision was the perhaps inevitable result of his predilection for European-style warfare, of his own ignorance of the Viet Minh and of war in northwestern Vietnam, and of believing what he wanted to believe and not what was variously reported by his staff.

According to an official investigation subsequently conducted by a French commission headed by General Catroux, Navarre seriously underestimated Viet Minh capabilities. He did not believe that the Viet Minh could concentrate more than one division in the area within a month, nor that the enemy could maintain more than a limited siege by two divisions. He discounted the possibility of the Viet Minh bringing up heavy artillery despite indications reported by French intelligence.

Navarre believed that French transport aircraft could supply the garrison while French fighter-bombers supported ground troops and effectively interdicted Giap's lines of communication. He also apparently placed considerable stock in Roger Trinquier's GCMA units, which had been causing the Viet Minh increasing concern and which, in the event,

30. Fall (*Hell*), *supra.*
31. Ibid.
32. Acheson, op. cit.

were supposed to cut Viet Minh supply lines.[33] Perhaps unconsciously, Navarre believed that the French Government would not allow a defeat at Dien Bien Phu—a mentality similar to that displayed by Gordon at Khartoum. Possibly he was unduly impressed by the new American doctrine of instant and massive retaliation against an aggressor—for example, China—announced by Dulles in late January 1954; later events suggest that he might have been promised American air support in case of trouble—in February 1954, the United States supplied B-26 bombers to his command along with 250 U. S. Air Force technicians, vanguard of an eventual twelve hundred men who would keep them flying. Finally, an inhibitive psychological factor in form of a "last-chance" philosophy might have been at work, as suggested by a lecture Navarre delivered four years later:

. . . We had no policy at all [in Indochina]. . . . After seven years of war we were in a complete imbroglio, and no one, from private to commander in chief, knew just why we were fighting.

Was it to maintain French positions? If so, which ones? Was it simply to participate, under the American umbrella, in the "containment" of Communism in Southeast Asia? Then why did we continue to make such an effort when our interest had practically ceased to exist?

This uncertainty about our political aims kept us from having a continuing and coherent military policy in Indochina. . . . This rift between policy and strategy dominated the entire Indochina war.[34]

---

33. McCuen, op. cit.: In late 1953, the designation changed to GMI (*Groupement Mixte d'Intervention*); by the end of the war, the GMI numbered 15,000 and ". . . required 300 tons of air-delivered supplies per month"; see also Tanham, op. cit.; Fall (*Hell*), *supra;* Trinquier, op. cit.

34. Devillers and Lacouture, op. cit.

Chapter 63

Vietnam: French and American estimates • Giap attacks Dien Bien Phu • Viet Minh tactics • The guerrilla effort • Crisis • Question of American military intervention • Dissenting voices • General Ridgway's warning • Eisenhower backs down • The fall of Dien Bien Phu

WHATEVER THE REASONS behind the tactical aberration of Dien Bien Phu, General Navarre was not the only one who erred. Western military conceit carried over to numerous members of his staff and to ranking commanders in Hanoi and Dien Bien Phu. The record does not show that any senior officer dissociated himself from his commander's decision, much less resigning either staff billet or command.

The error also overflowed area lines. In February 1954, the French Minister of National Defense, René Pleven, and the Chief of the French General Staff, General Paul Ély, visited Vietnam, including Dien Bien Phu. Although Pleven was critical of Navarre's "hedgehog" strategy, which, he feared, created "game preserves" for the Viet Minh,[1] Ély described Dien Bien Phu as an ". . . extremely strong position, which could only be attacked by a very powerful force," and, even then, he

---

1. Devillers and Lacouture, op. cit.

believed that the advantage would be with the defenders.[2] Also in February, the head of the American military advisory group, Lieutenant General O'Daniel, visited Dien Bien Phu and reported so favorably to Washington that President Eisenhower cabled Secretary of State Dulles, then attending the foreign ministers' conference in Berlin: ". . . General O'Daniel's most recent report is more encouraging than that given to you through French sources."[3]

By March 1954, the Dien Bien Phu garrison numbered some seventeen thousand troops, who occupied a sector system of defense and who were supported by artillery and aircraft. These troops were still digging in when, on March 13, the Viet Minh opened fire to begin a siege action that would last a little longer than two months. At this time, ". . . enemy combat strength in the Dien Bien Phu area was estimated at 49,500 men, with [an additional] 31,500 logistical support personnel. Another 23,000 Communist support troops and personnel were strung out along the communication lines."[4]

The reader will find a blow-by-blow account of this heart-rending battle in Bernard Fall's book *Hell in a Very Small Place*. We can only note that events swiftly disproved all of Navarre's suppositions, to result in tactical defeat that, despite limited proportions, brought resounding military and political repercussions.

Giap's most important success lay in secretly bringing up artillery and other heavy weapons through jungles and over mountains, a fantastic logistics effort that resulted in bombardment of French jerry-built positions by 75-mm. and 105-mm. howitzers, 75-mm. recoilless rifles, 120-mm. mortars, and, toward the end, Soviet multiple-rocket launchers:

. . . The French artillery specialists inside the fortress later estimated that they had been hit by approximately 30,000 shells of 105-mm. artillery and probably by over 100,000 of other calibers . . . thus roughly 1,300 to 1,700 tons of munitions delivered to the valley between December, 1953, and May,

2. Lancaster, op. cit.: Pleven later told Premier Laniel ". . . that he viewed the prospect of such an attack with misgivings, describing the Expeditionary Corps as 'exhausted' and the general military stiuation as essentially 'precarious'"; see also Devillers and Lacouture, op. cit.: Ély and two of his fellow generals later reported ". . . that no military solution could be achieved," that France ". . . had already reached the limits of its military effort," and that ". . . the most it could now hope to achieve was the optimum military conditions for a political settlement."

3. Eisenhower, op. cit.

4. Fall (*Hell*), *supra;* see also Lancaster, op. cit.: According to General Navarre, the Chinese provided military advisers to the Viet Minh at both high-command and division-command levels. Chinese soldiers also allegedly drove Soviet-supplied trucks and possibly manned 57-mm. anti-aircraft guns at Dien Bien Phu; P. E. X. Turnbull, "Dien Bien Phu and Sergeant Kubiak," *Army Quarterly,* April 1965.

1954. In addition, about 6,500 tons of other supplies were brought to the valley by the Viet-Minh.[5]

Aided by direct artillery fire (frowned on by Western officers as too simple), Viet Minh assault teams from four secretly concentrated divisions pinched off outer defense sectors until artillery interdicted the vital airstrip to render it inoperable. This disaster forced the French to drop ammunition and supply by parachute, but Giap now unleashed his second surprise, a ring of anti-aircraft guns which produced flak that, according to later testimony of American civil pilots flying C-119s under contract to the French, ". . . exceeded in intensity that met in Korea and 'was as dense as anything allied pilots had encountered over the Ruhr during World War II.' "[6] To evade flak, cargo planes resorted to higher altitudes, which meant widely dispersed cargo drops, with much vital supply falling to the Viet Minh.

Guerrilla activity behind French lines also took a major toll of French resources. In early March, Viet Minh teams struck three French airfields to destroy thirty airplanes and fifty-three thousand gallons of fuel; at heavily fortified Cat Bi Airfield, raiders crawled through sewers to reach and destroy eighteen transport aircraft![7]

French combat air support proved a disappointment. The distance of the target area from French fields gave the B-26s only limited time on target—fighters had only ten minutes!—while uncomfortably accurate flak coupled with extremely effective camouflage discouraged the direct support task. The interdiction task ran into problems also encountered in World War II and in Korea. Poor weather and jungle terrain hindered observation. French planes bombed roads and bridges by day, but Vietnamese coolies either repaired them or built bypasses at night. Interdiction, on occasion, halted the several hundred trucks at Giap's disposal; it almost never stopped thousands of coolies laboriously pushing bicycles loaded with ammunition and supply.[8] As with American air power in Korea, French air power impeded, but never halted, the flow of material.

Trinquier's GCMA teams also proved disappointing. Despite his later assertions to the contrary, they did not "seal off" the target.[9]

All was not smooth sailing for the Viet Minh, however. Giap also faced enormous problems. Early assaults on outer hill positions, carried out in a manner reminiscent of American marines attacking Pacific

5. Fall (*Hell*), *supra*. Some readers will perhaps recall a CBS television documentary, *The End of an Empire,* which recorded the battle of Dien Bien Phu from the Viet Minh side; see also Giap, op. cit.
6. Fall (*Hell*), *supra*.
7. Ibid.; see also McCuen, op. cit.
8. Fall (*Hell*), *supra:* Fall claimed that these specially made bicycles, which coolies pushed, not rode, carried 440 pounds; see also O'Ballance, op. cit., who suggests 150 pounds.
9. Trinquier, op. cit.; see also Fall (*Hell*), *supra;* Tanham, op. cit.

beaches in World War II, but lacking a sophisticated system of artillery and air support, cost so heavily that Giap changed his tactics to a trench warfare reminiscent of World War I. Viet Minh morale sagged, and was revived only with considerable difficulty. Largely untrained replacements were slow in arriving. Medical services were appallingly inadequate.

But transcending these problems was strategic and tactical surprise, which Giap had achieved and which caused the panic-stricken French high command to start thinking in terms of American air support.

The confusing and frightening events of this period were later pieced together by veteran Washington journalist Chalmers Roberts in a superb piece of reporting. According to his account, on March 20, the French army's chief of staff, General Paul Ély,

. . . arrived in Washington from the Far East to tell the President, Dulles, Radford [Chairman of the Joint Chiefs of Staff], and others that unless the United States intervened, Indochina would be lost. This was a shock of earthquake proportions to leaders who had been taken in by their own talk of the Navarre Plan to win the war.[10]

Admiral Radford took the lead. To what extent Arthur Radford was speaking for himself and to what extent for his government was not made clear. At fifty-seven years, the Iowa-born carrier admiral was a man of forceful action: In 1949, he had led the "revolt of the admirals," insisting that the B-36 bomber was a "billion-dollar blunder."[11] He now argued that carrier air strikes—presumably using atomic bombs—were necessary to retrieve the situation at Dien Bien Phu. His words caused a decided flurry in the National Security Council. Supported by Vice-President Nixon and Secretary of State Dulles, Radford argued ". . . that Indochina must not be allowed to fall into Communist hands lest such a fate set in motion a falling row of dominoes."[12]

On March 24, President Eisenhower ominously stated in a press conference that Southeast Asia was of the ". . . most transcendent importance." On March 29,

. . . Dulles, in a New York speech had called for "united action" even though it might involve "serious risks," and declared that Red China was backing aggression in Indochina with the goal of controlling all of Southeast Asia. He had added that the United States felt that "that possibility should not be passively accepted but should be met by united action."[13]

10. Chalmers M. Roberts, "The Day We Didn't Go to War," *The Reporter*, September 14, 1954.
11. *Time*, May 25, 1953.
12. Roberts, op. cit.
13. Ibid.; see also Anthony Eden, *The Memoirs of Anthony Eden—Full Circle* (Boston: Houghton Mifflin, 1960): Dulles told the British ambassador in Washington, Sir Roger Makins, that ". . . the United States was thinking in terms of a joint warning to China, by several countries, of naval and air action against the China coast; it would not threaten landing of American troops."

With this prelude, President Eisenhower called Congressional leaders to confer on April 3. He himself was not present. Dulles occupied the chair and was assisted by Admiral Radford and assorted officials and aides. The Secretary of State told the eight members of Congress that he wanted ". . . a joint resolution by Congress to permit the President to use air and naval power in Indochina":

. . . Then Radford took over. He said the Administration was deeply concerned over the rapidly deteriorating situation. He used a map of the Pacific to point out the importance of Indochina. He spoke about the French Union forces then already under siege for three weeks in the fortress of Dienbienphu.

The Admiral explained the urgency of American action by declaring that he was not even sure, because of poor communications, whether, in fact, Dienbienphu was still holding out. (The fortress held out for five weeks more.)[14]

Radford having duly raised hairs on Congressional heads, Dulles carried on:

. . . If Indochina fell and if its fall led to the loss of all of Southeast Asia, he declared, then the United States might eventually be forced back to Hawaii, as it was before the Second World War. And Dulles was not complimentary about the French. He said he feared they might use some disguised means of getting out of Indochina if they did not receive help soon.[15]

What kind of help?
Radford relieved Dulles:

. . . Some two hundred planes from the thirty-one-thousand-ton U. S. Navy carriers *Essex* and *Boxer,* then in the South China Sea ostensibly for "training," plus land-based U. S. Air Force planes from bases a thousand miles away in the Philippines, would be used for a single strike to save Dienbienphu.[16]

The Congressional leaders, Lyndon Johnson among them, determined by astute questioning that such an air strike would mean war, that if it did not succeed in relieving Dien Bien Phu, further action would have to follow, that none of the three service chiefs constituting the Joint Chiefs of Staff agreed with Radford, that Dulles had not gained allied approval of such a course, and that no one could say whether China or the Soviet Union would also go to war over the issue. Not all questions rang brilliantly; the domestic political factor showed in some. They collectively demonstrated, however, the administration's jerry-built plan that might well have precipitated an atomic war and the end of civilization as we know it.

14. Roberts, op. cit.
15. Ibid.
16. Ibid.

Democrats and Republicans, congressmen and senators—that raw, windy Saturday—earned their pay:

. . . In the end, all eight members of Congress, Republicans and Democrats alike, were agreed that Dulles had better go shopping for allies. . . .[17]

The Administration was not yet ready to yield. Key figures began to prepare the home front for American intervention. On April 7, President Eisenhower, at a press conference, parroted Radford by speaking of a "row-of-dominoes" to conjure to the American public a black-and-white picture of the conquest of Southeast Asia by "communists." Under the date of April 8, Richard Rovere wrote in a *New Yorker* "Letter from Washington" that ". . . Indo-China has become the most pressing of all problems here. . . ." Having decided that the loss of Indochina would prove a greater calamity than the loss of Korea, Secretary of State Dulles reasoned that

. . . the commitment of American ground forces and the sacrifice of American lives to prevent it would be fully justified. Realizing that public opinion has not up to now shared this view of the matter—in fact, the view seems to be of fairly recent origin in Mr. Dulles's own mind, and is certainly so in the mind of the President, who as late as February 10 told a news conference that he could scarcely imagine a tragedy greater than American intervention—the Secretary in the past couple of weeks has been conducting what must undoubtedly be one of the boldest campaigns of political suasion ever undertaken by an American statesman. Congressmen, political leaders of all shadings of opinion, newspapermen, and radio and television personalities have been rounded up in droves and escorted to lectures and briefings on what the State Department regards as the American stake in Indo-China. The somber word-portraits of the diplomats show Communist influence radiating in a semicircle from Indo-China to Burma, Malaya, and Thailand, and then across the South China Sea to the islands of Indonesia. They show Soviet Russia and Communist China economically and militarily strengthened by the strategic raw materials available to them in that region, and the United States and other anti-Communist powers correspondingly weakened by the loss of those materials. They show Nehru's India impressed more deeply than ever by Communist power and no longer offering any sort of resistance to Communist infiltration, and they concurrently show Pakistan, the Philippine Republic, South Korea, Formosa, and Japan disheartened and discouraged by an American failure to succor a threatened Asiatic people. Even Australia, Mr. Dulles's lieutenants argue, would find its security threatened by a Vietminh victory. Hearing this analysis, one gets the impression that they have grave doubts whether the United States could survive the establishment of Communist power in Indo-China. . . .[18]

17. Ibid.
18. Richard H. Rovere, *The Eisenhower Years* (New York: Farrar, Straus & Cudahy, 1956).

In mid-April, Admiral Radford publicly stated that loss of Indochina ". . . would be the prelude to the loss of all Southeast Asia and a threat to a far wider area." On April 16, Vice-President Nixon told a group of newspaper editors: ". . . The United States as a leader of the free world cannot afford further retreat in Asia. It is hoped the United States will not have to send troops there, but if this government cannot avoid it, the Administration must face up to the situation and dispatch forces."[19]

Meanwhile, Secretary of State Dulles was trying to win the allied approval for intervention demanded by Congressional leaders. Although talks went smoothly with France, Australia, New Zealand, the Philippines, Thailand, Vietnam, Laos, and Cambodia, he ran into a brick wall when it came to Great Britain.

In early April, President Eisenhower had written Prime Minister Churchill and asked him to join a coalition that would be prepared to intervene militarily in Indochina.[20] Churchill deferred the proposal until Dulles arrived in London, about a week later. Speaking for Churchill and the British Government, Foreign Minister Anthony Eden voiced three major objections: British military advisers did not believe that air action alone would be effective (it followed that ground troops would have to be committed); direct intervention would torpedo the Geneva Conference, for which Eden held great hopes; in view of the existing Sino-Soviet treaty, direct intervention might well lead to general war.

Despite Dulles' vigorous, heated, and repeatedly expressed arguments for intervention, neither Churchill nor Eden would yield except to agree to some sort of coalition security arrangement, which had been under discussion since 1952.[21]

From Dulles' standpoint, this was better than nothing, and, upon his return to Washington, he called in concerned ambassadors in order ". . . to set up an informal working group to study the collective defense of South East Asia."[22] Dulles' unilateral action ignored Burma and India, and Eden refused to allow his ambassador to attend. The conclusion of Eden's message to the British ambassador, Sir Roger Makins, was particularly significant in view of Dullesian wheeling-dealing peripatetic diplomacy:

. . . Americans may think the time past when they need consider the feelings or difficulties of their allies. It is the conviction that this tendency becomes more pronounced every week that is creating mounting difficulties for anyone in this country who wants to maintain close Anglo-American relations. We, at least, have constantly to bear in mind all our Commonwealth partners, even if the United States does not like some of them; and

19. New York *Times,* April 17, 1954; see also Eisenhower, op. cit.
20. Eisenhower, op. cit.
21. Eden, op. cit.
22. Ibid.

I must ask you to keep close watch on this aspect of our affairs, and not hesitate to press it on the United States.[23]

Dulles next flew to Paris for a NATO conference prior to the Geneva meeting. On April 23, the French foreign minister, Georges Bidault, showed him a cable from General Navarre: In Navarre's opinion, only a massive American air attack could save Dien Bien Phu. Dulles passed this information to Eden, explaining that, if Britain agreed, he, Dulles, would ask President Eisenhower to gain Congressional authorization for direct intervention. Eden had not changed his mind since the earlier talks: He doubted if intervention at this late stage would materially affect the situation; as palliative, he broached the notion of an Anglo-American guarantee of Thailand's frontier.[24]

Dulles tried once more. Bolstered by Admiral Radford's presence on the following day, he again put the issue to Eden. When Eden further demurred, Dulles handed Bidault an official letter that promised American intervention, including ground forces, should France and Western allies so desire. Eden, for his part, took the issue to Prime Minister Churchill, who, along with the Cabinet, refused to countenance direct intervention, preferring instead to attain a political settlement —some form of partition—at Geneva.

The British provided only one stumbling block. The reader may recall that, at the famous March conference, the three American service chiefs disagreed with Admiral Radford's tactical plan to launch an air strike at Dien Bien Phu. We know the feelings of one of these officers, General Matthew B. Ridgway, surely one of the most capable generals in history. Ridgway had never been impressed with the French defense of Dien Bien Phu, a fight, he believed, that ". . . could end in but one way—in death or capture for the defenders. . . ." But, in spring of 1954, the army's chief of staff was more alarmed

. . . to hear individuals of great influence, both in and out of government, raising the cry that now was the time, and here, in Indo-China, was the place to "test the New Look" [i.e., in American air-oriented military forces], for us to intervene, to come to the aid of France with arms. At the same time that same old delusive idea was advanced—that we could do things the cheap and easy way, by going into Indo-China with air and naval forces alone. To me this had an ominous ring. For I felt sure that if we committed air and naval power to that area, we would have to follow them immediately with ground forces in support.[25]

Ridgway had commanded in Korea, where he had extricated UN forces from MacArthur's catastrophic strategy, an experience that left

23. Ibid.
24. Eisenhower, op. cit.
25. Matthew B. Ridgway, *Soldier: The Memoirs of Matthew B. Ridgway* (New York: Harper & Brothers, 1956).

him with few illusions. War in Asia, he knew, was not a pinchpenny business:

. . . I also knew that none of those advocating such a step [intervention at Dien Bien Phu] had any accurate idea what such an operation would cost us in blood and money and national effort. I felt that it was essential therefore that all who had any influence in making the decision on this grave matter should be fully aware of all the factors involved. To provide these facts, I sent out to Indo-China an Army team of experts in every field: engineers, signal and communications specialists, medical officers, and experienced combat leaders who knew how to evaluate terrain in terms of battle tactics. . . .

Their report was complete. The area, they found, was practically devoid of those facilities which modern forces such as ours find essential to the waging of war. Its telecommunications, highways, railways—all the things that make possible the operation of a modern combat force on land—were almost non-existent. Its port facilities and airfields were totally inadequate, and to provide the facilities we would need would require a tremendous engineering and logistical effort.

The land was a land of rice paddy and jungle—particularly adapted to the guerrilla-type warfare at which the Chinese soldier is a master. . . .[26]

Neither Ridgway nor his army was afraid of a war in Indochina; his point was the immensity of the effort, for, ". . . if we did go into Indo-China, we would have to win. . . ."

. . . We could have fought in Indo-China. We could have won, if we had been willing to pay the tremendous cost in men and money that such intervention would have required—a cost that in my opinion would have eventually been as great, or greater than, that we paid in Korea. In Korea, we had learned that air and naval power alone cannot win a war and that inadequate ground forces cannot win one either. It was incredible to me that we had forgotten that bitter lesson so soon—that we were on the verge of making that same tragic error.[27]

The Ridgway report reached President Eisenhower, probably in late May, about the same time General Ridgway personally briefed him.[28] Eisenhower mentioned nothing of it in his memoirs, which are particularly ambiguous for this crucial period. So far as one can gather, the President was not steering a firm course toward intervention but, rather, was allowing his ship of state to be blown into it by Dullesian-Radford war winds. Eisenhower, all along, had objected to tactical aspects of the French stand at Dien Bien Phu; as an old soldier, he must have raised a tired eyebrow when still another airman claimed he could

26. Ibid.
27. Ibid.
28. Letter from General Ridgway to the author.

win a war with bombs alone. The Ridgway report must have made a considerable impact; as General Ridgway later wrote, ". . . to a man of his military experience its implications were immediately clear." It is probably safe to say that the report and its author steered Eisenhower to a more cautious course at an incautious time of government.[29]

While international diplomacy so ran the course, the plight of the Dien Bien Phu defenders grew steadily worse. On May 8, 1954, the beleaguered garrison surrendered to the Viet Minh. Over two thousand defenders had died; the remainder, including some five thousand wounded, marched forlornly into captivity.[30]

Here was a crushing defeat too great for the French to accept and still fight on. The Paris and Saigon governments fell; in June, General Ély replaced General Navarre. Although the French army in Indochina remained a cohesive unit, with 95 per cent of its strength intact, government and country had suffered enough. The Expeditionary Corps, since 1945, had suffered over 170,000 casualties including nearly seventy-five thousand missing (of whom nearly twenty-seven thousand were Vietnamese); the war had cost France nearly $7.5 billion (plus another $4 billion in U.S. aid).[31]

Despite American pressure, the new prime minister of France, Pierre Mendès-France, hastened to a political settlement that, had it been made in a yesterday, would have solved many problems of the morrow.

29. Ridgway (*Soldier*); *supra:* ". . . when the day comes for me to face my maker and account for my actions, the thing I would be most humbly proud of was the fact that I fought against, and perhaps contributed to preventing, the carrying out of some hare-brained tactical schemes which would have cost the lives of thousands of men. To that list of tragic accidents that fortunately never happened I would add the Indo-China intervention. . . ."

30. Jean Lartéguy, *The Centurions* (London: Hutchinson, 1961). Tr. Xan Fielding. The author offers a gripping account of subsequent treatment of prisoners; see also Giap, op. cit.; Fall (*Hell*), *supra.*

31. Fall (*Hell*), *supra;* see also Lancaster, op. cit.; O'Ballance, op. cit.

Chapter 64

The Geneva Conference • The American position • Dulles'
defeat • The agreements • SEATO • Ngo Dinh Diem • His
background • The refugee problem • American support •
Eisenhower's letter • The Collins mission • Diem takes over

I N SEPTEMBER 1953, sixty-five-year-old Secretary of State John
Foster Dulles told listening representatives at the United Nations that
U.S. leaders

. . . are ready to learn from others. Also we recognize that our views may
not always prevail. When that happens, we shall regret it, but we shall not
sulk. We shall try to accept the result philosophically. We know that we
have no monopoly of wisdom and virtue. Also we know that sometimes
time alone proves the final verdict.[1]

Dulles of that speech and Dulles at Geneva seven months later seemed
to be different persons. Arriving in the old Swiss city in a state of near
funk, his mood darkened when Anthony Eden reported the British Government's final decision against direct intervention at Dien Bien Phu.
When Dulles, backed by Walter S. Robertson, Assistant Secretary of

1. *Time,* September 28, 1953.

State for Far Eastern Affairs, continued to plead for military intervention, Eden argued that the problem was as much political as military, and thus would hinge on Asian support which was not forthcoming.

On May 1, Eden notified Churchill that ". . . only Mr. Bedell Smith [U. S. Under Secretary of State] seemed to have any real comprehension of the reasons which had led us to take up our present position." Robertson, he told Churchill,

. . . whose approach to these questions is so emotional as to be impervious to argument or indeed to facts, was keeping up a sort of "theme-song" to the effect that there were in Indo-China some three hundred thousand men who were anxious to fight against the Vietminh and were looking to us for support and encouragement. I said that if they were so anxious to fight I could not understand why they did not do so. The Americans had put in nine times more supplies of material than the Chinese, and plenty must be available for their use. I had no faith in this eagerness of the Vietnamese to fight for Bao Dai.[2]

Walter Bedell Smith provided the greatest surprise, however. In opposition to the administration's domino theory, so favored by Dulles, Smith thought

. . . that though it would be quite impossible to attempt to stop a communist advance on the border of Malaya, it was possible to find a position from which Thailand, Burma and Malaya could be defended. One of the difficulties was that they had never been able to sit down with the French over a map and examine the military possibilities of the situation.[3]

Coming from Eisenhower's wartime chief of staff and former head of the Central Intelligence Agency, Smith's opinion, along with those of Ridgway and the other service chiefs, undoubtedly helped President Eisenhower to decide against direct American military intervention.

Dulles' views having prevailed neither with allies nor Eisenhower, he went into a diplomatic sulk far removed from philosophical acceptance of recent events. He could not withdraw the American delegation from the conference, but he could pretend that the conference did not exist, just as he pretended, in refusing to acknowledge the presence of Chou En-lai, the Communist Chinese foreign minister, that Red China did not exist. Even before Vietnam appeared on the agenda, Dulles returned to the United States, leaving Walter Bedell Smith in charge of American representation.

Dulles did not lack supporters in the United States. Despite the unfavorable military situation—Dien Bien Phu had fallen and the French had made it clear that they would not continue the war—a good many Americans including some extremely influential Republican congress-

2. Eden, op. cit.
3. Ibid.

men were appalled at the thought of granting territorial and political concessions to the Communists. For five years, the Republicans had made
political capital by accusing Democrats of responsibility for the fall of
Chiang Kai-shek. Now, suddenly, a similar disaster loomed on their own
political horizon. As one result, American diplomacy, in Joseph Buttinger's splendid phrase, became "wildly incoherent":

. . . Dulles was still interested only in united action. Not discouraged by
growing British irritation with his concept, he stubbornly continued to propa-
gate the need for a Western alliance against the Communist threat to Southeast Asia, insisting that united action would become "imperative" if the
Communists did not halt their aggression. A few days later, both Dulles and
Eisenhower indirectly admitted that Washington had become reconciled to
a compromise settlement of the Indochina War. In a radio conference on
May 11 [three days after the fall of Dien Bien Phu], Dulles said that the
whole situation would not be hopeless if "certain events" occurred, meaning
a compromise situation in Indochina. That same day, President Eisenhower
discarded the domino theory, which had been an article of faith as long
as Washington had played with the idea of direct military intervention. The
domino theory could be "counteracted," he said, "if collective defense came
about," or, as Dulles put it: The rest of Asia could be held even if Indochina
fell. Had the American people been truly concerned with the manner in
which the foreign policy was conducted by Eisenhower and Dulles, it would
have been no less upset during these weeks than were Washington's European allies. On April 9, Eisenhower said that "the loss of Indochina will
cause the fall of Southeast Asia like a set of dominoes," and less than five
weeks later both he and his Secretary of State stated flatly that the retention
of Indochina was not essential for the defense of Southeast Asia. When were
they right? In April or in May?[4]

Dullesian boycott of the Geneva Conference changed neither the fact
of the conference nor the awkward situation faced there by Western
powers. Eisenhower's change of posture did not help matters, in that
it seemed to abandon Indochina to the Viet Minh, who, at this stage,
were riding high. Despite severe casualties, they correctly hailed the fall
of Dien Bien Phu as a decisive victory: They already controlled over
three fourths of Vietnam, and they now left no doubt in anyone's mind
that they believed themselves capable of totally evicting the French from
Indochina. So determined were Viet Minh representatives to continue
the war, that the Soviet Union and China, each wanting a settlement for
its own political purposes, restrained their ally only with considerable
difficulty. Tired though they were, high though their casualties, the Viet
Minh at Geneva were negotiating from strength, and they knew it. As
Professors Kahin and Lewis, among other observers, have pointed out,
the Viet Minh agreed to a settlement mainly because it transferred the

4. Buttinger, op. cit.; see also Gurtov, op. cit.

situation to the political plane, where they felt equally confident of victory.

The Geneva Conference produced two agreements, the first a bilateral armistice between Ho Chi Minh's DRV and France, the second a "Final Declaration." The armistice called for a general cease-fire in Indochina; in Vietnam, it established a ". . . provisional military demarcation line," the 17th parallel. Article 14 stated in part: ". . . pending the general elections which will bring about the unification of Viet Nam, the conduct of civil administration in each regrouping zone shall be in the hands of the party whose forces are to be regrouped there in virtue of the present Agreement." In other words, the document assigned administrative jurisdiction north of the line to Ho Chi Minh's DRV Government and jurisdiction south of the line to France during the interim period preceding country-wide elections. The agreement provided a three-hundred-day period in which military forces and any civilians who wished would regroup as appropriate in North and South. It also prohibited any form of external military reinforcements and established an International Control Commission to insure that neither side violated these provisions. Finally, ". . . the Vietminh's interests were further safeguarded by the provision that any administration succeeding the French prior to the 1956 elections would legally assume France's obligations and 'be responsible for ensuring the observance and enforcement of the terms and provisions' of the agreements entered into between the Vietminh and France."[5]

France and the DRV signed this agreement on July 20. On the following day, conference participants produced a "Final Declaration," a thirteen-point document that, in part, "took note" of the various articles and, in part, amplified them. Point 6, for example,

. . . recognizes that the essential purpose of the agreement relating to Viet Nam is to settle military questions with a view to ending hostilities and that the military demarcation line is provisional and should not in any way be interpreted as constituting a political or territorial boundary. The Conference expresses its conviction that the execution of the provisions set out in the present declaration and in the agreement on the cessation of hostilities creates the necessary basis for the achievement in the near future of a political settlement in Viet Nam.

Point 7 called for general elections, in July 1956 ". . . under the supervision of an international commission composed of representatives of the Member States of the International Supervisory Commission. . . . Consultations will be held on this subject between the competent representative authorities of the two zones from July 20, 1955, onwards."[6]

5. Kahin and Lewis, op. cit.
6. Ibid.; see also Douglas Pike, *Vietcong—The Organization and Techniques of the National Liberation Front of South Vietnam* (Cambridge, Mass.: MIT Press, 1967).

The "Final Declaration" evoked two important dissenting voices. The first belonged to Dr. Tran Van Do, who represented the Associated State of Vietnam. Titularly headed by Bao Dai, early in July its premier had become the redoubtable nationalist Ngo Dinh Diem. Diem now instructed Dr. Do

. . . to disassociate South Vietnam from the agreements that were signed, thereby laying the legal groundwork for his subsequent refusal to abide by them. He considered the division of Vietnam a personal betrayal and echoed Dr. Do's final Geneva declaration that South Vietnam "reserved to itself entire freedom of action to safeguard the sacred right of the Vietnamese people to territorial unity, national independence, and freedom."[7]

The second voice belonged to the American delegate, Walter Bedell Smith, who, instructed by Dulles, refused to sign.

Other participating governments—Great Britain, Communist China, the Soviet Union, Cambodia, Laos, DRV, and France—circumvented this contretemps by awarding the document "oral assent," the United States and Vietnam refusing. Smith "took note" of the Agreements and declared that the United States would ". . . refrain from the threat or the use of force to disturb them" and that it ". . . would view any renewal of the aggression in violation of the aforesaid Agreements with grave concern and as seriously threatening international peace and security"—an attempted face-saving declaration not unlike the "non-injury oath" familiar to the feudal period of history.[8]

The results of the Geneva Conference almost immediately drew American Congressional criticism, answered by, among others, Under Secretary of State Smith with a reasoned protest which concluded: ". . . I would like to point out, too, that when we analyze and discuss the results of Geneva it will be well to remember that diplomacy has rarely been able to gain at the conference table what cannot be gained or held on the battlefield."[9]

To dispute this truism is difficult, and further discussion is probably futile until concerned governments release pertinent documents. Even

7. Shaplen, op. cit.
8. Kahin and Lewis, op. cit.: Smith stated further that United States policy in the case of divided nations was ". . . to seek to achieve unity through free elections, supervised by the United States to ensure that they are conducted fairly"; he also reiterated America's traditional position ". . . that peoples are entitled to determine their own future"; see also S. Runciman, *A History of the Crusades* (New York: Penguin Books, 1965), 3 vols.: In the First Crusade, Raymond of St. Gilles, count of Toulouse, refused to take an oath of allegiance to the Byzantine emperor, Alexius. Under pressure from other crusader leaders, Raymond eventually ". . . swore a modified oath promising to respect the life and honor of the emperor and to see that nothing was done, by himself or his men, to the emperor's hurt. Such an oath of non-injury was often taken by vassals to their overlord in southern France; and Alexius was satisfied with it."
9. Kahin and Lewis, op. cit.

824 WAR IN THE SHADOWS

these may not totally clarify the American position, particularly since
Dulles was an exponent of vest-pocket diplomacy.

But it does seem reasonable to suggest that a more determined Dulles
practicing first-rate diplomacy could have come closer to a partition
arrangement similar to that of Korea, indeed similar to that contained
in a seven-point proposal sent to the French during negotiations.[10]
Even as drawn, the Agreement and Final Declaration smack of partition, and it is difficult to believe that the representatives of the major
powers did not foresee such an eventuality. Although Eden later up-
held the necessity for a general election, he admitted that the two-year
period allotted to prepare for it was inadequate. A British student of
Southeast Asia, P. J. Honey, later wrote that the Viet Minh representatives at Geneva ". . . privately expressed the opinion that the plebiscite
would never be held."[11]

Perhaps Dulles knew that neither the DRV nor the State of Vietnam
could accede publicly to a partition arrangement, or perhaps, in his
opinion, the concerned documents contained enough legal holes to
justify further partition action. Whatever the case, Dulles seemed to
regard the 17th parallel as a political boundary between two states. It
remained for him to pick up as many pieces as possible in the South,
and he attempted to do so in two ways: internal and external.

Dulles' external answer to the diplomatic defeat at Geneva was the
South-east Asia Collective Defense Treaty and Protocol, signed by the
United States, Great Britain, France, Australia, New Zealand, the Philippines, Thailand, and Pakistan, in early September 1954. The Southeast Asia Treaty Organization, or SEATO, bound its members to a
"security" pact which meant so many things to so many people as almost to vitiate logical meaning. The nub of the document occurs early
in Article IV:

. . . Each Party recognizes that aggression by means of armed attack in the
treaty area against any of the Parties or against any State or territory which
the Parties by unanimous agreement may hereafter designate, would endanger its own peace and safety, and agrees that it will in that event act to meet
the common danger in accordance with its constitutional processes. . . .

10. Eden, op. cit.
11. Shaplen, op. cit.; see also, Donald S. Zagoria, *Vietnam Triangle—Moscow,
Peking, Hanoi* (New York: Pegasus, 1967). Professor Zagoria points out
that ". . . in early 1957, Moscow proposed the admittance to the United Nations
of both North and South Vietnam, thus tacitly accepting the position"; *The Times*
(London), Hong Kong, July 28, 1971. Chou En-lai told American students
". . . that inexperience in matters of international diplomacy had allowed him to
permit the United States to avoid formally signing the 1954 Geneva agreement
ending the war in Indo-China."

An additional protocol extended the provisions of this article to Cambodia, Laos, and ". . . the free territory under the jurisdiction of the State of Vietnam."[12]

In short, SEATO was Dulles' jury-rigged answer to diplomatic defeat at Geneva. In Dulles' mind, SEATO existed to halt the spread of communism in Southeast Asia, and particularly in Vietnam:

> . . . In presenting the treaty to the United States Senate in late 1954, he argued that the treaty was designed to meet subversion, which was "most acute at the moment in Vietnam," and to build up in that country "a strong government which commands the loyalty of the people, and which has an effective police and constabulary at its command to detect and run down subversive activities.[13]

Even had signatories stood solidly behind SEATO, it would have had difficulty functioning as an effective regional security organization. Unlike NATO, no combined command existed, no country committed military forces to SEATO, and no country had to respond in case another was attacked.[14] The Geneva Agreements, at least for some time, prevented overt military action—but not covert political preparation—by the Viet Minh in Indochina, the area Dulles was most concerned about. As a psychological force, SEATO suffered from failure of major neutralist states, Burma, India, and Indonesia, to join. Still, it represented a common voice of sorts and, judging from the flood of counterpropaganda it loosed from DRV and from China and the Soviet Union, it obviously hit a Communist nerve.[15]

Simultaneously with organizing SEATO, Dulles and the State Department concerned themselves directly with developments inside Vietnam. This meant dealing with the new premier, Ngo Dinh Diem.

In 1954, the prime minister of Vietnam, Ngo Dinh Diem, was fifty-three years old. Robert Shaplen, who later knew him, described him as ". . . a short, broadly built man with a round face and a shock of black hair, who walked and moved jerkily, as if on strings. He always dressed in white and looked as if he were made out of ivory. . . ."[16] A bachelor and ascetic, he lived remote from his world. Surrounded by sycophants, he saw few strangers. Those received into his presence generally found themselves subject to a monologue that betrayed extreme egocentricity.

12. Kahin and Lewis, op. cit.
13. Ibid.
14. Rostow, op. cit., discusses this in detail.
15. Devillers and Lacouture, op. cit.: Psychologically, Ho Chi Minh was probably not far removed from Frederick William, the great Elector of Brandenburg, who deeply resented the treaty of Westphalia (1648), which robbed him of his gains—a fact duly respected by Frederick the Great.
16. Shaplen, op. cit.

Diem was the third child in an ancient family of Catholic aristocrats. His father served as court chamberlain to Emperor Thanh Thai at Hué; when the French deposed Thanh Thai, the elder Diem became a reasonably prosperous rice farmer. After elementary schooling, young Diem entered a monastery but later gave up the idea of the priesthood and graduated from the School of Public Administration and Law at Hanoi. Beginning imperial service as a mandarin, or court official, he rose to provincial-governor level and spent much of his time effectively countering Communist activities in his province.

In 1933, the French appointed him Minister of Interior in young Emperor Bao Dai's Annam Government. Unable to persuade French overlords to reforms he felt essential to combating communism, Diem resigned. For ten years he lived quietly, mostly in Hué, ". . . the reflective life of a scholar-revolutionist," but with little contact with the people. In 1942, he tried to interest the Japanese in establishing a free Vietnam, and when that failed, he remained in political limbo along with other nationalists. In September 1945, Viet Minh Communist agents arrested and imprisoned him. At about the same time, the Communists killed his older brother Ngo Dinh Khoi, who was governor of a northern province.[17]

In February 1946, Ho Chi Minh ordered Diem's release and brought him to Hanoi. Trying to corral nationalist figures, Ho offered him an important position in the new government. Diem refused, mainly because of his brother's death. He next tried to organize anti-Communist guerrilla activity but without success. After a short stay in a Hanoi monastery, he disguised himself as a monk and wandered around the country trying to work up anti-Communist activity among his contacts. Finally forced into complete hiding, he eventually went south and lived with his brother Thuc near Saigon.

In spring of 1947, Diem became a founding father of the National Union Front, a nationalist movement quickly and efficiently sabotaged by the French. Diem gained considerable prominence, however, and became go-between with the French in Saigon and Bao Dai in Hong Kong. The French wanted Bao Dai to return to Saigon and head a new government; Diem wanted him to hold out for a promise of Vietnamese independence. When Bao Dai chose to become puppet ruler, Diem dissociated himself from the new regime. Subsequent efforts to enlist him in the government failed because of French refusal to promise what Diem believed were essential reforms. Diem himself was unable to form a genuine nationalist movement to force these reforms. In 1950, the Viet Minh sentenced him to death *in absentia,* the French refused him police protection, and he wisely left for a trip that ended in the United States.

17. Robert Scigliano, *South Vietnam: Nation Under Stress* (Boston: Houghton Mifflin, 1964); see also Fall (*The Two Viet-Nams*), *supra.*

Diem lived for two years at Maryknoll Seminary, in Lakewood, New Jersey. In addition to lecturing at universities and writing articles pleading for an independent Vietnam, he won the ear of a number of influential Americans, including Francis Cardinal Spellman, Supreme Court Justice William Douglas, and various congressmen, among them Mike Mansfield, John F. Kennedy, and Walter Judd.[18] From time to time, Bao Dai tried to persuade him to return to Saigon and participate in his government. In mid-1953, when Diem was living in Europe, Bao Dai promised him full political powers if he would return to Vietnam, but the French would not agree to Diem's demand that ". . . the Vietnamese be allowed to conduct the war." Finally, in early July 1954, toward the final stages of the Geneva Conference, Diem accepted the premiership.

Although Diem had dissociated Vietnam from the Geneva Agreements, he was nonetheless compelled to work with the French in carrying out cease-fire provisions and trying to bring some order into the country south of the 17th parallel.

Neither task proved easy:

. . . The country was in ruins. Most bridges had been blown up. Canals, roads, railways, telephone and telegraph services had been either destroyed or were in disrepair. Dykes, too, were destroyed; vast regions of rice land were uncultivated; countless peasants who had fled the countryside found themselves unemployed in the cities. And Diem's administration, run by an incompetent civil service, politically hostile and disintegrating, had to provide the human and material resources for receiving, feeding, and temporarily settling hundreds of thousands of refugees. . . .[19]

In the months following the Geneva Conference, the armed forces of both sides had to be evacuated. About fifty thousand Viet Minh troops and twenty thousand Communist sympathizers went North. Following French evacuation of the Red River Delta, Vietnamese civilians, mostly Roman Catholics, began flooding South. With the help of American ships and planes, some 860,000 refugees eventually arrived; another four hundred thousand who wanted to come were prevented by the Viet Minh (in contravention of the Geneva Agreements).[20]

This influx of population would have taxed the resources of an efficient government. In Diem's case, it nearly brought ruin. He not only lacked experienced administrators and personal advisers, but he soon found himself in active opposition to Bao Dai, to Bao's army chief, General Nguyen Van Hinh, to many French officials and most French civilians, to powerful political-religious sects in the South, and to Viet Minh cadres that, at Ho Chi Minh's behest, remained in the South.[21]

18. Buttinger, op. cit.
19. Ibid.
20. Shaplen, op. cit.
21. Scigliano, op. cit., discusses the political situation of this period in detail.

About the only bright note at this critical time was American support. Diem found help both in Saigon and Washington, where President Eisenhower and Secretary of State Dulles had determined on a "security and reform" policy:

... With Diem as a nationalist fulcrum, the Americans wanted to build up a single army that would be trained by American officers and could serve as the instrument for pacification in the countryside, where a land distribution program and other social-economic reforms would be introduced.[22]

Such a policy conflicted with French desire to dump Diem in favor of a ruler more sympathetic to French interests. The French now turned to General Nguyen Van Hinh, in Saigon, who, in September, was ready to attempt a military coup. An American counterinsurgency expert from the Philippines, a forty-six-year-old Air Force officer on loan to Central Intelligence Agency, Colonel Edward Lansdale, deftly parried this threat with a counterthreat of having American aid stopped. Diem gained further strength from a U. S. Senate report of mid-October prepared by Senator Mike Mansfield, who praised him and called for total American support of his government.

In case anyone still doubted the Administration's intention, President Eisenhower wrote President Diem a cordial letter delivered in late October. This has subsequently become famous as the letter that "morally" committed successive American administrations to Diem's and South Vietnam's support. It did no such thing. It authorized the American ambassador to Vietnam, Donald R. Heath,

... to examine with you in your capacity as Chief of Government, how an intelligent program of American aid given directly to your Government can serve to assist Vietnam in its present hour of trial, provided that your Government is prepared to give assurance as to the standards of performance it would be able to maintain in the event such aid were supplied.

The purpose of this offer is to assist the Government of Vietnam in developing and maintaining a strong, viable state, capable of resisting attempted subversion or aggression through military means. The Government of the United States expects that this aid will be met by performance on the part of the Government of Vietnam in undertaking needed reforms. It hopes that such aid, combined with your own continuing efforts, will contribute effectively toward an independent Vietnam endowed with a strong government. Such a government would, I hope, be so responsive to the nationalist aspirations of its people, so enlightened in purpose and effective in performance, that it will be respected both at home and abroad and discourage any who might wish to impose a foreign ideology on your free people.[23]

22. Shaplen, op. cit.
23. U. S. Senate Committee on Foreign Relations, *Background Information Relating to Southeast Asia and Vietnam* (Washington: U. S. Government Printing Office, 1967).

These words represented challenge more than commitment. American moral involvement derived from an attempt to convert a political zombie into a rational human being. At no time was the involvement such in the eyes of the world that it could not have been abrogated with impunity.

Eisenhower followed his frank statement of American intentions by dispatching General J. Lawton Collins as ambassador. Upon arriving in Saigon, Collins stated: ". . . I have come to Vietnam to bring every possible aid to the government of Diem and to his government alone."[24]

Diem's immediate internal-security problem centered not on the Viet Minh who had remained in the South, but, rather, on the Vietnamese army first, the neo-military Binh Xuyên second, and the political-religious sects third.

Diem was relieved of the first problem by Collins' stated policy. The United States would not consider ". . . training or otherwise aiding a Vietnamese army that does not give complete and implicit obedience to its premier."[25] This effectively pulled the power rug from beneath the feet of Diem's main rival, General Hinh. There remained Hinh's fall: the American Government persuaded Bao Dai to order him to Paris and dismiss him as army head.

Collins, meanwhile, set up a combined American-French training command headed by General O'Daniel, who was also chief of MAAG. O'Daniel undertook the task of organizing and training an indigenous Vietnamese army. One of his four division heads, Colonel Lansdale, commanded the National Security division, ". . . the only one actually advising the Vietnamese on operations."[26]

The second and third problems were not so simple. The Binh Xuyên, a sort of oriental Mafia that controlled the vice and police in Saigon-Cholon, was a well-entrenched organization protected both by Bao Dai and by a private army of some twenty-five hundred thugs. As in any gangster activity, millions of dollars went into local payoffs that benefited numerous officials—French, Vietnamese, and Chinese.

The Cao Dai and the Hoa Hao were something else again. Offshoots of the Buddhist religion, they formed virtually separate states, the Cao Dai northwest of Saigon, the Hoa Hao southwest. The Cao Dai supposedly maintained twenty thousand men under arms, the Hoa Hao fifty thousand, but each sect claimed over a million supporters in its particular area.[27]

Diem moved very carefully against the sects. In September 1954, he appointed four leaders from the Cao Dai and four from the Hoa Hao to his Saigon cabinet. He then spent $12 million of American taxpayers' money in bribing these and other leaders to assimilate at least

24. Buttinger, op. cit.
25. Kahin and Lewis, op. cit.
26. Shaplen, op. cit.
27. Ibid.; see also Hammer, op. cit.; Fall (*The Two Viet-Nams*), *supra*.

some of their armed forces into the Vietnamese army. Thus prepared, he challenged the Binh Xuyên, in January 1955, by closing down gambling casinos.

This reads more smoothly than it happened. The confusion and intrigue of the day would have furnished Milton Caniff enough plots for fifty years—and should have furnished concerned American officials a caution sign in future relationships in South Vietnam. For, while Diem was attempting to consolidate his power, a great number of people, including Bao Dai and local French and Vietnamese officials, not to mention Viet Minh cadres, were doing their best to sabotage his every effort.[28]

Moreover, the important and powerful General Collins was becoming increasingly disillusioned with Diem, as were various sects that felt their powers slipping away. Diem, however, retained Lansdale's support in Saigon and that of the Dulles brothers, important State Department officials, and Congressional leaders in Washington.

The situation exploded in late March 1955, when Diem refused to give the sects more power in his government. Hoa Hao and Cao Dai cabinet members resigned, and the two sects joined with the Binh Xuyên to form the United Front of Nationalist Forces. A few days later, Binh Xuyên forces attacked the presidential palace.

Although the French arranged an uneasy truce, the new war widened the breach between Diem and Collins. Collins returned to Washington in mid-April determined to dump Diem. Backed by President Eisenhower, he had set the wheels in motion when, to the surprise of all, excepting possibly Colonel Lansdale, important units of Diem's army remained loyal and thrashed the Binh Xuyên. A month late, Diem had driven the Binh Xuyên out of Saigon (they eventually disintegrated) and had the Cao Dai and Hoa Hao forces either on the run or coming over to his side.

Diem's victory deflated Collins' effort to unseat him. But, far worse, Diem suddenly appeared to be the strong leader so desired by the American Government. Not only Senator Mansfield now reiterated his belief in Diem, but such as Hubert Humphrey joined the chorus:

. . . Premier Diem is the best hope that we have in South Vietnam. He is the leader of his people. He deserves and must have the wholehearted support of the American Government and our foreign policy. This is no time for uncertainty or half-hearted measures. . . . He is the only man on the political horizon of Vietnam who can rally a substantial degree of support of his people. . . . If we have any comments to make about the leadership in Vietnam let it [sic] be directed against Bao Dai. It is time we broke

28. Buttinger, op. cit., offers interesting details on the infighting; see also Scigliano, op. cit.

our ties with him and not with Diem. If the Government of South Vietnam has not room for both of these men, it is Bao Dai who must go.[29]

In Paris, during a NATO meeting in May,

. . . the French called Diem an American puppet and threatened that unless Diem was removed they would pull out their troops and cancel other forms of assistance they were still rendering Vietnam. Dulles called their bluff and told them to go ahead, and at one point threatened that if the French did leave, the Americans would get out, too. This upset the French so much that they subsided.[30]

Dulles unknowingly was touching on a solution that perhaps would better have served his own country's and Vietnam's best interests. At this time, Diem already was exhibiting those administrative traits that contrasted so strongly with promises made to President Eisenhower in return for American aid. This was the time for the President's ambassador—Collins or anyone else—to inform Diem that he either would rule as promised or he would rule alone until deposed by a more popular choice, Buu Hoi, for example, or another nationalist leader.

Unfortunately, powerful American voices, absurdly strengthened by a pathological fear of communism, already had elevated Ngo Dinh Diem as savior of Southeast Asia, an incorruptible Christian patriot who alone could guard his country from the Red Menace. Here was a peculiar concept well suited to the black-and-white thinking of that American day: Here was GOOD challenged by EVIL, the hero facing the villain.

In mid-May, Eisenhower relieved Collins in favor of Ambassador G. Frederick Reinhardt, who stated upon his arrival in Saigon: ". . . I come here under instructions to carry out United States policy in support of the legal government of Vietnam under Premier Ngo Dinh Diem."[31]

The stage was now set for old-fashioned melodrama. It remained for the United States cavalry, banners flying, bugles blowing, and hoofs thumping, to charge across the plain. Figuratively, this is what happened —and hereby melodrama changed to tragedy.

29. Kahin and Lewis, op. cit.
30. Shaplen, op. cit.
31. Buttinger, op. cit.

Chapter 65

Diem's early government • The Fishel mission • Diem's house of power • "Communist"-suppression campaigns • The Diem dictatorship • Failure of Diem's reforms • The Montagnard problem • Question of general election • The American role • ARVN • MAAG's influence • The result

WITH THE TROUBLESOME SECT PROBLEM temporarily under control, with the army temporarily loyal and daily being strengthened by American arms and equipment, Prime Minister Ngo Dinh Diem should have turned with a will to the major task of broadening his base of support by instituting greatly needed political, social, and economic reforms, particularly in the countryside.

Despite the turbulent events surrounding him, he had made a reasonable start in areas evacuated by the Viet Minh. Early civic-action programs had worked quite well, and by spring of 1955, local Self-Defense Corps and Civil Guards were coming into existence. The viability of these and other measures depended almost entirely on peasant co-operation, and this, in turn, depended on the validity of Diem's promised reforms.

Diem pretended to want these reforms. Shortly after becoming premier, he had named as civil adviser a young assistant professor of political science, Wesley Fishel, of Michigan State University, who had earlier befriended him in Tokyo and helped him in America. At Diem's request, Fishel, supported somewhat grudgingly by the U. S. Operations Mission in Saigon, was collecting a team of specialists to provide the Diem government with ". . . a massive program of technical assistance in four areas: public administration, police administration, public information, and economics and finance."[1]

Here was an ambitious program that, carried out effectively, might have resulted in a viable government. Unfortunately, almost from the outset of operations—Fishel's staff began arriving in spring of 1955— the effort faced major and often insurmountable obstacles. In a sense, the eighty-eight academicians, police experts, administrators (and a sprinkling of CIA types) who descended on Siagon in the first year resembled the experts who had arrived in Washington twenty years earlier to help Franklin Roosevelt implement the New Deal. Their intentions were honorable and their theories beautiful, but, alas, the theories too often failed to work, or, if they worked, they alienated the people concerned and were quickly sabotaged.

The almost inconceivable operational independence granted to the Fishel mission automatically brought it into conflict with other American civil and military missions. This could have been suffered in view of the importance of its task, but what neither Fishel nor his sponsors seemed to realize was that Diem did not want a democratic government. In spring of 1955, Diem eliminated the public-information mission and sharply curtailed the economics and finance effort. The mission subsequently did some good work in training civil administrators and policemen—but with results considerably different from those envisaged. In almost every respect, the group encountered obstructionism, with Diem's entrenched bureaucracy proving more than a match for the newcomers, the majority of whom were unfamiliar with the country, its peoples— and their language.[2]

Similar difficulties plagued other American aid programs. By spring of 1955, Diem was already dragging his feet when it came to devising and implementing economic and agrarian reforms, an attitude that brought him into continuing conflict with American officials in Saigon, particularly with General Collins.

The difficulty stemmed first from Diem himself, a mandarin born and raised, a man who had become incapable of recognizing a grass root, much less its importance to the garden of state. But, more than Diem, the problem stemmed from his family. A disgusted American diplomat once told the writer: "Half of our troubles in Vietnam would have vanished if Diem had been an orphan."

Diem's family shared his power. One brother, Monsignor Ngo Dinh

1. Robert Scigliano and Guy Fox, *Technical Assistance in Vietnam—The Michigan State University Experience* (New York: Frederick A. Praeger, 1965).
2. Ibid.

Thuc, a Roman Catholic bishop, had long been prominent in central
Vietnam and, with Diem's rise, grew increasingly powerful and rich.
Another brother, Ngo Dinh Luyên, a mechanical engineer and the
least troublesome, became Diem's ambassador to England. A third
brother, Ngo Dinh Can, became virtual ruler of central Vietnam. A
fourth, but scarcely runt of the litter, Ngo Dinh Nhu, a trained librarian-
archivist, became Diem's "personal adviser." To the discomfiture of all
concerned, Nhu's advice included that of his ambitious and venal wife,
Tran Le Xuan (Beautiful Spring)—as early as February 1955, Mme.
Nhu was accused in a Saigon court of extensive corruption resulting
from official connections.[3]

After occupying the choice suites in Diem's house of power, this
oligarchy rented remaining rooms to men of their own breed hastily
appointed to important key civil and military posts in Saigon and in the
provinces. A considerable number of appointees were Catholic Northerners whom Diem and Company felt they could "trust"—and who tram-
pled over regional and Buddhist customs to disrupt further an already
disrupted country.

Diem's first task was to consolidate his newly won control. His most
important target consisted of Viet Minh cadres who had remained in
the South—an incubus estimated by Professor Fishel to have numbered
ten thousand persons, most of whom were militant Communists, albeit
with a strong nationalist bias.[4] These cadres had been working among
the people for years, and had won an impressive number of supporters.
Viet Minh control, as Joseph Buttinger later wrote,

. . . remained unchallenged in vast regions of the South, and was near total
in such provinces as Quang Ngai, Binh Dinh, in the so-called Zone D, between Saigon and the Cambodian border, in the Plain of Reeds, on the
Camau Peninsula, and in numerous other districts, both in the highlands
and the Mekong Delta.[5]

In spring of 1955, Diem opened war on his opponents, a determined
effort aimed not only at Communist cadres and Viet Minh sympathizers,
but also at non-Communist nationalists whom Diem and his cohorts
feared politically. Professor Scigliano later described the slapdash
methods employed by the Department of Information and Youth, whose
chief, Tran Chanh Thanh, had learned political propaganda methods
from service with the Viet Minh:

. . . As government troops occupied Viet Minh and sect-controlled areas
in the spring and summer of 1955, Information agents swarmed in their
wake denouncing the triple evils of Communism, colonisation, and

3. Fall (*The Two Viet-Nams*), *supra*.
4. Pike, op. cit.
5. Buttinger, op. cit.; see also Jean Lacouture, *Vietnam: Between Two Truces*
(London: Secker & Warburg, 1966). Tr. K. Kellen and J. Carmichael.

feudalism, and extolling the Ngo Dinh Diem government. Those themes were pounded home in posters, banners, leaflets, radio messages, and rallies. . . .[6]

In mid-1955, Tran Chanh Thanh launched the first Denunciation of Communism campaign:

. . . In a typical denunciation ceremony, Viet Minh cadres and sympathizers would swear their disavowal of Communism before a large audience; the repentants would recount the atrocities of the Viet Minh and, as a climax to their performance, would rip or trample upon the Viet Minh flag and pledge their loyalty to Ngo Dinh Diem.[7]

In May 1956, Thanh claimed that the campaign had ". . . entirely destroyed the predominant Communist influence of the previous nine years."

. . . According to Thanh, in this short period 94,041 former Communist cadres had rallied to the government, 5,613 other cadres had surrendered to government forces, 119,954 weapons had been captured, and 75 tons of documents and 707 underground arms caches had been discovered.[8]

Had these figures been accurate, Diem's problems would have been largely solved. They were not accurate, and neither this attempt nor others launched by the National Revolutionary Movement and various youth and group movements could claim notable success. The most valid effort, a government-sponsored community-action program that brought young volunteers to the countryside to work with peasants, died an early death, presumably because of jealousies it aroused in other government agencies.[9]

Thanh's propaganda efforts might not have been wasted had Ngo Dinh Diem carried out political reforms and given his people something to be thankful for. Unfortunately, he held no intention of rebuilding South Vietnam in the image desired by Washington. In October 1955, Diem, strongly influenced by brother Nhu, proclaimed a referendum between himself and Bao Dai. After a campaign ". . . conducted with such a special disregard for decency and democratic principles that even the Viet Minh professed to be shocked,"[10] a limited electorate returned an improbable 98.2 per cent in favor of Diem, who became the new President of Vietnam. Brother Nhu followed this victory by expanding his personal political party, the Can Lao,

. . . that served primarily as a political intelligence agency for Nhu; he used it to detect Communists or anyone he suspected of Communist or other op-

6. Scigliano (*Nation Under Stress*), *supra*.
7. Ibid.
8. Ibid.; see also Pike, op. cit.
9. Scigliano (*Nation Under Stress*), *supra*.
10. Lancaster, op. cit.

positionist tendencies, and it was thus a powerful weapon in obtaining and maintaining loyalty to the Ngo family.[11]

Max Clos, a veteran French observer of the Vietnam scene who was expelled from Saigon in November, wrote in *Le Monde:*

. . . Oddly enough . . . M. Diem has borrowed from his enemies what is most reprehensible in their methods: the denial of freedom of opinion, the deification of the man who incarnates the regime and also that form of hypocrisy which attributes to the "people's will" measures taken against those whom one considers as political opponents. . . . The Viet Minh dictatorship is at least as odious as that of M. Diem. But it can show results in the political and economic fields. It is up to Diemism to show concrete achievements. That has not yet been done in South Vietnam.[12]

This insidious beginning of dynasty rule expanded during 1956. But, as opposed to decentralized rule practiced both by early emperors and by the French, Diem insisted on centralized rule:

. . . In place of the colonial regional system of government, whereby the central and southern parts of the country had been administered more or less separately, forty-one provinces were created, with a chief in each directly responsible to the President; in theory, the province chief controlled district and village officials below him, but in practice, especially under the watchful eye of Nhu, the central government dominated them, too, and sent direct orders down to them on virtually all matters.[13]

In spring of 1956, Diem took this a step further by eliminating village elections in favor of appointment by province chiefs—a disastrous error that installed many northern Catholic officials in the South, to alienate the peasant further from the new government.[14] The following October, he completed political carnage by forcing through a constitution in a vain attempt to legalize what already was a dictatorship. By the end of 1956, one observer concluded,

. . . South Viet Nam is today a quasi-police state characterized by arbitrary arrests and imprisonment, strict censorship of the press and the absence of an effective political opposition. . . . All the techniques of political and psychological warfare, as well as pacification campaigns involving extensive military operations, have been brought to bear against the underground.[15]

11. Shaplen, op. cit.; see also Buttinger, op. cit.; Duncanson, op. cit.
12. Lancaster, op. cit.
13. Shaplen, op. cit.
14. Buttinger, op. cit.: ". . . Village autonomy was one of the strongest Vietnamese political traditions, dating back to the fifteenth century and sanctioned both by tradition and precolonial law."
15. Kahin and Lewis, op. cit., quoting from William Henderson's "South Viet Nam Finds Itself," *Foreign Affairs,* January 1957.

In dictatorial tradition, Diem meanwhile was filling jails and concentration camps not alone with "communists" but with communist "sympathizers," which meant anyone seriously at odds with the regime. Philippe Devillers estimated that the Diem government was holding fifty thousand political prisoners by the end of 1956. Official figures listed between twenty and thirty thousand former Viet Minh cadres, but a British observer, P. J. Honey, himself no liberal, visited these concentration camps and reported that ". . . the majority of the detainees are neither Communist nor pro-Communist."[16]

As opposed to wiping out the Communist threat, Diem's promiscuous policy of repression destroyed an important bulwark against communism. In Ellen Hammer's prescient words,

. . . Nationalists who had once worked with the Viet Minh were evidently best equipped to rally the people against it. They understood both its mechanism of action and its popular strength as no outsider could and were able to turn its techniques and its professed principles against it; they had also come closer to the people than had most of the intellectual and middle-class Nationalists who had no experience of mass movements and whose sole contribution to the Nationalist cause was their insistence, especially among foreigners, that they were anti-French; and further, these men who had at one time worked with the Viet Minh benefited from the very real and favorable prejudice in their favor on the part of the majority of the population because they had participated actively in the struggle for independence.[17]

In the crucial years 1957–60, the Diem regime followed its earlier pattern with but few variations. By continuing dynasty rule, a cabal within a clique, a totalitarian regime cloaked with brother Nhu's mystique of Personalism,[18] Diem continued to alienate important nationalist elements that should have provided political leaders and administrators essential to stable government. He erred not only in ignoring these voices but by constantly suppressing them, by imprisoning or exiling or otherwise silencing them. He attempted to suppress all criticism by rigorous censorship and by a wide-ranging network of secret police. In early 1958, an official of one province reported that ". . . a five-week campaign . . . had resulted in the surrender of 8,125 communist agents and the 'denunciation' of 9,806 other agents, and 29,978 'sympathizers,' " surely a haul that would have won even Senator Joseph McCarthy's approval. In spring of 1959, the regime enacted legislation that gave special military courts the right to pass death sentences without

16. Buttinger, op. cit.; see also Scigliano (*Nation Under Stress*), *supra*.
17. Hammer, op. cit.
18. Lacouture, op. cit.

right of appeal for a host of political crimes including the spreading of anti-government rumors.[19]

The cumulative effects were disastrous, not alone in depriving the new state of both intelligent support and intelligent dissent, but in setting up brooding centers of dissension that eventually would lead to open rebellion, for example among students and Buddhists.

The full significance of Diem's strong-arm methods has been dulled in too many Western minds, whose pathological fear of communism has admitted the Communist philosophy of the end sanctioning almost any means. At a 1969 seminar of prominent British experts on insurgency warfare, this writer mentioned as a Western failure the lack of encouraging indigenous leadership in South Vietnam. Mr. P. J. Honey, who has written extensively on the country, replied:

. . . In 1945–46 when the Communists took over in North Viet-Nam, they systematically killed every nationalist non-communist leader, and the leadership of a whole generation went. There has been a big gap in the interval, and only now are we seeing young men from the next generation coming up.[20]

Mr. Honey's exaggerated explanation is only a half truth. Many nationalist non-Communist leaders and, far more important, many such *potential* leaders, as Mr. Honey was well aware, survived to languish later either in South Vietnamese jails or to lead precarious and embittered lives either underground or abroad. Nor was the repressive air conducive to education and emergence of younger leaders.

Neither did Diem's alleged reforms mollify the effect of these harsh measures. Particularly wanting were his land-reform laws. When Diem came to power in 1954, ". . . forty per cent of the nation's 2,300,000 hectares of riceland was owned by *a quarter of one per cent of the rural population;* about a fourth of the large landholdings were French, and the rest were owned by wealthy Vietnamese or by the Catholic Church."[21] The peasant farmed land under a short-contract, sharecrop system whereby he paid the landlord about 50 per cent of the crop in rent.

19. Kahin and Lewis, op. cit.; see also Scigliano (*Nation Under Stress*), *supra;* Lacouture, op. cit.: Special military tribunals could sentence to death ". . . anyone who intentionally proclaimed or propagated, by no matter what means, unfounded news on prices, or rumor contrary to the truth, or distorting the truth, on the actual or future economic situation in the country or outside, likely to provoke economic or financial disturbance in the country . . . anyone who committed or tried to commit the crime of sabotage or made an attempt against the security of the State or an attempt on the life or property of the population . . . anyone who adhered to an organization in order to aid in the preparation or execution of these crimes . . . etc."

20. Royal United Service Institution Seminar, *Lessons from the Vietnam War,* London: RUSI, 1969. (Hereafter cited as RUSI seminar.)

21. Shaplen, op. cit.

Diem's reform laws extended length of contract and brought rent down to a more reasonable 25 per cent of the crop. Unfortunately, the most liberal reform laws would have been unpopular in many areas because landlords had abandoned almost a third of the riceland—land sequestered by the Viet Minh and given to peasants rent free. The Diem government now allowed absentee landlords to begin collecting rent, and, if this was reduced to 25 per cent of crop value, it did not make the peasant any happier; neither did taxes freshly imposed from Saigon. In areas under strong Viet Minh influence, if not control, the peasant sometimes found himself paying two sets of taxes, one to the Viet Minh and one to Saigon. Moreover, some landlords continued to collect more than 25 per cent of the crop in rent, violations often overlooked by agrarian courts controlled by landowning officials.

In 1956, Diem's government introduced a land-purchase plan whereby the government purchased riceland and sold it to the peasant. Landlords were allowed to retain a hundred hectares, or nearly two hundred fifty acres; nevertheless, ". . . some seven hundred thousand hectares belonging to twenty-five hundred owners were declared subject to transfer."[22] The peasant could buy this land at an average price of two hundred dollars per hectare, an enormous sum to a peasant but one that he could pay off in six annual installments without interest, each installment being the estimated rough equivalent of 25 per cent of the crop value.[23]

This program encountered difficulties familiar to the rent-reform laws. First, it applied only to ricelands, and, as numerous observers have pointed out, the amount of land reserved to former landowners, two hundred fifty acres, was a tremendous area under the circumstances.[24] Other observers have criticized the limited time given the peasant to pay. Peasants who, in some instances, had already been "given" land by the Viet Minh naturally resented now having to pay for it. Finally, the government again dragged its heels while indulging corruption:

. . . Perhaps the most disturbing aspect of the land redistribution program was the manner in which influential politicians and members of Diem's family obtained huge amounts of land that had been taken over by the government from French or Vietnamese landlords but had not been distributed to the peasants. . . .[25]

Landowning officials found numerous ways to sabotage this not overly generous program.[26] When rural cadres of the powerful Confederation

22. Ibid.
23. Ibid.; see also Buttinger, op. cit.
24. Kahin and Lewis, op. cit.
25. Shaplen, op. cit.
26. Pike, op. cit.

of Vietnamese Labor attempted to explain the program to the peasants, they

. . . frequently found themselves in a hostile atmosphere because of the alliance that had grown up between the landlords and many government officials against the plan. In numerous places, union representatives were arrested; in one area, south of Saigon, where many of the farmers were union members, Buu [Tran Quoc Buu, who headed the union] later told me that the wife of the province chief had originally owned three-quarters of the land and that the chief had tossed all the union cadres into prison.[27]

Similarly, farmers' associations, which were supposed to help the peasant with credit and other aids, too quickly ". . . came to be dominated by local officials and landlords, and consequently were more paternalistic than progressive."[28]

Subsequent government measures did little or nothing to ameliorate these difficulties. In a situation demanding drastic action, the government refused to act—an intentional sabotage of a program the Diem regime never believed in and adopted only as a sop to American officials. Some evidence exists that the Eisenhower administration did not fully sympathize with proposed reforms, in that the American Government ". . . refused to provide the $30,000,000 needed to pay off the landowners. . . . It appears that the United States was unwilling to support the appropriation of private property openly. Similarly, the American government was long opposed to aiding public-controlled industrial development. . . ."[29]

Diem also alienated primitive Montagnard tribes of the central highlands. Unlike the Viet Minh, which had allowed Montagnards considerable autonomy, Diem incorporated their lands into the South Vietnamese state and also tried to assimilate what he held to be inferior peoples into the southern culture. In 1957, he worked further hardship on the primitives by transferring over two hundred thousand northern refugees to Montagnard areas, which made eventual conflict with the nomads almost inevitable. Moreover, by awarding security priority over other factors, he did much to defeat success of the highlands development program:

. . . the American economic aid mission was dismayed by the lack of careful planning by the Vietnamese authorities. Settlement sites were selected with little regard to soil fertility or water resources; the land allotments seemed too small to sustain the settlers; and the whole program was pushed with alarming speed while the Americans were still wondering whether it was economically feasible. The Vietnamese, however, saw the program primarily in military, not economic, terms. The development centers were de-

27. Shaplen, op. cit.
28. Ibid.
29. Scigliano (*Nation Under Stress*), *supra*.

signed to form a human wall against Communist North Vietnam, and President Diem himself selected many of the sites in flights over the area or from military maps.[30]

Diem's penchant for security, and the inefficiency of his administrators, similarly ruined the government's later attempts to create fortified hamlets and villages. By mid-1959, Viet Minh attacks forced the government to undertake the "agroville program," an attempt to regroup whole villages into "protected" settlements called *agrovilles,* both to offer the peasant security and to prevent him from supporting the guerrilla effort.

Directed by Diem's brother Nhu, the plan called for eighty to a hundred *agrovilles* of two to four thousand persons each, besides several hundred smaller communities. Each peasant was supposed to tear down his present house and carry the materials to the new area, where the government loaned him money to buy an acre and a half of new land.[31]

This scheme resembled one that the British imposed on Chinese villages in Malaya with considerable success. But a world of difference separated the two situations. In Malaya, the British were dealing with a largely "squatter" population, who attached little importance to a particular area. In Vietnam, the Diem government was dealing with centuries-old villages. Forsaking village graveyards, and thus abandoning one's ancestors, struck many peasants as a heinous crime. The government's arbitrary orders and pitiful resettlement allowances infuriated others, nor was the concentration-camp aspect popular. Diem's insistence on siting *agrovilles* along tactically important lines of communications brought immediate and destructive Viet Minh attacks.[32] Finally, corruption and inefficiency ruled the program from the beginning. Only about a score of *agrovilles* were built in a year and a half, before the government abandoned the effort.

Diem's concept of government would have been awkward enough for his American sponsors to justify, even had he neutralized the Communist threat. Not only did his dictatorial measures fail internally in this respect, but his diplomatic intransigence opened South Vietnam to reprisals from the North.

The reader will perhaps remember that the Geneva Agreements called for a cease-fire and regroupment of forces pending a country-wide general election to be held by July 1956. In mid-1955, as provided for in the agreements, the DRV sought to open talks with South Vietnam concerning arrangements for these elections. Diem categorically refused to discuss the matter. In July, he told the South Vietnamese people that his government was not bound by the Geneva Agreements. In August,

30. Ibid.; see also Pike, op. cit.
31. Shaplen, op. cit.; see also Scigliano (*Nation Under Stress*), *supra,* whose figures slightly differ.
32. Scigliano (*Nation Under Stress*), *supra.*

he denied that fair elections could be held in North Vietnam, an objection publicly sustained by Mr. Dulles. In September, Diem stated that ". . . there can be no question of a conference, even less of negotiations."[33]

The DRV continued to press for talks, and Diem, despite prodding by a few far-sighted American and South Vietnamese officials and by the governments of England and the Soviet Union—the cochairmen countries of the Geneva Conference—continued to refuse right through the July 1956 deadline. He did not act unilaterally: ". . . in this stand he continued to receive warm American encouragement and the fullest American diplomatic backing."[34]

This was a very serious action.

We have discussed earlier the ambivalent air that surrounded the Geneva Agreements and the principle of a general election. But that air did not hide the fact of the provisions from an interested world. As written, the provisions gave both sides option to insist on an election; perhaps neither side took this seriously, but, nonetheless, each side held the option. If either the DRV or France or a replacement government in the South refused to hold such an election, the other side could claim that the cease-fire, what was in effect an armistice, was null and void.

This was not so much legal mumbo-jumbo. Some of the staunchest allies of the United States so interpreted the situation. According to a British observer, Brian Crozier, at a SEATO meeting in February 1955, ". . . the United States was cautioned by its allies that SEATO would not function if a South Vietnamese refusal to hold the required elections resulted in an attack from the North."[35]

Nor did Diem's refusal to countenance the Geneva Agreements change matters. The reader may remember that France had guaranteed the election and ". . . that any administration succeeding the French prior to the 1956 elections would legally assume France's obligations. . . ." France turned the government over to Bao Dai in early 1955, Diem eliminated Bao Dai that autumn, and, in spring of 1956, the last formal vestige of French power, her troops, left South Vietnam. Two students of the area, Professors Kahin and Lewis, argued subsequently that Diem was now legally obliged to co-operate in holding a country-wide election.

Their conclusion seems specious to this writer. As head of a government that had refused to sanction the Geneva Agreements, Diem surely was within his rights to abstain from carrying out the provisions. *However*, in so doing he opened himself to punitive action from two sources. One was France, which, in the event, did not choose to alienate the United States by pressing the matter. The other was the DRV, which,

33. Kahin and Lewis, op. cit.; Lancaster, op. cit.
34. Kahin and Lewis, op. cit.
35. Ibid.

quite legally and certainly logically, broadcast Diem's action to the world as a *casus belli,* meanwhile making capital propaganda from it at home and abroad, including the hamlets of South Vietnam.

Diem would have been far more clever had he paid lip service to the DRV proposals, which good diplomacy could have spun out for years while simultaneously deriving excellent propaganda. Indeed, had Diem held proper confidence in his own government-making ability, he should have wanted an election eventually if somehow machinery could have been arranged to insure a fair and secret procedure in the North—admittedly doubtful. Considering Ho's economic and agrarian difficulties in 1956, he was not prepared to push the issue too hard—fertile ground here for an impressive victory had Diem correctly played his cards.

The American Government, or those officials who encouraged Diem in perversity, did him a great disservice. No matter how well-intentioned the advice, it was contrary to common sense. And not alone from the propaganda standpoint or the friction caused between allies. Far more important, it opened the way for renewed Viet Minh activity in the South at a time when the Diem government was particularly vulnerable.

Diem and his advisers, both Vietnamese and American, were also erring in another, but related, direction: South Vietnam's police and armed forces.

Here again the original American intention can scarcely be faulted. As Secretary of State Dulles explained to Mendès-France in November 1954, the United States wanted an autonomous Vietnamese army with about ninety thousand troops:

. . . the Vietnamese forces were not intended for the defense of South Vietnam against external aggression; their sole purpose was to preserve public order and suppress any attempts of subversion. There could be no question of raising funds sufficient to enable the Vietnamese Army to oppose a Vietminh attack that might well be supported by China. Only the Manila Pact (that is, SEATO) could provide the requisite deterrent against such an act of aggression.[36]

In late December 1954, Homer Bigart, of the New York *Times,* reported that a secret plan called for an army on the Philippine model, that is, one that would emphasize civil improvements in the countryside in an attempt to convert Viet Minh followers to the new regime.[37] General O'Daniel, who headed the Military Assistance Advisory Group in Saigon, stated:

. . . The [Vietnamese] Army will be, above all, according to American ideas on the subject, a police force capable of spotting Communist guerrillas and Communist efforts at infiltration.[38]

36. Devillers and Lacouture, op. cit.
37. Ibid.
38. Trager, op. cit.

O'Daniel reckoned without political aspects of the Vietnamese army, which Diem turned into the major prop of his regime and which offered his supporters lucrative and powerful roles; nor did O'Daniel appreciate the inability of French and many American military advisers to understand the essence of guerrilla warfare and train troops to counter the threat. During 1955, he had to put up with the incubus of the old French Expeditionary Corps, which influenced the Vietnamese army to a considerable degree. At the end of 1955, Lieutenant General Samuel ("Hanging Sam") Williams replaced O'Daniel, and MAAG received several hundred U.S. officers, who began reorganizing and training Diem's army. Although the Americans managed to reduce its bulk of some 270,000 men, they probably did not trim it to much below 150,000. Influenced by Diem's wishes and by the Korean war, they soon began converting the police role originally envisaged into more conventional terms: an army ". . . organized for conventional warfare in regiments, divisions, and corps. This military force was mechanized, motorized, and road-conscious. . . ."[39] While MAAG supplied American arms, including artillery, tanks, and aircraft, hundreds of young Vietnamese officers attended training courses at American bases in the Philippines, Okinawa, and the United States, where they learned conventional Western military doctrine.[40]

Concurrent with this shift to a more conventional, or "heavy," organization, the Diem government relieved the army of what O'Daniel had believed was its most important mission, that ". . . of spotting Communist guerrillas and Communist efforts at infiltration." Diem turned these functions over to the Civil Guard and the Self-Defense Corps, neither of which could conceivably carry them out.

This fundamental error was not altogether the fault of General Williams. At the time, Diem was the fair-haired boy of some very powerful American officials, notably Dulles and Dulles, and it would have taken someone as forceful as "Vinegar Joe" Stilwell to withstand his assault on logic. It would also have taken someone exceedingly knowledgeable in insurgency warfare, and here the American military plant suffered a surfeit of orthodoxy. Oblivious to lessons offered by history, they seemed unaware even of those inherent in such recent campaigns as China, the Philippines, Malaya, Greece, and, most importantly, Indochina itself.

In American military minds, the "communists," or "reds," having attacked overtly in Korea, would attack similarly in Vietnam. Thus Pentagon and Saigon planners deemed the problem that of defense against a conventional army spilling across the 17th parallel. The new Vietnamese army supported by its proud artillery, armor, and air units would rush forward to hold the breech until SEATO powers, or at least American forces, would land and "win" the war. General Williams' own think-

39. Ibid.
40. Scigliano (*Nation Under Stress*), *supra*.

ing is obvious from a statement made when he retired, in 1960, after five years as chief of MAAG: ". . . In 1954, the Communist army of North Vietnam could have crossed the seventeenth parallel and walked into Saigon standing up. Today if they tried it, they would have one nasty fight on their hands."[41]

This political-strategic-tactical concept stood at odds with the political-strategic-tactical problem. Direct invasion from the North was highly unlikely at this time: Korea had demonstrated to Moscow and Peking alike that the U.S.A. and her allies would respond to any such action with armed force, and Secretary of State Dulles quite recently had warned that this could include atomic weapons; the Soviet Union and China had shown reluctance to test American patience further by restraining North Vietnam at the Geneva Conference. Always a realist, Ho Chi Minh remained well aware of the international situation, but, discounting that, he was facing severe internal problems, problems undoubtedly known to Western intelligence agencies but evidently not appreciated by either Diem or his Western military advisers.

To build large and heavy units in South Vietnam worked a three-fold disaster: First, they were useless in that they deterred nothing, because the northern enemy had no intention of direct military invasion. They were also extremely expensive, and to build and maintain them, totally at American cost, necessarily reduced the amount of American funds available for essential civil projects. They were also destructive, in that, wherever based, they took without giving, whereas the original concept had called for them to work alongside civilians in the country's reconstruction. Generally commanded by inept and corrupt officers, they became a drain on the state, a monster exercising "squeeze" in a thousand forms on already disgruntled peasants. Flying the Saigon flag, they turned it in short order into a symbol as repressive as the old French tricolor.

Second, the new army contained the seeds of state destruction, an indirect objection that apparently escaped American civil and military minds. By creating regiments and divisions instead of light, mobile battalions, Diem brought into being an armed force that could either bolster or threaten his regime. To make it an ally meant installing politically safe senior officers in top-command and staff billets, a pernicious practice that reminded some observers of Chiang Kai-shek and the old war-lord concept. Senior commanders perforce demanded and received command autonomy, which too often meant flagrant failure to correct military deficiencies and widespread corruption in the military body itself. Diem thus created and condoned a disaster-prone army not far removed, despite Western window dressing of snappy uniforms, shiny weapons, and American quantitative tactics, from the old mainland armies of Chiang Kai-shek.

41. Ibid.

But, worse by far, army power soon spilled over into civil areas. Corps, division, and regimental commanders virtually ruled command areas and, almost without exception, refused to implement necessary civil reforms. Regular army officers had always occupied powerful positions, but with the growth of Viet Minh activity, Diem entrusted civil administration more and more to them. In 1958, according to Robert Scigliano's interesting analysis, ". . . 13 of 36 province chiefs were military officers and it was planned shortly to replace them with civilians. . . ." By autumn of 1960, however, regular officers ruled twenty-one provinces, with younger officers holding numerous interprovince positions, a disturbing trend that, by 1962, would result in total military administration.[42]

Third, Diem's military task was essentially pacification: securing the countryside under his control and extending that control to peripheral areas. The first steps in the process were to provide his peoples with security while rooting out Viet Minh cadres, an onerous and difficult task that would have taxed the efforts of a small army trained along lines recommended by O'Daniel. By assigning the all-important functions to the Civil Guard and the Self-Defense Corps, Diem virtually assured their non-fulfillment.

Diem's Department of National Defense administered the forty-thousand-man Self-Defense Corps. MAAG paid its members and furnished a few arms, but the Vietnamese regular army provided most of the officers and was responsible for training. In the event, this proved rudimentary, and many of its members were armed with ". . . sticks, clubs and other such makeshifts."[43]

The fifty-thousand-man Civil Guard, administered by Diem's Department of the Interior, became the responsibility of the Michigan State University group, to the extent of training and equipping its units. An operational dichotomy resulted almost at once. Police advisers of the group wanted to halve the Guard's size and equip and train it as a rural police organization, ". . . which should not live apart in military posts but among the villages it would protect."[44] Here was a key concept, ranking in importance only under political reforms. Had it been carried out effectively, as in Malaya and Kenya, had a rural police organization emerged to work in conjunction with national police and army units, many of Diem's security problems would have vanished.

Instead, the Diem government and MAAG rejected the group's recommendation, insisting that the Civil Guard become a paramilitary adjunct to the regular army. This led to conflict so bitter that, in 1957, the Michigan group began withholding considerable aid:

. . . In addition, the Vietnamese government did little to improve the efficiency or morale of the Guard during this period, using it as a dumping

42. Ibid.
43. Ibid.
44. Ibid.

ground for inferior army officers. The organization—poorly trained, poorly led, and lacking needed armament, transport and communications—was faced with the increasingly difficult job of maintaining security in an increasingly insecure countryside.[45]

In mid-1959, increased American aid somewhat improved the organization, but now the group abandoned this particular mission. MAAG eventually took it over, and, with that, any hope of a rural police force vanished.

By this time, the group's efforts to organize a viable national police force had also backfired. Instead of the organization envisaged—a country-wide network to aid the rural police force—a variety of police forces existed. Regular police operated under Department of Interior, but the Civic Action, Information, and Defense departments also supported police networks. The key agency was secret. Called the Social and Political Research Service, it was run by Doctor Tran Kim Tuyen, ". . . an able Catholic intellectual from Central Vietnam"—and a chum of Nhu's. Tuyen's American-trained agents, rather than ferreting out Viet Minh cadres, concentrated on collecting information ". . . on government officials, military officers, businessmen, intellectuals, students, and others," and preventing them from upsetting Diem's political applecart.[46]

Few, if any, of these failures caused an outcry from concerned officials. Persons who had promoted Diem continued to congratulate themselves on soundness of judgment. Yet, by the end of the decade, the Diem regime, aided by American advisers and vast American expenditures, had laid the groundwork for disaster. It remained for the Communists to exploit the target.

45. Ibid.
46. Ibid.

Chapter 66

Revolution in the South • Ho Chi Minh's problems • His attitude toward the South • Viet Minh tactics in the South • The National Liberation Front (NLF) • Non-Communist opposition to Diem • The 1960 revolt • Diem's refusal to effect reforms • His civil and military weaknesses • The American contribution

IMMENSE DEBATES in the West have centered on the extent of Ho Chi Minh's collusion with the Viet Minh in the South from 1954 onward. The American Government's position was a simple black-and-white insistence that the DRV, aided by China and the Soviet Union, totally controlled the Viet Minh movement in the South and concentrated almost exclusively in this period on fomenting revolution from within. Once subversive tactics succeeded, the official thesis argued, Hanoi called into being the National Liberation Front (NLF) and, later, the People's Revolutionary Party (PRP) to prepare the country for the forces of "external aggression" from the North that would bring about a general "people's uprising."

A number of qualified observers have taken vigorous exception to this position. Prominent are Philippe Devillers and Jean Lacouture, George Kahin and John Lewis, Bernard Fall, and Joseph Buttinger, whose reasoned arguments, buttressed by cited evidence, should not be ignored. These observers have argued that the revolutionary impetus derived from southern elements almost in spite of Ho Chi Minh and the DRV, that, indeed, on occasion, they were embarrassing to the North. Although Ho aided the movement in the South, the argument continued, it retained a distinctly regional independence throughout formative years.

The argument is important mainly because the simplistic position adopted by the American Government was fundamental to official performance. In maintaining its position, the American Government was indulging in deductive thinking in a situation demanding skillful appreciation of complex political factors. The use of the term *Viet Cong* (Vietnamese Communists) in the South from 1956 onward was significant: the abbreviation of *Cong-san*, or "Communists," it was (and is) used to describe any opponents to the regime and reminds one of Chiang Kai-shek's contemptuous term "Communist bandits." That the enemy did not use the term was apparently beside the point, as was its inaccuracy; Douglas Pike noted in his carefully documented work, *Viet Cong*, a book that in large part attempts to vindicate the official position:

. . . For Americans Vietnam has grown steadily as a crisis in perception, one that began with a failure in definition. It is both symbolic and significant that no appellation coined for the opposing insurgent forces was acceptable to all parties, including the insurgents themselves.[1]

Another astute observer, Professor Donald Zagoria, has emphasized the complexity of the situation in his most-interesting book *Vietnam Triangle—Moscow, Peking, Hanoi,* published in 1967:

. . . The idea that Hanoi set out, in the late 1950s or early 1960s, with a plan for the conquest of South Vietnam which they have been following ever since is a myth. Indeed, there is good evidence to suggest that Hanoi initially strove to restrain the Southern resistance fighters. The truth of the matter seems rather that as the anti-Diemist struggle in the South gained intensity, and as the North came to believe that the risks of outright intervention were minimal, it increasingly dropped its restraint. But throughout the period from 1959 to 1965, there were a number of signs of debate within the Hanoi leadership and between Hanoi and the NLF over the proper course of action to pursue in the South.

To this writer, it seems as absurd for the American Government to insist that either the NLF or the later PRP is a completely Hanoi-inspired and Hanoi-imposed organization (ultimately controlled from Peking and Moscow) as it does for more-liberal thinkers to argue that both the NLF and the PRP are totally home-grown in the South and practically had to blackmail Hanoi for support. The truth lies somewhere between, and it is regrettable that responsible American officials, civil and military, did not attempt to more closely determine the facts instead of basing a

1. Pike, op. cit.

position on the convenient but, in part, erroneous accusation of "external aggression."

The end of the war with the French left the DRV in an awkward position. The fighting had destroyed large areas in the North, which always depended on rice imports from the South in return for coal and electricity. Diem's refusal to commence limited trade with the North forced Ho to almost total dependence on Peking and Moscow. In 1954, they supplied economic relief, mostly food. A visit to the two capitals in summer of 1955 yielded Ho $350 million in economic credits—a considerable sum, but one not nearly sufficient to turn the North into an industrial-socialist state.

To further this aim, Ho embarked on "agrarian reforms" based on the Chinese model of collectivization and communal farming. Apparently the work of Truong Chinh, the Communist Party's secretary-general, the radical program caused widespread resentment in the countryside. Government officials summarily executed numerous "middle" and "rich" peasants and dispossessed thousands of hapless farmers of already marginal holdings. So ruthless were the reforms that, in 1956, peasants began organized uprisings. Ho put these down sharply with troops—all together, the regime probably executed between ten thousand and fifteen thousand peasants and deported and imprisoned between fifty thousand and a hundred thousand.[2] But Ho also dismissed concerned officials (including the powerful Truong Chinh), modified the program, and eventually restored order in the countryside. Ho's confidence in his remedial measures showed in late 1956, when he lifted press censorship only to find his regime inundated by complaints. As in China following the "Hundred Flowers Movement," the new freedom quickly gave way to an even more repressive air than existed formerly.

Internal difficulties notwithstanding, Ho began in mid-1955 to press Diem and the South Vietnam Government for a general election in accordance with the Geneva Agreements. Diem's refusal to even discuss elections placed Ho in a difficult position. Neither Moscow nor Peking seemed inclined to push the matter (other than, in the case of the Soviet Union, as one of the cochairmen of the Geneva Conference). Not only militant elements in Ho's government objected to the delay, but thousands of cadres and Viet Minh sympathizers in the South, who daily were losing ground to Diem's government, vociferously clamored for action from the DRV.

Despite the opening given him by Diem's refusal, Ho could not consider overt military action, for a variety of reasons. He was not strong enough, and in 1956 a drought further complicated the restive peasant

2. Buttinger, op. cit.: ". . . Many regained their freedom, though perhaps not their former rights and possessions"; see also Lancaster, op. cit.; Hammer, op. cit., states, ". . . at least 50,000 people were killed."

situation. But, more than this, he was intent on building an industrial-socialist state, a priority he made clear in a letter of mid-June 1956 to southern cadres:

. . . Our policy is: to consolidate the North and to keep in mind the South.
To build a good house we must build a good foundation. . . . The North is the foundation, the root of the struggle for complete national liberation and the reunification of the country. That is why everything we are doing in the North is aimed at strengthening both the North and the South. Therefore, to work here is the same as struggling in the South, to struggle for the South and the whole of Vietnam.[3]

Ho emphasized his intention when he later announced a Three Year Plan which, from 1958 to 1960, was to concentrate on agrarian and industrial growth in the North. Joseph Buttinger has cited some of Ho's impressive gains during these years and concluded that ". . . even before the Soviet Union in 1960 gave Hanoi a long-term loan for forty-three new industrial plants, North Viet-Nam was well on the road toward becoming the most industrialized country of Southeast Asia."[4] The DRV may not have won any awards as a model state, but, by 1960, as Bernard Fall has pointed out, foreign aid, principally from China and the Soviet Union, represented 21 per cent of the 1960 budget, as opposed to 65.3 per cent of the 1955 budget.[5]

Several other factors probably influenced Ho into soft-pedaling the situation in the South. One was training. Ho was Moscow-trained, and Moscow preferred the technique of self-sustaining revolution, as the Communist effort in Yugoslavia and Greece so well illustrated. This was common sense. As the Soviets knew from experience in World War II, central direction of guerrilla warfare is always difficult and sometimes impossible (see Chapters 34–35, Volume I). Regional revolution, further, brings immense problems in leadership, with only grudging acceptance of outsiders, as, for example, Zapata demonstrated in the Mexican revolution (see Chapter 18, Volume I).

Ho Chi Minh also faced a delicate and complex international situation. Chinese and Russian reluctance to stir up trouble overtly in Indochina grew rather than diminished, the inevitable result of basic differences that were emerging in late 1957,[6] but also the result of Dulles' announced intention to intercede in case of enemy invasion of the South.

Another factor was the increasingly turbulent situation in South Viet-

3. Ho Chi Minh (*Ho Chi Minh on Revolution*), *supra*.
4. Buttinger: ". . . For each factory built under Diem—there were less than two dozen—the Communist regime in the north built fifty"; See also Zagoria, op. cit.
5. Fall (*The Two Viet-Nams*), *supra*.
6. Richard Lowenthal, "Russia and China: Controlled Conflict," *Foreign Affairs*, April 1971.

nam. Despite massive injections of American aid, Diem was failing to build a viable state, a failure that not only opened the way to increased Viet Minh activity but also increased Viet Minh popularity, particularly in the countryside. In this respect, Diem, his imperial court, and his senior American advisers were doing Ho's job for him, rather like the earlier situation in China, in which Chiang Kai-shek & Company had so ably prepared the soil for Mao Tse-tung's destructive seeds.

Ho, perforce, concentrated on wringing a great deal of propaganda value from Diem's continued refusals while mollifying the South and continuing to build in the North. Like a good Communist, he encouraged southern dissidence where he could—for example, in the central highlands, where his agents were working actively with the Montagnards, and by allowing some Communist cadres that had returned North to go back South to help organize the revolutionary movement. In time, success of Viet Minh cadres would cause him, or perhaps force him, to lend a more forceful hand. Meanwhile, he seemed content to let Diem go his destructive way.

Diem's repressive measures in both city and countryside, without doubt, severely damaged the organization of Viet Minh cadres that had remained in the South in 1954. Enough of them survived, however, to instigate a campaign of propaganda and subversion that, in places, prospered as the inevitable result of Diem's inept government.

In the early years, the Viet Minh used mainly agitation-propaganda tactics to accomplish their purpose. As their strength grew and after Diem refused to consider elections called for by the Geneva Conference, the hard-core Viet Minh turned to more-violent tactics, which appeared as early as 1956. A year later:

. . . A campaign of terror, extortion, assassination, and guerrilla action was used to undermine village security. Targets of such activities always include local village officials, civil guards, the members of the Self-Defense Corps, teachers, and, especially, officials sent out from the capital as local administrators of one kind or another. Sometimes these officials were "put on trial" by the Communists, then "sentenced" to death; after execution the bodies were left exposed with a notice pinned on them to indicate that the sentence had been carried out by the "liberation Forces."[7]

Viet Minh terrorism was not as haphazard as some commentators have suggested. It was and remained subordinate to the propaganda effort. With few exceptions, the Viet Minh indulged in selective terrorism, that is, killing for a specific political purpose. The picture of a disemboweled body of a village headman or government official aroused deepest feelings in the West, but, all too often, local peasantry welcomed the killing in that it offered relief, if only temporary, from repressive gov-

7. Trager, op. cit.

ernment. At very least, the killing impressed the peasantry with Viet Minh power, and it often frightened other headmen and officials into accommodating to Viet Minh aims. Nothing is pleasant about terror, because man was put on earth to trust, not fear—but, to write it off as indiscriminate killing, as a form of warfare unacceptable to Western quantitative theories, is scarcely conducive to countering it successfully.

The Diem government's inability to prevent selective terrorism increased its importance as a weapon in these years. One observer has estimated that, ". . . by mid-1959, Viet Cong violence of this type accounted for between fifteen and twenty assassinations of provincial-government officials per month; how many less prominent villagers were similarly treated is not known, but many particularly brutal cases of beheading and disembowelment were reported."[8]

Terrorism formed only part of a process already familiar from the China campaign and from earlier Viet Minh resistance to the French:

. . . Insurrection took the form of guerrilla action against villages still under government control; it usually led to the surrender or the wiping-out of the local self-defense units and Civil Guards charged with ousting the guerrillas. Organized, indoctrinated, and led by Communist cadres, the Vietcong, as these guerrillas were henceforth called, soon controlled almost the entire countryside by night and about two-thirds of it in daytime. The Vietcong set up their own administration, imposed their own taxes, conscripted the local youth into military service, provided education and medical care, collected food supplies for their fighting units, dug bomb shelters, built defense works along the regions they controlled, and continuously trained new men for stepped-up military operations. For years, they increased the number of their fighting men (if not their cadres) entirely through local recruiting, and their arms supply more through the capture of arms from government units than through infiltration from the North. . . . From 1960 on, they began to operate in ever-larger groups, and to attack and overrun government outposts held by the army, as well as to ambush and destroy army units sent to relieve outposts under attack. . . .[9]

The Viet Minh effort naturally varied from area to area, but, in general, it was determined and effective, as in the case of the Montagnards, in the central highlands:

. . . Their vulnerability to Communist influence has been high, as a result of their distrust of Vietnamese settlers and government officials and the astute efforts of Communist agents to win their favor. These agents have adopted tribal customs, often speak the tribal dialects, have married tribal women, and have in many cases lived and worked for years among the tribal people. Young tribesmen have been sent to North Vietnam for political and guerrilla

8. Ibid.
9. Buttinger, op. cit.

training and have come back home. The tribal peoples have been promised autonomy. . . .[10]

As previously discussed (see Chapter 65), effective countermeasures might have won over the Montagnards, but the Saigon government repeatedly failed to promulgate them; indeed, Diem's officials seemed to go out of their way to antagonize these primitive tribesmen.

Neither Communist leadership nor Communist guerrillas, however, monopolized the resistance effort. Diem may have bested the Hoa Hao and Cao Dai sects, but he had not eliminated them. In places, the remnants made common cause with the Viet Minh; indeed, Fall has suggested that the bulk of early opposition came from the sects. Remnants of the Dai Viet party were also working against the government, as was another group, the National Salvation Movement, sponsored by Vietnamese dissidents in Paris.[11]

From this mélange of dissent arose the National Liberation Front, or NLF. Its birthdate is not definitely known in the West. Kahin and Lewis point out that a clandestine broadcasting station called itself the Voice of the South Vietnam Liberation Front as early as mid-1958. Robert Shaplen noted that, in 1958, the NLF flag was seen in Viet Minh-dominated areas of the South. Douglas Pike has argued that ". . . the initial organization phase was the period from mid-1959, when the decision was made to begin building an organization, to December 1960, when the new creation was first unveiled." While arguing that the NLF per se was a Communist-front organization imported from Hanoi, Pike readily admitted that it depended on indigenous, and not alone Communist, support:

. . . Members of the original NLF, and its most ardent supporters in the early years, were drawn from the ranks of the Viet Minh Communists; the Cao Dai and Hoa Hao sects; a scattering of minority group members, primarily ethnic Cambodians and montagnards; idealistic youth, recruited from the universities and polytechnic schools; representatives of farmers' organizations from parts of the Mekong delta, where serious land tenure problems existed; leaders of small political parties or groups, or professionals associated with them; intellectuals who had broken with the GVN (particularly members of a network of Peace Committees that had sprung up in 1954 in both the North and the South); military deserters; refugees of various sorts from the Diem government, such as those singled out by neighbors in the Denunciation of Communism campaign but who fled before arrest.[12]

In short, here was a genuine grass-roots opposition whose predominantly nationalist elements caused Hanoi and the Viet Minh in the South to act carefully, generally downplaying the Communist bias of the new

10. Scigliano (*Nation Under Stress*), *supra*.
11. Kahin and Lewis, op. cit.
12. Pike, op. cit.; see also Lacouture, op. cit.; Shaplen, op. cit.

organization while providing leadership and guidance essential to its control. Pike goes on:

. . . Many of the original participants in the NLF had turned to it because they had been denied participation in South Vietnam's political process, even in the role of loyal opposition; some felt that the NLF was the most promising route to power, believing as did many at the time that the Diem government would not prove viable. They had one thing in common, to bring down the Diem government.[13]

Opposition to Diem did not end with this heterogeneous bunch. In spring of 1960, before Hanoi had officially admitted NLF's existence, mounting criticism in Saigon civil and military circles found voice in a public protest—the Caravelle Manifesto—to Diem signed by eighteen prominent Vietnamese, ten of them former government ministers.

Their statement referred to "anti-democratic elections"

. . . and to "continuous arrests [that] fill the jails and prisons to the rafters," and it charged that "effective power" had been "concentrated in fact in the hands of an irresponsible member of the 'family' [Ngo Dinh Nhu, Diem's brother] from whom emanates all orders."[14]

Diem cracked down hard on this group, arresting all signatories.

A few months later, in November, a group of army officers rebelled. After considerable behind-the-scenes maneuvering, three paratrooper battalions surrounded Diem's palace in Saigon. Leaders of the revolt called on Diem ". . . to rid himself of his family advisers and follow a political course more sensitive to the country's needs." While stalling the rebels, Diem and Nhu called up loyal elements, which broke up the revolt. Once again, the government cracked down hard and arrested many civil and military opposition leaders. Others went underground or fled the country.[15]

Only after these developments did Hanoi officially announce the existence of NLF and a program calling for liberation of the South, departure of the Americans, and final reunification of the country. To what extent Hanoi voluntarily acted and to what extent Ho's hand was forced by the southern cadres is not known in the West. The Hanoi government did not seem in any hurry to recognize the southern movement. The sanction came only during the Third Congress of the Vietnam Communist Party, in September 1960. But the same Congress stressed the necessity for continued internal development of North Vietnam. Vo Nguyen Giap, DRV Minister of Defense, told the Congress:

. . . Today, the economic construction in the North has become the central task of the Party. Therefore it is necessary to cut down defense budget,

13. Pike, op. cit.
14. Kahin and Lewis, op. cit.
15. Ibid.

adequately reduce our army contingent so as to concentrate manpower and material in economic construction.[16]

Such a policy in no way abrogated the repeatedly stated goal of reunification of the country, but, considering the state of insurrection that existed in the South, the Hanoi government logically would have been in no hurry to act—not as long as Diem continued to do the job for the Communists, and not as long as guerrillas in the South, who cost Hanoi next to nothing, continued to exploit his errors.

Primarily for this reason, the exact extent of Hanoi's participation from 1954 to 1960 is relatively unimportant. Had Diem, with all the millions of dollars and expertise furnished by the United States built even a reasonable government in the South, he would have neutralized the Viet Minh threat and then some. No matter what the American Government, or its particular spokesmen in this matter, would have us believe, Ho Chi Minh did not bring about the attempted coup of 1960. The villains were and remain Ngo Dinh Diem, his imperial court, his ambitious and venal generals and officials, and his Vietnamese and senior American advisers.

This would have been an appropriate time for Diem to do an about-face and come to terms with his critics, not alone those in cities and towns and those in government and armed forces, but the dissident peoples in the countryside, and, most of all, the peasants—the vast majority that formed the "neither-nor" constituency whose support was vital both to viable government and to an NLF-inspired insurgency.

Unfortunately, Diem proved incapable of reversing his pernicious policies. By 1960, he was a prisoner of forces as strong as those that ever surrounded Chiang Kai-shek. Had his warders ably administered the country, Diem might have survived. They did not. Not only were they inefficient, but they were repressive and corrupt, and they could only keep the government on a collision course with disaster. In Joseph Buttinger's biting words:

. . . Opposed by the intellectuals, despised by the educated middle class, rejected by businessmen, hated by the youth and by all nationalists with political ambitions, and totally lacking in mass support, the Diem Government had to rely for its survival on an apparatus of coercion."[17]

And by coercion with little purpose: negative, soul-destroying coercion, the attempt of mediocre minds to preserve a status quo in a situation demanding imaginative and daring change.

The army was symptomatic of the regime. By 1960, its major faults were becoming all too clear to objective observers. Far from being a national force that offered protection and security to peasants, the army served the political purposes of Diem and the ruling oligarchy. As had

16. Ibid.
17. Buttinger, op. cit.

been the case with Chiang Kai-shek's mainland armies, officer promotion depended on political whim. As had been the case in Greece, location of units more often satisfied private interests than public welfare, the estates of prominent politicians, for example, being guarded while rural areas lay open to Viet Minh depredation. As in the case of all totalitarian countries, "palace guard," or trusted, units never ventured far from the capital's periphery and played little part in combating increasingly serious guerrilla attacks in the countryside.

In spring of 1960, the prominent Vietnamese who submitted a public manifesto to Diem included a separate clause covering and, indeed, condemning the army:

. . . The purpose of the army, pillar of the defense of the country, is to stop foreign invasions and to eliminate rebel movements. It is at the service of the country only and should not lend itself to the exploitation of any faction or party. Its total reorganization is necessary. Clannishness and party obedience should be eliminated; its moral base strengthened; a noble tradition of national pride created; and fighting spirit, professional conscience, and bravery should become criteria for promotion. The troops should be encouraged to respect their officers, and the officers should be encouraged to love their men. Distrust, jealousy, rancor among colleagues of the same rank should be eliminated. . . .[18]

Operationally, the army had failed to neutralize Viet Cong tactics. Too often, corps commanders either refused to fight or were forbidden to fight or were unable to fight effectively. Politically tainted command relationships often meant confused and lackadaisical operations in situations demanding immediate and forceful response. Almost total lack of identification with peasants meant corresponding lack of information on which to base operations. Fear and frustration entered the picture to cause the army to use increasingly repressive measures and thus further to alienate the peasantry. Morale remained low, desertions high.

As mentioned earlier, in 1955 the Diem government had transferred the village security task to the Civil Guard and Self-Defense Corps. Neither organization proved able to cope with it effectively. Uneven and usually corrupt administration had produced largely untrained and badly equipped units whose poorly paid militiamen seemed unable to keep the Viet Cong from the door. As one result, local officials, businessmen, and plantation managers made private deals with guerrillas, to whom they paid bribes in money or kind—a sort of rural protection racket with the Viet Cong representing the "mob." Unfortunately, Saigon insisted that its government controlled these "quiet" areas, when the opposite held true.

18. Marcus G. Raskin and Bernard B. Fall (eds.), *The Viet-Nam Reader—Articles and Documents on American Foreign Policy and the Viet-Nam Crisis* (New York: Random House, 1967).

At a crucial time, then, the Diem government was not meeting its responsibilities. Instead of offering the people legitimate government, it was wallowing in a self-created malaise made more dangerous by failure of Diem, his advisers, and senior American officials both in Saigon and Washington to face up to problems and take appropriate action.

The American response to Diem's deteriorating position was mixed. Not only did the two camps, official and unofficial, hold frequently opposing views, but individual opinions in each camp often radically differed. Among other things, this caused uneven reporting, both public and private, at a time when a thoroughly confused and dangerous situation demanded objective coverage in order to be understood either by concerned officials in Washington or by the American public.

The basic villain was ignorance, which prompted fear among officials at all levels. So long as American officials believed in the "domino theory," so long as they insisted that South Vietnam was a "strategic necessity" as opposed to a "strategic convenience," their vision remained myopic, unable to see beyond the day to recognize inherent fallacies in Diem's repressive policies. Part of this failure rested on misconception of enemy capabilities and intentions, part on ignorance of Vietnam—a natural ignorance compounded by an insulated and luxurious life in Saigon, where the true situation in the countryside was not to be learned. Whatever the reason, results were disastrous. Typical of misinformation broadcast by Eisenhower-administration officials was that contained in an emotive speech by Walter Robertson, Assistant Secretary of State for Far Eastern Affairs, in June 1956. Robertson told an American audience:

. . . And finally Vietnam today, in mid-1956, [is] progressing rapidly to the establishment of democratic institutions by elective processes, its people resuming peaceful pursuits, its army growing in effectiveness, sense of mission, and morale, the puppet Vietnamese politicians discredited, the refugees well on the way to permanent settlement, the countryside generally orderly and calm. . . .

Perhaps no more eloquent testimony to the new state of affairs in Vietnam could be cited than the choice of the people themselves, as expressed in their free election of last March. At that time the last possible question as to the feeling of the people was erased by an overwhelming majority for President Diem's leadership. . . .

William Lederer, an experienced participant in and student of the area and author of *The Ugly American,* quoted the above words in his recent book *Our Own Worst Enemy* and added:

. . . There is not one single true statement in this excerpt from Assistant Secretary of State Walter Robertson's address. I do not know of a single living historian or student of Vietnamese affairs, official or otherwise, who would disagree with me. In mid-1956, under President Ngo Dinh Diem, there was no democratic institution. The president was ruling the nation like a tyrant. The army was not growing in effectiveness. The so-called discrediting of puppet Vietnamese politicians simply meant that President Ngo Dinh Diem was murdering or jailing everyone who disagreed with him. The free election which Walter Robertson speaks of [for members of the National Assembly] was a total fraud. . . .

Lederer's findings were later supported by official dissembling in 1959, ". . . when the countryside was slipping rapidly away from the control of the Vietnamese government."[19] Major General Samuel Myers, deputy chief of MAAG, ingeniously reported that summer that ". . . the Viet Minh guerrillas . . . were gradually nibbled away until they ceased to become a major menace to the government." In July, Ambassador Elbridge Durbrow told a Senate committee: ". . . The [Vietnam] government is becoming more and more effective in curbing these terrorist acts . . . [and] the internal situation has been brought from chaos to basic stability."[20] Wesley Fishel, who headed the Michigan State University-CIA mission to Saigon, wrote in the autumn issue of *Yale Review* for 1959:

. . . On October 26, 1959, South Vietnam will celebrate its fourth anniversary of the Republic of Vietnam. The anticipated elections of 1956 have never been held, and the Communist capability in Vietnam, south of the 17th parallel, has been reduced to one of sheer nuisance activity. . . . It is one Asian area where Communism has been rolled back without war. . . . There is little likelihood of a revolution against the regime. . . .

Other important voices echoed these sentiments, including those of Admiral Arthur Radford and Admiral Felix Stump, who agreed that ". . . President Ngo Dinh Diem was the most brilliant and successful Asian leader of democracy since Chiang Kai-shek."[21]

These incredibly inaccurate statements played directly into Diem's hands. The optimism of American Pollyannas created an ideal blackmail situation ably exploited by experienced mandarins who surrounded Diem. American policy makers had been told for so long that Diem was the only man who could prevent Vietnam from falling to Communists that they believed it, and they did not stop to examine sources:

19. Scigliano (*Nation Under Stress*), *supra;* William Lederer, *Our Own Worst Enemy* (New York: W. W. Norton, 1968).
20. Scigliano (*Nation Under Stress*), *supra.* Ambassador Durbrow nonetheless indirectly supported the 1960 coup in that he failed to warn Diem—another example of officials telling the American public one thing while officially reporting another.
21. Lederer, op. cit.

frightened politicians, officials who had staked careers on the Diem regime, militarists who wanted to expand the armed forces, even an American public-relations agency hired by the Diem government to perpetuate the myth of his indispensability throughout the United States!

Ignorance existed in other areas, the MAAG mission typifying one. In 1960, MAAG advisers were only beginning to comprehend Viet Minh techniques, and then only in part. Civil-aid officials erred just as badly by continuing to back expensive projects either without realizing, or realizing but refusing to admit, that success of such projects hinged almost totally on political and social reforms that the Diem government refused to make.

Efforts to inform the American public of burgeoning disaster did not prosper, and for several reasons. At first, the relatively low-priority area from the news standpoint attracted but few reporters. Later, when French defeat and withdrawal brought more-extensive coverage, new-comers were impeded both by ignorance of the area and by suspicious and unco-operative American and Vietnamese officials.

Official hostility was not new. It had begun shortly after World War II, when French officials became incensed at factual reporting. News suppression is invariably one of the first devices chosen by a government operating from fear. The French continued to suppress news until their withdrawal. The Diem government picked up the ugly habit, and such were the emotional issues, and such the personal stakes, that a good many American officials subverted all that is brilliant in the American heritage and, from desks carrying the great seal of the United States Government and backed by the American flag, took refuge in lies that they wished reported to American taxpayers.

Personal and official hindrances sometimes prevented accurate reporting, as did confused issues and failure to identify the type of war being fought. This naturally contributed to American public apathy, but we must remember that, from the news standpoint, Vietnam continued to be a relatively low-priority area—it was difficult for the American public to identify with strange-sounding names in a country of which many had never previously heard and did not even know the exact location.

In 1960 and later, it was far easier to accept official pronouncements than to seek out issues and decide for oneself. In this sense, the Vietnam lobby in Washington had things largely its own way. Large blocs of the American public, if thinking about Vietnam at all, believed that, if South Vietnam fell to the "Communists," all of Southeast Asia would be overrun and Red hordes would shortly appear off the California coast. Preventing this, so they were told time and again, was the Christian savior, Ngo Dinh Diem; therefore the American Government had no option but to support the Diem regime.

This was the general picture when John F. Kennedy became President of the United States. His relatively brief administration would soon suffer the Vietnam problem and would greatly change its dimensions. At this juncture, however, we must interrupt the Vietnam story to look at contemporary insurgencies in Kenya, Cyprus, Algeria, and Cuba.

Chapter 67

The Mau Mau rebellion • Historical background • British colonization • Early native political movements • Rise of the KCA • Enter Jomo Kenyatta • Early Mau Mau activities • Government suppression • Mau Mau appeal • Organization and strength of Mau Mau • Kenyatta's arrest • The emergency begins

WHILE FIGHTING CONTINUED in French Indochina and Malaya, a new insurgency broke out in Kenya, the large British colony in East Africa (see map, p. 864). Unlike the other areas, communism did not fuel this boiling pot of trouble, which soon became known as the Mau Mau rebellion. Although the Kenyan political leader Jomo Kenyatta had fallen under Marxist influence during his long period of self-imposed exile in England, the instrument of rebellion that he fashioned in Nairobi after World War II bore but slight resemblance to other Communist-inspired and -directed guerrilla movements. For here the mantle of Marx soon slipped away to expose a primitive body of rebellion that fed on a weird admixture of religious-tribal cultism while performing violent deeds particularly abhorrent to the Western world.[1]

1. Colonial Office (F. D. Corfield), *Historical Survey of the Origin and Growth of Mau Mau* (London: HMSO, 1960) (Command Paper 1030). Hereafter cited as Corfield: The author suggests that Kenyatta learned Soviet Communist agit-prop and organizational techniques on short visits to the Soviet Union, first in

Most readers will probably associate the Mau Mau rebellion with Robert Ruark's best-selling novel *Something of Value*,[2] which stressed Mau Mau excesses. The historian cannot justify these, but he can explain them, just as he can explain moral aberrations among more-civilized races, for instance the wholesale slaughter of two world wars, and Nazi Germany's performance with the Jews. In the case of the Mau Mau, the explanation begins in the nineteenth century and might be called the story of an insurgency that need never have happened.

Dozens of tribes had occupied eastern Africa over the centuries. These pastoral bodies migrated to lush plains, and when they had killed the game and their cattle and goats had eaten the tender grass, they moved to greener pastures. Some fell prey to other, more warlike tribes, some to natural disasters and epidemics. Some tribes survived and even prospered; some disappeared.

The Bantu-speaking Agikuyu, or Gikuyu tribe, which we know as the Kikuyu, is probably seven or eight hundred years old. Toward the end of the sixteenth century, a population increase caused the tribe to advance into the Kiambu district and north to fertile plains of Nyeri and Mount Kenya. Here the Kikuyu settled to farm the land while protecting it from incursions of the warlike Masai, which, in the nineteenth century, stressed a warrior cult and terrorized such neighboring tribes as the Bantu, Taveta, and Kikuyu.[3]

Whether the tribal complex ever would have amalgamated into a peaceful state, we don't know. But anthropologists long since have exploded the popular conception of savage hordes living in an anarchic

1929–30 and later in 1933, when he attended the Lenin School. This suggestion appears impractical to me in view of Kenyatta's brief stay in the U.S.S.R. and the hiatus of thirteen years between techniques learned and techniques practiced. More logically, Corfield points to the lack of Communist bias in Mau Mau leadership and also that a Communist Party did not exist in Kenya: ". . . It can accordingly be concluded that Mau Mau had virtually no connection with Communism, but was developed by Kenyatta as an atavistic tribal rising aimed against Western civilization and technology and in particular against Government and the Europeans as symbols of progress"; see also L. S. B. Leakey, *Mau Mau and the Kikuyu* (London: Methuen, 1952); L. S. B. Leakey, *Defeating Mau Mau* (London: Methuen, 1954): Dr. Leakey awards the movement more of a religious-nationalist bias; Donald L. Barnett and Karari Njama, *Mau Mau from Within —Autobiography and Analysis of Kenya's Peasant Revolt* (New York: Monthly Review Press, 1966): ". . . My own investigation of Mau Mau ideology," Dr. Barnett wrote, "viewed as the unifying set of aims, interests and beliefs of the Movement, has shown it to be a rather complex phenomenon containing at least four major aspects or components; namely secular, moral-religious, African national and Kikuyu tribal."

2. Robert Ruark, *Something of Value* (London: Hamish Hamilton, 1955).

3. Leakey (*Mau Mau and the Kikuyu*), *supra;* see also Roland Oliver, and Gervase Mathew (eds.), *History of East Africa* (London: Oxford University Press, 1963), Vol. 1; Jomo Kenyatta, *Facing Mount Kenya—The Tribal Life of the Gikuyu* (London: Secker & Warburg, 1938).

SUDAN

ETHIOPIA

L. Rudolf

KENYA

UGANDA

Rift Valley

Central Province

Mt. Kenya

Aberdare

Nyeri

Naivasha

Lari

Kiambu

Nairobi

Lake Victoria

L. Natron

Mt. Kilimanjaro ▲

SOMALI REP.

TANGANYIKA

Mombasa

N

INDIAN

ZANZIBAR

OCEAN

AFRICA

KENYA

South Atlantic Ocean

KENYA
• Towns and Cities
∿ White Highlands
∿ African Reserve

0   100   200   300 miles

M.E.P.

state. We know that a *modus vivendi* often existed between tribes, and we also know that some tribes possessed a viable political structure as well as moral codes that, in result, often compared favorably with the Christian ethic—belief realized through feathers and blood instead of bread and wine, but belief just as firm and perhaps more so than that in the West.[4]

We also have a good deal of firsthand information about the Kikuyu from Jomo Kenyatta's early book *Facing Mount Kenya.* Those inclined to shrug away his words as obviously prejudiced will find much of what he wrote confirmed by independent scholarship and particularly by the works of Dr. L. S. B. Leakey. A son of missionaries, Leakey grew up among the Kikuyu, where he mastered the difficult language, became a member of a tribal age-group and later a first-grade elder of the tribe. He also became a distinguished archaeologist and historian. His books on Kenya and the Kikuyu should be read in order to understand the underlying grievances that allowed the insurgency to form and caused so many Africans to support it.[5]

The Kikuyu worshiped a god, angry old Murungu, or Ngai—". . . supreme, almighty, unseen but all pervading, having four 'homes' in the four sacred mountains of the Kikuyu."[6] Ngai forever required propitiating by animal sacrifice and a mumbo-jumbo that meant nothing to the Westerner but a great deal to the African. The Kikuyu also practiced ancestor worship and a form of animism in which they recognized spirits in trees, large rocks, waterfalls, and epidemic diseases. Ceremony played a vital role in their religion. So did the related all-important oath, which, varying from the supreme, or *githathi,* oathing ceremony to less severe forms, governed tribal society, economics, marriage, even tribal health. White magic was the province of the *mundu mugo,* or "medicine man," who functioned as doctor, seer, and protector against black-magic practitioners:

. . . It was this absolute fear of magic powers that was the foundation stone of all Kikuyu ceremonies of oath taking, and in consequence the taking of a solemn oath was an act never lightly undertaken, and once sworn, its effect upon the taker was very great.[7]

Animal sacrifice normally accompanied oath taking—". . . in the course of the life of an individual Kikuyu there were no less than 108 occasions

4. Leakey (*Mau Mau and the Kikuyu*), *supra.*
5. Ibid. and Leakey (*Defeating Mau Mau*), *supra;* see also the following three works by Leakey: "Colonial Administration from the Native Point of View." In *Comparative Methods of Colonial Administration* (London: Chatham House, 1930); *Kenya—Contrasts and Problems* (London: Methuen, 1936); *White Africa* (London: Hodder & Stoughton, 1937); Barnett and Njama, op. cit.; Corfield, op. cit.; Fred Majdalaney, *State of Emergency—The Full Story of Mau Mau* (London: Longmans, Green, 1962).
6. Leakey (*Mau Mau and the Kikuyu*), *supra;* see also Kenyatta, op. cit.
7. Ibid.

from birth to death which required the slaughter and sacrifice of a goat or a sheep." But ". . . the Kikuyu were a deeply religious people for whom life without religion was unthinkable."[8]

The Kikuyu governed themselves by regional, or "ridge," councils of elders—the *athamaki,* whose spokesmen and members had trained for the role since adolescent initiation into an age-group followed by specific *rites de passage,* each of which increased importance and responsibilities. Farming and animal husbandry were the main occupations. People lived in villages fortified for protection against Masai raids. Individuals owned farms and even estates worked by tenants. A strict moral code governed buying and selling of land. Tribal law preserved certain forest areas for purposes of hunting and beekeeping and also for fuel reserves. Early Western explorers, toward the end of the nineteenth century, were in general impressed with Kikuyu territory, which, according to one, ". . . as far as the eye could see . . . was one vast garden."[9]

Toward the end of the nineteenth century, manifold disaster struck the Kikuyu and other eastern African tribes. A smallpox epidemic tore through the land to decimate humans, as a rinderpest epidemic decimated cattle. Severe drought and a locust invasion followed. Leakey has estimated that the combined tragedy took from 20 to 50 per cent of the tribe. It also caused families to evacuate lands in the Kiambu country, where farms reverted to bush country.

As if this weren't sufficient, the Kikuyu now faced invasion from the West. Toward the end of the century, Germany and Great Britain carved out respective spheres of commercial influence in eastern Africa through the co-operation of the sultan of Zanzibar. In 1890, the British East Africa Company began moving inland, an effort soon taken over by the British Government, which established a protectorate over Kenya and, at the turn of the century, built a railroad from Mombasa to Uganda, nearly six hundred miles into the interior. To help justify this expensive project, the British began colonizing south-central Kenya, the supply railhead being the village of Nairobi. In this area, the government acquired sixteen thousand square miles of prime land, the White Highlands, for distribution to settlers.[10]

The colonizing task fell to two men: to the high commissioner, Sir Charles Eliot, a thirty-seven-year-old scholar and diplomat, and to an eccentric, adventure-loving nobleman, Lord Delamere. Considering natural hazards and costly discouragements involved in establishing and building farms, both men rate high from the technical standpoint.

The white man also brought numerous benefits to Africans. Tribal wars, in general, vanished. European doctors and veterinarians began

8. Ibid.
9. Ibid.
10. Ibid.; see also Marie de Kiewiet Hemphill, "The British Sphere 1884–94." In Oliver and Mathew, *supra;* Barnett and Njama, op. cit.

to eliminate dreadful epidemic diseases that had wiped out tribes and herds of cattle since time immemorial; Western methods and medicines brought general improvement in health and a lowering of the high infant-mortality rate. European farming methods brought bigger and better crops. European and Asian merchants filled market places with new and exciting wares. Missionaries, mostly Scottish preachers, established schools and spread the Christian gospel, which held considerable appeal to illiterate natives. Had the white man respected the native's identity, his traditions and beliefs, his dignity and natural ambition, he might still be in control of a prosperous Kenya.

Unfortunately, he did no such thing. Exercising an arrogance of ignorance that would persist in subsequent decades, he interpreted the situation as it fitted his convenience. In Leakey's words,

. . . this simple and yet highly effective organized system of decentralized control of religious, judicial, and secular affairs was not in the least understood by the British when they came to the country. The administrators believed that throughout Africa there was a system of "chiefs" and subchiefs and they believed wrongly that the spokesman of the senior ridge councils was the "chief" of that ridge. If he met with approval he was retained as "chief" whereas he had never before been a chief in our sense, and if he did not suit the British he was replaced by a "chief" chosen and appointed by the administration. Thus there was instituted a system wholly foreign to Kikuyu custom and tradition.[11]

The European also erred, perhaps intentionally, in land acquisition. Government officials assumed that large areas of "empty" land in the Kiambu district were for the taking. This was not always the case. As we have seen, calamity had forced widespread evacuation of Kiambu lands legitimately owned by individual Africans. In his mind, the African had not relinquished title, nor had the tribe yielded valuable forest reserves. Bushland that officials assumed was not being used was in reality serving as grazing land for the all-important cattle and goats. Governmental payments for land sold to white settlers (". . . a halfpenny an acre plus survey fees")[12] meant one thing to the government, another to the native, who regarded the deal as temporary since sale or transfer of privately owned land involved a host of tribal-religious rites essential to freeing it from evil spirits:

. . . so from the Kikuyu point of view none of the rights acquired in Kikuyu lands by the white settlers were considered as vesting ownership in the newcomers, while from the point of view of British law, and the country was now administered by the British, the transactions were wholly valid and had been made in absolute good faith.[13]

11. Leakey (*Mau Mau and the Kikuyu*), *supra.*
12. R. Meinertzhagen, *Kenya During 1902–1906* (London: Oliver & Boyd, 1957).
13. Leakey (*Mau Mau and the Kikuyu*), *supra.*

Here was the genesis of the later Kikuyu complaint that the land was stolen by the whites—a grievance fundamental to the rebellion, a grievance that arose from British arrogance of ignorance.

The white man's attitude, in general, was uncompromising. Our old friend Captain Richard Meinertzhagen (see Chapter 19, Volume I) was sent to Kenya as a young officer. In 1902, he met Eliot, whom he found capable but scarcely attractive:

. . . He is out of touch and harmony with the world in general. His pet hobby is the study of hudibranchs or sea slugs. Never did a man more closely resemble the objects of his hobby. He is invertebrate, with an icy cold nature, unsympathetic, but a scholar of the first rank.[14]

Their meeting upset the young subaltern. Eliot

. . . amazed me with his views on the future of East Africa. He envisaged a thriving colony of thousands of Europeans. . . . He intends to confine the natives to reserves and use them as cheap labor on farms. I suggested that the country belonged to Africans, that their interests must prevail over the interests of strangers. He would not have it; he kept on using the word "paramount" with reference to the claims of Europeans. I said that some day the African would be educated and armed; that would lead to a clash. Eliot thought that that day was so far distant as not to matter . . . but I am convinced that in the end the Africans will win and that Eliot's policy can lead only to trouble and disappointment.

A few months later, Meinertzhagen met Lord Delamere:

. . . He is an enthusiast about the future of East Africa and remarked: "I am going to prove to you all that this is a white man's country." "But," I humbly said, "it is a black man's country; how are you going to superimpose the white over black?" Delamere is a quick-tempered man; he said, rather impatiently, "The black man will benefit and co-operate."[15]

Eliot, Delamere, and most of their subordinates exemplified the concept of the Christian white man's burden. Under their aegis, an entire colony was developing to further this notion. In essence, the Africans existed for the white man's convenience (profit). In essence, the black was not a human being, and few white men in Kenya would have agreed with Meinertzhagen, who noted, upon his departure in 1904:

. . . I am sorry to leave the Kikuyu, for I like them. They are the most intelligent of the African tribes I have met; therefore they will be the most progressive under European guidance and will be more susceptible to subversive activities. They will be one of the first tribes to demand freedom from European influence and in the end cause a lot of trouble. And if white

14. Meinertzhagen, op. cit.
15. Ibid.

settlement really takes hold in this country it is bound to do so at the expense of the Kikuyu, who own the best land, and I can foresee much trouble.[16]

As presciently foreseen by Meinertzhagen, Eliot's policy led precisely to trouble, disappointment—and finally rebellion. Under Eliot's administration, the white man not only took land that was not his, but compelled the African to work this land under an arrangement close to slavery. He kept natives in large reserves and denied them identity to other than themselves and their employers. Although Eliot left Kenya in 1904, his legacy continued to rule: In 1915, for example, the Crown Lands Ordinance made all Africans "tenants at the will of the Crown," the government refusing to issue them land title deeds.[17]

The African's service in two world wars, his stumbling attempts, beginning in 1920, to gain a political voice, his efforts to educate himself (encouraged finally by the government, deprecated by white Kenyans), did not alter his status. Those blacks who demanded the return of "stolen lands" might as well have saved their breath; those who demanded a place in government were marked as agitators and carefully watched. Although the British Government made Kenya a colony after World War I and, in 1923, announced that it would respect African rights by a "trusteeship," matters changed but slightly.[18]

Education continued in the hands of Scottish missionaries, who too often taught form but not substance of Christianity. In their eagerness to learn to read and write at mission schools, many young Kikuyu embraced Christianity but

. . . did not accept the Christian doctrine or have any intention of really trying to live up to Christian standards of morality, honesty, and codes of behavior. At the same time, many of these young men—and as time went on young women too—learned enough to make them cease to have real faith in their own Kikuyu religious beliefs and practices, so that a body of people sprang into being who had abandoned one faith without accepting another in its place and who were thus without any real guiding principles in their lives.[19]

Secular education was limited in the extreme, the government failing to live up to its responsibilities by providing needed teachers and schools. The few educated blacks could not find jobs commensurate with ability. They were accepted neither into government nor into white society.

16. Ibid.: Meinertzhagen also disapproved of colonial administration. In 1904, he noted in his journal " . . . the low class of man who is appointed. . . . Few of them have had any education, and many of them do not pretend to be members of the educated class. One can neither read nor write. This is not surprising when one realizes that no examination is required to enter the local Civil Service."

17. Barnett and Njama, op. cit.

18. Ibid.; see also Leakey (*Mau Mau and the Kikuyu*), *supra;* Corfield, op. cit.; Majdalaney, op. cit.

19. Leakey (*Mau Mau and the Kikuyu*), *supra.*

The white man, long before, had closed the door to the evolutionary notion, and he was not now going to open it.

The black political movement in Kenya began in 1921, with the Young Kikuyu Association, which a few years later became the Kikuyu Central Association, or KCA. In the twenties and thirties this organization exploited the old grievance of "stolen lands," a sore point which survived even though a Royal Commission in 1932 investigated and awarded "appropriate" compensation. It also exploited new grievances such as the hated *kipande,* or compulsory black worker registration; low wages; a law that prohibited Africans from raising coffee; lack of African representation in the colonial legislature; and the color bar.

The KCA movement did not prosper. White settlers disrupted it whenever possible; older tribal chiefs, appointed by the new government and relatively well off, did not trust young Kikuyu leaders.

But neither did the movement die. Failure of the colonial administration to provide proper education, coupled with the Church of Scotland's insistence on banning such tribal rites as *irua,* or female circumcision, and festival dances, turned the Kikuyu to providing their own schools and religion, which soon became the main instruments of propaganda to serve the KCA's militant identity.[20]

World War II also played a role. The government declared the KCA illegal, which brought its leaders increased prominence among tribesmen. The war transported numerous Africans abroad, in some ways a broadening and awakening experience that made them more receptive to KCA propaganda when they returned. In their absence, Kenya had enjoyed considerable prosperity, and postwar years seemed to promise more. From a social-political-economic standpoint, however, the returning black veteran found but slight improvement. Although the government established a number of industrial training schools, openings for subsequent employment "were very limited." F. D. Corfield, in an official report published in 1960, noted:

. . . over and above these economic grievances there was a deeper sense of resentment, caused by the various forms of discrimination which were considered by the Kikuyu to be a barrier to his economic, political and social aspirations—the restriction on the planting of cash crops, such as coffee; the fact that Africans were not permitted to acquire land in the White Highlands; the different wage scales which applied to Europeans, Asians and Africans by the Government; the restrictive covenants which applied to housing in European areas, some municipalities, and the opposition to entry into some of the larger hotels.[21]

20. Ibid.; see also Kenyatta, op. cit., who explains the importance of female circumcision to tribal tradition and mores.

21. Corfield, op. cit.; see also Barnett and Njama, op. cit., who offer interesting comparisons between wages received by Africans, Asians, and whites.

To the returning veteran, the colony seemed as devoid of opportunity for the black man as formerly. But now the black man was finding his voice, and now appeared a formidable leader, Jomo Kenyatta, who, to many, resembled a latter-day Moses intent on leading his people from the wilderness.

Jomo Kenyatta was born on a tribal reserve outside Nairobi around 1893. Educated in a Church of Scotland mission school, he worked as a clerk in Nairobi, edited a newspaper, and, in 1925, joined the KCA, becoming secretary-general in 1928. A year later, the association sent him to London to present a list of grievances to the Colonial Office. Staying on, he joined the Communist Party and toured England and the Soviet Union; after a brief stay in Kenya, he returned to England, where he obtained a degree in anthropology at the London School of Economics, his thesis being published as a book, *Facing Mount Kenya*.[22] He also married an English woman, who bore him a son but remained in England when he returned to Kenya, in 1946.[23]

The first phase of what came to be called the Emergency began shortly after Kenyatta's return to Nairobi. Here he reorganized remnants of the illegal KCA into a militant party that operated under cover of the Kenya African Union, Kenyatta becoming its president in 1947. Inflammatory speeches now became the order of the day, as did ugly rumors of special oathing ceremonies along with talk of killing all Europeans. District officers began to report sinister activities of a new organization, the Mau Mau, in 1948, and missionaries, tribal chiefs, police, and civil officials began to confirm the reports.[24]

Neither governor nor government seemed unduly alarmed. In 1950, the government recognized the Mau Mau as ". . . an evil and subversive association" and brought a gang to court; found guilty, the nineteen Africans won an appeal on a slim technicality. Although this led to proscription of the Mau Mau and to more prosecutions, the government did not take further remedial action.[25]

Considerable blame must rest on the governor, Sir Philip Mitchell, who felt he knew more about Africans than some of his better-informed subordinates. If ever a man believed in the Christian white man's burden, it was Mitchell. An old Africa hand, he held that natural inferiority of Africans explained their dismal circumstances. An imperialist to the core, he saw England as the Trustee, whose major aim is

. . . now, as it has always been, to create conditions in which his wards can advance in civilization, knowledge and capacity, with all the help he can give, to the furthest point they can reach. But that cannot be done with-

22. *Supra.*
23. Majdalaney, op. cit.
24. Corfield, op. cit.
25. Ibid.

out effecting a radical transformation of the subsistence society in which the masses are still enmeshed, with its poverty, sorcery, superstition and ignorance, and all the other conditions which combine to chain the African to his dark and terror-ridden past.

Although he wanted certain reforms, African independence was not to be thought of. If England succeeded in its trust,

. . . there will be created here in East and Central Africa a Christian civilization, tolerant of course of other faiths, with "equal rights for all civilized men" as its major political principle.

Qualified Africans could play a part in the process:

. . . If these politically mature groups are willing to accept and to collaborate without reserve in the central policy of the Trustee, then they have a right to be associated closely—indeed, I would say to be entrusted—with the execution of it and the works will benefit greatly by their participation. But if they, or any one of them, reject that policy, then they are in effect taking a position in opposition to high policy and cannot expect to be accorded anything more than the representation reasonable for a minority.

The Trustee policy, ". . . administered by a strong and enlightened colonial power," was Kenya's only hope for the future.[26]

Poor old Mitchell. As he was writing these words, the rebellion had broken out to shatter his imperialist dreams. Whether he could have salvaged the situation by instituting needed reforms during his tenure (1944–52), admittedly a difficult task in view of white opposition, we shall never know. His reforms, at best, would have been mild, as witness excerpts from one of his dispatches relating to exclusive white ownership of the White Highlands:

. . . the land must, on no account, be simply thrown open for congestion and destruction by ignorant peasants following their ancestral agricultural practices and tenure.

. . . It is the general experience of mankind that a tolerably high standard of living in any community cannot rest solely upon peasant farming by primitive methods. . . .[27]

Mitchell did not dwell on the British Government's responsibility in changing these methods or improving the "peasant's" lot. He otherwise refused to act with vigor. Perhaps colonial bureaucracy was the real villain, as he suggests in his book, but it is difficult to deny that the function of a governor is to govern. Despite significant theft of arms and ammunition from government depots, security remained lax. Mitchell apparently did not reinforce the police function significantly, the main instrument for intelligence collection and collation. The police section

26. Philip Mitchell, *African Afterthoughts* (London: Hutchinson, 1954).
27. Corfield, op. cit.

responsible, a small and impoverished Special Branch, operated mainly in Nairobi and Mombasa, which severely limited its activities. Command channels remained muddled: Corfield concluded that most of the intelligence reports forwarded in the "formative" years ". . . just 'disappeared' into the Central Secretariat." As one result, the government lacked clear definition of the Mau Mau, of its origin, organization, methods, and goals; as another result, it failed to impede the spread of Mau Mau propaganda and recruitment.[28]

Official ignorance was startling. The anthropologist Dr. Donald Barnett has suggested that Mau Mau itself is a meaningless term that may have been corrupted by a European policeman from the word *muma,* or oath, or may have derived from a derogatory term for venal tribal elders. Africans did not use the term, any more than the Viet Minh in Indochina used the term Viet Cong. What some Africans called "The Movement" was in reality the work of the KCA, which was far more extensively organized than local authorities imagined.[29]

Beginning in 1950, the KCA ". . . underwent a dramatic shift . . . from a highly selective, elite organization to an underground mass movement."[30] From headquarters in Nairobi, organizers traveled the land recruiting new members and setting up cells and units. A ceremonial oath had been essential to membership for years, but the new underground movement ". . . demanded strict secrecy as well as total commitment and the oath was altered to meet these requirements."[31] Persons who would not voluntarily submit to the oath were forced to submit whenever possible, an unseemly business conducted at night with black-magic overtones.

The program worked for several reasons. The first and, according to Dr. Leakey, the foremost was legitimate grievances, which made Africans receptive to KCA "land and freedom" propaganda. The land grievance topped the list. In 1951, Mr. Eliud Mathu, member of the Legislative Council in Nairobi, told a meeting of Africans:

. . . It is on the land that the African lives and it means everything to him. The African cannot depend for his livelihood on profits made through trading. We cannot depend on wages. We must go back every time to the only social security we have—the piece of land. The land stolen must be restored, because without land the future of the African people is doomed. God will hear us because that is the thing he gave us.[32]

Another was the government's educational failure, both religious and secular: the one creating a group of confused Christians, the other maintaining a high level of ignorance and illiteracy. A third was the adminis-

28. Ibid.
29. Barnett and Njama, op. cit.
30. Ibid.
31. Ibid.
32. Corfield, op. cit.

trative system of government-appointed "chiefs," who often lacked popular following. Another was the peculiar psychology of the oath. In Dr. Leakey's words,

. . . We have already seen that a Kikuyu who takes a solemn oath is punished by supernatural powers if he breaks that oath, or if he has perjured himself. One of the phrases used in the Mau Mau oath ceremony is to the effect that "if I do anything to give away this organization to the enemy, may I be killed by the oath"! Having once made such an oath, even under pressure, no ordinary Kikuyu would dare to go and make a report to the police or to his employer, because, were he to do so, he would be breaking the oath and thus calling down upon himself, or upon members of his family, supernatural penalties.[33]

His only recourse was a "cleansing ceremony" to nullify the force of the oath, but

. . . participation in such a ceremony could not be kept quiet for long, since, to be effective, it must be carried out in public and before many witnesses. The Mau Mau people made it very clear to their victims that if they tried to get out of their obligations under the oath by such means, they would be victimized and even, if necessary, murdered.[34]

Some loyal Christian Kikuyu reported Mau Mau activities, and other Kikuyu, ". . . many of whom were afraid and shocked," refused to join the movement. The KCA approach nevertheless contained an inherent appeal, and the government continued to underestimate the movement's growth (an estimated quarter of a million by mid 1952).[35] A Central Committee, in Nairobi, ran the movment by means of seven district committees, each supporting division, location, and sublocation committees.[36] Although only a fraction of the Mau Mau were armed—Corfield estimates that, in 1952, the movement possessed between four hundred and eight hundred modern weapons, stolen from government arsenals —Mau Mau leaders grew increasingly bold. Early in 1952, terrorist gangs started burning huts of African officials and fields of some white farmers. The Mau Mau oath also continued to change and, by spring, included an ominous promise to kill on order.[37]

33. Leakey (*Mau Mau and the Kikuyu*), *supra.*
34. Ibid.
35. Corfield, op. cit.
36. Barnett and Njama, op. cit., explain the organization in detail.
37. Leakey (*Mau Mau and the Kikuyu*), *supra:* Both the First Oath, or Unity Oath, and the Second Oath, or Warrior Oath, derived from the traditional Kikuyu *githathi* oath but involved considerable black magic along with bestial practices that intentionally violated tribal taboos in order to separate further the militants from the tribe to create a class apart—not unlike the anti-Christian movement in England that employed the revolting Black Mass; see also Corfield, op. cit., who suggests that the *batuni*, or Warrior Oath, began being administered as early

In June the governor retired, and the interregnum proved no more energetic in coping with the deteriorating situation. Government itself was badly split. In July the commissioner of police told the government:

... If it is accepted that a general revolt among the Kikuyu people is being carried into effect, and I have no doubt that this is the case, the situation calls for immediate action, and action which must go far beyond that which lies in the hands of the police.[38]

But in August, in response to demands of a legislative group for action, the acting governor stated: ". . . I categorically deny that there is a state of emergency."[39]

Despite Jomo Kenyatta's alleged denunciation of the Mau Mau, reports of large-scale oathing ceremonies continued to reach Government House. In September, police reported the murder of fourteen Africans by Mau Mau gangs, who also burned some white farms and killed or mutilated several hundred cattle and sheep. At the end of the month, the new governor, Sir Evelyn Baring, arrived and inspected disturbed areas. While Baring was so engaged, the Mau Mau brazenly murdered a Kikuyu senior chief in daylight a few miles from Nairobi. Baring notified his government: ". . . It is now abundantly clear that we are facing a planned revolutionary movement. If the movement cannot be stopped, there will be an administrative break-down, followed by bloodshed amounting to civil war. . . ."[40] Whitehall authorized him to declare a state of emergency.

---

as 1948. By 1953, all Mau Mau terrorists were taking it—in the forest, it was called the *githaka;* see also Barnett, and Njama, op. cit., who write most interestingly on the subject and suggest that the Warrior Oath is a logical extension of the *githathi* oath: ". . . the sexual acts or symbols performed or invoked while swearing an oath were calculated violations of acknowledged taboos designed, in both traditional and modern usage, to revolt and inspire awe and fear in the initiates or accused. Second, that according to Kikuyu belief, the more vile or repulsive were the acts performed while swearing an oath—i.e., the more highly tabooed such acts would be in everyday life—the stronger and more binding did such an oath become. Third, that Karari [a terrorist] and others should have found the Second Oath both 'horrible' and 'typically Kikuyu' was, in light of the above, both a normal and highly predictable response"; to this writer, the Warrior Oath described by Karari would be no more perverted in Kikuyu minds than certain fraternal initiation rites experienced by many readers would be in American minds. The oath, at this stage, also brings to mind the *Blutbrüderschaft* indulged by members of the Luftwaffe in World War II, which was a logical if somewhat perverted extension of the commissioned officer's oath. But the oath early described by Karari is a far cry from later forest oaths, which involved violent sexual orgies and the drinking of ghastly concoctions, and which seem to this writer to have been indulged by illiterate and semihysterical commanders trying desperately to hold together a fragmenting organization.

38. Majdalaney, op. cit.
39. Ibid.
40. Corfield, op. cit.

On the night of October 20, a British battalion arrived by air from Egypt and a British cruiser sailed into Mombasa. Early the next morning, police arrested Kenyatta and 182 followers. A short time later, Baring broadcast a state of emergency and included a plea that emphasized the poverty of the administration he had inherited:

. . . Kenya has before it a bright future with a good prospect of a rising standard of living for people of all races, provided that there is peace and order. In peaceful conditions plans were being made for economic development and particularly for help to the poorer inhabitants of this country. There was, for example, good hopes of accelerating the pace of the construction of houses for Africans, of expanding African education, and of improving the positions of Africans in the Civil Service. All these things will be impossible of realization if conditions of disorder continue. . . .[41]

The words came seven years too late.

41. Ibid.

Chapter 68

Mau Mau terrorism • The government's response • British security forces • The tactical problem • British military tactics • Mau Mau mistakes • General Erskine's military solution • Forest guerrillas • Final operations • The tally

I F SIR EVELYN BARING, Kenya's new governor, hoped to disrupt the Mau Mau rebellion by forceful action, he was disappointed. Government had waited too long. Two weeks after the declaration of emergency in October 1952, a Mau Mau gang killed a white farmer and two of his African servants. Ugly incidents continued against Europeans and Africans alike. In late November, a Mau Mau gang killed a white retired naval commander and badly cut up his wife; four days later, terrorists in Nairobi murdered a leading African politician, a moderate. Although official reports noted "increasing lawlessness," the government apparently did not respect the implications of these murders: Arrests of Kenyatta and other Mau Mau leaders had not broken the insurgency.

Lacking positive identification of the organization and of its strength and objectives, the government adopted a defensive strategy, farming out its limited number of troops to support local police units. At the same time, it began to expand police forces; Baring also sent for an intelligence expert, Sir Percy Sillitoe, to reorganize the all-important but theretofore neglected police intelligence service, Special Branch. Finally, government began to organize a Kikuyu Home Guard cored by Tribal Police to protect native villages against Mau Mau depredations.

These measures, valid enough, suffered from several disadvantages. The first was the theater of operations, which comprised, in addition to Nairobi,

. . . the whole of the Central Province (which embraces the Kikuyu Reserve) and the three settler Districts of the adjoining Rift Valley Province [where some seventy thousand Kikuyu worked on European farms]: ten Districts in all, about 14,000 square miles or about one-sixteenth of the country.[1]

Two large areas of forests and mountains, the Aberdare Range of some six hundred square miles and the Mount Kenya area of about nine hundred square miles, provided natural sanctuary for Mau Mau guerrilla gangs. Since these forests bordered the African Reserve, they greatly eased the Mau Mau task of agitation and recruitment—much as jungle-based terrorists in Malaya gained sustenance from bordering Chinese villages.[2]

Extent and variety of terrain dictated difficult operations at best. But, at this time, security forces lacked a single commander to provide common plan and purpose. The official responsible for security operations, the Member for Law and Order, was also Attorney General, a latter-day Pooh-Bah who carried out his own orders, much as if the late Mr. J. Edgar Hoover had served simultaneously as Attorney General and chief of the FBI.

The major security instrument was the Kenya Police, a colonial force with mostly white officers. This group included a reserve force, soon mobilized. The Kenya Police Reserve, or KPR, consisted mostly of white settlers who wanted direct action and who were not inclined to respect legal niceties.

Still another security force existed: the Tribal Police, which was made up of Africans who operated under white District Officers and looked after security needs of the DOs and various chiefs and headmen. They were not, technically, police and had no official relationship with the Kenya Police (which helps to explain early intelligence failures).

Troops provided a further complication, in that most Europeans did not speak Swahili and were definitely not at home in a forest environ-

1. Majdalaney, op. cit.; see also P. M. Slane, "Tactical Problems in Kenya," *Army Quarterly,* October 1954.
2. Barnett and Njama, op. cit., offer details on composition and operation of forest gangs.

ment. Fred Majdalaney, in his excellent book *State of Emergency*, described the initial military problem:

. . . The degree of dispersion is indicated by one deployment of the British battalion which entailed a tour of 400 miles if the commanding officer visited each sub-unit of his three companies, and even a company commander traveled seventy miles on a tour of his three platoons. It was in the early stages a war of small sub-units operating very much on their own and improvising methods of cooperating with their police opposite numbers, with the nearest District Officer, with the settlers and police reservists (often the same man) in the European areas and with the chiefs and headmen in the Kikuyu locations. . . . Information was the crying need and when they were lucky enough to receive any that was accurate (a rare occurrence) they sometimes made a kill or a capture. It was a matter of following up reported acts of violence attributable to Mau Mau, and constant patrolling. It was a crime wave rather than a war.[3]

A political complication also existed. The arrest and deportation of Kenyatta and his lieutenants were neither as intelligent nor as effective as people believed at the time. If this action disrupted the movement's leadership, it also removed what might well have proved a restraining hand, and it removed a leader with whom the government in time might have been able to negotiate. In the event, lesser KCA members immediately took over the movement's leadership, and when these were arrested, still lesser members moved in. The ultimate result was a diluted thing called the Council of Freedom, which from Nairobi maintained liaison with district and locational committees. But, at some point, the Nairobi group, or "passive wing," lost control of terrorist gangs in Nairobi and in the forests, thus yielding to fanatical and ignorant leaders whose excesses horrified the civilized world and badly damaged the movement.[4]

Such was early support enjoyed by the movement, and such its organization, that Kenyatta's arrest did not seriously upset operations. Early in 1953, the Mau Mau opened a general offensive against Europeans and loyal Africans. Donald Barnett's and Karari Njama's excellent description of the period February–May 1953 may remind the reader of resistance days in France and other occupied countries in World War II:

. . . As the major patterns of resistance were being established within forest, town and countryside, this dual role was becoming fixed as a way of life for countless thousands of Kikuyu, Embu and Meru peasants, particularly the women, children and men too old to bear arms. At night, or with great care and secrecy during the day, they attended meetings and oathing ceremonies, carried food and material to supply depots near the forest boundary,

3. Majdalaney, op. cit.
4. Corfield, op. cit.

provided refuge and lodging for active fighters or new recruits passing through the village, purchased or stole weapons, ammunition, medical supplies, etc., for the guerrilla units, and performed numerous other tasks in support of the "fight for land and freedom." During the daylight hours, however, these same peasants feigned loyalty to the white man's Government and tried, under steadily mounting pressure and hardships, to carry out the normal tasks and duties of their everyday lives. Many willingly endured this ever dangerous and harsh double-life, filled increasingly with fear, anxiety, suspicion, hunger and brutality, for one, two and, in some cases, even three years. Others, whose existence was no less dangerous or miserable, endeavoured in very pragmatic fashion to play both sides against the middle, seeking to accommodate Government with one hand and the revolutionary forces with the other in a frequently vain effort to safeguard their own lives, loved ones and property. For still others, like Karari [who had taken the Warrior Oath], there was no room in the middle; their situation required that they openly declare, in actions as well as words, either for or against the revolution. Karari, whose recollections reflect the ambivalence inherent in his position, decided to throw in his lot with the revolution, though this decision was ultimately made for him by the flow of events. Others faced with a similar decision, and especially those who had achieved an education equal or superior to Karari's lined up on the Government side.[5]

Terrorist raids on farms to gain food and cattle and terrorist assaults that involved murder or attempted murder generally occurred at night, usually with the co-operation, willing or unwilling, of African servants. Although, in the first two weeks of the new year, the Mau Mau killed two Europeans and thirty-five Africans, other European farmers, including women, successfully beat off attacks, as did units of the expanding Kikuyu Home Guard. The murders nonetheless drove settlers into frenzy and, as undoubtedly planned by the Mau Mau, brought severe repression on Africans in general.

Continued attacks caused the government to make the administering of the Mau Mau oath a capital offense. At this time, security forces

. . . concentrated on breaking or at least neutralizing the popular base of the revolt among the peasant masses in the Kikuyu Reserve. In addition to curfews, movement restrictions, new pass requirements, collective fines and punishment, "cleansing" and counter-Mau Mau oathing campaigns and severe methods of interrogation, Government launched a strong anti-Mau Mau propaganda campaign, raised personal taxes and introduced a "communal" or forced labor scheme whereby damaged roads and bridges could be repaired, guard and police posts erected and new agricultural schemes enforced without cost.[6]

5. Barnett and Njama, op. cit.
6. Ibid.

Drawing on lessons of Malaya, the government declared the Kikuyu Reserve a Special Area, ". . . wherein a person failing to halt when challenged could be shot";[7] the Aberdare and Mount Kenya forests became Prohibited Areas—anyone found in them could be shot on sight. The government cleared some European areas of Kikuyu labor; in other areas, African farm workers voluntarily returned to the Reserve. The government also organized three-man committees—civil, police and military—to run operations at district and province levels. Finally, Baring brought in a senior military adviser, Major General W. R. N. Hinde.

Once again, these measures seemed valid enough, but did not immediately produce desired results. The influx of natives to the Reserve proved particularly unfortunate, since they could not be readily absorbed, which meant that the Mau Mau exploited their subsequent discontent. Raids and attacks continued, culminating, at the end of March, in a two-pronged operation against the native village complex of Lari and the police post at Naivasha. The night attack at Lari, carried out in the most bestial fashion, took eighty-four native lives; terrorists mutilated another thirty-one natives and burned a large number of huts. The Naivasha attack killed one policeman and gained the Mau Mau eighteen automatic weapons and twenty-nine rifles; the attackers also released 173 prisoners.[8] According to Barnett's informant, Karari, ". . . the Naivasha raid marked the rising power of *Mau Mau* and was followed by a flow of thousands of young men entering the Aberdare and Mt. Kenya forests."[9]

Although attacks were reasonably well co-ordinated, they succeeded as much from government errors as from Mau Mau skill. In the long run, they proved a serious mistake, because they tipped the Mau Mau hand and caused a good many *attentiste* Kikuyu to turn to the government, providing information or joining the Home Guard. They also brought Kenya into world focus with sympathy automatically given to the victims, and thus weakened the Mau Mau hand. They inspired Hinde to work out the committee system of operations, to start arming the Kikuyu Guard, and to conscript from the colony's 150,000 Asians, a move theretofore opposed by the white community. Finally, they brought military reinforcement, a brigade, from England and caused the War Office to establish a separate military command for East Africa under General Sir George Erskine.

Erskine did not accept prevailing defensive strategy, but instead sought a military solution. Wanting to eliminate or at least diminish contact between forest gangs and supporters in the Reserve, he cleared a one-mile-wide strip along the hundred miles of forest Reserve, a new Prohibitive Area occupied by police posts that were to create a sort of

7. Ibid.
8. Majdalaney, op. cit.
9. Barnett and Njama, op. cit.

WAR IN THE SHADOWS

cordon sanitaire. Although lacking troops, he managed to form an infantry force to protect the Reserve until the Kikuyu Guard was strong enough for the task. At the same time, he set the RAF to bombing forest areas in hope of trying to keep pressure on the gangs.

Matters remained touch and go for some time. Quite a few Kikuyus in the Reserve sympathized with and aided Mau Mau gangs; loyal natives in general were terrorized into keeping silent. Mau Mau also infiltrated the Home Guard, though probably not to the extent later reported by Karari.[10] Erskine nonetheless managed to establish a viable Home Guard, which subsequently served courageously and well.

Erskine now commenced operations in the forest itself. To carry out the new mission, his troops at first tried massive sweep operations, "grouse drives," which generally failed to catch any quarry. By this time, various terrorist gangs had become at home in the forest. Karari later wrote that various wild animals

. . . became accustomed to our presence and smell and, after a few months in the forest, they treated us as simply another form of animal life and we in turn learnt all their habits and calls. This proved extremely useful to us in detecting the presence or approach of strangers. Security forces entering the home of the animals smelling of soap, cigarettes and laundered clothing were greeted with many danger and warning signals or calls from the animals. . . .[11]

If an operation happened to blunder into a Mau Mau camp, or "hide," the Mau Mau quickly packed up and experienced little difficulty in snaking through "lines" of soldiers struggling awkwardly through heavy forest. Realizing, finally, that the soldiers themselves had to become at home in guerrilla environment, the high command ordered construction of roads leading some five or six miles into the forest. A troop unit moved to each terminal point, set up base, and fanned out patrols.

The forests held a vast number of surprises for troops. The two ranges, Aberdare and Mount Kenya, climbed steadily through belts of woods and bamboo split laterally into ridges and gulleys—cruel territory at best, but, with its strange sounds and hidden dangers, anathema to ordinary troops, no matter how well trained. The vast areas swallowed both Mau Mau gangs and troop units.[12] Erskine called for more and more troops. By late autumn of 1953, forest operations were claiming eleven infantry battalions supported by young officers from Kenya Regiment and by African trackers. A group of young Kenyan pilots flying light aircraft also worked closely with patrols, both in spotting Mau Mau targets and in relaying messages and dropping supply; the RAF

10. Ibid.
11. Ibid.
12. Ibid.: Karari describes in detail the life of his forest gang.

continued to bomb forest areas, using both the Harvard trainer and, later, the Liberator bomber (with generally poor results).[13]

By end of 1953, the government had deployed over ten thousand troops and expanded the police from seven thousand to fifteen thousand plus six thousand part-time auxiliaries. The Home Guard numbered some twenty thousand. Government forces claimed over three thousand Mau Mau killed and over a thousand captured. Security forces had arrested about 150,000 Kikuyu (including Embu and Meru) and brought sixty-four thousand to trial.[14]

Mau Mau gains were not so impressive. The gangs had killed sixteen Europeans and wounded five; eleven Asians, with seventeen wounded; 613 Kikuyu, with 359 wounded. Although killings would continue, the Mau Mau now realized that they had failed to unite the tribe in a general uprising. If gangs remained intact inside forests, communications between gangs and also with supporters in the Reserve and in Nairobi were becoming more difficult. Gang leaders faced increasingly severe morale problems, and leadership quarrels also developed. Dedan Kimathi's "Kenya Defense Council," in the Aberdare forest, operated independently of Mount Kenya, Nairobi, and Reserve organizations, as did his subsequent "Kenya Parliament," whose pretensions to government fell victim to lack of capability and communications.[15]

Early in 1954, the government scored a major victory: the capture of Waruhiu Itote, or General China, the thirty-two-year-old leader of the Mount Kenya gangs—some five thousand Mau Mau who operated independently of the Aberdare gangs. His patient interrogation by a Kenyan police officer, Ian Henderson, not only produced a wealth of intelligence, but Henderson also persuaded China to co-operate in trying to arrange a surrender of the Mount Kenya forces, a laborious process that, thanks to personal courage of Henderson and his assistants as well as a realistic government offer, came within a hair of success. Although, at the last minute, it failed, negotiations did result in surrender or capture of other important Mau Mau leaders, and the intelligence produced also dealt a blow to the support organization in the Reserve.[16]

The situation was still unfavorable from the government's standpoint, however. In January 1954, a parliamentary delegation concluded:

. . . It is our view based upon all the evidence available to us, both from official and responsible unofficial sources, that the influence of Mau Mau in the Kikuyu area, except in certain localities, has not declined; it has,

13. Frank Kitson, *Gangs and Counter-gangs* (London: Barrie & Rockliff, 1960); see also Slane, op. cit.; Barnett and Njama, op. cit.
14. Majdalaney, op. cit.; see also Corfield, op. cit.
15. Barnett and Njama, op. cit.
16. Ian Henderson (with Philip Goodhart), *The Hunt for Kimathi* (London: Hamish Hamilton, 1958); see also Barnett and Njama, op. cit., who suggest lesser results than claimed by security forces.

on the contrary, increased; in this respect the situation has deteriorated and the danger of infection outside the Kikuyu area is now greater, not less, than it was at the beginning of the State of Emergency. . . . In Nairobi, the situation is both grave and acute. Mau Mau orders are carried out in the heart of the city, Mau Mau "courts" sit in judgement and their "sentences" are carried out by gangsters. There is evidence that the revenues collected by gangsters, which may be considerable, are used for the purposes of bribery as well as for purchasing Mau Mau supplies. . . . There is [also] a passive resistance movement amongst Africans, an example of which is a "bus boycott" under which Africans for several months boycotted European-owned buses. . . .[17]

So grave had the situation in Nairobi and adjoining Kiambu District grown that General Erskine had been forced into a different operation: nothing less than wholesale removal of some hundred thousand Africans from the city and surrounding areas for screening purposes, the theory being that the forest gangs could not survive without this support. Operation Anvil began in late April. For several weeks, twenty-five thousand police and soldiers, the latter temporarily transferred from forest operations, screened Nairobi's Africans to send thousands of Mau Mau suspects to specially prepared detention camps.[18] The operation continued through most of May. Although criticized, particularly from liberal sources, as unduly harsh, it accomplished its mission: It broke up the Mau Mau support organization in Nairobi and Kiambu, which never recovered. It also eliminated a great deal of crime within the city, and, further, it yielded valuable intelligence.

Erskine exploited his victory in several ways: He tightened control of the civil population by a more rigorous identity-card system. Follow-up raids, known as "pepper-pots" and conducted by special intelligence teams, kept remaining Mau Mau off balance and continued to provide intelligence. The government also carried out a resettlement scheme that, by end of 1954, had moved about a million natives into villages that could be more easily protected and controlled.[19]

Although Erskine's strategy necessarily interrupted forest operations, a few units continued to press the gangs or at least to impede their contact with the Reserve. By now, some units were becoming quite skillful in forest environment, and new operational techniques also improved efficiency.[20] A young British regular officer named Frank Kitson had already introduced pseudo gangs; that is, small units led by Europeans

17. Barnett and Njama, op. cit.
18. Ibid., which cites 50,000 persons detained, a figure that perhaps included families of the detainees who were sent back to the Reserve; see also Majdalaney, op. cit., who states that the operation screened 30,000 Africans, with just over half sent to detention camps; Kitson, op. cit., states that 10,000 Africans were incarcerated.
19. Majdalaney, op. cit.
20. Slane, op. cit.

and consisting of captured Mau Mau and loyal Kikuyu fitted out to resemble real gangs. Pseudo gangs made contact with real gangs either in the Reserve or in the forest in order to get intelligence or to carry out offensive action against them if circumstances were favorable. Kitson had told his story well in his book *Gangs and Counter-gangs*.[21] As he points out, this is an old technique and variants of it were used in the Philippine insurrection and in Malaya, among other places. The disturbing fact is that a young British officer had to introduce it in Kenya, where it should have been standard operating procedure at once invoked by those responsible for the colony's security.

Erskine also improved his *cordon sanitaire* by building a fifty-mile ditch along eastern and southern borders of Mount Kenya forest:

. . . It was eighteen feet wide and ten feet deep, the most primeval of military obstacles, the fosse. Along its bed bristled thousands of sharpened stakes and these were augmented by miles of barbed wire which had been booby-trapped. At half-mile intervals there were police posts and the half-mile between them was continuously patrolled by night and by day. Massed African labor created this ditch and it proved a highly successful barrier to the barefoot Mau Mau terrorist. . . .[22]

Erskine also enforced a rigorous food-denial policy. Special laws required farmers to lock up cattle after dark and prohibited food crops being planted within three miles of forests.

Despite the success of all these measures, the gangs continued active, stealing or destroying cattle, burning homesteads, murdering natives and even a few Europeans. As soon as he could, Erskine returned to the task of suppressing their activities. In January 1955, the military opened Operation Hammer, a sweep of the Aberdares in approximately division strength. What military commanders fondly thought of as a "combing" operation unfortunately lacked teeth. Operation Hammer brought to earth just over a hundred fifty Mau Mau. This disappointing result produced a more sophisticated tactic known as "domination of areas":

. . . The essence of this was that instead of sweeping the forest, units would be given areas of it to dominate. Every unit and sub-unit would therefore have its own bit of forest to take charge of and get to know intimately so that the enemy would have difficulty in entering it without the fact becoming known.[23]

A two-month effort along these lines in the Mount Kenya forests netted 277 Mau Mau killed, captured, or prisoner, a meager result, consider-

21. *Supra.*
22. Majdalaney, op. cit.; see also Barnett and Njama, op. cit.
23. Majdalaney, op. cit.

ing the investment, which included airdrop of over one hundred thousand pounds of supply.

The key to productive counteroperations remained intelligence, and, increasingly, security forces concentrated on procuring good information. Erskine's successor, General Sir Gerald Lathbury, established a separate police section called Special Forces, which enlarged Kitson's pseudo-gang technique and proved probably the most successful of all methods employed. The Administration developed a related technique of considerable interest, from both psychological and operational standpoints. This involved forest sweeps by largely native lines; in one instance, seventeen thousand natives, mostly women, cleared a large area of forest, the Mau Mau either surrendering or being hacked to pieces. Although the army continued operations in certain parts of the forest, from late 1955 Special Forces increasingly took over the task of tracking down the two thousand terrorists who remained in Aberdare forest under command of Dedan Kimathi. This police action, thrilling in the extreme, demanded infinite patience and is well told in Ian Henderson and Philip Goodhart's book *The Hunt for Kimathi*. The hunt ended in October 1956, when the deranged terrorist was wounded and captured; he was later executed.

Kimathi's capture virtually ended Mau Mau resistance. All told, security forces had killed over eleven thousand Mau Mau (presumed) and captured some twenty-five hundred, at a cost of 167 dead (101 Africans) and over fifteen hundred wounded (1,469 Africans). Civilian casualties, including those of the Kikuyu Guard, totaled almost nineteen hundred dead (1,819 Africans) and almost a thousand wounded (916 Africans). By spring of 1959, the counterinsurgency had cost British and Kenya governments £55 million.[24]

At the height of the emergency, security forces detained seventy-seven thousand Africans. This figure shrank to about two thousand by end of 1958. Meanwhile, the government had held elections ". . . on a qualitative franchise for the eight African seats in the legislature." In the next two years, more Africans were brought into government until they formed a majority in the Legislative Council.

Kenyatta and his lieutenants meanwhile had been removed from jail and held under house arrest. The government freed Kenyatta altogether in 1961. Just over two years later, Kenya became a republic, with Kenyatta its first president.

24. Corfield, op. cit.; see also James Cameron, *The African Revolution* (New York: Random House, 1961).

Chapter 69

The Cyprus rebellion • *Historical background* • *The question of* enosis • *The 1931 rebellion* • *The postwar situation* • *Makarios and Grivas* • *Grivas' estimate of the situation* • *Origin of EOKA* • *Opening attacks* • *Early guerrilla operations* • *Harding's negotiations* • *He deports Makarios* • *His military solution* • *Organization and strength of EOKA* • *British counterguerrilla tactics* • *Grivas' critical analysis of British tactics* • *Attempts at a political solution* • *Fragile peace* • *The cost* • *Analysis of Grivas' tactics*

Britial TROOPS were still fighting guerrillas in Malaya and Kenya when a serious insurgency broke out in Cyprus, the eastern-Mediterranean island that the British had ruled for over seventy-five years and that, in 1954, had become British military headquarters in the Middle East (see map, p. 901).

The Cyprus rebellion had been a long time forming and was neither Communist-inspired nor Communist-directed. All elements of rebellion were present in 1878, when Disraeli, in furthering his Middle East strategy, wrested Cyprus from Turkish control.[1] Nominally Ottoman territory—it lies only forty miles from the Turkish coast—it held two distinct ethnic groups, which differed in race, religion, and language. The Turkish population, 18–20 per cent, accepted British rule amicably, but the Greek portion, 80 per cent, at once expressed desire for *enosis,* or union, with Greece. Whitehall refused, arguing that, under

1. Robert Stephens, *Cyprus—A Place of Arms* (London: Pall Mall Press, 1966).

terms of the Anglo-Turkish Convention, it was governing only by proxy. This argument vanished when Turkey joined the wrong side in 1914; Great Britain annexed the island and, in the following year, offered it to Greece if she would declare war against the Central Powers. Greece refused and Britain retained possession.

Greek Cypriotes argued after the war that Britain, free of treaty entanglements with Turkey, could grant enosis if she wished. Although Prime Minister Lloyd George seemed favorably disposed, ". . . the War Office opposed on strategic grounds any change in the island's status."[2] In 1925, the island became a crown colony, and British officials remained deaf to continued pleas for enosis. In 1931, Greek Cypriotes spontaneously rebelled against British rule.

Captain H. A. Freeman, who, at the time, commanded the British garrison of one infantry company—125 men—later described the chauvinistic temper of Greek Cypriotes and the wave of anti-British feeling during the 1931 financial crisis, when the administration imposed new taxes. In late October 1931, Greek Cypriote leaders met and, ". . . after inflammatory speeches by the Bishop of Kitium and Mr. Lanitis, an ex-member of the Legislative Assembly," decided to enforce a demand for enosis: ". . . This was telegraphed to Nicosia, where the church bells were rung—the usual method of collecting the people. The mob was addressed by its leaders . . . and, after being blessed by the priests, they marched on Government House."[3]

Here they stoned and broke windows and finally set the structure on fire. Police, in turn, opened fire, killing one Cypriote and wounding sixteen. Captain Freeman marched his company to the scene and successfully dispersed the crowd. Whitehall dispatched another company of troops from Egypt (by air!) and, two days later, two cruisers and two destroyers arrived to add to government muscle. The governor also declared Defense Order in Council, similar to martial law ". . . except that the Civil Government remains in control and the Civil Courts continue to function." Within a week, ". . . this badly organized rebellion" was broken:

. . . There were no government casualties but six Cypriots were killed, and over thirty wounded. The bishops of Kition and Kyrenia and eight other Greek Cypriot religious and political leaders were banished for life from the island. Two thousand others were sent to prison and fines amounting to £66,000 were imposed on the Greek Cypriots to pay for the damage. Constitutional government was suspended, the Legislative Council and local councils abolished, political parties banned and the press put under censorship. The governor was empowered to rule by decree. The Colonial Office

2. Ibid.
3. H. A. Freeman, "The Rebellion in Cyprus—1931," *Army Quarterly,* January 1933.

promised to review the constitutional future of the island but no new constitution was put forward until 1948.[4]

World War II somewhat relaxed political tensions on the island. As in 1914, so in 1940, numerous Greek Cypriotes volunteered to fight for the allies. The Anglo-Greek alliance, as opposed to Turkish neutrality and pro-Axis attitude, brought a softening in British attitude, and, in 1941, the administration allowed political parties to form once again. The war also created considerable prosperity for the people. Perhaps more important, Greek Cypriotes reckoned that self-determination of peoples promised by allied declarations would at last result in long-awaited enosis with Greece.

They reckoned without other factors, however. One was continuing antagonism of Turkish Cypriotes to enosis, a feeling strengthened by island Communists, both Turkish and Greek. Another was Greek civil war and cold war in general: Greece was in no position to effectively press either Great Britain or the United States for enosis while depending on them for survival. Once Greece and Turkey, as members of NATO, formed a strategic flank against the Soviet threat, the United States turned a deaf ear to Greek demands, since to respect them would mean a break with Turkey. Finally, loss of Palestine and unsettled conditions surrounding bases in Egypt and Iraq increased the strategic importance of Cyprus to Britain, though scarcely to the degree the War Office believed.

If the cumulative force of these factors prevented Greek Cypriotes from achieving their postwar goal, Mr. Clement Attlee's Labour government nonetheless allowed exiled Cypriote leaders to return to the island and attempted to substitute constitutional reforms for enosis. Had either party faced reality, a working arrangement might have resulted in 1948. But clouds obscured common sense: in the case of Greek Cypriotes, who now numbered some four hundred thousand, a political immaturity and naïveté—the result largely of British refusal to encourage indigenous political growth from 1931 onward—that prevented them from grasping opportunities inherent in the proposed constitution; in the case of the British, failure of the Labour government and particularly of Mr. Ernest Bevin and his advisers to respect the depth of Greek Cypriote feeling regarding this issue. Once negotiations lapsed, the gulf widened; in 1950, a plebiscite showed 96 per cent of Greek Cypriotes in favor of enosis. The plebiscite was allegedly inspired by the young and determined bishop of Kition, who, at thirty-seven years, became the new archbishop of Cyprus, Makarios III.[5]

New negotiations might now have commenced but for factors pre-

4. Stephens, op. cit.
5. Ibid.; see also Charles Foley, *Island in Revolt* (London: Longmans, Green, 1962); Doros Alastos, *Cyprus Guerrilla—Grivas, Makarios and the British* (London: William Heinemann, 1960).

viously mentioned and for the introduction of a new and in some ways
sinister character in the Cyprus drama: George Grivas. At fifty-three
years of age, Grivas was a good-looking man, short and broadly built,
". . . with a strong, unsmiling face and deep-set eyes under fierce brows;
his thin mouth . . . topped by a dark moustache."[6] A Cypriote born
and raised, son of a prosperous grocer, Grivas graduated from the
Athens Military Academy to become a professional officer in the Greek
army, where colleagues found him dour and determined, a Spartan
". . . tireless and demanding, a martinet who required no less of himself
than he did of the soldiers under him. . . ."[7] We earlier encountered
him briefly in the Greek civil war (see Chapter 57), when, as a colonel,
he commanded the irregular *Khi,* or X, organization, an extreme-rightist
movement dedicated to killing as many Communists as possible—an
experience that left Grivas impressed with the effectiveness of Communist subversive warfare in accomplishing limited goals. Retired because of extreme political views, he studied Communist methods of
warfare with the same intensity bestowed on his stamp collection; he
also ran for parliament on a promonarchist platform and was defeated.[8]
Adrift in the political caldron of Athenian politics, he brushed against
Greek nationalists and Cypriote exiles, finally to join the stew of enosis:
In 1951, the small but determined group decided that Grivas ". . .
should undertake the leadership of an armed struggle to throw the British out of Cyprus."[9]

Grivas has described the ensuing struggle in two books, *The Memoirs
of General Grivas* and the rather more technical but no less Zarathus-
trian work *General Grivas on Guerrilla Warfare.*[10] Grivas does not
emerge as a particularly attractive man in these works, but, rather, as a
man with a mission, a man who faced up to means at hand which he
used with great effect for a particular end.

His task was extremely difficult. He knew and respected the British
and had every reason to believe that they would fight and fight hard
to retain sovereignty over Cyprus. A conventional campaign was thus
hopeless, but so was a guerrilla campaign: Only the western, mountainous half of the relatively small island (some hundred forty miles long
and sixty miles wide) offered natural sanctuary, but good roads meant
rapid troop movement; a Royal Navy blockade would mean difficulty
in receiving arms and supply; only a relatively few Greek Cypriotes had

6. Foley, op. cit.; see also Dudley Barker, *Grivas—Portrait of a Terrorist* (London: Cresset Press, 1959); W. Byford-Jones, *Grivas and the Story of EOKA* (London: Robert Hale, 1959).
7. Charles W. Thayer, *Guerrilla* (New York: Harper & Row, 1965).
8. Stephens, op. cit.; Barker, op. cit.
9. George Grivas, *The Memoirs of General Grivas* (New York: Frederick A.
Praeger, 1964). Ed. Charles Foley. Hereafter cited as Grivas (*Memoirs*).
10. Ibid.; George Grivas, *General Grivas on Guerrilla Warfare* (New York:
Frederick A. Praeger, 1965). Tr. A. S. Pallis. Hereafter cited as Grivas (*Guerrilla*).

had military training, and most were skeptical about his plan, Archbishop Makarios himself seeming ". . . reserved and sceptical." These adverse conditions meant that ". . . the main weight of the campaign will be placed on sabotage," designed ". . . to draw the attention of international public opinion, especially among the allies of Greece, to the Cyprus question."[11] Essential to the plan was co-operation of the Greek Cypriote population, particularly its passive resistance to British rule and countermeasures. Grivas rightly guessed that he could exploit the general desire for enosis into support necessary for his operational plans.

Meager resources compelled him to spend the next three years in Athens collecting arms and smuggling them into Cyprus, where volunteers, recruited from two Christian Youth movements during his second visit, received and hid them. Progress remained slow: The new Prime Minister of Greece, Marshal Papagos, would not support the movement. Archbishop Makarios feared reprisal effects of violence and ran hot and cold on Grivas' preparations. By late 1954, when Grivas landed secretly on Cyprus, only one arms shipment, with a total value of £600, awaited him. Actual shooting stock amounted to seven revolvers, forty-seven rifles of assorted calibers and manufacture, and ten automatic weapons.[12]

Known now as Dighenis—a mythological Byzantine warrior-hero—Grivas began training saboteurs while organizing small guerrilla groups, distributing and hiding weapons and explosives and establishing intelligence and courier services. Leaning heavily on youthful volunteers, he organized sabotage groups of five or six persons and selected targets in principal cities. His was the qualitative approach: He selected only the most suitable men, each of whom swore to obey his orders while preserving utmost secrecy.[13]

Thus the origin of *Ethniki Organosis Kyprion Agoniston* (National Organization of Cypriot Fighters) or EOKA; at the start of the rebellion, April 1955, it numbered fewer than a hundred activists. The majority of the Greek Cypriote population, however, sympathized in whole or in part with its professed aims.

EOKA's greatest ally was the British Government. Continuing to misread the depth of Greek Cypriote feeling, the British military, in spring of 1954, moved Middle East land and air headquarters from Suez to the island. Throughout summer and autumn, various official spokesmen left no doubt that Britain would retain sovereignty over Cyprus, which, so the argument ran, was needed ". . . to fulfil her treaty obligations to the Arab states, NATO, Greece, Turkey and the United

11. Grivas (*Guerrilla*), *supra;* see also Lawrence Durrell, *Bitter Lemons* (London: Faber & Faber, 1959), for a good picture of island life before the rebellion.
12. Grivas (*Memoirs*), *supra.*
13. Alastos, op. cit., gives the oath; see also Barker, op. cit.; Durrell, op. cit.

Nations."[14] Greek willingness to guarantee her old ally military bases
on Cyprus was brushed aside, as was a Greek appeal to the UN to debate the case for the island's self-determination.[15] Having been forced
to leave Palestine and Egypt, the British were in no mood for compromise: In September 1953, a convalescent Anthony Eden allegedly had
told Marshal Papagos: ". . . For Her Majesty's Government there is
not and there cannot be a Cypriot problem which has to be discussed
with the Greek Government";[16] in July 1954, the Minister of State for
the Colonies told the House of Commons that Cyprus could "never"
hope to become an independent state.

Such sentiments further charged island air. The colonial government
was not popular, to start with. British intransigence now eliminated the
moderating force of Archbishop Makarios on Cyprus and Marshal
Papagos in Athens and brought them into Grivas' camp. It also helped
Grivas to arrange a series of demonstrations, strikes, and riots that effectively screened his own clandestine preparations. The opening of
the rebellion by EOKA attacks on government, police, and military
installations, early on April 1, 1955, caught the government completely
by surprise. Confused intelligence agents studied inflammatory leaflets
distributed by the thousands and frowned: What was EOKA? Who (or
what) was DIGHENIS?

Grivas continued the attacks for a few days. He then switched to
demonstrations, mostly by young students. In June, he opened a prolonged series of attacks that killed one policeman and wounded sixteen
others, besides causing considerable property damage and agitation
among the British population. Although disappointed in material results, Grivas exulted in international publicity (engendered in large
part by Radio Athens, which would continue to report the campaign to
the world); Grivas reasoned that this would force the UN to reverse its
earlier decision and debate the Cyprus question. He now moved to the
mountains to organize guerrilla groups prior to opening a new series of
attacks, intended ". . . to terrorize the police and to paralyze the administration, both in the towns and the countryside." His plan would
have won approval of Irish Republican Army leaders thirty-five years
earlier or Irgun-Sternist leaders in Palestine ten years earlier. By such
means,

. . . the army would be drawn deeper into the terrain of my choosing and
their strength dissipated; at present they were concentrating on guarding government buildings and on riot duty. My town groups would execute police
who were too zealous on the British behalf, while my countryside groups
would attack police stations, kill isolated policemen and ambush police patrols, which were already being stiffened by soldiers.[17]

14. Stephens, op. cit.
15. Ibid.
16. Alastos, op. cit.; Eden did not mention the meeting in his memoirs.
17. Grivas, op. cit.

UN refusal to reopen the Cyprus question, in September, brought a new spurt of EOKA activity. While guerrillas began striking primarily military targets in the countryside, selective terror tactics in cities and towns resulted in more police deaths, which, according to Grivas, soon ". . . shattered opposition to EOKA among the Greek police."

These tactics succeeded in part because the hostile population refused to co-operate with police and army. Grivas constantly exploited what often was only incipient hostility. He showered the population with leaflets and pamphlets, a propaganda campaign augmented by the technique of the Voice—megaphoned instructions to a village in the dead of night. While EOKA did not hesitate to kill informers and traitors, its members treated the people with great circumspection—for example, always paying for food or goods and maintaining strict sexual morality.[18]

The tactics succeeded for another good reason: police inefficiency. Charles Foley, a distinguished British newspaperman and publisher of the *Times of Cyprus* during the emergency, later wrote:

. . . Mr. Robins, the Police Commissioner, was soon at his wits' end to stop Greek resignations from the Force: it was obvious that "disloyal" elements at his H.Q. were reporting over-zealous colleagues to EOKA. He revealed no secret in saying, in a poignant moment, that things were virtually out of his control. Coming from Tanganyika a few months before, he had been asked to turn a weak peace-time force, used to trailing after pickpockets and erring motorists, into a body capable of dealing with armed terrorism. Negligence, meanness, stagnation over the years had sapped the spirit of his men long before EOKA appeared.[19]

Against this background of mounting terror, the British compounded an already confused situation by calling Greece and Turkey to a London conference—thus introducing Turkey into the Cyprus discussions. To ". . . avoid shaking hands with murder," the indignant government did *not* invite Cypriote representatives to hear Foreign Secretary Harold Macmillan present still another constitutional scheme: While offering Cyprus limited self-government, Macmillan refused to abandon or even question the right of British sovereignty. Before the Greeks could reject what, to them, was an unworkable plan, widespread anti-Greek riots in Izmir and Istanbul wrecked the conference.

Matters meanwhile were worsening on Cyprus, where EOKA, despite operational flaws, clearly held the initiative. In October, a distinguished soldier, Field Marshal Sir John Harding, arrived as the new governor, empowered both to negotiate with Makarios and, with help of substantial military reinforcements, to quell EOKA.[20]

18. Alastos, op. cit.
19. Foley, op. cit.
20. Stephens, op. cit.; see also Durrell, op. cit., who served as press adviser to the government during the early years of the emergency.

Negotiations with Makarios made some progress over the next few months: Harding yielded on the important question of self-determination—but in the unspecified future. He also dangled a £38-million development scheme before the people, a futile gesture in view of continued British political intransigence. The talks also suffered from disruptive forces already discussed, as well as from concomitant forces: from continuing EOKA successes, which placed uncomfortable pressure on Makarios to refrain from yielding on enosis, pressure increased by civil hostility engendered by British countermeasures; from a new administration in Athens, the Karamanlis government, which did not feel strong enough to intervene forcefully; from Prime Minister Anthony Eden's mistrust of Makarios; from the deteriorating position in Jordan, which, in British minds, increased further the strategic value of Cyprus.

In late February 1956, the British broke off the talks. A few days later, security agents intercepted Makarios on his way to Athens and, shades of 1931, deported him to the Seychelles Islands—thus leaving the field open to Grivas. Since Grivas was not willing to reveal himself, this, in effect, eliminated further negotiations. As Charles Foley later noted: ". . . Harding, by signing the deportation orders, had cut himself off from four-fifths of the population. No Greek Cypriot would enter Government House."[21]

Field Marshal Harding now removed the velvet glove to seek a military solution. At this time, his security forces amounted to some five thousand police and about twenty thousand troops with another five thousand scheduled to arrive. British intelligence did not know it, but Grivas commanded 273 "regulars," who shared about a hundred weapons and who were augmented by some 750 villagers armed with shotguns (from which he formed OKT, or ambush units)—a hard core that the Greek Cypriote population increasingly supported, though sometimes with sorrow and misgiving. By this time, Grivas had divided the island into sectors, which, at his order, undertook specific tasks and enjoyed support of two main groups, ANE, a youth organization, and PEKA, a covert civil organization. Although his later claim that ". . . every Greek Cypriot, from the smallest child to old men and women, belonged to our army . . ." was exaggerated, there is no doubt that he had fashioned an effective organization in a remarkably short time and with remarkably few materials at his disposal.[22]

Harding and his advisers apparently did not have a clue concerning the depth of EOKA. Convinced that he was up against a few terrorists who enjoyed the support of no more than 5 per cent of the popula-

21. Foley, op. cit.
22. Grivas (*Guerrilla*), op. cit.: Mines, for example, were made from stolen dynamite or explosive from old shells dumped off shore by the British at the end of World War II.

tion,[23] the field marshal "attacked" in two directions, a quantitative approach designed to eliminate terrorist attacks in the cities and guerrilla activity in the mountains. Continued EOKA raids already had caused him to proclaim a State of Emergency, and, following what Foley termed the Templer Bible of Malaya, to invoke stringent regulations governing the civil population. Anyone carrying firearms was subject to a death sentence; persons could be detained or banished without trial. Rewards were offered for information on terrorist activities; Dighenis carried a £10,000 price on his head. As extra measure, Harding proscribed the local Communist Party, AKEL, and locked up 129 of its members—a strange move, since the party *opposed* the rebellion.[24] Other measures involved not only such collective punishments as regional curfews and large community fines, but indiscriminate and often insulting search methods—a sort of military charging into the fog of a civil population soon turned very hostile.[25] Grivas later wrote:

. . . The "security forces" set about their work in a manner which might have been deliberately designed to drive the population into our arms. On the pretext of searching they burst into people's homes by day and night, made them stand for hours with their hands up, abused and insulted them. Soldiers would empty sacks of grain on the floor of a farmhouse and pour oil, wine or paraffin over it [sic], thus ruining enough food to keep a family for a year; or they would stop a lorry taking produce to market and tip the whole load of fruit and vegetables out on to the road. Anyone who protested had scant hope of getting justice.[26]

Whipping schoolboys and prolonged detention of hundreds of suspects continued to infuriate Greek Cypriotes. In spring of 1956, Harding executed two terrorists, which further antagonized the people (and caused Grivas to execute two captured British soldiers). Grivas, himself, was now on the run. A British patrol almost captured him in May—on May 25, he noted in his diary: ". . . This day is the worst of the struggle for me." In early June, he fled from another patrol in such haste that he left behind personal gear including his diary.[27]

Although the rebel leader remained free, British hopes for his capture or surrender soared. In autumn, Harding replied to a cease-fire called by Grivas with an insulting ultimatum to surrender. Grivas answered by renewing his campaign.

23. Foley, op. cit.: On one occasion Harding told him, ". . . Not five percent of Greek Cypriots are behind this evil organization. Not five percent!"
24. Alastos, op. cit.
25. Foley, op. cit.; Alastos, op. cit.
26. Grivas (*Memoirs*), *supra*.
27. Barker, op. cit.

Harding already had sent sizable task forces into the mountains to break up guerrilla bands, operations later criticized by Grivas:

. . . I had expected that a Field-Marshal would come out with a flexible military plan; if he did, it was hard to discern what it consisted of. Twice from my hiding place in the mountains I watched forces of up to 1,000 troops looking for me, with helicopters flying overhead. I did not even trouble to move off as they approached, so aimless was their search. Officers, remaining on the road, shouted orders as if on an exercise. In Limassol later the strong patrols which so often passed our house went by as though on a route march. This, then, was the "spider's web" which Harding said he was weaving for us.[28]

Harding tried to repair tactical poverty by a number of devices. One was tracking-dogs, which terrorists sabotaged by liberal use of pepper. Another was "Q patrols"—". . . small mobile units of strong-arm men from the Special Branch [police intelligence], both British and Turkish, which relied on Greek traitors and informers for their leads into the organization."[29] The patrols enjoyed only limited success, due to EOKA's excellent intelligence and courier system. A later tactic, of counterambushes, produced far better results, but to Grivas' relief the British failed to expand the technique.[30] Still later, the British began using helicopters, ". . . mostly for carrying out reconnaissance against guerrilla bands in the mountains and over inhabited areas where operations were proceeding."[31] Again to Grivas' relief, the British did not use them to exploit certain tactical situations. (In his later work, *Guerrilla Warfare,* Grivas stressed the importance of the helicopter to future guerrilla campaigns, and noted, in passing, ". . . its vulnerability because of its low speed and its proximity to the ground.")

Some of Harding's subordinates employed more-radical measures. According to Charles Foley and other observers, British intelligence officers used torture while interrogating captured terrorists. Security forces also seem to have frequently employed indiscriminate detentions. The hostile civil climate, without question, adversely affected some conscript or National Service soldiers, who mistreated not only "suspects" but ordinary citizens—stupid behavior that could only benefit the EOKA.

After early failure, British military tactics grew more sophisticated, but even the most carefully planned and executed operations left escape gaps for the guerrillas, although, on occasion, some were captured

28. Grivas (*Memoirs*), *supra;* see also Kenneth Diacre, "Cyprus, 1956," *Army Quarterly,* April 1956, who describes a raid on a mountain village.
29. Ibid.
30. Grivas (*Guerrilla*), *supra.*
31. Ibid.

or killed and, in time, whole groups were neutralized. Grivas himself remained unimpressed with general British military performance:

. . . The officers lacked initiative and judgement and the other ranks lacked training, dash and personal courage. This is a harsh verdict, and I think that this seeming indifference to duty, so unlike what I knew of the British Army, was due in part to the fact that many of them felt that they were fighting for an unjust cause; this view is supported by the fact that frequent instances of military disobedience occurred, and sometimes developed into mutinies.[32]

Nor did Harding's performance particularly impress the guerrilla leader. Although British operations became more co-ordinated in 1957, they never grew subtle, at least in Grivas' mind:

. . . Harding disliked changing a decision, once he had made it; if the results were not all he expected he would go on just the same, thus opening the way to a series of mistakes. His soldierly bluntness, which put the whole country against him, was also a valuable index to me of his military intentions. In speeches and broadcasts, and through newspaper interviews which he gave so prodigally, I was kept in constant touch with the way in which his mind was working. No less lavish were his assurances of early victory: did he believe them himself? It seemed that he did, and thus fell into what Napoleon called the biggest mistake a General could make: to paint an imaginary picture and believe it to be true.[33]

Grivas later placed his finger on Harding's real failure:

. . . he underrated his enemy on the one hand, and overweighed his forces on the other. But one does not use a tank to catch field-mice—a cat will do the job better. The Field-Marshal's only hope of finding us was to play cat and mouse: to use tiny, expertly trained groups, who could work with cunning and patience and strike rapidly when we least expected.[34]

Instead,

. . . the British flooded Cyprus with troops, so that one met a soldier at every step, with the only result that they offered plenty of targets and so sustained casualties. They completely ignored the principle of "saturation" of the terrain. In accordance with this principle, each separate kind of terrain has a limit to its capacity of absorption of means without risk. Beyond this limit, any increase in forces not only does not yield better results but, on

32. Grivas (*Memoirs*), *supra;* see also Foley, op. cit.
33. Grivas (*Memoirs*), *supra.*
34. Ibid.; see also Grivas (*Guerrilla*), *supra:* ". . . In various studies and handbooks on guerrilla warfare, mention is made of 'fast-moving, mobile units' etc. for use in operations against guerrillas, whereas in my opinion what is needed is a special organization of specialized forces corresponding to the general and special conditions of the struggle."

the contrary, increases casualties and complicates movements to the extent of placing the operation itself in jeopardy.[35]

Lacking "a special organization of specialized forces" to fight the terrorists, Harding perforce depended on quantitative tactics. The abortive Suez Canal operation, at the end of October, greatly facilitated Grivas' campaign by drawing off a large number of troops.[36] EOKA carried out 416 attacks in November alone[37]—"Black November" to embarrassed British authorities, who replied with even more stringent regulations, including the threat of a death sentence for a variety of offenses. The conflict now widened into fighting between Greek Cypriotes and Turkish Cypriotes, the latter recruited in considerable quantity by the British for the police force. When EOKA agents killed Turkish policemen, the Turks formed an underground terrorist organization, Volkan, for reprisal purposes.

In December, the British flew in a peace dove in form of the Radcliffe Constitution, which, although suggesting a division in low-level rule between Greeks and Turks, changed little at the top: ". . . Cyprus must remain under British sovereignty; . . . Britain must have the use of the island as a military base; . . . external affairs, defense and internal security were to remain in British hands."[38] The Greek Government rejected the proposals ". . . even before the Cypriots had seen them," and Makarios, a prisoner in the Seychelles, refused to discuss them until he was released.[39]

The rebellion continued in cruel intensity into 1957, with each side recording major gains and losses. The first real breakthrough came in March 1957: A renewed British military effort had cost Grivas the loss of over sixty hard-core fighters since the turn of the year; although plenty of fight remained in EOKA, Grivas now offered another ceasefire in return for Makarios' release.[40] The Suez fiasco had cost Anthony Eden his job, and his replacement, Harold Macmillan, urged on by President Eisenhower, agreed to the archbishop's release but refused to allow his return to Cyprus.

The turn of events nonetheless brought a welcome lull in fighting, which Britain followed with two additional moves, one secret and one not. The former consisted of a strategic reappraisal, the first step in abandoning the theretofore sacrosanct demand for continued British sovereignty over all of Cyprus. The Macmillan government next replaced Harding with Sir Hugh Foot, a ". . . colonial civil servant with

35. Grivas (*Guerrilla*), *supra.*
36. Barker, op. cit., suggests that Grivas was about finished at this point, a conclusion official in origin, and rather ludicrous in view of "Black November."
37. Stephens, op. cit.
38. Ibid.
39. Ibid.
40. Barker, op. cit., writes that "EOKA was virtually crushed" at this point—again, wishful thinking in view of subsequent events.

a liberal reputation."[41] The Greek Government, in turn, began to yield on the question of enosis—perhaps, her leaders reasoned, independence would be sufficient for the time being. The UN also came around to supporting, albeit mildly, the right of Cypriote self-determination. The Menderes government, in Turkey, continued to hold for partition.

A good bit of blood would spill before these discordant goals merged into a working plan. Grivas' cease-fire, fragile at best, gave way to renewed fighting in late 1957. Throughout 1958, pressures internal and external continued to influence involved parties. In March, Grivas added to guerrilla-terrorist tactics by launching a Gandhi-like campaign of "passive resistance," which included an island-wide boycott of all British goods. By year's end, British security forces seemed no closer to "winning" the war than they had three years earlier.

But if EOKA resistance had once gained considerable international sympathy, it was beginning to lose it, as the rift between Turkey and Greece widened to NATO's disadvantage and as danger of total civil war developed in Cyprus.

The home front was also feeling the pinch: ". . . Although the EOKA campaign could have been kept up for a long time, the economic repercussions of the boycott and the British counter-measures—curfews, mass detentions, dismissal of workers from military establishments— were beginning to be felt by the Greek Cypriot population."[42] The British were no happier: The boycott proved effective and thus expensive, and so was support of twenty-eight thousand troops (about one to every twenty civilians) plus greatly expanded police forces, all to control a few hundred terrorists; a civil war would prove even more costly and would produce severe international repercussions. Resumption of emergency measures, including wholesale round-up and detention of Greek Cypriotes, was bringing unfavorable international publicity without seeming to influence the military situation favorably.

The Macmillan government now decided that the whole of Cyprus was not a "strategic necessity" but, rather, a "strategic convenience," not worth the foreseeable cost of retention. Instead, Britain could yield sovereignty in return for base rights (which the Greek Government had suggested four years earlier), a decision aided by the fall of the Iraqi Government and that country's withdrawal from the Baghdad Pact. Turkey also indicated a new willingness to negotiate—the result of international pressure by countries, mainly the United States, on whom she depended for economic and military aid.

The effect of these shifting pressures enabled Britain to bring the Greek and the Turkish governments into direct negotiations toward end of 1958. Makarios recognized the changing situation and approved. With the political rug pulled from under him, Grivas, in early 1959,

41. Stephens, op. cit.
42. Ibid.

announced a final cease-fire. Conferences in Zurich and London followed, and Cyprus eventually emerged as a republic with its own constitution and a complicated series of treaties meant to protect British, Greek, and Turkish interests.

Though opposed to the settlement, Grivas disbanded EOKA and left the island. In Athens, he enjoyed a hero's welcome, including promotion to lieutenant general and a life pension[43]—exaggerated tribute, perhaps, considering the muddled fate that awaited Greek Cypriotes, a fate influenced in part by his subsequent mysterious and at times sinister machinations. Grivas had not gained his intended goal of enosis, nor had he forced the British from Cyprus. All things considered, however, he could claim the upper hand in this war that had taken five to six hundred lives, wounded over twelve hundred persons, and cost the British Government an estimated £90 million.[44] Starting from scratch, for four years he not only had fought a greatly superior force to a draw at an estimated financial cost of about £50,000,[45] but, at the end, he was prepared to carry on the battle, as witness the imposing amount of arms and ammunition finally surrendered by EOKA fighters at Grivas' orders.[46]

Most Western observers found it difficult to award more than grudging admiration to Grivas' employment of Byzantine tactics, and many of them spoke in terms of moral abhorrence. Such judgments seem to this writer to lack balance, in that they fail to weigh British culpability in the emergency; first by a myopic prewar policy; second by failing to adopt a mature and rational, as opposed to primarily an emotional, attitude concerning the future government of Cyprus; third by deporting Makarios and thus creating a political vacuum; and fourth by inviting the disputatious and disreputable Menderes government to debate the question and thus inflame already heated island passions. These and other actions were predicated on the assumption that force would rule. They thus invited counterforce (the potential of which the British Government failed to respect) and opened the way for a Grivas, unhappily an astute military professional able to adapt tactical thinking to the tactical problem.

Grivas was not deaf to cries of outrage from Western voices or from objections by Makarios and Papagos, or to distaste of island moderates. Rather, like Marion and his North Carolinians in the American revolution, like Lenin and his fellows before and during the Russian revolution, like Michael Collins and the IRA during the Irish revolution, and like Menachem Begin in Palestine, he was contemptuous. In defending

43. Ibid.
44. Foley, op. cit.; see also Barker, op. cit.
45. Barker, op. cit.
46. Foley, op. cit.

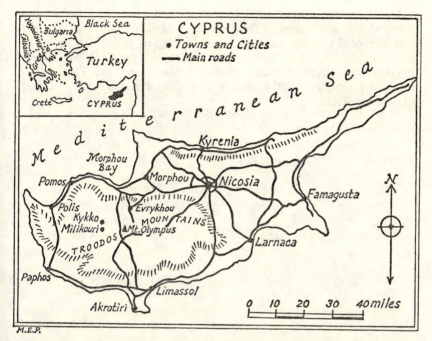

CYPRUS
• Towns and Cities
— Main roads

his techniques, he later wrote words that, despite translation, carry a Lawrentian ring:

. . . The British, who arm their commandoes with knives and instruct them to kill in just this way—from the rear—protested vociferously when such tactics were applied to themselves. It may be argued that these things are only permissible in war. This is nonsense. I was fighting a war in Cyprus against the British, and if they did not recognize the fact from the start they were forced to at the end. The truth is that our form of war, in which a few hundred fell in four years, was far more selective than most, and I speak as one who has seen battlefields covered with dead. We did not strike, like the bomber, at random. We shot only British servicemen who would have killed us if they could have fired first, and civilians who were traitors or intelligence agents. To shoot down your enemies in the street may be unprecedented, but I was looking for results, not precedents. . . . All war is cruel and the only way to win against superior forces is by ruse and trickery; you can no more afford to make a difference between striking in front or from behind than you can between employing rifles and howitzers. The British may criticize me as much as they like for making war in Cyprus, but I was not obliged to ask their permission to do so; nor can they now deny that I made it in the most successful way. For my part, I always drew the line at unnecessary cruelty.[47]

47. Grivas (*Memoirs*), *supra*.

Unfortunately, Grivas' ruthless methods and generally extremist political views badly damaged the people he allegedly wanted to help. His war disrupted Cypriote life to an alarming degree, and it also served to turn Greek Cypriotes against each other. In his fanatical single-mindedness, Grivas underestimated and exacerbated the Turkish nationalist factor, and left a volatile and divided island with civil war almost inevitable.

Chapter 70

The Algerian crisis • Historical background • The French conquest • French colonial policy • Growth of nationalism • The 1945 riots • Ahmed Ben Bella and the OS • Belkacem Krim's guerrillas • The internal situation • FLN emerges • Outbreak of rebellion • Soustelle's pacification strategy • Origin of SAS • French military and political errors • La guerre révolutionnaire

THE INK HAD SCARCELY DRIED on the Geneva Agreements, which extricated France from Indochina, when the Mendès-France government faced another major crisis, in Algeria (see map, p. 915). As in Indochina, trouble in this principal North African colony as well as in Tunisia and Morocco had been brewing for a long time.

The Maghreb otherwise resembled Indochina. Algeria was an older holding, the occupation having begun in 1830 (see Chapter 11, Volume I), but Tunisia did not become a protectorate until 1881 and Morocco only in 1912. Algeria occupied a colonial status similar to Cochin China, or southern Vietnam; Tunisia and Morocco retained their monarchs and something of their local administration, as did the other French Indochina kingdoms. Tunisia and Morocco claimed more-cohesive cultures than the semi-nomadic Algerians, but some Algerian tribes traced from antiquity, and all were proud: The French did not subjugate them until 1857, and active resistance continued until 1881. Tunisia submitted more readily to French rule; the pacification of Morocco continued until 1934 (see Chapter 28, Volume I).

In theory, French colonial policy in North Africa called for assimilation—a civilizing mission to convert Arab-Berber peoples into good and loyal Frenchmen. In practice, Paris allowed European colonizers to develop the countries on a double-standard basis, their local powers steadily increased by continuing dissension in the French Government. While the Moslems enjoyed certain benefits brought by the newcomers, most notably in health, trade, and administration, reactionary colonial governments dominated by *colons* soon brought conditions matching those in Indochina (see Chapter 42, Volume I): extensive land ownership by Europeans and a local Moslem elite who controlled the economic and financial structure while the bulk of the people were landless and hungry, a vast illiterate body suffering a pastoral-agricultural economy with distinct feudal overtones.[1]

With one result: although each North African country was said to be pacified, the French never ruled comfortably, and force was never far removed from government. An Arab Bureau with a strong military arm put down early, spasmodic resistance without much trouble, though often with considerable brutality. But the multiplying germs of nationalism that ultimately infected Indochina and the Far East also settled in North Africa and the Middle East.

The germs attacked variously. In Tunisia, a nationalist political party, the Neo-Destour, emerged in the early 1930s under Habib Bourguiba and, despite a host of vicissitudes, continued to grow and, finally, in 1956, to win a relatively peaceful battle for independence. Morocco reacted more slowly: In the 1940s, nationalists strongly influenced by Cairo nationalists founded *Istiq-lal,* which won the backing of Sultan Mohammed V and, as in the case of the Neo-Destour, overcame multiple obstacles to wage a successful campaign for independence, again a relatively peaceful transition, occurring in 1956.[2] The process in both cases involved considerable guerrilla-terrorist activity, but, like international liberal pressures, this proved contributory rather than fundamental. Both countries owed an immense debt first to the Indochinese insurgency, which drained France of so much of her strength, including troops from North Africa, and second to the Algerian rebellion, which began in late 1954.

Algeria was a late-comer to the Arab nationlist movement, primarily because of her special relationship with France. Unlike other colonies, Algeria constituted part of metropolitan France. Europeans had begun settling in coastal areas soon after Bugeaud had put down initial re-

1. Joan Gillespie, *Algeria—Rebellion and Revolution* (London: Ernest Benn, 1960); Edward Behr, *The Algerian Problem* (London: Hodder & Stoughton, 1961).
2. Stéphane Bernard, *The Franco-Morocco Conflict 1943–56* (New Haven: Yale University Press, 1968).

sistance, and in time grew to a heterogeneous colony of over a million Frenchmen, Italians, Spaniards, and Corsicans.

French culture affected Algeria more than Tunisia or Morocco; educated Algerian Moslems often regarded themselves as French rather than Algerian. Probably for this reason, no forceful leader such as Habib Bourguiba emerged from the educated classes during the fateful thirties and forties, nor did a monarchical symbol exist as a nationalist rallying point.

Despite wishful thinking of European Algerians who denied Moslems a national tradition, a latent nationalism existed: It stemmed from centuries before the birth of Christ, and it survived and gained from centuries of occupation by Phoenicians, Romans, Vandals, Byzantines, Arabs, Turks, and modern Europeans.[3] It began to emerge after World War I, but it was always factious, and intense internal rivalry made it easier to neutralize, if not suppress, from without.

Nationalist murmurings before World War I found voice shortly after the war, when Ferhat Abbas, representing a group of French-educated Moslems and former Moslem officers in the French army, unsuccessfully demanded social and political reforms. Returning Algerian soldiers—about one hundred thousand had served in France—and Algerian workers showed more interest in economic reforms, which, together with a demand for independence, became the rallying cry of the ENA (*Étoile Nord-Africaine*) movement, soon led by Messali Hadj, a Communist who subsequently left the party and, influenced by Chekib Arslan, became strongly pro-Islamic.[4] A small Communist Party also emerged, but was banned in 1929. In the mid-thirties, a religious movement called the Association of Ulemas (religious teachers) added to the cry for reforms and independence. Though alarmed, the administration and the powerful European community turned a deaf ear to all these voices. Shortly after the war, they had neutralized Clemenceau's effort to introduce parity in the French-Moslem relationship, and the next twenty years saw no change in their attitude.

In World War II, the European colony accepted Vichy rule and, in turn, gained a free hand to ban various nationalist movements and imprison such leaders as Messali.[5] Ferhat Abbas and other prominent Moslems nonetheless survived to present the Free French Government with an Algerian Manifesto—a demand for self-determination and specific rural reforms in return for Moslem participation in World War II.[6] While promising nothing specific, De Gaulle seemed sympathetic and, once again, Moslems fought on the side of France. Ferhat Abbas and his intellectual following, now supporting a party called the AML (*Amis du Manifeste et de la Liberté*), continued to press for reforms

3. Gillespie, op. cit.
4. Ibid.
5. SORO, op. cit.
6. Behr, op. cit.; see also Gillespie, op. cit.

within the system. The ENA, however, which had become the PPA (*Parti du Peuple Algérien*) ". . . advocated direct action in the country-side as the only way of achieving improvements."[7] On V-E Day, May 8, 1945, the PPA instigated Moslem riots that led to the death of perhaps a hundred Europeans in Algeria.[8] European "militia" forces, supported by police and army units, attacked Moslem settlements throughout Algeria; French authorities admitted fifteen hundred Moslem deaths, but more-realistic estimates varied from twenty thousand, reported by *Time* magazine, to forty-five thousand, claimed by Algerian nationalists.[9]

The slaughter quieted matters—temporarily. Under Governor General Chataigneau's rather liberal aegis, Ferhat Abbas converted his following to a new party, the UDMA (*Union Démocratique du Manifeste Algérien*), and continued to follow a moderate policy. Also in 1946, Messali Hadj converted the remnant PPA organization to a new party, the MTLD (*Mouvement pour le Triomphe de Libertés Démocratiques*). This party, too, seemed to follow a moderate policy despite militants who wanted to use force to fight the government.[10]

Decisive action by the French Government might now have steadied matters. Instead, the Algerian Statute of 1947 merely modified the existing system, with real power remaining in hands of a new governor general, a reactionary socialist, Marcel-Edmond Naegelen.[11] Although the new law provided for an Algerian Assembly with legislative powers, half of the one hundred and twenty elected delegates ". . . were elected by one-tenth of Algeria's population [i.e., the Europeans and upper-class Moslems], the remainder by the other nine-tenths."[12] Internal administration remained lopsided and corrupt. Rigged elections in 1948 offered flamboyant proof that nothing had really changed: precisely what the European colony intended.[13]

Their error lay in believing same.

As happened elsewhere, World War II had caused fundamental changes. The fall of France and the loyalty of Algeria's Europeans to Vichy had discredited the administration. Some Algerians had taken allied promises of self-determination seriously; returning veterans who had fought long and hard in Italy looked forward to overdue reforms. Instead, they found the Algerian people victims of reaction—and a few rebelled.

In 1947, a small group, which included a number of war veterans,

7. SORO, op. cit.
8. Edgar O'Ballance, *The Algerian Insurrection 1954–1962* (London: Faber & Faber, 1967).
9. *Time*, February 17, 1958.
10. Behr, op. cit.
11. Tanya Matthews, *Algerian ABC* (London: Geoffrey Chapman, 1961).
12. Behr, op. cit.
13. Gillespie, op. cit.; see also Matthews, op. cit.

splintered from the MTLD to launch a secret paramilitary movement, the OS (*Organisation Secrète*), under the titular control of handsome and magnetic Ahmed Ben Bella, a twenty-eight-year-old combat veteran and former sergeant major in the Free French army, where he had been decorated for bravery. Drawing on Mao Tse-tung's writings, lessons of the Sinn Fein movement, and Tito's World War II resistance, in three years Ben Bella and his fellows built the organization to some five hundred trained militants. In addition, the OS won new members from MTLD ranks and, in time, attracted another underground movement, Belkacem Krim's guerrillas already active in Kabylie.

The first important overt action by OS occurred in 1949, when Ben Bella, remembering Lenin's teachings, masterminded a robbery of the Oran post office, which yielded party coffers over three million francs.[14] Following this short-lived success, French police closed in, arrested Ben Bella and other leaders, and captured numerous caches of arms. Important lieutenants fled to Cairo, however, where Ben Bella joined them after escaping from jail, in 1952.

The young rebels now formed the League of Nine (*Club des Neufs*), which, early in 1954, became the CRUA (*Comité Révolutionnaire pour l'Unité et l'Action*). Ben Bella and three other members remained in Cairo as an External Delegation to drum up political and material support for the rebellion from sympathetic states. The other leaders returned to Algeria as an Interior Delegation, each to organize and train guerrilla forces in an assigned *wilaya,* or operational district. In October, the six wilaya commanders secretly met and decided to start the shooting.

The rebel decision cannot be justified, but it can be explained. It was a decision of desperation. The majority of Algeria's nine and a half million Moslems were living in abject poverty, devoid of either dignity or hope. A French official investigation in 1954 revealed the travesty of the comforting fiction that Algeria was France—"*L'Algérie, c'est la France*" (as a European living in Algiers would say with tears in his eyes, having just referred to his Moslem servant as *raton* [little rat] or *bicot* [nigger]). According to the Maspétiol report,

. . . 90 percent of Algeria's wealth was in the hands of ten percent of its inhabitants; nearly one million Moslems were totally or partially unemployed, and two more millions seriously under-employed; the average yearly income per head of the rural Moslem population stood at about 16 pounds sterling, and for another 1,600,000 Moslems living in towns the annual per capita income was about 45 pounds sterling. Eighty percent of all Moslem children did not go to school at all. The report stressed French achievements in road building, urban development and public health, but, taking account

14. Behr, op. cit.

of the changing value of the franc, it estimated that France was spending on Algeria, in 1953, about the same amount yearly as she had spent in 1913.[15]

Other authorities estimated that, in 1954, ". . . about three-quarters of the Moslem population was illiterate in Arabic, and about 90 per cent illiterate in French." Six and a half million Moslems owned some 615,000 small farms; 120,000 Europeans including dependents owned about twenty-two thousand farms. Nearly 6 million Moslem farmers claimed a per-capita annual income of about $45; European per-capita income from farming ranged from $240 to about $3,000.[16] A limited industrial plant employed only half a million Moslems; another half million worked in France. A galloping birthrate compounded this almost unbelievable poverty.[17]

The French Government, or, rather, a succession of divergent governments representing the controlled anarchy under which France labored for as long as one could remember, had recognized the unhappy situation and attempted without success to implement overdue reforms. Much of the failure rested on lack of stable government, with accompanying inefficiency, which in turn made it easier for the *colons,* some one million Europeans of whom about half were French, to sabotage reform measures in favor of rule by force, a policy in general approved by local French civil and military authorities.

The *colons* seem to have altogether misjudged the situation. Holding Moslems in general contempt, they had neutralized nationalist movements during and after World War II and apparently thought that this halcyon state of affairs could continue by their paying lip service through the Algerian Assembly to Moslem delegates derisively termed *Beni Oui Ouis* (yes men) by Abbas' and Messali's followers. As had happened to the British in Cyprus and Kenya, and to French and Dutch *colons* in Indochina and Indonesia, they refused to recognize the strength of nationalist feeling that contributed, in this case, to CRUA support. One of them, a liberal named Jean Daniel, wrote in *L'Express* in June 1955:

. . . These French of Algeria have more than one point in common with the Southerners of the United States: courage, dynamism, narrowness of views, the sincere conviction that they are born to be masters as others are born to be slaves.[18]

Such was their arrogance derived from ignorance that they failed to recognize and correct a collision course with disaster.

15. Ibid.
16. Gillespie, op. cit.
17. Germaine Tillion, *Algeria—the Realities* (London: Eyre & Spottiswoode, 1958); See also Tanya Matthews, op. cit.; Behr, op. cit.
18. Gillespie, op. cit.

In choosing force, however, the rebels also displayed an arrogance of ignorance:

. . . They underestimated both the umbilical cord linking Algeria to France in the minds of the great majority of public opinion in metropolitan France, and the diehard courage, tenacity and obstinacy of the European inhabitants of Algeria. They underestimated the military forces against them and the means France was prepared to place at the French army's disposal. Above all, they underestimated the sacrifices which nearly every single one of Algeria's nine million Moslems would have to endure. . . . They underestimated, too, Algeria's importance as a pawn in the Cold War, and naively failed to realize that France's allies, however disapproving, would neither interfere nor proffer advice until French public opinion had reconciled itself to the eventuality of Algerian independence.[19]

On November 1, 1954, rebel bands—perhaps a total of two to three thousand poorly armed guerrillas—struck more than thirty targets, the majority being gendarmerie posts in the Aurès Mountains of eastern Algeria.[20] Liberally scattered pamphlets announced that the National Liberation Front (*Front de Libération Nationale,* or FLN, the new name for the CRUA) and its army—soon to be called the National Liberation Army, or ALN—would lead Algerians to independence. If France were to grant this, the tract explained, European nationals would retain their rights and presumably France would enjoy a special relationship with the new nation.[21] Here was a basis for negotiation. French rejection automatically meant war.

French military force in Algeria numbered about fifty thousand. While armored columns struck out for the Aurès area to crush the rebels, the Mendès-France government rushed in three paratrooper battalions from France. The military showed no great concern; in minds of senior commanders, this was a local uprising, the work of Communist *fellaghas,* or bandits, who would quickly yield to superior power of the French army.

As any veteran of Indochina might have informed the military commander, mechanized columns accomplished little except to provide numerous targets of opportunity for lurking guerrillas. Nor should the reader be surprised to learn that simultaneous police measures only exacerbated the situation: for example, police arrested one hundred and sixty MTLD members, some of whom were moderates wanting to avoid war. Police brutality almost immediately provided another divisive issue: In December, forty-six Moslem members of the Algerian Assembly protested against ". . . illegal searches, arbitrary arrests and

19. Behr, op. cit.
20. Gillespie, op. cit.; O'Ballance (*Algerian Insurrection*), *supra.*
21. Gillespie, op. cit.

WAR IN THE SHADOWS

inhuman brutalities to which prisoners . . . are subjected." The vicious circle of terror and counterterror soon neutralized moderating forces such as those led by Ferhat Abbas. Revolution spread rapidly, the guerrillas ruthlessly killing or maiming any moderates ("traitors") who stood in the way. The new governor general, Jacques Soustelle, inspected the Aurès area in early 1955 and found a countryside frozen by fear: ". . . The population as a whole, without throwing in their lot with the rebels . . . remained frightened and noncommittal."[22] Soustelle told the Algerian Assembly that he intended to pacify the country, which would continue to ". . . form an integral part of France, one and indivisible."[23]

Within months, rebellion had spread north to coastal areas and then west. In April, the French Government declared a limited state of emergency and endowed certain local authorities with powers similar to those exercised by British forces in Malaya. But Soustelle's pacifying hand was checked by limited resources—in May, the army numbered only one hundred thousand.[24] The European colony also frustrated most of his administrative reforms. He did establish a new administrative corps, the SAS (*Sections Administratives Spécialisées*), which sent young French officers to remote parts of the country to function similarly to British civil district commissioners.

The SAS was still in the formative stage when Moslem uprisings in eastern Algeria brought another wave of terror. The ghastly killings and counterkillings of August 1955 led to three important developments. The first was the effect of Moslem terror on the new governor general. Soustelle, a young scholar and anthropologist who had served De Gaulle in an intelligence capacity during the war, arrived in Algeria with a liberal reputation. *Colon* hostility seemed to shake his limited assurance, as did Moslem savagery; in short order, his liberal intentions disappeared like gilt in the acid of reality. The second was the effect outside Algeria: The Afro-Asian bloc introduced the subject of the rebellion into the United Nations, much against France's will. The third was the effect on Algerian Moslem "moderates" such as Ahmed Francis and Ferhat Abbas, who published a manifesto addressed to the French Government and urging "the Algerian national idea," a document that ". . . both encouraged the rebels to continue and had a considerable effect on French public opinion in France."[25]

Inept countertactics remained the rebellion's best friend. In Edward Behr's words,

. . . Police and army activity against the rebels contributed to its very success: the lack of discrimination with which arrests were made and villages

22. Behr, op. cit.
23. Ibid.
24. O'Ballance (*Algerian Insurrection*), *supra.*
25. Behr, op. cit.

destroyed, the increasingly brutal interrogation measures practised by troops and police, the blind conservatism of most European settlers, all helped to turn the mass of the Moslem population into prudent "attentistes," intent on keeping out of trouble if possible but increasingly willing to support the rebellion.[26]

The French military build-up was still under way during 1955, and commanders did not possess sufficient troops to carry out traditional pacification tactics. Once troops occupied important towns and villages (the *quadrillage*), few units remained for the *ratissage* (cleaning out grid areas so that SAS units could proceed with pacification) or for the *bouclage* (sealing off and combing known insurgent areas). The FLN also benefited from Arab League support, particularly from Nasser's Egypt, and from Tunisian and Moroccan sanctuaries, which provided arms and supply.

French political weakness was even more serious. In early 1956, the new French premier, socialist Guy Mollet, appointed Soustelle's successor, seventy-nine-year-old General Georges Catroux. In Algiers to install his new minister resident, Mollet faced a hostile European mob, which pelted him with rotten vegetables while police stood idly by. Bowing to mob authority, Mollet cancelled the appointment and named a man acceptable to Algerian *colons,* Robert Lacoste.

Mollet's disastrous capitulation provided false strength to Europeans in Algeria and blinded them even further to political realities. In their own eyes, they had become a law unto themselves, an attitude that nullified further conciliatory efforts toward Moslems on the part of the Mollet government and thus widened the gulf between European and Moslem. But more than this: Mollet's political insouciance infuriated and frightened Moslem moderates and inevitably drove more of them into supporting and even joining the FLN.

By bowing to force, then, Mollet opened the way to force, which proved disastrous to all elements in Algeria. Mollet's action, as analyzed by Edward Behr, did not stem from cowardice but, rather, from ignorance derived by listening to the wrong people—a tragedy, since, ". . . on any number of occasions, civilians and officers alike could have gauged the true nature of the situation in Algeria by questioning men of proven experience whose testimony was not likely to be false."[27] Ignorant of ". . . the true nature of the situation," Mollet succumbed to military blandishments and agreed to let the army ". . . use political propaganda weapons" in addition to other pacification measures. With this decision, Mollet tacitly yielded control over the French military at a time when control was vital.[28]

26. Ibid.
27. Ibid.
28. Ibid.; see also Gillespie, op. cit.

The French army was in a particularly dangerous frame of mind at this time. Its collapse in 1940 and its defeat in Indochina had left it laboring under a gigantic inferiority complex. Although blaming the home front for the Indochinese disaster—the stab-in-the-back thesis so effectively enunciated by Hindenburg and Ludendorff in 1918—the army, in reality, had been greatly impressed by the Viet Minh intermingling of political and military factors to fight revolutionary warfare. Returning prisoners of war also had been indoctrinated in Viet Minh ways, and, in time, a powerful school of revolutionary warfare—*la guerre révolutionnaire*—had developed in the French army.

We are unable here to analyze it in detail; that has been done by Professor Peter Paret in his excellent book *French Revolutionary Warfare from Indochina to Algeria—The Analysis of a Political and Military Doctrine*.[29] In brief, the French school dissected Chinese and Viet Minh revolutionary doctrines and developed a counterrevolutionary doctrine that depended on powerful ideological and moral forces to produce a "dynamic strategy." If communism formed a strong ideology, then hatred of communism would form a stronger one. If Communists could indoctrinate soldiers and civilians with certain beliefs, the French could indoctrinate them with counterbeliefs.

Proponents of the new school recognized that the army would have to change its ways, relying heavily on psychological warfare in re-educating soldiers and target peoples to the glory and grandeur of a new crusade. But the nation, too, would have to change its ways: There would be no shirking, as in the case of Indochina; if government could not lead the people to support counterrevolutionary warfare, then the army would have to educate government and people!

The doctrine contained certain strengths. At a time of defeat and doubt, it offered a positive program, a splendid vision of a new France. Militarily, it admitted past errors and sought to correct them, in some cases successfully, as will be seen.

Its weaknesses, however, far outweighed strengths. Approaching the subject deductively, its proponents had gathered operational flowers from Mao's and Giap's works while ignoring thorny philosophical stems. The doctrine of *la guerre révolutionnaire* as applied to the Algerian rebellion failed from the beginning, because, as noted by that sound reporter C. L. Sulzberger, it ignored Mao's first lesson: ". . . If the political objectives that one seeks to attain are not the secret and profound aspirations of the masses, all is lost from the beginning."[30]

Nor is genius required to recognize the doctrine's fascist connotations. As Professor Paret asked: Is it accidental that so many of its

29. Peter Paret, *French Revolutionary Warfare from Indochina to Algeria—The Analysis of a Political and Military Doctrine* (New York: Frederick A. Praeger, 1964).

30. C. L. Sulzberger, *The Test: De Gaulle and Algeria* (London: Rupert Hart-Davis, 1962).

theorists and supporters ". . . are found among the leaders of the various putsches and rebellions that shook France during the past year?"
Its proponents made no secret of their disgust not alone for the Fourth
Republic, which they insisted had let down French arms so badly, but
also for the reigning political philosophy: In Colonel Hogard's words of
1958, ". . . it is time to realize that the democratic ideology has become
powerless in the world today."[31] In the minds of the new school, democratic ideology could only be replaced by totalitarian ideology, which
was and is foreign to political beliefs held by most Frenchmen.

The doctrine contained other weaknesses. In its civil application to
Algeria, it was far too ambitious, considering size and training of the
French army. It was also too negative: Its ideology pre-supposed a constant state of war with Communists, a war of no compromise, a fight to
the finish. This was repugnant to millions of Frenchmen, including hundreds of thousands of conscript soldiers who were tired of war and
held little respect for the professional army.

At this crucial time, proponents of *la guerre révolutionnaire* badly
overestimated the strength of appeal to fellow countrymen. They undoubtedly believed that the bulk of the army subscribed to their new
mission—that of preventing a Communist takeover of the world. Despite
the Communist threat and the anarchic quality of the home government,
the bulk of the army, not to mention that of the citizenry, did not believe
in the mission. Civil and military leaders, finding its proponents a bore,
shrugged off the new propaganda. This was a mistake: Boring it was,
but, as will be seen in the next chapter, it was also dangerous.

31. Paret (*French Revolutionary Warfare*), *supra.*

Chapter 71

FLN growth • Rebel weaknesses • French strength increases • The CNRA • The battle of Algiers • Jacques Massu and la guerre révolutionnaire • *French excesses • War in the country-side • Guerrilla organization • The counterinsurgency task: destruction and construction • French tactics • The Morice Line • Problem of sanctuaries • Failure of the* regroupement *program • SAS difficulties • De Gaulle takes over • The Constantine Plan • French tactical adaptation: the Challe Plan • Role of helicopters • De Gaulle's peace offensive • Origin of OAS • A mutiny fails • Algerian independence • The cost*

REVOLUTIONARY DOCTRINE OR NO, the French army continued to rely on traditional techniques in fighting the Algerian war. In March 1956, shortly after Mollet's abdication to the Algiers mob, the army executed two Moslem terrorists. The FLN replied by killing or wounding a number of Europeans—and the gulf between European and Moslem again widened, to FLN advantage.

The FLN also gained when the French granted independence to Morocco and Tunisia, thus easing the flow of arms into Algeria besides providing border sanctuaries and training areas for guerrilla forces. The abortive Anglo-French campaign in Suez, during summer of 1956, further helped rebel operations by drawing off French military units. The army's interception and arrest, a few months later, of Ben Bella and several associates who were flying from Rabat to a conference called by Habib Bourguiba in Tunis was a grave error; since the party was a guest of the Moroccan sultan, the act insulted Moslem hospitality and made Tunisian and Moroccan leaders even more sympathetic to the

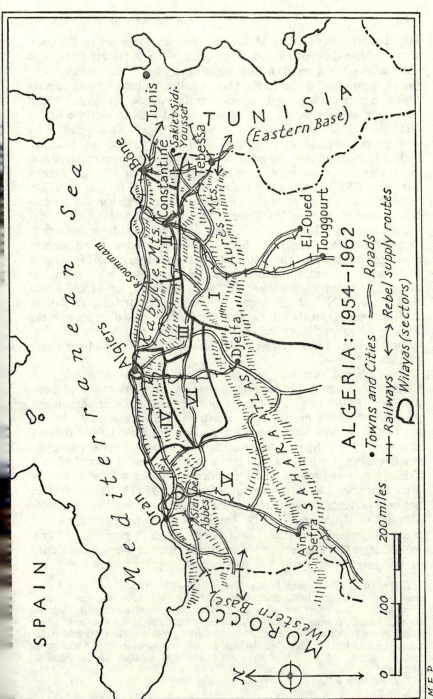

SPAIN

Mediterranean Sea

Kabylie Mts.

R. Soummam

TUNISIA
(Eastern Base)

Tunis
Bône
Sakiet-Sidi-Yousset
Constantine
Tébessa
Aurès Mts.
El-Oued
Touggourt
Algiers
Djelfa
ATLAS
SAHARA
Oran
Sidi bel Abbès
Aïn Sefra
MOROCCO
(Western Base)

ALGERIA: 1954–1962

• Towns and Cities   ══ Roads
+ Railways   → Rebel supply routes
▷ Wilayas (sectors)

200 miles

100

0

N

M.E.P.

Algerian rebel cause. The Mollet government acquiesced in the deed, thus compounding damage both by eliminating a powerful Algerian nationalist with whom to conduct negotiations, and by further alienating the most powerful leader in the Maghreb, Bourguiba, who was actively trying to promote a peaceful solution to the Algerian problem.[1] Taken with inept military tactics, these events helped FLN to increase during 1956 to an estimated eighty-five hundred guerrillas supported by twenty-one thousand auxiliaries, who greatly expanded the rebellion.

The French military, however, also enjoyed some important advantages. One was increasing strength: By April 1956, the forces in Algeria numbered 250,000, which, by utilizing conscript soldiers and reservists, would rise to four hundred thousand by autumn.[2] Another was the factious nature of the rebellion. Ferhat Abbas and other UDMA moderates did not leap into FLN arms, but, rather, displayed an independence that, properly exploited, might well have become an important and perhaps even decisive divisive force. Nor did Messali Hadj and the MTLD join FLN ranks. Instead, he reconstituted the party into the Algerian National Movement (*Mouvement National Algérien*), or MNA, which rivaled the FLN both in Algiers and in the countryside, as well as in France proper. Although the Communist PCA joined forces with the FLN in Algiers, neither organization trusted the other, a precarious relationship that ultimately resulted in almost total demise of the Communists.[3]

The FLN and its militant arm, the ALN, were also becoming divisive. Conflict would probably have developed between the two branches—the External Delegation, in Cairo, and the Internal Delegation, inside Algeria—even with proper communications. With messages taking up to three months to deliver by courier and with long delays in delivery of arms and supply, misunderstandings frequently occurred and rivalries flourished. Lack of internal cohesion also played a disruptive role. Tribes within one wilaya held little interest in other wilayas (precisely what Lawrence had discovered in Palestine in 1917). Tribal rivalries not only prevented co-ordinated operations, but also hindered equitable distribution of arms and supply. Ambitious and inexperienced guerrilla leaders began outright attacks on French units, a disaster that, according to Major O'Ballance, cost six thousand insurgent lives—about a third of the guerrilla army—in just two months, April and May of 1956;

1. Dwight D. Eisenhower, *Waging Peace 1956–1961* (London: William Heinemann, 1966): In late 1956, at President Eisenhower's request, the new ruler of Tunisia outlined a plan that called for France to grant independence to Algeria. As with Tunisia, it would be granted in stages—a plan that in the end, he believed, would prove beneficial to France. As for his own position: "The fighting in Algeria," he told the President, "holds back Tunisia and economic and social progress. I want to do everything to promote a happy solution of the Algerian problem."

2. O'Ballance (*Algerian Insurrection*), *supra*.

3. Ibid.

French authorities later claimed fourteen thousand insurgent deaths by year's end.

Leadership arrests and fatalities meant the rise of new leaders such as the young Kabyle, Ramdane Abbane, who soon challenged Ben Bella's leadership. In August 1956, Abbane arranged the Soummam conference, which brought together some two hundred and fifty wilaya rebels in a valley shown as "pacified" on French military maps. Members of the External Delegation (Cairo) were delayed and never did arrive, a confusion that some observers traced to Abbane's machinations.

Abbane was a rough but clever and forceful leader. At the Soummam conference, he established a new governing body, the CNRA (*Conseil National de la Révolution Algérienne*) which, together with its executive, the five-member CCE, was to challenge the Cairo group for leadership of the rebellion. Abbane charged the CCE with introducing a coherent administrative system in each wilaya as well as co-ordinating wilaya operations. He also persuaded his fellows that time was ripe for an all-out urban terrorist campaign—". . . A curfew in Algiers," he argued (in the Lenin tradition), "is worth two hundred dead in the mountains"[4]—a dreadful decision that not only would cost the FLN numerous sympathizers abroad but would nearly cost it its existence. Ironically, Ben Bella, who recognized the error and probably could have prevented the campaign from taking place, was arrested the following month.[5]

Abbane should have moved more cautiously. A new factor, discovery of valuable oil fields in the Sahara, had stiffened French determination to quell the insurrection. By end of 1956, French forces had grown to over four hundred thousand, and the home government had ordered conscript troops to fight. Moreover, the Mollet government had all but abrogated its authority over Algerian affairs when it allowed the army in Algeria to kidnap Ben Bella—and the leadership of that army was determined to eliminate the guerrillas.

Optimistic military reports from the field also had favorably impressed the civil representative in Algiers, Robert Lacoste. When Algiers police failed to cope with FLN's new terror campaign, Lacoste turned the suppression problem over to Major General Jacques Massu and the 10th Parachute Division. The battle of Algiers, which began in late January 1957 and lasted until September, left little doubt in Moslem minds of French military determination and strength and little doubt in colonial minds that the French military was in full control of French policy in Algeria.

In killed, wounded, and maimed, and in brutality and terror, the battle of Algiers compares to the 1944 battle of Warsaw (see Chapter 32,

4. Gillespie, op. cit.
5. Ben Bella subsequently condemned the action in letters sent from prison to FLN leaders. Abbane himself did not long remain in power; in June 1958, FLN newspapers announced his death—possibly arranged by the party.

Volume I). The rebels started the battle with the upper hand: They numbered about twelve hundred well-organized hard-core terrorists supported by perhaps forty-five hundred members of the FLN, an organization that provided a variety of skills and was financed by taxation and extortion, which yielded perhaps three hundred thousand dollars a month.[6] According to one French officer, Colonel Roger Trinquier, whom we met earlier in Indochina (see Chapters 55 and 63), they faced only about a thousand police, neither trained nor equipped for insurgency warfare. Moslems relied on terror in a score and more of forms —unrestricted, promiscuous terror that struck at innocent and guilty alike. Based in the notorious casbah, terrorists stole snake-like through the city to bomb and kill and then hide in the sympathetic Moslem quarter—one important rebel leader, Yassef Saadi, later lived within two hundred yards of army headquarters.[7]

When Lacoste turned the problem over to the army, Massu went after them. Massu was not very bright. A big man with enormous ears and a nose that brought to mind Cyrano de Bergerac, "Roughneck" Massu, as he was known, embraced excesses preached by younger proponents of the *guerre-révolutionnaire* school, colonels such as Trinquier, Ducasse, and Thomazo, who believed, like Communist leaders they had studied, that end justifies means—that fire must be fought with fire.

Lacking co-operation of the Moslem population, Massu depended on informers for intelligence. He established military "special police" units called DOPs (*Détachements Opérationnels de Protection*), which incorporated Moslem defectors; he used hooded informers to identify terrorists; he formed Moslem militia units. Major O'Ballance described another of his techniques, which Diem's government would later use in Vietnam:

. . . The paratroops started the "ilot" system of surveillance and checking personnel, by making one man responsible for a family, and another responsible for a building or house in which there were invariably many families, another for a whole alleyway or street, and so on. In this way they were able to lay their hands on any wanted Muslim in the Casbah within hours.[8]

In addition to informers, counterterrorist organizations flourished. Consisting of European *ultras,* these employed agent-provocateur techniques: blowing up Moslem and even European dwellings to provoke army reaction.

Most of all, Massu's people depended on fear and duress, and their activities soon equaled anything practiced by the Gestapo in France during World War II. In addition to beatings and killings, the paratroopers used torture—the famous *gégène,* by which field-telephone wires were

6. Gillespie, op. cit.
7. Trinquier, op. cit.
8. O'Ballance (*Algerian Insurrection*), *supra.*

attached to the victim's genitals and current shot through them. Massu and some of his officers openly defended the usage, Massu himself submitting to it.[9] His intelligence officer, Colonel Roger Trinquier, later argued that a terrorist cannot claim the same honors as a soldier if he rejects the same obligations; rather, he is beholden to yield vital information such as the name of his superior. If not, he can be tortured:

. . . No lawyer is present for such an interrogation. If the prisoner gives the information requested, the examination is quickly terminated; if not, specialists must force his secret from him. Then, as a soldier, he must face the suffering, and perhaps the death, he has heretofore managed to avoid. The terrorist must accept this as a condition inherent in his trade and in the methods of warfare that, with full knowledge, his superiors and he himself have chosen. Once the interrogation is finished, however, the terrorist can take his place among soldiers.[10]

Trinquier's philosophy, which was shared by most proponents of the doctrine of *la guerre révolutionnaire* and by a great many police both in Algeria and metropolitan France, represented a tragic reversion to medieval thinking. If Torquemada would have agreed, the Italian philosopher Beccaria would have disagreed; in a work published in 1764, he demolished the rationale behind torture: ". . . Torture, it was said, is *inhuman;* it is also inefficient; it is frequently used against innocent people and the confessions extracted by it have no validity."[11] Frederick the Great had already abolished torture in Prussia. Other civilized nations tended to follow Beccaria's lead, and, in 1957, most of French society agreed—particularly those who had suffered German barbarism in World War II. The bulk of French society, including a good portion of the army, had no idea that torture had become standard operating procedure in many army units. Greater was the shock, therefore, when such works as Jean-Jacques Servan-Schreiber's *Lieutenant in Algeria,* Lartéguy's *The Centurions,* and Henri Alleg's *The Question* revealed a military depravity that brought howls of liberal protest and a "crisis of conscience" to the army high command—a military depravity that in time would culminate in unsuccessful rebellion against legitimate government.[12] As Edward Behr later wrote, the French army, along with many

9. Pierre Vidal-Naquet, *Torture: Cancer of Democracy* (Harmondsworth, Middlx: Penguin Books, 1963); Behr, op. cit.: This grandstand play proved nothing, for, as Behr points out, Massu submitted only to limited pain, like going to a dentist, whereas torture derives much of its force from the victim's contemplation of prolonged pain; see also Henri Alleg, *The Question* (London: John Calder, 1958), for a vivid description of French army methods.
10. Trinquier, op. cit.
11. Vidal-Naquet, op. cit.
12. Jean-Jacques Servan-Schreiber, *Lieutenant in Algeria* (London: Hutchinson, 1958). Tr. Ronald Matthews; Jean Lartéguy, op. cit.; Henri Alleg, op. cit.; Vidal-Naquet, op. cit.; Servan-Schreiber published his work in serial form in *L'Express*

other armies, on occasion, had behaved badly; in the Algerian rebellion, however, ". . . police and army brutality became a permanent and quietly efficient instrument, a weapon of war of the same caliber as the grenade or the mortar-bomb."[13] Pierre Vidal-Naquet went further: ". . . The part played by torture throughout the Algerian war can be summed up in a few words; it started as a police method of interrogation, developed into a military method of operation, and then ultimately turned into a clandestine institution which struck at the very root of the life of the nation."[14]

French policy, which could be described as controlled genocide, seemed to work: By October 1957, the army had destroyed the FLN apparatus in Algiers; Larbi Ben M'Hidi was dead, Yassef Saadi surrendered, other leaders dead, captured, or fled; the city quiet. A massive French effort in the countryside also brought favorable results.

Or so it seemed.

The total campaign had not eliminated the FLN. Killings and arrests and tortures that affected thousands of innocent persons had shocked the population, as ice numbs a wound. As shock wore off, as people realized this was a fight to what the army intended to be their finish, they turned increasingly to the FLN. Moderate leaders such as Ferhat Abbas now not only joined the organization but became one of its leaders. Tunis and Morocco increased support of the rebellion, as did Arab League countries.

The situation in the countryside resembled a small-scale Vietnam. The Soummam conference had brought considerable order to rebel ranks. A rebel colonel now commanded each wilaya and was responsible for civil as well as military functions. A three-man military committee responsible for political affairs, military operations, and liaison/ intelligence assisted him, as did a civil committee of some five elected representatives concerned with ". . . civil, financial, economic and Islamic problems."[15] As with the Viet Minh in Indochina, administration carried down to village level, where possible. Small committees, the Popular Assembly, carried out propaganda, taxation, and recruiting functions necessary to maintain civil support of guerrillas, through an organization known as OPA.

Each wilaya consisted of operational zones and subzones, and each zone, in theory at least, supported a "regular" battalion of twenty officers and three hundred and fifty men. These were full-time soldiers, the *moujahidines,* who were paid. Part-time irregulars, the *moussebilines,* the equivalent of the Viet Minh "peasants by day—guerrillas by night,"

---

with the open support of one of Massu's generals: General de Bollardière commanded the Blida Atlas area and—brave and good man—forbade the use of torture in his command.

13. Behr, op. cit.
14. Vidal-Naquet, op. cit.
15. O'Ballance (*Algerian Insurrection*), *supra.*

assisted them, as did less-trained *fidayines,* many of whom belonged to the civil support system, the OPA, which also included women and probably children.[16]

Although FLN leaders claimed that the guerrillas acquired most arms by raids on French posts, the bulk of arms, ammunition, and supply probably came from neighboring sanctuaries: Morocco and Tunisia. In spring of 1957, the FLN's Exterior Delegation had moved from Cairo to Tunis at invitation of Habib Bourguiba, ambitious in his new-found freedom. What became known as the Eastern Base (as opposed to Morocco—the Western Base) would support some thirty thousand rebels by the end of the year.[17] Financed in part by Arab League countries, in part by taxes and extortions collected in Algeria and France, the FLN bought arms wherever possible; Egypt also sent arms captured from British stocks at Suez, and Syria supplied old French weapons. The system may have been rickety, but there was no doubt that it helped FLN forces inside and outside Algeria to grow during 1957.

The French faced a twofold counterinsurgency task: destruction and construction, as General Allard put it.[18] Security forces had to separate the guerrilla from the civil populace and destroy him along with the political infrastructure that supported him. The construction phase involved converting the population to the government's side in order to prevent re-emergence of the rebel organization.

To carry out the first phase, the French relied on the traditional concept of the *tache d'huile,* modified to circumstances. The *quadrillage* requirement—setting up garrison networks in specified areas—consumed the bulk of forces. Of three hundred thirty thousand troops assigned to rural pacification during 1957–58, three hundred thousand carried out more or less static duties while occupying towns and villages. Some thirty thousand elite troops—paratroopers, marines, and legionnaires—formed a Réserve Générale, a mobile force complete with helicopters to carry out the *ratissage,* or raking operations, and the *bouclage,* or encircling operations, designed to eliminate guerrillas in each area.

Several factors combined to lessen over-all effect of French tactics. One was the inhibiting influence of the garrison concept, which tended to leave the countryside to the guerrillas, a failing already familiar from Indochina. Another was inexperienced conscripts, who could scarcely be expected to understand intricacies of guerrilla warfare, particularly since few seniors understood those intricacies. A third was the old bugaboo from Indochina: an inadequate force for the mission. A fourth was guerrilla reinforcement from neighboring sanctuaries. A fifth was FLN determination: According to Colonel Antoine Argoud, in one small village, ". . . the OPA reorganized ten times in three years, despite public

---

16. Ibid.; see also Gillespie, op. cit.; Vidal-Naquet, op. cit.
17. O'Ballance (*Algerian Insurrection*), supra.
18. Paret, op. cit.

executions having been carried out in the village square."[19] A sixth was French barbarism: torture, summary executions, a disregard for civilians perhaps best exemplified by Colonel Argoud's order that children should search for mines![20] A seventh was the extent of the "destruction" phase, particularly in the Kabylie, areas of which experienced repression bordering on genocide.

The French defended the garrison concept on grounds that the flag had to fly in order to instill law and confidence and thus gain intelligence essential to fighting guerrillas. The conscript problem persisted to the end: An intense psychological program designed to convert the recruit either to *la mission civilisatrice* or to a "new France," failed almost completely.

The French expanded their forces with Moslems who either volunteered or were drafted for auxiliary service, usually in small *harkas* commanded by French officers and non-commissioned officers, and also in village defense forces. French intelligence agents also subverted "independent" guerrilla bands. None of these expedients proved entirely satisfactory. Moslem forces tended to be unreliable and undoubtedly supplied a great deal of intelligence to the FLN. As for tribal subversion, Professor Paret concluded:

. . . Promoting dissension among the nationalists was a useful policy, but the allies gained in the process were hardly reliable. The tendency to play off one side against the other appeared to be almost universal among Moslem chiefs; to keep them under control, their men had to be regularized to some extent, and with the coming of liaison officers, of uniforms and paratroopers, the bands lost the ability to blend into the countryside and merge with the population, which had been their most significant military asset.[21]

The French continued to use Moslem soldiers and eventually built up a force of about 150,000. But, as in Indochina, they did not succeed fully in exploiting the potential: ". . . The inadequacy, lateness, and contradictions of their political program prevented a sufficient rallying of the population."[22] By mid-1958, most of Mohammed Bellounis' and Belhadj Djilal's following had gone over to the ALN; Djilal's own men murdered him in April, and French soldiers killed Bellounis in July.

To neutralize Moroccan and Tunisian bases, the French navy maintained a patrol blockade that claimed right of intercept and involved the French Government in steady international imbroglio. France did not lack weapons here. As a senior member of NATO, she claimed powerful allies, and her later threat to publish a list of countries that were furnishing FLN support, including Switzerland and West Germany, effectively diminished the blockade-running operation. She could not,

19. Vidal-Naquet, op. cit.
20. Ibid.
21. Paret, op. cit.
22. Ibid.

however, blockade the Libyan coast, and arms continued to arrive in that country for road shipment to Tunis, and also cross-country from Egypt.

Simultaneously, the French Government carried on a diplomatic offensive designed to prevent other nations from supporting the FLN. She put particular pressure on Moroccan and Tunisian governments, which, due to natural sympathy for the rebels reflected in internal political pressures, were not inclined to co-operate. It was a difficult situation: Increased pressure would further alienate one of the best friends the West had in Africa, Habib Bourguiba.

The troops fighting in Algeria understandably did not appreciate diplomatic nuances. Commanders would spend months searching out and reducing a guerrilla unit only to find it reinforced from across the border; or, if action grew too hot for the guerrilla, he escaped across the border, precisely as had happened in Greece.

The army reacted in two ways: It began building a fortified barrier, a forty-meter-wide complex cored by an electrified fence that stretched two hundred and fifty kilometers (about 150 miles) from Bône to south of Tebessa. Surveyed by radar and human patrols and, in places, covered by searchlights and artillery, its approaches were mined, its avenues patrolled.[23] Like all static defenses, including the Maginot Line, the new Morice Line held disadvantages: It cost a great deal to build (one sixth of the total cost of French military operations for a year)[24]; it required thousands of troops to patrol the often tortuous terrain; in places, it was as far as fifty miles from the border, a disadvantage corrected in time by two expedients: clearing the natives from the area and burning off brush to make a free-fire zone (*zone interdite*) suitable for ground and air interdiction, and in places building a second parallel fence; finally, it could be outflanked.[25] The Morice Line, however, seriously impeded infiltration, though probably not to the degree claimed by military authorities.[26]

The army also moved operations closer and closer to the border until, in September, it exercised "the right of pursuit" into Tunisia, killing six Tunisian soldiers in the process. Instead of condemning the action, the Gaillard government defended it, which worsened already bad relations with Bourguiba's government.[27] A few months later, in February 1958, an air force colonel ordered a bombing and strafing mission against the Tunisian border village of Sakiet-Sidi-Youssef on the pretext that machine guns located there fired on French aircraft three miles away in Algerian skies! The raid killed eighty and wounded seventy-nine Tunisians, including children.[28] The Gaillard government again defended

23. O'Ballance (*Algerian Insurrection*), *supra*.
24. Ibid.
25. *Time*, March 3, 1958.
26. Ibid.; see also O'Ballance (*Algerian Insurrection*), *supra*.
27. *Time*, September 16, 1957.
28. *Time*, February 17, 1958.

the action, this time to hostile allies as well. Bourguiba broke off relations with France and protested to the United Nations, thus "internationalizing" the war—which France had tried to prevent.[29] Although a patchy truce emerged, the episode contributed to the fall of the Gaillard government, in April.

The army also ran into trouble in its *regroupement* program, which overlapped the constructive phase of *la guerre révolutionnaire*. Moving hundreds of thousands of people is a difficult task at best. Unfortunately, the French, for the most part, did it badly: Hastily organized and almost totally inadequate centers caused thousands of Moslem deaths from cold and hunger. Word quickly spread among the people, many of whom resisted removal and turned to the rebels.

Regroupement also had another purpose: to provide security for the people and then educate them to support the government. This task fell largely to two groups: to the psychological warfare, the 5th bureaus, of military units, and to SAS units, which, for some time, had been working in remote areas attempting to protect and mobilize the population.

Of the two organizations, SAS performed more satisfactorily, yet, in the end, failed in its task of converting the bulk of the population to the French cause. Several reasons explain the combined failure, but, basically, its fault lay in attempting to sell an inferior product, French hegemony, to people who had already tried and rejected it. Overcommitment also plagued the effort: The 5th bureaus held other major responsibilities, such as indoctrinating French troops into the blandishments of *la guerre révolutionnaire* and converting captured and surrendered guerrillas to the cause. The latter task alone involved organizing and administering internment camps before even approaching the major, brain-washing task. Shortage of qualified personnel meant reliance on people who too often replaced psychology with brutality. But here again, the chief problem lay in trying to sell a specious product with ersatz-communism methods. As Professor Paret concluded:

. . . Crude weekly crash programs stressing hygiene, patriotism, discipline, etc. and self-criticism meetings took their place; and it is difficult to believe that such directed mass-activities could produce any lasting effects in the prisoners' minds other than antagonism.[30]

SAS units encountered a host of difficulties. Although lieutenants and captains were supposed to concentrate on improving people's welfare, the security task usually claimed the bulk of their energy. Nor did their military bias prove popular. Their use of the *képi bleu*—the distinctive military headgear—and of the *bordj,* or small fort for militia forces, reminded many peasants of the old and unpopular Arab Bureau days of military administration.[31] The language barrier further reduced their

29. Sulzberger, op. cit.
30. Paret, op. cit.
31. Behr, op. cit.

effectiveness, as did military priorities—by shelling a village, the army often undid months of work. Still, SAS units proved a step in the right direction and helped to repair past damage caused by a top-heavy administration that kept thousands of civil servants in cities and few in the countryside. But the task was enormous and personnel in short supply: At its maximum strength, the program utilized fewer than thirteen hundred officers, administering some six hundred and sixty sections with the help of about six hundred and fifty non-commissioned officers and about three thousand civilians.[32] A confusion of mission also plagued the effort. Professor Paret concluded:

. . . The SAS officers were less concerned with understanding the Algerians than with turning them into docile collaborators.

From imposing French bureaucratic control and instructing the population in French principles of public health, it was a short step to advocating French social and cultural values while—implicitly or explicitly—condemning native traditions.

Far from uniting the two races, such paternalistic tactics were devisive and could easily recoil on their users.[33]

By end of 1957, then, grave faults were apparent in both the destruction and construction tasks of *la guerre révolutionnaire*. Although the army would repair some of these in time, it would not succeed in its most vital mission. In Paret's words:

. . . Despite its control of the machinery of government and administration, and despite its psychological-warfare armory, France was unable to match the diffused but continuous moral and physical pressure that a native, nationalistic revolutionary movement can exert on the people.[34]

In spring of 1958, political poverty of the Fourth Republic turned to bankruptcy, the catalyst significantly being an uprising of European ultras in Algiers. When Algerian rebels shot three French soldiers in reprisal for execution of three terrorists, the European colony spilled into Algiers' streets. With full military co-operation, angry mobs seized Government House and established a Committee of Public Safety—an insurrection seemingly blessed by thousands of Moslems, some of whom acted spontaneously, some under coercion. Failing to cope with this new crisis, the Fourth Republic fell under the weight of its own weakness. When dust settled, General Charles de Gaulle occupied the chair of power—the beginning of a curious dictatorship that, in repairing what De Gaulle termed "the degradation of the state," would bring numerous surprises to France and the world.

And to his supporters in Algeria. For, if generals and colonels hoped

32. Paret, op. cit.
33. Ibid.
34. Ibid.

that De Gaulle, one of their own, would underwrite the pernicious doctrine of *la guerre révolutionnaire,* they were doomed to disappointment. De Gaulle held no intention of supporting an "integration" policy that he reasoned had come too late. If the Algerian situation was to be salvaged, he warned soon after resuming power in June 1958,

. . . opportunities must be opened that, for many, have until now been closed. This means that a livelihood must be given to those who have not had it. This means that the dignity of those who have been deprived of it must now be recognized. This means that a country must be given to those who may have thought they had no country.[35]

De Gaulle moved slowly but steadily to re-establish state authority over the military. Dissident officers in Algeria received transfers to home commands. He ordered his new commander, General Salan, to begin replacing military administrators with civilians, and he also curtailed budget allotments for "psychological warfare," SAS, and *regroupement* activities. In September, he ordered Salan to terminate army participation in Committees of Public Safety: ". . . The moment has come," De Gaulle wrote, ". . . for the military to stop taking part in any organization which has a political character."[36] When Salan demurred, De Gaulle relieved him in favor of a civilian, Paul Delouvrier. The new army commander, General Maurice Challe, became subordinate to Delouvrier—at least in theory.

As De Gaulle consolidated his position, he moved more openly, calling for peace in Algeria. At first, he hoped to negotiate with Moslem moderates inside the country, but as he grew more aware of the real political situation, he extended overtures to the FLN, which meanwhile had established a provisional government-in-exile, the GPRA, in Tunis. Although not recognizing the new government, De Gaulle could scarcely ignore names such as Ferhat Abbas, its prime minister; Ben Bella (still in prison), its deputy prime minister; Belkacem Krim, its defense minister; and dozens of other persons representing just about every shade of Algerian nationalism. Moreover, Tunisia, Communist China, Pakistan, Morocco, Egypt, and a number of African nations had recognized it, and some were providing support.

In early October 1958, De Gaulle announced a five-year reform program for Algeria, the Constantine Plan.[37] A few weeks later, at a press

35. Behr, op. cit.; see also, Charles de Gaulle, *Memoirs of Hope* (London: Weidenfeld & Nicolson, 1970), Vol. 1 of 2 vols. Tr. Terence Kilmartin.
36. Sulzberger, op. cit.
37. Tanya Matthews, op. cit.: De Gaulle promised ". . . that wages in Algeria would be raised to levels comparable with those paid in France, that housing would be provided for a million people, that two-thirds of the Moslem children of school age would be sent to school, that more land would be provided for Moslem farmers and that . . . 400,000 new jobs would be found for Moslems in Algeria in the next five years"; see also Gillespie, op. cit.; see also De Gaulle, op. cit.

conference, he emphasized the continuing cost of the war, which, since November 1954, had taken the lives of seventy-two hundred French soldiers, seventy-seven thousand insurgents, fifteen hundred European civilians, and over ten thousand Moslems.[38] Offering rebels an amnesty, he called for a "peace of the brave" and even suggested, albeit cryptically, self-determination (". . . the political destiny of Algeria is Algeria itself") and a new Algeria, ". . . a vast physical and spiritual transformation," hopefully under French aegis.[39] Unfortunately, the FLN refused these overtures even though military pressure was beginning to hurt.

De Gaulle's words were no more welcome to European ultras or military commanders. Each group believed that a military "victory" was at hand—just as "victory" had been achieved in Algiers. The army held reasonable grounds for optimism. Increasing rebel strength had brought change in rebel tactics: Units up to battalion strength had begun attacking French positions, the prelude, according to some, of the third, or "mobile," phase of Mao-style warfare to be undertaken by the "regular" army training in Tunisia. But French strength also had increased; in 1959 it would reach 550,000 (including police and Moslem auxiliaries).[40] Considering French strength and armament, the rebel action proved premature and ALN units began suffering high casualties. By the time of the frontier battles in 1958, the French claimed thirty thousand insurgent dead and thirteen thousand wounded; in early 1958, they were claiming three thousand insurgent "kills" per month.[41] Allowing for normal military hyperbole—somewhere between 50 and 75 per cent —little doubt existed that the insurgents were being hurt.

French tactics, moreover, were becoming increasingly sophisticated. General Salan and his successor, General Challe, developed a more qualitative approach by organizing *commandos de chasse,* elite units of sixty to a hundred men that disappeared into rebel country for weeks at a time, in General Salan's words,

. . . moving always on foot and nearly always at night, carrying out surprise attacks on well-chosen targets, unexpectedly arriving in villages, attempting to gain maximum intelligence on FLN units and arrest or eliminate rebel personnel, setting up intelligence networks, ambushing local rebel bands, if necessary splitting up in groups as small as four men . . . perhaps calling on artillery and the air force to engage sizeable rebel concentrations, these units would create constant insecurity for the opponent while gradually giving the rural population a comforting feeling of constant security.[42]

Helicopters had also come into their own; they numbered about two hundred and, although air force retained operational control, which led

38. O'Ballance (*Algerian Insurrection*), *supra.*
39. Behr, op. cit.
40. O'Ballance (*Algerian Insurrection*), *supra.*
41. Ibid.
42. Paret, op. cit.

to late reaction, they were beginning to result in considerable operational gains.[43] Enemy resistance had caused the French to arm helicopters with machine guns and rockets and to protect pilots with armored seats and flak suits. Vulnerability to enemy fire—guerrilla fire—was still high, but improved tactics reduced it. In 1957, helicopter pilots flew fifty-six thousand combat hours and sixty-two machines were hit; in 1958, they flew sixty-four thousand hours and fifty machines were hit; in 1959, they flew sixty-six thousand hours and thirty-five were hit. In 1957, enemy fire killed nine crew members, in 1960 none.[44]

The Challe Plan, as it became known, continued to introduce more-mobile tactics. Large-scale *bouclage* operations also grew in size and intensity throughout 1959 to produce thousands of insurgent dead—according to French reports. Less-biased observers questioned that many of the dead were insurgents and that Challe's widely publicized plan was as productive as he claimed.

De Gaulle himself refused to share military optimism. Challe may have frustrated the final "mobile" phase of the insurgency, but that did not mean he had eliminated the guerrilla threat. Notwithstanding Challe's assertions, urban terrorism was increasing, and guerrilla action continued in the countryside. De Gaulle realized that the French could fight in Algeria for the next hundred years, a war that for some time had been costing France over a billion dollars a year. Military action, he realized, had become of subordinate importance—a necessary prelude to bringing the FLN to the negotiating table. The sooner he could accomplish this, the better, for the GPRA was steadily gaining international sympathy, including substantial Communist support, a fact exploited by French rightists, who forever argued that the rebellion in reality was a Communist putsch.[45]

In September 1959, De Gaulle made his famous "self-determination" speech: within four years after peace, he offered Algeria a choice of three courses: to continue as an integrated part of France; to become a federated member of the French Union; or to secede entirely from French control (in which case, France would retain the Sahara region).

Once again, De Gaulle probably did not expect instant action. Astute

43. Hilaire Béthouart, "Combat Helicopters in Algeria." In T. N. Greene (ed.), *The Guerrilla and How to Fight Him* (New York: Frederick A. Praeger, 1962).
44. Ibid.
45. O'Ballance (*Algerian Insurrection*), *supra*, estimated that, by the end of 1960, Communist China was supplying half of FLN's annual $80-million budget, with Moslem countries making up the other half. In addition, terrorists extracted large sums by blackmail and extortion from Moslem workers—perhaps as much as $30 million a year in France; see also Eisenhower (*Waging Peace*), *supra*: ". . . De Gaulle's concern over suspected Communist influence in Algeria was strong"—and it was one reason that he shied away, at first, from dealing directly with FLN leaders. Chancellor Adenauer of Germany ". . . seemed almost obsessed with the Algerian problem" and the fear that the entire area would fall under Communist control—a fear that Eisenhower claimed he did not share.

politician that he was, he probably hoped to clear the air further: to satisfy allies, particularly the United States; to cause militant FLN leaders some soul-searching—Ferhat Abbas had admitted a deterioration in the guerrilla campaign and was under considerable pressure from Tunisia and Morocco to come to terms with France; to let natural pressures exert themselves on the FLN, for instance the four hundred thousand Moslems working in France; to show European ultras and the army in Algeria his intention either to gain their acquiescence or provoke a showdown. At the time of his speech, he was aware of military recalcitrance, particularly on part of Challe and Massu, who, backed by a number of "activist" groups in Algiers, were increasingly hindering Delouvrier's reform attempts.

The crisis came in January 1960, when Massu openly criticized De Gaulle in a newspaper interview. De Gaulle promptly transferred him. A protest demonstration of European "territorial units" in Algiers exploded into an insurgency that gendarmerie could not contain and army refused to put down. "Barricades Week" was an incipient attempt to unseat De Gaulle. Fortunately for him, a good many units remained loyal and the action fizzled—but only after French soldiers had fired on French civilians, increasing the bitterness of the European population. The action left De Gaulle more determined than ever to re-establish state authority; in February, he obtained "special powers" for one year and, virtually in a dictatorial role, continued his peace offensive throughout 1960.

De Gaulle continued to meet obstructionism from the European ultras and his own military leaders. Certain of the latter insisted that the FLN rebellion had failed: they pointed to successful border suppression operations and to a marked decrease in size of guerrilla units and scope of guerrilla actions. They failed to understand that De Gaulle's promise of self-determination had moved rebellion to the political arena, a fact De Gaulle realized and one emphasized both by continuing guerrilla-terrorist actions where necessary to serve FLN political purposes and by massive Moslem pro-FLN demonstrations when De Gaulle again visited the country, in December 1960.

To strengthen his hand further, De Gaulle held a referendum, in January 1961, which overwhelmingly approved his Algerian policy. Thus armed, he secretly approached the FLN to arrange talks at Évian. FLN fears of a double cross had just been assuaged when De Gaulle faced another, and final, rebellion, the price of his refusal to take drastic action against dissident military commanders. Men such as Raoul Salan, André Zeller, and Edmond Jouhaud did not suffer retirement gracefully. Instead, with the help of Algerian Europeans and other senior military officers, they organized the OAS (*Organisation de l'Armée Secrète*), whose slogan was "French Algeria or Death." Early in 1960, the OAS had opened a terrorist campaign against the De Gaulle government *inside* France. The movement grew until, at some point, General Maurice Challe, De Gaulle's former military commander in Algeria who subsequently served at NATO headquarters, joined it. In April 1961, Challe and Zeller arrived secretly in Algiers. A few days later, the military junta proclaimed open rebellion and, for a few days, France stood in grave danger of falling under a military dictatorship.

As happened earlier, the bulk of conscripts remained loyal to De Gaulle, as did the commander in chief, General Gambiez, all of the navy, and most of the air force. Major O'Ballance has estimated that perhaps forty thousand troops opted for the junta, whose hard core numbered about eighteen thousand paratroopers and legionnaires. In addition, the army distributed an estimated thirty thousand arms to civilian supporters. But junta leadership seemed vague, and when other military units did not join the rebellion, the leaders lost heart. Within four days, Challe surrendered, Zeller followed suit; Jouhaud and Salan went into hiding.[46] De Gaulle arrested five generals and some two hundred officers, dissolved disloyal units—and carried on negotiations with the FLN.[47]

The rebellion now entered a new, and final, phase. The FLN and ALN, already on the defensive, responded favorably to conciliatory moves by further reducing guerrilla-terrorist activity while peace talks continued. Unfortunately, this did not stop the shooting. The De Gaulle government had to fight a take-over attempt by the OAS both in Algeria and in France, a seamy period, with Frenchmen killing Frenchmen, that lasted until spring of 1962. Shortly after the OAS collapsed, France agreed to Algerian independence, which, for better or worse, was proclaimed in July.

The rebellion cost both sides heavily. All told, the French army suffered perhaps twelve thousand troops plus twenty-five hundred Moslem auxiliaries killed. About three thousand Europeans lost their lives and thousands were wounded. Algerian Moslems suffered about 141,000 deaths, according to the French[48]; the FLN estimated six hundred thousand deaths.[49]

Twelve years after the rebellion, France is still recovering from the psychological effects—from shock experienced by millions of Frenchmen upon learning of their police and military proclivity for torture; from bitterness particularly rampant among military rightists, who regarded and still regard De Gaulle's acquiescence as a denial of traditional French values. Twelve years after the rebellion, Algeria is still

46. Behr, op. cit.; see also De Gaulle, op. cit.
47. O'Ballance (*Algerian Insurrection*), *supra:* Subsequent trials sent Challe and Zeller to prison for fifteen years; sentenced Salan, Jouhaud, and other fugitives to death *in absentia;* dismissed other officers from the service without pension; and summarily retired still others; see also De Gaulle, op. cit.
48. O'Ballance (*Algerian Insurrection*), *supra.*
49. Gillespie, op. cit.

struggling to establish legitimate government, let alone enjoy the fruits of independence—a struggle that has caused her on occasion to seek awkward political bedfellows, but a struggle that may yet lead to rapprochement with France and the West.

Chapter 72

The Cuban revolution • Special characteristics • Its psychological impact on the United States • Historical background • Early American presence • The Platt Amendment • American military intervention • Gerardo Machado and the strong-man tradition • Internal opposition mounts • Early rebellions • Washington intervenes • The Batista era • His strength and weakness • The political situation • The American position • Enter Fidel Castro • His background • The 26th of July Movement • Trial, imprisonment, release

A FINAL INSURGENCY and one of particular importance to the United States marked the end of this turbulent decade. The first phase of the Cuban revolution, fought from 1953 to 1959, replaced Fulgencio Batista with Fidel Castro as Cuba's ruler—the opening act of a drama that would soon raise a Communist flag over this large island lying only ninety miles from Florida's coast.

The rebellion was peculiarly Cuban. Its outbreak surprised both Cuban and American authorities, who seemed reluctant to admit the threat to government. Its suppression, even when that threat became real, seemed generally apathetic. The insurgency followed no particular precedent, combining, as it did, peasant, proletarian, and middle-class elements which finally fused to produce popular revolution. Castro's leadership proved important, but revolution might have occurred without it. It could not have occurred without Batista's government. It is not an easy revolution to understand: It was fought in a welter of confusion compounded by divisive movements inside and outside Cuba,

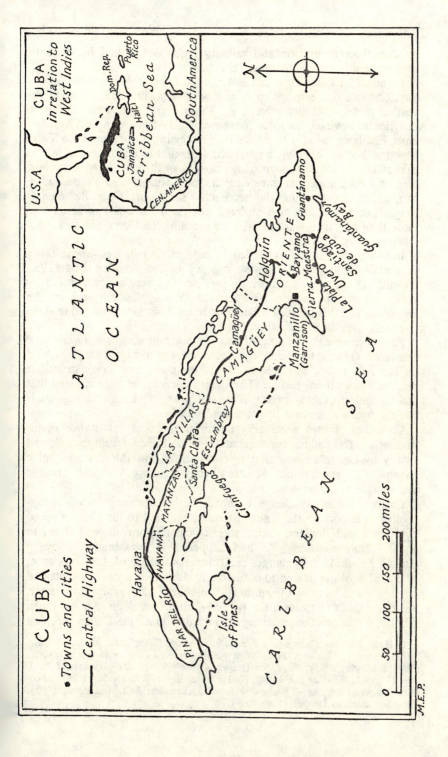

by American diplomatic and military ambivalence, and by dramatic and frequently erroneous press reports.

In terms of carnage, it did not approach other insurgencies of the day. Castro's first attempt to seize government, in 1953, failed at the cost of perhaps seventy rebel lives. Three years later, when he landed in Oriente province, his force numbered eighty-three men and, in a few days, had been reduced to twelve men struggling to survive in the Sierra Maestra. For months, he commanded a handful of guerrillas. As late as mid-1958, his columns counted no more than three hundred irregulars, some not even armed; at war's end, the rebel army totaled a thousand or two, with perhaps another thousand active supporters. Guerrilla columns fought but few battles and suffered minimum casualties—probably no more than fifty men were killed after reaching the Sierra Maestra sanctuary in early 1957.

Batista's small army expanded to only modest figures—about thirty thousand—despite the increasing urgency of the situation from 1957 onward. Though equipped with American weapons and supported by tanks and aircraft, in only one operation did it aggressively seek out the guerrillas, and this failed. Probably no more than three hundred soldiers lost their lives in the rebellion's last two years.

Far more casualties occurred in cities and towns, where a variety of resistance organizations employed selective terrorism answered in kind by Batista's police and soldiers. No one knows how many casualties resulted from urban warfare. The Castro government later claimed that the revolution exacted twenty thousand lives; more-realistic appraisals put the figure at around two thousand killed.[1]

Casualties do not necessarily determine residual importance of insurgencies. The sudden consummation of the Cuban rebellion, followed swiftly by Castro's conversion to communism, introduced catastrophic change to Cuban fortunes, besides directly affecting American strategic and commercial interests.

Castro's blatant challenge to hemispheric hegemony levied a psychological impact on the United States tantamount to those experienced by France and England during their colonial upheavals, and it led to equally futile reactions. As had happened in Washington following Chiang Kai-shek's fall, charges and countercharges filled the air. A score of biased books appeared to obfuscate further the analysis of events and any lessons to be drawn from them. Subsequent scholarship, fortunately, has done much to unravel the twisted skein of rebellion. An American scholar, Theodore Draper, early attempted to place the Cuban rebellion

---

1. Hugh Thomas, *Cuba or the Pursuit of Freedom* (New York: Harper & Row, 1971); Boris Goldenberg, *The Cuban Revolution and Latin America* (London: Allen & Unwin, 1965); Theodore Draper, *Castro's Revolution—Myths and Realities* (London: Thames & Hudson, 1962). Hereafter cited as Draper (*CR*); Theodore Draper, *Castroism—Theory and Practice* (London: Pall Mall Press, 1965). Hereafter cited as Draper (*Castroism*).

in honest perspective.[2] More recently, a British scholar, Hugh Thomas, has opened new vistas with his definitive history, *Cuba, or the Pursuit of Freedom*—a must for any reader interested in the island's past (and future).[3]

As with other insurgencies, the etiology of the Cuban revolution was old and complex, its roots growing from soil prepared by prolonged Spanish occupation, its early blooms the 1865 and 1895 uprisings, its growth from 1898 directly related to American policy deriving from the Spanish-American war (see Chapter 12, Volume I).

This war, which cost perhaps three hundred thousand Cuban lives, brought something akin to anarchy to Cuba.[4] The survivors, about a million and a half people living on an island roughly the size of Pennsylvania, were eager for independence but ill-prepared for self-government. Public services had broken down; people were ill and hungry; bands of Spanish counterguerrillas turned outlaws roamed the island in manner reminiscent of French *routiers* in the Hundred Years' War.

Convinced that Cubans could not govern themselves, President McKinley assigned the problem to the U. S. Army, which occupied and administered the war-torn country until 1902. As in the Philippines, most American civil and military officials tended to treat the native with contempt. General Young described García's veteran guerrilla army as ". . . a lot of degenerates, absolutely devoid of honor or gratitude. They are no more capable of self government than the savages."[5] American soldiers treated Negro guerrillas with open disdain. On the other hand, Americans got on well with Spanish survivors, and many of the latter continued to serve in official capacities. The uneven occupation produced a number of benefits to Cubans, particularly in health and education, and it also resulted in considerable U.S. commercial investment, about $100 million, mostly in tobacco, sugar, and railroads.[6] While this brought welcome prosperity to some, it also introduced a lopsided economy, whose expansion too often depended on bribery and corruption.

But for Congressional legislation (the 1898 Teller Amendment, which renounced American sovereignty over Cuba) and anti-administration pressures arising from the Philippine insurrection, McKinley

2. Draper (*CR*), *supra*.
3. Thomas, op. cit.
4. R. A. Chapman, *A History of the Cuban Republic* (New York: Macmillan, 1927); H. A. Herring, *A History of Latin America* (London: Jonathan Cape, 1955); Fulgencio Batista, *Cuba Betrayed* (New York: Vantage Press, 1962); Thomas, op. cit.
5. Thomas, op. cit.
6. Ibid.: The real figure is higher, since land bought in huge parcels by U.S. companies was so cheap; the American Government eventually rented the Guantánamo base area—45 square miles—at a rent of $2,000 a year!

might have annexed Cuba. Instead, the American Government secured indirect control through the Platt Amendment. This incredible document gave the United States the right to maintain military bases in Cuba and to intervene either to preserve Cuban independence or to maintain stable government. The United States also reserved right to ratify treaties Cuba made with other nations! Theodore Roosevelt's administration extended the legislation by forcing Tomás Estrada Palma's government to incorporate the amendment in the Cuban constitution and in the 1903 treaty between the United States and Cuba.[7]

The Platt Amendment disguised a commercial wolf in the sheep's clothing of strategic necessity. An attempt at colonialism on the cheap, this codicil to the Monroe Doctrine mocked the "manifest destiny" thesis so ably and forcefully expounded by Alfred Mahan, Henry Lodge, and Theodore Roosevelt. It tried to reap the fruits of colonialism without accepting responsibilities of colonialism. It was the opening chapter in the U.S.A's imperialistic fling, and no one quite knew how to interpret it. Secretary of War Elihu Root viewed it circumspectly, carefully differentiating between "formal action"—the use of force—and persuasive action. Secretary of State Philander Knox later chose force to further a "preventive policy." As succeeding administrations learned the limits of force as well as its expense, the Platt Amendment grew less attractive and even embarrassing.[8] But, by the time the American Government and people came to their senses, a great deal of damage had been done.

Cuban self-government proved disastrous. Although Estrada was honest, his administration was not; a weak man, he failed to check venal officials more interested in amassing personal fortunes than in weaving sound fabric of government. Opposition developed. Lacking an adequate army to defend his government, Estrada turned to the United States for support.

McKinley's and Roosevelt's refusal to annex Cuba should have left the island to work out its own political destiny. The Philippine experience had dampened Roosevelt's belief in "manifest destiny," and he would have preferred this. It possibly could have happened, had the commercial element been absent. But it was not absent. American investment soon doubled, to approximately $200 million, and the pot of gold lying beneath the Cuban rainbow seemed scarcely touched. When General Piño Guerra's guerrillas began threatening Estrada's government, Roosevelt found himself under severe pressure to intervene.[9]

7. Bryce Wood, *The Making of the Good Neighbor Policy* (New York: Columbia University Press, 1961); see also SORO, op. cit.

8. Wood, op. cit.

9. Thomas, op. cit.: To clarify matters, McKinley sent his Secretary of War, William Howard Taft, to Havana. Taft reported unfavorably on the rebel movement: ". . . It is not a government . . . only an undisciplined horde of men

He refused, but when Estrada resigned, in late September 1906, Roosevelt saw no alternative.[10] A few days later, a hastily improvised force of two thousand U.S. marines landed "to restore order," the vanguard of some five thousand U.S. army occupation troops, which remained for two and a half years. During the interregnum, a provisional governor, Charles Magoon, introduced political, administrative, and military reforms—a program only partially completed when he returned the country to its newly elected president, José Miguel Gómez, in 1908.

The Gómez government and its successor, the Menocal government, virtually legalized what the Estrada administration (but not Estrada) had practiced: wholesale corruption that made the two presidents and their senior lieutenants millionaires at the country's expense. At the same time, American investment increased. In 1912, to protect American interests against an uprising of Negro field hands, Secretary of State Philander Knox arranged a "preventive" landing of American marines.[11] In 1917, marines briefly landed in support of Menocal's regime, which was being challenged by a Liberal revolution. Menocal, who ". . . became known as a man more utterly committed to bribery and corruption than even Gómez,"[12] stood in high favor in Washington, partly because of Wilson's desire for a co-operative Cuba in World War I, partly because ". . . the general attitude in Washington had always been that Menocal was upright and that Gómez and the Liberals were corrupt."[13] At Menocal's request, the Wilson administration stationed twenty-six hundred marines in Cuba, where they remained until 1923, an important instrument in maintaining the fragile "stability" so sought by American commercial interests, particularly during the sugar crisis of 1920 and the election that placed Menocal's candidate, Alfredo Zayas, in the presidency.

Zayas changed nothing of Cuba's political pattern. A rich man by the end of his term, he had insured the growth of forces of discontent. Maintaining internal stability was to become ever more difficult. In early 1921, rebellious University of Havana students had organized a

---

under partisan leaders. The movement is large and formidable and commands the sympathy of a majority of the people of Cuba but they are the poorer classes and uneducated."

10. Ibid.: Roosevelt cabled Taft: ". . . If the Palma government had shown any real capacity for self-defense and ability to sustain itself and a sincere purpose to remedy the wrongs of which your telegrams show them to have been guilty, I should have been inclined to stand by them no matter to what extent, including armed intervention. But as things already are we do not have a chance of following any such course . . . [since] they absolutely decline either to endeavor to remedy the wrongs they have done or to so much as lift a hand in their own defense . . . we must simply put ourselves . . . in Palma's place, land a sufficient force to restore order and notify the insurgents that we will carry thru the program in which you and they are agreed. . . ."

11. Wood, op. cit.
12. Thomas, op. cit.
13. Ibid.

WAR IN THE SHADOWS

student federation, the FEU. In 1925, a trade union federation, CNOC, appeared, as did a small Communist Party. Faced with these and other opposition groups, Zayas' successor, General Gerardo Machado, turned increasingly to strong-arm methods, as befitted one whose hero was Benito Mussolini. Machado cunningly disguised his methods, at least sufficiently to fool the Coolidge administration. By this time, however, the American Government, influenced by various commercial interests, had become so wedded to the strong-man concept of Cuba government that little fooling was necessary. Even when Machado abrogated the constitution to extend his term of office, American apologists defended the action in interests of "stability"; nor did the Hoover administration seem entirely displeased. A U. S. State Department official later wrote:

. . . both the Department and the Embassy put a premium on "order" in Cuba. . . . President Machado had brought internal peace to Cuba for the first time since 1917. Both Ambassador Crowder and the Department indicated that their passivity to the constitutional amendments was due to their hope that under Machado peace, order, and "political cooperation" would continue.[14]

Secretary of State Stimson's experience in Mexico and Nicaragua had caused him to shy away from intervention elsewhere, and though he continued to "intermeddle," he would not intervene:

. . . Henceforth, the Department's policy became one of drift, punctuated by spasmodic and gradually feebler attempts to persuade Machado to satisfy the press, the public, and the opposition by legislative reforms and by permitting a larger measure of civil liberties.[15]

If Washington turned a blind eye, influential segments of the Cuban population did not. Continued opposition had long since caused Machado to compound wholesale corruption by the unpleasant expedient of imprisoning, torturing, and murdering political opponents. With the constitution defunct and the sugar market at an all-time low, Cuba faced political and economic bankruptcy.[16]

Underground opposition spread among students and middle-class citizens. An organization known as ABC undertook ". . . by the deliberate creation of terror to cause a break-down in governmental activities, so, they assumed, making action of some sort by Washington inevitable."[17] Machado blamed political assassinations of his *porristas* on "Communist" elements and replied with counterterror. Murder

14. Wood, op. cit.
15. Ibid.
16. Ruby Hart Phillips, *Cuba—Island of Paradox* (New York: McDowell, Obolensky, 1959).
17. Thomas, op. cit.; Phillips, op. cit.: ABC used a cellular organization based on a secret French revolutionary society.

became commonplace: ". . . Scarcely a night passed in Havana without some attempt at assassination, or some cruel measure of reprisal by the secret police."[18] Early in 1933, the CNOC called out twenty thousand sugar workers at beginning of harvest. In May, a rebellion broke out in Santa Clara.

The American Government intervened, but not quite in the way imagined by Cuban terrorists. Instead of marines, the newly elected president Franklin Roosevelt, sent Sumner Welles as his ambassador to "mediate." After studying the situation and consulting with various opposition groups, Welles attempted to force Machado to step down.

In addition to a bureaucratic apparatus whose senior officials would continue to benefit from his stay in office, Machado had two allies in his fight with Welles and the opposition groups. The Communists were one, but, at this time, the party was not even strong enough to ward off a general strike that brought life in the cities almost to a standstill. The army was the other. Here was Machado's Achilles' heel. By involving the military in state administration, Machado had opened its ranks to unseemly pressures. Graft permeated the twelve-thousand-man body. Senior officers were not reliable and were prone to back a new horse; junior officers, many trained in the United States, desired a military efficiency they believed could come only with change. Enlisted men resented inadequate food and clothing and were amenable to change. Machado's refusal to give the military a voice in his discussions with the opposition further weakened its loyalty, and, in the crunch, important elements refused to back him.

Machado abdicated in August. A ghastly period followed, in which ABC terrorists killed any *porristas* they could find. The blood bath, graphically described to American readers by Ruby Hart Phillips, wife of the New York *Times* correspondent in Havana, in her interesting book *Cuba—Island of Paradox,* probably took a thousand lives before the government restored precarious order.[19] Although Welles asked Washington to land troops, wiser counsels prevailed and held intervention to a naval fleet, which appeared in island waters and effectively strengthened Welles's hand.

Cuba's new ruler, Carlos Miguel Céspedes, was Sumner Welles's compromise selection. Too weak for the task, he almost at once succumbed to forces unleashed by the "sergeants' revolt": a small but powerful group of well-organized non-commissioned officers who, incredibly, led a bloodless coup that installed a thirty-two-year-old sergeant-typist, Fulgencio Batista, as army chief of staff!

An exceptional man, Batista. Son of a sugar worker, he was of mulatto-Indian extraction. At age eight, he was working in cane fields;

18. Sumner Welles, *The Time for Decision* (New York: Harper & Brothers, 1944); see also Wood, op. cit., for a detailed analysis of the Welles negotiations; see also Cordell Hull, *Memoirs* (New York: Macmillan, 1948).

19. Phillips, op. cit.; see also Wood, op. cit.

orphaned at thirteen, he attended a night school run by American Quakers.[20] He later held a variety of common-laborer jobs and finally enlisted in the army. Correspondence courses trained him in stenography; promoted to sergeant, he held a staff job that allowed him to participate in and soon lead the army rebellion.

Batista was young, smart, handsome in a way, charming when he wished to be. He possessed considerable charisma and was also a realist. Recognizing his limited strength and particularly Welles's opposition, he formed a military-student junta that replaced Céspedes with a provisional revolutionary government headed by the dean of the University of Havana's medical school, Doctor Ramón Grau San Martín.

Whether the Grau government would have effected the revolution it proclaimed is a moot question. Its radical intentions frightened Sumner Welles nearly to death, and if he failed in having marines landed to put things right, he succeeded in preventing Washington from recognizing the new government.[21] No Cuban government could long endure without Washington's approval, and no one recognized the fact more than Batista. After cementing his position as army chief—a nasty fracas that eliminated officer opposition—he installed a compromise president, Colonel Carlos Mendieta. He himself remained the real boss.

Thus began the Batista era. As with most dictatorships, a period of consolidation proved necessary to eliminate or at least neutralize active opposition. Batista possessed three allies during this crucial period: the Mendieta government, which he virtually ruled but which offered at least a façade of legitimate government; the army, which he did rule; and the Good Neighbor Policy, which caused the American Congress to abolish the Platt Amendment even while insuring American commercial dominance in Cuba.

Although Batista ruled as dictator, he somewhat mollified the Roosevelt administration (which had numerous other problems) by providing stability and continued protection of American investments. He also introduced a good many social reforms, including labor laws. If rule by army increased rather than decreased, he nonetheless permitted return of opposition groups; he not only allowed Communists a legitimate existence, but, in answer to middle-class and student opposition, he actively allied with them and with labor. Finally, he permitted election

20. Edmund A. Chester, *A Sergeant Named Batista* (New York: Henry Holt, 1954). This fulsome account must be read with care: Chester was Batista's public-relations adviser; see also, Herbert L. Matthews, *The Cuban Story* (New York: George Braziller, 1961). Hereafter cited as Matthews (*CS*); Herbert L. Matthews, *Castro—A Political Biography* (New York: Simon & Schuster, 1969). Hereafter cited as Matthews (*Castro*).

21. Wood, op. cit.: Grau called Welles's non-recognition policy ". . . a new type of intervention—intervention by inertia," that ". . . intensifies the very ills it claims to pacify, maintaining a condition of intranquillity in our social and economic structure."

of a constituent assembly, which wrote the 1940 constitution: ". . . a real attempt at social democracy. It was, however, rarely read after it was written."[22]

Elected president in 1940, Batista continued a warm alliance with the United States and Great Britain. In the fever of war, no one seemed to notice that the new constitution became as dead as yesterday's newspaper. Bolstered by U.S. loans and huge sugar crops, the economy surged forward. In 1944, Batista stepped down. When his presidential candidate lost to Grau San Martín, head of the rival Auténtico party, Batista retired to his Florida holdings and a personal fortune estimated at about $20 million.

But not for long.

His successors, Grau and, in 1948, another Auténtico leader, Carlos Prío Socarrás, ruled in the Batista mold but without Batista's effectiveness. Corruption appeared in a thousand new forms, and, from corruption, grew violence, until government became a riddled mass of competing forces, legitimate and illegitimate. Grau's and Prío's Auténticos remained the leading party. Eduardo Chibás, scion of a wealthy family, had splintered to form the Ortodoxos, which attracted a liberal middle-class and student following. Grau alienated the Communists, who formed a separate political entity, as did Batista's followers. In addition to legitimate parties, political pressure groups existed such as the trade unions (CTC) and the students (FEU); so did a host of gangster groups, which infiltrated and sometimes controlled segments of political parties and pressure groups.[23]

Batista returned to this political maelstrom in 1948, as a newly elected senator. Three years later, he declared himself a candidate for President and began campaigning against Auténtico and Ortodoxo candidates. Two months before scheduled elections, he stole the government in a bloodless coup d'état carried out by a group of army officers that had remained loyal to him.

Batista might have emerged a Salazar or a Franco—even a Bolívar or a Martí. A number of factors favored him. He enjoyed considerable personal popularity despite former excesses. In general, the army supported him and, in turn, he cosseted officers and non-commissioned officers with increased pay and other perquisites.[24] The twelve-thousand-man army was becoming reasonably well organized, trained, and equipped—the work, largely, of a U.S. military mission that operated under the terms of a hemispheric Mutual Security Pact.[25]

Batista soon installed his own followers in other key departments,

22. Thomas, op. cit.
23. Ibid.
24. Goldenberg, op. cit.
25. Thomas, op. cit.; the agreement somewhat unrealistically forbade use of armor and B-26 bombers ". . . except in agreement and in defense of the hemisphere."

particularly in the enlarged police force, and he made considerable progress in neutralizing activities of gangster elements. Promise of stable government appealed to wealthy businessmen and landowners and to the Catholic Church, but a large and reasonably articulate middle class also was tired of corruption and inept government and probably would have supported a progressive administration. The small Communist Party, the PSP, was well disciplined; its main strength lay in trade unions whose leaders Batista had paid off, and it readily assumed a working relationship with Batista.[26]

The American Government almost immediately recognized the new regime—according to some experts, a fatal error—and promised to continue supplying it with arms and military advisers.[27] This was the McCarthy era, and Batista knew how to whisper the magic phrase "Communist threat"—little fear of the neighboring horn of plenty drying up, and almost none after the U.S.S.R. broke diplomatic relations with Cuba. As a boon, in 1953 the new President, Dwight Eisenhower, sent Ambassador Arthur Gardner to Havana. Gardner was an ". . . unabashed admirer and ardent abettor of Batista."[28] According to Mrs. Phillips, he was so pro-Batista as to embarrass even Batista![29]

Cuba itself was prosperous enough, though with shocking inequities. The sugar market had remained healthy since the early 1940s, and the Korean war had sustained it. Ample labor and American capital existed to expand and diversify the lopsided sugar economy. Despite the financial drain of a half century of venal rule, urban dwellers—57 per cent of the population—fared reasonably well. In terms of per-capita income, Cuba's six and a half million people ranked fourth in Latin America and also ranked high in percentage ownership of such material possessions as cars and radios.[30] Trade unions were bringing social security and other advantages to the working man. With proper leadership, the country could probably have advanced to a level sufficient to support major social, economic, and political reforms.[31]

26. Goldenberg, op. cit.
27. Draper (CR), supra: In 1945–60, U.S. military aid to Cuba totaled "only" $10.6 million; see also Frank Tannenbaum, "The United States and Latin America," Political Science Quarterly, June 1961; Robert Taber, M-26—Biography of a Revolution (New York: Lyle Stuart, 1961): In 1956–58, Batista received from the United States 3,000 M-1 rifles, 50 machine guns, a large quantity of ammunition, several thousand rockets, and seven tanks.
28. Draper (CR), supra.
29. Phillips, op. cit.
30. Draper (Castroism), supra; but per-capita measure of income is often misleading; see also D. Seers, A. Bianchi, R. Jolly, and M. Nolff, Cuba—The Economic and Social Revolution (Chapel Hill, N.C.: University of North Carolina Press, 1964). Hereafter cited as Seers: In 1958, Cuba's per-capita income had risen from the 1952 figure, yet ". . . averaged about $500 or one-fifth as much as the average in the United States (far lower even than in any Southern state there)"; Goldenberg, op. cit.
31. Taber, op. cit.: ". . . Felipe Pazos, head of the Banco Cubano Continental, Cuba's largest private bank under the Batista administration, said that graft on

Batista nevertheless faced a number of problems that demanded urgent attention. Cuba's five hundred thousand peasants all too often lived in impoverished circumstances. Cuba's illiteracy rate was 11.6 per cent in the cities; in the countryside, it reached a shocking 41.7 per cent.[32] A team of non-Cuban economists later concluded:

. . . in the countryside social conditions were very bad. About a third of the nation existed in squalor, eating rice, beans, bananas, and root vegetables (with hardly any meat, fish, eggs, or milk), living in huts, usually without electricity or toilet facilities, suffering from parasitic disease and lacking access to health services, denied education (their children received only a first grade education, if that). Particularly distressing was the lot of the *precaristas*—those squatting in makeshift quarters on public land.[33]

C. Wright Mills's not-so-mythical Cuban cries plaintively to the reader:

. . . In our Caribbean paradise of violence and grief, of terror and misery, almost nine out of ten of the rural "homes" (although North Americans would scarcely call our *bohíos* "homes") had only kerosene lighting. Less than 3 per cent had water piped into them. More than half did not even have—perhaps it is difficult for you to imagine this—over half did not even have an *outdoor* privy; only about 3 per cent had toilets indoors.

Almost two-thirds of our children were *not* in any elementary school and most of those who did start in school soon dropped out. In 1950, for example, 180,000 children began the first grade, but less than 5,000 began the eighth grade. That figure is not for the countryside only; it is for the whole of Cuba, city and country.[34]

The peasants needed not only land, houses, schools, and hospitals, but also crop diversification to allow more than a few months' work each year harvesting the sugar crop. By ignoring the peasants' plight, Batista encouraged a rural dissidence that needed only to be harnessed to become a viable revolutionary force; perhaps as important, the peasants constituted the bulk of his army, a venal, corrupt, and factional body that offered the recruit no more pride in country than offered by his earlier, grim rural environment.[35]

Cuba also suffered a high rate of chronic unemployment and underemployment, with accompanying poverty in the towns:

. . . Here, too, there were squatters living in shacks, and of course there were slum tenements. In 1953, no less than one-fifth of these families lived

---

public works during the seven years of Batista's rule came close to 500 million pesos on a total public-works budget of less than eight hundred millions. . . ."

32. Draper (*Castroism*), *supra*.

33. Seers, op. cit.; see also Leo Huberman and Paul Sweezy, *Cuba—Anatomy of a Revolution* (London: Routledge & Kegan Paul, 1960).

34. C. Wright Mills, *Castro's Cuba* (London: Secker & Warburg, 1960).

35. Draper (*Castroism*), *supra*.

in single rooms, and the average size of those families was five, according to the census. Taking the urban and rural population together, 62 per cent of the economically active population had incomes of less than $75 a month.[36]

In cities, Batista faced considerable opposition from Auténticos, Ortodoxos, and students. His problem here was basically political. Batista seized power, he said, because Prío Socarrás was preparing his own *coup d'état*. He probably acted because it was the only way he could have gained office. He now faced the ugly fact that he, self-pronounced father of constitutional government, violated his own tenets. His pose as savior of democracy by rape possibly could have come off had he restored the 1940 constitution and implemented administrative reforms. He promised to do so. Pleading need for time, he promised elections in late 1953. But, in the interim, he abrogated civil rights and resorted to one-man rule. Although eventually permitting "cooked" elections, he retained authoritarian rule, his power dependent on police and army.[37]

But politics entered here as well. Batista's chief of staff, General Tabernilla Dolz, was a particularly unfortunate choice. Not only did he install sons and in-laws in senior command billets, but he actively engaged in the protection rackets, and the gambling and prostitution that made Havana, and indeed all of Cuba, a major tourist attraction, and here he collided with police interests.[38] Worse, however, was his administration of the army:

. . . Soon the army was dominated by a net of intrigue and distrust, exacerbated by Tabernilla's recall of all officers dismissed by Grau in 1944–45, who were given their back pay over seven or eight years as well. Tabernilla was concerned to establish a network of officers loyal to him—an activity which made enemies not only of the professional group of officers, the *puros,* who had joined since 1945 but of those—the *tanquistas*—who had begun the conspiracy against Prío and who now were increasingly disillusioned, having hoped for a tougher, stricter, and more puritanical regime.[39]

Batista would have had a difficult time solving these various problems even had he exerted his considerable abilities. He did not do this, and he accomplished very few reforms. The why of his failure is not clear. Professor Hugh Thomas suggests that years of exile had made him lazy

---

36. Seers, *supra.*
37. Batista, op. cit.: He attempted to gain a semblance of legitimacy from an appointive Consultive Council of 80 members and a smaller Council of Ministers.
38. Taber, op. cit.: ". . . The officers of the general staff—Tabernilla and the rest—were notoriously Cuba's greatest smugglers of automobiles, refrigerators, cigarettes, whiskey; the police fattened on the brothels and invested their illicit gains in apartment houses; Batista himself received a slice of everything, including the fantastic revenue of the great gambling casinos run by American gangsters."
39. Thomas, op. cit.

and petty. Economic prosperity probably added to his fecklessness, as did American support of his armed forces and regime. As long as he could offer "stable" government, he would continue to attract American capital and thus insure mounting prosperity.

Batista also seems to have underestimated opposition. Cuba's security problem was not the Communist threat to the American hemisphere posed by the Soviet Union and preached by the Pentagon. It was an internal threat, and, as in the Philippines, Vietnam, and other trouble areas, it called for accurate recognition and intelligent suppression by small, specially trained units, as opposed to shiny battalions supported by armor and air and taught conventional tactics by conventionally minded American officers.

Most of all, however, it called for solution by good government. But Batista, from the beginning, refused the task of democratic government. Instead, like some fat slug, he retired into the official cocoon of the Presidential Palace seemingly secured by martial trappings of police and troops. The trappings would hold for a while. Intimidation and arrest and beatings and torture and murder would mute but not calm breezes of dissidence. When breezes swelled to winds of change, the trappings would waver and begin to snap until a final hurricane swept them away to demolish the cocoon they supported.

Enter Fidel Castro Ruz.

Castro was born in 1927, the illegitimate and eldest son of Ángel Castro, a hard-working and shrewd peasant.[40] Although Ángel became a landowner sufficiently wealthy to leave each of seven children a considerable sum, his house lacked both bathroom and running water, as did nearly all houses in Birán, in Oriente province, an impoverished area dominated by American fruit and mining companies.

Fidel attended good Jesuit schools, and, in 1945, went on to study law at the University of Havana. A poor student, he concentrated on politics, associating with campus branches of two gangster groups, the MSR and the UIR, and finally joining Chibás' Ortodoxo party; he may have participated in two political assassinations.[41] In 1947, he joined an MSR-sponsored expeditionary force that planned to overthrow the neighboring Trujillo regime, a plot foiled by the government. A year later, he headed a delegation to an anti-imperialist student congress in Bogotá; serious riots broke out—an estimated three thousand deaths resulted—and Castro escaped the country only with difficulty.

Returning to the university, he married and became active in the Ortodoxo Youth Movement. He graduated in 1950, joined a law firm, defended impoverished Cubans, and also entered politics. In 1952—he was twenty-five years old—he ran for Congress as an Ortodoxo. He

40. Matthews (CS), supra; see also Matthews (Castro), supra.
41. Goldenberg, op. cit.

946

protested Batista's coup as unconstitutional by filing briefs with two courts, a right granted by the 1940 constitution. After this courageous but futile demonstration of dissent, he became a full-time revolutionary and emerged as leader of various underground organizations. He had flirted with Marxism, but he had flirted with a lot else; his briefs, though powerful indictments of tyranny, do not suggest that he was a Marxist or a Communist.[42]

Castro spent nearly a year organizing and training a heterogeneous armed group with which he hoped to overthrow Batista. On July 26, 1953, his force attacked two military posts in Oriente province: Fort Moncada in Santiago and a smaller one at Bayamo, an ill-advised effort that resulted in his capture along with most of his 150-man army. Only a few on either side fell in the brief actions.[43] Batista's soldiers and police, however, tortured and killed a large number of rebel survivors—perhaps sixty-eight of them. Castro barely escaped death. At his trial, in October, he defended himself, a spirited effort concluding with his famous "History Will Absolve Me" speech, which became the hallmark of the 26th of July Movement. Castro's appeal failed to move his judges, who sentenced him to fifteen years' imprisonment on the Isle of Pines; brother Raúl, who was a Communist at this time, received a thirteen-year sentence.

The episode may have frightened Batista, but he did not seem to realize that government overreaction swung a considerable number of persons to Castro's cause. In addition to abrogating various civil rights and exercising press censorship, he outlawed the PSP, a curious move in that Blas Roca's Communists had nothing to do with the rebellion and even criticized Castro's tactics. Batista was already riding the anti-Communist bandwagon so popular in Washington. He now became one of the drivers: At Ambassador Gardner's urging and with CIA help, he established, in 1954, a special police section, BRAC (*Buró de Represión a los Actividades Comunistas*), designed particularly to suppress Communist activity.[44] Batista's confidence showed in May 1955, when, in an attempt to gain goodwill from dissident liberal parties, he declared a general amnesty—which freed the brothers Castro.

Prison had diminished none of Fidel's fire. From the Isle of Pines, he had sent a flow of organizational missives to various leaders of the Movement. He read a great deal and, though he quoted Marx, he seemed to prefer José Martí's inspiration. He early concluded that unity was essential. As he wrote to a friend:

. . . I must in the first place organize the men of the 26th of July and unite, into an unbreakable bundle, all the fighters, those in exile, those in

42. Taber, op. cit., cites the briefs.
43. Draper (*Castroism*), *supra;* see also Taber, op. cit.; Thomas, op. cit.
44. Thomas, op. cit.

prison, those free, who together amount to over eighty men implicated in the same historic day of sacrifice. . . . Conditions indispensable for the integration of a true civil movement are ideology, discipline, leadership. All are desirable, but leadership is essential. . . .[45]

45. Ibid.

Chapter 73

*Castro in Mexico • Che Guevara joins • Return to Cuba •
Early disaster • The fugitives • Sanctuary in Sierra Maestra
• Castro's plan • Urban support • Early guerrilla operations •
Castro's problems • The Matthews interview • A myth begins
• Guerrilla tactics • Batista's countertactics • American army
influence • Dissension in Washington • Ambassador Smith*

IN LATE SPRING OF 1955, Fidel Castro traveled to the United States, where he raised several thousand dollars for "the cause."[1] In Mexico City, he rounded up other Cuban exiles, mostly middle-class dissidents belonging to the Movement, and put them on a ranch to train for invasion—the task of one Colonel Alberto Bayo, a former Cuban air force officer, a veteran of the Spanish civil war, and supposedly an expert in guerrilla fighting.[2]

Enter Ernesto Guevara Lynch.

Che Guevara was twenty-six years old when he met Castro, in Mexico. Son of a left-wing Argentinian architect, he had extended a medical career to revolutionary politics. He had participated in several unsuccessful attempts to depose Juan Perón, and the previous year had allegedly served in a minor capacity in Arbenz's Guatemalan Communist government. After Arbenz's overthrow, he went to Mexico and

1. Huberman and Sweezy, op. cit., put the figure at $50,000.
2. Taber, op. cit., offers details of this training.

was working either in a heart institute or as an itinerant photographer (the record is cloudy) when he met Castro. Politically, he was far left, though not necessarily a Communist. He was well read in Marx and Lenin—he carried their books with him—and he was anti-United States, mainly because of the CIA's role in Guatemala.[3] He enthusiastically joined the Movement and, despite chronic asthma, devoted himself to serious guerrilla training, serving also as the army's doctor.[4]

Castro himself paid little attention to operational matters. Instead, he continued to seek support both inside and outside Cuba. The internal situation was scarcely conducive to his plans. Batista seemed stronger than ever. After rigged elections returned him to the presidency, he received a fulsome Vice-President Nixon and, later, Allen Dulles, head of CIA. In early 1956, he offered an olive branch to opponents and began the short-lived *Diálogo Cívico*.[5] In Havana, ". . . there was widespread feeling among *Ortodoxo* and middle-class professional Cubans that negotiations with Batista were both possible and really the only viable way ahead."[6] Cuba's economy was expanding and, to the casual observer, Batista's government appeared stable.

Batista's refusal to negotiate in depth with opposition groups and to restore civil rights had created a good deal of dissidence, however, not only outside government but inside and particularly in the army. Serious incidents including assassination of Batista's intelligence chief plagued the government during 1955 and 1956. Splinter opposition groups formed and dissolved; students continued to protest through the FEU's newly formed militant group, the DR (Directorio Revolucionario), which agreed to support Castro. But most of these groups did not recognize Castro and the Movement as the key to Batista's overthrow. Commenting on the failure of Castro's later plan, Robert Taber noted:

. . . The [opposition] parties were fragmented, and irretrievably discredited. Thus failure is found in their disunity, their weakness, their intramural rivalries, in the jealousies and personal ambitions and venality of the politicos, and in the skill with which the Batista regime used the means at its disposal— bribery, intimidation, murder, diplomacy, and *a careful adherence to the outward semblance of constitutional procedure,* to render all legal opposition impotent.[7]

Castro did gain some new allies from the remnant MNR, notably Frank País, a Baptist and former teacher in Santiago, whom Castro named as

3. Goldenberg, op. cit., himself a former Communist, described Che as a Marxist closely linked to international communism; see also Daniel James, *Che Guevara— a Biography* (London: Allen & Unwin, 1970). Hereafter cited as James (*Che*).
4. Ernesto Che Guevara, *Reminiscences of the Cuban Revolutionary War* (New York: Grove Press, 1963). Tr. V. Ortiz. Hereafter cited as Guevara (*Reminiscences*).
5. Goldenberg, op. cit.
6. Thomas, op. cit.
7. Taber, op. cit.

head of all "action groups" in Cuba, and Armando Hart and Faustino Pérez in Havana. Cuban exiles in the United States and Mexico also supported him.

Castro was plagued by Batista's secret police, who arranged raids by Mexican police on his various headquarters and even arrested him.[8] But such were the vicissitudes of Cuban politics that Castro now gained an important temporary backer: Prío Socarrás, Cuba's former President, who was spending millions in trying to overthrow Batista, donated fifty thousand dollars to Castro.[9] Castro used fifteen thousand dollars to buy a battered yacht, *Granma;* he also procured arms and supply, the former including thirty-five rifles with telescopic sights. At end of November 1956, *Granma* sailed for Cuba with Castro and eighty-two guerrillas aboard.[10]

Castro's plan was slightly more complicated than either Wellington's expedition to Portugal in 1808 or MacArthur's return to the Philippines in 1944. Like these commanders, Castro planned to land with the help of local guerrillas. The new army would then attack Manzanillo garrison to capture arms and equipment. Simultaneously, urban terrorists would attack various targets, and finally a general strike would bring down the government. In case of a general uprising, Castro's force would arm the peasants and march on Havana; in case of trouble, it would escape to the mountain vastness of the Sierra Maestra to organize and train a volunteer army.[11]

This was an extremely optimistic plan. Frank País, Castro's agent in Santiago, had warned him against it. In the event, no local guerrillas met *Granma.* Badly overloaded, she landed late and off course, disgorging passengers in a swamp where much food and supply were lost. Even before she landed, País' people, some three hundred young rebels, had attacked various targets in Santiago, a fiasco, as it turned out. Most other "action groups" remained inactive.

8. Guevara (*Reminiscences*), *supra.*
9. Some accounts state more.
10. Guevara (*Reminiscences*), *supra;* see also Taber, op. cit.; Thomas, op. cit.
11. Taber, op. cit.; see also, Draper (*Castroism*), *supra,* who holds that Castro had no intention of achieving revolution by guerrilla warfare, but, rather, that events forced him into it. Taber argues that guerrilla training in Mexico, as well as purchasing rifles with telescopic sights, indicated the possibility of a guerrilla campaign in Castro's mind. I don't think the point is all that important. However, in refuting Castro's and Guevara's claim to having led an "agrarian revolution," Draper seems to me to denigrate Castro's abilities unnecessarily. Militarily (and even more, politically), Castro showed himself a flexible tactician, exploiting opportunities when they arose. I do not mention Wellington and MacArthur altogether with tongue in cheek. Each commander faced a disintegrating enemy army, as did Castro. It is farfetched to suggest that Castro shrewdly (albeit, perhaps, unknowingly) followed Wellington's lead: The French marshals, he said, ". . . planned their campaigns just as you might make a splendid set of harness. It looks very well, and answers very well, until it gets broken, and then you are done for. Now, I made my campaign of ropes. If anything went wrong, I tied a knot, and went on." Philip Guedalla, *Wellington* (New York: Harper & Brothers, 1931).

No general uprising—no local uprising.

A Cuban frigate spotted *Granma;* troops and planes rushed to the coast. With help of a turncoat guide, soldiers cornered the guerrillas in a cane field and killed or captured about seventy. Twelve men, including Castro, his brother Raúl, and Che Guevara, who was wounded, escaped to the Sierra Maestra.[12] For several weeks, they lived precariously, unable to trust most peasants, almost constantly hounded by army patrols.

But this was what Che later categorized as "favorable ground" for guerrillas, and though patrols often came close, they never captured the errants. The Sierra Maestra was too big, the terrain too difficult, for troops to plug all exits. Moreover, the peasants, including large numbers of *precaristas,* or squatters, were unusually impoverished and proved receptive to revolutionary propaganda, notably the old song Land to the Landless.[13] In time, Castro established a "safe" base and set to the task of revolution.

His original plan to overthrow Batista's government having failed, Castro now relied on a two-front strategy: warfare in cities and warfare in the country, the one (the *Llano*) to support the other (the *Sierra*)— or vice versa! Urban warfare—strikes, riots, and terrorism—fell to Civic Resistance (*Resistencia Cívica*) movements in Havana and Santiago, which forced the government to keep numerous army units in cities and thus ease pressure on guerrillas in the Sierra Maestra; urban units also sent money, arms, supply, and recruits to the mountain sanctuary.[14] Rural guerrillas, on the other hand, began to enlarge the mountain base by enlisting peasant co-operation while training a regular army. Simultaneously, Castro's guerrilla units began to strike small army outposts such as La Plata, which, in early January, yielded arms and ammunition. Just as important, this and other attacks goaded the army into ever more repressive measures that ensured revolutionary growth in both cities and countryside.[15]

As Theodore Draper has pointed out, for a long period the urban effort sustained the rebellion. The "peasant revolution" later claimed by Castro and publicized by Che Guevara, Régis Debray, and C. Wright Mills did not exist—neither at this time nor later.[16] The rural effort grew

12. Authorities differ on many of these figures: Thomas, op. cit., cites 15 survivors; Draper (*CR*), *supra,* cites 12, which ". . . dwindled at one point to only nine."

13. Guevara (*Reminiscences*), *supra;* see also Draper (*Castroism*), *supra.* The approximately 50,000 peasants in the Sierra Maestra represented one tenth of Cuba's rural population, but a group ". . . notoriously the poorest, the most backward, the most illiterate of the Cuban peasants."

14. Batista, op. cit., stresses the extent of terrorist activity.

15. Guevara (*Reminiscences*), *supra;* Taber, op. cit.

16. Guevara (*Reminiscences*), *supra;* see also Ernesto Che Guevara, *Che Guevara Speaks* (New York: Grove Press, 1967); Régis Debray, *Revolution in the Revolution?—Armed Struggle and Political Struggle in Latin America* (New York: Monthly Review Press, 1967); Huberman & Sweezy, op. cit.; Mills, op. cit.

very slowly. Unlike Mao Tse-tung and Ho Chi Minh, Castro had not prepared the peasantry; he and his lieutenants were intellectuals, and neither class easily identified with the other.[17] Rather than turning peasants of Oriente province into a grand army, Castro had all he could do to prevent peasants from turning him in. Life in the mountains also proved hard: morale plunged. Castro concerned himself more with security and sustenance than with fighting; three crimes, he declared, were punishable by death: insubordination, desertion, and defeatism. Che Guevara later wrote:

. . . Our situation was not a happy one in those days. The column lacked cohesion. It had neither the spirit which comes from the experience of war nor a clear ideological consciousness. Now one comrade would leave us, now another; many requested assignments in the city which were sometimes much more dangerous but which meant an escape from the rugged conditions in the countryside. Nevertheless, our campaign continued on its course. . . .[18]

In Castro's later words:

. . . We had yet to learn very bitter lessons in the months to come. We had to suffer the effects of the enemy's infiltration tactics. We had to suffer the consequences of treason and on more than one occasion our enemies were on the verge of exterminating us. It was a bitter apprenticeship, but it was a very useful apprenticeship.[19]

At this point, February 1957, the outside world knew little either of Fidel Castro or the rebellion. Taking the government's word, United Press and the New York *Times* had reported Castro's death in early December.[20] Batista, who, in private, referred to the guerrillas as "a bunch of bandits," seemed to control the situation, and the Eisenhower administration continued to bless him. An American military advisory group daily strengthened his army; Batista and his officers received American decorations, and American officers received Cuban decorations.[21] The Cuban economy was booming, with large increases in American investments. Batista's propaganda machine continued to insist that Castro was dead; his security forces added to the illusion by promptly and ruthlessly suppressing local outbreaks: On Christmas Day 1956, a provincial commander rounded up, tortured, and executed twenty-two men and boys at Holguín, a stupid act exploited by rebels as "Batista's Christmas Present."[22]

17. Guevara (*Reminiscences*), *supra*.
18. Ibid.
19. Matthews (*Castro*), *supra*.
20. Phillips, op. cit.
21. Draper (*CR*), *supra*.
22. Taber, op. cit.: Rebels later assassinated the responsible officer, Colonel Fermín Cowley.

To dispel the notion of security and to broadcast his intentions to the world (following Grivas' example in Cyprus), Castro arranged a rendezvous with a senior New York *Times* editor, Herbert Matthews, a fifty-seven-year-old peripatetic reporter nudging the Richard Harding Davis tradition. Matthews later described the meeting in his book *The Cuban Story*:[23] In mid-February 1957, Castro agents shepherded Matthews to Castro's camp in the mountains. Castro immediately impressed him: ". . . a powerful six-footer, olive-skinned, full-faced, with a shapely beard. He was dressed in an olive grey fatigue uniform and carried a rifle with a telescopic sight of which he was very proud."[24] They spent the night talking, or, rather, whispering, since, according to Matthews' dramatic account, Batista's soldiers were hovering nearby. Castro evidently whispered persuasively: Matthews, who was with him less than a day, became as pro-Castro as Ambassador Gardner was pro-Batista.

Matthews' articles proved sensational. The first of three opened:

Fidel Castro, the rebel leader of Cuba's youth, is alive and fighting hard and successfully in the rugged, almost impenetrable fastnesses of the Sierra Maestra. . . .

Matthews found Castro's personality ". . . overwhelming. It was easy to see that his men adored him. . . . Here was an educated, dedicated fanatic, a man of ideals, of courage and of remarkable qualities of leadership . . . one got a feeling that he is now invincible."

As for his aims:

. . . His is a political mind rather than a military one. He has strong ideas of liberty, democracy, social justice, the need to restore the Constitution, to hold elections. He has strong ideas on economy too, but an economist would consider them weak. . . .

Matthews informed his readers:

. . . Fidel Castro and his 26th of July Movement are the flaming symbol of the opposition to the regime. The organization, which is apart from the university students' opposition, is formed of youths of all kinds. It is a revolutionary movement that calls itself socialistic. It is also nationalistic, which generally in Latin America means anti-Yankee.

The program is vague and couched in generalities, but it amounts to a new deal for Cuba, radical, democratic and therefore anti-Communist. . . .

Matthews also relayed Castro's comforting message to his northern neighbors: ". . . You can be sure that we have no animosity towards the United States and the American people . . . we are fighting for a democratic Cuba and an end to the dictatorship."

23. Matthews (*CS*) and Matthews (*Castro*), *supra;* Phillips, op. cit.
24. Matthews (*CS*), *supra;* but see also Irving Pflaum, *Tragic Island—How Communism Came to Cuba* (Englewood Cliffs, N.J.: Prentice-Hall, 1961): The author found Castro shorter than six feet, pudgy, and with sloping chin.

WAR IN THE SHADOWS

Castro's strength was daily growing in Oriente province, Matthews wrote:

. . . Havana does not and cannot know that thousands of men and women are heart and soul with Fidel Castro and the new deal for which they think he stands.

Castro told the reporter:

. . . We have been fighting for seventy-nine days now and are stronger than ever. . . . The soldiers are fighting badly; their morale is low and ours could not be higher. We are killing many, but when we take prisoners they are never shot. We question them, talk kindly to them, take their arms and equipment, and then set them free.

Castro refused to tell Matthews his guerrilla strength:

. . . Batista has 3,000 men in the field against us. I will not tell you how many we have, for obvious reasons. He works in columns of 200; we in groups of ten to forty, and we are winning. It is a battle against time and time is on our side.[25]

The articles caused a furor in the United States. Batista had recently lifted censorship, and they were also published in Cuba. Government officials immediately denied that a meeting had taken place; the New York *Times* replied by publishing a photo of Castro and Matthews in the mountains. Cuban dissidents reacted enthusiastically to the story, with many townspeople joining Civic Resistance units. Like the poet Keats, Castro and the Movement awoke famous. A CBS television documentary filmed in the mountains a few weeks later added to Castro's now considerable fame in North America.

Matthews had bought a gold brick.

No one, probably including Castro, knew his political loyalties at this time. A complex man, Castro: In Theodore Draper's words, ". . . as much demagogue as idealist, as much adventurer as revolutionary, as much anarchist as Communist or anything else"—superficially a bright man, but an undisciplined man whose brain was not to cope with challenge of democratic government, whose quixotic personality was to take refuge in the role of twentieth-century Leader, with the disaster it entailed. But all this lay ahead. At the time of the Matthews visitation, Castro's background was known. Despite relatively moderate social, economic, and political reforms called for in the "History Will Absolve Me" speech, he obviously was an angry young man who stroked and sometimes embraced far-left philosophies. Matthews found Raúl Castro "slight and pleasant" but said nothing of his known Communist background, nor did he mention Che Guevara, much less *his* background.

Matthews also falsely reported Castro's strength. What seemed an

25. Matthews (*CS*), *supra*.

endless flow of guerrillas in and out of the Castro camp was the same group, herded by brother Raúl. This was the force that ". . . had been fighting for seventy-nine days"—fighting mainly to stay alive. By Castro's later admission, his "army" at this time consisted of eighteen men![26]

Thus the foundation of a myth: in part, the result of sensational, as opposed to in-depth, reporting. How to explain this monumental aberration on the part of a senior New York *Times* editor? Matthews helped us when he later wrote:

. . . I knew I had a sensational scoop. I exulted at the fact that at the age of fifty-seven I could still show a younger generation of newspapermen how to get a difficult and dangerous story, and how to write it. And I was moved, deeply moved, by that young man.[27]

Pride first, emotion second. But on what other grounds did Matthews justify his positive assertions? Where was the discipline of objectivity? Where were the follow-up investigations that accurate reporting demands? Matthews proved as biased as Gardner and as reluctant to discover and report facts conflicting with his bias. If Matthews had superiors on the newspaper, they were as lax as Gardner's superiors in Washington in not insisting on more objective appreciation, and the same may be said for superiors of other journalists and cameramen who subsequently reported on Castro. Matthews later tried to justify his reporting. The fact remains that it was cheap and tawdry stuff—a costly episode that should come to the minds of those persons who are fortunate enough to write words for publication and who are tempted to abnegate the tremendous responsibility involved.

Despite Matthews' publicity, Castro's situation remained precarious. Batista's new commander in Oriente, Colonel Barrera Pérez, had correctly analyzed the tactical problem and had started a pacification program designed to lure precarista and peasant loyalty. Once he had deprived Castro of their support, he planned to isolate the guerrillas in the mountains and eventually destroy them. He might have succeeded had command jealousies not brought his transfer, and had other military units, including the Rural Guard, ceased alienating the peasants. Not the least of his crosses was Senator Rolando Masferrer, an Oriente

26. Ibid.; see also Guevara (*Reminiscences*). This is scarcely an original *ruse de guerre*. While Castro at this time could have commanded a meaningful force, that was not proof that he *did* command one—and it was a reporter's responsibility to either discover the strength or report it with qualification.

27. Matthews (*CS*), *supra*; see also Thomas, op. cit.; Draper (*CR*), *supra*: On March 11, 1966, Draper wrote Matthews, ". . . I strongly doubt that your articles would have had such an electrifying effect if you had not personally vouched for Castro's large and winning force. You now claim that you 'guessed at the time that he had about forty men.' Then why did you report at the time, without any hint of skepticism, his boast that he had 'groups of ten to forty'? And you gave a different version of this matter in your book. . . ."

war lord whose private army of some two thousand uniformed thugs was particularly loathed throughout the province.[28]

Castro probably foresaw himself as commander of a vast peasant-guerrilla army. His cadres, however, remained middle-class city dwellers: The most marked reinforcement, fifty recruits (including three American youths) who joined Castro in March, came from Santiago—recruited, organized, and partially armed by his principal urban lieutenant, Frank País.[29] Castro now reorganized his force into platoons which often lived and fought independently. These units worked hard in winning over local peasants, but their support, including recruits, probably depended as much on repressive army counterguerrilla measures and on landlords seizing land temporarily vacated by precaristas (at army orders) as on Castro's blandishments. This does not detract from the work and accomplishments of the various columns, and Che Guevara's account of life in the mountains is well worth reading as a primer on guerrilla warfare.[30]

Castro and Che claim to have developed guerrilla techniques independent of either Mao's or Giap's teachings.[31] Whatever the truth, they bore a marked resemblance to these teachings. They concentrated on agitation and propaganda techniques to win over peasants and gain their support, both active and passive—what Guevara called ". . . dressing the guerrillas in palm leaves."[32] Small bands raided army outposts and ambushed army columns and convoys to gain arms and supply and prisoners (treated well and released) and to provoke the government to extreme countermeasures. In May, the guerrillas were strong enough to carry out a successful frontal attack in daylight against Uvero.

The main accomplishment, however, was survival during a critical period—what Guevara called the nomadic phase. Whether we like it or not, Castro was (and is) a charismatic figure with tremendous appeal to a large number of his countrymen. By keeping the standard of revolt flying in the Sierra Maestra, he succeeded in polarizing opposition elements that daily became more daring in the cities. But, as in the countryside, urban guerrilla tactics proved a two-edged weapon, particularly

28. Taber, op. cit.
29. Draper (CR), supra: 58 recruits ". . . many of them armed with weapons stolen from the U. S. Naval Base at Guantanamo . . ."; see also Guevara (Reminiscences), supra.
30. In addition to his works cited, see also, Ernesto Che Guevara, Che Guevara on Guerrilla Warfare (New York: Frederick A. Praeger, 1961). Ed. Harries-Clichy Peterson; see also Debray, op. cit., who repeats many of Che's axioms.
31. Debray, op. cit.: Castro relied politically on Marx, Martí, Lenin; militarily, on Engels and Hemingway's For Whom the Bell Tolls [see my Chapter 30, Volume I] ". . . not so much as sources as . . . coincidences; Fidel found in them only what he was looking for. Mao Tse-tung's Problems of Strategy in Guerrilla War Against Japan [sic] came into Fidel's and Che's hands after the 1958 summer offensive: to their surprise, they found in this book what they had been practising under pressure of necessity."
32. Guevara (Reminiscences), supra.

when they were unco-ordinated and lacked single political purpose, and various urban movements suffered some serious defeats. A senseless frontal attack on the presidential palace by a group of DR terrorists, in March 1957, not only failed but brought a great deal of influential support to Batista.[33] The government's reaction to this attempt to kill the President as well as to other acts of selective terrorism was so violent, however, that in time it lost the considerable support previously claimed. Batista later described the invidious process:

. . . As the crimes and cruelties of the terrorists grew, so did the necessary repressive measures. New excesses would take place, followed by another wave of slogan propaganda. Public sensibility would be offended, and corrective action would be the responsibility of the Batista government (always in his name) and not that of the provocateurs. . . . In this way the unscrupulous groups headed by Fidel Castro, who ordered assassinations and massacres, succeeded in being represented as fighters for the liberty which they themselves assaulted and mutilated.[34]

Matters thus seesawed into summer of 1957. Time favored the guerrillas only because Batista failed to cope intelligently with the situation. Political mistakes aside (though here lay the key to his ultimate defeat), his counterguerrilla tactics proved inept. Although he returned Barrera Pérez to the Sierra Maestra, he also approved Tabernilla's plan to evacuate peasants and create free-fire zones. Instead of winning over precaristas and thus depriving Castro of support while simultaneously keeping him on the run by small, mobile columns, Tabernilla thought to "seal" the guerrillas in the mountains and bomb and starve them into submission.[35]

The plan had more holes than a Swiss cheese. Summary evacuation of precaristas played into landlord hands and increased already widespread dissatisfaction, bringing more security, more recruits, and more aid to Castro. Tabernilla's five thousand soldiers could not seal the vast range from outside supply. Nor could Castro be bombed or starved to death. His strength amounted to only about two hundred guerrillas operating in small units that defied the keenest bombardier's eye. The guerrillas daily were growing tougher and, for some time, had existed, when necessary, on one meal a day. As with other guerrilla units throughout history, Castro's people were becoming increasingly self-sufficient. Small workshops appeared, a dispensary, armory, a shoe factory; the guerrillas printed and circulated a mimeographed newspaper and, in time, built

33. Batista, op. cit.
34. Ibid.; see also, Matthews (CS), supra: ". . . Americans had no conception in those last two years of the Batista dictatorship of the fierceness and viciousness with which the General was fighting back against the terrorism and the rising wave of revolutionary opposition. Death for plotters was not only the normal rule; in cases like this torture always came first. . . ."
35. Taber, op. cit.; see also, Guevara (Reminiscences), supra.

958 WAR IN THE SHADOWS

a cigar factory! And all in remote mountain valleys approachable only through most difficult and hostile terrain.[36]

No easy way existed to smoke out Castro. The situation called for conventional-force pressures augmented by specially trained counter-guerrilla units to go in after him. The troops who maintained checkpoints and outposts around the Sierra Maestra and who plodded without purpose through valleys and up ridges were the least satisfactory answer— next to the bombings, which were ludicrous. Cuban pilots were not sufficiently trained for this type of warfare (is anyone ever so trained?), and evidence exists that some of them did not wish to bomb fellow Cubans any more than Chiang Kai-shek's pilots wished to bomb fellow Chinese in 1946–47. As Castro not only survived but grew in strength, soldiers in Oriente grew discouraged and finally demoralized, their commanders at each other's throats, the men too often uncaring.

The American army cannot escape a certain amount of responsibility for this state of affairs. The role of the advisory mission at this crucial time is hazy, but American military advisers do not seem to have influenced the tactical situation favorably. Until relevant Pentagon files are released, we won't know the extent of the mission's participation in the Oriente campaigns. We do know that, in 1957, the lessons of Korea, as opposed to those of contemporary insurgencies, ruled American military thinking. The size and shape of Batista's army suggests that he was receiving conventional advice from American advisers.

More important was American political involvement. By early 1957, some U.S. officials were vigorously objecting to Batista's dictatorial government. Press and television coverage was making Cuba a domestic political issue, and Castro was rapidly emerging as Hero against Villain Batista. Writing of the period in his memoirs, President Eisenhower noted ". . . the universal revulsion against the Batista government."[37] That spring, Eisenhower removed Ambassador Gardner (no easy task) in favor of a generous Republican backer, Earl Smith, a fifty-four-year-old investment broker with Ivy League background—his first wife was Consuelo Vanderbilt—who lacked diplomatic experience.

Eisenhower's choice was unfortunate. The situation demanded a master, not a student. The American ambassador occupied a unique role. Smith later told a Senate committee that ". . . the American Ambassador was the second most important man in Cuba, sometimes even more important than the President."[38] To use this power wisely and to persuade the American Government to a sound course of action, the ambassador needed both a mind trained in professional diplomacy and considerable local knowledge to unravel the complex political snarl.

Even the best diplomat would have found the task difficult and frus-

36. Guevara (*Reminiscences*), *supra.*
37. Eisenhower (*Waging Peace*), *supra.*
38. Taber, op. cit.; see also Earl E. T. Smith, *The Fourth Floor—An Account of the Castro Communist Revolution* (New York: Random House, 1962).

trating. The Administration was veering toward what it called a "neutral" attitude. Smith was instructed to ". . . alter the prevailing notion in Cuba that the American Ambassador was intervening on behalf of the government of Cuba to perpetuate the Batista dictatorship."[39] Considering decades of involvement, American neutrality was as ludicrous as the attempted "neutral" role of the British in Palestine after World War II—a fact that a competent ambassador would have stressed to the Secretary of State. It perhaps would have done no good. The Administration, the State Department, and the military were split into pro- and anti-Batista factions, a split that carried to the Havana embassy, where the CIA was operating virtually independently of the ambassador. The situation called for a united stand on the part of his embassy—and perhaps no one could have achieved this, considering the military-political schisms of the day and the bewildered man in the White House.

Despite Eisenhower's later words, he apparently did not realize the rotten structure of Batista's government. Batista's crusade against "communism," his expanding economy and so-called stable rule were daily attracting diverse American investments, which only added to the strength of the pro-Batista lobby in Washington.[40] And yet American officials, diplomats, CIA agents, and newspapermen were reporting the sordid facts. Robert Taber later wrote that, despite the façade of business as usual in spring of 1957, ". . . it was impossible for the observer who made it his business to look behind the facade *not* to discover the truth."[41]

The Eisenhower administration continued to be friendly to Batista when it should have been suspicious. Positive action in mid-1957 might not have salvaged anything in the end, but it was the only hope: To let matters continue on a disaster course, to pursue a policy of diplomatic "neutrality" not only solved nothing but caused considerable harm. For "neutrality," as defined by the Administration, meant arms and shipments to Batista and harassment of anti-Batista forces in the United States; it meant continued presence of the American military mission in Havana—and all this, in Cuban minds, spelled support of the regime. This, in turn, produced two results: So long as Batista felt that he could count on continued American support, he refused to change his ways. Yet his regime was growing so distasteful that theretofore moderate and *attentiste* Cubans were veering toward the opposition, which meant that they would regard the American Government as hostile.

The American Government would not necessarily have had to come

39. Thomas, op. cit.

40. Draper (*Castroism*), *supra:* The Communist Party (PSP) played a minimal opposition role at this time and objected to Castro's revolutionary tactics; see also Matthews (*CS*), *supra.*

41. Taber, op. cit.

to terms with Castro at this time. As early as March 1957, Robert Taber, who was in Havana, noted in his notebook:

> . . . With regard to Batista's opposition, the U. S. Embassy in Havana feels that the oppositionists are divided among themselves principally by fear of the political demands that Fidel Castro might make, were he to emerge as the hero of a popular revolution. They don't want him on their team; they feel that he's too young, fiery, militaristic, anti-Yanqui; in their opinion, a potential dictator worse than the present one.[42]

Here was the nucleus of a reasonable third-party alternative, and the Eisenhower administration's failure to develop it was fatal. Theodore Draper later concluded:

> . . . It would appear that American policy in this period was so inept and ineffectual that it was pro-Batista to Castro and pro-Castro to Batista. On the whole, however, Batista was favored as long as he was capable of benefiting from favors, and this period constitutes a sorry and sometimes shameful interlude in the history of recent Cuban-United States relations.[43]

42. Ibid.
43. Draper (*CR*), *supra*.

Chapter 74

Pact of the Sierra • Urban guerrillas • War in the countryside • The balance sheet • The American position • Eisenhower's arms embargo • The climax approaches • Operation Summer fails • Castro's counterattack • The revolution spreads • Batista exits • Castro takes over • Che Guevara on guerrilla warfare • His heterodoxy • His exodus • Che's Bolivian expedition • Capture and execution • Che's failure anlayzed

THROUGHOUT SUMMER OF 1957, the threat to Batista's government steadily grew in scope. In July, two opposition leaders from Havana, Raúl Chibás, of the Ortodoxos, and Felipe Pazos, a respected economist, visited Castro to work out an alliance. The Pact of the Sierra called for a united revolutionary front to oust Batista in favor of free elections and democratic government. Significantly, it asked Washington to stop sending arms to Batista and otherwise not to intervene in Cuban affairs.[1]

Meanwhile, terror in the towns continued to do Castro's work for him. Toward the end of July, his chief organizer, Frank País, fell to police bullets in Santiago. The funeral brought a massive and impressive demonstration by Santiago mothers. Ambassador Smith witnessed this sad

---

1. Manuel Urrutia Lleó, *Fidel Castro and Company, Inc.—Communist Tyranny in Cuba* (New York: Frederick A. Praeger, 1964); see also Guevara (*Reminiscences*), *supra*, who details the program, a compromise that he and Castro later called a "minimal" program of social reform.

group, which Batista's police broke up with a violence that caused the new ambassador's public protest (and, in turn, elicited Batista's protest against Smith's statement). A strike followed, which police and troops savagely broke within a week.

By autumn of 1957, civil war existed in Cuba. In September, dissident naval elements working with the 26th of July Movement (and probably the CIA) attempted a mutiny, an abortive effort called off at the last minute. Not getting the word, Cienfuegos rebels rose, captured the base, and seized most of the town. Troops, supported by armor and aircraft, arrived in the afternoon and soon eliminated all opposition, killing perhaps three hundred rebels. The revolt made headlines in the United States. A small anti-Batista bloc in Congress objected to American arms being used to suppress internal disorders.[2] The State Department demanded an explanation from Batista. When none came, some officials began talking about prohibiting further arms shipments to Cuba. Influential voices spoke just as loudly in defense of such shipments, and there the matter rested—for the moment. The Washington *Post,* however, noted in a pertinent editorial:

. . . In the past few months, Cuba has witnessed an assassination attempt on the presidential palace, an abortive general strike, police terror in Santiago, midnight bombings and shootings in Havana, and a blackout of the Cuban press. General Batista deceives no one by blaming the unrest on the Communists. He has pledged a free election in June of 1958, but his repressive policies weaken faith in his promise. It seems clear that if Batista does not accede to an orderly transfer of power, trouble and revolt will continue to plague the freedom-hungry island of Cuba.[3]

Castro's guerrillas meanwhile were not idle and had made several successful, if small, attacks on outposts, and at least one ambush of a relief column. Castro now controlled about two thousand square miles of Oriente province and was strong enough to send two columns from the mountains: one, seventy men, of whom only twenty-eight were armed, under Juan Almeida, to work slowly toward Santiago; the other, sixty-five partially armed men under brother Raúl, to work north toward the Central Highway.[4] Local columns, one commanded by Che Guevara, continued to expand the Oriente base, striking at army outposts in fringe areas.

All was not roses for Castro, however. His people remained desperately short of arms, and supply was also difficult. In early 1958, the American reporter Dickey Chapelle visited Castro: ". . . at one point I lived on raw sugar cane for two days, and at another time I ate only

2. Taber, op. cit.: Senator Wayne Morse and Representatives Adam Clayton Powell and Charles Porter.
3. Ibid.
4. Ibid.

one meal a day for five days in a row."[5] Contrary to sensational reporting by American correspondents, Castro's total force numbered closer
to three hundred, than to the several thousand alleged. His army lacked
discipline, while a good many peasants refused his blandishments and
had to be coerced and (foreshadowing the future) sometimes executed.[6]
In December, he ordered widespread burning of the sugar crop, a mistake that caused considerable resentment and was later canceled. Finally, representatives of various opposition groups meeting in Florida
presented him with the Miami Pact, which called for a joint resistance
effort under a Council of Liberation, a notion he angrily rejected while
criticizing Prío Socarrás' followers for storing arms in Havana, where
they most likely would be captured, when they were needed in the countryside.

Batista, on the other hand, counted some positive gains. Despite
bombings and murders and the fighting in Oriente, the Cuban economy
continued to prosper and more capital to flow in, mostly from the United
States.[7] The U.S.A. was also providing weapons, and he had placed orders for more, including armored vehicles; he had also declared that the
army would recruit another seven thousand men.[8] Security forces in
cities kept terrorists splintered and frequently on the run. He was rapidly weaning Ambassador Smith from "neutrality." Though appalled at
Batista's strong-arm methods, Smith had always been impressed with
the dictator's peculiar anti-Communist organization BRAC. Its influence was evident a few months later when Smith, ". . . becoming rapidly less inclined to believe the State Department or his own embassy
advisers, telegraphed Allen Dulles, head of the CIA, recommending
the placing of an agent with Castro in the Sierra 'to discover the extent
of Communist control' in the 26 July Movement. Apparently this could
not be done and anyway the CIA in Cuba itself remained favorable to,
rather than opposed to, the 26 July. . . ."[9]

Neither CIA nor State Department officials favored Castro so much
as they condemned Batista. To what extent condemnation stemmed
from democratic bias, to what extent from realistic appreciation of the
power situation, we are not likely to learn. A black-and-white situation
probably did not exist. William Wieland, a Cuban specialist in the

5. Dickey Chapelle, "How Castro Won." In T. N. Greene (ed.), *supra*.
6. Guevara (*Reminiscences*), *supra*.
7. Matthews (*CS*), *supra*: ". . . in 1958, United States interests controlled 80
per cent of Cuban utilities, 90 per cent of the mines, 90 per cent of the cattle
ranches, all of the oil refining and distribution (with the Royal Dutch Shell)
and 40 per cent of the sugar industry"; see also Draper (*Castroism*), *supra*; Mills,
op. cit.
8. Taber, op. cit.
9. Thomas, op. cit.; see also Smith, op. cit.: The CIA sent an American journalist, Andrew St. George, to Castro's camp—surely an inferior effort, in that the
situation required a sophisticated intelligence operation, for example "turning" a
member of the Movement and having him infiltrate Castro's headquarters.

State Department, later greatly criticized for pro-Castro sympathies, told a *Newsweek* correspondent at this time:

> . . . I know Batista is considered by many as a son of a bitch . . . but American interests come first . . . at least he is our son of a bitch, he is not playing ball with the Communists. . . . On the other hand, Fidel Castro is surrounded by commies. I don't know whether he is himself a communist. . . . [But] I am certain he is subject to communist influences.[10]

Wieland and his superior, Roy Rubottom, U. S. Assistant Secretary of State for Latin American affairs, could not ignore field reports that showed Batista losing ground. Castro was no longer a semimyth to Cubans; he might have been weak in numbers and otherwise disorganized, but he was creating havoc in Oriente province. In February 1958, Radio Rebelde began broadcasting from the Sierra, and it was difficult, if not impossible, for the government to refute facts and figures that came over the air.

The key, however, remained Batista's reaction. While he burbled on about spring elections, police and troops continued to operate with such undisguised violence that theretofore-neutral agencies began to swing over to the revolutionary cause. The Communists, whom Batista had been blaming all along, only started to veer toward Castro's support in February 1958. Significantly, prominent church leaders and judges also began protesting. In mid-March, a Havana magistrate ordered indictment of two of Batista's hatchet men (and barely escaped with his life). Batista suspended constitutional guarantees, reimposed censorship, and postponed scheduled elections. The university long had been closed; secondary schools now closed. Urged by resistance leaders in the city, Castro ordered a general strike for early April, to be followed by a massive civil-disobedience campaign throughout the country.[11]

A blow to Batista far worse than these was about to fall. The American public had become increasingly upset by Batista's brutality; simultaneously, Herbert Matthews and other reporters had built Castro into a romantic figure of considerable appeal to liberal elements. Castro effectively played the liberator's role. According to an article in the February 1958 issue of *Coronet* magazine, he promised ". . . genuine representative government," ". . . truly honest general elections within twelve months," and restoration of all personal and political liberties guaranteed by the 1940 constitution.[12]

The 26th of July Movement had established a series of "clubs" in American cities that were disseminating pro-Castro propaganda while

10. Thomas, op. cit.
11. Draper (*Castroism*), *supra*, quotes the March manifesto; Castro would have been wise had he read Chorley on the efficacy of the general strike in the history of revolutionary warfare: K. C. Chorley, *Armies and the Art of Revolution* (London: Faber & Faber, 1943).
12. Draper (*CR*), *supra*.

collecting funds, and the Movement had also established a vociferous lobby in Washington, where Castro was already served by several congressmen and by a secret agent in the Cuban embassy.[13] Cuba had become a domestic political issue. Eisenhower no longer could watch, he had to act: Citing the charter of the Organization of American States, he placed an embargo on further arms shipments to Batista.

The arms themselves were not so important as the moral effect of the deed. Batista at once placed orders on the continent and in England.[14] He could not replace the tacit support of the Eisenhower administration, even though, ambiguously enough, the Administration bowed to Pentagon pressures and left the military advisory mission in Havana. Ambassador Smith remained close to Batista, and the U. S. Army tactlessly decorated Colonel Tabernilla with the Legion of Merit (for prior services on the Inter-American Defense Board).

The arms embargo nonetheless proved a welcome shot in the arm to the rebels, who hastened plans for a general strike. They may have moved too rapidly. Some evidence suggests that Castro himself did not really favor the tactic, perhaps because of its organizational difficulties, perhaps because success would have allowed a junta to take over.[15] Whatever the case, the strike failed. Trade-union leaders, most of them in Batista's pocket, refused to call out workers; urban leaders of the Movement did not consult Communist leaders and thus lost their cooperation. Failure in Havana and Santiago perforce nullified Castro's orders for country-wide civil disobedience.

Failure of the April strike, what Hugh Thomas more accurately calls an urban uprising, caused Castro to resume guerrilla tactics in both cities and countryside. Batista answered in two ways, the first being counterterror:

. . . The army and secret police struck back blindly, indiscriminately, senselessly. The students, blamed as the main troublemakers, were their chief victims. It became safer for young men to take to the hills than to walk in the streets. The orgy of murders, tortures, and brutalities sent tremors of fear and horror through the entire Cuban people and especially the middle-class parents of the middle-class students.[16]

The second way was Operation Summer, the biggest military operation in Cuban history, launched toward end of May and designed to eliminate Castro. Thirteen combat teams of about three hundred fifty men each—some forty-five hundred troops—supported by tanks, artillery,

13. Taber, op. cit.
14. Draper (CR), supra.
15. Ibid.: Draper vigorously dissents, citing Castro's March manifesto; see also Urrutia Lleó, op. cit.
16. Draper (CR), supra.

naval gunfire, and aircraft, and supplemented by Rural Guard units, pushed in from two directions toward Castro's headquarters.[17]

Although progressing satisfactorily for a few weeks, the attacks failed, for a variety of reasons. Batista's two senior commanders, Río Chaviano and Cantillo, loathed each other. Like Rennenkampf and Samsonov, who brought the Russian armies to disaster at Tannenberg in 1914, they refused to co-operate, either with each other or with the General Staff.[18] Batista's orders tied up about a quarter of the troops in guarding coffee and sugar plantations in Oriente. Army morale, in general, was poor; most units were untrained for guerrilla warfare: Upon leaving the lowlands, they succumbed to fatigue and disease; the rainy season slowed them even more.[19] They pushed on, however, and, by mid-June, had boxed Castro into a four-square-mile area; in his later words: ". . . Our territory was reduced and reduced until we could not reduce any further."[20] But now columns lacked sufficient strength to deliver a *coup de grâce*, nor were reinforcements available to help them.

Even worse, the push had not fragmented the guerrillas. Learning of Batista's plans in ample time, Castro had pulled in his outposts and his roving units. As soldiers advanced, he retreated. Knowing literally every move made by the army, he kept one step ahead.[21] When the columns reached the end of their tether, he attacked. One army column, nearly a thousand men, lost two thirds of its strength in killed and wounded, not to mention loss of arms, radios, and code books.[22] This success triggered a series of attacks in which Castro ably exploited intelligence and mobility and, in addition, rubbed salt in the wound by transmitting false orders in code on a captured radio. Rebel attacks shortly routed the army, with many soldiers and even some units deserting.[23] Besides deserters and prisoners (over four hundred, well treated and released to the Red Cross), the retreat yielded Castro rifles, machine guns, mortars and bazookas, even a 14-ton tank.[24] The entire action cost him perhaps twenty-seven killed and fifty wounded.

Batista's army was still extricating itself from the Sierra Maestra when guerrillas under Raúl Castro struck in the north. Toward the end of June, to protest American delivery of rockets to the army, his group kidnaped a number of American and Canadian mining employees, along with twenty-seven American sailors and marines from Guantánamo and several officials of United Fruit Company. This bold act caused ranking officials in Washington to argue for armed interven-

17. Taber, op. cit.
18. Batista, op. cit.
19. Jay Mallin, "Castro's Guerrilla Campaign," *Marine Corps Gazette,* January 1962.
20. Thomas, op. cit.; see also Matthews (*Castro*), *supra.*
21. Chapelle, op. cit.
22. Thomas, op. cit.
23. Batista, op. cit.; see also Taber, op. cit.
24. Thomas, op. cit.; see also Taber, op. cit.

tion against the guerrillas, but the storm blew over when Raúl released them and they reported that they had been well treated.[25]

Batista's failure in the countryside, graphically described to the Cuban people by Radio Rebelde, brought near panic in top government circles. He attempted to counter Castro's growing popularity with incessant propaganda and large rewards, such as a hundred thousand dollars offered for the capture of the bearded guerrilla leader. In cities, police rounded up thousands of "suspects" in a desperate attempt to quell growing revolution.

Castro's popularity continued to increase as his clandestine radio broadcast victorious communiqués, only some of which were true. In July, in Caracas, agents of the Movement brought together representatives of other underground groups (Communists excluded) to form a Junta of Unity (Frente Cívico Revolucionario Democrático), which designated Castro commander in chief of revolutionary forces and issued a revolutionary manifesto. Although Batista prevented publication in Cuba, it was published in the United States and elsewhere in the hemisphere and was broadcast in Cuba both from stations in Caracas and from Radio Rebelde.[26] About this same time, the Communists, who had been edging closer to Castro and the Movement since early in the year, saw the light and sent a representative to the Sierra, much to the delight, no doubt, of Raúl Castro and Che Guevara.[27]

Failure of Operation Summer sounded the knell to Batista's hope of restoring control in southern Oriente. A large part of the area now lay under Castro's direct or indirect command, to the extent that local mills paid him a tribute of fifteen cents per 250-pound bag of sugar shipped to Havana—an income, according to Batista, of millions of dollars, used to bribe more soldiers and buy more weapons.

In August, Castro established central headquarters in the hills above La Plata. A few weeks later, his units started toward the coastal city of Santiago. Simultaneously, Guevara and another lieutenant, Cienfuegos, led columns west, toward Las Villas province, where Guevara was to establish a new base and take command of Directorio guerrilla groups fighting in the Escambray area. Both Guevara and Cienfuegos have written graphically of the hardships of this forty-day march. Although the enemy shot up one of Guevara's units, the guerrillas received con-

25. Matthews (*Castro*), *supra;* see also Taber, op. cit.; Mallin, op. cit.: From the guerrilla standpoint, the kidnapings made sense: Raúl's idea was to force the United States to negotiate and thus grant the rebels a sort of diplomatic recognition important for propaganda purposes; the diverse kidnapings also demonstrated widespread geurrilla control of the area.

26. SORO, op. cit.: ". . . The agreement called for co-operation in the common cause, continued co-operation after victory, the arming of the people, and the co-operation of labor and business in a general strike to be called to aid the military front when needed. The manifesto called on the soldiers to desert, and on everybody else to support the revolution. Above all, it stressed the theme of unity."

27. Draper (*CR*), *supra.*

968   WAR IN THE SHADOWS

siderable help from local Communists; they may also have bribed Batista's local commander in Camagüey—the suggested figure is one hundred thousand dollars—to let them transit the province. By end of October, Guevara and Cienfuegos had absorbed the Directorio and Communist units and were controlling a large portion of Las Villas, even going so far as to distribute privately owned land to local peasants.[28] Guevara now began working across the island to sever the government's east-west communications.

Castro's columns meanwhile had snaked toward Santiago and other towns and were cutting communications and ambushing increasingly demoralized army units, a situation that brings to mind Mao's guerrillas in 1946, when they were isolating Chiang's garrisons in Manchuria. In camp at La Plata, Castro increasingly resembled an army theater commander more than a provincial guerrilla leader. Political envoys, couriers, and foreign correspondents arrived and left in a steady stream. The guerrillas were on the offensive and would remain so until Batista's fall.

Batista fell with surprising swiftness. He later wrote feelingly of conditions in that crucial autumn:

. . . Some of the sugar mills were not operating because the cane had been burned, and others because it was believed that, no matter how great the effort, labor crews would not be protected while trying to reconstruct the railways and the bombed-out roads. The ranchers could not transport their steers to the markets. . . . The coffee harvest faced the same risks. . . . A similar situation faced the miners and harvesters of rice, tobacco and other agricultural products.

These conditions brought about greater efforts for a fast settlement, and even hints that the Government yield its power to the rebels. . . .[29]

A rigged election of a new President in November, a Batista candidate, Rivero Agüero, fooled no one. Although Rivero attracted limited American support, mainly from the pro-Batista lobby, the government's situation was deteriorating beyond salvation. Batista later wrote:

. . . Panic was growing among the commercial interests and, apparently, in several important sectors of the Armed Forces. . . .

Military affairs went from bad to worse. . . .

With the elections over . . . Sabotage ran wild, people were slain and wounded by the rebels. Government forces were unable to stop them.

The military operations carried out in the Sierra Maestra and its valleys dragged along without satisfactory results. The Command and the Chief of Operations were changed several times. . . .

The delay in fighting the guerrillas with adequate tactics created anxiety in the population. Terrorism, indiscriminately and unscrupulously carried on

28. Thomas, op. cit.
29. Batista, op. cit.

in the whole country but especially in the capital, was the contagion that became known as "the cancer of the Sierra Maestra. . . ."[30]

To the uneducated observer, the crisis was not immediately apparent. A reporter, Irving Pflaum, later wrote:

. . . I remember Havana in the final months of 1958, while the thieves and gangsters prepared to flee, as a dying city, scarcely breathing, bruised and sullen behind a facade of wholly synthetic gaiety in the near-empty hotels and casinos.[31]

In the second week in December, Senator Ellender of Louisiana asked newsmen in Havana: ". . . Is there a revolution here?"[32]

Behind the scenes, Batista was desperately reshuffling senior commanders, but this was only riding tired horses. Che Guevara's campaign in Las Villas caught him and his commanders off guard. In a desperate attempt to keep roads open, the government expanded its highway patrol: ". . . patrol cars manned by a crew of four, each fully armed. They made their run in pairs, staying only one kilometer apart and communicating by radio-telephone."[33] The army backed this effort with another twelve hundred troops sent from Havana along with an armored train to protect repair crews. But, by mid-December, villages and towns were falling to guerrillas, the small army garrisons in most cases surrendering.

Panic in Havana washed over Washington. Eisenhower's later words unintentionally emphasized the poverty of his Cuba policy:

. . . During the rush of these last events in the final days of 1958, the Central Intelligence Agency suggested for the first time that a Castro victory might not be in the best interests of the United States. (Earlier reports which I had received of Castro's possible Communism were suspect because they originated with people who favored Batista.)

"Communists and other extreme radicals appear to have penetrated the Castro movement," Allen Dulles said. "If Castro takes over, they will probably participate in the government." When I heard this estimate, I was provoked that such a conclusion had not been given earlier.

One of my advisers recommended that the United States should now back Batista as the lesser of two evils. I rejected that course. If Castro turned out to be as bad as our intelligence now suggested, our only hope, if any, lay with some kind of non-dictatorial "third force," neither Castroite nor Batistiano.[34]

30. Ibid.
31. Pflaum, op. cit.
32. Taber, op. cit.
33. Batista, op. cit.
34. Eisenhower (*Waging Peace*); see also Matthews (*CS*), *supra:* The Deputy Director of CIA, General C. P. Cabell, testified to the Senate Internal Security Committee on November 5, 1959, that his organization believed that Castro was

Eisenhower was about five years too late. When Ambassador Smith flew to Washington in mid-December, he received only negative instructions ". . . instructions to disabuse Batista of any idea that Rivero Agüero might receive the backing of the U.S. government."[35] This effectively finished Batista. Castro's guerrillas had surrounded Santiago and were negotiating surrender of Batista's senior commanders. Guevara's guerrillas had isolated the armored train, whose garrison surrendered. Guevara now cut the island in half and continued to receive surrender of principal city garrisons.[36]

At year's end, Batista gathered wife and children and, with a personal entourage ". . . of bodyguards, retainers, and erstwhile military and political accomplices" who filled five airplanes, flew into an exile that would end in Florida—no great hardship, in view of a personal fortune estimated as high as $300 million.[37]

Batista's exodus was Castro's victory. In early January 1959, Che Guevara and his ragged band entered Havana and took control of government. A few days later, Castro triumphantly followed, the Liberator claiming the country for the Movement.

The political revolution was over, the social revolution about to begin—with results disastrous to Cuba and her long-suffering people.

From the standpoint of guerrilla warfare, Che Guevara's expedition to Bolivia constitutes an important postscript to the Cuban revolution. Daniel James, who translated and edited Che's captured diaries, offers an excellent account of this ill-fated expedition in his book *The Complete Bolivian Diaries of Ché Guevara,* on which the following brief account is largely based.[38]

Almost immediately upon assuming power, Castro began to alter facts of the multifaceted revolutionary experience. A combination of arrogance of ignorance and political opportunism caused him and cohorts to insist that they had carried off a "peasant revolution"—a vast oversimplification, as we have briefly discussed. As early as spring of 1959, Castro and Che were developing a theme that, by means of a peasant uprising, the rebels had established a peculiar "Latin American way"

---

not a member of the Communist Party, and did not consider himself to be a Communist; Draper (*CR*), *supra,* quotes Senators Eastland and Dodd of the Senate Internal Security Subcommittee: ". . . Cuba was handed to Castro and the Communists by a combination of Americans in the same way that China was handed to the Communists."

35. Thomas, op. cit.
36. Guevara, op. cit.
37. Thomas, op. cit.; see also Matthews (*CS*), *supra.*
38. Daniel James (ed.), *The Complete Bolivian Diaries of Ché Guevara—and Other Captured Documents* (London: Allen & Unwin, 1968). Hereafter cited as James (*Diaries*); see also James (*Che*), *supra;* Ernesto Che Guevara, *Bolivian Diary* (London: Jonathan Cape, 1968). Tr. Carlos Hansen and Andrew Sinclair.

to revolution.[39] In 1961, in a book called *Guerrilla Warfare*,[40] and in 1963, in a long article, "Guerrilla Warfare: A Method,"[41] in *Cuba Socialista,* Che Guevara developed the theme:

. . . We consider that the Cuban Revolution made three fundamental contributions to the laws of the revolutionary movement in the current situation in America [i.e., Central and South America]. They are: Firstly, people's forces can win a war against the army. Secondly, we need not always wait for all the revolutionary conditions to be present; the insurrection itself can create them. Thirdly, in the underdeveloped parts of America the battle-ground for armed struggle should in the main be the countryside.[42]

Che foresaw a continental struggle brought on by a series of local insurrections—the famous *foco insurreccional:*

. . . The prediction of the continental character of the struggle is borne out by analysis of the strength of each contender, but this does not in the least exclude independent outbreaks. Just as the beginning of the struggle in one part of a country is bound to develop it throughout its area, the beginning of a revolutionary war contributes to the development of new conditions in the neighboring countries.[43]

Here was a sort of revolutionary *tache d'huile* concept that, in time, Che supposed would result in a large revolutionary base from which to carry on the armed struggle:

. . . As Fidel said, the Andes will be the Sierra Maestra of America, and all the immense territories that make up this continent will become the scene of a life-and-death struggle against the power of imperialism.[44]

The United States inevitably would react to the threat, and the Southern Hemisphere, in time, would become a second Vietnam.

This grandiose dream might have died, except for a peculiar combination of factors. One was Castro's and Che's belief, probably genuine, in historical determinism:

. . . We cannot tell when this struggle will acquire a continental character nor how long it will last; but we can predict its advent and its triumph, because it is the inevitable result of historical, economic and political conditions and its direction cannot be changed.[45]

39. George Lavan (ed.), *Che Guevara Speaks—Selected Speeches and Writings* (New York: Grove Press, 1967). See his interview by two Chinese Communist journalists in April 1959.
40. *Supra.*
41. Lavan, op. cit.
42. Ibid.
43. James (*Diaries*), *supra.*
44. Lavan, op. cit.
45. Ibid.

Allied to this factor was Castro's determination to retain his own revolutionary personality, particularly as regards Soviet influence. Castro and Che's revolutionary thesis was a synthesis owing much more to Mao Tse-tung and Ho Chi Minh than to the Soviets. This was all right so long as Castro did not have to depend on the U.S.S.R. for survival. When that unhappy state of affairs arose, the unorthodox revolutionary line could scarcely be tolerated, and, indeed, from 1961 onward, Guevara found himself in nasty fights with doctrinaire Communists at home and abroad.

Add to this Che's own performance as president of the Cuban National Bank and as Minister of Industry. Dr. Guevara's treatment of the Cuban economy very nearly killed the patient. His ineptness both in economics and in politics brought him into increasing conflict with Castro, whom he was beginning to criticize, albeit guardedly, and who saw him as a rival in any event.

In late 1964, Che evidently fell from grace, leaving Havana and becoming a sort of revolutionary ambassador without portfolio, in some ways a romantic figure—a Walt Whitman with machine gun. In New York, he delivered a fiery address to the United Nations attacking both the United States and the Soviet Union as imperialist powers; he went on to Africa, made more bellicose speeches, and returned to Havana in March 1965, apparently impressed with the revolutionary possibilities offered by Congo troubles. He now went underground, resigning all official positions and renouncing Cuban citizenship, his goal to carry revolution abroad.[46]

Backed by Castro, he took 125 Cuban guerrillas to join the Kinshasa rebellion in the Congo. This effort totally failed, and he returned to Havana in autumn of 1965. He next decided to carry revolution to South America by establishing an insurrectional *foco* in Bolivia—a plan approved by Castro, who allowed him to recruit and train some twenty Cuban guerrillas and also supported him financially.

At first glance, Bolivia seemed just the country in which to launch an agrarian revolution. The population was predominantly peasant. Terrain favored guerrilla warfare. The Barrientos government was authoritarian and seemed to Che and Castro to resemble Batista's government. The army was small and ill-trained. A local Communist Party existed to carry revolution to the cities.

Disguised as a traveling salesman, Che arrived in Bolivia in November 1966. The young French Communist Régis Debray had arrived earlier ". . . to make a geopolitical study of the selected zone."[47] Che now organized a headquarters for his small group, which included twenty-nine Bolivians. After a short training program, he started his force, about fifty, on a training march designed to learn the terrain, to

46. Ibid.: See his "Farewell Letter to Fidel": ". . . Other nations of the world call for my modest efforts."
47. James (*Diaries*), *supra*.

perfect guerrilla tactics, and to recruit local peasants. In late March, the guerrillas successfully ambushed an army patrol, a success repeated in April.

But, also in April, an army patrol elsewhere captured Régis Debray and two followers, and the Barrientos government agreed to accept a sixteen-man team of American Special Forces advisers to train a regiment of Rangers in counterinsurgency tactics. By May, considerable steam had gone out of Che's operations. Che had been recording frequent quarrels in the ranks; lack of food and general illness were slowing his movements; he had recruited no peasants. Although he remained optimistic and, in July, briefly "captured" a town, he was forced to split his group and, in general, to keep moving. By now, army intelligence had closed in on his earlier headquarters and had identified him and most of his lieutenants. By August, he admitted he was in ". . . a difficult situation." Matters steadily worsened, and, in early October, units of the 2nd Rangers surrounded his small group. He was wounded, captured, and presumably summarily executed.

What went wrong?
Castro's and Che's estimate of the situation was nearly as faulty as

that made by Lyndon Johnson, Eugene Staley, Maxwell Taylor, and Walt Rostow in Vietnam in 1961 (see following chapter). The terrain in southeastern Bolivia favored guerrilla warfare only so long as one *knew* the terrain. Neither Che nor his Cubans nor his Bolivians knew the terrain, which meant that they had to depend largely on the peasants.

Che miscalculated badly here. The peasants, in this case Indians, who constituted more than two thirds of Bolivia's 4.25 million people, were not to be stirred. As Daniel James noted,

. . . The National Revolution had radically transformed the life of the Bolivian Indian . . . and that was probably its greatest single accomplishment. It had done so, first, through an agrarian reform law enacted in 1953, which made landholders of the virtually landless Indian peasantry and gave them pride of ownership, even if it was but a little plot they were given. Second, the whole body of revolutionary legislation had the effect of raising the Indian out of age-old serfdom and enabling him to exert his rights as a citizen. . . .[48]

Guevara's chief selling point of revolution—Land to the Landless—automatically fell flat when pitched to Indians with land. But, more than that, in Che's area of operations, his *foco insurreccional* in southeastern Bolivia, the Indians were a particular sort, parochial and suspicious of any outsiders. Che and his guerrillas had studied the dominant Indian language, Quechua, but, in the Southeast, the Indians spoke Guaraní: ". . . Not one of the guerrillas, including the Bolivians, could speak it. . . ."[49]

Lacking a valid sales pitch and easy communication, Che failed not only to win over peasants but to gain even limited co-operation. His monthly analysis for April included the ominous statement: ". . . The peasant base has not yet been developed although it appears that through planned terror we can neutralize some of them; support will come later. Not one enlistment has been obtained." The May analysis included this statement: ". . . Complete lack of peasant recruitment, although they are losing their fear of us and we are beginning to win their admiration. It is a slow and patient task. . . ." In June, he noted: ". . . The lack of peasant recruits continues. It is a vicious circle: to get this enlistment we need to settle in a populated area, and for this we need men." And the last analysis, in September: ". . . the peasants do not give us any help and are turning into informers."[50]

Peasants had been informing all along. Though no great shakes, the Barrientos government and the Bolivian army impressed the peasants far more than did Che's guerrillas. This was partly because of land reforms, partly an "ingrained fear and respect" of the army, and partly

48. Ibid.; see also J. E. Fagg, *Latin America—A General History* (London: Macmillan, 1969).
49. James (*Diaries*), *supra*.
50. Ibid.

because it was a peasant army and its recruits were aware that the government had been trying to help peasants. American army advisers had been on hand since 1958, their influence evident in a Civic Action Program which, by late 1963, had the army spending 20 per cent of its time in civil works, most in the countryside. When Che's early successes were reported,

. . . peasant organizations throughout the country held meetings at which they not only denounced the invaders but proceeded to organize armed peasant detachments to send into battle against them.

In July 1967 the Fourth Peasant National Congress was held, representing the vast majority of Bolivian peasants. It called upon its followers to back the government against the guerrillas with arms if necessary. This was supplemented by a formal "Pacto Campesino-Militar," an alliance of the peasantry with the Armed Forces, which itself is made up almost entirely of peasant conscripts.[51]

For this reason, the army gained intelligence it needed to run down guerrillas; guerrillas lacked intelligence needed to survive, prosper, and grow.

Che fared no better with local revolutionary groups. Two such could have helped him: the Communist Party, or PCB, headed by Mario Monje, with primarily an intellectual-student following; and the miners, helped by one Guevara (no relation).

Castro and Che alienated Monje with their initial decision to use Bolivia as a revolutionary comfort station, a decision taken without consulting the Communist chief. Che's words to his small guerrilla group were scarcely calculated to appeal to nationalism:

. . . Bolivia will sacrifice itself so that conditions [for revolution] can be created in neighboring countries. We have to make [Latin] America another Viet Nam, with its center in Bolivia.[52]

Debray added to conflict by dealing with miners instead of with Monje—a futile gesture that resulted in only a few, undesirable recruits for Che. Che's own insistence on leading a rural revolution with the military struggle predominant over the political struggle completed Monje's alienation. Monje ". . . saw the revolution in more orthodox Leninist terms, as emerging from a mass uprising in the cities."[53] In a December meeting with Che Guevara, he presented a plan that called for ". . . coordination of simultaneous actions in the cities, mines, countryside, and mountains," as soon as a national crisis occurred. Monje, moreover, felt that he should lead the effort, and, when Che refused to consider this, the two fell out—to Guevara's great cost.

51. Ibid.
52. Ibid.
53. Ibid.

Even had Monje remained co-operative, he could have offered only limited help. He could have supplied Bolivian recruits, but whether they would have known terrain and Indians any better than Che is problematical. He also could have kept open a line of communications to Che, but whether Fidel Castro would have filled that line with revolutionary needs—arms, supply, and money—is also problematical: Daniel James suggests that Castro was not sorry to be rid of his old lieutenant.

That his old lieutenant was failing, seems to have been the case. From his arrival in Bolivia, he had begun violating his own basic tenets of guerrilla warfare. By June, he was a sick man gradually losing control of himself and his group. It is possible that he wanted to die a martyr. He had seen his economic theories refuted. He might have believed that Castro was compromising Marxism-Leninism by accepting an imperialistic Soviet presence. He had failed in the Congo, and almost daily, despite various euphoric diary entries, he was seeing his theories fail in the Bolivian wilderness. Whether asthma and general debilitation dulled his senses or whether he underestimated the army, he refused to cut out for the border in time to avoid capture. On the basis of diary entries, not to mention his previous behavior and personality in general, we can conclude that Che's ego overcame his common sense. We don't know where his body lies, but, if ever a plaque is erected, it should bear only two words, as fatal to a guerrilla as to those who fight guerrillas: VANITAS VANITATUM.

Chapter 75

John Kennedy inherits a war • General Lansdale's estimate of the situation • Kennedy's strategic appraisal • His early errors • Lyndon Johnson's report • Hawks versus doves • Military versus political strategy • The Staley Plan • The Taylor mission • The military solution • Kennedy's reservations • Roger Hilsman dissents • De Gaulle's warning • Kennedy acts • His relations with Diem

SINCE 1951, John Kennedy had interested himself in the Vietnam scene, on several occasions pressing his views on fellow legislators and the nation.[1] For nearly ten years, protests of dissident officials had claimed his ear. He had listened to such Saigon veterans as Robert Blum and Edward Gullion, and he knew and approved of some of Colonel Edward Lansdale's views.

In June 1956, the young senator told a meeting of American Friends of Vietnam: ". . . What we must offer [the Vietnamese people] is a revolution—a political, economic, and social revolution far superior to anything the Communists can offer—far more peaceful, far more democratic, and far more locally controlled."[2]

1. John F. Kennedy, *The Strategy of Peace* (New York: Harper & Brothers, 1960).
2. Buttinger, op. cit.; see also Tanya Matthews, op. cit.: In July 1957, Senator Kennedy introduced a resolution in the Senate ". . . calling on the President and the Secretary of State to use American influence to achieve a solution which would recognize the independent personality of Algeria."

Kennedy's error, and that of hundreds of influential and well-intentioned Americans, was the assumption that President Ngo Dinh Diem both wished and was able to effect such a revolution—an assumption unfortunately voided by Diem's behavior, which increasingly caused some of his most enthusiastic American supporters to begin having second thoughts on his performance. Although the Eisenhower administration was preparing to send more advisers and more aid, Ambassador Durbrow ". . . had been required to bear so many messages of disapproval from the United States that he had not been welcome at the presidential palace in Saigon for several months."[3] Nor did Diem's belief that Durbrow was privy to the November 1960 coup attempt, and had failed to warn Diem, help matters.

Although Vietnam played no prominent role in 1960 U.S. presidential elections, Kennedy entered office displeased with the situation in Indochina. He was scarcely reassured when, in early February 1961, presidential assistant Walt Rostow handed him a memorandum prepared by Lansdale, now a brigadier general:

. . . Lansdale's paper, on the basis of his earlier experience in Vietnam, dealt with what he regarded as the American failures to use political power for what it was worth in backing the cause of real nationalism and in conducting the war in ways that would counter the increasingly successful guerrilla effort of the Vietcong. As a man who understood the nature of guerrilla warfare, and who at the time was recognized as the Pentagon's leading expert on the subject, Lansdale felt that the Vietnamese military structure and military methods of operation (which the Americans, in their pale advisory role, were countenancing) were all wrong. He felt that if the bitter conflict stood any chance of being won, we would have to be firm in insisting on a complete reorganization of the government's fighting machine; we would have to make it a force capable of dealing with Communist subversion in a meaningful and imaginative way, much as Magsaysay had done in the Philippines in 1951–52.[4]

Kennedy read the paper through and turned to Rostow: "This is the worst yet," he said. "You know, Ike never briefed me about Vietnam."[5]

3. Roger Hilsman, *To Move a Nation—The Politics of Foreign Policy in the Administration of John F. Kennedy* (Garden City, N.Y.: Doubleday, 1967).

4. Shaplen, op. cit.

5. Arthur M. Schlesinger, Jr., *A Thousand Days* (Boston: Houghton Mifflin, 1965). Hereafter cited as Schlesinger (*Days*); see also Hugh Sidey, *John F. Kennedy, President* (New York: Atheneum, 1963), for a slightly different version; but see also Clark M. Clifford, "A Viet Nam Reappraisal," *Foreign Affairs,* July 1969: As Kennedy's "transition planner," Clifford arranged a briefing on Southeast Asia on January 19, 1961. He later wrote: ". . . Most of the time, the discussion centered on Southeast Asia, with emphasis upon Laos. At that particular time, January 1961, Laos had come sharply into focus and appeared to constitute the major danger in the area.

No matter the new President's lack of information on Vietnam, he entered office fully aware of the deteriorating position in Southeast Asia, particularly in Laos. Kennedy did not regard this as an isolated problem area, but, rather, as symptomatic of a new strategic threat. He saw guerrilla warfare—what he called "internal" or "subterranean" war—as the real challenge of the sixties. As he was soon to tell the American Society of Newspaper Editors:

. . . it is clearer than ever that we face a relentless struggle in every corner of the globe that goes far beyond the clash of armies or even nuclear armaments. The armies are there, and in large number. The nuclear armaments are there. But they serve primarily as the shield behind which subversion, infiltration, and a host of other tactics steadily advance, picking off valuable areas one by one in situations which do not permit our armed intervention.[6]

Almost as soon as he took office, he ordered Secretary of Defense Robert McNamara to begin weaning the United States from dependence on the massive-retaliation strategy of nuclear warfare: ". . . I instructed the Secretary of Defense to reappraise our entire defense strategy, capacity, commitments and needs in the light of present and future dangers."[7]

The Lansdale report thus found a receptive mind. It so impressed Kennedy that he decided to send its author back to Vietnam as American ambassador, an intention shortly announced to a select group of officials. It would have been a healthy move. Although Lansdale had overrated Diem's potential, he had remained on good terms with the man and possibly could have separated him from the destructive embrace of the Nhus and persuaded him to a more productive course. He could also have spelled out the insurgency problem to the White House and recommended specific reforms needed in the South Vietnamese army (ARVN), MAAG, and perhaps even in various American civil-aid and intelligence missions. But the threat of Lansdale's disruptive presence to sacrosanct bureaucratic and particularly military empires caused a storm of protest from Washington and Saigon officialdom.[8]

"My notes disclose the following comments by the President [Eisenhower]:

At this point, President Eisenhower said, with considerable emotion, that Laos was the key to the entire area of Southeast Asia.

He said if we permitted Laos to fall, then we would have to write off all the area. He stated we must not permit a Communist take-over. . . ."

6. John F. Kennedy, *Public Papers of John F. Kennedy* (Washington: U. S. Government Printing Office, 1962), Vol. 1 of 2 vols. Hereafter cited as Kennedy (*Public Papers*); see also Hilsman, op. cit.

7. Kennedy (*Public Papers*), *supra.*

8. John Mecklin, *Mission in Torment* (New York: Doubleday, 1965); see also Hilsman, op. cit.: The State Department recommended sending Lansdale out on three subsequent occasions without success; in 1965, Lodge finally insisted on his presence.

Unfortunately, the young President succumbed to these forces (which he would never quite tame).

Uncertain as to the situation in South Vietnam—an uncertainty inherited from the Eisenhower administration, itself victim to false reports from the field regarding Diem's indispensability—Kennedy yielded to military and civil advisers, including Dean Rusk, and, in March 1961, sent out Frederick E. Nolting as his new ambassador. A soft-spoken Virginian, Nolting was a fifty-year-old former philosophy professor turned diplomat, a man without experience in Southeast Asia. Roger Hilsman later offered an interesting insight into the President's thinking at this time:

> . . . Nolting was a big, soft-spoken man who was so comfortable to be with that almost everyone used his nickname, Fritz. He was ideal for the job of restoring good relations with Diem and attempting to influence him toward concessions that would bring his regime wider support from within Vietnam and make it politically easier for the United States to give him the aid he requested.[9]

Instead of getting off to a good start, then, Kennedy, by these negative actions, kept the pot of South Vietnam bubbling as it had been for the previous five years. A change of faces and significant increases in personnel, both civil and military, meant no fundamental improvement of a worsening situation. Instead, it meant privately compounding past and present errors while publicly defending them as a viable program.

A number of reasons exist for Kennedy's disappointing performance in this troubled area, and we shall discuss them in due course. But first we must present in brief the turbulent events of these crucial years of the insurgency.

In spring of 1961, Kennedy and his advisers were still deeply concerned about the American role in Vietnam and particularly in Laos, where the Joint Chiefs of Staff (JCS) had recommended committing American ground troops. General James Gavin, whom Kennedy had appointed ambassador to France, later described a meeting with the President in mid-May:

> . . . The talk soon shifted to Southeast Asia, particularly Vietnam and Laos. At that time Laos appeared the more volatile situation of the two. I argued strongly against committing any U.S. troops to Laos. I pointed out that Laos was a landlocked area in which it would be very difficult to bring U.S. power to bear in any meaningful way, even if it should be in the U.S. interest to do so. I felt Laos would turn into a bottomless pit into which we would pour soldier after soldier. I recounted for the President the history of the debate inside the Pentagon after Dien Bien Phu and said I felt this new

9. Hilsman, op. cit.

situation was similar. There was little to be gained and a great deal to be risked by U.S. military action.

In the discussion President Kennedy indicated strongly that he believed sending U.S. troops to Laos was the wrong course of action. He also implied that if he asked the Pentagon for advice they would recommend dispatching troops. . . .[10]

While a special task force—the Attorney General, Robert Kennedy, State Department, Defense Department, and CIA and USIA officials—studied the problem, Kennedy sent Vice-President Lyndon Johnson on a general tour of Southeast Asia. In Saigon, the lanky Texan talked to Diem and his officials, promised increased aid, and stated the Administration's confidence in the Diem government. Ngo Dinh Diem, he told reporters, was the Winston Churchill of Southeast Asia—a remark that must have brought an interesting comment from Sir Winston.

Back in Washington, Johnson reported to Kennedy that

. . . the basic decision in Southeast Asia is here. We must decide whether to help these countries to the best of our ability or throw in the towel in the area and pull back our defenses to San Francisco and a "Fortress America" concept. More important, we would say to the world in this case that we don't live up to our treaties and don't stand by our friends. This is not my concept. I recommend that we move forward promptly with a major effort to help these countries defend themselves.[11]

Johnson told the President that

. . . he did not consider Southeast Asia lost, "and it is by no means inevitable that it must be lost." In each country, he said, it was possible to "build a sound structure capable of withstanding and turning the Communist surge." But this could only be done if the nations of Southeast Asia had "knowledge and faith in United States power, will and understanding. . . ."[12]

Johnson found Diem

. . . a complex figure beset by many problems. "He has admirable qualities, but he is remote from the people, is surrounded by persons less admirable than he. The country can be saved—if we move quickly and wisely."[13]

Johnson's mission produced varied, generally unfortunate results. Perhaps the most harmful was to reinforce the concept of South Vietnam as a "strategic necessity" to the United States, along with the notion of

10. James Gavin, *Crisis Now* (New York: Random House, 1968).
11. Schlesinger (*Days*), *supra;* see also L. B. Johnson, *The Vantage Point—Perspectives of the Presidency 1963–1969* (New York: Holt, Rinehart & Winston, 1971).
12. Schlesinger (*Days*), *supra.*
13. Ibid.

Diem's indispensability—not only in his and his intimates' minds but in those of the Administration and the American public. Johnson made plain his attitude, on the plane flying from Saigon, when a reporter started discussing Diem and his faults. ". . . Don't tell me about Diem," Johnson answered. "He's all we've got out there."[14]

Kennedy simultaneously fell victim to another pernicious influence, his Secretary of State, Dean Rusk, a small man in a big job:

> . . . While the President and a number of his advisers saw the insurgency primarily as a civil war . . . Rusk tended to ignore the highly complex causes and history of the insurgency and developed the theme of "aggression from the North," which was to become increasingly prominent as the American-sponsored efforts of the Saigon regime proved ineffective against the rebellion. As early as 1961, Rusk was speaking of "the determined and ruthless campaign of propaganda, infiltration, and subversion by the Communist regime in north Viet-Nam to destroy the Republic of Viet-Nam."[15]

Rusk's indignation was shared by Secretary of Defense Robert McNamara and, to a lesser degree, by Kennedy's national-security adviser, McGeorge Bundy. All apparently favored a military strategy. Bundy's deputy, Walt Rostow, was particularly hawkish. Forty-five years old, he was a Yale man, a Rhodes scholar, an economist and historian long associated with government; in World War II, he had served with the OSS in Burma. Rostow shared Rusk's belief in "aggression from the North" (or perhaps Rusk shared Rostow's belief). Rostow made his thinking known publicly at West Point, in spring of 1961, where he argued that emerging nations must be protected against external Communist aggression to the point that it might be necessary to ". . . seek out and engage the ultimate source of aggression."[16] Rostow's argument failed to respect internal differences in the emerging country; it was a lovely black-and-white interpretation in which GOOD would attack the forces of EVIL. Although Hanoi at this time was helping insurgents in the South, the effort nowhere near approached that claimed by Rusk and Rostow, and they were as much at fault for preaching this as others were for denying its existence.[17]

Still other presidential advisers, most of them close to Kennedy, though admitting the North's unsavory role in the South, wanted to counter it, along with the actual insurgency, with a political strategy that would have sharply subordinated military operations. This group, who could be called doves and of whom we shortly will hear more, included

14. David Halberstam, *The Making of a Quagmire* (New York: Random House, 1965).

15. Kahin and Lewis, op. cit.

16. W. W. Rostow, "Guerrilla Warfare in Underdeveloped Areas." In T. N. Greene (ed.), op. cit.

17. Pike, op. cit.

Robert Kennedy, Averell Harriman, George Ball, Roger Hilsman, and Michael Forrestal.

The hawks—Johnson, Rusk, McNamara, Rostow, and the JCS— formed a formidable pressure group. Although Kennedy, in general, favored a political strategy, he could not ride roughshod over those who favored a military strategy. Moreover, he grew increasingly incensed, as did many Americans, with Viet Cong terrorist tactics. Finally, implementing a political policy would probably involve military aspects, and this posed the problem of preparing the nation to follow him. Heretofore restrained in public utterances on the subject, he now began emphasizing the theme of Communist revolutionary warfare and external aggression. Speaking before a joint session of Congress in late May, the President sounded remarkably like an indignant Winston Churchill scorching Lenin's tactics in Poland in 1920 (see Chapter 23, Volume I):

. . . Yet their aggression is more often concealed than open. They have fired no missiles; and their troops are seldom seen. They send arms, agitators, aid, technicians and propaganda to every troubled area. But where fighting is required, it is usually done by others, by guerrillas striking at night, by assassins striking alone, assassins who have taken the lives of 4,000 civil officers in the last 12 months in Vietnam, by subversives and saboteurs and insurrectionists, who in some cases control whole areas inside of independent nations.[18]

Equally unfortunate, Johnson's visit, as Robert Shaplen later wrote, stiffened

. . . the resistance of the Vietnamese to carrying out a number of things we wanted them to do—things which the American Embassy had thought they were on the verge of doing as a result of patient pressure. This included the devaluation of the piastre and relinquishing of full Vietnamese control over income from American economic aid imports. After Johnson left, the Vietnamese would no longer even discuss these matters.[19]

Kennedy next dispatched Professor Eugene Staley, who spent summer of 1961 preparing a report on Diem's needs. Although not made public, Staley's recommendations included ". . . a number of changes in the administration of aid, as well as certain reforms of a political nature."[20] He also allegedly recommended increasing Vietnamese army strength to 170,000, doubling the Civil Guard to a total 120,000, equipping the Self-Defense Corps with modern small arms and radios, and constructing a network of fortified, or strategic, hamlets.[21] Kennedy was mulling over the Staley Plan when Diem sent an an-

18. Kennedy (*Public Papers*), *supra*.
19. Shaplen, op. cit.
20. Ibid.
21. Fall (*The Two Viet-Nams*), *supra;* see also Lacouture, op. cit.

guished plea for help. Kennedy now dispatched a larger mission, headed by sixty-year-old General Maxwell Taylor, a former army chief of staff whom he had consulted in the Bay of Pigs fiasco. Walt Rostow served as Taylor's deputy. Kennedy, in particular, wanted to know if the Diem government could be "saved." Taylor (and Rostow) reported that it could be, but Taylor

. . . was dismayed by a number of things he thought were wrong with the Diem regime and he recommended a tougher American approach. He drew up a list of some thirty subjects on which he suggested the Americans should act forcefully in its [sic] relations with the Diem regime. They include, among other things, recommendations that we stand firm on our demand that Diem and Nhu decentralize their administration, both in its civilian and its military aspects, and that we insist on a revamping of the muddled system of collecting and interpreting intelligence about the Vietcong. Taylor also felt strongly that certain political reforms should be instituted and that bona fide nationalist leaders who were in jail should be freed.[22]

On the positive side:

. . . their collective answer to Kennedy's question was that South Vietnam had enough vitality to justify a major United States effort. The trouble, as Taylor and Rostow diagnosed it, was a double crisis of confidence: doubt that the U.S. was really determined to save Southeast Asia; doubt that Diem's methods could really defeat the Viet Cong. To halt the decline, they recommended increased American intervention—in effect, a shift from arm's length advice to limited partnership. While only the Vietnamese could finally beat the Viet Cong, Americans at all levels, Taylor and Rostow argued, could show them how the job was to be done.[23]

Taylor's recommendations meant openly refuting the manpower ceiling laid down by the Geneva Agreements. The American role would be enlarged, ". . . essentially through the penetration of the South Vietnamese army and government by American 'advisers,' attached to Vietnamese military units or government offices and designed to improve the level of local performance"[24]; these included American helicopter and air-reconnaissance units for logistics-support purposes. The report also called for committing American ground troops (which the JCS had

22. Shaplen, op. cit.; see also, Halberstam, op. cit.; Hilsman, op. cit.; Kahin and Lewis, op. cit.

23. Schlesinger (*Days*), *supra;* see also Daniel Ellsberg, *Escalating in a Quagmire* (Boston: Center of International Studies, MIT, 1970), who points out that the report called for the short-run goal of "frustrating" the Communists; i.e. ". . . halting or reversing a current downward trend or spiral of deterioration," and the long-run goal of "defeating" them, i.e. the ". . . ultimate goal of eliminating the Communist threat."

24. Arthur M. Schlesinger, Jr., *The Bitter Heritage—Vietnam and American Democracy 1941–1966* (Boston: Houghton Mifflin, 1967). Hereafter cited as Schlesinger (*Bitter*); see also Hilsman, op. cit.

recommended a few months earlier): an eight-to-ten-thousand-man task force would be committed as "engineers" to help in flood-control work; such a force, in addition to raising Vietnamese morale and demonstrating United States determination to Hanoi, Peking, and Moscow, would be capable of conducting ". . . combat operations for self-defense and perimeter security and, if the Vietnamese Army were hard pressed, of providing an emergency reserve."[25] In case this force provoked invasion from the North, additional troops would be required. Moreover—and here was Catch-22—". . . Taylor and Rostow *hoped* that *this* program would suffice to win the civil war—and were sure it would *if only* the infiltration from the north could be stopped. But if it continued, then they could see no end to the war. . . ."[26] Finally, ". . . the whole program was only an important first step in the direction of the longer-run goal, eventually to contain and eliminate the threat to the independence of South Vietnam . . . for final victory the U.S. might have to strike the source of the aggression (though this decision could be deferred)."[27]

Here was a qualitative change in addition to a quantitative change of means to realize the grand ambition: *stop communism*. Maxwell Taylor, one analyst wrote,

. . . described it to the President at the time as "essential" if we were to reverse the present downward trend of events. In fact, he reported, "I do not believe that our program to save South Vietnam will succeed without it." Elsewhere his view is recorded that it was very doubtful that the remainder of the program, less the proposed U. S. Task Force, would even avoid a further deterioration of the situation in South Vietnam.[28]

Taylor's rationale was as fascinating as it was dangerous. Instead of appreciating the political nature of an insurgency, he was attempting to change the rules. As Roger Hilsman later noted,

. . . The mission of these American troops—revealing the continued focus in General Taylor's mind on the possibility of a conventional, Korea-type attack—would be to hold the ring against invasion from the north by regular

25. Schlesinger (*Days*), *supra;* see also Hilsman, op. cit.
26. Schlesinger (*Days*), *supra.*
27. Ellsberg, op. cit.; see also Hilsman, op. cit.
28. Ellsberg, op. cit.: ". . . Taylor underlined the urgency by making explicit his recognition of an impressive list of disadvantages of the proposed move, including weakness of the U.S. strategic reserve; increased engagement of U.S. prestige; difficulty of resisting pressure to reinforce the first contingent if it were not enough (with no limit to the possible commitment, unless we attacked the source in Hanoi, if we sought ultimately to clean up the insurgents); and the risk of escalation into a major war in Asia. It was in the face of all these possible drawbacks that he made his recommendation to introduce a Task Force without delay: made it on the grounds that a U.S. program to save South Vietnam simply would not succeed without it"; see also Hilsman, op. cit.

North Vietnamese divisions and to man the northern borders against infiltrators, while the South Vietnamese dealt with the guerrillas in the rear.[29]

Far from being the far-sighted strategist that Kennedy needed, Taylor might as well have donned an air force uniform and stood in the public pulpit to preach the virtues of massive retaliation. Far from approaching the problem with imagination and flexibility (and caution), he was thinking primarily in conventional-force terms.

Apparently, Taylor and his fellows were either ignorant of or oblivious to the estimate of the situation that General Matthew Ridgway had presented in 1954 (scc Chapter 63) and that emphasized incompatibility between the American military machine and the tactical environment of Vietnam. In 1961, highest American military councils unfortunately lacked any semblance of Ridgway's intelligent restraint. Only that spring, General Lyman Lemnitzer, chairman of the JCS, had returned from an inspection trip to Vietnam and, according to newspaper reports, ". . . felt that the new administration was 'oversold' on the importance of guerrilla warfare and that too much emphasis on counter-guerrilla measures would impair the ability of the South Vietnamese Army to meet a conventional assault like the attack on South Korea by the ten or more regular North Vietnamese divisions."[30] In early November, speaking at Fordham University, General Earle G. Wheeler, army chief of staff, told his audience

. . . that what the United States was committed to support in Vietnam was "military action. . . . Despite the fact that the conflict is conducted as guerrilla warfare," Wheeler went on to say, "it is nonetheless a military action. . . . It is fashionable in some quarters to say that the problems in Southeast Asia are primarily political and economic rather than military. I do not agree. The essence of the problem in Vietnam is military."[31]

Now Taylor was proposing a course of action consonant with Lemnitzer's and Wheeler's antiquated reasoning—a course of action that, if it did provoke the enemy to conventional counteraction, would lead to escalation noted by the JCS in a report on Laos: If landing American troops in Thailand, South Vietnam, and government-held portions of the Laotian panhandle did not produce a cease-fire, the JCS

. . . recommended an air attack on Pathet Lao positions and tactical nuclear weapons on the ground. If North Vietnamese or Chinese then moved in, their homelands would be bombed. If massive Red troops were then mobilized, nuclear bombings would be threatened and, if necessary, carried out. If the Soviets then intervened, we should "be prepared to accept the pos-

29. Hilsman, op. cit.
30. Ibid.
31. Ibid.

sibility of general war." But the Soviet Union, they assured the President, "can hardly wish to see an uncontrollable situation develop."[32]

Taylor's plan contained no less a number of "x" factors. Rostow was an even more outspoken advocate of escalation, arguing ". . . for a contingency policy of retaliation against the north, graduated to match the intensity of Hanoi's support of the Viet Cong. . . ."[33] Secretary of Defense Robert McNamara also reported to the President a conclusion shared by his deputy secretary Roswell Gilpatric, and by the JCS,

. . . that the chances were against, probably sharply against, preventing the fall of South Vietnam to Communism by any measures short of the introduction of U.S. forces on a substantial scale. McNamara explicitly judged, in agreement with General Taylor, that the various other measures proposed by Taylor short of this (i.e., the set of measures eventually accepted by the President) would not by themselves do the job of restoring confidence and setting Diem on the way to winning his fight.

Indeed, though of great help to Diem, even the initial U.S. task force of about 8,000 men, would not convince the other side that we meant business, unless we accompanied the introduction of the initial force with a clear commitment to the full objective of preventing the fall of South Vietnam to Communism and warned Hanoi through some channel that continued support of the VC would lead to punitive retaliation against North Vietnam. Lacking this commitment and warning, the initial force by itself (let alone, the program without this force) would probably not tip the scales decisively; we would be almost certain to get increasingly mired down in an inconclusive struggle.

If the proposed commitment and force deployment were undertaken, the President was warned of the possibility that Hanoi and Peiping might intervene openly, in which case as many as, but (given logistic difficulties of the other side) not more than six U.S. divisions, or about 205,000 men would be required.[34]

The Taylor-Rostow mission evoked several responses. Not long after the mission's return, President Kennedy met with his close friend and adviser Arthur Schlesinger:

". . . They want a force of American troops," he told me early in November. "They say it's necessary in order to restore confidence and maintain morale. But it will be just like Berlin. The troops will march in; the bands will play; the crowds will cheer; and in four days everyone will have forgotten. Then we will be told we have to send in more troops. It's like taking a drink. The effect wears off, and you have to take another." The war in

32. Theodore C. Sorensen, *Kennedy* (New York: Harper & Row, 1965).
33. Schlesinger (*Days*), *supra;* see also Halberstam, op. cit.
34. Ellsberg, op. cit.

Vietnam, he added, could be won only so long as it was *their* war. If it were ever converted into a white man's war, we would lose as the French had lost a decade earlier.[35]

Although pressured by the JCS and by ". . . all his principal advisers on Viet-Nam" to commit a task force of troops,[36] Kennedy refused. This is not surprising, and for three reasons. The Bay of Pigs fiasco had made Kennedy ". . . far more skeptical of the experts, their reputations, their recommendations, their promises, premises and facts. . . ."[37] Added to this was another school of thought, whose major teacher was Roger Hilsman, aided by Michael Forrestal and backed by Averell Harriman, Chester Bowles, and other important Kennedy advisers. A West Pointer ('43) from Texas, forty-one-year-old Hilsman had served with OSS in Burma; after the war, he had gotten a Ph.D. from Yale, left the army, and taught international affairs until entering the State Department, in 1961, as director of its intelligence section. Hilsman differed sharply with the Pentagon and with Rusk and Rostow as to Vietnam. He saw the challenge as political—as a war of ideas that demanded essentially a political strategy designed to gain popular support:

. . . that government existed for the benefit of the people, that a government could really *care,* was as revolutionary in most of Asia as anything the Communists had to offer. . . .[38]

He concluded that a viable strategy ". . . would require an emphasis on political, economic, and social action into which very carefully calibrated military measures were interwoven."[39] Militarily, guerrillas must be fought with guerrilla, rather than conventional, tactics. This opinion, shared by other experts, military and civil, struck a responsive note with the President, who long since had recognized the futility of a foreign power (France) trying to polarize national forces.

. . . "Without the support of the native population," he said, "there is no hope of success in any of the countries of Southeast Asia." To try to oppose

35. Schlesinger (*Days*), *supra;* see also Sorensen, op. cit.: ". . . He had watched the French, with a courageous well-equipped army numbering hundreds of thousands, suffer a humiliating defeat and more than ninety thousand casualties. Now the choice was his. If the United States took over the conduct of the war on the ground, he asked, would that not make it easier for the Communists to say we were the neo-colonialist successors of the French? Would we be better able to win support of the villagers and farmers so essential to guerrilla warfare—than Vietnamese troops of the same color and culture? No one knew whether the South Vietnamese officers would be encouraged or resentful, or whether massive troop landings would provoke a massive Communist invasion—an invasion inevitably leading either to nuclear war, Western retreat or an endless and exhausting battle on the worst battleground he could choose."

36. Sorensen, op. cit.
37. Ibid.
38. Hilsman, op. cit.
39. Ibid.

Communist advances "apart from and in defiance of innately nationalistic aims spells foredoomed failure."[40]

Finally—and this reason is speculative—Kennedy a few months earlier had received some frank advice from an elder statesman, Charles de Gaulle. The young President not only admired De Gaulle but also respected him, and his blunt words at their Paris meeting must at least have raised a caution flag in Kennedy's mind. In spring of 1961, as Charles de Gaulle wrote in recently published memoirs:

. . . John Kennedy made it clear to me that a breakwater would be set up in the Indo-Chinese peninsula to resist the Soviets. But instead of giving him the approval he desired I told the President that he was taking the wrong road.

"For you," I said to him, "to intervene in this region will be to catch yourself in the cogs of a machine. From the moment that a nation awakes to its nationalism no foreign State, no matter how great its power, has any chance of imposing its will. That you will discover for yourself. For, if you find a Government there ready in its own interest to take your orders, the people will not agree to it.

"Ideological reasons which you put forward will change nothing. Moreover the masses will think it is your desire for power and not your ideology which counts. That is why the more you become involved there fighting Communism, the more Communists will appear as champions of national independence. They will get more support; despair will bring them support.

"We, the French, have experience of that. You, the Americans, wanted to take our place in Indo-China. Now you want to take over where we left off and restart the war which we ended. I predict that you will sink bit by bit into a bottomless military and political swamp however much you pay in men and money.

"What we and others ought to do for unhappy Asia is not to interfere in her affairs but to give her the means to escape from misery and humiliation which are, as they are elsewhere, the causes of totalitarian regimes. I speak to you in the name of the West."[41]

Kennedy had turned down action recommended in the Laos report, both because its contents, in part, struck him as specious and because —and this is one of his greatnesses—he realized the catastrophe that an atomic war would create and had no intention of risking same over the strategic non-entity of Laos. As for the Vietnam recommendations, Sorensen tells us that the President

. . . wanted more questions answered and more alternatives presented. The military proposals for Vietnam, he said, were based on assumptions and predictions that could not be verified—on help from Laos and Cambodia to

40. Ibid.
41. *The Sunday Telegraph* (London), November 11, 1970. Tr. Ronald Payne; see also Charles de Gaulle, *Memoirs of Hope, supra.*

halt infiltration from the North, on agreement by Diem to reorganization in his army and government, on more popular support for Diem in the countryside and on sealing off Communist supply routes. Estimates of both time and cost were either absent or wholly unrealistic.[42]

Kennedy did accept the rest of the plan—though, for what purpose, remains something of a mystery. He probably hoped that the psychological effect of committing more "advisers" and logistics-support troops such as helicopter units would warn Hanoi that he meant business, would revive South Vietnamese morale, and would cause Diem to reform his government; he probably hoped that such action would satisfy administration hawks. He also retained the option of committing ground troops: ". . . He ordered the departments [of the armed forces] to be prepared for the introduction of combat troops, should they prove necessary."[43] In addition, he remained committed to a covert effort that in time would yield bitter fruit. We know now from the Pentagon Papers that, in June 1961, Kennedy authorized continued CIA support of agents infiltrated into North Vietnam and Laos to work up covert resistance against the Communists, a program started in the Eisenhower administration.[44]

What he did not do—and this is one of his great failures—was to pursue his doubts. What he did not do was to call for a re-examination of what was passing for political policy and military strategy. He badly needed a devil's advocate with intelligence and courage sufficient to question underlying assumptions held by the majority of his advisers. He turned down recommendations to commit troops in Laos and Vietnam partly because the JCS and CIA had misjudged the Cuban situation so badly. What made him think that prevailing notions of policy and strategy in Southeast Asia were any more valid, particularly in view of General Ridgway's earlier dissent? That the domino theory could hold up under intelligent analysis? That the Pentagon would be content to remain in an advisory role? That Diem was indispensable? That Nolting and Harkins could manage Diem? That he himself could foist the Diem regime on the world as free, democratic government? That, had the American people been properly informed, they would not have trusted him and backed him in a "risk" strategy necessary to straighten out the Diem regime?

Instead, he remained a prisoner to this regime, and to his own bellicose advisers. In late October, when Taylor was still in Saigon, Kennedy wrote Diem an extremely sympathetic letter: ". . . Let me assure you again that the United States is determined to help Vietnam preserve its independence, protect its people against Communist assassins, and build a better life through economic growth."[45]

42. Sorensen, op. cit.
43. Ibid.; see also Hilsman, op. cit.
44. *The Times* (London), June 23, 1971.
45. Kennedy (*Public Papers*), *supra*.

In December, he again wrote Diem to describe what an aide called
". . . the limited and somewhat ambiguous extent" of the American
commitment:

> . . . The United States, like the Republic of Viet-Nam, remains devoted
> to the cause of peace and our primary purpose is to help your people main-
> tain their independence. If the Communist authorities in North Viet-Nam
> will stop their campaign to destroy the Republic of Viet-Nam, the meas-
> ures we are taking to assist your defense efforts will no longer be neces-
> sary. We shall seek to persuade the Communists to give up their attempts
> of force and subversion. In any case, we are confident that the Vietnamese
> people will preserve their independence and gain the peace and prosperity
> for which they have sought so hard and so long.[46]

He also compounded earlier diplomatic failure, by ordering General
Paul D. Harkins, allegedly on Taylor's recommendation, to Saigon,
where he would arrive, in March 1962, as chief of the new Military
Assistance Command Vietnam, or MACV, and where he would prove
about as effective in the military field as Nolting was proving in the civil
field.

A more explosive response to the Taylor report came from the
Diem government in Saigon and the Vietnam lobby in the United States.
Stung by Taylor's criticisms and prompted by brother Nhu, the Vietnamese President huffed and puffed about his country's sovereignty.
In Shaplen's words, ". . . what followed over a period of several weeks
was a game of bluff, which the Vietnamese won hands down."[47] Instead of pressing the issue to final conclusions, the Administration
yielded and pretended to find solace in Diem's empty promises.[48]

This was a vital error. Diem had consistently refused to allow either
a political opposition or a coalition government in order to broaden his
support. Diem was incapable of understanding representative government, and, by 1962, this fact was obvious. The cult of "personalism"
preached by brother Nhu was a specious doctrine, a euphemism for an
authoritarianism as severe as anything practiced by Khrushchev, Mao,
Tito, Castro, or Trujillo. Theodore Draper's later words describing
Castro's and Trujillo's forms of government were equally applicable to
Diem:

> . . . At bottom all these "neo" and "direct" democracies rest on a simple
> proposition: that the Leader and his people are one and indivisible. Hence
> they need no representative institutions, no elections, no loyal or disloyal
> oppositions, no free or partially critical press, none of the rights and safe-
> guards traditionally associated with a democracy.

The horror of this thinking is that it wipes out the lessons to be learned

46. Ibid.
47. Shaplen, op. cit.
48. Halberstam, op. cit.

from the most desperate and tragic experiences of our time. If there is anything that should have burned itself into our consciousness, it is the excruci-
ating evil of the popular despot, the beloved dictator, the mass leader.[49]

As David Halberstam concluded:

. . . Eventually, South Vietnam became, for all intents and purposes, a
Communist-type country without Communism. It had all the controls, all
the oppressions and all the frustrating, grim aspects of the modern totalitarian state—without the dynamism, efficiency and motivation that Communism
had brought to the North. It was a police state, but it was unique in that
its priorities were so haphazard; as a result, it was hopelessly inefficient.
It was likely to pick up people for the wrong reasons; it had a strong enough
police force to shake the loyalty and allegiance of the population, but not
efficient enough to make them truly afraid.[50]

49. Draper (CR), *supra.*
50. Halberstam, op. cit.

Chapter 76

The situation in South Vietnam • NLF organization • The People's Revolutionary Party (PRP) • Hanoi's influence in the South • NLF aims • "The Struggle Movement" • Agit-prop techniques • Diem's failings • Increased American aid • American military influence • Viet Cong setbacks • American optimism • Tactical chimeras • The Viet Cong recovers • Disaster at Ap Bac • ARVN failures • The strategic-hamlet program • Diem's increasing intransigence • The American commitment increases • Buddhist revolts • Shifting NLF strategy • Washington changes direction • Diem's death

B Y 1962, THEN, the dismal picture in Vietnam had changed but slightly. Despite such sops as a National Economic Council and provincial councils, Diem and his ruling oligarchy had refused to relinquish any real powers.[1] Millions of American dollars continued to fall into their hands—$300 million in army credits alone in 1961[2]—and, either in cash or kind, precious little of these funds reached the countryside, where the war was being fought. U.S. protests aroused only further threats from Diem and his advisers. At Ambassador Nolting's urging, the Administration agreed to a "soft" approach in hope that Diem would change his ways.

Instead of political reforms, Diem pushed through his rubber-stamp assembly such restrictive legislation as the Public Meetings Law, ". . . a law that forbade all kinds of meetings unless they were authorized by the government,"[3] and the Bill for the Protection of Morality, a piece

1. Lacouture, op. cit.
2. Ibid.
3. Shaplen, op. cit.

of legislative nonsense sponsored by Mme. Nhu and one comparable to Chiang Kai-shek's New Life Movement. Total censorship prevailed and Nhu's secret police prowled everywhere to pounce on dissidence:

. . . by 1962 there were some thirty thousand prisoners in about fifty jails throughout the country, about two-thirds of whom were classified as political prisoners. Many were captured Vietcong insurgents, but there were also a lot of "suspects" who had languished in jails for months or even years. Among the prisoners were some three hundred non-Communist liberals arrested solely for having expressed anti-Diem views or for being suspected of having spoken out in favor of the abortive 1960 coup.[4]

The regime's suspicions extended to the army, which continued to stir restlessly despite Diem's efforts to control it:

. . . Promotion on the basis of personal loyalty rather than ability, the use of informers, the banishment of men of integrity and initiative, and the domination of all strategy had not made the Army more loyal; these methods had merely brought about a tenuous control, and badly compromised and diluted a military force which was in a fight to the death with a tough enemy.[5]

A confused and demoralized army not only could not fight a successful counterinsurgency, but its ranks became increasingly vulnerable to the enemy's proselyting effort, the *binh van* program, which one expert believed was ". . . the most deadly weapon" in the Viet Cong arsenal.[6] The regime's innate xenophobia had made suspect the American presence since 1954. Subsequent American attempts to pressure Diem into various reforms had only brought increased resentment.

The outlook, then, was bleak. As Halberstam concluded:

. . . a government was fighting a complicated war, suspicious of its own army and attempting to minimize its effectiveness; at the same time remaining suspicious of its major ally and attempting to minimize its influence.[7]

Halberstam might have added that in emphasizing the Communist and northern-aggression themes that so appealed to American officials, Diem steadfastly refused to recognize his real enemy, the NLF, and the emphasis it placed on the "armed struggle," particularly the political struggle. In Douglas Pike's words,

. . . The GVN [Government of Vietnam] had no national policy or even official attitude toward the NLF's struggle movement, nor was there any systematic effort at the district and village operational levels to develop techniques designed either to head off a struggle movement as it was being

4. Ibid.; see also Halberstam, op. cit.
5. Halberstam, op. cit.
6. Pike, op. cit.
7. Halberstam, op. cit.

launched or to blunt it once under way. The posture of the Diem government was to pretend it did not exist or, if forced to take notice, to characterize it as an insignificant and ineffectual Communist effort to create disorder. District and village officials were left to their own resources when confronted by a struggle movement, and their responses depended largely on their personalities. Some officials attempted to ameliorate the situation if in their power to do so; others simply ordered their police and troops to disperse the crowds. Occasionally an official was politically astute enough to regard the struggle movement as an opportunity to seize the initiative from the NLF and would alleviate a genuine grievance and turn the crowd's attitude from hostility to amity; this was a difficult manipulation for it involved both acquiescing to a demand without appearing to surrender in the face of force and structuring the solution so as to maneuver the NLF out of credit for the change.[8]

What of the enemy, which General Myers and Ambassador Durbrow had written off so comfortingly in 1959? As we have seen, in December 1960, the National Liberation Front, or NLF, appeared in the South, published a "Ten-Point Manifesto" that called for a democratic, coalition government, and embarked on an "action program" to achieve this end. A year later, it gained a leader in the person of Nguyen Huu Tho, a fifty-two-year-old Saigon lawyer and Marxist who had escaped after five years of imprisonment for political activities.

The interworkings of NLF leadership in these years are not particularly well documented in the West (despite the capture, in 1966, of some six thousand NLF documents). NLF leaders remained underground. They did not reside at a permanent headquarters, they met infrequently, and those of their records later captured are sketchy:

. . . The actual headquarters of the NLF was believed to be in Laos . . . deep in Pathet Lao country. Periodically, from 1961 to 1964, the Central Committee convened in the sparsely populated area of northern Tay Ninh province. When the central Committee was not in session, and this was most of the time, the NLF was managed by the Presidium and its Secretariat. The secretary-general undoubtedly was the most powerful individual in the NLF. The military high command, which was responsible for the violence program, reported directly to the Presidium. All other activity went through the Secretariat, dominated by the secretary-general.[9]

By the time Tho joined his comrades, Communists both in the South and in Hanoi apparently were worried about ultimate control of the liberation movement. In January 1962, militant Communist elements of NLF established a revolutionary front, the People's Revolutionary Party, or PRP—the old Lao Dong, or Communist Party—which now

8. Pike, op. cit.
9. Ibid.

became the radical branch of the movement, the "vanguard" of the revolution.

Hanoi's exact role in this development is not clear: Ho Chi Minh apparently blessed the PRP as a control instrument of the movement; he may, at China's insistence, even have ordered northern Communists to organize it. According to Donald Zagoria, and most experts agree, ". . . evidence is overwhelming that the People's Revolutionary Party (PRP) . . . is, in fact, the Southern branch of the Lao Dong Party which rules Hanoi."

. . . In sum, the main function of the PRP is to insure political control of the military arm of the NLF and to guide the movement's political struggle. According to captured NLF documents, PRP secretary-general, Tram Nam Trung [who came South in 1963], has overall responsibility for the NLF armed forces. PRP chairman Vo Chi Cong supervises agitprop and indoctrination, recruitment, and organization building. . . .

This does not mean, as asserted by South Vietnamese and American officials at the time, that Hanoi either absorbed the movement or thenceforth directly controlled it. Zagoria, among other experts, concluded that

. . . there are non-Communist individuals and forces in the Front, some of whom unquestionably believe that they can push the NLF toward democracy, and many of whom do not want to subordinate themselves to the North. . . . On several key issues, at any rate, there have been persistent signs of disagreement between the North and the NLF. . . .

Again,

. . . Notwithstanding this elaborate control machinery [of the PRP], whose threads all lead back to Hanoi, the NLF has emerged as a viable movement in its own right . . . Certainly the NLF includes very significant political forces that are not Communist and still harbor long-held apprehensions about both Communist domination and domination by Northerners.[10]

In other words, the NLF remained a specific political entity, and, despite the extent of Hanoi's control, it might have been wiser to recognize it as such if only to influence its non-Communist and even some of its Communist members.

Two months later, in March 1962, the NLF held its first congress, which elected Nguyen Huu Tho president and Nguyen Van Hieu, a mathematics professor believed by many to be the real driving force of NLF, secretary-general of the Central Committee. The congress also announced a new objective: independence of South Vietnam, an objective extended in July to making ". . . south Viet-Nam, Laos, and Cambodia a neutral zone with all three states enjoying sovereign

10. Zagoria, op. cit.; see also Pike, op. cit.; Shaplen, op. cit.

rights."[11] Simultaneously, the NLF continued appealing to all ". . . parties, sects, and groups representing all political tendencies, social strata, religions, and nationalities of South Vietnam."[12] The Geneva Agreements of 1962, which resulted in a neutralized Laos (in theory), strengthened the NLF (and Hanoi) in demands for a neutral, coalition government in the South.

No matter the ultimate NLF and PRP intention, which Communist leadership cunningly concealed during formative years: At a time when Diem was adamantly refusing representative government, his enemy was stressing its desire for such, a brilliant tactic in the propaganda war. Continued U.S. association with and support of the Diem regime also offered a superb propaganda target for Communists to exploit. In 1962, NLF leaders introduced the term *special war*—". . . described as a form of neocolonialism in which a colonial power, no longer able to use expeditionary forces to assert its control, worked through a clique of compradors whom it 'advised,' with the rank-and-file military force being supplied by the colonialized nation."[13]

The NLF, or anyway its Communist leadership, sought to gain either direct control of the South Vietnam Government through a general uprising, or to gain indirect control by establishing a coalition government and working on from there. Essential to the process was "the struggle movement," a two-pronged program well described by Douglas Pike:

. . . Within the generic term "struggle," there were two types of struggle movements: The political struggle (*dau tranh chinh tri*) and the armed, or military struggle (*dau tranh vu trang*). To the NLF, as to the Viet Minh and Chinese Communists before it, victory would be achieved through the proper balance of political and military activities or, in Communist terms, by the proper combination of the political struggle and the armed struggle.[14]

The political struggle, which, in accordance with Mao's teachings, gained primary ascendancy, called for a three-pronged program: consolidation of areas already controlled by Viet Cong; the "liberated areas" or base sanctuaries so essential to further revolutionary activity (the *dan van,* or "action among the people"); organization of the countryside under GVN control, the agit-prop task discussed earlier (the *dich van,* or "action among the enemy"); proselyting of ARVN and the GVN civil service (the *binh van,* or "action among the troops").

The military struggle, which at first remained subordinate to the political struggle, consisted ". . . not simply [of] guerrilla military attacks but kidnappings, assassinations, executions, sabotage"—what Pike succinctly calls the "violence program." Military organization strongly

11. Lacouture, op. cit.
12. Ibid.
13. Pike, op. cit.
14. Ibid.

resembled that of the Viet Minh earlier discussed (see Chapter 54). Operations remained the responsibility of the "People's Self-Defense Armed Forces Committee." As with other national committees, this extended downward through provincial and district organizations. The Liberation Army consisted of two parts: Main Force regiments, or what might be called regulars; the Guerrilla Popular Army or paramilitary forces—peasants by day, guerrillas by night—organized in small units that varied in function from village militia duty (generally covert) to active combat often in conjunction with Main Force or regional units. The Guerrilla Popular Army formed the reservoir of men that supplied the regular units. It also maintained three-man "special activity cells," which

. . . would strike anywhere at any time. From the roster of these cells were drawn the assassination teams, the volunteer grenade hurlers, the death or suicide squads. Most of the spectacular acts of sabotage, assassinations of province chiefs, or daring military escapades were the work of a special activity cell, sometimes working with demolition experts or other military specialists supplied by the provincial-level central committee.[15]

Although the importance of the political and military struggles would vary, each complemented the grand design.

. . . Vo Nguyen Giap wrote that if an uprising was an art, the chief characteristic of its leadership was the ability to change the struggle form in accordance with changed events. At the beginning, he said, the political struggle dominated and the armed struggle was secondary. Gradually the two assumed equal roles. Then the armed struggle dominated. In the end came the return to the political struggle. Struggle was *the word*. Its goal, toward which the cadres pledged themselves, toward which each Vietnamese was expected daily to contribute a little, was the General Uprising, the nationwide, simultaneous grand struggle movement.[16]

By 1962, the NLF controlled large areas of South Vietnam, including two rich areas in the Mekong Delta. While they busily converted these into "liberated areas," Viet Cong units continued to ambush ARVN columns and attack ARVN and police outposts. Terrorists struck at government officials whenever possible:

. . . They also made schoolteachers a prime target; hundreds were murdered. Between 1959 and the end of 1961, the Government was forced to close six hundred and thirty-six schools, either because of intimidation, or because the Vietcong were using them for propaganda. Again and again the story was the same: brutal murders, decapitation of village officials and teachers in front of an entire village; hidden Vietcong cadres coming slowly to the

15. Ibid.
16. Ibid.

surface. These spotlighted the corruption of officials, and by wholesale murders demonstrated that a government which could not protect its own officials certainly could not protect its people.[17]

Hideous tactics these, but not often promiscuous and no more hideous in final result than quantitative military tactics: mass artillery bombardment or aerial bombings. Above all, tactics with a purpose, tactics that formed part of a relentless propaganda war designed to consolidate and expand a peasant base that Communist leaders realized was essential to future operations.

The song had not changed, and now, after over twenty years of singing, the voices were good. The communism that Kennedy was endeavoring to stop did not enter the picture. Human misery did. John Mecklin later described the Communist target, a typical Vietnamese hamlet of fewer than a thousand people:

. . . a cluster of straw and bamboo huts with earthen floors and straw sleeping mats. The land between the huts was a quagmire of ankle-deep black mud in the rainy season, choking dust in the dry season. The peasant's wife or children often walked as much as three or four miles and then waited in line an hour or two for the daily drinking water. In the dry season the distance was often further because the regular well became saline. There was seldom electricity, frequently no road of any sort to the outside world, and no communication except by foot.

He was beset by insects, by rats that could literally make a hamlet uninhabitable and become fierce enough to attack humans (in one province alone, some five million rats were killed in a two-month, U.S.-sponsored drive in 1962), by floods and by droughts. He was seared by the sun and whipped by the rain, and his bare feet became calloused, unfeeling boards. The beauty of his women was destroyed by their mid-twenties, and by the mid-thirties they were hags, wracked by years of merciless burden, and often by disease.

And forever there were the flies, chiltering the stinking fish at the village market, swarming the open sores in the skin of his infant son, harassing his sleep. To survive his mind became numb, reconciled forever to submission and pain without end.[18]

17. Halberstam, op. cit.
18. Mecklin, op. cit.; see also Pike, op. cit.: ". . . Vietnamese villages vary greatly. There is the long narrow village strung out, one house wide, along a canal in the Mekong delta; the village of houses widely scattered through the deep shadows of a rain forest in the Massif Plain; the ancient village of Central Vietnam with its worn paths and closely grouped houses; the sun-baked village in the near-desert country of the west; the fishing village, resolutely turning its back on the land in favor of the South China Sea. Some were rich, a few poor, but almost all enjoyed a basic self-sufficiency. Life within the village may have been simple, but it was good." One may ask, were they in the same country? Other personal observations, my own included, not to mention sociological statistics, favor Mecklin's report.

Then strangers appeared. In the night, strangers came to the hamlet and to the peasant. They brought no gifts, no money, no food. Sometimes they asked for food, paying if they could. They sat by the fire, they talked, they listened, and because they had once been of these hamlets themselves, they soon did not seem strange. They identified with the peasant before they proselyted:

. . . They made every grievance theirs: long-standing historical antagonisms, whether against Asians or Caucasians, became *their* grievances, as were economic inequities, the division of land, the arbitrary system of tax collection—even the ravages of disease.[19]

The newcomers brought sympathy and understanding and compassion. They brought what no one had ever brought before: genuine interest in the peasant's welfare. They presented themselves ". . . as nationalists continuing the war against the foreigners and their lackeys." They explained that the fight was being carried on by the National Liberation Front. They preached

. . . not Communism, but "real" independence, peace, a neutral Vietnam, political freedom, extensive land reform, and other popularistic economic policies.[20]

They preached more. They carried a materialistic bible with thousands of appealing verses. Here is part of a directive to cadres of secret self-defense units:

. . . Show them [the peasants] how hard they are forced to work, from three o'clock in the morning until four o'clock in the afternoon, and for low wages . . . are forced to attend "Denunciation of Communism classes" and other Diem-sponsored meetings, are drafted into the army. Workers have poor and miserable working conditions. . . . Secret police follow workers and sometimes threaten them. . . . Show them that the wealth of a society is produced by the workers and the farmers and then taken by the imperialists [pure Marx, that]. Support the National Liberation Association [one of the many "tailored" fronts]. Show the great leadership role assumed by the Party in the NLF and describe its great prestige. Counter the distorting propaganda of the enemy against the Party and the Revolution. . . . Describe the successes of the socialist countries. . . . Use concrete details in talking with the masses. In rubber plantations point out the great burden of the workers in tapping up to 500 trees from early morning to noon and then having to carry ten kilos [twenty-two pounds] of latex for five to seven kilometers [3–4 miles], having to negotiate slippery slopes in the rain, and for which they are paid only 44 piasters [fifty cents] a day.[21]

19. Halberstam, op. cit.
20. Scigliano (*Nation Under Stress*), *supra*.
21. Pike, op. cit.

Propaganda agents did not hesitate to exploit targets of opportunity. Preparatory bombing and strafing offered natural subject matter, particularly when villagers were killed. If an epidemic suddenly broke out in an area (and epidemics frequently did) and if defoliants had been dropped in that area—well, then, they had caused the epidemic.

Agit-prop agents did not hurry to convert the listener. At first they settled for passive acceptance. Their continued interest and honeyed words of promise in time often produced the desired effect, and that was to arouse hope and, with it, new-found dignity. The peasant now had something to fight for.[22] Now he would lend his children to the Viet Cong, the younger as messengers, the older as fighters. Now he would donate to the cause, now he would pay taxes, now he would supply food and sanctuary and guides who would help guerrillas transit twenty-five miles of tortuous terrain in five hours of night marches. The agent recruited the female as well. He organized the guerrilla version of a Fem-Lib movement. He stressed the ghastly lot of woman during the French colonial regime and the Diem regime. The PRP pledged itself to liberate the Vietnamese woman from ". . . the life of the water buffalo": ". . . We stand for total liberation of women in every respect . . . for economic equality, political equality, cultural equality, social equality . . . and equality in the family."[23]

Having aroused the peasant, the Viet Cong kept him aroused: "struggle meetings," "denunciation meetings," "ceremonial meetings," "people's conventions"; dozens of front organizations, each tailored to a specific target; newspapers, leaflets, theatrical troupes, cultural teams, radio, motion pictures—an altogether-well-organized, massive propaganda effort almost constantly misunderstood and underrated by South Vietnamese and American officials.

As the American-Diem military effort provided weapons and supply to the Viet Cong, so did it sustain the propaganda effort. Each bomb dropped, each machine-gun bullet fired, each gallon of defoliant, was worth a thousand persuasive words.

Probably not one Viet Cong agent in a thousand could read English, yet each knew the truth long-before written by Lawrence of Arabia:

. . . A province would be won when we had taught the civilians in it to die for our ideal of freedom. The presence of the enemy was secondary. Final victory seemed certain, if the war lasted long enough for us to work it out.[24]

22. George Tanham, *War Without Guns* (New York: Frederick A. Praeger, 1966). Hereafter cited as Tanham (*Guns*): On one occasion, Dr. Tanham interviewed a guerrilla prisoner in Thailand. The man said he had become dissatisfied with his government in June 1959. Pressed as to why the date was so specific, he answered: ". . . A man told me I was unhappy with certain things and I suddenly realized he was right."
23. Pike, op. cit.
24. Lawrence (*Seven Pillars*), *supra*.

The prevailing political atmosphere in Saigon could hardly have engendered a national will so necessary to combating Communist influence in the countryside. Diem's continued failure to allow urgently needed economic, agrarian, and social reforms and to decentralize political control meant an apathetic peasantry who remained peculiarly prone to propaganda and blandishments offered by NLF and PRP cadres.[25]

So long as peasants remained apathetic or hostile, the military effort against the Viet Cong could not succeed—no matter how expansive it became. Unfortunately, this unpalatable truth, emphasized repeatedly since 1945 and preached by vigorous and intelligent voices, did not wash against the American military priesthood, who were well on their way to the fateful formula for disaster that combined arrogance of ignorance with arrogance of power. As Douglas Pike wrote:

. . . We assumed that the Vietnamese, because they were Vietnamese, would know how to defeat Vietnamese guerrillas if they had the means to do so. We assumed a charismatic leader was required. We assumed the solution was simply some combination of military force and welfare work. We assumed there was a high correlation between helping villagers in economic aid programs and their hostility toward the guerrilla. We assumed that methods used in other counterinsurgencies could be put to work in Vietnam. All of these assumptions, we discovered, were partially or wholly wrong. Error continued because of lack of information. . . .[26]

Kennedy's decision to go along at least in part with the Staley and Taylor-Rostow recommendations tipped an expansion that by early 1962 reached impressive proportions. The Vietnamese task force already existed. The Pentagon soon opened an Office on Counter-Insurgency and Special Activities, headed by Major General V. H. Krulak, a marine officer who enjoyed direct access to the Joint Chiefs of Staff and also to McNamara. The State Department set up a "counter-insurgency course" to train civil officials; the armed forces began similar specialized training.[27]

In Saigon, Ambassador Nolting headed the Country Team of civil and military officials, and he also headed the Country Task Force, which, in theory, functioned ". . . as an extension of the Vietnam Task Force in Washington." In reality, General Paul Harkins, who arrived in March 1962 as head of the new MACV, which absorbed MAAG, almost at once became the dominant figure, which meant, among other things, that the military effort continued to receive priority over the civil effort. John Mecklin, who arrived in Saigon in the spring of 1962

25. Tanham (Guns), supra, spells out some of these; see also Pike, op. cit.: Diem's land-reform program lasted only ". . . 3 years and aided only about 10 per cent of the landless."
26. Pike, op. cit.
27. Hilsman, op. cit.; see also Mecklin, op. cit.

as Public Affairs Officer and later wrote a disturbed book, *Mission in Torment,* that is well worth reading, also found ". . . a number of specialized, inter-agency committees to coordinate such activities as intelligence, economic development and psychological operations."[28]

By early 1962, the United States was funding a hefty increase in South Vietnam's armed forces, including the Civil Guard and Self-Defense Corps, and it was also financing what it hoped would prove to be a widespread "strategic hamlet" program. American army and marine helicopters began ferrying Vietnamese troops to and from "combat areas." By spring, some six thousand Americans were serving in Vietnam; a significant portion of field advisers and helicopter crews were being shot at; some military advisers were beginning to shoot back, as were armed helicopter crews. Special Forces teams working with the CIA were active in the central highlands and in the North, trying to woo heterogeneous Montagnards to fight on the government's side. Other advisers worked in the South, in the Mekong Delta area, where the Vietnamese began fighting a different kind of war, one much more in tune with contemporary American military thinking.

Here the infusion of weapons and material sparked a great series of "offensives," of "search-and-destroy" operations, of regimental and division sweeps supported by T-28 and B-26 aircraft strafing and bombing (too often on speculation) and burning out "enemy" complexes with napalm.

Communiqués sounded like those issued by the French in the late 1940s. According to one source, Vietnamese battle deaths were running between four hundred and five hundred a month, with another thousand men being wounded or taken prisoner. Mobility offered by helicopters allowed ARVN forces to catch numerous units off guard and posed a tactical challenge not immediately met by the Viet Cong. Captured NLF and PRP documents showed Communist consternation, as did increased terrorist tactics including kidnapings and assassinations. In some areas, the Viet Cong forcibly recruited guerrilla replacements and kept them in line by threatening reprisals against their families; they kept families in line by threatening to punish the sons.[29] Wilfred Burchett, the peripatetic Australian Communist reporter in Hanoi at the time, later wrote that the Viet Cong were on the point of yielding the Mekong Delta and withdrawing to the mountains.[30]

All this was heady stuff that impressed a good many American officials. Secretary of Defense Robert McNamara returned from Vietnam, in May 1962, and stated: ". . . Every quantitative measurement we have shows we're winning this war."[31] General Maxwell Taylor

28. Mecklin, op. cit.
29. Pike, op. cit.
30. W. G. Burchett, *Vietnam: Inside Story of the Guerrilla War* (New York: International Publishers, 1965).
31. Schlesinger (*Bitter*), *supra.*

returned from a second trip to Saigon impressed by "a great national movement" that would destroy the Viet Cong.[32] In January 1963—the American presence in Vietnam had increased to nearly ten thousand —President Kennedy, in his State of the Union message, said: ". . . The spearhead of aggression has been blunted in South Vietnam."[33]

Unfortunately, these statements and the reports on which they were based were unduly optimistic. Tactical gains amounted to little more than a gossamer sheen woven by temporary technological superiority. Despite intensification of fighting, it remained essentially guerrilla warfare, and, for this, the Vietnamese army and a large proportion of American advisers proved singularly ill-prepared, not only showing themselves unable to adjust tactically but, perhaps as important, unable to exploit tactical gains by a forceful and effective civil-affairs program.

Not understanding basic tenets of guerrilla warfare, Vietnamese and American senior officers converted fatalities into "victories." This was a great mistake: Dead bodies do not mean destroyed infrastructure. Dead bodies, particularly those of innocent peasants, mean a strengthening, not a weakening, of the insurgent cause. The NLF and PRP were down, but scarcely out. They may have been hurt, but a retreat to the mountains would not necessarily have spelled an end of insurgency. At the time retreat was being discussed, an NLF delegation headed by Nguyen Van Hieu, secretary-general of the NLF Central Committee, was touring Eastern Europe to introduce the NLF to the world. Also at the same time, southern cadres who had been living in the North took to what was to become famous as the Ho Chi Minh Trail to infiltrate back to the South. About thirty-seven hundred had arrived in 1961, according to Douglas Pike, who studied available evidence with great care; he suggests that in 1962 another fifty-eight hundred arrived.[34] More would arrive the next year.

As 1962 turned to autumn, the Viet Cong seemed more elusive than ever, and also began to display a new and disturbing aggressiveness. If they were not yet actively picking fights with ARVN troops, they were not avoiding them either. And they were continuing to strike Civil Guard and Self-Defense Corps outposts, both to supply themselves with new American arms and to prove their power to the peasants. Such was their success that, to American advisers, the outposts became known as Viet Cong PXs.[35]

Nor was ARVN showing well. As the Viet Cong recovered and began to shoot back, Diem's army seemed reluctant to fight. The battle of Ap Bac, in January 1963, exposed the awkward truth.[36] A task force of more than three South Vietnamese battalions, lifted in part by heli-

32. Ibid.
33. Ibid.
34. Pike, op. cit.
35. Mecklin, op. cit.
36. Hilsman, op. cit.

copters and armored personnel carriers, failed to destroy a Viet Cong battalion though having had it surrounded and greatly outgunned. David Halberstam, who covered the action for the New York *Times,* later wrote:

. . . To us [American reporters] and to the American military advisers involved, Ap Bac epitomized all the deficiencies of the [South Vietnamese] system: lack of aggressiveness, hesitancy about taking casualties, lack of battlefield leadership, a non-existent chain of command. The failures at Ap Bac had been repeated on a smaller scale every day for the past year.[37]

ARVN's big problem was trying to fight a guerrilla war with a conventionally organized and trained army that lacked both will and know-how essential to combat an insurgency. The U. S. Army's training program had denied it necessary flexibility. Armored personnel carriers and artillery had eliminated cross-country mobility. Confined to roads, ARVN units, just like French units formerly, remained vulnerable to ambush. Units lifted by helicopter could not long sustain themselves in the field without logistic support they had been taught to expect. ARVN staff work remained haphazard, particularly in vital intelligence sections. Operations remained unco-ordinated. Diem refused to establish a supreme commander and general staff. Instead, like Chiang Kai-shek, whose personal command on occasion extended to regimental level, he continued to run what virtually amounted to a war-lord arrangement:

. . . Operations were mounted in the field by President Diem, or by his immediate staff, more often by whim and hunch than by planning and co-ordination with the various corps commanders. Some of President Diem's favorite division commanders or province chiefs were able to persuade him to approve of actions that simply suited their particular needs or their egos.[38]

Such a command arrangement meant spotty military operations with slow response to hit-and-run guerrilla tactics. Intelligence, the vital ingredient in counterguerrilla warfare, was missing to a disastrous degree, the inevitable result of governmental failure to identify with peasants. Lacking intelligence on which to base small, selective, surprise raids, army units resorted to "sweeps," which often damaged and destroyed crops and hamlets but generally failed to kill or capture significant numbers of enemy. Troop looting and torture of villagers to obtain information nullified any psychological gain from show of force. If ARVN did clear an area of enemy, failure to occupy, consolidate, and protect villagers soon brought back the Viet Cong. U. S. Army advisers, with few exceptions and almost none at senior levels, could not be persuaded to adopt a proper counterinsurgency strategy: viable search-and-hold op-

37. Halberstam, op. cit.
38. Shaplen, op. cit.

erations with concomitant political and military pressure on Diem to force his government to initiate a genuine strategic-hamlet program.

Over-all failure only sapped ARVN of remaining will and made its ranks more prone to enemy propaganda—the *binh van* (proselyting) program. Although the Viet Cong sought to induce desertions whenever possible, they also relied on internal disintegration, on the process the French called *pourrissement*. Douglas Pike described one of their more invidious tactics:

. . . Particularly in insecure areas and especially to low-ranking civil servants, the NLF would convey the idea that it would not harm a GVN representative providing he arranged that the programs for which he was responsible were not implemented in any effective way. This could be done by a slowdown, by snarling the program in red tape, or by outright falsification of reports to higher headquarters. For instance, a strategic-hamlet chief could go through the motions of creating a village security apparatus that only appeared to have succeeded in separating the guerrillas from the villagers. Vietnamese Information Service posters and leaflets arriving from Saigon could be distributed only superficially, in areas where district officials would be likely to notice them, and the rest destroyed. A military patrol leader could lead his patrol noisily down a well-travelled path and after an hour return to the hamlet, never having made a serious effort to determine whether guerrillas were in the area but with his superiors being none the wiser. The effect was to place a premium on mediocrity in low-level administration at a time when excellence was vital. A civil servant would imagine he could enjoy the best of both worlds: He could perform well enough not to arouse the suspicions of his superior but not so well as to earn the hostility of the NLF. He might even be in contact with the NLF so as to be certain that they understood his position; many ARVN military operations were ruined by Vietnamese military or civil servants gratuitously passing on information to NLF agents or persons they presumed to be in contact with the NLF, simply in an effort to ingratiate themselves with the NLF—as a sort of life insurance policy.[39]

Neither did complementary governmental measures prosper.

The CIA and Special Forces found lucrative operational possibilities in the central highlands, where more than a hundred thousand Montagnards had fled their villages, the result of NLF failure to capture their loyalty.[40] American teams began recruiting and training Montagnard units to return to the hills to fight the Viet Cong. Initial successes here also proved illusory: The Montagnards, while willing in some instances to fight as mercenaries in American pay, refused to transfer loyalty to the Diem government; to the South Vietnamese, they were known as *moi*,

39. Pike, op. cit.
40. Ibid.

or savages, treated similarly, and responded predictably.[41] So long as Americans remained, the effort prospered; with their departure, it failed.

By the end of 1962, the highly touted "strategic hamlet" program, which aimed to fortify eleven thousand, or two thirds, of the country's hamlets by 1963, had also bogged down.[42] In theory, this was an excellent idea. Its genesis traces not to Eugene Staley but to the head of the British Advisory Mission to Viet-Nam, Robert Thompson, who arrived in Saigon in autumn of 1961.[43] A veteran of Orde Wingate's operations in Burma in World War II and of the later Malayan Emergency, Thompson had been instrumental in relocating Chinese villages in order to cut insurgents from intelligence, supply, and recruits (see Chapter 61).[44]

The idea was not original. As Gallieni and Lyautey realized, protection is an essential part of pacification. Area clearance had been used subsequently in emergencies, for example by General Weyler in Cuba, by the American army in the Philippines, by Kitchener in the Boer war, more recently by the French in Indochina and Algeria, and by the British in Malaya and Kenya. The present concept called for the army to clear and hold an area while the government helped villagers fortify hamlets into defensive complexes defended with militia, civil guards, and police, with regular troops on call. The Diem government refused Thompson's original suggestion, because brother Nhu did not like it. When Staley favored it, which spelled American financing, Nhu swung around and made it his own project—something quite different from what Thompson or Roger Hilsman had in mind.

Though valid enough, the concept, at best, was no panacea, which Thompson would have been the first to point out. Like most pacification measures, it called for a patient, methodical, and selective approach best illustrated by Lyautey's phrase *tache d'huile*. It had several drawbacks: The Mekong Delta, for example, was rich enough to feed guerrillas, fortified hamlets or no; the concept demanded efficient administration, and particularly effective internal and external security arrangements. But when it worked, it worked well. In Douglas Pike's words:

. . . This program not only forced NLF village leaders to flee but it offered alternative social and political organizations to the villagers. It eliminated the village as a base for guerrilla support. Moreover, since the program relocated villagers and thus mixed people from different villages, efforts by NLF agents to rebuild the network inside the strategic hamlet became increasingly complicated and less successful. It was difficult for an agent to

41. Mecklin, op. cit.: In 1963, Special Forces took over the program and eventually trained 20,000 troops with varying success; see also Pike, op. cit.
42. Scigliano, op. cit.
43. Robert Thompson (*Defeating Communist Insurgency*), *supra;* op. cit.; see also Mecklin, op. cit.; Tanham (*Guns*), *supra.*
44. Thompson (*Defeating Communist Insurgency*), *supra;* see also Clutterbuck, op. cit.

get into and operate inside a strategic hamlet, and the leadership could no longer simply send back to a village that was being organized a native whose only recommendation was that he had been born and raised there . . . in a mixed village the organizers faced strangers, and dealing with them required organizational and persuasive talents and skills that most of them did not possess. The drain on organizational and recruiter manpower was great, and the difficulties faced by the NLF grew steadily.[45]

Here was some real progress. Properly implemented, the program might have proved the key to solving the pacification problem. But two major defects marred the halcyon picture drawn by Pike.

The first was a failure to integrate the strategic-hamlet program into a single, over-all strategy evolved by Hilsman and others and discussed above. Thompson and Hilsman wanted the program to start in the heavily populated Mekong Delta and work slowly out from there. Instead, under Nhu's aegis, strategic hamlets sprang up like rice shoots. The government could not possibly provide enough civic action and security teams necessary to revamp hamlets and to organize and train peasant militia, nor did police exist in sufficient quantity to ferret out Viet Cong agents and sympathizers from within defended complexes. Once again, massive American aid, dollar and material, filtered through venal fingers to lose intended impact. In most areas, the program mired in ooze of bureaucratic corruption and ineptitude.

This was bad enough in its own right. But, as it was happening, the enemy was admitting the threat and, once again, was adjusting tactics. NLF leadership judged the threat of such proportions that it began subordinating the political struggle to the armed struggle and made the strategic-hamlet program a priority tactical target—at a time when ARVN and local militias were particularly vulnerable. Many of the hastily constructed complexes lacked adequate fortifications and remained physically vulnerable to Viet Cong propaganda, infiltration, and attacks. Rudimentary communications and regular army inefficiency slowed reaction time and thus lowered promised protection. Battery-operated transmitter-receiver radios copiously distributed by AID improved village-to-garrison communications, a slight gain, however, since ". . . calls for help were so rarely answered [by ARVN], or answered so slowly as to be useless."[46]

A second major defect centered on Nhu's ulterior motives. As with the previously unsuccessful *agrovilles* and "fighting hamlets," Nhu saw fortified hamlets as a convenient form of population control, with neighbor reporting on neighbor.[47] In places, they became little more than concentration camps full of unwilling guests. These were peasants who,

45. Pike, op. cit.
46. Mecklin, op. cit.; see also Tanham (*Guns*), *supra*.
47. Pike, op. cit.; see also Halberstam, op. cit.; W. R. Warne, "Vinh Binh Province." In Tanham (*Guns*), *supra*.

until the government-enforced move, had been listening to a siren song. No matter how false the notes, the peasant listened, his deception the greater because his ears had never before heard music. Then, suddenly, he was scooped up, placed in a strategic hamlet—and found the same miserable life of old, the same arrogant and corrupt officials, the same squeeze, the same sicknesses. A song became a nightmare and a program went to pot.

Here was the real failing, not alone of the strategic-hamlet program but of the entire counterinsurgency effort. The Diem government and its foreign advisers may not have known it, but they were fighting essentially an idea, and fortifications, in the long run, are invalid against ideas. As Hilsman had discerned, the only valid weapon against an idea is a better idea—and Ngo Dinh Diem's abortive doctrine of Personalism, which the Eisenhower and Kennedy administrations kept trying to insist was democracy, did not fill the bill. The Diem government may have given peasants barbed wire and advisers and even a civil-guard unit, but failure to provide vigorous counterideas—to give the peasant something to fight for—left hamlets and villages as vulnerable as ever to vigorous NLF and PRP propaganda. Unfortunately, much of this propaganda was based on fact. In 1962, a Vietnamese ". . . with a keen understanding of the peasant problem" told Robert Shaplen:

. . . To the peasants, the government is not what it says it is. Words are not enough. It's the people who represent the government in the peasants' daily life who count—the soldier, the village or district chief, the tax collector. They are the image of the government, as they always have been, and unfortunately most of them continue to put the government in a bad light. Because official pay is so low, corruption is customary and is accepted. Each man, all the way to the province chief, owes his job and influence to someone else, and favors and kickbacks are paid all the way along the line.[48]

The evil of the system transcended mere corruption. A later AID report noted:

. . . From the very inception it was apparent that many of the provincial officials did not fully understand the concept [of the strategic-hamlet program] and were so frightened by the pressures from the President [Diem] and his brother [Nhu] that they would employ any measures, from forced labor and confiscation to false reporting, to achieve the quantitative goals set.[49]

Far from protecting the peasant, the strategic-hamlet program frequently alienated him. Despite strenuous efforts of some American field advisers and a good many Vietnamese officers and officials, this unhealthy situation continued into 1963. Whether the situation could have

48. Shaplen, op. cit.
49. Halberstam, op. cit.

been retrieved then is debatable; if Diem could have brought himself to initiate legitimate reforms, it is possible that he still could have claimed the upper hand.

But this was not to be. Diem continued to rule on the basis of fear. A natural corollary of fear is dissembling, and this is what happened in these crucial years. In David Halberstam's words:

. . . Local officials and commanders became dependent on lying their way out of situations. For instance, because Diem did not want the ARVN to risk casualties and because Colonel Dam had reported that the war was going well, it became impossible for Dam to meet the enemy challenge. To do so would have required taking casualties, and then Diem would have demanded to know why there need be casualties in an area which, according to Dam, the Government had long controlled. Thus, potentially good men became prisoners of their past mistakes, and in the early months of 1963 the Vietcong took over the Delta countryside virtually unchallenged.[50]

Kennedy's kid-glove treatment of the Diem hierarchy, meanwhile, was also backfiring. Diem and his circle of intimate advisers grew increasingly difficult to deal with. At times, Diem held himself practically inaccessible; on other occasions, he granted audiences and then submitted ranking callers such as Nolting or Harkins to hours-long monologues. To most observers, he appeared firmly under the thumb of brother Nhu and Mme. Nhu, and, to some observers, the former was as mad as the latter was corrupt and ambitious.

What was the official American reaction?

In March 1963, the Secretary of State, Dean Rusk, stated that the war was ". . . turning an important corner . . . Government forces clearly have the initiative in most areas of the country."[51] In April,

. . . he discerned a "steady movement toward a constitutional system resting upon popular consent," declared that "the 'strategic hamlet' program is producing excellent results," added that "morale in the countryside has begun to rise," assured his listeners that "to the Vietnamese peasant" the Viet Cong "look less and less like winners" and concluded, "The Vietnamese are on their way to success. . . ."[52]

Roger Hilsman later reported an April meeting in Honolulu between Harkins and McNamara:

. . . General Harkins gave us all the facts and figures—the number of strategic hamlets established, number of Viet Cong killed, operations initiated by government forces, and so on. He could not, of course, he said, give any guarantee, but he thought he could say that by Christmas it would be

50. Ibid.; see also Staff of the Senate Republican Policy Committee, *The War in Vietnam* (Washington: Public Affairs Press, 1967).
51. Schlesinger (*Bitter*), *supra*.
52. Ibid.

all over. The Secretary of Defense was elated. He reminded me that I had attended one of the very first of these meetings, when it had all looked so black—and that had been only a year and a half ago.[53]

In May, when the NLF was collecting taxes in forty-one of South Vietnam's forty-four provinces, Harkins told Saigon reporters that the war would be won ". . . within a year." In Washington, a Defense Department spokesman announced that ". . . the corner has been turned in Viet-Nam." A month later—American troops in Vietnam now numbered over fifteen thousand—Ambassador Nolting told Saigon reporters: ". . . South Viet-Nam is on its way to victory over communist guerrillas."[54] To gain that victory, the administration had progressively raised its commitment from six hundred to thirteen hundred to six thousand to ten thousand to fifteen thousand troops; as an adviser had warned Dean Acheson in 1950: ". . . These things have a way of snowballing."

The brilliance of official statements suddenly dimmed in the flare of Buddhist revolts. The Buddhist problem had been building for a long time. Like the peasant problem, it was essentially political, although it held religious overtones. South Vietnam is overwhelmingly Buddhist, with some eleven million persons carrying the appellation. But, like all great religious movements, Buddhism had splintered into many variations, and perhaps four million could be called orthodox Buddhists.[55] The disillusionment of this majority bloc began when Diem installed northern, Catholic refugees in the more important and lucrative administrative posts and otherwise favored the minority (1.5 million) Catholic population. Buddhist grumblings grew increasingly severe in 1961. Instead of righting wrongs and admitting Buddhist leadership into his government, Diem, as usual, relied on repression:

. . . Sometime around mid-1962, as the Saigon regime grew more and more frightened, the campaign against the Buddhists did take on the aspect of persecution, religious as well as social and political. And where there had been only a smoldering discontent and a growing malaise, by the spring of 1963 a burning anger against the authoritarian actions and attitudes of the government had begun to roll across the countryside.[56]

Open rebellion broke out in May, in Hué, when government troops, attempting to disperse a Buddhist crowd, opened fire and killed nine Buddhists. Although the Diem government blamed this on Communist agitators, it gave in to some Buddhist demands. During negotiations, a Buddhist fanatic, following an ancient sacrificial custom, burned himself to death in a public ceremony in Saigon, an act photographed by Mal-

53. Hilsman, op. cit.
54. Schlesinger (*Bitter*), *supra*.
55. Shaplen, op. cit.
56. Ibid.

colm Browne and one that helped turn world opinion sharply against the Diem regime.[57] Subsequent immolations kept the issue alive and brought continuing demands from the Kennedy administration for a settlement. Instead, Nhu, prodded by his wife (who heartlessly described the suicides as "barbecues"), persuaded Diem, in August, to declare martial law, which he followed by police raids of Buddhist pagodas throughout South Vietnam—his police supplemented by Vietnamese Special Forces, a unit organized with CIA aid and one supposedly dedicated to counterguerrilla warfare.

With these acts, Diem and Nhu signed the death warrant of their government and, as it turned out, themselves. The raids brought thousands of protesting students into Saigon and Hué streets, where their arrest by army troops caused additional thousands of vociferous protests. Meanwhile, the NLF was shifting emphasis to the armed struggle. This was partly at the instigation of its own leaders and of the PRP, partly at Hanoi's instigation. Hopes in the South and in the North for an early settlement on Laotian lines had increasingly faded during the previous year. Once the NLF recovered from the tactical surprise of American intervention, it had turned increasingly to the military struggle. In April 1963, in Hanoi, the secretary-general of the Lao Dong, Le Duan, ". . . made the case for a violent versus a peaceful path to power [in the South]."[58] Hanoi also sent south a particularly skillful leader, Tran Nam Trung (an alias), who became secretary-general of the PRP, which held responsibility for the armed struggle. Probably on the advice of two generals from Hanoi, who allegedly came South in August

57. *The Times* (London), January 29, 1971: ". . . The ancient custom which Thich Quang Duc [the 73-year-old monk who burned himself to death] revived takes its origins in a Mahayana Buddhist text written in India in the first century A.D. Called the Saddharma-pundarika-sutra, it tells the story of Bhaishayja-raja, who ate incense, drank oils, and bathed in essences for 12 years before setting fire to himself as an offering to Buddha.

"This text was translated into Chinese (about 223 A.D.) and the cult first became established in China and Vietnam in the fifth century A.D. In the next 500 years there are records of at least 25 Buddhists (including two nuns and one layman) ceremonially burning themselves. The fanatics commonly dieted before igniting themselves, to make their bodies more combustible. Others made more modest offerings by cutting off and burning fingers or hands"; see also Lacouture, op. cit., whose authority is M. Folliozat, a specialist in the tradition of Indian Buddhism: ". . . One may see in these acts primarily an affirmation of eminent dignity and purification. By burning his arm—which is the most traditional gesture—or his body, the initiate, who is 'free' or 'awakened,' freely disposes of what he has come to know to be simple appearance. No longer attached to things, he heroically demonstrates that he understands real values, a deeper order, and in this fashion condemns the attitude of those who persecute his co-religionists.

"F. adds that such cremations could also be gestures of protest, condemnation, or vengeance; he states, too, that these acts constitute exploits of an extraordinary psychosomatic technique which, it seems, reduces the sufferings caused by the sacrifice. . . ."

58. Zagoria, op. cit.

or September, the NLF continued to step up guerrilla operations—the armed struggle was about to command the political struggle.[59] The situation was far from simple, and the exact power relationships are still not known in the West. At this time, however, dissident groups existed in the NLF and also in Hanoi. Moscow did not want the war escalated, but Peking did. Apparently, moderates in both South and North still controlled the situation—in any event, the NLF and Hanoi now released peace proposals sufficiently concrete to cause General de Gaulle to ask for neutralization of the area.

At the same time, President Kennedy dispatched a new ambassador, Henry Cabot Lodge, who was instructed to maintain a ". . . posture of silent disapproval" vis-à-vis the Diem government. Kennedy now suspended $12 million of monthly aid. As a particular snub to Nhu, Lodge arranged for recall of the CIA chief, John Richardson, who was overtly sympathetic to the regime.

The move toward neutralization, and the American government's new firmness, began jelling an incipient army revolt that had been brewing for over a year and now joined hands, albeit obliquely, with a more recently formed generals' plot.

Although the Kennedy administration, and the President himself, would willingly have continued to support Diem in return for sincere political and economic reforms, Diem's continued intransigence and particularly the anti-American raillery indulged in by Nhu and his vicious wife finally wore Kennedy's patience thin. In his famous speech of early October 1963, he told a television audience that ". . . a change of policy and perhaps personnel" was required in the Saigon government.

Rightly or wrongly, the generals plotting a coup regarded the President's words as a green light, and they seem to have been further encouraged by some American officials, both in Washington and Saigon, who had been made aware of their plans:

. . . On October 10th, the American go-between informed Minh that the United States would not stand in the way of a coup if it took place, and that if it was successful and if a new regime could improve military morale and effectiveness, could obtain popular support, and could deal on a practical basis with the American government, it would receive aid.[60]

Plots and counterplots developed during the next three weeks. The interested reader will find lucid recitals and analyses of these sordid events in several fine books such as Robert Shaplen's *The Lost Revolution,* David Halberstam's *The Making of a Quagmire,* and Roger Hilsman's *To Move a Nation.* Finally, on the first day of November, the coup began in earnest. Diem activists, such as Colonel Tung, who commanded the dreaded Special Forces, lost their lives on the first day;

59. Pike, op. cit.
60. Shaplen, op. cit.

Diem and Nhu refused Ambassador Lodge's offer of sanctuary and flight and, on the following day, were arrested and summarily executed by army officers.

The coup might have solved many problems, particularly had the American administration followed with a firm policy vigorously pursued. Unfortunately, less than three weeks after Diem and Nhu met their deaths, President Kennedy was assassinated.

Chapter 77

Kennedy's failure analyzed • The administration's ignorance concerning South Vietnam • Ambition versus policy • Vietnam's low priority • Pentagon and CIA influence • False reports • Kennedy's advisers • Guerrilla warfare and American armed forces • Special Forces (the Green Berets) • CIA's role • The tactical problem analyzed • General Griffith's warning • Quantitative versus qualitative warfare • The inevitable result

W HY DID JOHN KENNEDY fail in Vietnam?
The reasons are several and complex. Taken together, they do not compliment the man's historical image, nor do they present a comforting picture of American officialdom, military or civil, and the decision-making process. Taken together, they unfortunately emphasize the theme of this book—the arrogance of ignorance—and they must be analyzed, if only briefly, for us to understand subsequent events in Vietnam, the growing rift in present American political, diplomatic, and military circles, the resultant widening, and in many ways dangerous, schism between government and people, and the precarious moral position in which the United States finds herself vis-à-vis the world today.

Although Kennedy had interested himself in Indochina since 1951, his was a politician's interest, in his case a well-meaning, liberal desire to put matters right, but scarcely a profound understanding of basic issues. We have heard his plaintive comment to Rostow: ". . . You know, Ike never briefed me about Vietnam."

Kennedy never recovered sufficiently from initial ignorance to give Indochina the priority attention it required. The situation demanded a dynamic, imaginative, courageous, and even incautious policy on Kennedy's part. Instead, he remained wedded to what he had inherited: an ambition—what the Tasmanian Minister for External Affairs, Paul Haslack, later called a wish, when he warned fellow Australians:

. . . We need to see the difference between a wish and a policy. We all wish for peace, prosperity, world understanding and the peaceful settlement of disputes. These are not policies but wishes. A policy is a planned course of conduct devised by a government to serve an identified purpose and put into effect by its own efforts. If it is put into effect by the efforts of others it is not a policy but a hope. If it is proclaimed but not associated with any measures of any kind for putting it into effect it is a piece of humbug.[1]

A good many of the officially stated goals of the Kennedy administration were a sugar coating to the grand and inherited ambition: *stop communism*. This presupposed that communism is a physical thing like a tank or a division of troops or a bullet, and not an abstract idea so theoretically appealing as to survive elaborate corruptions placed upon it by a dozen pinchpenny dictators.

Much less a policy or even an objective, *stop communism* is an ambition—one that disallows occasional short-term "defeat" in the process of winning long-term "victory." Hinder communism while proving the virtues and strengths of democracy is a policy—one that realistically determines "strategic necessities" as opposed to "strategic conveniences" and one that accepts temporary setbacks, even "defeat" (whatever that means) in the process of insuring healthy survival.

Kennedy inherited the negative ambition of stopping communism as opposed to hindering it and letting it evolve into civilized society while further developing and strengthening his own political organism. A tense domestic political situation—in Theodore White's words: ". . . The margin of voices that proclaimed him President was so thin as to be almost an accident of counting"[2]—dissuaded him from disowning his inheritance. Instead, he bowed to forces of fear, both Republican and Democratic—and, almost to the end, remained prisoner to the Diem regime and to those officials who favored a predominantly military approach to a political problem.

Thus his early backdown on sending Lansdale to Saigon; the appointment of Mr. Nolting, a stranger to the Far East; the presence of Maxwell Taylor, an old man steeped in Western military convention, and of Walt Rostow, an academician and historian who, presumably from

1. A. Vandenbosch and M. B. Vandenbosch, *Australia Faces Southeast Asia— The Emergence of a Foreign Policy* (Lexington, Ky.: University of Kentucky Press, 1967).

2. T. H. White, *The Making of the President 1960* (New York: Atheneum, 1961).

OSS service, had fallen in love with force to the extent that Kennedy later referred to him derisively as the air marshal; the later appointment of General Harkins, like Taylor an old man, a military conventionalist, but, unlike Taylor, with no experience in the Far East.

Two other bonds added to ignorance.

The first was Vietnam's relatively low priority in international affairs. Kennedy no sooner entered the White House than, like Truman and Eisenhower before him, he faced a host of major international and domestic problems. Speaking to Congress on January 30, 1961—his State of the Union address—he reviewed some severe domestic problems, then told his audience:

. . . No man entering upon this office, regardless of his party, regardless of his previous service in Washington, could fail to be staggered upon learning—even in this brief 10 day period—the harsh enormity of the trials through which we must pass in the next four years. Each day the crises multiply. Each day their solution grows more difficult. Each day we draw nearer the hour of maximum danger, as weapons spread and hostile forces grow stronger. I feel I must inform the Congress that our analyses over the last ten days make it clear that—in each of the principal areas of crisis—the tide of events had been running out and time has not been our friend.[3]

Kennedy assumed office during the Laotian blow-up, with Vietnam a secondary problem. Before he could come to grips with Vietnam, he was involved in the Berlin crisis, with resultant political strains at home. Then the moratorium on nuclear testing, the Bay of Pigs fiasco, the missile challenge, the 1962 Congressional elections, the quarrel with Great Britain over Skybolt, the De Gaulle crisis, the civil-rights battle, the confrontation with the Soviet Union over Cuba—one followed the other, a political TV serial, a house of troubles with the Vietnam issue now and again popping in like an unwanted relative. Only with the Buddhist revolts in spring of 1963 did Vietnam become an administration "crisis area." Until late 1963, only three American news media— Associated Press, United Press International, and the New York *Times* —maintained full-time staff correspondents in Vietnam.[4]

A second bond strengthened the first. Kennedy, essentially, was a positive person. He entered office as a young and healthy man with a sincere belief in himself and his philosophy of government. This was one of the most appealing things about the man: his belief in America and America's greatness. Unfortunately, he had not yet defined the meaning of or need for humility. He had not yet defined sufficiently the word "force" to realize that, in addition to virtues, it contained defects; that it was a word of nuance and limit; indeed, that use of force is en-

3. Kennedy (*Public Papers*), supra.
4. Mecklin, op. cit.; Robert Shaplen also covered the area, for *The New Yorker* Magazine.

gendered by fear, a subtle truth that explains, among other things, the remarkable success of judo.

I have said that Kennedy refused to disown his inheritance of an impractical ambition. This was in part due to the tense domestic political situation—the genesis was the fall of Chiang Kai-shek—but it was also due in part to Kennedy's insistence on a crusader role. At a time when polarized communism was defrosting, Kennedy embraced the monolithic theory, which threatened the engulfment of the "free" world.[5] On April 28, 1961, for example, his words to Cook County Democrats sounded this alarmist note:

. . . The Russians and the Chinese, containing within their borders nearly a billion people, totally mobilized for the advance of the Communist system, operating from narrow, interior lines of communication, pressuring on Southeast Asia with the masses of the Chinese armies potentially ready to move. . . .[6]

The image is there—the Red Menace of yesteryear—the infidels to be destroyed by still another crusade, this one in the form of a "relentless struggle," a "no greater task": protect the "Free World" from EVIL: *stop communism.*

At this time, Kennedy was full of himself and his country, and insisted on having that confidence justified. He wanted to believe reports of responsible officials who, when it came to insurgency warfare, were as enthusiastic, confident . . . and ignorant as he himself—and for some time, for too long, he believed them.

Kennedy welcomed dissent no more than most of us. Despite severe and persevering contradictions offered by the historical record and presented by such able writer-participants as Jean Lacouture, Donald Lancaster, Ellen Hammer, Bernard Fall, George Tanham, and Matthew Ridgway; despite advice from such qualified persons as Chester Bowles, John Kenneth Galbraith, Arthur Schlesinger, Averell Harriman, Roger Hilsman, and George Ball; despite contemporary writings (and warnings) of such talented, courageous, and knowledgeable correspondents as Bernard Fall, Robert Shaplen, Homer Bigart, later David Halberstam, Neil Sheehan, Malcolm Browne, François Sully, and Jim Robertson—despite this cumulative body of intelligent opinion derived from historical and contemporary experience, President Kennedy refused what President Eisenhower had refused before him: to

5. Zagoria, op. cit.: ". . . During the decade in which the triangular relationship [between Moscow, Peking, and Hanoi] replaced the bipolar, the United States was slow to appreciate its own role in the triangle. Top American officials recognized the existence of the Sino-Soviet dispute only belatedly, then were extremely cautious about acknowledging it, and were always at a loss to know whether or how to exacerbate it."
6. Kennedy (*Public Papers*), *supra.*

force a political settlement to what was in essence a political, not a military, problem.[7]

In 1961, Kennedy was still under the Pentagon's and CIA's influence. The Bay of Pigs fiasco and the unsuitable report on Laos had begun a doubting, more than a disillusioning, process. In late autumn of 1961, when he accepted the Taylor recommendations in part, he was suspicious but still respectful of his senior military and intelligence advisers. As Roger Hilsman later pointed out, the Taylor mission was essentially military, not political:

. . . General Lansdale, for example, was a member of the mission, and his experience with the political undercurrents in Vietnam was probably greater than any other American's, as were his sources of information. But much to his disgust, he was put to work estimating the costs and number of men required to "seal off" the 250-mile borders of jungle and mountains through which the infiltrators came—a question that he thought itself revealed a misunderstanding of guerrilla warfare. Lansdale did in fact see Diem and Nhu while he was in Vietnam, and he noted that some of the disturbing signs that he had noticed on his January trip was [sic] aggravated.[8]

The man who was supposed to prepare a political assessment, Walt Rostow, unfortunately forsook academic objectivity in favor of deductive thinking. Rostow had sometime before embraced the "aggression from the North" school, as we have discussed. In Vietnam,

. . . he was preoccupied with the problem of the infiltration routes. His argument was that these routes of access made the situation different from the guerrilla terrorism that had been defeated in Malaya and the Philippines. He noted that the guerrillas in Greece had been beaten only after the Yugoslavs closed the border, and he argued that unless a way could be found to close the Vietnamese border political reforms would do nothing but buy a little time. This view, in fact, was a basic premise in Rostow's thinking. . . .[9]

If the reader will refer to Chapter 57, he will discover the trap that ensnared Rostow and so many of his associates, civil and military: The closing of the Yugoslav border was *not* the major factor in the Greek Communist defeat; failure of insurgents to identify with the Greek people was the primary cause. Rostow's specious conclusion was doubly

7. Ellsberg, op. cit.: ". . . In early 1962, writing to the President to argue against sending combat units to Vietnam or otherwise deepening our involvement, J. K. Galbraith spoke of his fears that the bright hopes of the New Frontier would be sunk in the ricepaddies of Southeast Asia"; see also Hilsman, op. cit.: Chester Bowles argued for extending the area of neutrality beyond Laos to include Vietnam, Burma, Thailand, and Malaya; although Kennedy took no action, he seemed to favor a neutral Southeast Asia as a long-term goal.
8. Hilsman, op. cit.
9. Ibid., but see also Otto Heilbrunn, "Counter-Insurgency Tactics: A Question of Priorities," *Army Quarterly*, January 1967.

unfortunate, for in finding facts to fit his thesis—a deductive approach surprising for one of his academic background—he neglected his real responsibility to ascertain the political environment of the target area, and this abetted a lopsided report whose military bias unduly influenced important minds.

By allowing the military mastiff to grow alongside the political cat, Kennedy erred egregiously. It was partly his own fault, in that he had appointed a man of limited stature as Secretary of State—"a hawk in sheep's clothing," as a critic, borrowing from Churchill, unkindly referred to him—thus insuring ". . . the State Department's inability to compete with the Pentagon."[10] This would have been difficult in any case; as Roger Hilsman has pointed out, Dean Rusk ". . . regarded Vietnam as essentially a military problem even though a number of his colleagues in the State Department disagreed."[11]

Neither McNamara nor Taylor served the President well. Not understanding the complexities of insurgency warfare himself, he could not know that they had escaped the conventional mind of Taylor and the computer mind of McNamara, both of whom accepted false reports that continued to come in from the field, quantitative reports presenting a dangerously inaccurate picture.

Perpetrators of these reports at first intended no deception. Alike untrained in insurgency warfare, military and civil advisers and observers, with some splendid exceptions, misread field developments to report extravagant tactical gains that so excited Washington officialdom in 1962. This is understandable if scarcely commendable. Top officials, military and civil, were putting careers on the line. Vanity was at work and so was ambition, but over these rode an appalling ignorance that produced an unhealthy, indeed fatal, arrogance that would admit of no error. When the bloom wore off, these people refused to accept that the tactical flower had died, and when mourners turned up for the funeral, they were brusquely advised there was no funeral.

Although several factors combine to explain this unfortunate fact, it was due primarily to American military ascendancy in Vietnam affairs since 1954 and concomitant insistence on seeking a military solution to an essentially political problem. Once the military began to rule the American presence, arrogance of ignorance asserted itself to begin eliminating rational thought. And when rational thought disappears, error multiplies finally to explode into catastrophe—which is what happened to the U.S. effort in Vietnam.

To understand this, is to understand something of the American military profile at the time. We discussed earlier some brief American forays into guerrilla actions, a generally unimpressive record that furnished no particular operational doctrine (see Chapters 12–14 and 30, Volume I).

10. Sorensen, op. cit.
11. Hilsman, op. cit.

This should not be surprising. Guerrilla warfare is an inevitable corollary of empire and expansion; thus, the American army fought guerrilla actions against Indians, Filipinos, and, to a lesser degree, Mexicans; American marines fought in the Philippine campaign as well, and then against Santo Domingan rebels, Haitian *cocos,* and Nicaraguan insurgents. That ended in 1932. World War II, as we have discussed, offered but slight opportunity for American armed forces to fight guerrilla warfare, and, in Korea, they encountered guerrillas only in secondary operations, ancillary to the conventional battlefield.[12]

No more did most senior American military commanders grasp the concept of limited war; their excursion into it in Korea, thanks largely to MacArthur's inept strategy, proved a disaster. Though holding to a "victory" claim, American military leaders privately agreed that a limited ground war in Asia must be avoided in the future, that the requirement demanded an all-or-nothing strategy.

The post-Korean international situation raised two challenges that the American armed forces deemed more important than guerrilla expertise. The first is difficult to fault: survival. In the government's pathetic search for cheap security, in the "bigger bang for a buck" days, the air force gained budgetary supremacy over the other three services to the extent of sharp curtailment of army, navy, and marine operating forces. Instead of joining hands to fight the airmen's voracious appetite, the other services continued to fight for the remaining dollars—an altogether unseemly demonstration (but one that continues). The upshot of this was a "massive retaliation" strategy, which continued into the 1960s. In Theodore Sorensen's words,

. . . Unfortunately in the 1950's, as the Communists increasingly achieved a military posture that made the threat of massive retaliation less and less credible, the United States had moved increasingly to a strategy based on that threat. Kennedy inherited in 1961 a 1956 National Security Council directive relying chiefly on nuclear retaliation to any Communist action larger than a brush fire in general and to any serious Soviet military action whatsoever in Western Europe. "If you could win a big one," Eisenhower had said, "you would certainly win a little one." Because NATO strategy had a similar basis, no serious effort had been made to bring its force levels up to full strength, and our own Army had been sharply reduced in size.[13]

The second challenge faced by the services was to fight in an atomic environment. The air force answered this challenge with Strategic Air Command, or SAC, the expensive counterforce weapon that claimed

12. Griffith (CPLA), *supra;* see also Lynn Montross, *U. S. Marine Operations in Korea 1950–53* (Washington: U. S. Government Printing Office, 1957), Vol. 3 of 3 vols.; R. B. Asprey, "Guerrilla Warfare" and "Jungle Warfare." In Encyclopaedia Britannica, 1969; R. B. Asprey, "Tactics." In Encyclopaedia Britannica, 1971.

13. Sorensen, op. cit.

so much of the military budget. The navy opted for submarines and supercarriers. The army sought to controvert the new danger by re- organization, at first into pentomic divisions, and when these proved unsatisfactory, into brigades and battle groups with troops protected by armor and shielded personnel carriers. The marines, which logically should have become the American counterguerrilla force, were ". . . not eager to rethink and regroup in terms of the limited, awkward problems of guerrilla operations and the smaller military units involved in them."[14] Indeed, they clung to amphibious expertise by developing what became the helicopter bandwagon and emerging with the "vertical envelopment" concept.

Kennedy did not take kindly to either the military strategy or the military plant that he inherited. He did not wish to rely entirely on mas- sive retaliation, which he feared would bring a nuclear war, and he did not trust so-called "tactical" nuclear weapons.[15] Prompted by Maxwell Taylor, who had argued against air force predominancy in a controversial book, *The Uncertain Trumpet*,[16] Kennedy returned to a conventional- force strategy:

. . . the new Kennedy-McNamara [and Taylor, it should be added] doc- trine on conventional forces—a more radical change in strategy even than the augmenting and defining of the nuclear deterrent. . . . A limited Com- munist conventional action, in short, could best be deterred by a capacity to respond effectively in kind.[17]

So far, so good.

At this stage of the cold war, however, the Communists no longer seemed interested in waging costly conventional actions such as that in Korea, a fact that seems to have escaped the attention of the Pentagon despite Communist involvement in some of the insurgencies we have earlier discussed, and despite declarations by Communist leaders. Ken- nedy, Sorensen later wrote, ". . . inherited a military policy which had left us wholly unprepared to fight—or even to train others to fight—a war against local guerrillas."[18] Kennedy directed the Department of Defense to a priority effort to repair this tactical ignorance.

Enter Special Forces.

Special Forces—the Green Berets—belonged to the army, a small unit

14. Rostow, op. cit.
15. Sorensen, op. cit.: ". . . some of these 'small' weapons carried a punch five times more powerful than the bomb that destroyed Hiroshima. Those ready for use in Europe alone had a combined explosive strength more than ten thou- sand times as great as those used to end the Second World War. If that was tactical, what was strategic . . . ?"
16. Maxwell D. Taylor, *The Uncertain Trumpet* (New York: Harper & Broth- ers, 1960).
17. Sorensen, op. cit.
18. Ibid.

operating under such a cloak of secrecy that, in the mid-1950s, it very nearly secreted itself out of existence.[19]

Special Forces was and is a valid operational concept. Without going into detail, it attempted to amalgamate the best features of SOE/OSS World War II guerrilla operations to come up with teams based on the Jedburgh and OG prototypes (see Chapter 33, Volume I). These teams varied in size, but each consisted of specialists trained to infiltrate into a target area and there contact and organize indigenous guerrilla forces either known, or believed by intelligence, to exist. In the mid-fifties, the U.S.S.R. and her satellites formed the major targets, but another Special Forces unit, based on Okinawa, was undoubtedly casting covetous eyes on China's hinterland. Despite some favorable publicity, Special Forces remained small and relatively unimportant until 1961.[20]

Special Forces skyrocketed to fame when President Kennedy recognized its elite status, authorized its unofficial emblem, the green beret, and increased its numbers and scope of responsibility. In effect, Kennedy made Special Forces what it was never intended to be and what it had not trained for, a counterinsurgency force.

The United States possessed still another agency concerned with guerrilla warfare. This was the CIA, which concurrently had been operating in Laos, clandestinely arming, supporting, and transporting pro-Western Laotian units to meet Pathet Lao guerrilla incursions supported by North Vietnam. In spring of 1961, by presidential authority, the CIA began infiltrating South Vietnamese forces into southeastern Laos ". . . to locate and attack Communist bases and lines of infiltration." The agency also began infiltrating agents into North Vietnam, where they were to form ". . . networks of resistance, covert bases and teams for light harassment inside North Vietnam." A historical evaluation of these operations cannot be made until CIA releases necessary documents; judging from results and from later events, they were not very successful, though better than other efforts.

Nor was CIA successful in the political field. The conflict between

19. The near disaster caused a change of public-relations heart, and in 1956 this writer was given an open-arms welcome as a military correspondent by the Special Forces unit headquartered in Bad Tölz, Bavaria.

20. In 1956, after a period in field and garrison at Bad Tölz, I wrote a favorable article for *Army* Magazine. Alas! the secrecy cloak had not lifted to mini-size: My relatively short article was returned with 55 security violations noted, one of which was a recommendation to give Special Forces units on-the-job training in Vietnam. My article was not published. In 1961, as special correspondent for *Army* Magazine, I revisited the scene of my earlier crime, was again welcomed and again impressed. Whether I was less perceptive or whether army security precautions had relaxed, my article was finally cleared and published and even elicited a congratulatory letter from the chief of the army's Information Section upon its inclusion in a volume on special warfare; see also Sorensen, op. cit.: Special Forces consisted of ". . . only eighteen hundred men . . . preparing for a wholly different kind of action in a general war in Eastern Europe. Their equipment was outmoded and insufficient, unchanged since the Second World War."

intelligence collection and analysis and executive operations had already emerged in the agency. The CIA in Laos and Vietnam was in the policy-making business to an alarming degree.[21] Among other disadvantages, this meant that, once it had taken a stand, its reports were likely to be less dispassionate than is desirable. In 1962, David Halberstam, of the New York *Times,* interviewed John Richardson, chief of the CIA in Vietnam:

. . . I remember distinctly: our discussion of the Nhus [Diem's brother and his wife]. Nhu, Richardson said, was a great nationalist. When I mentioned some of Nhu's anti-American remarks and the resentment many anti-Communists felt toward him, Richardson said that the anti-American was simply a product of Nhu's nationalism. He was a proud Asian, but he was also for us; more important, he was the one man who understood the strategic hamlet program. . . .[22]

At the beginning of the Kennedy administration, then, the country possessed precious little guerrilla expertise. The armed forces were operating in a state of flux, each more concerned with trying to maintain a state of readiness necessary to carry out conventional missions than in probing unconventional depths of insurgency warfare. A military correspondent in 1961 was asked to cover NATO Operation Wintershield, in Bavaria, not MAAG activities in Vietnam, and was ticked off by the air force for writing critically of its concentration on strategic bombers at the expense of tactical air support.[23] Insurgency and guerrilla warfare were not subjects of general military discussion. The *Marine Corps Gazette* scooped its competitors by devoting its January 1962 issue to guerrilla warfare: President Kennedy was so moved that he wrote the editor a personal letter of congratulation and directed the Pentagon to pay special attention. In spring of 1962, the President told the graduating class at West Point:

. . . This is another type of war, new in its intensity, ancient in its origins —war by guerrillas, subversives, insurgents, assassins; war by ambush instead of by combat; by infiltration, instead of aggression, seeking victory by eroding and exhausting the enemy instead of engaging him. . . . It requires in those situations where we must counter it . . . a whole new kind of strategy, a wholly different kind of force, and therefore a new and wholly different kind of military training."[24]

But, in spring of 1962, when the first American helicopter units were flying in South Vietnam, Kennedy nevertheless entertained the Shah-

21. Sorensen, op. cit.
22. Halberstam, op. cit.
23. I was the correspondent. Scene: U. S. Air Force PIO office, Pentagon. Serious Major Sunderman tapping copy of offensive article in *Army* Magazine: ". . . I must inform you, Mr. Asprey, that you have ruined General LeMay's afternoon."
24. Hilsman, op. cit.

in-Shah of Iran by taking him to Camp Lejeune, North Carolina, where hordes of marines performed a conventional amphibious landing. And in spring of 1962, a military correspondent could ask the chief of staff of Fleet Marine Force, Atlantic, what the immense command—some forty thousand ground and air troops—was doing about counterinsurgency, and could hear in reply: "What is it?"[25]

Kennedy would still have to learn that a presidential directive cannot work miracles. He failed to respect the soldier's fondness for tradition. It had taken a century to remove the soldier from the horse, once the rifle claimed the battlefield. A piece of paper could not overnight reorient armed forces that had grown up on gasoline. Special Forces could expand its command at Fort Bragg; the air force could train pilots to fly T-28s and B-26s and organize "Jungle Jim" commando-type ground units; the navy and marines could begin altering units and adapting amphibious tactics to meet the new challenge—but that did not mean that their leaders understood the essence of counterinsurgency warfare, any more than did the twenty-two American generals in Saigon.[26]

Convinced that the challenge was primarily military, commanders of all services began trying to convert an unorthodox area of operations into an orthodox theater of war. Not understanding the new rules, they could not tactically adapt. Whatever the President said about guerrilla warfare, these officers, in general, secretly believed that military professionalism would prove more than a match in any battle with "irregulars." Although, in time, some of the younger advisers would realize this error, the bulk remained convinced that professionalism—by which they meant adherence to Western military doctrines—would *win the war*. They had never heard of Major Callwell's writings on small wars, so they would never have pondered his sage advice to regard the native as the professional, the newcomer as the amateur (see Chapter 15, Volume I). They had never studied Gallieni's and Lyautey's pacification campaigns (see Chapter 17, Volume I). They had never heard of General Gwynn and so did not realize that, in countering an insurgency, the military was fulfilling a police role and had to apply *minimum,* not maximum, force; nor would they have known of his warning that a lull in guerrilla action is usually a danger sign, not a "victory" (see Chapter 30, Volume I).

Some of their own people tried to educate them—with no success. As early as 1950, a regular marine officer, an Annapolis graduate, wrote a series of articles on guerrilla warfare in the *Marine Corps Gazette*. This was Colonel Samuel B. Griffith, who had served in Nicaragua, had personally observed Mao Tse-tung's tactics in China and was the first to translate his writings into English, and had served with great distinction as a Raider commander in World War II. Griffith stressed that

25. Again, I was the correspondent.
26. Hilsman, op. cit.

". . . modern arms and techniques have greatly increased the capabilities of partisans":

. . . Powerful explosives, shaped charges, and light rocket firing weapons make it possible for small groups to attack and destroy heavy installations, such as structures of steel and reinforced concrete, that their predecessors were unable to cope with. Propaganda facilities which have been greatly improved by such things as light mobile presses make it easier than it has previously been for partisans to stage full dress propaganda offensives among the people.

Partisan operations are capable of redressing an unbalanced situation in respect to available military manpower. Ten thousand partisans organized into a number of columns can easily tie up 10, 20, or 30 times their own number of regular troops. Radio makes possible concerted partisan effort in widely separated areas. It also insures close strategic and tactical coordination between conventional and partisan forces and provides a means for the uninterrupted flow of information.

The partisan can be defeated, the author argued, but not by conventional military operations:

. . . Anti-partisan operations embrace political, economic, and psychological measures, as well as those of a military nature. Indeed, the latter are of the least significance. The basis of partisan operations is in the people, or at least in a proportion of them. It becomes the first task then to win away important segments of this support, a task which requires correct policies in the three fields named. These policies will also make it possible to recruit one's own partisans, who should constitute the major part of the anti-partisan forces.

Partisans must be beaten at their own game. This means that mobile columns must be the primary military agency. These columns should be equipped with the lightest weapons consonant with delivery of maximum fire effect. The 60 mm mortar and the light machine gun would probably be the heaviest organizational weapons carried. Light radios of varying ranges and characteristics will of course be essential.

These columns cannot be dependent upon supply trains; supply, replacement, and evacuation must be carried out by aircraft so that the columns need not be tied to a base. Equipment must be transportable by light aircraft and helicopters in order that an entire column may be moved from place to place within its operating area with the greatest possible rapidity. Two or three anti-partisan "flying columns" of several hundred men each would thus, even if operating in an area of one hundred miles square, never be out of mutually supporting distance.

Anti-partisan columns cannot be transferred from one area to another and be expected to operate effectively until some time has elasped after they have entered a new area. They must learn an area of operations so that they know it as well as do the partisans themselves. . . .

Too much centralization of control over operations of anti-partisan columns must be avoided. . . . Operational rigidity can result only in disaster.

The author concluded:

. . . It is abundantly clear that the problem posed by guerrilla operations on a vast scale is not susceptible to a military solution that is completely divorced from political reality. But given a reasonable political basis, military operations can be productive if they are properly planned and executed by ingenious and imaginative leaders. . . . [The problem] requires serious study of all available historical experience, and the formulation therefrom of realistic and flexible doctrine.[27]

Thus, in 1950, Griffith was emphasizing the truth of Lawrence of Arabia's dictum: ". . . Guerrilla warfare is more scientific than a bayonet charge."

Lacking suitable background, the American command did not realize that Western warfare is quantitative and that insurgency warfare is qualitative. To fight the latter successfully is frequently to reverse normal standards of measurement, just as trick mirrors in an amusement park make a fat person thin and a thin person fat.

From the beginning, the American command erred, in waging counterinsurgency warfare, first by trying to use maximum, not minimum, force, second by designating the guerrilla the primary target rather than the population that supported him. Dead guerrillas became "victories"—enough "victories" would "win" the war.

They did not understand that an insurgency is not "won"—except that it fades into relative quiescence. Unlike the Western battlefield, a rising body count in an insurgency is a danger sign. So is the necessity for "surprise" encounters, no matter how successfully fought. Progress is not made in an insurgency situation until local peasants are protected sufficiently and have sufficient reason to support government forces and supply necessary information on which to base operations. The oft-expressed American desire to persuade the Viet Cong "to stand and fight," a desire inherited from the French, was another pathetic fallacy. These were professional guerrillas, who would not stand and fight—except on their own terms.

The Americans also failed to understand that qualitative warfare calls for careful target selection—that "saturation" of a battle area contains a number of built-in booby traps in an insurgency situation. The more units involved, the more-attenuated the lines of communication, thus the more targets available to the enemy. The Pentagon and State Department could bleat their combined heart out about arms and supply from the North—the grim fact remained that the Viet Cong was deriving the bulk of its arms and supply from ARVN, exactly as Mao Tsetung had done from the armies of Chiang Kai-shek. Worse than this,

27. Griffith ("Guerrilla"), *supra*.

however, saturation of a battle area invariably damaged the peasants' crops and villages, frequently killing innocent people, and thus alienating the very persons the government needed to "win."

Our military commanders could not understand this. When General Harkins

. . . was asked about the political consequences when villages were hit with napalm, he replied that it "really puts the fear of God into the Viet Cong." "And that," he said, "is what counts."[28]

Even after the disaster at Ap Bac, in January 1963, Hilsman found ". . . General Harkins and Ambassador Nolting . . . strongly and quite genuinely optimistic." In a memorandum for the record at that time, Hilsman wrote:

. . . All this [the hamlet program, American aid, numerous advisers] gives them [the American command] a sense of movement and of progress. The trouble is, however, that the progress and movement is [sic] highly uneven. . . . The failure to provide a police program that is even remotely phased in with the provision of barbed wire and radios for the strategic hamlets is one example. Thus you have strategic hamlets going up enclosing Communists inside their boundaries with no provision for winkling out those Communists.

Other things are similar. You also have the impression that the military is still too heavily oriented toward "sweep" type operations. There is also still the same emphasis on air power as there was before. Almost every operation, so far as I can tell, still begins with an air strike which inevitably kills innocent people and warns the Viet Cong that they should get moving for the troops will be coming soon. I think all this indicates that the Americans are just as much to blame as the Vietnamese.[29]

28. Hilsman, op. cit.; see also Mecklin, op. cit.; Pike, op. cit. Harkins' attitude at times approached the incredible: In 1962, the highly respected and experienced *New Yorker* correspondent Robert Shaplen brought a CBS television documentary to Saigon. Called *The End of an Empire*, it was a photographic record of the Viet Minh fighting at Dien Bien Phu— ". . . by far the most graphic picture of its kind ever filmed." Harkins refused to let it be shown to either American advisers or South Vietnamese officers, because it would "frighten" them to see how well the Viet Minh had fought! (Private information in the author's files.)
29. Hilsman, op. cit.

Chapter 78

American military advisers • American dependence on technology • Helicopters • ARVN tactics • The war escalates • Nolting's and Harkins' dream world • Warnings from the field • Wishful thinking in Saigon • American Government versus the press • The Hilsman-Forrestal report • Kennedy condones the great deception • Pierre Salinger's warning • McNamara's volte-face • Kennedy's private doubts

A LARGE PART of the American failure in South Vietnam derived from ignorance of respective forces. A long time ago, Sun Tzu advised military commanders: ". . . Know the enemy and know yourself; in a hundred battles you will never be in peril. When you are ignorant of the enemy but know yourself, your chances of winning or losing are equal. If ignorant both of your enemy and of yourself, you are certain in every battle to be in peril."[1]

Prompted by Diem and Nhu, who, like Chiang Kai-shek, regarded guerrillas as "Communist bandits," American commanders in Saigon in large part oversimplified the enemy and particularly his goals. They would not accept that he was waging revolutionary warfare as defined by Mao and modified by Ho Chi Minh and Vo Nguyen Giap. Our senior officers refused to differentiate between the "political struggle" and the "armed struggle" or realize the importance of the former and its determinant influence on the course of war. They accepted militarily

1. Griffith (*Sun Tzu*), *supra*.

"quiet" areas as "won" areas, where, often, the reverse was true and they were politically "active" areas calling for the greatest concentration of government counteractivity.[2] Such was their arrogance, such their ignorance, that they refused to respect adverse reports filed by subordinates from the field—reports that frequently contradicted information being fed to Washington.

Conversely, they found it difficult, if not impossible, to understand the temperament and mentality of the ARVN troops they were advising. They did not understand the evolutionary requirement of making a military silk purse out of a native sow's ear—they did not realize the awful hold of ingrained tradition epitomized militarily by two Vietnamese words: the ". . . word for soldier stems from the root word for bandit, just as the word for general stems from warlord."[3] They would not admit that expensive American-trained ARVN was avoiding contact with the VC, not seeking it—that the Civil Guard and Self-Defense Corps, which were running on slim budgets, were taking the bulk of casualties in defending static positions against VC night assaults.[4] They failed to realize that the edifice had to be scrapped and rebuilt, with will a cornerstone, if a viable army was to result. As corollary to this failure, they did not understand that defectors gained by the government's Open Arms (Chieu Hoi) program did not necessarily mean loyal government supporters—that, in a larger sense, diminishing NLF strength did not mean added Diem strength.

With some splendid exceptions, American advisers did not understand very much. They came with confidence instead of caution; they started teaching before they had learned. From Nolting on down, too many of them resembled Alden Pyle—Graham Greene's Quiet American: ". . . He was impregnably armored by his good intentions and his ignorance."[5] The insurgencies of our time, not to mention those of history, might never have happened. The lessons they furnished weren't so much lost—they were never learned. To accomplish the military goal in Vietnam, to "win the war," to achieve "victory," the American military command sought to repair doctrinal deficiencies with machines. It relied on technology as opposed to motivation, on helicopters and jeeps and trucks and armored personnel carriers as opposed to men. It did precisely what the American military command in China had done nearly twenty years earlier. It attempted to remedy political, social, and economic deficiencies with metal.

The advisers were not discouraged, not at first, because the new technology brought illusory success. The initial impetus created by new weapons and new vehicles, by the helicopter and APC, frightened the Viet Cong. Greatly increased ARVN mobility led to disruption of a

2. Thompson (*Defeating Communist Insurgency*), *supra.*
3. Pike, op. cit.
4. Halberstam, op. cit.
5. Graham Greene, *The Quiet American* (London: William Heinemann, 1955).

good many guerrilla units; ARVN killed and captured impressive numbers of guerrillas and forced others to take sanctuary in Cambodia and Laos.

And yet . . .

The South Vietnam Government estimated that the Viet Cong began the year with about sixteen thousand hard-core guerrillas. They estimated that in 1962 they had killed about twenty thousand "guerrillas" (I use quotation marks because we shall never know how many innocents were included in the figure). And yet VC strength, they estimated, had increased to twenty thousand! ". . . At the same time," Roger Hilsman later wrote, "captured documents, interrogation of prisoners, and other intelligence indicated that *at the most* only three to four thousand infiltrators had come down the Ho Chi Minh trail."[6] The other replacements came from hamlets and villages, and if some arrived under duress, a great many others came freely.

Despite ARVN "victories" and diminishing enemy morale, the Viet Cong retained control of major areas. In summer of 1962, this writer flew several missions with marine helicopter squadrons operating out of Soc Trang, south of Saigon. Fuel for these machines came from Saigon by tank truck, the Saigon trucker paying the Viet Cong a "toll" in order to pass to Soc Trang. This meant that, at any moment, the Viet Cong could prevent marine helicopters from flying; indeed, on one occasion during my stay, the worst was feared, but, in the event, the precious fuel came through.

The fallacy of the new approach was already becoming evident at this time. ARVN may have killed a lot of Viet Cong, but the South Vietnam Government had not deprived survivors of peasant support— whether voluntary or under duress. Initial Viet Cong fright soon turned to bewilderment; analysis followed, to produce countertactics. Night operations increased, since helicopters at first did not fly at night. Assassinations and kidnapings greatly increased, the reasons being to enforce discipline, demonstrate determination, and gain recruits. By spring of 1962, the Viet Cong were beginning to fight back, and, by autumn, were not only pursuing active guerrilla tactics but were standing against ARVN units.[7] Once again, Viet Cong countertactics were immensely aided by intelligence derived from networks that, while on the defensive, were scarcely defunct. Marines at Soc Trang provided a case in point: They were living, in Bernard Fall's term, in a fishbowl, their every movement, their takeoff and landing, their resupply, noted and reported by Viet Cong agents.[8]

In June 1962, Homer Bigart, of the New York *Times,* reported a

6. Hilsman, op. cit.; see also Pike, op. cit.; Halberstam, op. cit.; A. H. Bushell, "Insurgency and the Numbers Game," *Army Quarterly,* April 1967.

7. Personal observation; see also Mecklin, op. cit.; Halberstam, op. cit.

8. A few months later, when U. S. Army helicopter units were occupying Soc Trang, the VC attacked with mortars.

Viet Cong ambush of an ARVN column and then put his finger squarely on the problem. The enemy, he pointed out, had laid an ambush three hours before the army unit approached, an effort witnessed by dozens and perhaps hundreds of peasants:

. . . Could this have happened if the peasants felt any real identification with the regime? . . . The Viet Cong probably would never have undertaken this action without full confidence that the peasants were with them, or at least indifferent.[9]

The new technology did nothing to repair the existing gap between Vietnamese army units and peasants; indeed, helicopter delivery widened the intelligence gap by flying troops *over* villages and thus eliminating personal contact with the peasants—admittedly a good thing in the case of rapacious army units. Both helicopters and armored personnel carriers, by tearing up ricelands, also alienated the peasants in major operational areas.

The new vehicles also proved expensive. Neither mechanism is simple; each requires large workshop and storage complexes, installations that in Vietnam demanded ground troops to provide security and nonetheless remained vulnerable to guerrilla attack, as did their lines of communication to major supply centers. Troops so assigned inevitably assumed a static role, to the guerrilla's benefit.

Finally, the new vehicles were only aids, not panaceas. The machines neither rectified command deficiencies nor removed the warlord command concept that prevented co-ordinated operations. Armor plate and motors did not erase poorly conceived plans. Prompted in part by American advisers, Vietnamese planners were trying to strike the enemy all over the place, and, all too often, these were random strikes, because the commands lacked proper intelligence on which to base specific and profitable operations. Where good intelligence existed, Viet Cong intelligence frequently countered it. Helicopters and APCs are noisy, and a black-pajama-clad Viet Cong did not take long to ditch his weapon and either commence work in the field or hide along the reeded bank of a nearby canal.

Already, by summer of 1962, frustrated American airmen had begun developing new tactics, for example "eagle flights," whereby helicopters landed a unit in a suspect area. If contact resulted, other, lingering helicopters immediately brought in reinforcements. The poverty of this tactic is too obvious for comment.

When the Viet Cong recovered from surprise and started to shoot —and they were shooting in summer of 1962, an unhappy fact visibly evident from holes in helicopter "skins"—helicopter crews shot back.[10] At first, this was primitive; a crew member firing from the cargo door-

9. Mecklin, op. cit.
10. Ibid.; by the end of 1962, American combat deaths numbered 21; in 1963, 97 were killed.

way. Then Vietnamese planes, T-28s, sometimes piloted by American advisers, began strafing missions prior to helicopter landings. In late 1962,

. . . the armed helicopters arrived, with four mounted machine guns and sixteen rocket pods; they were to escort the unarmed helicopters into battle and were not to fire until fired on. But this was too dangerous—it gave the enemy too many opportunities—and the rules of engagement were further broadened. By mid-1963 the armed helicopters were often serving as fighter planes, carrying out strafing missions.[11]

The net result was an increase in quantitative tactics—or escalation of the tactical effort.

CIA and Special Forces operations in the central highlands produced two results. One was a diminution of effort on part of the Vietnamese when left to their own resources. Once American teams moved on, Montagnard projects wilted and died to create tribal disillusionment and thus fertile ground for Viet Cong propaganda. The other was an extension of the war by building military outposts such as that at Pleiku, outposts that had to be defended, supplied—and finally evacuated.

At the same time, the civil effort burst forth into fresh bloom. This concentrated on the expensive strategic-hamlet program, which, as we have seen, was rapidly becoming dangerous in that false reports were endeavoring to prove it a success. Not only were the hamlets host to the sea of troubles already discussed, but they in no way answered the root problem of land reform. The reader will perhaps remember that highly restrictive land-distribution laws had made about 20 per cent of total ricelands available for peasant purchase. By the end of 1962, only about 25–30 per cent of the available land had been transferred to peasant hands. The former big landowners, rich Vietnamese, French *colons,* and the Catholic Church remained principal owners, with members of Diem's family and government claiming huge chunks of sequestered lands.[12] Despite Diem's promises to American officials, nothing had changed. John Mecklin later wrote of

. . . at least one area where we found tax collectors attached to military units. The idea was that this was a convenient way to collect back taxes for absentee landlords in hamlets where government authority had totally collapsed, often several years later.[13]

The fallacy of the American approach did not escape certain observers. A small press corps almost unanimously contradicted optimistic statements of various American officials. Official statements emanating from Saigon and Washington, they wrote, scarcely reflected

11. Halberstam, op. cit.; see also Frank Harvey, *Air War—Vietnam* (New York: Bantam Books, 1967).
12. Shaplen, op. cit.
13. Mecklin, op. cit.

true feelings of American advisers in the field. The war admittedly had
picked up speed, but, to what ultimate purpose, was not clear. Certainly
by the turn of the year, it was obvious that the South Vietnamese army
was not doing its share, the result of manacled command and poor
morale, and it was obvious that the strategic-hamlet program had bogged
down.

Nor did the small press corps stand alone in its pessimism. A good
many of its stories traced to complaints by field advisers. David Halberstam names one of these, Lieutenant Colonel John Vann, an army officer who later retired so he could tell the truth to the American public
—the first of several officers so motivated. Vann was adviser to ARVN's
IV Corps, commanded by Colonel Huynh Van Cao, a Diem appointee
whose zest for combat was shown by his earlier command of ARVN's
7th Division: From October to December, this division, in fourteen
operations against the Viet Cong, had suffered four killed.[14] Cao's behavior, along with that of other Diem appointees at Ap Bac, drew sharp
protests from Colonel Vann. Incredibly, General Harkins scorned
Vann's report. At a press conference in Saigon two days later, Harkins
told dumfounded reporters that he considered Ap Bac ". . . a victory.
We took the objective."[15]

Other field advisers were reporting adversely on complementary
pacification operations such as the strategic-hamlet program and the
effort in the central highlands. Ralph Harwood, who was in charge of
the strategic-hamlet program in the Mekong Delta, had warned Saigon
". . . that the program was not working and that in many of the low-
land areas the Vietcong were taking over virtually unchallenged."[16]

By 1963, the failure of the American program was evidencing itself
in a further and very sinister way: An increasing casualty rate of
American personnel—not from bullets but from mental illness. John
Mecklin later explained the problem:

. . . Young American Army officers who came to Vietnam as advisers were
set for hardship and extreme danger, and they accepted both with admirable
spirit. But they were not prepared for a system where incompetents were
given commands for political reasons, where a battle was lost because a company commander was a coward and was not then relieved, where there was
no authority, and no possible action but to appeal to commanders who would
not listen, because they had no authority from Saigon to listen, much less
act.

Intellectually it made sense to support the Diem regime, or this in any
case was the considered judgment of U.S. policy-makers, including President
Kennedy, who was deeply admired by most Americans in Saigon. This, in
turn, meant in effect that it was near blasphemy to be critical of the regime,

14. Halberstam, op. cit.
15. Ibid.
16. Ibid.

even in exclusively American company. Yet blasphemy there was, plentifully, with many a resulting guilty conscience. The bitter fact was that an overwhelming majority of all Americans in Vietnam disliked the regime, and many of them hated it for its uniform abuse of so many principles Americans believe in, like free speech, even though that same majority kept telling itself our policy was right.[17]

The result was disastrous: erroneous official reporting on such a scale that one seeks for a parallel; perhaps one occurred in 1933, during Sumner Welles's excursion in Havana at the time of the Batista takeover. In Vietnam, two factors prevented the bulk of American officials from objectively analyzing the situation. The first was ignorance—historical ignorance of guerrilla warfare. The second was subjectiveness—to an alarming degree. The myth of Ngo Dinh Diem's indispensability had been so well inculcated that many of our officials believed he was the only man we had—they could not let Diem fail. Mecklin later wrote:

. . . As mentioned earlier, a large portion of the American community in Vietnam privately disliked and distrusted the Diem regime, and doubted that it could prevail. Among those of us who felt that we nevertheless should keep trying, in the absence of an acceptable alternative, this tended to create a complex of defensiveness. I hope it is not presumptuous to suggest that this in turn created an underlying feeling, perhaps subconsciously, of guilt vis-à-vis the American people because we were politically bankrupt, failing to serve their interest well in a critical situation. This, in any case, was the way I felt. Failure became unthinkable.[18]

Mecklin amplified these words in a later paragraph:

. . . We were stuck hopelessly with what amounted to an all-or-nothing policy, which might not work. . . . The state of mind in both Washington and Saigon tended to close out reason. The policy of support for Diem became an article of faith, and dissent became reprehensible.[19]

This partly explains the difficulty between the U.S. mission in Saigon and its field advisers and American journalists. Saigon officials, not knowing the difference between right and wrong in insurgency warfare, continued to insist that the combined U.S.-Vietnam effort was right. Nolting probably meant what he said in a speech of 1962: that ". . . the Republic of Vietnam will take its place in history as the country where the tides of Asian Communism was reversed and the myth of Communist invincibility forever shattered."[20]

Unfortunately for Nolting and Harkins, some American field advisers, by no means all, in time had learned the difference between

17. Mecklin, op. cit.
18. Ibid.
19. Ibid.
20. Ibid.

right and wrong and had passed their observations to perceptive journalists. Hilsman later noted that ". . . every faction was so passionately convinced of the rightness of its cause that leaking to the press became a patriotic act."[21] As befits a democratic system, a number of these journalists avoided the subjective thinking that crowned the Saigon mission and attempted to report the situation objectively.[22] Their accounts of what was happening conflicted at almost every point with what Saigon *wanted* to be happening. The official reaction was attempted news management and suppression in the totalitarian tradition—thus, a State Department directive of February 1962 that virtually ordered reportage favorable to the regime.

Here was a hideous situation that was Administration policy, a pernicious policy that refused to trust the American people with the truth. John Mecklin, who was charged with carrying out the restrictive policy, later wrote:

. . . The Mission persisted in the practice of excessive classification, under the secret fraternity doctrine of State Department Cable No. 1006, to a degree that denied newsmen access to whole segments of U.S. operations in Vietnam.[23]

American reporters reacted predictably to the Administration's attitude and particularly to the dissembling behavior of American officials in Saigon, and a feud of massive proportions developed. Contradiction crowned contradiction until a veritable communications breakdown developed, with awesome results in the United States. A Congressional subcommittee later condemned the State Department's attitude:

. . . The restrictive U.S. press policy in Vietnam . . . unquestionably contributed to the lack of information about conditions in Vietnam which created an international crisis. Instead of hiding the facts from the American public, the State Department should have done everything possible to expose the true situation to full view.[24]

Nolting and Harkins could not altogether ignore adverse field reports, particularly when journalists were quoting "informed sources" in highly critical articles, and when, in some cases, the reports reached Washington.

Some evidence exists that President Kennedy was already worried about the Pandora's box of power he had opened. Faced with a pessi-

21. Hilsman, op. cit.

22. More-subjective reporting, e.g. by Halberstam and Browne, came later—induced in part, it should be added, by the hopeless corruption of the Diem regime, in part by obtuse and obdurate behavior of American civil and military officials.

23. Mecklin, op. cit.; but see also Pierre Salinger, *With Kennedy* (Garden City, N.Y.: Doubleday, 1966): Salinger points out that Cable 1006 was *intended* to help the press.

24. Ibid.

mistic report from Hilsman's office in late December 1962, he sent Hilsman and Michael Forrestal (son of the former Secretary of Defense) on still another "fact-finding" mission. The two emissaries found Harkins and Nolting ". . . strongly and quite genuinely optimistic," despite the battle at Ap Bac (which Harkins insisted was a "victory"). As for the strategic-hamlet program, the British expert Robert Thompson, though admitting certain shortcomings, was now ". . . the most optimistic" of all. Their report to the President began: ". . . The war in South Vietnam is clearly going better than it was a year ago." After a review of facts, the report continued:

. . . Our overall judgment, in sum, is that we are probably winning, but certainly more slowly than we had hoped. At the rate it is now going, the war will probably last longer than we would like, cost more in terms of both lives and money than we had anticipated, and prolong the period in which a sudden and dramatic event could upset the gains already made.

The report went on to object to a lack of an over-all plan, to an inadequate police system, and to a predominance of "search-and-destroy" and "elaborate, set-piece" tactics; it also questioned the ". . . increasing use of air power."[25]

Kennedy could scarcely have been reassured by the corpus of the report. But a top-secret, "eyes only" annex must have jolted him, particularly when he read:

*. . . no overall planning effort that effectively ties together the civilian and military efforts;

*. . . little or no long-range thinking about the kind of country that should come out of a victory and about what we do now to contribute to this longer-range goal;

*. . . among both civilians and military there is still some confusion over the way to conduct a counter-guerrilla war;

*. . . in general, we don't use all the leverage we have to persuade Diem to adopt policies which we espouse.

The "eyes-only" annex continued in damning words:

. . . The real trouble, however, is that the rather large U.S. effort in South Vietnam is managed by a multitude of independent U.S. agencies and people with little or no overall direction. No one man is in charge. What coordination there is results mainly from the sort of treaty arrangements that we arrived at in the country team meetings. . . . The result is that the U.S. effort is fragmented and duplicative. . . .

What is needed ideally is to give authority to a single strong executive, a man perhaps with a military background but who understands that this war is essentially a struggle to build a nation out of the chaos of revolution. . . .[26]

25. Hilsman, op. cit.
26. Ibid.

How much credence the President attached to this report is not known, but Hilsman's promotion to Assistant Secretary for Far Eastern Affairs seemed to lend it at least presidential grace. In spring of 1963, Colonel Vann returned to Washington to report his dissent, and it is unlikely that this bit of healthy heterodoxy escaped White House ears. In late April 1963, John Mecklin, at Pierre Salinger's instigation, personally reported to the President the unsavory relationship between officialdom and press in Saigon. William Truehart, Nolting's deputy, was beginning to express grave doubts about the Diem regime. In September, Rufus Phillips, who headed the $20-million Rural Affairs program in Vietnam, told President Kennedy that, despite Phillips' own earlier optimism, the program was failing. When Henry Cabot Lodge arrived in Saigon as the new ambassador, William Flippen, deputy chief of AID, who had been in South Vietnam for six years, ". . . delivered a bitter attack on our previous policy. Flippen added that the American military had been consistently wrong in its reports and interpretations ever since he arrived in Vietnam, and stated flatly that the war was being lost."[27]

Unfortunately, such dissidents formed a minority. MACV and Harkins still refused to admit that the American effort had turned sour, and Nolting and Richardson, despite impressive evidence to the contrary, chose to go along with this optimism. By spring of 1963, these people resembled company directors surrounded by charts and statistical reports showing favorable production and sales at a time when, unknown to them, the factory was shutting down.

Harkins and his principal staff officers were continuing an unhealthy tradition begun by Generals Williams and Myers, who could not or would not objectively analyze and report on the situation. Their obdurate attitude unfortunately found reflection in visiting officials, some of whom should have known better. At one point, Major General V. H. Krulak, an incisive little man jocularly known to his Marine Corps associates as "the Brute," arrived in Saigon as McNamara's counterinsurgency expert. At a time when the strategic-hamlet program was bursting at the seams, Krulak, although aware of Vann's strong feelings on this and other matters, reported favorably to McNamara. Later, when Rufus Phillips flew to Washington to acquaint Kennedy with disaster, he ". . . was immediately and bitterly challenged by Krulak, who doubted his veracity and his competence . . ."[28]—a courageous stand, considering Krulak's lack of background in guerrilla warfare.

The conflict between Saigon and the field—between wishes and facts —had already produced a chilling corollary: extreme intolerance, on the part of both the Saigon regime and the American mission, of journalists who questioned the validity of allied performance. In March

27. Halberstam, op. cit.
28. Ibid.; see also Hilsman, op. cit.

1962, Mme. Nhu had begun persuading President Diem to expel three troublemakers, the veteran news correspondents Homer Bigart of the New York *Times,* François Sully of *Newsweek,* and James Robinson of *NBC,* each of whom was increasingly harassed by the Saigon government, as were other correspondents. Joseph Buttinger later wrote:

. . . Sully was called a Vietcong spy, an opium smuggler, and a participant in sex orgies [and was expelled in August 1962]. Halberstam [who replaced Bigart], Neil Sheehan of the United Press International, and several others were accused of being part of an international Communist-inspired conspiracy to slander the regime. They were shadowed, and some of them were attacked and physically mishandled by Nhu's secret-service agents. Their telephones were tapped, and they were prevented from sending uncensored dispatches out of the country.[29]

What was the official American reaction to this attempt to keep the American public informed of events in Vietnam?

By 1962, the collective mind of the American civil and military high command in Saigon, with few exceptions, had closed itself to nuance: Vietnam was a matter of GOOD versus EVIL, Hero versus Villain, democracy versus communism:

. . . The U.S. mission was anything but forceful in defending these correspondents against abuse and ill-treatment, and almost apologetic in explaining that these men were merely trying to live up to the American concept of a free press. Ambassador Frederick E. Nolting, Jr., and General Paul Harkins in particular were incensed by the American newsmen's attacks on the regime. Both stanchly believed that there was no alternative to Diem, and were therefore on the whole inclined to accept as true the regime's claim that the Vietcong were on the way to defeat. They, as well as their superiors in Washington, spoke repeatedly of the "slanted" or even "irresponsible" press reporting out of Saigon, convinced not only that the correspondents who criticized the regime did harm to U.S.-South Vietnamese relations, but also that they were wrong. . . .[30]

Nolting and Harkins took it upon themselves to deny the democratic right of free speech. Dissent would not be tolerated. As David Halberstam, a dissenter, later wrote:

. . . The result was an outward rigidity and orthodoxy at the top that was unique among American missions overseas. Admiral Harry Felt, the commander of all American forces in the Pacific, summed up the attitude eloquently when, at a press conference in Saigon in late 1962, he became angered by a question from Malcolm Browne of the Associated Press, and snapped, "Why don't you get on the team?"[31]

29. Buttinger, op. cit.; see also Mecklin, op. cit.
30. Buttinger, op. cit.
31. Halberstam, op. cit.

Felt's direct violation of his authority, indeed his official mockery of everything sacred in the American heritage, did not draw a protest from the top. On April 20, 1961, President Kennedy had told the American Society of Newspaper Editors:

. . . The President of a great democracy such as ours, and the editors of great newspapers such as yours, owe a common obligation to the people: an obligation to present the facts, to present them with candor, and to present them in perspective. . . .[32]

Not only did this advocate of a free press allow Felt's outburst, which should have brought his immediate relief, to pass unnoticed (so far as we know), but he later attempted to muzzle the outspoken Halberstam by suggesting to his publisher, Arthur Hays Sulzberger, ". . . that he might give Halberstam a vacation to remove him from Vietnam."[33] Sulzberger refused, and Halberstam, along with Malcolm Browne, went on to win a Pulitzer prize. Another dissident, Charles Mohr, of *Time*, who reported pessimistically on the deteriorating situation, found his copy suppressed by senior editors, and resigned in disgust.[34] Reporters who wrote favorable accounts, among them Marguerite Higgins, Joseph Alsop, and Richard Tregaskis, received comforting little pats for their part in what was rapidly becoming the great deception. The Administration was running scared!

Kennedy's press representative, Pierre Salinger, had been monitoring the situation as it developed. To prevent a blow-up, he persuaded Kennedy to send a State Department representative, Bob Manning, to Saigon to investigate. Manning's report pinpointed the difficulty:

. . . The press problem in Vietnam is singular because of the singular nature of the United States involvement in that country. Our involvement is so extensive as to require public, i.e., press, scrutiny, and yet so hemmed by limitations as to make it difficult for the United States government to promote and assure that scrutiny. The problem is complicated by the long-standing desire of the United States government to see the American involvement in Vietnam minimized, even represented, as something less than in reality it is. The early history of the handling of the situation is marked by attitudes, directives, and actions in Washington and in the field that reflect this United States desire.[35]

Manning's report helped to change policy and ease tension, and Lodge's later arrival and fair treatment of the press did a great deal of good. But, again, a directive cannot change things overnight, and a good many bureaucrats and ranking military officers continued to lie to the press and otherwise antagonize journalists carrying out one of the most sacred

32. Kennedy (*Public Papers*), *supra*.
33. Salinger, op. cit.; see also Halberstam, op. cit.
34. Halberstam, op. cit.
35. Salinger, op. cit.

tasks of a democratic nation. Pierre Salinger later wrote presciently of the problem:

. . . The most important [lesson] is that despite all the motivations which exist to the contrary the government can never expect success for a press policy which does not rely on total candor. Thus, the government of the United States, as a free democratic society, may be faced with an impossible choice: that choice is between using any methods at its disposal, including some secret operations, to defend the national interest and doing everything out in the open with the accepted drawbacks that such a policy would produce.

I do not believe that such a choice should be forced on either government or press. It is at best an oversimplification and at worst unacceptable to a great nation locked in struggle around the world.

It is why I have suggested frequently that instead of walking away from a central problem of our time—and hoping that it will somehow go away—it should now have the attention of the most knowledgeable and creative people in both the government and the press.[36]

Salinger's efforts to bring about healthy conferences failed. What he was calling for was an educational effort to achieve a mature relationship that would benefit everyone, including the American public. Unfortunately, his dismal conclusion could have been written at the present time:

. . . The recitation of the events in Vietnam [1961 to early 1964] . . . cries out for a new start to such an approach. The question is whether the government and the press are content to limp through the rest of the twentieth century on the basis of unfortunate policies based on improvisation.[37]

The double standard of reporting continued into 1963. As each new allied effort flared and wilted, MACV continued to insist that the war was being won; the press, in general, continued to insist that it was being lost. If conditions were somewhat dicey in the Mekong Delta, briefing officers said, it was because ". . . the guerrillas had been pushed south by successful operations in northern areas."[38] If conditions were somewhat dicey in the delta, reporters wrote, it was because the strategic-hamlet program was failing—the inevitable result of a despot-ridden regime whose venality and corruption penetrated the entire command system of ARVN. (The reader should take note that almost every disclosure made by American reporters earlier and at this time was confirmed, and then some, by discoveries made after Diem's death!)[39]

36. Ibid.
37. Ibid.
38. Halberstam, op. cit.
39. Hilsman, op. cit.

The eye-opening Buddhist revolts favored the reporters, however. Throughout summer of 1963, some of the truths they had been writing began emerging in official reports. National Security Council meetings grew more tense and acrimonious as the civil-versus-military battle mounted in Administration circles. In September, the President sent out still another civil-military fact-finding team, consisting of Krulak, the Pentagon's expert on insurgency warfare, and J. S. Mendenhall, a veteran diplomat with extensive service in Vietnam. In due time, they returned to Washington and a meeting of the National Security Council. Krulak reported enthusiastically on the situation, Mendenhall unfavorably. So diametrically opposed were the reports that President Kennedy dryly commented, ". . . Were you gentlemen in the same country?"[40] The President was probably not impressed, either, with General Harkins, who stated in October: ". . . I can safely say the end of the war is in sight."[41]

The end of the war, though not as Harkins meant it, might have been in sight had President Kennedy lived. During 1963, Kennedy had been hearing increasingly disturbing minority reports such as those offered by Phillips and Mecklin, which must have brought De Gaulle's warning in spring of 1961 to mind. In September 1963, one of his most trusted advisers, Robert McNamara, theretofore an optimist, returned from Saigon to report a *volte-face* that brought Kennedy up short. On previous inspection tours, McNamara had been sold a bill of goods by Harkins and Nolting that bore but slight resemblance to facts. By now, however, Henry Cabot Lodge had replaced Nolting and was dissatisfied with what he found. Apparently, he pressed his views with considerable vigor on McNamara. Despite Harkins' continued whitewash, McNamara back in Washington ". . . reportedly told Kennedy that the military had been wrong, that the war was not going well and that the official version of military events was inaccurate."[42] McNamara and Taylor nonetheless continued to insist on a military approach:

. . . Secretary McNamara and General Taylor reported their judgment that the major part of the United States military task can be completed by the end of 1965. . . . They reported that by the end of this year [1963] the U.S. program for training Vietnamese should have progressed to the point that one thousand U.S. military personnel assigned to South Vietnam can be withdrawn.[43]

40. Schlesinger (*Days*), *supra.*
41. Schlesinger (*Bitter*), *supra.*
42. Halberstam, op. cit.; see also Hilsman, op. cit.: McNamara ". . . came back doubting the statistics he loved so well—or at least recognizing that unquantifiable political factors might be more important than he had been willing to believe before"; Kahin and Lewis, op. cit.
43. Hilsman, op. cit.

Despite this optimism, misplaced as usual, the situation continued to deteriorate, with such rapidity that, shortly after McNamara's return, Kennedy decided to dump Diem or at least not stand in the way of those who wished him dumped.

A former presidential aide, Kenneth O'Donnell, disclosed in 1970 that Kennedy, for some time, had been entertaining private personal doubts as to the American role in Vietnam. In late 1962, Senator Mike Mansfield had urged that the President stop escalating the American effort and withdraw all American forces from what was a civil war.

. . . A continued steady increase of American military advisers in South Vietnam, the senator argued, would lead to sending still more forces to beef up those that were there, and soon the Americans would be dominating the combat in a civil war that was not our war. Taking over the military leadership and the fighting in the Vietnam war, Mansfield warned, would hurt American prestige in Asia and would not help the South Vietnamese to stand on their own two feet, either.[44]

This was Kennedy's original position, and though he ignored the argument by implementing the Taylor-Rostow program in part, he had second thoughts in spring of 1963, when Mansfield continued to press the argument. Kennedy called Mansfield to the White House, a private meeting witnessed by O'Donnell:

. . . The President told Mansfield that he had been having serious second thoughts about Mansfield's argument and that he now agreed with the senator's thinking on the need for a complete military withdrawal from Vietnam.

"But I can't do it until 1965—after I'm re-elected," Kennedy told Mansfield.

President Kennedy felt, and Mansfield agreed with him, that if he announced a total withdrawal of American military personnel from Vietnam before the 1964 election, there would be a wild conservative outcry against returning him to the Presidency for a second term.

After Mansfield left the office, the President told me that he had made up his mind that after his re-election he would take the risk of unpopularity and make a complete withdrawal of American forces from Vietnam. "In 1965, I'll be damned everywhere as a Communist appeaser. But I don't care. If I tried to pull out completely now, we would have another Joe McCarthy red scare on our hands, but I can do it after I'm re-elected. So we had better make damned sure that I *am* re-elected."[45]

What the President thought is not what the President told the public. Neither doubts nor maturity embossed his statement given at a news conference in mid-September 1963: ". . . But we have a very simple policy in that area. In some ways I think the Vietnamese people and

44. Kenneth O'Donnell, "LBJ and the Kennedys," *Life,* August 7, 1970.
45. Ibid.

ourselves agree: we want the war to be won, the Communists to be contained, and the Americans to go home. That is our policy. . . ."[46]

As we said earlier, that is no policy but, rather, an ambition. What would have happened had the President lived and been re-elected is futile to speculate. We know that, until his death, he continued publicly to support the American commitment to Vietnam. Unfortunately, his successor, Lyndon Johnson, chose to expand it.

46. Hilsman, op. cit.

Chapter 79

Enter President Lyndon Johnson • Duong Van Minh's provisional government • Political anarchy in the South • Revolutionary pressures • Nguyen Khanh takes over • McNamara's report (I) • Operation Plan 34A • Intelligence experts dissent • JCS hawks • Nguyen Khanh's reforms • McNamara's report (II) • Renewed VC offensives • The situation deteriorates • The Lodge plan: "carrot and stick" • Johnson backs the hawks • CIA rebuttal • Seaborn's mission to Hanoi • Hanoi hawks • Taylor relieves Lodge: the military situation • The new Saigon team • The Tonkin Gulf incident • William Bundy's Congressional resolution

NOTHING in President Johnson's background presaged a healthy change of policy in Vietnam. So far as that dismal situation went, he assumed office with one foot in a trap, albeit a trap he had helped set.

Like John Kennedy, Johnson embraced a number of simplistic tenets. Unlike Kennedy, he was intellectually unable to outgrow them. He was wedded to the grand ambition: *stop communism.* He accepted the "aggression from the North" theory, and if the monolithic-Communist-conspiracy theme had developed a major crack, Peking conveniently replaced Moscow as master villain. The new President regarded South Vietnam as a military rather than a political problem; drawing on Prometheus and Robert Frost, he ". . . held with those who favored fire" for its solution.

But, unlike Kennedy, Johnson faced a presidential election within a year, and that, rather than personal doubts, at first checked his use of overt force. Instead, as Kennedy had done in 1961, Johnson ordered a program greatly enlarged from the earlier civilian effort. At the same time, however, Johnson accepted arguments for more overt action and allowed advisers to plan accordingly.

We know from events what these advisers generally had in mind. Many details of their thinking more recently have emerged in the celebrated Pentagon Papers, and the interested reader should study Neil Sheehan's analytical account of these crucial years.[1] Although not all principals have written memoirs, the present record, which includes President Johnson's version of these momentous events, indicates that the President increasingly embraced force to compel the North to stop the war.

In the case of the South, he behaved predictably, and what we have said of Kennedy's opening performance, we can say of Johnson's:

. . . A change of faces and significant increases in personnel, both civil and military, meant no fundamental improvement of a worsening situation. Instead it meant privately compounding past and present errors while publicly defending them as a viable program.

As with the Kennedy era, we shall attempt to analyze Johnson's actions once we examine the major happenings of these tragic years.

President Diem's demise had opened the way for a reform government that probably could still have retrieved the situation in South Vietnam. Unfortunately, the new provisional government showed itself weak and divided. Headed by a cardboard premier, it consisted of twelve generals, who formed a Military Revolutionary Council, chopped off as many pro-Diem heads as possible—and then sat still. In a situation that demanded firm and vigorous domestic policy carried out by trustworthy, trained, and confident officials, Duong Van Minh and his fellow generals proved themselves incapable of rule, indeed even of trusting one another.

Here was a power vacuum that a determined effort on the part of American advisers might have filled. But lack of viable American policy dictated inaction at a crucial time. As Robert Shaplen later wrote, instead of responding to a situation that American officials had helped create,

. . . we dealt repeatedly in tired shibboleths, in continued bland expressions of optimism; and in consequence our policy, if indeed we had one, was obscured in a welter of words that unfortunately soon became involved in a Presidential political campaign. The admission must be made that we had no more of a post-coup plan than the Vietnamese had.[2]

1. Neil Sheehan, Hedrick Smith, E. W. Kenworthy, and Fox Butterfield, *The Pentagon Papers* (New York: Bantam Books, 1971); see also L. B. Johnson (*The Vantage Point*), *supra;* Lyndon B. Johnson, *Public Papers of the President* (Washington: U. S. Government Printing Office, 1965–70), 10 vols. Hereafter cited as Johnson (*Public Papers*), with appropriate year.
2. Shaplen, op. cit.

The situation would have been difficult under normal circumstances. With government fragmented by Diem's death and daily challenged by the Viet Cong, it soon grew calamitous. In the cities, political parties proliferated—sixty-two of them within a month and a half of the coup![3] The factious bodies in no way influenced the junta government into framing and passing reform legislation. A Council of Notables, which was supposed to draft a new constitution (but never did), included ". . . no representatives of the peasantry or of the labor movement."[4]

Although the junta removed some important pro-Diem officials, a number of them survived in office, as did thousands of lesser bureaucrats imbued with mandarin philosophy. Part of the reason was necessity: Trained officials remained in short supply. But part was political: Each junta member held ties to the old regime, his power resting, in part, on cliques and cabals within the framework of Diem's government, including the army.

Nothing was unique about the situation. It was a typical coup setup, a palace revolution; it was familiar to history; in the previous half century, it had occurred dozens of times in the Near East and in South America. Power shifted from one house of rule to another, usually without improving the peasant's lot. The great powers normally condoned such shifts of power for reasons of "stability" essential to business —whether growing bananas or mining metals or pumping oil. Sometimes, however, they were endorsed for reasons of what statesmen like to call policy—by which they frequently mean pride and prestige—and that was the case in South Vietnam in that winter of 1963–64.

The Johnson administration would not accept a situation already experienced by the Wilson administration in Mexico—a political revolution being overwhelmed by demands for a social revolution. A nationalist leader, Dan Van Sung, had complained in mid-1963 that,

. . . By emphasizing anti-Communism rather than positive revolutionary goals and from lack of a better adaptation to the local situation, the United States has reduced its anti-Communist efforts in Viet Nam to the maintenance of an administrative machine and of an army. . . . The way out, to our mind, is not by an abandonment but, on the contrary, by going deep into every local revolutionary problem and helping solve them using principles of justice and freedom, and perhaps in fusing them with the revolutionary spirit of 1776.[5]

In autumn of 1963, the politically organized NLF-PRP was on hand to exploit the very real desire in the South for social revolution in cities and countryside. Within a month after the junta had assumed power,

3. Ibid.; see also Pike, op. cit.; George A. Carver, Jr., "The Real Revolution in South Viet Nam," *Foreign Affairs*, April 1965.
4. Shaplen, op. cit.
5. Edward G. Lansdale, "Viet Nam: Do We Understand Revolution?" *Foreign Affairs*, October 1964.

Viet Cong guerrillas opened carefully planned offensives throughout South Vietnam. By December, guerrillas had ARVN on the run; once again, a cloud of jeopardy covered the land.

The failure of Minh's junta government promoted increasing intrigue, which brought another coup at the end of January 1964. Using the pretext that De Gaulle was on the verge of persuading the junta to back his plan for a neutral Southeast Asia and come to terms with the NLF and Hanoi, the dissidents promoted a bloodless military coup that installed General Nguyen Khanh in place of Minh.

Shortly after taking office, President Johnson conferred with Ambassador Lodge and with CIA Chief John McCone. Johnson later described Lodge as "optimistic" (as opposed to McCone):

. . . I told Lodge that I had not been happy with what I had read about our Mission's operations in Vietnam earlier in the year. There had been too much internal dissension. I wanted him to develop a strong team; I wanted them to work together; and I wanted the Ambassador to be the sole boss. I assured him of full support in Washington. . . .[6]

We still don't know the exact relationship of that period. We do know that a stronger man than Lodge was needed to halt the internecine warfare being fought between not only American civil and military missions, but between sections within each. We also know that McCone's pessimism was justified. In December 1963, President Johnson sent Secretary of Defense Robert McNamara to Saigon for a two-day visit. McNamara reported that ". . . the situation is very disturbing. Current trends, unless reversed in the next 2–3 months, will lead to neutralization at best and more likely to a Communist-controlled state." In his opinion, the new Saigon government was ". . . the greatest source of concern. It is indecisive and drifting." The "second major weakness," McNamara reported, was the Country Team, or *ad hoc* civil-military U.S. committee that was supposed to co-ordinate the American effort (see Chapter 76):

. . . It lacks leadership, has been poorly informed, and is not working to a common plan. A recent example of confusion has been conflicting USOM [U. S. Operations Mission] and military recommendations both to the Government of Vietnam and to Washington on the size of the military budget. Above all, [Ambassador] Lodge has virtually no official contact with Harkins. Lodge sends in reports with major military implications without showing them to Harkins, and does not show Harkins important incoming traffic. My impression is that Lodge simply does not know how to conduct a co-ordinated administration. This has of course been stressed to him both by Dean Rusk and myself (and also by John McCone [chief of CIA]), and

6. Johnson (*The Vantage Point*), *supra*.

I do not think he is consciously rejecting our advice; he has just operated as a loner all his life and cannot readily change now.

Lodge's newly-designated deputy, David Nes, was with us and seems a highly competent team player. I have stated the situation frankly to him and he has said he would do all he could to constitute what would in effect be an executive committee operating below the level of the Ambassador.

As to the grave reporting weakness, both Defense and CIA must take major steps to improve this, John McCone and I have discussed it and are acting vigorously in our respective spheres.

McNamara also told the President that the situation has ". . . been deteriorating in the countryside since July to a far greater extent than we realize because of our undue dependence on distorted Vietnamese reporting." Infiltration of men and equipment from the North also played a part: ". . . The best guess is that 1000–1500 Viet Cong cadres entered South Vietnam from Laos in the first nine months of 1963." He was also concerned with ". . . the quality of the people we are sending to Vietnam. It seems to have fallen off considerably from the high standards applied in the original selections in 1962. . . ."

From the operational standpoint, he called for reallocation of South Vietnamese forces to challenge VC control in threatened provinces. His other recommendations perhaps unconsciously indicted the U.S.-Vietnamese performance to date:

. . . We also need to have major increases in both military and USOM staffs, to sizes that will give us a reliable, independent U.S. appraisal of the status of operations . . . realistic pacification plans must be prepared, allocating adequate time to secure the remaining government-controlled areas and work out from there.

He also discussed anti-infiltration measures, but noted:

. . . In general, the infiltration problem, while serious and annoying, is a lower priority than the key problems discussed earlier. However, we should do what we can to reduce it.

As for the North, McNamara reported:

. . . Plans for covert action into North Vietnam were prepared as we had requested and were an excellent job. They present a wide variety of sabotage and psychological operations against North Vietnam from which I believe we should aim to select those that provide maximum pressure with minimum risk. . . .

McNamara's report concluded:

. . . My appraisal may be overly pessimistic. Lodge, Harkins, and Minh would probably agree with me on specific points, but feel that January should see significant improvement. We should watch the situation very carefully, running scared, hoping for the best, but preparing for more forceful moves if the situation does not show early signs of improvement.[7]

Johnson was sufficiently impressed by this report to order significant changes in reporting methods from the field including direct ". . . detailed weekly reports from Ambassador Lodge which pulled no punches in describing problems as well as progress."[8] The President also authorized additional American personnel, both civil and military, for the Saigon missions, as well as covert operations in the North. The latter effort, known as Operation Plan 34A, called for a variety of actions ranging from U-2 flights to commando-type raids designed ". . . to result in substantial destruction, economic loss and harassment"—what the Pentagon called "destructive undertakings."

Two other covert operations complemented Plan 34A. One was an air effort directed by CIA in Laos, where a force of twenty-five to forty T-28 fighter-bombers interdicted Pathet Lao operations. The other consisted of U. S. Navy destroyer operations in the Gulf of Tonkin. Codenamed DeSoto patrols, they were mainly designed as a show of force, but

. . . the destroyers collected the kind of intelligence on North Vietnamese warning radars and coastal defenses that would be useful to 34A raiding parties.[9]

Along with other Administration officials, McNamara was apparently convinced from radio intercepts ". . . that Hanoi controlled and directed the Vietcong." McNamara recommended Plan 34A to the President in the hope that ". . . progressively escalating pressure from the clandestine attacks might eventually force Hanoi to order the Vietcong guerrillas to halt their insurrections." The President accepted the plan, which went into effect in February 1964.

Two important bodies remained unimpressed with the covert effort. The first was the intelligence community in general, which held that raids would not affect NLF operations in the South. The JCS also dissented, but for rather different reasons. A JCS memorandum signed by the chairman, General Maxwell Taylor, and submitted to McNamara in late January 1964, cited President Johnson's resolve ". . . to ensure victory over the externally directed and supported communist insurgency in South Vietnam." In JCS minds,

. . . our fortunes in South Vietnam are an accurate barometer of our fortunes in all of Southeast Asia. It is our view that if the U.S. program succeeds in South Vietnam it will go far towards stabilizing the total Southeast Asia situation. Conversely, a loss of South Vietnam to the communists will

7. *The Pentagon Papers, supra* (pp. 271–74); see also Johnson (*The Vantage Point*), *supra*.
8. Johnson (*The Vantage Point*), *supra*.
9. *The Pentagon Papers, supra* (p. 240).

presage an early erosion of the remainder of our position in that subcontinent.

This was the old domino theory, but to it was now added a prestige factor that would eventually overtake strategic factors originally cited. The memorandum continued:

. . . In a broader sense, the failure of our programs in South Vietnam would have heavy influence on the judgments of Burma, India, Indonesia, Malaysia, Japan, Taiwan, the Republic of Korea, and the Republic of the Philippines with respect to U.S. durability, resolution, and trustworthiness. Finally, this being the first real test of our determination to defeat the communist wars of national liberation formula, it is not unreasonable to conclude that there would be a corresponding unfavorable effect upon our image in Africa and in Latin America.

To defeat insurgency in South Vietnam, Taylor and JCS believed, demanded a predominantly military effort, carried out by an American military commander authorized to widen the war:

. . . In adverting to actions outside of South Vietnam, the Joint Chiefs of Staff are aware that the focus of the counter-insurgency battle lies in South Vietnam itself, and that the war must certainly be fought and won primarily in the minds of the Vietnamese people. At the same time, the aid now coming to the Viet Cong from outside the country in men, resources, advice, and direction is sufficiently great in the aggregate to be significant—both as help and as encouragement to the Viet Cong. It is our conviction that if support of the insurgency from outside South Vietnam in terms of operational direction, personnel, and material were stopped completely, the character of the war in South Vietnam would be substantially and favorably altered. Because of this conviction, we are wholly in favor of executing the covert actions against North Vietnam which you [McNamara] have recently proposed to the President. We believe, however, that it would be idle to conclude that these efforts will have a decisive effect on the communist determination to support the insurgency; and it is our view that we must therefore be prepared fully to undertake a much higher level of activity, not only for its beneficial tactical effect, but to make plain our resolution, both to our friends and to our enemies.

A "much higher level of activity" included raids into Laos, bombing the North with South Vietnamese and American aircraft, and committing American troops in sufficient numbers to meet the combat challenge in the South, including any specific response from the North such as invasion in the Korean style.[10]

In large part, this parroted JCS thinking on Laos in 1961 and also bore direct resemblance to the Taylor-Rostow plan of late 1961. It had at least one supporter in State Department. Walt Rostow, who now

10. Ibid. (pp. 274–77).

headed State Department's Policy Planning Council, continued to press his "aggression from the North" thesis, urging punitive action against Hanoi; as he stated in a memorandum to Dean Rusk in February, Ho Chi Minh ". . . has an industrial complex to protect: he is no longer a guerrilla fighter with nothing to lose."[11]

As with earlier plans, the new JCS plan glossed over the danger of escalating local insurgency into thermonuclear war:

. . . A reversal of [U.S.] attitude and the adoption of a more progressive program would enhance greatly our ability to control the degree to which escalation will occur. It appears probable that the economic and agricultural disappointments suffered by Communist China, plus the current rift with the Soviets, could cause the communists to think twice about undertaking a large-scale military adventure in Southeast Asia.

Whatever the danger, however:

. . . The Joint Chiefs of Staff consider that the strategic importance of Vietnam and of Southeast Asia warrants preparations for the actions above and recommend that the substance of this memorandum be discussed with the Secretary of State.[12]

In Saigon, meanwhile, General Nguyen Khanh was trying to rule through a mélange of vice-premiers, a Cabinet, and an enlarged Military Revolutionary Council. His top officials consisted mainly of Dai Viet nationalists, his government, in general, excluding other important nationalist groups and parties.

In March 1964, presumably prodded by American advisers, Khanh announced a Program of Action that included ambitious and bold political, social, economic, and military reforms. In place of Nhu's defunct strategic-hamlet program, Khanh substituted a concept called New Rural Life Hamlets. Theoretically a reversion to Lyautey's tache-d'huile concept of pacification, Khanh's plan called for clearing, consolidating, and defending specific rural areas. Unlike former programs, however, the new effort bowed to NLF success in mobilizing from the inside. Integral to it were Advance People's Action Groups:

. . . Directed by Vietnamese after being organized and trained by the United States Central Intelligence Agency, they were, specifically, guerrilla outfits of six men each who, dressed in black pajamas, like those worn by the Vietcong, surreptitiously entered a Vietcong-controlled hamlet, usually at night, engaged in direct armed counterinsurgency action against the Communists; and followed this up, once the Vietcong were dispersed, by staying on the scene and helping the people harvest their rice and repair whatever damage had been done.[13]

11. Ibid. (p. 241).
12. Ibid. (p. 277).
13. Robert Shaplen, *The Road from War* (New York: Harper & Row, 1970).

By going after what one counterinsurgency expert, Richard Clutterbuck, aptly terms "the man with the knife," the groups were attacking the fundamental fear that allowed Communist agitation/propaganda agents to organize the infrastructure essential to guerrilla operations. Once covert groups had removed Viet Cong agents, political and social action would consolidate the gain, new areas would be cleared and held . . . and so on until South Vietnam lived free of Viet Cong. To aid the process, Khanh wanted the Civil Guard brought up to strength, some eighty thousand, and joined to the regular army; the Self-Defense Corps would also be brought up to its authorized strength, seventy-two thousand. Specific land reforms would win over peasant groups, while "national mobilization" would eliminate inequities in conscription laws.[14]

To some American observers, Khanh appeared determined to lead South Vietnam out of chaos created by Diem and subsequent junta governments. Secretary of Defense McNamara, always on the lookout for a strong man, seemed particularly impressed. Reporting on still another trip to Saigon, which he made with General Taylor in mid-March 1964, McNamara, although upset at the general situation,

. . . found many reasons for encouragement in the performance of the Khanh Government to date. Although its top layer is thin, it is highly responsive to U.S. advice, and with a good grasp of the basic elements of rooting out the Viet Cong. . . .

McNamara advised Johnson to instruct appropriate government agencies:

. . . To make it clear that we are prepared to furnish assistance and support to South Vietnam for as long as it takes to bring the insurgency under control. . . . To make it clear that we fully support the Khanh government and are opposed to further coups. . . .[15]

The United States was already contributing directly $500 million a year to South Vietnam, not counting the cost of supporting her own military and civil units operating there; she now added another $50 million a year.[16]

Alas, the new strong man could not lift the weight of government. Not only did he fail to fuse dissident political and religious elements into a governing whole, but he also fell victim to a self-made legacy of quarreling, jealous, and ambitious generals, not to mention veteran nationalist politicians. In protecting his flanks of power, he slowed and ultimately doomed forward movement.

While Khanh was forming a government, announcing grandiose

14. Shaplen (*The Lost Revolution*), *supra;* see also McNamara's report, *The Pentagon Papers, supra* (pp. 271–74).
15. *The Pentagon Papers, supra* (pp. 277–83).
16. Shaplen (*The Lost Revolution*), *supra.*

plans and projects, and attempting to consolidate his power, the NLF-PRP became increasingly aggressive. Hanoi later distributed a balance sheet which stated:

. . . From the tactics of 1963, which consisted of taking the initiative in attacking and routing the enemy's Southern forces in entire sections, the Army of Liberation passed in 1964 to the tactic of conducting an uninterrupted offensive against the enemy, and of destroying a great number of his units on battalion and company level, and depriving him of all weapons. . . .

Efforts to kill Americans have developed with great vigor and on a large scale in all regions, and particularly in Saigon proper. . . .[17]

Black-clad agit-prop teams proclaimed Khanh another American lackey in the Diem tradition. They also made capital propaganda out of Khanh's attempts to cut losses by abandoning weak and isolated strategic hamlets. As government forces withdrew, Viet Cong forces advanced, the process accompanied by Communist cries of the inevitability of socialist progress. At the same time, Viet Cong cadres continued, as did outright VC attacks. ARVN remained the VC's major supply depot, contributing an average eight hundred weapons per month![18]

The South Vietnamese army seemed no more able under Khanh's aegis to halt the rot than previously. Although Khanh promised improvements such as a much needed pay raise, many internal abuses remained: political rather than professional commanders and staff officers, poor staff work, non-integrated field operations, corruption and inefficiency at all levels. In the spring of 1964, at a formal briefing in Saigon, an American adviser,

. . . a colonel with three years' experience in the field and famous for his frankness, condemned the whole Vietnamese military and administrative structure as being riddled with "second-raters" who, he said, had no ability for "management of the war" and who went about their business in the manner of "the blind leading the blind." In decrying "politics, corruption, and nepotism" at the top, and sheer incompetence or laziness at the middle and lower levels, the colonel reminded the Vietnamese that their Vietcong antagonists had become stronger and better in the last three years not only because they had better weapons, including such new things as electrically detonated anti-personnel and vehicular mines, but also because they went about their work of winning the war with dedicated ardor "twenty-four hours a day, seven days a week, convinced that their cause is right."[19]

17. Lacouture, op. cit.
18. Ibid.: ". . . Between January 1 and October 1, 1964, the Viet Cong took nine thousand arms from government troops, that is an average of eight hundred per month between January and July, and close to fifteen hundred per month between July and October."
19. Shaplen (*The Lost Revolution*), *supra*.

The deteriorating situation continued to cause deepest concern in Washington. Despite McNamara's guarded enthusiasm for Khanh, he and Taylor reported upon their return from Saigon in mid-March 1964 that ". . . the situation has unquestionably been growing worse." About 40 per cent of the countryside was ". . . under Viet Cong control or predominant influence." Civil and military morale was low, ARVN and para-military desertion rates high, draft-dodging extensive.[20]

The JCS memo of late January previously referred to seems to have influenced the Secretary of Defense toward a more aggressive course. In his report to the President of mid-March, he recited the domino theory and pointed to the "very modest 'covert' program" against the North—". . . a program so limited that it is unlikely to have any significant effect." Although deeming it vital ". . . that we continue to take every reasonable measure to assure success in South Vietnam," McNamara recommended contingency plans capable of putting ". . . new and significant pressures upon North Vietnam." These included limited ARVN incursions into Laos and Cambodia as well as "retaliatory bombing strikes" of the North by South Vietnamese and American planes. At the same time, however, McNamara cautioned:

. . . There were and are sound reasons for the limits imposed by present policy—the South Vietnamese must win their own fight; U.S. intervention on a larger scale, and/or GVN actions against the North, would disturb key allies and other nations; etc. In any case, it is vital that we continue to take every reasonable measure to assure success in South Vietnam. The policy choice is not an "either/or" between this course of action and possible pressures against the North; the former is essential without regard to our decision with respect to the latter. The latter can, at best, only reinforce the former.[21]

President Johnson accepted the bulk of McNamara's recommendations, and directed planning to ". . . proceed energetically." Despite JCS objections, Johnson agreed that it was too early to take overt military action against the North.[22] As he cabled Ambassador Lodge in late March, ". . . the immediate and essential task is to strengthen the southern base . . . for possible later action. There is additional international reason for avoiding immediate overt action in that we expect a showdown between the Chinese and Soviet Communist parties soon

20. *The Pentagon Papers, supra* (p. 279); see also Johnson (*The Vantage Point*), *supra.*

21. *The Pentagon Papers, supra* (pp. 278–83).

22. Johnson (*The Vantage Point*), *supra:* Chief of CIA John McCone, according to Johnson, also wished to escalate the action, believing that McNamara's measures were ". . . too little, too late."

and action against the North will be more practicable after than before
a showdown. . . ."[23]

Johnson's other immediate concern was the increasing indigenous
sentiment in Saigon for a neutralist settlement in form of a coalition
government with the NLF, a solution that he and his advisers deemed
tantamount to Communist victory, in view of Khanh's fragile government. In the same cable to Lodge, the President instructed:

. . . It ought to be possible to explain in Saigon that your mission is precisely for the purpose of knocking the idea of neutralization wherever it
rears its ugly head, and on this point I think nothing is more important
than to stop neutralist talk wherever we can by whatever means we can.[24]

Lodge, meanwhile, had been touting a carrot-and-stick plan as ingenious as it was impractical. This involved

. . . sending a secret non-American envoy to Hanoi with an offer of economic aid, such as food imports to relieve the rice shortages in North Vietnam, in return for calling off the Vietcong. If the North Vietnamese did not
respond favorably, the stick—unpublicized and unacknowledged air strikes,
apparently with unmarked planes—would be applied until they did.[25]

Various courses of action were discussed at a high-level strategy
meeting of American officials in late April in Saigon. In general, two
schools of thought were at work: a go-slow and a go-fast. The major
check on go-fast escalation, aside from American public opinion, was
lack of adequate information ". . . concerning the nature and magnitude" of infiltration from the North. Its appeal, however, to the bulk
of the President's top advisers, was only too obvious. In mid-April,
the JCS approved a plan submitted by Commander-in-Chief, Pacific
(CINCPAC) Admiral Harry Felt:

. . . It tabulated how many planes and what bomb tonnages would be required for each phase of the strikes, listed the targets in North Vietnam
with damage to be achieved, and programed the necessary positioning of
air forces for the raids. A follow-up operation plan, designated 32-64, calculated the possible reactions of China and North Vietnam and the American ground forces that might be necessary to meet them.[26]

At the same time, William Bundy, who headed Intelligence Security
Affairs—a sort of private State Department in the Department of Defense—was preparing a sixteen-point "scenario" for escalation. Bundy
and Rusk had questioned a tacit assumption that the insurgency's con-

23. *The Pentagon Papers, supra* (pp. 285–86); see also Johnson (*The Vantage
Point*), *supra,* whose stated reason later became the necessity to avoid massive
Communist intervention.
24. *The Pentagon Papers, supra* (pp. 285–86).
25. Ibid. (p. 244).
26. Ibid. (p. 247).

tinuing success hinged on aid from the North. Rusk sent a former New York *Times* correspondent, William Jorden, to Saigon to assemble available data. What became known as the Jorden Report apparently convinced Rusk and Bundy that sufficient infiltration existed to justify attacks against the North—sufficient, at least, to justify such attacks to the American public. In late May, Bundy drafted a resolution for Congress that would free the President's military hand, a resolution we shall examine shortly.[27]

But, also in May, Pathet Lao offensives in Laos heated up that situation and caused the Administration to commit American navy and air force planes to low-level reconnaissance flights. Although this crisis blew over, continuing deterioration in South Vietnam did nothing to dampen hawk enthusiasm. By early June, Ambassador Lodge, theretofore moderate, began arguing for bombing the North. A Pentagon analyst later wrote:

. . . In answer to Secretary Rusk's query about South Vietnamese popular attitudes, which supported Hanoi's revolutionary aims, the Ambassador stated his conviction that most support for the VC would fade as soon as some "counterterrorism measures" were begun against the D.R.V. [North Vietnam].

According to Admiral Felt, who was present, Lodge predicted that ". . . a selective bombing campaign against military targets in the North" would ". . . bolster morale and give the population in the South a feeling of unity."[28]

The Honolulu meeting resembled those portentous 1961 meetings when Kennedy and his advisers discussed sending American troops into Laos. In 1964, in discussing necessity for a Congressional resolution prior to escalating military action, McNamara noted that it might be necessary ". . . to deploy as many as seven [U.S.] divisions," while Rusk

. . . noted that some of the military requirements might involve the calling up of reserves, always a touchy Congressional issue. He also stated that public opinion on our Southeast Asia policy was badly divided in the United States at the moment and that, therefore, the President needed an affirmation of support.

According to William Bundy's memorandum:

. . . General Taylor noted that there was a danger of reasoning ourselves into inaction. From a military point of view, he said the U.S. could function in Southeast Asia about as well as anywhere in the world except Cuba.

27. Ibid. (p. 286).
28. Ibid. (pp. 250–51).

Although the assembled notables advised President Johnson to delay overt action in order to gain time ". . . to refine our plans and estimates,"

. . . Mr. [William] Bundy emphasized the need for an "urgent" public relations campaign at home to "get at the basic doubts of the value of Southeast Asia and the importance of our stake there."[29]

At a subsequent JCS meeting, enemy reaction to escalation was discussed. Admiral Felt asked for the option to use nuclear weapons, ". . . as had been assumed under various plans":

. . . Secretary McNamara then went on to say that the possibility of major ground action also led to a serious question of having to use nuclear weapons at some point. Admiral Felt responded emphatically that there was no possible way to hold off the Communists on the ground without the use of tactical nuclear weapons.[30]

During this crucial period, President Johnson continued to follow a wait-and-see policy, but one that held aggressive overtones. He permitted American aircraft to engage in combat operations in Laos; he evidently authorized official leaks to emphasize the Administration's determination ". . . to support its allies and uphold its treaty commitments in Southeast Asia"; he authorized military preparations for troop movements to the area.

But doubt apparently entered his mind, at least to the extent that he formally asked the CIA: ". . . Would the rest of Southeast Asia necessarily fall if Laos and South Viet-Nam came under North Vietnamese control?" Neil Sheehan, who studied these particular highly classified documents, later wrote that the CIA replied on June 9:

. . . With the possible exception of Cambodia, it is likely that no nation in the area would quickly succumb to Communism as a result of the fall of Laos and South Vietnam. Furthermore, a continuation of the spread of Communism in the area would not be inexorable, and any spread which did occur would take time—time in which the total situation might change in any number of ways unfavorable to the Communist cause.

. . . The C.I.A. analysis [Sheehan wrote] conceded that the loss of South Vietnam and Laos "would be profoundly damaging to the U.S. position in the Far East" and would raise the prestige of China "as a leader of world Communism" at the expense of a more moderate Soviet Union. But the analysis argued that so long as the United States could retain its island bases, such as those in Okinawa, Guam, the Philippines and Japan, it could wield enough military power in Asia to deter China and North Vietnam from overt military aggression against Southeast Asia in general.

Even in the "worst case," if South Vietnam and Laos were to fall through

29. Ibid. (p. 252).
30. *The Sunday Times* (London), June 27, 1971.

"a clear-cut Communist victory," the United States would still retain some leverage to affect the final outcome in Southeast Asia, according to the analysis.

It said that "the extent to which individual countries would move away from the U.S. towards the Communists would be significantly affected by the substance and manner of U.S. policy in the period following the loss of Laos and South Vietnam."[31]

The CIA analysis said, in effect, that South Vietnam was a strategic convenience, *not* a strategic necessity. If ever a green light flashed for a President and his advisers to accept facts, re-examine objectives, reform priorities, and realign effort—to change from a collision course to a crafty and intelligent course designed to attain national aims at a reasonable cost—it was in June 1964. We don't know Johnson's reaction to this reply prepared by the nation's top intelligence experts. Judging by subsequent events, he was unimpressed; at least, he appears not to have questioned sharply those spurious and dangerous postulates pleaded by those around him.

Instead, in mid-June, he sent a Canadian official, Mr. Blair Seaborn, on a secret visit to Hanoi in line with Ambassador Lodge's senseless carrot-and-stick approach. How much carrot Seaborn offered Premier Pham Van Dong, we don't know. In Neil Sheehan's words,

. . . The [Pentagon] analyst says Mr. Seaborn stressed to Premier Dong that while the United States' ambition in Southeast Asia was limited and its intentions "essentially peaceful," its patience was not limitless. The United States was fully aware of the degree to which Hanoi controlled the Vietcong, Mr. Seaborn said, and "in the event of escalation the greatest devastation would of course result for the D.R.V. [North Vietnam] itself."

The North Vietnamese Premier, the study relates, "fully understood the seriousness and import of the warning conveyed by Seaborn."[32]

It was a dangerous time to present an ultimatum in Hanoi, where moderate voices were having a difficult time surmounting clamor raised by such hawks as Vo Nguyen Giap, Nguyen Chi Thanh, and the premier himself. Viet Cong gains made it seem only a matter of time until the Saigon government collapsed. An ultimatum would have enjoyed a more prosperous reception had the Viet Cong been losing ground. Two German analysts writing of this period are probably correct in concluding that Chinese and North Vietnamese Communist leaders were convinced ". . . that the nuclear deterrent is not effective in South Asia and that the revolutionary war they are waging carries no risks and because of the superior morale and better organization of the Communist guer-

31. *The Pentagon Papers, supra* (p. 254).
32. Ibid. (p. 256); see also Johnson (*The Vantage Point*), *supra:* ". . . all he [Seaborn] heard from Hanoi's leaders was propaganda repeated many times since."

rilla forces can be waged without risk and brought to a victorious conclusion."[33] Had the NLF been contained or, better, dispersed and falling back, then Hanoi hawks would have had to look a bit harder at the situation. As it was, with a minimum of investment on the part of the North, a major political goal was about to be realized.

Hoping to forestall more-overt action, at least until after the presidential election, Johnson continued to approve massive doses of American aid to the South. In June, he recalled Ambassador Lodge, who had never quite made "the team" and now wanted to campaign for the Republican presidential nomination. He replaced Lodge with a powerful "team": General Maxwell Taylor as ambassador and U. Alexis Johnson, a hawkish career diplomat, as deputy ambassador—appointments that confirmed priority of the military over the political role. In July 1964, he turned his back on Hanoi and, sounding remarkably like Lloyd George voicing his dilemma in Ireland (see Chapter 21, Volume I), declared: ". . . If those practising terror and ambush will simply honor their existing agreements, there could easily be peace in Southeast Asia immediately. But we do not believe in conferences called to ratify terror."[34] On the military side, General William Westmoreland already had replaced General Harkins; Admiral Ulysses S. Grant Sharp would soon replace Admiral Harry Felt as CINCPAC. A corps of American military and civil specialists descended on Saigon to help Khanh realize his Program of Action.

Khanh's program unfortunately failed to get off the ground. Although a few reforms emerged and some pacification progress resulted in a few provinces, Khanh never tamed the political and social forces that had brought down Diem and the junta.

Nor did an influx of American advisers serve him as well as Washington had hoped. At Taylor's insistence, South Vietnamese officials directly controlled materials provided by American aid, which resulted in two major disasters: First, relatively little reached the essential target, the peasants, whose co-operation was vital to neutralizing VC operations; and second, in siphoning off and selling American arms, equipment, and material to make personal fortunes, GVN officials and ARVN officers (frequently the same) furnished the enemy with more equip-

33. Ernst Kun and Joseph Kun, "North Vietnam's Doctrine," *Survival,* The International Institute of Strategic Studies, London, February 1965. The authors do not seem to me, however, to prove their contention that ". . . for Peking and Hanoi the whole Chinese Communist conception of world revolution is at stake."
34. Adam Roberts, "Lessons of Geneva 1954," *The Times* (London), April 23, 1968. Reprinted in *Survival,* June 1968; in 1921, David Lloyd George complained, ". . . I recognize that force is itself no remedy, and that reason and goodwill alone can lead us to the final goal. But to abandon the use of force today would be to surrender alike to violence, crime and separation, and that I am not prepared to do."

ment than was arriving from Hanoi. Looking at the ships daily arriving
in the South, Ho Chi Minh might well have thought of Xerxes:

. . . While he was staying at Abydos, he saw some corn-ships, which were
passing through the Hellespont from the Euxine, on their way to Egina and
the Peloponnese. His attendants, hearing that they were the enemy's were
ready to capture them, and looked to see when Xerxes would give the signal.
He, however, merely asked, "Whither the ships were bound?" and when
they answered, "For thy foes, master, with corn on board." "We too are
bound thither," he rejoined, "laden, among other things, with corn. What
harm is it, if they carry our provisions for us?"[35]

From Taylor on down, the Americans found themselves enmeshed
in corruption and intrigue that made most thrillers read like nursery
stories. Lacking linguistic ability, not to mention an understanding of
insurgency warfare, they floundered while attempting to repair inadequate performance by quantitative methods: American agencies quickly
proliferated into numerous bureaucratic empires staffed by highly paid
civil servants who, like war lords of old, too often fought each other
instead of the common enemy. To add to Taylor's problems, as the
internal situation worsened during summer of 1964—at this time the
NLF-PRP correctly claimed to control much of South Vietnam—Khanh
sought to save his neck by carrying the war into North Vietnam, a
"March North" propaganda campaign squelched only with difficulty by
Taylor.

NLF-PRP gains during the summer scarcely calmed Administration
hawks. Although Johnson had forbidden overt action, covert operations
involving ". . . trained sabotage teams, electronic intelligence-gathering
equipment, C-123 transports for the airdrops and fast PT boats for the
coastal raids" mounted in scope and intensity.[36] At the end of July, one
of MACV's South Vietnamese naval commando teams raided two
North Vietnamese islands. Two days later, enemy patrol boats searching the area attacked a DeSoto patrol destroyer, USS *Maddox*. Her
guns and American carrier planes knocked out three of the boats, and
Maddox sailed South. The next day, President Johnson ordered *Maddox*
and another destroyer back North along with air cover[37]—gunboat
diplomacy that, considering the circumstances, was provocative enough.
But two other events fired the explosive situation: On August 1 and 2,
T-28 planes bombed North Vietnamese villages on the Laotian border;
and on the night of August 3, MACV launched two more covert attacks
by South Vietnamese-manned PT boats. On the following night, North
Vietnamese patrol boats attacked the two American patrol destroy-

35. Herodotus, op. cit.
36. *The Pentagon Papers, supra* (p. 259).
37. Ibid.; see also Johnson (*The Vantage Point*) and (*Public Papers 1963–
1964*).

ers.[38] Washington reacted promptly. Planes from two U.S. aircraft carriers struck DRV naval installations along a hundred miles of coast. At the same time, President Johnson ordered previously alerted aircraft squadrons to South Vietnam, as called for in JCS strike plans; he also alerted army and marine ground forces for deployment against North Vietnamese or Chinese reaction to the raids. In announcing these momentous events that night on television, the President assured his audience, ". . . we still seek no wider war."

This might have been so, but Johnson nonetheless wanted authority to wage wider war if necessary. Bundy's resolution was now dusted off, altered slightly, and introduced into Congress.[39] In secret and hastily held Congressional hearings, Robert McNamara threw up a verbal dust screen to inquisitive senators. To Senator Wayne Morse, who had learned of the August 3 raids and suggested that McNamara was aware of them and that the American navy had been involved, he replied:

. . . First, our Navy played absolutely no part in, was not associated with, was not aware of, any South Vietnamese actions, if there were any. . . .

I did not have knowledge at the time of the attack on the island. There is no connection between this patrol and any action by South Vietnam.

The Secretary went on to explain that whatever action had occurred was part of an anti-infiltration program run by a South Vietnamese fleet of junks for some years. He did not explain that the junk patrols had nothing to do with Plan 34A operations, nor did he confide the fact of the August 3 raids, much less that the destroyer skippers had been notified. Neither did he explain the air action against North Vietnamese border villages.[40]

Partly on the basis of this and presumably other false, distorted, and incomplete testimony from top American officials, an alarmed and emotional Congress passed the Southeast Asia resolution, which authorized the President ". . . to take all necessary steps, including the use of armed force, to assist any member or protocol state of the Southeast

38. *The Pentagon Papers, supra* (p. 305); a number of qualified observers, including a senior marine intelligence officer, have argued that it is doubtful if the North Vietnamese attacks ever occurred. While I do not wish to argue the case here, I would suggest that we have not heard the end of this episode. (Confidential information in the author's files.)

39. Ibid. (p. 264); see also Johnson (*Public Papers 1963–1964*), *supra;* William P. Bundy, "The Path to Vietnam," *Survival,* October 1967. On August 15, 1967, Mr. Bundy offered this version to a National Student Association audience: ". . . [The Tonkin Gulf action] led President Johnson to seek, and the Congress to approve overwhelmingly on 7 August, 1964, a resolution—drafted in collaboration with Congressional leaders . . ."; see also Johnson (*The Vantage Point*), *supra,* who later wrote that Rusk and George Ball ". . . in consultation with the congressional leaders of both parties" had worked out the resolution during Johnson's one-day absence from Washington.

40. *The Pentagon Papers, supra* (pp. 265–66).

Asia Collective Defense Treaty requesting assistance in defense of its freedom." Although some critics, including two senators, dissented on the grounds that DRV attacks were shrouded in mystery and that the resolution partially abrogated Congressional responsibility for placing the nation in war, the bulk of American people seemed to accept it with equanimity and trust—even with pride.

Chapter 80

General Taylor reports from Saigon • Seaborn's second mission to Hanoi • William Bundy's program of escalation • Admiral Sharp's recommendations • Taylor's operational plans • Pentagon voices • Johnson: ". . . we still seek no wider war" • September meeting in the White House • Enemy estimate of the situation • Douglas Pike's analysis • Bias of the insurgency • Enemy strategic adjustments • Edward Lansdale's analysis • The Bien Hoa attack • John McNaughton's adjusted aims • "Fast full squeeze" and "hot-blood actions" • Rostow on power • George Ball's doubts • Taylor's pessimism • The intelligence panel dissents • Khanh's dictatorship • Dissent in Saigon • Tran Van Minh takes over

CONGRESSMEN AND CITIZENS might have been upset had they known of behind-the-scenes communications shortly after American bombs fell on North Vietnam.

The situation already had alarmed Premier Nikita Khrushchev and the Kremlin sufficiently to involve them in the imbroglio. Professor Donald Zagoria later wrote:

. . . Just after the Tonkin Gulf incident, Hanoi, with apparent Soviet encouragement, relayed a message to Washington through U.N. Secretary-General U Thant, who, in turn, dispatched it to Washington through Adlai Stevenson, then U.S. Ambassador to the U.N. The message continued Ho Chi Minh's response to U Thant's suggestion of a private meeting with U.S. envoys. Thant, after hearing from Ho, arranged for such a meeting at an estate outside Rangoon. Washington, however, refused to participate and reportedly also rebuffed a second invitation to meet with Ho.[1]

1. Zagoria, op. cit.; see also New York *Times*, December 6, 1966; Mario Rossi, "U Thant and Vietnam: The Untold Story," *The New York Review of Books*, November 17, 1966.

The action had also raised international pressures for a Geneva-style conference on the Laotian problem, a conference that undoubtedly would have considered the Vietnam situation as well. On August 7, Secretary of State Rusk queried various U.S. embassies as to the desirability of such a conference. Two days later, Ambassador Taylor replied from Saigon:

. . . Rush to conference table would serve to confirm to Chicoms [Chinese Communists] that U.S. retaliation for destroyer attacks was transient phenomenon and that firm Chicom response in form of commitment to defend NVN [North Vietnam] has given U.S. "paper tiger" second thoughts. . . .

Intensified pressures for Geneva-type conference . . . would appear to us to be coming almost entirely from those who are opposed to U.S. policy objectives in [Southeast Asia] (except possibly UK [Great Britain] which seems prepared to jump on band wagon).[2]

Nor would Congress and the American public have been relieved to know of a second secret visit by Mr. Seaborn to Hanoi on August 10. This time, Johnson's message, drafted by John McNaughton and delivered to Premier Pham Van Dong, apparently offered nothing of carrot and plenty of stick. It said, in effect, you have seen what we can do; now if you don't stop your nonsense and call off your offensives in Laos and South Vietnam, we are going to clobber you. According to the Pentagon report, Mr. Seaborn noted that Pham Van Dong, in August as in June,

. . . showed himself utterly unintimidated and calmly resolved to pursue the course upon which the DRV was embarked to what he confidently expected would be its successful conclusion.[3]

All this might have upset congressmen and citizens, but worse was to come: While Mr. Seaborn was speaking to Premier Pham Van Dong, Ambassador Taylor was preparing a detailed report for Secretary McNamara and the JCS. Taylor had canvassed ". . . responsible U.S. advisers and observers" throughout South Vietnam on a score of pertinent questions:

. . . In broad terms, the canvass results are surprisingly optimistic at the operational levels of both the civil and military organizations. The feeling of optimism exceeds that of most senior U.S. officials in Saigon. Future reports should determine who is right.

Taylor reported that the Khanh government

. . . is ineffective, beset by inexperienced ministers who are jealous and suspicious of each other.

2. *The Pentagon Papers, supra* (p. 346).
3. Ibid. (pp. 268–69 and 289 ff.); see also Johnson (*The Vantage Point*), *supra.*

Khanh does not have confidence or trust in most of his ministers and is not able to form them into a group with a common loyalty and purpose.

Taylor estimated ". . . that Khanh has a 50/50 chance of lasting out the year," but there is ". . . no one in sight to replace Khanh." Accordingly, we must ". . . do everything possible to bolster the Khanh Government." Among other courses of action, the American Government must ". . . be prepared to implement contingency plans against North Vietnam with optimum readiness by January 1, 1965."[4]

At the same time, William Bundy, now working in the State Department, where he replaced Roger Hilsman as Undersecretary of State for Far Eastern Affairs, was drawing up an action memorandum calling for

. . . a combination of military pressures and some form of communication under which Hanoi (and Peiping) eventually accept the idea of getting out. Negotiation without continued pressure, indeed without continued military action, will not achieve our objectives in the foreseeable future. . . .

Bundy and McNaughton agreed with Taylor that the United States must not consent to an international conference on Vietnam, at least until North Vietnam was "hurting" from retaliatory pressures.[5] Bundy's program called for "military silence" for the rest of August, then for "limited pressures," both covert and overt, until the new year, then "more serious pressures" such as interdicting ". . . infiltration routes and facilities" leading up to bombing oil depots, bridges, and railroads and mining Haiphong harbor.[6]

Flashed to CINCPAC for comment, this memorandum drew a predictable response. The effect of recent American actions, Admiral Sharp replied on August 17,

. . . was to interrupt the continually improving Communist posture, catch the imagination of the Southeast Asian peoples, provide some lift to morale, however temporary, and force CHICOM/DRV [China/North Vietnam] assessment or reassessment of U.S. intentions. But these were only steps along the way. What we have not done and must do is make plain to Hanoi and Peiping the cost of pursuing their current objectives and impeding ours. . . .

"Military silence" for the rest of August, Sharp argued,

. . . is not in consonance with desire to get the message to Hanoi and Peiping. Pierce Arrow [Tonkin bombing attacks] showed both force and restraint. Further demonstration of restraint alone could easily be interpreted as period of second thoughts about Pierce Arrow and events leading thereto as well as sign of weakness and lack of resolve. . . .

4. *The Pentagon Papers, supra* (pp. 291–94).
5. Ibid. (p. 295).
6. Ibid. (pp. 294–98).

Sharp agreed

. . . that we make clear to all that military pressure will continue until we achieve our objectives. Our actions must keep the Communists apprehensive of what further steps we will take if they continue their aggression. In this regard, we have already taken the large initial step of putting U.S. combat forces into Southeast Asia. We must maintain this posture; to reduce it would have a dangerous impact on the morale and will of all people in Southeast Asia. And we must face up to the fact that these forces will be deployed for some time and to their need for protection from ground or air attack. RVN [South Vietnam] cannot provide necessary ground security without degraduation of the counterinsurgency effort and has little air defense capability. A conference to include Vietnam, before we have overcome the insurgency, would lose U.S. our allies in Southeast Asia and represent a defeat for the United States.

Sharp next got to the nub of his and Saigon mission's desires:

. . . In considering more serious pressures, we must recognize that immediate action is required to protect our present heavy military investment in RVN. We have introduced large amounts of expensive equipment into RVN and a successful attack against Bien Hoa, Tan Son Nhut, Da Nang, or an installation such as a radar or communication site would be a serious psychological defeat for U.S. MACV reports that [sic] inability of GVN to provide requisite degree of security and therefore we must rely on U.S. troops . . . consideration should [also] be given to creating a U.S. base in RVN [to] provide one more indication of our intent to remain in S.E. Asia until our objectives are achieved. . . . Such a base should be accessible by air and sea, possessed of well developed facilities and installations, and located in an area from which U.S. operations could be launched effectively. Da Nang meets these criteria. . . .

Sharp concluded that

. . . our actions of August 5 have created a momentum which can lead to the attainment of our objectives in S.E. Asia. We have declared ourselves forcefully both by overt acts and by the clear readiness to do more. It is most important that we not lose this momentum.[7]

Sharp's recommendations introduced a sinister note into the proceedings. The general Administration view at this time, at least as outlined in a joint State and Defense departments publication, did not call for committing American combat troops, and for good reasons:

. . . The military problem facing the armed forces of South Viet Nam at this time is not primarily one of manpower. Basically it is a problem of acquiring training, equipment, skills, and organization suited to combating

7. Ibid. (pp. 298–300).

the type of aggression that menaces their country. Our assistance is designed to supply these requirements.

The Viet Cong use terrorism and armed attack as well as propaganda. The government forces must respond decisively on all appropriate levels, tasks that can best be handled by Vietnamese. U.S. combat units would face several obvious disadvantages in a guerrilla war situation of this type in which knowledge of terrain, language, and local customs is especially important. In addition, their introduction would provide ammunition for Communist propaganda which falsely proclaims that the United States is conducting a "white man's war" against Asians.[8]

Some military hawks agreed with this altogether-sound analysis. On August 18, General Taylor, in Saigon, cabled a reappraisal of the situation that called for a carefully limited commitment of ground troops. He agreed with the "apparent assumption" of the State Department

. . . that the present in-country pacification plan is not enough in itself to maintain national morale or to offer reasonable hope of eventual success. Something must be added in the coming months.

His cable cited four objectives:

. . . The first and most important objective is to gain time for the Khanh government to develop a certain stability and to give some firm evidence of viability. . . . A second objective in this period is the maintenance of morale in South Viet Nam particularly within the Khanh Government. . . . Thirdly while gaining time for Khanh, we must be able to hold the DRV in check and restrain a further buildup of Viet Cong strength by way of infiltration from the North. Finally, throughout this period, we should be developing a posture of maximum readiness for a deliberate escalation of pressure against North Viet Nam, using January 1, 1965 as a target D-Day. . . .[9]

To accomplish these objectives, the mission recommended a three-part general course of action:

. . . the first, a series of actions directed at the Khanh government; the second, actions directed at the Hanoi Government; the third, following a pause of some duration, initiation of an orchestrated air attack against North Viet Nam.[10]

Specifically, Taylor nominated two operational plans. The first, a go-slow plan—U-2 overflights of North Vietnam, resumption of 34A coastal raids and DeSoto destroyer patrols, and air and ground strikes

8. Department of State Publication 7724 (Department of Defense, Gen.-8), *Viet Nam: The Struggle for Freedom* (Washington: U. S. Government Printing Office, 1964).
9. *The Pentagon Papers, supra* (pp. 349–52).
10. Ibid.

against infiltration routes in Laos—which the United States would implement in return for Khanh's promise ". . . to stabilize his government and make some progress in cleaning up his operational backyard." This, Plan A, called for a specific "precautionary military readiness": ". . . Hawk [anti-aircraft] units to Da Nang and Saigon, landing a Marine force at Da Nang for defense of the airfield and beefing up MACV's support base." Course B, a go-fast plan, would ask ". . . virtually nothing from the Khanh Government, primarily because it is assumed that little can be expected from it. It avoids the consequence of the sudden collapse of the Khanh Government and gets underway with minimum delay the punitive actions against Hanoi. Thus, it lessens the chance of an interruption of the program by an international demand for negotiation by presenting a fait accompli to international critics." Taylor added, however,

. . . it increases the likelihood of U.S. involvement in ground action since Khanh will have almost no available ground forces which can be released from pacification employment to mobile resistance of DRV attacks.

Taylor recommended adopting Course A, ". . . while maintaining readiness to shift to Course of Action B."[11]

The Joint Chiefs of Staff duly considered this appraisal. Echoing Admiral Sharp's earlier message, the JCS, in a memorandum to McNamara on August 26, showed a preference for Taylor's Course B: ". . . an accelerated program of action with respect to the DRV is essential to prevent a complete collapse of the U.S. position in Southeast Asia." They approved various pressures, covert and overt, as part of an escalating program of action. Holding that ". . . more direct and forceful actions" would be required, the memorandum went on:

. . . We should therefore maintain our prompt readiness to execute a range of selected responses, tailored to the developing circumstances and reflecting the principles in the Gulf of Tonkin actions, that such counteroperations will result in clear military disadvantage to the DRV.[12]

These and other top-secret messages stood in stark contrast to President Johnson's ". . . we still seek no wider war" theme, which he was laboring against his Republican opponent, Senator Barry Goldwater, who was calling for all-out air strikes against North Vietnam. In late August, Johnson told a crowd at an outdoor barbecue in Texas:

. . . I have had advice to load our planes with bombs and to drop them on certain areas that I think would enlarge the war and escalate the war, and result in our committing a good many American boys to fighting a war that I think ought to be fought by the boys of Asia to help protect their own land.

11. Ibid.
12. Ibid. (pp. 354–55).

Although the American presence in Vietnam had cost fewer than two hundred lives, ". . . we think it better to lose 200 than to lose 200,000. For that reason we have tried very carefully to restrain ourselves and not to enlarge the war."[13]

While Johnson was soothing Texas constituents, one of his top officials, John McNaughton, in the Pentagon, was working on still another operational memorandum. Dated September 3, this paper described the seriously deteriorating situation in South Vietnam and spelled out specific Administration objectives:

. . . to reverse the present downward trend. Failing that, the alternative objective is to emerge from the situation with as good an image as possible in U.S., allied and enemy eyes.

McNaughton outlined measures for action inside South Vietnam, including consideration of a proposal ". . . to enlarge significantly the U.S. military role in the pacification program . . . e.g., large numbers of U.S. special forces, divisions of regular combat troops, U.S. air, etc., to 'interlard' with or to take over functions of geographical areas from the South Vietnamese armed forces. . . ." Simultaneously, he called for actions against North Vietnam that would cause the enemy to react in such a way as to give the American Government initiative to escalate the action at will.

At best, McNaughton suggested, this program would cause Hanoi to call off its support, thus allowing pacification of the South. It might result in either "explicit settlement" or "tacit settlement":

. . . If worst comes and South Vietnam disintegrates or their behavior becomes abominable, to "disown" South Vietnam, hopefully leaving the image of "a patient who died despite the extraordinary efforts of a good doctor."

The American Government had to be particularly careful, however, in implementing such a program:

. . . During the next two months, because of the lack of "rebuttal time" before election to justify particular actions which may be distorted to the U.S. public, we must act with special care—signalling to the DRV that initiatives are being taken, to the GVN that we were behaving energetically despite the restraints of our political season, and to the U.S. public that we are behaving with good purpose and restraint.[14]

Various Administration points of view met on September 7 at the White House, where, after considerable debate, the principals agreed that air attacks against North Vietnam would have to be employed, but on a go-slow, "low-risk" basis, since Khanh's government was too weak to withstand probable enemy reaction to rapid escalation by Amer-

13. Ibid. (p. 311); see also Johnson (*Public Papers—1964*), *supra*.
14. *The Pentagon Papers, supra* (pp. 355–57).

ican forces. Undoubtedly with the rapidly approaching election in mind, Johnson agreed to this course, but approved various covert actions already recommended, including U.S. air operations—"Yankee Team"—in Laos, as well as resumption of naval patrols in Tonkin Gulf. He also approved a significant increase in expenditures inside South Vietnam, including overdue civil-service raises for the South Vietnamese and other urgent projects.[15]

Hanoi did not react passively to the continuing American counter-offensive. In mid-September, North Vietnamese patrol boats attacked DeSoto patrol destroyers, an action that President Johnson let slide. Administration nerves again jangled in October, when Communist China exploded a nuclear pile. Also in October, Saigon observers reported an increase in infiltration, including a GVN claim that ARVN had captured four North Vietnamese soldiers in South Vietnam. The administration, however, was not particularly worried by action from the North. A Special National Intelligence Estimate (SNIE), of October 9, read in part:

. . . While they [Hanoi and Peiping] will seek to exploit and encourage the deteriorating situation in Saigon, they probably will avoid actions that would in their view unduly increase the chances of a major U.S. response against North Vietnam (DRV) or Communist China. We are almost certain that both Hanoi and Peiping are anxious not to become involved in the kind of war in which the great weight of superior U.S. weaponry could be brought against them. Even if Hanoi and Peiping estimated that the U.S. would not use nuclear weapons against them, they could not be sure of this. . . .

In the face of new U.S. pressures against the DRV further actions by Hanoi and Peiping would be based to a considerable extent on their estimate of U.S. intentions, i.e., whether the U.S. was actually determined to increase its pressures as necessary. Their estimates on this point are probably uncertain, but we believe that fear of provoking severe measures by the U.S. would lead them to temper their responses with a good deal of caution. . . .

If despite Communist efforts, the U.S. attacks continued, Hanoi's leaders would have to ask themselves whether it was not better to suspend their support of Viet Cong military action rather than suffer the destruction of their major military facilities and the industrial sector of their economy. In the belief that the tide has set almost irreversibly in their favor in South Vietnam, they might calculate that the Viet Cong could stop its military attacks for the time being and renew the insurrection successfully at a later date. Their judgment in this matter might be reinforced by the Chinese Communist concern over becoming involved in a conflict with U.S. air and naval power.[16]

15. Johnson (*The Vantage Point*), *supra;* see also *The Pentagon Papers, supra* (pp. 357–60).
16. *The Pentagon Papers, supra* (pp. 419–20).

The American intelligence estimate fell considerably wide of the mark, as did American insistence that the fulcrum of insurgency lay in Hanoi. The NLF-PRP had by no means decided on a specific course of action during these momentous months. Ever since major American intervention, in 1962—the beginning of what the NLF called Special War—the enemy had been debating how to win the war. As Douglas Pike has pointed out, this was a major doctrinal problem that occupied enemy minds during 1963 and 1964.

Three options existed:

. . . the military ending, or third stage; the social ending, or General Uprising; and the political-infiltration and takeover ending, or the negotiated settlement. All three were doctrinally acceptable. It was abundantly clear from both the nature of the NLF struggle movement and the priorities employed, as well as from NLF documents, that the early doctrinaires believed the General Uprising and not the Giap third-stage military assault would be the culmination of the action programs and deliver final victory. It is true that the Giap thesis of "first political struggle, then mixed political and armed struggle, then armed struggle, and finally again political struggle" continued as an ikon motif; but within this sort of generalized approach there was room for great latitude of interpretation.

Pike's analysis is the more interesting since it was made before the Tet offensive of 1968:

. . . Among the earlier theorizers armed struggle was conceived of not as a military effort but as a series of violent actions, some of a military cast, that sought to achieve those goals that the political struggle movement could not achieve alone. The emergence of a military force for the purpose of fighting a more or less conventional war, similar to the final stages of the Viet Minh war, was considered highly risky and quite unnecessary. The Giap armed struggle phase was conceived of not as regiments or divisions openly confronting the enemy but as an explosion of small-unit acts of violence across the country. The end of the struggle then would be marked by a multitude of guerrilla-unit assaults, in unit force of perhaps 500 men, erupting simultaneously and in coordinated fashion throughout the country. ARVN revolts would break out in every unit as the result of the *binh van* [proselyting] movement. GVN [South Vietnamese Government] officials would be assassinated in numbers. But most of all the people of the country, by the millions, would have taken to the streets in one grand struggle movement that would paralyze what remained of the GVN administrative and military power. This was the General Uprising, which could be accomplished without use of military or paramilitary units larger than a battalion.

I know of no other writer who has defined the fulcrum of the Vietnam insurgency in clearer terms than Douglas Pike and, in so doing, has demonstrated what must be the proper counterinsurgency effort:

. . . The NLF originally saw itself as an agency of social control, not as a military force. It sought to channel rural Vietnamese activities in certain directions and in line with its own purposes. Its control instruments were individuals, especially the natural leaders in villages, the so-called influentials; institutionalized organizations, the various liberation associations and special-interest groups; and social pressure, that is, its own social norms and mores. Its social inducements included superiority in the form of praise, flattery, and prestige; and deterrents were in the form of punishments, coercion, social ostracism, humiliation, physical injury, or death. The process of social control was suggestion and example, argument, persuasion and exhortation, inducement, deterrence, encouragement, and discouragement. These were the social bases for its efforts. In its revolutionary guerrilla warfare a three-pronged attack was employed: the political, use of the united front; the social, fomenting and instigating class strife; and the violence program, use of paramilitary and military war, assassinations, and various other acts of violence. The instrument throughout was the organization. Now this gigantic effort suggested something far beyond the traditional three stages of revolutionary guerrilla warfare. It suggested strongly that the ultimate objective was not Stage Three but, assisted perhaps by the General Uprising, assumption of power by means of the conference table.

The overt American military response in 1962 raised doubts as to the validity of this approach, and was one reason that the PRP came into being to bring increasing emphasis on a military approach. In 1964, according to Douglas Pike,

. . . an open division occurred at the Central Committee level and perhaps higher, in which the then dominant doctrine of the General Uprising was openly questioned. Defending it were the original NLF founders and the older more indigenous elements from the South; in opposition to it were the regulars from the North. The first group held that an intensification of the *dich van* [rural] and *binh van* [proselyting] programs, and perhaps with a step-up in the armed struggle, eventually could completely destroy the GVN's administrative and military apparatus, and thus a frontal assault would never be necessary. The regular cadres from the North held for increased militarization of the effort, a calculated military challenge to the ARVN, and greater emphasis on military assaults, including assaults on exclusively American military installations in Vietnam. For a time, as the debate raged, the armed struggle took on a schizoid character: NLF activities for a few weeks would be predominantly military, then switch to political approaches, and then back to military actions.

The heart of this debate was whether it would be possible to win through to victory in revolutionary guerrilla warfare by means of the political and armed struggles, whose basic objectives were mobilization of the civilian population and attrition, and immobilization but not physical destruction of the enemy's military establishment. . . . Both Mao and Giap, of course, adamantly insisted that no revolutionary guerrilla war could end as a guerrilla war, that it must evolve into a more or less conventional war in which the opposing armed forces are defeated or destroyed in direct combat. In the end the Northerners won the NLF debate, and military activities increased in scope, tempo, and nature. . . .[17]

Though allowing that the fulcrum of insurgency lay in the South, the Johnson administration continued to believe that its *raison d'être* came from the North. They could not understand the true situation as explained, for example, by Edward Lansdale. After discussing favored Administration options, he wrote: ". . . The anomaly in these reactions is that each falls short of understanding that the Communists have let loose a revolutionary idea in Viet Nam and that it will not die by being ignored, bombed or smothered by us. Ideas do not die in such ways." He then called for essentially a political approach, which would

. . . oppose the Communist idea with a better idea and to do so on the battleground itself, in a way that would permit the people, who are the main feature of that battleground, to make their own choice. A political base would be established. The first step would be to state political goals, founded on principles cherished by free men, which the Vietnamese share; the second would be an aggressive commitment of organizations and resources to start the Vietnamese moving realistically toward those political goals. In essence, this is revolutionary warfare, the spirit of the British Magna Carta, the French "Liberté, Egalité, Fraternité" and our own Declaration of Independence.

South Vietnam had to have a "cause," and the American effort primarily had to go ". . . on helping the Vietnamese leadership create the conditions which will encourage the discovery and most rapid possible development of a patriotic cause so genuine that the Vietnamese willingly will pledge to it 'their lives, their fortunes, their sacred honor.'" After suggesting a number of ways in which this could be done, Lansdale warned that the most urgent function is ". . . to *protect* and *help* the people":

. . . When the military opens fire at long range, whether by infantry weapons, artillery or air strike, on a reported Viet Cong concentration in a hamlet or village full of civilians, the Vietnamese officers who give those orders and the American advisers who let them "get away with it" are helping

17. Pike, op. cit.: Pike does not emphasize that these were NLF, or Viet Cong, attacks. Although he asserts that militarizing the effort in late 1964 ". . . included ordering thousands of North Vietnamese regular army soldiers to the South," he cites no evidence for this statement. Administration officials subsequently claimed that regular North Vietnam army (PAVN) units appeared in the South in late 1964, but these contradictory and confusing claims tend to validate contrary assertions that regular PAVN units did not appear in appreciable numbers until after mid-1965 and then mainly in the central highlands and in the North.

defeat the cause of freedom. The civilian hatred of the military resulting from such actions is a powerful motive for joining the Viet Cong.[18]

On November 1, whether acting on orders from Hanoi or independently, the Viet Cong launched a surprise mortar attack against Bien Hoa, the American airbase outside of Saigon, killing four airmen and destroying a number of B-57 aircraft. Although Lyndon Johnson was elected President two days later by a large majority, he did not use the Bien Hoa attack as an excuse to escalate the war—despite urgings by the JCS for extensive reprisal action and by Ambassador Taylor for a lesser program.[19] Instead, he directed an interagency working group, under William Bundy, to once again examine the problem.

Although quite a wide range of options remained open to the American Government at this point, Administration minds seemed in no more a receptive mood to face reality and act accordingly than formerly. In a draft paper dated November 5, William Bundy perhaps unwittingly disclosed the Administration's temper:

. . . Bien Hoa may be repeated at any time. This would tend to force our hand, but would also give us a good springboard for any decision for stronger action. The President is clearly thinking in terms of maximum use of a Gulf of Tonkin rationale, either for an action that would show toughness and hold the line till we can decide the big issue, or as a basis for starting a clear course of action under the broad options.[20]

Subsequent talks remained hawkish, with compromise options discussed only briefly if at all. The Pentagon Papers reveal, beyond question, that ranking officials of the Department of Defense, the State Department, and the American mission in Saigon, and members of the JCS intended to escalate the war; it was a matter of when and how, as it had been for some months. From the standpoint of the American public, the record is one of dissembling, if not outright fraud. Thus, in the draft paper of November 5, quoted above, William Bundy continued:

. . . Congress must be consulted before any major action, perhaps only by notification if we do a reprisal against another Bien Hoa, but preferably by careful talks with such key leaders as Mansfield, Dirksen, the Speaker, Albert, Halleck, Fulbright, Hickenlooper, Morgan, Mrs. Bolton, Russell, Saltonstall, Rivers, (Vinson?), Arends, Ford, etc. He [the President] probably should wait till his mind is moving clearly in one direction before such a consultation, which would point to some time next week. Query if it should be combined with other topics (budget?) to lessen the heat.

18. Lansdale, op. cit.
19. *The Pentagon Papers, supra* (p. 322); see also Johnson (*The Vantage Point*), *supra*.
20. *The Pentagon Papers, supra* (pp. 363–64).

We probably do not need additional Congressional authority [to that granted in the Tonkin Gulf resolution], even if we decide on very strong action. A session of this rump Congress might well be the scene of a messy Republican effort.

We are on the verge of intelligence agreement that infiltration has in fact mounted, and Saigon is urging that we surface this by the end of the week or early next week. Query how loud we want to make this sound. Actually Grose in the Times had the new estimate on Monday; so the splash and sense of hot new news may be less. We should decide this today if possible. . . . In general, we all feel the problem of proving North Vietnamese participation is less than in the past, but we should have the Jorden Report updated for use as necessary. . . .[21]

Apparently as a result of this thinking, the State Department sent another representative, Chester L. Cooper, to Saigon to report on infiltration, meanwhile stressing the fact of mounting efforts from Hanoi by means of "leaks."[22]

McNamara's assistant secretary, John McNaughton, was also drafting a paper that adjusted Administration aims in South Vietnam. The task now became, according to McNaughton and presumably McNamara:

. . . (a) To protect U.S. reputation as a countersubversion guarantor.
   (b) To avoid domino effect especially in Southeast Asia.
   (c) To keep South Vietnamese territory from Red hands.
   (d) To emerge from crisis without unacceptable taint from methods.

Although admitting that the real problem of South Vietnam lay in the South, McNaughton noted:

. . . Action against North Vietnam is to some extent a substitute for strengthening the government in South Vietnam. That is, a less active VC (on orders from DRV) can be matched by a less efficient GVN. We therefore should consider squeezing North Vietnam.

McNaughton offered a three-option plan. Option A called for continuing the present course of action: In essence, go-slow, low-risk operations against the North with reprisals when necessary ". . . but not to a degree that would create strong international negotiating pressures. Basic to this option is the continued rejection of negotiating in the hope that the situation will improve." Option B called for:

. . . Fast full squeeze. Present policies plus a systematic program of military pressures against the north, meshing at some point with negotiation, but with pressure actions to be continued at a fairly rapid pace and without interruption until we achieve our central present objectives.

21. Ibid.
22. Ibid. (p. 338); see also Chester L. Cooper, *The Lost Crusade—The Full Story of U.S. Involvement in Vietnam from Roosevelt to Nixon* (London: Mac-Gibbon & Kee, 1970).

Option C called for:

. . . Progressive squeeze-and-talk. Present policies plus an orchestration of communications with Hanoi and a crescendo of additional military moves against infiltration targets, first in Laos and then in the DRV, and then against other targets in North Vietnam. The scenario would be designed to give the U.S. the option at any point to proceed or not, to escalate or not, and to quicken the pace or not. The decision in these regards would be made from time to time in view of all relevant factors.

In McNaughton's opinion, reaction from the North was not a vital worry:

. . . The DRV and China will probably not invade South Vietnam, Laos or Burma, nor is it likely that they will conduct air strikes on these countries. The USSR will almost certainly confine herself to political actions. If the DRV or China strike or invade South Vietnam, U.S. forces will be sufficient to handle the problem.

McNaughton showed considerable concern for the effects of escalation on South Vietnam:

. . . Military action against the DRV could be counterproductive in South Vietnam because (1) the VC could step up its activities, (2) the South Vietnamese could panic, (3) they could resent our striking their "brothers," and (4) they could tire of waiting for results. . . .

However, McNaughton continued,

. . . Should South Vietnam disintegrate completely beneath us, we should try to hold it together long enough to permit us to try to evacuate our forces and to convince the world to accept the uniqueness (and congenital impossibility) of the South Vietnamese case.[23]

Apparently, neither Department of Defense nor State Department senior officials seriously considered holding the line with Option A. William Bundy and McNaughton were said to favor Option C. The JCS, however, preferred Option B—". . . fast full squeeze," with what the Pentagon called "hot-blood actions"—". . . with something like Option C as a fall-back alternative."[24]

Still another voice sounded a cry for escalation. In mid-November, Walt Rostow wrote McNamara his feeling that the American Government must clearly "signal" Hanoi its intentions, including escalation if desired. Rostow was ". . . convinced that we should not go forward into the next stage without a U.S. ground force commitment of some kind." A few days later, he expanded his thinking in a memorandum to Secretary of State Rusk. Convinced that Hanoi wished to avoid de-

23. *The Pentagon Papers, supra* (pp. 365–68).
24. Ibid. (pp. 368–70).

struction of its industrial plant (as postulated in the October SNIE),
Rostow wrote:

. . . Our most basic problem is, therefore, how to persuade them that a
continuation of their present policy will risk major destruction in North Viet
Nam; that a preemptive move on the ground as a prelude to negotiation
will be met by U.S. strength on the ground; and that Communist China
will not be a sanctuary if it assists North Viet Nam in counter-escalation.

Calling for retaliation against the North ". . . for continued violation
of the 1954–1962 [Geneva] Accords" and ". . . the introduction of
some ground forces in South Viet Nam and, possibly, in the Laos cor-
ridor," Rostow wanted to go further:

. . . Perhaps most important of all, the introduction into the Pacific Theater of massive forces to deal with any escalatory response, including forces
evidently aimed at China as well as North Viet Nam, should the Chinese
Communists enter the game. I am increasingly confident that we can do this
in ways which would be understood—and not dangerously misinterpreted—
in Hanoi and Peiping.

But deployment of forces and ". . . even bombing operations in the
north" would not form a "decisive signal." The situation called for
". . . that kind of Presidential commitment and staying power" familiar
to the Berlin and Cuba crises. In Rostow's mind, the danger existed
that Hanoi would either ". . . pretend to call off the war in South Viet
Nam, without actually doing so," or would ". . . revive it again when
the pressure is off." American troops in South Vietnam, as well as an
American naval blockade, were essential to prevent this and to force
Hanoi to stop supporting the NLF and the PRP. Rostow continued:

. . . As I said in my memorandum to the President of June 6, no one can
be or should be dogmatic about how much of a war we still would have—
and for how long—if the external element were thus radically reduced or
eliminated. The odds are pretty good, in my view, that, if we do these things
in this way, the war will either promptly stop or we will see the same kind
of fragmentation of the Communist movement in South Viet Nam that we
saw in Greece after the Yugoslav frontier was closed by the Tito-Stalin
split. . . .

This was Rostow's old thesis, with the same fundamental flaws we have
already discussed (see Chapters 57 and 77). Rostow himself may have
felt the ice of logic cracking under his words, for he continued:

. . . But we can't proceed on that assumption. We must try to gear this
whole operation with the best counter-insurgency effort we can mount with
our Vietnamese friends outside the country; and not withdraw U.S. forces
from Viet Nam until the war is truly under control. . . .

Although this course of action would probably lead to a demand from allies of the United States to admit Communist China into the UN, Rostow continued, the Administration could live with this in return for resolving ". . . the Laos and South Viet Nam problems." In summing up, Rostow wrote:

. . . Considering these observations as a whole, I suspect what I am really saying is that our assets, as I see them, are sufficient to see this thing through it we enter the exercise with adequate determination to succeed. I know well the anxieties and complications on our side of the line. But there may be a tendency to underestimate both the anxieties and complications on the other side and also to underestimate that limited but real margin of influence on the outcome which flows from the simple fact that at this stage of history we are the greatest power in the world—if we behave like it.

"The greatest power in the world," according to Rostow, could bring limited Utopia to ". . . the Asian community," provided that it acted swiftly and surely. Among other deeds, he called for:

. . . immediate direct communication to Hanoi to give them a chance to back down before faced with our actions, including a clear statement of the limits of our objectives but our absolute commitment to them.

Should this fail, as was likely, physical actions were in order.[25]

In late November, a select committee of the National Security Council (NSC) met to discuss the working group's draft proposals. Present at this meeting of ranking Administration officials was Under Secretary of State George Ball, who challenged basic Administration postulates, a brave act, considering the prevailing temper of his associates. According to William Bundy's memorandum of this meeting,

. . . Mr. Ball "indicated doubt" that bombing the North in any fashion would improve the situation in South Vietnam and "argued against" a judgment that a Vietcong victory in South Vietnam would have a falling-domino effect on the rest of Asia.[26]

The reader perhaps will remember that this was the stand taken by CIA analysts in the report made for President Johnson the previous spring. Instead of a policy of military escalation, Ball favored Option A. However, as Neil Sheehan later wrote,

. . . While the working-group sessions had been in progress, the [Pentagon] study discloses, Mr. Ball had been writing a quite different policy paper "suggesting a U.S. diplomatic strategy in the event of an imminent GVN collapse."

In it, he advocated working through the U.K. . . . who would in turn

25. Ibid. (pp. 418–23).
26. Ibid. (pp. 325–26).

seek cooperation from the U.S.S.R., in arranging an international conference
. . . which would work out a compromise political settlement for South Vietnam. . . .

Although Ball alone stood for this particular approach, other dissent
emerged during the meeting. Secretary of State Rusk said

. . . that while he favored bombing North Vietnam, he did not accept an
analysis by Mr. McNaughton and William Bundy that if the bombing failed
to save South Vietnam "we would obtain international credit for trying."

"In his view," the [Pentagon] analyst writes, "the harder we tried and
then failed, the worse our situation would be."

McGeorge Bundy [the President's special assistant for national security
affairs] demurred to some extent, the account goes on, but Mr. Ball "expressed strong agreement with the last Rusk point."

General Wheeler [who had replaced Maxwell Taylor as chairman of the
JCS], reflecting the viewpoint of the Joint Chiefs, argued that the hard, fast
bombing campaign of Option B actually entailed "less risk of a major conflict before achieving success," in words of the study, than the gradually
rising air strikes of Option C.[27]

The meeting ended with no decision as to which option would be
recommended to the President. On the following day, Ambassador Taylor joined the select group of officials to report on the Vietnam situation.
His words could not have been more gloomy: The Viet Cong everywhere had advanced and were threatening to cut the country in half.
Despite heavy casualties produced by an increasingly stronger and professionally competent ARVN, the Viet Cong not only were making good
their losses but were adopting new and improved tactics. A new, civilian
government in Saigon was proving no more effective than the old, military government, either in the capital or in the provinces. Indeed,

. . . As the past history of this country shows, there seems to be a national
attribute which makes for factionalism and limits the development of a truly
national spirit. Whether this tendency is innate or a development growing
out of the conditions of political suppression under which successive generations have lived is hard to determine. But it is an inescapable fact that
there is no national tendency toward team play or mutual loyalty to be
found among many of the leaders and political groups within South Viet-
Nam. . . .

The ability of the Viet-Cong continuously to rebuild their units and to
make good their losses is one of the mysteries of this guerrilla war. We
are aware of the recruiting methods by which local boys are induced or
compelled to join the Viet-Cong ranks and have some general appreciation
of the amount of infiltration personnel from the outside. Yet taking both
of these sources into account, we still find no plausible explanation of the

27. Ibid.

continued strength of the Viet-Cong if our data on Viet-Cong losses are even approximately correct. Not only do the Viet-Cong units have the recuperative powers of the phoenix, but they have an amazing ability to maintain morale. Only in rare cases have we found evidences of bad morale among Viet-Cong prisoners or recorded in captured Viet-Cong documents.

One reason for continued Viet Cong growth, Taylor continued, was increasing infiltration from the North. Although the real problem lay in the South, where effective government had to be established in order to run an effective counterinsurgency, pressure also had to be brought on the North by a combination of methods already discussed. Not only could escalating American military operations cause Hanoi to back off from the war, but they could also be used to gain the South Vietnamese Government's promise to provide more-effective government. Taylor added ominously, however,

. . . In any case, we should be prepared for emergency military action against the North if only to shore up a collapsing situation.[28]

For the moment, he favored carrying on with Option A; once Saigon leaders promised to reform, he favored the first actions in Option C.

Thus Ambassador Taylor suggested still another course of action, one that seemed acceptable to most concerned principals. One more voice remained to be heard from, however. Bundy's working group included an "intelligence panel" composed of representatives from CIA, the State Department's Bureau of Intelligence and Research, and the Pentagon's Defense Intelligence Agency. This panel faulted the prevailing desire for air strikes against the North. It did not believe the chances were great of ". . . breaking the will of Hanoi"; it suggested that such strikes would cause a much wider war; and it did not attach much weight to Walt Rostow's thesis, embraced by a good many top military officers, that Hanoi would back down in order to preserve its industrial base:

. . . We have many indications that the Hanoi leadership is acutely and nervously aware of the extent to which North Vietnam's transportation system and industrial plant is vulnerable to attack. On the other hand, North Vietnam's economy is overwhelmingly agricultural and, to a large extent, decentralized in a myriad of more or less economically self-sufficient villages. Interdiction of imports and extensive destruction of transportation facilities and industrial plants would cripple D.R.V. industry. These actions would also seriously restrict D.R.V. military capabilities, and would degrade, though to a lesser extent, Hanoi's capabilities to support guerrilla warfare in South Vietnam and Laos. We do not believe that such actions would have a crucial effect on the daily lives of the overwhelming majority of the North Vietnam population. We do not believe that attacks on industrial tar-

28. Ibid. (pp. 370–73).

gets would so greatly exacerbate current economic difficulties as to create unmanageable control problems. It is reasonable to infer that the D.R.V. leaders have a psychological investment in the work of reconstruction they have accomplished over the last decade. Nevertheless, they would probably be willing to suffer some damage to the country in the course of a test of wills with the U.S. over the course of events in South Vietnam.[29]

No one seems to have respected the intelligence panel's doubts, which (correctly) refuted official thinking, particularly Rostow's optimistic thesis. Ignoring professional opinion, the principals agreed on a course of action more or less as outlined by Taylor, and one more or less consonant with William Bundy's "escalation scenario" of May. But, for the moment, the go-slow school prevailed, and William Bundy's intention ". . . to publicize the evidence of increased DRV infiltration" at the earliest feasible date was shelved. The plan presented to the President in early December, in essence, called for a two-pronged course of action: Phase I—go-slow, low-risk until the South Vietnamese Government swung around to making a real war effort; then Phase II—increasing air strikes against the North while concentrating on the pacification program in the South. The President seems to have accepted the plan, at least sufficiently to brief Prime Minister Wilson on its operational aspects and send various emissaries off to inform other allies.[30]

The Tonkin Gulf action served Khanh well. In mid-August, he submitted a constitutional charter ". . . that gave him virtually complete powers"; the Military Revolutionary Council approved it and elected him President of South Vietnam.[31] But the new charter immediately brought protests from such important elements as students and Buddhists. Instead of trying to placate them, Khanh chose imperial aloofness. Dissenters responded with mass demonstrations against the government. Catholic groups spilled out to fight them. Viet Cong infiltrators effectively fanned rampant hatreds. Riots in Saigon spread to Hué and Da Nang. Khanh refused to accept dissident demands, summoned the Military Revolutionary Council, and resigned as president! He was reinstalled as prime minister in a caretaker government headed by himself and Generals Minh and Khiem—a deceptively simple solution for a most complex problem.[32]

The new government brought a shaky end to demonstrations by promising a better constitution than the one framed by Khanh. The new constitution would be written by a new High National Council; as soon as possible, government would return to civilian hands.

29. Ibid. (pp. 331–32).
30. Johnson (*The Vantage Point*), *supra*.
31. Shaplen (*The Lost Revolution*), *supra*.
32. Ibid.; see also George Carver, op. cit. This article, by a CIA official, examines political compatibilities in the South, where, the author stresses, a social revolution was occurring, as distinct from a northern-imposed insurgency.

The dust had not settled when a group of disgruntled generals attempted another coup. This failed, in part because some younger and powerful officers remained loyal to Khanh, notably the head of the Vietnamese air force, Air Commodore Nguyen Cao Ky, a former pilot in the French air force and an ambitious young man whose slick mustache, purple scarf, and Captain Midnight flight suit would soon become prominent on the Vietnamese scene.

Civil government succeeded no better than military government. The new premier, a sixty-year-old former schoolteacher and mayor of Saigon, Tran Van Huong, quickly fell prey to now-familiar dissident elements. Although he received American backing, his hands were tied, in part by General Khanh, who retained real power in the form of ARVN. Beset by various demonstrations in cities and by military reverses in the countryside, the new government soon foundered. The High National Council splintered into opposing cliques, and, in December, the young generals "purged" it in favor of an Armed Forces Council. This was not to Ambassador Taylor's liking. On Christmas Eve, he assembled a group of errant officers, including General Nguyen Van Thieu and Air Commodore Nguyen Cao Ky. ". . . Do all of you understand English?" the ambassador asked. When the officers indicated that they did, the ambassador-general lowered the boom:

. . . I told you all clearly at General Westmoreland's dinner we Americans were tired of coups. Apparently I wasted my words. . . . I made it clear that all the military plans which I know you would like to carry out are dependent on governmental stability. Now you have made a real mess. We cannot carry you forever if you do things like this. . . .

After elaborating this theme and stressing need for a functioning High National Council, Taylor concluded: ". . . You people have broken a lot of dishes and now we have to see how we can straighten out this mess."[33]

Taylor could not understand the mess, let alone straighten it out. He now backed Huong, who backed down. General Khanh next launched a virulent anti-Taylor, anti-American campaign, at a time when the American Government was attempting to preserve South Vietnam's identity by spending $1.5 million per day. Although Taylor advised Huong to defy the purge, the premier instead reached a shaky compromise with the young generals. Khanh allied himself briefly with the Buddhist cause, the Buddhists opened their own anti-American campaign, the young generals ousted the Huong government—and Khanh again was in power.

But not for long. His new government, headed by Premier Phan Huy Quat, proved no more stable than its predecessors. Plots and

33. *The Pentagon Papers, supra* (pp. 379–81).

counterplots swirled through the capital.[34] On February 19, 1965, an attempted military coup succumbed to counterforces. But Taylor notwithstanding, the young generals had had enough of Khanh. They now deposed him as army commander in chief in favor of General Tran (Little Minh) Van Minh.

34. Shaplen, in *The Lost Revolution,* offers a splendid account of this political maelstrom.

Chapter 81

Fresh Viet Cong offensives • William Bundy's dilemma • McGeorge Bundy's memorandum • The attack at Pleiku • McGeorge Bundy's report • Sharp's "calculated risk" • The White Paper • American marines land • Early results • Westmoreland demands more troops (I) • Johnson's Baltimore speech • Hanoi's investment in the South • ARVN offensives • More American aid • The enemy retreats • More American troops • Taylor dissents • Rostow's optimism • Renewed guerrilla offensives • The Thieu-Ky dictatorship • Westmoreland demands more troops (II) • Senator Fulbright's analysis • George Ball's secret warning • Clifford's and Mansfield's pessimism • Ball's solution • Johnson's intransigence • The deception continues

THE INTERNECINE WAR in Saigon scarcely benefitted the real war. Each crisis and each coup expended untold amounts of energy that could better have been used in the countryside. Even optimum government would have made the outcome "a near-run thing." Instead, inept government resulted in continuing VC gains of such importance as to decide Hanoi and the NLF-PRP to launch the third, or all-out offensive, phase of the insurgency.

Fresh VC offensives caused something akin to panic among American officials in Saigon and Washington. By end of December 1964, the Saigon trinity—Taylor, Alexis Johnson, and Westmoreland—apparently despaired of rigging a stable South Vietnamese government and notified Washington that the air campaign should start ". . . under any conceivable alliance short of complete abandonment of South Vietnam."[1] Although President Johnson still held off, continuing VC attacks brought

1. *The Pentagon Papers, supra* (p. 337).

renewed recommendations from top officials for overt action. In early January, Johnson received a report from Taylor that concluded, ". . . we are presently on a losing track and must risk a change. . . . To take no positive action now is to accept defeat in the fairly near future." According to President Johnson,

. . . That was the view of every responsible military adviser in Vietnam and in Washington. Painfully and reluctantly, my civilian advisers were driven to the same conclusion by the hard facts.[2]

The thought processes of some of these advisers may be gathered from a memorandum written in early January by William Bundy to Secretary of State Rusk:

. . . The alternative of stronger action obviously has grave difficulties. It commits the U.S. more deeply, at a time when the picture of South Vietnamese will is extremely weak. To the extent that it included [sic] actions against North Vietnam, it would be vigorously attacked by many nations and disapproved initially even by such nations as Japan and India, on present indications. Most basically, its stiffening effect on the Saigon political situation would not be at all sure to bring about a more effective government, nor would limited actions against the southern D.R.V. in fact sharply reduce infiltration or, in present circumstances, be at all likely to induce Hanoi to call it off.

Nonetheless, on balance we believe that such action would have some faint hope of really improving the Vietnamese situation, and, above all, would put us in a much stronger position to hold the next line of defense, namely Thailand. Accepting the present situation—or any negotiation on the basis of it—would be far weaker from this latter key standpoint. If we moved into stronger actions, we should have in mind that negotiations would be likely to emerge from some quarter in any event, and that under existing circumstances, even with the additional element of pressure, we could not expect to get an outcome that would really secure an independent South Vietnam. Yet even on an outcome that produced a progressive deterioration in South Vietnam and an eventual Communist takeover, we would still have appeared to Asians to have done a lot more about it.[3]

This attitude gained currency among administration officials in January. Both William Bundy and McNaughton openly favored air strikes and the possibility of committing "limited" numbers of American ground troops to South Vietnam. Secret preparations for more-overt action continued during the month, as pessimistic reports continued to roll in. In late January, McGeorge Bundy sent a memorandum to the President stating that he and McNamara were ". . . pretty well convinced that our current policy can lead only to disastrous defeat."

2. Johnson (*The Vantage Point*), *supra.*
3. *The Pentagon Papers, supra* (pp. 341–42).

. . . The Vietnamese know just as we do that the Viet Cong are gaining in the countryside. Meanwhile, they see the enormous power of the United States withheld, and they get little sense of firm and active U.S. policy. They feel that we are unwilling to take serious risks. In one sense, all of this is outrageous, in the light of all that we have done and all that we are ready to do if they will only pull up their socks. But it is a fact—or at least so McNamara and I now think.[4]

President Johnson later wrote:

. . . Bundy and McNamara saw two alternatives: either to "use our military power in the Far East and to force a change of Communist policy" or to "deploy all our resources along a track of negotiation, aimed at salvaging what little can be preserved with no major addition to our present military risks." They said that they were inclined to favor the first alternative —use of more military power—but they believed that both courses should be studied carefully and that alternative programs should be developed and argued out in my presence.

"Both of us understand the very grave questions presented by any decision of this sort," the memo continued. "We both recognize that the ultimate responsibility is not ours. Both of us have fully supported your unwillingness in earlier months, to move out of the middle course. We both agree that every effort should still be made to improve our operations on the ground and to prop up the authorities in South Vietnam as best we can. But we are both convinced that none of this is enough, and that the time has come for harder choices."

The January 27 memo concluded by pointing out that Dean Rusk did not agree with the McNamara-Bundy assessment. Rusk knew things were going badly, and he did not claim that the deterioration could be stopped. "What he [Rusk] does say," the memo stated, "is that the consequences of both escalation and withdrawal are so bad that we simply must find a way of making our present policy work. This would be good if it was [sic] possible. Bob [McNamara] and I do not think it is."[5]

President Johnson responded by asking ". . . Rusk to instruct his experts once again to consider all possible ways for finding a peaceful solution." In addition, he sent McGeorge Bundy and a team of experts to Saigon to make still another report.

In early February, Viet Cong guerrillas attacked two American camps in the central highlands, Pleiku and Camp Holloway, killing nine and wounding a hundred and forty American troops (see map, p. 1091). While helicopter-borne troops pursued and killed a substantial number of guerrillas, American naval aircraft and South Vietnamese bombers carried out Operation Flaming Dart I, an attack on North Vietnamese barracks and staging areas at Dong Hoi, some forty miles north of the

4. Johnson (*The Vantage Point*), *supra*.
5. Ibid.

17th parallel. The President also ordered American dependents withdrawn from South Vietnam.

A few days later, Viet Cong guerrillas struck again, attacking both American and South Vietnamese installations on the central coast. Once again, naval jet fighter-bombers and bombers attacked North Vietnamese "installations," a heavier raid, code-named Flaming Dart II.

Political confusion in Saigon largely negated morale benefits derived from this new and tough line. While South Vietnamese politicians continued to behave as if no national crisis threatened, Viet Cong guerrillas continued to strike in the central highlands. Johnson earlier had authorized Westmoreland to commit combat aircraft in support of ARVN. Now, to prevent the enemy from slicing off the northern provinces, Westmoreland released U. S. Air Force F-100 fighter-bombers and B-57 light jet bombers to bomb and strafe alleged VC concentrations in support of South Vietnamese troops.[6]

Meanwhile, arguments for escalation continued within the Administration. McGeorge Bundy and his team of experts were in Saigon when the VC attacked Pleiku. On his way back to Washington, he wrote a memorandum for the President that began,

. . . The situation in Vietnam is deteriorating, and without new U.S. action defeat appears inevitable—probably not in a matter of weeks or perhaps even months, but within the next year or so. There is still time to turn around, but not much.

Bundy then went on to assess the situation:

. . . The stakes in Vietnam are extremely high. The American investment is very large, and American responsibility is a fact of life which is palpable in the atmosphere of Asia, and even elsewhere. The international prestige of the United States, and a substantial part of our influence are directly at risk in Vietnam. There is no way of unloading the burden on the Vietnamese themselves, and there is no way of negotiating ourselves out of Vietnam which offers any serious promise at present. . . .[7]

Arguing that a negotiated withdrawal of American forces would mean ". . . surrender on the installment plan," Bundy instead proposed a policy of ". . . graduated and continuing reprisal" against North Vietnam, as outlined in an annex. He also pointed to specific courses of action in the South, ". . . such as helping to strengthen the Vietnamese political structure and improving pacification," and concluded:

. . . There are a host of things the Vietnamese need to do better and areas in which we need to help them. The place where we can help most is in the clarity and firmness of our own commitment to what is in fact as well as in rhetoric a common cause. There is one grave weakness in our posture

6. Ibid.
7. Ibid.

in Vietnam which is within our own power to fix—and that is widespread belief that we do not have the will and force and patience and determination to take the necessary action and stay the course.

This is the overriding reason for our present recommendation of a policy of sustained reprisal. Once such a policy is put in force, we shall be able to speak in Vietnam on many topics and in many ways, with growing force and effectiveness.

One final word. At its very best the struggle in Vietnam will be long. It seems to us important that this fundamental fact be made clear and our understanding of it be made clear to our own people and to the people of Vietnam. Too often in the past we have conveyed the impression that we expect an early solution when those who live with this war know that no early solution is possible. It is our own belief that the people of the United States have the necessary will to accept and to execute a policy that rests upon the reality that there is no short cut to success in South Vietnam.[8]

The annex, apparently written by John McNaughton, proposed ". . . a policy of sustained reprisal against North Vietnam—a policy in which air and naval action against the North is justified by and related to the whole Viet Cong campaign of violence and terror in the South." The costs of such action, particularly the air aspect, would be "real," ". . . yet measured against the costs of defeat in Vietnam, this program seems cheap. And even if it fails to turn the tide—as it may—the value of the effort seems to us to exceed its cost."[9] Although the object of a reprisal policy was not to "win" an air war against Hanoi but, rather, ". . . to influence the course of the struggle in the South," the United States would have to fight an air war. Moreover, such a reprisal policy might lead to advanced air action—the Option C earlier discussed:

. . . It may even get us beyond this level with both Hanoi and Peiping, if there is Communist counteraction. We and the GVN should also be prepared for a spurt of VC terrorism, especially in urban areas, that would dwarf anything yet experienced. These are the risks of any action. They should be carefully reviewed—but we believe them to be acceptable.

The authors sought a final rationale:

. . . Action against the North is usually urged as a means of affecting the will of Hanoi to direct and support the VC. We consider this an important but longer-range purpose. The immediate and critical targets are in the South —in the minds of the South Vietnamese and in the minds of the Viet Cong cadres.

Sustained reprisal action would raise South Vietnamese morale and thereby ". . . should offer opportunity for increased American influence

8. Ibid.
9. Ibid.; see also *The Pentagon Papers, supra* (p. 423).

in pressing for a more effective government—at least in the short-run."
Simultaneously, according to CIA analyses from Saigon, the action would
lower VC morale. The argument concluded:

. . . We cannot assert that a policy of sustained reprisal will succeed in
changing the course of the contest in Vietnam. It may fail, and we cannot
estimate the odds of success with any accuracy—they may be somewhere
between 25% and 75%. What we can say is that even if it fails, the policy
will be worth it. At a minimum it will damp down the charge that we did
not do all that we could have done, and this charge will be important in
many countries, including our own. Beyond that, a reprisal policy—to the
extent that it demonstrates U.S. willingness to employ this new norm in
counterinsurgency—will set a higher price for the future upon all adventures
of guerrilla warfare, and it should therefore somewhat increase our ability
to deter such adventures. We must recognize, however, that that ability will
be gravely weakened if there is failure for any reason in Vietnam.[10]

Other Administration hawks, particularly Rostow and members of
the JCS, did not adopt such a pessimistic attitude regarding use of air
power. This school held that strategic bombing of the North would
"win" the war.[11] What it could not ignore was that strategic bombing
of the North could well lead to a nuclear war. Primarily for this reason,
President Johnson adopted a lesser course of action, ". . . a policy of
sustained reprisal" against North Vietnam. In his later words,

. . . The decision was made because it had become clear, gradually but
unmistakably, that Hanoi was moving in for the kill. Its leaders had sent
in regular North Vietnamese army units. They had directly attacked not only
our ships but our barracks, our airfields, and our men. They had asked for
and received increased aid from Moscow. They were exerting maximum
pressure on the military and political situation in South Vietnam. The best
advice available to me indicated that if we did not act against the North
Vietnamese, they soon might achieve their objectives in the South. Also our
forces in the South were increasing and I felt strongly that our men de-
served all the support and protection we could give them. . . .[12]

The Administration's justification for escalation rested fundamentally
on the aggression-from-the-North theme. The State Department now
added a diplomatic exclamation point to military plans by publishing
a fourteen-thousand-word treatise called "Aggression from the North—
The Record of North Viet-Nam's Campaign to Conquer South Vietnam." The White Paper, which William Bundy had called for in his
"escalation scenario" of May and which the State Department had been
preparing for some months, made it clear that the Johnson administra-

10. *The Pentagon Papers, supra* (pp. 423–27).
11. Johnson (*The Vantage Point*), *supra;* see also U. S. Grant Sharp, "We
Could Have Won in Vietnam Long Ago," *Reader's Digest,* May 1969.
12. Johnson (*The Vantage Point*), *supra.*

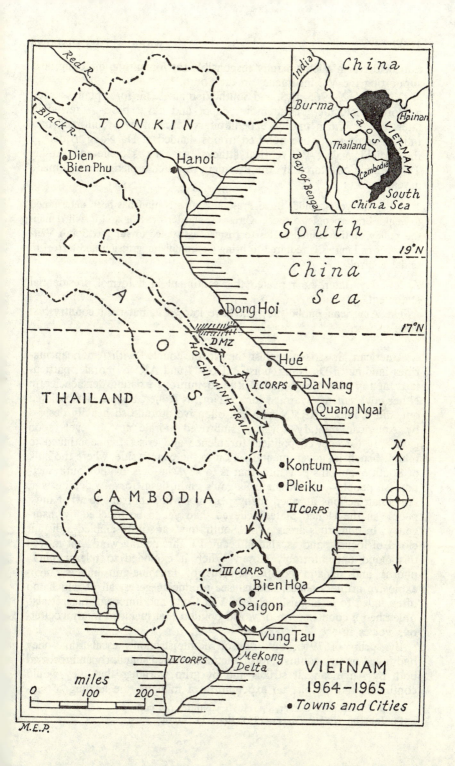

VIETNAM
1964–1965
• Towns and Cities

tion held North Vietnam fully responsible for fomenting, directing, and supporting the VC insurgency in the South.[13]

On March 2, 1965, U.S. and South Vietnamese air force planes struck a North Vietnamese ammunition depot and naval base. A few days later, an American marine expeditionary force of two reinforced battalions—some thirty-five hundred troops—landed at Da Nang to defend the airfield against VC reprisal attacks. At a news conference at his Texas ranch on March 20, the President repeated a pledge he had made a year before:

. . . For ten years, under three Presidents, this Nation has been determined to help a brave people to resist aggression and terror. It is and it will remain the policy of the United States to furnish assistance to support South Viet-Nam for as long as is required to bring Communist aggression and terrorism under control.

A few days later, he repeated this sentiment in a formal presidential statement.[14]

The American public may not have known it, but their country had gone to war.

American air strikes against the North, coupled with American marines landing in Da Nang, bolstered GVN and ARVN morale, particularly at top echelons, but did little to improve existing deficiencies in either government or armed forces. Nor, as Robert Shaplen has pointed out, did it imbue ARVN with the offensive attitude so heavily desired by American military advisers. Improved morale at top levels soon gave way to renewed political turbulence and crises that continued to inhibit beneficial governmental action in the countryside, where the bulk of South Vietnam's peasants—that is to say, the bulk of the South Vietnamese people—did not share Saigon's enthusiasm for a widening war. American actions alarmed many peasants who, contrary to what most people in the United States believed, had yet to be touched by insurgency: In numerous areas of the South, the war still resembled a distant cloud of locusts, and escalation seemed a threatening wind that moved this cloud uncomfortably closer. When it exploded to release phosphorus and napalm bombs, streams of machine-gun bullets, high-explosive artillery shells, and nausea-producing gases, all of which too often failed to distinguish between Viet Cong and innocent folks, it also unleashed a counterstorm of world opinion that included many vociferous voices in the United States.

By spring of 1965, the Johnson administration's escalation policy had failed on two counts: North Vietnam seemed singularly unimpressed both by American air strikes and by grim warnings that they would continue. And, despite an expenditure of millions, the landing of sev-

13. Ibid.; see also, Carver, op. cit.; Lacouture, op. cit.
14. Johnson (*Public Papers*—1965, Book I), supra.

eral thousand troops, and the presence of over twenty-five thousand advisers, the American Government seemed as far from accomplishing the necessary task of establishing viable government in South Vietnam as it ever had.

As one result, President Johnson faced a situation familiar in embryo to Presidents Eisenhower and Kennedy. Reduced to simplest terms, it called for the American Government to demand that the Saigon government produce or else stand (or fall) alone. It was not an easy ultimatum, but it was the one action, short of arbitrarily terminating aid and withdrawing, that might have fused dissident elements sufficiently to fight a counterinsurgency.

But where Eisenhower and Kennedy failed, so did Johnson. Instead of demanding an about-face from the Saigon government, instead of confining the war to the South and treating it for what it was, a politically motivated civil conflict, the President attempted to convert it to an international ideological conflict that had to be resolved by American arms with or without the tacit co-operation of either the South Vietnamese or American people.

Throughout March, air strikes called for by Operation Rolling Thunder mounted in intensity. Although President Johnson authorized use of napalm early in the campaign, he imposed such restrictions as confining air strikes to south of the 19th parallel, which infuriated service chiefs as well as Ambassador Taylor in Saigon. Pressures mounted during March for a sustained bombing program north of the 19th parallel. Also in March, the JCS and General Westmoreland began calling for SEATO ground forces (which would have to be predominantly American) both to hold coastal enclaves and to patrol northern and northwestern border areas. Westmoreland wanted about seventy thousand troops by June ". . . and indicated that more troops might be required thereafter if the bombing [of the North] failed to achieve results." The JCS recommended sending in three divisions, two American and one Korean, ". . . for offensive combat operations against the guerrillas." Ambassador Taylor argued against the requests,

. . . because he felt the South Vietnamese might resent the presence of so many foreign troops—upwards of 100,000 men—and also because he believed there was still no military necessity for them.[15]

McNamara tended to support the requests, but his deputy, John McNaughton, wanted them integrated into a specific course of action. By late March, McNaughton had concluded that the chief U.S. aim in South Vietnam was ". . . to avoid a humiliating defeat (to our reputation as a guarantor)":

. . . It is essential—however badly SEA [Southeast Asia] may go over the next 1–3 years—that U.S. emerge as a "good doctor." We must have kept

15. *The Pentagon Papers, supra* (p. 399).

promises, been tough, taken risks, gotten bloodied, and hurt the enemy very badly. We must avoid harmful appearances which will affect judgments by, and provide pretexts to, other nations regarding how the U.S. will behave in future cases of particular interest to those nations—regarding U.S. policy, power, resolve and competence to deal with their problems. . . .[16]

Pointing to the Administration's "trilemma" and its inability for various reasons either to achieve aims by all-out bombing of the North and large troop deployments, or to exit by negotiations, he suggested slowing the escalating air effort in order to avoid "flash points" with the Soviet Union and China, preparing phase deployments of limited numbers of troops, and opening preliminary talks immediately with the U.S.S.R., a diplomatic offensive that hopefully would lead to a resumption of the 1954 and 1962 Geneva Accords. If this plan failed, then the United States would have to escalate accordingly.

CIA chief John McCone held still other ideas. In line with Walt Rostow's thesis, McCone believed that ". . . forcing submission of the VC can only be brought about by a decision in Hanoi." A decision in Hanoi, in turn, could only result from a massive air campaign that would impose "unacceptable damage" and threaten the DRV's "vital interests." He did not object to committing ground troops, but

. . . I believe our proposed track offers great danger of simply encouraging Chinese Communists and Soviet support of the DRV and VC cause, if for no other reason than the risk for both will be minimum. I envision that the reaction of the NVN [North Vietnamese] and Chinese Communists will be to deliberately, carefully, and probably gradually, build up the Viet Cong capabilities by covert infiltration of North Vietnamese and, possibly, Chinese cadres and thus bring an ever-increasing pressure on our forces. In effect, we will find ourselves mired down in combat in the jungle in a military effort that we cannot win, and from which we will have extreme difficulty in extricating ourselves.

Therefore it is my judgment that if we are to change the mission of the ground forces, we must also change the ground rules of the strikes against North Vietnam. We must hit them harder, more frequently, and inflict greater damage. Instead of avoiding the MIG's, we must go in and take them out. A bridge here and there will not do the job. We must strike their airfields, their petroleum resources, power stations and their military compounds. This, in my opinion, must be done promptly and with minimum restraint. . . .[17]

President Johnson and his top advisers met at the White House in early April. Although VC guerrillas had just blown up the American embassy in Saigon, the President declined to take drastic overt action (other than asking Congress for a million dollars in order to build a

16. Ibid. (p. 438).
17. Ibid. (pp. 440–41).

new one), but instead set the stage further. Among other decisions, he now authorized two more marine battalions and one marine air squadron for the Da Nang enclave, and a further eighteen to twenty thousand support troops for South Vietnam. More important, he authorized marines to change from defensive to offensive operations in Da Nang area. The order embodying these decisions concluded:

. . . The actions themselves should be taken as rapidly as practicable, but in ways that should minimize any appearance of sudden changes in policy, and official statements on these troop movements will be made only with the direct approval of the Secretary of Defense, in consultation with the Secretary of State. The President's desire is that these movements and changes should be understood as being gradual and wholly consistent with existing policy.[18]

On April 7, 1965, in his famous Baltimore speech, the President set forth the Administration's position in Southeast Asia. Like Kennedy before him, he was Prometheus on the podium. He left no doubt as to the villains:

. . . The first reality is that North Viet-Nam has attacked the independent nation of South Viet-Nam. Its object is total conquest. Of course, some of the people of South Viet-Nam are participating in attack on their own government. But trained men and supplies, orders and arms, flow in a constant stream from North to South.

Hanoi, however, was not acting unilaterally: ". . . Over this war—and all Asia—is another reality: the deepening shadow of Communist China. The rulers in Hanoi are urged on by Peiping. . . . The contest in Viet-Nam is part of a wider pattern of aggressive purposes."

As for American presence in South Vietnam:

. . . We are there because we have a promise to keep. Since 1954 every American President has offered support to the people of South Viet-Nam. We have helped to build, and we have helped to defend. Thus, over many years, we have made a national pledge to help South Viet-Nam defend its independence.

And I intend to keep that promise.

To dishonor that pledge, to abandon this small and brave nation to its enemies, and to the terror that must follow, would be an unforgivable wrong. We are also there to strengthen world order. Around the globe, from Berlin to Thailand, are people whose well-being rests in part on the belief that they can count on us if they are attacked. To leave Viet-Nam to its fate would shake the confidence of all these people in the value of an American commitment and in the value of America's word. The result would be increased unrest and instability, and even wider war. We are also there because there are great stakes in the balance. Let no one think for a moment that

18. Ibid. (pp. 442–43); see also Johnson (*The Vantage Point*), *supra*.

retreat from Viet-Nam would bring an end to conflict. The battle would be renewed in one country and then another. The central lesson of our time is that the appetite of aggression is never satisfied. To withdraw from one battlefield means only to prepare for the next. We must say in Southeast Asia—as we did in Europe—in the words of the Bible: "Hitherto shalt thou come, but no further."

What did the United States wish to accomplish?

. . . Our objective is the independence of South Viet-Nam and its freedom from attack. We want nothing for ourselves—only that the people of South Viet-Nam be allowed to guide their own country in their own way. We will do everything necessary to reach that objective, and we will do only what is absolutely necessary. . . .

Increased American participation in the war did not signify a change in purpose but, rather,

. . . a change in what we believe that purpose requires.
We do this in order to slow down aggression.
We do this to increase the confidence of the brave people of South Viet-Nam who have bravely borne this brutal battle for so many years with so many casualties.
And we do this to convince the leaders of North Viet-Nam—and all who seek to share their conquest—of a simple fact:
We will not be defeated.
We will not grow tired.
We will not withdraw, either openly or under the cloak of a meaningless agreement. . . .

God was clearly on the side of the big airplanes:

. . . I wish it were possible to convince others with words of what we now find it necessary to say with guns and planes: armed hostility is futile—our resources are equal to any challenge—because we fight for values and we fight for principle, rather than territory or colonies, our patience and our determination are unending. . . .

Having applied the stick, the President offered the carrot that General de Gaulle had recommended to President Kennedy four years earlier. The United States had been and remained ready ". . . for unconditional discussions" in order to bring an end to the fighting. If fighting stopped, he would ask Congress to fund a billion-dollar investment program in Southeast Asia that would bring a new and better life to the peoples of Southeast Asia, including those of North Vietnam.[19]

19. Johnson (*Public Papers*—1965, Book I), *supra;* see also his statement to the press, "Tragedy, Disappointment, and Progress" in Vietnam, April 17, 1965.

If President Johnson expected his words to propel Ho Chi Minh to the conference table, he was quickly disappointed. Although, at one time, the United States might have influenced the Communist leader to conciliatory action, since 1950 the U.S.A. had emerged as archenemy in northern eyes. Even had Ho been inclined to deal with capitalist Satan, forces around him—Hanoi's hawks—would probably have been able to prevent it.

It is doubtful if Ho or any of his more moderate colleagues entertained such a desire, particularly since President Johnson's offer meant virtual capitulation, with attendant destruction of the NLF in the South. Someday we may learn Hanoi's estimate of the situation at this time. Considering the factors at work, it was probably neither unanimous nor inflexible. Like Japan prior to World War II, North Vietnam's high command included leaders who could not envisage American industrial and military might and whose arrogance derived from this ignorance was compounded by Viet Minh victory over France. Hanoi was probably impressed by American refusal to intervene militarily at Dien Bien Phu, and continued to be impressed by divisive voices in the 1960s sounding with greater frequency and volume from within the United States and from around the world. Finally, a number of Ho's colleagues, probably all of them, also felt cheated by results of the Geneva Conference. They had not relinquished the notion of a unified Vietnam, and, in one way or another, would continue to pursue that goal.[20]

That did not mean that they stood ready to rush army divisions to the South. Thanks to Pentagon and State Department fulminations, we tend to forget that, at this time, Hanoi's investment in the southern rebellion was minimal. Hanoi had contributed by training Southerners who had come North and who returned South to work up the insurgency. During 1964, Hanoi began infiltrating *northern* cadres, at the most probably twenty-five hundred. These people joined an extremely viable organization that was Communist-dominated in part by means of the PRP, but one that was largely self-supporting. For years, the NLF had controlled large areas of the South; they collected taxes, sold war bonds, extorted money, captured arms, ammunition, medical supplies, and other material from ARVN—all this to a remarkable degree, described in detail by Douglas Pike.[21] Pike estimated that the 1964 NLF budget was $7.5 million with Hanoi contributing about 20 per cent, a minimum investment that kept the pot of rebellion not only boiling but daily growing more savory.

In this respect, President Johnson was aiming at the wrong target. As Jean Lacouture has pointed out, not only was the NLF-PRP carrying on the war, but Hanoi would have had its hands full in persuading the southern organization to stop fighting. Put another way: successful ne-

20. Zagoria, op. cit., discusses these various factors in detail.
21. Pike, op. cit. (Chapter 16); see also Robert J. O'Neill, *Vietnam Task* (Melbourne: Cassell Australia, 1968).

gotiations with the NLF-PRP could have stopped the war. At this point, Hanoi was still conforming to standard Communist revolutionary doctrine as determined by both Moscow and Peking, whose leaders believed that a rebellion had to come from within although it could be helped from without. We have seen this principle at work in Yugoslavia, Greece, Indonesia, the Philippines, and Malaya. It is a wait-and-see policy, and Communists have no monopoly on it: Woodrow Wilson practiced it during the Mexican revolution.

Perhaps because it is so simple, Western experts seem unable to understand it. Douglas Pike, for instance, wrote:

. . . It is the thesis of this book that the DRV was indeed the godfather of the NLF, that its support over the years was developmental, from lesser to greater, that until mid-1964 this aid was largely confined to two areas— doctrinal know-how and leadership personnel—and after mid-1964 it supplied antiaircraft weapons and certain other types of military hardware not available through capture, but at all times from 1960 on *it stood ready to help the NLF in any way that was absolutely necessary.*[22]

But what Pike fails to add, and what Rostow and various hawks in Washington, Honolulu, and Saigon failed to heed, was that Hanoi's help remained contingent on satisfactory progress of the southern insurgency. This is the essence of protracted revolutionary warfare; it is a political axiom derived from a tactical tenet: If an insurgency fails, back off, wait, and try again. This is very important to understand, for it means that the fulcrum of insurgency is interior, not exterior.

By spring of 1965, Hanoi's commitment to the southern insurgency was remarkably slight and for good reason. Years of toil had produced a formidable southern guerrilla force. In Douglas Pike's words:

. . . The ARVN reported in early 1965 that the NLF army consisted of some 47 battalions, which it said were organized on paper into five regiments. The battalion was planned for 500 men but most had fewer, some as few as 250 men; the NLF Main Force company averaged about 85 men. There were an estimated 94 such companies as part of the 47 battalions. Of the total Main Force units in South Vietnam, approximately one third was in the ARVN's First and Second Corps areas and two thirds in the Third and Fourth Corps areas.

A characteristic of a guerrilla war is that the government side never knows how many of the enemy it faces—every cyclo driver, every Vietnamese who passes in the street could be a guerrilla—but by early 1965 at least 55,000 and perhaps as many as 80,000 "hard hats" were fighting in South Vietnam. Some of them had been fighting for more than a decade and were perhaps the toughest, most experienced guerrilla fighters to be found anywhere on earth. . . .[23]

22. Pike, op. cit. (Chapter 16).
23. Ibid. Chapter 13 offers excellent detail on Viet Cong organization and tactics.

Considering the growth of this force from some five thousand in 1959, Hanoi would have been foolish to interrupt local dynamics, the more so because, as Hanoi waited, the insurgency continued to prosper. Although Diem's demise proved inconvenient in some ways—his government was so corrupt and ineffectual as to prosper the NLF-PRP-Hanoi cause—the resultant fragmentation of Saigon government seemed worthy of exploitation and resulted in a 1964 decision to concentrate on a military solution. This did not mean seriously involving North Vietnam's fourteen regular infantry divisions (though this army might have been tempted into overt invasion had the American military acted wisely). It was to be a southern-based military solution, as it had to be if only some twenty-five hundred Northerners came South in all of 1964.

In 1965, Hanoi infiltrated an estimated eleven thousand Northerners, but this figure must be qualified: Considering NLF-PRP strength, it was not impressive; moreover, Administration testimony is contradictory and confusing. Dean Rusk, in April 1965, told the Senate Foreign Relations Committee that a North Vietnamese division, the 325th, had moved across the border ". . . as a division" between November 1964 and January 1965[24]—a presence repeatedly referred to by Lyndon Johnson in his memoirs as justification for subsequent attacks against the North.[25]

But Rusk and Johnson apparently were not using William Bundy's intelligence sources, because, on August 15, 1967, in "a major policy address," he told a meeting of the National Student Association that

. . . Multiple and conclusive evidence which became available from spring 1965 onwards seems to me to refute these contentions. As has been repeatedly made public over the past two years, we know that one North Vietnamese regiment entered South Vietnam by December 1964, and we know that several other regiments entered in the spring of 1965 on timetables of infiltration that can only have reflected command decisions taken in Hanoi prior to the beginning of the bombing.

From the standpoint of the basis for US decisions, this evidence simply reinforces the February picture that Hanoi was moving for the kill. Native North Vietnamese alone or in regular units, were in themselves no more and no less aggressive than the earlier native South Vietnamese who had gone north and become North Vietnamese nationals. The point is that Hanoi, as we suspected then and later proved, had taken major steps to raise the level of the war before the bombing began.[26]

According to Johnson and Rusk, rather than suspecting this presence, the Administration *knew* of it, nor do the figures cited jibe with those claimed by Johnson and Rusk. Now enter Westmoreland, who told an

24. William R. Corson, *The Betrayal* (New York: W. W. Norton, 1968); see also U. S. Senate, *The Vietnam Hearings* (New York: Vintage Books, 1966).
25. Johnson (*The Vantage Point*), *supra*.
26. William Bundy, op. cit.

interviewer, in November 1966, that ". . . in 1965 he [the enemy] began to move regular North Vietnamese Army units into Vietnam through Laos. . . ."[27]—but Rusk said that the enemy began to do this in 1964! Now enter McNamara, who apparently was relying on still other intelligence sources, for, in the same month that Rusk testified before the Senate Foreign Relations Committee, that is, April 1965, McNamara revealed that

. . . it was not until the end of March [1965]—four weeks after the systematic bombing of North Vietnam was initiated and three weeks after the Marines had landed—that intelligence confirmed the presence of North Vietnamese troops in South Vietnam. Moreover, McNamara indicated, the unit was only one battalion of 400 to 500 men from the North Vietnamese Army's 325th Division. Tacitly it was noted that the 325th Division was still in North Vietnam.[28]

By August 1965, according to General Wheeler, chairman of the Joint Chiefs of Staff, approximately fourteen hundred North Vietnamese troops were serving in the South (as opposed to seventy-five thousand American troops); by year's end, North Vietnamese troops numbered fourteen thousand, U.S. troops two hundred thousand![29]

President Johnson's speech aroused more consternation in South Vietnam than in the North. In Saigon, the Quat government hastened to assure Hanoi that while the United States may have been ready ". . . for unconditional discussions," the GVN would not even consider a cease-fire until certain preliminaries were carried out, namely the ". . . previous withdrawal of the Viet Cong armed units and political cadres."[30]

American reinforcements, which followed the President's reassuring speech, once again seemed to breathe new life into the Saigon government and ARVN. After blunting the Viet Cong's winter offensives, ARVN had moved against the enemy in the Mekong Delta area, the central coastal areas, and the north; government troops, in some actions, had killed impressive numbers of guerrillas and, in some areas, had opened major roads.

In April, another three thousand American marines reached the Da Nang area, to build the commitment to some eight thousand men supported by artillery, armor, aircraft, and naval gunfire. Marine patrols were now fanning out from Da Nang, the first steps in contesting Viet Cong control of that area. After a necessary experimental period, as Ambassador Taylor explained to Premier Quat, marine units could fulfill a strike role ". . . as a reserve in support of ARVN operations"

27. *U. S. News and World Report,* November 28, 1966.
28. Corson, op. cit.
29. Ibid.
30. Kahin and Lewis, op. cit.

in the area.[31] McNamara and the JCS subsequently persuaded President Johnson to enlarge the ground role by committing an American airborne brigade to the Bien Hoa-Vung Tau areas, outside of Saigon, ". . . to secure vital U.S. installations."[32]

Despite these reinforcements, the situation in South Vietnam remained fragile in the extreme. As usual when ARVN forces made substantial gains, they failed to exploit them by consolidating operational areas. Instead, they withdrew to defensive positions.

If the Viet Cong had failed to gain tactical objectives and divide South Vietnam, it did not mean that they were defeated. Instead, in the best guerrilla tradition, and as they had done repeatedly in fighting the French and also in 1962 following the first impressive American reinforcement, they withdrew to the hills, fortified villages, licked wounds, and reorganized units with replacements and supply obtained locally and from the North. Fresh American efforts once again had caused them to think twice about the war. An ominous portent of their thinking emerged in a CIA report of late April, which identified a regiment of the North Vietnamese army (PAVN) in the province of Kontum, in northeastern South Vietnam.[33]

Though inducing a certain optimism in the American camp, the lull in the fighting, in general, was regarded as temporary. Most concerned principals now agreed that bombing the North was not going to bring "victory" (but most agreed that it should nonetheless be intensified). At a high-level meeting in Honolulu on April 20, Assistant Secretary of Defense John McNaughton noted general agreement that the decision would be gained in the South:

. . . Progress in the South would be slow, and great care should be taken to avoid dramatic defeat. The current lull in Vietcong activity was merely the quiet before a storm.

The victory strategy was to "break the will of the D.R.V./VC by denying them victory."

Impotence would lead eventually to a political solution.[34]

The aggressive school of tactical thought dominated the Honolulu meeting. Members of the JCS, Westmoreland, and other hawks continued to argue for aggressive tactics to bring the war home to the enemy. They accordingly asked for more troops from the United States and other countries. Ambassador Taylor, according to the Pentagon study, although not opposed to an American troop build-up, preferred a go-slow escalation based on enclaves until the American military machine had satisfactorily identified the tactical problem and adapted accordingly.

31. *The Pentagon Papers, supra* (p. 402).
32. Ibid. (p. 403).
33. Ibid. (p. 409); statements of Administration officials aside, this would appear to be the first major PAVN unit in the South.
34. Ibid. (p. 407); see also Johnson (*The Vantage Point*), *supra*.

Something of his attitude was revealed in a cable to McGeorge Bundy shortly before the Honolulu conference, when Taylor ". . . protested the 'hasty and ill-conceived' proposals for the deployment of more forces with which he was being flooded" and called for ". . . a clarification of our purposes and objectives."[35]

The Honolulu conference ended in a clear victory for the Pentagon, which recommended a 100 per cent increase in American troop strength, raising the total from about forty thousand to over eighty thousand; in addition, another seventeen battalions, eleven American and six South Korean, could be deployed at a later stage. The whole package, according to the JCS, was

. . . to bolster GVN forces during their continued counter-insurgency combat operations in coordination with the RVNAF, and prepare for the later introduction of an airmobile division to the central plateau, the remainder of the third M.E.F. [the Third Marine Expeditionary Force] to the Da Nang area, and the remainder of a ROK [Korean] division to Quangngai.[36]

This deployment was underway when the Viet Cong struck in early May, a regimental attack that captured and briefly held a provincial capital with heavy losses to government forces.

Although the attack caused considerable alarm in Saigon and the Pentagon, it did not signal a new Viet Cong offensive, in Administration minds. The President was still hopeful that extraneous action would force the North to call off the war. On May 10, he proposed a bombing halt of the North to coincide with Buddha's birthday. A paragraph in a message sent to Ambassador Taylor offers an interesting insight into presidential thinking at this stage:

. . . You should understand that my purpose in this plan is to begin to clear a path either toward restoration of peace or toward increased military action, depending upon the reaction of the Communists. We have amply demonstrated our determination and our commitment in the last two months, and I now wish to gain some flexibility.[37]

Three days later, the President suspended air strikes, a four-day halt that brought no response from Moscow, Hanoi, or Peiping. Although he resumed Operation Rolling Thunder, he refused to authorize strikes in the vicinity of Hanoi. His obdurate attitude infuriated the JCS, just as his cryptic statement that ". . . a military victory is impossible" alarmed one of the more bellicose of his civil advisers, Walt Rostow. Rostow informed Rusk in late May that there was no reason the U.S.A. could not win a clear victory in South Vietnam. In Rostow's mind,

35. *The Pentagon Papers, supra* (pp. 406–7, 443–46).
36. Ibid. (p. 408).
37. Ibid. (pp. 446–47).

Hanoi, which in February had hoped to obtain victory through political collapse and subsequent coalition government in Saigon, was now

. . . staring at quite clear-cut defeat, with the rising U.S. strength and GVN morale in the South and rising costs in the North. That readjustment in prospects is painful; and they won't in my view, accept its consequences unless they are convinced time has ceased to be their friend, despite the full use of their assets on the ground in South Viet-Nam, in political warfare around the world, and in diplomacy.[38]

While Rostow was writing this remarkable prognosis, the situation in South Vietnam was deteriorating at an alarming pace. In late May, VC guerrillas ambushed an ARVN battalion to open an action that ". . . completely decimated" two ARVN battalions. In June, two VC regiments attacked an ARVN outpost and then ambushed reinforcements. Around Da Nang, U. S. Marine Corps patrols had encountered increasing numbers of enemy, and in April and May suffered about two hundred casualties. Johnson's decision to widen the bombing effort in the North by way of reprisal brought still another ominous reaction, when Britain's Prime Minister Harold Wilson "dissociated" his country from it.[39]

In Saigon, the political situation remained as confused and torn as ever. Renewed fighting between Buddhist and Catholic factions led to the generals' ousting Premier Quat in early June. In place of civil government appeared a National Leadership Committee headed by forty-two-year-old General Nguyen Van Thieu. The ten-man committee included most of the familiar military faces, among them thirty-five-year-old Nguyen Cao Ky, the airman who now became premier. Although Ky imposed a number of dictatorial measures including summary trial and execution of terrorists, black marketeers, speculators, and corrupt officials, government remained weak and ineffective.[40]

With a Viet Cong offensive obviously developing, General Westmoreland reported to the JCS, via CINCPAC, on June 7:

. . . In pressing their campaign, the Viet-Cong are capable of mounting regimental-size operations in all four ARVN corps areas, and at least battalion-sized attack in virtually all provinces. . . .

ARVN forces on the other hand are already experiencing difficulty in coping with this increased VC capability. Desertion rates are inordinately high. Battle losses have been higher than expected; in fact, four ARVN battalions have been rendered ineffective by VC action in the I and II Corps zones. . . .

38. Ibid. (p. 448); see also Roswell W. Gilpatric, "Vietnam and World War III," New York *Times,* May 30, 1965. Gilpatric's recital of American strengths and weaknesses was tempered only by the possibility that the American people would not want to fight a prolonged war.
39. *The Pentagon Papers, supra* (pp. 448–49).
40. Shaplen (*The Lost Revolution*), *supra.*

Force ratios on which earlier estimates had been made were thus upset, Westmoreland continued. His solution was to become a MACV theme song:

. . . I see no course of action open to us except to reinforce our efforts in SVN with additional U.S. or third country forces as rapidly as is practical during the critical weeks ahead.[41]

Westmoreland now requested a whopping increase in outside troop strength, to a total of forty-four battalions. Admiral Sharp (CINC-PAC) endorsed the request with approval and noted: ". . . We will lose by staying in enclaves defending coastal areas." The JCS were not antagonistic to the request but wanted to know ". . . where Westmoreland intended to put this force in Vietnam." Westmoreland's reply, according to a Pentagon analyst,

. . . was extremely important, for in it [he] spelled out the concept of keeping U.S. forces away from the people. The search and destroy strategy for U.S. and third country forces which continues to this day [1967–68] and the primary focus of RVNAF (ARVN) on pacification both stem from that concept. In addition, Westmoreland made a big pitch in this cable for a free hand to maneuver the troops around inside the country.[42]

Westmoreland's request aroused considerable controversy inside the government. At the same time, however, Johnson's decision to allow American troops to indulge in combat operations had slowly leaked to the public, segments of which were already uneasy by a supplementary appropriation of $700 million authorized by Congress in early May ". . . for military needs in Viet-Nam." Mounting intensity of fighting due to the Viet Cong's monsoonal offensive now caused some critical questioning of Administration policy. In mid-June, Senator J. W. Fulbright addressed his fellow senators:

. . . It is clear to all reasonable Americans that a complete military victory in Viet-Nam, though theoretically attainable, can in fact be attained only at a cost far exceeding the requirements of our interest and our honor. It is equally clear that the unconditional withdrawal of American support from South Viet-Nam would have disastrous consequences. . . . Our policy therefore has been—and should remain—one of the determination to end the war at the earliest possible time by a negotiated settlement involving major concessions by both sides.

The senator went on to echo the President's speech at Johns Hopkins:

. . . I am opposed to an unconditional American withdrawal from South Viet-Nam because such action would betray our obligation to people we

41. *The Pentagon Papers, supra* (pp. 409–10); see also Johnson (*The Vantage Point*), *supra*.
42. *The Pentagon Papers, supra* (p. 413).

have promised to defend, because it would weaken or destroy the credibility of American guarantees to other countries, and because such a withdrawal would encourage the view in Peiping and elsewhere that guerrilla wars supported from outside are a relatively safe and inexpensive way of expanding Communist power.

However, he saw a great danger in further escalation of the war, because

. . . the bombing thus far of North Viet-Nam has failed to weaken the military capacity of the Viet-Cong in any visible way; because escalation would invite the intervention—or infiltration—on a large scale of great numbers of North Vietnamese troops; because this in turn would probably draw the United States into a bloody and protracted jungle war in which the strategic advantages would be with the other side; and, finally, because the only available alternative to such a land war would then be the further expansion of the air war to such an extent as to invite either massive Chinese military intervention in many vulnerable areas in Southeast Asia or general nuclear war.

In view of the then-current Viet Cong offensive and advantages derived by them from the monsoonal season, Fulbright warned of American setbacks:

. . . As the ground war expands and as American involvement and American casualties increase, there will be mounting pressure for expansion of the war.

Indeed, such pressures already existed, and the President must continue to ignore them in favor of "restraint and patience." After reviewing American errors, the senator noted recent American desire for settlement, as opposed to continuing North Vietnamese and Chinese intransigence, and offered two goals:

. . . First we must sustain the South Vietnamese Army so as to persuade the Communists that Saigon cannot be crushed and that the United States will not be driven from South Viet-Nam by force; second, we must continue to offer the Communists a reasonable and attractive alternative to military victory. For the time being it seems likely that the focus of our efforts will have to be on persuading the Communists that they cannot win a complete military victory. . . .[43]

In other words, once the monsoonal offensive ended and ARVN remained intact, the Communist powers would presumably see the error of their ways and be more inclined to negotiate.

Fulbright's tolerance was shared neither by the JCS nor by Westmoreland, whose hand was steadily being reinforced by the deteriorating situation, political and military, in South Vietnam. In May, President

43. Raskin and Fall, op. cit.

Johnson authorized Westmoreland ". . . to use his forces in combat support if it became necessary to assist a Vietnamese unit in serious trouble." In June, the President authorized the general to use his forces "independently" of South Vietnamese forces. At the end of June, Westmoreland committed an airborne brigade to a search-and-destroy operation in conjunction with an ARVN battalion and an Australian battalion northwest of Saigon, in War Zone D. Meanwhile, General Wheeler, chairman of the JCS, asked Westmoreland ". . . if the 44 battalions were enough to convince the enemy forces that they could not win." According to the Pentagon study, Westmoreland replied

. . . that there was no evidence the VC/DRV would alter their plans regardless of what the U.S. did in the next six months.

The 44-battalion force should, however, establish a favorable balance of power by the end of the year. If the U.S. was to seize the initiative from the enemy, then further forces would be required into 1966 and beyond. . . .[44]

A few days later, the JCS approved a planned deployment of nearly two hundred thousand American troops in South Vietnam. In mid-July, impressed by a new and optimistic report from McNamara, President Johnson authorized this build-up and also gave Westmoreland authority to commit American troops to combat at his discretion.[45]

Although these measures remained secret, at least for the moment, they caused considerable consternation within the Administration. On July 1, Under Secretary of State George Ball submitted a lengthy memorandum to President Johnson. Ball bluntly opened:

. . . The South Vietnamese are losing the war to the Viet Cong. No one can assure you that we can beat the Viet Cong or even force them to the conference table on our terms, no matter how many hundred thousand *white, foreign* (U.S.) troops we deploy.

No one has demonstrated that a white ground force of whatever size can win a guerrilla war—which is at the same time a civil war between Asians— in jungle terrain in the midst of a population that refuses cooperation to

44. *The Pentagon Papers, supra* (pp. 413–14).
45. Johnson (*The Vantage Point*), *supra*. McNamara, according to the President, reported a seriously deteriorating situation that could be met with one of three courses of action: cut losses and withdraw under the best conditions that could be arranged; continue at present level; expand promptly and substantially. McNamara recommended the third course. ". . . With the force that he and the others were proposing, McNamara was convinced that the South Vietnamese and allied armies could reverse the downward trend and move to the offensive. He said that the military commanders planned to locate, engage, and destroy the North Vietnamese and Viet Cong main-force units. At the same time, they believed we should press our anti-infiltration campaign by hitting enemy supply lines by air and on the sea. We would also carry the air war more intensively into Viet Cong base areas in the South . . ."; see also Johnson (*Public Papers*—1965, Book I), "The President's News Conference of July 13, 1965."

the white forces (and the South Vietnamese) and thus provides a great intelligence advantage to the other side. . . .

The President, Ball stated, had one question to decide:

. . . Should we limit our liabilities in South Vietnam and try to find a way out with minimal long-term costs?

The alternative—no matter what we may wish it to be—is almost certainly a protracted war involving an open-ended commitment of U.S. forces, mounting U.S. casualties, no assurance of a satisfactory solution, and a serious danger of escalation at the end of the road.

The President, Ball believed, had to decide on the answer now:

. . . So long as our forces are restricted to advising and assisting the South Vietnamese, the struggle will remain a civil war between Asian peoples. Once we deploy substantial numbers of troops in combat it will become a war between the U.S. and a large part of the population of South Vietnam, organized and directed from North Vietnam and backed by the resources of both Moscow and Peiping.

The decision you face now, therefore, is crucial. Once large numbers of U.S. troops are committed to direct combat, they will begin to take heavy casualties in a war they are ill-equipped to fight in a non-cooperative if not downright hostile countryside.

Once we suffer large casualties, we will have started a well-nigh irreversible process. Our involvement will be so great that we cannot—without national humiliation—stop short of achieving our complete objectives. *Of the two possibilities I think humiliation would be more likely than the achievement of our objectives—even after we have paid terrible costs.*

Ball then went on to examine the costs of a compromise solution ". . . in terms of our relations with the countries in the area of South Vietnam, the credibility of our commitments, and our prestige around the world":

. . . In my judgment, if we act before we commit substantial U.S. troops to combat in South Vietnam we can, by accepting some short-term costs, avoid what may well be a long-term catastrophe. I believe we tended grossly to exaggerate the costs involved in a compromise settlement. . . .

Ball did not recommend a unilateral withdrawal from South Vietnam. Instead, he proposed a total troop commitment of seventy-two thousand men to support restricted combat operations; he also agreed to the present bombing program. Simultaneously, he called for a diplomatic offensive by unilateral approach to Hanoi, the general idea being that Johnson could pressure the Saigon government and Ho the NLF to the conference table to hammer out ". . . a multi-national agreement guaranteed by the U.S., the Soviet Union and possibly other parties, and providing for an international mechanism to supervise its execution."[46]

46. *The Pentagon Papers, supra* (pp. 449–54).

Ball next examined short-term costs of a compromise solution. Astute diplomacy could hold these to a minimum. The United States had good allies in Southeast Asia and would continue to support them. If South Vietnam fell to Communist control, Burma, Cambodia, and Indonesia would probably enter the Eastern orbit—but they were scarcely in the Western orbit at this time. Other nations could be expected to hold, with proper backing from the U.S.A. As for Thailand: ". . . Providing we are willing to make the effort, Thailand can be a foundation of rock and not a bed of sand in which to base our political/military commitment to Southeast Asia."

As for U.S. world-wide credibility: With the possible exception of West Germany,

. . . In my observation, the principal anxiety of our NATO allies is that we have become too preoccupied with an area which seems to them an irrelevance and may be tempted in neglect to our NATO responsibilities. Moreover, they have a vested interest in an easier relationship between Washington and Moscow. By and large, therefore, they will be inclined to regard a compromise solution in South Vietnam more as new evidence of American maturity and judgment than of American loss of face. . . . On balance, I believe we would more seriously undermine the effectiveness of our world leadership by continuing the war and deepening our involvement than by pursuing a carefully plotted course toward a compromise solution. In spite of the number of powers that have—in response to our pleading—given verbal support from feeling of loyalty and dependence, we cannot ignore the fact that the war is vastly unpopular and that our role in it is perceptively eroding the respect and confidence with which other nations regard us. We have not persuaded either our friends or allies that our further involvement is essential to the defense of freedom in the cold war. . . .[47]

We do not know how much credence the President invested in this memorandum, which outlined a bold, imaginative, and courageous policy that had been needed since 1954. Ball further dissented from Administration thinking during a late-July session with Johnson.[48] At Camp Aspen a few days later, Johnson also found his close adviser Clark Clifford ". . . in a reflective and pessimistic mood":

". . . I don't believe we can win in South Vietnam," he said. "If we send in 100,000 more men, the North Vietnamese will meet us. If North Vietnam runs out of men, the Chinese will send in volunteers. Russia and China don't intend for us to win the war."

He urged that in the coming months we quietly probe possibilities with other countries for some way to get out honorably. "I can't see anything but catastrophe for my country," he said.[49]

47. Ibid.
48. Johnson (*The Vantage Point*), *supra.*
49. Ibid.

Senator Mike Mansfield, who had dissented from Johnson's February decision to begin bombing North Vietnam, also expressed ". . . serious doubt and opposition" to the present course.[50]

Refined and properly applied, this dissentient thinking, echoed variously by influential citizens throughout the country, might have led to a solution that would have given Lyndon Johnson that place in American history he so obtrusively desired. Instead, he rejected compromise in favor of a "win" strategy. At the end of July, at a press conference, he said: ". . . The lesson of history dictated that the U.S. commit its strength to resist aggression in South Vietnam."

. . . I have asked the commanding general, General Westmoreland, what more he needs to meet this mounting aggression. He has told me. We will meet his needs.

I have today ordered to Vietnam the Air Mobile Division and certain other forces which will raise our fighting strength from 75,000 to 125,000 men almost immediately. Additional forces will be needed later, and they will be sent as requested. . . .

Having declared a collision course with disaster, the President still thought it was necessary to deceive the American public. A reporter asked,

. . . Mr. President, does the fact that you are sending additional forces to Vietnam imply any change in the existing policy of relying mainly on the South Vietnamese to carry out offensive operations and using American forces to guard American installations and to act as an emergency back-up?

At a time when an American airborne brigade had already sharply engaged the Viet Cong in a search-and-destroy mission, at a time when marines were seeking out Viet Cong and were planning a major search-and-clear operation, at a time when McNamara, Westmoreland, and the JCS were flexing military muscles to "come to grips" with the enemy[51]—at this time, the President of the United States replied:

. . . It does not imply any change in policy whatever. It does not imply change of objective.[52]

50. Ibid.
51. *The Pentagon Papers, supra* (pp. 457–58).
52. Johnson (*Public Papers*—1965), *supra,* "The President's News Conference of July 28, 1965."

Chapter 82

The fighting escalates • Viet Cong setbacks • American and ARVN gains • The air war • Westmoreland's strategy • Search-and-destroy tactics • The American build-up • Westmoreland's four wars • The "other war" • American arms and equipment • Army operations in the central highlands • Westmoreland's "spoiling" tactics • Operation Crazy Horse • Marine operations in I Corps area • Walt's pacification program • PAVN crosses the DMZ: Operation Hastings, Operation Prairie • Operations in III Corps area • The air war escalates • The naval war • The "other war": the Honolulu conference • Ky's Revolutionary Development program • Elections in the South • The Manila conference • General allied optimism

ONCE AGAIN, American infusion of strength steadied the fibrillating heart of South Vietnam's Government and army. Although, in vicious fighting in summer and autumn of 1965, the Viet Cong nowhere accomplished its major objective of permanently dividing the country, its battalions and regiments, increasingly reinforced by PAVN units from the North, cut road and rail communications, attacked ARVN outposts almost at will, ambushed ARVN forces sent to relieve beleaguered garrisons, and continued a campaign of sabotage and terror against South Vietnamese and American installations and personnel.

But ARVN units, in some cases supported by American forces, also generally fought hard, and new American units showed every willingness to fight.[1] A sort of monsoonal counteroffensive developed. In August, American marines based on Da Nang mounted Operation Starlight, a

1. William G. Leftwich, "Decision at Duc Co," *Marine Corps Gazette*, February 1967; Shaplen (*The Lost Revolution*), *supra;* Robert Thompson, *No Exit from Vietnam* (London: Chatto & Windus, 1969).

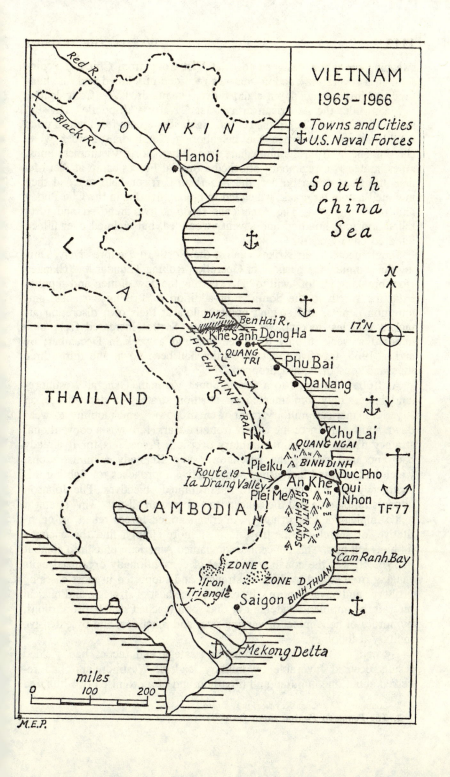

sweeping operation designed to evict Viet Cong from Chu Lai Peninsula. In a several-day action, marines recorded fifty killed and one hundred and fifty wounded, but claimed over five hundred Viet Cong deaths.

Meanwhile, the American army's 1st Cavalry (Airmobile) Division set up shop at An Khe, in the central highlands—a base from which units would attempt to screen the neighboring Cambodian border while clearing enemy from the immediate area. When North Vietnamese units, an estimated two regiments, attacked a Special Forces camp at Plei Me, near the Cambodian border, the American garrison held out and then mounted a counterattack, which led to bloody fighting in the Chu Phong and Ia Drang area. The Americans recorded two hundred and forty killed and four hundred and seventy wounded, but claimed over fifteen hundred enemy deaths.[2]

Simultaneously, air strikes against the North rose impressively. During the summer, the purpose of Operation Rolling Thunder had changed from breaking Hanoi's will to ". . . cutting the flow of men and supplies from the North to the South."[3] In addition to striking barracks, ammunition depots, and staging points, pilots at their own discretion attacked vehicles, locomotives, and barges. Sorties increased from nine hundred a week in July to fifteen hundred a week in December; by end of 1965, fifty-five thousand sorties had been flown and thirty-three thousand tons of bombs dropped.

As troops continued to arrive in South Vietnam, General Westmoreland increasingly implemented an attrition strategy—a dependence on superior American military manpower, firepower, and mobility to wear down and finally force the enemy from the war. Here was a conventional strategy designed to gain a military decision. Precedents for it already had appeared during the Eisenhower and Kennedy administrations, which had adopted increasingly quantitative approaches for fighting this insurgency but had managed to retain limited objectives. The Johnson administration enlarged the concept to embrace an all-out "win" strategy.

To implement this strategy, American armed forces relied on quantitative, or search-and-destroy, tactics: more simply, find the enemy—fix him—kill him. This concept accompanied American units into combat in 1965. It was the conventional goal of conventionally organized units ranging from squad to division strength and supported in most cases by artillery (and naval gunfire), by an awesome host of strategic and tactical aircraft, by an inland-waters navy that soon reached sizable proportions, by hordes of helicopters of varying sizes and functions, and by extensive military technology.

By end of 1965, Westmoreland's strategy and tactics had yielded results deemed favorable by military leaders. Westmoreland had received about one hundred and fifty thousand of a promised two hundred

2. Shaplen (*The Lost Revolution*), *supra.*
3. *The Pentagon Papers, supra* (p. 468).

thousand troops. New units were arriving daily, as were tons of equipment and supply needed to support them. Energetic commanders were slowly sorting out initial logistics confusion while simultaneously pushing the enemy on several fronts. American commands were working around the clock. American planes were striking enemy units in North and South. American patrols were seeking contacts, and fighting when possible. A pervasive air of aggression was pushing aside stale air of defeatism. A RAND report based on interviews of refugees also read favorably:

. . . We find that villagers increasingly tend to ask the Viet Cong unit to leave, refuse to sell them rice, refuse to allow them to sleep in their houses. In some cases, the villagers simply leave the area when the Viet Cong unit arrives. Criticism of irresponsible and provocative actions on the part of the guerrillas is fairly widespread, not only among the villagers but also among defectors from hard-core (Communist) units. Despite Viet Cong propaganda, there is no belief that the Vietnamese government or the Americans are deliberately bombing harmless villages. The villagers more often take the view that the attacks are part of the unavoidable existence of war. . . .[4]

It was just as well the villagers felt that way, because, whether they liked it or not, war was coming to them. That winter in South Vietnam, even the most cynical observer had to admit that the Americans were obviously determined to impose their will on the enemy.

The man chosen to command the American military effort in Vietnam, General William Childs Westmoreland, seemed ideally fitted for the task. A South Carolinian and West Pointer (1936), he had served as an artillery commander in World War II in Africa and Europe. He had commanded an airborne regiment in Korea. Promoted to brigadier general at thirty-eight years, he had served subsequently as secretary of the general staff, commanding general of the 101st Airborne Division, and superintendent of West Point, adding a star for each new billet. Now fifty-one years old, he stood nearly six feet tall, a rugged, fit man of one hundred and eighty pounds, a devout Episcopalian who frowned on swearing, smoking, and hard drinking, and who was said to keep a Bible on his desk and to read it.[5]

General Westmoreland soon found himself fighting four distinct, though intimately related, shooting wars: the "original" guerrilla, or counterinsurgency, war that challenged the NLF-VC organized in regular and paramilitary units throughout the country; the quasi-conventional ground war in the central highlands and south of the Demilitarized

Zone (DMZ) that was fought against VC and regular units of the North Vietnamese army (PAVN); the naval war; and the air war.[6] Each of these efforts bred certain political, economic, and psychological problems, which, taken together, influenced what some called "the other war," the contest to win people's "hearts and minds"—what a few persons accurately called "the only war."

To fight the shooting wars, General Westmoreland disposed of a force so impressive as to bring to mind the prophet Jeremiah's description of the ancient army that would irrupt into Judah: ". . . his chariots shall be as a whirlwind: his horses are swifter than eagles. . . . Their quiver is as an open sepulchre. . . ." From the standpoint of technology, the world had never seen a more sophisticated armed host than that committed by the Americans in South Vietnam. Literally, no expense had been spared in equipping and training these infantry and airborne and marine divisions and air units and naval armadas before committing them to combat in Vietnam.

In addition to standard arms and equipment, troops received rapid-firing Armalite rifles, at first the controversial M-16, later the improved M-14 which fired a lighter, 7.62-mm. round. Each squad carried flame throwers, light machine guns, and grenade launchers; in addition to fragmentation and smoke grenades, troops were equipped with a variety of nauseous gases and rocket launchers. Platoons and companies carried such organic support weapons as 60- and 81-mm. mortars and 90- and 106-mm. recoilless rifles. Supporting artillery units carried 4.2-inch mortars and 105-mm., 155-mm., and eight-inch howitzers. More effective artillery shells appeared, for example the 105-mm. "Beehive," which, upon detonation, released eight thousand steel "fléchettes," or tiny darts, to tear through whatever body got in the way. Small-unit communications were vastly improved, as were tropical clothing, boots, ancillary equipment, field rations. Combat troops also received such sophisticated identity aids as electronic sensory devices, or "man sniffers," infrared night-sighting equipment, short-range ground radars. A galaxy of specialist units—medical, engineer, communications—supported ground operations, and, where necessary, commanders could count on heavy-artillery, armor, and, along the coast and inland waterways, naval-gunfire support.[7]

Commanders also relied on armored personnel carriers and on large numbers of helicopters for improved mobility. The U. S. Marine Corps,

6. Hugh A. Mulligan, *No Place to Die* (New York: William Morrow, 1967): The author describes enemy forces in detail; see also Shaplen (*The Lost Revolution*), *supra;* Pike, op. cit.; S. L. A. Marshall, *Battles in the Monsoon* (New York: William Morrow, 1967); O'Neill, op. cit.; General Westmoreland described the war as he saw it in an interview published in *U. S. News and World Report,* November 28, 1966.

7. Francis J. West, "Small Unit Action in Vietnam. Summer 1966." Washington: Headquarters, U. S. Marine Corps, 1967; see also Mulligan, op. cit.; Donald Duncan, *The New Legions* (New York: Random House, 1967).

a pioneer in helicopter "vertical assault" tactics, brought its own "chopper" squadrons as integral components of its air wings. The U. S. Army, which employs helicopter companies organic to the ground division, went so far as to build two divisions around this machine! Each "airmobile" division consisted of approximately sixteen thousand troops equipped with 434 aircraft, mostly helicopters, and sixteen hundred land vehicles (compared to a normal army division's one hundred organic aircraft and over three thousand vehicles).

A vast armory escorted troop-carrying helicopters into action. Conventional aircraft often "prepared" the "target": F-100, F-104, F-105, F-4C, and F-5 planes, to name a few, not only bombed and machine-gunned with great expertise but also carried a varied and highly destructive kit that included conventional high-explosive bombs, delayed-action bombs, white-phosphorus bombs, napalm, and rockets. Some of these were tailored for the tactical situation, for example "daisy-cutters"—bombs fitted with a delayed fuse so as to detonate in water and destroy by concussion any Viet Cong hiding there; and CBUs, or Cluster Bomb Units, which contained thousands of small metal balls released on impact and scattered lethally by compressed air.

Huey gunships—helicopters armed with 7.62-mm. machine guns, rockets, and grenades—usually accompanied troop-carrying helicopters (also armed with machine guns) to furnish immediate fire support in case of enemy fire during approach and landing or in later retrieval operations. Ground commanders also were supported by specially fitted aircraft, old and slow-flying Douglas DC-3s and C-47s, for night defense. These relics, known as Puff the Magic Dragon and Smokey the Bear, circled for hours, dropping magnesium flares and pouring in thousands of rounds from three electrically operated rapid-fire machine guns, each capable of firing six thousand rounds per minute.

Helicopters also played an immensely important support role. Small, fast machines that land most anywhere whipped commanders around extended battle areas to give a tactical cohesion unfamiliar since Napoleonic warfare. Larger machines landed reinforcements and supply to hard-pressed units, and evacuated wounded. Medical evacuation (Med-Evac) techniques became so polished that the American army claimed a "save" ratio of eighty-two out of a hundred men wounded (as opposed to seventy-one out of a hundred in World War II); the Marine Corps pointed out that no wounded man was ". . . more than 30 minutes . . . from a fully staffed and equipped hospital."[8]

The quasi-conventional ground war at first centered north of Saigon, specifically in the central highlands of II Corps area and the northern coastal provinces of I Corps area. Having foiled the enemy's 1965 plan to cut South Vietnam in half, Westmoreland now turned to the task of,

8. U. S. Air Force, "The U. S. Air Force in Southeast Asia." Washington: Headquarters, U. S. Air Force, 1967; see also Frank Harvey (*Air War—Vietnam*), *supra;* R. B. Asprey ("Tactics"), *supra.*

first, preventing the enemy from resuming the offensive, and, second, eventually isolating and destroying him in detail while energetically pacifying areas reclaimed from enemy control. To accomplish the first task, Westmoreland depended primarily on a wide variety of search-and-destroy missions, or what he called "spoiling" tactics, that is, blocking and enveloping actions designed to keep the enemy off-balance and thus "spoil" his plans.

Operations in the central highlands centered on the 1st Cavalry (Airborne) Division, based on An Khe. The reader may remember that this division deployed here in autumn of 1965 and fought a sharp and generally successful series of actions culminating in the Chu Phong and Ia Drang area. A veteran American military correspondent, S. L. A. Marshall, visited the division in spring of 1966 and later wrote an excellent, if sometimes alarming, description of its operations, in his book *Battles in the Monsoon.*[9]

Based at Camp Radcliffe, a huge complex protected by ". . . a seventeen-kilometer-long barrier around Hon Kong mountain," the division "fed" a variety of permanent and temporary fortified bases in the surrounding area. These, in turn, supported numerous operations ranging from small patrols to task-force "sweeps" but including special missions by other units, for example Civilian Irregular Defense Groups (CIDG) composed of Special Forces teams and friendly Montagnard tribesmen.

In winter and spring of 1966, the division was carrying out a threefold mission: countering enemy operations in the central highlands; interdicting border areas where six or seven PAVN regiments were believed to be hovering (across the line, in Cambodia); protecting communications from Pleiku along Highway 19 to the sea.

Division operations almost always utilized helicopters. The American army believed that extreme mobility offered by these machines was the key to fighting successful counterinsurgency warfare. Early in the division's operations, Major General W. E. DePuy told Frank Harvey: ". . . The VC need ten days to transfer three battalions. We manage five battalions in a day."[10]

Standard operating procedure in the highlands called for extensive patrolling designed to find the enemy. Although information derived from several sources, for example from aerial observation, Special Forces units such as CIDG, and friendly local peasants, preliminary action generally fell to a special Reconnaissance Squadron, ". . . formed of three cavalry troops . . . and one ground troop. In each air troop there is a scout platoon, a weapons platoon and an infantry platoon. They mount up in armored Huey Bravos [helicopters]

9. S. L. A. Marshall, op. cit.; see also Mulligan, op. cit.; Duncan, op. cit.
10. Harvey, op. cit.

with a mixed bag of rockets and machine guns. The scouts go forth and find the enemy; the infantry element then lands to exploit."[11]

Exploitation assumed a number of forms. One was an ambush patrol, usually carried out by specially trained teams infiltrated into the target area by helicopters using appropriate deceptive techniques. Another was the combat patrol, which sought out and engaged the enemy. If action developed favorably, division could escalate it to a major operation, thanks to mobility offered by helicopters and to fire support supplied by base artillery, helicopters, and tactical (and even strategic) aircraft. If a fire fight developed adversely, the local commander could usually evacuate his patrol, including wounded and dead, by helicopter under cover of supporting fire.

These actions were generally very confused, and co-ordinating them into a meaningful whole taxed the ability of competent senior commanders. Marshall described one such operation, known first as Crazy Horse, later as the battle of Vinh Thanh Valley, in detail. The action began when a CIDG patrol surprised an enemy patrol and killed five PAVN soldiers, including a lieutenant. Captured documents indicated that PAVN had moved 120-mm. mortars into the area and was probably going to attack the CIDG base camp in battalion strength (as had been rumored by local villagers). The division commander, Major General Jack Norton, turned the problem over to First Brigade, which was tactically responsible for the area. Although strapped for troops, its commander, Colonel John Hennessey, committed a company-strength patrol into an area "fed" by Landing Zone (LZ) Savoy and, beyond that, by LZ Hereford. When the patrol encountered substantial resistance—it was ambushed and mauled—another company joined the action. Suspecting a lucrative target, Norton enlarged the operation to brigade strength.

According to Marshall, who monitored the action, its purpose was two-fold: ". . . to purge the mountain country beyond LZ Hereford of Communist forces and to make it so costly to them that they would be loath ever again to attempt using it as a sanctuary."

Hennessey now moved his Tactical Operations Center (TOC)—". . . a capsulated headquarters shaped like a Quonset hut" and lifted by a Flying Crane helicopter—to LZ Savoy. From this forward defended base, the colonel dispatched various companies to LZ Hereford, from where they fanned out through the rugged terrain.

Marshall offers several splendid descriptions of these units. Of a thirty-one-man patrol scheduled for a three-day action, he wrote:

. . . Every soldier carried 800 rounds for his M-16, most of them slung in crossed bandoliers around their shoulders, Mexican-guerrilla style. All carried six meals in C rations and four hand grenades. Then there were two M-60 machine guns with 800 rounds per weapon, nine claymore mines in

11. S. L. A. Marshall, op. cit.

each squad, three M-79 grenade launchers with 24 rounds for each, twelve
smoke grenades and twelve trip flares.

These are nigh incredible loads for any patrol. With their canteens, aid
packs, bayonets, pill bottles, etc., they must have weighted out with an average carry between sixty-five and seventy pounds.

The patrol could be expected to take care of itself, but, in addition to
organic armament, the commander could call down a host of supporting
fires on whatever unfortunate enemy unit he encountered.

Unfortunately, he did not encounter many enemy units, at least not
on favorable terms. Although captured enemy documents soon confirmed that the Americans were fighting elements of five battalions from
two PAVN regiments, as well as local Viet Cong units, none of the
patrols captured prisoners or attracted defectors, who could have offered precise enemy locations, strength, and intentions.

As one result, operations continued on a hit-and-miss basis. Although
patrols sometimes "found" the enemy, too often by virtue of stumbling
into ambushes, they rarely succeeded in "fixing" and "destroying" him.
Although the "kill" ratio at times was favorable, it was never decisive.
Apparently at home in the terrain, the enemy seemed to have little
difficulty in breaking off an action at will and in evading pursuit forces.
Hennessey's units could not hope to cover the entire area, and other,
substitute measures proved ineffective. Lacking troops to probe the
northern arc of the range, Hennessey attempted to neutralize it with
tear-gas crystals, but these quickly dissolved in the rainy climate. B-52
strikes in the same area probably did about as little damage as tear gas.

Within two weeks, the operation bogged down. In Marshall's words,

. . . So there, for the most part, they stood and waited, or patrolled, and
in either case served. The highland interior was no longer being prowled
and pounded. The wishful hope was that the enemy, deprived of his stores,
driven by hunger, would emerge, poking through the holes in large numbers looking for rice.

Hennessey did the best he could with the forces at his disposal. Parts
of the operation were very professional—for example, an ambush set
by an experienced and specially trained platoon of twenty-nine men
infiltrated into the area by helicopters using appropriate deceptive techniques. General Marshall described the action:

. . . They went well loaded. Every man carried ten full magazines for his
M-16, four fragmentation grenades, one claymore mine and one trip flare.
Of food, there was enough in C rations to take care of six meals, since
they figured they might be on their own for two days. Counting his rifle,
bayonet and clothing, each soldier was carrying about fifty-five pounds. . . .

It took them not more than thirty minutes to walk from the landing zone
to the ambush site. They had hoped to have about an hour of daylight after

arrival, affording time to choose the best possible concealment, but had cut things a bit short, as dark comes early in that latitude. Still, their passage had been both swift and silent . . . they were quite sure they had not been detected.

. . . Beyond the grass were two small fields framed by closely clipped, low hedges. Here they would set their deadfall, extending somewhere between thirty and forty meters. The clearing to their front was more than adequate.

There was no need for talk about how to dispose themselves. Having rehearsed the exercise and discussed their plan numerous times, they went to their stations automatically, silently.

They divided into two lines. The eleven riflemen in the rear rank were to about-face and point weapons across the hedges, with one machine gun in the center. Here was the insurance against counter surprise.

The twelve men in the front line were to spring the ambush. Here, too, was a machine gun in the center, pointed leftward along the trail toward the village. The violence and fury of this trap lay, however, in the twenty claymore mines evenly distributed along it frontally. The closest claymore was about twenty meters from the trail. The blast of this mine approximately equals that of a 60 mm. mortar round and its maximum effective range is about fifty meters. So as to concentration, the setup was superlative.

This particular ambush yielded fifteen enemy killed, with one slightly wounded American. But this was one ambush in a large area. As Marshall noted,

. . . The enemy too frequently declined to react sensibly when he was getting away, and it is axiomatic that if any escape route was left unguarded, he would invariably find it. Evasion was his one great talent. The net cast around the mountains was not only very large but very loose, one wide sector going wholly unmanned for lack of troops. So there were large hopes and small expectations.[12]

The battle of Vinh Thanh Valley, which did not yield spectacular results, was only one of dozens of such operations. Not all resulted in battle. Task forces ranging from reinforced companies and battalions to brigades and even divisions tramped through the highlands and border country to the west in almost constant pursuit of the elusive enemy. So successful did MACV deem search-and-destroy tactics, that over sixty operations a month were mounted in South Vietnam in the first six months of 1966, an effort that, according to MACV, yielded a "kill" figure of over sixteen thousand PAVN/VC troops.[13] Marshall has described several of these, and, from the standpoint of mobil-

12. Ibid.
13. Edgar O'Ballance, "Strategy in Viet Nam," *Army Quarterly,* January 1967; see also Dennis J. Duncanson, "The Vitality of the Viet Cong," *Encounter,* December 1966.

ity and organizational flexibility, they are indeed impressive. In one instance, in August, helicopters lifted most of one division to the Cambodian border area—sixty miles to the west—in less than twelve hours, to kick off a campaign that yielded 861 enemy dead (confirmed) and over two hundred prisoners. Still another operation, Hawthorne Two, yielded 459 enemy dead (confirmed) at a cost of thirty-nine U.S./ ARVN dead and 196 wounded. In support of Hawthorne Two, artillery units fired 15,250 rounds of light shells and 4,020 rounds of heavy stuff. The attached helicopter battalion had transported 8,657 men and 395 tons of cargo in 1,579 flight hours—enemy fire struck fifteen of the machines.[14]

An equally impressive effort simultaneously was occurring in the more heavily populated I Corps areas on the coast. Here the build-up of III Marine Amphibious Force had been rapid and efficient. Commanded by Major General (soon to be Lieutenant General) Lewis Walt, the force soon numbered nearly sixty thousand troops, including air units.

We have already discussed the marines' early and, in some ways, successful clearing of Chu Lai Peninsula. Unfortunately, before that area could be pacified—that is, the Viet Cong infrastructure rooted out and replaced by government authority—Walt had been forced to expand his command area: In just over a year, it would grow from eight square miles to eighteen hundred-plus square miles, mostly under Viet Cong control. His mission also had altered: In addition to defending airfields at Da Nang, Chu Lai, and Phu Bai, he was supposed to destroy PAVN and main-force Viet Cong units in the area and root out VC infrastructure, as part of an extensive pacification program.[15]

Tactical operations at first remained at small-unit level and consisted primarily in patrol and ambush work essential to command security. By summer of 1966, marine units had carried out thousands of patrols, while helicopters and marine fixed-wing aircraft had flown thousands of sorties, an activity that, all together, resulted in several thousand confirmed enemy dead[16]—though how many were enemy and how many were peasants is a moot question.

For some time, marines relied on search-and-destroy tactics favored by the American army. Two reasons explained the choice. One was command ignorance. General Walt later explained that, when he assumed command in Vietnam, he did not understand the nature of the

14. S. L. A. Marshall, op. cit.
15. Lewis W. Walt, *Strange War, Strange Strategy* (New York: Funk & Wagnalls, 1970; see also Russel H. Stolfi, *U. S. Marine Corps Civic Action Efforts in Vietnam—March 1965–March 1966* (Washington: U. S. Marine Corps, 1968). Captain Stolfi describes this transition period in detail.
16. U. S. Marine Corps, "III Marine Amphibious Force—The Mission—And How It Is Fulfilled." Headquarters, U. S. Marine Corps, October, 1967; see also West, op. cit.

war, a failing we shall later discuss in detail.[17] Senior marine commanders echoed Walt's confusion (with some exceptions) and attempted to fight the war with conventional methods.

The second fact was I Corps area, which had been under VC control for a long time. I Corps area comprised five provinces (about ten thousand square miles) and over 3 million people, 90 per cent of whom lived in the narrow coastal strip. Although the South Vietnamese Government exercised some control in the cities, the countryside, in general, belonged to the Viet Cong. Marine units sent to outlying areas such as Duc Pho, in Quang Ngai province, lived in a sea of hostility provoked both by regional resentments of Saigon government and by fear of the Viet Cong. Jonathan Schell, who later centered a series of *New Yorker* articles on this coastal area, met a marine who had served in Duc Pho:

. . . He said that for the first month they had been unable to travel five hundred yards beyond their camp without running into heavy enemy fire. After receiving reinforcements, they had moved out farther but had still been unable to penetrate many areas.[18]

One result, an important one, was lack of intelligence on which to base operations—a complaint common to all allied commands in Vietnam, and one generally met by random destruction of "suspected" VC hideouts. Schell, who was appalled at the amount of destruction in Quang Ngai province, explained its etiology:

. . . The villages had been destroyed in many ways and in a great variety of circumstances—at first by our Marines and later by our Army. In accordance with the local policy of the 3rd Marine Amphibious Force, a village could be bombed immediately and without the issuing of any warning to the villagers if American or other friendly troops or aircraft had received fire from within it. This fire might consist of a few sniper shots or of a heavy attack by the enemy. Whatever the provocation from the village, the volume of firepower brought to bear in response was so great that in almost every case the village was completely destroyed. A village could also be destroyed if intelligence reports indicated that the villagers had been supporting the Vietcong by offering them food and labor, but in such a case the official 3rd Marine Amphibious Force rules of engagement required that our Psychological Warfare Office send a plane to warn the villagers, either by dropping leaflets or by making an airborne announcement. Because it was impossible to print rapidly enough a leaflet addressed to a specific village and specifying a precise time for bombing, the Psychological Warfare people had largely abandoned leaflet drops as a method of warning, and had begun to rely almost completely on airborne announcements. There was no official ruling on when troops on the ground were permitted to burn a village, but, generally speaking, this occurred most often after fire had been received

17. New York *Times,* November 18, 1970; see also Walt, op. cit.
18. Jonathan Schell, *The Military Half* (New York: Alfred A. Knopf, 1968).

from the village, or when the province chief had given a specific order in advance for its destruction. In some cases, the villagers had been removed from an area in a big-scale operation and then the area had been systematically destroyed. . . .[19]

Such tactics did not endear the allied cause to local populations. So long as peasants remained hostile or apathetic, marines were not going to obtain information on enemy locations and movements, which they needed in order to fight successfully. In a relatively short time, the marines set about obtaining this information.

They approached the task in two ways: Area commanders instituted civic programs designed to win over local people. These varied considerably in effectiveness. Some of them proved outstanding. In August 1965, one enterprising commander instituted the Golden Fleece program, wherein marines guaranteed four villages a secure rice harvest in return for information on local Viet Cong.[20] Other programs seemed to prosper, but progress remained slow, due both to interruptions caused by enemy attacks and to widespread xenophobia and peasant apathy, perhaps the inevitable result of this particular civil war.

The second method was better. Beginning with villages south of Da Nang, marines provided medical services and began assisting in various construction projects. This necessitated working with I Corps commander Lieutenant General Nguyen Chanh Thi, a suspicious Buddhist nationalist who, in March 1966, would be involved in a minor civil war with the Saigon government.

Walt nonetheless persuaded Thi to co-operate in establishing a joint area-pacification council of civil and military members, under whose aegis the pacification program slowly spread to a nine-village area. Not content with creeping progress, Walt borrowed a page from the old Nicaraguan campaign and persuaded Thi to go along in establishing a Combined Action Group—an integrated company of marines and Popular Forces (local militia) designed to provide village security. First tried at Phu Bai, the experiment worked almost at once. Shaplen, who visited the village in early 1966, observed marines and militia working together and even learning each other's language:

. . . As a result of these joint patrols, the Vietcong network in four villages around Phu Bai has been measurably damaged, though the Communists still slip in eight or ten armed agents at a time to collect food and taxes from the population and nothing as advanced as a Census/Grievance and Aspiration unit can yet function safely. Road traffic in this area has picked up noticeably, and hamlet markets now attract buyers and sellers from as

19. Ibid. The author points out that printed warnings often failed in purpose, because villagers were illiterate. We have pointed out that a similar situation existed in the Rif Rebellion (see Chapter 28, Volume I).
20. Stolfi, op. cit.

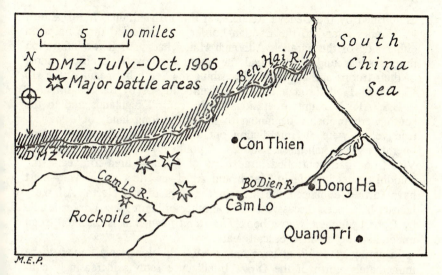

far off as two kilometers, which may not sound like much but is a lot compared with what the safe-travel radius was six months ago.[21]

Such was the impact of Combined Action Groups that Walt extended the program as rapidly as possible. In September 1966, the commandant of the Marine Corps, General Wallace Greene, reported his favorable impression:

. . . The people, in turn, are casting out the Viet Cong from their hamlets and telling us where the enemy is hidden. And the people in the villages are defending their homes with Combined Action Companies composed of a team of US Marines and local militia. The success of these Combined Action Companies has surpassed our expectations. There are over 40 of these units now operating and we expect to have a total of about 75 by the end of this year.[22]

Two events now occurred to interrupt the burgeoning pacification program. In March, Buddhist riots, which involved Thi and brought an eyeball-to-eyeball confrontation between ARVN and Walt's marines, seriously impeded the pacification program.[23] By the time this crisis ended, intelligence was reporting indications of a planned North Vietnamese attack through the DMZ. This was the so-called "neutral strip,"

21. Shaplen (*The Road from War*), *supra;* see also Mulligan, op. cit.; Corson, op. cit.; R. K. Stanford, "Bamboo Brigades," *Marine Corps Gazette,* March 1966; D. L. Evans, "Civil Affairs in Vietnam," *Marine Corps Gazette,* March 1968; Stolfi, op. cit.
22. (Editorial), "Marines in Viet-Nam," *Marine Corps Gazette,* September 1966.
23. Walt, op. cit.

established by the Geneva Accords, at the 17th parallel. It ran almost sixty miles inland to the Laotian border and extended three miles on either side of the parallel. Although Hanoi had used it for infiltration purposes (as undoubtedly had the South for covert purposes), most of their troops and supply were reaching the South by means of the Ho Chi Minh Trail through Laos and Cambodia, or by the sea route.

U.S./ARVN counteroperations in the central highlands and to the south were probably beginning to make the long land route less attractive, as were air interdiction operations, which, along with naval operations, we shall discuss shortly. A political factor also entered: The Viet Cong had controlled large parts of I Corps area for years; the Buddhist riots in Hué in March and April—in effect a civil war—must have further enhanced the area in the eyes of the North. All these factors have been discussed in still another brilliant *New Yorker* article by Robert Shaplen, whose book *The Road from War* is essential to an understanding of these crucial years.[24]

In spring of 1966, at least four PAVN divisions were known to be immediately north of the DMZ. Intelligence reports increasingly confirmed that PAVN units were crossing the line and busily ". . . preparing the battlefield" for subsequent operations. Communist movement began in late May, when vanguard units of Division 324B crossed the DMZ into the rugged terrain of northern Quang Tri province. This was a "regular" army division, some ten to twelve thousand troops well armed and equipped, though perhaps not so well fed. Soldiers carried Chinese copies of Soviet weapons, the AK-47 assault rifle with fifty to a hundred rounds of 7.62-mm. ammunition, RPD light machine guns, SKS carbines, RPG-2 rocket launchers, grenades. Shaplen later wrote:

. . . Each man's supplies further consisted of two khaki, green, or purple uniforms, a canteen, a canvas bag, a raincoat, a pair of rubber sandals, a pair of boots, a hammock, a blanket, a mosquito net, some halazone water-purification tablets, some quinine tablets, some vitamin pills, a small can of chicken or shrimp, a kilogram and a half of salt, and seven kilograms of rice. According to information obtained later from prisoners and from captured documents, food, especially rice, was in very short supply, and several of the battalions had to be pressed into service as transport units, going back and forth a number of times to bring more rice down from North Vietnam before crossing the Ben Hai River for good.[25]

General Westmoreland, in Saigon, had been keeping a close eye on the situation, as had General Walt in Da Nang, and had worked out contingency plans that involved both Marine Corps and ARVN units. In July, a small marine reconnaissance team landed by helicopter but was soon spotted, and quickly evacuated by the same means. A few

24. Shaplen (*The Road from War*), *supra*.
25. Ibid.

days later, it tried again, and, this time, reported enemy presence in strength, reports confirmed by ARVN units who had taken some prisoners in the same area. Operation Hastings, designed to intercept and disrupt the North Vietnamese units, now began.[26]

Operation Hastings called for "spoiling" operations by a marine force of seven battalions plus artillery units—Task Force Delta, some eight thousand troops, commanded by Brigadier General Lowell English. While Delta operated well to the northwest, an ARVN force of five infantry and airborne battalions—about three thousand men—moved into the eastern and southcentral zones.

English landed two battalions by helicopter at either end of a valley about a mile south of the DMZ and northeast of a prominent terrain feature known as the Rockpile. Shaplen later wrote that English's battle plan ". . . was brilliantly conceived to take the enemy by surprise on his key trails and behind his own lines and to smash and destroy him before he had a chance to regain his balance and his momentum." Unfortunately, the enemy did not seem sufficiently surprised to prevent his reacting furiously and effectively. He first prevented a juncture of the two battalions; by the time they did join, fighting was so intense that English decided to break it off in favor of a new attack from the south. The marine withdrawal provoked more severe fighting. English meanwhile committed other battalions to block the southern portion of the area, and, for several days, marines fought a series of hot actions ranging from squad to battalion strength. Throughout this period, a small reconnaissance team occupied the Rockpile to call in air, artillery, and naval gunfire on nearby PAVN columns. ARVN units to the south and east also, on occasion, engaged enemy units, and claimed several hundred enemy lives.

Operation Hastings ended in early August with a general backing off of PAVN regiments. Pointing to enemy losses—nearly nine thousand confirmed killed, with another eight hundred estimated killed and several thousand wounded—Marine Corps spokesmen claimed a "victory" of major proportions. In some respects, however, it was a Pyrrhic victory: The marines lost over two hundred killed and several hundred wounded. If PAVN division 324B had been knocked out, it was temporary, and three other divisions remained in the immediate area. Finally, as General Walt later noted, the enemy accomplished two major objectives: ". . . they had slowed the pacification of the I Corps area by forcing me to commit men into the largely barren north, and they had made many headlines in the United States about escalation and American casualties."[27]

Operation Hastings gave way to Operation Prairie. Increasingly bloody contacts soon confirmed that Division 324B, despite its pum-

26. Ibid.; see also Walt, op. cit.
27. Walt, op. cit.

meling, was still active in the DMZ, where it was fortifying the area in the vicinity of the Rockpile. In frustrating this plan, the marines fought another series of bloody actions, in some cases using tanks. The description of the fighting at the time in various papers and magazines reminded more than one marine veteran of both World War II and Korean actions, particularly the assault and capture of Hills 400 and 484, which dominated the enemy's main line of resistance in the DMZ and forced him once again to withdraw to the North.

Operation Prairie terminated in early October. The marines claimed over twelve hundred "counted" dead, with another sixteen hundred "probable," at a cost of about two hundred marine lives.[28] Unfortunately, the area would remain a hot spot; further action would center on Khe Sanh, not many miles to the south.

While army and marine units fought in the central highlands and coastal areas, Westmoreland continued to build up forces and to undertake operations in III Corps area, which included Saigon, and in IV Corps area, the Mekong Delta, which was almost completely a guerrilla challenge.

The enemy was strong in both these corps areas. In III Corps area, Zones C and D and the Iron Triangle had been Viet Minh centers of resistance and were extremely well fortified and organized. Early in 1966, a combined ARVN-U.S. force had swept part of Zone D in Binh Duong province to capture over six thousand enemy documents and large amounts of supply and munitions.[29] Probing efforts continued during the year and consisted both of search-and-destroy and more-permanent, clear-and-hold operations such as those undertaken by an Australian task force southeast of Saigon and very well described in a book by an Australian soldier and scholar, Robert O'Neill, *Vietnam Task*.[30]

Throughout 1966, allied troops, including Australians, a few New Zealanders, and the vanguard of a Korean division, continued to arrive in South Vietnam. Once sufficient numbers were on hand, the American command directed a series of giant "sweeps" through sanctuary zones. Toward the end of 1966 and in early 1967, such operations as Attleboro, Cedar Falls, and Junction City uncovered and destroyed miles of tunnel defenses, underground hospitals, and supply depots.

Simultaneously, other troops were fighting other wars.

The air war consisted of two parts. One was the out-country war already familiar to us: the continuance of Operation Rolling Thunder— the strategic bombing of North Vietnam and tactical interdiction of supply routes leading to and running through Laos and Cambodia. Rolling Thunder utilized both B-52 bombers (carrying 500- and 750-pound

28. Shaplen (*The Road from War*), *supra*.
29. Pike, op. cit.
30. O'Neill, op. cit.

bombs) flying from Thailand and Guam, and a host of air force, navy, and marine planes flying from immediate land and carrier bases. In spring of 1966, President Johnson yielded to pleas of military advisers and authorized strikes against oil-storage depots, including those around Hanoi and Haiphong. This effort continued throughout the summer: ". . . By the end of July, the Defense Intelligence Agency reported to Secretary McNamara that 70 per cent of North Vietnam's original [oil] storage capacity had been destroyed."[31] In December 1966, President Johnson again yielded to pleas of military advisers and authorized strikes against the theretofore prohibited inner ring of Hanoi, an act that brought repercussions we shall discuss in the next chapter. The year's bombing tally was impressive: In 1965, planes had flown 55,000 missions, which dropped 33,000 tons of bombs in the North; in 1966, they flew 138,000 missions to drop 128,000 tons of bombs on targets in the North. In December, the President also agreed that, beginning in February 1967, B-52 flights would increase from sixty to eight hundred monthly (including missions over South Vietnam).[32]

Air force, navy, and marine planes, including giant B-52 bombers, also carried on an in-country aerial war consisting of conventional strategic bombing of VC base areas and defensive complexes, tactical interdiction of supply routes along borders and inside South Vietnam, and tactical and logistic support of ground units. During 1966, air force pilots alone ". . . flew more than 70,000 attack sorties in South Vietnam," an effort that, according to an air force writer, ". . . denied the insurgents the initiative. The enemy no longer can mass for sustained attacks, and the sanctuary he once knew in the darkened jungles is a thing of the past." During the first three days of Operation Attleboro, air force planes delivered three hundred thousand pounds of rations, ammunition, and other supplies to the ground forces.[33]

The air war also involved a host of special missions including around-the-clock rescue of downed airmen. High-flying planes bombarded Vietnam with millions of Chieu Hoi (Open Arms) amnesty leaflets, which exhorted the enemy to surrender (and prosper thereby)—according to the air force, these leaflets brought in over nineteen thousand "ralliers" by end of 1966.[34] RB-57s, RB-66s, ". . . supersonic RF-101 Voodoos and double-sonic RF-4C Phantoms" patrolled the skies on thousands of reconnaissance missions, each utilizing highly sophisticated techniques to photograph targets that ranged from the immediate ground battle scene to enemy lines of communication and suspected enemy concentration areas. During 1966, air force technicians were processing four million feet of film a month, while aerial reconnaissance

31. *The Pentagon Papers, supra* (p. 480).
32. Ibid. (p. 523); see also U. S. Air Force, op. cit.
33. U. S. Air Force, op. cit.
34. Harvey, op. cit.; see also U. S. Air Force, op. cit.

was furnishing ". . . 85 per cent of all immediate intelligence data in Southeast Asia."[35]

Still another aerial effort involved chemical defoliation, the theory being to deprive the enemy of natural cover as well as of food in his base areas. This mission fell to the Ranch Hand Squadron, whose motto, according to one correspondent, Frank Harvey, was: "Only You Can Prevent Forests." The squadron's motivation was noteworthy for its brevity:

. . . Dresser showed me around the squadron rooms. It was a spartan place. The familiar sign, FUCK COMMUNISM, which was painted horizontally in stripes of red, white and blue, was tacked to one wall. . . .[36]

Ranch Hand pilots performed the hazardous duty of spraying from a hundred fifty feet at a slow speed over generally enemy-infested areas. An eleven-thousand-pound pay load, which cost five thousand dollars, took four minutes to spread and killed everything green over three hundred acres.[37]

The American navy was also fighting two wars: an out-country effort, which attempted to intercept coastal junks bringing arms and supply from North to South, and the in-country effort, which involved coastal and inland-waterway patrols to intercept supplies intended for the Viet Cong. The out-country naval war also included a support role for American marines and ARVN units in I Corps area, a role later expanded southward to include operations in the Mekong Delta. A flotilla of cruisers, destroyers, and smaller craft furnished on-call naval-gunfire support, while other craft landed amphibious teams as necessary to fight coastal operations.

Both efforts quickly escalated to majestic proportions. The out-country interdiction task fell to Task Force 77, an armada of five aircraft carriers, four hundred aircraft, about twenty-five support ships, and over thirty thousand men operating from "Yankee Station," in Tonkin Gulf. A pamphlet issued by Seventh Fleet described the mission in precise-enough terms. Besides aerial bombardment (planes were soon flying thousands and even tens of thousands of missions), TF 77's surface arm—

. . . the guided missile cruisers, frigates and destroyers—are prowling the Vietnamese coast, foiling attempts to infiltrate by sea and pumping tons of ordnance into shore battery positions and coastal supply routes.[38]

Interdiction of coastal operations north of the DMZ became the task of destroyers charged with Operation Sea Dragon, which, in its first six months, destroyed or damaged more than one thousand barges and

35. U. S. Air Force, op. cit.
36. Harvey, op. cit.
37. Ibid.; see also U. S. Air Force, op. cit.
38. U. S. Seventh Fleet, "Task Force 77." No place, no date.

junks that were allegedly carrying supplies South. Still another armada, of radar-picket escorts and smaller craft, both navy and coast guard, carried out Operation Market Time, below the DMZ, in an effort to disrupt infiltration of supplies along the thousand miles of coastline. Naval-gunfire support hinged on another armada, of heavy and light cruisers, guided-missile destroyers and frigates, destroyers, destroyer escorts, and radar-picket escorts. This combined might could send eight-inch 55-caliber shells, each weighing over 250 pounds, some fifteen miles, or six-inch, five-inch, or three-inch shells to a lesser range.[39] This effort would soon be garnished with a battleship, USS *New Jersey,* removed from mothballs and reconditioned at a cost of $40 million.

The in-country, or riverine, warfare also quickly grew. Fought mainly in the Mekong Delta, it introduced a host of specially adapted craft ranging from PGM patrol gunboats to PBR river patrol boats and ". . . unsinkable styrofoam and fiber-glass swimmer support boats, Swift Boats, patrol air cushion vehicles (capable of traveling over 65 knots, combat loaded, over land or water), and an impressive list of modified amphibious craft, including monitors and armored troop carriers, sampans and junks." These operated either on their own or in conjunction with American and ARVN troop units: sea-air-land, or SEAL, teams extended the offensive aspect of river patrol operations inland, and the Navy-Army Mobile Riverine Force, an amphibious strike force of two army battalions, eventually began to penetrate fortified Viet Cong areas.[40]

There remained the final war: the "other war"—the war for people's "hearts and minds"—the real war. This had also gained impetus in mid-1965, when the new American ambassador, Henry Cabot Lodge, brought with him, as principal assistant, a counterinsurgency expert, veteran of the earlier Philippine and French Indochina campaigns, Edward Lansdale. Lansdale had always advocated grass-roots pacification as the key to revolutionary warfare. As opposed to centralized direction of the program from Saigon down to hamlet level, Lansdale wanted to begin at hamlet level and work outward and upward—a decentralized, horizontal concept practiced with such telling effect by the National Liberation Front.

Like previous regimes, the Thieu-Ky government opposed such an approach, since it would force Saigon to yield partial control not only of provinces and of pacification cadres but of immensely valuable supplies daily arriving from the United States and daily adding to personal fortunes of South Vietnamese officials. In addition to Vietnamese bureaucracy, Lansdale also found himself at odds with a vast number of

39. U. S. Seventh Fleet, "Cruisers and Destroyers in Vietnam." No place, no date; see also, U. S. Navy, "Riverine Warfare," Washington: U. S. Government Printing Office, 1967.
40. U. S. Navy, op. cit.; see also Asprey, op. cit.

American agencies, a proliferation of bureaucracy, civil and military, so ably described by Robert Shaplen.[41]

The end result was a sluggish pacification program. Thanks mainly to Lansdale, the Johnson administration was not allowed to forget this vital failure, and pressure continued on the Thieu-Ky government to take necessary action. In January 1966, Prime Minister Ky, in a major speech,

. . . set three primary goals for his country and for the government: to defeat the enemy and to pacify and rebuild the countryside; to stabilize the economy; and to build a democracy. He advanced specific programs to help achieve each objective.[42]

In early February 1966, President Johnson met with South Vietnamese leaders in Honolulu, where Ky impressed the President by his determination to build ". . . a really democratic government, one which is put into office by the people themselves and which has the confidence of the people." The pacification program, Ky promised, would go ahead full steam; in return, Johnson promised a priority effort from Washington and by the American mission in Saigon. In the President's later words,

. . . I remember Ambassador Lodge saying: "We have moved ahead here today in the fight to improve the lot of the little man at the grassroots. That is what this is all about."[43]

The President himself expected rapid results: By the next meeting between the South Vietnamese and Americans, he wanted ". . . coonskins nailed to the wall." He later wrote,

. . . As a result of the Honolulu conference, the government of Vietnam under Thieu and Ky was pledged to an all-out effort to win "the other war" in their country. We were equally pledged to help them in that struggle. I ordered a reorganization of our Mission in Saigon to reflect this new emphasis on nonmilitary programs. At the meeting in Hawaii, I selected our Deputy Ambassador to Vietnam, William J. Porter [who had replaced U. Alexis Johnson in 1965] to take charge of this drive. During the next month I established a special office in the White House headed by Robert W. Komer of the National Security Council staff. As my special assistant, he coordinated and supervised Washington support for pacification and other nonmilitary campaigns.[44]

To fight the other war, Thieu and Ky already had established a Ministry of Revolutionary Development, headed by Major General Nguyen Duc Thang, whose principal assistant was Major Nguyen Be.

41. Shaplen (*The Road from War*), *supra;* see also Corson, op. cit.
42. Johnson (*The Vantage Point*), *supra.*
43. Ibid.; see also Johnson (*Public Papers—1966*, Book I), *supra.*
44. Johnson (*The Vantage Point*), *supra.*

The reader will perhaps remember that past South Vietnamese governments had tried a number of pacification programs involving cadre administration: the Agroville cadre, Mobile Administration cadre, Rural-Political cadre, and Armed Propaganda cadre. The Khanh government had instituted a new pacification program cored by Advance People's Action Groups, and this had been expanded into People's Action Teams.

General Thang and Major Be had recognized for some time the short-comings of earlier programs. As early as summer of 1965, Be and an American adviser, Richard Kriegel, had worked out a pacification program in conjunction with an American marine battalion whose tactical area of responsibility (TAOR) comprised two hamlets ". . . which had been under VC control for nearly one year." Kriegel later wrote,

. . . As a result of the Marines' efforts in support of the GVN plan over 2,000 people returned to the two hamlets within a period of 45 days. Hamlet government was reactivated and the people openly demonstrated their support of the GVN. Thus the first successful pacification effort was completed in Binh Dinh [province] after nearly one year of VC military and political victories.[45]

The experience impressed Be and Thang, who agreed that the government's principal pacification instrument of the time, the forty-man People's Action Team, was neither large enough nor sufficiently motivated to provide ". . . sufficient guidance to the hamlet people in the essential areas of hamlet administration, construction and motivation." The result was a fifty-nine-man Revolutionary Development Group, trained at a special center run by Be.

In theory, little fault could be found with the new program, which emulated existing Communist doctrines. Its over-all objective was twofold: to pacify the hamlet and to help build a better life for its people. Revolutionary Development Groups were to be guided by four principles:

. . . 1. The cadre are to be the link between the people and the government of Viet-Nam.

2. The people are the main force and the cadre are to be their guides.

3. The old life is to be destroyed, and in its place, a new life is to be created. The result of the creation of a new life will be the New Life Hamlet (Ap Doi Moi).

4. The cadre are guided by the Ministry of Revolutionary Development's policy and doctrine and by the people's will.

Once a hamlet was militarily secure, government forces would concen-

45. Richard Kriegel, "Revolutionary Development," *Marine Corps Gazette*, March 1967.

trate on rooting out VC infrastructure, while simultaneously helping
the people to build a viable "community of responsibility." Two of
seven "basic techniques" were particularly to the point:

. . . More reliance will be placed upon the people's ability to provide local
resources. When the people have done their utmost to tackle a particular
problem, including the construction of buildings, etc., and are unable to
progress on their own, then and only then will the Government of Viet-
Nam step in to help. New Life Hamlets will not become beggars.

Again,

. . . The people build; the cadre guide and assist; and the soldiers defend.
In 1967, it is planned that each of the ARVN divisions will be assigned
a TAOR which will provide the outer protective shield behind which the
pacification program can be carried out.

All this was good common sense, but more was to come. The RD program spelled out eleven steps necessary to create a New Life Hamlet.
The first four were essential to building a community of responsibility:
eliminating the Communist infrastructure *as well as* ". . . hamlet bullies,
grafters, thieves and corrupt village officials"; clearing away ". . . the
petty grievances and problems: the distrust and suspicions which exist in the hearts and minds of the hamlet people . . ."; instituting
hamlet elections; organizing local militia forces. However, seven more
steps were spelled out to turn a "community of responsibility" into a
"community of prosperity." In Kriegel's words, ". . . The newly reactivated forces of cooperation, understanding and love must be channeled
into a positive program—into a socio-economic program": a program
built on educational, health, and economic reforms.

The instrument to do all this, the fifty-nine-man RD cadre consisting
of men and women recruited by province chiefs on a two-year basis,
consisted of a thirty-nine-man People's Action Team, which provided
security for the work of Census-Grievance, Civil Affairs, and New Life
Development cadres. Census-Grievance teams were trained to identify
and classify hamlet population and also to take swift action on important
local grievances. Civil affairs work followed, in which village administration was reorganized and elections held. New Life Development
cadres simultaneously began helping people to help themselves. Large
doses of political propaganda accompanied cadre efforts.[46]

The new program faced a number of difficulties, which we shall discuss later. Buddhist riots in spring of 1966 added to manifold problems
already faced by the RD program, and it failed to make significant
headway during the summer.

46. Ibid.; see also W. L. Traynor, "The Political War in Viet-Nam," *Marine
Corps Gazette*, August 1967; Shaplen (*The Road from War*), *supra*.

An effective pacification program depended, as always, on an effective government, and here some progress seemingly did appear. At American urging, in September 1966, the junta held elections for a constituent assembly that would write a new constitution. Although polls opened in only 55 per cent of the country, American officials applauded a turnout of ". . . 81 per cent of over 5 million registered voters, in spite of Vietcong intimidation and terrorism."[47] In general, American observers commented favorably on electoral procedures. If the mechanism appeared clumsy and in places questionable, no one could deny that the elections introduced the "democratic idea" to the South Vietnamese.

And few denied that definite progress was being recorded in general. The enthusiasm of both governments was plain at a conference in Manila in October 1966. One of President Johnson's most intimate advisers, Clark Clifford, later wrote:

. . . In 1966, I served as an adviser to President Johnson at the Manila Conference. It was an impressive gathering of the Chiefs of State and Heads of Government of allied nations; it reassured me that we were on the right road and that our military progress was bringing us closer to the resolution of the conflict.[48]

Johnson's other advisers apparently agreed. One result of the conference was ". . . specific plans for the postwar and long-term civil development of Viet Nam." To accomplish these, a Joint Development Group soon came into being, ". . . an organization composed of a private American company, Development and Resources Corporation, and a group of Vietnamese professionals," with ". . . the task of postwar planning, of creating a design and a strategy for the transition from a wartime to a peacetime footing, and of making an objective assessment of the prospects of South Viet Nam's economy in the years ahead."[49]

As the year ended, a new optimism seemed to have emerged in South Vietnam, and with some justification. ARVN forces totaled 285,000, with another 284,000 Regional and Popular troops, plus about 130,000 police and some thirty thousand Revolutionary Development cadres. The infusion of American strength was daily freeing ARVN units for pacification duties. Although the Viet Cong continued to control over half of the countryside, American counteraction, without doubt, had blunted their offensive plans. American troops numbering 350,000 had

47. Thompson (*No Exit*), *supra;* see also Shaplen in *The Road from War,* who questions the 81 per cent figure as optimistic; Tran Van Dinh, "Elections in Vietnam," *The New Republic,* July 2, 1966, offers interesting background on electoral problems.
48. Clifford, op. cit.
49. David E. Lilienthal, "Postwar Development in Viet Nam," *Foreign Affairs,* January 1969.

now arrived in South Vietnam, and more were on the way—though not as many as Westmoreland and the JCS would have liked. The ground, naval, and air wars continued to escalate. More than ever, the U.S.A. seemed determined to win the war.

Chapter 83

Blurs on the operational canvas • Failure of Operation Rolling Thunder • Increasing cost of aerial warfare • Shortcomings of attrition strategy and search-and-destroy tactics • The refugee problem • Manpower facts • The numbers game • Russian and Chinese aid to the North • The ground war • Increasing American costs (I) • The logistics picture • The Jurassic dinosaur

A NUMBER OF BLURS unfortunately marred the operational canvas in Vietnam. One was the failure of Operation Rolling Thunder —bombing North Vietnam—to accomplish its objectives (already being variously changed by Administration officials). The reader will perhaps remember that the theory advocated by the JCS and such presidential advisers as Walt Rostow was to hurt the North sufficiently to cause Hanoi to call off the war in the South. Although planes flew fifty-five thousand sorties in 1965, to drop thirty-three thousand tons of bombs and otherwise shoot up military targets, top-level intelligence reports at end of 1965 confirmed that bombing had indeed ". . . reduced industrial performance." But: ". . . the primary rural nature of the area permits continued functioning of the subsistence economy." Moreover, reports agreed, Hanoi seemed as determined as ever to support the war in the South.[1] The effort expanded during 1966, when planes flew 138,000 missions to drop 128,000 more tons of bombs. According to Bernard

1. *The Pentagon Papers, supra* (pp. 462, 469, 494).

Fall, who quoted McNamara, the 1966 "bombing plan" called for expending 638,000 tons of "aerial munitions"—thirty-eight thousand tons *more* than dropped in the Pacific theater in *all* of World War II[2]—yet the Pentagon report quoted CIA estimates that the bombing ". . . accomplished little more than in 1965."[3]

But operational costs were nonetheless enormous. In 1965, Rolling Thunder cost 171 planes and a direct operational expense of $460 million; installation of Russian surface-to-air missile (SAM) sites in the Hanoi-Haiphong areas insured higher losses. In 1966, American planes encountered ". . . the most sophisticated and concentrated air defense network ever faced in any war."[4] Although American fliers shot down thirty-six MIGs and otherwise carried out bombing and interdiction missions, the effort cost another 147 American aircraft—a total of 318 lost. Direct operational costs rose from $460 million to $1.2 billion in 1966.[5]

Operation Rolling Thunder also continued to reap heavy criticism both within and without the Administration. Although raids in June and July knocked out an estimated 70 per cent of North Vietnam's oil-storage capacity, it soon became clear that the North Vietnamese could get by on fuel dispersed in drums, which meant that the flow of men and supply to the South did not diminish. This failure added to McNamara's disillusionment. According to the Pentagon report,

. . . The Secretary was already in the process of rethinking the role of the entire air campaign in the U.S. effort. He was painfully aware of its inability to pinch off the infiltration to the South and had seen no evidence of its ability to break Hanoi's will, demoralize its population or bring it to the negotiation table.[6]

Escalation of bombing, in December, to the theretofore prohibited inner ring of Hanoi brought two major consequences: First, reports of civilian casualties raised an uproar in the world press, the more so since Harrison Salisbury, of the New York *Times,* was reporting directly from Hanoi at the time. Although the Johnson administration denied the accusation, top-secret CIA estimates, according to the Pentagon report, put the casualty figure in North Vietnam at thirty-six thousand for 1965 and 1966; of this figure, about 80 per cent were civilians.[7]

2. Bernard Fall, "Viet Nam in the Balance," *Foreign Affairs,* October 1966.
3. *The Pentagon Papers, supra* (p. 523; see also pp. 502–9, 518, 522).
4. U. S. Air Force, op. cit.
5. *The Pentagon Papers, supra* (p. 523).
6. Ibid. (pp. 480–81); see also p. 499: arguing from a World War II bias, Walt Rostow wrote in a memorandum to Rusk and McNamara in May 1966, ". . . I nevertheless feel it is quite possible the military effects of a systematic and sustained bombing of POL [petroleum-oil-lubricants] in North Vietnam may be more prompt and direct than conventional intelligence analysis would suggest. . . ."
7. Ibid. (pp. 513, 515, 523).

Second, the new effort may have caused Hanoi to back off from talks that some hoped would lead to negotiation. According to John Hightower, AP diplomatic correspondent in Washington, the Soviet Union and European satellites brought considerable pressure on North Vietnam at the Bulgarian Party Congress in mid-November 1966 to open the way for a peace conference. Negotiations by Polish intermediaries were allegedly proceeding favorably when American planes bombed Hanoi's outskirts, on December 13–14, causing Hanoi to break off proceedings. President Johnson later made light of this effort in his memoirs; Mr. Hightower, however, suggested that, in reality, the bombing was a major blunder, recognized as such by the President, and was the major reason for the later, four-month halt in bombing Hanoi as well as for a secret peace initiative (admitted, in part, by Johnson).[8]

The second blur centered on the ground war and emerged from Westmoreland's choice of attrition strategy and search-and-destroy tactics.

The problem faced by allied forces was essentially pacification. It demanded a qualitative and selective approach. The tactical task was to clear an area of Viet Cong so that civil teams could move in to build a viable and secure community. The military tactic thus required was clear-and-hold. The first task was to free an area from main-force guerrilla control. This called for fragmenting, dispersing, and destroying main-force units.

But that was only the beginning. Having cleared an area, military units had to "hold" it—that is, they had to provide area security while helping police forces to root out the all-important Viet Cong infrastructure, while, simultaneously, other specialized government forces undertook area rehabilitation and established viable government. Military strength was insufficient to clear and hold *all* enemy-infested, or even challenged, areas simultaneously. This meant that priority areas of operation had to be established, along with "economy of force" areas, which received only limited military pressure. Some challenged areas would perforce have had to be ignored until later in the pacification process. The real target was the peasant, not the guerrilla, and the only way the peasant's support could be gained was by establishing secure and viable local-area government—a slow and difficult task.

American strategy and tactics did not respect this essential requirement. Large "sweeps" through an area, though uncovering supply dumps and killing a few enemy, essentially answered nothing. The marines learned this in mid-1965, in their first major aggressive action, Operation Starlight. When combat units left the area for more-urgent duties, Viet Cong cadres and units slipped back to prevent civil teams from carrying out the vital pacification mission. The marines had not

8. Zagoria, op. cit.; see also Johnson (*The Vantage Point*), supra; Henry Brandon in *Anatomy of Error: The Secret History of The Vietnam War* (London: André Deutsch, 1970), discusses this in detail.

realized that Operation Starlight, while allegedly killing some seven hundred Viet Cong, did not kill the NLF-PRP village infrastructure that made Viet Cong existence possible.

Neither did search-and-destroy tactics respect the essential military task. If such tactics had a place, it was a specialized place: On rare occasions, enemy concentrations, such as those in certain areas of the DMZ, could be countered by conventional-warfare methods. As a rule, however, such methods inflicted grievous damage on people whose co-operation was necessary if the over-all mission was to be accomplished. Instead of clearing and holding small areas as first essential steps in winning peasant support, marine and army units pushed out in all directions in huge, awkward attempts to "kill" the enemy. The results were several, and each contained the seeds of important failure.

The first was to widen the war. Up to spring of 1965, fighting in South Vietnam had remained selective, on the whole. Douglas Pike, an official and careful observer and analyst, later wrote:

. . . To those outside Vietnam there was a general perception, one shared neither by Vietnamese nor by foreigners within the country, that South Vietnam was a place of terror and sudden death, of coups d'état and bombings, of alarms and excursions by night. These things did exist. Yet somehow they remained in perspective and did not dominate the lives of either Americans or Vietnamese, in or out of Saigon. . . . Thousands of Vietnamese villagers lived through the entire 1960–1965 period without being involved in, and hardly ever being inconvenienced by, either the NLF's armed struggle or the GVN's military operations. Although subjected to great NLF organizational and political attention, the average rural Vietnamese was seldom if ever a direct victim of its violence program. The mental picture held by most Americans of rural Vietnam as a vast, boiling battlefield, of innumerable military engagements by day, of villages again and again torn apart by ARVN-guerrilla clashes, of a people in the midst of constant fighting and bloodshed, with no place to hide, living in a sort of no man's land between two contending armies—that picture simply does not hold up under scrutiny.

A villager of course would be monumentally affected if his village found itself under guerrilla attack, was the scene of a battle between ARVN troops and the guerrillas, or, if in a liberated area, was bombed or napalmed. But the odds of this happening in the 1960–1964 period were not much greater than the odds of being hit by lightning. If, on a statistical basis, a single rural villager was selected at random and studied in terms of how much the war impinged on his life, how often he witnessed combat or even saw combatants, it is most likely that he never would have been directly affected to any degree. The author talked to innumerable villagers in all parts of Vietnam, and most of them spoke of the effects of the war on others but admitted that it had never fallen on them.

The average rural Vietnamese could plant his rice, watch it grow, harvest it, and begin the cycle again, placidly unconcerned, unaffected by the swirl around him. The result was that he did not perceive the situation in Vietnam as a "war" in the same way that Americans regard the Vietnam "war." Thus the frequently stated observation that the Vietnamese peasant "has known nothing but war for twenty years," although technically accurate, is also misleading. An American reading this formed a mental picture of the peasant in "war" under circumstances quite different from reality.[9]

Escalation inevitably changed this low-key situation. By July 1965, over four hundred thousand refugees had fled South Vietnam's country-side. The bulk of these unfortunates either ended in ghastly shanty-towns around larger cities or in hastily constructed and very primitive camps. Their potential importance was tremendous. Roger Hilsman testified before the Senate in late 1965:

. . . The refugees are, in my judgment, a key [to an effective counter-guerrilla program]. . . . What I am suggesting is that the refugee program should not be just to feed, house, and care for these people, but to train them for the job of making their villages guerrilla proof when they return—to train them as village defenders, as school teachers, medical technicians, agricultural advisers and so on. If an imaginative, positive effort is made, in sum, the refugees can become the vanguard of a peaceful revolution in the Vietnamese countryside sponsored by the free world—which is the only way that the bloody, Communist revolution can be circumvented.

Wesley Fishel, who was originally involved in Ngo Dinh Diem's government, warned the same Senate committee:

. . . If this refugee problem is badly handled, these people . . . could further intensify the political instability of South Vietnam and create even greater problems for the Government than it now faces.
If this situation is treated with some intelligence, then these 600,000 refugees of the moment could become a major asset to the Vietnamese Government. . . . If these people are handled well the Saigon government is going to secure the manifest loyalty which it needs. . . .

Alas, the refugees were not being well handled. Fishel, who visited the area in summer of 1965, told the committee that ". . . thus far I believe the military regime in Saigon has failed to grasp the tremendous implications of this flood of humanity which now threatens to engulf it." The Americans performed no better. AID had estimated a hundred thousand refugees and was unprepared to cope with a larger number. GVN's 1965 budget called for 370 million piasters for refugees, but, as of July, just less than 25 million piasters had been spent. The results were perhaps inevitable. Fishel testified:

. . . I think one generally is surprised by the aimlessness of much that goes on in the camp, by the fact that it is not the kind of planning for these people which would quickly restore them to some useful position in society.

9. Pike, op. cit.

The committee concluded that the refugee program

. . . reflected the absence of an overall strategic concept and program which fully integrates the political, economic, and social aspects of the Vietnamese conflict with the needed military effort.[10]

The second result of promiscuous search-and-destroy tactics, equally unfortunate, was frequent damage to either person or property or both of peasants who remained and whose strength was necessary to effectively counter the insurgency. The third result was frequently to tire the troops with "Yorkish" operations that produced no real benefits:

> The noble Duke of York,
> He had ten thousand men,
> He marched them up to the top of the hill,
> And he marched them down again.

The fourth result was to flood the country with foreign troops. The fifth result was to increase the troop commitment and eventually relieve ARVN of combat duties, which, in turn, called for a larger American military investment, which compounded incipient failures.

By end of 1966, it was becoming clear that American troops had undertaken a task for which they were neither organized nor trained, a task that they did not understand—indeed, a task that could only have been accomplished by the South Vietnamese themselves. Such was the nature of the insurgency, the weakness of the South Vietnamese Government and army, and the limitations of American armed force, that search-and-destroy tactics *had* to fail in Vietnam.

It is a great pity that the innate ineptness of Westmoreland's strategy and tactics was not more obvious. Unfortunately, the "indicators," or criteria selected by the military, to judge progress in Vietnam seemed reasonable to many Americans, who, bless them, at first trusted their government and armed forces. But, as any number of experts had earlier pointed out and as Bernard Fall once again emphasized in 1966, MACV and the JCS continued to judge progress by such military indicators as troop increases, expended ammunition, enemy dead, structures destroyed, rice confiscated, and weapons captured—conventional criteria meaningless in a counterinsurgency.[11]

The military's chief criterion was "kill" figures; pointing to seven to eight hundred enemy deaths a week or forty to fifty thousand a year as well as thousands of wounded and thousands of deserters, they argued that enemy morale would have to crumble. As James Reston wrote, ". . . Death became the official measure of success."

10. U. S. Senate, *Refugee Problems in South Vietnam* (Washington: U. S. Government Printing Office, 1966).
11. Fall ("Viet Nam in the Balance"), *supra*.

But enemy morale showed little sign of crumbling. One qualified British observer, Dennis Duncanson, writing at the end of 1966, pointed out:

. . . Perhaps the day is not far off when it will happen; and yet, for the moment, Viet Cong surrenders do not exceed Government desertions, and the visible, overwhelming might of US armament, though it sustains the Government forces, has made only some—very few—guerrillas think again.[12]

Despite optimistic field reports from American commands, the enemy did not seem to have much difficulty in keeping units up to strength or bringing in new ones from the North. Despite an estimated sixty thousand battle deaths, local VC recruitment continued at thirty-five hundred a month; by mid-1966, VC-PAVN forces had increased within a year from 110,000 to 270,000.[13] The bulk of the increase came from the South: In January 1966, Senator Mansfield had reported that, although total enemy strength in South Vietnam numbered 230,000, the figure included only fourteen thousand North Vietnam regular troops (versus 170,000 American troops in the country)[14]; of an estimated 230,000 enemy at end of 1966, only fifty thousand were North Vietnamese (versus three hundred thousand American troops).[15]

If American marines had thwarted enemy plans in the DMZ and had given Division 324B a bloody nose, Division 324B had shortly reappeared in action—and the enemy had four divisions deployed north of there, nine more divisions farther north, and the Chinese army north of there. If American army units had hurt him in the central highlands and along the Cambodian border, he still had numerous units in reserve, with replacements coming down the Ho Chi Minh Trail through Laos.

Manpower facts alone fatally opposed attrition theory. As one analyst, Herman Kahn, has pointed out:

. . . as long as morale is not too eroded the NLF and the North Vietnamese clearly can replace their losses at the present rate for the rest of history. About 250,000 young men come of age each year in North Viet Nam and about 200,000 in South Viet Nam. In principle, the NLF could replace the 50,000 or so losses that it has been suffering each year, either by drawing on the rural half of this pool or by substituting North Vietnamese. North Viet Nam by drawing on its large pool not only can replace its casualties indefinitely but can also provide "recruits" for the NLF.[16]

12. Duncanson ("The Vitality of the Viet Cong"), *supra*.
13. Fall ("Viet Nam in the Balance"), *supra*.
14. Howard Zinn, *Vietnam—The Logic of Withdrawal* (Boston: Beacon Press, 1967).
15. Corson, op. cit.; see also Edgar O'Ballance, "The Ho Chi Minh Trail," *Army Quarterly*, April 1967.
16. Herman Kahn, "If Negotiations Fail," *Foreign Affairs*, July 1968.

A more subtle difficulty also existed. This was the fallacy inherent in the numbers game. Ever since Dorothy Parker's classic remark ". . . If all the girls at Vassar were laid end to end, I wouldn't be surprised," American analysts had become slaves to statistical studies. Testifying before the Senate Foreign Relations Committee in February 1966, Maxwell Taylor stated:

. . . Encouraging though the results have been in increasing the Vietnamese strength, during the year cited, our intelligence authorities believed that the Viet Cong increased their total strength by some sixty thousand. In other words, we were advancing at a rate only a little better than two to one in our favor. Since history has shown that the government forces successfully opposing a guerrilla insurgency in the past have required a much greater preponderance of strength, ten to one or twelve to one for example, it was quite clear the Vietnamese could not raise forces fast enough to keep pace with the growing threat of the Viet Cong in time. It was this sobering conclusion that led to the decision to introduce American ground forces with their unique mobility and massive fire power to compensate for the deficiency in Vietnamese strength. With such forces available, it was felt that the ratios of required strength cited above would lose much of their validity.[17]

Taylor was trying to mount cannons in sand. As Richard Clutterbuck, the British counterinsurgency expert, has argued, the 12:1 or 10:1 soldier vs. guerrilla ratio is virtually meaningless, since the guerrilla's strength derives from the people, and his numbers must include not only those persons sympathetic to his aims but those too frightened or too apathetic to contest those aims. Successful Roman commanders in Spain had realized this before the birth of Christ. In 1775, General Gage had warned that American rebels would not be easily subdued (see Chapter 7, Volume I):

. . . Since other colonies would undoubtedly come to the aid of the north, ". . . he urged that the Ministry estimate the number of men and the sums of money needed, and then double their figures."

When another realist, William Tecumseh Sherman, was asked how many men he would need to pacify the Cumberland area during the Civil War, he replied: "Two hundred thousand" (see Chapter 11, Volume I).

A further difficulty existed: The enemy, both South and North, was not standing alone. Although Soviet aid in 1965 amounted to only about half a billion dollars, it substantially increased during 1966, after Alexander Shelepin's mission to Hanoi in January, when he promised ". . . ground-to-air missiles, 'complex' antiaircraft guns with radar

17. J. William Fulbright (ed.), *The Vietnam Hearings* (New York: Vintage Books, 1966).

guidance systems, and antiaircraft automatic guns of 'large caliber' ";
the U.S.S.R. quickly furnished these, along with some fighter aircraft.
Later in the year, at an October conference of Communist countries,
the Soviet Union agreed to contribute $800 million of a proposed billion
dollars of additional aid. Hanoi, meanwhile, was successfully playing
off Moscow against Peking, which was also supplying arms and equipment[18] and probably stood ready to supply "volunteers" if necessary.[19]

American bombing and interdiction of supply routes in the North
and Laos and in South Vietnam were only partially successful in interrupting the flow of supply south. Planes could bomb and strafe roads
and railroads and warehouses and vehicles, but thousands of peasants
repaired roads and bridges, and trucks continued to travel at night.
Moreover, enemy supply did not depend entirely on the Ho Chi Minh
Trail or on vehicles. An experienced American marine observer pointed
out in March 1966

. . . that South Viet-Nam is fronted by over 500 miles of penetrable national boundary. Though the general trace of the Ho Chi Minh trail does
exist, the actual points of entry into South Viet-Nam are subject to the latest
VC intelligence. It is still more difficult to comprehend the number of personnel involved in logistic transportation. Of primary impact is the individual
carrying capacity of the Vietnamese people. Eighty-pound women can carry
100-pound loads for long distances; children easily carry their own weight.
Viewed as a military application, 100 pounds is four 75mm recoilless rifle
rounds or 33 60mm mortar rounds. If each supply column is composed
of at least 100 persons, and over 100 columns are in motion in different
areas at the same time, the potential "pipe-line" is shown in realistic perspective. Security is provided by local guerrilla forces. Coordination is facilitated
by restricting supply columns to fragmented routes of march. Group One
moves only from town A to town B and return. At town B, Group Two
picks up the load and moves it on to town C where the next Group takes
over. Though this method requires more time and personnel than Western
organizations, it is not dependent on any specified or vulnerable routes, or
is there any threat of mechanical failure. People are the only required item
of equipment. Even if five columns are interdicted, others are simultaneously
rerouted and the ant-like procession continues.[20]

The Viet Cong also received supply from sampans sailing from the
North, from peasants sympathetic to the rebel cause, from corrupt
South Vietnamese officials, and, not least, from attacks on government
outposts and hamlets and villages. Such was the extent of local support

18. Zagoria, op. cit.
19. Albert Parry, "Soviet Aid to Vietnam," *The Reporter*, January 12, 1967.
20. Lane Rogers, "The Enemy," *Marine Corps Gazette*, March 1966.

and participation, that Dennis Duncanson has called Vietnam a *symbiotic insurgency:*

> . . . one, that is, in which, for the great bulk of its resources, the revolutionary movement draws its requirements from the supplies of its adversaries.[21]

Kill figures contained two other weaknesses: First, they were suspect. Such was the tactical environment, that "body counts" were often hasty even when taken from the ground. When made from a helicopter or even an aircraft, they were generally fraudulent. "Probable kills"—usually exceeding "confirmed kills" and generally complemented by two or three times the number of vanished wounded—represented more wishful thinking than corpses. Far more sinister, however, was the almost constant gap between enemy dead and number of weapons captured; we shall never know how many civilians were included in "kill" figures.

We do know that American tactics had been used countless times in history, as earlier chapters have demonstrated. Whether called search-and-destroy or burn-and-bolt (see Chapter 29, Volume I), they amounted, too often, to indiscriminate use of force against peasants, some of whom were armed and a great many of whom were not. These tactics made about as much sense as early Cornish law, or, as Browne put it:

> I oft have heard of Lydford law,
> How in the morn they hang and draw—
> And sit in judgment after. . . .

Search-and-destroy tactics replaced the Lyauteyan concept, of winning hearts and minds, with the Western concept quoted by one senior American commander in Vietnam: ". . . Grab 'em by the balls and the hearts and minds will follow."[22] Too often, it was warfare at its most violent and stupid, and those who ordered it and condoned its excesses were placing themselves in a dangerous legal and moral position.[23]

Even when senior officers controlled the tactic, operations generally hurt or destroyed peasants, whose support was necessary if the government was ever to counter the insurgency. So long as peasants remained hostile or apathetic, American and ARVN forces were operating largely in the dark (despite intelligence furnished by the air force). Senior American commanders were only too well aware that, although American infusion of combat strength had blunted the enemy offensive, American "spoiling" tactics had not claimed the initiative except in isolated tactical instances and then only rarely.

21. Duncanson ("The Vitality of the Viet Cong"), *supra.*
22. Corson, op. cit.
23. Telford Taylor, *Nuremberg and Vietnam: An American Tragedy* (New York: Quadrangle Books, 1970).

The choice of search-and-destroy tactics was perhaps inevitable, considering the tactical "shape" of American units—and this introduces still another blur. Despite emphasis placed on counterinsurgency warfare since 1961, U.S. divisions, regiments, and battalions were more suitably formed for conventional than for irregular warfare. This meant, among other things, a quantitative approach that proved expensive in manpower and resources. In 1965, U.S. officer death rate in South Vietnam soon rose above the 5 per cent of World War II and Korea; U.S. casualty figures for 1966 totaled four thousand killed and twenty-one thousand wounded by spring, cumulative totals that would rise sharply by year's end. Also upsetting, of 240,000 U.S. troops in South Vietnam, ". . . only 50,000 at most were actual combat troops"—and those suffered the bulk of casualties.[24] Westmoreland perforce developed an insatiable appetite for troops, only a relatively small percentage of whom could undertake combat/pacification tasks. Added to this was a personnel policy that limited a tour of duty to one year: thus, those who fought the enemy did so for only twelve months before returning to the United States—in the case of draftees, for discharge.[25] But, such was (and is) the American military's administrative requirement, that roughly three months was spent coming, three months going. And such was the peculiar nature of the war, as we shall shortly examine, that a man needed the other six months to learn how to fight it. If he survived enemy mines and booby traps and ambushes and pungi stakes and jungle rot and malaria—if he lived and remained intact in body and mind—he was just becoming valuable when he went home.

An enormous logistics requirement also existed and adversely affected the situation in several ways. Search-and-destroy tactics in a hostile country utilized an expenditure of ammunition that is difficult to comprehend. The official explanation for abrogation of what older soldiers know as "fire discipline" is to the effect that, lacking sufficient numbers to fight the war (the old shibboleth 10:1 or 12:1 was constantly invoked by such as Maxwell Taylor), American forces had to compensate by increased mobility and firepower. The true explanation is far more complex and stems from fear derived from ignorance of the enemy. Versions of the army's "mad minute" described in the next chapter existed throughout American operations in South Vietnam. In describing one patrol action in mid-1966, Captain West wrote:

. . . Less than two minutes after reception of the message, the guns were firing. So swift was the reaction that the message alerting the patrol of an impending fire mission reached the patrol via the relay station after the shells had fallen. The battery fired 1,188 pounds of high explosives to discourage the trackers. It did.

24. Fall ("Viet Nam in the Balance"), *supra.*
25. C. N. Barclay, "The Western Soldier Versus the Communist Insurgent," *Military Review,* February 1969.

Twenty minutes later, from task force headquarters came the order to blanket the entire target area. At higher headquarters, the thinking was that, if the North Vietnamese had organized a pursuit, they must have returned to their base camp and been in the process of digging out. The battery fired another area saturation mission, dropping 10,692 pounds of high explosives in the stream bed, base camp, and hill complex.[26]

This was theater policy, and, far too often, it amounted to promiscuous firing that accomplished very little, oftentimes damaged a great deal— and, in any event, was very expensive.

Quasi-conventional operations were equally expensive. To field what amounted to nearly a marine division during Operation Hastings required a supply effort that suggested a World War II amphibious landing. Robert Shaplen, who was on the scene, later described the combined arms effort utilized against a North Vietnamese division of ten to twelve thousand troops:

. . . Between July 15th and August 3rd, the day Hastings ended, some seventy helicopters made more than twelve thousand sorties, lifting more than seventeen thousand troops about and delivering thirteen hundred tons of cargo. During this period, twelve hundred tons of ordnance—bombs, napalm, rockets, and other forms of ammunition—were either fired or dropped by helicopter into the battle zones, and fighter-bombers based at Danang and Chu Lai, south of Danang, made more than twelve hundred sorties. During some of these attacks—particularly at night or in poor weather —targets were hit by radar control, the bombs being dropped when buttons were pushed in Dong Ha. In some respects, the most amazing job was that performed by the lumbering, awkward-looking C-130 transport planes, which during the Hastings period flew ten and a half million pounds of cargo from Danang into Dong Ha, which at the outset had only a small dirt airstrip. . . .[27]

To give the 1st Cavalry (Airmobile) Division helicopter mobility meant supplying five hundred tons of material a day.[28] Such was the appetite of conventionally organized American units that a division required a logistics "tail" of over forty thousand troops. Put another way, of every hundred thousand troops committed in South Vietnam, perhaps twenty thousand would serve in a combat role, and, of the twenty thousand, a significant percentage would be performing service and logistic duties.

Another factor, meanwhile, inexorably exacerbated the supply problem. With exception of a few elite units, American armed forces had grown used to comfort, and even elite units expected amenities pro-

26. West ("Small Unit Action in Vietnam—Summer 1966"), *supra*.
27. Shaplen (*Road*), *supra*.
28. Jac Weller, "The U. S. Army in Vietnam: A Survey of Aims, Operations, and Weapons, Particularly of Small Infantry Units," *Army Quarterly*, October 1967.

vided by no other armed forces in the world or in history. This disturbing trend began after World War II and stemmed in part from a national pride of an affluent society buttressed by swollen defense budgets. By the time of Korea, it had grown sufficiently for one commander, General Mark Clark, to complain. Shortly after assuming command in Korea, he later wrote,

. . . I felt strongly that we would have to pull in our belts, cut off some fat. We have always wanted the best of everything for our men—the best medical care, the best equipment, the best-stocked post exchanges, the best service clubs, the best entertainment, the best in food and clothing. In Korea that search for the best went so far as to make ice cream an item of regular distribution to front-line units.

Our rotation system in Korea sent hundreds of thousands of our men home after nine to twelve months service in the front line. . . .

The experience strongly impressed Clark, who concluded:

. . . I always insisted that my men in battle have the finest care that our medical profession can provide. The same goes for fighting equipment, clothing and food.

But the amenities in the American Army will have to be the first casualty in any big war with communism.[29]

By the end of 1966, the amenities in South Vietnam had not gone, and they added heavily to the logistics requirement.

Aside from expense, the logistics burden influenced the situation in two ways: First, as General Ridgway's 1954 report had emphasized, the theater of war was not compatible with support of conventional forces. Base development, as Ridgway forecast, proved an enormous task. Westmoreland himself later wrote that, lacking ". . . a fully developed logistic base" to support combat units rushed into South Vietnam, he had to use ". . . backed-up ships as floating warehouses."[30] What he did not point out was the large number of combat troops initially tied up in base-construction tasks during this crucial period. But conventional organization also meant undue reliance on mechanical transport and on supporting weapons that tended to "tie" small units to centralized operations and also consumed "combat troops" in administrative and support duties. Each new installation produced a new security requirement, both to protect the installation and to provide security for convoys carrying material to combat units, and this, in turn, demanded more troops.

A second result was more indirect but equally invidious. To supply the insatiable hunger of a few combat divisions, base supply areas developed and rapidly expanded. Each held thousands of troops who

29. Mark W. Clark, op. cit.
30. *U. S. News and World Report,* November 28, 1966.

could not but influence local economies—too often, adversely. A heavy expenditure of piasters contributed to an already ugly inflation. A black market invariably sprang up, one not alone fed by PX and commissary supplies but often by combat equipment and arms—significant quantities of each ultimately ending in Viet Cong hands. Bored garrison soldiers also constituted a problem: bars, dance halls, whorehouses, each multiplied to exacerbate already difficult community relations, particularly between American and ARVN soldiers.[31] Large numbers of Vietnamese employees—around a hundred thousand, many in servile occupations—inside American bases not only upset local economies but insured that Americans continued to live inside a fish bowl.

All these factors combined to produce a highly unsatisfactory military profile. By the end of 1966, Westmoreland's military plant, which should have been lean and fit, resembled the Jurassic dinosaur, which became weaker as it grew larger.

31. Malcolm W. Browne, "Why South Viet Nam's Army Won't Fight," *True Magazine,* October 1967.

Chapter 84

More blurs on the canvas • American tactical problems • The failure of Operation Crazy Horse • Colonel Emerson defines the tactical challenge • U. S. Marine Corps operations • Captain Miller's observations • The intelligence failure • Mines and booby traps • VC intelligence network • Captain Cooper's discovery • The pacification failure • Continued governmental abuses • ARVN's failure • Dissent in the U.S.A. • The Vietnam hearings • The thoughts of James Gavin and George Kennan • The secret thoughts of Robert McNamara • Escalation pressures • The hawks win again

THREE OTHER BLURS had appeared on the allied operational canvas by the end of 1966: One was the difficulty of American combat units in adapting to the tactical challenge; one, the continued inept performance of South Vietnam's government and army; and one, the influence of these on American opinion, both official and public.

American combat units faced severe tactical problems in South Vietnam, most of which resulted from trying to impose Western tactical doctrines on an insurgency environment. Contemporary accounts of fighting in 1965 and 1966 leave little to be desired regarding individual and unit bravery. Young officers, non-commissioned officers, soldiers, marines, sailors, and airmen generally fought hard and gave as much as, and more than, they got.

But were they fighting wisely?

Let us return for just a moment to Operation Crazy Horse, so well described by S. L. A. Marshall and cited briefly in Chapter 82. Did anyone at corps or division or brigade level consider the possibility of accomplishing the mission by beating the enemy at his own game? The CIDG had made a good start by bushwhacking an enemy patrol—a prosperous tactic that should have impressed senior commanders. Marshall does not suggest alternate plans. No mention is made of carrying on as usual while setting a trap for the enemy lurking up in the mountains.

Estimate of enemy intentions is relatively simple: He is going to attack the CIDG camp—a small and minor installation—or he is going to shell Camp Radcliffe with mortars, or he is going to do nothing until more reinforcements reach him by means of routes shown on the captured map. To accomplish either of the first two objectives, he would have to bring forward his units and thus subject them to ambush. What would have been the result had not one ambush team of the type described by Marshall (which is larger than necessary) but a score or forty or eighty such teams spotted the few routes of approach? What would have happened had similar teams staked out ingress routes?

Put another way, why hurry to ferret out the enemy on other than your own terms? The war was not going to end the next day. Corps, division, and brigade commanders knew enough of the area to know their ignorance concerning enemy strength and locations. Intelligence had furnished some reasonable indications of enemy presence in strength. By this time, senior commanders knew that the enemy rarely acted impulsively—that he prepared the battlefield, in this case his mountain base. Lacking patience to prepare a reception for the enemy, did no one want to find out more before committing a company? What was the matter with using the CIDG force, which operated extremely well in the mountains? Lacking this force, where were the small guerrilla teams that were needed to work the area? Why an orthodox approach, when, from beginning to end, the units would be operating in the blind? Marshall's only explanation is unsettling in the extreme:

. . . So it became agreed, as it was later done, an inspiration of which nothing better can be said than that it seemed to look good at the time. At the top level of the cavalry division there was still no firm belief that the hills so close to home base were loaded with big game.[1]

According to Marshall—traditionally pro-army—the company patrol was committed in an incredibly casual fashion: ". . . First Brigade had been looking for a low-grade operation of company size in enemy country, with small risk," for the purpose of "conditioning" a new company commander and first sergeant, neither of whom had had combat experience. ". . . Every platoon sergeant was without experience at fighting in Vietnam." The company was not properly alerted—". . . they thought of the outing as a training exercise." The company was also understrength by thirty-one men. Two more men collapsed at LZ Here-

1. S. L. A. Marshall, op. cit.

ford, where helicopters landed them in daylight, and two more came down on pungi sticks and had to be evacuated. The remainder landed in channeled terrain in full view of whatever enemy occupied the area.

What was the kit for people moving in mountainous terrain, in very hot humid weather, where mobility was all-important?

. . . Every man carried at least twenty magazines, or 400 bullets for his M-16. There were 1000 rounds apiece for the six machine guns. All hands had a minimum of two, but most of them carried four hand grenades. There were two M-79 grenade launchers per squad, with fifty rounds for each weapon. Also they carried food for six meals, in C rations. For the one 81 mm mortar that was carried along there were twenty-six rounds. This last was useless weight. The mortar crew never found a spot where they could fire the tube without hitting the jungle mass in the immediate foreground.

Whether the presence of pungi sticks, not a few but hundreds, was reported back to brigade commander Colonel John Hennessey is not related, but the presence of communications wire was reported. At LZ Hereford, they left a platoon in defense and took off on a single jungle trail for the top of the mountain. Midway, they discovered more communications wire and reported this to Hennessey. Pungi sticks, not a few but hundreds, and communications wire—either one suggested trouble. The enemy hit them at the top of the slope, at the same time blocking their retreat. Forming a small perimeter, they called in Huey gunships and held until a reinforcing company arrived. Throughout the long night, Puff the Magic Dragon dropped flares and Huey gunships plastered the area with rockets. At first light, the force staged a World War I tactic called the "mad minute":

. . . all hands fire all weapons around the perimeter and keep the blast going for sixty seconds, the central idea being that if the enemy is preparing to charge as the darkest hour ends, the shock fire will turn him about.

The enemy did attack, but then withdrew pursued by guns firing from LZ Savoy. Hennessey landed the vanguard of a reinforcing battalion, and the veterans of the night evacuated with some twenty dead and fifty-four wounded.

Very little of the above suggests tactical mastery or even excellence. In subsequent actions, PAVN units used both ambushes and envelopment with telling effect. American units twice walked *through* areas holding sizable numbers of enemy, hidden, weapons zeroed in, patiently waiting for a propitious moment to strike. They paid for their carelessness.[2]

And if they replied in kind, that does not erase the unpalatable fact that the enemy had made friends with the terrain and had either won

2. Ibid.

over or neutralized most of its inhabitants. The Americans may have been technologically superior, but, despite a panoply of firepower, despite magic dragons and mad minutes, they never owned more than the ground they walked on or fought from. They were operating in the blind, and they continued to pay for it, and the debt did not lessen because ten times as many or twenty times as many (or whatever ratio MACV claimed) of the enemy died as well. As one disillusioned veteran, Donald Duncan, told one of his mates: ". . . Sure we have the skills—and thousands of dollars worth of sophisticated radios, helicopters, C-47s to fly contacts, choppers to stand by in case we get in trouble, helicopters to bring us home. With all that going for us, if we survive the first couple of hours [of a patrol], we have a fifty-fifty chance of getting out five days later. We have to be skillful with our equipment, because it's all we've got. As we've learned the hard way, nobody living in the area will help us. The VC have the people, we have our helicopters. I don't call that effective, and I don't think it's the same game."[3]

A veteran lieutenant colonel commented feelingly on the problem to Jac Weller:

. . . We can use some sophisticated detection devices, but we must rely mainly on the eyes and ears of the foot soldier. He is the best source of useful intelligence. I feel that we do not always employ the foot soldier to his maximum capability. Properly trained and led, small reconnaissance patrols could roam the country in depth and could provide a wealth of information. Our old Ranger companies of Korean days and Special Forces mercenary patrols *under U.S. command* could do a superior job along this line. We could, and should, enhance their ability by introduction of the "Katusas" (Koreans in U.S. units serving in South Korea) system.

The colonel touched on another major deficiency:

. . . Night operations don't require comment; they require doing. The average American seems to have an innate fear of darkness and will avoid night operations whenever possible. This applies alike to new recruits and officers in high commands. Moving and fighting at night takes training and professional expertise, but some U.S. units have developed this capability. . . . until we can teach every U.S. soldier to consider darkness an advantage, the night will belong to the V.C.

If I were C/S [chief of staff], I would see that the work of one month in three was done entirely at night. All training including classroom exercises, close order drill, and so on would be done during darkness and with a minimum of artificial light. When we conquer this fear of the night, we will minimize our defensive thinking and move out of our camps at sundown, not into them.[4]

3. Duncan, op. cit.
4. Weller, op. cit.

Lieutenant Colonel Henry Emerson, who commanded a battalion of 101st Airborne paratroopers, early recognized the tactical challenge and adapted accordingly. Emerson told a *Newsweek* correspondent:

. . . It is a fast-moving, exhausting, subtle style of war, requiring heavy firepower even in a small unit patrol. The men in the Second Battalion are walking arsenals, carrying everything from light-weight M16 automatic rifles and M60 machine-guns to grenade launchers, hand-grenades and sharp-bladed Bowie knives. As often as possible, they operate by darkness. Each soldier carries one or two cans of meat rations and 2½ lb. of rice—enough for five days. "I try to get my men to sustain themselves for five days without resupply," says Emerson. "My effort is to try to beat the damned guerrilla at his own game."[5]

Up north, marines also found the tactical going extremely difficult, be it in fighting guerrilla warfare south of the DMZ or in fighting larger, quasi-guerrilla operations in and around the DMZ. Part of the problem was normal: that of adapting to a new tactical environment. An experienced veteran of these early days, Captain John Miller, later offered a remarkably candid analysis of small-unit actions and problems encountered by the newcomers. Miller found the climate to be hostile:

. . . The constant heavy rains of the wet monsoon can swell rifle stocks to the point where the trigger cannot be depressed completely and where disassembly and assembly are out of the question. Rust and corrosion of metal surfaces are, of course, accompanying side effects.

Terrain, too, posed immense problems:

. . . The unit leader must constantly fight the recurring problem of canalization. Both the thickly wooded highlands and the open paddy areas tend to force his unit—be it squad or company—into a column, vulnerable to directional mines, ambushes, and similar evils. His choices are limited. If he departs from a jungle trail, he must cut his own—and pay the price in terms of slow movement plus wear and tear on his trailbreakers. If he leaves the paddy dikes, he can count on the same slow pace in moving through the muck and (sometimes) high water and high grass. In deciding, he must constantly weigh the requirements of his mission against his vulnerability, adopting whatever dispersion and security measures he can effect.

Rains frequently altered terrain to an amazing degree. Like Alexander's forces in Bactria,

. . . Coils of line and flotation material for improvised rafts become standard patrol accessories during this period. More than passing attention must be devoted to stream-crossing techniques and to security measures which must

5. Ibid. quoting *Newsweek,* May 23, 1966.

be employed during crossings. At times, small boats must be bought, borrowed, or commandeered in an attempt to match the enemy's sampan mobility.

Marines had to learn how to keep as dry as possible and avoid omnipresent evils such as immersion foot (from wet socks) and flu/pneumonia (from generally wet surroundings). Miller also commented feelingly about "the load":

. . . It is still too heavy. A Marine wearing a flak jacket [body armor] will not match the cross-country speed of a guerrilla who is not wearing one. Unit commanders, through judicious pacing of their moves, can avoid excessive heat casualties, but the box score of heat-evacs does not tell the whole story. The biggest hazard is the sluggishness and slow reaction of an overheated, overtired Marine to a fast-breaking combat situation. Without question, the jackets have saved many lives. The heavy preponderance of wounds sustained by Marines are still of the fragmentation type. Because of these undisputable facts, the unit commander will usually find that the jackets-or-no-jackets decision has already been made for him. The issue then becomes a "leadership problem."[6]

Another marine officer, Captain West, later described a patrol with the 9th Marines:

. . . The Marines wore helmets and flak jackets. Each rifleman carried 150 rounds of ammunition and 2 or more hand grenades. The men of the two machine gun crews were draped with belts of linked cartridges totalling 1,200 rounds. The two 3.5-inch rocket launcher teams carried five high explosive and five white phosphorus rockets. Four grenadiers carried 28 40mm shells apiece for their stubby M79s. Sergeant Cunningham had given six LAAWs [a 66 mm one-shot disposable rocket launcher for use against tanks] to some riflemen to provide additional area target capability. . . .

The platoon moved out at 1100. There was no breeze and no shade. The temperature was 102 degrees. Within five minutes, every Marine was soaked in sweat. . . .[7]

Although the patrol acquitted itself well, the weight problem continued to bother unit commanders. Captain Miller noted that company commanders could lighten loads by replacing bulky C rations with dehydrated and lightweight foods, and that a lighter radio also helped. The problem nonetheless remained:

. . . Heavy loads, heat, canalizing terrain, and flooding combine to create significant dilemmas of movement for the unit leader who is constantly attempting to trap an elusive enemy. The company commander can assist in

6. John G. Miller, "From a Company Commander's Notebook," *Marine Corps Gazette,* August 1966.
7. West, op. cit.

resolving these dilemmas at squad and platoon level by deploying his forces—when possible—in a manner to provide mutually supporting maneuver units. This requires careful preliminary study of the area of operations and some degree of anticipation of the "danger spots" within each area—when time is available.[8]

Other accounts substantiated Miller's observations as marines familiarized themselves with various areas of operation. One of the most difficult problems faced was enemy use of mines. Whether planted passively or electrically detonated by guerrillas, they extracted a heavy toll, not alone from the initial explosion but often in subsequent pursuit actions that involved enemy-prepared terrain and ambush. Discussing small-unit operations in spring of 1966, Captain West pointed out that of ten marines killed and fifty-eight wounded in one company in five weeks, ". . . two men were hit by small arms fire, one by a grenade. Mines inflicted all the other casualties."[9]

These and other substantial problems usually stemmed, at least in part, from a supreme problem: lack of intelligence. Marine patrols, more often than not, were operating in the dark, trying to guess enemy locations while keeping oriented with unsatisfactory, 1:50,000 maps. Marines were not long in the field before they agreed with Captain Miller's conclusion that the enemy presented ". . . a constantly changing face in small unit tactics and techniques, as he seeks to counter Marine methods of operation."

Lack of intelligence told in a number of ways. Captain Miller noted that:

. . . target acquisition is one of the rifleman's biggest problems. The presence of civilians on the battlefield requires each Marine to exercise the finest degree of judgment in applying any number of local rules of engagement. This situation sometimes puts Marines in the unhappy position of having to "lead with their chins" in order to make contact with the enemy.[10]

Leading with their chins was exactly what the enemy wanted marines to do. They reacted in one of several ways. Sometimes they slipped away, usually leading the marine unit a merry chase before so doing. Sometimes they fought and, though suffering themselves, usually inflicted relatively high casualties on the marine units involved; but, more important than that from the enemy standpoint, he usually arranged the firefight so that peasants tasted marine wrath.

Examples in each category abound. Only too often, patrol radios crackled out this type of bad news:

. . . This is Bound-3, let me speak to Blade-2 . . . we have just drawn another nothing-zero-blank! Delta and Bravo [companies] cordoned off the

8. Miller, op. cit.
9. West, op. cit.; see also O'Neill, op. cit.
10. Miller, op. cit.

area and we've been searching for two days. No sign of the VC. No indication that there have ever been any VC in this area.

Again,

. . . Blade 00 this is Blade-3. Nothing! We have searched every inch of that hamlet and there's no sign of the VC. Somebody is passing us bum dope . . . this is the third time in two weeks.[11]

Sometimes marine patrols were fired on from hamlets or had visual evidence of VC occupation. Captain West described one such occasion, a platoon patrol of the 5th Marines:

. . . Occasionally they saw the Viet Cong. Some were carrying weapons, some wore packs, some were dressed in black peasant shirts and shorts, some in green uniforms. They traveled freely in small groups of from two to eight men. They crossed the rice paddies, chatted with the women hoeing or the boys herding cows, and entered various hamlets, without any apparent military pattern or plan to their movements. The enemy seemed unaware that the shells which fell sporadically near them were observed fire missions [called by the marine patrol], although some were hit and dragged away.

Monroe requested that a Marine company sweep the area. From his observation post, he could direct their movements. Charlie Company arrived by foot two hours later and the platoons spread out on line to sweep the hamlets.

A quarter of a mile in front of the company, Robinson saw a group of armed VC in uniforms run across a rice paddy and enter a large house. They reappeared moments later, wearing black pajamas, straw conical hats, and carrying hoes. They split up and waded into the rice paddies.

"Look at them—the innocent farmers. They're going to get the surprise of their lives when they're scoffed up—hoes and all—in a few minutes," Monroe said.

It was Monroe who was surprised; the company was ordered back to base camp to perform another mission.

"We'll get that hooch [native house] ourselves on our way in tomorrow morning," he said.[12]

On occasion, similar patrols walked into enemy ambush and, though fighting valiantly and well, were often badly hurt. Even where ambushes were avoided, other dangers constantly lurked. Mines and booby traps (minbotraps) are always difficult to detect, but were particularly so in

11. John P. Murtha, "Combat Intelligence in Vietnam," *Marine Corps Gazette,* January 1968; see also Otto Heilbrunn, "Counter-Insurgency Intelligence," *Marine Corps Gazette,* September 1966; Leon Cohan, "Intelligence and Viet-Nam," *Marine Corps Gazette,* February 1966.
12. West, op. cit.

Vietnam. One experienced adviser later discussed various clues as to presence of mines, for example soil disturbance:

. . . Another signal that should arouse suspicion is the change of the natural scene in any form. A small branch of a tree blocking the jungle trail may be the actuator for an explosive. The hand that casually brushes it aside is the objective.

The means that the enemy uses to identify the minbotrap is closely allied to detection. The branch mentioned above might also indicate to the VC that a mine is buried in the trail ahead. Broken sticks, a dead snake, a worn out conic [head gear], a piece of cloth, and an old sandal have all been used in the past for identification purposes. It's a battle of wits and no matter how insignificant, all suspected means used by the insurgent for recognition of minbotraps should be reported. This is an enemy code and the best source of information to break the code is the man in daily contact with the VC.

Once again, war reverted to the peasant: ". . . The peasantry often know about the enemy's minbotrap tactics; everything from restricted areas to actual MBT locations."[13] As one senior intelligence officer pointed out to this writer, the peasant *invariably* knew the location of booby traps and mines, but, for one or more reasons, usually fear of the VC, would not warn the intended victim, thereby further eliciting American fury.

What allied forces in Vietnam refused to recognize, at least for some time, was what Callwell had pointed out nearly a hundred years earlier: In a guerrilla situation, the guerrilla is the professional, the newcomer the amateur. A veteran marine intelligence officer later wrote of a VC intelligence officer, ". . . a wizened little man wearing black pajamas and tire-tread sandals":

. . . Ai No U does not have aerial observers; no infra-red, no SLAR, no TV; no digital data "real time" readout computerized equipment. But he is successful. This confounds Americans. The result is a communist psychological operation by accident; more effective than if by design. How does he do it?

Ai No U relies upon two things: (1) the People's Military Intelligence Concept, and (2) the American Military penchant for the SOP [standard operating procedure], a commander's tactical signature.

The peasant formed the core of the VC intelligence organization,

. . . a form of reconnaissance broadly participated in by the masses. The concept consists of organizing the population, teaching them how to take advantage of their normal activities to perform reconnaissance. It is visualized as an immense information collection network with thousands of ears and eyes concentrated upon all enemy activities—military, political, and social.

13. R. E. Mack, "Minbotrap," *Marine Corps Gazette,* July 1967.

Reconnaissance is only one function, however:

> . . . this vast network provides commo-liaison agents, warning services, and a pipeline for agent infiltration; conducts military proselyting, participates in psychological operations; and takes diversionary action to provide security for cadre personnel.

Cellular organization makes it particularly difficult to penetrate:

> . . . An elaborate apparatus known as commo-liaison provides communication between intelligence cells. Together these form an integrated intelligence system extending through every province and district, city and town, village and hamlet. Intelligence cadre actively supervise each of these echelons.

Much of the success of this effort, in turn, rested on American tactical predictability, or SOP operations. Fragmentary reports (frequently from VC sympathizers) too often tipped the American commander's hand and allowed a VC unit to disperse. The ensuing operation, while accomplishing no concrete result, often further antagonized the peasants, strengthening VC control over them.[14]

The key remained the peasant. Despite the aggression-from-the-North theme, constantly hammered home by senior American officials and officers, the real enemy was indigenous to the area; as Viet Minh, he had fought the French; as Viet Cong, he was fighting ARVN and the Americans. He had lived in this area for a long time; he had devoted his every effort to his task. Here is one marine description of a VC complex, by no means extraordinary:

> . . . All the tunnels had well-concealed entrances located in the heavy vegetation, generally in close proximity to the houses. In one area, six caves were located in what appeared to be a graveyard. The entrances were well concealed under cactus plants. It was noted that almost all the tunnels were dug on a bank or on high ground to afford good drainage. They were well constructed and thoroughly waterproofed. Despite heavy rain only two tunnels were found with water in them. Tunnels were reinforced with concrete and almost all had a corrugated tin roof. In addition to the enemy killed and captured, numerous weapons, 62 mines, various equipment and many documents were discovered by the search force.

> It is significant to remember that the Viet Cong were hidden within 500 meters of the original cordon, and could have easily ex-filtrated during the night. The Viet Cong did not actually believe the Marines could find them. . . .[15]

Nor could marines have found them without valid intelligence procedures. Once the area intelligence concept was refined and became productive, tactical success resulted. The above position was uncovered

---

14. S. L. Grier, "Black Pajama Intelligence," *Marine Corps Gazette*, April 1967.
15. West, op. cit.

in a cordon operation in October 1966, in which twenty-two VC were killed and forty-three captured.

Here, then, was the real problem: The enemy profited from detailed knowledge of most operational areas, knowledge gleaned from personal reconnaissance, often over the years and sometimes even decades, and from information supplied either by guerrillas or local peasants who either sympathized with the VC cause or were coerced into co-operation. The enemy also profited from an adaptive ability noted by one experienced marine officer: ". . . His techniques and tactics are not exotic innovations; his strength lies only in the ability to apply fundamentals and to adjust his tactics to those of his opponent."[16]

This was precisely the challenge faced by marines. They were fighting to clear an area infested by gophers: For too long, their answer was to rip up terrain in an attempt, vain of course, to kill the gophers rather than to make that terrain sufficiently unpleasant for the gophers to go away. Some commanders twigged the essential problem and tried to do something about it. In mid-1966, one company commander, Captain Jim Cooper, saw the futility of operating from an isolated combat outpost on top of a hill:

. . . After a few weeks of fruitless forays and grimy living, Echo Company changed its tactics and position. "I just got plain sick and tired of baking on top of some hill while the VC ran the villagers down in the valleys. So I decided to move," Captain Cooper said.

Cooper moved his people into a hamlet of about three hundred fifty peasants, one of several in a village complex of some six thousand population, set up proper security, increased patrols and ambushes, and slowly integrated a theretofore isolated Popular Forces unit into hamlet life:

. . . The hamlet chief moved from the ARVN fort back into his own home. . . . Cooperation followed friendship. The hamlet chief showed the Marines the favorite ambush and hiding places of the Viet Cong.

Cooper was on to the real secret of fighting an insurgency. But, despite his impressive success, he learned by a cunning maneuver that VC sympathizers and informers continued to live *in the hamlet*. What had happened, in other words, was that surrounding VC units had shifted operations elsewhere. Converting the village to the government's side would have taken a major effort and much patience and time. And here is what happened:

. . . Less than a month after their arrival, the Marines did leave to go on an operation. They left the marks of their influence behind in the village

16. Rogers, op. cit.; see also R. E. Mack, "Ambuscade," *Marine Corps Gazette*, April 1967.

and especially in the hamlet. The Vietnamese had reopened two schools and a pagoda. They were washing. Their medical ills had been treated. A Vietnamese public health nurse and two school teachers had come to the village. The hamlet and village chiefs had returned. The Popular Forces were acting more like disciplined troops.

What would happen in the future, Cooper was not about to guess. . . .[17]

What happened to that particular village, we are not told. What frequently happened both in I Corps area and elsewhere was a return of the VC the moment allied troops departed.[18] Once again, the situation cried for clear-and-hold tactics followed by a viable pacification or rehabilitation campaign. General Walt and his marines finally came to understand this, at least in part, and were on the right track with Combined Action Groups. In time, marines might have overcome the language obstacle and even innate corruption of most Saigon and I Corps area officials, who did not want viable government in the villages and sabotaged the American effort at almost every turn.[19] But marines lacked time and, so long as Giap sucked marine units into quasi-conventional warfare, they lacked men. The marine pacification effort was never more than a drop in the bucket. In 1966, the Viet Cong controlled about three quarters of I Corps area, either outright or through parallel hierarchies. By mid-1966, of 169 villages within the marine area, only thirty-seven were regarded as 80 per cent or more pacified; less than half of the area's nine hundred thousand people lived therein.[20]

Even in areas where local South Vietnamese officials performed well, such as the Australian TAOR southeast of Saigon, the task demanded patient, low-key (and economical) operations. The Australians, who were not blessed with prodigious logistic support, learned faster than the Americans what Lyautey long ago had taught: Pacification is a slow business.

Pacification was a particularly slow business in South Vietnam. Ky's highly touted Revolutionary Development program, so fervently embraced by President Johnson, suffered from two perhaps irreconcilable difficulties.

The first was a definition of terms. The democracy that the Johnson administration wanted in South Vietnam was an ambition, not a feasible goal; the assumption that this was a form of government also wanted by Thieu and Ky and the special interests they represented was false.

17. West, op. cit.
18. O'Neill, op. cit., writes feelingly on the subject.
19. David A. Clement, "Le May—Study in Counter-Insurgency," *Marine Corps Gazette,* July 1967; see also Corson, op. cit.
20. U. S. Marine Corps ("III MAF"), *supra.*

Here was a dual failure, as later noted by the *enfant terrible* of the Marine Corps, Colonel Corson:

> . . . My own reaction to the Honolulu Conference [of February 1966] was that our leaders, outside of a very few, did not know what they were talking about. The Great Society was hardly fit for domestic consumption let alone export. I felt sure that the semantic differential between our officials and the smiling Vietnamese officials was overlooked once again, that is, we call it democracy–they call it obedience. Honolulu left unanswered the questions "What is pacification?" and "What are we really trying to do?" The generalized and idealized statements about a "better world," "hearts and minds," and such are not, and were not then, operational. You can't sell a product if you can't define it.[21]

Corson had a good point. The situation in South Vietnam did not fit the picture being reported by Lodge and Westmoreland, whose claims of significant pacification progress were frequently broadcast to the nation by its President, despite his being informed to the contrary by Robert McNamara (among others), as we shall see shortly. While Johnson promised Thieu and Ky the moon and a piece of cheese at the Manila conference in October 1966, *all* governmental abuses so far discussed continued in force. No matter who was elected to the constituent assembly or what type of constitution would result, neither Thieu nor Ky nor the ruling junta of generals intended to liberalize government, much less institute a representative government that would appeal to either peasants or dissident sects or Buddhist or minorities or classes or professions–that would appeal to those complex elements constituting the political invention of South Vietnam. The generals stood as far removed from peasant aspirations as their American counterparts: ". . . only one [of them] . . . had fought for Vietnamese independence against the French. The others had either fought with the French or, like Ky, spent the war period being trained by the French."[22] As with former regimes, a preponderance of northern Catholics occupied major posts both in Saigon and the countryside. The peasants were as badly off as formerly, and in some cases worse. Land reform was a dead issue: Landlords continued to accompany troops to claim back taxes from peasants, and to invoke heavy, usually illegal rents.[23] Friction continued, not only with increasingly militant Buddhists, but with other dissident southern groups such as remnant Cao Dai and Hoa Hao. GVN failure to live up to promises made to the Montagnards also cost heavily: More than two thirds of the two-hundred-fifty-man Montagnard garrison at Plei Me had defected the day prior to the Viet Cong attack! And some Montagnards had subsequently gone over to the enemy.[24] Divi-

21. Corson, op. cit.
22. Zinn, op. cit.
23. Fall ("Viet Nam in the Balance"), *supra*.
24. Corson, op. cit.

sive elements within the Military Revolutionary Council also constantly jockeyed for power positions.

Government failure meant that old abuses continued. The administration's chief hatchet man, General Nguyen Ngoc Loan, used the most violent methods to eliminate political opponents.[25] Jails remained jammed with political prisoners; favored sons remained exempt from military duty; bribery and corruption claimed almost every transaction. At virtually each level of government, officials extracted "squeeze." Peasants bringing vegetables and fish to market paid squeeze to the police for protection; people buying and selling commodities paid squeeze for necessary licenses; students wanting scholarships to the U.S.A. paid for them; sick people wanting treatment on American hospital ships paid for it; peasants and refugees wanting food and clothes supplied by American funds paid for them.

This would have been bad enough under normal circumstances, but, considering South Vietnamese needs, it proved catastrophic. A dangerous political climate suppressed intelligent opposition and discouraged worthy Vietnamese who had fled abroad from returning at a crucial time. As one example, of the country's eight hundred doctors, five hundred served the army, a hundred fifty served private patients, and a hundred fifty treated fifteen million people[26]; yet, over seven hundred Vietnamese doctors were in Paris and refused to return![27]

Continuing VC gains in the countryside and the infusion of American troops exacerbated the situation. Rampant inflation developed, as did an enormous black market—an economically confused situation ably exploited by VC resident agents and infiltrators in two ways: by buying or stealing military needs from American stockpiles (while MACV and the JCS continued to worry about enemy supply lines from the North), and by agitation and propaganda among the hundreds of thousands of refugees generated from search-and-destroy tactics—from fighting in villages, and from bombing and shelling and burning them as part of an attrition strategy.

Governmental failure inevitably influenced ARVN, which contained nearly as many organizational and operational flaws as previously. The advisory system, in which so much hope had been placed, had already backfired—just as it had in the case of Chiang Kai-shek's Kuomintang army. A good many American army advisers were ill-equipped for the task and proved ineffective and, in some cases, dishonest and dangerous. The turbulent military situation, language deficiencies, and a one-year tour of duty combined to thwart the hard work of a good many capable and courageous Americans. Try as they would, they could not

25. Karl H. Purnell, "The Man Who Fired the Shot . . . ," *True Magazine*, July 1968.
26. U. S. Senate, *Refugee Problems in South Vietnam* (Washington: U. S. Government Printing Office, 1966).
27. Corson, op. cit.

overturn a ruling mandarin philosophy and get ARVN units into the boondocks and keep them there. Bernard Fall pointed out in the article in *Foreign Affairs* quoted above that the bulk of ARVN casualties, allegedly eleven thousand dead and 21,600 wounded in 1965, ". . . are suffered passively, i.e. by units garrisoned in forts or ambushed on roads rather than engaged in offensive operations." ARVN increased in 1965 from 493,000 to 640,000, but it counted ninety-three thousand desertions for the year.

Continued government and ARVN failures explained the second difficulty of the Revolutionary Development program, which was operational. Few GVN officials and ARVN officers shared Major Be's expressed idealism (see Chapter 82). Although ARVN units became increasingly available to provide hamlet security (as American units—army and marines—took over virtually the entire combat role), and at the same time reorganized themselves, they proved, in general, as unsatisfactory in pacification as in combat. One American adviser, Dwight Owen—a highly motivated and sincere young man who left a postgraduate course to serve in Vietnam, where he would shortly die—wrote of this period:

. . . At present the ARVN has little or no responsibility or responsiveness to the people of Vietnam. They fight but do not build. . . . Garrisons in towns and villages are notoriously inactive in CA [civic action] work. Often this is because they lack initiative and spirit. . . . Good pay, promotions, decent quarters, good rations, leave, and many other benefits most armies enjoy are lacking in many respects in the Vietnamese army. This undercuts morale and thus troop effectiveness. . . .[28]

ARVN officers, from corps commanders down, received squeeze to the extent that peasants saw little difference between friends and enemies. A veteran correspondent, Malcolm Browne, wrote that ARVN's most serious fault was corruption, but running a close second was ". . . mutual distrust and even hostility between most American soldiers and most Vietnamese soldiers." Viet Cong infiltration was another major fault, as was an inadequate officer corps and also inept tactical influence levied by American advisers. Browne pointed out that ARVN's pay scale, when taken with inflation, made it mandatory for officers and men to steal or otherwise profit whenever possible. This also helped to explain widespread desertion—24 per cent in 1966. Putting hungry soldiers among the hamlets was putting foxes among geese: ". . . the peasants learn to dread the coming of government troops worse than the plague."[29]

Ky's Revolutionary Development program presupposed that the South Vietnamese Government wished to establish a genuinely demo-

28. Dwight Owen, private letter in the author's files.
29. Malcolm Browne ("Why South Viet Nam's Army Won't Fight"), *supra*.

cratic government that would benefit South Vietnamese peasants, some 85 per cent of the population. Nothing could have been farther from the truth. The RD program's national training center could fire up thousands of cadres, but, without governmental co-operation, these could do nothing. Major Kriegel noted that, by mid-1967, Be's national training center had oriented about a thousand provincial officials, including twenty-seven province chiefs, into the new program in a series of two-day seminars. He could have held two-year seminars, which also would have been without effect so long as the Saigon government continued to condone excesses noted by observer after observer, for example landlords accompanying ARVN troops to reclaim land and levy unfair rents. Neither was the subsequent political aspect satisfactory, bringing to mind, as it did, brother Nhu's earlier efforts to control the peasant population rather than win it to the government's side (see Chapter 76). William Corson, who was intimately involved in the pacification effort in I Corps area, later wrote:

. . . The 30,000 members of the Armed Combat Youth (ACY) are a bargain-basement mob of thugs who counterterrorize the Vietnamese people while promoting "democracy" GVN style. The ACY units—or as they are being renamed, the Revolutionary Development Peoples' Groups (RDPG) —are organized to promote Nguyen Cao Ky's "strength through joy" approach to individual liberty. Through this borrowed Hitlerian concept Ky is attempting to build up an absolute form of political control that makes Nazi Germany look like Thomas More's "Utopia."

The ACY, or RDPG, organized into armed gangs of twenty-five to fifty hooligans, are used to enforce "support" for the GVN in the village-hamlet environment. Their techniques effectively blended to promote uniformity and obedience. The fear generated by the presence of the ACY in a hamlet is exceeded only by presence of one of the "elite" ARVN units such as the Rangers, Airborne, or Vietnamese Marines.[30]

Nor did the American mission reorganization result in streamlined operations that were needed. Province advisers at all levels found themselves enmeshed in bureaucratic and military corruption that sometimes defied imagination. Some of these advisers were conscientious, hard-working, and brave persons. Others were not. Most did not speak the language and had to rely on interpreters. Most knew little of customs of the people they were trying to help, and their aid estimates frequently lacked practicality or proper priority. Most were also endowed with the desire to do the job themselves. In the same letter quoted above, Dwight Owen wrote:

. . . Our pacification effort is not making significant headway. The first major problem is a lack of realistic appraisal by U.S. officials of what is needed. Plans have been grandiose and have not considered the realities of

30. Corson, op. cit.

the situation—too much and too fast. We have not allowed pacification cadre adequate time in hamlets by assigning them a quota of so many hamlets a year, which allows them about 2–3 months per hamlet. The plans have lacked follow-through. After the cadre leave, the job is considered finished, when, in reality, it is only beginning. . . .

In our estimation of the war we must realize that the Vietnamese populace wants a revolution and a better life. They will not be satisfied with less and are willing to fight for that revolution. We must help GVN win over the peasants and thus win the war. But the Vietnamese must do it. We are foreigners—always will be—and thus can not perform this function with other than a colonial administration, which is unacceptable to the Vietnamese (in spite of what some Americans maintain).

In addition to these deficits, agency infighting frequently ruled an American camp, and agencies often fought with the military, both ARVN and American. A British expert on counterinsurgency, Sir Robert Thompson, later told a seminar audience, ". . . when I added up the intelligence organizations which were operating in Saigon in 1966 against the Vietcong, there were seventeen, both American and South Vietnamese, and none of them were talking to each other!" Thompson continued:

. . . Having no Police Force, and an Army facing in rather the wrong direction, it then became a matter of building up other forces to deal with the insurgency, and there was a complete proliferation of these forces. Every little problem that came up resulted in a force being created. None of them knew what they were doing and none of their operations were co-ordinated. The net result was a tremendous waste of manpower and effort.

Similarly, on the civilian side, there was no emphasis at all on administration. Americans do not understand administration in the sense that we do and, as you know, in a counter-insurgency environment there are many things that require to be done, which can only be done effectively and without causing further problems due to unpopularity or resentment, by a very efficient administration. There was no great effort paid to this. . . .[31]

What should have been, and possibly could have been, a viable pacification program became just another in a long series of flaccid efforts—a development incessantly harped on by NLF-PRP-Hanoi propaganda, which exhorted South Vietnamese peasants to fight against U.S. imperialists and their Saigon lackeys.[32]

Unlike MACV and the Saigon government, the enemy fully realized the importance of the "other war"—to them, the "only war"—and de-

31. RUSI Seminar, op. cit.
32. Vo Nguyen Giap, "The Strategic Role of the Self-Defense Militia Force in the Great Anti-U.S. National Salvation Struggle of Our People." Foreign Broadcast Information Service, April 1967; see also Vo Nguyen Giap, *Big Victory, Great Task* (New York: Frederick A. Praeger, 1968).

voted top priority to its prosecution. If Hanoi ever displayed nervousness, it was over the allied pacification effort. In a major speech delivered in January 1967, Vo Nguyen Giap returned to the subject[33] with the reluctant persistence of Raskolnikov returning to his evil deeds in Dostoevsky's *Crime and Punishment*. And well he might: Pacification was the key to combat in the South, a fact repeatedly proved by history, ancient and modern, a fact never understood by American military planners who refused to fight a complex war of nuance and subtlety in preference to a good old black-and-white shooting match, a fact never understood by Johnson or his hawkish advisers who refused to formulate objectives consonant to fact in preference to wild ambition that demanded an undefinable and thus unrealizable nothing called "victory."

By early 1966, a good many doubts had risen in public and private minds within the United States as to the wisdom of American actions in Vietnam. Taken together, they began to suggest that the Johnson administration had bought a gold brick made the more fraudulent by size and weight.

In February, *Harper's Magazine* published a letter-article from a retired soldier with a fine World War II combat record and a lengthy postwar record of distinguished public and private service. This was General James Gavin, who now challenged the logic of escalation. What became unfairly known as a demand for "enclave strategy" was an intelligent attempt to reassess a complex situation, and fit limited resources to realistic goals.

Gavin's article was published shortly before the Senate Foreign Relations Committee, whose chairman was William Fulbright, opened what became the famous Vietnam hearings. These televised sessions left little doubt that the situation was not as black-and-white as the Johnson administration proclaimed. The Administration's position was presented by Dean Rusk and Maxwell Taylor, each of whom reaffirmed the domino theory and aggression-from-the-North-under-Peking-aegis thesis (and each of whom was pretty well worked over in question periods).

As devil's advocates, the Senate called on General Gavin and Ambassador George Kennan. Gavin warned the Foreign Relations Committee and the listening American public of dangers inherent in further expanding the war, particularly since no tactical need existed. As he had already written in *Harper's Magazine:*

. . . Today we have sufficient forces in South Vietnam to hold several enclaves on the coast, where sea and air power can be made fully effective. By enclaves I suggest Camranh Bay, Danang, and similar areas where American bases are being established. However, we are stretching these resources beyond reason in our endeavours to secure the entire country of South Viet-

---

33. Giap ("Strategic Role"), *supra*.

nam from the Viet Cong penetration. This situation, of course, is caused by the growing Viet Cong strength.

To expand the American presence and the war would create new problems, for example Chinese intervention or a new war in Korea. Instead, the United States should pursue a strategy compatible to the area's importance and to the tactical challenge:

. . . if we should maintain enclaves on the coast, desist in our bombing attacks in North Vietnam, and seek to find a solution through the United Nations or a conference in Geneva, we could very likely do with the forces now available. . . .

Frederick the Great, in speaking of his foray from Silesia against the Austrians, noted that ". . . this plan was simple, proportionate to the possibility of execution, and adapted to circumstances; there was therefore every reason to hope it would succeed." The same could be said of the Gavin plan, but such was the power of the hawks that it became perverted into a strategy of defeat and would not soon have the chance to prove itself. Further, such was the Administration's outcry against the "enclave theory," that few persons paid attention to what possibly was Gavin's most important point. As Mao Tse-tung had suggested some years before, Gavin believed that warfare had radically changed:

. . . Since the advent of the Space Age, there has been a revolution in the nature of war and global conflict. The confrontation in Vietnam is the first test of our understanding of such change, or our lack of it. The measures that we now take in Southeast Asia must stem from sagacity and thoughtfulness, and an awareness of the nature of strategy in this rapidly shrinking world.[34]

Ambassador Kennan already had challenged the wisdom of American commitment to South Vietnam.[35] Once again, he contradicted Administration hawks who proclaimed that South Vietnam was of vital strategic interest to the United States:

. . . if we were not already involved as we are today in Vietnam, I would know of no reason why we should wish to become so involved, and I could think of several reasons why we should wish not to. Vietnam is not a region of major military, industrial importance. It is difficult to believe that any decisive developments of the world situation would be determined in normal circumstances by what happens on that territory.

After expatiating on this statement, which must have shaken thoughtful senators, Kennan suggested that, since we had become militarily in-

34. James M. Gavin, "A Soldier's Doubts," *Harper's Magazine*, February 1966; see also J. William Fulbright (ed.) (*The Viet Nam Hearings*), *supra*.
35. M. G. Raskin and Bernard Fall, op. cit.: See, for example, Ambassador Kennan's testimony before the House Committee on Foreign Affairs, May 1965.

volved, we could not hastily abandon our posture. But that was no reason to enlarge the posture. The political situation in the South permitted no easy solution; American military might could not overcome such factors as enemy space and manpower, and an attempt to subdue the North by invasion would probably draw China into the fray. As it was, the war was severely damaging American relations with the U.S.S.R. and Japan. Kennan wanted the American presence liquidated as soon as possible:

. . . In matters such as this, it is not, in my experience, what you do that is mainly decisive. It is how you do it, and I would submit that there is more respect to be won in the opinion of this world by a resolute and courageous liquidation of unsound positions than by the most stubborn pursuit of extravagant or unpromising objectives.

As for the "obligation" maintained by Johnson and his advisers, Kennan, sounding like a diplomatic Socrates, continued:

. . . I would like to know what that commitment really consists of, and how and when it was incurred.

What seems to be involved here is an obligation on our part not only to defend the frontiers of a certain political entity against outside attack, but to assure the internal security of its government in circumstances where that government is unable to assure that security by its own means.

Now, any such obligation is one that goes obviously considerably further in its implications than the normal obligations of a military alliance. If we did not incur such an obligation in any formal way, then I think we should not be inventing it for ourselves and assuring ourselves that we are bound by it today. But if we did incur it, then I do fail to understand how it was possible to enter into any such commitment otherwise than through the constitutional processes which were meant to come into play when even commitments of lesser import than this were undertaken.

Although Kennan felt the deepest personal sympathy for the South Vietnamese and repugnance toward the Viet Cong, he nonetheless maintained that

. . . our country should not be asked, and should not ask of itself, to shoulder the main burden of determining the political realities in any other country, and particularly not in one remote from our shores, from our culture, and from the experience of our people. This is not only not our business, but I don't think we can do it successfully.[36]

Three months later, another hard-charging soldier spoke up. This was David Shoup, a retired four-star Marine Corps general, winner of the Medal of Honor at Tarawa, former commandant of the Marine Corps, member of the Joint Chiefs of Staff, and unofficial military ad-

36. J. William Fulbright (ed.) (*The Viet Nam Hearings*), *supra*.

viser to President Kennedy. Speaking in Los Angeles in May 1966, Shoup denied South Vietnam's strategic importance:

. . . The Administration, he said, has never realistically assessed whether the United States' own self-interest is at stake in Southeast Asia. The Administration has never presented a timetable proving that there would be "irreparable effects upon this nation at the end of five, ten, fifteen, fifty years" if South Vietnam were overrun by the Communist Vietcong guerrillas.

Pointing to drastic changes in the world Communist order, Shoup declared that Administration reasons for American intervention in South Vietnam ". . . are too shallow and narrow for students, as well as other citizens. Especially so, when you realize that what is happening, no matter how carefully and slowly the military escalation has progressed, may be projecting us toward world catastrophe." In case any one missed the point, General Shoup stated: ". . . I don't think the whole of Southeast Asia, as related to the present and future safety and freedom of the people of this country, is worth the life or limb of a single American."[37]

Although President Johnson publicly treated these and other dissentient voices with insouciance tinged with contempt, members of his own inner circle continued to express certain doubts that could not altogether be ignored. These were occasioned mainly by the increasing expense of the war as fought by Westmoreland and the JCS.

No sooner had President Johnson authorized committing nearly two hundred thousand troops by the end of 1965 than Westmoreland, in July of that year, informed McNamara that these would suffice only to stop the enemy offensive by the end of the year. In order to resume the offensive in priority areas and to continue the pacification program, Westmoreland requested another 112,000 troops for the first half of 1966; he also warned McNamara that he would need even more troops to defeat the enemy by the end of 1967.

McNamara at this point—summer 1965—apparently entertained some doubts as to the wisdom of an attrition strategy, but he nonetheless recommended approval of the new request to the President. But, in November, McNamara, once again in Saigon, received further disturbing information. According to MACV estimates, the enemy had increased in strength from 48,550 combat troops, in July, to 63,550, in November, a figure that included an ominous increase from one to eight North Vietnamese (PAVN) regiments. To offset this development, Westmoreland wanted another 154,000 troops. After more soul-searching, McNamara again agreed: If a bombing pause failed to produce a satisfactory reaction from Hanoi, he recommended a troop increase to seventy-four battalions, or about 400,000 men, by the end of 1966, but warned that at least two hundred thousand additional troops would perhaps be

37. James Deakin, "Big Brass Lambs," *Esquire,* December 1967.

needed in 1967! McNamara concluded his memorandum to the President in somber but ambivalent words that bring to mind the western-front syndrome of World War I:

. . . We should be aware that deployments of the kind I have recommended will not guarantee success. U.S. killed-in-action can be expected to reach 1000 a month, and the odds are even that we will be faced in early 1967 with a "no-decision" at an even higher level. My over-all evaluation, nevertheless, is that the best chance of achieving our stated objective lies in a [bombing] pause followed, if it fails, by the deployments mentioned above.[38]

McNamara's recommendation for a bombing halt touched off an intra-Administration quarrel that would continue to the end of Johnson's administration. Westmoreland in Saigon, Sharp in Honolulu, the JCS, and numerous presidential advisers in Washington continued to argue that the cumulative effect of American air blows against the North and air and ground blows against PAVN/VC forces in the South would eventually tell.[39]

President Johnson later wrote that he viewed McNamara's proposal to halt the bombing with a "deep skepticism" shared by McGeorge Bundy, Dean Rusk, and Ambassador Lodge, not to mention military chiefs and advisers. Slowly, however, pertinent factors brought some of these persons around. Undoubtedly, McNamara's pessimistic words raised doubts in the presidential mind. In private discussions, McNamara went so far, according to the President, as to question ". . . assurance of military success in Vietnam," stating that ". . . we had to find a diplomatic solution":

. . . I asked him whether he meant that there was no guarantee of success no matter what we did militarily. "That's right," he answered. "We have been too optimistic. One chance in three, or two in three, is my estimate."[40]

Other factors existed. One was McNamara's argument that if the pause failed to move Hanoi to the conference table, ". . . it would at least [demonstrate] our genuine desire for a peaceful settlement and thereby temper the criticism we were getting at home and abroad."[41] International diplomatic activity, particularly from the U.S.S.R. and Hungary, also seemed to promise negotiations if the bombing halted. In the end, according to the President, McGeorge Bundy and Rusk joined McNamara and George Ball in urging the halt. Against JCS advice, the President stopped the bombings in late December. When Hanoi showed no inclination to come to the conference table—critics of the Administra-

38. *The Pentagon Papers, supra* (pp. 487–89).
39. Ibid. (pp. 490–91); see also Sharp, op. cit.; Johnson (*The Vantage Point*), *supra*.
40. Johnson (*The Vantage Point*), *supra*.
41. Ibid.

tion pointed to Johnson's intractable conference position as one reason
—the President ordered bombing resumed at the end of January.

The hawks were now definitely in the ascendancy. In February 1966,
The New York *Times Magazine* published an article, "The Case for
Escalation," by veteran military analyst Hanson Baldwin.[42] Arguing
that the domino theory was valid, Baldwin seemed willing to accept war
with China if that was necessary to defeat North Vietnam; meanwhile,
he called for declaration of a national emergency and a greatly expanded
war.

The next round started with the Buddhist revolts in March 1966,
which precipitated a new crisis and forced the Thieu-Ky government
to use ARVN units to recapture the cities of Hué and Da Nang.[43] Again
the Washington administration split on the issue. Pessimists argued that
Ky could never form an effective government, which meant that he could
not maintain a viable pacification program; optimists pointed out that
he commanded enough loyalty, at least in the army, to settle the issue
and that, as a bonus, the government and Buddhists agreed to elections
for a constituent assembly to draw up a new constitution. Although the
crisis occasioned another fierce argument within the Administration
(with Under Secretary of State Ball once again calling for disengagement), President Johnson sided with those who favored pursuing the
current program, escalating as necessary. With the appointment of Walt
Rostow as presidential assistant (replacing McGeorge Bundy as presidential adviser on national security in deed if not in word), the hawks
won a major round, and the American commitment continued to increase.

The doubts that had already formed in Secretary of Defense Robert
McNamara's mind now began to develop dramatically. In August of
1966, the Secretary received an unpleasant, if not entirely unexpected,
surprise: a report from forty-seven of the nation's top scientists whom
he had secretly mobilized to study the effects of Operation Rolling Thunder and to consider alternate means of stopping enemy infiltration from
the North. Their report stated that not only had the twin objectives of
Rolling Thunder—to reduce infiltration and to force Hanoi to call off
the insurgency—failed (a conclusion previously reached by CIA reports), but that an expanded bombing program would probably fail to
accomplish either objective.

Instead, the group recommended building a sophisticated barrier
across the southern border of the DMZ and curling on the Laotian panhandle—all together some forty to sixty miles—this to comprise new and
secret mines and sensors that would locate infiltrators, who would then
be destroyed by patrolling troops and supporting arms. The system

42. Hanson Baldwin, "The Case for Escalation," New York *Times Magazine*,
February 27, 1966.
43. Shaplen (*Road*), *supra;* see also Walt, op. cit.

would cost perhaps a billion dollars to build and about $800 million a year to operate.[44]

McNamara was still digesting the morbid contents of the scientists' findings when he received another unpleasant surprise: a new request from General Westmoreland to provide a total 570,000 troops in South Vietnam by end of 1967. A few weeks later, the JCS, which approved Westmoreland's newest request (favorably endorsed by Admiral Sharp), ". . . urged what the Pentagon study calls 'full-blown' mobilization of 688,500 Army, Navy, Air Force and Marine reservists to help provide more troops for Vietnam and also to build up the armed forces around the world."[45]—a move pressed on the American public by Hanson Baldwin in the October *Reader's Digest*.[46]

The Westmoreland-Sharp-JCS-Baldwin thinking was not to McNamara's liking. In October, he again flew to Saigon (where an attempt was made on his life). Upon his return to Washington, he reported in detail to President Johnson:

. . . In the report of my last trip to Vietnam almost a year ago, I stated that the odds were about even that, even with the then-recommended deployments, we would be faced in early 1967 with a military stand-off at a much higher level of conflict and with "pacification" still stalled. I am a little less pessimistic now in one respect. We have done somewhat better militarily than I anticipated. We have by and large blunted the communist military initiative—any military victory in South Vietnam the Viet Cong may have had in mind 18 months ago has been thwarted by our emergency deployments and actions. And our program of bombing the North has exacted a price.

My concern continues, however, in other respects. This is because I see no reasonable way to bring the war to an end soon. Enemy morale has not broken—he apparently has adjusted to our stopping his drive for military victory and has adopted a strategy of keeping us busy and waiting us out (a strategy of attriting our national will). He knows that we have not been, and he believes we probably will not be, able to translate our military successes into the "end products"—broken enemy morale and political achievements by the GVN.

Although the enemy was probably suffering more than sixty thousand battle deaths a year,

. . . there is no sign of an impending break in enemy morale and it appears that he can more than replace his losses by infiltration from North Vietnam and recruitment in South Vietnam.

44. *The Pentagon Papers, supra* (pp. 483–85, 502–9).
45. Ibid. (p. 517).
46. Hanson Baldwin, "To End the War in Vietnam, Mobilize!" *Reader's Digest*, October 1966.

The September elections in South Vietnam were healthy enough, he opined, but the South Vietnamese Government had not come to terms with the real problem:

. . . Pacification is a bad disappointment . . . [and] has if anything gone backward. As compared with two, or four, years ago, enemy full-time regional forces and part-time guerrilla forces are larger; attacks, terrorism and sabotage have increased in scope and intensity; more railroads are closed and highways cut; the rice crop expected to come to market is smaller; we control little, if any, more of the population; the VC political infrastructure thrives in most of the country, continuing to give the enemy his enormous intelligence advantage; full security exists nowhere (not even behind the U.S. Marines' lines and in Saigon); in the countryside, the enemy almost completely controls the night.[47]

In McNamara's opinion, the United States had to ". . . continue to press the enemy militarily" and also to make "demonstrable" progress in pacification. But

. . . we must add a new ingredient forced on us by the facts. Specifically, we must improve our position by getting ourselves into a military posture that we credibly would maintain indefinitely—a posture that makes trying to "wait us out" less attractive.

McNamara now called for ". . . a five-pronged course of action": contrary to Westmoreland's, Sharp's and JCS desires, he wished to limit troop increases to seventy thousand which, in the current round, would give a total of 470,000—enough, he believed, to neutralize enemy operations and get on with pacification; to save troops, and thus avoid mobilizing reserves, and to find an effective substitute for expensive and relatively useless bombing of the North, he recommended building an electronic barrier across the DMZ as suggested by the earlier-mentioned scientists' report; he called for stabilizing Operation Rolling Thunder: eighty-four thousand attack sorties had failed to attain stated objectives:

. . . It is clear that, to bomb the North sufficiently to make a radical impact upon Hanoi's political, economic and social structure, would require an effort which we could make but which would not be stomached either by our own people or by world opinion; and it would involve a serious risk of drawing us into open war with China.

We were then flying twelve thousand attack sorties per month (at an operational cost of $250 million per month), which was sufficient to

47. *The Pentagon Papers, supra* (pp. 542–51); see also Giap ("Strategic Role"), *supra.*

". . . continue the pressure and would remain available as a bargaining counter to get talks started (or to trade off in talks)." Moreover,

. . . At the proper time . . . I believe we should consider terminating bombing in all of North Vietnam, or at least in the Northeast zones, for an indefinite period in connection with covert moves toward peace. Pursue a vigorous pacification program—if necessary, reorganize. Press for negotiations.

He did not believe that either military action or negotiations offered more than a "mere possibility" of ending the war. As opposed to Westmoreland and the JCS, McNamara believed that

. . . The solution lies in girding, openly, for a longer war and in taking actions immediately which will in 12 to 18 months give clear evidence that the continuing costs and risks to the American people are acceptably limited, that the formula for success has been found, and that the end of the war is merely a matter of time. All of my recommendations will contribute to this strategy, but the one most difficult to implement is perhaps the most important one—enlivening the pacification program. The odds are less than even for this task, if only because we have failed consistently since 1961 to make a dent in the problem. But, because the 1967 trend of pacification will, I believe, be the main talisman of ultimate U.S. success or failure in Vietnam, extraordinary imagination and effort should go into changing the stripes of that problem.

President Thieu and Prime Minister Ky are thinking along similar lines. . . . They expressed agreement with us that the key to success is pacification and that so far pacification has failed. They agree that we need clarification of GVN and U.S. roles and that the bulk of the ARVN should be shifted to pacification. Ky will, between January and July 1967, shift all ARVN infantry divisions to that role. . . . Thieu and Ky see this as part of a two-year (1967–68) schedule, in which offensive operations against enemy main force units are continued, carried on primarily by the U.S. and other Free-World forces. At the end of the two-year period, they believe the enemy may be willing to negotiate or to retreat from his current course of action.

Neither Westmoreland nor the JCS agreed with McNamara's conclusions. The JCS vigorously dissented from stabilizing the air campaign against the North, calling instead for a radical expansion of the effort along with an increase in targets and additional naval action.[48] Other hawks agreed, and President Johnson was inclined to agree with the hawks.[49]

McNamara did persuade Johnson to limit troop increases, but only for a short time. At the Manila conference in late October, Westmoreland agreed to a top of four hundred eighty thousand men by end of

48. *The Pentagon Papers, supra* (p. 552–53).
49. Johnson (*The Vantage Point*), *supra.*

1967 and five hundred thousand by end of 1968.[50] According to John McNaughton, Westmoreland said ". . . that those forces would be enough 'even if infiltration went on at a high level' but that he wanted a contingency force of roughly two divisions on reserve in the Pacific."[51] McNamara shaved the figure even further and in November, obviously with presidential assent, informed the JCS that Westmoreland could have 469,000 troops at his disposal by mid-1968.[52]

50. *The Pentagon Papers, supra* (pp. 520–21).
51. Ibid.
52. Ibid.

Chapter 85

The war continues • President Johnson's optimism • The February bombing halt • Operation Cedar Falls • Task Force Oregon • Fighting in the highlands • The marine war • New tactical techniques • Khe Sanh defended • Air and naval wars • "The new team": Ambassador Bunker and pacification • South Vietnam's political progress • Allied profits for the year • ". . . Light at the end of a tunnel"

IN HIS STATE OF THE UNION MESSAGE in early January 1967, President Johnson once again justified American presence in Vietnam in the strongest possible terms. Once again he spoke of specific "commitments" and the evil that would follow should the United States fail to uphold them. He promised no easy way out of what he called this "limited war":

. . . I wish I could report to you that the conflict is almost over. This I cannot do. We face more cost, more loss, and more agony. For the end is not yet. I cannot promise you that it will come this year—or come next year. Our adversary still believes, I think, tonight, that he can go on fighting longer than we can, and longer than we and our allies will be prepared to stand up and resist.

The answer to that was to continue Westmoreland's attrition strategy:

. . . Our men in that area—there are nearly 500,000 now—have borne well "the burden and the heat of the day." Their efforts have deprived the Communist enemy of the victory that he sought and that he expected a year ago. We have steadily frustrated his main forces. General Westmoreland reports that the enemy can no longer succeed on the battlefield.

So I must say to you that our pressure must be sustained—and will be sustained—until he realizes that the war he started is costing him more than he can ever gain.[1]

Although problems continued to plague the American effort—pacification, for example, was not showing the "desired progress"—that effort already had ". . . created a feeling of confidence and unity among the independent nations of Asia and the Pacific." Even while war continued, the Administration was working on an Asian development plan that the President had outlined in his famous Baltimore speech.

The President's words reflected optimism current among the hawks; as he later wrote in his memoirs:

. . . By early 1967 most of my advisers and I felt confident that the tide of war was moving strongly in favor of the South Vietnamese and their allies, and against the Communists.[2]

His speech made it clear that he was committed to a hawk strategy and did not want to change.

The President continued to place great faith in Operation Rolling Thunder, the bombing of the North. He approved none of McNamara's "stabilizing" suggestions made the previous autumn and, indeed, drastically raised the number of authorized B-52 missions, to take effect in late February. Although international pressures caused him to halt bombing the North for a few days in February, he ignored the British prime minister's plea to hold off until the Soviet premier could discuss negotiations with Hanoi. How much this was due to his own belief and how much to the work of hawks is anyone's guess. The President made his attitude clear in two documents, however. In a secret letter of early February to Ho Chi Minh, his moral indignation at Hanoi's transgression is apparent—it is all he can do to swallow it and offer to stop bombing the North if Hanoi would stop infiltration into the South. Ho replied, in effect, that the U.S.A. had no right to bomb the North in the first place and that discussions between the two countries could occur only when bombing and other unjustified acts of war ceased.[3]

Not only was bombing the North morally and legally justified in the President's mind, but, contrary to reports from the nation's top intelligence analysts, he insisted that the bombings were producing very real

1. Johnson (*Public Papers*—1967, Book I), *supra*.
2. Johnson (*The Vantage Point*), *supra*.
3. The letters are quoted in *Survival*, June 1967.

effects. President Johnson wrote Senator Henry Jackson, upon resuming bombing of the North in February:

> . . . Our attacks on military targets in North Viet Nam have diverted about half a million men to cope with effects of our attacks. They are repairing the lines of supply and are engaged in anti-aircraft and coastal defense. This figure approximates the total number of men we now have fighting in Southeast Asia. It is not much less than the number of men South Viet Nam has had to mobilize to deal with the guerrilla attack in the South.
>
> At the cost of about 500 gallant American airmen killed, captured, or missing, we are bringing to bear on North Viet Nam a burden roughly equivalent to that which the Communists are imposing through guerrilla warfare in the South—and we are doing it with far fewer civilian casualties in the North.
>
> Finally, the bombing of North Viet Nam has raised the cost of bringing an armed man or a ton of supplies illegally across the border from the North to the South. Substantial casualties are inflicted on infiltrators and substantial tonnages of supplies are destroyed en route. Those who now reach the South arrive after harassment which lowers their effectiveness as reinforcements.[4]

The President was not as confident in deed as in word, for the air campaign, Operation Rolling Thunder, became a subject of grave dispute within top Administration echelons, as we shall discuss in the next chapter—dispute that showed in the on-again off-again half-again orders emanating from the White House throughout the year. Although Johnson emphasized in his memoirs that he did not expect bombing of the North to win the war, the record strongly suggests that he regarded air power as his chief punitive weapon and could not understand why Hanoi did not submit in order to call off the punishment. In any event, the air war, both North and South, escalated to frantic proportions in 1967.

The President did not exercise such active control over the ground war in the South as he did over bombing of the North. He nonetheless vigorously supported Westmoreland. Without acceding to maximum requests levied by Saigon and the JCS, he still authorized substantial increases in American troop commitment and in over-all expenditure. By year's end, South Vietnam's armed forces climbed to over seven hundred thousand (at least on paper); American troop strength approached half a million with 525,000 authorized; Korea supplied forty-five thousand troops; Australia, six thousand; Thailand, twenty-five hundred, with the promise to furnish a division; New Zealand, a few hundred. Direct operational costs for the year zoomed to over $25 billion. By October 1967,

4. Johnson (*Public Papers*—1967, Book I), *supra*.

. . . 40 percent of our combat-ready divisions, half of our tactical airpower, and at least a third of our naval strength . . . were waging full-throated war on the Southeast Asian peninsula.[5]

One analyst aptly called it more of the same.

In January, Operation Cedar Falls—an allied force spearheaded by the American army's 1st Division—began to sweep through a B-52-bomb-plastered Iron Triangle, northwest of Saigon. In this traditional Viet Cong defense complex, troops discovered an "underground city" and seized half a million enemy documents and enough rice to feed ". . . an estimated 13,000 soldiers for one year."[6] More sweeps followed to push the enemy from the Iron Triangle and from Zones C and D and keep him on the defensive while bringing alleged stability to surrounding provinces (see map, p. 1187). An active and tactically profitable year in vital III Corps area: by December, U.S.-ARVN-allied forces claimed 22,500 enemy dead; more important, Viet Cong main-force units had retreated north to Cambodian border areas. Summarizing the war at year's end, *Newsweek* magazine quoted Lieutenant General Frederick Weyand, commanding U.S. forces in III Corps area: ". . . The three enemy divisions that used to ring Saigon are now 80 and 90 miles away from the capital, where their targets are outside the key areas. . . . The enemy can't suck me out of the populated areas now by attacking an outpost. We now have the strength to respond to such attacks and still maintain control of the population."[7]

Farther south, in IV Corps area, U.S.-ARVN forces also reported significant gains and claimed to be destroying one thousand Viet Cong guerrillas per month. Where once enemy units had proved elusive, contacts now were frequent: ". . . The units we fight now will break and run," says one general. "Two years ago you couldn't pry them out."[8] Particularly productive in this corps area were riverine warfare operations conducted by U. S. Navy personnel often in conjunction with American and Vietnamese ground units.

Similarly, large-scale "spoiling" operations in II Corps area, both along the coast and in the central highlands, were said to be keeping the enemy temporarily off balance. These sophisticated operations differed only in quantity and location from ones earlier discussed. Task Force Oregon operations, in the spring of 1967, as described by Robert Shaplen, might have happened in 1966:

. . . we continued north by helicopter to the headquarters of Major General William B. Rosson, in command of Operation Oregon, a large combined

5. Townsend Hoopes, *The Limits of Intervention* (New York: McKay, 1969).
6. Johnson (*The Vantage Point*), *supra.*
7. *Newsweek*, January 1, 1968.
8. Ibid.

action by the 101st, the 25th, and the 196th, co-ordinated with that of the 1st Cavalry to the south. Since Oregon had begun, on April 20th, our officers had claimed seven hundred enemy dead at the cost of fifty-one dead Americans. Oregon consisted of a lowlands and a highlands effort. In the lowlands, where a brigade of the 25th Division was operating, the campaign was designed to root out the Vietcong and to get a major pacification effort started in what had been solid Communist territory for many years. General Rosson described this lowlands region as "a big island of hope." General Westmoreland agreed, but emphasized the difficulties that still lay ahead in bringing permanent peace to the region and persuading the Vietcong to quit—a task that indeed did loom as enormous. The enormity was emphasized when we flew back into the hills, where part [an airborne brigade] of the 101st was trying to root out two regiments of the N.V.A. 3rd Division, breaking them up and pushing them down toward the area of operations of the 1st Cavalry or east into open areas where they could be more readily attacked. The 101st has established the remarkable record in Vietnam of moving twenty-five times in twenty months. With the help of a Special Forces team on the mountains far to the west, among the Montagnard Re tribesmen, the 101st was discovering a number of enemy infiltration routes and, as its briefing officers said, was forcing N.V.A. company- or battalion-size elements to move about in smaller numbers. There were still plenty of enemy soldiers about, though, and one of the battalion officers said, "We feel surrounded out here."[9]

American army operations continued in the two coastal provinces throughout summer and autumn. The correspondent Jonathan Schell found operations virtually unchanged from previous months. American army units continued to sweep hostile areas and to call in air and artillery strikes on suspect villages. Each operation strongly resembled the others; each depended on the quantitative approach that had now become the hallmark of American tactics.[10]

In October, enemy forces again became active in the northwest. To prevent them from seizing the provincial capital of Kontum, Westmoreland broke off coastal operations to fight a number of fierce actions in the vicinity of Dak To. Then, in mid-November, in III Corps area, in the south, two enemy regiments attacked an allied outpost at Loc Ninh, a town only nine miles from the Cambodian border, a fierce action that claimed 926 confirmed North Vietnamese dead, with another two or three thousand wounded. Another attack, against Dak To, was beaten back with five hundred Communist dead claimed; week-long fighting cost 177 American dead and 761 wounded, and 279 ARVN dead.[11] In early December, the enemy again attacked the base camp

9. Shaplen (*Road*), *supra*.
10. Schell, op. cit.
11. Reuters, Saigon, November 16, 1967; see also Shaplen (*Road*), *supra*, for details of these actions.

at Dak To, a vicious five-day battle that again resulted in heavy Communist casualties: 1,599 confirmed dead at a cost of 150 U.S. paratrooper lives and 250 wounded. Another attack, a week later, at Bo Duc was also beaten off.

In the North, in I Corps area, Walt's marines had been kept busy fighting three wars: one against main-force Viet Cong and PAVN units in and around the DMZ, one against VC units south of the DMZ, and finally, the "other war," that which involved protecting hamlets and villages while trying to win peasants to the government's side.

One marine commander aptly defined the war against main-force Viet Cong and PAVN units:

. . . This is the one against the NVA [North Vietnamese Army] regular— Mr. Charles, because he is a lot more sophisticated than his VC cousin. He operates with all supporting arms except air and naval gunfire. He'll dig in and stay to fight. He'll counterattack and try to fractionalize units as large as a battalion. When he has had enough he'll break contact, drag off his dead and lick his wounds. If he has been hurt badly he'll be returned to North Vietnam and replaced by a fresh unit.[12]

Marines fought this war from a series of strong points designed to prevent infiltration south by PAVN units crossing the DMZ or entering from Laos. The effort involved screening enemy movements and harassing or disrupting them by ground action and/or artillery, air, and naval fire when possible. Although major fire fights continued to exact heavy enemy casualties, the enemy seemed no less strong, and as the year wore on, he began employing ". . . sophisticated Russian howitzers, artillery, mortars and rockets"—the result of increasing Soviet aid.[13] Marines replied by increasing ground, air, and naval action. General Walt, who returned to the United States from Vietnam in spring of 1967, told an audience: ". . . we are looking forward to the arrival of *New Jersey* [a battleship taken out of mothballs] on station so that we can start sending some of those one-ton shells into the enemy's heavily fortified bunker areas. There is nothing to match them for the accurate reduction of deeply dug in positions."[14]

Action flared variously in the area, in general the marines reacting rather than acting. One marine strong point was at Khe Sanh, a scrubby, isolated combat base with airstrip, originally the home of a CIDG—

12. J. W. Hammond, "Combat Journal," *Marine Corps Gazette,* July and August 1968.
13. Robert Shaplen, "Viet-Nam: Crisis of Indecision," *Foreign Affairs,* October 1967. Hereafter cited as Shaplen ("Crisis").
14. L. W. Walt, "The Navy in Vietnam." Headquarters, U. S. Marine Corps release, n.d.: Walt was forgetting Marine Corps experience in World War II and Korea, when naval gunfire and aerial bombing "preparation" of enemy targets frequently produced minimum results.

some two hundred Vietnamese irregulars and Special Forces advisers.[15] A few miles from the Laotian border, the base had been occupied by a marine battalion during Operation Prairie, in autumn of 1966, and subsequently was held by a reinforced company. As with other combat bases, Khe Sanh filled a dual role: Patrols constantly issued forth to observe and sometimes interdict enemy movement, and to respond, along with base supporting weapons, to calls from neighboring Combined Action units.

In April 1967, a marine patrol from Khe Sanh had set up an observation post on Hill 861, part of a nearby triangular terrain feature. Unknown to marines, elements of two PAVN regiments had been moving to these hills, presumably in preparation for an attack on Khe Sanh itself. When enemy attacked the marine patrol on Hill 861, a fire fight of major proportions developed, to culminate in a marine counteroffensive: violent assault and capture of Hills 861, 881 North, and 881 South, actions that reminded older marines of World War II operations. The twelve-day battle ended in a marine "victory" in that the PAVN regiments retired, having lost, according to marine figures, nine hundred lives with two or three times that number wounded. Marine casualties numbered 138 dead and 397 wounded.[16]

An even more frustrating war continued against VC units south of the DMZ:

. . . a gruelling tedious war. It is characterized by long patrols, occasional quick fights with some confirmed kills, and monotony. The enemy employs mortars and is nasty with his propensity for mines and other explosive devices. He uses the terrain and its concealment well—he moves at night, but rarely stays and fights. When he does, it is usually a delaying action to protect something valuable or at least to allow it to be moved.[17]

Although marines fought this war with grim determination, they possessed neither tactics nor strength essential to clear and hold areas that, long since, had been dominated by VC cadres. Every time a quasi-conventional action developed in the DMZ area, the effort to the south suffered. In early spring of 1967, VC units were sufficiently strong to open a general offensive, shelling Hué and Da Nang and even overrunning Quang Tri, while other units struck at pacification teams throughout the provinces.

VC gains led to important reorganization of the area. Marine units, now some seventy-five thousand strong, concentrated in the three northern provinces. South of them, a new army unit moved in, the American Division, whose four brigades were reinforced with a fifth, airmobile

15. L. W. Walt, "Khe Sanh—The Battle That Had to Be Won," *Reader's Digest*, August 1970.

16. U. S. Marine Corps, "The Battle for Hills 861 and 881." n.p., n.d.; see also, Corson, op. cit. who cites 155 dead and 425 wounded.

17. Hammond, op. cit.

brigade. ARVN troops were increased to some thirty thousand, and units began fighting in conjunction with American troops. In June, Lieutenant General Robert Cushman, U. S. Marine Corps, replaced General Walt in command of III MAF, whose operational area had grown to over two thousand square miles in I Corps area (which comprised five provinces and some three million people and was commanded by Lieutenant General Huong Xuan Lam). In addition to troops listed above, the area held a Korean brigade, CIDG units, eighteen thousand American sailors, and seven thousand American airmen, not to mention countless civil and military advisers.

That summer and autumn, fast and furious actions continued to be fought throughout the long coastal area and in the north. In summer, marine and ARVN units began Operation Beau Charger, designed to root out VC forces in and south of the DMZ prior to making it a "free fire zone"—a complicated and costly task that, among other things, meant relocating some thirteen thousand civilians, to add to refugee hordes already crowding Da Nang and Hué.[18] In autumn, as engineers began surveying terrain as the first step in constructing McNamara's "fence" across the southern boundary of the DMZ, marine units fought frequent savage actions in defending strong points such as Cam Lo and Con Thien—"spoiling" operations that bore heavy price tags: In September alone, marine casualties totalled over twenty-two hundred.[19]

A marine battalion commander has given an excellent account of operations at this time in vicious jungle country west of the piedmont:

. . . The battalion marched for twenty-two of the first twenty-four hours. The going, once inside the heavy canopy, was slow. The lead elements actually had to break trail. The point was relieved frequently and rested. The remainder of the battalion was strung out in company columns. By 1800 on the second day, the battalion had marched 7,000 meters and had penetrated the canopy only 1,000 meters. It bivouacked on a piece of high ground for the second night after marching 22 of the first 24 hours. Despite the commanding feature of the high ground, actual visibility and observation were nil. There was no contact.

Next morning, at first light, the lead company moved out. An attached company from ⅓ [battalion] was sent off to the flank to search for enemy trails and camp sites.

Ensuing progress will perhaps put some readers in mind of the British fighting Thibaw's guerrillas in Burma eighty years earlier (see Chapter 16, Volume I):

. . . During the next two days movement was slow, in column, and characterized by brief fights at the point. Charlie would delay along a trail, fire at the point hoping to inflict casualties. The VC know the American pro-

18. Corson, op. cit.
19. *Time*, October 6, 1967.

cedure for casualty evacuation. If the VC can fire from concealment, kill, or better still, wound a Marine, it is their hope to immobilize the entire column as it waits for the Medevac helicopter. In this instance at least seven VC paid with their lives for such an assumption. Aggressive counter-fire and pursuit made the difference.

After four days and five nights and some hunger (CH-46 helicopters were grounded and supply interrupted), this battalion destroyed three VC base camps but no VC. At the second camp, marines destroyed four hundred Chinese Communist grenades.

. . . Unfortunately, the enemy himself had evacuated the area after a small rear guard action. Everything which he had which was mobile, including some cattle, accompanied him.

This battalion had scarcely rested from its jungle foray when it received orders to proceed to Con Thien, from where it would conduct patrols and spoiling operations against PAVN units. The author wrote feelingly on effective enemy tactics and on the difficulties of operating in strange terrain and difficult climate. Almost at once, his battalion blundered into a major fight, which, as usual, saw courageous fighting by individual marines but cost heavy casualties: ". . . The toll of the day was counted and 2/4 was down under 500 effectives in the field, including walking wounded." Two hundred enemy dead were claimed for the inconclusive fire fight. Of a good many conclusions drawn by the battalion commander, one read as follows:

. . . Search and destroy is a proper mission against irregulars; it is a poor mission assignment against regulars engaged in conventional warfare. Assigning a large area to be swept vice specific objectives to be attacked is asking for trouble. Better intelligence is mandatory; and moving large units through an area without a specific objective is capricious.[20]

The scope of fighting, not only in I Corps area but throughout South Vietnam, is difficult to comprehend. By August 1967, marine units had mounted over three hundred thousand patrols—over 1,200 a day since early 1967!—set 114,000 ambushes, and fought over two hundred battalion-size or larger actions. Marine fixed-wing aircraft had flown 128,000 missions; marine helicopters registered a total of 859,000 flights. Marines claimed an impressive cumulative confirmed enemy kill—". . . we have buried more than 28,455 [enemy]" read one bulletin—with 2,344 enemy captured, along with 3,952 weapons. At year's end, the claimed kill figure for I Corps area would reach thirty-eight thousand.[21]

Pacification also showed impressive gains. Of 219 villages (with a population exceeding 1.2 million) in the marine area, forty-three (with

20. Hammond, op. cit.
21. *Newsweek,* January 1, 1968.

a population of five hundred thousand) were declared 80 per cent or more pacified by late autumn. ARVN units had been working in the area for over a year, and Combined Action Platoons now numbered seventy and were to expand to 114—all together, a program that would provide ". . . security for an estimated 400,000 Vietnamese people or in percentage figures 15 percent of the entire population of I Corps area."[22] Navy doctors attached to marine units had treated over two million Vietnamese, dentists over a hundred thousand. Marines had distributed over four million pounds of food, had helped build or rebuild a hundred five schools and a hundred other buildings such as churches and dispensaries; they had dug a hundred thirty wells, built forty-nine bridges, and serviced four hundred miles of roads.[23] Pacification techniques were improving, as witness this account of an operation called County Fair:

. . . A Marine unit in cooperation with Vietnamese units surrounds a hamlet or village usually before dawn and cordons it off to prevent anyone from leaving. After the people are assembled, Vietnamese officials with Marine support begin a series of actions to gain their confidence. A census is taken. A field dispensary is set up and medical attention given to those who need it. Sometimes a dentist accompanies the party. Meals are cooked and served. Lectures and movies are presented. A Marine band may play for an hour or so. Much of this activity takes place under canvas which probably accounts for the name County Fair. A careful house-to-house search is aimed at VC guerrillas and VC political personnel who may be part of the local cadre. . . . The County Fair technique has had excellent results and is now a routine type operation, although each one varies in its specifics.[24]

The marines also improved techniques in an attempt to repair intelligence deficiencies. A long-overdue step involved recruiting scouts from enemy defectors, the Kit Carson Scout Program, variations of which had proved so successful in Malaya and Kenya (see Chapters 61 and 68), indeed in the Philippines at the turn of the century (see Chapter 14, Volume I). Marine intelligence officers recruited these people from Viet Cong and North Vietnamese who had surrendered under the Chieu Hoi program. After training, they were normally assigned in pairs to an infantry battalion deployed in search-and-destroy missions. The former enemy soldiers proved invaluable in detecting ambush sites and booby traps, and also in acting as interpreters when needed. When possible, they were employed in areas where they were familiar with the terrain, people, and their former units. Marines initially

22. David H. Wagner, "A Handful of Marines," *Marine Corps Gazette,* March 1968.
23. U. S. Marine Corps ("III MAF Force . . ."), *supra;* see also Wagner, op. cit.
24. Keith B. McCutcheon, "Air Support for III MAF," *Marine Corps Gazette,* August 1967; see also L. W. Walt (*Strange War, Strange Strategy*), *supra.*

procured fifty per division, later a hundred; the program was so successful that the army adopted it. One marine division commander, Herman Nickerson, later told an audience in the United States:

. . . I had two scouts killed and several wounded during the performance of their duties with the First Marine Division. . . . The use of these "Kit Carson" scouts pays great dividends. For example, I have had many marines at night on counterguerrilla patrols or ambushes saved by the quick eyes, the knowledge and understanding, the ability of the scouts to recognize the V.C. booby traps in the dark and remove them or avoid same.

Unit commanders used two Vietnamese and two marine scouts as a point fire team. Nickerson described one incident:

. . . One night one of the scouts noticed, in the dark now, along an area that he was familiar with—that the little branches were picked off or broken off the bushes along the trail at more and more frequent intervals. He signaled the patrol. They got off the trail, and they discovered that this seemingly meaningless action of taking cover triggered a Viet Cong ambush prematurely. The scout knew the V.C. had an ambush set ahead. It takes a long while, especially in the low visibility of the dark, to train an occidental to recognize those kind of signs! In other words, it takes one to know one! I am a great believer in the Kit Carson scouts. . . .[25]

A complementary solution involved developing a unit's own scouts in the form of small, long-range patrols that came to be known as Sting Ray operations. Such a patrol consisted of a few highly trained men equipped to find the enemy, then call in and adjust friendly air, artillery, or naval gunfire by radio. A patrol infiltrated an area believed to hold enemy forces either on foot or by helicopter. It operated normally for five days, during which it fulfilled one or more missions: One was gathering intelligence that a tactical commander could exploit either in future plans or more immediately by flying in additional forces. The patrol could also employ disruptive tactics, in which case it sought out enemy supply trails and established appropriate ambushes. If a fire fight developed unfavorably, a patrol sought to extricate itself either by guerrilla tactics of fading into the terrain, or by helicopter call-in; one enterprising marine lieutenant, when greatly outnumbered, ordered his men to don gas masks, then saturated the area with tear gas, which held off the enemy until helicopters arrived.

This same officer, who led patrols over a period of several months, obtained a final kill ratio of 226 confirmed VC dead to the loss of a few wounded marines, a figure he believed would have been five times greater had an assault company, controlling its own helicopter trans-

25. Herman Nickerson, "Address." Headquarters, U. S. Marine Corps release, n.d.

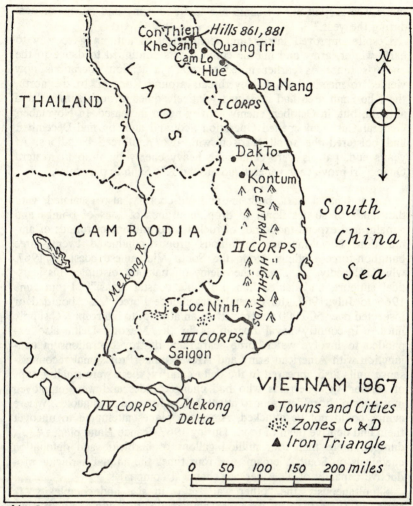

M.E.P.

port, been instantly available to exploit numerous chances for severely
punishing observed enemy units.[26]

Still another tactic involved two-man sniper teams that were especially trained to stake out a position and wait for opportunity. The 1st
Marine Division claimed that, in eight months, its ninety snipers recorded over four hundred fifty confirmed kills against four marine dead.
Called "13-cent killers," because of the price of a rifle cartridge, the

26. Private information in the author's files; see also Asprey ("Guerrilla Warfare" and "Tactics"), *supra;* West, op. cit.

tactic was carried out by some five hundred army and marine snipers during the year.[27]

Despite improved tactics and techniques, as autumn gave way to early winter, army and marine commanders continued to dance to the enemy's tune. As earlier noted, coastal pacification operations now yielded to meeting new enemy threats around Kontum. In the north, the Khe Sanh area had remained relatively quiet through summer and autumn, but, in October, enemy activity again increased. In November, General Cushman opened Operation Scotland and, by mid-December, had bolstered the small garrison with two reinforced battalions. At year's end, patrols were confirming heavy enemy build-up in western Quang Tri province in general and around Khe Sanh in particular.

Air and naval wars, both in- and out-country, also escalated, with thousands of sorties flown to drop thousands of tons of bombs and napalm and expend thousands of rockets and millions of rounds of ammunition. Naval-marine amphibious groups conducted twenty-three battalion-force landings along the South Vietnamese coast in 1967, which allegedly ". . . kept the enemy off balance, disrupted his logistical support, and denied him profitable coastal areas."[28] From June 1966 to July 1967, the Coastal Surveillance Force ". . . boarded or inspected over 500,000 watercraft" in an attempt to interrupt VC supply lines.[29] In-country naval operations in the Mekong Delta also expanded to involve water-borne search-and-destroy operations in conjunction with American army and ARVN units. Provisional reconnaissance units also appeared in the delta country; these were small groups of former VC guerrillas who had changed sides and were employed mostly as night raiders sent to attack VC camps and strongholds. Where camps could not be attacked, American planes attempted to uncover them and deprive them of food: During 1967, Ranch Hand planes ". . . dumped more than four million gallons of herbicide and defoliation chemicals on South Vietnam . . . four times the annual herbicide productive capacity of *all* American chemical companies."[30]

Simultaneously, the "other war" grew in size and complexity. In spring of 1967, the new American ambassador to South Vietnam, Ellsworth Bunker, once again reorganized the pacification program, at least from the American standpoint. Called now Civil Operations and Revolutionary Development Support (CORDS), it was headed by a deputy ambassador, former presidential aide Robert Komer, who administered it under MACV's jurisdiction with large amounts of funds going directly to the South Vietnamese Government. The general idea was to co-

27. *Time,* October 27, 1967.
28. Department of the Navy, "Chinfonote 5721." Washington: U. S. Navy, March 28, 1968.
29. U. S. Navy ("Riverine Warfare"), *supra.*
30. Corson, op. cit.

ordinate military aspects, particularly security, which had always been a weak point, with civil aspects. During 1967, the Revolutionary Development program grew to some fifty-five thousand cadres, including nearly five hundred Revolutionary Development Teams. Their work was measured by Komer's people, using an elaborate computerized system called Hamlet Evaluation System (HES). Data furnished by U.S. advisers, who monthly reported on eighteen criteria, went into computers, which then graded villages anywhere from totally secure ("A") to VC-controlled ("V"). By year's end, Komer claimed that two thirds of the population now lived under government control—". . . only one South Vietnamese in six now lives under VC control."[31]

Administration voices also emphasized substantial political progess in South Vietnam. At Guam, in March, Thieu and Ky had unveiled their new constitution, a document heralded by President Johnson as slightly more important than Magna Carta, particularly since he secretly exacted a pledge from the two Vietnamese not to break up the fragile South Vietnamese Government by reason of personal vendettas. Spring elections followed in about eight hundred villages and four thousand hamlets. An autumn presidential election placed Thieu in power, with Ky as vice-president; voters also elected a sixty-man senate and a 137-man house of representatives.

The Administration's line was clear: By continuing to pursue a winning strategy, the President was going to give the American people a well-deserved victory in South Vietnam. In various speeches around the country, Lieutenant General Walt, returned, in June 1967, from commanding III MAF, assured audiences that we were "winning" (at least in I Corps) and that it would be folly to stop now: ". . . wise or unwise, we have committed ourselves in Vietnam; weakness, vacillation, irresolution here at home are being paid for on the battlefields of Vietnam with the lives and blood of our fighting men."[32] MACV spokesmen in Saigon continued to report positive gains during the summer. In October, General Westmoreland told newsmen that ". . . the enemy is in the worst posture he has been in since the war started." Year-end figures seemed to confirm his optimism: a weekly enemy kill rate of nearly seventeen hundred (241,300 enemy killed since 1961),[33] a drop in infiltration from the North of twelve thousand, a decrease in VC recruitment in the South from seven thousand to thirty-five hundred a month,[34] an enemy desertion figure nudging twenty-five thousand for the year,[35] a half million persons (including a hundred thousand

31. *Newsweek*, January 1, 1968.
32. L. W. Walt, "Our Purpose in Vietnam" and "Are We Winning the War in Vietnam?" Headquarters, U. S. Marine Corps release, n.d.
33. UPI, Saigon, December 14, 1967.
34. *Newsweek*, January 1, 1968.
35. *The Economist*, November 18, 1969.

Chinese) repairing bomb damage in the North,[36] northern ports all but closed and supplies to the South drastically reduced as a result of the new aerial "choke-and-destroy" strategy, "victories" one after the other in all corps areas.

Prior to leaving for Washington, in November, General Westmoreland told newsmen that he was ". . . more encouraged than at any time since I arrived here."[37] Ambassador Bunker and Robert Komer, Bunker's pacification chief, reflected Westmoreland's optimism; indeed, according to *Time,* ". . . all three brimmed with confidence." At a White House meeting, Bunker told the President, ". . . It's going to be all right, Mr. President. Just let's keep on, keep on."[38] Also at the White House, Westmoreland told newsmen, ". . . I have never been more encouraged in my four years in Vietnam."[39] After citing various favorable statistics, Westmoreland explained that, having gotten his logistics plant in order, he had succeeded in driving enemy main-force units to border areas, where they would be contained. At President Johnson's request, Westmoreland addressed a joint session of Congress, which learned ". . . that the war was being won militarily. He outlined 'indicators' of progress and stated that a limited withdrawal of American combat forces might be undertaken beginning late in 1968."[40] Robert Komer offered equally good news. According to *Time,*

. . . The profile of war and pacification was sketched for the President from meticulously gathered statistics, Communist reports, prisoner interrogations, and U.S. and South Vietnamese intelligence sources. In almost all the country's provinces, the reports suggest, the Viet Cong is suffering increasingly from lack of food, recruiting difficulties, and the steady movement of the people from Viet Cong held areas to the security of government-controlled territory . . . many Viet Cong troops are sick and tired of the fighting.[41]

The combined report reminded a few observers of the French general Henri Navarre, who, in 1953, had spoken of ". . . light at the end of a tunnel" (see Chapter 62).[42]

General optimism continued to be expressed by Administration officials as the year closed. In mid-December, Admiral Sharp, while visit-

36. Shaplen ("Viet-Nam: Crisis of Indecision"), *supra.*
37. *Time,* November 17, 1967.
38. *Time,* November 24, 1967.
39. Ibid.; see also AP, Washington, November 15, 1967.
40. Henry Kissinger, "The Viet Nam Negotiations," *Foreign Affairs,* January 1969; see also Johnson (*The Vantage Point*), *supra:* Westmoreland told the President that his "central purpose" over the next two years was to transfer additional responsibility to the South Vietnamese. Westmoreland, the President wrote, ". . . was convinced that within that time—that is, by the end of 1969—we could safely begin withdrawing American forces. . . ."
41. *Time,* November 24, 1967.
42. UPI, Washington, November 21, 1967; see also Brandon, op. cit.; Hoopes, op. cit.; Johnson (*The Vantage Point*), *supra.*

ing Malaysia, pointed to a 50 per cent increase in Communist casualties in Vietnam for the year: ". . . The enemy can no longer feel safe in much of South Viet Nam," he said, qualifying his words by also pointing out that ". . . Communist forces in South Viet Nam retain a dangerous capability for terrorism and guerrilla warfare."[43] On December 19, President Johnson said, ". . . General Abrams tells me that the ARVN is as good as the Korean Army was in 1954."[44] At the turn of the year, Secretary of State Rusk spoke optimistically of ". . . a clear . . . turn of events on the ground."

Although the President later wrote in his memoirs that the tactical situation was very crucial at this time, and that he had warned of "kamikaze tactics" to come, the record does not show that he disapproved of Westmoreland's strategy or was in any mind to heed warning voices. Shortly before the new year, he stated that the Communists ". . . can't point to one single victory" in Vietnam. His State of the Union address in January 1968 implied satisfactory progress, with more of the same to come. General Westmoreland's annual report, delivered on January 27, included the following paragraph:

. . . Interdiction of the enemy's logistics train in Laos and NVN [North Vietnam] by our indispensable air efforts has imposed significant difficulties on him. In many areas the enemy has been driven away from the population centers; in others he has been compelled to disperse and evade contact, thus nullifying much of his potential. The year ended with the enemy increasingly resorting to desperation tactics in attempting to achieve military/psychological victory; and he has experienced only failure in these attempts.[45]

43. *Time,* December 15, 1967.
44. Corson, op. cit.
45. *The Pentagon Papers, supra* (p. 593).

Chapter 86

More blurs on the canvas • Allied losses • Failure of Operation Rolling Thunder • The numbers game • Increasing American costs (II) • The fallacy of attrition warfare • The "other war" examined • The communications deficiency • Search-and-destroy versus pacification • "Have we killed all the enemy?" • Failure of the Revolutionary Development program • Komer's "indicators" • Government corruption • Failure of land reforms • Electoral restrictions and irregularities • Increasing opposition at home and abroad • Press and TV coverage • The experts dissent • Behind-the-scenes dissent • Westmoreland demands more troops (III) • John McNaughton: ". . . A feeling is widely and strongly held that 'the Establishment' is out of its mind." • McNamara's new policy paper • The President's "middle course" • The Clifford mission • Johnson's San Antonio offer • Westmoreland demands more troops (IV) • McNamara's final effort

As WESTMORELAND'S OPERATIONAL CANVAS expanded in 1967, the blurs that had appeared in 1966 grew more prominent. One resulted from increasing cost and extensive physical loss. During 1967, nine thousand Americans were killed in Vietnam and over sixty thousand were wounded, to make cumulative totals of about sixteen thousand dead and one hundred thousand wounded since 1961.[1] Other allies lost fifteen hundred killed. South Vietnamese deaths were reported at sixty thousand, of which ten thousand were ARVN deaths. Steadily improving anti-aircraft defenses in the North exacted increasing toll of aircraft. On December 15, the Reuters news agency quoted an official American spokesman who put cumulative U.S. losses at 1,822 planes and 1,416 helicopters.[2]

1. The Institute for Strategic Studies, "The United States Strategic Survey, 1967," *Strategic Survey, 1967* (London: Institute for Strategic Studies, 1968).
2. Reuters, December 15, 1967; see also Hoopes, op. cit.: From February 1965 to December 1967, the United States lost, from all causes, in Vietnam some 3,000 aircraft (including helicopters), at a cost of $2.9 billion.

Yet the air war was proving no more effective than in 1966, despite official claims to the contrary. Testifying before a Senate subcommittee in August 1967, Robert McNamara pointed out that North Vietnam had the capacity to import fourteen thousand tons of supply per day, but was importing only fifty-eight hundred tons. North Vietnam and Viet Cong forces in the South, he told senators, required under one hundred tons of supply per day from the North.[3] American air power was not preventing this small amount from reaching the enemy, nor would it do so.

Townsend Hoopes later wrote that, by October 1967, ". . . the cold, unhypothetical fact remained that the flow of men and supplies from North Vietnam to South Vietnam had definitely increased in absolute terms."[4]

At the same time, as in 1965 and 1966, the bombing, far from breaking Hanoi's will, was increasing its intransigence. Just as unfortunate, it was drawing increasing criticism, from critics both within and without the United States. And, as in previous years, it continued to frustrate well-intentioned efforts by intermediaries to bring both sides to a conference table. Prime Minister Wilson, of Great Britain, was particularly offended by Johnson's attitude in February during behind-the-scenes negotiations. Wilson ascribed the hard-line attitude to "mentally confused" hawks and later wrote, undoubtedly with Rostow in mind, ". . . The more I saw of certain White House advisers, the more I thought Rasputin was a much maligned man."[5]

Despite official claims that enemy units could not win a major tactical victory in the South and could not maintain main-force units close to cities, the Viet Cong seemed more active than ever, while PAVN forces continued to call the play in the highlands and in the North. Despite severe losses—MACV claimed some eighty thousand enemy dead and three or four times that wounded in 1967—the enemy seemed to have ample ammunition and resources, not to mention open supply lines from both China and the U.S.S.R. and to the South. VC terrorists murdered 3,820 people, double the count for 1966, and kidnaped nearly six thousand as part of a determined effort to display continuing strength in and control of specific areas. If enemy morale suffered, as captured soldiers attested and as MACV claimed while pointing to twenty-five thousand deserters, it did not show in less-determined fighting, whether in defense or attack. Confusion also surrounded MACV figures. Where,

3. Hoopes, op. cit.
4. Ibid.
5. Harold Wilson, "The Night LBJ Wrecked Our Secret Manoeuvres for Peace," *The Sunday Times* (London), May 16, 1971; see also Johnson, in (*The Vantage Point*), *supra*, who offers a different interpretation but with interesting similarities; Hoopes, op. cit., and Brandon, op. cit., who tend to confirm Wilson's version. Personalities aside, one is inclined to accept Wilson's conclusion that ". . . an historic opportunity had been missed."

in 1966, this headquarters had stated that 280,000 enemy were fighting in South Vietnam, in 1967 the figure had risen to 378,000, a dramatic increase scarcely in keeping with official claims and one weakly explained in Saigon, where spokesmen argued ". . . that last year's figures had been deceptive. In November, after months of haggling among intelligence experts, the U.S. drastically revised its method of calculating enemy strength. As a result, meaningful comparisons with previous manpower estimates have now become all but impossible."[6]

Casualty figures aside, the war was also very expensive. Direct war expenditures totaled $24–27 billion in 1967 and billions more in indirect costs. Part of the expense was due to the technology of war as Americans fought it. Airplanes, helicopters, APCs, self-propelled artillery, tanks, vast naval armadas—all cost a great deal of money to maintain and replace if destroyed. Part of the expense also stemmed from the vast logistics effort, which tied up some 80 per cent of the armed forces in supporting about 20 per cent combat troops. Finally, a large part of the expense was due to Westmoreland's quantitative strategy, whereby commanders defended vast ammunition expenditures on grounds of saving lives.

At times, figures approached the fantastic. At Dak To, in November, a *single* B-52 raid dropped one hundred and fifty thousand pounds of bombs.[7] Jonathan Schell summed up a search-and-destroy operation, not a particularly big one, that in two weeks destroyed an estimated 65 per cent of the houses of perhaps seventeen thousand natives. Operation Benton was undertaken by an airborne brigade in the Chu Lai area:

. . . On August 28th, when Operation Benton came to a close, Task Force Oregon announced that the troops taking part in it had killed, and counted the bodies of, three hundred and ninety-seven of the enemy, and that forty-seven American soldiers had been killed. Into an area of ten by twenty kilometres they had dropped 282 tons of "general-purpose" bombs and 116 tons of napalm; fired 1,005 rockets (not counting rockets fired from helicopters), 132,820 rounds of 20-mm. explosive strafing shells, and 119,350 7.62-mm. rounds of machine-gun fire from Spooky flights; and fired 8,488 artillery rounds. By the end of the operation, the Civil Affairs office had supervised the evacuation of six hundred and forty of the area's seventeen thousand people, to the vicinity of government camps.[8]

During the twelve-day battle for Hills 861 and 881, in the marine area, gunners fired over eighteen thousand artillery rounds,[9] tactical aircraft dropped 1,375 tons of bombs, and B-52 aircraft dropped 1,750 tons of bombs.[10] Small-unit commanders relied on supporting artillery and

6. *Newsweek*, January 1, 1968; see also Shaplen ("Crisis"), *supra*.
7. *Time*, November 17, 1967.
8. Schell, op. cit.
9. U. S. Marine Corps ("The Battle for Hills 861 and 881"), *supra*.
10. Shaplen (*The Road from War*), *supra*.

aircraft fire as probably no commanders in history. The "mad minute" previously described became standard operating procedure in many units. A marine battalion commander later wrote of a 1967 operation outside Con Thien:

. . . Tuesday morning, before dawn, artillery was called on likely enemy mortar positions, i.e. positions within 2000 meters of where Mr. Charles [Marine Corps euphemism for sophisticated, PAVN troops, as opposed to Charlie, for less-sophisticated, Viet Cong troops] could have effectively mortared the battalion perimeter. This pre-dawn artillery shoot was continued every morning while 2/4 [battalion] remained around Con Thien. The net effect was that the battalion was never subjected to a surprise early morning mortar attack.[11]

American supporting arms, particularly from warships and B-52 bombers, responded to later Communist attacks of Con Thien with what Westmoreland called the heaviest concentration of firepower ". . . on any single piece of real estate in the history of warfare."[12]

Most accounts of army and marine operations in this period stress use of supporting weapons, which commanders employed to rectify tactical disadvantages caused by inadequate intelligence. Spoiling tactics were scarcely the precise operations implied by MACV, but, rather, for the most part, were "encounter" battles, which the enemy broke off when he wished, as in the case of Hills 861 and 881 or the fighting around Con Thien. Valiant as was the American effort to hold defensive outposts or "capture" prominences, it didn't really solve anything. It proved once again that an enemy was hard put to stand against either a determined defense backed by co-ordinated supporting fires (the major tactical lesson of the 1905 Russo-Japanese war and of World War I) or against a determined offense also backed by co-ordinated supporting fires (the major tactical lesson of World War II)—but in South Vietnam damage inflicted on the enemy was scarcely decisive, particularly when that enemy held ample reserves and reasonably secure lines of communication.

These actions continued to demonstrate the fallacy of American attrition strategy. At times, Westmoreland's highly vaunted "spoiling tactics" led to outright disaster: The ambush in October of a combat patrol of the 1st Infantry Division by the 271st VC Regiment sounds like 1952–54 Red River Delta fighting all over again. So long as American commanders lacked good intelligence, they would have to fight in the most expensive possible way. Trumpeted to the world as American "victories," encounter battles, in view of cost in human lives and suffering and in material versus tactical results did little more than illustrate the truth of an ancient axiom: ". . . from no victory shall the ass's kick

11. Hammond, op. cit.
12. *Time*, October 6, 1967; perhaps the general forgot Hiroshima and Nagasaki?

be missing." Or, as Captain Roeder had put it while watching Napoleon's army invade Russia: ". . . Every victory is a loss to us."

It is doubtful if they even achieved claimed enemy casualties: Marine commanders would have been hard put to explain the discrepancy between a claim of 28,455 "confirmed enemy dead" and 3,952 weapons captured.[13] Assuming, however, that the enemy lost nine hundred men in the fight for Hills 861 and 881 in April, he apparently could stand the loss without too much difficulty. His reserve strength remained sufficient to retain the tactical initiative, and his morale did not seem unduly low if the marine figure of a total 371 Chieu Hoi returnees is considered.[14]

Similarly, American army units may have badly hurt various attacking forces, but their claims were made suspect not alone by various factors discussed in earlier chapters, but by tactical surprises such as that at Bo Duc in early December. The previous month, at Loc Ninh, the American army claimed a unique victory, as reported by *Time* magazine:

. . . U.S. intelligence estimated that perhaps half that many again [of 926 North Vietnamese dead] had been dragged away for burial by their comrades, and that another 2,000 to 3,000 had been wounded. This high casualty rate (roughly 50%) for the two ill-fated Red regiments, who were ordered to take the town at all costs, made Loc Ninh one of the war's most significant Allied victories.[15]

Major General John Hay, commanding the 1st Infantry Division, ". . . predicted that it would be three to six months before the 9th V. C. Division [to which the two regiments belonged] . . . would be able to fight in force again."[16] Yet, one of the decimated regiments attacked at Bo Duc less than a month later!

Granting that enemy casualties were heavy, the enemy nonetheless initiated the actions that caused the casualties—and for good reason. His attacks in the central highlands caused Westmoreland to divert units from pacification operations in the coastal provinces. His continued presence in and around the DMZ, his attacks at Khe Sanh and Con Thien, his continued probes in the general area—all slowed marine pacification efforts in two ways: by causing General Cushman to commit battalions and resources needed for pacification duties, and by adding to a refugee flow that, in late 1967, numbered some five hundred thousand in I Corps area alone.

13. U. S. Marine Corps ("III MAF Force"), *supra.*
14. Ibid.
15. *Time,* November 17, 1967.
16. *Time,* December 8, 1967.

Thus we return to the "other war." Despite the barrage of statistics fired by MACV and III MAF against all visitors, pacification was not going well anywhere.

The marines in I Corps area erred in several respects. As elsewhere in South Vietnam, search-and-destroy tactics continued to antagonize people who had to be won over. Marines were operating in a vast sea of fear that could easily turn to hatred, and frequent fire fights, no matter how carefully conducted, could not but exacerbate the situation—moving bullets are promiscuous. Marine bands could play, and marines could distribute food and clothing, and doctors could help villagers, but these advantages paled when one, two, or more villagers were killed in a fire fight or by bombs, rockets, naval shells, or napalm.

Marines attempted to prevent this in two ways: either to evacuate villages or to help them to protect themselves. In 1967, nearly three hundred thousand of half a million refugees were living in hastily constructed camps, sometimes in appalling conditions. Far from being rehabilitated and trained for the day when they could return to their hamlets, they were fortunate to survive, considering the rapacious officialdom that surrounded them. Further, since numerous Viet Cong agents had accompanied refugee groups, they presented a bewildering security problem, as did 176 villages that were under 80 per cent pacified.

In attempting to protect villages, marines erred by trying to do the job themselves: Marines could hold "county fairs" until doomsday, but, unless carried to fruition, they were not only meaningless but dangerous, in that they brought forward either friendly or potentially friendly villagers who were subsequently exposed to VC wrath. Nothing was new about the county-fair technique; Lyautey used almost an identical procedure, but Lyautey was smart enough to back it with reasonably honest administration that improved tribal life, at least initially. Moving in government development teams too often subjected villagers to rents and various forms of squeeze that soon neutralized attendant advantages. As far as the psychological approach went, the Viet Cong did it better: Few Vietnamese peasants would prefer to hear a marine band in preference to Vietnamese acting out dramas and operas in their own tongue and their own cultural traditions.

Civil relations, what marines called personal response, were at best difficult and demanded not alone patience and determination, but intelligence—which is why counterinsurgency demands a qualitative approach. Captain Williamson, a marine with extensive civil-affairs experience, later wrote:

. . . One of the chief factors making warfare so difficult as it exists in Vietnam is the unhealthy climate of mutual suspicion and fear between the civilian and the military. The Marine encounters a Vietnamese civilian where he does not expect him to be and thinks of him first as a Viet Cong. He is considered a friend and ally only after the proper papers are produced and satisfactory answers received to certain questions. The civilian in return understandably resents this continuous threat of invasions to his privacy and person as well as the subordination of his individual interests to the sacred cow of military necessity. The military never ventures forth without arms, the civilian never has arms with which to venture forth.

The situation would be difficult enough with a common language. Without communications, it at times became impossible. A communications deficiency could be repaired only in part, by extreme common sense. But, too often, nervous and inexperienced marines lacked such:

. . . On one occasion, a Marine patrol dispatched to search for suspects of a mortar attack picked up two local villagers who lacked proper identification papers (an error of omission the VC assiduously avoid). The villagers stated that the local chief could vouch for their identity and innocence, which he did. But they were brought in for interrogation anyway—just to be safe. The village chief, a duly elected official approved by the central government, was less than happy over being rated a liar in public, and cast as a leader without sufficient status or power to save his townsmen from a humiliating experience. How easy military courtesy became the sacrificial lamb of military necessity.

On another occasion,

. . . members of a local village were denied scarce and valuable grazing land for their livestock by the erection of barbed wire. A compromise was worked out which allowed them to establish and operate a marketplace inside the perimeter. This arrangement was cleared through appropriate channels and the market proved quite satisfactory to all concerned. Months later, after numerous personnel changes and reorganization of area responsibilities, it was decided that the market *might* become a dangerous point of infiltration for V.C. The local emporium was promptly and unceremoniously wrecked. However compatible that decision was with military necessity, it did little to enhance free enterprise as a desirable way of life.

More was to come to this village when "military necessity," in this case for defensive positions, dictated bulldozing ancestral burial grounds, which automatically made village inhabitants ". . . unworthy and virtually non-beings." The result was a decided VC gain:

. . . These two incidents created an atmosphere of embarrassing hostility. Reprisals [by villagers] were carried out in the form of cutting barbed wire, harassing work details and scavenging Marine scrap piles.

Captain Williamson did not so state, but the hostile air undoubtedly aided the VC in more ways than one.[17]

17. R. E. Williamson, "A Briefing for Combined Action," *Marine Corps Gazette*, March 1968.

Although marines made better progress in pacification than either the American army or ARVN, their program left considerable to be desired, and, in view of South Vietnamese civil and military corruption, it is doubtful if it would ever have succeeded. One of the most tragic cameos to come from I Corps area is this, related by a senior marine intelligence officer:

. . . one day [in 1966] the commanding general remarked to me, "We've been doing well lately. Don't you think we are now really eliminating the enemy? Haven't we just about killed them all?" Looking out the window, I thought of the hundreds of thousands of peasants living on that vast rice plain; of the patient and thorough way in which a highly-motivated enemy for decades had been organizing that society at all levels. I answered only, "No, sir. We haven't killed all the enemy."[18]

The pacification effort elsewhere in South Vietnam caused the largest blur to occur on Westmoreland's operational canvas. The reader may remember that one reason for an extensive American build-up was to replace ARVN combat units with American units, so that ARVN could reorganize while undertaking the major task of protecting the pacification program. This program worried the enemy more than any other action, because, where it worked, it seriously challenged his presence. Unfortunately, it did not work in many places. In June 1967, Robert Shaplen noted:

. . . Estimates of how much of the [Mekong Delta] region is under Allied control vary, but even the most optimistic ones don't claim more than a quarter of the total land space, though this includes much of the arable land. The government and the Americans consider ten of the sixteen Delta provinces as priority areas this year; the others—mostly along the Cambodian border and on the Ca Mau Peninsula, in the far south—will have to wait. More than half of the fifty-four hundred hamlets in the Delta are still outside government control, and many of those considered "safe" are subject to constant attack or harassment, especially at night. The target for 1967 is to pacify two hundred and eighty-seven hamlets in all—a modest ten-per-cent improvement and a figure that, perhaps more than anything else, reveals the difficulty of the Delta problem.[19]

Although the Revolutionary Development program had expanded drastically during 1967, under Robert Komer's aegis, the performance of ARVN units assigned to protect the teams proved disappointing, and VC terrorism increased substantially in some areas during the year. Increased South Vietnamese control of funds and materials added to already widespread corruption, which further hindered the program's effectiveness.

18. Private information in the author's files.
19. Shaplen (*Road*), *supra;* see also, Shaplen ("Crisis"), *supra;* Hoopes, op. cit.

Despite widespread failures noted and reported by a host of observers, Komer continued to claim substantial progress based on "indicators" that, like those used by the American military, were not always pertinent to a counterinsurgency situation. A particularly hostile critic of Komer, William Corson, later wrote concerning one of CORDS's projects:

. . . When the General Accounting Office (GAO) reviewed AID/CORDS stewardship of the funds for War Relief and Support [about $70–75 million annually], it was not misled by Komer's reports. Under Komer, progress is indicated by the amount of money pushed into the hands of the GVN. However, the GAO noted that in the October 1967 report only one out of ten "scheduled" houses had been rebuilt, one out of eight "New Life" hamlets constructed, one out of nine public-health sanitation facilities erected, and more than half of the refugees had received *no* assistance. Senator Edward Kennedy, in commenting on the GAO report, said that the findings "show that the refugee program and the medical program in South Vietnam are a scandal." . . .[20]

Komer also claimed substantial progress in regaining control of hamlets, his indicator here being the Hamlet Evaluation Estimate program. But William Lederer noted that ". . . the evaluation of the conditions in approximately 13,000 hamlets is made by U. S. Army officers who are advisers to Vietnamese district chiefs. They send in Hamlet Evaluations monthly. I estimate that 99 percent of the U. S. Army advisers have neither language facility nor the knowledge of Vietnamese culture to know what is happening in their own district." Lederer continued:

. . . I have seen samples of the Hamlet Evaluation Estimates sent to headquarters by U. S. Army advisers. These estimates are fraudulent, or, to be charitable, they are distorted with errors. Under the present system they can be no other way. It is not only that the U. S. advisers and their interpreters are intellectually and culturally unable to make accurate estimates, but the taint of dishonesty has swept through the entire United States government reporting system in Vietnam. This pollution sinks down from the top. In Washington, Walt Rostow (who advises President Johnson) suggests—sometimes even insists—that his colleagues de-emphasize unfavorable facts. Occasionally when his assistants refuse to alter facts Rostow goes into tantrums. Once he threw a water pitcher at a colonel who showed that Rostow's figures were biased. Unwillingness to face unwelcome facts has spread throughout the government, and it has of course reached Saigon and down to the Army advisers in remote South Vietnamese districts.[21]

20. Corson, op. cit.: He offers numerous illustrations of gross incompetence, maladministration, and corruption—all bad enough in their own right as damaging American aid programs—but damage *always* compounded by a high percentage of missing items and supplies ending in the enemy's camp.
21. Lederer (*Our Own Worst Enemy*), *supra;* see also Hoopes, op. cit.

A RAND analyst, Konrad Kellen, included the pacification program as one of eleven American fallacies, ". . . perhaps the most deeply ingrained and therefore the most pernicious of all." The basic factor was identification: Whether we liked it or not, the VC identified more completely with the peasants than either Americans or South Vietnamese working to reshape the country in an American image:

. . . but aside from the fact that Pacification is impossible because our Pacification aims and methods are unacceptable to the people in the Vietnamese countryside, there is another aspect to this which makes Pacification a doubly impossible aim: the choice of Americans entrusted with it. . . . One need only to have met a member of AID and Army representatives to know that all these men, despite their great goodwill, and ample knowledge of local detail, can never do anything but confuse and antagonize any foreign population, and disorganize, if not destroy, its social fabric. And there are no other men to do the job, which cannot be done in the first place.[22]

Unfortunately, the people who should have taken on the pacification task could not accomplish it. As in former years, government inefficiency and pervasive corruption stultified South Vietnam's economy. Horrified senators sitting on a judiciary subcommittee learned that only half of an estimated four million refugees received the fourteen ounces of rice and five cents a day that the South Vietnamese Government was supposed to be providing—at U.S. expense. The same report alleged that numerous refugees never received a $42 resettlement allowance and a six-month rice supply.[23] One American official, John Vann, senior adviser in IV Corps area, ". . . managed to have 75 GVN officials removed for corruption, only to find all of them reinstated within six months in equal or better jobs."[24] William Lederer concluded, from personal investigations, that the black market in South Vietnam involved about $10 *billion* a year, all American goods and moneys, an incredible situation that ". . . could not exist without American collusion." He described a visit to a black-market warehouse in Saigon:

. . . The place looked like a U. S. Army Ordnance Depot. Everything seemed to be painted brown and to smell of either oil or fresh paint. Ordnance equipment was arranged in orderly lines, and neatly printed price tags hung from everything. Automatic rifles were $250. A 105 mm mortar . . . was priced at $400. . . . There were about a thousand American rifles of different kinds standing neatly in racks. M16s cost $80. On one side of the loft were uniforms of all services. . . .

22. Konrad Kellen, "Fourth Round or Peace in Vietnam?" RAND Corporation, 1968.
23. *Time,* October 20, 1967.
24. Kellen, op. cit.

So much American military transport had been stolen, that ". . . the American military has been renting its own stolen jeeps from black-market operators at $250 a month. The same double indignity and multiple cost applies to U.S. government trucks."

Lederer pointed out that, in three years, South Vietnam's gold reserves increased from $130 to $450 million (all at American expense) and that, according to Swiss and Chinese informants, approximately $18 *billion* ". . . has been sent to foreign banks by private Vietnamese individuals since 1956. Not so long ago, Madame Nhu, through a silent partner, purchased outright the second largest bank in Paris, for cash."[25]

The same blatant corruption pervaded the pacification program. Land reform remained a bad joke. As two congressmen, John Moss and Ogden Reid, informed Secretary of State Rusk in December 1967, ". . . Land distribution in South Vietnam has been at a virtual standstill since 1962."[26] Their letter continued:

. . . Of 2.47 million acres acquired by the Government of Vietnam only 667,000 acres have been distributed to 128,000 families since 1954, including 51,800 acres to 12,000 families in 1967.

Of 566,000 acres of choice rice land acquired by the government in 1958 from French owners, 240,000 have been rented to small farmers, but no actual distribution was made until October 1966, eight years after the land was expropriated. . . .[27]

Landlords frequently violated rent-control laws. Although limited by law to paying 25 per cent of the principal crop as maximum rent, ". . . four out of five peasants pay a land rent equal to more than fifty per cent of the crop because there is no valid attempt to enforce the provisions of the land-rent law."[28]

Aid programs similarly suffered: Almost without exception, South Vietnamese officials and ARVN officers sold food and material to hamlets and villages, a shocking corruption freely admitted by American personnel in the field and in Saigon.[29] While admitting these and other violations, MACV and embassy spokesmen applauded political progress as demonstrated by elections. But other observers pointed to specific electoral irregularities and suggested that, though satisfying certain American officials, the elections were, in many ways, meaningless.[30] Townsend Hoopes later wrote that official American efforts to produce a South Vietnamese constitution and elections

25. Lederer, op. cit.
26. Corson, op. cit.; Lederer, op. cit.
27. Corson, op. cit.
28. Ibid.
29. Lederer, op. cit.; see also Corson, op. cit.; Hoopes, op. cit.
30. Lederer, op. cit.; see also Tran Van Dinh, op. cit.

. . . were of a piece with the underlying, only half-veiled, determination to press for a military victory, for U.S. endorsement of a constitution that specifically barred all Communists from participation in the GVN could only greatly narrow our military and political options. In the eyes of the world, such an endorsement transferred our commitment from the people as a whole to a particular form of government and a particular group of men. Moreover, the carefully drawn electoral laws and the Thieu-Ky group's full use of its inherent leverage on behalf of its own cause precluded anything but a victory for the existing military government. Some candidates were barred because their advocacy of peace was considered to be evidence of Communist sympathies (one man thus eliminated had been the GVN Finance Minister until 1966). No militant Buddhist could be a candidate, and no run-off elections were permitted, as it was feared that these might produce a "civilian victory." Several oppositionist newspapers in Saigon were closed down during the campaign. As Robert Kennedy later wrote: "it was in these and many similar ways, and not in the crude stuffing of ballot boxes, that the election . . . was such a disappointment."

The result was to legitimize military rule in a way that tended to push civilian nationalist groups, like the Buddhists, toward the only viable opposition, the NLF. . . .[31]

If the Johnson administration expected immediate advantages to occur, it was disappointed. Robert Shaplen warned, in November, ". . . The assumption—primarily an American one—that the Vietnamese elections . . . have had, or are likely to have, any salutary effect on the war or on the internal political situation here [Saigon] is regarded by most Vietnamese as unwarranted and unrealistic."[32] A postelection imbroglio between Thieu and Ky almost immediately lent substance to this and other pessimistic observations. Thieu would thenceforth rule by means of an uneasy executive oligarchy consisting of: Ky; Thieu's hatchet man who headed the secret police, General Nguyen Ngoc Loan; and ranking generals. Elections or no, the government would remain authoritarian in structure; bureaucratic inefficiency would continue, and so would widespread corruption, which, in large part, accounted for the dismal performance of ARVN and the pacification program.

Thus it was that, despite escalation, despite increasing costs in lives and money, despite optimism frequently expressed by Administration spokesmen and by the President, the U.S.A. and South Vietnam were no closer to "winning" the war than ever and, in some respects, were even farther from this ambition. As Robert Shaplen wrote in October 1967: ". . . There are indications that the long and difficult conflict is in a state of irresolution, or what the communists describe as 'indecisive-

31. Hoopes, op. cit.
32. Ibid.

ness.' "[33] An otherwise favorable article in *The Economist* (November 18, 1967), included this realistic, if damaging, appraisal:

. . . The hardest fact to face is that, whatever level of military security is achieved, the really difficult job of rooting out the Vietcong's local organization depends on the Vietnamese themselves. They have barely started this long task. Military control of the main areas of population may be only a year away, or twice that if things go wrong. But at the present rate of progress it could be at least a decade before the government and people of South Vietnam are strong enough to fend for themselves. . . .

President Johnson's expressed determination to persevere unto "victory" was also in jeopardy. Increasingly influential voices were questioning the conduct of the war, a debate characterized in Prime Minister Harold Wilson's words by ". . . great passion, great feeling, and great emotion." Despite a fiscal-year defense budget of an unprecedented $75 billion, American military forces seemed strangely impotent to cope with the Vietnam challenge. As the Institute for Strategic Studies noted in its *Strategic Survey 1967*,

. . . What concerned a growing number of Americans . . . was not the cost of military strength but whether that strength was capable of being applied both wisely and effectively. Nowhere did that concern seem more urgent than in Vietnam. Other strategic issues during the year had greater objective importance for United States security, but Vietnam continued to fill a growing area of the national vision.

Looked at objectively, the situation in South Vietnam presented a dismal picture. Although the President and Administration officials continued to emphasize bright colors, an increasing number of Americans were studying manifold blurs. In the minds of an increasing number of American citizens, Lyndon Johnson had lost control of the situation—the praying mantis of earlier portraits had become a preying menace to common sense. *Time* magazine noted in October, ". . . Until recently, most of the opposition has come from intellectuals and the young, from college professors and clerics. But now the ranks have been swelled by apolitical businessmen and uneasy politicians eying the antiwar sentiment in the polls. . . . Congress is in a rebellious mood."[34]

Capable journalists were continuing to report adversely, their copy often reflecting dissident views of American civil and military officials, particularly at lower levels, with official policy. Similarly, TV coverage of battle areas increasingly brought home the agony of war in all forms. What some American officials liked to call distorted camera coverage, in reality emphasized stupidity of search-and-destroy tactics and, at the same time, questioned optimistic claims of military spokesmen. Embar-

33. Shaplen ("Crisis"), *supra*.
34. *Time*, October 6, 1967; see also Brandon, op. cit.

rassed Administration officials continued to blame press and television correspondents for distorting news, an accusation frequently implied by President Johnson and one that scarcely modified the growing antagonism between press and government. Johnson refused to realize that the protesting press was accurately reflecting increasing doubts in many American minds. Although a few correspondents did allow personal emotion to overcome objective reporting, a great many did not, and the Administration erred grievously in attempting to cast doubt on the veracity of many courageous and intelligent observers whose analyses often contained constructive criticism. In early 1967, for example, Walter Lippmann, writing in *Newsweek,* challenged the desire of such Congressional hawks as Mendel Rivers ". . . to flatten Hanoi if necessary and let world opinion go fly a kite." If the United States adopted genocide as a national policy, Lippmann wrote, it would find itself dangerously isolated. It would not only earn the suspicion and hatred of neutrals but even of allies: ". . . We would come to be regarded as the most dangerous nation in the world, and the great powers of the world would align themselves accordingly to contain us." The President, Lippmann went on, found himself confronted

. . . with the agonizing fact that limited war has not worked because *limited war can be effective only for limited objectives.* The reason why the President is confronted with the demand for unlimited war is that he has escalated his objectives in Vietnam to an unlimited degree.[35]

Interested and experienced observers such as Generals Gavin, Ridgway, and Shoup added to the criticism, as did portions of the business world—thenceforth, the BEM (Business Executives Move for Peace in Vietnam), whose military board included one of the United States' few genuine guerrilla-warfare experts, Brigadier General S. B. Griffith, would become increasingly influential and, through its publication, *Washington Watch,* hostile to Administration policy. Other new voices were heard: In mid-November, General Lauris Norstad, former NATO chief and subsequently a top business executive, told a Los Angeles audience that Washington should seriously consider such moves as an unconditional halt of bombing and unilateral cease-fire in South Vietnam if these would move Hanoi to the conference table.[36]

Writing in the New York *Times,* John Kenneth Galbraith pointed to a shifting tide of feeling within the United States and within Congress:

. . . For I next assume that public opinion in the United States has turned very strongly against the war—and especially against those who hope to bring it to a military solution. The public opinion polls show it. So do the altered stands of political and other leaders—Senators Frank Lausche, Thruston Morton, Clifford Case, by gradual movement George Romney, numerous

35. *Newsweek,* January 16, 1967.
36. *Time,* November 17, 1967.

Congressmen of both parties, the Republican governors, Bishop Fulton J.
Sheen, and, conceivably one day soon, since he has never shown any quixotic
tendency to stand on principle against the publicly expressed preference of
the voters, Richard Nixon. . . .

The Administration's credibility, Galbraith continued, was rapidly approaching ground zero:

. . . The consequence of this ghastly sequence of promise and disappointment is that now nearly everything that is said in defense of the war is
suspect. This, in turn, nullifies the natural advantage of the Administration
in access to press and television. There isn't much advantage in being able
to get your side before the people if they no longer believe what you say
or do not listen.

In Galbraith's opinion, the situation could only worsen for the Johnson
administration:

. . . Those who must defend the war have a second and potentially even
more serious handicap than this conflict between promise and circumstance.
Increasingly, as the base of support narrows, the case for the war is made
by conservative Republicans, conservative Democrats, or high members of
the military services. (Even within the Administration itself support is far
from universal.) The defenders have a strong base in the Armed Services
Committees of the two houses of Congress, both of which are headed by
conservative supporters of the war. So the tactical position is strong; Congressional action can be obtained or blocked as required. But John Stennis,
Everett McKinley Dirksen, Mendel Rivers, and the Joint Chiefs do not
electrify the country. On the contrary, theirs is a combination that can only
repel public support. The Armed Services will themselves one day realize
with sorrow that one of the costs of the Vietnam war has been the widespread alienation of public opinion on which they too depend.

Since ". . . it now seems reasonably clear that our involvement in Vietnam was the result of a massive miscalculation—perhaps the worst miscalculation in our history," it was essential, Galbraith argued, for the
Administration to change objectives and reverse present policy.[37]

Senator Eugene McCarthy was equally critical: In his best-selling
book *The Limits of Power,* the senator from Wisconsin called for a fundamental change in general foreign policy and as swift an exodus as possible from Vietnam.[38] At year's end, Senator Fulbright told constituents
that national pride, not national security, is the reason that Americans
are fighting in Vietnam. As opposed to the President's statements concerning Communist aggression and danger to U.S. security, the senator

37. John K. Galbraith, *How to Get Out of Vietnam* (New York: Signet, 1967).
38. Eugene McCarthy, *The Limits of Power* (New York: Dell, 1967).

held that here was ". . . a civil war between two factions of Vietnamese. . . ."[39]

Experts added persuasive testimony: Douglas Pike, in his quasi-
official work *The Viet Cong,* identified the real enemy; George Tanham,
in his quasi-official work *War Without Guns,* pointed to some errors in
American aid programs in Vietnam. Foreign experts also contributed:
Richard Clutterbuck's *The Long Long War* and Robert Thompson's
Defeating Communist Insurgency threw considerable, if not always pertinent, light on the Vietnamese challenge as seen by two veterans of the
Malayan emergency. The British strategist Alastair Buchan, in the January 1968 issue of *Encounter,* warned that Vietnam was the greatest tragedy that had befallen the U.S.A. since the civil war. By diminishing
American influence, it was giving superb diplomatic advantage to its ad-
versaries while destroying the confidence of its own people in their vision of law and order and international justice.[40] In December, a group
of scholars and former Administration officials and officers that included
General Ridgway and Roger Hilsman produced a short analysis, the
"Bermuda Statement," which urged the Administration to de-escalate
the war and start giving it back to the South Vietnamese Government.
A week later, a larger group of scholars, mostly Asian specialists, published a lengthy statement that defended American armed presence in
Vietnam but called for increased restraint in its use:

. . . They said that U.S. withdrawal from Vietnam under conditions of Communist victory would be "disastrous for free people everywhere," but that
an escalation of the war into a regional or global conflict would be "equally
ruinous." Their principal advice to the Administration was couched in these
words; Vietnam is a "crucial test of whether we can stay the course with
a limited war involving extremely important but limited objectives. It is a
part of the broader test of whether in this nuclear age we have the wisdom,
maturity, and patience to avoid totalistic policies. . . . Nothing would do
more to strengthen American support for our basic position than to show
a capacity for innovation of a de-escalatory nature, indicating that there is
no inevitable progression upwards in the scope of the conflict."[41]

This and other important testimony and criticism influenced increasingly large segments of public opinion against the American effort. People began questioning the war in intelligent terms, and this particularly
applied to campuses, to students and teachers, and if emotion sometimes colored the questioning process, it was usually genuine emotion
expressed by youngsters who eventually would probably wind up in
Vietnam fighting a war for which, more and more, they saw less and
less reason.

39. UPI, Washington, December 21, 1967.
40. Reuters, London, December 20, 1967.
41. Hoopes, op. cit.

The situation was not new. Over two centuries earlier, Frederick the Great wrote on the bloody war of the Spanish succession:

. . . Conflicting events alter the cause of dispute; effects however continue, though the motive has ceased; fortune rapidly flies from side to side, but ambition and the desire of vengeance feed and maintain the flames of war. We seem to view an assembly of gamesters who demand their revenge, and who refuse to quit play till they are totally ruined.

So Johnson and the majority of his advisers either ignored what they regarded as minority voices or, when these spoke too powerfully to be ignored, brushed them aside with considerable petulance that too often questioned the dissenter's loyalty to his country. Communications between government and people continued to break down, and at a crucial time. As Townsend Hoopes later wrote,

. . . Above all, through riots, protests, and the fateful merging of antiwar and racial dissension, it [the war] was polarizing U.S. politics, dividing the American people from their government, and creating the gravest American political disunity in a century.[42]

Internal dissension within President Johnson's close circle of advisers and officials continued into 1967, the hawks, in general, remaining dominant. McNamara had already touched off a first-class row by suggesting de-escalation. Johnson's resistance to international attempts, in February, to end bombing of the North and get both sides to a conference table had caused further rupture.

Then, in March 1967, the matter of more troops again arose. In less than two months after Westmoreland, the JCS, and McNamara had worked out a troop ceiling, Westmoreland pointed to a sharp rise in enemy strength—in this case, some forty-two thousand during 1966, despite known losses.[43] Among other things, this meant that in the three military regions north of Saigon, ". . . the enemy can attack at any time selected targets . . . in up to division strength." To regain the "tactical initiative," Westmoreland once again requested more troops: a "minimum essential force" of about one hundred thousand; an "optimum force" of about two hundred thousand, which would have meant a total of some 670,000 Americans in South Vietnam—a radical increase from the figure agreed on in November. The JCS passed this request on, with favorable endorsement, to McNamara. According to the Pentagon study, the JCS now proposed

. . . the mobilization of the reserves, a major new troop commitment in the South, an extension of the war into the VC/NVA sanctuaries (Laos, Cambodia and possibly North Vietnam), the mining of North Vietnamese ports

42. Ibid.
43. *The Pentagon Papers, supra* (p. 525).

and a solid commitment in manpower and resources to a military victory. The recommendation not unsurprisingly touched off a searching reappraisal of the course of U.S. strategy in the war.[44]

In late April, Westmoreland returned to the United States and, accompanied by Wheeler, argued his case before the President. According to notes made by John McNaughton, the President was not pleased at future prospects:

. . . When asked about the influence of increased infiltration upon his operations the general [Westmoreland] replied that as he saw it "this war is action and counteraction. Anytime we take an action we expect a reaction." The President replied: "When we add divisions can't the enemy add divisions? If so, where does it all end?"

Westmoreland explained that VC and DRV strength in South Vietnam now totaled 285,000 men and that, last month, it appeared that, except in the two northern provinces, the enemy is losing more men than he is gaining. On the other hand, he is maintaining eight divisions in South Vietnam but could deploy twelve and undoubtedly would react to a significant American increase. Johnson then asked: ". . . At what point does the enemy ask for volunteers?" Westmoreland allegedly answered, ". . . That is a good question."[45] Westmoreland explained that, with the minimum increase he requested, the war could continue for three years; with the maximum increase, for two years. Wheeler warned that American troops would possibly have to invade Cambodia, Laos, and North Vietnam; he also pointed out that the air effort had nearly run out of targets and would have to be extended to port areas.

Almost none of the ranking civilian officials agreed with the proposed new and aggressive strategy. Townsend Hoopes, who had been promoted to Under Secretary of the Air Force, argued that, despite American bombing, Hanoi, ". . . in absolute terms," was sending more, not fewer, men and materials to the South. He himself had concluded ". . . that the Administration's Vietnam policy had become a quietly spreading disaster from which vital U.S. interests could be retrieved only if the policy were reversed or drastically altered."[46] William Bundy argued strongly against extending ground operations to North Vietnam, ". . . asserting that the odds were 75 to 25 that it would provoke Chinese Communist intervention."[47] He also warned that an attack on

44. Ibid. (p. 528); see also Johnson (*The Vantage Point*), *supra;* Hoopes, op. cit.

45. *The Pentagon Papers, supra* (pp. 567–68); see also Johnson (*The Vantage Point*), *supra:* According to Johnson, Westmoreland ". . . pointed out that heavy infiltration and continuing recruitment in the South were making up for battle casualties, but he was hopeful that the 'crossover point'—when losses exceeded the ability to replace those losses—might be reached reasonably soon. . . ."

46. Hoopes, op. cit.

47. *The Pentagon Papers, supra* (pp. 530–31).

northern ports could bring Soviet counteraction, a position supported by CIA reports. A call-up of reserves, in Bundy's opinion, was to be avoided for domestic political reasons.

Walt Rostow, theretofore as hawkish as the generals, did not agree with mining North Vietnamese harbors or bombing ports; in his opinion, this would make Hanoi more dependent on China and would increase United States tensions with the Soviet Union and China.[48] Instead, he wanted to concentrate the air effort ". . . on the 'bottom of the funnel,' the lines of communication and infiltration routes in southern North Vietnam and through Laos. . . ."[49]

Dr. Alain Enthoven, Assistant Secretary of Defense for Systems Analysis, argued that the troop increases requested by Westmoreland and the JCS would not produce proportionate enemy casualties. Dr. Enthoven wrote in a memorandum of early May:

. . . On the most optimistic basis, 200,000 more Americans would raise [the enemy's] weekly losses to about 3,700, or about 400 a week more than they could stand. In theory we'd wipe them out in 10 years.[50]

John McNaughton, slated to become Secretary of the Navy, was equally firm. Hoopes described him at this time as

. . . physically exhausted and deeply disenchanted with the Administration's Vietnam policy . . . [he was] appalled by the catastrophic loss of proportion that had overtaken the U.S. military effort in Vietnam. "We seem to be proceeding," he said to me in barbed tones, after returning from a particular White House session, "on the assumption that the way to eradicate Viet Cong is to destroy all the village structures, defoliate all the jungles, and then cover the entire surface of South Vietnam with asphalt."[51]

McNaughton wanted the air war shifted to lines of communication south of the 20th parallel, a definite cutback, designed primarily to save American pilots and planes. He argued against any significant troop increase as ". . . more of the same," which would not resolve anything. In early May, McNaughton advised McNamara (belatedly)

. . . that the "philosophy" of the war should be fought out now so everyone will not be proceeding on their own major premises, and getting us in deeper and deeper; at the very least, the President should give General Westmoreland his limit (as President Truman did to General MacArthur). That is, if General Westmoreland is to get 550,000 men, he should be told, "That will be all, and we mean it."

48. Ibid. (p. 533).
49. Ibid. (pp. 573–77); see also Johnson (*The Vantage Point*), *supra*.
50. *The Pentagon Papers, supra* (p. 531).
51. Hoopes, op. cit.

McNaughton, who was to die shortly in an air crash, continued:

. . . A feeling is widely and strongly held that "the Establishment" is out of its mind. The feeling is that we are trying to impose some U.S. image on distant peoples we cannot understand (any more than we can the younger generation here at home), and we are carrying the thing to absurd lengths.

Related to this feeling is the increased polarization that is taking place in the United States with seeds of the worst split in our people in more than a century.[52]

On the basis of these and other arguments, Robert McNamara submitted a major policy paper to President Johnson on May 19.[53] Mc-Namara recommended a scaling down of the air effort and very limited troop increases. Even more important, however, he called for a change in American policy: He recommended that the ambitions enunciated by President Kennedy and carried on by President Johnson in National Security Action Memorandum 288 be changed to reasonable political goals. He attempted first to quiet unreasonable fears by abolishing the domino theory he himself had once embraced:

. . . The fact is that the trends in Asia today are running mostly for, not against, our interests (witness Indonesia and the Chinese confusion); there is no reason to be pessimistic about our ability over the next decade or two to fashion alliances and combinations (involving especially Japan and India) sufficient to keep China from encroaching too far. To the extent that our original intervention and our existing actions in Vietnam were motivated by the perceived need to draw the line against Chinese expansionism in Asia, our objective has already been attained, and COURSE B [a continuation of the present effort] will suffice to consolidate it.[54]

McNamara continued in words made the more intelligent, bold, and courageous in that they reflected his own reversal of thought at a time when the President was embracing force more than fact:

. . . The time has come for us to eliminate the ambiguities from our minimum objectives—our commitments—in Vietnam. Specifically, two principles must be articulated, and policies and actions brought in line with them: (1) Our commitment is only to see that the people of South Vietnam are permitted to determine their own future. (2) This commitment ceases if the country ceases to help itself.

It follows that no matter how much we might *hope* for some things, our *commitment* is *not*:
—to expel from South Vietnam regroupees [Viet Cong], who are South Vietnamese (though we do not like them),
—to ensure that a particular person or group remains in power, nor that

52. *The Pentagon Papers, supra* (pp. 534–35).
53. Ibid. (pp. 577–85); Johnson (*The Vantage Point*), *supra.*
54. *The Pentagon Papers, supra* (p. 583).

the power runs to every corner of the land (though we prefer certain types and we hope their writ will run throughout South Vietnam),
—to guarantee that the self-chosen government is non-Communist (though we believe and strongly hope it will be), and
—to insist that the independent South Vietnam remain separate from North Vietnam (though in the short-run, we would prefer it that way).
(Nor do we have an obligation to pour in effort out of proportion to the effort contributed by the people of South Vietnam or in the face of coups, corruption, apathy or other indications of Saigon failure to co-operate effectively with us.) We *are* committed to stopping or off setting the effect of North Vietnam's application of force in the South, which denies the people of the South the ability to determine their own future. Even here, however, the line is hard to draw. Propaganda and political advice by Hanoi (or by Washington) is presumably not barred; nor is economic aid or economic advisors. Less clear is the rule to apply to military advisors and war matériel supplied to the contesting factions.

The importance of nailing down and understanding the implications of our limited objectives cannot be overemphasized. It relates intimately to strategy against the North, to troop requirements and missions in the South, to handling of the Saigon government, to settlement terms, and to US domestic and international opinion as to the justification and the success of our efforts on behalf of Vietnam.[55]

McNamara, in effect, was recommending a dramatic shift to viable policy; he was recognizing (after a long hiatus) that South Vietnam was a "strategic convenience" and should be treated as such. If it could be held with a limited effort, fine; but its retention was not worth a world war and was not worth a deepening schism inside the U.S.A. If the South Vietnamese could not come to terms with themselves, the country would be "lost" and could be "lost" without undue damage to American interests in Southeast Asia (which had never "owned" it, to start with).

McNamara recognized that he was asking the President to adopt a difficult course of action, which would be sharply criticized and possibly would cause a government crisis in South Vietnam:

. . . Not least will be the alleged impact on the reputation of the United States and of its President. Nevertheless, the difficulties of this strategy are fewer and smaller than the difficulties of any other approach.[56]

President Johnson did not agree with Secretary McNamara, and this document probably marks the beginning of McNamara's decline and fall from presidential grace. Indeed, the Secretary allegedly offered to resign at this time. His own doubts were reflected the following month, when he commissioned what since has become known as the Pentagon

55. Ibid. (pp. 583–84).
56. Ibid. (p. 585).

report—a highly secret attempt to explain how and why the United States became and remained involved in South Vietnam.

Neither did the President altogether agree with hawks who refuted McNamara's conclusions and recommendations with practiced fervor and ability similar to those of Viet Cong agit-prop agents. Although he refused to alter what he liked to call Administration policy, he did not authorize troop increases requested by Westmoreland, Sharp, and the JCS. Instead, he sent McNamara to Saigon to work out still another compromise with Westmoreland. Early in August, he announced an increase of fifty-five thousand troops, to bring total American commitment to 525,000. He did, however, authorize expanding the air war to include targets in Hanoi and in the China buffer zone.[57]

But now he received further bad news. In late summer, he had sent one of his closest advisers, Clark Clifford, and Maxwell Taylor on a tour of Southeast Asia, an informal attempt to persuade concerned countries to increase troop support of the war. In Saigon, MACV played the visitors its favorite record: ". . . Our briefings in South Viet Nam were extensive and encouraging. There were suggestions that the enemy was being hurt badly and that our bombing and superior firepower were beginning to achieve the expected results."[58] But the dominoes that had played such a major role in shaping the American commitment seemed unusually inert. Thailand, South Korea, Australia, and New Zealand showed no interest in increasing minimal contributions (which, in the case of Korea and Thailand, were subsidized by the United States); the Philippines Government asked President Johnson to avoid sending the team to Manila, for political reasons! The experience deeply impressed Clifford: ". . . It was strikingly apparent to me that the other troop-contributing countries no longer shared our degree of concern about the war in South Viet Nam." In his later words:

. . . I returned home puzzled, troubled, concerned. Was it possible that our assessment of the danger to the stability of Southeast Asia and the Western Pacific was exaggerated? Was it possible that those nations which were neighbors of Viet Nam had a clearer perception of the tides of world events in 1967 than we? Was it possible that we were continuing to be guided by judgments that might once have had validity but were now obsolete? In short, although I still counted myself a staunch supporter of our policies, there were nagging, not-to-be-suppressed doubts in my mind.[59]

57. Johnson (*The Vantage Point*), *supra*: ". . . I rejected the suggestion that we use air power to close the port of Haiphong and knock out part of the dike system in the Red River delta. I felt that there was too grave a risk of Communist Chinese or even Soviet involvement if those measures were carried out, and I wished to avoid the heavy civilian casualties that would accompany destruction of the dikes. . . ."
58. Clifford, op. cit.
59. Ibid.

What portion of these doubts brushed against President Johnson is problematical, but, in late September, at San Antonio, he did offer to halt bombing in the North if Hanoi wished to negotiate (an offer already made privately to Hanoi by Henry Kissinger, acting as presidential agent). Although Clifford and other advisers found this a step in the right direction, their optimism was brief:

. . . As I listened to the official discussion in Washington, my feelings turned from disappointment to dismay. I found it was being quietly asserted that, in return for a bombing cessation in the North, the North Vietnamese must stop sending men and matériel into South Viet Nam. On the surface, this might have seemed a fair exchange. To me, it was an unfortunate interpretation that—intentionally or not—rendered the San Antonio formula virtually meaningless. The North Vietnamese had more than 100,000 men in the South. It was totally unrealistic to expect them to abandon their men by not replacing casualties, and by failing to provide them with clothing, food, munitions and other supplies. We could never expect them to accept an offer to negotiate on those conditions.[60]

Thus, bombing continued and so did the ground war. In late September, General Westmoreland asked Washington to speed the arrival of promised troops. Worried by reports of a general enemy build-up, Johnson agreed. Once again, McNamara tried to prevent further escalation. As he had done the previous year, in early November he sent the President a general analysis of the war. Rejecting increased military actions because of the risks they entailed in widening the war, he wrote:

. . . The alternative possibilities lie in the stabilization of our military operations in the South (possibly with fewer U.S. casualties) and of our air operations in the North, along with a demonstration that our air attacks on the North are not blocking negotiations leading to a peaceful settlement.[61]

He wanted Johnson to halt bombing in the North by end of the year, to stabilize operations in the South with no increase in American troop strength, and to reshape the southern effort in order to give the South Vietnamese a larger share of responsibility in fighting the war.

Once again, the proposal set off an Administration row. Johnson later wrote that, after careful consideration of the views of various advisers, he decided against the proposal, in view of an increasing enemy build-up. Unfortunately for his case, the record contradicts the carefully drawn self-portrait of studied calm presented in his memoirs. If his public utterances are to be believed, he ended the year as firmly convinced of a pending American victory as at year's beginning. In discussing the President's performance at one point, the British Prime Minister evoked the image of the czar's court. That was wrong: In 1967,

60. Ibid.
61. Johnson (*The Vantage Point*), *supra*.

Johnson did not sound so much like Czar Nicholas as he did George III, who, during the American revolution, forever demanded "total submission" of American colonists.

But even George III could not match Johnson's ideological motivation. The President spoke and wrote at this time and later as if he were St. George bent on destroying the dragon of communism. Whether writing to Senator Jackson to explain resumption of bombing the North, or addressing the Tennessee legislature and announcing "a new team" for South Vietnam, or in introducing David Lilienthal and Robert Komer to discuss their optimistic appraisal of the situation in South Vietnam, or in lengthy news conferences where star performers such as Robert McNamara or William Westmoreland or Ellsworth Bunker confirmed his expressed optimism, or at Guam or Canberra or Cam Ranh Bay—whenever and wherever possible, in discussing the war, the President sounded like Thwackum and Square discussing Tom Jones's frequent aberrations. And if he identified Ho's intransigence without understanding it, he nonetheless made it clear to any who would listen that the transgressor would be punished—no matter the time, no matter the effort, no matter the cost.

Chapter 87

The Pueblo *fiasco • The Tet offensive • Enemy aims and accomplishments • Defeat or victory? • The Johnson-Westmoreland stand • General Wheeler's report • MACV objectives • Westmoreland demands more troops (V) • Hawks versus doves • Dean Acheson: ". . . With all due respect, Mr. President, the Joint Chiefs of Staff don't know what they're talking about." • The Clifford Group • Action in the North • The other war • Dissension within America • Johnson's compromise • Westmoreland is relieved • Johnson steps down • Paris peace talks • Saigon's intransigence • The war continues • Increasing American costs (III) • Johnson quits*

THE CONFIDENT if not ebullient pose maintained by the Johnson administration was transmitted to Congress and the American people by the President in his annual State of the Union message in mid-January 1968. In this major speech, the President listed what he regarded as major gains in South Vietnam. Although he noted that ". . . the enemy continues to pour men and material across frontiers and into battle, despite his continuous heavy losses," he left little doubt that the situation was under control: ". . . Our patience and our perseverance will match our power. Aggression will never prevail."[1]

The President later wrote, in his memoirs: ". . . Looking back on early 1968, I am convinced I made a mistake by not saying more about Vietnam in my State of the Union report. . . . I did not go into details concerning the build-up of enemy forces or warn of the early major combat I believed was in the offing. . . ."[2]

---

1. Johnson (*Public Papers*—1968, Book I), *supra.*
2. Johnson (*The Vantage Point*), *supra:* Johnson here characteristically attempted to shift blame to the press corps: ". . . I relied instead on the 'background'

This would have been well-advised. The first of a series of military disasters had already struck by the time General Westmoreland's comforting report reached the White House in early 1968 (see Chapter 85). In late January, patrol boats of the North Korean navy attacked and captured an American ship, the USS *Pueblo*. Although the *Pueblo* carried highly sensitive and top-secret electronic gear, with which she was intercepting North Korean communications, she was sailing in international waters, her mission common to both American and Soviet ships. As her captain, Lloyd Bucher, later made clear in his book, neither officers nor crew were fully trained in destruction procedures, and her armament was virtually non-existent; Bucher's messages to higher authorities elicited no response—no planes, nothing.[3]

The Western world was still stunned with this act of piracy and seeming American impotence to contest it, when tragedy reverted sharply to Vietnam.

Despite official optimism, MACV and the marines had been worried about a continuing enemy build-up in the South. Since the turn of the year, the enemy had repeatedly struck positions in III and I Corps areas, attacks beaten off only with fighting described by Westmoreland as ". . . the most intense of the entire war."[4] In the first two weeks of 1968, VC units had shelled forty-nine district and provisional capitals, attacking eight of them and twice occupying two within thirty miles of Saigon—activity suspiciously at odds with General Weyand's comfortable claims of superiority made less than a month before (see Chapter 85). However, during those two weeks, MACV claimed to have killed five thousand enemy; in Saigon, Westmoreland announced that ". . . the Communists seem to have run temporarily out of steam."[5]

Westmoreland nonetheless was carefully watching Khe Sanh, where the enemy was daily building up attacking forces. The importance of Khe Sanh can be gathered from later official statements. General Walt regarded the place ". . . as the crucial anchor of our defenses along the demilitarized zone."[6] General Wheeler would shortly stress its strategic and tactical importance as the Western anchor of the American defensive line. ". . . To lose it," Wheeler said, "would allow a deep

---

briefings that my advisers and I, as well as the State and Defense departments, had provided members of the press corps for many weeks. In those briefings we had stressed that heavy action could be expected soon. . . ."

3. Lloyd M. Bucher, *Bucher: My Story* (Garden City, New York: Doubleday, 1970); see also Trevor Armbrister, *A Matter of Accountability—The True Story of the Pueblo Affair* (London: Barrie & Jenkins, 1970); Daniel V. Gallery, *The Pueblo Incident* (Garden City, New York: Doubleday, 1970). Although the North Koreans released the crew eleven months later, they kept the ship and her secrets.

4. *Time*, January 19, 1968.

5. Ibid., January 26, 1968.

6. L. W. Walt, "The Nature of the War in Vietnam." Headquarters, U. S. Marine Corps release, n.d.

Communist penetration into South Vietnam."[7] Not all commanders agreed. General Cushman allegedly was not happy about tying up several marine combat battalions in a static defense of a position vulnerable to long-range enemy artillery fire, tactically dominated by heights, some of them enemy-held, and at the fog-shrouded end of a twenty-seven-mile supply line that guerrilla interdiction made dependent solely on air delivery. In any event, Westmoreland expected a major attack against the garrison either before or after the Tet holiday, and, at his instigation, Cushman continued to build up the garrison while other units moved north to bolster defenses in the DMZ area. By month's end, the Khe Sanh garrison comprised four marine infantry battalions, one marine artillery battalion, one ARVN ranger battalion, U. S. Air Force and Seabee detachments. Armament included 105-mm. howitzers, 90-mm.-gun tanks, and 106-mm. recoilless rifles. During the final twelve days of January, the garrison fired thirteen thousand artillery and mortar rounds and was supported by nearly four thousand tactical air missions and 288 B-52 bomber missions.[8] Meanwhile, Westmoreland was said to have moved over half of his combat battalions north.

That was not, however, the tragedy referred to, though it would play a significant part. At the end of January, with allied eyes anxiously watching Khe Sanh, the enemy opened what soon became famous to the world as the Tet offensive—so named because it began during the Tet, or lunar new year, holidays, when a truce had been established and large numbers of South Vietnamese soldiers were on leave.

For some days prior to January 31, Viet Cong and North Vietnamese commando squads had infiltrated areas around allied bases and in principal cities and towns, where they were hidden by VC sympathizers. Simultaneously, battalion-size units had worked into the surrounding countryside. Numbering between fifty and sixty thousand, the attack force consisted predominantly of Viet Cong units reinforced by about six thousand PAVN soldiers. Early in the morning of January 31, the commandos attacked key targets in cities and towns while their fellows attacked from without. In addition to Saigon and Hué, the enemy struck thirty principal towns and seventy district towns. The targets included human beings: Special squads sought out and executed military and police officers, civil officials, and their families. In Saigon, a VC commando (whose ranks included Vietnamese working for the U. S. Government) penetrated American Embassy grounds while other units captured the radio station and attacked Joint General Staff Headquarters (where Westmoreland was), near the airport, and naval headquarters near the Saigon River. Extensive damage included some 125 planes and helicopters fully or partially destroyed.

In most places, heavy fighting lasted a week or two. As perhaps fore-

7. UPI, Washington, February 5, 1968.
8. U. S. Marine Corps, "Khe Sanh Wrap-Up." n.d.

seen by the enemy, ARVN and American counterattacks caused tremendous damage; in Hué, where the enemy held out almost to the end of February, allied counterattacks destroyed perhaps half the city and inevitably added to civilian casualties. About four thousand American and South Vietnamese troops lost their lives, and some twelve thousand were wounded.[9] Thousands of civilians were killed or wounded and thousands more made homeless. Continuing rocket and mortar attacks from surrounding countryside added to general carnage. But the enemy did not escape unscathed; according to government figures, thirty-six thousand Communists were killed by February 18, a figure that probably included large numbers of non-Communists.[10]

We still do not know what prompted the enemy to this particular course of action. Qualified analysts have pointed to a number of reasons, including a major factional dispute between Vo Nguyen Giap and Le Duan, first secretary of the Communist Party.[11] We know also that elements of the NLF and PRP for years had entertained notions of a general uprising; possibly southern and northern commands agreed that the time had come to bring this about; possibly it represented a compromise between north and south and between factions in each camp. Whatever the case, the NLF-PRP-VC seem to have held great expectations:

. . . On the eve of the attack, a general order of the day was issued to all participants by the headquarters of the National Liberation Front. It began with a special Tet poem written by Ho Chi Minh. Then came a statement that the assault on South Vietnamese and American installations was designed to "restore power to the people, liberate the people of the South, and fulfill our revolutionary task of establishing democracy throughout the country." The order continued, "This will be the greatest battle ever fought in the history of our country. It will bring forth worldwide changes, but will also require many sacrifices." An additional order, which referred to "the confused Americans, who are bogged down and hurting badly" and to "the expected disintegration of the Puppet Army," called on the troops to punish drastically all high-level traitors and all tyrants and to "establish a people's revolutionary government at all levels." All the attacking commando units were told that there would be a popular uprising, and that large elements of the South Vietnamese forces would desert and join them.[12]

If enough troops deserted and if sufficient persons rose in the cities and towns, then the Thieu-Ky government would fall and the NLF/VC would either take over direct control or join a coalition that eventually would lead to Communist control of South Vietnam.

9. Shaplen (*The Road from War*), *supra*.
10. Ibid.
11. Victor Zorza, "Vietnam—Long or Short War," *The Guardian* (England), February 15, 1968; see also Pike, op. cit., especially Chapter 20, which, written before the Tet offensive, could well provide the most reasonable explanation; Giap (*Big Victory, Great Task*), *supra*.
12. Shaplen (*Road*), *supra*.

If this was the case, the enemy failed to realize his objective (just as Algerian and Cuban guerrillas had failed to bring off urban uprisings). Despite the surprise and ferocity of attacks, most ARVN and militia units fought stubbornly and well, as did the police. Although the VC sought out and murdered or maimed known government supporters, no mass uprising occurred, either in cities and towns or in the countryside, nor did troops desert as anticipated. Communist hierarchies in South Vietnam and Hanoi might well have falsely assessed the situation in an attempt to retain guerrilla morale. Wholesale assassination campaigns probably cost the VC considerable sympathy, as did widespread house-to-house fighting that could not but hurt the average person. Guerrillas also err, and it could be that the VC forgot the dangers inherent to a guerrilla cause in use of mass terror methods.

But most analysts agreed that a general uprising represented the optimum Communist goal, and that a number of secondary goals existed. NLF officials told an Italian correspondent, Alessandro Casella, who was captured during the Tet offensive and later released, that

. . . Our aim . . . was to establish military and political bases around the towns. This enables us to keep closer to the enemy and therefore facilitates our attacks. However, we do not feel that we can liberate the country in one go, and victory will come only through a succession of offensives. The second aim of the Tet offensive was to liberate the countryside and destroy the pacification program, forcing the Americans to bring all their pacification forces back to the towns.

In Saigon our aim is to encircle the town through the suburbs, not to take the center. Moreover, we are continually waging a double struggle, political and military. Bringing the struggle to the doorsteps of the urban areas is an important weapon in our political campaign. As for the Tet attack on the American Embassy, it is important to understand that to us this is not an ordinary embassy but the headquarters and symbol of the American presence in Vietnam, which is why we attacked it. . . .[13]

From the Hanoi viewpoint, the Tet offensive was probably multipurposed. It represented a positive striking-back against enemy air offensives in the North and ground-air offensives in the central highlands and DMZ. By emphasizing the extent of Communist support in the countryside, where peasants sheltered guerrilla infiltration, and in cities and towns, where Communists or Communist sympathizers supported the surprise effort, the attack substantiated enemy claims being made in Paris. Such support also impressed progovernment urbanites (many of whom were murdered during the attacks) and *attentistes,* or fence-sitters, who would not soon forget that Big Brother was watching. The attacks also threw immense weight on the Saigon government and, not

13. Alessandro Casella, "The Militant Mood," *Far Eastern Review,* May 16, 1968. Quoted in *Survival,* July 1968.

least, brought a general halt to the pacification program—the one effort that Communists north and south seemed always to have feared.

To what extent Hanoi approved the offensive is not known, and estimates differ. A limited commitment—perhaps half of all main-force VC units, or some sixty thousand men, and perhaps six thousand of some sixty thousand PAVN soldiers in South Vietnam—suggested that Hanoi viewed the effort in terms of limited goals, although, had a general uprising resulted, Giap undoubtedly would have hastened to exploit it.

In commenting on Giap's change of strategy from a long war to a general counteroffensive, a French general and military analyst, André Beaufre, was

. . . inclined to think that the real reason . . . is the massive injection of modern war material by the Russians. . . . I have the impression that what the Tet offensive was really aimed at was what has in fact been achieved: to confer international political significance upon the Vietcong, to ruin the prestige of the Americans and of the South Vietnamese government, and to restore better control over the countryside. In sum, the Tet offensive appears to have been much more of a psychological than a military operation.[14]

Ambassador Bunker, in Saigon, also believed this to be the case. A few days after the offensive had begun, he reported ". . . he thought it likely that the primary purpose of the Tet offensive was psychological, not military. He believed that the campaign might well have been designed to 'put Hanoi and the [National Liberation] Front in a strong position for negotiations by demonstrating the strength of the Viet Cong while shaking the faith of the people in South Vietnam in the ability of their own government and the U.S. to protect them.' President Thieu had expressed a similar view in a talk with Ambassador Bunker that same day. . . ."[15]

Whatever the motivation, the attacks accomplished a number of things. Many readers will remember the force of surprise and shock that hammered America—the futility that one felt upon seeing blood-spattered bodies, friendly and enemy, in the American Embassy compound, or the famous black-and-white photograph of General Loan about to shoot a manacled VC officer through the head, or the statement made by an unwitting American army major to the Australian correspondent Peter Arnett as the two looked over the smoking ruins of Ben Tre: ". . . The city had to be destroyed in order to save it." The sum formed an overdraft on the meager balance of credibility maintained by the Johnson administration, ". . . seriously damaging," as the prestigious Institute of Strategic Studies later noted, "the reputation

14. André Beaufre, "Prospects for the New General," *The Sunday Times* (London), March 24, 1968.
15. Johnson (*The Vantage Point*), *supra*.

of those analysts who had concluded that the ability of the enemy to organize military action on a national or regional scale had been eliminated during 1967."[16] In Henry Kissinger's later words,

. . . On January 17, 1968, President Johnson, in his State of the Union address, emphasized that the pacification program—the extension of the control of Saigon into the country—was progressing satisfactorily. . . . A week later [sic], the Tet offensive overthrew the assumptions of American strategy.[17]

Not only did the Tet attacks emphasize the bane of American military operations in Vietnam—lack of intelligence—but they also brought home to the American people that, despite official optimism, the war was likely to continue *ad nauseam*. And, as surely foreseen by Hanoi, they added a particularly volatile fuel to the already blazing row within top echelons of the Johnson administration. Perhaps the main accomplishment of the Tet offensive, from enemy standpoint, was to finally polarize existent but theretofore divergent opposition to Administration policy in Vietnam.

Johnson, the JCS, Sharp, Westmoreland, and other hawks at once adopted a simplistic stand on the attacks. At a news conference in early February, the President told correspondents:

. . . We have known for several months, now, that the Communists planned a massive winter-spring offensive. We have detailed information on Ho Chi Minh's order governing that offensive. Part of it is called a general uprising.

We know the object was to overthrow the constitutional government in Saigon and to create a situation in which we and the Vietnamese would be willing to accept the Communist-dominated coalition government.

Another part of that offensive was planned as a massive attack across the frontiers of South Vietnam by North Vietnamese units. We have already seen the general uprising. . . .

After emphasizing maximum enemy and minimum American casualties, the President announced that ". . . the biggest fact is that the stated purposes of the general uprising have failed." However, he warned,

. . . we may at this very moment be on the eve of a major enemy offensive in the area of Khe Sanh and generally around the Demilitarized Zone.

Further, the enemy's second objective was to attain a psychological victory, and Johnson was taking pains to prevent that from being achieved. In this lengthy conference, he implied that nothing of the situation was surprising and that matters were firmly under control; as for further deployment of U.S. troops: ". . . There is not anything in any

16. The Institute for Strategic Studies, "The United States." In *Strategic Survey, 1968* (London: Institute for Strategic Studies, 1969).

17. Kissinger, op. cit.

of the developments that would justify the press in leaving the impression that any great new overall moves are going to be made that would involve substantial movements in that direction."[18]

The salve of this business-as-usual approach comforted almost no one, and the President probably would have been wiser to share some of his apprehensions with the American people. If his later writings are to be believed, these must have been considerable:

. . . This is not to imply that Tet was not a shock, in one degree or another, to all of us. We know that a show of strength was coming; it was more massive than we had anticipated. We knew that the Communists were aiming at a number of population centers; we did not expect them to attack as many as they did. We knew that the North Vietnamese and the Viet Cong were trying to achieve better co-ordination of their countrywide moves; we did not believe they would be able to carry out the level of co-ordination they demonstrated. We expected a large force to attack; it was larger than we had estimated. Finally, it was difficult to believe that the Communists would so profane their own people's sacred holiday.[19]

In Saigon, Westmoreland went Johnson one better. The American commander's ebullience reminds one of Lord Cornwallis insisting that the battle of Guilford Courthouse (see Chapter 8, Volume I) was a "victory"—(a victory, perhaps, responded the Annual Register's scribe, but a victory ". . . productive of all the consequences of defeat"). In reviewing dispatches of the time, one would suppose that the American general had himself planned the Tet offensive. On February 2, he told newsmen that there was evidence to suggest that the enemy ". . . is about to run out of steam."[20] Westmoreland interpreted the attacks as designed to drive American troops from Khe Sanh, which was the enemy's real objective: The Communist attacks, he told newsmen, were prelude to a "go-for-broke" attack on Khe Sanh and the two northern provinces.[21] This plan would fail, as had the rest of the enemy plan—by February 6, Westmoreland believed that enemy losses, which he put at 21,330 dead, ". . . may measurably shorten the war."[22] Westmoreland, in short, viewed the attacks as a desperate move of a dying enemy: He went so far as to tell a disbelieving André Beaufre ". . . that he compared this decision [of Giap's] with that of Hitler on the eve of the Ardennes offensive in the autumn of 1944, that is to say a decision of despair by an enemy at his wit's end."[23]

18. Johnson (*Public Papers—1968*, Vol. I), *supra.*
19. Johnson (*The Vantage Point*), *supra.*
20. AP, UPI, Saigon, February 2, 1968.
21. UPI, Saigon, February 2, 1968.
22. UPI, Saigon, February 6, 1968.
23. Beaufre, op. cit.

The plot now thickens, and an account can only be hazarded until the time that additional pertinent papers and personal testimony are available for study. Existing accounts—the President's memoirs, the Pentagon study, works such as Marvin Kalb and Elie Abel's *Roots of Involvement* and Townsend Hoopes's *The Limits of Intervention,* and contemporary reportage—differ considerably.[24] The record suggests, however, something like the following.

Apparently, early in the Tet offensive the President asked Westmoreland how he could help him—a reasonable and sympathetic request confirmed in part by a presidential news conference on February 2, when White House correspondents learned that the President was ". . . in close touch with all of our Joint Chiefs of Staff to make sure that every single thing that General Westmoreland believed that he needed at this time was available to him, and that our Joint Chiefs believe that his strategy was sound, his men were sure, and they were amply supplied."[25] According to Kalb and Abel, who quote official communications, General Wheeler pressed Westmoreland to request substantial troop reinforcements at this time. On February 3, Wheeler allegedly cabled Westmoreland: ". . . The President asks me if there is any reinforcement or help that we can give you." On February 8, having received no reply [!] from Westmoreland, Wheeler cabled:

. . . Query: Do you need reinforcement? Our capabilities are limited. We can provide 82d Airborne Division and about one-half a Marine Corps division, both loaded with Vietnam veterans. However, if you consider reinforcements imperative, you should not be bound by earlier agreements [i.e., a troop limit of 525,000]. United States Government is not prepared to accept defeat in Vietnam. In summary, if you need more troops, ask for them.

According to Kalb and Abel, Westmoreland immediately requested the units named by Wheeler and also asked ". . . that the President authorize an amphibious assault by the marines into North Vietnam as a diversionary move." A day later, he outlined his need for additional troops to contain the enemy's "major campaign" in the north and ". . . to go on the offensive as soon as his attack is spent," to otherwise carry out previous campaign plans, to bolster a weakened ARVN, and ". . . to take advantage of the enemy's weakened posture by taking the offensive against him." Wheeler ambiguously replied: ". . . Please understand that I'm not trying to sell you on the deployment of additional forces which in any event I cannot guarantee. . . . However, my sensing is that the critical phase of the war is upon us, and I do not believe

24. M. L. Kalb and E. Abel, *Roots of Involvement—the U.S. in Asia, 1784–1971* (New York: W. W. Norton, 1971). (Hereafter cited as Kalb.)
25. Johnson (*Public Papers—1968,* Vol. I), *supra.*

that you should refrain from asking for what you believe is required under the circumstances."[26]

How much of this background was known to the President has not been disclosed. Johnson later wrote that, on February 12, Westmoreland sent the JCS the following assessment, which the President read:

. . . Since last October, the enemy has launched a major campaign signaling a change of strategy from one of protracted war to one of quick military/political victory during the American election years. His first phase, designed to secure the border areas, has failed. The second phase, launched on the occasion of Tet and designed to initiate public uprising, to disrupt the machinery of government and command and control of the Vietnamese forces, and to isolate the cities, has also failed [!]. Nevertheless, the enemy's third phase, which is designed to seize Quang Tri and Thua Thien provinces has just begun.[27]

Westmoreland expected the enemy to make a "maximum effort" in the northern provinces in the third phase, and also to try to regain initiative elsewhere. According to the President, Westmoreland

. . . saw the situation as one of heightened risk but of great opportunity as well.

"I do not see how the enemy can long sustain the heavy losses which his new strategy is enabling us to inflict on him," he reported. "Therefore, adequate reinforcements should permit me not only to contain his I Corps offensive but also to capitalize on his losses by seizing the initiative in other areas." He believed that exploiting the opportunity "could materially shorten the war."

Accordingly, he requested early delivery of troops, presumably as proffered by Wheeler; that is, the ". . . 82d Airborne Division and about one-half a Marine Corps division." Although the President remained mute on the subject in his memoirs, this was probably the requirement brought forward at a presidential conference on February 12. According to the Pentagon study, the JCS now pointed out that such a deployment would compromise the strategic reserve and should be deferred—a tactic that allegedly was designed to cause Johnson to call up the reserves, a major step in full-scale mobilization, which the JCS so long had desired. According to Johnson, debate centered on sending Westmoreland six maneuver battalions, or about ten thousand men, and all agreed to do this while holding off on the subject of a reserve call-up.

The JCS also requested presidential authority to bomb closer to the centers of Hanoi and Haiphong—a request opposed by McNamara and by Paul Warnke, who had replaced John McNaughton as Assistant Secretary of Defense for International Security Affairs, and one finally turned down by the President.

26. Kalb, *supra;* see also *The Pentagon Papers, supra* (pp. 594–95).
27. Johnson (*The Vantage Point*), *supra.*

Johnson now sent General Wheeler to Saigon ". . . to go over the entire situation with Westmoreland." Toward end of February, Wheeler reported that ". . . the current situation in Vietnam is still developing and fraught with opportunities as well as dangers." In MACV's opinion, the enemy's general offensive was designed to bring a general uprising. To attain this initial objective, he committed eighty-four thousand troops: ". . . He lost 40,000 killed, at least 3,000 captured, and perhaps 5,000 disabled or died of wounds." With a total force of 240,000 in the South, this meant that he had lost a fifth of his strength. He nonetheless possessed the ". . . will and the capability to continue" the fight.

The enemy offensive, Wheeler continued, hurt ARVN more psychologically than physically. Nonetheless, two to three months were needed to recover equipment losses; three to six months to regain pre-Tet strength. The worst damage occurred to the Rural Development Program; in many areas, the VC now openly controlled the countryside.

MACV objectives, Wheeler reported, were:

. . . First, to counter the enemy offensive and to destroy or eject the NVA invasion force in the north.

Second, to restore security in the cities and towns.

Third, to restore security in the heavily populated areas of the countryside.

Fourth, to regain the initiative through offensive operations.

In addition to the 525,000 troops, now nearly all deployed in South Vietnam, Westmoreland wanted a ". . . 3 division-15 tactical fighter squadron force"—a whopping levy of over two hundred thousand more troops to be deployed by end of 1968.[28]

The President later wrote that the Westmoreland-JCS request came to slightly more than 205,000:

. . . With forces of that size, Westmoreland believed he could not only resist anything the enemy attempted but could move quickly to the offensive and take advantage of heavy Communist losses suffered during the first weeks of the Tet offensive. He also wanted to be prepared in case a change in our strategy permitted operations against enemy sanctuaries in Cambodia and Laos and across the DMZ.[29]

A later study, by John Henry in *Foreign Policy*, alleges that Westmoreland had rather more specific plans at this time:

. . . General Westmoreland, the report states, saw the Tet offensive as a "golden opportunity," which would enable the United States to change from

28. *The Pentagon Papers, supra* (pp. 615–21); see also Hoopes, op. cit.; Shaplen (*Road*) *supra:* ". . . American officials estimate that the whole [pacification] program, which was just beginning to make some small headway, has lost three or four months, and maybe more."
29. Johnson (*The Vantage Point*), *supra.*

a policy of "creeping escalation" to a more "dynamic strategy." He did not believe he would receive the entire force of 206,000 men, but hoped to obtain half that number.

With these additional troops he felt that he would be able to strike at communist sanctuaries in Laos and Cambodia and launch "amphibious-airmobile operations against North Vietnamese bases just north of the demilitarized zone."

Later the article quotes him as saying: "Once I Corps [area] was cleaned up, and the north-east monsoon had dissipated, an amphibious hook, an Inchon-type operation around the DMZ and into North Vietnam, could be staged."[30]

We do not know how much President Johnson was told of these plans. According to his memoirs, he learned from Wheeler that responsible commanders regarded 1968 as "the pivotal year." Wheeler also warned that, without the troop increase, ". . . we might have to give up territory, probably the two northernmost provinces of South Vietnam. . . ."

Aggressive plans aside, the troop increase requested by Westmoreland and the JCS placed the President in an extremely awkward position. Hawk that he was, he was also politician, and he was naturally upset at the national furor generated by the Tet offensive. In his later words,

. . . I did not expect the enemy effort to have the impact on American thinking that it achieved. I was not surprised that elements of the press, the academic community, and the Congress reacted as they did. I was surprised and disappointed that the enemy's efforts produced such a dismal effect on various people inside government and others outside whom I had always regarded as staunch and unflappable. Hanoi must have been delighted; it was exactly the reaction they sought.[31]

It was also a reaction justified in large part at higher echelons by specific facts. Hanson Baldwin, parroting the official line, may have concluded in an article in the March *Reader's Digest* that ". . . the enemy can no longer find security in his South Vietnamese sanctuaries,"[32] but the enemy seemed to be doing pretty well without security. Meeting the Westmoreland-JCS request for over two hundred thousand American reinforcements, meant increasing American armed forces by over five hundred thousand men, which, in turn, meant calling up at least two hundred fifty thousand reserves, extending present enlistments by six months, spending an additional $10 billion in fiscal year 1969 and an additional $15 billion in fiscal year 1970.[33] Astute advisers also questioned Westmoreland's and the JCS interpretation of

30. Ian McDonald, *The Times* (London), Washington, August 31, 1971.
31. Johnson (*The Vantage Point*), *supra.*
32. Hanson W. Baldwin, "The Foe Is Hurting," *Reader's Digest*, March 1968.
33. Johnson (*The Vantage Point*), *supra.*

the attacks as a desperation move on the part of the NLF-PRP-VC and Hanoi. Costly though the attacks proved to the enemy, the NLF still disposed of over sixty thousand hard-core guerrillas, augmented by twice that many active supporters and by some sixty thousand more PAVN troops, with impressive reserves untouched in North Vietnam (not to mention China, which, as James Reston once noted, was down to her last 700 million men). Some advisers, such as Clark Clifford, questioned the magic number of 205,000, where perhaps a half million to a million men would be required. Some advisers, such as Philip Habib, pointed to divided opinions in the Saigon mission as to the wisdom of sending *any* large reinforcement as opposed to insisting on the South Vietnamese doing the job.[34] Subordinate but influential voices added to the general protest. Townsend Hoopes later wrote:

. . . In the Pentagon, the Tet offensive performed the curious service of fully revealing the doubters and dissenters to each other, as in a lightning flash. Nitze suddenly spoke out on "the unsoundness of continuing to reinforce weakness," and wrote a paper that argued that our policy in Vietnam had to be placed in the context of other U.S. commitments in the world. Warnke thought Tet showed that our military strategy was "foolish to the point of insanity." Alain Enthoven . . . confided that, "I fell off the boat when the troop level reached 170,000." In various ways, the Under Secretary of the Army, David McGiffert, the Assistant Secretary of Defense for Manpower, Alfred Fitt, the Deputy Assistant Secretary for Far Eastern Affairs (ISA), Richard Steadman, and other influential civilians expressed their strong belief that the Administration's Vietnam policy was at a dead end.

One thing was clear to us all: The Tet offensive was the eloquent counterpoint to the effusive optimism of November. It showed conclusively that the U.S. did not in fact control the situation. . . .[35]

At this point, Johnson was so insulated, by Rostow, from dissident opinions, that it is doubtful if these attitudes reached him. Nonetheless, he remained keenly aware of the national mood, and he was also brought abruptly to heel by a senior adviser, Dean Acheson. Acheson had no love for Johnson and did not eagerly accept his summons to the White House in late February. Townsend Hoopes later described the meeting:

. . . When the President asked him his opinion of the current situation in Vietnam, Acheson replied he wasn't sure he had a useful view because he was finding it impossible, on the basis of occasional official briefings given him, to discover what was really happening. He had lost faith in the objectivity of the briefers: "With all due respect, Mr. President, the Joint Chiefs of Staff don't know what they're talking about." The President said that was a shocking statement. Acheson replied that, if such it was, then perhaps the President ought to be shocked.[36]

34. Ibid.
35. Hoopes, op. cit.
36. Ibid.; see also Brandon, op. cit.

The sum of these factors persuaded the President to two important moves. One, he asked Acheson to make an independent study, drawing on expert testimony at subordinate levels of government. Two, he ordered his new Secretary of Defense, Clark Clifford, to convene his most responsible officials to study the Westmoreland-JCS request, indeed to appraise fully the situation in Vietnam.

Sixty-two years old, Clark Clifford had recently replaced the disillusioned McNamara. A well-known Washington attorney, a close friend of the President and loyal supporter of Johnson's Vietnam policy, he had served for years as a confidential adviser. The previous summer, as we have related, he had undertaken a presidential mission to persuade Asian countries to increase troop support in Vietnam, an unsuccessful effort that caused him to entertain certain doubts concerning the war.

What became known as the Clifford Group included Secretary of State Dean Rusk, Secretary of the Treasury Henry Fowler, Under Secretary of State Nicholas Katzenbach, Deputy Secretary of Defense Paul Nitze, General Wheeler, CIA director Richard Helms, presidential assistants Walt Rostow and Maxwell Taylor, and numerous other ranking officials. To no one's surprise, subsequent meetings merely accentuated the current rift between hawks and doves. General Maxwell Taylor presented the prevailing JCS view in a memorandum both to the group and directly to President Johnson:

. . . We should consider changing the objective which we have been pursuing consistently since 1954 [!] only for the most cogent reasons. There is clearly nothing to recommend trying to do more than we are now doing at such great cost. To undertake to do less is to accept needlessly a serious defeat for which we would pay dearly in terms of our worldwide position of leadership, of the political stability of Southeast Asia and of the credibility of our pledges to friends and allies.[37]

Doves did not agree. Prompted by CIA reports, most civilian members of the group apparently argued that any substantial increase of American forces could be easily offset by North Vietnamese troops. Dr. Alain Enthoven typified the realistic pessimism of the doves:

. . . While we have raised the price to NVN [North Vietnam] of aggression and support of the VC [Viet Cong], it shows no lack of capability or will to match each new U.S. escalation. Our strategy of "attrition" has not worked. Adding 206,000 more U.S. men to a force of 525,000, gaining only 27 additional maneuver battalions and 270 tactical fighters at an added cost to the U.S. of $10-billion per year raises the question of who is making it costly for whom. . . .

We know that despite a massive influx of 500,000 U.S. troops, 1.2 million tons of bombs a year, 400,000 attack sorties per year, 200,000 enemy

37. *The Pentagon Papers, supra* (p. 600); see also Johnson (*The Vantage Point*), *supra*; Hoopes, op. cit.

K.I.A. [killed in action] in three years, 20,000 U.S. K.I.A., etc., our control of the countryside and the defense of the urban areas is now essentially at pre-August 1965 levels. We have achieved stalemate at a high commitment. A new strategy must be sought.[38]

Enthoven and other experts argued that Westmoreland should call off search-and-destroy attrition strategy in favor of protecting population centers while the South Vietnam Government and armed forces developed effective capability—which was more or less what General James Gavin had recommended in 1965.

Nothing illustrates the abject poverty of Administration thinking, and thus of prevailing attitudes of political and military executive instruments, than Clifford's later account of these high-level meetings:

. . . In the colloquial style of those meetings, here are some of the principal issues raised and some of the answers as I understood them:

"Will 200,000 more men do the job?" I found no assurance that they would.

"If not, how many more might be needed—and when?" There was no way of knowing.

"What would be involved in committing 200,000 more men to Viet Nam?" A reserve call-up of approximately 280,000, an increased draft call and an extension of tours of duty of most men then in service.

"Can the enemy respond with a build-up of his own?" He could and he probably would.

"What are the estimated costs of the latest requests?" First calculations were on the order of $2 billion for the remaining four months of that fiscal year, and an increase of $10 to $12 billion for the year beginning July 1, 1968.

"What will be the impact on the economy?" So great that we would face the possibility of credit restrictions, a tax increase and even wage and price controls. The balance of payments would be worsened by at least half a billion dollars a year.

"Can bombing stop the war?" Never by itself. It was inflicting heavy personnel and matériel losses, but bombing by itself would not stop the war.

"Will stepping up the bombing decrease American casualties?" Very little, if at all. Our casualties were due to the intensity of the ground fighting in the South. We had already dropped a heavier tonnage of bombs than in all the theaters of World War II. During 1967, an estimated 90,000 North Vietnamese had infiltrated into South Viet Nam. In the opening weeks of 1968, infiltrators were coming in at three to four times the rate of a year earlier, despite the ferocity and intensity of our campaign of aerial interdiction.

"How long must we keep on sending our men and carrying the main burden of combat?" The South Vietnamese were doing better, but they were

38. *The Pentagon Papers, supra* (pp. 600–1).

not ready yet to replace our troops and we did not know when they would be.

When Clifford asked for a military plan, he was told that no plan for victory existed ". . . in the historic American sense" due to presidential limitations that prohibited invading North Vietnam, pursuing into Laos and Cambodia, and mining Haiphong Harbor. Clifford now asked:

. . . "Given these circumstances, how can we win?" We would, I was told, continue to evidence our superiority over the enemy; we would continue to attack in the belief that he would reach the stage where he would find it inadvisable to go on with the war. He could not afford the attrition we were inflicting on him. And we were improving our posture all the time.

I then asked, "What is the best estimate as to how long this course of action will take? Six months? One year? Two years?" There was no agreement on an answer. Not only was there no agreement, I could find no one willing to express any confidence in his guesses. . . .

A disturbed man now asked a disturbed question:

. . . "Does anyone see any diminution in the will of the enemy after four years of our having been there, after enormous casualties and after massive destruction from our bombing?"

The answer was that there appeared to be no diminution in the will of the enemy. . . .

The total experience was salutary if dismal. It had reinforced Clifford's earlier doubts:

. . . I was convinced that the military course we were pursuing was not only endless, but hopeless. A further substantial increase in American forces could only increase the devastation and the Americanization of the war, and thus leave us even further from our goal of a peace that would permit the people of South Viet Nam to fashion their own political and economic institutions. Henceforth, I was also convinced, our primary goal should be to level off our involvement, and to work toward gradual disengagement.[39]

The Clifford report attempted to resolve the contretemps by compromise. Although Clifford later wrote that he favored a reversal of strategy, the hawks proved sufficiently strong to prevent this recommendation. The final document did not question present strategy except by indirection, in that it recommended limiting troop reinforcement to a maximum twenty-two thousand. It did not recommend a new peace initiative or a proposed cutback in the bombing of the North.[40]

Clifford's group paid considerable attention to the air question. The JCS submitted three general plans for consideration: an increase in bombing, including expansion of targets around Hanoi and Haiphong

39. Clifford, op. cit.
40. *The Pentagon Papers, supra* (pp. 601-3); see also, Hoopes, op. cit.

to include railroad equipment in the Chinese buffer zone and the dike system that supported the North's agriculture, and mining Haiphong Harbor; a shift in bombing away from the Hanoi-Haiphong area in favor of striking roads and supply trails in the southern part of North Vietnam, including the Laotian panhandle; an interdiction campaign in the South ". . . designed to substitute tactical airpower for a large portion of the search-and-destroy operations currently conducted by ground forces, thus permitting the ground troops to concentrate on a perimeter defense of the heavily populated areas."[41]

Wheeler, Taylor, and Rostow wanted the first course of action; other principals held for the second and third.

Since the report left matters largely as they were, it pleased no one. It reached the President in one of his optimistic moods, and he accordingly scorned the prevailing pessimism expressed by his advisers, particularly the civilians. The report had changed no one's mind: Ensuing discussions accentuated hawk and dove positions.

It nonetheless performed a valuable interim service: first, by suggesting limited troop reinforcement; second and more subtly, by generating new ideas.

One of the President's objections to the document centered on its negative approach to negotiations. The CIA had reported to the Clifford group that if the United States were to call off bombing of the North, ". . . Hanoi would probably respond to an offer to negotiate, although the intelligence agency warned that the North Vietnamese would not modify their terms for a final settlement or stop fighting in the South."[42] In discussing the possibility of renewed negotiations, Secretary of State Dean Rusk now suggested a bombing halt in the North except ". . . in the area associated with the battle zone. When Johnson expressed interest, Rusk said that '. . . we could stop most of the bombing of the North during the rainy season without too great a military risk.'"[43] This fitted nicely with one segment of Pentagon thinking —the suggestion to shift the aerial interdiction effort to the southern part of North Vietnam—and now Clifford apparently endorsed the notion to confine bombing to south of the 19th parallel. Rusk's suggestion continued the argument already being waged within Administration circles, one that would intensify during the rest of March.

The Clifford report served an even more subtle purpose, by reinforcing with impressive statistics and marshaled thoughts major doubts held by important men including Clifford, who personally, privately, and probably forcefully imposed them on the President, an action that, in Clifford's case, started his relegation to the wilderness but was consonant with later developments.

41. Hoopes, op. cit.
42. *The Pentagon Papers, supra* (p. 599).
43. Johnson (*The Vantage Point*), *supra.*

The Clifford report kicked off what proved to be an exciting, exasperating, and, finally, crucial month in American affairs. The military situation was by no means as favorable in Vietnam as Westmoreland was reporting. Although enemy attacks had been beaten back, enemy units surrounding towns and cities continued to strike and to interdict road communications while rebuilding bases in the countryside. At Khe Sanh, the marine-ARVN garrison continued to withstand severe buffeting while the greatest aerial bombing effort in history pounded the besiegers. The President later wrote that, on March 9, the enemy had withdrawn about half his attacking troops; that might have been so, but the remainder continued probing efforts and larger attacks throughout the month while artillery and rocket fire continued around the clock. Westmoreland might have been moving toward what he fondly termed "a general offensive," but his preoccupation with Khe Sanh did not lessen the real and devastating importance of the other war. In contrast to claims advanced by MACV and Washington, Robert Shaplen offered an eyewitness account of the scene:

. . . Since the Tet attack, the Communists have maintained their countrywide harassment of cities, airfields, and various Allied installations, primarily with rocket and mortar fire. They have made occasional fresh ground assaults against about a dozen cities, mostly in the Delta, and particularly on March 3rd and 4th, when it seemed that a second wave of the offensive might be beginning. They have recruited as many as thirty thousand new troops, ranging in age from fifteen to forty. Most of the recruiting has been done in the Delta, where the Communists moved in to fill the vacuum in the countryside following the withdrawal of American and government troops to positions of defense around the cities and the towns. Hanoi has continued to infiltrate troops both to reinforce the North Vietnamese forces now totalling a hundred and twelve thousand men in South Vietnam (five more North Vietnamese divisions are said to be alerted to move south) and to build up the main-force Vietcong units that suffered the heaviest losses during Tet. . . .

The attacks had not only badly hurt ARVN and halted the pacification program, but had further splintered the Saigon government, widening the dangerous rift between Thieu and Ky. Once the emergency had passed, a sense of shock set in. Shaplen noted

. . . a continuing erosion of morale and a growing sense of foreboding. Vietnamese I have known for many years are as frank as they are sad these days in their prognoses; they sound more and more like men who know they are suffering from an incurable malady.[44]

Pessimism so prevalent in Saigon found ample voice throughout the United States. At the end of February 1968, George Kennan told a

44. Shaplen (*Road*), *supra.*

Newark audience that we ". . . have pushed stubbornly and heedlessly ahead, like men in a dream, seemingly insensitive to outside opinion, seemingly unable to arrive at any realistic assessment of the effects of [our] acts."[45] Large numbers of influential Americans, including leading business executives, agreed. Throughout the country, campus demonstrations, draft-card burnings, and civic protestations were becoming the order of the day. Congress was becoming increasingly rebellious. Toward mid-March, the Senate Foreign Relations Committee opened televised hearings on the Foreign Aid Bill and called Dean Rusk before it. Almost at once, the hearings became a debate on Vietnam. For almost two days, a beleaguered Rusk fielded generally hostile questions with what many persons believed were less than candid answers—altogether a performance that further fueled nationwide fires of dissent.

The pressure was telling on the President. The veteran British correspondent Henry Brandon later wrote:

. . . Anyone who had the opportunity of seeing President Johnson around March 11, 1968, in person and in private, was taken aback by the near-exhaustion that had overcome him. He was a man in torment as I had never seen one before. His face was ashen, his eyes sunken, his skin flabby, and yet, underneath, his expression was taut.[46]

The President was to find little relief ahead. Almost no one agreed with anyone else. Ambassador Bunker, for example, although a hawk who agreed with the necessity of supplying Westmoreland with a reserve force, wanted it limited to seven battalions, since he felt that more men would dissuade the South Vietnamese from putting their own army right. Rusk and Clifford pointed to a practical difficulty: The United States could not supply an additional half million men with weapons and at the same time furnish modern arms to an expanding ARVN.[47] Civilian dissension was also increasing: Paul Nitze, Clifford's deputy, allegedly asked to be excused from appearing before the Senate committee to defend Administration policy in Vietnam. Then came Eugene McCarthy's near victory in the New Hampshire primary elections—McCarthy was a dove and outspoken critic of Johnson's Vietnam policy. A few days later, the President received another unpleasant surprise, in the form of Dean Acheson, who, as earlier agreed, had been conferring with numerous officials on the Vietnam question. Acheson had shocked Johnson in their discussion in late February with the blunt statement: ". . . With all due respect, Mr. President, the Joint Chiefs of Staff don't know what they're talking about." And now, at a private luncheon,

45. Kellen, op. cit.: Kennan was introducing Senator Eugene McCarthy, February 29, 1968.

46. Brandon, op. cit.; see also Louis Heren, *No Hail, No Farewell* (London: Weidenfeld & Nicolson, 1971).

47. Johnson (*The Vantage Point*), *supra*.

. . . Acheson told the President he was being led down a garden path by the JCS, that what Westmoreland was attempting in Vietnam was simply not possible—without the application of totally unlimited resources "and maybe five years." He told the President that his recent speeches were quite unrealistic and believed by no one, either at home or abroad. He added the judgment that the country was no longer supporting the war. . . .[48]

The President was still digesting his lunch when a memorandum arrived from UN Ambassador Arthur Goldberg; following a line suggested by U Thant in late February, Goldberg now suggested a total bombing halt in the North. The following day, the President's real political nemesis, Robert Kennedy, announced his candidacy for the Democratic nomination.

It was all too much for tired old Johnson. After a final show of truculence, he decided to accept facts and act accordingly. On March 22, he announced Westmoreland's imminent relief. He also convened a senior advisory group of prominent civil and military officials, past and present, including Dean Acheson, George Ball, Arthur Dean, Henry Cabot Lodge, McGeorge Bundy, and Matthew Ridgway. Meeting for two days in late March, this group, known as the Wise Men, heard a special briefing delivered by an interdepartmental executive team that included the army's Major General DePuy, the State Department's Philip Habib, and CIA's George Carver. Although opinions differed in detail, only three of fourteen members agreed with Administration policy; seven, including former hawk McGeorge Bundy, argued for a basic change; four expressed grave doubts. Johnson's reaction to this new dissension, particularly on the part of McGeorge Bundy, brings to mind Mrs. Western's furious words to her brother, the squire: ". . . Thou art one of those wise men whose nonsensical principles have undone the nation; by weakening the hands of our Government at home, and by discouraging our friends, and encouraging our enemies abroad." Johnson was allegedly so upset that he insisted on hearing the same briefing, which he later said contained information that he had been receiving all along.[49]

Johnson now decided to send only a token troop reinforcement to South Vietnam, although he did ask Congress for an additional $4-billion defense appropriation. He also announced that the American Government would concentrate on building up ARVN (a task theoretically begun thirteen years earlier!) so that it could relieve American forces of

48. Hoopes, op. cit.
49. Ibid.; see also Matthew B. Ridgway, "Indochina: Disengaging," *Foreign Affairs*, July 1971; Brandon, op. cit.: ". . . To Acheson's surprise, his views were shared by more among those present than he had expected. The one who mattered most, because he too had been a strong supporter of the war, was McGeorge Bundy. He summed up for those supporting Acheson's views and admitted, in self-flagellating mood, that 'for the first time in my life I find myself agreeing on this issue with George Ball.' "

major combat tasks. Finally and more important, he summarily halted bombing of North Vietnam beyond the 20th parallel. At the same time, he asked Hanoi to begin talks that would lead to peace, and he attempted to underline his sincerity by withdrawing from coming presidential elections.[50]

In this dramatic speech, President Johnson offered to meet the enemy "anywhere." When Hanoi responded favorably, American officials rejected one place after another, to settle finally on Paris, where peace talks opened officially on May 13. Meanwhile, however, renewed fighting in Vietnam flared in the background like an ancient omen of evil, and while American and North Vietnamese delegations argued about protocol—who would sit where—many thousands of human beings bled and died.

Once again, ARVN and allied forces pushed from beleaguered cities and towns to try to reclaim the countryside from the VC or at least open communications between cities. Once again, MACV announced "successful" offensives with such improbable code names as "Complete Victory"; once again, MACV stressed enormous enemy losses: fifteen thousand dead at Khe Sanh alone; seventy-one thousand dead since Tet began.

And once again, in early May, the enemy launched another, a second Tet offensive, that undeniably hurt the South, first psychologically, by again demonstrating a strength he wasn't supposed to have, second by causing more casualties and destruction.

The total carnage was ghastly: The two offensives resulted ". . . in 13,000 civilians killed, 27,000 wounded, 170,000 homes destroyed or damaged; and created 1,000,000 refugees with property damage estimated at $173,500,000."[51] American and allied casualties shot upward and would continue at high level.

Despite these figures, Westmoreland, about to leave for the United States, again claimed that the offensives had hurt the enemy worse than he admitted. He pointed to some impressive facts: Nowhere had the enemy succeeded in realizing military objectives. Having failed to take Khe Sanh, in early April he had lifted the siege and stolen away—at a cost of an estimated ten to fifteen thousand dead (an action we shall discuss later). Elsewhere he was neutralized by American "spoiling" tactics, which were effectively keeping him off balance. Although damage done by the Tet offensives was great, the Saigon government and country had survived. Meanwhile, pacification operations slowly revived, as did Operation Phoenix, a long-overdue effort to identify, infiltrate, and destroy Communist political networks in the south.[52] In late March, General Abrams, Westmoreland's deputy, who, for over a year,

50. Johnson (*Public Papers*—1968, Vol. I), *supra*.
51. Personal letter from General Walt to the author.
52. The Institute for Strategic Studies ("The United States"), *supra*.

had been working with ARVN, had reported considerable progress. Asked by the President to compare the South Vietnamese effort with the earlier, Korean effort, Abrams replied, ". . . I would say the Vietnamese are doing as well, if not better, than the Koreans."[53] In Washington in early April, General Westmoreland delivered a more than favorable report to the President, including the comforting news that ". . . militarily, we have never been in a better relative position in South Vietnam."[54]

Westmoreland continued to display the optimism so admired by the President. Shortly before his return to the United States to take up the post of army chief of staff—surely the most extraordinary appointment since King James I knighted a piece of beef—he launched into a vigorous defense of his generalship. Dismissing enclave strategy as "defeatist," and "oil-spot" strategy as impractical in view of a limited number of troops [!], Westmoreland told reporters: ". . . Our strategy in Viet Nam is most definitely not a search-and-destroy strategy, and it is unfortunate that it has been so characterized by some. Search and destroy is merely an abbreviated version of a time-honored infantry mission: 'Find, fix, fight and destroy the enemy.' It is not a strategy or a tactic; it is a mission. . . ." The general repeated what he had told the President:

. . . The allies are in the strongest relative military position in Viet Nam today that we have yet achieved.[55]

At this point, a good many Americans refused to take Westmoreland or his pronouncements seriously. Not only Westmoreland but Pentagon "spokesmen" had become a supreme embarrassment to the Democratic Party and its leading candidate, Hubert Humphrey. While unable to dissociate himself from Vietnam policy, Humphrey attempted to chart a cunning course that elevated Vietnam tactical issues to world strategic issues, where he could say more without almost automatically being contradicted by unpalatable fact. The leading Republican contender, Richard Nixon, on the other hand, blasted American policy in Vietnam and spoke mysteriously of a "new plan" to end the American involvement and regain American "superiority" in strategic matters.

While political debate claimed the American scene in summer and autumn of 1968, fighting continued sporadically in Vietnam, with Saigon frequently under rocket bombardment. Despite claims of American officialdom to heavy enemy casualties, VC/PAVN troops showed little hesitation in attacking where and when they wished. Although the enemy was hurting and infiltration from the North had slowed, it nonethe-

53. Johnson (*The Vantage Point*), *supra.*
54. Johnson (*Public Papers—1968*, Vol. I), *supra.*
55. *Time*, May 10, 1968.

less continued at an estimated ten thousand men per month,[56] a figure that allegedly, on occasion, approached thirty thousand.[57] In addition to firing rockets at random from peripheral countryside, VC terrorist units continued active in Saigon and other cities—counting the Tet offensives, terrorist action claimed approximately five thousand lives in 1968.[58] In the country, some hope appeared in a fundamental tactical change reportedly made by Westmoreland's successor, fifty-three-year-old Creighton Abrams, a West Pointer (1936) and World War II tank commander. As later reported in *Time:*

. . . Abrams has found that forays by sub-battalion-size units—companies, platoons, even squads—can be mounted more quickly, more often and in more places [than battalion and brigade actions]. Such surprise sweeps also achieve better results. Thus the general's sting-ray tactics, designed to interdict the movement of North Vietnamese units and supplies, involve the same number of men but hundreds and sometimes thousands more of what Abrams prefers to call "initiatives" rather than "offensives." As Abrams explained it . . . ". . . all our operations have been designed to get into the enemy's system. Once you start working in the system that he requires to prepare his offensive operations, you can cause him to postpone his operations or to reduce their intensity or length."[59]

As we shall see, this was a diluted version of sting-ray tactics, which the Marine Corps and also some army units had been using for over two years—a qualitative approach calling for small, highly trained patrols experienced in guerrilla tactics, as opposed to a quantitative approach, yet one that still tied units to artillery protection. Unfortunately, what Abrams ordered and what army and marine unit commanders did were frequently two different things. So wedded were some commanders to search-and-destroy tactics that they sabotaged the new directives in favor of the old.[60] Elsewhere, the tactical environment defeated them. In early July, Abrams abandoned the Khe Sanh position (a sensible move that nonetheless further bewildered an already bewildered American public, who, thanks to Westmoreland and Walt, regarded it as of Verdun-like importance). But other fire bases remained, and so did the problem of keeping open communications: So long as units were tied up in static defenses and line-of-communication guard duties, they were not available for clear-and-hold missions essential to pacification.

Nor did Hanoi appear in any hurry to sit down at the Paris conference table and hammer out the longed-for peace. In retaliation for Hanoi's refusal to admit the Saigon government to the talks, as well as

56. Shaplen (*Road*), *supra.*
57. *Time,* June 21, 1968.
58. Shaplen (*Road*), *supra.*
59. *Time,* June 6, 1969.
60. Brian Jenkins, "The Unchangeable War." RAND Corporation, n.d.

to stop fighting in the South, Johnson continued limited bombing in the
North. He later wrote his attitude at this time:

. . . I said [to Abrams] that we had reached the crucial stage of both
military and diplomatic operations. We would never achieve the kind of
peace we wanted unless the enemy was kept on the run, unless he realized
he could never win on the field of battle. I instructed Abrams to use his
resources and manpower in a maximum effort to achieve that goal and to
inspire the South Vietnamese army to do the same.[61]

Matters were still at a standstill when the two presidents met in Honolulu in mid-July. Prior to the meeting, Secretary of Defense Clifford flew
in from Saigon. The Secretary was

. . . oppressed by the pervasive Americanization of the war: we were still
giving the military instructions, still doing most of the fighting, still providing all the matériel, still paying most of the bills. Worst of all, I concluded
that the South Vietnamese leaders seemed content to have it that way.[62]

Johnson seems to have been more impressed with President Thieu, who
". . . was more confident than I had ever seen him"[63] Thieu spoke of
the splendid job of reorganizing ARVN and privately told Johnson that
the United States would be able to start withdrawing forces in mid-1969,
perhaps sooner.

Johnson's honeymoon with Thieu was short-lived. In October, the
North Vietnamese delegation in Paris quietly signaled that they would
admit Saigon to the talks in return for a bombing halt. Johnson and his
advisers, including the JCS, went along with this. But now Saigon refused to send a delegation, and was persuaded to do so only with considerable difficulty and delay—an attitude that reinforced Secretary of
Defense Clifford's belief that ". . . the goal of the Saigon government
and the goal of the United States were no longer one and the same, if
indeed they ever had been. . . ."[64] Although the President was inclined to blame this development on Republican machinations, he nonetheless later wrote, ". . . It was one of those rare occasions, in my years
of dealing with them, that I felt Thieu, Ky, and their advisers had let me
down. More important, I felt that their action put in peril everything
both governments had worked so long and sacrificed so much to
achieve. . . ."[65] The President scarcely veiled his annoyance in a major
speech at the end of October, when he announced a total bombing halt

61. Johnson (*The Vantage Point*), *supra*.
62. Clifford, op. cit.; see also Johnson, in *The Vantage Point, supra*, who did
not find Clifford so pessimistic.
63. Johnson (*The Vantage Point*), *supra*.
64. Clifford, op. cit.; see also, Kissinger, op. cit., who questioned the advisability
of American insistence on Saigon's participation in the first place.
65. Johnson (*The Vantage Point*), *supra*.

of the North and implied that South Vietnam would henceforth take over a larger share of the fighting.[66]

But, as American voters went to the polls to elect Richard Nixon the thirty-seventh President of the nation, American and North Vietnamese officials in Paris continued to argue over the shape of the conference table, a momentous issue still unsettled by year's end.

Whatever the results in Paris, the United States would not rejoice. At the end of 1968, a tally offered by a responsible organization read as follows:

From 1961 to 1967, 16,022 American troops had been killed in action in Vietnam. 14,592 more were killed during 1968. When deaths from accident and disease were added, 35,724 Americans had lost their lives in Vietnam since 1961. Communist casualties were far greater still: the United States claimed over 191,000 of the enemy killed during 1968 alone. In all, the war had caused more than half a million deaths in South Vietnam within eight years. Even the high Communist casualties had cost the United States dearly. Allied forces used conventional munitions in Vietnam during 1968 at a rate of nearly $14 million a day. The value of equipment destroyed was hardly less remarkable. Since 1961, combat action had claimed 919 American aircraft and 10 helicopters over North Vietnam, together with 327 aircraft and 972 helicopters over South Vietnam. 1,247 aircraft and 1,293 helicopters had been destroyed on the ground or in accidents. The cost of this attrition of aircraft alone was at least $4,800 million. Figures for the complete cost of the war to the United States were incalculable, but $27,000 million [i.e. $27 billion] was a reasonable estimate for 1968.[67]

These figures, which are conservative, represented only part of the price paid. The direct result of escalation and attrition strategy, they did not include the cost of a nation torn, with no visible means of immediately repairing the damage, and at a peculiar historical time of particular stress from within and without. The human and material costs, however, emphasized the poverty of a strategy founded on ignorance and executed in arrogance, a strategy we shall examine in the following chapter, a strategy whose failure drove a President from the White House—a defeated man, ". . . unwept, unhonored and unsung."

66. Johnson (*Public Papers*—1968, Vol. I), *supra*.
67. The Institute for Strategic Studies ("The United States"), *supra*.

Chapter 88

The summing up (I): the Bible and the Sword • Not "reason good enough" • Communists and dominoes • Inside South Vietnam • Economics • Government versus press: America— the communications failure

WHY DID LYNDON JOHNSON fail in Vietnam?

He failed for many of the same reasons that John Kennedy failed (see Chapters 77 and 78). As in Kennedy's case, the key to failure lay in substituting ambition for policy. *Stop communism* appealed to Johnson, a man of ". . . little background and much uncertainty in foreign affairs" (in the words of one subordinate),[1] even more than it had appealed to Kennedy. A Texas Baptist, Johnson had been raised in shadows of GOOD and EVIL. He was a great believer in the Bible and the Sword, and while he quoted one, he wielded the other. When neither faith nor force served him well, he was lost.

Johnson's downfall began before he was elected President. Like other worthy but myopic Americans, he accepted the "strong man" thesis that resulted in the American Government's prostrating itself before the pudgy form of Ngo Dinh Diem. As a Democrat, a southern Demo-

1. Hoopes, op. cit.

crat, Johnson wore scars from the Republican excoriation that followed the loss of Nationalist China to Mao's Communists. In spring of 1954, following the Geneva Conference, he said, ". . . American foreign policy has never in all its history suffered such a stunning reversal. . . . We stand in clear danger of being left naked and alone in a hostile world."[2] He did not believe that his party could survive another such loss, and when Diem—whom he had called the Winston Churchill of Southeast Asia—failed him, he turned to force.

The President early displayed his line of thought in a National Security Action Memorandum which he approved shortly after assuming office and which read in part:

. . . It remains the central objective of the United States in South Vietnam to assist the people and Government of that country to win their contest against the externally directed and supported communist conspiracy. The test of all U.S. decisions and actions in this area should be the effectiveness of their contribution to this purpose.[3]

Johnson greatly expanded this relatively mild statement in his famous Baltimore speech of April 1965 (see Chapter 81), where he repeated misplaced ambition emphasized by misdirected appeal, neither to change during the next three years. His eloquence not only failed to propel Ho Chi Minh to the conference table, but it prompted a rather negative reaction both in the United States and throughout the world.

This should have warned Johnson and his advisers. In his peroration, he had asked the American people: ". . . Have we, each of us, all done all we can do? Have we done enough?"

The true leader leads by example. Had Johnson asked himself this question, he would have had to reply no. In his crusading zeal, the President was forgetting wise Demades' admonition to the assembly ". . . to have a care lest in guarding heaven they should lose earth." Instead, like an emperor of old, he was crying, "Justice must be done, even if the world should perish."[4] The President should have respected the dissident opinions of those who attempted to warn him of Demades' words. Critics with such credentials as George Kennan, James Gavin, and David Shoup should not have been lightly dismissed. Sufficiently disturbing currents were at work at the beginning of Johnson's administration to call for the most penetrating examination of policy. The President might have asked himself, as for example Edward Lansdale, an expert on Vietnam, later asked *himself,* ". . . What is it exactly, that we seek in Viet Nam? . . . We have to answer the question *fully.* . . . Without a sound answer, the seemingly endless war in Viet Nam be-

2. New York *Times,* May 7, 1954; quoted in Anthony Eden, *Towards Peace in Indo-China* (London: Oxford University Press, 1966).

3. Johnson (*The Vantage Point*), *supra.*

4. *Fiat justitia, pereat mundus.*

comes just that—seemingly endless. Alternatively, it may be headed for an end that could be dishonorable, with profound consequences."[5] He could have listened to intelligent and courageous officers such as General Matthew Ridgway, who in 1967 warned:

. . . A war without goals would be most dangerous of all, and nearly as dangerous would be a war with only some vaguely stated aim, such as "victory" or "freedom from aggression" or "the right of the people to choose their own government." Generalities like these make admirable slogans, but authorities today must be hardheaded and specific in naming exactly what goal we are trying to reach and exactly what price we are willing to pay for reaching it. Otherwise, we may find that, in spite of ourselves, the whole conduct of the war will be left in the hands of men who see only victory as the proper objective and who have never had to define that word in terms plain enough to be understood by all the world's people.

Ridgway continued in words strengthened by simplicity:

. . . A limited war is not merely a small war that has not yet grown to full size. It is a war in which the objectives are specifically limited in the light of our national interest and our current capabilities. A war that is "open-ended"—that has no clearly delineated geographical, political and military goals beyond "victory"—is a war that may escalate itself indefinitely, as wars will, with one success requiring still another to insure the first one. . . .[6]

Had Johnson pursued this question of specific goals, had he demanded that civil and military advisers answer it fully, had he taken counsel not so much of fears as of unpalatable facts, he would not have weakened his position, as he did, by basing it on arguable premises. To pursue the strategy foisted by his military and civil advisers, demanded "exquisite reason," but, unlike Sir Andrew, the President lacked even "reason good enough." At a time when he and his advisers should have been questioning, they were accepting. Townsend Hoopes, who became Deputy Assistant Secretary of Defense for International Security Affairs in January 1965, discerned no ". . . central guiding philosophy" in American foreign policy, but, rather, hit-and-miss efforts motivated by the belief of Johnson and his principal advisers in a monolithic Communist threat, despite both Russia's traditional disinterest in Southeast Asia and her current quarrel with China (indisputably the most significant international development since Tito's defection and Chiang Kai-shek's fall). Dean Rusk, McGeorge Bundy, Robert McNamara, Walt Rostow, Maxwell Taylor, William Westmoreland, members of the JCS

5. Edward G. Lansdale, "Viet Nam—Still the Search for Goals," *Foreign Affairs,* October 1968. This article demonstrates only a few contradictions that occur when ambition is substituted for policy.
6. Matthew B. Ridgway, *The War in Korea* (London: Barrie & Rockliff, 1968).

—each spoke frequently and feelingly of "Communist aggression," while never fully defining the term or fitting the facts to the precise situation in Vietnam. Hoopes later wrote that ". . . to the President's men in early 1965, there seemed no logical stopping point between isolationism and globalism." Perhaps even more dangerous, he found these men supremely confident of militarily stopping the North Vietnamese and, with that, all "wars of national liberation."[7]

The President and his advisers grossly erred in trying to make a complex problem so simple. Unduly influenced by American economic and military power, frightened by the bogeyman of international communism, they accepted shibboleths bequeathed by Eisenhower and Kennedy and polished them with perfervid rhetoric made the more specious by crusade-like appeal. With one or two exceptions, they were yesterday's men living in tomorrow's world—like great-power exponents of another century, they tried to stop the clock of history and succeeded only in producing cacophonous chimes. Listen to Lyndon Johnson writing on the September 1964 White House meeting:

. . . As one gloomy opinion followed another, I suddenly asked whether anyone at the table doubted that Vietnam was "worth all this effort." Ambassador Taylor answered quickly that "we could not afford to let Hanoi win in the interests of our overall position in Asia and in the world." General Wheeler strongly supported the Ambassador's view. It was the unanimous view of the Chiefs of Staff, he said, that if we lost South Vietnam we would lose Southeast Asia—not all at once, and not overnight, but eventually. One country after another on the periphery would give way and look to Communist China as the rising power of the area, he said. John McCone agreed. So did Secretary Rusk, with considerable emphasis.[8]

Johnson failed to add that a great many experts, including top CIA analysts, did not agree with these views.

During the next two years, opposing voices, many of them expressing experience and study of decades, made it clear that the issues at stake were anything but black-and-white. With one or two exceptions, presidential advisers refused to listen. Here is Maxwell Taylor testifying before the Senate Foreign Relations Committee in February 1966:

. . . Our purpose is equally clear and easily defined. In his Baltimore speech . . . President Johnson did so in the following terms: "Our objective is the independence of South Vietnam and its freedom from attack. We want nothing for ourselves—only that the people of South Vietnam be allowed to guide their own country in their own way." This has been our basic objective since 1954. It has been pursued by three successive administrations and remains our basic objective today. . . .

7. Hoopes, op. cit.
8. Johnson (*The Vantage Point*), *supra.*

Taylor echoed the international-Communist-plot theory: ". . . Their leadership has made it quite clear that they regard South Vietnam as the testing ground for the 'war of liberation' and that, after its antici-pated success there, it will be used widely about the world. . . ." Amer-ican ground forces were needed, he explained, to create a favorable ratio: ". . . Since history has shown that the Government forces suc-cessfully opposing a guerrilla insurgency in the past have required a much greater preponderance of strength, 10 to 1 or 12 to 1, for exam-ple, it was quite clear that the Vietnamese could not raise forces fast enough to keep pace with the growing threat of the Viet Cong in time." Strategic bombing was necessary, not so much because it would stop in-filtration but because, ". . . in a very real sense, the objective of our air campaign is to change the will of the enemy leadership." As for Gavin's heresy of "holding strategy":

. . . I am obliged to conclude that the so-called "holding strategy" is really not an alternative way of reaching our objective of an independent South Vietnam free from attack; . . . it amounts to the modification and erosion of our basic objective and hence appears to me to be unacceptable.[9]

As late as 1967, William Bundy told a meeting of the National Student Association:

. . . Moreover, the wider implications for our commitments elsewhere ap-peared no less valid than they had ever been. Vietnam still constituted a major, perhaps even a decisive, test case of whether the Communist strategy of "wars of national liberation," or "people's wars" could be met and countered even in the extraordinarily difficult circumstances of South Viet-nam. Then as now, it has been I think rightly judged that a success for Hanoi in South Vietnam could only encourage the use of this technique by Hanoi, and over time by the Communist Chinese, and might well have the effect of drawing the Soviets into competition with Peking and Hanoi away from the otherwise promising trends that have developed in Soviet policy in the past ten years.[10]

Here, in but slight disguise, was the monolithic-Communist thesis that produced the domino theory: If one falls, all fall. Johnson and most of his advisers persisted in this belief despite demonstrable facts: that a good many insurgencies of two decades stood remote from commu-nism; that insurgency in South Vietnam could not have lasted a month without peasant support; that by threatening Hanoi's existence, Ameri-can arms had nearly brought rapprochement between China and Soviet Russia, they had brought an internal political development inside China whose full effects cannot yet be judged vis-à-vis America's best inter-ests, and they had brought the Soviet presence, probably permanently,

9. J. William Fulbright (ed.) (*The Viet Nam Hearings*), *supra*.
10. William Bundy, op. cit.

into an area in which, historically, Russia had displayed little interest.[11]

None of the above facts are original with the writer. The President and his advisers could have heard them from a score of highly qualified and eminently patriotic observers at home and abroad. C. P. Fitzgerald, for example, a distinguished scholar who lived in China for twenty-five years, demolished the domino theory (as others had done earlier): His article in *The Nation,* June 28, 1965, "The Fallacy of the Dominoes," should have been required Administration reading. Fitzgerald pointed out that since if one falls, all fall, then it follows that if one stands, all stand. But this was patently false at a time when Indonesia was in more danger of being taken over by Communists—their own—than Vietnam. He denied the validity of regional protective pacts, for clearly stated historical reasons; he argued, in short, that here was an immensely complicated political situation with deep historical roots:

. . . All these ancient claims and quarrels are more important, more real and more urgent to the peoples of South-East Asia than the conflict of communism backed by China and anti-communism backed by the United States. That contest is seen essentially as the quarrel of two great outsiders, to be used for promoting national ambitions or thwarting those of traditional foes, but in itself extraneous to the countries themselves. The Asians may well be wrong to take such an attitude, but the West is also much deluded when it thinks of these states as being without personalities of their own, willing to enlist on one side or the other in a global conflict, obedient to the behests of Washington or Peking.

The real appeal in these countries, evidence suggests, is nationalism, and this is one reason why the presence of Western armed forces, which provide an anti-nationalist target, is so dangerous. The challenge calls for a much more subtle approach and for extremely limited objectives: ". . . it must be remembered that this area is the region adjacent to China, in which its influence through the centuries has always been present, sometimes powerful and active, at other times dormant, but by the mere facts of geography, never extinct."[12]

Not a word do we find of such heretical notions either in official state-

11. Zagoria, op. cit.
12. Quoted in *Survival,* September 1965; see also C. P. Fitzgerald, *The Chinese View of Their Place in the World* (London: Oxford University Press, 1965); Donald S. Zagoria, "Who Fears the Domino Theory?" New York *Times Magazine,* April 21, 1968; Owen Harries, "Should the U.S. Withdraw from Asia?" *Foreign Affairs,* October 1968, offers a dissenting opinion; but see Edwin O. Reischauer, *Beyond Vietnam* (New York: Alfred A. Knopf, 1967); Dr. Reischauer is an acknowledged expert on the Far East and Asia, and his telling arguments as to the minimal importance of a Communist "victory" in Vietnam cannot be dismissed out of hand; Soedjatmoko, "South-East Asia and Security," *Survival,* October 1969; Richard Harris, "How the Chinese View South-East Asia," *The Times* (London), September 8, 1970; Harrison Salisbury, "Image and Reality in Indochina," *Foreign Affairs,* April 1971, discusses distorted viewpoints of both sides.

ments of the day or in the Pentagon papers. Were similar opinions reported by American diplomats throughout the area? Were such opinions debated in high councils? Perhaps someday we shall know the answers. Some argument must have existed, though Johnson's memoirs are lacking substance in this respect. Still, in the January 1967 issue of *Foreign Affairs,* for example, we find McGeorge Bundy carefully disclaiming the theretofore sacrosanct domino theory, but, by then, Bundy had left the government[13]; we also find indirect confirmation in later disillusionment expressed by Clark Clifford and Townsend Hoopes. In 1965, however, and for the next two years, any government official daring to question the cornerstone of Administration policy would have been tagged a "nervous Nellie" and relegated to limbo.

The President's personal advisers and top civil and military officials equally could insist on Hanoi's dominant role in the war as proclaimed in the 1965 White Paper.[14] But this did not wash with a good many American and international observers and experts, who were aware of the early minimum role played by Hanoi, particularly in troop and supply categories. If a "constant stream" of trained men and supplies was flowing from North to South, a veritable flood of such had already flowed from West to East.[15]

Similarly, Communist China's participation in the conflict had been minimal, despite menacing growls from Peking. The partnership between Ho and Mao implied by the President did not exist. Writing in 1967, Donald Zagoria pointed out that

. . . any careful study of Chinese foreign policy during the past fifteen years would have to conclude that although China is a revolutionary power oppos-

13. McGeorge Bundy, "The End of Either/Or," *Foreign Affairs,* June 1967.

14. See, for example, Maxwell Taylor, *Responsibility and Response* (New York: Harper & Row, 1967): ". . . as early as 1961 when I headed a mission to Vietnam at President Kennedy's directions, the mission called attention to the fact that the real source of the guerrilla strength in South Vietnam was not in South Vietnam but in North Vietnam. It was perfectly clear that the direction, the supplies, the reinforcements, and the leadership came from the North. . . ."

15. David Horowitz, *Containment and Revolution* (Boston: Beacon Press, 1967): Hans Morgenthau commented: ". . . Let it be said right away that the (State Department) white paper is a dismal failure. The discrepancy between its assertions and the factual evidence adduced to support them borders on the grotesque"; see also U. S. Department of Defense, "Working Paper on the North Vietnamese Role in the War in South Vietnam," Washington: 1968. This study asserts, rather than proves, Hanoi's dominant role from the beginning; George K. Tanham and Dennis J. Duncanson, "Some Dilemmas of Counterinsurgency," *Foreign Affairs,* October 1969: ". . . In reality, the Marxist-Leninists of the East not only take pride in winning power with a minimum contribution from their own side, but have found from experience that this is a more reliable road to victory. Besides concealing the directing hand, it leaves the door open to repudiation of unsuccessful insurgencies . . ."; Lacouture, op. cit., cites Pentagon advice ". . . that the deliveries from the North were . . . on the order of fifteen to twenty percent [of Viet Cong needs]. . . ."

ing the present status quo, it does not aim to bring about change by its
own military force.

. . . [It is] one of the key messages in Lin Piao's article [September 3,
1965] and one of the basic principles of "liberation wars"—that Communist revolutionaries throughout the world must make their revolutions on
their own. Far from giving any notice of any intention to intervene aggressively in Vietnam or in other "people's wars," Lin Piao was rationalizing
Peking's unwillingness to intervene directly and massively in such wars. He
was reiterating what is essentially a "do-it-yourself" model of revolution for
foreign Communists.[16]

Five years later, an expert on counterinsurgency warfare, in discussing
Chinese aid to Thailand guerrillas, noted:

. . . Current Chinese doctrine stresses that the indigenous apparatus must
carry out the revolution itself with only limited support from other socialist
nations. This policy, which makes a complete turnabout from Mao's 1949
position that outside aid was the critical factor, culminated in Lin Piao's
speech in 1965 when the current theory of do-it-yourself was fully expounded.[17]

In 1965, Ho was walking a tightrope between Chinese and Soviet
camps, and President Johnson's attempts to stress the Chinese threat
while not mentioning the theretofore prominent villain, the Soviet
Union, did not impress intelligent auditors.

The President's "national pledge" was equally specious: ". . . We
are there because we have a promise to keep." What promise? When?
President Eisenhower said that the United States would supply limited
aid to South Vietnam, providing Diem carried out essential reforms.
Here was a reasonable proposition. Nothing was new about it. It was
the beginning of a temporary alliance with attendant advantages to each
party. Such alliances crowd the pages of history, and such have been
commented on through the ages as, for example, by Spinoza, who, as
Leopold Ranke noted,

. . . starts from the principle that states permanently subsist in a state of
nature with respect to one another, and does not hesitate to assert that a
treaty has force only so long as the causes of it—fear of injury or hope of
gain—exist; that no ruler is to be reproached with faithlessness for breaking
an alliance he had formerly concluded, as soon as any of the causes which
determined him to it should have ceased, since that condition is equal for
both parties.

16. Zagoria, op. cit.; this does not deny Chinese expansionist aims—see also H. L.
Duncan, "Does China Want War?" *Army Quarterly,* July 1967; Owen Harries,
op. cit.
17. George K. Tanham, *Trial in Thailand* (New York: Crane, Russak, 1974).

This is little more than common sense. Yet, in less than a decade, Eisenhower's casual alliance became promoted, mostly by military voices, into a "promise" and now into "a national pledge to help South VietNam defend its independence." Listen to Maxwell Taylor, writing in 1967:

. . . If we are convinced, as I am, that the stake is important, that we are honor-bound to obtain for the people in South Vietnam the right to freedom, then every dollar and every man we have committed in my opinion is justified.[18]

By right to freedom, Taylor undoubtedly included rule by Diem and Nhu and Thieu and Ky and whatever other national war lords will appear in the future—neither Taylor nor any of the other ancient citizens who surrounded the President, with the possible exception of Clifford, realized that Administration ambitions for South Vietnam bore almost no resemblance to the relatively simple goal of the Saigon government, which was (and is) to maintain and enlarge its own power structure while yielding minimum freedoms to its peoples. And if the U.S.A. was honor bound to intervene in South Vietnam, then why not in Rhodesia, South Africa, Greece, most of the South American and all the Iron Curtain countries, indeed in any country whose government did not conform to American system or desire?

Attempting to put the record in proper perspective, in 1967 Senator Eugene McCarthy wrote:

. . . It is argued that we have a legal obligation [in Vietnam] under the SEATO treaty and other commitments. But the SEATO treaty itself has not been brought into operation in the Vietnam War. South Vietnam has never requested action under SEATO, and any joint action, as provided for in that treaty, would be impossible because of the positions of France and Pakistan, and possibly Britain. The argument of legal obligation is one which the Administration sought to bolster by securing the passage of the Tonkin Gulf Resolution by the Congress in 1964, although the Secretary of State, in testimony before the Foreign Relations Committee, said that even without the Tonkin Gulf Resolution, commitment in Vietnam was defensible and did not depend on the resolution for its legal basis.

It is said that we fight to ensure the credibility of our commitments, to show the world that we honor our treaty obligations. This is the rationale of our politico-military prestige. Yet we have already demonstrated our reliability in Korea and in the protection of Taiwan as well as in Europe.

It is said that we must carry on the war in Vietnam in order to preserve and defend our national honor. Our national honor is not at stake, and should not so readily be offered. In every other great war of the century, we have had the support of what is generally accepted as the decent opinion of mankind. We do not have that today. We cannot, of course, depend only

18. Maxwell Taylor (*Responsibility and Response*), *supra*.

on this opinion to prove our honor; it may not be sound. But always in
the past we have not only had this support, but we have used it as a kind
of justification for our action.[19]

As for the unforgivable wrong of abandoning ". . . this small and
brave nation to its enemies, and to the terror that must follow," the
President again was indulging in fiction. The homogeneous national
picture that he implied did not exist. Viet Cong cadres had controlled
large areas of South Vietnam since 1954; in 1965, the enemy controlled
probably 90 per cent of the countryside. In 1965, as in 1955, Saigon
rule was remote in some areas, ruthless in other areas. A large percentage of peasants did not care who ruled so long as they could till crops
and get a fair shake in the market place. The peasants' main concern
was not democracy but survival with dignity, and the splendid rhetoric
that burbled from Washington and Saigon officialdom was virtually
meaningless to bent bodies laboring in rice paddies and on rubber plantations. No one had shown peasants that democracy was worth fighting
for, because no one had shown them democracy. As Johnson spoke, the
gulf between the Saigon government, the sects, and the peasants was as
wide as ever, growing wider.[20]

People who would have directly suffered terror of a Communist takeover constituted, for the most part, a rapacious ruling minority whose
greed and intransigence were keeping the nation, such as it was, in its
turbulent, impotent condition. And here was Johnson, like Kennedy
and Eisenhower before him, compounding the damage by unfounded
fears and loose rhetoric. Once again, Johnson was saying that the West
could not survive without this geographical neutrino, this whirling nothing of a country. So many Americans had insisted that a dubious political entity called South Vietnam was an indispensable ally in the war
against communism, that South Vietnamese Catholics, Buddhists, mandarins, generals, landowners, merchants, intellectuals, and students began to believe it—so indispensable, that, on occasion, South Vietnamese
Government leaders such as Khanh could indulge the most virulent
language and defiant behavior to the country that was keeping them
alive. About this time, a Vietnamese political observer told Robert
Shaplen: ". . . In a way, after all the pent-up years under the French
and under Diem, we are like children letting off steam. Maybe there
will have to be yet another half-dozen coups before we settle down—
even though we know we can't afford them."[21] He was wrong. South
Vietnam could afford them—as long as the United States insisted on
bestowing unqualified support on a rump government whose totalitarian
characteristics contradicted a heritage held sacred by thoughtful American citizens.

19. McCarthy (*The Limits of Power*), *supra*.
20. Duncanson (*Government and Revolution in Vietnam*), *supra*.
21. Shaplen (*The Road from War*), *supra*.

In spring of 1965, a firm threat to abandon South Vietnam was perhaps the only action that could have produced the social-political cohesion necessary to make a nation. The Vietnamese politicians may not have admitted it, but they were in a classic "backs-to-the-wall" position. President Johnson's "solution," his Baltimore speech, removed the wall.

His words caused similar psychological damage in other countries that the United States was trying to help. A serious threat to abandon South Vietnam might have produced some interesting soul-searching in these other areas. Instead, the President's words insured the continued flow of golden eggs from the increasingly tired Western goose. Almost to the very end of his administration, the President continued to promise unqualified American support to the Thieu-Ky regime.

No one could fault the President's assertion of great stakes in play in the international power game. But if retreat from Vietnam would not bring an end to conflict, neither would "victory" in Vietnam. The President was trying to produce a black-and-white center-ring act from a multicolored sideshow. Neither Moscow nor Peking particularly wanted the war to escalate: Moscow did not want to upset her détente with Washington; Peking did not want a strong American military presence on the Asian mainland.

However, once the United States made a major commitment in South Vietnam, Moscow and Peking rolled with the punch and moved to exploit the situation. No matter how big, powerful, and rich the U.S.A., no nation could be everywhere at once. While President Johnson was talking to the world, Chinese money and Chinese technicians were on their way to Tanzania to begin construction of a sixteen-hundred-mile railroad into the interior of Africa; Soviet money and Soviet technicians were working in Cairo's defense ministry; satellite money and satellite technicians were scouring underdeveloped parts of the world for investment and prestige purposes. While American priority effort went to a strategically unimportant country, the Soviet Union and China reinforced their presence in Africa and the Middle East—indeed, anywhere they wished—to the detriment of the West and with the knowledge that the U.S.A. could not launch a maximum countereffort.

The President's stated objective of "independence" for South Vietnam also rang hollow. Whether the United States or South Vietnam liked it or not, the tragic rump would remain economically and militarily dependent on the United States, just as had Cuba and the Philippines for so many decades, just as Taiwan and Korea were doing.

The economic factor is of particular importance because a great deal of woolly thinking has surrounded and obfuscated it. In 1968, a Joint Development Group report read:

. . . For several years well over a million men on both sides have been fighting in the country, but physical destruction is minimal and, in spite of many pressures, the economic wealth of the country in physical facilities has increased.

South Vietnam has a system of modern ports that will not require major renovation and is capable of expansion; an agriculture that is diversifying, that is beginning to benefit from the potentials of new types of rice and that has a basis for absorbing other technological improvements; an industrial structure that has not seriously suffered and that has investment funds available when the risk-reward calculation is favorable; and a labor force that has acquired useful skills.

In economic terms, Vietnam does not have a large debt or debt service burden, and its foreign exchange reserves are sufficient to finance six months of imports even at inflated import levels.

By many measures South Vietnam is in an enviable position in relation to the experience of other countries at the end of a war, including Korea more than a decade ago. There are serious problems in the number of refugees, the dependence on United States aid, and distortions in the economy, but overall, economically the country is fortunate.[22]

This happy conclusion ignores a good many peripheral but pertinent factors.[23] Almost all of its physical plant was financed gratis by American citizens, a contribution that, taken along with the war, was helping to bankrupt "the richest and most powerful nation" in the world. Some of the fine print is also damning. David Lilienthal, who quoted the above report in an article in *Foreign Affairs,* went on to point out that "land reform" still constitutes a major problem, one that must be solved by the South Vietnamese Government (which has to date shown little intention of solving it).

But that is only the beginning.

Transition from war to peace would demand heavy public and private investments beyond South Vietnam's ability to provide: ". . . it seems inevitable that even heroic measures will not provide sufficient domestic resources to fill the need; the gap must be filled by external aid." Lilienthal continues:

. . . After the initial transition period, import requirements should slacken, but there will still be an annual gap of $300 to $400 million in the commodity balance of trade. Even if, as seems indicated, private capital will be attracted to the country, from $250 to $350 million per year will still be required in aid. Some of this might be in the form of soft currencies, but about $200 million annually will be needed in hard currencies. Since annual averages are often deceptive, it is better to say that aid on the order of $2 billion spread over a ten-year period will be needed.

22. David E. Lilienthal, "Postwar Development in Viet Nam," *Foreign Affairs,* January 1969.
23. Reischauer, op. cit.; for a brilliant analysis of the Mekong Delta area, see also Robert L. Sansom, *The Economics of Insurgency in the Mekong Delta of Vietnam* (Cambridge, Mass.: MIT Press, 1970).

Lilienthal did not mention that official estimates have also often been deceptive and that economic aid would probably amount to at least twice the predicted sum. But no matter,

. . . This is not a burden which the United States can or, I believe, will shoulder alone. It must be shared among many, not the least being those nations in the Pacific Basin itself. The American pledge to support the development of Southeast Asia needs to be matched by others who have been involved directly or indirectly in the events of the past years—as allies, as economic beneficiaries of the war (notably Japan) and, indeed, as critics. Ally and critic alike have a responsibility to help find a viable and lasting path of development for Viet Nam and for Southeast Asia as a whole.

Unfortunately for Lilienthal's argument, ally and critic alike did not recognize a responsibility proclaimed by the American Government, and did not jump aboard the financial-aid train, no more than local dominoes had jumped aboard the military-aid train.

And with good reason. Lilienthal continued:

. . . The corollary to the need for external aid in achieving economic independence is the need for South Viet Nam to adopt appropriate policies of growth. Understandably, after 20 years of war, during the last few years of which large numbers of foreigners have been prominent and influential in the country, various forms of xenophobia have appeared, inspired by a sense of nationalism and pride of culture. In the economic field, this has created a preference for import substitution rather than export promotion, for the public sector to assume responsibility over wide areas of economic activity and exercise tight controls over the private sector, and for direct controls rather than competitive market processes. In general, this attitude looks inward and is conservative rather than outward-looking and expansive.

It is clear, even now, that Viet Nam cannot successfully make the transition to a peaceful footing if such autarchic policies are dominant in its economy. Ultimately, they meet neither the need for efficiency in the use of resources nor the requirements of social justice. If carried to an extreme, they would make it difficult if not impossible for Viet Nam to attain or enjoy economic independence. Long-continued economic dependence on foreigners would make a tragic travesty of the sacrifices made in the cause of political independence.[24]

Economic health cannot be divorced from political health. President Johnson's desire ". . . that the people of South Vietnam be allowed to guide their own country in their own way" would have been reasonable enough except that the United States was supporting a minority segment that, by refusing to tolerate political opposition, had increasingly alienated major social groups and significantly reduced the country's determination to give battle to its foes.

24. Lilienthal, op. cit.

Unable to state this fact, yet having to offer reasons for the American action, the President resembled a boy whistling his way past a cemetery on a dark night. The most cursory reader of American newspapers, magazines, and books knew that the President's stated resolution was not shared by an increasingly influential portion of the nation, including legislators who were beginning to hold second thoughts about the Tonkin Gulf Resolution. Leaving aside domestic problems that were crying for enormous expenditures of expertise and money, nothing in the American character suggested the qualities of patience that Lyndon Johnson claimed in pursuing his ambitions:

. . . We will not be defeated.
We will not grow tired.
We will not withdraw, either openly or under the cloak of a meaningless agreement. . . .

Here again the President was dreaming. These statements presupposed a national interest and stamina that did not exist—and for several reasons. The first was a failure in communications that we have already discussed with regard to the Kennedy era. Johnson himself, in spring of 1954, speaking as a congressman, had said: ". . . We will insist upon clear explanations of the policies in which we are asked to cooperate. We will insist that we and the American people be treated as adults, that we have the facts without sugar coating."[25]

When, during the Kennedy administration, the press attempted to give the facts, a good many senior American officials bridled and a minor war developed. As Vice-President, Johnson must have been aware of the dangerous situation, yet, as President, he did not bear Pierre Salinger's warning (see Chapter 78) in mind, and relations between press and officialdom continued to deteriorate. In an article in *Foreign Affairs* in July 1966, veteran correspondent James Reston again warned of a communications breakdown. Far from heeding him, Johnson increasingly scorned the press (which he criticized throughout his memoirs).

As one result, a good many senior officials both in Saigon and Washington continued to dissemble; some reporters continued to distort. So complex was the Vietnamese scene that even highly talented correspondents had their hands full covering it and communicating its complex turbulence to the American public. With a few splendid exceptions, not many, publishers unfortunately did not present the war in depth. A British expert on counterinsurgency, Major General Richard Clutterbuck, after visiting South Vietnam, accused three journalist friends ". . . of reporting only what occurred above 12,000 feet. If you put cloud over the world at 12,000 feet, the only things that stick up are rugged and spectacular, and that is what gets reported. They

25. Deakin, op. cit.

agreed that that was what they did, and said that if they reported anything below 12,000 feet, it would not get into their papers anyway; no one would read it if it did, and they would lose their jobs. We had to leave it at that, and so the real blame falls on the public."[26]

While newspaper publishers, TV-station owners, and public admittedly are culpable, the statement is not altogether true. Reporting in depth (by far the most accurate and intelligent coverage came from Robert Shaplen of *The New Yorker*) was well received by impressive segments of the public, who became aware that the situation scarcely resembled the black-and-white situation described in presidential platitudes.

But, for every informed American citizen and even vaguely informed American citizen, dozens existed who had only the foggiest notion of what was going on in Vietnam. The Administration could not alleviate national ignorance by a well-conceived and well-executed educational program, because it had already decided that the issues were black and white, and that it was a question of imposing American will on Hanoi. Unlike many Americans, the President refused to grow in four years. He refused to abandon pubescent dreams promulgated by persons unable either to understand or accept political realities in a complicated world. Like Count Bestuzhev in dealing with Prussia, he had ". . . changed passion into principle," and was a prisoner of the process, for, unlike Bestuzhev, he could not swallow his hatred to alter an intransigence clearly and frequently repeated. In February 1968, we hear a typical Johnsonianism: ". . . As near as I am able to detect, Hanoi has not changed its course of conduct since the very first response it made. Sometimes they will change 'will' to 'would' and 'shall' to 'should,' or something of the kind. But the answer is all the same." But, as Henry Kissinger later pointed out: ". . . A different kind of analysis might have inquired why Hanoi would open up a channel for a meaningless communication, especially in the light of a record of careful planning which made it extremely unlikely that a change of tense would be inadvertent."[27]

The communications problem, which resulted in continuing national ignorance (thus frustration and resentment), gave rise to an even more serious condition. Johnson had embarked on a crusade that the American public did not understand but at first supported, though by no means eagerly, because it trusted its national leaders and its military and civilian officials and because it shared, at least in part, their arrogance of

26. RUSI Seminar, *supra:* Brigadier Kenneth Hunt of The Institute for Strategic Studies also complained of a press deficiency: ". . . The most dispiriting thing is to go to a Press conference in Saigon. It is not merely because the quality of the briefing is kindergarten, that it comes out in a dead-pan American style. The quality of the questions asked by reporters is also often poor and amateurish. That is reflected in what comes back and is printed."

27. Kissinger, op. cit.

ignorance. But, not very long after the Tonkin Gulf Resolution, a tradition began quietly to assert itself. As Bill Moyers, Johnson's press man, later pointed out, the American democratic concept embraces not only a tradition of dissent, but also of consent:

. . . Our system assumes a sense of participation by the people in the making of critical national decisions. When that sense of involvement is absent, when the public feels excluded from the judgments that are made in its name, a policy is doomed from inception, no matter how theoretically valid it may be.[28]

Translating this to Vietnam, Moyers continued:

. . . War is clearly one of those questions on which a government—a democratic government—dare not act without evidence of genuine support. In this case, that support was not deliberately withheld—it simply was not sought. And it was not sought, because few if any officials anticipated the war would ever reach the proportions that would require a declaration.

Rather than "leveling" with the American people, Johnson and his advisers continued in the hope that they could clean up matters—that they could "win"—before the American public realized quite what had happened. That this hope was doomed by a false military strategy did not at first occur except to a very few advisers, and these Johnson ignored and later banished. When truth began leaking out, when casualties and expenses rose out of all proportion to gained results, the American public, or, anyway, impressive portions of it, rebelled.

Parts of the United States were already rebelling at the time of Johnson's Baltimore speech in the spring of 1965. Although Communist leaders in South and North Vietnam were provincial and often naïve, they sensed currents at work in the United States that suggested France of an earlier day. These leaders had experienced protracted warfare, many had been fighting since 1943 and even earlier (some since 1932), and from 1946 onward, they had witnessed the pressures of protracted guerrilla warfare at work on Western countries. In their minds, protracted warfare had gained one victory. It could now gain another. An American President could proclaim that his nation would not be defeated or would not grow tired—but Communists had only to read American newspapers and magazines to realize that this was proclamation without solid national support. Throughout his later memoirs, the President repeatedly stressed Hanoi's unwillingness to negotiate a peace in these crucial years. Never once, apparently, did it occur to him to ask himself why; never once does he suggest that, being human, he was fallible and his basic precepts could have been fallacious.

28. Bill D. Moyers, "One Thing We Learned," *Foreign Affairs,* July 1968.

Chapter 89

The summing up (II): use of air power • The Douhet theory • Strategic bombing in World War II • The paradox of nuclear stalemate • Lessons of the Korean War • American expectations in North Vietnam • Historical factors • Harrison Salisbury reports from the North • Bombs and international diplomacy

THE PRESIDENT'S DECISION to carry the war to the North undoubtedly came as an unpleasant surprise to Hanoi. But the President's decision could not change the axis of war, which remained in the South. Moreover, his intention to alter enemy will by use of aerial bombardment introduced several factors that seem to have escaped official cognizance.

The use of air power produces both moral and material results, and the tally means one thing to the user, another to the receiver.

On advice of his military chiefs, Johnson was embracing a modified Douhet theory of aerial bombing when he agreed to send American planes over North Vietnam. This theory emerged in 1921, when Giulio Douhet, an Italian air officer, wrote a small book, *The Command of the Air*.[1]

1. Giulio Douhet, *The Command of the Air* (London: Faber & Faber, 1943). Tr. D. Ferrari. (First edition published in 1921, second edition in 1927.)

Douhet correctly foresaw the importance of the new arm:

. . . By virtue of this new weapon, the repercussions of war are no longer limited to the farthest artillery range of surface guns, but can be directly felt for hundreds and hundreds of miles . . . the battlefield will be limited only by the boundaries of the nations at war, and all of their citizens will become combatants since all of them will be exposed to the aerial offensives of the enemy. There will be no distinction any longer between soldiers and civilians. The defenses on land and sea will no longer serve to protect the country behind them; nor can victory on land or sea protect the people from enemy aerial attacks unless that victory ensures the destruction, by actual occupation of the enemy's territory, of all that gives life to his aerial forces.

All of this must inevitably effect a profound change in the form of future wars. . . .

Air power, Douhet argued, would prove omnipotent:

. . . Thus were born anti-aircraft guns, and reconnaissance and pursuit planes. But subsequent experience demonstrated that all these means of defense were inadequate, despite the fact that aerial offensives in the last war [World War I] were of minor importance, haphazardly planned and executed. Every time an aerial offensive was carried out resolutely, it accomplished its purpose. Venice was bombed repeatedly from beginning to end of the war; Treviso was almost razed under our eyes; and Padua had to be abandoned by the Supreme Command. . . .

Douhet made no claim to selectivity or subtlety:

. . . The complete destruction of the objective has moral and material effects, the repercussions of which may be tremendous. To give us some idea of the extent of these repercussions, we need only envisage what would go on among the civilian population of congested cities once the enemy announced that he would bomb such centers relentlessly, making no distinction between military and non-military objectives.

In Douhet's mind, as in Foch's before him, the moral was as important as the physical:

. . . We should always keep in mind that aerial offensives can be directed not only against objectives of least physical resistance, but against those of least moral resistance as well. For instance, an infantry regiment in a shattered trench may still be capable of some resistance even after losing two-thirds of its effectives; but when the working personnel of a factory sees one of its machine shops destroyed, even with a minimum loss of life, it quickly breaks up and the plant ceases to function.

Professional airmen in the West such as Billy Mitchell in the United States and Hugh Trenchard in England, who were attempting to build air forces and were obstructed at every turn by army and navy traditionalists, embraced Douhet's theory as another argument in favor of the new arm. In the late twenties, Mitchell demonstrated that bombs could sink a battleship; as we have seen, the British claimed strategic-tactical successes in Iraq and in northwestern frontier provinces in India, as did U. S. Marines in Nicaragua (see Chapters 29 and 30, Volume I). Goering's Luftwaffe experimented with the theory during the Spanish civil war, at one point eliminating the town of Guernica; at another, testing results of carpet bombing.

Variations appeared early in World War II. Older readers will remember horrendous pictures of Stuka dive bombers preparing cities such as Rotterdam for paratroop invasion and later attacking refugee columns in France in order to cause panic and impede military movement. The Battle of Britain raised the psychological level of the theory, but the Luftwaffe failed to bring England to its knees. When skillful and determined RAF opposition produced heavy German losses in aircraft and pilots, which could not easily be replaced, Hitler terminated the campaign.

The theory did not die with this failure. RAF and American strategic air bombings attempted to destroy Hitler's industrial plant and thereby force Germany from the war. RAF saturation bombings culminating in the destruction of Dresden attempted to break the German people's will; American fire bombings of Tokyo and the final destruction of Hiroshima and Nagasaki by atomic bombs did play a major role in breaking Japanese will to continue war.

Thus the Douhet theory: At its nicest, strategic bombing; at its ugliest, genocide. And this is why the theory is fallacious: first, the more bombs dropped, the lower the morale—but not necessarily a significant lessening of will to resist. This is a challenge situation familiar to psychology. Challenge, discipline, and incentive all play major roles; resistance is never easily analyzed. These factors help to explain why medieval fortresses held out against overwhelming odds, why, in World War I, neither side would yield on the western front, why men in battle, for example American marines on Guadalcanal in those black days of late 1942, tolerated weeks of bombing and shelling by Japanese aircraft and ships without losing their will to fight. Civilians of London, Berlin, Tokyo, and numerous other cities reacted similarly. Aerial bombings subverted civil will to resist only by killing the holders of that will. Conventional strategic bombing did not kill enough holders of that will fast enough; atomic bombing did.

The advent of the atomic bomb seemed to fructify Douhet's theory, but only as long as one side held a monopoly. Even then, moral aspects outweighed the practical: Premeditated genocide is not an acceptable clause in the Western code of civilization, as the Germans discovered. And not only the Germans. At the height of allied bombing in World War II, the American air force general Carl ("Tooey") Spaatz caviled at the RAF's saturation bombing program. The American people's reaction to the atomic bombings of Hiroshima and Nagasaki was also disturbed, and if those of us who were training for the invasion of Japan proper were pleased with the war's sudden termination, this did not erase a feeling of guilt, however nebulous, in the national conscience. As General Matthew Ridgway wrote in 1956, when discussing the use of strategic air power:

. . . Furthermore, to my mind, such mass destruction is repugnant to the ideals of a Christian nation. It is incompatible with the basic aim of the free world in war, which is to win a just and enduring peace.[2]

Once the Soviet Union broke atomic monopoly, the atomic bomb's omnipotence evaporated in an air of retribution. The paradox of nuclear stalemate—of destructive impotence—resulted. Both moral and practical aspects prevented American use of atomic bombs in Korea and in North Vietnam. At the height of the bombing of North Vietnam, in October 1967, Robert McNamara laid the issue on the line in a top-secret memorandum to President Johnson:

. . . It is clear that, to bomb the North sufficiently to make a radical impact upon Hanoi's political, economic and social structure, would require an effort which we could make but which would not be stomached either by our own people or by world opinion; and it would involve a serious risk of drawing us into open war with China.[3]

Material results of strategic bombing are something else again. Strategic-bombing proponents have frequently overstated their case, which is usual with minority arguments. World War II offered excellent examples of bombing's strength and weaknesses. Any interested reader can find myriad statistics in the postwar *Strategic Bombing Survey,* whose directors included George Ball, John Galbraith, and Paul Nitze.[4] The survey cited impressive accomplishments of allied air forces, giving fliers their due and then some; but it also established that workers did not flee an area when first bombs fell, as Douhet and later strategic-bombing proponents had it, but, rather, that bombing, although interrupting production, rarely halted it, at least until the very end, when allied ground forces already had invaded Germany. Permanent damage was not nearly so great as current estimates had suggested, and in some areas production even increased, while in others reserve stocks and emergency measures provided short-term compensation for havoc wrought. Bombing raids in July and August 1943 on Hamburg killed some sixty to a hundred thousand people and destroyed 55–60 per cent of the city, including three hundred thousand homes. Yet

2. Ridgway (*Memoirs*), *supra.*
3. *The Pentagon Papers, supra* (pp. 542–51).
4. U. S. Government, *The United States Strategic Bombing Survey—Over-all Report* (Washington: U. S. Government Printing Office, 1945).

. . . Hamburg as an economic unit was not destroyed. It never fully recovered from the bombing but in five months it had regained 80 per cent of its former productivity, despite the fact that great areas of the city lay, and still lie, in dust and rubble. As in the case of industrial plants where it was found much easier to destroy the buildings than the machines within, so also it is much easier to destroy the physical structures of a city than to wipe out its economic life.

Industrial damage lowered and even halted priority production while massive allied air attacks against Germany's communications system hindered supply from reaching her armies. But her armies did not crumble from lack of supply, the Wehrmacht retaining considerable fighting spirit even at the end, as most allied veterans will attest.

Saturation bombings, what the RAF called "area raids," also provided startling "kill" figures. The Strategic Bombing Survey estimated that bombs eliminated 3.6 million homes, or approximately 20 per cent of Germany's total dwelling space; bombs killed about three hundred thousand people and injured some 780,000. Although ". . . bombing appreciably affected the German will to resist," bombs did not crumble that will:

. . . War production is the critical measuring rod of the effects of lowered morale in the German war effort. Allied bombing widely and seriously depressed German civilian morale, but depressed and discouraged workers were not necessarily unproductive workers. As has been seen, armaments production continued to mount till mid-1944. . . .

The survey asserted that continuous, heavy bombing of a town did not further lower morale:

. . . In the first place, the cities undergoing heavy raids lost a considerable part of their population through evacuation, and these evacuees were in some cases the faint-hearted, the less patriotic; in short, the people with lower morale. In the second place, very severe bombing changed active dissension to apathy about political matters, and to preoccupation with keeping alive. In a police state with totalitarian controls, an apathetic, passive people has better morale from the point of view of the existing regime than an actively disgruntled people. Such passivity facilitates their control and manipulation. Intense bombing, moreover, made it more difficult for undercover oppositional movements to operate, since their limited resources for communication and organization were frequently disrupted.

Strategic bombing also received a setback from a cost-analysis standpoint. It proved very expensive in both lives and cost of bombers and bombs. The establishment required to operate a peak twenty-eight thousand combat planes numbered 1.335 million men. Nearly eighty thousand American and eighty thousand British airmen were lost in action, while eighteen thousand American and twenty-two thousand British planes were lost or damaged beyond repair. Up to VE-day, the American air effort in Europe alone cost over $43 billion! A final factor emerged after the war: Industrial complexes that had been damaged and destroyed, not to mention surrounding urban areas, had to be rebuilt, with the victors, primarily the U.S.A., picking up the tab.

Strategic-tactical bombing and interdiction also proved chimerical. Lavish claims advanced by proponents of air power were often matched by lavish failures. Few, if any, interested persons disputed tactical advantages derived from command of the air. We have glanced at these in the 1920s and 1930s. But, as Gwynn pointed out in 1934, air power was not a tactical panacea and could not apply in all places at all times. In World War II, tactical air power proved a tremendous boon to allied armies, not only in clearing skies of enemy aircraft but in close air support, a fine art developed particularly by U. S. Marines. But such accomplishments did not obliterate shortcomings: Tactical air power did not "win" ground battles, any more than strategic air power "won" the war. Writing years later, General Matthew Ridgway recalled that limitations of air power ". . . were never better illustrated in World War II, when the Germans were able to maintain some twenty-six divisions south of the Alps in Italy, using a few mountain passes to keep them supplied for two years, regardless of uncontested Allied air supremacy."[5]

The Korean war added to lessons already learned (but either ignored or forgotten by proponents of aerial warfare). As General Mark Clark later wrote:

. . . The Air Force and the Navy carriers may have kept us from losing the war, but they were denied the opportunity of influencing the outcome decisively in our favor. They gained complete mastery of the skies, gave magnificent support to the infantry, destroyed every worthwhile target in North Korea, and took a costly toll of enemy personnel and supplies.

But as in Italy [in World War II], where we learned the same bitter lesson in the same kind of rugged country, our air power could not keep a steady stream of enemy supplies and reinforcements from reaching the battle line. Air [power] could not "isolate" the front. . . .[6]

Lieutenant General James Gavin was even more critical:

. . . For the Air Force, Korea had been a disillusioning and frustrating experience. Air Force leaders had assumed that air superiority, air surveillance and air attacks would smash the North Korean drive and demolish the North Korean military establishment. They had trumpeted this point of view both to the public and to the President. When the bombing failed to halt the North Korean war effort they developed the myth of the Yalu sanctuary. If only they could bomb Red Chinese Manchuria, which lay beyond

5. Ridgway (*The War in Korea*), *supra*.
6. Mark Clark, op. cit.

the Yalu River, they said, everything would turn out all right. Thus the Air Force was able to avoid, at least in public, confronting the evidence that in Korea both strategically and tactically air power had failed. Unfortunately from their frustration sprang a readiness to answer any challenge to American power with threats of total nuclear war.[7]

In those momentous months of 1964 and 1965, Johnson and his advisers displayed massive historical ignorance of air power. Johnson himself had fallen victim to a powerful civil-military lobby that preached virtues of air power without mentioning its severe limitations. Ignorant of the true nature of the war in Vietnam, frustrated at lack of progress in "winning" it, and frightened by recent and substantial reverses, Johnson proved particularly prone to panaceas.

Judging from later events, he probably also believed that he could control the action, that he needn't place all military eggs in one basket. In his mind, he could turn air power on and off like a water tap, and if this did not succeed, he could follow with ground and sea power. The Joint Chiefs of Staff and some top civil advisers assured that, if necessary, American military might could "win" the war in Vietnam—it was a matter of application. These were essentially the same voices that had tried to persuade President Kennedy to fight a war in Laos. In 1961, they failed. In 1965, they succeeded.

Their rationale is of interest, first, because as bombing began and failed, it changed; second, because the Nixon administration brought it back to life. Maxwell Taylor early wrote:

. . . by February, 1965, it had become perfectly apparent that we must strike at this external base [North Vietnam] and do so for three reasons . . . to let the people of South Vietnam feel that for the first time, after eleven years of bitter warfare, they were striking back against the source of all their troubles [!] . . . to utilize our superiority in the air to strike military targets which, if destroyed, would have the effect of restraining or making more difficult the infiltration of men and supplies from North Vietnam into South Vietnam . . . to remind the leadership in Hanoi, the men who were directing this war in the South, that little by little through the progressive, restrained application of force by bombing, they would pay an ever-increasing price for a continuation of their aggression in the South. In other words, we were following the basic military principle applicable to all wars—that the objective of military action is the will of the enemy—in the conviction that, by the use of our air power, we could operate on that will and eventually create in the minds of the leadership of Hanoi a picture of the inevitability of defeat and the realization of the prohibitive cost of continued aggression. . . .[8]

7. Gavin (*Crisis Now*), *supra.*
8. Maxwell Taylor (*Responsibility and Response*), *supra.*

Some hawks went even further. Admiral Sharp wrote in 1969 that the secret to "winning" the war in Vietnam was relatively simple: ". . . All that we had to do to win was to use our existing air power—properly."[9] Sharp, as well as members of the JCS and other hawks, argued from the beginning for the Pentagon's Option B: ". . . fast full squeeze" with "hot-blood actions" (see Chapters 80 and 81). He and his "colleagues in the field" wanted ". . . to bring the economy of North Vietnam to a halt," naturally by bombing. Parroting Rostow's earlier thesis, Sharp argued that ". . . the primary purpose of the air campaign against North Vietnam should have been to disrupt the enemy's economy and thus destroy his ability to wage war." Sharp wanted ". . . a sustained, maximum-effort attack on all of the enemy's war-supporting industries, transportation facilities, military complexes, petroleum-storage depots . . ."; he wanted Haiphong Harbor mined and the port closed. Although he understood that ". . . the Joint Chiefs of Staff supported my position 100 percent," most of his requests were denied by Secretary of Defense McNamara, who ". . . arbitrarily and consistently discarded the advice of his military advisers."

About all the reader can say is thank God he did, for Sharp goes on:

. . . It may well be that our civilian leadership believed that to use our military tools properly, to eliminate the enemy's ability to make war would have been to risk a nuclear confrontation with the Soviet Union. Personally, I believe the risk was minimal; in any case, a nation which is not willing to take calculated risks to achieve its objectives should never go to war in the first place. Further, I believe that once a political decision is made to commit American troops to battle, we are morally obliged to use our military power in such a way as to end the fighting as quickly as possible.[10]

If Taylor and other advisers did not go as far as Rostow, Sharp, and the JCS, they nonetheless erred, not only in estimating strategic effects of air power but also in estimating tactical effects of air power in guerrilla warfare. It is a great pity that these influential experts had never studied such recent insurgencies as those in Indonesia, the Philippines, Malaya, Cyprus, and French Indochina, where interdiction air raids played about as effective a role in the ground action as Drake's naval raids on the Spanish Main played in England's war against Spain. In the same work quoted above, Taylor pointed to

. . . the inability of the enemy to maintain and keep in action an indefinite number of men supported only by a clandestine logistic system. Their logistic problem increases if we continue to conduct air attacks against their lines of supply. It grows if, by the use of our mobile offensive capability, our heliborne forces keep attacking the main forces of the Vietcong, requiring them to defend themselves, to consume ammunition and supplies, and to suffer

9. Sharp, op. cit.
10. Ibid.; see also Johnson (*The Vantage Point*), *supra*.

heavy casualties. Under such pressures, they probably cannot maintain much larger forces than they have now.[11]

Taylor was seeing the enemy in Taylor's terms: He failed to realize that PAVN had not attained Western military sophistication and that its logistic demands were not to be compared with American demands. Tactical bombing against conventional armies brings meager rewards—against quasi-guerrilla armies, it brings virtually no rewards. American intelligence estimated that the *entire* Viet Cong needed twelve tons of outside supply per day[12] (versus five hundred tons daily needed to support operations by the 1st Cavalry [Airmobile] Division alone!) to carry on. How are you going to interdict effectively such a meager supply requirement?

President Johnson's decision in 1965, then, ignored two primary lessons concerning air power furnished by the past. The first was that chances were virtually nil of bending Hanoi's will to the extent of bringing a cringing North Vietnam Government to the conference table. Unless, it should be added, atomic bombs were employed—but this was unacceptable from both moral and practical viewpoints, and the President knew this.

The second was that aerial interdiction could impede but not stop passage of men and supplies from North to South. Neither could it noticeably halt production in North Vietnam, because the industrial complex essential to furnishing targets to bombers did not exist. To halt cottage production meant eliminating cottages, a lengthy, repugnant, and expensive task, as we learned in the strategic-bombing effort against Japan in World War II. To stop arms and equipment from entering North Vietnam meant risking war by interdicting Chinese and Soviet supply lines, and since the Administration wished to avoid war with either nation, this meant that supply lines would remain open.

These lessons proved valid.

Almost everything that history either had suggested or confirmed about aerial bombing was demonstrated in North Vietnam and along the Ho Chi Minh Trail by end of 1967.

The first outstanding fact was expense in American lives and machines. Although North Vietnam possessed neither an air force nor early-warning systems nor sophisticated anti-aircraft weapons, in response to early American raids the Soviets and Chinese vied in supplying anti-aircraft guns and missiles. Soviet SAM missile sites soon appeared around priority objectives. As early as 1966, American pilots were reporting that North Vietnam bridges were protected by ". . . an awe-

---

11. Maxwell Taylor (*Responsibility and Response*), *supra*.
12. Browne, op. cit.; see also McNamara's analysis, *The Pentagon Papers*, *supra* (pp. 550–51 and 577–85); Hoopes, op. cit.; Weller, op. cit.

some curtain of exploding steel,"[13] words similar to those used by American pilots flying over Dien Bien Phu in 1954. Hundreds of aircraft were shot down; pilots and crews were killed; pilots and crews were to languish in North Vietnamese prison camps.

The second fact was operational cost compared to results obtained.

It is difficult even for a student of warfare to comprehend the vastness of the American air effort. By end of 1967, American airplanes—air force, navy, and marine—had dropped more bombs on Vietnam than the allied total expended on Germany in World War II. We must add to this hundreds of thousands of rockets and machine-gun bullets and tons of napalm. Initial operational costs shot upward and continued to rise, not a matter of millions of dollars, but of billions, which does not include more billions of indirect cost.

The third fact was international opprobrium wrought by bombings. In Ramsey Clark's words,

. . . Few people in Asia, Africa or Latin America can identify sympathetically with well-fed representatives of a rich society journeying ten thousand miles to pilot multimillion dollar B-52s and drop death and destruction on underfed Indochinese in miserable villages or along jungle trails.[14]

In early 1966, George Kennan warned the Senate Foreign Relations Committee that strategic bombing would jeopardize American relationships with Japan and other nations:

. . . Our motives are widely misinterpreted, and the spectacle . . . of Americans inflicting grievous injury on the lives of a poor and helpless people, and particularly a people of different race and color, no matter how warranted by military necessity or by the excesses of the adversary our operations may seem to us to be or may genuinely be, produces reactions among millions of people throughout the world profoundly detrimental to the image we would like them to hold of this country.[15]

International voices soon confirmed the validity of this warning. In Charles de Gaulle's words, ". . . We find it totally detestable that a small country should be bombed by a very big one." Arthur Schlesinger has concluded that bombings have brought

. . . the rise of a new form of anti-Americanism, emotional rather than ideological, leading toward a serious estrangement between Europe and America. . . . When we began to bomb the oil deposits, James Reston wrote, "There is now not a single major nation in the world that supports Mr. Johnson's latest adventure in Hanoi and Haiphong. . . ."[16]

13. Harvey, op. cit.
14. Ramsey Clark, "On Violence, Peace and the Rule of Law," *Foreign Affairs*, October 1970.
15. U. S. Senate (*The Vietnam Hearings*), *supra*.
16. Schlesinger (*Bitter*), *supra*.

Other difficulties, unique to Vietnam, also existed. Townsend Hoopes, who was Assistant Secretary of the Air Force in 1967, later listed ". . . four adverse and intractable factors" when it came to bombing effectiveness in the North. One was relatively small supply needs of the North, both for its own purposes and to pursue war in the South. Another was the North's ability to keep going under heavy bombardment. The third was poor weather for most of the year: From late September to early May, ". . . visual bombing attacks were possible on the average of only five days per month, and were frequently precluded for from two to three weeks at a time." This meant not only diminution of attacks, but, the fourth factor, inaccurate bombing: ". . . in bad weather the bombs fell, on the average, between 1,500 and 1,800 feet from the target center." Due to the military policy of "massive retaliation" during the Eisenhower era, ". . . bombing accuracies had improved hardly at all in the period between Korea and Vietnam."[17]

What was the net accomplishment?

Very little, except once again to disprove the Douhet theory and confirm Sir Robert Thompson's later suggestion that ". . . the bombing of the North was probably the greatest of the strategic errors of the war."[18] In fairness to Douhet, and as any number of American air force officers and other hawks have repeatedly stated, the American effort was selective (in theory, anyway) and not a saturation-bombing program. At President Johnson's insistence, planes bombed and strafed "military" targets only. Major targets at first consisted of forward supply depots and installations and of "choke points," for example key bridges or railroad yards or warehouses and oil depots. As these were neutralized or destroyed, air intelligence officers furnished secondary targets, usually smaller depots and railheads. Planes flying "armed reconnaissance" also fired on targets of opportunity, such as convoys and trains, repair parties, occasional troop units; if nothing else, planes dropped bomb loads on roads and rail lines.

As bombs and bullets killed more bridges and culverts and roads, then exploded on factories and refineries, then crept around and into Hanoi and killed and wounded thousands of civilians, and as General Curtis LeMay spoke of bombing the North Vietnamese back to the stone age—the moral and material fallacies were becoming more apparent. Harrison Salisbury, veteran correspondent of the New York *Times,* visited Hanoi in December 1966 and January 1967. He found the city in a state of defense, with thousands of individual concrete shelters ". . . spaced three or four feet apart along every boulevard and street

17. Hoopes, op. cit.
18. RUSI Seminar, *supra.*

in the city, round dark cavities with concrete lids."[19] Rather than shocked and frightened, the people struck him as determined:

. . . I seldom talked with any North Vietnamese without some reference coming into the conversation of the people's preparedness to fight ten, fifteen, even twenty years in order to achieve victory. . . . I began to realize that this was a national psychology. It might have been inspired by the regime, but it certainly was entirely natural. And, I believed, it suited the North Vietnamese temperament. . . .

The regime had little trouble in exploiting this feeling into strength. Mr. Salisbury was shown what could hardly have been a staged scene: the wreck of the Vandien truck park, on the outskirts of Hanoi,

. . . listed as one of the major targets of our December 13 [1966] attack. It was not a formidable target when I viewed it from Route Nationale No. 1 —just a half-dozen loading sheds, blasted by American bombs. But in attacking these the bombers had wrecked what was called the Polish Friendship School, probably half a mile distant on the other side of the highway. . . . I could accept the bombing of the school as an accident. But I was not surprised to find that the North Vietnamese thought it was deliberate. . . .

The "major" target, incidentally, contained twelve or fourteen broken-down buses and trucks. As Salisbury rhetorically asked: ". . . For this kind of target was it worth jeopardizing $2-million planes and the precious lives of American pilots?"

The North Vietnamese Government constantly exploited, from the propaganda standpoint, other bombing mistakes, such as destruction of Namdinh village in an attempt to neutralize its rail yards. Even without mistakes, the government would have had little difficulty in exploiting the people's hatred. Fixed installations were few in North Vietnam; they had been built by personal sacrifice, and the people could hardly refrain from hating that which destroyed them. The government went so far as to arm factory workers and some citizens in Hanoi with ordinary rifles, which they fired at attacking planes. David Schoenbrun, the respected CBS correspondent, later confirmed Salisbury's findings:

. . . Anyone who drives down Mandarin Road, as this correspondent did, learns how cruelly futile American bombing has been, for it has only wrought physical destructions and failed utterly to accomplish any military or psychological purpose.

It has filled people with hatred and redoubled their determination to fight on harder than ever.[20]

19. Harrison E. Salisbury, *Behind the Lines—Hanoi* (New York: Harper & Row, 1967); see also David Schoenbrun, "Journey to North Vietnam," *The Saturday Evening Post,* March 1968; see also David Schoenbrun, *Vietnam* (New York: Atheneum, 1968).
20. Quoted in Gavin (*Crisis Now*), *supra.*

A Communist diplomat in Hanoi told Salisbury: ". . . I think something like this happened in England . . . in the days when the German Air Force attacked the British. As a Communist I have been interested to see the ideological propaganda gradually being replaced by national patriotic appeal. Maybe you remember something like this in the Soviet Union during the critical days of the German attack."[21]

Bombings also lent strength to a burgeoning youth cult who already preached hatred of the United States. Salisbury wrote of a hero cult that centered on Nguyen Van Troy, a Saigon teen-ager executed for attempting to assassinate Secretary of Defense Robert McNamara in 1965. In a neighborhood theater in Hanoi, he witnessed

. . . a kind of variety hall performance, songs, dances and skits. Of the fourteen acts twelve were devoted to epics of bravery. In one a group of ferrymen pulled their craft across a river in the face of fierce attack by United States planes. Several were killed, but they shot down an American aircraft. In a dance number a Red Cross nurse whose husband had been killed tore from her head the traditional Vietnamese white mourning veil and used it to bind up the wounds of an antiaircraft gunner. In another a Vietcong detachment stormed an American strongpoint and captured it despite terrible losses. . . .

The theme of the songs and the ballets was patriotism. The portraits of heroism were simple and humorless. The audience, judging by the intense and serious expressions I saw on the faces around me, took the tableaux with complete literalness. They lived the little sketches of war—their war. These were their heroes. They saw nothing naive or made-up about these schoolboy vignettes. They themselves were mostly schoolboys. North Vietnam was a very young country. This, in large measure, was a teen-age war. I was impressed by the fact that again and again the same theme was repeated—that of fighting back against the American bombers, of shooting down American aircraft. . . .

If the reader thinks this is patriotic schmaltz, he is correct. He should remember, however, that Salisbury's description was not far removed from the American scene created by the Japanese bombing of Pearl Harbor: a scene dominated by emotion, by the song "Praise the Lord and Pass the Ammunition," by Colin Kelly allegedly dropping bombs down the smokestack of a Japanese cruiser—by a national reaction that jammed recruiting centers in every state of the union. It is perhaps superfluous to add that the scene described by Salisbury did not discourage recruitment into the North Vietnamese army.

Not only did Hanoi's will survive bombing, but substantial material gains failed to result. As expert and experienced voices soon pointed out, interdiction was not materially influencing the flow of men and supply to the South. A bomb can hit a train or a truck only with difficulty;

21. Salisbury, op. cit.

it can rarely hit a coolie pushing a loaded bicycle along a narrow jungle trail. A bomb can interdict a bridge, which a mass labor force can either repair, replace, or bypass in a night. A bomb can interdict roads and slow traffic. But, as the French learned, mass labor can repair roads quickly; supply will get through and so will small guerrilla forces marching at night or under jungle cover to evade eyes flying overhead.

If air strategists such as Taylor, LeMay, Sharp, and Wheeler had studied Harrison Salisbury's report, they might have had second thoughts. Salisbury personally saw what past experience and present photographic reconnaissance already had demonstrated: that bombs had closed neither roads nor railroads to traffic:

. . . We had certainly destroyed sections of the railroad time and again. I could see bridges that had been blasted beyond repair. I bumped over stretches of highway that had been relaid several times. Yet traffic was moving. It was moving in very large quantities. And this, I quickly learned, was not just because a Christmas truce was on. . . . Never, so far as I could learn, had it been seriously impeded. Difficulties, yes. Barriers, no.

Mr. Salisbury attributed this to ". . . a massive investment of manpower, labor and matériel and a careful utilization of national resources." This was Korea all over again: Bombed roads offered only slight repair problems. Bridges were more difficult, but could be replaced by pontoons:

. . . They were made by lashing together the required number of shallow flat-bottomed wooden canal boats. . . . A surface of cut bamboo poles was laid across them, without even being lashed or nailed in many cases. Or, if available, a surface of bamboo planks. The trucks lumbered over the pontoons with a roar as their wheels hit the loose poles, but the pontoons seemed sturdy enough to bear the heavy traffic. In most cases where a permanent bridge was knocked out, two pontoons were pressed into service—one to handle traffic moving south, the other to accommodate the empty trucks returning north.

Foreigners who had watched the pontoons being put into place said this seldom took more than a couple of hours. The boats and bamboo poles were kept available at every bridge, the expectation being that sooner or later the bridge would be knocked out.

Railroad bridges provided the most difficult repair or replacement problem:

. . . But here, too, native ingenuity was called into play. If the rail line was blocked by destruction of a bridge or trackage, bicycle brigades were called up. Five hundred men and women and their bicycles would be sent to the scene of the break. They would unload the stalled freight train, putting the cargo on the bikes. Each bicycle would handle a sixty-pound load, balanced across the frame with a bar. The bicycles would be wheeled, not ridden, over a pontoon bridge, and on the other side of the break a second train would be drawn up. The cargo would be reloaded and moved on south.

So much effort went to keeping the railroads functioning that Mr. Salisbury wondered why the North Vietnamese did not abandon it in favor of roads:

. . . The answer was not readily forthcoming. It was obvious that the North Vietnamese took enormous pride in keeping the railroad going. It was a symbol of their ability to overcome the enormous technological advantage of the Americans. . . .

A more practical consideration also came into play: North Vietnam produced its own coal, but gasoline and oil to feed motor vehicles had to be imported.

A further factor also helped to explain the Vietnamese success. The logistic load necessary to keep the war going in the South was nowhere near what Saigon or Washington estimated. American planners, accustomed to logistic "tails" of forty thousand men per seventeen thousand man division, of POL (petroleum-oil-lubricant) requirements measured in thousands of tons did not envisage the simplicity of the enemy's supply system. Once American planes had blown up oil storage tanks around Haiphong and Hanoi, that should have ended the flow of trucks to the South. Instead, the enemy dispersed fifty-five-gallon drums at various supply points. Bombing could not eliminate these depots; they slowed, but they did not stop, traffic. Mr. Salisbury noticed this dispersal technique:

. . . I saw crates and bits of machinery, large weapons cases, huge boxes which contained, I guessed, shells and munitions, hardware of the most diverse sort, simply staked out in fields, let down beside rural roads, cluttering paths that led to rice paddies—indeed, in all the time I rode about the countryside I think I was never more than two or three minutes out of sight of some kind of supplies and equipment which had come to rest in the most unlikely setting.[22]

Even by the time of Mr. Salisbury's visit, the maximum effect of American bombing had been achieved, and it was little enough. It had not stopped Chinese and Soviet supplies from entering Vietnam, and it had slowed, but in no instance stopped, those supplies from going south. Escalation of the air war and a change of emphasis from North to South and then back again—from the Hanoi area to the Laotian border back to Hanoi—resulted in few substantial accomplishments, with almost no effect on the war in the South. The greatest accomplishment of the air war in the North lay in the reconnaissance field: On occasion, infrared radar cameras spotted troop build-ups such as that north of

22. Ibid.

the Demilitarized Zone in the spring of 1967, and resulted in profitable bombing operations. But such isolated instances cannot alter the program's destructive failure.

Like a medicine that failed to cure a disease, bombing of the North resulted in unpleasant side effects. An important one was propaganda value derived by Hanoi. Some of the world detected and did not like the paternalism evident in the President's words: You stop fighting in the South, North Vietnam, or Daddy will spank. When Daddy did spank, some of the world, and a great portion of the underdeveloped world, identified with the child. Unfortunately, selective bombing did not prevent civil casualties, which Hanoi, from the beginning, exploited internationally. North Vietnam had no air force and at first only primitive air defenses to counter American planes, and to some, the United States appeared as an aggressive bully, a posture exploited by Communist propaganda everywhere.

Another side effect concerned Hanoi's relations with Moscow and Peking. In late 1964 and early 1965, the U.S.S.R. cautiously favored another Geneva conference, a notion rejected by Peking, which was posing as friendly protector to Hanoi. In February 1965, Premier Kosygin made an important bid to replace Chinese influence in the North Vietnamese capital. He led a strong delegation to Hanoi, where he found some support for settlement by negotiation—despite American air attacks, which Washington hastily explained were taken in "retaliation" for an NLF attack against Pleiku. The situation was later analyzed by a particularly astute observer, Professor Donald Zagoria:

. . . It thus appears that as of early 1965, Moscow was anxious to bring about negotiations, Peking was trying to forestall them, and the Hanoi leadership was somewhere in the middle—ready to listen to American proposals, but internally divided on whether to continue applying military pressure on the south or to negotiate.[23]

The March bombings, followed by a massive commitment of American troops, placed Hanoi moderates in an impossible position and thus altered the diplomacy of the U.S.S.R. As Zagoria wrote, ". . . Hanoi's position began to harden and the Russians became increasingly sensitive to Chinese criticism that they were anxious to make a deal with the United States to end the war on terms disadvantageous to Hanoi." The Soviet Union, in other words, had to react to the new set of rules imposed by the American Government, and so did China. Where, formerly, aid to Hanoi was spasmodic and never particularly generous, now it became a token in the Sino-Soviet conflict—to Hanoi's profit. And along with that, Moscow ditched any hope for a negotiated settlement, or, as Zagoria wrote, ". . . the Russians moved to the diplomatic sidelines, letting initiatives pass to North Vietnam and the NLF."

23. Zagoria (*Vietnam Triangle*), *supra.*

But that was only one facet of this complicated situation. By spring of 1965, the rift between Peking and Moscow had grown very wide. Officials in both capitals displayed a loquacious virulence that has few parallels in historical non-shooting situations. American diplomacy had played almost no part in developing this rift. So far as the West was concerned, it came as a bonus from the historical process; it was the greatest boon to the West since Tito's defection, in 1947, and was far more momentous, and it should have been carefully nurtured and exploited by American diplomacy. As we have seen, the Kennedy administration seemed surprisingly unaware of the developing rift. The Johnson administration seemed almost bewildered by it. Far from appreciating its importance, Johnson continued with the one policy that could have led to rapprochement between the two titans. Khrushchev's departure from the Soviet Government, coupled with the March bombings, touched off a political quarrel in Peking, where influential members of the army argued for a common front with the U.S.S.R. to resist American aggression. The quarrel exploded into civil war, which Mao Tse-tung won only with the greatest difficulty. Had he lost—and the issue may not yet be decided—a very grave shift in the present balance of power might well have occurred, with difficult consequences for the West.

All this was bad enough, but, whatever the attitude of the Soviet Union and China, Hanoi could not have remained complacent in response. Whether Ho Chi Minh and his advisers wanted the North to participate more actively in the South is not known. We do know that, at the time (and later), the Hanoi power group contained hawks and doves, just as did the NLF in the South. This was only natural: The war in the South had created definite stresses in the North, and there were those who wished to terminate it and those who wished to escalate it and those who wished to pursue a middle course. By reducing and even eliminating these intraparty stresses, American bombings gave Hanoi hawks virtually a free hand to escalate the action further.

Chapter 90

The summing up (III): the war on the ground • Westmore-
land's strategy • Westmoreland, Walt, and the enemy • The
helicopter • Khe Sanh • The tactical challenge • Never the
twain shall meet • King An Ya: ". . . The peasant despises
nothing more than a fool" • The school solution • CAP: Bel-
isarius versus Narses

THE STRATEGY CHOSEN to fight the war in South Vietnam was another major reason for President Johnson's failure. It was not altogether his fault: President Kennedy had yielded to military control in Vietnam, and Johnson also supposed he could trust the knowledge and judgment of such responsible military advisers as the Joint Chiefs of Staff, theater commanders, and special advisers such as Maxwell Taylor.

This was a mistake.

A long time ago, Clausewitz noted that ". . . the most important single judgment a political or military leader can make is to forecast correctly the nature of war upon which the nation is to embark. On this everything else depends." Johnson's military advisers failed to forecast correctly the nature of this war; Johnson held neither knowledge nor experience to question their judgment, and he lacked inclination to consult those who could have helped him. Once he had erred, first by bombing the North, second by committing a large number of conventional American troop units, he compounded error by permitting further escalation. It would have taken a much more intelligent and courageous man to withstand surrounding pressures and do otherwise. He did otherwise only when a greater pressure—American public opinion—forced him to it.

The United States armed forces were relatively well organized for either nuclear or non-nuclear war when they were committed in strength to Vietnam, in spring of 1965. Unfortunately, they were neither well organized, properly equipped, nor adequately trained to cope with insurgency warfare.

We have already discussed Westmoreland's attrition strategy—a dependence on superior U.S. military manpower, firepower, and mobility to wear down and finally force the enemy from the war. In the July 1968 issue of *Army Quarterly,* a retired American army lieutenant colonel, J. J. Haggerty, undertook to explain this strategy to a British audience. Although grammatically and stylistically deficient, his words are of interest in that they reflect a wide stratum of belief within the army and indeed the American military establishment. Once Westmoreland landed his troops and tidied up logistics, Haggerty explained, he

. . . planned to use the United States superiority in mobility and firepower to strike the enemy concentrations with a spoiling attack. The latter would keep the enemy off balance and gradually wear him down to the point of exhaustion and desperation.

Upon completion of the build-up, United States ground forces, in conjunction with air and naval strikes, would launch sustained offensives directed against the enemy and enemy bases. War is extremely expensive and luckily the United States is wealthy enough to bear the cost of a large-scale continued pressure against the Viet Cong. The constant harassment by United States and South Vietnamese forces is seriously hurting the North Vietnamese conventional forces and is impairing their logistical system. It is hoped that if such tactics were successful the North Vietnamese and the Viet Cong would be forced from the populated fertile areas into the mountains. If this were the case, the enemy would be denied food, intelligence and recruits without which the resistance movement would wither and die. The people are a flexible lot, and once the yoke of Viet Cong terror control is lifted from their necks, and once they believe the Government can protect them, they will quickly sever their connections with the hated assassins.

The ever-present Allied pounding from ground, sea and air, the loss of the support of the civilian population, the guerrillas suffering more and more casualties, and the North Vietnamese and Viet Cong lack of noticeable victories—all will take their toll of the fighting heart. Morale will suffer horribly and will dip markedly and this will open the door to greater defections and surrenders. The pages of military history are strewn with examples of once proud military units crumbling under continual defeats and retreats.[1]

1. J. J. Haggerty, "South Vietnam and the Munich Crossroad," *Army Quarterly,* July 1968.

Westmoreland's conventional strategy, one with which the JCS and Johnson's military advisers concurred, was designed to gain a military decision, and it must be faulted on several counts.

It was a quantitative, as opposed to a qualitative, or selective, strategy: an open-ended strategy in a challenge that called for task-force strategy. If so many men and machines could not "win," its proponents argued, more men and machines could "win." Writing in the *Marine Corps Gazette,* in March 1966, Colonel Norman Stanford, ". . . a Japanese and French linguist who has served ten years in Asia in a variety of military and diplomatic billets," argued that the recent French concept of pacification in Indochina was a sound idea:

. . . the French effort, a gallant one with some 75,000 French Union troops killed in action (US KIA in Korea were about 29,000), failed not because of a faulty concept but because insufficient personnel and equipment were available to accomplish the combined combat/pacification mission.[2]

This was the Hindenburg-Ludendorff argument of post-World War I. Instead of admitting to errors of judgment, to mistaken political, strategic, and tactical concepts, the German commanders sought to blame military defeat on civil failure: the stab-in-the-back thesis.

This has happened before in history where commanders have erred in judgment, a major failure that generally is explained by ignorance of and resultant contempt for an enemy. Did Westmoreland and the JCS and other hawks really expect Hanoi to sit quietly by and allow American forces to defeat the Viet Cong in the South? If they did, they were as short-sighted as both the Romans and the French in Spain. If they did not, then they wittingly deluded the American people—a form of military blackmail practiced on a lesser scale by Gordon of Khartoum and Lyautey of Morocco.

In 1965, American ground hawks were as arrogant as air hawks. Roswell Gilpatric, for example, noted in May of that year that ". . . U.S. military power is greater, in a higher state of readiness, and better disposed than it ever has been on the eve of a possible major conflict."[3] Considering size and weight of the American military machine, commanders probably felt much as Roman commanders had felt when setting out to subdue recalcitrant Iberian tribes, or as French commanders felt two thousand years later when leading armies into Spain. Our command confidence was as misplaced. It is a great pity that our officers and officials had not analyzed these and other irregular campaigns, that they had not heeded warnings such as that delivered by Jomini:

. . . All the gold of Mexico could not have procured reliable information for the French [in Spain]; what was given was but a lure to make them fall more readily into snares.

2. Stanford, op. cit.
3. Gilpatric, op. cit.

No army, however disciplined, can contend successfully against such a system applied to a great nation, unless it be strong enough to hold all the essential points of the country, cover its communications, and at the same time furnish an active force sufficient to beat the enemy wherever he may present himself. If this enemy has a regular army of respectable size to be a nucleus around which to rally the people, what force will be sufficient to be superior everywhere, and to assure the safety of the long lines of communication against numerous bodies?

The Peninsular War should be carefully studied, to learn all the obstacles which a general and his brave troops may encounter in the occupation or conquest of a country whose people are all in arms. . . .[4]

American command ignorance was not justified in Vietnam. The Viet Cong repeatedly had demonstrated that they could fight and fight well. They had also shown tactical flexibility. When American armored personnel carriers and helicopters gained the upper hand in spring and summer of 1962, the enemy folded fighting wings until they adjusted to new instruments of war. In 1963, the Viet Cong began gaining tactical ascendancy to the extent that, in 1964, Hanoi intervened more openly and the third stage of the insurgency commenced.

Hanoi's failure to panic when American bombs started dropping in the North was surely significant, as was Vo Nguyen Giap's statement, in June 1965, that the Viet Cong would fight ". . . only to the point that the enemy could be brought to the conference table and there defeated"—which was the position of the Viet Minh vis-à-vis France in 1954.[5] The Viet Cong offensive in summer of 1965 added weight to Giap's words, as did the first appearance in strength of North Vietnamese (PAVN) regiments. When the American build-up blunted the enemy effort—essentially a VC effort—still another cautionary voice sounded from the enemy camp. This was Mao's top general, Lin Piao, who, in September 1965, wrote a lengthy and somewhat ambiguous article on liberation wars. If some persons interpreted his words as warning to Hanoi not to expect active Chinese involvement in Vietnam, he nonetheless made it clear that Hanoi held the option of changing strategy and fighting a protracted war.[6]

Such was the initial success of American arms in the South that this thought seemingly did not intrude itself into American strategic thinking. The military bias of American strategy effectively shielded the political bias of enemy strategy. Westmoreland and other military leaders, and civilians as well, could not but see the war in conventional terms despite its guerrilla trappings. They consistently underestimated the enemy's military potential. Westmoreland believed that the enemy was unimaginative and inflexible. In November 1966, he was asked: "What are the

4. Jomini, op. cit.
5. Shaplen (*The Road from War*), *supra*.
6. Zagoria (*The Viet Nam Triangle*), *supra*.

chances of the Viet Cong main-force units reverting to strictly guerrilla warfare?" He made this incredible reply:

. . . Of course, if the enemy did this, he would be going contrary to his doctrine. He has rigidly followed Mao Tse-tung's three-phase doctrine for Communist insurgency warfare. Under this doctrine, phase one provides the political structure, phase two the guerrilla force, and phase three large, conventional-type formations that can fight open warfare. If he moved back to phase two, it would be admitting defeat. And I think this would be hard on the morale of the leadership and the troops.[7]

Westmoreland's words suggest that he had never studied either Mao Tse-tung's writings (see Chapter 27, Volume I) or Giap's campaigns against the French (see Chapters 52–56 and 62–63). His confusion was matched only by the first marine commander in Vietnam, Lieutenant General Lewis Walt, who, according to the New York *Times*, told newsmen in Washington, in November 1970,

. . . that when we went to Vietnam in the summer of 1965, he did not understand that this was primarily a guerrilla war. Like many officers who were over-optimistic in the early years of the war, he thought in terms of World War II and the Korean War, when the enemy was easy to identify.
    To illustrate what he termed his naiveté, he said he had once interviewed a man in a Vietnamese village who claimed to be the village chief and who gave him an optimistic report. Later he felt a tug at his pocket and found that a village woman had slipped a note into his pocket warning him that he had been talking to the regional chief of the Vietcong.[8]

Walt further expressed his confusion in his book *Strange War, Strange Strategy,* and explained it in these extraordinary words:

. . . Before our involvement in Vietnam we knew practically nothing of its people. As late as 1958 there was no history of them printed in the English language. There are only two or three today, none widely read.[9]

If the reader will turn to my bibliography (Volume I), which does not include extensive intelligence studies of Indochina available to the author in the early 1950s (and surely to General Walt), he will note that the general errs. As for Walt's stigmatization of Giap as an inept commander (in the same book), this is a matter of criteria. One thinks of Foch walking in his garden at critical times in World War I and asking himself, "De quoi s'agit-il?"—What is the problem? One suggests that Giap held a rather more fundamental grasp of the problem than either Walt, Westmoreland—or the JCS.
    Having committed the military crime of underrating the opponent,

7. *U. S. News and World Report,* November 28, 1966.
8. New York *Times,* Washington, November 18, 1970.
9. Walt (*Strange War, Strange Strategy*), *supra.*

our military leaders fell victim to tactical panaceas occasioned by technology. Early ground actions caused a good many commanders, not all, to believe that they had found the key to fighting insurgency warfare. The key was the helicopter, which furnished mobility essential to locating the enemy and bringing superior firepower to bear on him. So impressed was Secretary of Defense Robert McNamara with early operations of the 1st Cavalry (Airmobile) Division, that he said the helicopter marked ". . . the beginning of a new era in land warfare."

But dissident voices also spoke. As early as February 1966, Sir Robert Thompson, a veteran counterinsurgency campaigner, complained of American misuse of helicopters in general, pointing out that they should primarily support clear-and-hold operations rather than chase ". . . Viet Cong guerrilla units around the jungle." Thompson astutely observed that extensive availability of helicopters ". . . has exaggerated two great weaknesses of the American character in counter-insurgency—impatience and aggressiveness."[10] The Australian army's manual on counter-revolutionary warfare warned: ". . . Any tendency to do something rather than nothing must be avoided if the something involves precipitate military action."[11]

What American commanders failed to realize was what the British learned in Borneo: that the helicopter is another form of transport and cannot replace tactical necessities including need for intelligence. As General Sir Walter Walker later explained:

. . . Our intelligence was such that we always knew when the Indonesians were about to attack across the frontier. The problem was to get troops to positions to ambush them, or to attack them before they got back to their side of the frontier. The only way in which we could get troops there in time was by helicopter. If we had used the helicopters as cavalry we would never have succeeded in intercepting them, because we would have lost surprise. So we used helicopters in the same way as we would use other means of mobility to close the gap between us and the enemy, and to land troops quietly so that no one knew where they were. Having done so, the troops got out and searched for and trapped the enemy. When they found them they ambushed them or attacked them. So they were used as a method of preventing the enemy from escaping to their safe sanctuary across the frontier. . . . We did not use our helicopters to get our troops on to the objective, but to close the distance between us and the enemy.[12]

Other shortcomings in American tactics soon appeared. Increased mobility proved expensive. The army's airmobile concept, while sacrificing armor, armored personnel carriers, and firepower heavier than the

10. Robert Thompson, "Feet on the Ground," *Statist,* February 4, 1966.
11. W. S. Tee, "Solutions in Counter-Insurgency Operations," *Army Quarterly,* October 1967.
12. RUSI Seminar, *supra;* see also Walter Walker, "How Borneo Was Born," *The Round Table,* January 1969.

105-mm. howitzer, nevertheless demanded hefty logistic support—
". . . as much as 500 tons per day if the entire division is in combat"
—and could be met by air transport delivery only at virtually prohibitive
cost.[13] Thus land communications, in this case from the coast to An
Khe, had to be kept open—a supporting operation that neither broke
up guerrilla units nor brought relief to peasants, yet furnished targets
to guerrillas. The security requirement of the base camp, a huge area
essential to house and feed the helicopters, also proved onerous, as did
security requirements of outlying bases, permanent or temporary. If a
hundred thousand troops were needed to maintain twenty thousand
combat troops, then fifteen thousand combat troops were needed to produce five thousand troops actively pursuing the enemy.

Further, the initial impact of the helicopter did not last long. Guerrillas heard and recognized helicopters, which meant that the user often
forfeited tactical surprise. Donald Duncan, a Special Forces soldier, later
wrote of this period:

. . . American pilots, having never worked with our [Special Forces] teams,
had no concept of what it was like to be on the ground. They had a propensity for arguing when our directions conflicted with the book. Working
close in, they like to use gun ship escorts—fine for them but lousy for us.
The VC know the pattern of U.S. choppers: a "slick ship" escorted by gun
ships means a landing, so they immediately take position on likely LZs [land-
ing zones]. . . .[14]

Although commanders, on occasion, used decoy techniques and low-
level approaches, the deception nonetheless alerted the enemy that
something was up. More often than not, helicopter operations left tactical initiative to the enemy: He slipped away before the machines landed,
or he fired on machines and then slipped away, or he engaged landing
parties and then slipped away. Sometimes American soldiers and marines killed, wounded, or captured him, but he also shot down a great
many helicopters, ambushed a great number of ground units, and killed
a great many soldiers and marines.

The increase in command communications offered by the helicopter
also proved a mixed blessing. Properly exploited, it helped bring a new
cohesion to the battlefield. But, as one disgruntled colonel told me,
". . . In a tactical environment where the company and battalion commanders should rule, the command helicopter often brought the brigade
or division commander to the small unit tactical scene before either the
company or battalion commander could arrive—the net result was to
dissipate further the lower level commander's already tenuous operational control."

At the same time, American units wasted time, effort, and money

13. Weller, op. cit.
14. Donald Duncan, op. cit.

in blindly pursuing the enemy. Noise limitation combined with excellent enemy intelligence caused a veteran if disillusioned marine combat officer to claim that ". . . less than two percent of all U.S. offensive operations produce any contact whatsoever with the Viet-Cong."[15]

While this figure has been criticized as pessimistic and was raised in 1968, the contact percentage undeniably remained low. Time after time, giant sweeps, either by helicopter or ground operations or both, produced minimum dead or captured Viet Cong. Unfortunately, in a good many instances the operations resulted in civil deaths, which unduly influenced reported "body counts," and in village destruction, which continued to swell casualty and refugee lists.

Neither did blocking operations prosper. Units along Cambodian and Laotian borders expended great effort in blocking Viet Cong lines of communication only to find, as commanders had discovered throughout history, that they expended the bulk of their strength in static defense duties while the enemy made end runs around them. The United States could not furnish enough troops to seal off borders, and strength in one area meant weakness in another. If defense concentrated on a particular zone, the Viet Cong, unburdened by maintenance of large barrack areas and supply depots, ceased operations in favor of striking elsewhere.

Blocking actions in the north, in I Corps area (see map, p. 1187), proved no more decisive. Lacking intelligence, marines blundered into costly fire fights in and south of the DMZ, where they defended strong points such as Khe Sanh only at considerable effort and cost. The Khe Sanh defense, headlined for so long in American newspapers, has been hotly debated. General Westmoreland and Lieutenant General Lewis Walt, commanding III MAF, originally chose to defend Khe Sanh in autumn of 1966, during Operation Prairie, which utilized the airstrip in this inhospitable terrain. What Walt later called ". . . the crucial anchor of our defenses along the demilitarized zone,"[16] played an extremely minor tactical role—a reinforced company formed its defense—until spring of 1967, when it became the focus of battles for Hills 861 and 881, inconclusive actions broken off by the enemy. Quiet again reigned until late autumn of 1967, when garrison reinforcement began under Operation Scotland. Khe Sanh, from that time, was rarely out of the news until overshadowed by the Tet offensive; it then briefly reclaimed the spotlight until the enemy broke off "siege" operations, at end of March 1968.

General Walt subsequently called the siege of Khe Sanh the most important battle in the war.[17] As he explained to a *Reader's Digest* audience, but for the "holding" action at Khe Sanh, two North Vietnamese divisions would have been able to attack Hué during the Tet offensive.

15. Corson, op. cit.
16. Walt ("The Nature of the War in Vietnam"), *supra.*
17. Walt ("Khe Sanh—The Battle That Had to Be Won"), *supra.*

Walt's claim seems meaningless to this writer. At the time of the Khe Sanh build-up, no one in the American or South Vietnamese camp, with the possible exception of some newspaper correspondents, dreamed of a massive Tet offensive against cities and towns. This offensive did not depend on PAVN troops, whether in the Khe Sanh area or elsewhere: The enemy used only a few thousand of an available sixty thousand PAVN troops *already in* South Vietnam. What neither Walt nor Westmoreland nor their planners nor other hawks seemed to appreciate was Giap's momentum tactics: If a battle prospered, pursue it no matter the cost; if a battle did not prosper, take your losses and get out. (Giap had learned this the hard way while fighting the French.) Had the Tet offensive succeeded (assuming that Giap was calling the signals), had the South Vietnamese people risen, Giap had no less than four divisions immediately north of the DMZ that he could, and probably would have committed, along with a substantial troop reserve in South Vietnam. During the fighting at Khe Sanh, marines discovered a secret road *south* of Khe Sanh, which the enemy was using to infiltrate men from Laos. Giap could have contained the Khe Sanh garrison with far fewer troops than he used—according to President Johnson, he had withdrawn half of his force by March 9!

Khe Sanh was one more American effort in a chimerical series to create a battle of Dien Bien Phu, one that American firepower would "win." It was a confession of inadequate intelligence, but, worse, it bespoke a low estimate of Giap's tactical judgment. Despite Giap's having repeatedly adjusted to new tactical challenges since 1946 and repeatedly regained the initiative (which he generally lost only locally), we know that Walt and Westmoreland thought little of his ability.[18]

Did American military leaders really expect Giap to make an all-out assault on Khe Sanh in view of the limited gains of Tet and of overwhelming American supporting arms—a situation totally different from that at Dien Bien Phu? What was in it for Giap? Very little: If he overran the garrison, he stood a good chance of reversing the strong anti-war movement in the United States; in attempting to do so, he undoubtedly would have encountered tactical atomic bombs, which would have introduced a new and dangerous dimension to the war—as it was, American planes dropped over 100,000 tons of bombs around Khe Sanh, more ". . . than had been dropped on any other single target in the history of warfare, including the atomic drop on Hiroshima."[19]

American leaders could term Khe Sanh's defense a "victory," but the word was corrupt. One day, perhaps, we shall learn exactly what Giap had in mind. Evidence suggests that he was using Khe Sanh as a tactical convenience. In the best Sun Tzu and Mao Tse-tung tradition, he was

18. Walt (*Strange War, Strange Strategy*), *supra;* see also Giap (*Big Victory, Great Task*), *supra.* (In this work, General Giap discusses American tactics in detail.)
19. Hoopes, op. cit.

fighting indirect warfare: ". . . Cause an uproar in the east, strike in
the west," as Mao had written, echoing Sun Tzu. Giap's encirclement
of Khe Sanh not only drew marine units from screening northern cities,
but it diverted allied attention during the Viet Cong build-up for the
Tet offensive.

American claims of Khe Sanh's great strategic value are founded
solely on wishful thinking. Khe Sanh was neither "blocking" nor "holding." It was a tactical excrescence and was recognized as such three
months after the American "victory"; in July, marines evacuated the
place, which, according to a marine division commander, Major General
Ray Davis, was ". . . a yoke around my neck."[20] Despite heavy enemy
casualties, Giap continued to hold the initiative in and around the DMZ
and tie down thousands of marines and ARVN troops needed for
counterinsurgency operations.[21]

Westmoreland's "spoiling" and "blocking" tactics may have unbalanced the enemy on occasion, but they did not gain the Americans the
initiative. Moreover, as quantitative tactics, they contained the seeds of
their own destruction. They called for combat troops that Westmoreland
did not have and could not have so long as the American military machine yielded one combat soldier per ten soldiers.[22] They produced
maximum casualties for results obtained. They proved incredibly expensive in supporting arms, and, in the end, they proved unacceptable to
the American people, whose support was necessary if the war was to
continue to escalate.

Why did Westmoreland use "spoiling" tactics, and why did the JCS
condone them?

The first reason was ignorance both of irregular and counterinsurgency warfare. Attrition strategy and search-and-destroy tactics defied
historical precedent. One has to search no farther than Marshal Lyautey's *tache d'huile* concept, which employed clear-and-hold tactics.
Whether moving against an active or a potential enemy, the commander's strength limited his ambition. He had to move slowly, forcing him-

20. UPI, Saigon, July 5, 1968.
21. Neither did McNamara's fence solve anything. Fences, walls—barriers of
all kinds—had been tried from the dawn of history, and most had been found
wanting even in favorable terrain. The difficult terrain of the DMZ, ground hotly
contested and often controlled by VC and PAVN units, ground interdicted by
long-range artillery, made such a project initially impractical. Neither was sensor
technology so advanced as scientists claimed. Finally, the enemy had never infiltrated through the DMZ to the extent reported, but, rather, through Laos by
the Ho Chi Minh Trail, which it continued to use: See Edgar O'Ballance, "The
Ho Chi Minh Trail," *Army Quarterly,* April 1967. In the event, McNamara's
project was quietly dropped—after an expenditure of several million dollars.
22. *Newsweek,* July 5, 1971: An American army officer and veteran of the
Vietnam War, Colonel Hackworth, pointed out that, although the American military force in Vietnam numbered 546,000, ". . . you never had more than 43,000
out in the boonies [boondocks] at one time."

self to build a "show-piece" community of such dimensions as to attract
loyalty and support of people on the spot and the attention of peoples
yet to be pacified. Successful application of the concept called for a slow
and methodical approach—the will to resist encroachment into "asleep"
areas until means became available to clear and hold them.

Contemporary insurgencies, which we have examined previously, emphasized the validity of Lyautey's pacification concept. American command failure to respect these historically proven lessons displayed itself
in Indochina from 1954 onward. In the words of Colonel David Hackworth, an American army ". . . combat veteran of five years in Vietnam
and the most decorated U.S. officer of the Indochinese war,

. . . Westmoreland's over-all strategy was one of search and destroy. He
didn't understand guerrilla warfare, in which the main tenet is protracted
war. When the enemy sees an overwhelming force drop in on his battlefield,
he's going to run away to fight another day. We were just a blind, clumsy,
superstrong giant fighting a swift little midget that was nickel and diming
us to death."[23]

Most of Westmoreland's contemporaries would probably have so
erred—the inevitable result of "molding" American officers to staff and
command norms as if they were some kind of human dough. It was
an attempt to solve an unconventional tactical situation with conventional weapons and tactics, an attempt to make ordinary war out of
extraordinary war. The Joint Chiefs of Staff, Westmoreland, and various
planning staffs did not and possibly could not understand that this was
a war to be fought for the people rather than against a physical enemy.
No matter that information was available to prove this a thousand times
over—one had only to read Douglas Pike's *Viet Cong*—our people would
not accept it. In contrast, in 1968 a senior North Vietnamese leader,
Hoang Quoc Viet, was asked for the secret of revolutionary success in
the South. A British observer, P. J. Honey, later quoted his answer in
part:

. . . In the first place, in order to conduct a successful revolution, you have
got to involve the entire people. It is no use trying to run a revolution with
the Communist Party alone. In order to involve the entire people you must
devise a revolutionary program embodying objectives which will appeal to
the entire people. This necessitates the division of the population into classes,
the study of the interests of each class, and the building of a program from
those which are common to all classes.

The resulting program contains little if any Marxism/Leninism and you
may not like this as a revolutionary communist, but you have to do it if
you are to have any hope of success. This will be known as the "Minimum
Program."

23. Ibid.

During the French domination of Vietnam the construction of a program was not difficult. Our "Minimum Program" called for the ending of French rule and the establishment of national independence, which appealed to everybody.

Honey went on to explain: ". . . The 'Minimum Program' wins mass support and the revolution may then begin, under the clandestine direction and control of the Communist Party but ostensibly a spontaneous national uprising. When the revolution has progressed to a certain stage, then, according to Hoang Quoc Viet, it is essential for the Communist Party to assume overt control of the movement. It does so by moving from this 'Minimum Program' to the 'Maximum Program' which simply means adding the unmistakably Communist goals to the original 'Minimum Program.' "[24]

Little was new about the situation, either politically or tactically. Throughout history, aggressors and defenders have been faced with extraordinary political and military challenges. Those who responded wisely, those who adapted to meet the task at hand are the great captains; the others rest in Valhalla, or, hopefully, in Limbo, where they bore only their fellows with tales of battles almost but not quite won.

Having gotten priorities wrong, Westmoreland and his fellows in the Pentagon failed to realize that a quantitative effort in the highlands and the North was counterproductive. Despite manifold lessons of history, American commanders (always with some splendid exceptions) failed to realize that conventional firepower possessed little validity or effectiveness in an insurgency situation. Conventional weapons "killed" without question—but they killed quantitatively. "Free fire zones" were but an admission of tactical poverty. The tactical problem was one of identifying and neutralizing enemy and reversing the political orientation of a peasantry motivated by terror, if not conviction, to anti-Western attitudes. When weapons killed the innocent, they contributed positively to the insurgent cause. And when weapons were used in such abundance as they were used in Vietnam in 1965–68, they killed many innocents. Sixteen-inch naval shells, 500-pound B-52 bombs, 105-mm. howitzer shells, heavy mortar shells, napalm, aerial strafing, bombs, rockets, bullets—if they hit specific targets, they still could not discriminate what political and ideological motivations were there.

The problem of enemy identification constantly plagued American commanders. Lacking an enemy actually firing a weapon or attempting to hide same, the American soldier was forced to identify on the basis of observation (a patrol, for example, sighting an enemy unit) and interrogation. His best intelligence source remained the peasant, but, in addition to usual hazards of obtaining military intelligence from civilians and of obtaining exact information from Orientals, the linguistic block

24. RUSI Seminar, *supra*.

asserted itself in nearly all cases, as did fear, distrust, and general xenophobia.

The collection process is difficult enough under the most favorable circumstances, but, in South Vietnam, the American soldier's distrust of the native complicated it. His superiors could speak loud and long about "hearts and minds," and President Johnson could continue to praise those true democrats, Thieu and Ky, but the words didn't mean very much. Excepting a few isolated instances, Americans did not readily identify with South Vietnamese, an attitude well illustrated when, during the Tet offensive, two marine generals trooped about the U.S.A. making speeches in defense of Administration policy. On February 1, 1968, Lieutenant General Victor Krulak rhetorically asked a California audience:

. . . How is it, after several years of war, where we are ostensibly making progress, that the enemy can get away with suicide raids in major cities such as Saigon?

Krulak ingeniously answered:

. . . The answer is simple. The raids, and the enemy's ability to launch them, are a product of the strange war we are fighting. There are 16 million people in South Vietnam, and they all look alike. There is no great trick to transporting arms and ammunition in a heavily populated urban area. A bundle of rice conceals a mortar. A push-cart load of vegetables hides a submachine gun. A basket of charcoal covers a dozen grenades. And there is no certain way to ensure against it. It is a frustrating reality that we must face. . . .[25]

General Leonard Chapman, commandant of the Marine Corps, enlarged this theme in a speech to a Texas audience in May. Prior to the Tet offensive, he told the good citizens of Harlingen,

. . . the security precautions taken by the enemy were absolutely amazing —until you remember that there are 16,000,000 people in South Vietnam; and they all look alike—they all talk alike—even though some of them may be guerrilla soldiers; and some of them may be North Vietnamese.[26]

These statements are as incredible as those made by Westmoreland and Walt cited above. Chapman and Krulak are personal friends of the author (as is Walt)—they are bright, intelligent, and courageous men. Why they would speak such palpable nonsense remains a disturbing question. Their statements sound like southern plantation owners talking about niggers or British officers talking about wogs. Sixteen million South Vietnamese do not "all look alike"—to start with, approximately half are men and half women. Nor do they talk alike, no more than a

25. V. H. Krulak, "Address to Western Newspaper Industrial Relations Bureau. . . ." U. S. Marine Corps release, n.d.
26. Leonard Chapman, "Remarks." U. S. Marine Corps release, n.d.

New Englander and a Texan. They represent a number of religious and political creeds, their aspirations are as genuine and probably more basic than most, and had the Saigon government and American officialdom attempted to respect, much less realize, these aspirations, the Tet offensive would never have occurred. Krulak aside, it is very difficult to smuggle arms anywhere *if the general population is opposed to the smuggling.* Krulak and Chapman were voicing basically a "gook philosophy."

Nor were they alone. Not one in a thousand soldiers or marines or sailors or airmen or civilians would have disagreed. At best, such a philosophy was reflected in daily contempt, sometimes genial, sometimes not, displayed toward South Vietnamese officials, officers, and servants. At worst, it was reflected in such tactical savagery as that occurring at My Lai.

The young soldier could not be blamed for this attitude. It was more an exuberance of confidence than of innate arrogance, more a blind belief in the American way of life and a rejection of another way of life. These were the sons of an affluent generation, and it probably had not occurred to them that over five eighths of the world's population are hungry. The monthly pay of an American private exceeded that of senior South Vietnamese officials and army officers. The young American raised in a technological society could not be expected to respect Vietnamese peasants, the more so since he could not even communicate with them. The bulk of American servicemen regarded peasants as gooks or slopeheads; they were human beings, yes, they should be fed and protected where possible, yes—but they were an inferior race.

This produced two important results: It often led to arrogant behavior on the part of officers and men. General Chae Myung-shin, who commanded forty-five thousand South Korean troops in Vietnam, commented on this in an interview published in *U. S. News and World Report.*[27] After stressing the importance of separating the Viet Cong from the rest of the people, the general described the Korean attitude:

. . . We don't discriminate. We have many neutral social activities. My soldiers have an easier time of it [than Americans] becoming friends with the Vietnamese. And we exploit our similarities to the maximum.

We are Oriental. Our political circumstances and those of Vietnam are the same. My soldiers sincerely sympathize with the Vietnamese, as if they were their own people.

Asked how to make friends in Vietnam, the general spoke of various civic-military programs and added:

. . . Our soldiers always try to mix with the people, play with the children, chat with the older people, give haircuts. The most important thing is to be sincere and peaceful. We must respect the people. That's a fundamental.

27. *U. S. News and World Report,* May 15, 1967.

The general liked Americans but was aware of some serious errors, such as giving children cigarettes:

. . . we scold them if they ask for cigarettes. The children are very impressed by this. But that's an Oriental custom. Americans don't understand that.

American generosity was a splendid thing, ". . . but they must not throw things off trucks, as if they're being generous to beggars."

Such American behavior probably did not surprise the peasant. He had suffered decades of it from the French and from his own people: the ruling mandarins and the army. It added, however, to a fundamental xenophobia that further widened the gulf, helping the enemy.

The other result was related. Not respecting the peasant and finding communication with him an onerous task, the American often failed to exploit him for information. Corson tells a story that was repeated a thousand times in battle areas. During the fighting for Hill 861, in the spring of 1967, a Vietnamese civilian approached a marine major to suggest that he use a tunnel that ran through the mountain to attack the enemy defenders from the rear.

. . . The major learned the location of the tunnel but by this time Hill 861 was taken. He snarled at the Vietnamese, "Why didn't you tell us about the tunnel before?" The Vietnamese answered, "Because you never asked me, Major," turned on his heel and walked away.

What the major did not know at the time was that the Vietnamese in question was a man named An Ya, who happens to be the hereditary king of the Bru, a tribal group with some 50,000 subjects. . . . He said, "Colonel, I have tried to reach you for five days, your sergeants in the CAPs (Combined Action Platoons) have also tried, but the battle was too important. My people—the children and the women are starving, we have no food. The hamlet chief left a week ago. The food your government has given the GVN [South Vietnam Government] to sell us is locked in a warehouse and the guards won't release it, even at a price double what you and your men have told me is the legal price. It was my belief that if you were dumb enough to trust the GVN to worry about what happened to the poor Bru people, then, why should I bother to tell your people anything?"

Corson liberated the rice and received a warning as payment: ". . . Colonel, try as hard as you can to teach your people that with us you will defeat the VC very quickly, but without us you will never win —remember we are not easily deceived and never ever forget: The peasant despises nothing more than a fool."[28]

Here was a truism that most American commanders failed to respect, and the intelligence-collection process suffered, and with that so did the troops. The less intelligence available to the commander, the less tactical success he enjoyed and the more he was forced to stab in the dark. This

28. Corson, op. cit.

CHAPTER 90   1289

meant that troops, fighting in strange and uncomfortable circumstances a long way from home for reasons that, though explained by officers, were less than convincing, were tiring themselves, often with no visible results, or were taking heavy casualties, often with minimum or inconclusive results.

In time, and not a very long time, the young soldier began to feel that anyone not in American uniform was against him. As jungle environment told, as fevers appeared, as sores opened and festered, as men fell victim to mines and booby traps, as units walked into ambush, tired and nervous men grew more tired and more nervous and, if fired upon, sometimes did not hesitate to invoke the available total wrath of the American equivalent of Zeus. Commanders who were enjoined to kill as many enemy as possible at cost of the fewest American lives, too often failed to delimit the target before committing the vast armory at their disposal. When such fury failed to evoke expected results, tempers flared further and sometimes innocent people suffered as a result. Early denunciations of ARVN cruelty to villagers horrified many Americans.[29] Yet, as the war continued, American forces sometimes indulged in the fatal error of promiscuous brutality. One disillusioned marine combat officer, Lieutenant Colonel Corson, charged that ". . . search-and-destroy tactics against VC-controlled areas have degenerated into savagery. The terrorism of the enemy has been equally matched by our own."[30] Corson's indignant cry was dismissed by hawks as that of a malcontent. Unfortunately, his words soon gained currency when My Lai became a part both of the American vocabulary and American shame.[31]

As the war continued, the collection process suffered. Where military action terrified the peasant, or where his home was destroyed and his loved ones killed by American firepower, or where American troop behavior otherwise put him off, he was apt to furnish either erroneous information or no information. Finally, and very important, where the Americans or his own government failed to protect him from the Viet Cong—from the man with the knife—he was too frightened or too wise to offer information, no matter his sympathies.

The reader may well ask: Was there a way around this difficulty, a solution? The answer is yes, and it is not an answer of hindsight, since, in part, it was demonstrated with favorable results.

The first solution would have been to choose civil and military commanders who understood insurgency warfare and were mentally and morally equipped to report realities, not dreams, to Washington. This would have dictated two complete turn-arounds in American policy: It would have resulted in a supreme commander, a single director of

29. See, for example, Donald Duncan, op. cit.
30. Corson, op. cit.
31. Seymour M. Hersh, "My Lai 4," *Harper's Magazine*, May 1970.

civil and military operations—a temporary dictator, if you will, but a qualified one. It would also have resulted in a clear-and-hold pacification strategy, a qualitative approach demanding more time and less physical and financial investment as onus was transferred to local, indigenous authority.

Search-and-destroy tactics can never win an insurgency, because they hurt and eliminate people on whom governmental authority depend for intelligence, the peasants. General Walker, who commanded the small but successful Borneo campaign, told a seminar audience in 1969:

. . . My aim in Borneo was to prevent the conflict from escalating into open war, similar to that in Vietnam today. That was my primary aim.

To do this it was vital to win not only the opening rounds of the jungle battle, but also at the same time, the psychological battle in the Kampongs and villages of the up-country tribal people. Therefore, the first and foremost principle was—and I believe always will be—to win the battle for hearts and minds. . . .

It was indelibly inscribed on our minds that one civilian killed by us would do more harm than ten killed by the enemy, and if the price a village had to pay for its liberation from the enemy was to be its own destruction then the campaign for hearts and minds would never have been won. It was because we won and kept the affection, and nothing less than the affection, of the local peoples that we were able to hold one thousand miles of jungle frontier against guerrilla forces always superior in number without once dropping a bomb or firing a rocket.[32]

On the tactical level, a primary solution would have been to utilize native talent. Robert Shaplen has pointed out to the writer that, whereas Americans find the Vietnamese language difficult to learn, the Vietnamese learn English fairly well and quickly, if properly taught.[33] Unfortunately, a viable teaching program did not develop, and as one result, most ARVN soldiers did not speak English, which made it even more difficult to integrate them into American units. Moreover, thanks to early American army influence, most ARVN units were not as guerrilla-oriented as American combat soldiers. Finally, the South Vietnamese soldier did not respect the peasant and often failed to identify with him.

One answer was the Kit Carson scout program, which, in general, worked very well. The surprising fact, in view of the historical precedent of such programs, is that it took so long to initiate and remained so limited.

The army and marines were also on the right track with long-range reconnaissance patrols, probably the most successful tactic employed by either service in Vietnam. It remained to go a step farther and cut the umbilical cord to artillery and air support—in other words, to fight

32. RUSI Seminar, *supra;* see also Walker, op. cit.
33. Private letter to the author.

guerrillas with guerrillas, as Roger Hilsman, among others, had recommended years earlier. The potential existed, and in some ways the CIDG program realized it. But as Donald Duncan, a Special Forces noncommissioned officer, pointed out:

. . . Special Forces enlarged the CIDG program, which means that the people they trained were essentially minority ethnic groups within the country, such as the Montagnards. These so-called Strike Forces did not live off the land; their food was supplied. They lived not in villages but in camps surrounded by barbed wire and land mines—and since they lived in camps that had to be protected, they lacked the mobility of guerrillas and could never stray far. Their weapons were not captured but given to them, and the camps and the Strikers were actually an additional source of weaponry for the enemy. Their pay and allowances usually exceeded the regular forces', and because they were mercenaries—seldom recruited by ideological appeals, and exempt from army conscription—their loyalty to Saigon was doubtful. They were trained and deployed as conventional small units, not as guerrillas, and their training usually lasted only six to eight weeks before they went on a "live" action. . . .[34]

To fight guerrillas with guerrillas would have dictated an entirely different tactical approach—that adopted, for example, by Carlson's long-range Raider patrol on Guadalcanal (see Chapter 39, Volume I) or by the French Commandos de Chasse in Algeria (see Chapter 71)—one that called first for decentralized operations (but directed toward specific goals), second for a sound political base. General Walker later hit on this in discussing his successful handling of the Borneo insurgency. After stressing the "cardinal principle" of gaining reliable intelligence, he went on:

. . . The next principle is domination of the jungle. We in Borneo would never have achieved the results we did had we merely attacked the enemy, and then returned to base, as the Americans have done. Our objective was to dominate and own the jungle week in and week out, day and night. In other words, clear and hold, and not search and destroy.

We played the guerrilla at his own game and we learnt to live as close to the animal as it is humanly possible to do. We insisted on rigid security of all our operations and plans. Therefore, our forward troops were never allowed in any shop, café or bar. When they rested they did so in their firm bases, where there were no bright lights. By our relentless patrolling and ambushing by day and night we were able to seize the initiative, and unit and sub-unit commanders and platoon commanders conducted what I called a person to person war against the particular enemy leader concerned, and it became a blood feud.

The last principle is security of our bases. Wherever they may be, in front or so-called rear areas, whether patrol base, or air field or a logistic installa-

34. Donald Duncan, op. cit.

tion, or whatever. In jungle warfare there can be no front in the accepted sense. Therefore, everyone had to be responsible for his own protection, and every man in uniform must be a potential front-line infantry soldier, wherever he happens to be. The same applies to the civilians. Every man has to be his own vigilante, as we called them in Borneo. Only in this way can you conduct a successful offensive defense, and avoid tying up your soldiers in static defense. You must have more teeth in the mouth and less length in the tail.[35]

Unfortunately, American military doctrine does not accept decentralized tactical control. Reluctance of senior commanders, from Pentagon to battalion level, to turn this war over to small-unit commanders was a major tactical deficiency that neither time nor experience repaired. Young soldiers, both officers and non-coms, often resented the doctrinaire approach, especially in such a variegated combat environment. Young, active, confident, and often imaginative, they respected without fearing the enemy. My friend Lieutenant X, cited in a previous chapter, like dozens of others, proved time and again that he and his men were as capable of sneaking through and fighting in the boondocks as the Viet Cong—just as marines in World War II proved that they were as capable of fighting in jungle as the Japanese. Had such men been encouraged to perfect appropriate tactics, the war could have been fought with minimum expenditure to gain maximum results.

They were not encouraged. Higher echelons of the American military, particularly the army, had no intention of departing from traditional command and staff doctrines. They not only ignored lessons of general history, but they refused to heed those derived from contemporary insurgencies. Each insurgency may be different and may post different problems, but, as we have attempted to point out, universals do exist. French and British experiences in the 1950s were germane in part to Vietnam of the 1960s. The Borneo campaign of 1965, though minute when compared to the Vietnam struggle, contained interesting parallels, yet the British commander of this successful campaign, General Walker, was not allowed to enter South Vietnam, much less advise MACV. At a later seminar on Vietnam, Walker made an excellent point:

. . . Where the Americans have made a big mistake, is in sending the wrong seniority of officer to our jungle warfare school in Malaya to be trained. They sent their most junior officers, whereas we send first our senior officers and NCO's followed by our junior officers. No British Brigadier took command of a brigade unit until he had been through the jungle warfare school, no commanding officer until he had done the course; so each knew what he was asking his men to do; the teaching, therefore, came from the top. Who did the Americans send? Their second lieutenants. When they got back

35. RUSI Seminar, *supra;* compare with Field Marshal Slim's teachings (see Chapters 47, 48, and 49, Volume I).

to Vietnam and tried to spread the gospel, the CO said: "You can forget all that and do it my way." This was their big mistake: had they sent their senior officers this would not have happened, for they would have been properly indoctrinated from the outset.[36]

The inevitable result was reliance on what the military calls "the school solution." Secondary operations such as Sting Ray patrols were tolerated but not particularly encouraged. The writer attempted to discuss the success of small, long-range patrols with a senior marine officer only to be told, ". . . Oh, we have dozens such patrols—one's the same as the other." Had other patrols scored the tactical success of the ones the writer was attempting to discuss, half of General Walt's tactical problems would have been solved. But as Frederick the Great sagely pointed out, ". . . The jackass who experienced twenty of [Prince] Eugene's campaigns was none the better tactician for it."

But small-unit tactics, no matter how well conducted, would have been wasted without the other essential: a strong political base from which they could be launched and which could be expanded as they succeeded—in effect, Lyautey's *tache d'huile* concept.

Nothing illustrated the disparity in thought in top military and civil echelons than this requirement. Despite MACV's authority, it did not command a unified effort. The Saigon government and ARVN remained outside its administrative and operational control, as did such allied units as the Koreans. This meant a variety of pacification efforts, each with its own administrative complex. But MACV also faced internal problems. U. S. Army commanders did not see the pacification task in the same light as Foreign Service officers in CORDS. The U. S. Air Force, U. S. Navy and U. S. Marine Corps, which reported directly to CINCPAC, generally did not agree with the army concept. So far apart were the U. S. Army and U. S. Marine Corps on the pacification issue, that the situation became reminiscent of nineteenth-century warfare, when commanders, separated and out of touch, waged the type of campaign each deemed best.

MACV held for occupation of "liberated" areas by ARVN units working in conjunction with the Saigon government's Revolutionary Development program—an inadequate solution (as discussed earlier) in that ARVN units furnished neither adequate military security nor economic sustenance to peasants, with whom they did not seem able to identify.

The marines approached the problem differently, and made some substantial progress. William Lederer pointed out that, during 1967, the number of villages under NLF-PRP control increased ". . . except in one small area where the United States Marine Corps combined action platoons (CAP) are operating." In his opinion, it was ". . . the only

36. Ibid.; see also J. E. Heelis, "Triumph in Malaysia," *Marine Corps Gazette,* January 1967.

successful American project of any kind whatsoever in Vietnam."[37] One experienced British observer, Major General Richard Clutterbuck, who played a prominent role in the Malayan insurgency and later wrote an excellent book on counterinsurgency, found that the marine effort represented one of "two grains of encouragement" in Vietnam in 1968. Clutterbuck was impressed because the CAP tackled the basic village problem of VC intimidation—in his effective phrase, ". . . the man with the knife":

. . . The normal popular force [militia] in Vietnam now does not live in the village at night, but outside. In the village at night the man with a knife can get in. If 15 Marines and 35 Popular Forces live inside the village at night, you get somewhere, and you can also patrol the village street at night.

At the time of Clutterbuck's visit, eighty CAPs had been formed, and in 80 per cent of the concerned villages ". . . the hamlet chief can sleep, whereas he can only do so in 20 per cent of the villages in the rest of Vietnam."[38] Although CAPs suffered high casualties, ". . . they are only 50 per cent of the casualties of the normal infantry or marine battalions being flown around by helicopter on large scale operations." Clutterbuck did not add that casualties would radically lower as village complexes were consolidated, policed, and redeveloped.

What went wrong with CAP?

A number of things. By mid-1968, the program included nearly two thousand Americans and twenty-seven hundred Vietnamese militia working in a hundred different hamlets. These figures are not impressive: I Corps area comprised five provinces, with a total 2.7 million population. The prototype program could only expand if additional combat personnel were made available. These would have had to come from one of two sources: from operational units, which would have meant adopting a defensive posture, in other words severely limiting or even ending search-and-destroy or "spoiling" tactics; or from fresh units sent from the United States.

But Westmoreland (later Abrams), MACV, and the JCS held no intention of abandoning large-scale actions. Another British observer, Brigadier K. Hunt of The Institute for Strategic Studies, was also favorably impressed with the CAP program, but ". . . when I went down to MACV and referred to this, they said that I had been fixed by the Marines, been brain-washed! They did not agree and said that in any case it would be too expensive."[39] MACV refused to accept early successes and went out of its way to sabotage the program by forcing Walt to commit increasing numbers of combat units to the DMZ fighting. To emphasize displeasure, Westmoreland created a new command in the north

---

37. Lederer, op. cit.
38. RUSI Seminar, *supra;* see also Mulligan, op. cit.
39. RUSI Seminar, *supra.*

under an army general, which exacerbated already tense command relations between the two services.[40] Tactical abilities aside, it was Belisarius fighting Narses at the expense of both.

But even MACV's attitude was not the major stumbling block to a pacification program. Walt and Westmoreland could have committed a hundred thousand American troops to the effort and still drawn a blank—so long as the South Vietnamese Government failed to govern properly.

By end of 1968, then, American tactics continued to provide mobility without purpose and purpose without mobility. They continued to expend American lives and dollars for minimum combat results, and, in addition, to destroy the vital ingredient of counterinsurgency warfare: peasant co-operation. In trying to win the shooting war, American military strategy was contributing to the loss of the real war. How to reverse the situation or at least to salvage some semblance of national self-respect from it was perhaps the chief problem inherited by Richard Milhous Nixon.

40. Saipan all over again! See Vandegrift and Asprey, op. cit.

Chapter 91

Richard Nixon's promise • His position on Vietnam • Enter Henry Kissinger • His plan for disengagement • Combat operations continue • Abrams' tactics • The war escalates • Dissent on the home front • The military and the Hellespont • Soedjatmoko speaks out • Stalemate in Paris • Secret talks with Hanoi • Saigon obstructionism • The President's new plan • First troop withdrawals • The Midway meeting • The Clifford plan (I)

A S THE KOREAN WAR had influenced 1952 presidential elections, the Vietnam war produced heated debate throughout 1967 and to the November elections of 1968.[1] Richard Nixon not only severely criticized President Johnson's Vietnam policy, but implied that he had a secret plan to win the war. As he told prospective voters in New Hampshire early in the year: ". . . I pledge to you the new leadership will end the war and win the peace in the Pacific. . . . I do not suggest withdrawal from Vietnam. I am saying to you that it is possible if we mobilize our economic and political and diplomatic leadership it can be ended. The failure in Vietnam is not the failure of our fighting men in Vietnam but the failure of our leadership in Washington, D.C., to back them up."[2] In his inaugural address, he spoke of moving from ". . . an era of confrontation to an era of negotiation."

1. U. S. Congress, "The Candidates' Views," *Congressional Quarterly*, May 3, 1968. Quoted in *Survival*, July 1968; see also T. H. White, *The Making of the President 1968* (New York: Atheneum, 1969).
2. U. S. Congress, "The Candidates' Views," *supra*.

If Nixon supporters imagined that he was going to pull an Eisenhower
—visit Vietnam and bring about a cease-fire (a dramatic effort, with disappointing results, in the case of Korea)—they were doomed to disappointment. Nixon was and is a man of covert compromise, and, in his
mind, Vietnam called for a particularly careful political approach.[3]

Nixon entered office a prisoner of three major forces: his own fears
of communism, which he had repeatedly emphasized by provocative
and even bellicose statements and actions in refuting the idea of negotiation as a proper basis for ending the Vietnam war; a hawkish military
strategy, which he had favored; the South Vietnamese Government,
which he had helped build. He could not summarily cut the bonds of
these forces. Rather, he had to shift and wiggle, hoping to free himself
sufficiently to gain his political ends.

Shortly after taking office, Nixon relieved negotiator Averell Harriman in favor of Henry Cabot Lodge, whom he instructed to avoid private negotiations at the Paris talks. At the same time, he permitted
General Creighton Abrams, Westmoreland's successor in South Vietnam, to continue attrition strategy by keeping pressure on the enemy.
So far, this was "more of the same," but the new President also made
an appointment that surprised a great many persons: he named Professor Henry Kissinger to the influential post of presidential adviser on
national security affairs.

Kissinger's appointment would have raised eyebrows under normal
circumstances. Forty-five years old, he had come to America in 1938, a
German Jewish refugee who studied at Harvard and subsequently became a professor of government there. Within the Establishment, he was
well known as a theoretician and writer on national strategy and limited
war—indeed, about the only Republican with such a background in
depth. A brilliant and controversial man, he had advised three administrations on international affairs; he had long been involved in behind-
the-scenes diplomacy concerning Vietnam; and he held some positive
ideas on action in the South, having worked the previous summer on
Governor Nelson Rockefeller's four-point escalation formula.

From the hawk standpoint, Kissinger was a disappointing selection.
He was not a military man, nor did he necessarily embrace force as a
proper solution to political problems. He was willing to listen to those
who favored a military solution, but he did not suffer fools gladly, and
he had an annoying habit of producing facts and figures that weighed
heavily against those cited by various hawks. The latters' fears were
greatly increased when the January 1969 issue of *Foreign Affairs* carried his work "The Viet Nam Negotiations" as its lead article.[4]

In a brief review of the situation in South Vietnam, Kissinger discounted American attrition strategy, which ". . . failed to reduce the

3. Richard M. Nixon, "Asia After Viet Nam," *Foreign Affairs,* October 1967.
4. Kissinger, op. cit.

guerrillas and was in difficulty even with respect to the North Vietnamese main forces." A predominant military influence ". . . caused our military operations to have little relationship to our declared political objectives. Progress in establishing a political base was excruciatingly slow; our diplomacy and our strategy were conducted in isolation from each other. . . ." This explained, among other things, the failure of the pacification program. The Tet offensive, which, militarily, Kissinger judged an American "victory," was ". . . a political defeat in the countryside for Saigon and the United States." This action

. . . marked the watershed of the American effort. Henceforth, no matter how effective our actions, the prevalent strategy could no longer achieve its objectives within a period or with force levels politically acceptable to the American people. This realization caused Washington, for the first time, to put a ceiling on the number of troops for Viet Nam. Denied the very large additional forces requested, the military command in Viet Nam felt obliged to begin a gradual change from its peripheral strategy to one concentrating on the protection of the populated area. This made inevitable an eventual commitment to a political solution and marked the beginning of the quest for a negotiated settlement. . . .

Kissinger then went on to review earlier, behind-the-scenes negotiations, and emphasized the difficulties that had to be overcome before meaningful talks could occur. A variety of factors were at work in each of the interested countries, and these combined in a dozen ways to affect internal and external relationships, thereby limiting each country's freedom of maneuver. At best, Kissinger believed, the United States could expect ". . . prolonged negotiations progressing through a series of apparent stalemates."

Negotiations surrounding the bombing halt showed a situation so tense, a distrust so deep, Kissinger went on, writing from personal experience, that each country was going to have to adjust its understanding of its own and the other's position. In the case of the United States, ". . . before we go much further in negotiations, we need an agreed concept of ultimate goals and how to achieve them." Lacking such a concept, all the United States could do was negotiate over interim items, such as a cease-fire and coalition government—a course fraught with hidden dangers.

Instead, Kissinger wanted to seek agreement on ultimate goals first, then work back to details. To achieve this, he called for a realistic evaluation of strengths and weaknesses in each country's position in order to obtain

. . . a clear definition of objectives. The limits of the American commitment can be expressed in two propositions: first, the United States cannot accept a military defeat, or a change in the political structure of South Viet Nam brought about by external military force; second, once North Vietnamese forces and pressures are removed, the United States has no obligation to maintain a government in Saigon by force.

American objectives should therefore be (1) to bring about a staged withdrawal of external forces, North Vietnamese and American, (2) thereby to create a maximum incentive for the contending forces in South Viet Nam to work out a political agreement. The structure and content of such an agreement must be left to the South Vietnamese . . .

Details would have to be negotiated, but

. . . the withdrawal should be over a sufficiently long period so that a genuine indigenous political process has a chance to become established; the contending sides in South Viet Nam should commit themselves not to pursue their objectives by force while the withdrawal of external forces is going on; in so far as possible, the definition of what constitutes a suitable political process or structure should be left to the South Vietnamese, with the schedule for mutual withdrawal creating the time frame for an agreement.

The United States, then, should concentrate on the subject of the mutual withdrawal of external forces and avoid negotiating about the internal structure of South Viet Nam for as long as possible. . . .

Kissinger called for three-tiered negotiations. Washington and Hanoi would work out ". . . mutual troop withdrawal and related subjects such as guarantees for the neutrality of Laos and Cambodia"; Saigon and the NLF ". . . would discuss the internal structure of South Viet Nam"; a third forum ". . . would be an international conference to work out guarantees and safeguards for the agreements arrived at in the other committees, including international peacekeeping machinery."

While Hanoi pondered such an approach, the United States should adopt ". . . a less impatient strategy—one better geared to the protection of the population and sustainable with substantially reduced casualties." If Hanoi spurned the effort,

. . . we should seek to achieve as many of our objectives as possible unilaterally. We should adopt a strategy which reduces casualties and concentrates on protecting the population. We should continue to strengthen the Vietnamese army to permit a gradual withdrawal of some American forces, and we should encourage Saigon to broaden its base so that it is stronger for the political contest with the communists which sooner or later it must undertake.

The newly elected President was not familiar with this article, so the story goes, when he tapped its author for the new and responsible job of national security adviser. His final choice implied tacit acceptance of Kissinger's thinking.

Kissinger's appointment, however, spelled no immediate or dramatic action. Several of his points had been raised over a year earlier by a proven authority on Indochina, Robert Shaplen, also writing in *For-*

eign Affairs.[5] Instead of a specific program, Kissinger offered general guidelines. The dissident factors he had discussed that existed in Hanoi, Saigon, and Washington exerted themselves on the new Administration just as they did on Saigon and Hanoi governments. Top American officials, civil and military, were still divided into hawks and doves. Three months after Nixon assumed office, *Newsweek* reported that a canvass of the Pentagon, the State Department, the American Embassy in Saigon, and the American team in Paris made it clear

. . . that none of these governmental "satrapies" could agree on the facts of the Vietnam conflict, much less on what conclusions to draw from those facts. As a result, at the first full-dress National Security Council meeting devoted to Vietnam, the participants were asked to consider no fewer than nine possible courses of action to end the war—four military and five political. . . .[6]

Nor did the enemy pause while the new American President debated a course of action. Although his 1969 Tet offensive in no way approached the 1968 effort, it nevertheless showed a capability of launching rocket and mortar attacks against ". . . more than a hundred towns, cities, and American installations" while variously launching small ground attacks, a total effort that, in a few days, killed some four hundred Americans and six hundred South Vietnamese, at an estimated enemy cost of six thousand.[7]

Shortly after Abrams relieved Westmoreland, American tactics had begun to alter. Although Abrams was a World War II tank commander wedded to conventional Western military thinking, he apparently entertained some doubts about Westmoreland's attrition strategy with emphasis on large-unit search-and-destroy operations. As stated in a previous chapter, he converted in part to Sting Ray tactics—small patrols instead of battalion and brigade actions. As we have noted, such tactics are essential to successful prosecution of this type of war. But, in Abrams' case, three factors tended to lessen beneficial effects on tactical changes.

The first was that Abrams did not seem to understand the nature of this war any more than had Westmoreland. He insisted on gaining a military solution by keeping "maximum pressure," so-called "pile-on" tactics, against an enemy willing to fight back. A RAND analyst who worked in Vietnam from 1966–69, Brian Jenkins, put his finger on the problem in a later report:

. . . The lack of a clear, attainable or decisive objective makes it difficult to assess the progress of the war in Vietnam. Enemy soldiers continue to die at a greater rate than our own but we do not know how many enemy

5. Shaplen ("Crisis"), *supra.*
6. *Newsweek,* April 7, 1969.
7. Shaplen (*The Road from War*), *supra.*

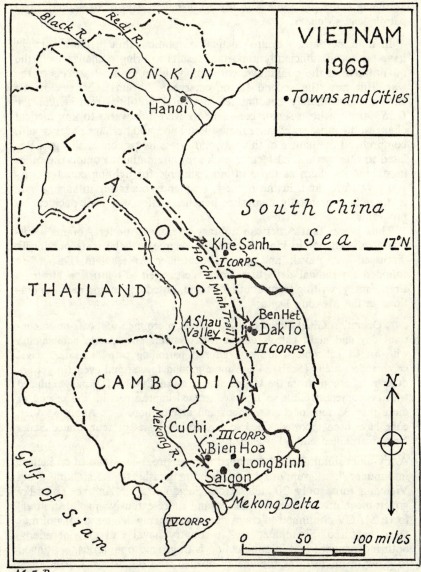

VIETNAM
1969
• Towns and Cities

M.E.P.

soldiers must die before the enemy's will cracks or his army begins to disintegrate. Frequently, increases in the amount of our military efforts are measured and this is called progress. On this basis, if twice as many bombs are dropped per month in 1969 as were dropped per month in 1967, we are doing better—the same with leaflets, battalion days of operations, night patrols, and so on.

In time, perhaps, Abrams' tactical adaptation, though limited, might have produced sufficiently important results to bring a change from the quantitative to the qualitative, with emphasis on political aspects of the war. But now the second factor emerged: Abrams' changes, minor enough, immediately encountered doctrinal hostility from *within the U. S. Army,* whose senior commanders were lukewarm to any tactical changes, the more so because they still did not, and perhaps never would, comprehend the nature of this war, much less its tactical challenges. Related to this was a final factor: each arm attempting to outdo the other in staking its claim as the arm most suitable for fighting counterinsurgency warfare, and, in the process, frequently operating in such a way as to reduce or totally neutralize beneficial effects of civil pacification programs.

Thus it was that American military operations under Abrams' command differed not in kind, but only in degree. All the wars previously discussed—air, naval, and ground—continued to escalate. Dispatches sounded no radical departure from Westmoreland's attrition strategy. Fred Emery, writing from South Vietnam, noted expanding naval operations in the Mekong Delta:

. . . Operation Giant Slingshot . . . had put more than 65 boats on to constant day and night patrols on the river system. They act in combination with armed helicopters, artillery, aircraft patrolling with "sensors," naval commando squads (Seals), Vietnamese ground forces, and even (in yet another role) troops from the United States 1st Air Cavalry Division, equipped with helicopters. Results so far have seemed impressive with the seizure of more than 35 tons of new weapons and ammunition. . . . About 55 Vietcong have been reported killed so far, against losses of four United States Navy men killed and 50 wounded. . . .[8]

Army units simultaneously combed suspect areas—we read of one effort in January ". . . supported by helicopter gunships . . . stalking a big Vietcong force only 20 miles from Saigon. . . ."[9] As the Thieu-Ky government promised new reforms and more-extensive pacification efforts, MACV continued to claim numerous enemy dead and tons of material captured. Simultaneously, in-country naval and air operations, both independent and in conjunction with ground operations, continued to grow in intensity as the enemy opened new offensives. Correspondents wrote of new and fearsome weapons systems such as those employed in hovercraft operations:

. . . The ACVs are one of the weapons systems most dreaded by the Vietcong. With fearsome-looking shark teeth painted across their bow skirts, the

8. Fred Emery, *The Times* (London), January 21, 1969.
9. Fred Emery, *The Times* (London), January 29, 1969.

spray all around them and the tremendous noise of their aircraft-type pro-
pellors, the psychological impact is dramatic. . . .

ACVs are able to sweep over much treacherous territory, destroying as
they go Vietcong sampans loaded with arms and supplies and flushing out
VC when they hide under swamps by using protruding hollow reeds to
breathe through. . . .[10]

The correspondent did not say how hovercraft gunners identified the
sampans or went about flushing Viet Cong guerrillas. The air war also
escalated in the South, with army and marine fliers flying thousands of
sorties per day. In late April, one read that B-52s ". . . dropped 2,000
tons of bombs on Tay Ninh province in the biggest raid of the Vietnam
war"; the province ". . . is riddled with infiltration routes leading from
the Cambodian border to Saigon, the [U.S.] officials said."[11]

As Abrams' version of attrition strategy continued, as search-and-
destroy operations blossomed throughout South Vietnam, so did attendant evils we discussed earlier. Sometimes these remained in small print.
Thus, in discussing U. S. Navy operations in the Mekong Delta, Emery
noted:

. . . one section of the river is already known to the sailors as "blood alley,"
and their machine guns rake the banks as we pass over a reach barely concealing well-built earth bunkers from which the patrol boats have been repeatedly fired upon. Any sampans encountered are stopped and checked for
papers, but at night this invariably means opening fire and sinking
them. . . .[12]

Some escaped notice until a later time. One of the most heavily decorated officers in the army, Lieutenant Colonel Anthony Herbert, later
testified, for example, that, in mid-February 1969, he witnessed a battle
with the Viet Cong near Cuu Loi:

. . . after the fire fight, I walked up on these [civilian] detainees—there were
about 15 of them—and they were in the custody of an ARVN unit and
an American lieutenant.

There were four dead already, and when I walked up, they had a knife
at the throat of a woman. Her baby—there were several kids in the bunch—
her baby was screaming and grabbing at her leg, and her other child . . .
was being suffocated by an ARVN who was pushing its face into the sand
with his foot.

I ordered them to stop, but with me just standing there looking, they proceeded to slit the woman's throat. I asked the lieutenant what the hell was
going on and then I ordered him to get his tail out of the area and take
his ARNV with him. They left and I sent one of my sergeants with the

10. Anthony Rowley, *The Times* (London), April 2, 1969.
11. *The Times* (London), April 24, 1969.
12. *The Times* (London), January 21, 1969.

detainees to the L.Z. [Landing Zone]. I told him to get them out and back
so they could be processed.

Well, it wasn't long after he left that I heard firing in the direction he'd
taken them. He came running back, yelling, mad as hell. He told me the
American lieutenant and the ARVN's had jumped him, overpowered him
and killed all the detainees. I followed him back and found the bodies. All
of them. The children, too.[13]

Herbert subsequently witnessed torture of prisoners by American military intelligence personnel. His insistent reports of these criminal activities won him only opprobrium of his seniors, Lieutenant Colonel J. Ross
Franklin and Major General John Barnes, and he was shortly relieved
of his command and sent to military limbo.[14]

Other evils appeared. Despite intense security, Viet Cong guerrillas
continued to penetrate American base areas such as that at Cu Chi,
where special raiding teams, covered by rocket and small-arms fire, destroyed nine and severely damaged three Chinook helicopters in a brief
night action, an estimated $16-million loss, described by MACV as
"light material damage."[15] In warding off a Tet attack on the big American base at Long Binh, American aircraft were forced to level the village
of Bien Hoa, a frantic action that resulted in heavy enemy casualties and
was, once again, claimed by MACV as a "victory."

As one perceptive correspondent, Nicholas Tomalin of *The Times*
(London), noted:

. . . NOW: who won the battle of Bien Hoa? Except that it was fought
in daylight, it was an archetype of virtually all the significant battles in Vietnam. The side that won Bien Hoa wins the war. . . . The Americans and
SVN [South Vietnamese] claim it as a great victory. . . . Hanoi also claims
the battle . . . as a victory. . . .

Tomalin went on to compare criteria. MACV pointed out that the attack failed to attain a military objective and cost 234 enemy dead and
eighty prisoners taken, at minimal cost of U.S.-ARVN forces. Opposed
to this was enemy penetration of an area supposedly "secure," with an
HES rating of "B," the second highest—yet the people not only gave *no*
warning to local authorities but obviously participated in digging tun-
nels and other preparatory enemy measures. A similar situation occurred in the Cu Chi area, where American officers were so careful to
avoid "incidents" that in-camp guards had to telephone a superior for
permission to open fire in order to avoid killing innocent civilians. As
in other areas, the army concentrated on civil relations. The command
was alerted to the possibility of attack,

13. James T. Wooten, "How a Supersoldier was Fired from His Command,"
New York *Times Magazine*, September 5, 1971.
14. Ibid.
15. Nicholas Tomalin, *The Times* (London), February 26, 1969.

. . . yet 80 Vietcong sappers managed to spend three and a half hours cutting through the 10 barbed wire fences that protect Cu Chi perimeter, without any of the American ambush patrols, sentries and bunker defense units detecting them. . . .[16]

Again the peasants knew of strangers among them—and kept silent.

Matters did not greatly improve in I Corps area, where marines seem to have learned few lessons. In February, 3rd Marine Division in conjunction with ARVN units had kicked off Operation Dewey Canyon, an immense sweep of tortuous terrain running west to the Laotian border. Although few enemy contacts resulted, marine spokesmen called the operation one of ". . . the most successful of the war" and insisted on the importance of captured weapons and material (some 450 tons) to justify 121 killed, several hundred wounded, and units exhausted. Marines followed this with sweeping operations around Khe Sanh while air and naval units continued to pound enemy positions in and around the DMZ, a gigantic effort that included USS *New Jersey* firing one-ton shells on suspected bunker positions.

In late May, paratroopers of 101st Airborne Division, while carrying out Operation Apache Snow, a sweep of A Shau Valley, south of the marine area of operations, "surprised" an enemy force dug in on Ap Bia Mountain. Rather than surround the complex and eliminate or at least badly damage the enemy by air strikes, the local commander ordered an assault in force. For several days, well-disciplined and terribly brave paratroopers fought up what became known as Hamburger Hill. They "captured" it at a cost of eighty-four dead and 480 wounded. A few days later, they evacuated. When North Vietnamese troops again occupied it, the division commanding general, John Wright, Jr., announced ". . . that if ordered to take the hill again, 'I am prepared to commit everything that it takes, up to the entire division, to do the job.' "[17] Fortunately for his troops, he was not so ordered. (Perhaps some senior remembered the warning given by Belisarius to his army: ". . . Remember that even intrepidity must be restrained within certain and moderate limits, and, when it becomes pernicious, ceases to be honorable.")

While paratroopers were bleeding and dying on Hamburger Hill, Giap, as usual, was preparing another unpleasant surprise for allied forces. This time, he chose the old battlegrounds around Dak To and Ben Het, the latter defended primarily by ARVN units. In May, South Vietnamese patrols had attempted to upset Giap's plans, but the newly reorganized army that American advisers were boasting about did not hold together. By early June, the South Vietnamese were dug in at Ben Het. By mid-June, PAVN units had cut off the strong point from the American garrison at Dak To, besieged it for a month, and disappeared,

16. Ibid.
17. *Time*, June 27, 1969.

an inconclusive action once again underlining Giap's retention of tactical initiative.

The Administration had already suggested that matters were not going to improve radically overnight. In early March, the President defended his policy, blaming it on the enemy:

. . . we had no other choice but to try to blunt the offensive. Had General Abrams not responded in this way, we would have suffered far more casualties than we have suffered, and we have suffered more than, of course, any of us would have liked to have seen.[18]

In view of the current offensive, the President said, ". . . there is no prospect for a reduction of American forces in the foreseeable future." In mid-March, Secretary of Defense Melvin Laird warned that the United States could not reduce troop commitment until North Vietnam withdrew its troops; according to military commanders in South Vietnam, another two years would be required to bring the situation "in hand."[19]

The Administration's "more of the same" attitude unleashed increasingly vocal and hostile voices in the United States. In late March, a protesting congressman placed the names of 31,379 American dead in the Congressional Record. In early April, Henry Niles, chairman of the increasingly influential BEM (Business Executives Move for Peace in Vietnam), complained that ". . . over 2,000 Americans have been killed in Vietnam since President Nixon took office. . . . The honeymoon is over. We want peace."[20] A New York *Times* dispatch of May 22, from Saigon, stated that U.S. commanders in Vietnam

. . . are still under orders to pursue the enemy relentlessly, using every tactic and weapon at their command, to deny the North Vietnamese and Vietcong troops any strategic advantage as a result of the halt in bombing. The United States commanders in the field have followed the order to the letter, and have dramatically stepped-up the number of offensive operations initiated by the allies.[21]

In the Senate, Edward Kennedy reminded fellow senators that Nixon had not ordered or intended to order any reduction of military activity in Vietnam; he continued:

. . . President Nixon has told us, without question, that we seek no military victory, that we seek only peace. How then can we justify sending our boys against a hill a dozen times or more, until soldiers themselves question the

18. Richard M. Nixon, *Public Papers of the President* (Washington: U. S. Government Printing Office, 1970), Vol. 1.
19. *The Times* (London), Washington, March 19, 1969.
20. *The Times* (London), April 9, 1969.
21. *Washington Watch*, May 26, 1969.

madness of the action? The assault on "Hamburger Hill" is only symptomatic of a mentality and a policy that requires immediate attention. . . .[22]

A month earlier, in the April issue of *The Atlantic,* a former marine commandant, General David Shoup, warned the public of a new and dangerous American militarism, "a poisonous weed" that would have to be exterminated.[23]

Shoup's article caused a major furor in Administration circles, as did continued press criticism of military actions in Vietnam. Assistant Commandant of the Marine Corps General Lewis Walt charged that ". . . news coverage of the war, assessment of the caliber of the South Vietnamese army and allegations of corruption in the Saigon government" were "inadequate or misleading." Admiral Moorer, Chief of Naval Operations, ". . . complained of the reporting on American military morale and the 'so-called existence of an evil military-industrial complex.'" The Washington *Post* noted: ". . . Criticism of press and television has joined ABM [anti-ballistic missile] boosterism as a predictable ingredient in top Defense Department speeches."[24]

Military hawks were fighting a losing battle, however. In taking on the national press, they were going to prove as effective as Xerxes when he tried to punish the Hellespont for destroying his bridge.[25] Like the Hellespont, the nation's press was too big, powerful, and insensitive, particularly when intelligent and politically influential observers around the world were pointing out fallacies that had underlain American policy in Vietnam. One of the most intelligent voices belonged to the Indonesian ambassador in Washington, Soedjatmoko, who told a Honolulu audience, on the same day President Nixon addressed the nation, that ". . . the future of the South-east Asian region will not be determined solely by the outcome of that war."

. . . Firstly, the population of Vietnam, or even of the whole of erstwhile Indo-China together, constitutes less than one-third of the total population of South-east Asia. On the other hand, Indonesia's population alone accounts for almost half of that total. In keeping the Vietnam war in its proper proportions, it is important to realize that if Indonesia had become a Communist country, any military gains in the Vietnam war would have been nullified.

22. Ibid.
23. David M. Shoup and James A. Donovan, "The New American Militarism," *The Atlantic,* April 1969; see also James A. Donovan, *Militarism, U.S.A.* (New York: Charles Scribner's Sons, 1970).
24. *Washington Watch,* June 23, 1969.
25. Herodotus, op. cit.: Xerxes ". . . straightway gave orders that the Hellespont should receive three hundred lashes, and that a pair of fetters should be cast into it. Nay, I have even heard it said, that he bade the branders take their irons and therewith brand the Hellespont."

The domino theory, so popular in American administration circles, was fallacious, because it did not respect regional facts:

. . . It is, therefore, not the political color of a regime that counts in the end, but its capacity for nation-building and development. More important than the question whether a country will turn towards Communism—however important that may be to the country concerned—is the question whether in doing so it will become a satellite of outside forces or not. For underlying my whole argument is the conviction that in the present world situation no outside power can for long force any South-east Asian country to do its bidding. The South-east Asian nations do not constitute lifeless entities that automatically fall one way or the other, depending on which way their neighbor falls. History does not operate that way. What matters is the will, the political will, the determination of a nation to preserve its own identity. Out of our own national experience, we in Indonesia more than ever believe that this is the crucial element in the equation. Without such a will and determination, the infusion of external power will fail to make much difference. The domino theory, therefore, is to us rather a gross over-simplification of the nature of the historical processes that go on in the area. It obscures and distorts rather than illuminates our understanding and offers no guidelines for realistic policy.[26]

So long as China pursued her present policy, the ambassador continued, the primary threat to Southeast Asian nations ". . . is one of internal subversion and insurgency." But:

. . . It is not primarily a nation's military capability that will determine its capacity to overcome these threats to internal security, but rather the cohesion of its political system, the viability and the effectiveness of its government in dealing with the problems of poverty, social inequalities and injustices, in bringing about economic development and in continually expanding its base for popular participation. Here again it is not only factors of economic growth, but beyond that the elements of will and determination that are decisive, as well as the people's loyalty to the government and faith in its purposes. . . .[27]

At some point in this spring of 1969, President Nixon decided to abandon hawkish desire for military victory in favor of negotiated settlement. Unfortunately, his decision did not make the deed. Although some observers drew comfort from the limited action of the 1969 Tet offensive —mainly indiscriminate shelling of South Vietnamese cities—the action showed an unhealthy enemy strength, as did expensive encounter actions in the DMZ and particularly along the Cambodian border, which continued to take a high toll of American lives. Enemy intransigence also

26. Soedjatmoko, op. cit.
27. Ibid.; see also Eugene R. Black, *Alternative in Southeast Asia* (London: Pall Mall Press, 1969).

showed in Paris, where it was complemented by President Thieu's luke-warm attitude, until virtually an impasse had been reached. Mounting criticism at home alarmed Administration officials, while Nixon's continued silence infuriated critics.

Finally, in a speech in early April, the President hinted that secret talks were taking place with Hanoi:

. . . We think we are on the right track but we are not going to raise false hopes. We are not going to tell you what is going on in private talks. What we are going to do is our job and then, a few months from now, I think you will look back and say what we did was right.[28]

Meanwhile, he told his audience, he wanted time. As for Administration intentions, Secretary of State William Rogers told a Senate committee two days later, ". . . We're prepared, if the other side is prepared, to have a [troop] withdrawal over a very short period of time."

The other side, or, rather, three other sides—the Saigon government, the Communists in the South, and the Hanoi government—still did not seem in a hurry to begin productive talks. About the last action that the Thieu regime wanted was an American withdrawal, and, as it had attempted to sabotage every major American effort toward de-escalating the war in the previous three years, so now it obfuscated major issues with dreary dilatory procedures that tried American officials nearly as much as the NLF's and Hanoi's repeated mouthings of all or nothing. Hanoi seemed equally obdurate. Writing from Paris in early May, Stewart Alsop concluded that the Communists ". . . presently have no intention whatever" of agreeing to mutual withdrawal:

. . . to believe that the Communists have any interest in a reasonable settlement it is necessary, like the Red Queen, to "believe six impossible things before breakfast."[29]

Nixon was in a position where he had to believe more than six impossible things before breakfast, and he chose to make the best of a difficult situation. Administration spokesmen pointed to indications of a possible breakthrough: The enemy was sitting at a table in Paris along with Saigon government representatives. That government had tabled a six-point peace proposal; Hanoi had countered with a four-point plan. In May, the NLF proposed a ten-point plan. If all this seemed relatively meaningless, particularly to the combat soldier in Vietnam, the Nixon administration accepted it as a necessary prelude to real negotiations that might even reverse the enemy policy of fighting before talking to that of talking before fighting.

Just how far the Nixon administration had moved from the U.S.A.'s previous bellicose attitude became apparent in mid-May, when the Presi-

28. *Newsweek*, April 7, 1969.
29. *Newsweek*, May 5, 1969.

dent appeared on television to make a major policy speech ". . . on our most difficult and urgent problem."[30] The President defended the American presence in Vietnam as necessary to accomplish the American objective, which he now defined as ". . . the opportunity for the South Vietnamese people to determine their own political future without outside interference." This and other bromides (". . . we seek no bases . . . we insist on no military ties . . .") were to be expected. But he also ". . . ruled out attempting to impose a purely military solution on the battlefield," committed the Administration (and, by implication, the Thieu-Ky government) to negotiation, formal or informal, and offered a one-year plan for mutual troop withdrawals under international supervision. Once a final cease-fire was negotiated, national elections could be held.

Although *Time* magazine greeted the plan as a sort of political Sermon on the Mount, its importance did not lie in the relatively vague proposals to the enemy, or even in Nixon's expressed willingness to negotiate theretofore *verboten* points such as the Saigon-NLF relationship and an interim provisional government. Its importance lay in Nixon's determination to proceed with negotiations, a not-so-hidden message that the Administration had no intention of maintaining the status quo; thenceforth the South Vietnamese would begin to share the combat burden and would search for a satisfactory internal political solution. Prior to the speech, Administration officials leaked the existence of a plan for unilateral withdrawal of American troops.

Although Nixon's speech had been shown to Thieu, who allegedly stated no objections, the Saigon government reacted quickly and sharply. Thieu at once rejected any talk of coalition government, and, in so doing, emphasized his respect for democratic procedures by banning distribution of American magazines that covered the speech. In Seoul, he persuaded South Korea's President, Chung Hee Park, to denounce both coalition government in South Vietnam and unilateral American withdrawal—not a difficult task, considering Park's own authoritarian government.

But the Administration refused to budge. At Midway, where Thieu and Ky met with Nixon in early June, they learned that Washington not only intended to push for elections in South Vietnam, but that it intended to emphasize desire for negotiated settlement by slowly withdrawing American combat support: The Administration, Nixon announced, was unilaterally withdrawing twenty-five thousand troops to evidence pacific intentions: ". . . We have opened wide the door to peace," Nixon announced, back in Washington, in words sounding as if Billy Graham had written them, "and now we invite the leaders of North Vietnam to walk with us. . . ."[31]

30. Nixon (*Public Papers*), *supra*.
31. Ibid.

Again, the message was intended for both North and South Vietnam. Although Thieu, at Midway, had promised the usual reforms (including still another land-reform program) and spoken optimistically of ARVN's increasing ability to take over the military load, the Nixon administration emphasized its intentions when Secretary of Defense Laird suggested that further withdrawals would be considered in August.

The President's action did not silence important critics at home. Writing in the July 1969 issue of *Foreign Affairs*, Clark Clifford, former Secretary of Defense in the Johnson administration, called for a complete reappraisal of American policy in Vietnam. Pointing to profound and, from the Western standpoint, favorable political changes in Southeast Asia and in Asia generally, Clifford argued that South Vietnam could stand increasingly on its own feet and should be left with minimum American logistic and air support. Clifford wanted a hundred thousand American soldiers withdrawn by end of 1969, the remainder by end of 1970.[32] Stung by this and other criticism, Nixon suggested further imminent troop withdrawals: ". . . I would hope that we could beat Mr. Clifford's timetable."[33] Although White House aides nervously suggested that the President had not committed himself, Nixon privately spoke of a desire to virtually end American military participation by end of 1970.

32. Clifford, op. cit.
33. Nixon (*Public Papers*), *supra*.

Chapter 92

The Hanoi scene • Emergence of the PRG • Combat action drops • General Wheeler's stand • The doves reply • Nixon's decision • Increasing American costs (IV) • Administration problems • CIA and Special Forces • Ho Chi Minh's death • Further troop withdrawals • Progress in South Vietnam • The President's November address • The Thompson report • Blurs on the canvas • Hanoi's position • Increasing dissent at home • Pacification problems • Thompson's report examined • The Saigon government • End of a year

W E DO NOT KNOW the exact effect of President Nixon's June 1969 overtures in Hanoi or in enemy ranks in the South. They could not have been unwelcome, however. Considerable friction existed in party ranks both in Hanoi and in the South prior to the 1967 Tet offensive. As Giap's heavy losses over a decade earlier, when fighting the French, had caused party dissonance, so must heavy losses in 1967. While hawks such as Truong Chinh, Vo Nguyen Giap, and probably Le Duan continued to demand total victory in the South, more moderate voices, including those of Ho Chi Minh and Premier Pham Van Dong, could point to devastating losses, to morale problems occasioned by heavy casualties, to severe economic difficulties in part brought on by floods, and suggest that some form of negotiated settlement was in order, particularly if it would result in an American exodus, which would leave the North free to undermine the Thieu-Ky government and eventually take over the South.

Apparently, dissident factions compromised in June, when the National Liberation Front (NLF) announced creation of a new ". . . provisional revolutionary government of the Republic of South Vietnam," the PRG, which was quickly recognized as a legitimate government by the Soviet Union and twelve other nations. The announcement created a brief flurry of interest, which subsided when the North Vietnamese delegation in Paris failed to follow with specific proposals.

That something was astir, however, became apparent in early July, when the enemy suddenly broke off a major attack against an ARVN post, Ben Het; action elsewhere faded, and American killed-in-action dropped to the lowest in 1969, a hundred fifty a week. Three North Vietnamese regiments reportedly withdrew north across the DMZ, while intelligence also reported a significant drop in infiltration via the Ho Chi Minh Trail. Although enemy guerrilla units continued spasmodic attacks, including those against American installations at Bien Hoa and north along the coast, the action continued to de-escalate until, in late July, American fatalities decreased to under a hundred a week.

The over-all trend set off an explosive, if secret, debate in Washington. Pentagon and State Department hawks argued that enemy disengagement was meaningless. On July 20, General Earle Wheeler, chairman of the JCS, announced in Saigon, at the end of a four-day inspection tour, that the recent lull did not appear to be politically significant; he disputed reports that PAVN regiments had withdrawn north and seemed to imply that an American military de-escalation was not justified.[1] Wheeler praised the continued development of ARVN—the U. S. Army had been "developing" ARVN since 1954, the current project costing over $6 *billion*—and said that allied forces ". . . are well prepared for any new military initiatives the enemy may attempt." He also said, in words undoubtedly intended for presidential ears, ". . . that the [South] Vietnamese could not take over the full war effort by the end of 1970."[2] In a secret briefing of the Senate Armed Services Committee at month's end, he allegedly said ". . . that the Nixon plan to de-Americanize the war had been dropped. He inferred a more aggressive strategy was needed to win the war."[3]

Doves retorted that the lull was politically significant, just as it had been after President Johnson halted the bombing. The military had erred then, the argument ran, by keeping up military pressure after Hanoi had withdrawn three PAVN divisions north of the DMZ. This time, doves insisted, Hanoi must be given a chance to show true intentions, particularly since it apparently had forsaken military conquest and reverted to political struggle, as suggested by the creation of the new Provisional Revolutionary Government (PRG) in the South in June.[4]

1. *The Times* (London), July 20, 1969.
2. Ibid.
3. *Washington Watch*, August 7, 1969.
4. Shaplen (*Road*), *supra,* offers an excellent analysis of these conflicting positions.

WAR IN THE SHADOWS

Nixon had already decided to wind down the shooting war. Hanoi's reactions aside, he was in serious political trouble. Early in July, the figure of American dead in South Vietnam had gone over the thirty-seven thousand mark. Official figures admitted loss of 5,666 aircraft, including nearly 2,900 helicopters—a total financial loss of above $3 billion.[5] The American people, not only students and other "troublemakers," were slowly realizing that an era of militarism was bankrupting the United States both spiritually and financially. More than two thirds of federal expenditure since World War II—over $1 *trillion*—had gone to armaments and armed forces. The 1970 defense budget topped $80 billion. Military leaders were clamoring for new weapons systems, new bombers, strategic missiles, tanks, aircraft. While poverty claimed large areas of the United States, while the population was outgrowing schools and social services, while American cities were coming apart at the seams, the Vietnam war would take $28 billion in *direct* costs in the new fiscal year. As David Calleo, of the Washington Center of Foreign Policy Research, put it:

... It is not isolationism that is reviving in the United States but humanism. Prodded by the prolonged agony of Vietnam many Americans now perceive grotesque distortions in their Government's values. The United States, they believe, is sacrificing the quality of its national life to the demands of a military empire.[6]

Widespread dissent continued to show itself, not only in draft-card burning and student demonstrations, but in the intellectual fabric of America and increasingly in Congress. In that summer of 1969, Nixon, in many ways, was facing an incipient rebellion, and it is a great argument for the worth of democracy that, though he favored force—he promised to respect what he called U.S. "commitment" to Thailand under the SEATO treaty, which some observers interpreted as including use of U.S. troops—public opinion was pushing him toward disengagement.

In late July, Nixon sent orders to Abrams not only to cut down offensive missions but to begin withdrawing American units from combat positions as rapidly as ARVN units could replace them. In late July, the President undertook a tour of Asia to spread a new gospel, which can be summarized as Nixon helps those who help themselves. Although the United States would honor its commitments in Southeast Asia, the President explained to leaders in Djakarta, Saigon, and Bangkok, it would thenceforth emphasize economic rather than military action. The time had come, Nixon proclaimed, to end a war and build a peace.[7]

5. *The Times* (London), July 25, 1969: 2,545 destroyed by enemy action; 3,121 destroyed by crashes or other accidents. I have not been able to determine the exact number of planes destroyed or badly damaged by guerrilla actions, but, in view of numerous successful raids, the figure must be high.
6. *The Times* (London), July 29, 1969.
7. Nixon (*Public Papers*), *supra*.

If Nixon hoped to quiet American critics by such oratory, he was quickly disappointed. A series of shocks now befell the Administration, and particularly the armed forces. In late July, a Congressional sub-committee, in a report on the *Pueblo* disaster (see Chapter 87), rapped the military soundly on the knuckles:

. . . The inquiry reveals the existence of a vast and complex military structure capable of acquiring almost infinite amounts of information but with a demonstrated inability, in these two instances, to relay this information in a timely and comprehensible fashion to those charged with the responsibility for making decisions.[8]

Further adverse publicity spilled over the U. S. Navy a month later, when it announced that USS *New Jersey,* the battleship that had been refitted for service in Vietnam waters at a cost of $40 million, was being put back in mothballs after eighteen months' service.[9]

In early August, a scandal broke in Saigon with the arrest of one Huynh Van Trong and some fifty associates. Trong was special assistant and confidant on political affairs to President Thieu. He was charged with running an espionage ring for North Vietnam! The American public was still digesting this upsetting development when MACV announced the arrest of eight Special Forces soldiers, including the Green Beret commander in South Vietnam, Colonel Robert Rheault, for murdering a Vietnamese civilian. The victim, who allegedly worked for both CIA and Special Forces, was said to have been "doubled" by the Communists. When this was discovered, CIA ordered him "terminated with extreme prejudice"—a death sentence allegedly carried out by Special Forces.

The case was important for three main reasons: First, it caused tremendous speculation, mostly critical, concerning American policy; NBC, for example, reported that Special Forces had committed over three hundred political assassinations in South Vietnam, including those of senior Vietnamese officials.[10] Second, it raised problems in the Phoenix program, the joint American-South Vietnamese effort that had been trying to root out VC infrastructure in liberated areas. The covert part of this program involved assassination of enemy agents by American-Vietnamese Provisional Reconnaissance Units (PRUs). Nearly five hundred American "advisers" now wondered if they were to be tried for murder.[11] Third, CIA's refusal to produce witnesses for prosecution of Rheault and his fellows caused the army to drop the case. Instead of airing policy, CIA claimed executive privilege and Nixon allowed the claim: But this did not repair damage done to the prestige of Special

8. *The Times* (London), July 28, 1969.
9. Los Angeles *Times,* September 2, 1969.
10. *The Times* (London), September 11, 1969.
11. *The Times* (London), August 21, 1969.

Forces, nor did it quiet critics who did not like the idea of CIA's "terminating" people with or without "extreme prejudice." To a good many intelligent Americans, the terminology belonged to SMERSH and James Bond, not to a democracy that claimed to embrace the principle of trial by jury.

More was to come. An article by two American scientists in the August issue of *Scientific Research* condemned the defoliation program in South Vietnam and directly challenged U. S. Army claims that herbicides caused only minimum damage. Pointing to established decreases in rice and rubber production caused in part by killing plants and trees, the scientist-authors claimed that herbicides were causing long-term ecological damage, as was B-52 bombing. In 1968, they pointed out, American bombs had created 2.6 million craters ". . . with currently incalculable consequences for the countryside."[12]

Still more criticism broke over the Administration when President Thieu replaced his civilian prime minister, the rather gentle Tran Van Huong, with General Tran Thien Khiem, generally considered a hawk. Administration critics bluntly accused Saigon of pursuing a militaristic policy at a time when the United States was trying to negotiate a peace. In late September, Averell Harriman, whom Nixon had relieved as envoy at the Paris peace talks in favor of Henry Cabot Lodge, stated that the United States must ignore Saigon and forge an agreement with North Vietnam and with the National Liberation Front in the South. The Nixon administration was acting ". . . as though it is some sort of a satellite of the Saigon government. A government should not be imposed on the south but the personal interests of President Thieu and Vice President Cao Ky should not be allowed to become the premises of American policy."[13] Also in late September, Senator Mike Mansfield returned from a tour of Asia and stated ". . . that the American involvement in Laos had grown to such an extent that it could lead to another Vietnam war."[14] Citing Nixon's new Asian doctrine, he ". . . added that present tendencies in Laos were running directly counter to what should be expected."[15] Mansfield's remarks brought correspondents to the Laotian scene like bees to honey. In late October, the New York *Times* reported details of the private war being run by CIA in Laos. Once again, critics had a field day, and not a few Americans agreed with Senator Stuart Symington, a one-time hawk, who now expressed worry about extensive American commitments in light of a worsening domestic situation: ". . . We spend $44 for every child's education up to college age, but in Vietnam we spend $21,600 in ammunition alone to kill one enemy soldier."[16]

12. *The Sunday Telegraph,* August 10, 1969.
13. *The Times* (London), September 18, 1969.
14. *The Times* (London), September 21, 1969; see also Zalin B. Grant, "What Are We Doing in Thailand?" *The New Republic,* May 24, 1969.
15. *The Times* (London), September 21, 1969.
16. *The Sunday Times* (London), November 2, 1969.

Meanwhile, other prominent Americans were questioning Administration efforts to negotiate a peace. Cyrus Vance, who had been deputy of the American delegation at the Paris peace talks until the previous February, announced his own six-point peace program, which called for a "standstill cease fire," that is, an admission that the NLF/VC controlled large areas of South Vietnam and would have a share in determining a new government.[17] This was scarcely original—Robert Shaplen had suggested it two years earlier, in an article in *Foreign Affairs*[18]; it was still anathema to the Nixon administration, and especially so to the Thieu-Ky government.

President Nixon did not accept this and additional criticism passively, and, indeed, a few streaks of light appeared in somber skies. Some were transitory. Ho Chi Minh's death, in early September, brought hopeful prophecies from some Hanoi-watchers of a power struggle that would probably end in a peace party's gaining dominance.[19] It did nothing of the sort. The transition appeared orderly, and the new government, in less than a month, admitted severe problems, not the least being its dependence on China and the political price entailed,[20] a problem scarcely new and one admitted by Hanoi representatives in Paris to Ambassador Harriman the previous year.[21]

Nixon did send two specific signals to the new government. One was a three-day halt of B-52 raids in South Vietnam; when this evoked no response from the enemy, the raids were resumed. Another was an announcement, in mid-September, that he was withdrawing at least another thirty-five thousand American troops from South Vietnam before the end of 1969, an occasion used to place the onus again on North Vietnam with an appeal to begin "meaningful negotiations." Nixon also canceled draft calls for November and December and dismissed General Hershey, octogenarian subject of extreme criticism particularly from students objecting to the draft's bias.

Nixon also continued his partial-withdrawal policy in South Vietnam, and here he scored a major gain. By late September, most American combat units had been withdrawn from the Mekong Delta area. To the surprise of all but genuine counterinsurgency experts, pacification now proceeded much more rapidly than it had when the military was tearing up the countryside with futile search-and-destroy missions. A veteran British correspondent, Murray Sayle, found village elections ". . . going on all over the Delta. . . . Every Delta village is being paid 400,000 piasters for village deployment. . . . Villages prepared to elect a village chief are paid one million piasters. The money, which comes ultimately

17. *The Times* (London), New York, September 22, 1969.
18. Shaplen ("Crisis"), *supra.*
19. But see also Richard Hughes, "After Ho, Watch for Giap and a Tougher Line in Hanoi," *The Sunday Times* (London), September 7, 1969.
20. *The Times* (London), September 28, 1969.
21. *The Times* (London), September 18, 1969.

from American sources, is paid into a bank account operated by the
village chief and his six-man council." Although assassinations by VC
terrorists continued—". . . more than 30 village chiefs and minor government officials have been assassinated in the province around Mytho
this year"—the Phoenix program at last was taking hold. Provincial
Reconnaissance Units (PRUs) were ferreting out VC infrastructure,
killing VC where necessary, bribing where possible with rates that varied
from a thousand piasters for identification of a VC courier to fifty thousand piasters for a VC district chief.[22] Although military hawks argued
that such progress was the result of attrition strategy including the 1968
Tet "victory," other observers insisted that the key lay in withdrawing
American combat units. Nixon accepted the arguments of the latter
group, and MACV turned to a strategy not dissimilar to that recommended by General James Gavin in 1965—an enclave strategy derided
by hawks at the time. If nothing else, however, casualties dropped significantly, despite the warnings of military experts who said they would
rise!

Nixon was walking a political tightrope during this autumn and early
winter of 1969. Faced with increasing dissent, including a nationwide
moratorium, his major pitch continued to be a plea for time. In late
September, he pointed to some hopeful facts, for example that North
Vietnamese infiltration into the South was down two thirds from the
previous year, American casualties had decreased one third, combat remained at a minimum level. If the American people formed a popular
front behind his peace proposals, the President predicted, the Vietnam
war would end the next year.[23]

In early November, the President made another major policy speech
designed to calm an impatient electorate: ". . . The American people
cannot and should not be asked to support a policy which involves the
overriding issues of war and peace unless they know the truth about
that policy."[24] The situation was particularly grim, the speaker went
on, when he assumed the presidency:

. . . The war had been going on for four years; 31,000 Americans had
been killed in action; the training program for the South Vietnamese armed
forces was behind schedule; 540,000 Americans were in Vietnam with no
plans to reduce the number; no progress had been made at the negotiations
in Paris, and the United States had not put forth a comprehensive peace
proposal; the war was causing deep division at home and criticism from many
of our friends as well as our enemies abroad.

In short, and the President carefully pointed this out, the Democrats
had left him an unholy mess.

22. *The Sunday Times* (London), September 28, 1969.
23. *The Times* (London), September 26, 1969.
24. Nixon (*Public Papers*), *supra;* see also *The Sunday Times* (London), November 5, 1969.

What had he done?

He had refused to accept defeat:

. . . For the United States, this first defeat in our nation's history would result in a collapse of confidence in American leadership, not only in Asia but throughout the world.

For this reason, he refused to withdraw all of America's military forces in South Vietnam:

. . . I chose instead to change American policy on both the negotiating front and the battle front.

After repeating his peace proposals, he stressed his flexibility: ". . . anything is negotiable except the right of the people of South Vietnam to determine their own future."

The President next reviewed the Administration's public and private attempts to work out a *modus vivendi* with Hanoi; unfortunately, ". . . no progress whatever has been made except agreement on the shape of the bargaining table." This effort having failed, he was concentrating on a contingency plan:

. . . At the time we launched our search for peace I recognized we might not succeed in bringing an end to the war through negotiation. I, therefore, put into effect another plan to bring peace—a plan which will bring the war to an end regardless of what happens on the negotiating front.

This was turning the war back to the people most intimately concerned:

. . . In the previous Administration, we Americanized the war in Vietnam. In this Administration, we are Vietnamizing the search for peace.

The President's approach appeased a good many Americans, as did continuing favorable news from the war-torn country. In early November, the Saigon government announced that, in October, over five thousand Viet Cong rallied to the government's side, to make a total of nearly forty thousand defectors for the year. In late November, Lieutenant General Julian Ewell, commanding a large allied force in III Corps area north of Saigon, told reporters that ". . . the Vietcong were rapidly becoming non-existent, the North Vietnamese were being forced to write off certain units to be withdrawn." The general claimed that 97 per cent of the rural population in his area was ". . . under nominal Government control"; 82 per cent of the remaining sixty-one thousand enemy, he continued, were North Vietnamese.[25] The British correspondent Fred Emery, who reported the above, wrote in a dispatch the following day that VC defectors had climbed to twenty-six thousand this year, that Regional and Popular Forces recruitment had doubled, and

25. *The Times* (London), November 24, 1969.

that a million peasants had joined the People's Self-Defense Forces.[26] High percentages of Mekong Delta villages and hamlets had elected their own officials.

. . . None of these figures, it is true, supports the contention that people have been swung behind the Government. The "geometric progression of confidence" some Americans detect is still mainly on their charts.

Yet there is little doubt that many people are living freer from direct harassment than they can perhaps remember, and many more are directly committing themselves against the Vietcong by shooting at them.[27]

A month later, a *Time* correspondent, Mark Clark, reported from Saigon that, although ". . . statements of optimism are far more muted than in the halcyon days that preceded *Tet* in 1968, there is an unmistakable air of confidence." The Thieu regime, Clark reported, ". . . is a going concern. While Thieu is not a popular hero, he heads a government that is stable."[28]

A similar report was made to the President in late December, by a British counterinsurgency expert, Sir Robert Thompson, whom Nixon had sent to Vietnam to "reassess" the situation. The corpus of Thompson's report, based on a five-week tour, remained secret, but in articles, interviews, and private conversations, he displayed enthusiasm made the more impressive by contrast to the critical and pessimistic tone of his book *No Exit from Vietnam,* published in March 1969.

In an interview with Brian Crozier in London, Thompson optimistically discussed pacification progress: ". . . In this last year there has been a race back into the countryside which has been won by South Vietnamese, helped by the Americans." The South Vietnamese and Americans were working much more effectively together than formerly, and as a result the Viet Cong's position in the countryside was being eroded. The enemy had also suffered so badly that the balance of power had changed in favor of the allies:

. . . In last year's battles, the North Vietnamese lost the cream of their regular army and are having great difficulty now in restoring the strength of their units. The recruits are much younger, so that their morale and their capability is [sic] much lower than it was [sic]. This means that though they may be in a position, as a result of the infiltration that is now occurring, to mount an offensive again in the coming months, it is unlikely that they will be able to sustain any such offensive, and its targets will necessarily be limited.

26. *The Times* (London), November 25, 1969.
27. Ibid.
28. *Time,* December 26, 1969.

Thompson was also impressed with the South Vietnamese Government's performance:

> . . . The war is not, of course, solely a military issue. There is the political side, and one thing that definitely impressed me was that the present Government in South Vietnam is not only more stable than any government we have had for a number of years, but is also becoming more effective and its performance is improving. There is a much more relaxed atmosphere, and the confidence of the Government in its capacity to carry on the war is increasing daily.

Thompson concluded:

> . . . The war in South Vietnam can therefore be won, in the sense that a just peace can be obtained, whether negotiated or not, and that the South Vietnamese people will be in a position to determine their own future without any interference or compulsion from the North. This after all is the limit of the American aim, and has been very clearly laid down by the President, particularly at the Paris peace talks. To requote this paragraph in my report which President Nixon quoted last Monday: "A winning position in the sense of obtaining a just peace, whether negotiated or not, and of maintaining an independent non-Communist South Vietnam, has been achieved but we are not yet through."[29]

Nixon could not have invested in a better report, and he proudly quoted from it in a major speech in mid-December, at the same time announcing that he was withdrawing another fifty thousand American troops, mostly combat units, before April 1970[30]; in early January, the President cited Thompson's "positive appraisal" of the situation.[31] A month later, in Saigon, President Thieu emphasized his claim of controlling 93 per cent of the South Vietnamese countryside by staging a 475-mile bicycle race, whose seventy-three contestants pedaled the course without VC opposition.

As with optimistic pictures previously drawn by Saigon and Washington administrations, a few blurs marred this canvas.

The first was the Administration's negotiating position. Nixon's wounded tones in discussing Hanoi's intransigence bore little semblance of reality. Whatever his hopes, he had few reasons to expect Hanoi to negotiate an unfavorable peace after fighting a war that had destroyed much of North Vietnam and, by the American administration's own figures, taken the lives of over 450,000 enemy soldiers, not to mention those of thousands of civilians, within the previous six years.

29. Robert Thompson, "On the Way to Victory," *The Sunday Times* (London), December 21, 1969.
30. Nixon (*Public Papers*), *supra*.
31. Fred Emery, *The Times* (London), January 17, 1970.

Did the President expect Hanoi to be frightened? intimidated? contrite? In August 1969, a Canadian broadcasting correspondent, Michael Maclear, visited North Vietnam. American bombing, he reported, had made Highway One, 250 miles south of Hanoi, ". . . like one continuous, bone-jarring pothole." American planes had leveled five North Vietnamese cities and eighteen towns with a total population of 2 million: ". . . Urban civilization has ceased to exist in most of Viet-Nam's southern provinces—a region containing one-third of North Vietnam's 17 million people." Maclear found a bombed-out wasteland:

. . . as far as I could see, and certainly according to local officials, there is not a single modern school, hospital, factory or administrative building remaining. It is a world of clay and thatch. . . .[32]

The President could resume bombing of the North, it was true, but, short of people, little remained to bomb. And bombing people out of existence—Giulio Douhet's strategic-genocide theory—would not be permitted either by American or world opinion.

What Nixon and his advisers, and a good many American citizens, failed to realize was that Hanoi could not be further hurt. She had suffered—but she had survived. Peking continued to vie with Moscow to supply essential needs and, in Moscow's case, to guarantee general postwar rehabilitation. American bombing had long since given the North Vietnamese people a genuine stake in the war. They would continue to exist on a subsistence level—a disciplined people is as essential to protracted war as flexibility in tactics and strategy. Whatever methods chosen to fight the war so far, Hanoi never forgot the requirements of portracted war: As Callwell had pointed out nearly a century earlier (see Chapter 15, Volume I), the "savages" were the professionals in their own environment.

Other factors entered. Hanoi was on the brink of winning a tremendous psychological victory by chasing American forces from the scene. Decades before, Lyautey had protested regarding the Spanish withdrawal in Morocco: ". . . My God! An army retreats when it must but it does not announce the fact to the enemy in advance." Nixon was forced to make this very announcement, which increased the influence of Hanoi hawks, who, negotiations or no, saw themselves on the verge of obtaining a major objective. Why should Hanoi hurry to negotiate when continuing criticism of the war in the United States and throughout the world would force Nixon's hand further and further? In mid-November, the scandal of the My Lai killings had broken, and though the full effect of the shock on the American people had not yet been wrought, cacophonous voices were already shrilling the shameful facts. Also in November, Senator Fulbright, a long-time critic of the war, publicly criticized growing presidential power to involve the United

32. *The Sunday Times* (London), November 9, 1969.

States in such areas as South Vietnam, where ". . . the United States has no vital security interest."[33] Fulbright kept up his attack in December, stating that Nixon's Vietnamization policy meant ". . . a continuing war of stalemate and attrition." Other legislators reacted adversely to reports of a secret war in Laos, and, in mid-December, the Senate voted to bar American combat troops from Laos and Thailand.[34] Dissension, in short, now ruled Washington counsels as it ruled the nation—all to Hanoi's benefit.

What about the optimistic situation in the South Vietnamese countryside?

Here, again, the Administration exhibited considerable naïveté, by treating a lull in guerrilla activity as if it were a major victory—precisely what Sir Charles Gwynn had warned against in 1934. American commanders would have been wise to respect the Spartan admonition to Philip of Macedon: ". . . If you imagine that your victory has made you greater than you were, measure your shadow." If parts of South Vietnam were being cleared of enemy, large numbers of enemy remained. In early November, the respected Washington correspondent of *The Times* (London), Louis Heren, reported that, of PAVN's 430,-000 troops, about 130,000 were in the South or in border sanctuaries. He placed VC strength at sixty thousand trained guerrillas, ninety thousand in political cadres, and perhaps fifty thousand in local irregular forces.[35] Fred Emery reported from Saigon in mid-November that the enemy was launching sporadic attacks:

. . . Less eye catching but more important is continued VC terrorism. Against all the rosy claims for the Government's accelerated pacification—which undoubtedly has taken it into occupation of ever expanding areas—must be set the one ineradicable statistic of terrorist incidents which has barely gone down at all with last year.

Over the past fifteen months, there has been a rough average of 19 incidents a day throughout the country, and today's Government bulletin, covering a 24-hour period of delayed reports, is a particularly grim example, showing 32 civilians killed and 45 wounded. The worst incidents were buses running over mines, but the killed included no fewer than five village and hamlet officials, and two Government revolutionary development cadres, all attacked inside hamlet areas.

It is of little comfort to assert, as some do, that this shows the success of the pacification program, which has so discomfited the Vietcong that they are making a special target of these kind [sic] of people. It is precisely because, whatever the military lull, they can inflict retribution on this scale,

33. *The Times* (London), November 13, 1969; see also Senator Fulbright's statement, on February 3, 1969, announcing a senatorial ad hoc subcommittee on United States Security Agreements and Commitments Abroad. Quoted in *Survival,* April 1969.

34. *The Times* (London), December 15, 1969.

35. *The Times* (London), November 3, 1969.

discriminately and indiscriminately, that pacification is shown to be rarely the same thing as security. And the difference is vital.[36]

In a later dispatch, quoting optimistic reports of General Ewell concerning eleven provinces north of Saigon, Emery also noted that the American general envisaged ". . . a war around here somewhere for the next 50 to 150 years."[37] President Nixon, in his mid-December speech, also noted ". . . one disturbing new development," which was a substantial increase in infiltration—some eight thousand a month from the North.[38]

Sir Robert Thompson's expressed optimism also glossed over some disturbing facts. Thompson had been enthusiastic before—in 1963, for example—and had been wrong. Whatever the total content of his report to the President, he had to admit to grave deficiencies in the scene that he had surveyed as paid consultant to the Nixon administration. Thompson had always deemed a constable force necessary for defeating an insurgency and maintaining the peace. At a London seminar in early 1969, he had pointed to the South Vietnamese failure to build a viable rural police force: ". . . In fact the Police Force in South Vietnam today is, from the point of view of numbers, just about the size the country would require in peace time, and it is not even trained for that."[39] This deficiency continued to exist. Another deficiency, to which he privately admitted, was a lopsided economic position, by which a country of 17.5 million people, with an estimated GNP of $2.5 billion (in large part, U.S.-subsidized), was supporting an armed force over one million strong (including 472,500 regular troops). This condition could scarcely improve under what Thompson called ". . . a long-haul, low-cost strategy" (with South Vietnam increasingly assuming the military burden) that would be necessary for at least three to five years, ". . . before Hanoi is compelled to give up her purpose and to negotiate a real settlement."[40]

We don't know what Thompson privately reported to President Nixon concerning President Thieu and his government. Publicly, he shared *Time* magazine's enthusiasm, and spoke admiringly of Thieu, whom he considered a real politician.

Thieu might have been a real politician—whatever that meant—but he had already proved himself a strong man in the worst totalitarian tradition: As someone disparagingly remarked, ". . . The Brown Sahib has replaced the White Sahib." His officials censored newspapers as frequently as his secret police arrested political dissidents. Magazines disavowing any of his acts were suppressed, such as *Time* and *Newsweek;*

36. *The Times* (London), November 11, 1969.
37. *The Times* (London), November 24, 1969.
38. Nixon (*Public Papers*), *supra.*
39. RUSI Seminar, *supra;* The reader perhaps will remember that Diem subverted the Michigan State University training effort to gain a national Gestapo-like police force. See Chapter 65.
40. *Time,* December 26, 1969.

he filled jails with political prisoners—Communists, yes, but also non-Communists; his secret police arrested and held opponents without charge. Some of his legislation was as oppressive as that dreamed up by the Diem-Nhu regime. The evils of earlier Saigon governments were carried over to the Thieu-Ky regime, and American efforts to put them right proved futile. General Duong Van Minh, leader of the revolt against Diem, returned from a four-year exile in Thailand and almost immediately denounced the minority basis of Thieu's government, stating, according to Fred Emery, ". . . that the Government has cut itself off from the people, and he adds that this cannot be. . . ."[41]

Government ineptness and corruption had been the Viet Cong's secret weapon since 1954, and so it remained. In enemy minds, North and South, Nixon could de-escalate at will, but the target remained the South Vietnamese people, and the VC were still adept at persuading or intimidating or otherwise preventing peasants from supporting established government.

So long as this government remained authoritarian, so long as Thieu's political base rested on force, so long as a gulf existed between mandarin bureaucracy and peasants, the Viet Cong would continue to operate. In the enemy's mind, American presence or no, the Saigon government would eventually fall. So the problem for Hanoi and the PRG was what it had always been: helping the process along with flexible tactics of revolutionary warfare.

This was what neither Nixon nor his advisers seemed to understand at the close of the Administration's first year. And this is what Thompson apparently failed to understand, a failure made the more dangerous because of his reputation as counterinsurgency expert.

Those fortunate enough to know either Sir Robert personally or his works on counterinsurgency are generally impressed with his genial presentation of a complicated subject. *Defeating Communist Insurgency* and *No Exit from Vietnam* should be read by anyone interested in the subject, since Thompson is undoubtedly more capable than most of examining a counterinsurgency environment to determine the degree of governmental success in prosecuting a campaign.

But, like many of us, Thompson is also a prisoner of his background. At the time of his mission, he was fifty-three years old, an English public school-Cambridge product, Malayan civil service, wartime service with the RAF and with Wingate in Burma, then civil service and a prominent role in the suppression of the Malayan insurgency. This background helps explain his expertise in counterinsurgency. Unfortunately, it did not endow him with deep political understanding, either of Asia or of the world, either in general or in revolutionary particulars. Once Thompson leaves the nuts and bolts of an insurgency situation for the machinery of political theory, he is a doomed mechanic, as witness his latest

41. *The Times* (London), November 14, 1969.

book, *Revolutionary War in World Strategy 1945–1969*,[42] in which he pleads (among other things) the theory of monolithic communism. As one reviewer unkindly put it, ". . . One can easily be 'the world's greatest expert' on the art of killing Asian revolutionaries without having the slightest idea of what Asian revolution is all about."[43]

Thompson unavoidably carried certain preconceptions with him to Vietnam in late 1969. One was an approach to counterinsurgency based largely on his Malayan experiences. While agreeing in general with this approach, we point out that what was good for counterinsurgency in Malaya was not always good for counterinsurgency in South Vietnam, where a far more complex situation called for a more selective and decentralized approach.[44] Thompson also took with him a strong belief in a "win" policy. In early 1969 he told a seminar, ". . . The moment you say that you will negotiate in a situation like this, it means that you are prepared for less than victory. In insurgency less than victory means defeat. In other words, you are prepared to settle for defeat."[45]

Thompson presumably is talking about "victory" of the type achieved in Malaya, a claim forever made by British authorities despite Ch'en P'ing's escape, his subsequent guerrilla operations in the North, and, perhaps more important, Malaya's current internal troubles.[46] Rather than resulting in clear-cut "victory," Britain's campaign in Malaya provided local government with breathing space in which to remove or ameliorate basic frictions and build a viable state. This is laudable—it has happened before—but it is not "victory," which, even in a conventional sense, is at best ephemeral.

In denying the validity of negotiation as a way to end the war, Thompson indirectly was condemning the efficacy of the Saigon government (which, indeed, he should have done). Presumably, he expected this government to continue to strengthen, while the American Government carried out ". . . a long-haul, low-cost strategy." But this term was surely relative; one might have asked: "How long and how low?" Fifteen billion a year? Ten billion? Five billion? Three years? Five years? Ten years? Twenty years? This type of "long-haul, low-cost strategy" scarcely respected either the state of American finances or the temper of the American people. The time for a long-haul, low-cost strategy was 1965. In 1969, the situation demanded settlement.

Finally, Thompson did not point out, at least publicly, another continuing deficiency: the old quarrel between civil and military control

---

42. Robert Thompson, *Revolutionary War in World Strategy 1945–1969* (London: Secker & Warburg, 1970).

43. John Gittings, *Survival*, March 1971.

44. Heilbrunn, op. cit., discusses this in detail.

45. RUSI Seminar, *supra;* see also Robert Thompson, "My Plan for Peace in Vietnam," *Reader's Digest*, March 1970.

46. John Slimming, *Malaysia: Death of a Democracy* (London: John Murray, 1969).

of the American mission. In theory, seventy-four-year-old Ambassador Bunker was running the show. In fact, the civil effort continued to diverge from the military effort, which at times was independent and usually in conflict. Although Nixon attempted to bolster the ambassador's authority, he erred, as had Kennedy and Johnson, in allowing the military effort to assume operational predominance.

Neither Nixon nor his advisers seemed to understand, at the close of the Administration's first year, that they were grappling with a political problem. Kissinger already had sounded the key word: *honor*. The Administration was embracing Comines's dictum, ". . . he who has success has honor," while overlooking Talleyrand's remark: ". . . Honor in our age of corruption has been invented in order to make vanity do the work of virtue." Nixon failed to see that victory could come only from within a country whose government was attuned to the demands of its peoples. Failing to see this, he made the fatal error of yielding to military advisers who forever believed that the threat was external and who, if they had had their way, would have enlarged the action to nuclear-warfare proportions.

As we shall see, the military got their way sufficiently to reverse the trend set by the President and to carry the war to Cambodia and Laos.

Chapter 93

Confused U.S. objectives • Congressional opposition mounts • Involvement in Laos • President Thieu's stand • President Nixon's dilemma • The Cambodian invasion • Disappointing results • Clark Clifford's new plan (II) • Renewed action in South Vietnam • Nixon's dominoes • Administration reverses • Paris: peace plan versus peace plan • The situation in South Vietnam: fact or fiction? • Enemy offensive moves

CONGRESSIONAL DISAPPROVAL of President Nixon's course in Vietnam continued into 1970. In mid-February, the President submitted a foreign-policy report to Congress that contained no specific statement of international objectives—". . . a disappointment to those who looked for an ordered definition, as opposed to a declamation, of American interests."[1] In the same month, a staff study published by the Senate Foreign Relations Committee concluded that ". . . the assumptions on which American policy [in Vietnam] are based are ambiguous, confusing, and contradictory." Nixon's policy depended on three factors, the study suggested: progressive Vietnamization, the stability of the Saigon government, and lack of enemy interference.

. . . We believe that the evidence presented in this report leads to the inference that the prospects for a successful outcome of any of the aforemen-

1. The Institute for Strategic Studies, "The Super-Powers." In *Strategic Survey, 1970* (London: Institute for Strategic Studies, 1971).

tioned three factors, much less all three, must be regarded as, at best, uncertain.

Dilemmas thus seem to lie ahead in Vietnam, as they have throughout our involvement in this war that appears to be not only far from won but far from over.[2]

In public hearings, individual senators bluntly made clear their hostility. Charles Goodell spoke of "illusions" entertained by the Administration and concluded: ". . . We have not Vietnamized the war: we have cosmetized it." Senator Fulbright cogently asked: ". . . In what exact ways have we advanced toward peace? The war, as we know, is still going on. Replacements are still being sent to Vietnam; we are still suffering about 750 casualties a week; and the war is still costing the American people about $70 millions a day." Senators Harold Hughes and Thomas Eagleton proposed a resolution calling on the Saigon government for immediate reforms; in lieu thereof, ". . . the President of the United States should declare officially that our commitment to the present Government of South Vietnam is ended."[3]

Adding to legislative dissatisfaction was the increasingly serious Laotian situation. Nixon's refusal to deny or confirm alleged American involvement drew strong criticism from Senator George McGovern in early March. Requesting that the Senate secretly debate the subject, McGovern condemned the notion of a secret war:

. . . It is absolutely incredible that a great nation such as ours could be waging a major military operation in a foreign country without the knowledge of either citizens or its Congress. But that is the fact.

We don't know the truth about our heavy involvement in Laos. We are increasingly in the dark about what is really going on in Vietnam. Indeed, the entire southeast Asia involvement is more and more riddled with confusion and contradiction.[4]

Although Nixon assured Congress that no American ground troops would be sent to Laos, he did not explain the presence of those already there—estimated from one to five thousand. Two weeks later, Secretary of State Rogers scarcely mollified worried congressmen by stating ". . . that the possibility of using American ground troops in Laos could not be ruled out, although there were no plans to do so at present."[5]

Even more alarming than these dissembling statements was the tack taken by President Thieu in an interview published in the March 9 issue

2. Louis Heren, *The Times* (London), Washington, D.C., February 2, 1970.
3. Ian McDonald, *The Times* (London), Washington, D.C., February 3, 1970.
4. Louis Heren, *The Times* (London), Washington, D.C., March 3, 1970; see also Roland A. Paul, "Laos: Anatomy of an American Involvement," *Foreign Affairs,* April 1971, for an analysis of the reasons for (and fallacy of) American official silence.
5. Louis Heren, *The Times* (London), Washington, D.C., March 17, 1970.

of *U. S. News and World Report*. Thieu reverted to the domino theory: If the United States withdrew from the Asian mainland, the Chinese would take over Laos, Cambodia, Malaysia, and Indonesia. South Vietnam, Thieu insisted, was the key to the whole area: ". . . We have to contain the rush of the communists right here—not in the U.S., not at Midway or Hawaii or in mid-ocean, but right here on the Asian mainland." Thieu insisted ". . . that there was no fixed timetable for the withdrawal of American troops. The South Viet-Namese forces must be given sufficient and adequate means to fight the communists. . . ."[6]

Some observers read this as a desire to widen the war to Laos and, with Sihanouk's fall, to Cambodia. Thieu had every reason for maintaining a state of emergency: It was his principal justification for running one of the most repressive and corrupt governments in the world.

Unfortunately, the American military, both MACV and the JCS, agreed, in part, with Thieu. The well-informed correspondent of *The Times* (London) in Washington, Louis Heren, wrote that ". . . the [American] Army is resisting further cuts [in South Vietnam]. General William Westmoreland, the Chief of Staff, is reported to be pressing for a six-month delay ostensibly because the rate of 'Vietnamization' is too fast for safety and comfort."

In spring of 1970, Nixon was caught between two powerful forces: public opinion at home, military opinion at home and abroad. If for no other than domestic political reasons, he had to continue winding down the war in Vietnam. At the same time, MACV and the Pentagon were pointing to forty thousand Communist troops active in Cambodia and renewed enemy activity in South Vietnam, and were violently arguing against further troop withdrawals.

In trying to satisfy everybody, Nixon satisfied no one. He further erred by reintroducing the bogey of atomic warfare, which alarmed and enraged other countries, friendly, neutral, and enemy.

On April 21, the President told the nation that he had based his troop-withdrawal program on three criteria. Two had been met: Training and equipping South Vietnamese forces had ". . . substantially exceeded our expectations"; and there had been "extensive progress" in pacification (including a new land-reform bill that, in theory, would provide over 3 million acres for distribution).[7] No progress, however, had been made on the negotiating front. Despite that disappointment and despite threatening Communist activity both in Cambodia and South Vietnam, he was continuing the withdrawal program—115,500 troops having already returned home. He was now planning to withdraw another 150,000 by spring of 1971—more, if progress was made in negotiations.

6. *The Times* (London), Washington, D.C., March 9, 1970.
7. *Time*, April 6, 1970.

Having thrown this bone to the political dogs, he tossed a biscuit to the military mastiffs:

. . . Viewed against the enemy's escalation in Laos and Cambodia and the stepped-up attacks this month in South Viet-Nam, it [further troop withdrawal] clearly involves some risks. But I again remind the leaders of North Viet-Nam that, while we are taking these risks for peace, they will be taking grave risks should they attempt to use the occasion to jeopardize the security of our remaining forces in Vietnam by increased military action in Vietnam, in Cambodia, or in Laos. . . . If I conclude that increased enemy action jeopardizes our remaining forces . . . I shall not hesitate to take strong and effective measures.[8]

In case anyone missed the point, James Reston noted in the New York *Times:*

. . . what the President *says* should be taken with the utmost seriousness. For if he personally takes the responsibility for withdrawing troops against the advice of General Abrams, and the enemy then launches an attack that threatens a major military defeat or even the destruction of General Abrams' command, it is not too much to say that he will use any weapon at his command, repeat *any* weapon, to avoid the destruction of his remaining soldiers.[9]

The threat of either atomic warfare or bombing the North was implicit in the President's words, but hawks paid little attention. For the biscuit tossed to them formed but an appetizer for a carcass soon to follow. Paradoxically, while Nixon was speaking of further troop withdrawals, MACV was completing plans to invade Cambodia.

In mid-March, a coup in Phnom Penh had ousted the querulous playboy-mystic Prince Norodom Sihanouk, in favor of General Lon Nol, who became prime minister and acting chief of state. Whether American-inspired or not, the coup seemed to MACV and Pentagon planners a heaven-sent opportunity. Administration hawks at once began demanding substantial support for the new ruler, who was vociferously protesting the presence of some forty thousand Communist Vietnamese troops on Cambodian soil. Henry Brandon noted from Washington that ". . . those favoring American aid claim that the North Vietnamese forces are already in such disarray along the South Vietnam-Cambodian border that American aid would have a decisive effect in ending the war especially as the North Vietnamese are over-extended."[10]

President Nixon apparently agreed. In response to a request from Premier Lon Nol, never a man to think small—a fuming Senator Ful-

---

8. *The Times* (London), April 22, 1970.
9. James Reston, *The Times* (London), New York, April 21, 1970.
10. Henry Brandon, *The Times* (London), Washington, D.C., April 25, 1970.

bright said that his request was for ". . . hundreds of millions of dollars worth of arms"—the President authorized MACV to send several plane-loads of arms from Saigon to Phnom Penh; these were said to have been AK47 rifles captured from the enemy. At about the same time, the President must have agreed to a MACV-JCS proposal for a combined South Vietnamese-American invasion of Cambodia.

Unfortunately, this was only the beginning. MACV, the Pentagon, and the CIA had been supporting a clandestine war in Laos for four years, and had long been wanting to strike enemy sanctuaries across the six-hundred-mile-long Cambodian border. Planners now dusted off previous contingency plans to emerge with an operation said to have been recommended to the President by a special task force, the Washington Special Action Group, which included Chairman of the JCS Wheeler, Richard Helms of the CIA, and presidential assistant Kissinger.

Operation Toan Thang (Complete Victory) kicked off on April 29.[11] American artillery, prepositioned inside South Vietnam, opened preparatory fire while South Vietnamese fighter-bombers further softened the target area. Three ARVN armored columns—some twelve thousand men, with perhaps fifty American "advisers"—then invaded a border area known as Parrot's Beak. American helicopters, including gunships, supported the operation, as did various logistic and medical-evacuation personnel.

Shortly after Vietnamese columns began clanking into Parrot's Beak, a combined task force commenced Operation Prometheus, north of Parrot's Beak. After suitable preparatory air and artillery fire, some five thousand American troops pushed into an area known as Fish Hook, a two-pronged operation that included three South Vietnamese paratroop battalions landed by American helicopters, and one that was designed to close a trap around the enemy. Military spokesmen described the total operation as a "quick-strike" pincers movement converging on the enemy headquarters known as the Central Office for South Vietnam (COSVN).

The offensive came as a surprise to nearly everyone (except the enemy). A Pentagon spokesman sounded the Administration's line: The purpose of the action was ". . . to destroy an extensive complex of North Vietnamese and Vietcong bases and depots in Cambodian territory, barely 25 miles from Saigon . . . the action is a necessary and effective measure to save American and other free world lives and to strengthen the Vietnamization program."[12] Lieutenant General Do Cao Tri, who commanded Operation Toan Thang, told correspondents that his mission was ". . . to kill as many Viet-cong as possible, destroy

11. More precisely, Complete Victory 42 and 43, following forty-one earlier Complete Victory operations begun after the 1968 Tet offensives.
12. Ian McDonald, *The Times* (London), Washington, D.C., April 29, 1970.

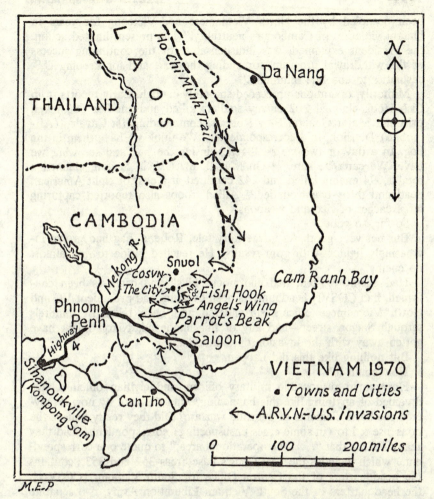

M.E.P

their supply depots and neutralize their activities."[13] President Nixon appeared on television to explain, somewhat ingeniously, that the invasion was not an invasion. Sounding not a little like Louis XIV's minister of war, Louvois, when undertaking the destruction of the Palatinate, in 1689, ". . . with the intention of destroying forever the war potential of the enemy,"[14] the President explained that the Cambodian operation was intended to eliminate ". . . the headquarters for the entire communist military operation in South Vietnam. This key control center has

13. Fred Emery, *The Times* (London), Phnom Penh, April 30, 1970.
14. Alfred Vagts, *Defense and Diplomacy. The Soldier and the Conduct of Foreign Relations* (New York: Kings Crown Press, 1956).

been occupied by the North Vietnamese and Vietcong for years in
blatant violation of Cambodia's neutrality." The present limited action,
the President explained, was indispensable for the continuing success
of the withdrawal program, for ending the war, and for keeping U.S.
casualties to absolute minimum.[15]

Militarily, operations proceeded smoothly enough. Early reports from
Fish Hook claimed 202 enemy soldiers killed and another 166 taken
prisoner. Major General Elby Roberts, commanding 1st Cavalry (Airmobile) Division, told correspondents: "We think we have them in the
bag. In a day or two we shall reach inside the bag and see what we
have. We can't be sure."[16] On May 3, MACV, in Saigon, claimed a
total 1,094 enemy killed and 242 captured at a cost of eight American
dead and thirty-two wounded.[17] Allied troops also reported capturing
large caches of rice and weapons.

So far, so good.

But not very good. As in the fairy tale, Roberts' bag had grown increasingly lighter—with grim results: He reached inside to find almost
no enemy.

Had enemy existed, had enormous "kills" and captures been confirmed, had COSVN headquarters been overrun, had prominent VC and
North Vietnamese officers surrendered and been taken in tumbrels
through Saigon streets—had any of this happened, Nixon might have
gotten away with the invasion of Cambodia.

But nothing like this did happen.

How could it?

How could responsible military officers and civilian officials have
dreamed of anything like this happening? Had they not by now discovered the basic elements of guerrilla warfare? Did they really believe the
nonsense fed to (in some cases unsuspecting) correspondents? Did they
really believe that ". . . the operational area," to quote one correspondent, "which includes the Viet Cong's base areas 352 and 353, 'contains
the headquarters of the Central Office for South Vietnam [COSVN],
the headquarters of the South Vietnam Liberation Army, two separate
regiments, an artillery command headquarters and a separate reconnaissance battalion' . . . a command complex said to be the nerve center
for the enemy war effort in the southern half of South Vietnam . . ."?

Did they really believe that there, in primitive Cambodian jungles,
they were going to find the North Vietnamese version of the Pentagon
and Fort Myer? Did they believe that Viet Cong and North Vietnamese forces were going to stand quietly by to await a pitched battle
in circumstances overwhelmingly favorable to enemy firepower? Did
they believe that, in an ARVN and a Saigon government known to be

15. Reuters, Washington, D.C., May 1, 1970.
16. Terence Smith, *The Times* (London), May 1, 1970.
17. Murray Sayle, *The Sunday Times* (London), May 3, 1970.

penetrated with Communist agents, this operation would surprise the enemy?

Apparently, responsible persons believed all this and more. The invasion of Cambodia was a conventional military operation intended to win a great "victory." Dispatches of that day read like those of World War II and Korea. Terence Smith, of *The Times* (London), who accompanied the American task force, wrote under a dateline of May 1:

. . . A total of 82 heavy artillery pieces had been positioned along and across the border. General Roberts [commanding the American 1st Cavalry (Airmobile) Division] said it was the greatest massing of artillery he had seen in one area since the Second World War. During the night, waves of B-52 bombers pounded the target in preparation. The heavy artillery began firing at dawn.

Early this morning, American F4 and F100 fighter-bombers began the first of 148 pre-planned air strikes, designed, together with the continuing artillery barrage, to soften up the area before the tanks and armored personnel carriers attacked. . . .[18]

All units apparently advanced on schedule. From Saigon, John Draw, of *The Times* (London), reported that ". . . sources from the battle area attributed the lack of big actions to 'the slow advance of allied troops that were instructed to take it carefully in tightening the noose around an estimated 7,000 Communist troops guarding this area.'" Although ". . . American troops, led by tanks, reached the headquarters zone of the Communist command yesterday and overran several North Vietnamese and Viet Cong base camps with little resistance . . . they were still searching for the underground headquarters itself."

Despite MACV's eulogistic communiqués, correspondents soon began to express doubts that made them unpopular with MACV. James Sterba, of the New York *Times*, for example, pointed out that, as opposed to Administration claims of an immense Communist build-up in South Vietnam, enemy activity, according to American intelligence officers, had been quite normal. Michael Hornsby, of *The Times* (London), reported from Saigon that observers were questioning the discrepancy between large numbers of enemy killed and captured versus the small number of weapons taken—were dead civilians being mistaken for dead enemy? By May 3, military leaders were backtracking. Reports to Washington from the Fish Hook area were "not encouraging"; in Washington, Ian McDonald, of *The Times* (London), wrote that ". . . military commanders now hint that the enemy might have had advance word of the operation . . ."[19]

By this time, President Nixon was undoubtedly sorry that he had ever heard of either the American army or Cambodia. A significant portion

18. Terence Smith, *The Times* (London), May 1, 1970.
19. Ian McDonald, *The Times* (London), Washington, D.C., May 3, 1970.

of Congress, on the other hand, was sorry that they had ever heard of Nixon. Not having seen fit to take the nation's legislators into his confidence, the President reaped Congressional wrath. Senator Fulbright called the operation ". . . a major expansion of the war. . . . If you accept the premises on which our justification and objectives have been based, this is consistent with our war policy. It is not consistent with any plan for ending the war."[20] Senator Mike Mansfield said: ". . . We're sinking deeper into the morass. The feeling of gloom in the Senate is so thick that you could cut it with a knife. . . ."[21] State Department officials who had not been advised of the action joined the chorus of disapproval, pointing out that Lon Nol's bellicose stand, taken without an adequate army at his disposal, had brought many of his troubles on himself.[22] Just as had Nixon, who had ". . . isolated himself from his State Department and depended almost entirely on military advice and White House staff work. His decision [to invade Cambodia], when announced, led several officials to resign, while 300 others in the State Department signed memoranda of protest."[23] Senators from both parties quickly moved ". . . to introduce legislation barring the use of funds to support American troops in Cambodia for any reason."[24]

Lon Nol also proved embarrassing. President Nixon reportedly had not seen fit to take the little general into his confidence, but Lon Nol rolled easily with the punches. He protested mildly against outright invasion: From Phnom Penh, Fred Emery, of *The Times* (London), reported that ". . . there is no hiding the strong feeling that the Government would have preferred it done another way." Having gotten one up, Lon Nol next used the rationale of the Nixon doctrine for Southeast Asia by appealing ". . . for arms for 250,000 men, for helicopters, and equipment for a national army." Lon Nol envisaged an army of some four hundred battalions. Mr. Emery reported that ". . . as for capacity they say their present forces strength is already up from the initial 35,000 to over 80,000, and they reckon they can have the full 250,000 in service within no less than five months."[25]

Nixon also faced considerable public hostility, sometimes more vague than concrete. By May 1970, the government's overdraft on credibility was considerable, and though large numbers of Americans still listened to their President and in general wanted to believe what he told them, a mean cynicism was pervading the country, particularly when it came to Pentagon and MACV communiqués. Some hostility was not so vague. The nation's college and university bodies spilled out in protest: Violent

20. Ian McDonald, *The Times* (London), Washington, D.C., May 1, 1970.
21. *Time*, May 11, 1970.
22. Ian McDonald, *The Times* (London), Washington, D.C., April 30, 1970.
23. John Franklin Campbell, " 'What Is to Be Done?' Gigantism in Washington," *Foreign Affairs*, October 1970.
24. Ian McDonald, *The Times* (London), Washington, D.C., April 30, 1970.
25. Fred Emery, *The Times* (London), Phnom Penh, April 30, 1970.

demonstrations erupted on nearly eight hundred campuses. Student protests in Ohio and Mississippi so alarmed authorities that police and national guardsmen shot twenty-seven and killed six students—we shall not tolerate dissent.

We will not tolerate dissent—but dissent swirled around the Administration, and around an uncomfortable President who had ingeniously de-escalated war by invasion and who was now in trouble. Such was Congressional hostility—increased by Kent State and Mississippi killings —that Nixon promised Congressional leaders, significantly of both parties, ". . . that all American forces would be pulled out of Cambodia within six weeks and that troop withdrawals from South Vietnam would proceed as planned." Meanwhile, Nixon not only wanted, but had to have, a "victory."

Victory was nowhere in sight—the invasion was not going at all the way the generals had promised. COSVN was not to be found. In searching for it, MACV had launched new incursions into Cambodia; one report estimated that fifty thousand troops were now involved.[26]

As invasion became non-invasion, so now non-victory became victory. Military communiqués described in glowing terms the capture of enemy complexes such as "the city," a group of huts twenty miles west of the Fish Hook area. By May 7, MACV claimed that 3,244 North Vietnamese and VC soldiers had been killed, with 529 captured, versus twenty-nine Americans killed and seventy-eight wounded, 163 South Vietnamese killed and 840 wounded.[27] Three days later, the figures rose to 3,740 enemy killed and 1,041 captured, along with over three thousand tons of ammunition.[28]

Developments in Hanoi also seemed favorable. The perennially optimistic Hanoi-watcher P. J. Honey pointed to ". . . the present perilous position of North Vietnam," where, since Ho Chi Minh's death, ". . . Communist leadership had been locked in an internal power struggle from which Le Duan now appears to be emerging the victor."[29] Le Duan, Honey continued, on April 25 ". . . ordered a large-scale purge of the Communist party—the first in its 40 years' existence—which cannot but weaken it in the immediate future." Honey also pointed to ". . . a desperate manpower shortage" in the North, the result of five hundred thousand North Vietnamese casualties in the South, a figure admitted by North Vietnam, which is ". . . unable to replace troop loses even though she conscripts males from 16 to 40 years of age. . . ."

These happy thoughts disguised neither over-all failure of allied action in the South nor an unpleasant political complication. Nixon, like

26. Michael Hornsby, *The Times* (London), Saigon, May 6, 1970.
27. Michael Hornsby, *The Times* (London), Saigon, May 7, 1970.
28. *The Sunday Telegraph*, May 10, 1970.
29. Ibid.

Napoleon after the "conquest" of Vitebsk, might have asked, ". . . Do you think I have come all this way just to conquer these huts?" Despite continuing communiqués claiming capture of Communist huts, arms, and rice, Communist prisoners seemed in short supply. On May 21, the Pentagon explained that COSVN, the elusive headquarters, ". . . had moved back into Cambodia beyond the 21-mile limit set up for U.S. ground operations."[30] This did not mean the end of the operation, however. Vice President Ky had stated that ARVN troops would remain in Cambodia after the American withdrawal on June 30. How long would they remain? For ". . . several months at the least . . . until the Cambodians were strong enough to defend themselves against North Vietnamese and Viet Cong. . . ."[31] Ky's statement further depressed Administration officials—as well it might, considering Indochinese historical evolution.

To add to Nixon's woes, on May 25 *Life* magazine published a lengthy article by Clark Clifford, President Johnson's disaffected Secretary of Defense, a one-time hawk who had become a powerful critic of the Vietnam war. Clifford now accused Nixon of contradicting stated policy with positive action—of widening the war to American and world detriment. After denying validity of the domino theory, and pointing to American lack of contributing allies in Southeast Asia, he accused the President of holding a "curious obsession" about Asia in general and Indochina in particular. To consider South Vietnam a strategic necessity—an arena where the future of the world would be decided—made no sense:

. . . The war in Vietnam is a local war arising out of the particular political conditions existing in southeast Asia. I consider it a delusion to suggest that it is part of a world-wide program of common aggression.

As to the war's nature,

. . . our problem in Vietnam is due not only to our inability to attain the military goals, despite our great effort, but to the fact that the struggle is basically a political one. The enemy continues to symbolize the forces of nationalism. The regime which we support is a narrowly based military dictatorship.

The Cambodian venture, Clifford went on, was meaningless militarily. The enemy would stay beyond our reach no matter how long troops remained in the area. Once troops were withdrawn, the enemy would return to old haunts. Despite this inevitable result, ". . . a determined effort will be made to portray the entire adventure as a success, even though no major engagements will have taken place and the number of enemy casualties will be woefully small."

30. *The Times* (London), Washington, D.C., May 21, 1970.
31. Michael Hornsby, *The Times* (London), Saigon, May 12, 1970.

If military results were negligible, the action created a new set of political problems. More than ever, a political settlement was needed to end the war. Clifford offered a three-point program that called for total disengagement from combat by end of 1970 and total withdrawal by end of 1971.

The Nixon administration remained seemingly oblivious to this and other outspoken criticism. In early June, the President told the nation ". . . that the Cambodian intervention was the most successful operation of a long and difficult war."[32] This might well have been, but it still failed to count for much. Administration arguments that the operation had deprived the enemy of rice for three months and ammunition for nine months fell on tired ears—legislators and public had heard all this before. Nor were feelings mollified by an announcement that Cambodia was to receive $7.9 million worth of small arms—the Nixon doctrine for Asia had called for emphasis on economic, not military, aid.

Twist and wiggle as he did, Nixon could not evade the fact that he had enlarged the war without accomplishing the stated mission of eliminating enemy operational headquarters in Cambodia. MACV could talk all it wanted about weapons and rice. Since 1932, the Vietnamese had proved that they could go without either and still fight. Hanoi-watchers could discern crisis in Hanoi and point to a manpower shortage. But, considering gains in the South in particular and political reality in general, neither Moscow nor Peking would abandon Hanoi in the crunch: In June, diplomats in Moscow warned Washington that the drain on North Vietnam in Cambodia and Laos was again turning her toward China; to counter that, the U.S.S.R. agreed to furnish more weapons and material to the DRV, thus continuing the vicious circle of escalation.

Thus enemy strength in the South remained basically unaltered: about a hundred thousand North Vietnamese either in the border areas or in South Vietnam and perhaps a hundred thousand "regular" Viet Cong supported by sixty thousand provincial guerrillas and a civilian network of supporters and sympathizers. As General Abrams reportedly stressed to the President and his advisers, the real challenge remained in South Vietnam.[33] Abrams' worries were particularly well founded, for ARVN, of which he had spoken so optimistically, was beset with troubles. Colonel David Hackworth, an experienced ARVN adviser and heavily decorated combat officer quoted in a previous chapter, later wrote,

. . . Vietnamization is a word which must be a product of Madison Avenue. It's a public-relations dream. I haven't seen an improvement in ARVN. . . .

32. Louis Heren, *The Times* (London), Washington, D.C., June 4, 1970.
33. Henry Brandon, *The Sunday Times* (London), Washington, D.C., June 7, 1970.

Perhaps from a cosmetic viewpoint they look a little better in that they wear their helmets and keep their equipment on.[34]

Returning to the main challenge was not so easy. Once again, inept military strategy had created more problems than it had solved. Having supported Lon Nol's regime without being requested to do so, Nixon could not leave the country open to enemy vengeance. The Administration now veered to supporting a continued ARVN presence in Cambodia and even requested Congress to extend the deadline for American troop withdrawal.

Congress was having none of it. Not only did a Senate vote defeat the amendment, but, on June 24, the Senate formally repealed the Tonkin Gulf Resolution in a belated attempt to curb the President's military powers.[35]

The Administration ignored the rebuff. American planes were already overflying "limits" stated by Nixon and were attacking Communist supply routes in western Cambodia. MACV quietly assured the Saigon government of continued support of its troops in Cambodia. When the last American troops headed for the border, in late June, ". . . leaving behind a lingering form of tear gas, blown bridges and damaged roads in an effort to slow communist reoccupation of the area," thirty thousand ARVN troops remained behind. The Administration continued to insist that it had gained an impressive victory. In late June, Fred Emery, of *The Times* (London), reported from Saigon that ". . . the Americans' conviction of the success of the Cambodian operation remains undiminished. The first seven weeks of the campaign are said to have produced 11,872 communist forces killed, 1,587 captured, 21,966 individual weapons seized, 1,640 crew-served weapons seized. American casualties are put at 323 killed, 1,446 wounded."[36]

But Louis Heren reported a gloomy assessment in Washington, where officials admitted that the enemy controlled one third of Cambodia, moved freely in another third, and was expected to reoccupy its old border sanctuaries within a few months.[37]

President Nixon completed the last act of a play within a play by appointing a new ambassador to the Paris peace talks, seventy-three-year-old David Bruce, and by again making a public appeal to Hanoi: ". . . We are prepared, by negotiation, to bring out all of our forces and have no forces at all in South Vietnam if the enemy . . . will withdraw theirs." The American Government attached only two conditions, the President continued: The South Vietnamese must remain free to determine their own future, and the United States would not impose a coalition government. What if the people chose a Communist government? Nixon would

34. *Newsweek*, July 5, 1971.
35. Louis Heren, *The Times* (London), Washington, D.C., June 24, 1970.
36. Fred Emery, *The Times* (London), Saigon, June 24, 1970.
37. Louis Heren, *The Times* (London), Washington, D.C., June 29, 1970.

accept their judgment. He was sure that this would not happen: No Communist government had ever been freely elected. However, he would not hand South Vietnam to the Communists. The domino theory, the President insisted, was still valid:

. . . Now I know there are those that say, "Well, the domino theory is obsolete." They haven't talked to the dominoes. They should talk to the Thais, Malaysians, to Singapore, to Indonesia, to the Philippines, to the Japanese, and the rest.

And if the United States leaves Vietnam in a way that we are humiliated or defeated, not simply speaking in what are called jingoistic terms but in very practical terms, this will be immensely discouraging to the 300 million people from Japan clear round to Thailand and in free Asia.

And even more important, it will be ominously encouraging to the leaders of Communist China and the Soviet Union who are supporting the North Vietnamese. It will encourage them in their expansionist policies in other areas. . . .[38]

So the presidential voice sounded on that first night in July 1970. It might have been Eisenhower in 1956, Kennedy in 1962, Johnson in 1966. The record was the same. After ten years, thirty-five thousand American lives, and perhaps $100 billion, the United States was returning to square one.

More of the same followed.

In early July, the American chief of the Vietnamization program in the Mekong Delta, John Paul Vann, personally reported to President Nixon that the enemy effort had been reduced to ". . . dispersed and dispirited units of five North Vietnamese regiments." Citing the NLF's latest directive, the report spoke of waning enemy confidence. The NLF now admitted the possibility of a cease-fire, in which case ". . . only continuing guerrilla warfare can achieve our purpose in the ensuing complicated situation."[39] The directive continued:

. . . Strike now at only a few objectives over a wide area. Where necessary and so directed, local cells will go into retirement and await opportunity and orders.

Several developments tempered the optimism of Vann's report. One was increasing enemy activity inside South Vietnam. As early as June, MACV reported that, in the last two weeks of May, 221 Americans had been killed in South Vietnam, compared to 138 in Cambodia.[40] Two weeks after Vann had submitted his report, an American military

38. Louis Heren, *The Times* (London), Washington, D.C., July 2, 1970.
39. Richard Hughes, *The Sunday Times* (London), Hong Kong, July 5, 1970.
40. Louis Heren, *The Times* (London), Washington, D.C., June 2, 1970; Vann, himself, would be killed in a helicopter crash in the central highlands, in June 1972.

spokesman warned of a pending Communist offensive in the central highlands. Five thousand ARVN troops and some fifteen hundred American marines pushed west from Da Nang in a search-and-destroy mission designed to disrupt the enemy build-up. While this action was occurring, enemy units attacked a 101st Airborne Division base camp eleven miles from the Laotian border, killing at least thirty-two Americans, wounding 148, and forcing evacuation of the area.[41] The action continued to build until, in mid-August, MACV launched one of the heaviest air interdiction efforts of the war: Nearly a hundred B-52 bombers, each carrying tons of bombs, struck ". . . North Vietnamese supply and staging areas on both sides of the Laotian border."[42] In early September, enemy reinforcements were coming down the Ho Chi Minh Trail, while local cadres were reoccupying old border bases in Cambodia.

Cambodia itself was proving a sink-hole. The $7.9 million in arms hastily authorized in May did not go very far. The Nixon administration slated $25 million for military aid in fiscal year 1970–71, but, in early July, several members of the Foreign Intelligence Advisory Board visited Phnom Penh to survey Cambodia's needs. A week later, proposed military expenditure for the fiscal year shot to $75 million. Discounting South Vietnamese troops in Cambodia (supported by the United States), this was virtually a unilateral program. Despite not-so-subtle hints from American officials, SEATO and other Asian nations proved reluctant to help erect a new Cambodian bulwark against communism. These were the "dominoes" to whom President Nixon had referred—the ones who stood in fear and trembling of the Communist threat: Domino Australia sent a little civil aid, dominoes New Zealand and Korea sent some medicines, and domino Thailand refused a request from Lon Nol to send troops. In late July, domino Cambodia, in the form of its prime minister, ". . . rejected the idea of Cambodian membership in SEATO. Reiterating his Government's policy of neutrality, he said Cambodia had no intention of taking arms against her enemies if they withdrew from Cambodian territory."[43]

Undeterred, Nixon continued generously to support Lon Nol. In late August, Vice-President Spiro Agnew said that it would be "impossible" to withdraw American troops from South Vietnam if Cambodia fell to the Communists: ". . . We are going to do everything we can to help the Lon Nol government."[44]

Southeast Asian leaders could not have received better news. In Bangkok, at month's end, Thailand's prime minister, Marshal Thanom Kittikachorn, proposed to Agnew that the United States underwrite a "South-East Asianization" program—long-term United States economic,

41. *The Times* (London), AP, and Reuters, Saigon, July 23, 1970.
42. *The Times* (London) and AP, August 17, 1970.
43. *The Times* (London), Bangkok, July 23, 1970.
44. N. Y. Times News Service, *The Times* (London), August 23, 1970.

military, and financial assistance to build up Southeast Asian countries so that American ground forces will no longer be needed to fight in the area.[45] Though he did not achieve this goal, he did win Agnew's promise of substantial financial aid.

The Nixon administration fared no better on either the Saigon or the home front. Fighting in Cambodia had returned Vietnam to national and international front pages, and little escaped notice. In early July, the story of appalling conditions in South Vietnamese prisons—the inhuman "tiger cages"—broke. This led to a rash of survey stories, many of which openly criticized Thieu's increasingly authoritarian regime. If the war shifted into low gear, some observers remarked, Thieu's government, caught in rampant inflation and corruption, would probably flounder and fall. A vast black market flourished, as did profiteering, but beyond this was the seeming inability of Thieu and his lieutenants to control the shaky economy, which depended almost entirely on continued American aid.

Also in early July, a Congressional committee investigating the My Lai massacre concluded

. . . that all details of the killings were covered up at the divisional level. There was, the investigation states in a report released tonight, "a concerted effort among military and State Department officers to suppress all evidence of the allegation and its investigation."

It said that senior officers in both the American Division and the State Department were guilty of casting "a blanket of silence" over the massacres. . . .[46]

This adverse report further reduced Administration credibility, now at its perigee.

September brought more unfortunate news. Although the Senate rejected an amendment that would have forced the President to withdraw all American troops from Vietnam by end of 1971, stories broke on widespread use of marijuana by American troops. Then Vice-President Ky announced that he would visit the United States to speak at a right-wing rally—". . . my voice in the United States will be of one warrior to another, of one ally to another ally." After an uncomfortable seven weeks, in which he reiterated his plan several times, by means unknown he was persuaded to postpone the trip and finally to reduce considerably its dimensions.

Nor did progress enlighten the gloom of what, to many Americans, was becoming the Hundred Years' War. As James Reston noted in the New York *Times,*

. . . the Nixon Administration finds itself in a familiar bind. What it calls its successes do not produce the results it expected. It keeps winning almost

45. *The Times* (London), Bangkok, August 20, 1970.
46. Ian McDonald, *The Times* (London), Washington, D.C., July 14, 1970.

every military battle, but ironically, the weaker the enemy gets, the less the enemy seems willing to negotiate. Hanoi now seems determined merely to carry on the war until a new situation is created by the withdrawal of the majority of the American troops.

In early October, Ramsey Clark argued against the Administration's continued reliance on force and violence to gain ". . . solutions of international problems." Vietnamization was one more demonstration of muscle, while the Cambodian incursion

. . . manifests as clearly as does the continued and increasing bombing that American leadership still seeks to solve problems by violence. But while it may show we have a flexible and fierce striking power, it also demonstrates that we have no knockout punch. We can only go on fighting. It tells us American leadership has learned nothing from Vietnam. We want to walk out the victors by killing, by leaving a prolonged war in our wake. We cannot win that way.

Instead,

. . . Our purpose in Vietnam now must be the end of violence. We should immediately act to remove our military presence. All bombing should halt. For Vietnamese who want sanctuary, it should be offered. The most ardent and relentless effort possible directed at Moscow, Peking, Paris and Hanoi should seek a political solution—a government reflecting the interests and needs of the people as comprehensively as possible. We should announce a firm, speedy schedule for complete military withdrawal and adhere strictly to it. Six months is ample. We should announce now that there will be no offensive, aggressive military action. We will return fire when fired upon and protect our evacuation by military action as necessary, but we will not initiate military engagements.

Simultaneously, we should offer rehabilitation and development: billions for food, health, construction and economic assistance. . . .[47]

Meanwhile, in Paris, in mid-September, the Communist delegation put forward a new, eight-point peace plan, which David Bruce dismissed as new wine in old bottles.[48] In early October, with mid-term U.S. elections less than a month away, President Nixon offered what he fondly described as a "peace offensive." Addressing the nation on television from Savannah, Georgia, the President announced that his new initiative had been made possible by the remarkable success of the Vietnamization policy of the past eighteen months, and that it had won the concurrence of the South Vietnam, Laos, and Cambodia governments.[49] As for his plan, vintner Nixon was offering old wine in old bottles. He

47. Ramsey Clark, "On Violence, Peace and the Rule of Law," *Foreign Affairs*, October 1970.
48. (Editorial), "Documentation," *Survival*, December 1970.
49. Ibid.

was like the magician who promised to produce an elephant and came up with a mouse. His proposals were a diluted version of Henry Kissinger's plan outlined in *Foreign Affairs* in January 1969, a plan that itself remarkably resembled Robert Shaplen's plan presented as long ago as 1967. Nixon now called for a cease-fire in place, to be "effectively supervised" by international observers (a qualification Shaplen had realistically dismissed, a new international conference, negotiated troop withdrawals, and immediate release of all prisoners of war.[50]

Nixon's proposal won varied reception. *The Sunday Times* (London) noted that

. . . in a sense the Nixon speech takes him back to where he was in May of last year [1969] when he first put forward some ambiguous offers that could have opened up the route to a compromise political settlement if Hanoi had been willing. Now he has added the ceasefire and, noticeably, omitted any reference to elections as the route to a settlement.[51]

The analyst then put his finger on the weakness of Nixon's stand: It supposed that the North was willing to negotiate the Americans out of South Vietnam:

. . . Washington has persisted for years in thinking that such a day would come. But at present the Communists have opted for protracted war, both militarily and diplomatically, and it will be a big surprise to most of those who have lived through the Vietnam problem if they decide this is the time to switch.[52]

The Communist delegation in Paris shortly and sharply rejected a cease-fire in place—as Shaplen had said they would if inhibited by international supervision. In October 1967, he had warned:

. . . It is the writer's opinion that almost any policing plan that would include such straight-jacketed mechanisms as the International Control Commission is doomed to failure. . . . What the Viet Nam situation desperately demands is a more free revolutionary expression of its own ethos, something which, during the long and tragic postwar period when the French refused to let go in the South, was denied it, and which, under Diem and since, has continued to be precluded. If the South is to rediscover its own revolutionary traditions, and to preserve or modify them in relation to the communist North, it must be as unmolested and even as unsupervised as possible. This naturally involves risk of communist domination or subversion, but the risks must be taken in a true revolutionary atmosphere and milieu, and not under the gaze of an ineffective international police element.

This does not mean that the Americans and the Russians and possibly

50. *The Times* (London), Washington, D.C., October 9, 1970.
51. *The Sunday Times* (London), October 11, 1970.
52. Ibid.

other powers should not play a role, but in so far as possible the role should be of a "good offices" nature. . . .[53]

In Saigon, President Thieu made it known that he violently disagreed with President Nixon: He did not want a cease-fire; he would not accept neutrality; he wanted the Communists to leave his country and American troops to remain; and he would not release forty thousand Communist prisoners.[54] To some observers in the United States, the proposal seemed so politically inspired as to deserve contempt. As James Reston wrote in the New York *Times,*

. . . All governments operate on two levels—the moral and the political— but seldom in recent history has any administration matched the Nixon Administration's spectacular combination of priggish moralizing and political expediency.

One day it sounds like Billy Graham and the next it acts like Machiavelli. . . .[55]

Considering election results, Nixon failed to derive much political profit from his diplomatic ploy. Too many factors were operating against him. For some time, the momentous issue of Vietnam had been tearing Americans from normal loyalty. We saw the beginning of this process in the early sixties, when pro and anti sides steadily leaked classified information to suit their purposes (see Chapter 78). A certain amount of official leakage has always been a part of American Government—a case can be made for it as integral to the system of checks and balances. But major leakages—leakages of what are called "state secrets"—were now developing. For example, in May the CIA circulated a top-secret report on South Vietnam that contained devastating information. Concerned government officials took it upon themselves to inform the New York *Times* of this report. In mid-October, the New York *Times* broke the story by a veteran reporter we have earlier encountered, Neil Sheehan.

According to the CIA report, shortly after the Tet offensive of 1968 the Communists

. . . decided to shift their long-range strategy from intense military activity to political erosion. They stepped up their infiltration of secret agents into various branches of the South Vietnamese Government.

Most of the agents were natives of the southern part of divided Vietnam, and they were infiltrated into the armed forces, the police force and the South Vietnamese intelligence organizations whose task it was to eradicate the Vietcong and their North Vietnamese allies.

53. Shaplen ("Crisis"), *supra.*
54. *The Sunday Times* (London), October 11, 1970.
55. James Reston, N. Y. Times News Service, *The Times* (London), October 15, 1970.

The Communists had infiltrated over thirty thousand agents into the South Vietnamese Government ". . . in an apparatus that has been virtually impossible to destroy." Some twenty thousand of the agents operated in ARVN. According to the report,

. . . the enemy network could not exist without the tacit complicity whether from fear, sympathy or apathy, of the majority of South Vietnamese soldiers and policemen and [the report] says that such feelings provide evidence that the Saigon government could not command the deep loyalty of the men on whom it depends to defend itself.

With virtually unlimited intelligence at its disposal, the enemy would have little trouble in surviving military pressures to emerge (and presumably take over control) once the United States had withdrawn her troops.[56]

White House officials downplayed the importance of the report. It was "overly pessimistic" and plainly contrary to present progress. President Thieu insisted that 98 per cent of South Vietnam's population was under government control, and if this figure contradicted an American official estimate of 75 per cent, no one could deny that progress was being made in pacification. American troops were daily withdrawing from actual combat—U.S. deaths were down to about forty a week. Over-all troop withdrawal was proceeding on schedule: Forty thousand more troops were to leave by year's end, and, by spring of 1971, all combat troops would be gone, leaving some 270,000 "support" troops in the area. President Thieu, Administration spokesmen insisted, was actively widening his political base for presidential elections scheduled for autumn of 1971. Thieu's seat already promised to be challenged by General Duong Van Minh, who reportedly would campaign on a "peace" ticket—if that wasn't democracy, then what was?

A pretty picture, but more blurs.

Ninety-eight per cent of the population under government control? 75 per cent? This was fine, except, as one correspondent noted, some qualified observers suggested that ". . . the indices upon which such assessments are based . . . [are] largely meaningless."[57] Until villages were properly policed, no one would know the depth of relationship between peasants and enemy who still controlled large areas of South Vietnam. So long as guerrilla units continued to strike, virtually at will, without peasants warning government authorities, government did not either command peasant support or control peasants. And what of White House silence following Sir Robert Thompson's *second* visit, in the autumn? What of New York *Times* reports ". . . asserting that Sir

56. Neil Sheehan, N. Y. Times News Service, *The Times* (London), October 19, 1970.
57. Michael Hornsby, *The Times* (London), Saigon, October 26, 1970.

Robert had reported on the continuing failure of the South Vietnamese to uproot the Viet Cong's underground political structure"?[58]

The Administration's definition of combat forces was also suspect. American aircraft ostensibly were interdicting Communist supply lines in Cambodia. In reality, they were also furnishing close air support to Cambodian forces. Although South Vietnam was building an air force, it had a long way to go: As of November, its helicopter fleet counted two hundred and fifty machines, compared to some four thousand American machines in the area. In early November, Secretary of the Air Force Robert Seamans admitted that U. S. Air Force units would have to remain in Indochina for years.[59] Plans to remove all combat forces also changed: Two combat divisions, the 101st Airborne in the north and the 1st Cavalry (Airmobile) in the south, would now remain to provide security for bases such as Da Nang and Cam Ranh Bay.

Nor did the Administration confine MACV entirely to a defensive posture. American deaths may have been reduced, but they did not cease. Installations suffered guerrilla attacks, and patrols suffered casualties. The enemy shot down an American reconnaissance plane in North Vietnam and, in late November, the President authorized bombing strikes—"protective reaction"—to resume south of the 19th parallel. At the same time, MACV launched a helicopter raid on an alleged prisoner-of-war camp near Hanoi. Ostensibly designed to free American prisoners of war, it also demonstrated American ability to penetrate North Vietnamese defenses. It failed on the first count, and in so doing, symbolized the over-all intelligence failure of American arms: No prisoners were in the camp. As for psychological effect, Hanoi already knew that American arms were capable of invading the North, just as her leaders knew that American atomic bombs could eliminate Hanoi. That wasn't the crux of the situation: Hanoi also knew that what happened subsequently might well end civilization.

Renewed bombing of the North was something else again. Besides retaliation for the lost reconnaissance plane, it undoubtedly was an attempt to influence intractable North Vietnamese negotiators in Paris. It brought general outcry from around the world. In defending it, indeed in threatening to resume it in earnest, Secretary of Defense Laird cited what he insisted was an "understanding" with the North when President Johnson stopped the bombing in November 1968. Hanoi predictably denied that any "understanding" existed. Laird should have read Kissinger's analysis of these negotiations in his celebrated *Foreign Affairs* article and respected the devastating effect of morbid linguistic behavior induced by the two countries' inability to identify with each other.

A more valid reason for threatening to resume bombing was embar-

58. Fred Emery, *The Times* (London), Washington, D.C., January 17, 1971.
59. *The Times* (London) and AP, Saigon, November 5, 1970.

rassing: American intelligence was reporting indications of a build-up from the North that scarcely jibed either with Hanoi's alleged exhausted state or Administration claims of "victory" in Cambodia. An Institute for Strategic Studies analysis of the Cambodian incursion concluded:

. . . The immediate effect was to reduce pressure on American forces in Vietnam and thus to ease the course of American withdrawal and "Vietnamization." But the North Vietnamese had not been crippled. Other supply routes, based not only on expanding the "Ho Chi-minh trail" but also on the Mekong and Sekong rivers, were developed with some speed to replace that through [the port of] Kompong Som. At the same time, military efforts in both southern Laos and eastern Cambodia were stepped up.[60]

The same analysis concluded that, in South Vietnam, ". . . the leadership in Hanoi had openly reverted to a policy of 'protracted struggle' by guerrilla forces and organised activity by major Viet Cong and North Vietnamese units was increasingly restricted to the sparsely populated fringes of the country. . . ." In mid-December, however, a Brazilian journalist, Louis Wiznitzer, reported from Hanoi in the *Christian Science Monitor* that the North Vietnamese were preparing ". . . a new and perhaps decisive round of fighting on the ground." He continued:

. . . There is every evidence to the visitor here that, for all the reports out of Washington and Saigon and even Moscow that the Viet Cong are exhausted and the North Vietnamese over-extended, preparations are under way for another push.[61]

As the year drew to a close, the enemy was fighting hard in Laos and Cambodia and remained uncomfortably evident in South Vietnam. His negotiators in Paris showed little inclination to negotiate. In mid-December, Hanoi radio predicted "more complex" and "more violent" fighting throughout Indochina during 1971.

60. Institute for Strategic Studies, "Eastern Asia." In *Strategic Survey, 1970* (London: The Institute for Strategic Studies, 1971).
61. Henry Brandon, *The Sunday Times* (London), Washington, D.C., December 13, 1970.

Chapter 94

The Nixon administration's new strategy • Hanoi's position • The war in Cambodia • Opposition at home • ARVN invades Laos: "the golden opportunity" • Battlefield alchemy: disaster • Reasons why • Picking up the pieces • Flies in the Nixon ointment • The Calley case • Captain Daniels writes the President • Thieu and Ky fall out • The Pentagon Papers • South Vietnamese elections: Thieu versus Thieu leaves Thieu • Enemy gains • Nixon's new stand • Stalemate in Paris • Operation Rolling Thunder resumes • Giap's spring offensive • ARVN reverses • The war escalates • Nixon's new peace plan • ARVN's problems • Saigon's losses • No win, no victory

IN EARLY 1971, two voices sounded words as prophetic as those uttered by Shakespeare's witches dancing around another devil's brew. One belonged to Secretary of Defense Melvin Laird, who announced that the U.S. combat role in South Vietnam would end within twelve months. More time would be needed, however, for the South Vietnamese ". . . to replace Americans in air support, logistics and administration." By May, American strength in Vietnam would be reduced to 285,000 men.[1]

Laird's brave words continued Nixon's effort to close a political coffin before it claimed what rapidly was becoming an administrative corpse. Militarily, his statement was as flaccid as the rest of the Nixon doctrine. Primarily a political ploy designed to ease anti-Administration pressures within the United States, it also was intended to allow the Administration certain strategic and tactical flexibility within South Vietnam. By tying American troop withdrawals to the progress of Viet-

---

1. Patrick Brogan, *The Times* (London), Paris, January 6, 1971.

namization, it enabled the Administration to plead that overt military action against the enemy within South Vietnam, Cambodia, Laos, and North Vietnam was necessary to save American lives, a dubious argument that perhaps favorably impressed duller elements of American society but adversely impressed the rest of the world. It also established the notion of a residual force remaining in South Vietnam after the bulk of American troops had left. Politically it was cheap, militarily it was unsatisfactory, diplomatically it was meaningless.

The other voice emanating from the devil's brew belonged to Prime Minister Pham Van Dong, who, in Hanoi, announced that ". . . the Vietnamese people would insist on unconditional withdrawal by the Americans and that this point was not negotiable."[2] The prime minister reiterated that Hanoi would not give in, an intransigence reflected in Paris, where Ambassador David Bruce continued to report no progress in peace talks, and in Laos, Cambodia, and South Vietnam, where guerrillas and PAVN units continued brisk, if isolated, actions. Le Duan, first secretary of Hanoi's Communist Party, emphasized this stand by announcing that the North's ". . . strategic guideline is to fight a protracted war, gaining strength as one fights." ". . . To engage in military struggle under unfavorable circumstances," he said, echoing Sun Tzu, "is a serious mistake."

Le Duan's words seemed to some Western observers to be an admission of defeat, and in a sense they were. But they scarcely were tantamount to capitulation. Instead, they marked a shift in strategy, one predicated primarily on the realization that American public opinion was forcing disengagement. Where, two years earlier, Hanoi was ignoring internal damage in favor of prosecuting the war in the South, it now turned to repairing this damage as part of growing strong internally in order to carry on protracted warfare. A visiting Canadian journalist, Michael Maclear, found that the government had pulled all stops in the North. Not only were conscription-age men and women now assigned to labor brigades, but the government was even offering such incentives as cash bonuses and home-building loans to further its program of repairing war damage and rebuilding the economy.[3]

Internal stress did not end combat operations in the South. Despite U.S.-ARVN attacks of the previous spring, the Communist position in Cambodia remained strong. Supplies continued to flow south via the Ho Chi Minh Trail, in defiance of American air interdiction. In November, Communist units had occupied a strategic pass in Cambodia to cut Highway 4, the single road connection between Phnom Penh, the capital, and Kompong Som, the single deepwater port (see map, Chapter 93). The capital soon suffered a fuel shortage. Convoys carrying

2. Ibid.
3. Michael Maclear, *The Times* (London), January 19, 1971; see also Robert M. Shaplen, "We Have Always Survived," *The New Yorker*, April 15, 1972, who discusses developments in the North after Ho's death.

fuel from South Vietnam on the Mekong River fell victim to guerrilla ambushes. In early January, undoubtedly inspired by MACV planners, a combined Cambodian-ARVN task force, heavily supported by American planes, moved to reopen the highway. When ground attacks bogged down, American helicopter gunships joined the action. Although Cambodian troops captured the target pass, a few days later Viet Cong suicide squads attacked Phnom Penh's airport, virtually eliminated the fledgling Cambodian air force, and shelled the capital, sending morale plunging. The American Government responded with massive airlifts of barbed wire, sandbags, and more arms and ammunition to Phnom Penh. At the same time, North Vietnamese units knocked out a series of guerrilla outposts in southern Laos, in the important Bolovens Plateau area—outposts secretly organized by CIA personnel (see map, p. 1354).

The new action caused a furor in Congress, whose opposition members, including Republicans, interpreted it as violation of the Cooper-Church amendment, which prohibited the Administration from using funds for U.S. operations in Cambodia. Senator William Fulbright held that ". . . our actions in Cambodia are clearly inconsistent with the spirit and intent of the amendment. Whether they are technically and legally in violation is another matter."[4] Senator George McGovern stated that ". . . any Senator who talks about sending American forces into Cambodia should lead the charge himself. I'm fed up with old men sending young men out to die, particularly in stupid wars of this kind."[5] With that, he introduced another bill calling for a specific date for total withdrawal of U.S. forces from Vietnam.

The Administration justified the action as necessary to protect American troops, as well as, in the words of Melvin Laird, ". . . to supplement the efforts and the armed forces of our friends and allies who are determined to resist aggression."[6] A British correspondent wrote from Saigon on January 21:

. . . A military spokesman expressing it another way said any action is justified to prevent activities that might "ultimately endanger" the U.S. Vietnamization (withdrawal) program or the safety of U.S. troops remaining in Vietnam.

American air strikes, an air force spokesman said, are technically limited to the tri-border area (where Cambodia, Laos, and Vietnam come together), and the area east of the Mekong river including the Parrot's Beak and Angel's Wing.

But it is safe to assume, officials said, that American planes will go wherever there are Communists in Cambodia. And, as was vividly demonstrated

4. *The Times* (London), Washington, D.C., January 25, 1971.
5. *Time,* February 8, 1971.
6. Ibid.

along Highway 7 in December, they will destroy towns and villages if it is felt necessary.[7]

In Washington, Secretary of State Rogers repeated the theme to an angry Senate Foreign Relations Committee and to a bewildered American public. The Administration, he said, was prepared to use air power in Indochina ". . . to the fullest possible extent necessary." The primary objective was to protect American forces: ". . . It is the least costly way to protect our men, and why shouldn't we?"[8]

Prior to this outburst, the Washington *Post* had expressed an attitude scarcely unique throughout the country. The prevailing crisis of confidence begins

. . . with solemn pledges from the highest government officials which are not fulfilled. Then comes the fine print and fancy rhetoric and the political finagling which cannot quite be put down—and probably shouldn't be—as lies or even calculated deceit, but yet have that look. And so the value of the next pledge depreciates.[9]

Commenting on the situation in *The Times* (London), Fred Emery sensibly wrote:

. . . This could all have been avoided, and the use of American air power very probably accepted with minimal disquiet, had the Administration come clean and admitted that the situation had changed to require it.

Instead, the American Government, like most, is reluctant to confess changes of policy, clings to the dubious insistence that the "Nixon doctrine" all along foresaw such developments. The suspicion is deep that the White House is simply gambling on the acquiescence of most Americans in bombing one's way out of South-East Asia—so long as American casualties are kept low.[10]

The powerful fumes of Congressional and public dissent had not yet dissipated when reports of another Nixon surprise began to reach Western readers. Despite a news blackout imposed by MACV and the White House, the public learned that some twenty thousand South Vietnamese soldiers, the elite of ARVN, were moving toward southern Laos. This task force, backed by an impressive armored task force of some ten thousand American troops, was said to be reoccupying once-familiar terrain in northwestern reaches of South Vietnam. A second ARVN task force was reportedly moving into eastern Cambodia.

On February 8, an uneasy world learned that South Vietnam had invaded the panhandle of southern Laos. American planes and artillery had prepared the way; American helicopters supported the action; an

7. Peter Osnos, *The Guardian*, Saigon, January 21, 1971.
8. *The Times* (London), Washington, D.C., January 29, 1971.
9. Fred Emery, *The Times* (London), Washington, D.C., January 28, 1971.
10. Ibid.

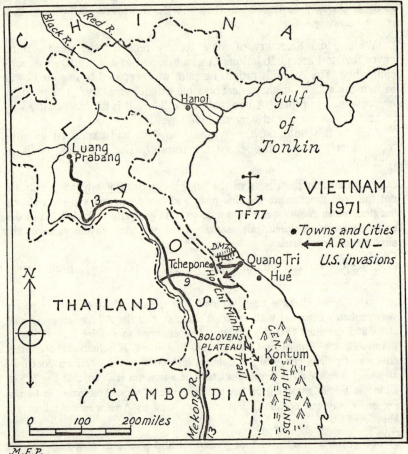

M.E.P.

American task force backed the effort but remained in South Vietnam. ARVN Operation Lam Son 719 and U. S. Operation Dewey Canyon II were designed to sever the Ho Chi Minh Trail leading to Cambodia— still another "golden opportunity," according to advocates including Abrams, to eliminate enemy supply lines and shorten the war accordingly.[11] In Saigon, Vice-President Nguyen Cao Ky told correspondents that ARVN forces would probably remain in Laos until the end of the dry season, in May, and would probably repeat the operation the next year.[12] It might be necessary, he said, to bomb North Vietnam in the

11. The operation was named after a Vietnamese victory over China in the seventeenth century, a belated attempt to profit psychologically as the North had been doing all along; Dewey Canyon was a misspelled code name.

12. Alvin Shuster, *The Times* (London), Saigon, February 10, 1971.

process. According to President Nixon, the operation was ". . . consistent with international law." It was as well that attorney Nixon did not have to debate the legal issue. Congressional opponents such as Senator Mansfield deplored the action as a ". . . deepening of the tragedy." The Royal Laotian Government condemned it; at United Nations headquarters, Secretary-General U Thant condemned it ". . . in strong terms."[13] In Washington, a columnist, Joseph Alsop, described the move as President Nixon's ". . . second great Southeast Asia gamble," which he hoped would prove "decisive." According to Mr. Alsop, President Nixon believed that the operation, by cutting Communist supply lines to the South, would force Hanoi ". . . to take the hardest kind of new look at their own situation and future prospects." Now that a precedent had been established, Alsop suggested, ARVN could cut the trail again next year.[14]

Speculation filled world newspapers, while front-line communiqués, as in the case of the Cambodian invasion the previous spring, told of slight resistance with impressive captures of food and ammunition. On February 15, Michael Hornsby of *The Times* (London) cabled from Quang Tri that, according to General Hoang Xuan Lam, ARVN commander of the invasion, ". . . the southward flow of North Vietnamese men and supplies down the Ho Chi Minh trail which is normally at its height during the last three months of the dry season—February to May—has been completely halted." The general claimed that his forces were deployed along Highway 9 fifteen to twenty miles inside Laos and that seven hundred fifty North Vietnamese had been killed at a cost of forty to fifty ARVN troops.[15]

Ugly rumors were already creeping into newsrooms, however. *Time* magazine noted that, in the first five days, twenty-nine thousand troops supported by ". . . 493 gunship attacks, 216 air cavalry missions, and 4,025 separate lifts of troops and supplies . . . destroyed two trucks, exploded one ammunition storage area and found one 57-mm. recoilless rifle, the mount for a mortar and a few dozen 105-mm. artillery shells."[16] Although MACV announced the loss of twelve helicopters, Michael Hornsby suggested that as many as fifty had been damaged or destroyed. If this was true, it followed that enemy resistance must be more than sporadic. Sure enough, two days later President Nixon repeated a report from General Abrams that although ARVN was fighting in ". . . a superior way," it had ". . . run into very heavy resistance."

Abrams' words preluded battlefield alchemy: In the harsh crucible of tactical reality, the "golden opportunity" was turning into base disaster; Operation Lam Son 719 was coming apart at the seams. Instead of vanishing, as early reports suggested, Communist forces had fallen

13. *The Times* (London), New York, February 8, 1971.
14. *The Times* (London), Washington, D.C., February 10, 1971.
15. Michael Hornsby, *The Times* (London), Quang Tri, February 15, 1971.
16. *Time*, February 15, 1971.

back only to snake around clanking ARVN armor columns to strike lines of communication—a tactic as old as the war. Once ARVN units occupied various positions, usually in battalion strength, VC and PAVN units joined to launch "suicide" attacks, exactly as they had done at Dien Bien Phu. And, as at Dien Bien Phu, they sprang a tactical surprise, this time in the form of tanks, old Russian PT-76s, whose presence had gone undetected by American fliers and planes (but was undoubtedly known to local peasants).

Washington attempted to break the truth as painlessly as possible. On February 22, the South Vietnamese Government, which earlier had spoken of minimum enemy forces in the area, now changed its tune: President Thieu said the invasion was to prevent a North Vietnamese invasion of South Vietnam's five northern provinces. While Secretary of Defense Laird, two days later, insisted that ARVN units were ". . . achieving their objective of major disruption of enemy supply routes," the enemy not only had shifted to western arteries beyond ARVN's reach but was overrunning ARVN positions in the vicinity of Highway 9. By February 25, the battle so wished for by MACV and ARVN was on. Once again, conflicting reports reached the outside world. For ten days, ARVN seemed to be holding its own and then some. On March 7, Saigon proudly announced the capture of Tchepone, a major Communist staging and supply area, and on that same day, Derek Wilson reported in *The Times* (London): ". . . The North and South Vietnamese now appear irretrievably committed to a decisive, full-scale showdown in Laos, each aiming at attrition of the other through mass-slaughter." Vice-President Ky, never at a loss for the dramatic, told correspondents that his government was looking for a ". . . Dien Bien Phu in reverse." A day later, General Lam claimed that his forces had cut ". . . the main portion" of the Ho Chi Minh Trail; Hanoi was taking casualties twenty times heavier than his own and had lost about six thousand killed and hundreds more by air strikes, as well as 112,000 tons of ammunition, 245 vehicles including seventy-four tanks, and thirteen hundred tons of food.[17] In a dramatic Pentagon press conference, Secretary of Defense Laird and Lieutenant General John Vogt, Jr., proudly displayed a piece of enemy pipeline used to bring down gasoline from the North—but failed to mention that it had been captured weeks earlier by a commando raid![18] But ARVN losses reportedly were heavy: In the week ending March 4, they amounted to 898 killed and over two thousand wounded; American deaths numbered sixty-nine; *Time* magazine reported that ". . . in three weeks, no less than five ARVN battalions had, for all practical purposes, been knocked out of action."[19] Derek Wilson reported fourteen helicopters shot down

17. Derek Wilson, *The Times* (London), Khe Sanh, March 8, 1971.
18. *Time*, March 15, 1971.
19. *Time*, March 8, 1971.

in one day; an American pilot had told him: ". . . We're being knocked off like flies."

ARVN still seemed to claim the upper hand, however, as it slogged into battered Tchepone, twenty-five miles inside Laos. President Nixon continued to insist that the operation was a success; according to General Abrams, the fighting proved that ARVN could "hack it" against top PAVN units. But suddenly, on March 11, General Lam began pulling units out of Tchepone only five days after they had occupied it. And now ARVN units began yielding artillery fire bases one after the other, often destroying guns and vehicles to prevent capture by the enemy, before being evacuated by helicopters—or killed. American efforts to save ARVN units reached frantic proportions: One day's operations cost thirty-seven out of forty helicopters engaged![20] By March 21, only four thousand of twenty-four thousand ARVN soldiers remained in Laos. A day after television viewers around the world had watched desperate ARVN soldiers clinging to helicopter skids in order to save themselves, Secretary of Defense Laird admitted that "withdrawal" was underway but that it was according to plan.[21] Three days later, ARVN had left Laos. A week later, enemy trucks were driving down the Ho Chi Minh Trail.

But now Administration spokesmen began singing new tunes: Lam Son 719 was not alone designed to cut enemy supply lines; Lam Son 719 was designed to mass enemy troops and make them vulnerable to American air power: Official spokesmen claimed over eleven thousand enemy dead and ten PAVN battalions annihilated in an operation that also relieved enemy pressure on Cambodia!

Almost no one was listening to such arrant nonsense. The cost of Lam Son 719 was tremendous: The Saigon government admitted to five thousand ARVN casualties (some observers thought ten thousand more likely) plus seventy American lives, perhaps a hundred forty helicopters, thirty tanks, and scores of armored personnel carrier and artillery pieces lost. Even worse was the morale factor. Lam Son 719 forfeited meager gains extracted from the Cambodian invasion of the previous spring with little to show for the sacrifice. ARVN units never reached western arteries of the Ho Chi Minh Trail, and scarcely had they left the area when trucks again began moving south.

What happened? Overconfidence played a major part. The earlier Cambodian invasion, which did not provide an accurate test of ARVN's tactical effectiveness, had misled military commanders and experts into once again painting dreams. Sir Robert Thompson, Nixon's paid consultant on counterinsurgency, had given ARVN high marks: ". . . The fact that you're able to keep withdrawing troops at the current rate, that U.S. casualties are down to well under fifty a week, that even South

20. *Time*, March 15, 1971.
21. *The Times* (London), Washington, D.C., March 22, 1971.

Vietnamese casualties are down—this is the measure of it." Thompson went on: ". . . The balance of power has shifted as between the enemy's capability and the South Vietnamese capability."[22] According to the same source, in Saigon ". . . Abrams likes to tell visiting firemen . . . that 70% of South Viet Nam's army is 'on a fighting par with U.S. troops.' " Abrams, Thompson, and a good many others were continuing to confuse quantity with quality, and were again ignoring General Gwynn's teaching that a lull in guerrilla warfare did not necessarily mean enemy weakness. ARVN found a flexibly organized enemy who was willing to yield a branch or two of the Ho Chi Minh Trail until the tactical position became clear. They found an enemy who had secretly brought down tanks and SAM missiles; an enemy that reinforced itself during battle with units from the DMZ; an enemy that skillfully employed guerrilla tactics to bewilder, slow, and isolate ARVN columns and outposts until they were ready for assault.

Divided command also apparently came into play, as noted by a particularly astute commentator, James Reston. ARVN and MACV together seem to have underestimated enemy strength—scarcely a new failing. Abrams allegedly urged Thieu to send in more forces than proposed, but Thieu refused: Thanks largely to U. S. Army indoctrination, ARVN commanders at this time held almost mystical belief in efficacy of air and artillery power, and this undoubtedly influenced Thieu's decision. Once opposition developed, Abrams is said to have again urged Thieu to commit more troops, but the South Vietnamese President, probably for domestic political reasons, refused and, instead, terminated the action.

Although Nixon and aides attempted to paint a satisfactory picture, the operation itself, let alone its obvious failure, brought heavy criticism from within the United States. Concurrent with its confused and contradictory course came a variety of other ills resulting from American involvement in Indochina. Despite reduction of American forces in the area and a claim that direct military expenditures in Indochina had decreased to $16 billion for the current fiscal year, over-all defense expenditures were to rise to $76 billion for Fiscal Year 1972. Even before the operation began, the American army reaped widespread opprobrium by dropping charges against Major General Samuel Koster for attempting to cover up the My Lai massacre: Koster was reduced in rank, given a letter of censure, and allowed to retire, the first of a series of mild punishments for major dereliction of duty.[23] The operation was only just underway when a heart attack felled the Cambodian prime minister, Lon Nol, to confuse that already confused situation further. Then the story of bribery and corruption in American military clubs

22. *Time*, February 15, 1971.
23. Seymour M. Hersh, "Coverup," *The New Yorker*, January 22 and January 29, 1972.

and post exchanges in Indochina (and elsewhere) broke; it would involve a brigadier general and the Sergeant Major of the Army.[24] The
public was further disturbed by an almost constant chorus of dissent.
Senator Edward Kennedy told an audience that ". . . Vietnamization
means war and more war; it has nothing to do with an end to violence,
it is a policy of violence." Senator McGovern accused President Nixon
of ". . . flirting with World War Three." ARVN's most able general,
Do Cao Tri, was killed in a helicopter crash along with veteran *Newsweek* correspondent, able François Sully; Larry Burrows, of *Life,* was
killed in another one. On February 22, Lieutenant William Calley began
a recital to a military court of his shocking actions at My Lai. A few
days later, the army decided to court-martial his brigade commander,
Colonel Oran K. Henderson. While fighting in Laos increased, four
VC guerrillas blew up 75 per cent of Cambodia's oil-refinery system.
The American people next learned that so zealous was its army as to
keep card files on 25 million American citizens. Sounding more like a
police-state official than an American public servant, Assistant Secretary
of Defense Robert Froehlke stated, on March 2, that

. . . surveillance designed to cope with civil violence that might eventually
require the use of army troops would continue.

To protect people and property in an area of civil disturbance with the
greatest effectiveness, he said, "military commanders must know all that can
be learnt about that area and its inhabitants."[25]

Army agents might better have been employed studying their own
establishment. While PX scandals mounted, the General Accounting
Office accused American defense contractors of making wildly excessive
profits. The public was also forcefully reminded that some soldiers in
Vietnam, in addition to insubordination including refusal, on occasion,
to fight, and drug addiction, had picked up the quaint habit of "frag-
ging": eliminating overzealous officers with a hand grenade; in a word,
murder. Writing of an army he had once considered ". . . the best Army
the United States ever put into the field," Colonel Robert Heinl, a retired
marine turned journalist, concluded, in May 1971, that the ". . . United
States armed forces, wrenched by seemingly insurmountable problems
within and without, appear to have reached their lowest point in this
century in morale, discipline and battleworthiness." After citing numer-

24. *The Times* (London), Washington, D.C., March 3, 1971; see also Shaplen
("We Have Always Survived"), *supra:* ". . . a conservative estimate is that fifteen
thousand Americans, in uniform or out, have been involved in this process of
corruption. These Americans have encouraged the black-marketing of all sorts of
goods, have encouraged pilferage for payoffs, have raked huge profits from the
smuggling of drugs and other goods, from the illicit trade in dollars, from the
operation of night clubs, from the importation of American call girls and so
on. . . ."
25. Ian McDonald, *The Times* (London), Washington, D.C., March 2, 1971.

ous incidents within and without Vietnam, Heinl quoted General Matthew Ridgway: ". . . Not before in my lifetime . . . has the Army's
public image fallen to such low esteem. . . ."[26] While army intelligence agents continued to cover public gatherings in the United States
and record covertly the words of American citizens, Lieutenant Colonel
Anthony Herbert confirmed army practice in Vietnam of torturing prisoners. And at the end of March, a military court found William Calley
guilty of callously murdering South Vietnamese civilians and sentenced
him to life imprisonment.

The verdict set off still another internal domestic row. People had
heard Calley describe the massacre at My Lai; yet some of them held
that the young lieutenant was no more guilty than others. Bowing to
pressures, President Nixon called the court to task and mitigated Calley's
sentence to twenty years. Captain Aubrey Daniels, the twenty-nine-year-
old army officer who had prosecuted, now wrote an open letter to his
commander in chief. After expressing shock and dismay at the reaction
of many people to the sentence, Daniels suggested that ". . . the war
in Vietnam has brutalized us more than I care to believe" and that it
must therefore cease. He continued:

. . . But how much more appalling it is to see so many of the political
leaders of the nation who have failed to see the moral issue or, having seen
it, to compromise it for political motive in the face of apparent public displeasure with the verdict.

Mouse Daniels then took lion Nixon to task:

. . . In view of your previous statements concerning this matter, I have been
particularly shocked and dismayed at your decision to intervene in these
proceedings in the midst of the public clamor. Your decision can only have
been prompted by the response of a vocal segment of our population, who
while no doubt acting in good faith, cannot be aware of the evidence which
resulted in Lieutenant Calley's conviction.

Not only had the President ". . . damaged the military judicial system"
and ". . . subjected a judicial system of this country to the criticism
that it is subject to political influence," but

. . . the image of Lieutenant Calley, a man convicted of the premeditated
murder of at least 21 unarmed and unresisting people, as a national hero
has been enhanced. . . .

And he concluded:

. . . I would expect that the President of the United States, a man whom
I believed should and would provide the moral leadership for this nation,

    26. Robert D. Heinl, "The Armed Forces: Are they 'near collapse'?" Detroit
Sunday News, May 23, 1971.

would stand fully behind the law of this land on a moral issue which is so clear and about which there can be no compromise.

For this nation to condone the acts of Lieutenant Calley is to make us no better than our enemies. . . .

These were difficult times for the Administration, but, as an experienced observer of the Washington scene, Henry Brandon, pointed out:

. . . In many ways the Nixon administration must assume responsibility for the credibility gap that now exists between the public and the Press, for anybody who has attended the background briefings given at the outset of the Laotian operation knows what its targets were and where high official expectations stood. Perhaps one of the most serious weaknesses of the administration—and it explains why it does not get the credit it should for some of its achievements—is that it suffers from a compulsive desire to oversell.[27]

To try to bolster waning popularity, the President, in early April, announced another large troop withdrawal, and began to hint at a new diplomatic offensive, which, by restoring ". . . the common purpose," would create ". . . a new national unity." The words sounded forlorn in view of massive anti-war demonstrations including those by Vietnam veterans who flung medals onto the White House lawn. Nor was the President's posture strengthened by Saigon, where Vice-President Ky broke openly with President Thieu and not only called for a political solution based on coexistence with North Vietnam but questioned Thieu's integrity and compared the country to a "sinking ship."[28] In the polemics that followed, he stated what all critics had been saying for years: ". . . There is no social justice [in South Vietnam] right now."[29]

Nor was military news any better. A benumbed American public was now informed that large numbers of American troops in South Vietnam were using drugs. Although units continued to leave the country, other units were still fighting in conjunction with ARVN forces. In late May, Viet Cong guerrillas attacked American installations only twenty-five miles from Saigon. At the same time, the enemy in Cambodia attacked ARVN's border force at Snuol and forced it to evacuate, a minor disaster that reportedly claimed a hundred ARVN killed and three hundred wounded and loss of eighty vehicles including tanks and armored personnel carriers.[30]

As if the situation were not sufficiently depressing, in mid-June the nation began reading extracts from theretofore-top-secret documents delivered to public media by a former Pentagon analyst and RAND em-

27. Henry Brandon, *The Sunday Times* (London), March 28, 1971.
28. Derek Wilson, *The Times* (London), Saigon, May 2, 1971.
29. Ibid., May 16, 1971.
30. Keyes Beech, Chicago *Daily News,* Saigon, June 7, 1971.

ployee, Daniel Ellsberg. These revelations of official dissembling, depressing in the extreme, were still rebounding when the General Accounting Office suggested that nearly two billion dollars budgeted for South Vietnam pacification from 1968 to 1970 could not be accounted for and listed ominously, among the problems, ". . . misappropriation of funds."[31]

Not surprisingly, the President's popularity had been steadily declining and he was in serious political trouble. His Administration had recorded a fiscal-year deficit of over $23 billion, the second-largest deficit since World War II and one estimated to increase in the current fiscal year. The balance of trade also measured an unhealthy deficit, which meant, among other things, that the dollar's value stood in jeopardy. No less an authority than former chief presidential economic adviser Gardner Ackley warned

. . . that failure to act to stem inflation and unemployment "can threaten the stability of the social and political order." He said that inflation and unemployment were exaggerating the poverty problem to the point where current policies could provoke outright revolution.[32]

Although the Administration gained some relief from Henry Kissinger's secret mission to Peking, little encouraging news arrived from Indochina. As American, Thai, and Australian troop units continued to depart, President Thieu left no doubt that he headed a military dictatorship, a fact shortly emphasized when he alone ran for election. Prime Minister Lon Nol, in neighboring Cambodia, added to the authoritarian air in mid-October by declaring a state of emergency and appointing ". . . a new government to rule by 'ordinance' rather than by constitutional law. He said that he no longer would 'play the game of democracy and freedom' since it stood in the way of victory."[33] Less than a month later, Field Marshal Thanom Kittikachorn overthrew Thailand's parliamentary government in favor of rule by revolutionary council.

Political issues seemed more clearly, if unhappily, settled than military issues. In Paris, the enemy, in early July, proposed a new, seven-point peace plan, a series of demands unacceptable to either Washington or Saigon.[34] As fighting receded inside South Vietnam, it continued to mount in Laos, where, according to Senator Stuart Symington, the American Government was secretly spending hundreds of millions in fighting a clandestine war.[35] In supporting a thirty-thousand-man irregular force supplemented by Thai mercenaries, the American Govern-

31. *The Times* (London), Washington, D.C., July 11, 1971.
32. Harlow Unger, *The Sunday Times* (London), August 1, 1971.
33. *Time*, October 21, 1972.
34. "Text of the North Vietnam Seven-Point Peace Plan," *Survival*, September 1971.
35. *The Times* (London), Washington, D.C., June 6, 1971.

ment spent over $230 million in fiscal year 1970.[36] In Cambodia, about thirty thousand PAVN troops supplemented by perhaps fifteen to twenty thousand Cambodian Communists, the Khmer Rouge, claimed control of about half the country, and, as 1971 drew to a close, guerrillas were bombarding the capital, Phnom Penh, a threat that caused Saigon to send some twenty-four thousand troops across the border to bolster ARVN units already in Cambodia.

Inside South Vietnam, the situation remained in flux. In September, a combined ARVN-U.S. task force hastily moved north against enemy activity in the demilitarized zone. Some two hundred American helicopters lifted thousands of ARVN troops to Quang Tri province, where three brigades, backed by about two thousand American troops, began a giant "sweep" of the area. Enemy forces inside Cambodia continued to contest the border area. In the Mekong Delta, about forty thousand VC continued active. In mid-October, VC guerrillas slipped into an American base eight miles from Saigon and blew up two helicopter gunships and damaged three others.[37]

The turbulent situation again brought dangerous Congressional antagonism. In late October, the Senate Foreign Relations Committee approved an amendment that limited ". . . all spending in Indo-China to the single goal of withdrawing American troops."[38] The Administration replied that it would continue operations necessary to protect American forces. In early November, waves of B-52 bombers supplemented by naval gunfire worked over enemy positions in the demilitarized zone. About the same time, Secretary of Defense Melvin Laird announced, in Saigon, that American troops might still be fighting long after the bulk of American forces had been withdrawn. He told reporters that he found the progress of Vietnamization "most encouraging." ". . . He said that Saigon's position was militarily strong and the main problem facing South Vietnam was economic. It was one of strengthening and stabilizing the economy so that the country could support its armed forces."[39] President Thieu complemented this pretty speech by devaluing the piaster and once again promising "economic reforms."[40] A few days later, President Nixon announced that another forty-five thousand American troops would be withdrawn, ". . . and proclaimed the end of the U.S. offensive role in the war." His decision would cut American troop strength to 139,000 by February 1, 1972. Further withdrawals ". . . would be determined by the level of enemy infiltration and combat activity, the success of Vietnamization, progress in securing release of American prisoners in North Viet-Nam and obtaining an Indo-China cease-fire." If no progress resulted from the Paris talks, ". . . it will be

36. *The Times* (London), Washington, D.C., August 2, 1971.
37. *The Times* (London), Saigon, October 13, 1971.
38. *The Times* (London), Washington, D.C., October 20, 1971.
39. Derek Wilson, *The Times* (London), Saigon, November 7, 1971.
40. Ibid., November 15, 1971.

necessary to maintain a residual force" of American troops in the country, he said.[41] ". . . Air power, of course, will continue to be used," the President told newsmen. "We will continue to use it in support of the South Vietnamese until there is a negotiated settlement or, looking farther down the road, until the South Vietnamese have developed the capability to handle the situation themselves." If the enemy increased infiltration, ". . . we will have to not only continue our air strikes; we will have to step them up."[42]

No progress resulted from the Paris talks, one reason probably being that General John Lavelle, commanding the U. S. Air Force in Vietnam, had taken it upon himself to open a secret air offensive against the North—in defiance of orders.[43]

With that avenue closed, the President had to play for time until overtures to Peking and Moscow came to fruition. With the approach of an election year, he could not renege on repeated promises to withdraw the bulk of American troops from South Vietnam. But neither could he risk collapse of Thieu's government. Instead, he chose a middle course: He would continue to use the American presence, particularly American air and naval power, to buttress ARVN until Vietnamization reached the point where Hanoi would see the light and come to the peace table.

The President was fishing deep in diplomatic waters. To help Hanoi make up its mind, he wished to demonstrate that bigger issues were at stake in the world: From December 26 to 30, 1971, American planes made over a thousand raids on North Vietnam—an act uncontested by either Peking or Moscow (but one that drew international opprobrium).

No matter the Chinese or Soviet attitude, no matter the raids, no matter severe air interdiction in all areas, the enemy continued operations in Laos and Cambodia while ARVN and U.S. commanders reported intense preparations for what appeared to be another Tet offensive.

Nixon put a brave face on failure to bring the enemy around. To demonstrate determination, he now recommended bombing the North. His insistence on the progress of Vietnamization brought dissembling echoes from Administration officials; in late February 1972, for example, Secretary of Defense Laird, testifying before the House Appropriations Committee, assured congressmen

. . . that the other side had been forced to switch from main-force to low-level guerrilla activity because of the "buildup of the South Vietnamese

41. Ian McDonald, *The Times* (London), Washington, D.C., November 12, 1971.

42. *Time,* November 22, 1971.

43. *Time,* June 26, 1972: Lavelle's action, which, by disrupting peace talks, may well have prolonged the war and which, at the very least, lent credence to enemy charges of American dissembling, was severely punished: He was retired as a three-star general with a pension of $2,250 a month.

forces" and could not "conduct a large-scale military operation for a substantial period of time" because "they do not have the logistic support" or
the "personnel."[44]

Five weeks later, Giap opened a spring offensive that involved elements of ten enemy divisions, or some 150,000 troops, whose armament
included ". . . missiles, radar-guided anti-aircraft guns, MIG-21 aircraft, and wire-controlled, heat-seeking missiles for use against tanks and
low-flying aircraft."[45] In the North, two divisions spilled through the
DMZ to fragment a defending ARVN division and chase it from Quang
Tri. Units of two more divisions pushed in from the Ho Chi Minh Trail
toward Hué, while a fifth remained north of the DMZ in close reserve.
In the central highlands, elements of three North Vietnamese divisions,
already in control of the northern portion of II Corps area, began to
push on Kontum. Another three divisions operated in III Corps area,
besieging An Loc and controlling large areas north and west of Saigon.

The most serious threat existed in the northern part of the country.
To defend Hué, President Thieu moved in his best units, while Washington rushed naval and air units to the area. Nixon was determined
that the new offensive not succeed: If he had been withdrawing ground
troops—there were only sixty-five thousand left in South Vietnam when
Giap's drive started—he had simultaneously been building up peripheral
strengths. Within five weeks of the beginning of the offensive, the U. S.
Seventh Fleet was maintaining a task force in the Gulf of Tonkin that
included six carriers, five cruisers, and forty destroyers, a task force
manned by forty-one thousand men. While air armadas including B-52
bombers struck enemy units throughout South Vietnam, MACV hastened to repair Thieu's material losses and to assure him and the world
of continuing American support. Nixon's answer seemed to produce a
favorable result: At Moscow's urging, Henry Kissinger flew to Paris to
meet with Hanoi's top negotiator, Le Duc Tho. When this attempt to
find peace failed, Nixon decided on the risky but dramatic move of mining North Vietnam's ports and increasing air strikes on North Vietnamese targets. This was necessary, he told the American people, to
protect remaining American troops in Vietnam. As for total withdrawal
of those troops, this would be to admit ". . . an American defeat,"
which would ". . . encourage aggression all over the world. . . ."
Sounding not unlike Lyndon Johnson at Baltimore seven years earlier,
the President pointed to Hanoi's intransigence, which could only be sur-
mounted by ". . . decisive military action to end the war." At the same
time, he offered a new peace plan: total withdrawal of U.S. forces within
four months in return for an internationally supervised cease-fire, return

44. I. F. Stone, "Why Nixon Won His Moscow Gamble," *The New York Review of Books,* June 15, 1972.
45. Robert M. Shaplen, "Letter from Vietnam," *The New Yorker,* May 13,
1972: As usual, Mr. Shaplen offers an excellent and detailed account of this action.

of American prisoners of war, and a political settlement negotiated between the Vietnamese themselves.

This was the sort of dramatic move that the Nixon-Kissinger psyche favored. As had past escalations, notably the Cambodian and Laotian excursions, it brought national and international recriminations. Politically it was far more meaningful than militarily, and politically it produced no real effect. Hanoi already had girded itself for resumption of bombing. Claiming decided military advantages, the Paris delegation spurned the President's latest proposals.

About all the escalation accomplished was to cheer a morose Saigon government. Gone was the early bravado. As reported by *Time* magazine,

. . . Saigon's 492,000-man regular army is suffering from more than battered morale. There are fewer than 150,000 Communist soldiers committed to the invasion; nonetheless they have not only tied up all of ARVN's reserve strength but have also knocked out an ever-growing list of South Vietnamese units—one full infantry division, a third of another division, five infantry regiments, six armored regiments, three artillery battalions, nine ranger battalions, two airborne brigades and three battalions of marines, Saigon's best troops. The South Vietnamese have admitted to heavy casualties: 4,610 dead and 14,093 wounded. U.S. military men hope that, with unstinting American air support and Nixon's morale-boosting moves, ARVN can hold up at least through May, when monsoon rains are expected to dampen the action in the southern two-thirds of the country.[46]

To some observers, it seemed like Chiang Kai-shek and China all over again. Like General Lon Nol in Cambodia and Field Marshal Thanom Kittikachorn in Thailand, General Thieu now threw off the light cloak of Western-imposed democracy to declare martial law and ask the national assembly for emergency powers. Simultaneously, his new commander in the north, Lieutenant General Ngo Quang Truong, started probing attacks toward Quang Tri.

Having focused allied eyes on Quang Tri and Hué, in late May Giap opened a new offensive against An Loc, in the south, a furious action that again isolated the town's six thousand ARVN defenders. When a relief force stalled some miles south of the town on Highway 13, a helicopter lift brought in two regiments to reinforce the battered garrison.

As battle slowed and partial lull claimed various areas, the American bombing effort intensified, with thousands of tons of television- and laser-guided bombs, "smart" bombs, dropping on North Vietnam, complemented by thousands of sorties that hammered enemy forces around Hué, Kontum, and An Loc.

As in the past, ranking American officers claimed enormous damage

46. *Time*, May 22, 1972.

to the enemy, who seemingly was expected to yield to American might. But hard facts scarcely justified optimism expressed by Washington and Saigon officials. If ARVN was holding, it was only because of American air and naval power. Giap's offensives had caused Saigon to strip the vital Mekong Delta of troops. Once again, the pacification effort virtually ceased, Viet Cong cadres appeared, and government control yielded throughout the vast area. By end of June, the offensives had generated over one and a half million refugees and had cost ARVN over seventy thousand casualties. Thieu's secret police had arrested thousands of "suspected Viet Cong sympathizers" and would continue to arrest some fourteen thousand a month. Thieu would continue to invoke emergency measures, and, in September, like Diem before him, would abolish hamlet elections, thereby returning South Vietnamese government to the stone age.

Still, his government had held together, and in July, ARVN units had begun the arduous task of reclaiming control of captured areas. In September, an ARVN task force finally reoccupied Quang Tri, a city of rubble evacuated by the enemy, who continued to hover nearby. Similarly, key cities and towns in center and south felt the hot breath of enemy, which controlled perhaps 50 per cent of South Vietnam and operated almost without opposition in Laos and Cambodia. Giap had taken heavy casualties, but he had achieved his primary goal of disrupting the highly vaunted Vietnamization and pacification of the South.

As President Nixon's first term drew to a close, thirty-nine thousand American troops remained in South Vietnam, with another hundred thousand based in peripheral areas. North of the DMZ, American planes, some of them allegedly pilotless, continued to hammer a country already flattened. But North Vietnam continued to receive arms, ammunition, and fuel, and to send them south. Air attacks, both ARVN and American, continued to pound suspected enemy positions throughout South Vietnam. While thousands of people fled contested areas to jam reception centers and hospitals, the enemy continued probing ARVN defenses and extending control in the countryside.

In Washington, Administration officials overlooked facts to point optimistically to heavy enemy casualties and to resumption of peace talks in Paris. To rumors of a supervised coalition government in the South in return for peace, President Thieu predictably responded: ". . . I severely warn the colonialists against interfering in the general affairs of the South Vietnamese people and providing comfort to the North Vietnamese invaders, either by words or deeds."[47] As he spoke, American intelligence reported that new PAVN units were moving south. Once again, the world watched an overlay pattern only too familiar to this cloth of impasse.

47. *Time*, October 9, 1972.

In late autumn 1972, a favorable end of war in Vietnam seemed almost as remote as when Richard Nixon became President. One thing only remained certain: No matter the end, neither side could justifiably use words like *win* and *victory*. There would be no win, no victory, in either the North or the South.

In attempting to claim what it believed it had won on the battlefield in 1954, the Hanoi government had subjected its peoples to over ten years of agrarian, economic, and military disasters that would scar at least two generations. Over half a million North Vietnamese soldiers had been killed in the South, with hundreds of thousands wounded; thousands of civilians in the North had been killed by bombing, and thousands had died from hunger and disease. The burgeoning industrial plant, once the pride of the North, lay in ruins. The government itself was beholden to Moscow and Peking and would remain so for at least a decade. No matter aid provided, no matter possible gains in the South, the North Vietnamese people would suffer a bleak existence, with uneasy independence as a traditional border satrapy.

In the South, similar disaster: half the area under Viet Cong domination, a government and army riddled with dissent, a torn countryside, a false and fragile economy, a military dictatorship as repressive as anything existing in the North. Nearly half a million South Vietnamese soldiers had died, probably a half million civilians had died, over a million people were living in refugee camps, millions more in urban slums where they breathed an air of hopeless xenophobia as American planes continued to plaster a defoliated landscape.

In the United States, similar disaster: To keep Thieu in power had cost some fifty thousand American lives, with 150,000 wounded, thousands of amputees, thousands of Negro soldiers dead (some of them those leaders so desperately needed at home), a financial expenditure so vast as to seriously damage the Western world economy, an internal quarrel so deep as to outlast a generation of Americans.

If fighting stopped tomorrow, no matter the terms: No win, no victory, but, rather, battered peoples and bleeding lands—a scene noted long ago by Tacitus, who said of the Romans in Britain: ". . . You have made this a desolation and you call it peace."

Chapter 95

The American failure • The public's role • Communications and education • Citizen apathy • New voices searching • The public trust • Official responsibility • Discretion versus dissembling • Commager on power • Galbraith on duplicity • The Department of State • Force versus diplomacy • Departmental problems • Reorganization and reform • The Department of Defense • Major deficiencies • The Tuchman message • Anomaly and autonomy • The Clearchos element • Interservice strife • Stab-in-the-back • Congress and the press • The tyranny of conformance • Mene, mene, tekel, upharsin

IF THE UNITED STATES is to avoid the shattering experience of another Vietnam and yet remain a leading international power, she must reshape her thinking, civil and military, toward a more mature and flexible philosophy. She emerged from World War II with enormous credits in the international bank of goodwill. She has slowly dissipated these until, today, she occupies a semi-isolated position vis-à-vis the rest of the world. Moreover, by thoughtless pursuit of frantic alarms and excursions, she has squandered a considerable portion of her own inheritance and, in so doing, has jeopardized that incalculable asset of government— the people's trust—to an alarming degree.

Much of the reason for what perhaps can be collectively described as the current American illness is the Vietnam experience, although it is symptomatic rather than causal. Deficiencies exposed in Vietnam existed, if only in incipient form, before Vietnam; the past unhappy decade has but raised them to prominence.

The major reason for American failure in Indochina is as old as history. Commencing with President Truman's original intervention on behalf of France, the American Government embarked on a course of action with nebulous ambition replacing specific (and limited) political and military goals. Never in the Indochina experience did an American administration chart an intelligent course through a tangled map of military crossroads imposed on political intersections; never did an administration formulate specific objectives or declare a policy compatible to the political-military force that it was able to apply (and retain) in the target area. Instead, under a blanket ambition, *stop communism,* five successive administrations contributed to a military attempt to "defeat" an enemy. One after the other encountered dilemmas that had confronted and confused nations throughout history; one after the other succumbed to forces as historically familiar as they were variable in influence. The experience, by no means ended, nonetheless indicts national leadership.[1]

National leadership is always an easy target until one remembers that, in a democracy, to indict national leadership is to indict a majority of the people. In a democracy, the electorate is demonstrably more responsible for governmental behavior than in a totalitarian form of government. The American electorate, for over twenty years, has continued to elect Presidents and legislators, too many of whom have refused to take a long, hard look at facts and act intelligently and courageously.

Reasons abound for this major aberration, but ignorance heads the list. The American public refused to study the issues of the Vietnam insurgency, an attitude partly due to a natural parochial outlook familiar to most nations and understandable considering America's size and location, and one partly due first to paucity of reliable analysis, then to surfeit of conflicting information on the area. These initial failures were due in large part to a communications deficiency—to a refusal of newspaper and television networks to assign a correct priority to Vietnam, a refusal in part occasioned by clandestine governmental activities, that is, official refusal to inform the public of the extent of national involvement and to allow it to share the burden. That ignorance continued to exist is an educational failure brought about by citizen apathy and fear but compounded by erroneous and distorted reporting, primarily on the part of responsible federal departments, but at times shared by correspondents, editors, and publishers who allowed personal animosities and political preferences to overcome professional objectivity.

The onus must fall primarily on citizen apathy, however. If a sufficient number of citizens demand objective, in-depth reporting, publishers will respond or go out of business, particularly if citizen consumer groups apply appropriate pressure on retail advertisers. Citizens similarly can

1. Henry Steele Commager, "A Limit to Presidential Power?" *The New Republic.* Quoted in *Survival,* July 1968.

influence Congressional representatives to demand communication reforms on the part of federal executive agencies, which will respond—or have budgets chopped. This is easy to suggest, difficult to accomplish. Citizen participation in government is always a difficult question. In some ways, citizen trust of elected leaders and representatives is comforting; in other ways, dangerous. If trust is borne out, then government is strengthened; if, as in the case of Vietnam, trust is misplaced, then government is weakened. Too often forgotten in a government of checks and balances is the fact that citizens must form the final check and the final balance.

In the case of Vietnam, which, despite the proportions of its disaster, is still only a ramification of a larger problem, a significant portion of American citizens, particularly the affluent and influential middle class, accepted a black-and-white analysis of what was and is an incredibly complex international scene. For good and forceful reasons, these generally well-meaning folk sincerely believed that the American way of life is superior, the only way of life that matters. Anything that helped other countries emulate such a way of life was GOOD, anything that carried countries from it was EVIL. Democracy was GOOD, communism was EVIL. The majority of American taxpayers willingly supported a foreign-aid program of unprecedented dimensions—but only so long as it respected this simplistic axiom.

Unfortunately, the axiom falls victim to major error. Such is the gulf between East and West that the average well-meaning American could not put himself in a peasant's position sufficiently to recognize a fundamental difference in outlook—no more than the average well-meaning Westerner today can realize that over five eighths of the world are hungry. To the Westerner, communism meant EVIL; to the peasant, it too often meant someone seeming to care about him for the first time in memory. To the Westerner, democracy meant GOOD; to the peasant, it too often meant continuation of appalling misery experienced originally under his own kings, then under colonial overlords.

Education may not be able to bridge this gap. It probably will not, so long as the Westerner of whom I speak refuses to question his own concept of democracy, indeed, his own notion of the American goal. One of the most odious phrases in history became current in the early 1960s when Americans, citizens and leaders, frequently referred to their country as "the richest, most powerful nation in the world." This arrogant, aggressive, and inaccurate phrase thankfully has grown tired. Increasing numbers of Americans are questioning the national course. Younger, educated citizens in particular are questioning lopsided federal priorities. These persons are asking themselves and are beginning to ask leaders and representatives how a country can be rich when many of its citizens, white and black, carry a second-class status? when millions of its peoples live financially and spiritually impoverished? when millions want for gainful employment? when millions cannot afford proper medical and dental care? when millions lack adequate educational facilities? when jails bulge with prisoners living in degradation while awaiting long-overdue trial? when citizens are frightened to walk a city after dark or even in daylight? where prevalence of weapons and violence of thought and deed have bred an anti-culture whose germs daily incubate and grow from a television fare insulting to an adult mind? where what once was an arsenal of democracy has become an arsenal of violence? where dissenting protesters are arrested and sometimes shot? where air in large cities is dangerous to breathe? where streams, rivers, and lakes are daily poisoned with industrial waste?

Rich?

Powerful?

Is it even a civilized country?

In taking a new and critical look at their country, in admitting these and other faults, some Americans have gained refreshing humility. Some are beginning to believe that their government should stop trying to re-shape other countries in the American image, at least until that image visibly brightens. Some citizens are heeding questioning voices from within—generally young voices of dissent, now a stream, but, when controlled and harnessed, able to power such civic dynamos as Ralph Nader. Held at one time to be only disruptive and thus inimical to established social order, these voices now are accepted by increasing numbers as searching for something lost from the American heritage.

The educational gap will not be bridged until influential citizens attempt to reorient existing values by asking themselves difficult questions. Those posed by philosophers from Plato to Marcuse—why is the human being on earth? what is the goal of government?—are still important. So is the difference between evolution and revolution—and the historical importance of dissent in human progress. In a sense, does not all progress result from dissatisfaction and dissent? Would the wheel otherwise have been invented? Does this not hold true politically? By permitting and even encouraging dissent, has the Western democratic tradition not freed the individual from a good many uncomfortable and harmful chains? Has it not enabled him to lead a fuller, more productive, and more rewarding, therefore a more meaningful, life? What is change? What are human aspirations today? What is pride and what is dignity? Why is rebellion different today from what it was in 1775? Why is the United States devoted to maintaining regional status quos so often incompatible to the needs of emergent nations? Why has she become the watchdog of reaction, when a troubled world demands change? What is a democracy? What is a citizen's proper function in a democratic form of government? If democracy is superior to communism, then why is a democratic nation reacting from fear as opposed to acting from belief? As Ramsey Clark has noted, ". . . In a world of such sweeping change, causing greater differences in daily human experience in one generation than in all previous history, the old rules have limited relevance."[2]

If answers are not easy, and important answers rarely are, an attempt to find them at least suggests a reawakening of national consciousness, a welcome detour and perhaps even a new highway away from a tiresome road of conformity that has so discouraged healthy dissent and imaginative national leadership.

Fear of dissent, perhaps more than any other national characteristic, explains feckless American leadership. By blindly accepting, indeed worshiping, such sacred cows as "the Communist threat," the electorate has tended to place representatives in political strait jackets. A "Communist threat" exists—but so does an "excess-population threat," a "poverty threat," an "ecology threat," an "education threat." Never has man been free of "threats," but even the ancients, hidebound to susperstition and worship, did not continue to fear past storms in preference to those approaching. The paranoiac fear of a "threat" that has radically changed form in the past decade is only stultifying: Where need has existed for intelligent examination and appraisal of cloudy but vital international issues, the American electorate too often has refused to allow elected representatives this vital freedom to examine and appraise, on pain of political death.

This demand for conformity of thought, this insistence on bowing to nebulous fears, this rejection of democratic strengths and goals in favor of rule by force, has resulted in still another unfortunate trend: It has allowed ignorant but extremely positive voices within the executive branch of government an unnatural and unhealthy strength. Solution by diplomacy has always been more subtle and difficult (but never more expensive) than solution by force. Stilling voices of dissentient diplomats by threats of career purgatory has increased the power of those who are wedded to solution by force. American militarists, the hawks of Vietnam, have forged a weapon from a national demand for conformity (based on unanalyzed fear), and, so long as that demand exists, they will wield it with skill. Never has blackmail been so ennobled as in the past twenty years of executive performance at the highest levels of American government.

The shortcomings of the American electorate may mitigate faults of American leaders, representatives, and officials, but they do not absolve them. One of the most reprehensible national faults today is personal reluctance to accept responsibility, in this case for the public trust, without hedging the acceptance. Past-Administration figures are vying with each other to blame the Indochina disaster on anyone but themselves; Professor Arthur Schlesinger, Jr., has told us that ". . . it is not only

2. Ramsey Clark, op. cit.; see also J. William Fulbright, "In Thrall to Fear," *The New Yorker*, January 8, 1972.

idle but unfair to seek out guilty men. . . . The Vietnam story is a tragedy without villains. . . ."[3] Clark Clifford has written that ". . . I see no profit and no purpose in any divisive national debate about whether we were right or wrong initially to become involved in the struggle in Viet Nam. . . ."[4]

What abject nonsense!

A leader cannot abrogate responsibility of leadership, a fact accepted even by reactionary kings. After the battle of Tournay, Louis XV led the dauphin onto the field of slaughter and told him: ". . . Here behold victims sacrificed and political hatred, and the passions of our enemies. Preserve this in mind, that you may not sport with the lives of your subjects, and be prodigal of their blood in unjust wars."

Nearly two hundred and fifty years ago, a French writer, Voltaire, introduced his life of King Charles XII of Sweden with this sharp (and to himself dangerous) observation:

. . . If any princes or ministers should find disagreeable truths in this work, let them remember that, being public men, they owe the public an account of their actions; that this is the price at which they buy their greatness; that history is a witness, not a flatterer; and that the only way to compel men to speak well of us, is to do good.[5]

Andrew Jackson put it more succinctly: Each President remains ". . . accountable at the bar of public opinion for every act of his administration." Thomas Jefferson warned that, if citizens ". . . became inattentive to the public affairs," the government ". . . shall all become wolves." Even President Nixon expected ". . . the American people to hold me accountable" for failure "to end this [Vietnam] war in a way that would increase our chances to win time and lasting peace in Vietnam, in the Pacific and in the world."

In a democracy, a candidate seeks office; he is neither born in nor driven to it. A cabinet member, an ambassador, a general: Each wants to hold his prestigious rank—no one has forced him so to serve. In theory, a public official's intelligence, education, qualifications, and experience have fitted him to hold the public trust in a manner more worthy and able than his fellows. In turn, the public supports him, enhances his position with privileges and perquisites, endows him with honors not offered to ordinary mortals. But, in return, the public is entitled to expect able performance. Part of able performance in a democracy, we should add, lies in instructing the public as honestly and forcefully and fully as possible on those issues of vital importance to the nation.

Not all issues can be so aired, and leaders must be allowed considerable discretion in conducting the nation's business. But discretion differs

3. Schlesinger (*Bitter*), *supra*.
4. Clifford, op. cit.
5. Theodore Besterman, *Voltaire* (London: Longmans, Green, 1969).

from dissembling, and if an official withholds information unnecessarily or distorts information intentionally, then, as Lord Mahon said of Narses, he is ". . . careless of the public cause."

But, in a democracy, this remains largely the fault of the public. In 1968, an American historian, Professor Henry Steele Commager, came to uncomfortable grips with basic facts:

. . . Abuse of power by Presidents is a reflection, and perhaps a consequence, of abuse of power by the American people and nation. For almost two decades now we have misused our vast power. We misused our economic power, not least in associating economic with military assistance and military with economic support, and in imposing economic sanctions against nations who did not see eye to eye with us about trade with our "enemies." We misused our political power by trying to force neutrals onto our side in the cold war and by bringing pressure on the nations of Latin America to support our shortsighted policy of excluding China from the United Nations. We have grossly misused our political power—if it may be called that —by planting the CIA in some 60 countries to carry on its work of subversion. We have misused our military power in forcing our weapons on scores of nations around the globe, maintaining military organizations and alliances like NATO and SEATO—the first of which has outlived its usefulness, the second of which never had any usefulness to begin with. And we are now engaged in a monstrous misuse of power in waging war on a distant people that does not accept our ideology. We have even misused our moral power, by bringing pressure on former allies and associates to join us in the cold war against the Soviet Union and China; and history may yet find the United States chiefly responsible for exacerbating the disunity of Germany and the division between East and West by exploiting Germany for cold war purposes. That seems to be the de Gaulle interpretation of our role in Europe, and de Gaulle is more often right than wrong.

As we have greater power than any other nation, so we should display greater moderation in using it and greater humility in justifying it. We display neither moderation nor humility, but immoderation and that arrogance of power which Senator Fulbright has so eloquently denounced.

In the long run, then, the abuse of the executive power cannot be separated from the abuse of national power. If we subvert world order and destroy world peace we must inevitably subvert and destroy our own political institutions first. This we are now in the process of doing.[6]

In 1971, John Galbraith added a warning exclamation point. Commenting on President Johnson's duplicity as revealed in the Pentagon Papers, he wrote:

. . . To the knowing, those of us who were making the speeches [for Johnson's re-election] were patsies serving usefully because of our ignorance. What we have learned is that a small group of professionally assured, morally

6. Commager, op. cit.

astigmatic and—a point to be emphasized—intellectually myopic men had undertaken deliberately to mislead the Congress, the public and the people of the world at large.

Galbraith concluded:

. . . In these past years we have allowed soldiers and civilian strategists—the most bizarre of authorities to entrust with such a matter—to divert us with the doctrine that because the communist countries do not have public debate on public issues neither should we.

Let us now accept the lesson. What may work for the communists may work disaster for us. The worst policy is one made in secrecy by the experts.

Our safety lies, and lies exclusively, in making public decision subject to the test of public debate. What cannot survive public debate—as the experience of Vietnam shows—we must not do.[7]

President, Congress, and people aside, the tragedy of Vietnam stemmed primarily from inadequate performance by two executive departments: the Department of State and the Department of Defense.

As we have discussed (Chapter 53), the Department of State's authority in conducting foreign affairs has steadily eroded since 1940. This is not an exclusively American phenomenon. Throughout history, diplomat has competed with general; one need only glance at Alfred Vagts's excellent study *Defense and Diplomacy* to note that, where force has usurped the diplomatic function, nations have suffered—often needlessly. American history contains a number of such instances. So prevalent was fear of militarism in the eighteenth century, that our founding fathers attempted to erect barriers against what they rightly believed had brought untold suffering to European millions. James Madison noted that ". . . a standing force . . . is a dangerous, at the same time that it may be a necessary provision." George Washington believed that

. . . Overgrown military establishments are under any form of government inauspicious to liberty, and are to be regarded as particularly hostile to republic liberty.

Samuel Adams held that a ". . . standing army, however necessary it may be at some times, is always dangerous to the liberties of the people. Soldiers are apt to consider themselves as a body distinct from the rest of the citizens. . . . Such a power should be watched with a jealous eye." Successive administrations generally heeded these words, and if, on occasion, the military establishment became "overgrown," it was to meet a particular challenge that diplomacy had failed to answer.

But the diplomatic function also posed problems to Presidents. An appointive tradition resulting from misplaced economy and a desire to reward political followers hindered effective growth and productive op-

7. Michael Leapman, *The Times* (London), New York, June 17, 1971.

erations of what eventually became the U. S. Department of State. Career diplomats, on the other hand, tended toward a generally conservative and unhealthy elitism that hindered objective reporting from foreign capitals. Secularism has often tainted American diplomacy, partly because some Secretaries of State have held personal political ambitions and have tended to compete with, rather than serve selflessly, President and nation, and partly because either inadequate knowledge of an area or personal political beliefs too often resulted in deductive reporting inimical to departmental objectivity.

A cumulative result has been a presidential tendency to circumvent the department, in higher reaches of diplomacy, by use of extra-departmental presidential "agents." Woodrow Wilson favored this system (which nearly precipitated war with Mexico). So did Franklin Roosevelt, who neither liked nor trusted diplomats. We have noted the questionable results of his personal diplomacy when he sent Pat Hurley to China in 1943. Roosevelt's antipathy to professional diplomacy continued in the 1940s: The war's global nature, the efficient performance of General George C. Marshall, the threat posed by German development of an atomic bomb, and presidential ego all combined to emphasize the importance of military operations at expense of State Department prestige. As allied conferences grew in size, as issues became more important, professional diplomats exercised less and less influence, a far from satisfactory development that helped to explain a good many postwar friction points.[8]

Ensuing cold war posed a unique threat to the diplomatic establishment. So long as the cold war was interpreted in primary terms of military threat, militarism remained dominant in American government councils. What many leaders unfortunately failed to realize is that history, in one sense, has been a prolonged cold war. Astute diplomacy has been necessary to minimize frictions and retain the chill. Application of force has yielded to friction to produce heat. Where force became a way of life, where a philosophy of militarism reigned, as during the Hundred Years' War and the Thirty Years' War and World Wars I and II, countries turned to wastelands—bloody, dreary soil suitable only for spawning more wars.

Since 1945, American leaders have allowed solution by force to assume precedent over solution by diplomacy, a trend perhaps understandable, considering the first decade of Soviet intransigence. But application of force, as history sadly demonstrates, is habit-forming. It always seems easier to fight than to negotiate. And the less efficacious the negotiations, the stronger becomes this illusion.

Unfortunately, the Department of State did not intelligently react to the military threat to its traditional hegemony in international affairs.

8. Kennan (*Memoirs*—Vols. 1 and 2), *supra,* offers a detailed and interesting discussion of this point.

It could have done so. The Foreign Service Act of 1946 recognized the need for, and indeed authorized, a single professional service to ". . . represent the United States abroad, a service responsive to the needs of all the agencies in foreign affairs, open to new ideas and talents, and self-improving."[9] A large part of the aberration stemmed from internal deficiencies that, for decades, have produced mediocre departmental leaders (always with some splendid exceptions) who have seemed unable to dominate military colleagues. Contributory reasons existed: The department took an awful pommeling in McCarthy days, and its aloof attitude has never endeared it to the public. That does not excuse internal failure exemplified in a promotion system that too often produces diplomats of studied mediocrity—and some not so studied.

The Vietnam experience has exposed this weakness to all eyes. Since 1950, the military has run roughshod over civil representation in Indochina. Part of this was due to a volatile international situation, but part was due also, as we discussed in Chapter 53, to ineffectual departmental understanding and representation. Military emphasis in Vietnamese affairs grew steadily through the 1950s and into the 1960s, the military voice always growing stronger—a volume increased by ineffectual State Department performance.

Almost everyone concerned with foreign affairs recognizes the problem. A staff officer in the department's executive secretariat, Lannon Walker, wrote in *Foreign Affairs* of January 1969: ". . . Recommendations for fundamental reforms in the organization and administration of foreign affairs have been made by high-level committees and task forces on the average of every two years since World War II. Despite the near unanimity of diagnosis, little has been done to deal with the serious problems uncovered; they are still with us, unsolved and debilitating."[10] A foreign-service officer, John Campbell, explored this problem further in a lengthy article in *Foreign Affairs* in October 1970.[11]

The major problem faced by the State Department then and now is lack of professional leadership in a professional day. If the American Government wants able diplomatic performance, its people and leaders must learn that a national interest does override a domestic political interest in the conduct of foreign affairs; as a British prime minister, Lord Palmerston, once cautioned: ". . . We have no perpetual allies and we have no perpetual enemies. Our interests are perpetual." It is not only unproductive, but also dangerous, to tolerate a bilateral foreign policy. Under the American system of government, the chief executive is entitled to appoint a Secretary of State as well as ambassadors. If effectual performance is to result, the political bias must diminish in favor of professional bias. Congress does retain an approval authority over

9. Lannon Walker, "Our Foreign Affairs Machinery: Time for an Overhaul," *Foreign Affairs*, January 1969.
10. Ibid.
11. John F. Campbell, op. cit.; see also Reischauer, op. cit.

presidential appointments, and if tradition dictates that these appointments receive courtesy approval—then we must challenge tradition.

Appointments aside, the department must be reorganized so that, while an appointive Secretary of State can contribute to its improvement, he cannot harm an essentially professional and objective performance of these most delicate duties. The Department of State must become apolitical to the greatest possible degree.

Part of any reform, a large part, will be dismissal of political patronage in form of ambassadorships. To place non-qualified persons in these seats of what should be awesome responsibility is tantamount to placing butchers in operating theaters. Not only do amateur diplomats fail to understand professional requirements; they cannot understand qualifications essential to persons who conduct positive diplomacy. Expense cannot enter into the argument: If the United States cannot afford to keep a career ambassador comfortably, it cannot afford to place a man on the moon.

Similarly, if a President or a Secretary of State does not trust a career ambassador, he must relieve him rather than circumvent his function. Along with abolition of amateur ambassadors must go the roving ambassador or superambassador or presidential agent—call him what you will. If the White House is not securing ambassadorial co-operation, if it is dissatisfied by a particular diplomatic activity, then it must change from within, not tread on from without. A brave American diplomat, Mr. John Alden Bovey, counselor in the American Embassy at The Hague, recently wrote that ". . . interfering ministers and high officials" have made "mail-boxes" out of ambassadors:

. . . Telephone calls can be forgotten and telegrams filed but ministers and presidents pouncing out of the sky are not lightly dismissed. Most such visits are a waste of time. They disrupt the business of an embassy; they cheapen the image of prestige; they lead to fatigue, and often to serious misunderstanding or even hostility.

Diplomacy, Mr. Bovey suggests, is a private matter to be conducted by ". . . honest men, each of whom enjoys the confidence of the other and of his own government."[12] Mr. Bovey might have added that "honest" men should be young, bright, and imaginative, not old men, physically and mentally dulled, able only to indulge in "prostate diplomacy," where a more virile approach is necessary. It is very difficult to grow younger —which is why private companies under old, "traditional" management so frequently find themselves in trouble. An aging body too often means a moribund mind. Some people are capable of absorbing new, fresh notions that emanate from organic world growth—Justice Douglas and Senator Fulbright would be two. Most minds cannot so grow, particu-

12. *The Times* (London), November 9, 1971.

larly in an environment where it is professionally safer to be cautious than bold.

The department, on the other hand, in order to justify new responsibility, will have to institute major internal reforms. In many ways, the department is responsible for more-severe failings, despite shaky senior leadership provided by a series of non-professional Secretaries. Lannon Walker noted some major deficiencies:

. . . One, related directly to the growth of competing services arising out of new ideas and new techniques, has been an overwhelming hostility to anything novel. The old ways, by definition, were the best. Another is that in a system threatened with irrelevance and in which the really good jobs are increasingly rare, the race goes to the loner who travels fast, who best manipulates the guild structure for personal ends, who has a friend who can get him out of the unpleasant job. And the collective well-being has gone glimmering: the old esprit de corps is still being invoked, but by the mid-1960s nobody was making a serious contribution to it.[13]

Other major faults exist. Department seniors have allowed increasing alienation to develop between the department and the rest of government, and between department and press and thus the public—too often forgetting that the department is to serve the nation and not itself. Department seniors have too long tolerated and even encouraged lackadaisical and inept performance; they have countenanced too many internal cabals and intrigues (indeed they have often headed them); they have for too long indulged subordinates in human failings that had no place in government. Demagogue Joseph McCarthy enlarged and exploited departmental failure—but the failure was there. Eisenhower's refusal to protect professional diplomats whose crime was accuracy allowed an era of fear to ensue and further corrode department performance. As John Campbell noted,

. . . The purge was followed by the Wriston Program, which trebled the number of Foreign Service officers in 1954–56 by bringing in 2,500 new personnel at the middle grades. The atmosphere of that period is best recalled by the motto of Security Chief Scott McLeod: "An ounce of loyalty is worth more than a pound of brains." Most of State's senior career men today are veterans of that era; and if honesty and brilliance are in short supply, it is partly because honesty and brilliance were not rewarded in the fifties.[14]

Internal reform is primarily a matter of education, both general and specific. The above-mentioned diplomat, Mr. Bovey, cites a need for diplomats ". . . to resist the defamations of their own profession." Mr. Bovey suggests ". . . systems of recruitment, examination and promotion, which combine rigorous competition with strictest anonymity."

13. Lannon Walker, op. cit.
14. John F. Campbell, op. cit.

The department also needs ". . . a new code of government behavior in relations with press and public, based on rigorous honesty as well as discretion."

The department needs all this and more. In an attempt to reclaim traditional roles, missions, and prerogatives from other agencies, especially from the military, it has chosen a quantitative approach that has resulted in interdepartmental duplication and confusion (and waste), and thus contributed again to a decline in the effectiveness that it needs to regain stature. John Campbell, among others, has discussed the dangers of "gigantism" and suggested, along with other cures, "bureaucratic surgery" not alone for State Department personnel but for those ancillary organizations that too often feed from the diplomatic function, confusing and frequently neutralizing the work of professionals.

The size, function, and authority of these ancillary organizations, which frequently operate independently of an embassy, should be drastically curtailed and, in some cases, eliminated. They explain, in large part, the ludicrous size of American embassies around the world, a cumulative ostentation that frequently does more harm than good. According to John Campbell, over 80 per cent of our diplomatic staff are not State Department employees but, instead, work for the military or USIA or AID or CIA or dozens of other agencies. Lannon Walker has pointed out that there are ". . . 23 agencies crowded under the umbrella of the American Embassy in Paris, each persuaded that it represents the national interest, many often at cross-purposes with the activities of an agency down the hall. In mid-1968 there were reportedly 56 agencies represented at one or more posts abroad."

Internal conflicts produced by this quantitative approach necessarily dilute an ambassador's effectiveness and are further reducing ambassadorial authority, at a time when it has become dangerously weak at best. Presidents Kennedy, Johnson, and Nixon concerned themselves with this problem, and each, in the case of South Vietnam, attempted to strengthen the ambassadorial hand.

These attempts failed for two reasons. The first was ambivalent presidential policy, which paid lip service to diplomacy while basically relying on force, that is, belief in and preference for military rather than political solution. A good example is Nixon's letter to Ambassador Leonard Unger, in Thailand, an embassy at the time, incidentally, second in size (one thousand people) only to the American embassy in Saigon (four thousand). On December 9, 1969, Nixon wrote Unger:

. . . As Chief of the United States Diplomatic Mission, you have full responsibility to direct and coordinate the activities and operations of all of its elements. You will exercise this mandate not only by providing policy leadership and guidance, but also by assuring positive program direction to the end that all United States activities in Thailand are relevant to current realities, are efficiently and economically administered, and are effectively interrelated so that they will make a maximum contribution to United States interests in that country as well as to our regional and international objectives.

So far, so good. But now Nixon added two Catch-22 paragraphs:

. . . I will reserve for myself, as Commander-in-Chief, direct authority over the military chain of command to United States military forces under the command of a United States area military commander, and over such other military activities as I elect, as Commander-in-Chief, to conduct through military channels.

However, I will expect you and the military commanders concerned to maintain close relations with each other, to keep each other currently informed on matters of mutual interest and in general to cooperate in carrying out our national policy. If differences of view not capable of resolution in the field should arise, I will expect you to keep me informed through the Secretary of State.

This effectively watered Unger's control, but was only part of the problem. As Unger's deputy for counterinsurgency, George Tanham, later wrote:

. . . With the best will in the world, it is difficult for an Ambassador to orchestrate the activities of the diverse agencies in his Mission. The confusion in the Nixon letter, already mentioned, is compounded by practical administrative problems. Each of the Mission elements has its own institutional loyalties, each of the parent agencies in Washington has its own goals and interests, and each has a congressional constituency to serve. Even when the Mission can speak with a single voice from the field, there is no single listener in Washington—there is a mixed audience which can respond only after a process of negotiation and compromise. Then too, Mission elements tend to build up client relationships with the various agencies of the host government; in time, this symbiotic relationship becomes very strong indeed. Of course, separate budgetary processes, outside ambassadorial control, contribute to all of this.[15]

Since this situation can be faulted by performance and results in a number of critical problem countries, it is going to have to be studied and reformed, particularly as regards unity of command, a deficiency that perhaps more than any other produced our national failure in Vietnam. But unity of command, as armies have discovered through the centuries, is useless if the commander is not up to the task.

To do his job properly, a modern-day ambassador, particularly in an insurgency situation, has got to be an extremely bright, efficient, forceful, and courageous executive, and it is this professional aspect in the Department of State that must be elevated by any reform. Diplomacy,

15. George K. Tanham, *Trial in Thailand, supra.*

in essence, is international political science, and so specialized has the discipline become that a general education no longer suffices. It probably never did: Even Napoleon attached the greatest importance to recruiting and training promising young men, the *auditeurs,* to hold high civil positions. Today a pragmatic approach is probably desirable: a solid liberal-arts degree with tested fluency in at least two foreign languages, followed by a specialized academic course to teach technical requirements and procedures and to instill in the future diplomat a pride in diplomacy; at some point in his early career, a year or two of cross-training in the military establishment would not be a bad idea, nor would a degree in business management be out of place. We train doctors, lawyers, and professors lavishly; surely international affairs, which bring us peace or war, deserve similar devotion.

Integral to the training process must be the inculcation of an inductive approach to diplomacy, particularly in analyzing and reporting an area situation. Objective reporting is imperative. This is professionalism, as opposed to particularism, and until the department can claim apolitical objectivity, it cannot claim superior professional performance. So difficult is this to achieve—and, without professional leadership at the top, it is impossible—that the transition period may have to employ various aids. One should be a modification of the Communist technique of parallel hierarchy—in this case, a devil's advocate trained to understand and present an opponent's position without fear of tainting his career.

Finally, the department itself is going to have to be decentralized to a greater degree than at present, in order to allow diplomats to concentrate on what is important. Perhaps the soundest advice ever given a diplomat was that offered by Secretary of State Marshall to George Kennan: "Avoid trivia." Diplomats should not have to worry about administrative details of running an embassy. On the other hand, no operational detail of that embassy should exist outside the ambassador's cognizance. The intelligence function, the military function, the aid function, the information function—each must remain subordinate to the diplomatic function. But that halcyon state of affairs will not result until reform has embraced the department, producing professional leadership able to accept and uphold the responsibility.

Able leadership, however, can emerge only with radical change in present philosophy and concept. As Lannon Walker has pointed out,

. . . The system and the people will produce if the new President [Richard Nixon] understands that reform is not accomplished by the submission of reports, by comprehensive legislation or by delegations of authority. Real reform requires, first and foremost, the will to change and the commitment to clearly enunciated goals on the part of the President and his top appointees in foreign affairs. The President must appoint reformers if he wants reform—and he must fire them if they do not produce. The reformers already have available to them all the resources and legislative authority that they require.

The options are not the poles of unordered decentralization on the one hand and total integration on the other. The options, rather, are centered on the practical, yet revolutionary, middle ground of flexibility and innovation—of integrated planning and decentralized operations.

If internal deficiencies have eroded the Department of State's traditional authority, the Department of Defense has not failed to exploit the situation whenever possible. It is this department which, having made itself the primary executive instrument in Vietnam, must accept primary blame for the tragedy.

As suggested earlier, the major villain here has been arrogance of ignorance compounded by arrogance of power—for so long and to such an extent that far too many of our military men can, like Bohemund, be accused of acquiring ". . . perjury and treachery as a species of ancestral heritage." The problem is to cure ignorance and curb power without sacrificing necessary components of the defense machine. (It can be done, and Congress, in its present militant mood, may possess courage and determination necessary to clip the bellicose tail that, for too long, has been wagging the national dog. After abrogating their share of responsibility for the public trust by passing the Tonkin Gulf Resolution, ". . . in a moment, in a fit of passion," the nation's legislators seem to have awakened and even to have realized that, thanks to clever forefathers, executive operations depend, in the final analysis, on money authorized by Congress).

That would be the first step in a difficult process, but no real gain will result until, along with the American electorate, the armed forces become sufficiently educated to gain maturity and humility. In a dangerous age, they have not come of age. Despite manifold lessons of history, teachings of their own and other professionals, the recent examples of Korea and of insurgencies one after the other, Pentagon and service leaders refused to recognize a limited species in the genre of war, insisting, instead, on an all-out black-and-white performance remote from either national interest or technical problems of the challenge. As one army general recently concluded: ". . . We haven't learned how to wage that which will be the most likely form of war in the coming decades . . ."—what a British brigadier, Frank Kitson, has aptly termed low-intensity operations.[16]

Almost nothing good can be said about the American military performance in Vietnam except the sadly misplaced willingness of youngsters to fight and die while using obsolete tactics to pursue impossible strategy. Never did civil and military hawks offer an intelligible definition of Indochina's strategic importance, except to bleat on about dominoes and Red hordes in Hawaii. Never did civil and military hawks offer

16. Ward Just, *Military Men* (New York: Alfred A. Knopf, 1971); Frank Kitson, *Low-Intensity Operations* (London: Faber & Faber, 1971).

a plan of political-military containment that would have utilized limited resources and minimum force to accomplish particular goals within an established objective.

Instead, commencing in 1950, they demanded a military solution to a political problem. When this failed, they did not pause to ponder and reorient thinking to a different sort of strategic and tactical challenge— but one scarcely new. Instead, they organized, equipped, and trained a conventional army inadequate to cope with an internal challenge—indeed, under the special circumstances, one that could only exacerbate that challenge. As the problem grew and variously manifested itself, they continued to misread it and to report erroneously, until a disastrous course of action resulted. Napoleon once wrote: "A general should never paint pictures, it is the worst thing he can do." Our generals and admirals and civilian hawks were painting pictures; as mistakes became evident, as strategic poverty grew in proportion to inept tactics, they sought increasing refuge in dissembling, distorted reports designed solely to justify an escalating military role. While facing a fluid situation, American hawks became enslaved by the western-front syndrome of World War I, and, more than once, they nudged the possibility of atomic war. Thanks to presidential confusion, Congressional apathy, and State Department weakness, their voices assumed unwarranted volume, to the extent that they mistakenly believed themselves to be representing the national will. In time, they ceased acting as rational human beings; they became discordant gods beating out their own version of *Götterdämmerung*. They were the villains without whom, Schlesinger aside, a tragedy has never existed.

The dismal military performance in Vietnam stems from a permissiveness not only authorized, but encouraged, by a Congress bowing to importunate demands of a series of administrations. The nation's military leaders have played upon a national fear of a monolithic Communist threat to justify building, maintaining, and frequently expanding an armed plant whose consuming nature is as alarming as the rapacious tendencies it demonstrates. When this threat demonstrably turned out to consist of bits and pieces that enjoyed brief historical prosperity before fragmenting, the military continued to insist that the threat had not changed and continued to approach it with strategic and tactical thinking unblemished by realistic analysis.

This would have been all right in normal circumstances, if only because executive and legislative branches would have slapped military fingers from the jam of power and allowed the Department of State its traditional hegemony in foreign affairs. Unfortunately, a bellicose Stalin and a victorious Mao Tse-tung introduced panic into top American Government echelons at a time when, as we have discussed, the Department of State was in a weakened and confused condition. In those turbulent years, when American policy relied on force, the military could not but grow and continue to establish itself as a major instrument of foreign policy.

The result has been anomalous and autonomous. Continued growth and influence in highest levels of government has changed a healthy and necessary national organism into a fear-producing and very wasteful specter remote from both American tradition and desire of a good many American citizens. As the Pulitzer prize-winning historian Barbara Tuchman recently and courageously told senior-officer students at the Army War College:

. . . It is true that in America the military has never seriously challenged civilian rule, but in late years it hardly needs to. With a third of the national budget absorbed by military spending, with the cost of producing nuclear and other modern weapons having evidently no limits, with 22,000 defense contractors and 100,000 subcontractors operating in the United States, with defense plants or installations located in 363 out of 435 Congressional districts, the interlocking of military-industrial interests grips the economy and pervades every agency of government.

The new budget of 83.4 billion for defense represents five times the amount for control of pollution (our Government having failed to notice that pollution by now is a graver threat to us than the Russians). It costs an annual average of about $10,000 to maintain each man in uniform compared to a national expenditure of $1,172.86 for each person in the United States, in other words the man in uniform absorbs ten times as much. The Pentagon, where lies the pulse of all this energy and activity, spends annually $140,000,000 on public relations *alone,* nearly twice as much as the entire budget of the National Endowment for Arts and Humanities. When military and military-connected interests penetrate government to that extent, the Government becomes more or less the prisoner of the Pentagon.[17]

Herein lies the anomaly. The American military establishment in 1974 occupies a more powerful position in the American Government than equivalent military plants in either China or the U.S.S.R. In fighting authoritative governments founded on force, the American Government is gradually succumbing to that form of government itself—and this is frightening. If the pursuit of international relations can be regarded historically as a carrot-and-stick proposition, those countries which have pursued the most successfully have used more carrot and less stick. But the American Government is increasingly using more stick and less car-

17. Barbara Tuchman, "Generalship." Speech delivered before the Army War College, April 1972; see also Donovan, op. cit.; George Thayer, *The War Business* (London: Weidenfeld & Nicolson, 1969); Ralph E. Lapp, *Arms Beyond Doubt: The Tyranny of Weapons Technology* (Chicago: Cowles Book Company, 1970); William Proxmire, *Report from the Wasteland: America's Military-Industrial Complex* (New York: Frederick A. Praeger, 1970); William McGaffin and Erwin Knoll, *Scandal in the Pentagon: A Challenge to Democracy* (Greenwich, Conn.: Fawcett, 1969); Alain C. Enthoven, and K. Wayne Smith, *How Much Is Enough?* (New York: Harper & Row, 1971).

rot. An increasing reliance on force as the major instrument of diplomacy has brought about a series of confused commitments any one of which can be used to justify military action. As two able analysts have pointed out:

... Our commitments are, in fact, a series of legal and historical abstractions obligating us, in often obscure phraseology, to come to the defense of over forty nations. But the trouble with our foreign commitments is that they have acquired an independent life transcending the US security interest that brought them into being. Collectively, our commitments remain what they have tended to become: an undifferentiated mass which defies discriminating analysis for defense planning purposes. . . .

As a basis both for avoiding senseless confrontations and for sound defense planning, the cardinal need today is a searching analysis of what these commitments should commit us to in the light of our genuine national interests.

The propensity to regard our commitments as 40-odd blank checks has contributed not to our security but to a defense budget disproportionate both to the military threats we face and to the domestic problems we cannot avoid. Our defense forces have achieved a size and versatility that far exceed the limited opportunities for their effective use. . . .[18]

This would perhaps be acceptable, providing that military leaders accept the trend of international affairs and tailor the military plant to a realistic appraisal of what military challenges are likely to affect American security.

But there enters the factor of autonomy. Once a body considers itself independent of a corporate state, it must ensure survival by continued growth. When one limb becomes useless, another grows. Thus, when national sentiment forces reduction of manpower, other instruments grow in importance: $30 billion worth of fighter-bombers for long-range interdiction; billions more for thirteen attack aircraft carriers that could not survive twenty-four hours of warfare; new, bewildering, and terribly expensive weapons, extensions of those systems which failed in Vietnam; finally, Westmoreland's supreme folly (which is saying a lot)—a non-man army of body-smelling sensors costing only a few billions (to start with) for use in a war that will never happen if civilization is to survive. Concomitant to the process is interservice rivalry, which can only continue to result in wasteful duplication. Many Americans do not realize the intensity of competitive feeling between the services. In Vietnam, army, navy, marines, and air force not only pursued separate and frequently unco-ordinated courses, but often contradicted theater policy, both military and civil, to further slow and confuse overall effort. In spring of 1968, senior Marine Corps officers were called

18. Paul Warnke and Leslie Gelb, "Security or Confrontation," *Foreign Policy,* Winter 1970–71.

together in secret session to hear a speech by Lieutenant General Victor Krulak, who was about to retire. Far from imparting wisdom on waging insurgency warfare, Krulak's major thesis was the necessity of thenceforth proving marine tactics in Vietnam correct, thus blunting the army's efforts to put marines out of business!

From these two factors, anomaly and autonomy, comes a spin-off of justification that could prove disastrous if it goes unchecked. Where bellicose ambitions of past American leaders were usually thwarted by limited means, the combination of Congressional indulgence, diplomatic impotency, and enemy intransigence has opened the door to a militaristic philosophy only too familiar to the ancients, as noted by wise Xenophon:

. . . Clearchos was a true soldier and war was his passion. . . . When he could have kept at peace without shame or damage, he chose war; when he could have been idle, he wished for hard work that he might have war; when he could have kept wealth without danger, he chose to make it less by making war; there was a man who spent upon war as if it were a darling lover, or some other pleasure.

Most armies have suffered a Clearchos element, and those governments and nations which have survived through history have successfully dampened its aspirations. Unfortunately, the Clearchos element in the American military grew steadily stronger in the 1950s, finally to erupt in Vietnam. Like the Clearchos element of old, the latter-day version was characterized by bellicose ambition stemming from political ignorance. The American military had not been trained to understand political subtleties, which is primarily why, in international affairs, it should follow, not lead. During and since World War II, the military has had its way for so long that it has grown used to making blanket assertions without having to justify them. The strategic necessity of Vietnam and the concomitant domino theory are prime examples of superficial thinking. So is the insistence on awarding priority to North Vietnam as the enemy in order to support a World War I strategy in a 1965 world. Presidential, Congressional, and public neglect to demand justification of military reasoning and performance further spoiled military minds, to the extent that, in time, they believed their own illogic.

When strategy and tactics failed, when the American armada was forced to come about and make for home, the Clearchos element turned to the task of justifying its actions. Not only did it refuse to admit severe shortcomings in respective services and an over-all failure of strategy and tactics in Vietnam, but it attempted to claim "victory" by indirection. Scarcely had the flesh of reputation been stripped from ranking bodies, when bones started knocking like a stork's knees. Older Germans recognized what was happening, because they had been through it all with Kaiser Wilhelm and Field Marshal Hindenburg and General von Ludendorff, whose 1918 tale had the German army winning but the home front surrendering. Beginning in 1967, the American President, American generals, and lesser fry went stumping about the country with a similar refrain.

The United States can and has survived Presidents and generals, but, unfortunately, in the Johnson and Nixon eras these have aided and abetted an intolerance within the armed forces, particularly among career officers, that too often approaches sedition and even mutinous intent. Only recently, the writer listened to an air force regular, a lieutenant colonel, condemn Congress in the most savage terms, concluding with, ". . . as for that stupid son of a bitch Fulbright. . . ." Only recently, the writer received a letter from a young marine officer, an Annapolis graduate and Vietnam veteran, who vociferously complained of the press role in Vietnam and ominously added, ". . . other traitorous acts by the press in and out of Vietnam has [sic] resulted in some dangerous talk. I have heard numerous rumblings among several officers that the biggest casualties in the next war will be reporters. Most young officers are very suspicious of [members of] the press and consider them an overt threat. . . ."[19] Hundreds and perhaps thousands of similar examples doubtless exist. Fortunately, so do compensating factors. Aside from lawful machinery of government, which must force internal military reforms if only by cutting appropriations, each service contains thousands of courageous and meritorious officers and non-commissioned officers anxious for legitimate reforms but heretofore powerless to effect them.

As in the State Department, this impotency probably represents the most severe internal deficiency. The armed forces have each embraced a doctrinaire philosophy that disallows public interservice dissent, particularly because a solid front is believed essential to maintaining a strong position vis-à-vis other services and thus the defense budget. Each service selects and trains officers as one would fit bread dough into a standard mold. Dissentient voices are not only not invited, but soon find themselves beyond the pale, shunted to unimportant billets, passed over for promotion and subsequently retired. If conformance has become a feature of American middle-class life, then it is the *sine qua non* of the American military profession.

As one result, we have bred a generation of conformist generals and admirals, few of whom had either the professional knowledge or the moral courage to dissent when it became obvious that the Administration was about to embark on a catastrophic course of military action. A few men who recognized and condemned this course of action thenceforth found themselves in limbo; the men who encouraged it won promotions and honors. Conformance thus continued to breed personal

---

19. Private information in the author's files.

rewards while sacrificing national assets in a strategic-tactical orgy unbelievable except that it happened.

In discussing the army's refusal to adapt tactics as desired by General Abrams, a RAND analyst pointed out various reasons. One was ". . . the belief held by many that the change recommended simply would not work or that they would not work better, or that they would work but at the expense of victory which would be exchanged for an economical stalemate."[20] A more important reason was

. . . the conviction that what we are doing now is successful. It *is* successful —according to criteria that the institution itself has established. And the only way that this "success" can be challenged is by challenging the criteria. By that I mean that it is possible to measure winning as a continuing process, but it is not possible to measure progress toward an ultimate victory because that goal has never been clearly defined. *The operations are the strategy.* In the absence of a goal or a strategy to reach that goal if we had one, the operational criteria remain valid by default and by those criteria, we are winning. One does not change a winning strategy.

Another reason was ". . . the belief that what was needed was simply more of the same, bolstered by the view, at least until recently, that Washington really would supply more." Still another reason was

. . . the wide-held myth that organizational changes cannot be made in the midst of a war. Military planners are prepared to think and talk about new concepts of strategy, tactics, and operations as long as this does not entail organizational changes. I found this true even in the "radical" Long Range Planning Group. . . . In rejecting changes in organization, the institution has thereby rejected changes in its operations since *the operations are what the organization is.*

Related to this reason was another, ". . . the feeling among many [army officers] that the war in Vietnam is irrelevant to the institution." (Or, as a senior army officer put it to the author of this book in 1971, ". . . Thank God we are leaving Vietnam. Now we can get back to the type of warfare we know how to fight.")

These reasons help explain the disastrous relationship that has developed between military and press. Like the State Department, the military has been its own worst enemy. Unwilling or unable to repair administrative and operational deficiencies, particularly in Vietnam, it has attempted to transfer blame to an outside agency, the press, which it frequently criticizes for distorted reporting.

The present military rank structure will not permit this philosophy to change voluntarily. American generals and admirals are so insulated as to be living in an unreal world. Command egos have to be experienced to be believed. The difference between the rank of colonel and brigadier

20. Jenkins, op. cit.

general is immense and perhaps is the gravest deficiency in the present rank structure. One of our most able marine generals once described the transition, to this writer, as going from a land of knowing to a land of dreaming. One day an ordinary mortal, the next a demigod who rates free servants, private limousines, special aircraft—all the paraphernalia formerly reserved for heads of state. A traditional argument for increasing military pay and perquisites has been to attract top men to top jobs. Are the services developing top leaders by continuing to demand sacrifice of independent thought, and frequently of integrity, in subordinates?

As part of returning military men to their world, service academies must review present curricula to enlarge the humanities program. The career officer must be encouraged in non-military reading, to a degree that promotion examinations cover this category. The promotion system for each service must be exhaustively examined and provision made for dissentient voices to be heard without prejudice to promotion. Such is the present strangulating personnel policy of both Defense and State departments that an extraneous promotion-review board must be established along lines similar to a civil appeals court.

These measures are going to have to be forced on the services. It is unfortunate that this is the case, but such are the issues, such the Vietnam record, that the nation must now challenge the policy-making abilities of executive departments.

If the United States continues to function internationally along present lines, disaster will probably result. Then it will benefit no one to believe that Vietnam was "a tragedy without villains." It will benefit no one to understand the meaning of arrogance of ignorance. It will prove only of academic interest to archaeologists, who, ages and ages hence, uncover burned and buckled Pentagon walls, there to find words once written in a Chaldean temple:

Mene, mene, tekel, upharsin.
Thou art weighed in the balance, and art found wanting.

Works Cited in This Volume

Acheson, Dean. *Present at the Creation—My Years in the State Department.* New York: W. W. Norton, 1969.

Alastos, Doros. *Cyprus Guerrilla—Grivas, Makarios and the British.* London: William Heinemann, 1960.

Alleg, Henri. *The Question.* London: John Calder, 1958.

Armbrister, Trevor. *A Matter of Accountability—The True Story of the Pueblo Affair.* London: Barrie & Jenkins, 1970.

Asprey, R. B. "Guerrilla Warfare." In Encyclopaedia Britannica, 1969.

———. "Jungle Warfare." In Encyclopaedia Britannica, 1969.

———. "Tactics." In Encyclopaedia Britannica, 1971.

Baldwin, Hanson. "The Case for Escalation," New York *Times Magazine*, February 27, 1966.

———. "The Foe Is Hurting," *Reader's Digest*, March 1968.

———. "To End the War in Vietnam, Mobilize!" *Reader's Digest*, October 1966.

Barclay, C. N. "The Western Soldier Versus the Communist Insurgent," *Military Review*, February 1969.

Barker, Dudley. *Grivas—Portrait of a Terrorist.* London: Cresset Press, 1959.

Barnett, Donald L.; and Njama, Karari. *Mau Mau from Within—Autobiography and Analysis of Kenya's Peasant Revolt.* New York: Monthly Review Press, 1966.

Batista, Fulgencio. *Cuba Betrayed.* New York: Vantage Press, 1962.

Beaufre, André. "Prospects for the New General," *The Sunday Times* (London), March 24, 1968.

Begin, Menachem. *The Revolt.* London: W. H. Allen, 1951. Tr. Samuel Katz.

Behr, Edward. *The Algerian Problem.* London: Hodder & Stoughton, 1961.

Bernard, Stéphane. *The Franco-Moroccan Conflict 1943–56.* New Haven: Yale University Press, 1968.

Besterman, Theodore. *Voltaire.* London: Longmans, Green, 1969.

Béthouart, Hilaire. "Combat Helicopters in Algeria." In Greene, T. N. (ed.). *The Guerrilla and How to Fight Him.* New York: Frederick A. Praeger, 1962.

Black, Eugene R. *Alternative in Southeast Asia.* London: Pall Mall Press, 1969.

Brandon, Henry. *Anatomy of Error: The Secret History of the Vietnam War.* London: André Deutsch, 1970.

Browne, Malcolm. "Why South Viet Nam's Army Won't Fight," *True Magazine*, October 1967.

Bucher, Lloyd M. *Bucher: My Story.* Garden City, N.Y.: Doubleday, 1970.

Bundy, McGeorge. "The End of Either/Or," *Foreign Affairs*, June 1967.

Bundy, William P. "The Path to Vietnam," *Survival,* October 1967.

Burchett, W. G. *Vietnam: Inside Story of the Guerrilla War.* New York: International Publishers, 1965.

Bushell, A. H. "Insurgency and the Numbers Game," *Army Quarterly,* April 1967.

Buttinger, Joseph. *Vietnam: A Dragon Embattled.* New York: Frederick A. Praeger, 1967. 2 vols.

Byford-Jones, W. *Grivas and the Story of EOKA.* London: Robert Hale, 1959.

Cameron, James. *The African Revolution.* New York: Random House, 1961.

Campbell, Arthur. *Jungle Green.* London: Allen & Unwin, 1953.

Campbell, John Franklin. "'What Is to Be Done?' Gigantism in Washington," *Foreign Affairs,* October 1970.

Carver, George A., Jr. "The Real Revolution in South Viet Nam," *Foreign Affairs,* April 1965.

Casella, Alessandro. "The Militant Mood," *Far Eastern Review,* May 16, 1968.

Chapelle, Dickey. "How Castro Won." In T. N. Greene (ed.), *infra.*

Chapman, Leonard. "Remarks." U. S. Marine Corps release, n.d.

Chapman, R. A. *A History of the Cuban Republic.* New York: Macmillan, 1927.

Chester, Edmund A. *A Sergeant Named Batista.* New York: Henry Holt, 1954.

Chorley, K. C. *Armies and the Art of Revolution.* London: Faber & Faber, 1943.

Clark, Mark W. *From the Danube to the Yalu.* New York: Harper & Brothers, 1954.

Clark, Ramsey. "On Violence, Peace and the Rule of Law," *Foreign Affairs,* October 1970.

Clement, David A. "Le May—Study in Counter-Insurgency," *Marine Corps Gazette,* July 1967.

Clifford, Clark M. "A Viet Nam Reappraisal—The Personal History of One Man's View and How It Evolved," *Foreign Affairs,* July 1969.

Clutterbuck, Richard L. *The Long Long War—Counter-Insurgency in Malaya and Vietnam.* New York: Frederick A. Praeger, 1966.

Cohan, Leon. "Intelligence and Viet-Nam," *Marine Corps Gazette,* February 1966.

Colonial Office (Corfield, F. D.). *Historical Survey of the Origin and Growth of Mau Mau.* London: HMSO, 1960. (Command Paper 1030.)

Commager, Henry Steele. "A Limit to Presidential Power?" *The New Republic.* Quoted in *Survival,* July 1968.

Cooper, Chester L. *The Lost Crusade—The Full Story of U.S. Involvement in Vietnam from Roosevelt to Nixon.* London: MacGibbon & Kee, 1970.

Corson, William R. *The Betrayal.* New York: W. W. Norton, 1968.

Costigan, G. "The Anglo-Irish Conflict, 1919–1922," *University Review,* Dublin, Spring 1968.

Deakin, James. "Big Brass Lambs," *Esquire,* December 1967.

Debray, Régis. *Revolution in the Revolution?—Armed Struggle and Political Struggle in Latin America.* New York: Monthly Review Press, 1967.

de Gaulle, Charles. *Mémoires d'Espoir*. Paris: Plon, 1970. 2 vols.

——. *Memoirs of Hope*. London: Weidenfeld & Nicolson, 1970. Volume 1 of 2 volumes. Tr. Terence Kilmartin.

——. *War Memoirs* (Vol. 3–Documents). Collins, 1955. 6 vols. Tr. R. Howar.

Department of Information, Federation of Malaya. *Communist Banditry in Malaya*. Kuala Lumpur: n.d.

Department of the Navy. "Chinfonote 5721." Washington: U. S. Navy, March 28, 1968.

Department of State Publication 7724 (Department of Defense, Gen.-8). *Viet Nam: The Struggle for Freedom*. Washington: U. S. Government Printing Office, 1964.

Devillers, Philippe; and Lacouture, Jean. *End of a War; Indochina, 1954*. New York: Frederick A. Praeger; London: Pall Mall Press; 1969.

Diacre, Kenneth. "Cyprus, 1956," *Army Quarterly*, April 1956.

Donovan, James A. *Militarism, U.S.A.* New York: Charles Scribner's Sons, 1970.

Douhet, Giulio. *The Command of the Air*. London: Faber & Faber, 1943. Tr. D. Ferrari.

Draper, Theodore. *Castroism—Theory and Practice*. London: Pall Mall Press, 1965.

——. *Castro's Revolution—Myths and Realities*. London: Thames & Hudson, 1962.

Duncan, Donald. *The New Legions*. New York: Random House, 1967.

Duncan, H. L. "Does China Want War?" *Army Quarterly*, July 1967.

Duncanson, Dennis J. *Government and Revolution in Vietnam*. London: Oxford University Press, 1968.

——. "The Vitality of the Viet Cong," *Encounter*, December 1966.

Durrell, Lawrence. *Bitter Lemons*. London: Faber & Faber, 1959.

Eden, Anthony. *The Memoirs of Anthony Eden—Full Circle*. Boston: Houghton Mifflin, 1960.

——. *Towards Peace in Indo-China*. London: Oxford University Press, 1966.

Eisenhower, Dwight D. *Mandate for Change 1953–1956*. London: William Heinemann, 1963.

——. *Waging Peace 1956–1961*. London: William Heinemann, 1966.

Ellsberg, Daniel. *Escalating in a Quagmire*. Boston: Center of International Studies, MIT, 1970.

Enthoven, Alain C.; and Smith, K. Wayne. *How Much Is Enough?* New York: Harper & Row, 1971.

Evans, D. L. "Civil Affairs in Vietnam," *Marine Corps Gazette*, March 1968.

Fagg, J. E. *Latin America—A General History*. London: Macmillan, 1969.

Fall, Bernard. *Hell in a Very Small Place: The Siege of Dien Bien Phu*. Philadelphia: J. B. Lippincott, 1967.

——. *Street Without Joy*. Harrisburg, Pa.; Stackpole, 1961.

——. *The Two Viet-Nams—A Political and Military Analysis*. New York: Frederick A. Praeger, 1967.

——. "Viet Nam in the Balance," *Foreign Affairs*, October 1966.

Falls, Cyril. *A Hundred Years of War*. London: Gerald Duckworth, 1953.

Fischer, Louis. *The Story of Indonesia.* New York: Harper & Row, 1959.

Fitzgerald, C. P. *The Chinese View of Their Place in the World.* London: Oxford University Press, 1965.

Foley, Charles. *Island in Revolt.* London: Longmans, Green, 1962.

Freeman, H. A. "The Rebellion in Cyprus—1931," *Army Quarterly,* January 1933.

Fulbright, J. William. "In Thrall to Fear," *The New Yorker,* January 8, 1972.

—— (ed.). *The Vietnam Hearings.* New York: Vintage Books, 1966.

Galbraith, John K. *How to Get Out of Vietnam.* New York: Signet, 1967.

Gallery, Daniel V. *The Pueblo Incident.* Garden City, N.Y.: Doubleday, 1970.

Gavin, James. *Crisis Now.* New York: Random House, 1968.

——. "A Soldier's Doubts," *Harper's Magazine,* February 1966.

Gettleman, Marvin E. (ed.) *Viet-Nam—History, Documents, and Opinions on a Major World Crisis.* New York: Fawcett, 1965.

Giap, Vo Nguyen. *Big Victory, Great Task.* New York: Frederick A. Praeger, 1968.

——. *People's War, People's Army.* New York: Frederick A. Praeger, 1967.

——. "The Strategic Role of the Self-Defense Militia Force in the Great Anti-U.S. National Salvation Struggle of Our People." Foreign Broadcast Information Service, April 1967.

Gillespie, Joan. *Algeria—Rebellion and Revolution.* London: Ernest Benn, 1960.

Gilpatric, Roswell W. "Vietnam and World War III," *New York Times,* May 30, 1965.

Goldenberg, Boris. *The Cuban Revolution and Latin America.* London: Allen & Unwin, 1965.

Grant, Zalin B. "What Are We Doing in Thailand?" *The New Republic,* May 24, 1969.

Greene, Graham. *The Quiet American.* London: William Heinemann, 1955.

Greene, T. N. (ed.). *The Guerrilla and How to Fight Him.* New York: Frederick A. Praeger, 1962.

Grier, S. L. "Black Pajama Intelligence," *Marine Corps Gazette,* April 1967.

Grivas, George. *General Grivas on Guerrilla Warfare.* New York: Frederick A. Praeger, 1965. Tr. A. S. Pallis.

——. *The Memoirs of General Grivas.* New York: Frederick A. Praeger, 1964. Ed. Charles Foley.

Guedalla, Philip. *Wellington.* New York: Harper & Brothers, 1931.

Guevara, Ernesto Che. *Bolivian Diary.* London: Jonathan Cape, 1968. Tr. Carlos Hansen and Andrew Sinclair.

——. *Che Guevara on Guerrilla Warfare.* New York: Frederick A. Praeger, 1961. Ed. Harries-Clichy Peterson.

——. *Che Guevara Speaks—Selected Speeches and Writings.* New York: Grove Press, 1967. Ed. George Lavan.

——. *Reminiscences of the Cuban Revolutionary War.* New York: Grove Press, 1963. Tr. V. Ortiz.

Gurtov, Melvin. *The First Vietnam Crisis—Chinese Communist Strategy and United States Involvement 1953–1954.* New York: Columbia University Press, 1967.

Haggerty, J. J. "South Vietnam and the Munich Crossroad," *Army Quarterly,* July 1968.

Halberstam, David. *The Making of a Quagmire.* New York: Random House, 1965.

Hammer, Ellen J. "Genesis of The First Indochina War: 1946–1950." In Gettleman, *supra.*

———. *The Struggle for Indochina 1940–1955.* Stanford: Stanford University Press, 1966.

Hammond, J. W. "Combat Journal," *Marine Corps Gazette,* July and August 1968.

Harries, Owen. "Should the U.S. Withdraw from Asia?" *Foreign Affairs,* October 1968.

Harris, Richard. "How the Chinese View South-East Asia," *The Times* (London), September 8, 1970.

Harvey, Frank. *Air War–Vietnam.* New York: Bantam Books, 1967.

Heelis, J. E. "Triumph in Malaysia," *Marine Corps Gazette,* January 1967.

Heilbrunn, Otto. "Counter-Insurgency Intelligence," *Marine Corps Gazette,* September 1966.

———. "Counter-Insurgency Tactics: A Question of Priorities," *Army Quarterly,* January 1967.

Heinl, Robert D. "The Armed Forces: Are they 'near collapse'?" Detroit *Sunday News,* May 23, 1971.

Hemphill, Marie de Kiewiet. "The British Sphere 1884–94." In Oliver and Mathew, *infra.*

Henderson, Ian (with Goodhart, Philip). *The Hunt for Kimathi.* London: Hamish Hamilton, 1958.

Henderson, William. "South Vietnam Finds Itself," *Foreign Affairs,* January 1957.

Heren, Louis. *No Hail, No Farewell.* London: Weidenfeld & Nicolson, 1971.

Herring, H. A. *A History of Latin America.* London: Jonathan Cape, 1955.

Hersh, Seymour M. "Coverup," *The New Yorker,* January 22 and January 29, 1972.

———. "My Lai 4," *Harper's Magazine,* May 1970.

Higgins, Marguerite. *Our Vietnam Nightmare.* New York: Harper & Row, 1965.

Hilsman, Roger. *To Move a Nation–The Politics of Foreign Policy in the Administration of John F. Kennedy.* Garden City, N.Y.: Doubleday, 1967.

Ho Chi Minh. *Ho Chi Minh on Revolution. Selected Writings 1920–1966.* New York: Frederick A. Praeger, 1967. Ed. Bernard Fall.

———. *Ho Chi Minh: Selected Articles and Speeches, 1920–1967.* London: Lawrence & Wishart, 1969. Ed. Jack Woddis.

———. *Prison Diary.* Hanoi: Foreign Languages Publishing House, 1962. Tr. Aileen Palmer.

Hoopes, Townsend. *The Limits of Intervention.* New York: McKay, 1969.

Horowitz, David. *Containment and Revolution.* Boston: Beacon Press, 1967.

Hosmer, S. T. (Chairman). *Counterinsurgency: A Symposium–April 16–20, 1962.* Santa Monica, Calif.: RAND Corporation, 1963.

Huberman, Leo; and Sweezy, Paul. *Cuba–Anatomy of a Revolution.* London: Routledge & Kegan Paul, 1960.

Hughes, Richard. "After Ho, Watch for Giap and a Tougher Line in Hanoi," *The Sunday Times* (London), September 7, 1969.

Hull, Cordell. *Memoirs*. New York: Macmillan, 1948.

Institute for Strategic Studies, The. "The Super-Powers," *Strategic Survey, 1970*. London: Institute for Strategic Studies, 1971.

———. "The United States," *Strategic Survey, 1967*. London: Institute for Strategic Studies, 1968.

———. "The United States," *Strategic Survey, 1968*. London: Institute for Strategic Studies, 1969.

Isaacs, Harold. "Independence for Vietnam?" In Gettleman, *supra*.

James, Daniel. *Che Guevara—a Biography*. London: Allen & Unwin, 1970.

——— (ed.). *The Complete Bolivian Diaries of Ché Guevara—And Other Captured Documents*. London: Allen & Unwin, 1968.

Jenkins, Brian. "The Unchangeable War," RAND Corporation, n.d.

Johnson, Lyndon B. *Public Papers of the President*. Washington: U. S. Government Printing Office, 1965–70. 10 volumes.

———. *The Vantage Point—Perspectives of the Presidency 1963–1969*. New York: Holt, Rinehart & Winston, 1971.

Just, Ward. *Military Men*. New York: Alfred A. Knopf, 1971.

Kahin, George M. *Nationalism and Revolution in Indonesia*. Ithaca, N.Y.: Cornell University Press, 1952.

———; and Lewis, John W. *The United States in Vietnam—An Analysis in Depth of America's Involvement in Vietnam*. New York: The Dial Press, 1967.

Kahn, Herman. "If Negotiations Fail," *Foreign Affairs*, July 1968.

Kalb, M. L.; and Abel, E. *Roots of Involvement—the U.S. in Asia, 1784–1971*. New York: W. W. Norton, 1971.

Katz, Samuel. *Days of Fire*. London: W. H. Allen, 1968.

Kellen, Konrad. "Fourth Round or Peace in Vietnam?" RAND Corporation, 1968.

Kennan, George F. *Memoirs 1925–1950*. London: Hutchinson, 1968. Vol. 1.

———. *Memoirs 1950–1963*. London: Hutchinson, 1973. Vol. 2.

Kennedy, John F. *Public Papers of John F. Kennedy*. Washington: U. S. Government Printing Office, 1962. Vol. 1 of 2 vols.

———. *The Strategy of Peace*. New York: Harper & Brothers, 1960.

Kenyatta, Jomo. *Facing Mount Kenya—The Tribal Life of the Gikuyu*. London: Secker & Warburg, 1938.

Kissinger, Henry. "The Viet Nam Negotiations," *Foreign Affairs*, January 1969.

Kitson, Frank. *Gangs and Counter-gangs*. London: Barrie & Rockliff, 1960.

———. *Low-Intensity Operations*. London: Faber & Faber, 1971.

Koestler, Arthur. *Promise and Fulfilment: Palestine, 1917–1949*. London: Macmillan, 1949.

Kriegel, Richard. "Revolutionary Development," *Marine Corps Gazette*, March 1967.

Krulak, V. H. "Address to Western Newspaper Industrial Relations Bureau. . . ." U. S. Marine Corps release, n.d.

Kun, Ernst; and Kun, Joseph. "North Vietnam's Doctrine," *Survival*, February 1965.

Lacouture, Jean. *Vietnam: Between Two Truces*. London: Secker & Warburg, 1966. Tr. K. Kellen and J. Carmichael.

Lancaster, Donald. *The Emancipation of French Indochina*. London: Oxford University Press, 1961.

Lansdale, Edward G. "Viet Nam: Do We Understand Revolution?" *Foreign Affairs,* October 1964.

———. "Viet Nam—Still the Search for Goals," *Foreign Affairs,* October 1968.

Lapp, Ralph E. *Arms Beyond Doubt: The Tyranny of Weapons Technology*. Chicago: Cowles Book Company, 1970.

Lartéguy, Jean. *The Centurions*. London: Hutchinson, 1961. Tr. Xan Fielding.

Leakey, L. S. B. "Colonial Administration from the Native Point of View." In *Comparative Methods of Colonial Administration*. London: Chatham House, 1930.

———. *Defeating Mau Mau*. London: Methuen, 1954.

———. *Kenya—Contrasts and Problems*. London: Methuen, 1936.

———. *Mau Mau and the Kikuyu*. London: Methuen, 1952.

———. *White Africa*. London: Hodder & Stoughton, 1937.

Lederer, William. *Our Own Worst Enemy*. New York: W. W. Norton, 1968.

Leftwich, William G. "Decision at Duc Co," *Marine Corps Gazette,* February 1967.

Leopold, Richard. *The Growth of American Policy*. New York: Alfred A. Knopf, 1965.

Lilienthal, David E. "Postwar Development in Viet Nam," *Foreign Affairs,* January 1969.

Lippmann, Walter. *The Cold War—A Study in U.S. Foreign Policy, 1947*. New York: Harper & Brothers, 1947.

Lorch, Netanel. *The Edge of the Sword: Israel's War of Independence, 1947–1949*. New York: G. P. Putnam's Sons, 1961.

Lowenthal, Richard. "Russia and China: Controlled Conflict," *Foreign Affairs,* April 1971.

Mack, R. E. "Ambuscade," *Marine Corps Gazette,* April 1967.

———. "Minbotrap," *Marine Corps Gazette,* July 1967.

Majdalaney, Fred. *State of Emergency—The Full Story of Mau Mau*. London: Longmans, Green, 1962.

Mallin, Jay. "Castro's Guerrilla Campaign," *Marine Corps Gazette,* January 1962.

Mao Tse-tung. *Basic Tactics*. New York: Frederick A. Praeger, 1966. Tr. with Introduction by Stuart R. Schram.

"Marines in Vietnam" (editorial), *Marine Corps Gazette,* September 1966.

Marlowe, John. *The Seat of Pilate—An Account of the Palestine Mandate*. London: Cresset Press, 1959.

Marshall, S. L. A. *Battles in the Monsoon*. New York: William Morrow, 1967.

Matthews, Herbert L. *Castro—A Political Biography*. New York: Simon & Schuster, 1969.

———. *The Cuban Story*. New York: George Braziller, 1961.

Matthews, Tanya. *Algerian ABC*. London: Geoffrey Chapman, 1961.

McCarthy, Eugene. *The Limits of Power.* New York: Dell, 1967.

McCuen, John J. *The Art of Counter-Revolutionary War.* London: Faber & Faber, 1966.

McCutcheon, Keith B. "Air Support for III MAF," *Marine Corps Gazette,* August 1967.

McGaffin, William; and Knoll, Erwin. *Scandal in the Pentagon: A Challenge to Democracy.* Greenwich, Conn.: Fawcett, 1969.

Mecklin, John. *Mission in Torment.* Garden City, N.Y.: Doubleday, 1965.

Meinertzhagen, R. *Kenya During 1902–1906.* London: Oliver & Boyd, 1957.

Miller, John G. "From a Company Commander's Notebook," *Marine Corps Gazette,* August 1966.

Mills, C. Wright. *Castro's Cuba.* London: Secker & Warburg, 1960.

Mitchell, Philip. *African Afterthoughts.* London: Hutchinson, 1954.

Montross, Lynn. *U. S. Marine Operations in Korea 1950–53.* Washington: U. S. Government Printing Office, 1957. Vol. 3 of 3 vols.

Moyers, Bill D. "One Thing We Learned," *Foreign Affairs,* July 1968.

Mulligan, Hugh A. *No Place to Die.* New York: William Morrow, 1967.

Murtha, John P. "Combat Intelligence in Vietnam," *Marine Corps Gazette,* January 1968.

Myrdal, Gunnar. *Asian Drama—An Inquiry into the Poverty of Nations.* London: Allen Lane the Penguin Press, 1968. 3 vols.

Nasution, Abdul Haris. *Fundamentals of Guerrilla Warfare.* New York: Frederick A. Praeger, 1965.

Navarre, Henri. *Agonie de l'Indochine.* Paris: Librairie Plan, 1956.

Nickerson, Herman. "Address." Headquarters, U. S. Marine Corps release, n.d.

Nixon, Richard M. "Asia After Viet Nam," *Foreign Affairs,* October 1967.

——. *Public Papers of the President.* Washington: U. S. Government Printing Office, 1970. Vol. 1.

"Noll." "The Emergency in Malaya," *Army Quarterly,* April 1954.

O'Ballance, Edgar. *The Algerian Insurrection 1954–1962.* London: Faber & Faber, 1967.

——. *The Greek Civil War, 1944–1949.* London: Faber & Faber, 1966.

——. "The Ho Chi Minh Trail," *Army Quarterly,* April 1967.

——. *The Indo-China War, 1945–1954.* London: Faber & Faber, 1964.

——. "Strategy in Viet Nam," *Army Quarterly,* January 1967.

O'Donnell, Kenneth. "LBJ and the Kennedys," *Life,* August 7, 1970.

Oliver, Roland; and Mathew, Gervase (eds.). *History of East Africa.* London: Oxford University Press, 1963. Vol. 1 of 3 vols.

O'Neill, Robert J. *Vietnam Task.* Melbourne: Cassell Australia, 1968.

Paget, Julian. *Counter-Insurgency Campaigning.* London: Faber & Faber, 1967.

Palmier, Leslie, *Indonesia and the Dutch.* London: Oxford University Press, 1962.

Paret, Peter. *French Revolutionary Warfare from Indochina to Algeria—The Analysis of a Political and Military Doctrine.* New York: Frederick A. Praeger, 1964.

Parry, Albert. "Soviet Aid to Vietnam," *The Reporter,* January 12, 1967.

Paul, Roland A. "Laos: Anatomy of an American Involvement," *Foreign Affairs,* April 1971.

Pflaum, Irving. *Tragic Island—How Communism Came to Cuba.* Englewood Cliffs, N.J.: Prentice-Hall, 1961.

Phillips, Ruby Hart. *Cuba—Island of Paradox.* New York: McDowell, Obolensky, 1959.

Pike, Douglas. *Viet Cong—The Organization and Techniques of the National Liberation Front of South Vietnam.* Cambridge, Mass.: MIT Press, 1967.

Proxmire, William. *Report from the Wasteland: America's Military-Industrial Complex.* New York: Frederick A. Praeger, 1970.

Purnell, Karl H. "The Man Who Fired the Shot . . . ," *True Magazine,* July 1968.

Pye, Lucian W. *Guerrilla Communism and Malaya—Its Social and Political Meaning.* Princeton: Princeton University Press, 1956.

Raskin, Marcus G.; and Fall, Bernard B. *The Viet-Nam Reader—Articles and Documents on American Foreign Policy and The Viet-Nam Crisis.* New York: Random House, 1967.

Ray, J. K. *Transfer of Power in Indonesia, 1942–1949.* Bombay: P. C. Manaktala & Sons, 1967.

Reischauer, Edwin O. *Beyond Vietnam.* New York: Alfred A. Knopf, 1967.

Ridgway, Matthew B. "Indochina: Disengaging," *Foreign Affairs,* July 1971.

———. *Soldier: The Memoirs of Matthew B. Ridgway.* New York: Harper & Brothers, 1956.

———. *The War in Korea.* London: Barrie & Rockliff, 1968.

Roberts, Adam. "Lessons of Geneva 1954," *The Times* (London), April 23, 1968.

Roberts, Chalmers M. "The Day We Didn't Go to War," *The Reporter,* September 14, 1954.

Robinson, R. E. R. "Reflections of a Company Commander in Malaya," *Army Quarterly,* October 1950.

Rogers, Lane. "The Enemy," *Marine Corps Gazette,* March 1966.

Rossi, Mario. "U Thant and Vietnam: The Untold Story," *The New York Review of Books,* November 17, 1966.

Rostow, W. W. *The United States in the World Arena.* New York: Harper & Brothers, 1960.

Rovere, Richard H. *The Eisenhower Years.* New York: Farrar, Straus & Cudahy, 1956.

Royal United Service Institution Seminar. *Lessons from the Vietnam War.* London: RUSI, 1969.

Ruark, Robert. *Something of Value.* London: Hamish Hamilton, 1955.

Runciman, S. *A History of the Crusades.* New York: Penguin Books, 1965. 3 vols.

Salinger, Pierre. *With Kennedy.* Garden City, N.Y.: Doubleday, 1966.

Salisbury, Harrison E. *Behind the Lines—Hanoi.* New York: Harper & Row, 1967.

———. "Image and Reality in Indochina," *Foreign Affairs,* April 1971.

Sansom, Robert L. *The Economics of Insurgency in the Mekong Delta of Vietnam.* Cambridge, Mass.: MIT Press, 1970.

Schell, Jonathan. *The Military Half.* New York: Alfred A. Knopf, 1968.

Schlesinger, Arthur M., Jr. *The Bitter Heritage—Vietnam and American Democracy 1941–1966.* Boston: Houghton Mifflin, 1967.

———. *A Thousand Days.* Boston: Houghton Mifflin, 1965.

Schoenbrun, David. "Journey to North Vietnam," *The Saturday Evening Post*, March 1968.

——. *Vietnam*. New York: Atheneum, 1968.

Scigliano, Robert. *South Vietnam: Nation Under Stress*. Boston: Houghton Mifflin, 1964.

——; and Fox, Guy. *Technical Assistance in Vietnam—The Michigan State University Experience*. New York: Frederick A. Praeger, 1965.

Seers, D.; Bianchi, A.; Jolly, R.; and Nolff, M. *Cuba—The Economic and Social Revolution*. Chapel Hill, N.C.: University of North Carolina Press, 1964.

Servan-Schreiber, Jean-Jacques. *Lieutenant in Algeria*. London: Hutchinson, 1958. Tr. Ronald Matthews.

Shaplen, Robert M. "Letter from Vietnam," *The New Yorker*, May 13, 1972.

——. *The Lost Revolution*. New York: Harper & Row, 1966.

——. *The Road from War*. New York: Harper & Row, 1970.

——. "Viet-Nam: Crisis of Indecision," *Foreign Affairs*, October 1967.

——. "We Have Always Survived," *The New Yorker*, April 15, 1972.

Sharp, U. S. Grant. "We Could Have Won in Vietnam Long Ago," *Reader's Digest*, May 1969.

Sheehan, Neil; Smith, Hedrick; Kenworthy, E. W.; and Butterfield, Fox. *The Pentagon Papers*. New York: Bantam Books, 1971.

Shoup, David M.; and Donovan, James A. "The New American Militarism," *The Atlantic*, April 1969.

Sidey, Hugh. *John F. Kennedy, President*. New York: Atheneum, 1963.

Slane, P. M. "Tactical Problems in Kenya," *Army Quarterly*, 1954.

Slimming, John. *Malaysia: Death of a Democracy*. London: John Murray, 1969.

Smith, Earl E. T. *The Fourth Floor—An Account of the Castro Communist Revolution*. New York: Random House, 1962.

Snow, Edgar. *The Other Side of the River: Red China Today*. New York: Random House, 1961.

Soedjatmoko. "South-East Asia and Security," *Survival*, October 1969.

Sorensen, Theodore C. *Kennedy*. New York: Harper & Row, 1965.

Special Operations Research Office. (American University, Washington, D.C.). *Casebook on Insurgency and Revolutionary Warfare*. Washington: The American University, 1962.

Stanford, R. K. "Bamboo Brigades," *Marine Corps Gazette*, March 1966.

Stephens, Robert. *Cyprus—A Place of Arms*. London: Pall Mall Press, 1966.

Stolfi, Russel H. *U. S. Marine Corps Civic Action Efforts in Vietnam—March 1965–March 1966*. Washington: U. S. Marine Corps, 1968.

Stone, I. F. "Why Nixon Won His Moscow Gamble," *The New York Review of Books*, June 15, 1972.

Sulzberger, C. L. *The Test: De Gaulle and Algeria*. London: Rupert Hart-Davis, 1962.

Sykes, Christopher. *Cross Roads to Israel*. London: Collins, 1965.

——. *Orde Wingate*. London: Collins, 1959.

Taber, Robert. *M-26—Biography of a Revolution*. New York: Lyle Stuart, 1961.

Tanham, George K. *Communist Revolutionary Warfare—From the Viet-minh to the Viet Cong* (rev. ed.). New York: Frederick A. Praeger, 1967.

——. *Trial in Thailand.* New York: Crane, Russak, 1974.

——. *War Without Guns.* New York: Frederick A. Praeger, 1966.

——; and Duncanson, Dennis J. "Some Dilemmas of Counterinsurgency," *Foreign Affairs,* October 1969.

Tannenbaum, Frank. "The United States and Latin America," *Political Science Quarterly,* June 1961.

Taruc, Luis. *He Who Rides the Tiger.* New York: Frederick A. Praeger, 1967.

Taylor, Alastair M. *Indonesian Independence and the United Nations.* London: Stevens & Sons, 1960.

Taylor, Maxwell. *Responsibility and Response.* New York: Harper & Row, 1967.

——. *The Uncertain Trumpet.* New York: Harper & Brothers, 1960.

Taylor, Telford. *Nuremberg and Vietnam: An American Tragedy.* New York: Quadrangle Books, 1970.

Tee, W. S. "Solutions in Counter-Insurgency Operations," *Army Quarterly,* October 1967.

Thayer, Charles W. *Guerrilla.* New York: Harper & Row, 1965.

Thayer, George. *The War Business.* London: Weidenfeld & Nicolson, 1969.

Thomas, Hugh. *Cuba or the Pursuit of Freedom.* New York: Harper & Row, 1971.

Thompson, Robert. *Defeating Communist Insurgency—The Lessons of Malaya and Vietnam.* New York: Frederick A. Praeger, 1966.

——. "Feet on the Ground," *Statist,* February 4, 1966.

——. "My Plan for Peace in Vietnam," *Reader's Digest,* March 1970.

——. *No Exit from Vietnam.* London: Chatto & Windus, 1969.

——. "On the Way to Victory," *The Sunday Times* (London), December 21, 1969.

——. *Revolutionary War in World Strategy 1945–1969.* London: Secker & Warburg, 1970.

Tillion, Germaine. *Algeria—The Realities.* London: Eyre & Spottiswoode, 1958.

Trager, Frank. *Why Viet Nam?* New York: Frederick A. Praeger, 1966.

Tran Van Dinh. "Elections in Vietnam," *The New Republic,* July 2, 1966.

Traynor, W. L. "The Political War in Viet-Nam," *Marine Corps Gazette,* August 1967.

Trinquier, Roger. *Modern Warfare—A French View of Counter-Insurgency.* New York: Frederick A. Praeger, 1964.

Truman, Harry S. *Year of Decisions 1945.* London: Hodder & Stoughton, 1955.

——. *Years of Trial and Hope.* Garden City, N.Y.: Doubleday, 1955.

Tuchman, Barbara. "Generalship." Speech delivered before the Army War College, April 1972.

Turnbull, P. E. X. "Dien Bien Phu and Sergeant Kubiak," *Army Quarterly,* April 1965.

Uris, Leon. *Exodus.* London: Allen Wingate, 1959.

Urrutia Lleó, Manuel. *Fidel Castro and Company, Inc.—Communist Tyranny in Cuba.* New York: Frederick A. Praeger, 1964.

U. S. Air Force. "The U. S. Air Force in Southeast Asia." Washington: Headquarters, U. S. Air Force, 1967.

U. S. Congress. "The Candidates' Views," *Congressional Quarterly,* May 3, 1968.

U. S. Department of Defense. "Working Paper on the North Vietnamese Role in the War in South Vietnam." Washington: 1968.

U. S. Government. *The United States Strategic Bombing Survey—Over-all Report.* Washington: U. S. Government Printing Office, 1945.

U. S. Marine Corps. "III Marine Amphibious Force—The Mission—And How It Is Fulfilled." Headquarters, U. S. Marine Corps, October 1967.

——. "The Battle for Hills 861 and 881." N.p., n.d.

——. "Khe Sanh Wrap-Up." N.p., n.d.

U. S. Navy. "Riverine Warfare." Washington: U. S. Government Printing Office, 1967.

U. S. Senate. *Refugee Problems in South Vietnam.* Washington: U. S. Government Printing Office, 1966.

U. S. Senate Committee on Foreign Relations. *Background Information Relating to Southeast Asia and Vietnam.* Washington: U. S. Government Printing Office, 1967.

U. S. Senate Republican Policy Committee. *The War in Vietnam.* Washington: Public Affairs Press, 1967.

U. S. Seventh Fleet. "Cruisers and Destroyers in Vietnam." N.p., n.d.

——. "Task Force 77." N.p., n.d.

Vagts, Alfred. *Defense and Diplomacy. The Soldier and the Conduct of Foreign Relations.* New York: Kings Crown Press, 1956.

Valeriano, N. D.; and Bohannan, C. T. R. *Counter-Guerrilla Operations. The Philippine Experience.* New York: Frederick A. Praeger, 1962.

Vandenbosch, A.; and Vandenbosch, M. B. *Australia Faces Southeast Asia —The Emergence of a Foreign Policy.* Lexington, Ky.: University of Kentucky Press, 1967.

Vidal-Naquet, Pierre. *Torture: Cancer of Democracy.* Harmondsworth, Middlx.: Penguin Books, 1963.

Wagner, David H. "A Handful of Marines," *Marine Corps Gazette,* March 1968.

Walker, Lannon. "Our Foreign Affairs Machinery: Time for an Overhaul," *Foreign Affairs,* January 1969.

Walker, Walter. "How Borneo Was Won," *The Round Table,* January 1969.

Walt, L. W. "Are We Winning the War in Vietnam?" Headquarters, U. S. Marine Corps, n.d.

——. "Khe Sanh—The Battle That Had to Be Won," *Reader's Digest,* August 1970.

——. "The Nature of the War in Vietnam." Headquarters, U. S. Marine Corps, n.d.

——. "The Navy in Vietnam." Headquarters, U. S. Marine Corps, n.d.

——. "Our Purpose in Vietnam." Headquarters, U. S. Marine Corps, n.d.

——. *Strange War, Strange Strategy.* New York: Funk & Wagnalls, 1970.

Warne, W. R. "Vinh Binh Province." In Tanham (*Guns*), *supra.*

Warnke, Paul; and Gelb, Leslie. "Security or Confrontation," *Foreign Policy,* Winter 1970–71.

Wehl, David. *The Birth of Indonesia.* London: Allen & Unwin, 1948.

Weller, Jac. "The U. S. Army in Vietnam: A Survey of Aims, Operations, and Weapons, Particularly of Small Infantry Units," *Army Quarterly,* October 1967.

Welles, Sumner. *The Time for Decision.* New York: Harper & Brothers, 1944.

West, Francis J. "Small Unit Action in Vietnam." Headquarters, U. S. Marine Corps, 1967.

Westerling, Raymond. *Challenge to Terror.* London: William Kimber, 1952.

White, T. H. *The Making of the President 1960.* New York: Atheneum, 1961.

———. *The Making of the President 1968.* New York: Atheneum, 1969.

Williamson, R. E. "A Briefing for Combined Action," *Marine Corps Gazette,* March 1968.

Wilson, Harold. "The Night LBJ Wrecked Our Secret Manoeuvres for Peace," *The Sunday Times* (London), May 16, 1971.

Wood, Bryce. *The Making of the Good Neighbor Policy.* New York: Columbia University Press, 1961.

Woodhouse, C. M. *Apple of Discord.* London: Hutchinson, 1948.

Woodhouse, J. M. "Some Personal Observations on the Employment of Special Forces in Malaya," *Army Quarterly,* April 1955.

Wooten, James T. "How a Supersoldier Was Fired from His Command," New York *Times Magazine,* September 5, 1971.

Wren, C. S. "A Sunday with Westmoreland," *Look,* October 18, 1966.

"X" (Kennan, George F.). "The Sources of Soviet Conduct," *Foreign Affairs,* July 1947.

Zagoria, Donald S. *Vietnam Triangle—Moscow, Peking, Hanoi.* New York: Pegasus, 1967.

———. "Who Fears the Domino Theory?" New York *Times Magazine,* April 21, 1968.

Zinn, Howard. *Vietnam—The Logic of Withdrawal.* Boston: Beacon Press, 1967.

Zorza, Victor. "Vietnam—Long or Short War," *The Guardian* (England), February 15, 1968.

Index

NOTE: *"Postwar" refers to post World War II.*

Abbane, Ramdane, 917 *and* n
Abbas, Ferhat, 905, 908, 910, 920, 926, 929
Abd-el-Kader, 152, 153, 156, 157
Abd-el-Krim, Mohamed, 370, 373–79, 381–82; army, 381; France, 382ff.; Great Powers, 380–81, 383; problems, 380–81; surrender, 384
Abd-er-Rahman, Emp., 155
Abel, Elie: *Roots of Involvement*, 1224
Abetz, Otto, 438
Abrams, Creighton, 1191, 1236–39, 1314, 1331, 1354ff.; tactics, 1300ff., 1390
Abyssinia, 497; Italy, 376
Accountability, 1373–74
Acheson, Dean, 800, 1011, 1235 *and* n; Indochina, 717ff., 726–27, 729–30, Kennan warning, 718; on Joint Chiefs of Staff, 1228, 1235; Johnson, 1228, 1234; Vietnam, 694–95; *Present at the Creation*, 690
Ackley, Gardner, 1362
Acre, siege of, 63
Adams, Samuel, 1376
Adcock, F. E., 9n, 28
Aden, 388
Adenauer, Konrad, 928n

Adrianople, battle of, 39 *and* n, 43
Advisers, military.
 See Military advisers *and under* names of Presidents
Aegean Islands, 739
Aëtius, Gen., 42
Aetolians, 5
Afghanistan, 206
Afghan War, 200
Africa, *xvi*, 26, 36, 92, 160, 1251, *map*, 254; England, 223, 369, 379; France, 369, 379; Kaffirs, 159; Southwest, 250
Africans, 20; white benefits, 866–67
 See Carthaginians
Afro-Asian bloc, 910
Agathias, 46
Aggression, 150
Agincourt, battle of, 67
Agnew, Spiro, 1342
Agriculture, 160, 226, 282; guerrilla warfare, *xii*
Agrovilles, 841
Aguinaldo, Don Emilio, 182–83, 185–87, 188–89, 191, 192–93, 196, 756; surrender, 193
Air power, 268, 378, 384–90, 583, 882–83, 1257–73; air control vs. ground control, 386–90; air drops, 589, 594, 595, 604;

bombings (mass attacks), 440; civilian bombings, 1259–60; cost, 1136; defense (*see* Battle of Britain); Douhet theory, 1257–59; fire bombings, 1259; helicopters (*see* Helicopters); Hump, 585, 595; international diplomacy-bombs, 1272–73; "kill" figures, 1261; Korean War, lessons, 1262; nuclear stalemate, paradox, 1260; psychological effect, 389; psychological value, 601; Salisbury reports from North Vietnam, 1267–72; saturation bombing, 1259; strategic, 1270; testing (Spanish Civil War), 402; World War II, 1259–62

Aitken, Gen., 253
Alaric, 41
Alaska, 638; oil fields, 800
Alba, Victor, 231
Albania, 62, 467, 469, 496, *map,* 501; communism, 734; Greece, 735, 738; World War II, 465, 488, 496–502: accomplishments, 501–2, *chetas,* 497ff., Communists (LNC), 497ff., Italy, 488, 496–97, politics, 497
Albert, Carl, 1075
Alcuin, 54
Alden, John R., *xvi,* 105, 109–10
Alexander I, Emp. of Russia: Napoleon, 139; strategy, 141, 142
Alexander II, Czar, 285, 286
Alexander III, Czar, 288; *okhrana,* 288
Alexander the Great, *xi,* 3, 5–9, 388, *map of route,* 9; guerrilla wars, 5–9; political philosophy, 8 *and* n
Alexandra, Czarina, 296, 310
Alexius, Emp., 62–63, 64 *and* n, 823n

Alfonso, King of Spain, 371; exile, 384
Alfred, King, 56
Algeria, *xiii,* 177, 206, 228, 374, 903–13, 914–31, 1007, 1291, *map,* 915; Arab Bureau, 156; Challe Plan, 928; *colons,* 904, 908–11; communism, 905, 916, bandits, 909, 928 *and* n; CNRA, 917; Constantine Plan, 926; CRUA, 907–9 (*see* FLN); De Gaulle, 925–31; ENA, 905; FLN (*see* FLN); France, 151–56, 166, 169, 201, 223, 224–25, 228, *map,* 154, 157; insurgency, 861 (*see* rebellion); Kennedy, J. F., 977n; Manifesto, 905; Moslems, 905, 906, 907, 908, 910, 922; nationalism, 693, 905, 908, 925, 926–27; OS (*Organisation Secrète*), 907; rebellion, 904ff., 909–31: Army, 916–18, 919ff., cost, 930, counterinsurgency, 921ff., French, 905–31 passim, historical background, 904ff., independence, 905, 908, 916n, 930–31, "internationalization," 924, leaders, 917, nature of, 916, outside support, 920–23; SAS, 910–11, 924–26; *smala,* 243; Statute (1947), 906; Turkey, 151; World War I, 905; World War II, 426, 429, 905, 906
Algiers, battle of, 917
Allard, Gen., 921
Alleg, Henri: *The Question,* 919
Allenby, Gen., 265, 267
Alliances, 1248–49
Allies, 27n, 695; *socii,* 21
Almeida, Juan, 962
Alps: guerrilla tactics, 10–11; passes, 10n, 11
Alsop, Joseph, 617, 1040, 1355

Alsop, Stewart, 1309

Alsop and Braden: *Sub Rosa,* 541, 608

Ambushes, 73, 74

America, 92, 93, 118; colonies, 97–98; Continental Congress, 98, 113, 114
See American Revolution; North America *and* United States

American Revolution, *xii,* 98, 100–17, 159, 170, 281, 900, *map,* 101; commanders, 101–2; guerrilla tactics, 99, 109, 112, 114; POWs, 104

American Society of Newspaper Editors, 979, 1040

Amery, Julian, *xvi,* 500; *Sons of the Eagle,* 497

Ammianus, 38, 39

Amnesty, 79, 108, 192

Analysts.
See Military analysts

Anarchism, 286

Anarchy, 227; semi-, 278

Anastasius, Emp., 46

Ancient cultures, 92

Anders, W., 423

Andes Mts., 971

Andrewes, A., *xvi*

Ángeles, Felipe, 243

Anglo-Norman expeditions, 72

Anglo-Turkish Convention, 888

Animism, 865

Annam, 542, 544, 551, 678, 683, 686; China, 322; uprisings, 558; Viet Minh, 806

Annapolis (U. S. Naval Academy), 618, 1025, 1389

Annexation, 183, 185

Anthropology (ists), 863, 871, 873, 910

Anti-Imperialist League, 186

Antioch, 64

Anti-Semitism, 768, 777; 1870s, 768; Hitler, 769

Anti-Yanqui, 960

An Ya, King, 1288

Appian, 18, 19, 24, 25

Aquitaine, 55

Arabia, 305

Arab-Israeli War: 1948, 780

Arab League, 780, 911; Algerian rebellion, 921

Arabs, 153, 905; camel corps, 261; Greeks, 466; handling, 269n; leaders, 259; nationalism, 904; Palestine, 769; revolt, 258ff., 269; tribes, 259; will, 264; World War I, 258–71, aim, 262, 265

Arab states, 891

Arbenz Guzmán, Jacobo, 948–49

Archaeologists, 865

Archers, 7, 49, 70

Architecture, 331

Argentina, 948, 949

Argoud, Antoine, 921–22

Aristocracy, 58, 59

Armenians, 66

Armies, 139, 391–93; Continental, 93; Europe (1815), 146; as positive social force, 224–25; professional, 85
(*See* Force: vs. diplomacy *and under* country)

Arms embargo, 965

Armstrong, John A., *xvi; Soviet Partisans in World War II,* 448

Army magazine, 1023n

Arnett, Peter, 1221

Arnold, Henry, 603

Aron, Robert, 439, 441

Arp Arslan, 51

Arrian, 5–6 and n, 7n

Arrogance, 383; imperialistic, 22; Japanese military, 526
See also under Ignorance *and* Power

Arslan, Chekib, 905

Arthurian legends, 58

Ascalon, battle of, 63
Asia, 34, 36, 92, 170; De Gaulle on, 989; domino theory (*see* Domino theory); economy, 799; "for the Asiatics," 522, 564, 588; independence movements, 695; Japan, 304, 334; leaders, 34; Mongols, 69, 70–72; postwar, 781; regionalism, 718; revolution, 688; revolutionary organizations, 557; symbols, 34; "Triple A" movement, 535; United States, *xv;* war, 817
Asia Youth Conference (1948), Calcutta, 782–83
Asprey, Peter, *xvii*
Asprey, Winifred, *xvii*
Asquith, Herbert, 273
Assassination, 282, 296, 421, 784, 939, 1031; Russia, 288, 292–93
Assimilation, 770
Associated States, 693, 694, 717, 720, 823; evolution, 726; independence, 722; U.S. aid, 696
See Cambodia; Laos *and* Vietnam
Asturians, 16
Atcheson, George, 633
Atheism, 316
Athenians, 5
Athens Military Academy, 890
Atkin, Ronald, 242, 244; *Revolution Mexico*, 238
Atlantic Charter, 565, 624, 690, 781
Atomic bomb, 413–16, 485, 628, 648, 812, 1071, 1259, 1260; U.S. monopoly, 672, 696; Soviet Union, 696
Atomic environment, 1021–22
Atomic warfare, 989–90; threat, 1330–31
Atrocities, 21, 59, 111, 132, 190, 193–94

Attila the Hun, 40–41, 42, 373; death, 42 *and* n; "scourge of God," 40; tactics, 41–42
Attlee, Clement, 739, 775, 777, 889
Attrition.
See under Strategy
Auchinleck, Gen., 584, 603
Augustus Caesar, 28
Aumale, Duc d', 155
Aung, Maung Htin, *xvi*, 210, 586n, 587, 610, 612
Aung San, Maung, 588, 610–12, 782
Auriol, Vincent, 693
Austerlitz, battle of, 142
Australia, 69, 1016, 1342; SEATO, 824; UN, 764; U.S., 815; Vietnam, 1126, 1160, 1178, 1213; World War II, 408, 488, 504, 509–12, 514, 515: coastwatchers, 504–5, 620, independent companies, 507–8, 575, Timor, 510–12
Austria, 87, 89; Balkans, 467; communism, 673; France, 135–36; Russia, 299; World War II, 464, 469
Austro-Hungarian Empire, 468–69
Autocracy, 289
Avars, 47, 48
Axelrod, Paul, 289

Babylon, siege of, 32
Bactria, 7, 7n, 8
Badian, E., 8n
Baghdad Pact, 899
Bakunin, Michael, 236, 285, 286; *Cause of the People*, 286
Baldwin I, king, 63
Baldwin, Hanson, 1171, 1227
Balfour Declaration, 769
Bali, 531, 761
Balkans, 13, 36, 672; "cockpit of Europe," 468; Germany, 488; guerrillas, military value, 494–

95; history, 466–68; World
War I, 468; World War II, 412,
485
Ball, George: Vietnam, 983, 1018,
1079, 1170, 1171, warning,
1106–8
Balliol, John, 77, 78
Baltic coast, 672
Ba Maw, Dr., 610, 611
Banditry (brigandage), 13
"Bandolerismo statue," (1902),
196
Bannockburn, battle of, 80
Bao Dai, 555, 568, 570, 686, 716,
717, 726, 820, 823, 826; Diem,
835, 842; "government," 694,
provisional, 689; puppet ruler,
826–27, 829–31, 842
Barbarians, xii, 46, 96, 153; decline
of threat, 57; defense against,
116, Emp. Maurice, 47–48;
organization and tactics, xii;
pattern (4th and 5th centuries),
53; political naiveté, 41; weak-
nesses, 56
Barbarian tribes, 13, 36, 40–41;
leaders, 39; political structure,
40
Barclay, C. N., 56n
Baring, Evelyn, 875–76, 877, 881
Barker, Gen., 776
Barnes, John, 1304
Barnett, Donald L., 863n, 873, 879,
881
Barr, David, 647–48
Barrett, David D., xvi, 620, 625, 626
Barrientos government, 972, 973,
974
Basil II, Emp., 58
Basil II, "The Bulgar Killer," 466
Basques, 16
Bataan, 513, 521–22
Batavia, 529
Batista, Fulgencio, 932, 934, 939,
957 and n, 961–70, 1035;

background, 939–40; BRAC,
963; era, 940–46, 949, 952,
954ff., 961; exile, 970; fall,
949, 968, 970; Operation
Summer, 965–67; staff, 966;
tactics, 955, 957, 965;
United States, 942, 952, 958–
60, 962
Battle of Britain, 408, 1259
Battle order, standard, 63
Battles: De Saxe on, 265; "en-
counter," 86; Lawrence on,
264; "orthodox," 68; set-piece,
158, 199; tactical stupidity,
252
See also under name of battles
Batu Caves, 579
Bavaria, 89, 135–36, 1023n, 1024;
Magyars, 57
Bay of Pigs, 984, 988, 1017, 1019
Bazaine, Marshal, 234
Be, Nguyen, 1130–31, 1163
Beaufre, André, 1221, 1223
Beccaria (Italian philosopher), 919
Beckett, J. C., 273
Beeler, John, xvi, 58n, 59
Begin, Menachem, 772, 773, 777,
778, 900; The Revolt, 773
Behr, Edward, 910, 911, 919 and n
Belfield, Charles, 253
Belgium, 58; UN, 764; World War
I, 251; World War II, 417, 424
Belisarius, 44–46, 47; quote, 47;
tactics, 44–46
Bell, Gen., 194
Bellounis, Mohammed, 922
Bell trade agreement, 747
BEM (Business Executives Move for
Peace in Vietnam), 1205, 1306
Ben Bella, Ahmed, 907, 914, 917
and n, 926; background, 907;
kidnaping, 917
Beneš, Eduard, 421
Bengalese, 201
Ben-Gurion, David, 770, 776

Ben M'Hidi, Larbi, 920
Bentham, Jeremy, 285
Berber Tribes, 151, 152, 155
Berenguer, Dámaso, 370–72, 374–76
Beresford, Gen., 129, 130
Berlin airlift, 691, 1017
Berlin Conference, Foreign Ministers, (February 1954), 807
Bermuda Conference, 803
"Bermuda Statement," 1207
Bessières, Marshal, 133
Bessus, 5, 6
Bevin, Ernest, 775, 776, 780, 889
Bible: *Exodus,* 772; Ten Commandments: sixth, 772
Bidault, Georges, 803, 816
Bigart, Homer, 843, 1018, 1031–32, 1039
Bigelow, John, 166; *Principles of Strategy,* 166
Big Three, 671, 689
Big Four, 617
Biltmore Program (Resolution), 771, 772, 774
Binh, Nguyen, 682, 699
Binh Xuyên, 829–30
Bishop of Kition, 888, 889
   See Makarios III, Archbishop
Bishop of Kyrenia, 888
Bismarck, 302
Blackburn, Don, *xvi*
Blackett, Dr., 413
Black magic, 865, 873, 874n
Blackmail, 1373; military, 201, 225 *and* n, 1276
Black political movement.
   See KCA
Black Sea, 46
Blackwell, Miles, *xvi*
Blair, C. N. M., 425
Blanc, Louis, 285
Bland, Humphrey: *Treatise on Military Discipline,* 93
Bleda (brother of Attila), 40

Blenheim, battle of, 86, 87
Bloemfontein, 211; conference (1899), 210
Blount, Charles, 87
Blow, Rex, 518–20
Blücher, Vasily, 306, 340
Blum, Robert, 717, 719, 720–21, 977
Bodleian Library, *xvi*
Boers, *xii,* 251, 255
Boer War, 202 *and* n, 351, 410, 788, 1007; 1st, 200, 210; 2nd, 206, 210; commandos, 214; cost, 216–17; tactics, 278
Bogotá, 945
Bohannan, Col., 750, 753, 755
Bohemia, 71, 82, 89
Bohemond, Gen., 62, 63–64 *and* n, 65, 396, 1384; characteristics, 62; tactics, 63
Bohlen, Charles, 629; on Yalta, 629, 630–31
Boissieux, Count de, 90
Bokhara, 5
Bolívar, Simón, 941
Bolivia, *map,* 973; Che Guevara expedition, 970, 972ff.
Bollaert, Émile, 688
Bolsheviks(vism), 470, 480; Nazis, 448, 451
   See also Russia *and* Soviet Union
Bonaparte, Joseph, 125, 131, 133
Bonaparte, Napoleon.
   See Napoleon
Booty, *xii,* 34, 40, 41, 54
Borneo, 531, 788, 1290, 1291; West, 763
Borodin, Mikhail, 340, 342
Borodino, battle of, 142
Boswell, James, 90, 91, 92
Botha, Louis, 213, 214
Bouchier, E. S., 16n
Bouquet, Henri, 94–96 *and* n, 204
Bourguiba, Habib, 904, 905, 914, 916, 921, 923, 924

Bourmont, Louis de, 152
Bovey, John A., 1379
Bowles, Chester: Vietnam, 988, 1018, 1019n
Boxer Rebellion, 194, 250, 335–36
Boyce, George, *xvi*
Boycotts, 899
Braddock, Gen., 93, 94n, 114
Bragg, Gen., 162, 163
Branche, Lesley: *The Sabres of Paradise,* 156
Brandon, Henry, 1234, 1331, 1361
Brayne, Pat, *xvi*
Brazzaville Conference, 565, 691
Breasted, Prof., 4
Brest-Litovsk, treaty of, 302
Bretons, 81; rebel "Chouans," 123
Briand, Aristide, 381
Bribery, 47, 55, 56, 57, 376; *Danegeld,* 56
Briggs, Henry, 788–89, 790
Briggs Plan, 788
Britain, 56; *burhs* (fortified towns), 56, 57; Caesar, 13–15, *map,* 14; *Danegeld,* 56; Vikings, 53, 55–56
   See England
British East Africa, *map,* 254
British East Africa Co., 866
British East India Co., 93, 325, 576
Brittany, 123; England, 81
   See Bretons
Brooke, Alan, 599, 601
Browne, Malcolm, 1011–12, 1018, 1040
Browne, Thomas, 113
Broz, Josip, 470
   See Tito
Bruce, David, 1340
   See Paris Peace Talks
Bruce, Robert, 78, 79–80
Brunschwig, Henri, 546
Brussels Conference (1874), 167
Buchan, Alastair, 1207

Buchan, John, *xiv*
Bucher, Lloyd, 1217
Buck, Pearl, 323
Buddhism, 1011; China, 322–23, 333; immolation custom, 1012 *and* n; nationalism, 586; offshoots, 829
Buell, Gen., 162, 163
Bugeaud, Gen., 153–56, 169, 177, 206, 904
Bulgaria, 3, 39, 47, 58, 466; Party Congress, 1137; World War I, 468; World War II, 408, 465, 477, 487, 488
Buller, Redvers, 211
Bullitt, William C., 630, 799; China report, 644–46
Bundoola, 158
Bundy, McGeorge, 982, 1080, 1086–89, 1170, 1235 *and* n, 1247
Bundy, William, 1057, 1075, 1086, 1099, 1209; Congressional resolution, 1057, 1062–63; escalation "scenario," 1056, 1066, 1082, 1090; State Department, 1066
Bunker, Ellsworth, 1188, 1190, 1215, 1221, 1234, 1327
Burchett, Wilfred, 1003
Burgoyne, Gen., 98
Burma, 160, 206, 538, 539, 782, 799, 815, 1183; China, 321; communism, 695; England, 158–59, 206–10, 332, 585–87; historical background, 586–87; independence, 612; nationalism, 586, 588, 610; Thibaw's guerrillas, 207–8; Wingate, 804; World War II, 408, 413, 503, 504, 512, 572ff., 591, 594ff., 1007, 1073, 1078: Arakan offensive, 594, 600, 605, 606, Chindits, 601, 602, 606, Kachin guerrillas, 607–9, OSS/SOE, 588–

89, 609, resistance, 589, Saya San rebellion, 586–87, Theater *map*, 593

Burma Road, 561, 585, 588; *map*, 593

Burn, A. R., *xvi*, 4, 4n, 6n, 7n, 9n

Burrows, Larry, 1359

Bury, J. B., 3n–4n, 4, 6n, 46n

Butler, J. R. M., 428

Buttinger, Joseph, *xvi*, 548, 551, 566n, 731, 799, 821, 834, 848, 851, 856, 1039; *Vietnam, A Dragon Embattled*, 220, 542

Byrnes, James, 690

Byzantine Empire, 51–52, 62, 823n, 900, 905; Army, 50; leadership, 51; warfare, 62

Caesar, Julius, 3, 13–14, 28; Britain, 13–15; France, 96, *map*, 14; Spain, 28

Cairo Conference, 386, 388, 565

Cairo Declaration, 629

Calabria, 124

Caliphs of Fatima, 152

Calleo, David, 1314

Calley, William, 1359, 1360–61

Callinan, Bernard, 510; *Independent Company*, 508–12

Callinicum, Gen., 44

Callwell, Charles E., 123, 202ff., 218, 391, 1025, 1322; *Small Wars —Their Principles and Practice*, 202–6

Calvert, Michael, 599, 601

Cambodia, 334, 538ff., 544, 550, 559, 568, 689, 717, 1231, 1352ff., 1362; "associated state," 693; Geneva Conference, 823; Giap, 804; United States, 696, 815, 1327, coup, 1331, invasion, 1331ff., 1342, 1349, 1350, 1352

Camden, battle of, 109, 110, 113

Campbell, Archibald, 158–59

Campbell, Arthur: *Jungle Green*, 793

Campbell, John, 1378, 1380

Can, Ngo Dinh, 834

Canada (ians), 97, 278, 281n, 602

Cannae, battle of, 39, 41

Cannibalism, 144, 449

Cantabrians, 16

Cantillo, 966

Cao, Huynh Van, 1034

Cao Dai, 559, 674, 679, 830, 854

Caravelle Manifesto, 855

Caribbean, 92, 172

Carlson, Evans, 359 *and* n

Carlson's Raiders, 506, 1291

Carnot (decree), 121

Carolingian Empire, breakdown, 55

Carpathians, 4n

Carpentier, Gen., 710, 712, 716

Carpetanians, 16

Carr, E. H., 284

Carrington, George C., *xvi*

Cartagena (New Carthage), 20

Carthage, 18; conqueror, 25

Carthaginians, 11, 16, 17, 18, 19, 20, 28, 41

Carus, Gen., 33

Carver, George, 1235

Casella, Alessandro, 1220

Cassivellaunus, 15

Castriotes, George "Scanderbeg," 467

Castro, Fidel, 932–34, 945–46, 948–60, 961–76, 991; army, 946; background, 945–46; characteristics, 953 *and* n, 954, 956, 972; communism, 934, 946, 964, 969 *and* n, 970n; "death," 952; fame, 954; imprisonment, 946; influences on, 956n, 972; leadership, 956; Liberator, 970–71; Matthews interview, 953–55; myth, 955; Pact of the Sierra, 961; Sierra Maestra, 950, 951, 953, 956;

strategy, 951–52, 956; support, 950; tactics, 950 *and* n, 951 *and* n, 962ff., 965; thesis, 959–60; United States, 959–60; yacht *Granma*, 950–51

See Che Guevara; Cuba *and* 26th of July Movement

Castro, Raúl, 946, 951, 954, 962, 967; communism, 967

Casualties, 24, 263, 267

See cost *under* name of war

Caswell, Richard, 101

Cate, James, 64

Catherine the Great, 137, 138

Catholic Church, 92, 182, 235, 747

Cato the Elder, 19, 23n, 28, 30

Catroux, Georges, 561, 807, 911

Caulaincourt, Armand de, 139, 140, 143

Cavour, 554

Cédile, Jean, 675

Celebes, 531, 762

Celtiberians, 31, 126, 279–80

See Spain

Celts, 12, 16

Censorship, 190

CIA (Central Intelligence Agency), 799, 820, 828, 859, 981, 990, 1012, 1023, 1033, 1048, 1052, 1079, 1094, 1229–32, 1235, 1381; Cuba, 946, 959ff., 963 *and* n, 969 *and* n; Guatemala, 949; Kennedy, J. F., 1019; Vietnam, 828, 1059, 1315–16, 1346

Céspedes, Carlos de, 172, 173, 939, 940, *map*, 175

Ceylon, 603

Chaffee, Adna, 193, 195

Challe, Maurice, 926, 927, 929, 930; Challe Plan, 928

Chalons-sur-Marne, battle of, 42

Chamberlain White Paper (1939), 770, 771, 772, 774

Chambrun, Gen., 381

Championnet, Gen., 124

Chang Hsueh-liang, Marshal, 353–54

Chang Yü, 35

Chapelle, Dickey, 962

Chapman, Leonard, 1286

Chariot warfare, 14–15, 34

Charisma, 41, 86, 162, 182, 225, 242, 249, 269, 506, 574n, 597, 598, 676–77, 712, 940, 956; guerrillas, 205; hereditary, 373

Charlemagne, 40, 54, 55; Spain, 58

Charles IV, King of Spain, 125

Charles V, King of France, 81, 82

Charles X, King of France, 151

Charles X, King of Sweden, 87

Charles XII, King of Sweden, 86

Charles the Bald, 55

Chataigneau, Gov-Gen., 906

Chau, Phan Boi, 555

Cheetham, Nicolas, *xvi*, 232; *History of Mexico*, 231

Chen Kai-ming, Gen., 620

Chennault, Claire, 566, 614, 615, 617, 620, 623, 627; Stilwell, 618

See Flying Tigers

Ch'en P'ing, 579, 782–84, 794; army (MRLA), 786, 790, 792; guerrilla army, 783–84, 786ff., 782, 793; tactics, 786

Ch'en Yi, Gen., 647, 648

Chernyshevsky, 285; *Unaddressed Letters*, 285

Chiang Fa-kwei, 568

Chiang Kai-shek, *xv*, 340ff., 350–67 passim, 568, 577, 585, 589, 594, 608, 968; army, 341–42, 350, 351, 365, 641, 845, 857, 1005; "bandits," 350, 352, 784; characteristics, 343, 617, 635; communism, 346, 353, 558, 596, 617, break, 341 (*see* Mao Tsetung), fall (defeat), 614, 648, 649, 674, 696, 799, 934, 1018, 1243; Formosa, 648, 696;

France, 678; Indochina (French), 689, 801; Kuomintang, 347, 350, 352, 616 (*see under* China); Mao Tse-tung, 347, 354, 367; Nationalists, 614, 618, 623; New Life Movement, 617, 994; postwar, 636ff.; Soviet Union, 340, 365; Stalin, 353; Stilwell, 584ff., 594ff., 603, 607ff., 624, coalition, 623–39 passim; Sun Yat-sen, 340; U.S., 820–21 (*see under* United States); Vietnam, 676; war-lord concept, 845; Whampoa Military Academy, 340, 557–58; World War II, 409, 413, 585ff., 594–95, 600, 605ff.: adviser (*see* Stilwell), Army, 594ff., 615–37 passim, attitude, 613–14, 618–20, strategy, 614, 618, 627–28

See also China (Nationalist)
Chibás, Eduardo, 941, 945
Chibás, Raúl, 961
Chicoms (Chinese Communists), 1065

See China (Communist)
China, *xii,* 34ff., 36, 69, 72, 183, 321ff., 324, 332, 572, 594–96, 672, 691, 793, 845; Annan, 321; army, 331, 345, 359, 594–96 (*see* Stilwell), regional, 330, 331; Autumn Uprising, 343, 346; awakening, 321ff.; Boxer Rebellion, 194, 250, 335–36; "buffer" states, 332; Burma, 322; Ch'ing dynasty, 324; Chou dynasty, 328; civil war, 632ff.; commanders, 34; "The Commentators," 35; communism, 316, 339, 340–42, 345ff., 366, 472, 557–58, 577, 615, 687, 969, leader, 355 (*see* Mao Tse-tung); DRV (*see* DRV); feudalism, 34; foreign interven-

tion, 324–34 passim, uprisings against, 335–36; France, 547; Germany, 335; government, 321–26, 332–33, 334, 337, 343; Great Wall, 69, 321, 638; Green Gang, 340; Hakkas, 326 *and* n; "Hundred Flowers Movement," 850; Indochina, 690; Japan, 322, 334, 338; Korea, 322; Kuomintang, 337ff., 342, 556, 569, 577, leaders, 784; lobby (U.S.), 617, 635, 644; Manchuria, 322; Manchus, 324ff., 336, 554, fall, 337, 340, 345; military academy (Pao-ting), 340; military establishment, 35, 1386; Ming dynasty, 324; Mongols, 69, 71, 324; Nationalists vs. Communists, 636 (*see* Chiang Kai-shek *and* Mao Tse-tung); North Vietnam, 850, 851; Opium War, 325; peasants, 345, -ruler conflict, 323ff.; People's Republic, 648; philosophy, 322; queue (pigtail), 327; Red Guards, 347; revolts, 324ff., 339; revolution, 669; "rice-bowl Christians," 334; Shensi, 351, 353; "sleeping giant," 321, *map,* 322; Soviet Union, 350ff.; sphere of influence, 1246; Summer Palace, 330–31; Sung dynasty, 69, 324; Taiping rebellion, 238, 239, 326–32, 343, 347; Tao, 323; Tibet, 322; Tientsin massacre, 335; Turkestan, 322; United Front, 353, 356, 364, 365 (*see* World War II); U.S., *xv,* 505, 632–49, 1030, analysis, 648–49, "old China hands," 619, 625, postwar, 636–49, White Paper, 648; Vietnam, 554, 674, 675ff.; war lords, 338, 340ff., 351, 568;

Warring States, 34; White Terror, 342; World War I, 339; World War II, 354ff., 408–9, 429, 503, 538, 577–631 passim, coalition problem, 623–31, "puppet troops," 622 (see Yünnan); Yuan dynasty, 69; Yünnan, 566 and n, 585, 594–608 passim, 676

See Chiang Kai-shek; Mao Tse-tung and Stilwell

China (Communist), 820, 1211, 1251; aggressiveness, erroneous estimate of, 798; atomic bomb, 1071; FLN, 926, 928n; foreign policy, 1247; Geneva Conference, 821, 822; Ho Chi Minh, 694; Korean War, 796, 806; Viet Minh, 707, 797, 806; Vietnam, 1012, 1105, 1247, 1251

See also Korean War and Mao Tse-tung

China (Nationalist), 694; Greece, similarities, 737; Viet Minh, 705–6

China, Gen., 883

Chinese-Vietnamese similarities, 802–3

Chinh, Truong, 1312

Chivalry, 51, 771n; code, 58

Chodjend, 6

Chou En-lai, 349, 353, 628, 631, 641; diplomacy, 824n; Dulles, 820–21; Geneva agreement, 824n

Christ, Jesus, xi, 328

Christian "civilization," 872

Christianity, 51, 57, 281, 333–34, 539, 543, 546, 865, 867, 869; missionary, 327; "rice-bowl Christians," 334; white man's burden, 868, 871

Christiansen, Eric, xvi

Christison, Philip, 760–61

Chroniclers, 81

Churchill, Peter: Of Their Own Choice, 431

Churchill, Winston S., 87n, 176, 279, 311, 313, 385, 386–87, 485, 981, 1020; characteristics, 415–16, 603n; colonialism, 565; on Dunkerque, 588; Eden, 820; Eisenhower re: Indochina, 815, 816; friends, 474; Greece, 734; Indochina, 689; Palestine, 774–75, 778–79; Roosevelt, F. D., 565; United States, 617; Wingate, 602–3, 606–7; World's Crisis, 314, 316; World War II, 410, 412, 413–16, 421, 437, 599, 601, 628, strategy, 475, 485; Yalta, 629

Church-warfare relationship, 57

Chu Teh, Gen., 347, 349, 350, 351, 365, 631, 633

Ciano, Count, 449

Cienfuegos, Lt., 967–68

Cinque Ports, 74

Cisalpine Republic, 124

Cities: garrisoned, 6; walled, 7

Citizen apathy, 1370

Citizen soldiers, 67

Civil disobedience, 675, 964, 965

Civil war, dilemma of, 105–6

Clark, Mark, Gen., 803, 1147, 1262

Clark, Mark, 1320

Clark, Ramsey, 1266, 1344, 1372

Clausewitz, Karl von, xiii, 141, 144, 147–49, 150, 151, 170, 262, 772, 1274; influence, 149; Mao Tse-tung, 357; On War (Vom Kriege), 147–48, 170

Clauzel, Bernard, 153

Clayton, Gen., 258

Clearchos element, 1388

Clemenceau, Georges, 905

Clemens, Martin, 504–5

Clement, Pope, 80

Clery, C. V.: *Minor Tactics*, 202 *and* n

Cleveland, Grover, 172

Clifford, Clark, 1108, 1133, 1213–14, 1228–29, 1239, 1374; Group, 1229–33; Vietnam Plan (1), 1311, (2), 1338

Clinton, Henry, 102ff., 115, 116, 117; characteristics, 105, 106, 108, 111, 112; occupation policy, 103–6
See Cornwallis

Clive, 118

Clos, Max, 836

Clutterbuck, Richard, *xvi*, 782, 787–90, 792–93, 1053, 1142, 1254; *Long, Long War*, 1207

Coalitions, failure of, 149

Coastwatchers (Australian), 504–5, 620

Cochin China, 542, 543, 544, 549, 568, 678, 679, 683, 686, 699, 903; *can tu* tactic, 699; France, 679, 683; Trotskyist movement, 559

Cochran, Philip, 606

Cogny, Gen., 805, 806

Cold War, 671, 759, 889, 909, 1022, 1375; United States, 692

Collaborators, 418, 442, 459–60, 516; value, 478

"Collective responsibility" principle, 220

Collins, J. Lawton: Diem, 833; Vietnam mission, 829–31

Collins, Michael, 274–75, 277, 774n, 900; strategy, 278

Colonialism, *xiv*, 151, 389, 531–32, 547, 576, 714, 903, 904; backlash, 317; "double standard," 550; East Africa, 866–69; economic myth, 547; Far East, 576; Great Powers, 557; neo, 997; "on the cheap," 936; Pacific, 504, 528, 529–31; post-

war, 672, 688, 691–93; responsibilities, 547–48; rivalry, 546, 547; Roosevelt, F. D., 565; *tache d'huile* technique, 685–86; undermining, 773; uprisings, 384
See under name of country

Colonial wars, 151, 158–59, 160, 307, 714–15, 717; characteristics, 198–200; European convention, 201; European-American difference, 169; mistakes, 201–2
See also small *under* Wars *and under* country

Colonization, 65, 69, 86, 92ff., 118, 156, 158, 194, 227–28; air-control concept, 388; armies, 158, 198–99; characteristics, 281; England, 69; European-U.S. differences, 170; French of Algeria, 151–56, *map*, 154; leaders, 158, 218; New World, 529; policy, 370–71; political problems, 218, 221; powers, accomplishments, 545; Romans, 12ff., 16ff., 26–30; Spain, 231–32, 369ff.; tactical problems, 167; techniques, 224

Colons, 904, 908, 910, 911

Columbus, Christopher, 92

Cominform, 673, 692, 741

Comintern (Communist International), 315, 316; agents, 339, 556; Cominform, 673; Fourth Congress (Moscow, 1922), 557; front for Far East, 557; Southeast Asia Bureau, 557; Spanish Civil War, 402, 405

Comitatus concept, 40

CRUA (*Comité Révolutionnaire pour l'Unité et l'Action*), 907, 908, 909
See FLN

Commager, Henry Steele: on power, 1375

Command, 1005; adaptability, 592; confusion, 484–85; division of, 106; egos, 1390; ignorance, 1120, 1277; large, 604; Napoleon on, 1385; policy, 371; tasks, 105; "three-man committee" concept, 493; training for, 270; unity of, 1382

Commanders, *xii, xiii, xiv, xv,* 9, 11, 23, 26, 62, 67–68, 85, 86–87, 92, 97, 98, 123–24, 158, 218, 574n, 590; ancient, 30, 31, 33; European, 82–83, -Asian differences, 34; "finger generals," 243; guerrilla, 17, 23, 146; importance, 742; memoirs, 574n (*see also under* name of commander); "modern major generals," 590; Napoleon's advice, 897; philosopher-general, 572; qualifications, 33–34, 148–49, 252, 590, 604; Sun Tzu advice, 1029; Western-Chinese, 594; World War II, 787

See also Leaders

Commercial "companies," 92–93

Communications, 29, 36

See Press; Radio *and* Television

Communism, *xiii,* 303, 339, 486, 784n, 862, 942; Catholics, 748; containment policy, 808; criticism/self-criticism session, 755; CTs, 784n; dualism, 405; Dulles, 798; fear of, 418, 928n; guerrilla organization and operations, 580–83; *gung ho* psychology, 581; ideology, 580, 648; Kennedy, J. F., 1016, 1018; monolithic theory, 798, 1245, 1326, 1385; nationalism, 698; Nazis, 420; Nixon, 1297; "parallel hierarchy," 783, 789;

postwar, 673, 696, 781; post World War I, 315–17; primitive, 328; rebellion doctrine, 1097; resistance movements, 503; Rolling Red Horde theory, 803; spread, 672, 673, deterrents, 825; *stop communism* ambition, 1016, 1018, 1045, 1241, 1370; teachings, 743–44; United States, 831, 942; vs. free world, 696; Vietnamese (*see* Viet Cong); West: fear of, 838; world threat, 913, 942; World War II, 413, 419, 424

See under country

Communist bloc, 798

Communist Manifesto, 289

Comnena, Anna, 62 *and* n, 63

Compromise, 311

Concentration camps, 177, 179, 197, 216, 420, 423, 770, 837; survivors, 775n

Condé, Gen., 85

Confidence, crisis of, 984

Conformity, demand for, 1373

Confucianism, 323, 327, 330, 333, 335, 344, 543; *Analects,* 346n; reformers, 337

Congo, 972, 976

Congress of Vienna, 146

Conquest, political purpose, 40

CNRA (*Counseil National de la Révolution Algérienne*), 917

Constantine Plan, 926

Constantinople, 40, 46, 47, 51, 62, 139; defense, 47

Containment, policy of, 691, 809

Convention of Cintra, 127

Conway, treaty of, 75

Cookridge, E. H.: *Inside SOE,* 409

Coolidge, Calvin, 397, 938

Cooper, Chester L., 1076

Cooper, Jim, 1159

Co-Prosperity Sphere, 503

Cordon sanitaire, 882, 885

Corfield, F. D., 863n, 870, 873, 874
Corinth, Isthmus of, 46
Cornwallis, Charles, *xii*, 99, 103 *and*
  n, 104ff., 110ff., 281, route
  map, 101; characteristics, 106,
  109; Clinton, 104ff., 112, 114–
  16, policy, 106, 110 *and* n,
  112–13; strategy, 110ff., 116–
  17; tactics, 114–15
Corregidor, 513; province, 946,
  952, 954
Corruption, 324
Corsica, 90–91
Corson, William, 1164, 1200, 1289
Cortés, Hernán, 231, 232
Cossacks, 143, 147
Costa Rica, 174
Coste-Floret, Paul, 693
"Cottage production," 705–6
Counterinsurgency warfare, *xiii and*
  n, 177, 276, 790–91, 794, 1025;
  experts, 782, 1052, 1129, 1142,
  1165, 1248, 1325–27; intelli-
  gence, 791, 1005; key ingre-
  dient, 113
Counterrevolutionary doctrine, 912
Coup d'état, 941, 1048
Coup nul (a draw), 796
Court-martial, 195, 273; field, 295
Cowpens, battle of, 114
Cox, Percy, 388
Crassus, 13
Crawfurd, John, 530
Crécy, battle of, 67
Cressingham, 74 *and* n
Crete: World War II, 408, 488
Crimea, 155
Crimean War, 156, 201
Croatia, 465
Crook, Gen., 169
Crossbow, 57
Crosthwaite, Charles, 209–10
Crozier, Brian, 842, 1320
Crusades, 57, 64–65, 66, 149; first
  (1095–99), 57, 59–61, 62,

map, 60; political weakness, 65
CTs, 784n
Cuba, 171, 186, 194, 802, 932,
  934–47, 949–60, 961–70,
  1007, *map,* 933, Army, 939ff.,
  944, 949, 952, 955ff.; communism, 932ff., 937–38, 939,
  942, 963, 969–70n; exiles,
  948, 950; FEU (students),
  937–38, 941, 949; heros, 174;
  leaders, 173, 174; Operation
  Summer, 965–67, Oriente,
  955, 962–63, war lords, 955–
  56; politics, 950; revolution,
  172 *and* n ff., 174, 860, 932–35,
  950–60, 961–70, *map,* 175,
  civil war, 962, CNOC, 938,
  939, historical background,
  935–47 (*see* Batista, Fulgencio; Castro, Fidel, *and* Guevara,
  Ernesto); Revolutionary Party,
  174; Spain, 172–74; U.S., 171,
  172, 173, 178, 179, 183, 958,
  1035, CIA, 990, Soviet Union
  confrontation, 1017
Cuesta, Gen., 126
Cult: of the hero, 34; "personalism,"
  991; warrior, 863
Cultism, 862
  See Mau Mau rebellion
Cunningham, Alan, 598, 775, 778
Curzon, Lord, 311
Cushman, Gen., 1218
Custer, George A., 169 *and* n, *map,*
  168
Cyprus, 801, 887–902, 953, *map,*
  901; communism, 889: AKEL,
  905; England, 887ff., 892, 893–
  94, 908; *enosis,* 887, 889, 890,
  891, 894, 900; EOKA, 891–
  902; ethnic groups, 887–89;
  Harding, 893; historical background, 887–88; Radcliffe Constitution, 898; rebellion, 861,
  887, 888–89, 892–93; Repub-

lic, 900; self-determination, 892, 893; World War II, 889, postwar, 889

See Greek Cypriotes; Grivas, George; Makarios *and* Turkish Cypriotes

Cyrus, 32

Czechoslovakia, 316, 403, 414, 417; World War I, 304–5; World War II, resistance, 421–22, 424

Dacoity (brigandage), 611

Dalat conference, 679

Dalat Military Academy, 719

Dallin, Alexander, 464: *German Rule in Russia*, 448

Dalmatians, 11

Dalton, Dr. Hugh, 409, 410

Da Nang airfield, 1092, 1095, 1100, 1102, 1110

Danegeld (bribe), 56

Daniel, Jean, 908

Daniels, Aubrey, 1360–61

Dao, Tran Hung, 71; *Essential Summary of Military Arts*, 71

D'Argenlieu, Thierry, 678–79, 682

Darius, *xi, xii,* 3–4, 32; march, *map,* 9

Davidson, Basil, 483

Davies, John Paton, 626

Davies, "Trotsky," 498–500

Davis, Richard Harding, 953

Davydov, Denis, 143: *Journal of Partisan Actions*, 143

Deakin, F. W., 473–74

Dean, Arthur, 1235

De Beer, Gavin, 10, 10n, 11n, 33

Deception, 47

Decius, Emp., 36

Declaration of the rights of man, 150

Decoux, Jean, 561, 562–64

Defoliation, 1316

De Gaulle, Charles, 565, 644, 677, 678, 910, 925; Algeria, 905, 926ff.; on bombing, 1266;

BCRA, 427; characteristics, 929; "dictatorship," 925; Kennedy, J. F., 989, 1042, 1096; Roosevelt, F. D., 691; Southeast Asia, 1048; Truman, 690; U.S. role in Europe, 1375; Vietnam, 1013; World War II, 426–36 passim, 437, 440

De Kalb, Gen., 107 *and* n

Delamere, Lord, 866, 868

De Lanessan, Gov., 219

De Lattre, Jean, 712–21 passim, 722–23, 725, 728, 796; death, 726; "Line," 715, 731, 797, 804

Delouvrier, Paul, 926, 929

Democracy, 336, 339, 1375; leadership indictment, 1370

Demosthenes, 5, 221

Denmark, 53, 55, 56, 58, 86; World War II, 407, 408, 424

Deportation, 216

De Puy, Gen., 1235

De Saxe, Marshal, 87, 96, 203, 262, 264; dictum, 265; *Mes Rêveries,* 87

Desertions, 595

Despotism, benevolent, 323

Destiny, arrangement with, 201

Deterrence, theory of, 389, 750

De Tham, "The Tiger of Yen Tre," 554, 555

Deutsch, Leo, 289

De Valera, Eamon, 274, 275

Devillers, Philippe, 682, 714, 837, 848

Dewey, George, 171, 180, 182–83, 186; Manila Bay, 183

Dewey, Thomas E., 646

Díaz, Juan Martín, 130, 131; *El Empecinado*, 131

Dickens, Charles, 283

Dictatorship, 338, 381, 488, 940, 991; of the proletariat, 291, 302

Diem, Ngo Dinh, 555, 688, 823–27, 832–47, 850, 852, 854–60, 979, 991, 1007, 1009–14, 1248; "agroville" program, 841; army, 994, 1005; background, 825ff., 833–34; Caravelle Manifesto, 855, 857; characteristics, 826, 830, 834, 1013; communism, 835–36; death, 1013, 1046, 1099; dictatorship, 836ff., 852–58; doctrine of Personalism, 1009; Eisenhower, 828; election, 841–43, 850, 853, 859; failings, 1002; family, 833, 835, 839, 855; Johnson, 981, 982; Kennedy, J. F., 983, 990, 1012, 1014, 1043; Montagnard problem, 840; myth, 1035; NLF, 995; opposition, 855–57; power, 834; regime, 826ff., 832, 835ff., 918, 991–92, 1099, 1139, 1324 and n; U.S., 827, 830–31, 833, 840, 856, 858–61, 978–80, 993–95, 1009–14, 1029, 1033, 1034

See South Vietnam Dien Bien Phu, 728, 805–18, 980, 1097; allied intervention, 819–20; fall, 818, 821

Dighenis, 891, 892, 895
See Grivas, George
Diocletian, 38
Diplomacy, 35, 47, 55, 80, 167, 196, 225, 259, 304, 305n, 339, 474, 538, 624, 644, 687, 692, 718, 923, 958–59, 1107; dexterous, 690; Dixie Mission, 620, 625–26; force: as instrument, 1387, versus, 1376–84; gunboat, 386, 1061; imperative, 678; international, 486, 818, 824n, bombing, 1266, 1272–73, political science, 1382–83; language, 310 and n; personal, 624, 1377; solution, 1373; truism, 824;

vest-pocket, 824; wheeling-dealing, 815
Dirksen, Everett M., 1075, 1206
Disciplina militaris, 64
Discretion vs. dissembling, 1374
Disease, 177, 212
Disobedience, 227
Displaced persons, 775; camps, 775
Disraeli, Benjamin, 887
Dissidence, 758
Divided nations, 823n
Dixie Mission, 620, 625–26
Djilal, Belhadj, 922
Do, Tran Van, 823
Doc-lap (independence), 701–2, 705
Dodge, T. A., 10, 10n
Dogma, 149
Dolz, Tabernilla, 944
Dominion status, 278
Domino theory, 645, 812, 814, 820, 821, 858, 990, 1051, 1166, 1211, 1246–47, 1330; genesis, 799; Nixon, 1341
Dong, Pham Van, 1059, 1065, 1312, 1351
Donovan, William J., 411
Don Quixote, 151
Doolittle, James, 601
Dorn, Gen., 596
Dorylaeum, battle of, 62
Dostoevsky: Crime and Punishment, 1166
Douglas, William O., 78, 80, 827, 1379
Douchet, Giulio, 1257, 1260; Command of the Air, 1257; theory of aerial bombing, 1257–60, 1267
Doumer, Paul, 548
DPs.
See Displaced persons
Draper, Theodore, xvi, 934, 951, 954, 960
Draw, John, 1335

Dreiser, Theodore, 283
Dresden, 440
DRV, 848, 849, 850, 851, 855–56;
    elections, 841–43; Geneva Con-
    ference, 822; NLF, 1098; Ton-
    kin Gulf, 1062–64; U.S. posi-
    tion on, 848, 849
    See also Ho Chi Minh *and* North
    Vietnam
Dr. Zhivago, 306
Ducasse, Col., 918
Du Guesclin, Bertrand, 81–82
Dulles, Allen, 949, 963, 969; Diem,
    830, 844
Dulles, John Foster, 644, 802, 810,
    819ff., 843, 844; Diem, 828,
    830, 842, 844; diplomacy, 815;
    Geneva defeat, 824; Indochina
    (French), 798, 803, 812–15,
    819–21, 823–25; massive re-
    taliation, 809; policy, 851; UN,
    819
Duncan, Donald, 1152, 1291
Duncanson, Dennis, 1141
Dunkerque, 407–8, 431, 588
Durbrow, Elbridge, 859 *and* n, 995
Durrell, Lawrence, 891n, 893n
Dutch East India Co., 93, 528–29
Dutch East Indies: World War II,
    408, 503, 603, *map,* 536
    See Indonesia
Dynastic feuds, 82
Dynastic states, 84
Dzerjinsky, 300, 302

Eagleton, Thomas, 1329
East: migrations, 69; tactics, 69;
    -West, differences, 34, 47, in
    military philosophy, 51
    See West
East Africa, 248, 862; colonization,
    866ff.; independence, 872;
    tribes, 863, 865–66 (*see* Ki-
    kuyu tribe)
    See Kenya

East Asia, 799
East India Co., 201
Economics (economy), 86, 125;
    laissez-faire, by-products, 282;
    oil, 769; revolution, 286; rice-
    paddy, 586; sugar, 942; war-
    fare, 125
Eden, Anthony, 428 *and* n, 565, 730,
    807, 815, 816, 819–20, 892;
    Geneva, 824; Greece, 733;
    Makarios, 894; Suez, 898
Edmonds, James E., 147, 149
Edward I, King of England, *xi,* 78;
    campaigns, *map,* 77; Scotland,
    76–80; Wales, conquest of, 72,
    74–76, *map,* 73, cost, 76
Egypt, 36, 48, 59, 65, 216, 393,
    911; Algeria, 921; army, 211;
    England, 201, 225, 369, 889,
    982; FLN, 926; France, 369;
    Soviet Union, 1251; World
    War II, 472, 473, 484, 488
Ehrlich, Blake: *The French Re-
    sistance,* 431
Eichelberger, Gen., 520
Einstein, Albert, -Roosevelt, F. D.,
    414
Eisenhower, Dwight D., 729, 898,
    1380; Cuba, 942, 952, 958–
    60, 965, 969–70; Diem, 828–
    29, 840, 858; Indochina
    (French), 798, 802ff., 810,
    812–18, 820, 821, 828–31,
    Ridgway report, 917–18;
    Korea, 1297; Vietnam, 978–79
    and n, 980, 1009, 1015, 1018,
    1093, 1248; strategy, 1112
Elgin, Lord, 330
Eliot, Charles, 866, 868
Elizabeth I, Queen of England, 87
Ellsberg, Daniel, 1362
Ély, Paul, 809–10 *and* n, 812, 818
Élysée Agreements, 693, 694, 712,
    715
Emerging nations, 982

Emerson, Henry, 1153
Emery, Fred, 1319, 1323, 1340
Emigration: "pig trade," 326
Emmet, Robert, 774n
Engels, Friedrich, 669, 956n
England, *xii, xvi*, 74, 78, 82, 92,
    104, 146, 157, 172, 183, 198,
    203, 257, 280, 281n, 283, 484,
    587, *map*, 73; Africa, 369,
    379; Albania, 496–501 passim;
    American Revolution, 100ff.;
    Arab Bureau, 258; Arab
    policy, 775–76; army, 158,
    258, 391ff. (*see under* specific
    wars); BBC, 394; Burma, 158,
    206–10, 332, 334, 612, 1183;
    China, 325–26 *and* n, 330,
    539; colonialism, *xiv*, 380,
    385, 389, 530, 544, 546, 547,
    549, 576–77, 586, 866, 934;
    Colonial Office, 871; colonial
    wars, 118ff., 146–47; coloni-
    zation, 92ff., 118ff., 388; com-
    munism, 316; crown colonies,
    576, 888; Cuba, 941, 965;
    Cyprus, 887–902: EOKA,
    891; Dutch East Indies, 760–
    63; East Africa, 862, 866–76,
    877–86; Egypt, 201, 225, 369,
    889, 891–92; empire, 380, 385,
    389, 391–92; Establishment,
    474, 602; failures, 200; foreign
    policy, 815–16, 819–20, 824;
    France, 86, 225 *and* n, 379;
    Geneva Conference, 823; gov-
    ernment, 78, 130, 278, 280,
    474; Great Power status, 86;
    Greece, 309n, 488–96, 735,
    737, 739, 889, 891, 893, 897;
    India, 118–21, 199, 200 *and* n,
    201, 325, 388, 393–96, 549,
    Afghan War, 202; Indochina,
    689, 819–20; Indonesia, 528–
    29; Industrial Revolution, 282;
    invasion (1066), 56; Ireland,
69, 87, 248, 272, 273–78;
"Irish Question," 276; Malaya,
688, 781–94, 841, policy, 790;
Marx on, 283; Mexico, 240,
241; military establishment,
206, 585, pre-World War II
attitude, 574–77; Ministry of
Defence Library, *xvi;* "most
favored nation," 326; Napoleon, 125; Navy, 260, supremacy, 171; North America, 97;
Palestine, 388, 389, 768–80,
786, 889, 892, Jewish Brigade,
771, Mandate, 769, 780, postwar, 959, White Paper (*see*
Chamberlain White Paper),
withdrawal, 780; Parliament,
76, 474; Portugal, 126ff.; RAF,
275, 384–90, 408, 434, 485n,
675, 882; Russia, 138, 316;
Sandhurst, 498; Scotland, 77–
80; SEATO, 824; SOE (*see
under* England, World War
II); South Africa, 206, 210–
17, command team, 211;
Southeast Asia, 782; "strategic
key area," 800; Thailand,
538–40, 541; Trans-Jordan,
388; treaty obligations, 891;
Turkey, 891, 893; United
States, 815–16, 1017 (*see*
American Revolution and
World War II); Vietnam, 674,
675, 679, 1103; Wales, 75–76;
World War I, 249–56, 273,
297, 304–6, 769; World War
II, 407–8, 412ff., 541, 770,
773, 799: Africa, 590, 599,
North, 408; Arabs, 769; Asia,
572–79, 582–83, 584, 588–89,
590, 591, 594, 599–601,
strategy, 592, 602; com-
mandos, 410, 499, 507; Far
East, SOE, 564, 565; Jewish
Brigade Group, 771; Middle

East, 591; Pacific: SOE, 541,
542, 575, 577–78, 609, strategy,
504, 535–37, 538, 541; postwar, 672; SOE (Special Operations Executive), 409–12,
415, 421, 424n, 425, 426–34,
435–41, 743, 1023; Yugoslavia,
470ff., 484–86
See Britain; Chamberlain White
Paper *and* Churchill, Winston S.
English, Lowell, 1125
Enosis, 887, 889, 890, 891, 894,
899, 900
Enthoven, Dr. Alain, 1210, 1228–
30
Environment: adaptation to, 787,
878–79; atomic, 1021–22; as
enemy, 71; forest, 878–79,
882, 884, jungle, 190–91,
572ff., 604–5; national wars,
150; North American, 95
EOKA (National Organization of
Cypriot Fighters), 891–900;
organization and strength, 894
Epidemics, 865, 866
Erskine, George, 881; Operation
Anvil, 884
Erwin, James, 246
Escalation, genesis, 390
Escoffier, 557
Espionage, 35, 70, 89; atomic, 648;
double agents, 290, 293
Essex, Earl of, 87
Estonia, 302
Estrada Palma, Tomás, 936–37
and n
Ethiopia: World War II, 597–98
ENA (*Étoile Nord-Africaine*)
movement, 905
Eurasia, 171, 282, 324, 531; com-
munism, 316
Europe, 67; anti-Semitism, 768;
armies, 93; Central, *xii,* 53;
"cockpit," 468; dynastic states,

84; Eastern, postwar, 672;
history, 34; law, 97–98; lead-
ers, 34; Mongol invasion, 69–
71; nationalism, 554; postwar,
672, 695; post World War I,
540; stability, 692; symbols, 34;
Thailand, 539–40; U.S. aid,
postwar, 646; warfare after
1815, 146; Western: political
influence, 286; World War II,
588 (*see* World War II)
Évian Talks, 929
Ewell, Julian, 1319
Excommunication, 80
Execution, 273, 401; methods, 246;
summary, 177
Exile(s), 296, 384, 465, 534;
Cuban, 948, 950
Exodus, 1947, 780
Expatriates, 557
Exploitation, 389
Extermination camps, 770

Fabian tactics, *xi,* 82
Fabius Maximus, Quintus, 33, 114
Falkenhausen, Gen. von, 350
Fall, Bernard, *xiii,* 71n, 547, 549,
562, 566n, 570, 687, 710,
724, 848, 851, 854, 1018, 1031,
1140, 1163; death, 563; Dien
Bien Phu, 805; on French de-
feat in Indochina, 710; *Hell
in a Very Small Place,* 810;
Street Without Joy, 683; *The
Two Viet-Nams,* 546–47
Falls, Cyril, 671
Famine, 11, 315, 551
Far East, 34; communism, 316;
nationalism, 904; power pic-
ture, 560–61; World War II,
412
"Far Eastern Agreement," 629
Fascism, 317, 405, 497; anti-, 418
Feisal, Prince, 259–60, 261–62,
270, 373, 382, 386

Feldt, Eric, 504
Fellowes-Gordon, Ian, 600, 608;
    Amiable Assassins, 608
Felt, Harry, 1039–40, 1060
Fêng Yü-hsiang, 341
Ferdinand, King of Naples, 124
Ferdinand, Prince of Spain, 125
Ferdinand I, Emp., 86
Ferguson, Patrick, 111, 113
Fergusson, Bernard, *xvi,* 606; *Be-
    yond the Chindwin,* 599, 601
Fermi, Enrico, 413
Fertig, Wendell, 517, 518, 519
Feudalism, 56, 282, 530; basis,
    280; China, 34; *haciendas,*
    235; military, 57; "non-injury
    oath," 823 *and* n
Feudal warfare, 67; chivalric code,
    58; rise, in West, 57–59
Feuerbach, 285
Fez, treaty of, 226
Fichte, Johann, 285
Fifth Columns, 404, 411, 588
"Finger salients," 18
Finland, 299, 304, 672
Fischer, Louis, 534, 762
Fishel, Wesley, 832, 859, 1139;
    Vietnam mission, 833
Fitt, Alfred, 1228
Fitzgerald, C. P., 1246
Fitzgibbon, Constantine: *Out of
    the Lion's Paw,* 277
Flanders, 78
Fleming revolt, 82
Flippen, William, 1038
Florida, 104, 159
Flying Tigers, 614, 617
Foch, Marshal, 264, 314, 635,
    1258, 1278
Foley, Charles, 893, 894, 895, 896
Folklore, 147
Foot, Hugh, 898
Foot, Michael, *xvi,* 419; *SOE in
    France,* 409, 411
Force: as instrument of diplomacy,

1387; -politics, interplay, 226;
    vs. diplomacy, 1376–84
Ford, Gerald, 1075
Foreign affairs, conduct of, 1378
Foreign Ministers Conference:
    Berlin (February 1954), 807,
    810
Foreign Policy Research, Washing-
    ton Center, 1314
Forest environment, 882, 884, 885
Formosa, 588, 696
Forrest, Nathan Bedford, 162, 163,
    164, 165, 166, 213
Forrestal, Michael: -Hilsman Re-
    port, 1037; Vietnam, 983,
    988
"Fortress America" concept, 981
Forum-Trebonii, battle of, 36
Fourier, Charles, 236, 285
Fowler, Henry, 1229
Fox, Charles James, 115
Fox, Robin Lane, *xvi,* 6n
France, *xi, xii,* 59, 67, 81, 82, 85,
    86, 90–91, 92, 121ff., 157,
    183, 187, 198, 199, 201, 203,
    283, 312, 919, 930; Africa,
    369, 379; Algeria, 151–56,
    158, 169, 201, 223, 224, 903,
    913, *map,* 168; Arab Bureau,
    924; army, 158, 218–19, 224,
    912–13, 914, 920, 930, Grand
    Army of 1812, 139ff., *la
    guerre révolutionnaire,* 912–
    13, 914, 918, 919, 924, 925,
    philosophy, 228; Burma, 539;
    Caesar, *map,* 14; China,
    330; colonialism, *xiv,* 118ff.,
    540ff., 544, 546–52, 576, 679,
    691, 692 *and* n –93, 714–15,
    802, 903–4, 934; commanders,
    121, 124, 218; communism,
    387, 557, 673; Crimea, 155;
    Dreyfus affair, 419; Egypt,
    369; -empire, relationship,
    227–28; England, 80–81, 86,

225 *and* n; failures, 200; Foreign Legion, 371, 730; Geneva Agreements, 842; government, 280: Directory, 124, Third Republic, 227, 548, Fourth Republic, 913, fall, 925, Provisional (1945), 691, Second Coalition, 124, Vichy (*see under* World War II); Greece, 487; India, 118, 120; Indochina (*see* Indochina [French]); Italy, 85, 123–24; Japan, 334n; Madagascar, 200; Mexico, 233–35, 241; military: behavior, 152, 153, 155, "crisis of conscience," 919; Morocco, 380–84, 903–5; North Africa, 151ff.; political philosophy, 913, 914; political weakness, 911; politics, 227; Portugal, 126, 129; postwar, 673, 696; Prussia, 219; Quai d'Orsay, 732; Revolution, 121, 284, 401; Roosevelt, F. D., 565–66; Russia, 297, 308; St. Cyr, 218; scandals, 155; SEATO, 824; Spain, 125–26, 131–32, 141, 150, Civil War, 402; Switzerland, 124; Tunisia, 903–5; Tyrol, 135–37; U.S., 677, 815; Vendée rebellion, 121–23; Vichy (*see under* World War II); Vietnam, *xiii*, 332, 334, 540–44, 675–76, 677, solution, 678, withdrawal, 842; Vikings, 53, 55–56; war, theory of, 264; World War I, 297, 304, 401n, 905, strategy, 264; World War II, 407–8, 412ff., 426ff., 692, 912, *map* (1940–45), 441, Communists, 432, 436, fall of, 507, 560, FFI, 437, German occupation, 918, 919, liberation, 565, *maquis,* 420, 433, memoirs, 430, resistance, 417, 419–20, 424, 426–42, 678, 879, cost, 438–42, Vichy, 472, 584, 692, 905, 906, Japan, 561–62, laws, 563, occupation, 433

See De Gaulle, Charles; Indochina (French) *and* Napoleon
Francis, Ahmed, 910
Francis, David, 304
Franco, 377, 379, 383, 941; Civil War, 400, 403, 404, 405
Franco-German War (1870), 403
Franke, Wolfgang, 327n, 329
Franklin, J. Ross, 1304
Franks, 40, 48–49, 56, 61, 62, 64, 65, 66, 69
Frederick II, Emp., 70
Frederick the Great, 86, 87, 89, 90, 93, 94n, 137, 603, 825n, 919, 1167, 1208; *Instructions to His Generals,* 87; Russia, 137; tactics, 96, 243
Frederick William, Elector of Brandenberg, 87, 825n
Freedom, 510
Free French, 426ff., 564, 565, 644; Vietnam, 566, 571, 675
Freeman, H. A., 888
Freikorps, 90
French and Indian War, 93, *map,* 94
French Revolution, 121, 284, 401
Fridigern, 39 *and* n, 40, 41
Friedman-Yellin, David, 772
Froehlke, Robert, 1359
FLN (*Front de Libération Nationale*), 909, 911, 914, 916–17, 918, 920ff.; army (ALN), 909, 916, 922, 927, 930; De Gaulle, 926–31; government-in-exile, 926, 928; leaders, 921; recognition, 926; support, 921–22, 928 *and* n
Fry, Christopher, *ix*
Fuchs, Klaus, 648

Fulbright, William, 1075, 1166,
    1322, 1329, 1352, 1375, 1379;
    Vietnam, 1105, 1206
Fuller, J. F. C., 4n, 5, 6n, 7n, 8n,
    34, 39n
Funston, Frederick, 193, 756
Furneaux, Rupert, 376

Gage, Thomas, 94n, 97, 98, 1142
Gaillard, 923
Galba, Servius, 23 *and* n, 28
Galbraith, John Kenneth, 1018,
    1019n, 1205–6; on duplicity,
    1375–76
Gallieni, Col., 221, 227, 554, 679–
    80, 686, 687, 1007, 1025
Gallipoli, 590
Gambiez, Gen., 930
Gandhi, Mahatma, 393, 899
Gapon, Georgi, 290, 293
García, 935
Gardner, Arthur, 942, 946, 953,
    955, 958
Garibaldi, 554, 774n
Gates, Horatio, 107–9, 110, 112,
    113
Gaul, 10, 16
Gaullists, 563, 712
    See De Gaulle, Charles
Gauss, Clarence, 617
Gavin, James, 980, 1166–67, 1230,
    1242, 1262
Geneva, 286, 298
Geneva Agreements (Accords)
    See under Geneva Conference
Geneva Conference, 815, 816,
    819ff., 827, 842, 845, 1097;
    Agreements (Accords), 822,
    825, 841, 842, 850, 852, 903,
    984, 997, 1094, 17th Parallel,
    Dulles boycott, 820–21; "Final
    Declaration," 822–23; origin,
    807; U.S. position, 823–24 *and*
    n, Vietminh, 822
Genghis Khan, 69, 70

Genocide, 155, 390, 922, 1205,
    1259; controlled, 920; Nazis,
    451; premeditated, 1259; tribal,
    169
Genoese, 90–91
Gent, Edward, 784
George II, King of Greece, 487,
    488, 489–90, 491, 496
George III, King of England, 103,
    104, 106
Georgia, 100, 104, 110, 116
Germain, George, 102, 103, 106,
    117
German East Africa, 224, 248–56,
    866–67, *map*, 254; *askaris*
    (natives), 249, 250; World
    War I, 249–56, 689–90
    See also Tanganyika *and*
    Tanzania
Germanic tribes, 43
    See Barbarians
German-Russian Non-Aggression
    Pact (1939), 470, 577
Germany, 90, 183, 187, 260, 285;
    army, 170, 252; China, 335,
    338, 547; East Africa (*see* Ger-
    man East Africa); Japan, 334n;
    Luftwaffe, 875n, 1259; Mexico,
    242; Russia, 298, 302, 306–7,
    Non-Aggression Pact (1939),
    470, 577; South Africa, 211;
    Spanish Civil War, 402, 406;
    Thailand, 541; World War I,
    373, 912, 1388, Hindenburg-
    Ludendorff position, 912, 1276,
    1388–89; World War II,
    407ff., 426–42, 496–502, 613,
    974–75n: Albania, 496–502,
    end, 671, Greece, 487–96,
    New Order, 478, occupation,
    419–25, 430ff., 487 (*see also*
    under country), policy, 776,
    reparations, 774, reprisals,
    420, satellites, 465, Soviet
    Union, 443–64, 470, strategy,

464, 465, tactics, 572, 686, Yugoslavia, 465–86
See Hitler *and* Nazis
Giap, Vo Nguyen, *xiii,* 558, 569, 680, 683, 697, 701ff., 722, 727, 796–97, 798, 804, 998, 1029, 1059, 1073, 1160, 1166, 1312; characteristics, 698; Chinese troops, 798; Laos, 728, 731–32; Minister of Defense (DRV), 855–56; Operation Le-Loi, 709; strategy, 698, 709, 713, 727, 729, 731–32, 1221, 1365ff.; tactics, 722, 804, 805–6, 810ff.; teachings, 956; on VC, 1277; *War of Liberation and the People's Army,* 698
See Dien Bien Phu *and* Viet Minh
Giau, Tran Van, 675
Gibraltar, 800
Gilpatric, Roswell, 987, 1276
Giraldus Cambrensis (Gerald de Barri), 72 *and* n –74
Giraud, Gen., 426, 429
Giskes, H. J.: *London Calling North Pole,* 430
Gladstone, William, 201
Godoy, Manuel de, 125
Goebbels, Joseph, 448
Goering, Hermann, 448, 449, 451, 1259
Goldberg, Arthur, 1235
Goldwater, Barry, 1069
Gómez, José Miguel, 937
Gómez, Máximo, 173, 174, 176
Goodell, Charles, 1329
Goodhart, Philip: *Hunt for the Kimathi,* 886
Good Neighbor Policy, 940
Gordon, C. D., 36n, 41
Gordon of Khartoum, 200–1, 225n, 227, 808, 1276
Gosselin, Capt., 544

Goths, *xii,* 36, 38, 39, 40, 41, 44, 46, *map,* 37; origins, 36; tactics, 39
Government, 226, 280, 530, 869; asset: the people's trust, 1369; authoritarian, 1386; citizen participation, 1370–71; civil, 192–96, 209; competition in, 788; constitutional monarchy, 293; democratic: basic mission, 749, concept of, 280; dictatorship (*see* Dictatorship); dominion, 278; feudal (*see* Feudalism); "flat" Confucianist concept, 323, 334; ideas post World War I, 540; -in-exile, 470, 489, 927; *officier-administrateur,* 228; policy: defined, 1016, -wish/difference, 1016; self-, 380, 389; semianarchic, 280; sovereignty, 546; strong-man concept, 938; Western development, 280–81; world, 630
Goya, 376; *Dos de Mayo,* 401; *Los Desastres de la Guerra,* 279
GPRA, 926
Gracchus, Gaius, 25, 28, 30, 33
Gracchus, Tiberius, 23
Gracey, Douglas, 674–75 *and* n
Graham, J. J., 147n, 148
Grant, A. J., Jr., 4n
Grant, U. S., 162, 163, 164, 165, 172, 213
Grau San Martín, Ramón, 940, 941, 944
Great Britain.
See England
Great Depression (1929), 534, 586
Greater East Asia Co-Prosperity Sphere, 562, 568
Great Northern War, 86
Great Powers, 389, 557; concept, 185

Greece, 4n, 62, 649, 695, 793, 894;
  Arabs, 466; army, 488, 735,
  737, 738–39, 740, 741, 857;
  civil war, 734–45, 889, 890,
  Khi or X organization, 890,
  map, 743; communism, 488,
  498, 673, 741, 851, EAM/
  ELAS, 733, 734ff., 743, KKE
  Central Committee, 734–35,
  737, 738ff., 743; Cypriotes
  (*see* Greek Cypriotes); England, 309n, 735, 736–37, 739;
  enosis (*see under* Greek
  Cypriotes); guerrillas, 1019;
  insurgency, 795, 844, 1098;
  monarchy, restoration, 737;
  postwar, 733ff.; Soviet Union,
  673; Spain, 16; Truman Doctrine, 673; Turkey, 899; United
  States, 673, 735, 739, 740,
  742, 889, JUSMAPG (Joint
  U. S. Military Advisory and
  Planning Group), 740–41;
  War of Independence (1821),
  488; World War I, 888; World
  War II, 408, 487–96 passim,
  501–2, 733–35, 741, *map*,
  501: Communists, 493, Operation Noah's Ark, 495, 496, 502,
  "Plaka Agreement," 495, politics, 489, 493–94, resistance,
  418, 487ff., 502
  See also Cyprus *and* Greek
  Cypriotes
Greece, Ancient, 4–5, 19, 31, 40;
  strategy (*epiteichismos*), 221
Greek Cypriotes, *xiii*, 887–902;
  enosis, 887, 889, 890, 891,
  894, 899, 900; EOKA, 891–
  900; leaders, 888; World War
  II, 889
"Greek fire," 48
Greek-Turkish War, 202
Greene, Nathanael, 113–15, 116,
  117

Greene, Wallace, 1123
Greenwood, Hamar, 276
Griffith, Dr. (CPLA), 357, 613,
  622
Griffith, Arthur, 274
Griffith, Belle, *xvii*
Griffith, S. B., *xvn*, *xvi*, 34n, 35,
  400, 1025–27, 1205
Grivas, George, 890–99, 900–2,
  953; characteristics, 890–91,
  900; goal, 900; *Memoirs*, 890;
  On Guerrilla Warfare, 890,
  896; tactics, 891ff., 900–2;
  "X" group, 736
GCMA (*Groupements de Com-
  mandos Mixtes Aéroportés*),
  716
GAMO (*Groupes administratifs
  mobiles opérationnels*), 724
Groves, Leslie: *Now It Can Be
  Told*, 413
Grüner, Dov, 778, 780
Guadalcanal, 359n, 1259, 1291;
  World War II, 504–6, 512
Guam, 186, 1189; World War II,
  408, 504
Guantánamo Bay, 802, 966
Guatemala, 948
Gubbins, Colin, 410
Guernica, 402, 1259
Guerre révolutionnaire, la, 912–13,
  914, 918, 919, 924, 925;
  philosophy, 228
Guerrillas, 31, 130–31, 157, 607–
  9, 881, 884, 886; bands, genesis,
  142; "Communist bandits,"
  1029; *ladrones* (outlaws), 196;
  lawful belligerents, 167; lead-
  ers, 28–29, 78, 81, 90, 130,
  131, 469 (*see also under*
  name); meaning of word, *xi*;
  neutralizing, 132–34; POWs,
  165; survival ability, 479
  See also Guerrilla warfare

Guerrilla warfare, *xii, xiv–xv*, 3ff., 13, 84, 135–37, 158–59, 204, 530, 572ff., 862; analysis, 147–51, American, 792–93; central direction, 851; Communist organization and operation, 580–83; cost, 440; current status, *xii;* defense against, *xiv*, 158; defined, *xi–xii;* development, *xi–xiv;* expansion, 1021; experts, 978, 1205 (*see also under* Counterinsurgency); Fitzgibbon on, 277; Griffith, 1025–27; ignorance of, 649; Kennedy, J. F., 979; leaders, 90, 118, 120 (*see also under* Guerrillas); Lenin, 303–4; lull, meaning of, 1358; Mao Tse-tung, 356, 357; orthodox army, 89, 499; political element/aim, *xii, xiii,* 248; post World War I, 384; primer (Che Guevara), 956; purest form, 327; purposes, *xii–xiii;* qualitative theory, 599; regulars' vulnerability, 162; roles, *xi–xii; ruses de guerre,* 193; saturation theory, 599; society and, 159; strength, bases, 29; tactics, *xii,* 4, 31, 793, counter-, *xii,* 123, quasi-, 36; vertical command concept, 580, 581; World War II, 538
  See also Counterinsurgency; Guerrillas *and under* rebellion *or* insurrection *under* name of country
Guerrilleros, xi
Guevara, Ernesto Che, 948–49, 951, 952, 962, 970–76; background, 948–49; Bolivian expedition, 970, 972–76; Castro (and Cuba), 948, 949, 951–52, 956 *and* n, 967–68, 969, 970, 971–76; communism, 967, 972; execution, 973; on guerrilla warfare, 956, 971–72, 973–74
Guilford Courthouse, battle of, 115
Guiscard, Robert, 62
Gullion, Edmund, 718–19, 720, 721, 731, 977
Gunboat, 151
Gunpowder, 67, 70, 84, 156, 264; invention, 82
Gurkhas, 785–86
Gurney, Henry, 789
Gustavus Adolphus, 86
Guthrum, 56
Guzmán, Martín, 243
Gwynn, Charles, 395–96, 1323, 1358; *Imperial Policing,* 391–93

Habersham, Joseph, 100
Habib, Philip, 1228, 1235
Habsburgs, 135, 234
Hackworth, David, 1284
Haganah (Defense Organization), 770, 771, 774–75, 776, 780; Palmach, 771, 774, 775; refugee issue, 775; terrorists, 774
Haggerty, J. J., 1275
Hague Conference on land warfare, 281 *and* n
Haiphong Harbor, mining, 1231
Haiti, 1021: United States, 396, 400, 411, 488
Halberstam, David, 992, 994, 1005, 1010, 1018, 1024, 1034, 1040
Halleck, Gen., 162–63
Hamburg bombing, 1260
Hamilcar, 20
Hamilton, Ian, 215
Hammer, Ellen, *xvi,* 563, 837, 1018; *Struggle for Indochina,* 545, 547
Ham Nghi, 553
Han Fei-tzu, *xv*

Hannibal, *xi*, 3, 10, 17, 39, 41, 113, 116; army, size, 10, 10n; march, 10–11, *map*, 12; tactics, 10, 33
Hanoi, 676; bombing, 1136–37 *See* North Vietnam
Harding, John, 893–98
Hardy, Mrs. Thomas, 271
Hargreaves, Reginald, 11n, 13n
Harkins, Paul, 991, 1002, 1010, 1017, 1028, 1034, 1035, 1037, 1039, 1042, 1048, 1060
Harriman, Averell, 634; Nixon, 1297, 1316; Vietnam, 983, 988, 1018; Yalta, 629
Harris, Townsend, 540
Harrison, D. J. A., *xvi*
Harrison, John A., 324, 329
Harrison, Prof., 353, 614
Hart, Armando, 950
Hart, Basil Liddell, 68 *and* n, 69, 82, 269
Hart, Robert, 333, 334
Harvard University, 1297; Law School, 540
Harvey, Frank, 1116, 1128
Harwood, Ralph, 1034
Haslack, Paul, 1016
Haspinger, Joachim "Redbeard," 135
Hastings, battle of, 56, 68
Hatred, 182, 186, 197, 457; Communists, of West, 315; -vengeance corollary, 282
Hatta, Dr. Mohammed, 534, 535, 541, 760, 761, 762, 766
Hattin, battle of, 66
Hawaii, 171, 336, 813; annexation, 183
Hayes, Rutherford B., 172
H-bomb, *xiii*
Heath, Donald, 717, 718–19, 828
Hebrew Committee of National Liberation, 773
Hedges, Col., 518

Hegel, Georg Wilhelm Friedrich, 285
Hegemony, hemispheric, 934
Heilbrunn, Otto, 485, 760
Heinl, Robert, 1359
Helicopters, *xiii*, 896, 921, 928, 1031, 1279–81; Algerian rebellion, 927–28; "vertical assault" tactics, 1115; "vertical envelopment" concept, 1022 *See also* Air power
Helms, Richard, 1229, 1332
Hemingway, Ernest: *For Whom the Bell Tolls,* 401, 404, 406, 956n
Henderson, G. F. R.: *Stonewall Jackson,* 164
Henderson, Ian, 883; *Hunt for the Kimathi,* 886
Henderson, Oran K., 1359
Henriques, Robert: *No Arms, No Armour,* 200n
Henry, Duke of Saxony, "The Builder," 57
Henry, John, 1226
Henty, G. A., 155
Heraclius, 51
Herbert, Anthony, 1303–4, 1360
Heren, Louis, 1323, 1330
Hero, 383, 602; individual, cult of, 34
Herodotus, 3, 4, 4n, 5, 5n, 32
Hershey, Gen., 1317
Herzen, Alexander, 285
Herzl, Theodor, 768
Hessians, 110
Heydrich, Reinhard, 421 *and* n
Heymann, Frederick, 83
Hickenlooper, Bourke, 1075
Hidalgo, Miguel, 232–33
Hieu, Nguyen Van, 996, 1004
Higgins, Marguerite, 1040
Hightower, John, 1137
Hilsman, Roger, *xvi*, 980, 983, 985, 988, 1007, 1009, 1010, 1018, 1028, 1031, 1139; background,

988; on guerrilla warfare, 1290–91; -Forrestal report, 1037ff.; State Department, 1038, 1066

Himalayas, 38; American airlift over "Hump," 585

Himmler, Heinrich, 448, 450, 452

Hinde, W. R. N., 881

Hindenburg, Paul von, 912, 1276, 1388

Hindu Kush, 6, 388

Hindus: Marathas, 118

Hinh, Nguyen Van, 827, 829

Hiong Nu, 360

Hiroshima, 440, 1259, 1260

Hiss, Alger, 648

Historians, 3, 4, 5, 7n, 11, 18, 21, 43, 59, 104, 210, 237, 439, 473, 531, 546, 714, 865, 1368, 1375, 1386; ancient, 20; Bolshevik, 289; military, 428; officer, 200; revisionist theory, 586n; Roman, 38

Historical determinism, 971

Historical process, 772, 1273

History: symbols, 34; Voltaire on, 1374

Hitler, Adolf, 353, 365, 405, 407ff., 414, 415, 434, 435, 443, 450, 456, 466, 1223, 1259; allies, 487; anti-Semitic policy, 769; extermination policy, 449, 457; Russia, 448, 449, 464, 470, 577; secret weapons, 628; strategy, 465, 487, 488
  See Germany; World War II and Nazis

Hoach, Le Van, 679

Hoa Hao, 559, 674, 679, 830, 854

Hoc, Nguyen Thai, 556

Hoche, Lazare, 122, 123

Ho Chi Minh, xiii, 413, 568, 569–70, 674ff., 677–78, 680, 684ff., 697–99, 795, 850–52, 952, 972, 1029, 1097, 1222, 1247–48; background, 556–58; characteristics, 678–79, 845; China, 558, 559, 568, 569; colleagues, 559; Comintern, 568; communism-nationalism, 699; death, 1317, 1337, 1351n; Diem, 826, 850; diplomacy, 692; DRV, 795, 822, recognition, 694, 696; France, 556–57, 678–82, 688, 691, Indochina, 803; French Colonization on Trial, 557; goals, 729; government (Hanoi), 676ff., 683, 850–51; Johnson, 1177; Lenin, 557; poetry, 568–69; problems, 676–77, 850; PRP, 996; quote, 669; South Vietnam, 851; Soviet Union, 558; strategy, 1312; supporters, 569, 850, 851; training, 851; UN, 1064; United States, 1064; Viet Minh, 568, 569, 848, 849
  See Viet Minh

Ho Chi Minh Trail, 1004, 1031, 1124, 1141, 1143, 1351, 1354, 1355

Hofer, Andreas, 135–36

Hogard, Col., 913

Holland, 92, 158, 198; China, 325; colonialism, 118ff., 547 (see Indonesia); Dutch East Indies, 408, 503, 603, map, 536, pacification, 763, postwar, 759–67 (see Indonesia); France, 87; Indonesia, 528–37 passim, 547, 576, 577, 688, colonialism, 528–31, 536–37, Forced Cultivation System, 531, World War II, 537 (see Indonesia); politics-religion relationship, 762; postwar, 672, 759–60; United States, 766, 767; World War II, 407, 408, 424, 430, 506ff., fall, 560

Homonoia, concept of, 8, 8n
Honduras, 398
Honey, P. J., 824, 837, 838, 1337
Hong Kong, 325, 336, 614
Honolulu Conference (South Viet-
    nam-United States), 1130,
    1161, 1239
Honor, 1327
Hoopes, Townsend, 1193, 1202,
    1209–10, 1228, 1244; *Limits
    of Intervention,* 1224
Hoover, Herbert, 624, 938
Hornsby, Michael, 1335
Horse archer, 43–44, 48
Hostages, 19, 87, 92, 123, 164
Hostility, official, 859–60
Hottentots, 250
Howard-Johnston, James, 50, 51n
Howe, William, 97, 102n
Hoxha, Enver, 498, 499, 738
Hoyt, R. S., 38n, 40, 58n, 59
Hsiung Shih-hui, Gen., 642
Htin Aung, Maung, *xvi,* 210, 586n,
    587, 610, 612
Hudson, Capt., 471, 473
Hughes, Harold, 1329
Huks, 747–54; BUDC, 748;
    strength, 755; tactics, 748ff.
Hull, Cordell, 541, 561, 566, 690
Humanism, 1314
Human rights, 323
"Hump," 595, 614
Humphrey, Hubert, 1237; Diem,
    830
Hundred Years' War, 81, 146, 306,
    546, 935, 1377
Hungary, *xii,* 87, 137, 316, 467;
    Mongols, 69, 70; origin, 56;
    World War II, 465, 488
Hung Hsiu-ch'üan, 326–31, 347
Huns, *xii,* 36, 38–39, 43, 49, 56,
    map, 37; origin, 36, 38; tactics,
    38–39
    See Attila
Hunt, K., 1294

Huong, Tran Van, 993–94
Hurley, Patrick, 624–25, 628, 633,
    634, 635, 636, 639, 1377;
    China mission, 624ff., 628, 631,
    633, 635–36, 646; resignation,
    639; Roosevelt, F. D., 630;
    Stalin, 633–34; Stilwell, 627;
    Yalta, 630–31
Hussite wars, 82 *and* n
Hyder Ali, 120

Iberia, 16, 130, 131–32
Iberian Peninsula: Napoleon, 125ff.;
    Romans, 280
Ibsen, Henrik: *An Enemy of the
    People,* 419
Ideologies, clash of, 759
Ignorance, 858: arrogance of, *xii,*
    30, 130, 214, 253, 310, 464,
    637, 734, 866, 867, 909, 970,
    1002, 1015, 1017, 1022, 1029,
    1030, 1097, 1240, 1384, 1391;
    command, 1120, 1277; of
    guerrilla warfare, 649; political,
    416, 502
Illiteracy, 371, 378, 677
"Ilot" system of surveillance, 918
Imamura, Gen., 535
Immigration: Biltmore Program,
    771; DPs, 775; Jewish, to
    Palestine, 768–69, 770, 771,
    774–75
Immolations, 1012 *and* n
Imperialism, 186n, 695, 871–72,
    936; Che Guevara, 971, 972;
    communism, 339; defenders,
    587; limited, 171; opponents,
    197
Indemnities, 18, 124
Independence, 872
    See under country
India, 5, 69, 118, 121, 160, 170,
    207, 209, 410, 547, 590, 815,
    map, 119; Amritsar riots,
    393–94; communism, 557;

England, 118–21, 199, 200 *and* n, 201, 388, 549; France, 118, 120; guerrilla leaders, 118, 120; Moplah rebellion, 393–95; Mutiny, 199ff.; Mysore, 120; United States, 1211; World War I, 249, 252; World War II, 503, 538, 584ff., 594, 595, 596, 606, SOE, 577–78

Indian Ocean, 384

Indians (North America), 93, 94–96, 97 *and* n, 108, 114, 167–69; Seminole War (Florida), 159–60; tactics, 168, 169–70

Indibilis (guerrilla leader), 17, 19

Indochina (French), 219–20, 228, 529, 542, 554, 649, 674ff., 684–96, 697–708, 709–21, 722–32, 783, 793, 908, 921, 1007, *map* (1945–54), 681; allies: intervention, 819–20, occupation, 674, 675 *and* n; Army, 726, 730–31, National Vietnamese, 716, 717; "associated state," 693; Cao Dai (*see* Cao Dai); Catholic League, 689; China, 678; communism, 550, 552, 557–60, 568; Dalat Conference, 679, 680, 699; division (*see* Geneva Conference); domino theory, 799, 812; Élysée Agreements, 693, 712, 715; France, 219–22, 542–44ff., 576, 710–21, 722–32, 795–97, 803–18, 904: "double standard," 549–50, failure, 547, 688–92, 699, policy, 807, postwar, 675–83, 685ff., 709ff., 721, resistance to, 553–60, withdrawal, 712–13, 821, 903; Geneva Conference, 822; Hoa Hao (*see* Hoa Hao); independence, 568, 689, 691, 719, 725 (*see* Vietnam); influences, 554–55; insurgency, 844, 904; Japan, 560–62; *la sale guerre*, 712; military history, 220; nationalism (*doc-lap*), 552, 555–56, 557, 559, 564, 674, 688, 904, -communism tie, 694; nationalists (*attentistes*), 689; Navarre Plan, 803, 804; O'Daniel mission, 803; Opération Atlante, 806; pacification, 725–26, 727, 1276; polarization, 694; politics, 559, 688; postwar, 787 (*see also under* France); power groups, 559; religious sects (*see* Cao Dai *and* Hoa Hao); "strategic convenience," 802; United States, 689–96, 715, 716: aid, 717, 722, 797–98, 803, 808, 812–18, -French position, 690–96, 715, 718–19, 722, position, 798–99, 803; VNQDD (National Party), 556; World War II, 408, 538, 560–71, 584, 603, 614–15, Free French, 565, Vichy French, 584; Yen Bay Mutiny, 556, 558

See Dien Bien Phu; Geneva Conference; Ho Chi Minh; Viet Minh *and* Vietnam

Indochinese Union, 544

Indonesia, 69, 541, 649, 672, 695, 717, 763, 793, 799, 1098, *map*, 761; Allied occupation, 760; army (*Peta*), 535, 536, 760, 766; Chinese, 533; communism, 533, 557, 577, 673, 695, 762, 763, 765; East, 763; history, 528–35; Holland, 576, 695, 908 (*see* Holland); independence, 536–37, 760, 762, 767; insurgency, 795; Japan, 760; Java War, 530–31; language, 536; National Front, 763;

nationalism, 533, 535, 536, 760; PNI, 533, 534 (*see* Sukarno*)*; politics, 765; postwar, 672, 759–67, 787; Renville Agreement, 764, 765; Surabaya, battle of, 761–62; U.S., 762, 764, 766, 1211; World War II, 528, 534–37, *map,* 536

Industrial Revolution, 146, 160, 282, 283, 289–90, 317; Eurasia, 324

Inflation, 500, 611, 644

Informers, 581, 582

Institute for Strategic Studies, 1221–22, 1294, 1349; *Strategic Survey, 1967,* 1204

Insurgencies, *xi, xiv,* 750, 795, 838, 844, 861, 1264; complexities, 1020; *foco insurreccional,* 971; fulcrum, 1099; symbiotic, 1144; unnecessary, 863 (*see* Mau Mau rebellion)

Intelligence, 28, 113, 225, 430, 591, 626

Intelligentsia, 421, 422; China, 336; Russia, 285, 286

International affairs, training for, 1383

International Control Commission, 822

International diplomacy.
  See under Diplomacy

Internationale, 583

International politics, 412, 820, 851, 1243, 1272–73, 1386; goodwill, 1369; honor, 1327; post-Korea, 1021; "strategic keys" vs. "strategic conveniences," 799–803
  See Domino theory

Intervention, 309 *and* n; allied (Russia), 314; foreign (in China), 323–27, 330–34; by inertia, 940n; wars of, 149

I.R.A., 294–95, 277–78, 774n, 892, 900

Iran, 624, 1024

Iraq, 772, 889, 899; England, 385, 388; World War II, 588

Ireland, *xii,* 272ff., 778; Black and Tans, 276, 277, 278; England, 69, 86–87; home rule, 273; Irish Free State, 278; Norman Conquest, 68–69; partition, 278; rebellion, 87, 248, 272–79, 410; Republican Brotherhood (IRB), 272, 273–74; Royal Irish Constabulary (RIC), 275, 276, "Auxies," 276, 277, 278; Vikings, 53, 55; World War I, 273
  See I.R.A. *and* Sinn Fein

Irgun, 771–78, 780; goal, 777; ideological climate, 771n; origin, 771 *and* n; -Stern terrorism, 773; strategy, 773

Irish Revolution, 900
  See under Ireland

Iron Curtain, 673, 1249

Irregulars, 90, 116, 118, 121, 137
  See Guerrillas

Irua, 870

Isaacs, Harold, 339

Islamism, wars of, 149

Isle of Pines, 946

Isolationism, 1314

Istanbul, 893

Istiq-lal, 904

Istrians, 11

Italy, 9, 11, 32, 41, 44, 46, 123; Abyssinia, 376; Albania, 488, 496ff.; communism, 425, 673; France, 85, 124; guerrillas, 124, 125; *lazzaroni,* 124, 125; Magyars, 56; postwar, 672, 673; Russia, 297; Spanish Civil War, 402, 405; unification, 554; World War I, 304; World War II, 408, 412, 413, 465,

472ff., 487, 490, 497, 590, 597–98, collapse, 474, 479, 495, 498, resistance, 417, 424
Iwo Jima, 281n, 504, 628
Izmir, 893

Jabotinsky, Vladimir, 771
Jackson, Andrew, 1374
Jackson, Henry, 1178
Jackson, Thomas J. "Stonewall," 164
Jacoby, Annalee (*and* T. H. White): *Thunder Out of China*, 615
Jacquerie, 82
Jäger battalions, 170
James, Daniel, 970, 974, 976; *The Complete Bolivian Diaries of Ché Guevara*, 970
James, Henry, *xiv*
Jamestown, 93
Japan, 183, 242, 334n, 538, 586; army, 360, 365, 366, 367, pre-war, 574–75; China, 321, 334, 338, 339, 353, 360, 365; Dutch East Indies, postwar, 759–60; Greater East Asia Co-Prosperity Sphere, 564; Indochina, 560–63; Korea, 332; Manchuria, 366, 614; postwar, 675n; "preeminent position," 561; Russia, 293, 554; Southeast Asia, 536; "strategic key area," 800; Thailand, 540; "Triple A" movement, 535; United States, 1211, 1266, invasion, cost, 629, 630 (*see under* World War II); Vietnam, 555, 569, 676; World War I, 304; World War II, 281n, 408, 503–12, 513–27, 528, 534–37, 538, 541ff., 562–71, 577–83, 584, 588–89, 591–92, 600, 605–12, 613, 614, 688: counterguerrilla operations, 578–79, 591, Indochina, 711,

occupation policy, 505, 511, 516–17, 526–27, 528, 534–36, 610, 613ff., 781, propaganda, 510, strategy, 524, 535ff., 622, surrender, 542, 568, 583, 637, 689, aftermath, 671, 781, tactics, 505, 522, 572, 574, 591–92, 596, 751
Java, 69, 529, 530, 531, 533, 760–61, 763, 764, 766; War, 530–31; West, 763; World War II, 506
Jefferson, Thomas, 1374
Jenkins, Brian, *xvi*, 1300
Jerusalem, 63, 65, 248
Jesup, Thomas, 159
Jewish Agency, 770, 771, 772, 774, 779, 780; goal, 777; immigration, 774–75; Irgun, 774
Jews, 75, 563, 768ff., 1297; American, 769; "colored," 771n; international, 769, 770; "national home," 768; Nazis, 420, 423, 448, 451, 863; oriental, 771n; state, antagonisms to, 770; survival, World War II, 775 *and* n See Anti-Semitism; Irgun *and* Palestine
Jihad (holy war), 152, 156
Joffe, Adolf, 339–40
Johnson, Lyndon B.: ambitions/goals, 1211; Baltimore speech, 1095–96, 1104, 1177, 1242, 1256, 1365; characteristics, 1177, 1375–76, 1381; critics, 1242–43 (*see* dissent *under* Vietnam); Diem, 980, 981; election, 1075, withdrawal, 1236, 1240; Great Society, 1161; Guam meeting, 1189; Honolulu Conference, 1130; Kennedy, J. F. comparison, 1045; *Memoirs*, 1224; "national pledge," 1248–49; press, 1254 (*see* Press); pressure on, 1234,

1240; Senator, 813; State of Union Message (1967), 1176 (1968), 1191, 1216; Vice-President, report on Southeast Asia, 974, 981, 983; Vietnam, 983, 1044, 1045–46, 1047–63, 1064–84, 1085–1109, 1110–34, 1135–48, 1149ff., 1160ff., 1176–1215, 1216–56, 1257: advisers, 1108, 1133, 1135, 1170, 1193, 1208, 1213, 1228, 1235, 1274 (*see under* name); aim, 1093, 1160; Bundy Congressional resolution, 1057, 1062–63; credibility, 1206, 1221, 1254ff.; dissent, 1204–5, 1222, 1228, 1233ff.; doves, 1229–30, 1234; errors, 1327; escalation, 1088, 1090, 1092, 1093, 1171, de-, 1208; failure, 1241ff., 1274; hawks, 1090, 1098, 1101, 1167, 1171, 1172, 1174, 1177, 1193, 1205, 1208, 1213, 1222, 1229, 1235, 1264, 1276 (*see under* name); ideological motivation, 1215; intelligence experts, 1050–52; Operation Plan 34A, 1050; policy, 1046, 1050, 1055, 1058, 1060, 1069, 1090, 1095, 1105–6, 1109, failure, 1092–93; strategy, 1109, 1112, 1127, 1133, 1166, 1205ff., 1230, 1235, 1274ff., "win" objective, 1203, 1263; "trilemma," 1094; war, 1092; "Wise Men," 1235
Johnson, U. Alexis, 1060, 1085ff., 1130
Johore Empire, 576
Joint Development Group, 1251
Joliot-Curie, Dr., 413
Jomini, Baron de, 148–51, 170; *A Treatise on the Art of War,* 148–51
Jones, Gwyn, 53n, 55

Jonnart, Gov.-Gen., 223–24, 225, 227
Jordan, 894
Jorden, William, 1057; Report, 1057, 1076
Jouhaud, Edmond, 929
Judd, Walter, 799, 827
Jungle warfare, 572ff., 591, 592, 593, 604
See Slim, William
Junot, Gen., 125
Junta of Unity, 967
Justinian, 43, 44, 46–47; Empire, *map,* 46; Long Wall, 46

Kabylie, 907
Kachins, 607–9
Kahin, George M., 760, 848, 854; *Nationalism and Revolution in Indonesia,* 529
Kahin and Lewis, 693, 694, 821
Kahn, Herman, 1141
Kalb, Marvin: *Roots of Involvement,* 1224
Kamikaze tactics, 1191
Kaminski band, 456
Kangleon, Ruperto, 514 *and* n –16, 517
Kant, Immanuel, 148, 285
Karamanlis, Premier, 894
Karen tribesmen, 610–11
Katz, Samuel, 774, 777
Katzenbach, Nicholas, 1229
Keitel, Gen., 450
Kellen, Konrad, 1201
Kelly, Colin, 1269
Kennan, George, *xvi,* 718, 800, 802, 1266; Indochina warning, 718; Johnson, 1242; Marshall advice, 1383; *Memoirs,* 690; Soviet-China policy, warning on, 633–34; "strategic key areas," 800; on Vietnam, 1166, 1167–68, 1233–34; X article (*Foreign Affairs*), 691

Kennedy, Edward, 1306; on Vietnam, 1359
Kennedy, John F., 827, 1263, 1273; ambitions vs. policy, 1016, 1017, 1144, 1211; assassination, 1014; characteristics, 990, 1017, 1381; De Gaulle advice, 989, 1042, 1096; Diem, 983, 990; friends, 987; Indochina, position, 721, 722; President, 860; Senator, 971–72; State of the Union address (1961), 1017; Vietnam, 978–91, 998, 1002, 1004, 1009–15, 1036ff., 1092–93: advisers, 982, 987, 988, 990, 1018–20, 1022, 1042–43, 1168–69; CIA, 990; experts, 988; failure, 1015–28, 1029, 1241, 1327; Green Berets, 1022–23; policy, 1043–44; strategy, 1022–25, 1034, 1112, 1274
Kennedy, Robert: Attorney General, 981; Johnson, 1235; Vietnam, 983
Kent State, 1337
Kenya, xiii, 846, 861ff., 881, 1007, map, 864; Asians, 881; black political movement (see KCA); communism, 862n–63n; Emergency, 871, 875, 876; England, 866ff., 871–72, 908; insurgency (see Mau Mau rebellion); KCA, 870, 871, 873–74, 879; KPR (Police), 878; Republic, 886
Kenyatta, Jomo, 862, 871, 879; arrest, 876, 877, 879; background, Facing Mount Kenya, 865, 871; Mau Mau, 875; President, 886; Soviet Union, 862n–63n; techniques, 862n–63n
Képi bleu, 924
Kerensky, Alexander, 297, 298–99, 303

Khanh, Nguyen, 1048, 1052–54, 1055, 1056, 1065, 1068, 1070; dictatorship, 1082–84; reforms, 1052–53, 1060
Khartoum, 200–1, 225n, 808
Khe Sanh, 1281–83
Khiem, Tran Thien, 1316
Khoi, Ngo Dinh, 826
Khrushchev, Nikita, 444, 991, 1064, 1273
Khwarazm Empire, 69
Kibbutzim (co-operative settlements), 774
Kidnaping, 966, 967n, 1031
Kierkegaard, Søren, 648
KCA (Kikuyu Central Association), 870, 871, 873–74, 879; oath, 873–74
Kikuyu tribe, 863 and n –76, 877–86; Home Guard, 878, 881, 883; oath, 873–74, 874n–75n, 879; Reserve, 878, 880; rites, 870
Kilimanjaro, Mount, 250, 252, 257
Kimathi, Dedan, 883, 886
Kimche, Jon, 778
King, D. W., xvi
King, Ernest, 620
King Philip's War, 93
King's Mountain, 111, 112, 113
Kipande, 870
Kipling, Rudyard, 194
Kirkpatrick, F. A., 231
Kissinger, Henry, 1222, 1255, 1327; background, 1297; disengagement plan, 1298–1300; Johnson aide, 1214; Le Duc Tho, 1365; Nixon aide, 1332; Peking mission, 1362; writings, 1298, 1345, 1348
Kitchener, Horatio, 199, 211, 214, 215, 366, 1007; Lawrence, 258; tactics, 214–15

Kitson, Frank, *xvi*, 884–85, 886, 1384; *Gangs and Counter-gangs*, 885

Kittikachorn, Thanom, 1342, 1362

Kléber, Gen., 121, 123

Knightly warfare: chivalric concept, 82; cost, 57; decline, 82; fact vs. fiction, 58–59; tactic, 82

Knights, 57, 64, 83; mounted, 57, 58, 67

Knox, Philander, 240, 936

Kochan, Lionel, 292: *Russia in Revolution*, 289–90

Koestler, Arthur, *xvi*, 776; *Promise and Fulfillment—Palestine, 1917–1949*, 769

Komer, Robert, 1130, 1188, 1190, 1199–1200, 1215

Korea, 69, 673, 1342; China, 321–22; communism, 557; Japan, 332; partition, 824; Vietnam, 1126

See South Korea

Korean War, *xvi*, 648, 714, 730, 796, 803, 806, 811, 844, 942, 1147; air power, lessons, 1262; cease-fire (July 1953), 797; China, 711, 713, 717; "Katusas," 1152; lessons, 817, 958, 1262; outbreak, 696; political settlement, 807; United States, 719–20, 726, 844, 1020–21, command, 816–17, lessons, 817

Kornilov, Gen., 299

Kosta Nadj, 483–84

Koster, Samuel, 1358

Kosygin, Alexei N., 1272

Kriegel, Richard, 1131

Krim, Belkacem, 907, 926

Kropotkin, Peter, 289

Kruger, President, 210, 212, 213, 214

Krulak, Victor H., 1002, 1038, 1042, 1286, 1388

Kuala Lumpur, 579

Kublai Khan, 69, 70, 71, 529

Kun, Béla, 316

Kuriles, 629

Kutuzov, Gen., 142–43, 144

Ky, Nguyen Cao, 1129–30, 1161, 1171, 1354, 1356; appearance, 1083; Johnson, 1130, 1160; Revolutionary Development Program, 1130, 1160, 1163; -Thieu dictatorship (*see* Thieu-Ky government); vice-president, 1189, 1233

See Thieu

Lacedaemonians, 5

Lacoste, Robert, 911, 917

Lacouture, Jean, 714, 848, 1018, 1097

Ladas, Justice, 741

Laffan, R. G. D., 57n

Laird, Melvin, 1311, 1348, 1350, 1352, 1363ff.

Lai Teck, 579, 782

Lakewood, N.J., 827

Lancaster, Donald, 679, 1018

"Land for the landless," 757, 951, 974

Landon, Gen., 90

Laniel, Premier, 795, 807, 810n

Lanitis, Mr., 888

Lansdale, Edward, 828, 829, 830, 977, 978, 1016, 1242; Diem, 979–80; Report, 978, 979, 1019; Vietnam analysis, 1074–75

Lao Dong, 713

Laos, 334, 541, 542, 544, 550, 568, 689, 795, 1141, 1231, 1349, 1362; "associated state," 693; Giap, 804, 805–6; Kennedy, J. F., 989; NLF, 995; Pathet Lao, 728, 732; U.S., 696, 979 *and* n, 980, 1057, 1316, 1322–23, 1327, 1329ff., 1350, 1362–63,

CIA, 1023, invasion, 1353ff.; Viet Minh, 728–29, 732

Lartéguy, Jean: *The Centurions*, 919

Lateran councils, 57

Lathbury, Gerald, 886

Latin America, 174, 942; "way" to revolution, 970–71

Latrocinium, 13

Latvia, 302

Lavelle, John, 1364

Law, 97, 867; martial, 395; *okhrana*, 288; rule by, 281; tribal, 866; Vichy, 563

Lawrence, T. E., 257–71, 305, 386, 388, 410, 596, 618, 901, 916; accomplishment, 265–71; analysis, 263–65; background, 257–58; goal, 271; on guerrilla warfare, 1027; illness, 262; *Revolt in the Desert*, 259; *Seven Pillars of Wisdom*, 259, 270–71; theories, 599; tragedy, 270

Lazzaroni, 124, 125

Leaders, *xiv*, 343, 604, 612, 789, 907; African, 871 (*see* Kenyatta); disobedience and, 227; by example, 1242; guerrilla, 205 (*see under* country); mass, 992; natural, 182, 214, 259, 467, 757; Zionist, 770

See under country *and* Leadership

Leadership, 28, 199, 249, 269, 506, 794, 838; American, 1373ff.; Arab, 258; Byzantine, 51; Castro on, 946; emperor-generals, 52; failures in, 312–13; flexibility, 306; formula, 605; indictment, 1370; inspired, 772; international, 672; political-military, 193; post World War I, 317; responsibility, 1373–75

See also Charisma

League of Nations, 405, 769

League of Oppressed Peoples of Asia, 557

Leakey, L. S. B., 863n, 865, 866, 867, 874

l'Échelle, Gen., 121

Lechfeld, battle of, 57

Leclerc, Gen., 675 *and* n, 679, 682, 685n, 693

Lederer, William: *Our Own Worst Enemy*, 858; *The Ugly American*, 958

Le Duan, 1312, 1337

Le Duc Tho, 1365

Lee, "Light Horse Harry," 113, 116

LeMay, Curtis, 1270

Lemnitzer, Lyman, 986

Lenin, V. I., 289, 290, 291, 293, 298–300, 301–16 passim, 339, 345, 522, 669, 672, 705, 900, 917, 949, 956n; aim, 315; brother, 292; characteristics, 298, 302, 306, 311; guerrilla warfare, *xii;* heritage, 1–317; Ho Chi Minh, 557; leadership, 306; legacy, 249; Orders of, 461–62; program, 298, 315ff.; *quote,* 1; on revolution, 975; soviets, 295; success, 308, 315; tactics, 306ff.; teachings, 907

See Comintern

Lenin School, 863n

Lentaigne, W. D. A., 607

Leopold, Richard: *Growth of American Foreign Policy*, 629

Leo VI, 50–51; *Tactics*, 47, 48

Leo the Wise, 63

Lermontov, Mikhail, 285

Leslie, Maj. Gen., 113

Leslie's Weekly, 191

Letourneau, Jean, 712, 725, 726–27, 729, 730, 732, 803

Lettow-Vorbeck, Paul von, 249–56, 257, 689; march, *map,* 254

Levée en masse, 145, 147

Lewis, John, 848, 854

Leyte, 514, 515
Liberation, wars of, 783
Libya, 26
Li Ch'üan, 35
Lidice, 421
Life magazine, 644
Lilienthal, David, 1215, 1252–53
Li Li-san, 349
Lillington, Alexander, 101
Lincoln, Abraham, 164
Lindbergh, Charles, 388
Linggadjati negotiations, 763
Lin Piao, 366, 638–39, 642, 647,
    1248, 1277; "Seventh Offen-
    sive," 646–47
Lippmann, Walter, 695, 716–17,
    1205
Literature, 401–2, 419; China, 344;
    military, 47, 48–49, 50, 200n,
    202, 203; protest, 181–82; rev-
    olutionary, 286, 287; Russian,
    285, 286
Lithuania, 82, 302, 312
Litvak, Anatole: *Night of the Gen-
    erals,* 420
Liu Po-ch'eng, Gen., 647, 648
Livy, 19
Llewellyn (Prince of Wales), 72,
    74–76; *map,* 73
Lloyd George, David, 227, 274, 276,
    278, 888; on Balfour Declara-
    tion, 769
Loan, Nguyen Ngoc, 1162
Lockhart, Bruce, 428
Lockhart, William, 200
Lodge, Henry Cabot, 171, 186n,
    936, 1048, 1235; ambassador,
    1170; carrot-and-stick plan,
    1056, 1059; Nixon, 1297; Paris
    Peace Talks, 1316; Vietnam,
    979n, 1013, 1014, 1038, 1040,
    1042, 1048ff., 1060, 1129
Logistics, 148, 574, 575, 713, 810;
    "tails," 160
Lohbeck, Don, 625

Lombards, 48
London: Conference (on Cyprus),
    893, 900; Library, *xvi;* School
    of Economics, 871; Tower, 76
London, Jack, 283
Long, Nguyen Phan, 716
Longbow, 67, 79
Long March, 351–52, 355, 359
Longo, Luigi, 424
Lon Nol, Premier, 1331, 1336, 1340,
    1342, 1358, 1362
Loudoun, Lord, 97
Louis XIII, King of France, 86
Louis XIV, King of France, 85, 86,
    539
Louis XV, King of France, 1374
Louis, King of Holland, 125
Louis Philippe, King of France, 152,
    155
Louis the Pious, 55
Loyalty, to person, 40
Luce, Henry, 644
Lucullus, Lucius, 23 *and* n, 28
Lucullus, M., 13
Ludendorff, Gen., 912, 1276, 1388–
    89
Lunacharsky, Anatoli, 299
Lusitanians, 16, 22, 26
Luyên, Ngo Dinh, 834
Luzon, 513, 514, 521–22; USAFIP,
    524
Lyautey, Hubert, 218, 221–28 pas-
    sim, 370, 378, 380–81, 383,
    433, 680, 685, 687, 1007, 1025;
    Indochina, 554; Morocco,
    1276, 1322; tactics, 701; tech-
    niques, 224–28, 685

MAAG, 829, 844, 845–47, 859, 860,
    979, 1002
MacArthur, Arthur: Philippines
    (1899), 189, 192–93
MacArthur, Douglas, 950 *and* n;
    on Allies' use of Japanese sol-
    diers, 675n; Bullitt, 645; Korea,

711, 816, strategy, 798, 1021; Philippines, 747; Truman, 1210; World War II, 513, 515, 525, Japanese surrender, 636, "Lay Low Order," 524, 525

McCarthy, Eugene, 1234, 1249–50; *Limits of Power,* 1206

McCarthy, Joseph, 648, 1043, 1378, 1380; Era, 942

McCone, John, 1049, 1094

McCuen, John, 685, 724–25

McDonald, Ian, 1335

Macedonia, 3, 4, 6, 8, 11, 39, 466, 736, 743

Maceo, Antonio, 173

Maceo, José, 173, 174, 176, 178

McGiffert, David, 1228

McGovern, George, 1329, 1352, 1359

Machado, Gerardo, 938–39; abdication, 1039

Machiavelli, Niccolò, *xiii,* 84–85

Mack, Gen., 124

MacKenzie, A. M., 79

McKinley, William, 172, 178–79, 184, 186, 935, 936 *and* n; on Cuba, 183; Philippines, 186–87, 192–93

Maclean, Bill, 497, 498–99, 500

Maclean, Fitzroy, 474–77, 482, 484, 485

Maclear, Michael, 1322, 1351

McLeod, Scott, 1380

Macmillan, Harold, 893, 898, 899

MacMurrogh, Dermot, 68

McNamara, Robert, 979; attempted assassination, 1269; characteristics, 1020, 1053; replacement, 1229; Vietnam, 982, 983, 987, 1002, 1003, 1020, 1038, 1050, 1062, 1086–87, 1100ff.: de-escalation, 1208, new policy paper, 1211–14, pessimism, 1169–73, 1193ff., recommendations, 1116n, Report (1), 1048–

49, (2), 1053–55, *volte-face,* 1042

McNaughton, John, 1065, 1070, 1076–77, 1086, 1089, 1209–11

Macready, Nevil, 276, 279

Madagascar, 158, 200, 222–23

Madison, James, 1376

Madura, 763, 764

Maghreb, 903, 916

Maginot Line, 923

Magoon, Charles, 937

Magsaysay, Ramon, 757–58, 978

Magyars, *xii,* 53, 56–57; invasion, *map,* 54

Mahan, Alfred T., *xiii,* 171, 183, 674, 936; *Influence of Sea Power upon History,* 171 *and* n

Maharbal, Gen., 41

Maillebois, Marquis de, 90

Maine, USS, 179

Majdalaney, Fred: *State of Emergency,* 879

Maji-Maji rebellion, 224 *and* n

Makarios III, Archbishop, 889, 891, 892, 894, 898, 899; deportation, 894, 900; release, 898

Makins, Roger, 815

Makron Teichos (Long Wall), 46

Malaya, 69, 574–76, 649, 673, 717, 788, 792, 799, 846, 1007, *maps,* 573, 791; Briggs Plan, 788; Chinese, 782, 783; communism (MCP), 557, 576–77, 673, 695, 782–83, 785, 786, 793, front (AEBUS), 577, 579, *kempetai,* 579, organization, 760–64; England, 781, 784–94, 841, 881, policy, 790; government, 781, 784–85; guerrillas (*see* Ch'en P'ing); history, 576–77; independence, 784n, 790; insurgency, 795, 844, 885, 1098, 1207, 1325; Min Yuen, 783, 790, 792; pacification, 793; postwar, 781–94; terrorists,

878; Thailand border, 794; World War II, 408, 413, 504, 572, 576–83, 584, 603, 614, Anti-Japanese Union, 783, SOE, 575, 577–78, 579, 583

Malayan Races Liberation Army (MRLA), 786, 790

Malraux, André, 312; *Days of Hope*, 402; *Man's Estate*, 312–13

Manchuria, 629, 643, 644, 968; Chiang-Mao conflict, 636–42 passim, 646–47; China, 322; Japan, 366, 614; Russia, 332; Soviet Union, 638–39, 640, 673

Mandalay, 586; fall of, 610

Mandates, 769

Mangu Khan, 69

Manila Conference, 1133, 1161, 1174

Manila Pact, 843
   See SEATO

"Manifest destiny" thesis, 936

Mankind, unity of, 8

Manning, Bob, 1040

Manpower, 85, 156, 160, 163, 211

Mansfield, Mike, 1075, 1141, 1316, 1336; Diem, 830; Kennedy, J. F., 1043; Vietnam, 827, 828, 1109

Manzikert, battle of, 51

Mao Tse-tung, 341ff., 344–54, 355–68, 522, 556, 558, 585, 907, 952, 972, 991, 1027, 1029, 1073, 1273, 1277, 1385; aim, 345; army, 348, 359–60, 364, 636, 638–39, 647–49; background, 344–45; Changsha defeat, 349; communism, 345, 632; guerrillas, *xiii*, 356–64, 366, 367, 749, 767; Ho Chi Minh, 677, 697, 698, 704; Japan, 353; Long March, 351–52, 355, 359; Manchuria, 968; methodology, 596, 912–13, 927; military organization, 703;

Northwest base, 559 (*see* Yenan); philosophy, 348, 350; President, 350; Red Army, 350, 352; on revolution, 319, 346; "people's war" theory, 355ff.; "Sinicization," 669; Stalin, 353, 636; strategy, 347–49, 352, 357–58; "identification," 365; teachings, 743, 956, 997; theory of protracted warfare, 697–98, Vietnamese version, 698; three-step plan, 783; "three unities" concept, 358–61; timetable, 353; war, theories on, 319, 363, 697; wife, 351; World War II, 409, 413: attitude toward, 613–14, 621–23, coalition problem, 623, 628, 631, Dixie Mission, 625–26, guerrillas, 620, 622, Hurley, 628, strategy, 614, 619–20, 621, strength, 626, 631, Yenan, 559, 620, 621, 623, 628, 631, 641; writings, 356ff., *Basic Tactics*, 356, *Problems of Strategy in Guerrilla War Against Japan*, 956n

Marabout (holy man), 152

Maracanda (ancient Samarkand), 7

Marceau, Gen., 123

Marcellus, Claudius, 23

Marchand, Gen., 132

Marching order, 63–64

Marching square, early version, 63

Marcius, Gen., 20

Marco Polo, 70, 71

Marcuse, Herbert, 1372

María Luisa, Queen of Spain, 125

Marion, Francis "Swamp Fox," 108, 109, 110n, 112, 113, 116

Marius, 25

Markos Vaphiadis, 736–44; defeat, cause, 743; tactics, 737

Marlborough, Duke of, 86, 87 *and* n

Marshall, Bruce: *The White Rabbit*, 431

Marshall, George C., 1377; Chiang Kai-shek, 640–41, 643; China mission, 639–41, 643, 644, 646; Indochina, 690; Kennan, 1383; Secretary of State, 641; Stilwell, 627

Marshall, S. L. A., 1116, 1117–19, 1149–50; *Battles in the Monsoon*, 1116

Marshall Plan, 691, 766

Martí, José, 174, 941, 946, 956n, *map*, 175

Martinet, Jean, 85

Martínez de Campos, Arsenio, 174, 176

Martyrdom, 976

Marx, Karl, 236, 283, 286, 291, 328, 345, 669, 672, 949, 956n; *Das Kapital*, 286

Marxism, 239, 288, 862, 946

Marxism-Leninism, 976; refutation of, 349; urban bias, 743

Marxist-Leninist-Maoist tradition, 580

Marxists, 315, 345

Maryland, 113

Masaryk, T. G., 295

Masferrer, Rolando, 955

Maspétiol report (on Algerian Moslems), 907

Massacres, 23, 471, 761

Massegetae ("Asiatic Scythians"), 6, 7

Masséna, Gov., 124, 130

Massive retaliation doctrine, 808

Massu, Jacques, 917–19, 929

Masters, John, 200n

Mathu, Eliud, 873

Matthews, Herbert, 964; Castro interview, 953–55; *Cuban Story*, 953

Mau Mau, *xiii;* rebellion, 860, 862, 871–76, 877–86: aspects, 863n, communism, 863n, England, 875, 877–78, 887, grievances, 867, 870, 873, historical background, 863ff., ideology, 863n, leadership, 879, 883, 886 (*see* Kenyatta), mistakes, 881, oath, 873–74, 874n–75n, 880, strength, 874, tally, 886, terrorism, 877–81

Maurice, Emp., 47–48, 50, 51, 203; *Artis Militaris*, 47; *Treatise*, 62

Maurice of Nassau, 86

Maximilian, Archduke, 234, 235

Maximus, Quintus Fabius, *xi*

Mazour, A. G., 287

Mazzini, 554, 774n

Mecca, 157, 259

Mecklin, John, 999, 1002, 1033, 1034, 1035–36, 1038, 1042; *Mission in Torment*, 1003

Medicine men, 224n

Medieval wars, 59

Medina, 265

Mediterranean, 29

Meijerink, J., 763

Meinertzhagen, Richard, 253–55, 868–69

Mekong Delta. *See* Vietnam

Melikov, Gen., 288

Mende, Tibor, 351, 352

Mendenhall, J. S., 1042

Menderes, Premier, 899, 900

Mendès-France, Pierre, 712, 818, 903; Algeria, 909; Dulles, 843

Mendieta, Carlos, 940

Menocal government, 937

Mercenaries, 48, 57, 67, 78, 110, 331; German, 90; Grand Companies (*routiers*), 81; Indian (North America), 93; Swiss, 94; Zouave, 153

Merino, Gerónimo (*El Cura*), 131

Merrill, Frank: Marauders, 607, 608

Merritt, Wesley, 184–85, 186

Merseburg, battle of, 57

Mesopotamia, 258, 267, 385, 386, 590; England, 388, 498
See Iraq

Messali Hadj, 905, 906, 908, 916

Messervy, Frank: Gazelle Force, 590

Metaxas, Gen., 488 *and* n

Metellus, Gen., 26

Mexican Revolution, *xiii*, 242ff., 851, 1047; background, 229, 230–31, 239; cost, 246; goals, 243, 244

Mexico, 229ff., 398, 938, 948, 1021, *map*, 230; Castro, 948; Cuban exiles, 950; *encomienda* (settlement system), 232; father of, 232; guerrilla leaders, 237, 242; politics, 234, 235; Porfiriate, 235, 236, 237; rebellions, 231ff., 236, 237; recognition, 242; Revolution (*see* Mexican Revolution); Spain, 231, Civil War, 402; U.S., 234; War of the Reforms, 234

Miami Pact, 963

Michigan State University, 832, 846, 859, 1324n

Middle Ages, 53, 67, 82, 280

Middle East, *xiv*, 57, 257, 385, 390, 533, 1251; British military headquarters, 887, 891; communism, 316; feudal system transplant, 65; nationalism, 904; oil, 769, 800; World War I, 257–71, *map*, 266; World War II, 412, 507, 591, 771

Midway: Vietnam talks, 1310–11

Migrations, East, 69

Mihailović, Draža, 469–74, 480, 484; collaboration, 473

Miles, M. E., 617, 618–21; *A Different Kind of War*, 618; Stilwell, 617, 618, 620

Militarism: philosophy of, 1377; Prussian, 170

Military academies: Athens, 890; Dalat, 719; Pao-Ting, 340; St. Cyr, 218; Sandhurst, 498; West Point, 164, 520, 521, 594, 628, 982, 988, 1024, 1113, 1238; Whampoa, 340, 557–58

Military advisers, 269n
See under name of leaders *or* Presidents

Military analysts, 147, 148, 798, 1171, 1221

MACV (Military Assistance Command Vietnam), 991

Military coup, 233
See also Coup d'état

Military doctrine, conventional Western, 844

Military principles: concentration of force, 268

Military stalemate, 767

Military thinking, 420; orthodox, 267

Military writings, *xiii*, 62, 71, 72, 87, 93, 140, 141, 143, 144, 147–52, 170, 219, 222, 249, 259, 262, 385, 391, 400, 413, 427, 514, 521, 577, 594, 601, 615, 734, 772, 810, 848, 912, 919 *and* n, 935, 1018, 1025–27; theorists, 147

Mill, John Stuart, 285

Millán Astray, José, 371

Millar, George: *Horned Pigeon*, 430–31

Miller, John, 1153, 1155

Mills, C. Wright, 943, 951

Milner, Arthur, 215

Mindanao, 514, 517–18

Mindon Min, 207

Minh, Duong Van, 1046–48

Mirabeau, Marquis de, 11

Missionaries, 542–43, 867, 869, 871; in China, 333; as terror weapon, 281

Mitchell, Billy, 1258

Mitchell, Philip, 871–72

Moesia, 36

Mogul Empire, 118

Mohammed II, 467

Mohammed V., Sultan, 904

Mohammedans: Moros, 519; priest (mullah), 156

Mohr, Charles, 1040

Moldavia, 3n

Mollet, Guy, 911, 914, 917

Molotov, 633; Yalta, 629

Mommsen, Theodor, 21, 22n, 23n, 25, 27

Monasteries, 71; Monte Cassino, 56; raids on, 54

Mongols, *xii*, 529, *map* (invasions), 70; armies, 71; Central Europe, 57; invasion of Europe, 69–71; strategy, 70

Monje, Mario, 975

Monks: Buddhist, 208; English, 78

Monroe Doctrine, 234; codicil (*see* Platt Amendment)

Monsoon, 121, 592

Montagnard tribes, 840

Moore, James, 101

Moore, John, 127 *and* n

Moore, Julia A., *xiv*

Moors, 371, 373

Morale, 509, 618, 711, 712, 1259; national, 601

Moravia, 71, 89

Mordant, Gen., 566

Morelos, José, 233

Morgan, Daniel, 113, 114

Morgan, John, 162, 163, 164–65, 166

Morice Line, 923

Morison, S. E., 172, 619

Morocco, 155, 174, 225, 496, 903–4, 905, 911, 920, 923, *map*, 395; Berber tribes, 225; *colons*, 228; FLN, 926; French, 223, 225–26, 228, 380–84; independence, 904, 914; nationalism, 693; Spain, 369ff., 383

Morris, J. E., 74n

Morse, Wayne, 1062

Mosby, John, 162–63, 166

Moscow: Napoleon, 143–44

Moses, 871

Moslems, 58, 66; China, 332; generals, 50; rulers, 65
  See Algeria

Mosley, Leonard, 252; *Duel for Kilimanjaro*, 249

Mountbatten, Louis, 536, 565, 603, 610, 612, 628, 675n; South-East Asia Command, 760; Wingate, 602, 605–6

Moyers, Bill, 1256

Moyne, Lord, 774

Mufti of Jerusalem, 769

Mukden, siege of, 647

Munro, D. C., 59 *and* n

Murat, Gen., 125, 126

Mus, Paul, 566

Musso, 765

Mussolini, Benito, 405, 408, 496, 938; Greece, 488

Mutiny, 227

Mutual Security Pact (hemispheric), 941

Myers, Gen., 995

Myers, E. C., 490, 491, 493, 494

Myers, Samuel, 859

My Lai, 1289, 1322, 1343, 1358, 1359, 1360

Myrdal, Gunnar, 799, 802

Mysore wars, 120

Mystique, oriental, 35–36

Nader, Ralph, 1372

Naegelen, Marcel-Edmond, 906

Nagasaki, 440, 1259, 1260

Nanking, treaty of (1842), 326n

Napier, "Fagin," 199

Napoleon, *xii*, 91, 123ff., 130, 131, 141, 159, 201, 264, 321, 401, 404, 897; Army, 139ff., 139n.; *auditeurs*, 1383; Balkans, 467; characteristics, 124–25, 137, 139; on command, 1385; "continental system," 125; guerrillas, 135ff., 146; health, 139; hero, 137; Iberia, 125ff. (*see also* Spain); marriage, 139; peasants, 141; political errors, 125; Prussia, 145; Russia, 138–45, *map*, 140; Spain, 133; strategy, 125, 143; "total wars," 146

Napoleon III, Emp., 234

Napoleonic wars, 170, 232, 529, 772

Narses, Gen., 44, 46

Nasser, Gamal, 911

Nasution, Abdul Haris, 766

Nationalism (ists), 91, 149–50, 173, 210, 219, 339, 373, 443, 480, 514, 520, 531, 532, 693, 759, 826, 1246; Arab, 258, 261; Buddhism, 586; communism, 694, 698; De Gaulle on, 989; growth/spread, 904–5; Iberia, 128; revolutionary, 554; Southeast Asia, causes, 586; strength, 908

See also under country

NLF (National Liberation Front), 848, 849, 855, 994–97, 1000, 1003ff., 1030ff., 1061, 1072ff., 1098ff., 1312–13; congress (1st), 996; leaders, 995; objective, 996; origin, 854–55; pacification, 1130; Special War, 1072; "The Struggle Movement," 997, 1001

National Student Association, 1099

Nation-in-arms concept, 48, 50, 51

Natives: *askaris*, 249, 250; mass psychology, 224n

Naulin, Gen., 383

Naval guerrillas, 13

Naval power, 171

Navarre, Henri-Eugène, 795–97, 803, 1190; errors, 807; Opération Atlante, 806; "Plan," 803, 804, 812; tactics, 796, 797, 804–5, 806–8, 809–10, 816, 818

Nazis, 411, 418, 420, 448, 454, 456, 465, 478; characteristics, 450; *Einsatzgruppe*, 449, 451; Gestapo, 435, 478, 610, 918; Japanese, 525; Jews, 420, 422, 448, 451, 863; SS, 448

Neave, Airey, *xvi*

Negotiation, 763; from strength, 821

Negroes, 164

Nehru, 814

Nelson, Adm., 124, 125

Nelson, Donald, 624

Neo-Destour, 904

Nero, Claudius, 17

Nes, David, 1049

Netherlands.

   See Holland

Neutrality, 250, 889; "diplomatic," 959

Neutralization, 1048

New England, 93, 98

New Guinea, 503, 531; World War II, 408, 503, 506, 512

New Jersey, USS, 1315

New York *Times*, 188

New World, 92

New Zealand, 159, 1342; SEATO, 824; United States, 624, 815; Vietnam, 1126, 1178, 1213; World War II, 488, 507

Nhu, Mme., 834, 994, 1010, 1012, 1013, 1039

Nhu, Ngo Dinh, 834, 835, 837, 841, 847, 855, 991, 994, 1007, 1008–9, 1012, 1013, 1029;

execution, 1014; nationalism, 1024

Nicaragua, 938, 1025, *map,* 395; United States, 396–400, 411, 506, 1259

Nicholas I, Czar, 156, 284, 285, 287; assassination, 288

Nicholas II, Czar, 289, 293, 296, 310; abdication, 297

Niemen River, 140

Nihilism, 285, 286, 288

Nikephoros Phokas, Emp., 50, 51; *On Shadowing Warfare,* 50

Nimitz, Chester, 621n

Nitze, Paul, 1228, 1229, 1234

Nixon, Richard M., 1237, 1296ff., 1328ff., 1350ff., 1362, 1381; accountability, 1374; crisis of confidence, 1353; peace plan, 1365–66; President, 1240; Vice-President, 812, 815, 949; Vietnam: dissent, 1306ff., 1335ff., 1343ff., doves, 1300, 1313ff., errors, 1327, Hanoi talks, 1309, hawks, 1300, 1313ff., 1331, policy, 1306ff., 1316–19, 1328ff., 1338, 1345, 1350ff. (*see* Cambodia), problem, inherited, 1295; promise, 1296, strategy, 1263, 1297ff., 1313, 1350, Washington Special Action Group, 1332

Nixon-Kissinger psyche, 1366

Njama, Karari, 879, 882

Nolting, Frederick E., 980, 990, 993, 1002, 1010, 1016, 1028, 1035, 1037, 1038, 1039

Nomads, 7

Non-appeasement, 760

Non-combatants: in jungle warfare, 592

Normandy, 56, 475

Normans, *xi,* 68–69

Norstad, Lauris, 1205

North Africa, 44; France, 151ff., 903; nationalism, 904; Vikings, 55; World War II, 408, 489 *See also under* name of country

North America, 92ff.

North Carolina, 100, 101, 102, 104, 105; Cornwallis, 110, 112, 115

North Korea: *Pueblo,* 1217

North Vietnam, 822, 827, 838, 848, 849, 1071ff., 1085ff., 1239, 1263, 1272, 1312, 1322, 1337ff., 1350ff., *maps,* 711, 796; bombing, 1135, 1214, halt, 1236, 1239–40 (*see* Operation Rolling Thunder); China (Communist), 1143; communism, 713; Da Nang, 1092, 1095, 1100, 1103; DRV, 1062–63 (*see* DRV); foreign aid, 1322, 1368; hawks, 1059, 1097, doves, 1273, 1312; insurgency phases, 1085; invading, 1231; leadership, 838; manpower, 1141; morale, 1141; NLF (*see* NLF); peace negotiations (*see* Paris peace talks); power struggle, 1337; PRP (*see* PRP); reunification, goal, 855; Salisbury reports, 1268–72; in South, 1097, 1099ff.; Soviet Union, 1142–43 (*see also* foreign aid); Tonkin Gulf, 1062–63; United States, 1062, 1064, 1090, 1135, 1351 *See* Ho Chi Minh; South Vietnam *and* Vietnam

Norway, 53, 281n; World War II, 407, 410, 414–15, 417, resistance, 419, 425

Nuclear deterrent, 1059

Nuclear stalemate, paradox, 1260

Nuclear warfare, 1069

Nuechterlein, Donald E., 539, 540, 541

Numantians, 16
Nuremberg trials, 423, 447, 450, 462

"Oath of non-injury," 823 *and* n
Oaths, 23: *Blutbrüderschaft*, 875n;
   KCA, 873–74, 874n–875n;
   muma, 873; "of non-injury,"
   823 *and* n; tribal, 865
O'Ballance, Edgar, 738, 742, 916,
   930; *The Greek Civil War*, 734
Occupation, 18, 103ff., 110, 126,
   408; limited, 376
O'Daniel, J. W. (Iron Mike), 803,
   810, 829, 843, 846
O'Donnell, Kenneth, 1043
OSS (Office of Strategic Services).
   See under United States, World
   War II
Ogdai Khan, 69, 71
O'Hara, Charles, 107
Oil, 769; Sahara fields, 917; super
   tankers, 800
Okamura, Gen., 367, 622
Okinawa, 844, 1023
Oman, C. W. C., 38n, 39n, 51n, 56,
   58–59, 62, 69, 132
O'Neil, Robert: *Vietnam Task*, 1126
Operation Cedar Falls, 1179
Operation Crazy Horse, 1117–19,
   1149
Operation Rolling Thunder, 1135,
   1171, 1177–78, 1213–14, 1235,
   1239–40, 1364; failure, 1192–
   93
Operation Toan Thang (complete
   victory), 1332–33
Opinion, wars of, 149
Opium, 609, 676; trade, 325 *and* n,
   547, 551; War, 325
Oporto, 131; capture of, 128
Oppression, thought and, 285
OAS (Organization of American
   States), 965
OAS (*Organisation de l'Armée Se-
   crète*), 930

OS (*Organisation Secrète*), 907
Orient: achievements, 4; commer-
   cial rivals, 187; psychology,
   576; tactics against, 50
Orlando Furioso, 281
Osmeña, Sergio, 746
Ostrogoths, 39, 39n, 43
Otis, Elwell, 185, 186, 188–91, 192
Ottoman Empire, 384, 466–67, 887
Otto the Great, 57
Outer Mongolia, 629
Overseas Workers Association, 557
Owen, Dwight, 1163, 1164
Oxford University, 257, 414, 473
Oxus River, 6
Oxyartes, 8

Pacification, 159, 192, 375, 724,
   911, 1007; Burma, 208; campaigns, *xi–xii*, 72, 77, 199,
   1025; Dutch East Indies, 761,
   762; England, 105, 109–10,
   120; grassroots, 1129; Lyautey
   on, 223; Malaya, 793; pogroms,
   586; political task, 206; protection, 1007; qualitative approach, 685; Romans, 16ff., 25,
   26; tache-d'huile concept, 1052;
   totalitarian concept, 227; village
   resettlement program, 209
   See Lyautey; Vietnam *and under*
   country
Pact of the Sierra, 961
País, Frank, 949, 950, 956, 961–62
Pakistan: FLN, 926–27; SEATO,
   824
"Palace guard," 857
Paladea, Juan (El Médico), 128
Palestine, 386, 410, 497, 759, 900,
   map, 779; Anglo-American
   Committee of Inquiry, 775ff.;
   Arabs' rebellion (1936–39),
   770–72 (*see also under* Jews);
   background, 768ff.; England,
   388, 498–99, 596–97, 769,

775–80, 889, 892, mandate, 769; German reparations, 774; Haganah, 771; insurgency, 795; Irgun-Stern, 892; Jews (Yishuv), 770: vs. Arabs, 769–70, 771–72, 777, 780, British conflict, 775–80, resistance movement, 775, state antagonisms to, 770; partition, 770, 777; postwar, 672, 959; statehood, 771, 772–73, 774; UN: intervention, 780, partition, 780; World War I, 265

Palmerston, Lord, 326n, 1378
Palmier, Leslie: *Indonesia*, 531
Panama, Isthmus of, 171
Panama Canal, 800
Panmunjom, 719
Paoli, Pasquale, 90–92
Papagos, Alexander, 488, 742, 891, 892, 900
Papandreou, Prime Minister, 733, 734
"Paper tiger," 1065
Papua, New Guinea, 504, 512
Pares, Bernard, 284–85
Paret, Peter, xvi, 228, 912–13, 922, 924–25; *French Revolutionary Warfare from Indochina to Algeria—The Analysis of a Political and Military Doctrine*, 912
Paris: commune, 286; Danes, 55; invasion, 55, 56; Vietnamese expatriates, 557
Paris peace conference.
See Versailles *under* Treaties
Paris peace talks (on Vietnam), 1236, 1238, 1240, 1297ff., 1308ff., 1317, 1318–45, 1348, 1349, 1351, 1362ff.; Bruce, 1340, 1344, 1351
Parker, H. M. D., 18n
Parsons, Charles, 515
"Parthian" tactics, 7

Partisans, *xi;* auxiliary role, 148
See Guerrillas
Passive resistance, 891, 899
Paternalism, 138, 185
Pathet Lao, 728, 732
Patriotism, 92, 132, 135, 219, 296, 412, 497, 615; quixotic, 771n
Patronage, political, 1379
Patton, George C., 594; Mexico, 245
Paul, Elliott: *Life and Death of a Spanish Town*, 402
Pavelić, Ante, 465
Pazos, Felipe, 961
Peace: "petitioners," 33; probability of, 546; Tacitus on, 1368; world, postwar, 671ff.
Peace of Tipitapa, 397
"Peace petitioners," 33
Peach, Capt.: *Handbook of Tactics —Savage Warfare*, 202
Pearl Harbor, 367, 408, 541, 562, 1269
Pearse, Padhraic H., 272, 273
"Peasant revolution," 951, 970
See Che Guevara
Peasants, 135–36, 137, 147, 231, 1288; armed, 58, 147–48; China, 323; folklore, 147; Poland, 139; "preparation," 952; revolts, 121, 123; Russia, 139ff.; separatist movements, 141; uprisings, 82, 137–39
Pečanac, Kosta, 649
Peking, 69
See China (Communist)
Peloponnesian War, 221
Pentagon papers, xv, 990, 1075, 1361, 1375
Pentagon report, 1212–13, 1224
PRP (People's Revolutionary Party), 848, 849, 996ff., 1001, 1003ff., 1061, 1071ff., 1073, 1097–98
See NLF *and* North Vietnam
"People's war," *xiv*
Pérez, Barrera, 955, 957

Pérez, Faustino, 950
Perón, Juan, 948
Pershing, John, 245, 411
Persia, 3–5, 31, 32, 47, 48, 53, 69, *map,* 14; Bactria, 5; leaders, 5, 6; Mongols, 69; Scythians, 4; tactics, 48; World War II, 591 *See* Darius
Pétain, Marshal, 383, 408, 419; National Revolution, 563; Vichy France, 426, 427, 431, 432
Pétainism, 563
Peter, King of Yugoslavia, 465, 474, 484
Peter III, Emp. of Russia, 137
Peter the Great, 86
Pflaum, Irving, 969
Pham Van Dong, 558
Pharnuches, 7
Philip, King of France, 79, 80
Philippines, 69, 178, 181ff., 549n, 649, 691, 717, 793, 843, 935, 936, 978, 1007, 1021, *maps,* 195, 754; Army, 756, 757; communism, 673, 747–48, 757, 758, popularity basis, 748 (*see* Huks); constitution, 186; Greece, similarities, 737; independence, 746, 747, Declaration of, 183; insurgency (Huk), 672, 748ff., 755–58, 795, 844, 885; insurrection, 181ff., 187–96, 281n, 411, 1098; internal threat, 945; Katipunan (Patriots' League), 181, 182; Luzon, *map,* 754; Moros, 181, 757; postwar, 746–58, 787; Scouts, 193, 196; SEATO, 824; Soviet Union, 673; Spain, 181, 183, 185, 186; United States, *xv,* 180, 183–97 passim, 223, 400, 746–47, 751, 753, 756, 757, 813, 815, 935, commissions: (1), 185, (2), 193; Viet Minh, 706; Vietnam, 1213; Visayan

Republic, 183; World War II, 408, 413, 503, 513–27, 610: communism, 514, 520, Huks, 520–21, Japanese attitude, 526–27, religions, 519, resistance, 513ff., 521ff.
Phillips, Gen., 115, 117
Phillips, Ruby Hart: *Cuba–Island of Paradox,* 939
Phillips, Rufus, 1038
Philosophy (-ers), 148–49, 264, 285, 308, 648, 863, 919, 1325, 1372; "flat" concept of existence, 323; "gook," 1287; government, 540; Greco-Roman military doctrines, 34; *guerre révolutionnaire,* 228; imperialist, 281; "last-chance," 808; mandarin, 1047; of militarism, 1377, 1388; military: East-West difference, 51; Nihilism, 285, 286, 288; political, 10, 10n, 29, 40, 219, 235, 236, 912, 914, 989–90; poverty-pride, 186; of rebellion, 522; religious, 322–23; reprisal, 420; of revolution, 92; of terror, 288; *Untermensch,* 448, 450; utilitarian, 285; of war, 31, 34ff.; white man's burden, 547, 548
Phoenicians, 16, 19, 32, 905
Pibul Songgram, 541
Pickens, Andrew, 102, 109, 110
Picton, Thomas, 131
Pignon, Léon, 712
Pike, Douglas, 854–55, 994, 1002, 1004, 1006, 1007–8, 1138; *Viet Cong,* 849, 1207; Vietnam analysis, 1072–74, 1098
Pilsudski, Marshal, 308
Piño Guerra, 936
Piracy, 1217
Pirates, 26, 151, 220, 221
Plague, 85
Plato, 1372; *Republic,* 323

Platt Amendment, 936; abolition, 940

Pleiku, 1033, 1088

Plekhanov, G. V., 287, 288, 289, 291

Pleven, René, 712, 809, 810n

Plutarch, 13; *Lives,* 13n

Pogroms, 295, 768, 770

Pokrovsky, M. N., 289

Poland, 82, 86, 139, 302, 629; invasions, 87; Mongols, 69, 70; revolutionary tradition, 771n; Russia, 306, 308; Vietnam, 1137; World War II, 407, 410, 417, 420, 421, 488, 917–18: army, 407, Jews, 774, resistance, 423, 435, Warsaw, 423, 430

Polavieja, Gen., 182

Political documents, 769

Political ends: errors, *xiii;* guerrilla warfare, *xii*

Political growth, concept, 228

Political ideology (Communist), 580

Political naïveté, 41

Political opportunism, 799, 970

Political patronage, 1379

Political philosophy, 219, 235, 912–13, 914; Alexander the Great, 8, 8n; in conquest, 40; De Gaulle, 989; *divide et impera,* 29; Roman, 29

Political power: religion as pretext, 149

Political science: international diplomacy, 1382

Political settlements, 807, 816, 818

Political theory, 1325

Political vacuum, 900; -Japanese defeat, 870

Politics: -force, interplay, 226; -guerrillas, relationship, 494–95; idealism-reality collision, 690; -military affairs, 358; power, 270; pragmatism, 769; religion, 762; theorists, 285, 286

(*see also under* name); violent, 487; war, 86, 149

Polybius, 9, 9n, 10n, 20

Pompey, 3, 13, 27–28, 30; -Caesar wars, 28

Ponomarenko, P. K., 458, 462

Pope, Gen., 164

Popes, 57

Popov, Col., 496

Port Arthur, 629

Porter, William J., 1130

Port Moresby, 504, 505

Portugal, *xi,* 92, 203, 506, *map,* 127; China, 324–25; England, 126ff.; France, 126, 128–30; guerrillas, 121, 127; Indonesia, 528, 529; Malaya, 576; Napoleon, 125; *ordenanzas,* 129; Thailand, 539; World War I, 251, 254; World War II, 510

Portuguese East Africa, 251

Possessions, 746

Postwar disillusionment, *xvi*

Potsdam Agreement, 638

Potsdam conference, 565, 674

Potter, Mary, *xvi*

Power, 245; arrogance of, *xii,* 30, 201, 215, 420, 464, 534, 537, 1002, 1375, 1384; balance of, 171, 1273; Commager on, 1375; Great, concept, 185; international game, 1252; military putsch, 744; political, 149, Mao on, 348; politics, 270; Rostow on, 987–89; vacuum, 759, 956

POWs, 144, 165, 220; American Revolution, 103, 105 *and* n; Boer, 216; camps, 514, 595; execution, 243; guerrillas, 165; Japanese camps, 514; Soviet, 449, 456; Vietnam, 1366; West Pointers, 164; World War II, 432

Prado Museum, 401

Prejudice, 186
Press, 601, 602; Australia, 1126, 1221; Britain, 210, 292, 893, 1234, 1304, 1317, 1323, 1335; Burma, 586; Canada, 1322, 1351; censorship, 675, 1036 *and* n; clandestine, 432n; Cuba, 962; deficiency, 1370–71; free, 1039; France, 836; Indonesia, 535; Ireland, 273; Italy, 1220; -military, relationship, 1390; news suppression, 860; New York *Times:* Matthews' Castro interview, 953–55, 964; -public credibility gap, 1361; responsibility, 955 *and* n; Spain, 375; United States, 245, 695, 803, 812, 814, 843, 859, 962, 964, 1024 *and* n, 1028, 1039, 1121, 1136, 1335; China, 633, government vs., 1254ff., Johnson, 1216n, military correspondents, 1116, Vietnam, 1017: problem, 1036–41, restriction, 1036; as weapon, 264; yellow, 178
   See also under name of correspondent
Preston, R. A., 44 *and* n
Prevost, Augustine, 102
Pridi Phanomyong (Luang Pradit Manutam), 540–42
Priests, 135, 150; agents, 290, 293; guerrillas, 128, 131, 232, 233; Mohammedan (*mullah*), 156; nationalism, 91
Primitive peoples, *xi, xii*
Primo de Rivera, 378–79, 380, 384; "Line," 379
Prío Socarrás, Carlos, 941, 944, 950, 963
Priscus, 39, 42n, 56
Prisoners, political, 558, 564
Privateers, 26
Procopius, 43
Propaganda, 225, 286, 431, 484, 494, 512, 550, 674, 695; agitation, 706, 852, 862n; agitation teams, 701; agit-prop techniques, 1001, 1054; anti-white, 510; *binh van,* 1006; British, 769; China, 348; Communist guerrilla, 582; counter, 271; Germany, 373, 478; grass-roots, 753, 754–55; Japan, 522; "land and freedom," 873; one's own, believing, 601; political, methodology, 834; political weapons, 911; revolutionary: Land to the Landless, 951; Russia, 291, 293, 294, 460; victory, 780
Protectorates, 186, 370, 388, 543, 866
PRG (Provisional Revolutionary Government of South Vietnam), 1313
Prussia, 87; army, 89, 90; boundaries, *map,* 88; France, 219, 234; *levée en masse,* 145; militarism, 170; Napoleon, 145
Psychology, 601; *gung ho,* 581; native mass-, 224n; oriental, 576; warfare, 598
Ptolemy, 9
Publicity, international, 892, 899
Public opinion, 159, 171, 614, 756, 1374; against Vietnam involvement, 1207; England, 283; international, 891; United States, 240, 1056, 1275, 1351
Public trust, 1373, 1384
Pueblo, U.S.S., 1217; Congressional report, 1315
Pugachev rebellion, 137–39
Pulitzer Prize, 1386
"Punic faith," 33
Punic Wars: casualties, 21; second, 11, 17, 20
Pushkin, A. S., 285; *The Captain's Daughter,* 138
Pye, Lucian, *xvi,* 577, 579

Pyrenees, 10; bandits (Miquelets), 133
Pyrrhic victory, 25, 315, 370

Quat, Premier, 1100, 1103
Quebec, 97
Quebec Conference, 602–3
Quezon, President, 756
Quirino government (Philippines), 757
Quisling, Vidkun, 419
Quislings, 465

Radcliffe Constitution, 898
Radetzky, Marshal, 146
Radford, Adm., 812–16, 859
Radio, 473, 1026; Athens, 892; BBC, 484; Kol Israel, 775; Radio Free Yugoslavia, 473; Rebelde, 964, 967
Raffles, Thomas Stamford, 576
Ragnar, 56
Rance, Hubert, 612
RAND, 1113, 1201, 1300, 1361, 1390
Rangoon, 585, 586, 588; fall, 599
Ranke, Leopold, 1248
Rasputin, Grigori, 296
Rawdon, Lord, 116
Rawlinson, George, 4n
Raymond of Antioch, 64
Raymond of Toulouse, 63
Raziel, David, 771–72, 774n; death, 772
Raziel, Esther, 774n
Razin, Stepan, 137
Rebellion, 280; genesis, 1098; Lawrence on, 269; treachery, 268
Recto, Claro M., 526–27
Red Cross, 966
Redmond, John, 273
Reform, 532, 586
Refugees, 592; Jews to Palestine, 768, 770, illegal, 772, 775, 780; South Vietnam, 1139

Regino, 56
Regionalism, 718
Regional security organizations, 825 See NATO and SEATO
Régis Debray, 951, 972–73
Regroupement, 924, 926
Reinhardt, G. Frederick, 831
Reischauer, Edwin O., 1246n
Religion: atheism, 316; freedom of, 286; philosophy, 323; as political instrument, 328; politics, 762; war, 57, 85, 149
Reno, Major, 169
Renville agreement, 764, 766
Reparations, 334
Resettlement plans, 788, 791
Resistance, 440, 524 See under World War II and under name of country
Resources, 793
Reston, James, 1140, 1228, 1254, 1266, 1331, 1343, 1358
Restrictive covenants, 870
Réunion (island), 384
Revenge, 442
Revers, Gen., 687, 710
Revolution: Asian, 688; economic, 287; emotions, 98; Land to the Landless, 974; "Latin American way," 970; Leninist terms, 975; palace, 284, 296, 1047; "peasant," 951, 970 (see Che Guevara); by persuasion, 286; philosophy, 92; political aim, 284, 286; "principle of the small number," 295; regional, 851; self-sustaining, 851; Siantos theory, 738; world, 315, teachers, 669 See also Bakunin, Michael, and Marx, Karl
Revolutionaries, hard-core, 680
Revolutionary doctrine: standard Communist, 1098
Revolutionary ideas, 497

Revolutionary warfare, *xiii and* n,
  xiv, 306, 912, 1029, 1098, 1129;
  countermeasures, *xiv;* essence,
  1098; French school (*see
  Guerre révolutionnaire, la*);
  -grass-roots pacification, 1129;
  Mao on, 319; political/military
  factors, 912
Rhineland, 41
Rhine valley, 800
Rhodes, Cecil, 210
Rhodes scholars, 982
Richardson, John, 1013, 1024
Ridgway, Matthew B., *xvi,* 820,
  1235, 1260, 1360; Dien Bien
  Phu, 816–17; Indochina, 817;
  Korea, 816; Vietnam, 986,
  990, 1018, 1147
Ridley, Sidney, *xvi*
Rif rebellion, 369–81, 382ff.
Riga, treaty of, 306, 308
Rigg, Robert, 638–39
Río Chaviano, 966
Rivero Agüero, 968, 970
Rivers, Mendel, 1205, 1206
Rizal, José, 181–82, 188
Roberts, Adam, *xvi*
Roberts, Chalmers, 812
Roberts, Elby, 1334
Roberts, Field Marshal Lord, 211–
  16
Robertson, Jim, 1018
Robertson, Walter S., 819–20, 858
Robinson, James, 1039
Rochejacquelein, Henri de La, 122
Rockefeller, Nelson, 1297
Roeder, Franz, 141, 143
Roger of Antioch, 64
Rogers, Robert, 97 *and* n
Rogers, William, 1309, 1329, 1353
Roman Empire, *xi,* 9, 20, 22, 23, 39,
  47–48, 905, *map,* 14; army, 18,
  21, 25, 28, 29, 89; barbarian
  invasions, 36ff., 41, 48; Britain, 1368; Celtiberians, 126; colonization, 11ff., 16–26 passim,
  28; defensive phase, 47; Eastern, 43, 47, 48, 50, 51, 53,
  map, 37; Hannibal, 9–11, 32;
  leadership, 28, 31; legions, 13,
  21–22, 24, 28, 39, 279 (*see
  also* army); policy, 21; political
  philosophy, 29; praetors
  (governors-general), 18, 19, 22,
  23, 26; "Punic faith," 33; revolts against, 26; Senate, 19, 22,
  23, 24, 25, 29, -army, 28–
  29; Spain, 16–30, 33, 119, 159,
  map, 17; *strategos,* 47; strategy,
  116; war, waging of, 23n, 24;
  Western, 43, *map,* 37, destruction, *xii,* 40
Romania, 3n, 202, 312; World War
  II, 408, 488
Romanization, 27
Romanus, 51
Rome, sack of, 41
Rommel, Erwin, 408, 489, 490
Roosevelt, Franklin D., 624, 625,
  628, 630, 644, 672, 833,
  1377; anti-colonialism, 565;
  characteristics, 415–16, 603n,
  630; Chiang Kai-shek, 616–17,
  623, 625; China, 614, policy,
  617, 624; critics, 630; Cuba,
  939, 940; death, 565, 632, 633,
  689; De Gaulle, 428, 691;
  Einstein, 414; Executive Order
  (Japan), 562; Indochina, 689,
  690, 691; Stalin, 628, 630;
  World War II, 412, 413–16,
  603 *and* n; Yalta, 628–30
Roosevelt, James, 359n, 603n
Roosevelt, Theodore, 171, 179,
  936, 937 *and* n
Root, Elihu, 297, 936
Rose, Hugh, 199
Rosenberg, Alfred, 448
Rostow, Walt, 1090, 1102, 1210;
  "aggression from the North,"

1019, 1052; background, 982;
Clifford Group, 1229–33;
Johnson, 1228; Kennedy,
1015; on power, 1077–79,
1081; -Taylor plan, 1043;
Vietnam, 974, 978, 981–82,
984–85, 987, 1002, 1016, 1019,
1077, 1135ff.
Rousseau, Jean Jacques, 91
Routiers, 81
Rovere, Richard, 814
Roxas, President, 749, 751
Ruark, Robert: *Something of Value,*
863
Rubber, 800
Rubottom, Roy, 964
Rumania. *See* Romania
Runciman, S., 59n
Rusk, Dean, 1020, 1170, 1234;
"aggression from the North,"
982; Clifford Group, 1229–33;
Vietnam, 980, 982, 1010,
1048, 1052, 1057, 1077, 1079–
80, 1087, 1099, 1166
Russia, *xii*, 36, 69, 82, 86, 137, 138,
156, 183, 200, 203, 285, *map*
(1918–19), 305; army, 137,
158, 296, 301, conscription,
307, Red, 303–7ff.; Austria,
299; Bloody Sunday, 293;
Bolsheviks, 291ff., 295, 297,
298, 299, 301, 306, 307, 342;
Caucasus, 156, *map,* 157;
China, 330; civil war, 301ff.,
308, 309–15; Comintern, 315–
16; commune system, 289;
Cossacks, 137, 293, 301, 312;
Duma, 294, 295, 296, 297;
England, 316; failures, 200;
famine, 315; France, 308;
Frederick the Great, 137;
Georgia, 301, 312; Germany,
307; guerrillas, 137, 142, 143,
303ff.; Japan, 293, 334n;
Kerensky, 297–99; Manchuria,

332; Marxism, 288, 289; Men-
sheviks, 294, 298; Mongols,
69, 70; Napoleon, 136, 139–
45, 147, *map,* 140; nobles,
138, 141, 143; October Manifesto, 294; *okhrana,* 288; peasants, 285, 286, 288, 291, 293,
294, 302; pogroms, 770;
Poland, 306, 308; Pugachev's
revolt, 313; Red Guards, 302–
3; Red Terror, 302; soviets,
294, 297; strikes, 289, 293,
294, 296, 297; Tartars, 137,
156–57; Turkey, 138, 302;
Ukraine, 301, 308, 312, independence, 302; White armies,
301, 304, 305, 306, 307, 308,
310; White Terror, 295; World
War I, 295, 296–300 passim,
301–2, 304, 309, 966, allied
intervention, 304–6, 308–9,
315
See Pugachev rebellion; Russian
Revolution *and* Soviet Union
Russian-German non-aggression
pact (1939), 470, 577
Russian Revolution, 248–49, 284ff.,
298–300, 301, 308, 309, 339,
403, 900; background, 284ff.
(1905), 294 (1917), 295ff.;
Decembrists, 284; justification,
289; Lenin on, 315; revolutionary parties, 290–91;
tragedy, 293
See also Russia
Russo-Japanese War, 293, 294, 296,
554; lessons from, 245

Saadi, Yassef, 918, 920
Sabotage, 431, 435
Saboteurs, 423
Sahara Desert, 917
Saint-Arnaud, Gen., 154–55
Sainteny, Jean, 677, 678, 680; Ho,
680

St. George, Andrew, 963n
Saint-Simon, Comte de, 285
Saladin, 59, 63, 65, 66
Salan, Raoul, 724, 725, 727, 728–
    29, 730–32, 796, 798, 804,
    926, 927, 929
Salazar, 941
Sale guerre, la, 712
Salisbury, Harrison, 1136; reports
    from North Vietnam, 1267–72
Salinger, Pierre, 1038, 1040, 1254;
    Vietnam press problems, 1040–
    41
Saltonstall, 1075
Salvian, 28
"Salvius the Soothsayer," 11
Samar, 514
Samarkand, 7
Samuel, Czar of Macedonia, 466
Sánchez, Julián, 128, 132
Sandford, Daniel, 598
Sandino, Augusto César, 397–99
Santa Anna, 233
Santo Domingo, 174, 1021; United
    States, 396, 399
Saracens, 48, 50, 53, 56, 75
Saraphis, Col., 491, 493, 495
Sartre, Jean Paul, 308
"Saturation"-of-terrain principle,
    897
Saunders, Joan, *xvi*
Saxons, 86
Saya San, rebellion, 587
Sayf al-Dawla, Gen., 50
Sayle, Murray, 1317
Sayre, Francis, 540
Schell, Jonathan, 1121, 1180, 1194
Schelling, 285
Schevill, Ferdinand, 466, 468
Schlesinger, Arthur M., 179
Schlesinger, Arthur M., Jr., 1266–
    67, 1393; Vietnam, 987–88
    and n, 1018
Schnee, Heinrich, 250
Schoenbrun, David, 1268

Schönbrunn, Treaty of, 136
Schram, Stuart, 355
Schulten, A., 19n, 20
Schuman, Maurice, 718, 729–30
Schurman, Jacob, 185
Scientists, 413–15
Scigliano, Robert, 834, 846
Scipio Aemilianus, 25, 26, 28, 29,
    30, 604; tactics, 33–34
Scipio Africanus, 28, 177
Scipio, Gnaeus, 17
Scipio, Publius Cornelius, 10, 17–19
    and n, 20
Scobie, Lt. Gen., 733–34
Scorched-earth policy (*razzia*),
    4, 79, 98, 121, 133, 138, 141,
    155, 764
Scotland, *xi*; England, 76–80, cam-
    paigns, *map*, 77; independence,
    78
Scullard, H. H., 18 *and* n
Scythians, *xi*, 3, 3n–4n; "Asiatic,"
    6–7; Persians, 4
Seaborn, Blair, mission to Hanoi:
    (1), 1059, (2), 1065
Seamans, Robert, 1348
"Search-and-destroy" operation,
    165, 751, 1105–6, 1113, 1120,
    1137–38, 1140, 1144, 1145
Secret agreements, 339
Secret weapons, 41
SAS (*Sections Administratives
    Spécialisées*), 910, 911
"Security" pacts, 824
Segregation schemes, 788–89
Self-determination, 892
Self-government, 187
Seljuk Turks, *xi*, 59–61, 62
Senegal, 221
Separatism, 278
Sephardis, 771n
Serbia, 465, 466, 468–69; Russia,
    470; World War I, 469
    See Yugoslavia
Sergei, Grand Duke, 292–93

Sertorius, Quintus, 26–27 *and* n
Servan-Schreiber, Jean-Jacques, 919n; *Lieutenant in Algeria,* 919
Service, John, 626
17th parallel, 822–23, 824, 827, 844, 1124
Seven Years' War, 90, 118, 146, 201
Seychelles Islands, 894, 898
Shamyl, 156–57, 373
Shaplen, Robert, *xvi,* 679, 699, 714–15, 719, 731, 825, 854, 983, 991, 1018, 1028n, 1046, 1124, 1130, 1146, 1179, 1250, 1299, 1317, 1345; *Lost Revolution,* 688
Sharp, Ulysses S. Grant, 1060, 1066–68, 1104, 1190, 1213, 1222, 1270
Shaw, George Bernard, 273
Sheean, Vincent, 374n, 377, 379
Sheehan, Neil, 1018, 1039, 1046, 1058, 1059, 1079, 1346
Shelepin, Alexander, 1142
Sheridan, Gen., 164, 169
Sherman, William T., 162, 165, 166, 170, 176, 216, 595, 1142
Shimonoseki, treaty of, 334
Shipping, 151
Shoup, David, 1168–69, 1242, 1307
Shute, Nevil, 512
Siam, 538, 576; U.S., *xv;* World War II, 408, 603 *See* Thailand
Siantos, Yioryios, 734, 738, 744
Siberia, 137, 285, 295, 301, 302, 313; Japan, 304, 309; strikes, 296
Sicily, 11, 44, 124; World War II, 492, 502
Sihanouk, Norodom, 568, 1331
Sikorski government (Poland), 423
Silesia, 89, 1167
Silesian Wars, *xii,* 87, 90
Sillitoe, Percy, 878

Silvestre, Manuel, 371–73, 374–75; "Line," 377
Sinclair, Upton, 283
Singapore, 576, 579; fall, 577, 579; fortifications, 573; SOE, 575
Sinn Fein (Ourselves Alone), 272, 274, 275, 276, 277, 907
Sino-American Co-operative Organization (SACO), 619, 620
Sino-Soviet conflict, 851, 1018n, 1243, 1272–73
Sino-Soviet treaty, 638, 815
Sivaji, 118, 120
Sjahrir, Sutan, 761, 762, 764
Sjarifuddin, P. M., 764, 765
Slavery, 20, 869; industrial, 282
Slaves, 11, 18, 20, 92
Slave trade, 92
Slavs, 47, 48, 53, 56, 466ff.
Slessor, John, 385, 386, 389; *The Central Blue,* 385
Slim, William, 574, 585, 590–94, 595, 596, 601, 602, 609, 611–12, 782; accomplishments, 595, 603–5; characteristics, 590, 591, 604; command, 603–4, 611; *Defeat into Victory,* 574n; Japanese tactics, analysis, 591–92; Stilwell, 595; tactics, 592–94, 600, 604; Wingate, 596, 605
Smail, R. C., 59 *and* n, 63, 65, 66; *Crusading Warfare,* 59 *and* n
Smala (mobile headquarters), 152, 155
Smith, Arthur, 334
Smith, Earl, 958, 962, 963, 970; Batista, 963, 965
Smith, Harry, 159
Smith, John, 93
Smith, Terence, 1335
Smith, Walter Bedell, 820; Geneva Conference, 823
Smolensk, 142, 144
Smuts, Jan, 214, 251, 255, 612

Snipers, 259, 387

Snow, Edgar, 354: *Red Star over China,* 364–65

Socialism, 286

Socrates, 282

SOE.
See under England, World War II

Sogdians, 6

Solomon Islands, 504, 505; World War II, 408, 503, 505, 506

Somaliland, 384

Somme, battle of, 252

Song of Roland, The, 58

Sorensen, Theodore, 989, 1021, 1022

Soummam conference, 917, 920

Soustelle, Jacques, 910, 911

South Africa, 210, 211, 214, 366, *map* (1899), 213; England, 206, 210–17; Transvaal, 211, 214

South Carolina, 102, 103, 104, 105, 106, 107–8, 110, 114, 116

South China Sea, 813

Southeast Asia, 799, 1362–63, *map* (1941), 567; China, 69; colonialism, 674; Co-Prosperity Sphere, 503; De Gaulle plan, 1048; England, 539; Japan, 535, conquest, 688; Johnson report, 981; nationalism, causes, 586; solution to problems, 807; United States, 812, 1065, 1095–96, 1108; "wars of liberation," 731; World War II, 408, 538–39, 542, 565, 584ff., 588–89, Command (SEAC), 603, 606, 607

SEATO (Southeast Asia Treaty Organization), 824–25, 843, 844, 1314, 1375; signatories, 824; U.S. resolution, 1062; Vietnam, 1094, election, 842

South Korea: Vietnam, 1178, 1213, 1287

South Seas Communist Party (Nan Yang), 557, 577

Southwest Africa: Hottentots, 250

South Vietnam, 822–23, 827–31, 832–48, 849–61, 903, 993–1014, 1133–34, 1293–95, 1341ff., 1367–68; "aggression from the North" theory, 1045, 1090; allied forces, 1126, 1179, 1213, 1240, 1274ff., 1356, 1362, losses, 1192–93, 1240; Ap Bac, 1004, 1028, 1034, 1037; armed forces, 1178, 1358–59; army (ARVN), 829, 843–46, 855, 857–58, 859n, 979, 994, 997, 998, 1003, 1004–5, 1027, 1041, 1101, 1110, 1313, American advisers, 1030, 1034, problems, 1005, tactics, 1005, 1031; body counts ("kill" figures), 1140, 1144; Buddhists, 938, 1124, -Catholics relationship, 833–34, 1011ff., 1103, revolts, 1011–13, 1042, 1171; Catholics, 826, 827, 836, 838, 1033 (*see also under* Buddhists); Collins mission, 829–31; communism (*see* NLF); defoliation, 1316; elections, 841, 850, 1133, 1189, 1202–3, 1310; France, 828; goals, 1249ff.; "gook" philosophy, 1286; government, 991, 993, 1082ff., 1093, 1103, 1110, 1130, 1162, 1189, Minh's provisional, 1046–48, 1049–50, post-Diem, 1046ff., PRG, 1313; independence, 827, 928, 837; Iron Triangle, 1179; Khe Sanh, 1281–83; Mekong Delta, 1003, 1007; Montagnards, 852, 854, 1006; My Lai (*see* My Lai); nationalism (ists), 826, 828, 830, 831, 834, 837; neutralization, 1013, 1056; NLF (*see* NLF); Operation Plan 34A, 1050, 1062; pacification, 1034, 1037, 1130ff., 1177, 1188, 1199, 1201–2, 1222, 1320, 1362, failure, 1160–66; Pleiku, 1088; refugees, 827, 1139–40; resistance, 854 (*see* NLF); sects, 830, 832 (*see under* name); "strategic convenience," 1212; strategic-hamlet program, 916–19, 1131–32; Tet Offensive, 1072; United States, 978–91, 1002–14, 1015–28, 1029–44, 1045–63, 1064–84, 1085–1109, 1110–34, 1145–48, 1155: AID, 1038, armed forces, 1146–48, 1149ff., 1180–99, Army, amenities, 828, 1023–24, CIA, 1058, command errors, 1027–30, cost, 1145, 1169, 1313, 1341, 1368, Dulles, 824 (*see* Dulles, John Foster), escalation, 1033, 1052, 1055n, 1056, 1066, 1075, 1302, government vs. press, 1036–41, great deception, 1040, hawks, 1060, 1068, 1075, "moral" commitment, 828, "other" war, 1188, policy, 828–31, 840, 1034–36, 1043–44, presence, 1095–97, strategy, 1137ff., 1209ff. (*see* Westmoreland), wind-down, 1313ff., 1330; Viet Cong, 1001, 1003, 1004, 1005–6; Viet Minh, 848, 852–54; village, 999 *and* n

See also Diem, Ngo Dinh; Eisenhower, Dwight D.; Kennedy, John F.; Johnson, Lyndon B.; Nixon, Richard M.; North Vietnam; Viet Cong; Viet Minh *and under* United States

Soviet Union, 316, 460, 558, 862n, 1251; atomic bomb, 648; Belorussia, 447, 451, 454; China, 341, 349–50, 636, 798, "Far Eastern Agreement," 629; Comintern, 470, 488, 498; Cuba, 942; expansionism, 672; German Non-Aggression Pact (1939), 577; Geneva Conference, 821, 823; Ho Chi Minh, 677, 694; Kremlin, 464; military establishment, 1386; NKVD, 443, 445, 458; North Vietnam, 848, 850, 851, 1064, 1142, 1143, 1272; Order of Lenin, 462; political aims, postwar, 672ff.; Red army, 443ff., father of, 444; guerrilla warfare, 445ff., 462; Spanish Civil War, 402, 405; sphere of influence, 485, 672; "strategic key area," 800; Vietnam, 1013, 1251; World War II, 408, 422ff., 424n, 443–57, 458ff., 577, 686, 851, *map*, 446: Germany, 470, 488, Greece, 495–96 *and* n, Manchuria, 638–39, resistance, 417, 443ff., 458ff., effect, 462–64; Yugoslavia, 688, 798

See Comintern; Russia; Stalin, Joseph, *and* Ukraine

Spaatz, Carl, 1259

Spain, *xi, xii,* 10, 16, 20, 81, 198, 203, 377, 383–84, 604, *map*, 127; Africanistas, 370, 377, 379, vs. Abandonistas, 377, 378; army, 158, 371 *and* n, 374, 383; "bad Spaniards," 133; Charlemagne, 58; China, 324–25; civil war (*see* Spanish Civil War); colonization, 16–17, 92, 370–71, 373, 376, 378 (*see* Rif); Communists, 401; conquest, 231;

Cuba, 172–79; France, 126, 128–29, 130, 141, 150, 152–53, 158–59 (see Napoleon); Further, 18, 23, 24, 28; guerrillas, 121, 128, 129, 130–34, 153, 159; history, 16ff.; Indonesia, 528; Madrileños, 125; Mexico, 231–32, 242; Morocco (Rif rebellion), 228, 369–84 passim; Napoleon, 125–26, 128, 135, 159; Nearer, 18; "paternal authority," 181; Philippines, 181, 183, 185, 186; Romans, 16–30, 33–34, 119, 159; "Spanish ulcer," 135, 137; status, 370; United States, 179–80, 186

Spanish-American War, 167, 172, 178–80, 240, 370, 935

Spanish Civil War, 384, 400–1, 424, 948, 1259: communism, 402, 405–6; cost, 401; foreign intervention, 402; guerrillas, 400, 402; international brigades, 402, 405–6, 470; La Pasionaria, 401; literature, 401–2

Spanish succession, war of, 1208

Spartacus, 3, 13

Speckbacker, Joseph, 135–36

Speer, Albert, 415

Spellman, Francis Cardinal, 827

Spencer-Chapman, F., xvi, 507, 575, 577–78, 580–83; Jungle Is Neutral, 577–78

Spheres of influence, 485, 672, 866

Spinoza, Baruch, 1248

Spitamenes, Gen., 6, 7, 8

Spoor, Gen., 767

"Stab-in-the-back" thesis, 912

Stalemate: military, 767; nuclear, paradox of, 1260

Staley, Eugene, 974, 1007; Plan, 983, 1002

Stalin, Joseph, 299, 315, 341, 342, 416, 565, 669, 671–73, 1385; aims, 672ff., 691; characteristics, 671, 672; Chiang Kai-shek, 633, 636, 638; Greece, 739; Hurley, 633–34; Indochina, 689; Kennan warning, 634; Kuomintang, 353; purges, 405, 558; Spanish Civil War, 405; Tito, 485–86; United States, 624; World War II, 475–76, 477, guerrillas, 445, 458ff., effect of, 463–64; Yalta, 629–31

Stanford, Norman, 1276

Starvation, 302, 315, 676, 677

Statesmen, 148, 200; allied, 311

Stauffenberg, Claus von, 457

Steadman, Richard, 1228

Steinbeck, John: The Moon Is Down, 419

Stennis, John, 1206

Stenton, F. J., 40n

Stephen of Blois, 63

Stephens, Robert, xvi

Sterba, James, 1335

Stern, Abraham, 772–73; death, 772; FFI, 772; Gang, 772–73, 777, 778; terror, 774–75

Stettinius, Edward, 634

Stevenson, Adlai, 1064

Stilwell, Joseph "Vinegar Joe," 584, 585, 589, 590, 600; accomplishments, 595, 636; background, 594–95; characteristics, 643; Chennault, 617; on Chiang Kai-shek, 627–28 (see under Chiang Kai-shek); China, 594–96, 603, 646; army, 594–96, 616, 636, mission, 617; dismissal, 618, 620, 628, 631; M. E. Miles, 617; Northern Combat Area Command, 607–8; road, map, 593; Roosevelt, F. D., 624; strategy,

623; syndrome, 632; writings, 595; "Yoke Force," 596, 608 See Chiang Kai-shek
Stimson, Henry L., 397, 938
Stipendium, 19
Stirling, battle of, 78
Stolypin, Premier, 296
Storrs, Ronald, 258
Stoughton, Gen., 163
Strategic Bombing Survey, 1260
Strategic-hamlet program, 1005–7, 1024, 1034, 1037
"Strategic key" vs. "strategic convenience," 800–3
"Strategic necessity"/"strategic convenience," 858, 899
Strategic values, 800
Strategy, 35, 116, 141, 148, 153, 845; artillery, 82; attrition, 29, 102, 1112, 1137, 1141, 1176, 1240, failure in Vietnam, 1195; "cage policy," 367; codification, 202; defense, 139: active/passive, 215, static, 923; defined, 269; division of force, 169 *and* n; "dynamic," 912; enclave, 1166–67, 1237, 1318; end justifies means, 918; *epiteichismos,* 221; Fabian, 350; "hedgehog," 809–10; indirect approach, 35, 362; Irgun, 773; Lawrence on, 269; *levée en masse,* 145; limited war, 65; massive-retaliation, 979, 986, 1021, 1022; "meat-grinder," 723, 728; NATO, 1021; *offensive à outrance* (all-out offensive), 264; -operations, relationship, 1390; -policy rift, 808; *pourrissement* (rotting away), 731; quantitative approach, 787; *razzia* (*see* Scorched-earth policy); Rolling Red Horde theory, 803; search-and-destroy,

165, 205, 1105; *tache d'huile* (oil-spot) technique, 224, 1237; *Wagenburg,* 82; wait-and-see policy, 1098; "withering on the vine," 512
See also Dien Bien Phu *and under* name of commander, period *and* war
Strauss, Lewis: *Men and Decisions,* 413, 415
Strayer, J. R., 59 *and* n
Strobel, E. H., 540
Stuart, Dr. J. Leighton, 640, 641
Stuart, Jeb, 163
Students, 128, 166, 587
Stump, Felix, 859
Subutai, Gen., 69, 70
Subversion, 825
Sudan, 201, 211, 221, 597
Suez Canal, 800, 891, 898; crisis (1956), 899, 914
Sukarno, Achmed, 533, 534, 535, 536–37, 541, 760–62; army, 535; government, 765; PNI, 533, 534
Sulla, 26
Sully, François, 1018, 1039, 1359
Sulus, the, 186
Sulzberger, Arthur Hays, 1040
Sulzberger, C. L., 912
Sumatra, 513, 534, 761, 763, 764, 766
Sumter, Thomas, 109
Sun Tzu, *xiii,* 34n, 47, 73, 85, 203, 572, 1029; *Art of War,* 34n, 34–36, 51; Mao Tse-tung, 362
Sun Yat-sen, 336, 337, 338, 339–40, 364, 616; aim, 338; attempts at revolt, 337; characteristics, 341; Chiang Kai-shek, 340; Communists, 340–41; death, 341; teachings, 340; *Three Principles of the People,* 338, 621
Surabaya, battle of, 561–62

Sutherland, C. H. V., 18 *and* n, 24–25

Swahili (language), 878

Sweden, 53, 86

Sweet-Escott, Bickham, 492

Switzerland, 94, 148, 289, 541, 922; France, 124; peasant revolts, 123

Sykes, Christopher, 601, 602, 778; *Orde Wingate*, 597

Symington, Stuart, 1316

Syria, *xi*, 48, 59, 257, 262, 267; Algeria, 921; Christians, 66; Franks, 65; Palestine, 771; Palmach, 771; World War II, 591

Szilard, Leo, 413

Taber, Robert, 949, 960

Tabernilla, 957, 965

Tache d'huile (oil-spot) technique, 224, 685–86, 921, 1007
See Lyautey

Tacitus, 1368

Tactical adaptation, 32, 34, 43, 65, 68–69, 97–98, 151, 177, 592, 786–87, 927

Tactical thinking: realignment re guerrilla warfare, 793

Tactics, *xii*, 31ff., 35, 86–87, 148, 159, 162, 223, 243; adaptation, 32, 34, 43, 65, 151, 592, 787, 927; ambush, 154, 159; ancillary units, 603n; *Blitzkrieg*, 572; *bouclage*, 685, 921; brutality, 128–29; burn-and-bolt, 1144; Byzantine, 900; Callwell on, 204; carrot-and-stick, 1096; cavalry vs. infantry, 42n; *cheng*, 35; *ch'i*, 35; coast-watchers, 504–5, 515; codification, 202; coercion, 856; colonial, 151; *commandos de chasse*, 927; *cordon sanitaire*, 882; counterguerrilla, 452;

defense, 170; "de Lattre Line," 715; Dinaussauts, 716; divide-and-conquer, 302; "domination of areas," 885–86; dormant period, 146–47; encirclement, 686; environmental adaptation, 787; European, 200 *and* n; Fabian, 33; fluid, 592; flying columns, 153, 154–55, 206, 215–16; in forest environment, 878–79; forest sweeps, 886; fortification, 85, 86, 93; garrison concept, 921–22; GCMA (*Groupements de Commandos Mixtes Aéroportés*), 716; genesis, 31ff.; *un golpe terrífico* (terrible blow), 243; *Groupes Mobiles*, 715; guerrilla (*see* Guerrilla warfare); helicopters (*see under* Air power); heterodoxy, 596; hook, 591, 592; "human sea," 713; "ilot" system of surveillance, 918; impasse, 170; independent raiding companies, 507–9; infiltration and penetration, 744; interior lines, 307 *and* n; invincibility myth, 505; jungle, 190–91, 572ff., 591–94, 604–5; "kamikaze," 1191; Lawrence on, 269–70; long-range penetration concept, 599, 600, 605; "mad minute," 1161; "mass," 22; "meat-grinder," 807; minbotrap, 1156–57; minor, 170; "nomadization," 724; oil-spot (*see Tache d'huile*); *pa* (fortified stockade), 159; paradox, 505; "parallel pursuit," 144; patience, 793–94; patrolling, 592, 597, 604, 756; qualitative approach, 891; quantitative approach, 895; quasi-guerrilla, 36ff., 39; *ratissage*, 921; "ratline," 470; "ring of steel," 752; "saturation"-of-terrain principle, 897; scorched-earth (*razzia*), 4, 79, 98, 121, 133, 138, 141, 155, 764; "sealing off" (*bouclage*), 685, 921; search-and-destroy, 165, 751–52, 1106, 1112, 1120, 1137–38, 1140, 1144, 1145; siege-craft, 49, 86; *smala,* 152, 155; "spoiling," 1236, 1283ff.; stronghold concept, 605, 728; stupidity, 252; subversive, 848; surprise, 591; "the sweep," 132, 886; *tache d'huile* (oil-spot), 224, 685–86, 921, 1007 (*see* Lyautey); "territorial offense," 685; terror, *xii,* 274; trends, 170; *trochas,* 174, 178; "wagon-city," 39; "water cure," 190; whirlwind-type (*tourbillon*), 685; *zona,* "sealing off," 751, 752, 758

See also under name of commander military and/or political, period *and* war, *and* Strategy

Tada Hayao, Gen., 366

Taft, William Howard: on Cuba, 937 *and* n; Philippines, 193, 196–97, 747; President, 240

Tai Li, Gen., 618–19, 620–21 *and* n

Talleyrand, 1327

Tamerlane, 139

Tancred, Prince, 65

Tanganyika, 249

See also German East Africa

Tangier, Treaty of, 156

Tanham, George K., *xvi,* 698, 707, 1018, 1382; *Communist Revolutionary Warfare,* 689; *War Without Guns,* 1207

Tan Malaka, 762, 765

Tannenbaum, Frank, 237–38

Tanzania, 249, 1251

See also German East Africa

Taoism, 322, 327, 333

Tarawa, 504

Tarleton, Banastre, 103–4, 106, 107, 110 *and* n, 112, 113, 114, 117; "Tarleton's Quarters," 104, 111

Tarn, W. W., 6n, 8, 8n

Tartars, 87

Taruc, Luis, 521, 747, 751–52, 753, 755; defeat of communism, 753

Taxes, 19, 20, 531

Taylor, Maxwell: on air power, 1264; ambassador, 1060–61, 1065–66ff., 1083ff., 1142; characteristics, 1020; Clifford Group, 1229–33; Kennedy, J. F., 1022; -Rostow plan, 1043; Vietnam, 974, 990, 1004, hearings, 1166, report, 984–87, 991, 1002, 1016, 1019, 1042, 1050–51, reappraisal, 1068–69ff., 1080–81

Taylor, Zachary, 159

Technology, 85–86, 146, 160, 169, 199, 408, 793; challenge to orthodoxy, 170; influence, 160; -strategic values, 800; Vietnam, 1130, 1114–15, cost, 1194

Tehran Conference, 474, 565, 605

Television, 484, 954, 1039; deficiency, 1369; documentary, 1028n; Vietnam, 1166, 1234

Teller, Dr. Edward, 413

Teller Amendment, 935

Templer, Gerald, 790, 791

Terminology, 873

Terror, 38, 282; counter-, 280, 282, 910; defined, 279; Lenin, 1, 302; Mao Tse-tung, 347; Nazi, 450, 451; paradox of, 279–81; philosophy of, 288, "prophylaxis by," 450; reign of,

283, 611, 783; rule by, 389;
Russia, 138, 139, 285ff., 287,
288, 291; selective, 460; tactics, *xii*, 274; as weapon, 279,
741; White (Russia), 295
See also Terrorism
Terrorism, 181, 246, 784n, 898;
counter-, 965; instruments of,
224; Irgun-Stern, 772–74; Mau
Mau, 877, 879, 880–81; Philippines, 756; quantitative, 110n;
selective, 110n, 688, 749, 852,
934; Viet Minh, 852
See Terror
Terry, Gen., 169
Tet offensive, 1072, 1218–25,
1227–28, 1286, 1298, 1300,
1308, 1346, second, 1236
Teutons, 40, 42
Thailand, 560, 717, 799, 1362,
1381; China (Communist),
1248; government, 540–41;
historical background, 538–
41; name, 541; SEATO, 824;
United States, 815, 1090,
1323, 1342; Viet Minh, 705;
Vietnam, 1178, 1213; -Viet-
namese rivalry, 799; World
War I, 540; World War II,
538, 541–42, 584, 614
Thakin movement, 587
Thames River, 15
Thang, Nguyen Duc, 1130–31
Thanh, Nguyen Chi, 1059
Thanh, Tran Chanh, 834
Thanh Thai, Emp., 826
Thant, U, 1064, 1235, 1355
Theodoric, 42
Theodosius, Emp., 40, 43
Theorists, 231
Thermopylae, pass at, 46
Thessalians, 32
Thi, Nguyen Chanh, 1122–23
Thierry, Amédée, 41
Thieu, Nguyen Van, 1221, 1233,

1362–63, 1366ff.; Johnson,
1161, 1239; -Ky regime (*see*
Thieu-Ky government); negotiations, 1308, 1316; position,
1330; reputation, 1324
Thieu-Ky government, 1103, 1129,
1161, 1251, 1302, 1309ff.,
1312ff., 1320, 1322ff., 1343;
constitution, 1189; scandals,
1315
"Thin red line," 151
Thirty Years' War, 85, 146, 244,
546, 1377
Tho, Nguyen Huu, 995, 996
Thomas, Hugh, *xvi*, 401, 944, 965;
*Cuba, or the Pursuit of Free-
dom,* 935
Thomazo, Col., 918
Thompson, Robert, 1007, 1037,
1267, 1357; *Defeating Com-
munist Insurgency,* 1207, 1325;
No Exit from Vietnam, 1320,
1325; *Revolutionary War in
World Strategy, 1945–1969,*
1326; Vietnam Report, 1320–
21, 1324–27
Thompson, Dr. Virginia, 799
Thrace, 3, 4, 36, 47, 57
Thuc, Monsignor Ngo Dinh, 833–
34
Thucydides, 5, 5n
Tibet, 69; China, 321
Tientsin, treaty of (1885), 219, 544
"Tiger cages," 1343
Timor, 510–12, *map,* 508
Tippu, 120
Tito, Josip (Broz), 470, 471, 472–
85 passim, 496, 496n, 623,
692, 991; accomplishments,
484; army, 472, 479, 485;
communism, 469, 480, 498;
defection, 692, 1243, 1273;
England, 473–76; Greece, 738,
740, 741–42, 744; guerrillas,
470ff., 480–83, 485; *Hausparti-*

sanen, 481; politics, 472, 475, 477, 480; Russia, 470, 473, 477, 485–86; strategy, 475–76, 481ff.; World War II, 686, 707, 906, allied aid, 484–86

Tojo, Prime Minister, 535

Tokyo: Doolittle raid, 601

Tolstoy, Leo, 144, 283

Tomalin, Nicholas, 1304

Tonkin, 222, 551, 555, 678, 682; Operation Léa, 686, 693; resistance to French, 553ff.; Viet Bac, 684, 686, 687

Tonkin Gulf, 71, 1061, 1062–64, 1065, 1071, 1082, 1128; rationale, 1075; Resolution (*see* Tonkin Resolution)

Tonkin Resolution, 1076, 1249, 1340, 1384

Topi, Tantia, 199

Torture, 1304; Algerian rebellion, 920; *gégêne,* 918; rationale behind, 919

Totalitarianism, 486; ideology, 913

Totila, 44

Tourism, 944

Tracy, Benjamin, 171

Trade(ers), 171, 183, 398, 528, 529–31, 539, 543, 547, 576; China-West, 325–26; opium, 325 *and* n, 547, 551; pacts, Soviet, 316; "pig," 326

Trade unionism-revolution, 290

Trafalgar, battle of, 125

Traitors, 418; "traitor-killing" camps, 582

Tran Phu, 558

Trans-Jordan, 388

Transport, 267–68

Tran Van Giau, 698

Treachery, 268, 581

Treason, 276

Treaties, 369: of Brest-Litovsk, 302; Conway, 75; Fez, 226; Nanking

(1842), 326n; Paris, 186, 187; Riga, 306, 308; Roman, 22–23, 24–25; Shimonoseki, 334; Tientsin (1885), 219, 544; trade, 539–40; Utrecht, 86; Versailles, 270, 310–11, 339, 469, 550, 557, 769; Westphalia, 825n

Tregaskis, Richard, 1040

Trenchard, Hugh "Boom," 384, 386–87, 1258

Trepov, Gen., 290

Trevelyan, George, 103, 108

Tribes, 19, 92, 259, 922

Tribute, 23, 41, 72, 322, 325

Trinidad, 131

Trinquier, Roger, *xiii and* n, 716, 918, 919; GCMA, 807, 811

Trong, Huynh Van, 1315

Trotsky, Leon, 182, 294, 299, 303–4, 304n, 309, 315, 342; characteristics, 298; soviets, 295

Trotskyites, 559

Truehart, William, 1038

Trujillo, 945, 991

Truman, Harry S, 746, 776, 1370; Bullitt, 644; China, 635, 639, 640, 643, 646, 648, embargo, 640, 644; De Gaulle, 690; doctrine, 673, 691, 739, 744; Greece, 735, 739, 744 (*see* doctrine); Indochina, 690, 695–96, 725; MacArthur, 1210; NATO, 695; postwar, 673; President, 632; Wedemeyer, 643

Truong, Ngo Quang, 1366

Truong Chinh, 558, 698, 850

Trusteeship, 565, 869; interim, 689

Tsaldaris government, 736

Tsitas, Gen., 63

Tuchman, Barbara, 617; on military establishment, 1386; *Stilwell and the American Experience in China,* 594, 596

Tulagi, 359n; World War II, 506

Tu Mu, 35–36

Tunisia, 228, 903–4, 905, 911, 920, 923; FLN, 926; independence, 904, 914, 916n; nationalism, 693

Turcopoles, 63

Turenne, Gen., 85

Turgenev, Ivan, 283, 291; *Fathers and Children*, 285

Turkestan, 5, 69; China, 321

Turkey (Turks), 47, 48, 49, 905; Algeria, 151; army, 202; Balkans, 466–67; Cyprus, 887–88, 898, 899, Volkan, 898; Greece, 488, 899; Menderes government, 899, 900; Russia, 138, 302; United States, 889, 899; World War I, 258–71, 888; World War II, 889

Turkish Cypriotes, 889, 898, 902

Turkomans, 200

Tuyen, Dr. Tran Kim, 847

Tu Yu, 35

Tu Yu-ming, Gen., 642

Twain, Mark, *xiv*, 186n

26th of July Movement, 946, 948, 949, 953, 954, 962, 967, 970; communism, 963–64; in United States, 964–65

Two-edged sword, 30

Tyler, Wat, 82

"Tyranny of the dead," 273

Tyrol, 135–37, *map*, 136

Tyrone's rebellion, 87

Tz'ŭ Hsi, Dowager Empress, 333, 335, 336; death, 337

Ukraine, 479; Cossacks, 87; Germans, 528; World War II, 366, 444ff., 447, 451, 456

Ulster, *xiv*

Underprivileged peoples: guerrilla warfare, *xiii*

Unger, Leonard, 1381

United Fruit Co., 966

United Nations (UN), 630, 643, 671, 672, 766, 824n, 924, 1355; Che Guevara, 972; "Committee of Good Offices," 764; Cyprus, 891–92, 893, 899; Greece, 737, UNRRA, 734, 735, 736; Indonesia, 764, 766; Korea, forces in, 816; Palestine: UNSCOP, 780; rebellion in Algeria, introduction of, 910; Security Council, 764, 766; United States, 1235; Vietnam, 1064

United States (U.S.), 171–72, 178, 199, 240–41, 273, 282, 283, 315, 316, 384, 1254–56: AID, 1381; Air Force, 603, 614, 617, 1021; American ideal, 630; Army, 159, 166, 167, 168ff., 179–81, 184, 186, 751, 757, 935, 1021–22, bases, 844, Green Berets (*see* Special Forces), guerrilla warfare, 1021 (*see* Special Forces *and under* Marines *and* military policy), influences on, 171, public image (Vietnam), 1359–60, 1361; Army War College, 1386; Asia, *xv*; Burma, 539–40; Caribbean, 396–400, 506, *map*, 395 (*see also under* country); Castro, 949, 961, psychological impact, 934–35; Central America, 396–400, *map*, 395; China, 326, 330, 506, 632–49, lobby, 617, 635, 644, "old China hands," 625, postwar, 636–48, White Paper, 648; CIA (*see* CIA); Civil War, 160–65, 166–67, 176, 184, 213, 234, 595, 1142: guerrillas, 162ff., 166, leaders, 162–63, strategy,

166, theaters, *map,* 161; colonialism, 389, 396ff., 719; Congress, 159, 179, 746, 798, 813, 827, 1076, Cambodia, 1391, Southeast Asia resolution, 1062–63, Vietnam: opposition, 1311ff., 1335, 1352; credibility, world-wide, 1108; Cuba, 171, 172, 173, 179, 183, 935ff., 940ff., 949–50, 952, 959–60, 962–63, 965, 966, 969–70 *and* n (*see also* Batista, Fulgencio, *and* Castro, Fidel); Defense Department, 981, 1021–22, 1048, -press, 1390, strategy: "Fortress America" concept, 981, Vietnam, 1376, 1384ff.; democratic concept, 1256; diplomacy, 617, 624, 821, 1273 (*see* Geneva Conference); elections: (1948), 644, (1952), 1296, (1968), 1296; England, 899 (*see* Churchill *and* World War II); expansionism, 171–72, 183, 186, 229, continental, 167, 281n; foreign policy, 171 *and* n –72, 179, 183, 229– 30, 234, 240ff., 561, 562, 565– 66, 629–31, 632, 674, 678, 690–91, 694, 718–19, 798, 812–18, 820 passim –25, 828– 31, 851, 858–61, 935–38, 940–42, 959, 962, 965, 969– 70 *and* n, 1062–63, 1385, China, 632, containment, 691 (*see* Domino theory; Truman Doctrine *and under* names of presidents *and* wars); France, 678, 690–93, 694–96, 715, 717–19, 722, 729, Indochina strategy, 717; government: leakage, 1346ff., -people schism, 1015, 1208ff., 1221, 1228, 1233ff., vs. press, 1255ff.;

Greece, 688, 737, 739, 889 (*see* Truman); hawks/doves (*see under* Kennedy, John F.; Johnson, Lyndon B., *and* Vietnam); imperialism, 186, 192– 93, 197, 240, 936; Indian Wars, 167–70, 184, *map,* 168 (*see also* Indians (North America)); Indochina (French), 689–96, 715–17: aid, 717–20, 722, 725–27, Geneva Agreement, 822–23, 824n–25, intervention, 819–20 (*see* Dulles, John Foster), policy, 719, 727, 730; Indonesia, 762, 764; Industrial Revolution, 282; Japan, 562 (*see* World War II); JCS (Joint Chiefs of Staff), 812, 813, 980ff., 990, 1002, 1056, 1100, 1206–9 passim, 1222, Acheson statement, 1229, hawks, 1050–52, 1090, Vietnam, 1062, 1069; leadership, 1373ff.; lobbies, 965, 968, China, 617, 635, 643–44, Vietnam, 991; manifest destiny, 184; Marines, 193, 359 *and* n, 396–400, 600, 603n, 628, 637, 742, 811, 937, 1022, guerrilla warfare, 1021, 1025, Vietnam, 1092, 1100, 1120ff.; Marshall Plan, 691, 766; Mexico, 229, 233–34, 240–42, 244, 245; militaristic philosophy, 1373, 1388; Military Academy (West Point), 164, 520, 521, 594, 628, 982, 988, 1024, 1113, 1238; military establishment, 945, 1315, 1385–86, interservice rivalry, 1387; military policy, 979, 1021, 1022; guerrilla warfare, 1020–24, massive retaliation, 1267; military position, postwar, 673; military thinking, 793, 958; moral position, 1015; National Security Action Memorandum 288, 1211; National Security Council (NSC), 812, 982, 1021, 1042, 1079, 1130; Naval Academy (Annapolis), 618; Navy, 171, 182, 504ff., 512, 618, 813, 1022, "revolt of the admirals," 812; OSS, 677 (*see under* World War II); Palestine, 778; Pearl Harbor, 367, 408, 541, 562, 1269; Pentagon, 1019, 1102, 1136, insurgency expert (*see* Krulak); Philippines, 180, 183–97 passim, 746–47, 754, 756; philosophy, 1369ff.; polarization, 1211; politics, 192, 673, 1237; postwar, 673–74; presidential "agents," 1377, 1379; press, 179, 188, 189, 191, -government antagonism, 1205; Reconstruction, 197; Russia, 297, 315 (*see* Soviet Union); SEATO, 824; Senate, 186, 1323, 1336, Foreign Relations Committee, 636, 1100, 1142, 1166, 1234, 1266, 1353, 1363, Internal Security Committee, 969n; service academies, 1391 (*see under* name); Soviet Union, 644, 673, 691; Spain, 180, 186; Spanish-American War (*see* Spanish-American War); Special Forces (Green Berets), 973, 1022–23 *and* n, 1025, 1033, 1291, 1315ff.; State Department, 183, 626, 628, 629, 690, 729, 819–20, 825, 858, 938, 959, 962, 963–64, 979n, 981, 988, 1002, 1020, 1038, 1040, 1051, 1066, 1075: Cable Number 1006, 1036, China, 632, 633–35, 636, Diem, 830, Foreign Service Act (1946), 1377–78,

Nixon, 1336, personnel, 718, purge, 1380, Viet Minh, 694, Vietnam, 1376–84, 1390, Wriston Program, 1380; "strategic key," 799; Thailand, 539, 540, 541; Turkey, 889, 899; USIA (Information Agency), 981, 1381; Vietnam: dissent over, 1166, 1306ff., experience, analysis, 1369ff., failure, 1370ff., 1382, "other war," 1188, 1197, tragedy of, 1376, 1384 (*see* South Vietnam; North Vietnam *and* Vietnam); war—public opinion on, 1103n; World War I, 297, 304–5, 1028; World War II, 359n, 412ff., 485, 811–12, 1377: China, 566, 584–85, 594ff., 613–31, Dixie Mission, 619–20, 626–27, Hurley mission, 624–25, 627–28, lend-lease, 625, 627, OSS, 608–9, 617, 619, 620, SACO, 619; command, 820; Japan, cost of invading, 629, 630; OSS, 409, 411, 424, 425, 429–30, 441, 494, 982, 988, 1023; Pacific, 367, 408, 504–6, 513–27, 535–36, 541, 569: OSS, 541, 565, 569, 570, Philippines, 513–27, strategy, 541, 542, 564, 569, 570

See Domino theory; Korean War; North Vietnam; South Vietnam; Vietnam *and under* Presidents Roosevelt, Franklin D.; Truman, Harry S; Eisenhower, Dwight D.; Kennedy, John F.; Johnson, Lyndon B. *and* Nixon, Richard M.

Universal military service, 72
University of Havana, 937, 940, 945

UNRRA (United Nations Relief and Rehabilitation Administration): Greece, 734, 735, 736

Upton, Emory, 170–71, 179, 180; *Military Policy of U.S.*, 170

Usborne, C. V., 152

Utrecht, Treaty of, 86

Václav I, 71

Vacuum: political, 870, 900; power, 759, 1046

Vagts, Alfred: *Defense and Diplomacy*, 1376

Valée, Gen., 153; Great Wall, 154

Valens, Emp., 39

Valeriano, Col., 750, 753, 754n, 755, 756; and Bohannan: *Counter-Guerrilla Operations— The Philippine Experience*, 750, 753, 755

Valley Forge, 99

Valluy, Étienne, 682, 686, 693; *bouclage*, 686

Valor, 34

Vandals, 44

Vandegrift, Alexander, 504–5, 506, 603n

Vandenberg, Sen., 644

Van den Bosch, 531

Van Deventer, Gen., 251, 255

Van Fleet, James, 740

Van Hinh, Nguyen, 725

Van Mook, Dr. Hubertus J., 760

Vann, John, 1034, 1038, 1341

Van Poll, Max, 762

Van Tam, Nguyen, 730

Van Tinh, Nguyen, 679

Varkiza Agreement, 734

Vatican, 196

Vegetius: *Summary of the Art of War*, 62

Veliamonif, 156

Vendée, 206

Vendée rebellion, 121–24, *map*, 122

Venezuela, 172

Venice (state), 467

Versailles, treaty of, 270, 311, 339, 469, 550, 557, 769

Veterans, *xvi*

Vetilius, Gaius, 23

Vettones, 16

Victory, 271; Pyrrhic, 25, 315, 370

Vidal-Naquet, Pierre, 920

Viet Cong (Vietnamese Communists), 849, 853, 857; ARVN, 1027, 1031ff.; Bien Hoa, 1075: *binh-van* program, 994; intelligence network, 1157–59; manpower, 1141; propaganda, 1032; tactics, 983, 999, 1003, 1005–6, 1031ff., 1054ff., 1080

Viet Minh, 566, 568, 569–71, 674, 675–76, 677, 680–82, 684ff., 697–708, 709ff., 722–32, 795–97, 805–8, 920, 1028n, *map*, 700; army, 684, 703–4; China, 708, 713, 797, 809; code names, 709n; doctrine, 698; foreign aid, 705–6, 713; France, 678, 684ff., 692, 707–8, 713ff.; GAMO, 724; Geneva, 821–23; independence (*doc-lap*), 701–2, 705; methodology, 912; organization, 699–706; OSS, 677; Pathet Lao, 728, 732; problems, 676–77; strategy, 698; tactics, 677, 693–94, 697–98, 700ff., -Ho Chi Minh, 680; terminology, 873; terrorists (*Dich-Van*), 705, 707

See Dien Bien Phu; Giap, Vo Nguyen *and* Ho Chi Minh

Vietnam, *xi, xiii, xv, xvi*, 69, 71, 281n, 539, 568, 669, 795–808, 918, *maps* (1964–65), 1091, (1965–66), 1111, (DMZ), 1123, (1967), 1187, (1969), 1301, (1970), 1333, (1971), 1354: "aggression from the North" theme, 982, 983, 1158; "associated state," 827ff.: creation, 693, division, 822–23, 17th parallel, 822–23, 824, 827, 845, 1124 (*see* Dien Bien Phu *and* South Vietnam); American Friends of, 977; Binh Xuyên, 829–30; China (Communist), 798; communism, 557; DMZ, 1123–26, *map,* 1123; England, 1103; flag, 675; France, 332, 540, 542, 545, 551, 674, 675n, 678, Viet Minh, 795–808 passim; Free French, 571; government: Democratic Republic (DRV), 570, premier (*see* Diem, Ngo Dinh), provisional, 569; Haiphong, 72, 1127; hearings, 1166–69; history, 542–44; independence, 568; internal threat, 945; Japan, 569, 674; Manila Conference, 1133; Mekong Delta, 1126; nationalism, 569; *no win, no victory,* 1368; pacification, *xiii,* 220, 1137; postwar, 1133; precolonial, 549n; summation: air power, 1257–73, the Bible and the Sword, 1241–56, ground war, 1274–95; Tet offensive, 1072, 1218–25, 1227–28, 1286, 1298, 1300, 1308, 1346, second, 1236; United States, 677–78, 696, 860–61, 974, 977–92 passim, 1017, 1020, 1073, 1096, 1124–26, 1156–57: air war, 1112, 1126–28; armed forces, 1387; arms/equipment, *xv,* 1114–15; command ignorance, 1120; cost, *xiv;* escalation, 986–87, 1106–7, 1139, 1366; four wars, 1113–14, 1126–27; Hanoi bombing, 1127; hawks, 1373,

1384ff.; hawks/doves, 982ff., 988; Iron Triangle, 1126; Johnson report, 981; Lansdale report, 978, 979; MACV (Military Assistance Command), 991; military machine/tactical environment: incompatibility, 986; naval war, 1128–29; objectives, 1328ff.; opposition to involvement, 1166, 1204, 1222, 1228, 1233ff., 1306ff., 1314–18 passim, 1328ff., 1336ff., 1343, 1350ff.; "other war," 1114, 1129–30, 1188, 1197; POWs, 1366; Staley Plan, 983; "strategic keys" vs. "strategic conveniences," 799–803; strategy, 1112, 1138, 1153–54; Taylor-Rostow mission, 984–87; troop withdrawals, 1310, 1317, 1321, 1330, 1347, 1350, 1363 (*see also* listings *under* United States); World War I, 550; World War II, 412, allied occupation, 570–71, 674
See Diem, Ngo Dinh; Ho Chi Minh; *under* Eisenhower, Dwight D.; Kennedy, John F.; Johnson, Lyndon B.; Nixon, Richard M.; North Vietnam; Paris Peace Talks; South Vietnam *and* Viet Minh
Vietnamese-Thai rivalry, 799
Vietnamization, 1329, 1341, 1344, 1349, 1350, 1359, 1364
Vikings, *xii,* 53–56; *Gokstad* ship, 53 *and* n; invasion *map,* 54
Villa, Pancho, 237, 238, 240, 242, 243, 244–45, 246; aides, 243, 245; tactics, 243
Vincent, John, 634
Violence, Lenin on, 1
Virginia, 93, 103, 104, 113, 115, 117

Viriathus, 23–25, 26, 29
Visigoths, 46
Vitebsk, 141
Vlasov, Gen., 456
Vogt, John, Jr., 1356
Volckmann, R. W., 521–25; *We Remained,* 521
Voltaire, 138, 672, 1374
Vong, King Sisavang, 568
Von Rundstedt, Marshal, 434, 435–36
Von Steuben, Gen., 99

Wagenburg, 82
Wake: World War II, 408
Walachia, 3n
Wales, *xi,* 72, 73–76
Walker, Lannon, 1378, 1380, 1383
Walker, Walter, 1279, 1291–92
Wallace, Henry, 623
Wallace, Major, 494
Wallace, William, 78–79
Waller, W. T., 194
Walpole, Horace, 115
Walt, Lewis, 1120–24 passim, 1160, 1181, 1189, 1217, 1222, 1278, 1286, 1293, 1307; *Strange War, Strange Strategy,* 1278
Wapshare, Gen., 253
War criminals, 165
Warfare: *Art of War* (*see under* Sun Tzu); atomic, 1330–31; bases, 35; *Blitzkrieg,* 407; -church, relationship, 57; colonial, 151; counterinsurgency (*see* Counterinsurgency warfare); counterrevolutionary, 912–13; crusading (*see* Crusades); defensive, 51, 177; development, 67, 146, 170; economic, 125; European, 807, -American differences, 170; Fabian tactics, *xi;* feudal (*see* Feudal warfare); guerrilla

(*see* Guerrilla warfare); history, *xii;* Homeric tradition, 34; irregular (*see* OSS *and* SOE *under* United States *and* England); insurgency (*see* Insurgency warfare); jungle, 191; knightly, 58; land, Western rules, 592; nuclear, 979; offensive, 86; orthodox, Mao Tse-tung and, 363; pacification campaigns, *xi–xii* (*see also* pacification *under* Vietnam); philosophy, 31; political, 674; political-military approach, 249; protracted, Mao Tse-tung theory, 697; psychological, 252, 275, 598, 912, 924–25, 926; quantitative vs. qualitative, 1027–28; resistance (*see under* World War II *and under* country); retraining, 594; revolutionary, *xiii and* n, *xiv,* 306, 912, 1098, 1129, countermeasures, *xiv,* essence, 1098, French school (*see Guerre révolutionnaire, la*), Mao Tse-tung on, 319; small, 198–99, 203–6, 395, 410, 1025 (*see* Callwell); treatises on, 34 (*see* Sun Tzu, *Art of War*); trench, 812; West-East contrast, 32
See also Guerrilla warfare *and* Sun Tzu, *Art of War*
Warnke, Paul, 1225, 1228
War of Succession, 86
War(s), 85; absolute, 262, 263; art of, 205, 270; axioms, 199; bionomics, 263; clandestine, 1362; Clearchos element, 1388; colonial (*see* Colonial wars); cost, 85; *coup nul* (a draw), 796; criminals, 165; desert, formula, 261–63; global, 408–9; historians, 147; history of, 39n;

holy (*jihad*), 152; indirect approach, 264; insurgency, 189, 265; "internationalizing," 924; intervention, 149; liberation, principles, 1248; limited, 263, 1176, 1205, 1243, concept, 1021; "low-intensity operations," 1384; national, 150; "of national liberation," *xiv;* nature of, forecasting, 1274; "open-ended," 1243; of opinion, 149; orthodox, 203; "people's," 144, 147, Clausewitz on, 148 (*see* Mao Tse-tung); principles, basic, 149; as profession, 84–85; psychological, 264; reasons for waging, 262; religion, 57, 85, 149; secret, 1329; small, 395, 410, 1025, Callwell's classic, 202–6, characteristics, 198–99, *genre,* 205, -guerrilla difference, 204; *special,* 997; theories, 148, 264; thermonuclear, 1052; total, 164; tribal, 866
  See Warfare
"Wars of national liberation," *xiv*
Warsaw, battle of, 917
Washington, George, 93, 97, 98, 102, 103, 107, 112, 113, 774n, 1376; tactics, 98–99
Washington Watch, 1205
Wavell, A. P., 268, 584, 599; Wingate, 598–600, 601
Wayne, Anthony, 113
Weapons, 34, 38, 82, 85, 199, 228, 267, 281; development, *xiii,* 30, 67, 82, 85, 160; napalm, 1028; -partisans, 1026; proscription, 57; secret, 41; systems, *xiv,* 1302; technology, 43n; training, 604; Vietnam, 1114–15
  See also Terror
Weber, Max, 291
Webster, Graham, 25n
Wedemeyer, Albert, 628, 632, 637; Chiang Kai-shek, 636, 637–38, 639; on China, 634–35; China mission, 643; Hurley, 634; on postwar Russia, 634; Roosevelt, F. D., 629, 640; Stilwell, 620, 628; *Wedemeyer Reports,* 628, 646
Weed killers, *xiii*
Weigley, Russell F., *xvi,* 93, 94n, 97n, 99, 106, 159, 169
Weizmann, Chaim, 770, 774
Weller, Jac, 1152
Welles, Sumner, 939–40 *and* n, 1035
Wellesley, 127 *and* n, 129
  See Wellington
Wellington, Duke of, *xi,* 120, 127, 129, 132, 950 *and* n; guerrillas, 129–30; strategy, 133, 141; tactics, 120, 129–30
Wemyss, Rosslyn, 260
West, the: Alliance, 695 (*see* NATO); boons, 1273; China, 325, 330–31, 332, 333–34, 341; civilization, 695, code of, 1259; Communists' hatred, 315; containment policy, 691; *direction* of war, 84–85; East: differences, 34, gulf, 694, 1371, postwar, 672ff.; Greek civil war, failure to analyze, 742; hypocrisy, 281–82; influence, 158; -Jewish survivors of World War II, 775n; land warfare, rules, 592; "limited" wars, 84; military doctrines, 1025; military structures, 307; political behavior, 185; professional airmen, 1258; quantitative theories, 853; social malaise, 283; -Soviet Union, conflict, 759; supremacy, myth, 534; as symbol of progress, 863n; tactics, 69; traditions, 47; victory for, 744
Westerling, Capt. "Turk," 763
Westermann, Gen., 121

West Germany, 922, 1108
West Indies, 102, 105
Westmoreland, William, 1060, 1083ff., 1094, 1099ff., 1112ff., 1124; background, 1113–14; Chief of Staff, 1237, 1330; failure, 1387; Johnson, 1178, 1190, 1191, 1209, 1224, 1237; logistics, 1147; strategy, 1104, 1112–13, 1126, 1137, 1140, 1176, 1191, 1194, 1208ff., 1237, 1275ff., fallacy, 1195; successor, 1235, 1238 (*see* Abrams, Creighton); troop build-up, 1169ff., 1172–75
Westphalia, treaty of, 825n
West Point, 164, 520, 521, 594, 628, 982, 988, 1024, 1113, 1238
Weyand, Frederick, 1179
Weygand, Maxim, 308
Weyler, Gen., 176–78, 194, 1007
Whampoa Military Academy, 557–58
Wheeler, Earle G., 986, 1217ff., 1224, 1229–32, 1270, 1313, 1332
White, George, 208
White, Lynn, Jr., 39n
White, T. H., 594, 595, 1016; *and* Annalee Jacoby: *Thunder Out of China*, 615
White magic, 865
"White man's burden," 171–72, 546, 547, 548; Christian concept, 868, 871
White supremacy, myth, 688, 781
Wickman, J. T., 190
Wickwire, Franklin and Mary, 104, 110 *and* n
Wieland, William, 963
Wilcken, U., 6n
Wilhelm, Kaiser, 1388
Willcox, William B., 102n, 105
William, Duke of Normandy, 56, 68

Williams, Samuel, 844
Wilson, Derek, 1356
Wilson, Harold, 1103, 1193, 1204, 1214
Wilson, Henry Lane, 241
Wilson, Woodrow, 229–30, 304, 309, 540, 1377; China, 337; Cuba, 937; Fourteen Points, 557; Mexico, 241, 243, 244, 245, 1047
Wingate, Orde, 596–601, 605–6, 607, 608, 609, 1007; Burma, 804; characteristics, 598–99; death, 607; fame, 602–3; long-range-penetration concept, 599, 600, 605; Palestine, 771; "strongholds" concept, 605, 728; tactics, 596–99
Wingate, Reginald, 260
Witte, Sergius, 289
Wiznitzer, Louis, 1349
Wohlstetter, Roberta, xvi
Wolfe, James, 97
Wolfert, Ira: *American Guerrilla in the Philippines*, 514
Womack, John: *Zapata*, 237, 238
Woodhouse, C. M., xvi, 418, 488n, 489, 490–94, 496
Woolman, Prof., 376, 382
World War I, 227, 229, 273, 279, 283, 317, 370, 401n, 469, 540, 557, 586, 590, 689, 863, 888, 905, 912, 1278, 1377; Africans, 869; allied powers, 297, 301–2, 304, 309–10; armistice, 251, 310; Balkans, 468; casualties, 279; Central Powers, 248, 888; England, 769; generals, 308; German East Africa, 249–56; guerrillas, 248; heros, 383; Middle East, 257–71; nature of, 248; Palestine, 265; peace treaty, 270, 310–11, 314; results, 248–49; strategy, 264,

308–9; tactics, 812; Vietnam, 550, 555
See also under country
World War II, xvi, 406, 407–16, 417–25, 426–42, 443–57, 733–34, 735, 742, 770, 776, 811, 863, 889, 918, 941, 1223, 1377; Africa(ns), 597–98, 869, 871; aftermath, 688–89; "agents" (see SOE under England and OSS under United States); Allies: conferences, 565 (see also under name of conference), policy, 412, SHAEF, 437, strategy, 409ff, 412–16, 430ff., 436ff., 475, 483–86, 491, 493, 494, 497, 502, 561, 565–66, 601, 1259–61 (see Churchill, Winston S.; Roosevelt, Franklin D. and under country and theater); AMM (Allied Military Mission), 494, 495; Arabs, 769; Asia, 408, 409; Balkans, 412; Big Four, 617; Big Three, 671, 689; China-Burma-India theater, 584–85; D-Day, 436, 437, 438, 525 (see Normandy); Europe, 407–8, 560, 588, 628, 918, analyzed, 417–25; Far East, 584–89, 590, 591, 599–601, 613–31, allied strategy, 585, 589, 595, 603, 605; guerrillas, 408ff., aid to, 404; Indochina (French), 563–71; Middle East, 412, 771; Normandy, 436, 475; North Africa, 408, 433; Operation Animals, 493; OSS (see under United States); Pacific theater, 281n, 359n, 408, 503–12, 513–27, 534–37, 538, 541, 628, 811–12, 1136, allied strategy, 503–4, 512, 538, 541–42, 561, 564–65, guerrillas, 511–12, 538, resistance, 503–4 (see

under country); postwar disillusionment, xvi; resistance, 408–16, 879 (see also under country and theater); results (sequelae), 671ff.; SOE (see under England); South-East Asia Command (SEAC), 603, 606, 607; Soviet Union, 443–57, 458–64, -Japan, 630; Spanish Civil War, 402; technology, 800; Tehran Conference, 474; West: attitude, 613
Wriston Program, 1380
Writings. See Military writings

Xenophobia, 229, 693, 994, 1368
Xenophon, 351, 1388; diathetic, 264

Yale University, 982, 988; in China, 333
Yalta Conference, 565, 628–31, 638, 644, 674, 689
Yamashita, Gen., 525
Yeats, William Butler, 278
Yeliu Chutsai, 69
Yemenites, 771n
Yenan, 559, 621, 623, 628, 631, 641; Dixie Mission, 620–21, 625–26
See also under Mao Tse-tung and China
Yeo-Thomas, Commander, 434, 437
Yorktown, battle of, xii, 116
Young, Gen., 935
Yugoslavia, 623, 1019, 1098, map, 476; communism, 734, 851; Greece, 735, 738; nationalism, 480; radio, 473; statehood, 470; World War II, 408, 412, 465–77, 478–86, 487, 686: army, 469, fall, 497, government-in-exile, 470, 471, 480, guerrillas, 469ff., 480–86, 487
See Tito

Yünnan, 566 *and* n, 585, 594–608
passim, 676

Zacharias, Ellis, 630
Zagoria, Donald S., *xvi*, 824n, 996,
1064, 1246, 1272; *Vietnam
Triangle—Moscow, Peking,
Hanoi,* 849
Zakhariadis, Nikos, 735, 741, 742,
744
Zanzibar, sultan of, 866
Zapata, Emiliano, 237–39, 241, 242,
243, 244, 246; Plan of Ayala,
239; tactics, 240
Zasulich, Vera, 289
Zayas, Alfredo, 937
Zeller, André, 929
Ziegler, Philip, *xvi*

Zionism (ists), 597, 598, 768–72;
Biltmore Program, 771, 772,
774; England, 770–71, pledge,
769; goals, 774; Jewish Agency,
770, 771; leaders, 770, 771;
militants, Revisionist Party, 771
(*see* Irgun); World War II, 771
Zizka, John, 82–83
Zog, King of Albania, 496
Zola, Émile, 283
Zona technique, 751, 752
Zones excentriques, 804
Zouri, Eliahu Bet, 774n
Zubatov, Col., 290
Zulus, 250
Zulu war, 200
Zurich, conference (on Cyprus),
900